Introduction

to the

Law of Scotland

BY

The late W. M. GLOAG, K.C., LL.D.

AND

The late R. CANDLISH HENDERSON, Q.C., LL.D.

EIGHTH EDITION

EDITORS

A. B. WILKINSON, M.A.(ST. AND.), LL.B.(EDIN.)

Advocate
Professor of Private Law in the University
of Dundee

AND

W. A. WILSON, M.A., LL.B.(GLAS.)

Lord President Reid Professor of Law
in the University of Edinburgh

ASSISTANT EDITORS

J. A. D. HOPE, Q.C., M.A.(CANTAB.), LL.B.(EDIN.)

AND

R. N. M. MACLEAN, Q.C., B.A.(CANTAB.), LL.B.(EDIN.), LL.M.(YALE)

AND

ANN PATON, M.A., LL.B.(GLAS.)
Advocates

EDINBURGH
W. GREEN & SON LTD.
Publishers
1980

First Published *1927*
Second Edition *1933*
Third Edition *1939*
Fourth Edition *1946*
Fifth Edition *1952*
Sixth Edition *1956*
Seventh Edition *1968*
Eighth Edition *1980*

©

1980   W. Green & Son Ltd.

ISBN 0 414 00625 9

Printed in Great Britain
by
Thomson Litho Ltd.
East Kilbride, Scotland.

TABLE OF CONTENTS

PREFACE TO EIGHTH EDITION

THE first edition of this work was conceived as a successor to Erskine's *Principles* which for more than a century and a half had been the leading introductory text-book in Scots Law. It has now itself achieved something of the classic status of its predecessor and we have approached the work of revision in the spirit which that status enjoins. Alterations have been made where the development of the law made that necessary or where views once held have ceased to be tenable, but we have refrained from any major recasting or from the gratuitous substitution of our own views for those of the original authors; a measure of comment and criticism is implicit in a work such as this and should sometimes be explicit, but, following the pattern of previous editions, we have not essayed wider issues of criticism and comment such as are developed in Professor T. B. Smith's justly celebrated *Short Commentary* which, it seems to us, is a work in many respects complementary in character to this; much new material has been added but continuity with the original has, we hope, been maintained and its merits of succinctness, accuracy and lucidity preserved.

The extent of necessary new material has been such that the whole could no longer have been contained within the bounds of one reasonably manageable volume if substantial excisions had not been made. It was accordingly decided at an early stage to delete the chapter on the National Insurance (Industrial Injuries) Act and the section on Criminal Procedure, which are alien to the general scope of a work essentially concerned with substantive private law. We believe that these were in any event among the least used parts of previous editions although no doubt consulted by some as a convenient summary. New chapters on Consumer Protection and Consumer Credit Transactions have been written by Professor Wilson and within the broad aim of fidelity to the original text much rewriting, some of it extensive, has been done. Although we have had to forego the substantial expansion of the treatment of some subjects, such as Criminal Law, for which at one time we had hoped, we trust that throughout the book the effect of the considerable revisions which have been made has been to enhance its utility. The initial work of revision was done in part by our assistants and in part by ourselves, but having as joint editors read and considered the whole text we are solely responsible for any deficiencies which remain.

Mr. Hector MacQueen of the University of Edinburgh revised the tables of cases and statutes. Mr. W. C. H. Ervine and Mr. J. W. R. Gray of the University of Dundee, Mr. Hamish Henderson of the University of Edinburgh, Mr. Matthew Clarke, Advocate and Mr. Alexander Sim of the Scottish Law Commission read parts of the text in draft and we have benefited greatly from the suggestions which they made. Our secretaries,

Mrs. Sheila Summers and Mrs. Betty Ferguson, have coped skilfully and uncomplainingly with the many demands which have been put on them, and, at all stages of preparation, the ready help and advice of Mr. R. R. Shaw of Messrs. W. Green & Son have been invaluable.

We have endeavoured to state the law as at 1st January 1979 but industrial action on the part of Government printers and other delays have made that a matter of more than usual difficulty. In a few instances, it has been possible to incorporate changes in the law since then. The length of the interval between the final revision of the text and publication has been due to circumstances beyond the control both of ourselves and our publishers.

A. B. W.
W. A. W.

February, 1980.

PREFACE TO FIRST EDITION

SINCE its publication in 1754 Erskine's *Principles,* as revised and brought up to date by various editors, has held a leading place as a textbook in the classes of Scots Law in the Universities. The latest edition, issued in 1911 under the editorship of Sir John Rankine, is now out of print: and accordingly, in order to meet the requirements of students, it became necessary to consider the preparation either of another edition or of an entirely new book.

On the whole it appeared to us that it would be unwise to attempt a new edition. In the later editions Erskine's original work had been extensively altered by the inclusion of new material rendered necessary by the development of the law: and the addition of this new material in a book within the compass of a student's textbook was possible only at the cost of such compression as to make it extremely difficult for readers at the outset of their legal studies. As the present book is less comprehensive in its scope, we have been enabled to treat more fully the subjects embraced.

We have confined our work to those branches of the law which are usually dealt with in classes of Scots and of Mercantile Law. Conveyancing, Evidence and Procedure, Private International and Administrative Law are, therefore, only incidentally referred to.

It is hoped that few of the leading decisions have been omitted, but no attempt has been made at such fullness of citation as the practitioner, as distinguished from the student, might expect.

We have to acknowledge the valuable assistance in the preparation of the work given by Mr. N. M. L. Walker and Mr. T. B. Simpson, Advocates.

W. M. G.
R. C. H.

October, 1927.

CITATION OF CASES

SCOTTISH CASES

THE older Scottish cases are reported in Morison's *Dictionary*, consisting of 22 volumes. These cases are cited by their year and the page on which they appear: thus, (1703) Mor. 1062. There are five supplementary volumes, known as Brown's *Supplement*. In addition, there are other collections of cases, such as Elchies' *Decisions* (2 vols., 1733–54), Hume's *Decisions* (1 vol., 1781–1822), and Bell's octavo and folio *Cases* (2 vols., 1790–5).

The Faculty Collection contains cases from 1738 to 1841. The volumes most frequently referred to are those covering the years between 1808 and 1825. These reports are cited by the date of the decision: thus, 10th January 1812, F.C.

The Session Cases were in the hands of private reporters until 1907, when they were acquired by the Faculty of Advocates. From 1907 onwards they are cited thus: 1907 S.C. 15. The earlier Session Cases consist of five series, which, strictly speaking, should be referred to by the year (in brackets) and the initial letter of the editor's, or a reporter's, name, although in practice the date or the bracketing is frequently omitted.

The citation is as follows:—

   (1831) 10 S. 82 refers to the first series (16 volumes, from 1821 to 1838), edited by Shaw.

   (1847) 10 D. 82, to the second series (24 volumes, from 1838 to 1862), edited by Dunlop.

   (1871) 10 M. 82, to the third series (11 volumes, from 1862 to 1873), edited by Macpherson.

   (1882) 10 R. 82, to the fourth series (25 volumes, from 1873 to 1898), edited by Rettie.

   (1903) 5 F. 82, to the fifth series (8 volumes, 1898 to 1906), referred to as Fraser.

There are also other contemporaneous reports, viz., the *Scottish Jurist* (running from 1829 to 1873), referred to as Sc. Jur. or J. or S.J.; the *Scottish Law Reporter* (61 volumes, from 1865 and ending in 1924), referred to as S.L.R.; and the *Scots Law Times* (beginning in 1893, and referred to as S.L.T.). The *Session Notes*, a series of short reports of cases not yet reported at length elsewhere, began in 1925 and ended in 1948; these reports are referred to by the year with S.N. added. A similar series of short reports has appeared since 1949 in the *Scots Law Times*, referred to as S.L.T. (Notes). A series of reports of cases decided in the Land Court was begun in 1912; the mode of reference is 1953 S.L.C.R. 40. Land Court decisions have also been reported, since 1964, in the *Scots Law Times,* referred to as, e.g., 1964 S.L.T. (Land Court) 4.

Decisions in the Sheriff Court are reported in the *Scots Law Times* (e.g. 1955 S.L.T. (Sh. Ct.) 100) and also in the *Scottish Law Review* (e.g. (1885) 1 Sh. Ct. Rep. 6).

The reports of decisions of the House of Lords in Scottish cases appear at the beginning of the Session Cases, and are cited thus: 10 M. (H.L.) 4; 1907 S.C. (H.L.) 4. The older cases are to be found in private reports.

These are:—

Robertson's Reports (1 vol.), 1707–1727.
Paton's Reports (6 vols.), 1726–1821.
Dow's Reports (6 vols.), 1813–1818.
Bligh's Reports (6 vols.), 1819–1821.
Shaw's Reports (2 vols.), 1821–1824.
Wilson and Shaw's Reports (7 vols.), 1825–1835.
Shaw and M'Lean's Reports (3 vols.), 1835–1838.
M'Lean and Robinson's Reports (1 vol.), 1839.
Robinson's Reports (2 vols.), 1840–1841.
Bell's Reports (7 vols.), 1842–1850.
Macqueen's Reports (4 vols.), 1851–1865.

Criminal (Justiciary) Cases are reported in the Justiciary reports, viz.:— Shaw, 1819–1831 (1 vol.); Syme, 1826–1830 (1 vol.); Swinton, 1835–1841 (2 vols.); Broun, 1842–1845 (2 vols); Arkley, 1846–1848 (1 vol.); J. Shaw, 1848–1851 (1 vol.); Irvine, 1851–1868 (5 vols.); Couper, 1868–1885 (5 vols.); White, 1885–1893 (3 vols.); and Adam, 1893–1916 (7 vols.). From 1874 to 1917 Justiciary Cases are also included in the volumes of Session Cases, and the reference to these reports is, e.g., (1892) 10 R. (J.) 1, 1916 S.C. (J.) 1. From 1917 onwards the criminal reports are referred to as e.g., 1917 J.C. 100, and are usually bound with Session Cases.

ENGLISH CASES

The earlier English cases appear in private reports. These are generally cited by the initials of the reporters' names, but there are a few in which this is not so. Thus: Q.B. stands for Adolphus and Ellis's Reports (1841–52, 18 vols.); H.L.C. for Clark's Reports (1846–66, 12 vols.); Exch. for Welsby, Hurlston and Gordon's Reports (1848–56, 11 vols.).

In 1865 the Council of Law Reporting undertook the issuing of reports and their publications are called "Law Reports" (L.R.). The Courts were separate until the Judicature Act, when they became Divisions of the High Court. Hence the Court of Queen's Bench (or Q.B.) in 1875 became Queen's Bench Division (or Q.B.D.). From 1865 to 1875 the letters L.R. are therefore prefixed in the citation of these Reports, followed by the number of the volume and the name of the court: thus, L.R. 3 H.L.; L.R. 5 Q.B.; L.R. 5 Ch.; L.R. 5 C.P. (i.e., Common Pleas); L.R. 3 Ex. (i.e., Exchequer); L.R. 3 Eq. (i.e., Equity); L.R. 3 P. & D. (i.e., Probate and Divorce).

From 1876 to 1890 L.R. is omitted and D. added for the Divisions, and the volumes are cited consecutively according to the courts; thus 2 App. Cas.; 2 Q.B.D.; 2 Ch.D.; 3 C.P.D.; 2 Ex.D.; 2 P.D. In 1881 the Queen's Bench, Common Pleas, and Exchequer Divisions were consolidated into the Queen's Bench Division—hence C.P.D. and Ex.D. appear only between 1875 and 1881.

After 1890 the year is inserted in square brackets and D. omitted: thus, [1891] A.C., or Q.B., or Ch., or P. After 1971, the Probate Division was replaced by the Family Division and the Reports are cited thus: [1972] Fam. 40. In 1953, the series known as the *Weekly Law Reports* began, replacing the *Weekly Notes*. It is cited thus: [1955] 1 W.L.R. 100; cases reported in volumes 2 or 3 of the *Weekly Law Reports* are intended for publication in the "Law Reports" series in due course.

In addition to the Law Reports, there are other series of English reports of considerable importance. Those of a general nature are the *All England Reports* (cited thus, for example: [1952] 2 All E.R. 100), the *Times Law Reports* (ended 1953, and cited latterly thus, for example: [1952] 1 T.L.R. 100), the *Justice of the Peace Reports* (cited thus, for example: 50 J.P. 100). There are, in addition, several series of specialised reports such as the *Tax Cases* (50 Tax Cas. or T.C. 100); *Reports of Restrictive Practices Cases* ((1958) L.R. 1 R.P. 76) which was in 1972 incorporated in the *Industrial Court Reports* ([1972] I.C.R. 129), known since 1975 as the *Industrial Cases Reports*; *Lloyd's List Reports* ([1952] 1 Lloyd's Rep. 100) renamed *Lloyd's Law Reports* after 1967; *Knight's Industrial Reports* ((1972) 12 K.I.R. 135) which became after 1974 *Knight's Industrial Law Reports*. The important series of the *Law Times Reports* ran from 1859 to 1947 and the *Law Journal Reports* from 1832 to 1949. Decisions of the Court of Justice of the European Communities are reported in *European Court Reports* ([1973] E.C.R. 27) and, along with decisions of the courts of member-states on community law, in *Common Market Law Reports* ([1962] C.M.L.R. 28).

TABLE OF CASES

TABLE OF STATUTES

INTRODUCTION TO THE LAW
OF SCOTLAND

CHAPTER I

STATUTE AND COMMON LAW

Stair, *Institutions* (1681, edited by More, 1832), I., 1; Bankton, *Institute* (1753), I. 1; Erskine, *Institute* (1773, edited by Nicolson, 1871), I., 1; *The Sources and Literature of Scots Law* (Stair Society, 1936); Maxwell, *Interpretation of Statutes* (12th ed., 1969); Craies on *Statute Law* (7th ed. 1971); Mitchell, *Constitutional Law* (2nd ed., 1968).

1. Enacted Law.—The Law of Scotland consists partly of enacted law, which has the authority of some body having legislative powers, and partly of common law, which is recognised by the Courts as binding on some ground other than express enactment. Enacted law may include a Royal proclamation or order; an Act of Parliament; a provision of a European Community treaty; a regulation, directive or decision of the European Community Council or Commission; an Act of Sederunt; an Act of Adjournal; a bye-law or regulation issued either by a department of State or by some local authority or body having statutory powers.

2. Legislative Authority of the Crown.—The legislative authority of the Crown, acting either through the Privy Council, or by some official, civil, naval or military, is a subject on which there is no direct authority in Scotland. Decisions of the House of Lords in English appeals cannot be taken as universally binding in questions of constitutional law in Scotland,[1] but the following rules, enunciated in a leading English decision,[2] seem to be consistent with the Scottish approach: (1) In the absence of any national emergency,[3] the Crown has no legislative authority, and therefore a Royal proclamation infers no obligation; (2) The Crown, in virtue of the Royal prerogative, has legislative powers in cases of national emergency, e.g., invasion, and may delegate that power to a particular officer; (3) The validity of an order issued under the Royal prerogative depends on the gravity of the emergency, and therefore, as no emergency can demand the seizure or the destruction as a precautionary measure of private property without payment of compensation, the person whose property is seized or commandeered may demand compensation as a right and not merely as an act of grace[4]; (4) If a particular act (e.g., seizure of private property) is done which might be

[1] *Glasgow Corporation* v. *Central Land Board*, 1956 S.C. (H.L.) 1; see also *MacCormick* v. *Lord Advocate*, 1953 S.C. 396, per Lord President Cooper at p. 411.
[2] *Att.-Gen.* v. *De Keyser Hotel Co.* [1920] A.C. 508.
[3] See Emergency Powers Act 1920 (10 & 11 Geo. V. c. 55), as amended by Emergency Powers Act 1964 (c. 38).
[4] See *Burmah Oil Co. (Burmah Trading) Ltd.* v. *Lord Advocate,* 1964 S.C. (H.L.) 117; note also War Damage Act 1965 (c. 18).

1

lawfully done either under the Royal prerogative or under the provisions of a statute it will be presumed that it was done under the statutory power and, therefore, under the statutory conditions.

3. Acts of Parliament.—A statute may be either a public general statute or a local or personal Act. There is a general presumption, in the absence of any express provision on the point, that a public general statute applies generally to Great Britain and Northern Ireland. This presumption may be rebutted, and the statute held not to be applicable to Scotland, either on the ground that it is expressed as an amendment of a statute in which Scotland was expressly excluded[5]; or, with less force, that it is expressed in technical terms of English law without an interpretation clause giving the equivalents in the law of Scotland.[6] A provision that the statute shall not apply to Ireland is a strong indication that it does apply to Scotland.[7] Historically, a division may be noted between statutes passed by the Scots Parliament prior to the Union in 1707 (usually termed Scots Acts) and statutes passed subsequently. Statutes of the English Parliament prior to 1707 are of no authority in Scotland, unless, as in the case of 25 Edw. III., relating to high treason, they have been applied to Scotland by a later Act.[8] The date at which a statute comes into force is generally stated; if not, it comes into force on the day when it receives the Royal Assent.[9]

4. Private Legislation Procedure Acts.—Local and personal, also called private, Acts are statutes conferring powers on some local authority, body or company, or regulating the rights or status of some private individual. By the Private Legislation Procedure (Scotland) Act 1936,[10] where any public authority or persons desire a private Act, they may apply to the Secretary of State for Scotland for a provisional order. If, after advertisement, no opposition is offered, the provisional order, after certain procedure detailed in the Act, will be issued; if objections are lodged, a local inquiry is held by commissioners. If their report is favourable, the provisional order is issued. A provisional order has no legislative force and it has to be confirmed by a Confirmation Act.[11] Provisions, for which reference must be made to the Act, are made excluding procedure by provisional order in projects which do not relate exclusively to Scotland or raise questions of public policy of novelty and importance.[12]

5. European Community Acts.—The European Communities Act 1972,[13] s. 2 (1), provides that "All such rights, powers, liabilities, obligations and

[5] *Levy* v. *Jackson* (1903) 5 F. 1170.
[6] *Scottish Drug Depot* v. *Fraser* (1905) 7 F. 646.
[7] *Scottish Drug Depot,* supra.
[8] See 7 Anne, c. 21, s. 1.
[9] Interpretation Act 1978 (c. 30) s. 4.
[10] 26 Geo. V. & 1 Edw. VIII. c. 52.
[11] ss. 8, 9.
[12] s. 2.
[13] c. 68.

restrictions from time to time created or arising by or under the Treaties, and all such remedies and procedures from time to time provided for by or under the Treaties, as in accordance with the Treaties are without further enactment to be given legal effect or used in the United Kingdom shall be recognised and available in law, and be enforced, allowed and followed accordingly." "The Treaties" are those specified in Part I of Schedule 1 to the Act, those specified in section 1 (2) of the Act and others specified in Orders in Council. The first effect of this provision is that the provisions of the treaties, e.g. Articles 85 and 86 of the Treaty of Rome relating to competition, are part of the law of the United Kingdom.[14] Secondly, a regulation made by the Council of Ministers or the Commission of the European Community has general application, is binding in its entirety and is directly applicable in all member states of the Community.[15] A directive is binding as to the result to be achieved upon each member state to which it is addressed but the choice of form and methods is left to the national authorities.[16] However, in certain circumstances, an individual litigant may invoke a directive.[17] A decision is binding in its entirety upon those to whom it is addressed; again, it may be invoked to affect legal relations between the addressee and a third party.[18] The Court of Justice of the Communities may review the legality of a regulation, directive or decision and declare it void; proceedings must be instituted within two months of the publication of the measure, or of its notification to the plaintiff or, in the absence thereof, of the day on which it came to his knowledge.[19]

6. Statutory Instruments.—There is a great deal of legislation (now often referred to as "subordinate legislation") by other authorities under powers conferred by Parliament, such as Orders in Council, orders by ministers, rules of procedure made by Courts, and bye-laws by local authorities and other corporations. Where an Act gives a power to Her Majesty in Council, exercisable by Order in Council, or to a Minister, exercisable by "statutory instrument", any document by which the power is exercised is a "statutory instrument".[20] Thus Orders in Council made under the Royal prerogative and some subordinate legislation made by ministers are not statutory instruments. An order or regulation made by a Minister is liable to be attacked as ultra vires.[21]

---

[14] *SpA S.A.C.E.* v. *Italian Ministry of Finance* [1970] E.C.R. 1213; *Firma Alfons Lütticke GmbH* v. *Hauptzollamt Sarrelouis* [1966] E.C.R. 205; *Eunomia di Porro eC.* v. *Italian Ministry of Education* [1971] E.C.R. 811; *Reyners* v. *Belgian State* [1974] E.C.R. 631; *Defrenne* v. *Sabena* [1976] E.C.R. 455.

[15] Treaty of Rome, Art. 189; *Politi S A S* v. *Italian Minister of Finance* [1971] E.C.R. 1039.

[16] Art. 189.

[17] *SpA S.A.C.E.* v. *Italian Ministry of Finance,* supra; *Van Duyn* v. *Home Office* [1974] E.C.R. 1337.

[18] *Franz Grad* v. *Finanzamt Traunstein* [1970] E.C.R. 825.

[19] Art. 173.

[20] Statutory Instruments Act 1946 (9 & 10 Geo. VI. c. 36); see Mitchell, *Constitutional Law,* pp. 273 et seq.

[21] *Alexander & Sons* v. *Minister of Transport,* 1936 S.L.T. 553; *Islay Estates* v. *Agricultural Executive Committee for South Argyll,* 1942 S.L.T. 174; *Forster* v. *Polmaise Patent Fuel Co.,* 1947 J.C. 56.

7. Acts of Sederunt and Acts of Adjournal.—Acts of Sederunt are rules passed by the Court of Session, under powers originally conferred at its foundation.[22] In the seventeenth and eighteenth centuries the Court took a wide view of its powers and promulgated Acts of Sederunt amounting to general legislation, e.g., ordaining parties to a strike to resume work.[23] In modern times Acts of Sederunt relate exclusively to procedure, and are usually passed in virtue of a specific authority in some particular statute. In such cases the repeal of the statute impliedly repeals the Acts of Sederunt which have been passed under it.[24] If the provisions of the statute admit of two interpretations, that consistent with the Act of Sederunt must be adopted.[25] In 1913 the existing Acts of Sederunt relating to procedure were collected, with amendments, in the Codifying Act of Sederunt, but in 1934 this, so far as regards procedure in the Court of Session, was in turn superseded by new Rules of Court made consequently upon the passing of the Administration of Justice (Scotland) Act 1933. In 1965 an Act of Sederunt[26] approved new consolidated rules, repealed the provisions of any statute or Act of Sederunt inconsistent with them,[27] and empowered the Court to relieve any party from the consequences of failure to comply with the rules due to mistake, oversight or other cause, not being wilful non-observance.[28] An Act of Adjournal is an Act passed by the High Court of Justiciary for regulating procedure in that Court and in inferior criminal Courts.

8. Orders and Bye-laws.—If a bye-law passed by a local authority or by a company has legislative force it must derive that force from a statute by which power to make bye-laws is conferred. So a bye-law issued by a company registered under the Companies Acts may be binding on the shareholders; if so, it is binding on principles of contract and because they have agreed to be bound by it; whereas a company founded on statute may have power to issue bye-laws which have legislative force, and are binding on the general public as well as on the shareholders. The exact degree of legislative force possessed by an order or bye-law depends on the terms of the statute by which the power to issue it was conferred. If it is there enacted that the bye-law, when passed, is to be read as part of the statute it is still open to the objection that it is inconsistent with a section of the statute, or that the official empowered has gone completely beyond his province; any objections less weighty are excluded.[29] If there is a mere power to make bye-laws for some particular

---

22 College of Justice Act 1532 (c. 2). The Law Reform (Misc. Provs.) (Scotland) Act 1966, s. 10, provided that Acts of Sederunt and Acts of Adjournal made after that Act under enabling statutes enacted after the commencement of the Statutory Instruments Act 1946 are to be statutory instruments unless the enabling statute provides to the contrary.
23 A.S. 1725. See Alexander, *Acts of Sederunt*.
24 *Inglis' Trs.* v. *Macpherson*, 1910 S.C. 46.
25 *Tonner* v. *Baird & Co.*, 1927 S.C. 870; *Carron Co.* v. *Hislop*, 1931 S.C. (H.L.) 75.
26 S.I. 1965 No. 321 (replacing S.I. 1948 No. 1691).
27 See *Graham* v. *Paterson & Co.*, 1938 S.C. 119.
28 *Dalgety's Trs.* v. *Drummond*, 1938 S.C. 709.
29 *The King* v. *Minister of Health* [1931] A.C. 494, explaining *Institute of Patent Agents* v. *Lockwood* (1894) 21 R. (H.L.) 61. And see *M'Ewen's Trs.* v. *Church of Scotland General Trs.*, 1940 S.L.T. 357, as to validity of a "scheme" made under an Act of Parliament; *Cheyne* v. *Architects' Registration Council*, 1943 S.C. 468.

object, these, when made, are valid only if they are intra vires, i.e., if they relate to the object referred to;[30] if they are reasonable;[31] and if they are not repugnant to the general law of the country.[32] There is, however, a strong presumption in favour of the validity of a bye-law passed by a local authority, especially if it has been confirmed, in accordance with the provisions of the statute, by some public official, such as the Secretary of State for Scotland or the sheriff.[33] In such a case the function of the confirming authority is to determine the expediency of the bye-law and not merely to consider its legality.[34] A bye-law falls if the statute authorising it is repealed.[35]

9. Repeal of Statutes: Desuetude.—A statute may be repealed by a later Act, either expressly, or by the enactment of provisions inconsistent with it.[36] Repeal is not to be presumed if, consistently with the later statute, it is possible to give any reasonable meaning to the earlier.[37] The repeal of a repealing statute does not revive the statute repealed.[38] Statute Law Revision Acts, providing for the express repeal of statutes or sections impliedly repealed, have been passed at various dates. A statute may also be impliedly repealed by falling into desuetude, with the result that if appealed to the Courts will decline to give effect to it. This rule, probably, is not applicable except to Scots Acts, at least there is no case where a statute passed since 1707 has been held to have fallen into desuetude, and no analogous rule is recognised in England.[39] Mere age is not a sufficient ground for holding an Act to be in desuetude; it requires in addition the consideration that there is no recent case reported in which the Act has been given effect to, that it has for a long period been disregarded in practice, or that its provisions are out of accord with modern conditions.[40] A large number of Scots Acts were repealed by the Statute Law Revision (Scotland) Act 1906, and there is a presumption, not conclusive, that Acts not included in the Schedule thereto are still in observance.[41] The Statute Law Revision (Scotland) Act 1964[42] repealed about 145 other Acts which were obsolete, spent or unnecessary, or had been superseded, and deleted obsolete matter from many others; it also provided short titles for the remaining Acts, which may be used without prejudice to any other mode of citation.[43]

[30] *Shepherd* v. *Howman*, 1918 J.C. 78; *M'Alister* v. *Forth Pilotage Authority*, 1944 S.L.T. 109.
[31] *Saunders* v. *South-Eastern Ry.* (1880) 5 Q.B.D. 456; *De Prato* v. *Magistrates of Partick*, 1907 S.C. (H.L.) 5.
[32] *Dunsmore* v. *Lindsay* (1903) 6 F. (J.) 14.
[33] *Aldred* v. *Miller*, 1925 J.C. 21; *Baird* v. *Glasgow Corporation*, 1935 S.C. (H.L.) 21. See Local Government (Scotland) Act 1973 (c. 65), ss. 201-204.
[34] *Glasgow Corporation* v. *Glasgow Churches Council*, 1944 S.C. 97.
[35] *Watson* v. *Winch* [1916] 1 K.B. 688.
[36] See for example *Angus County Council* v. *Magistrates of Montrose*, 1933 S.C. 505.
[37] *Lang* v. *Munro* (1892) 19 R. (J.C.) 53.
[38] Interpretation Act 1978 (c. 30) s. 15.
[39] See opinion of Lord Deas, *Bute* v. *More* (1870) 9 M. 180.
[40] *M'Ara* v. *Magistrates of Edinburgh*, 1913 S.C. 1059; *Brown* v. *Magistrates of Edinburgh*, 1931 S.L.T. 456.
[41] *Brown* v. *Magistrates of Edinburgh*, supra.
[42] c. 80.
[43] s. 2 and Schedule 2. Further repeals were made by the Statute Law Repeals Act 1973 (c. 39) Sch. 1, Pt. XIII.

10. Interpretation of Statutes: Scots Acts.—The general rules applicable to the interpretation of statutes are not applicable to Scots Acts. These, expressed in nearly all cases briefly and without detailed provisions, have been interpreted in a very liberal spirit, sometimes in terms which cannot be reconciled with the words of the Act. In their construction it is a recognised rule that, whatever the literal meaning of the statutory words, they are to be read as interpreted by decisions pronounced shortly after the Act was passed.[44]

11. Interpretation: Unambiguous Terms.—In modern statutes[45] the most general rule is that if the meaning of the statute is plain and unambiguous it must receive effect. Arguments as to resulting inconvenience or injustice or anomaly[46] are irrelevant. If injustice would result from a statute, it is the province of the legislature, not of the Court, to amend it.[47] The rule probably yields to cases where a literal interpretation would result in positive absurdity.[48] "Nothing short of impossibility should allow a judge to declare a statute unworkable."[49] Any ambiguity will admit of the construction of the statute in a sense which will not render it nugatory, or result in obvious injustice or inconvenience, although it may not be the most obvious meaning of the words used.[50]

12. Considerations Relevant in Construction.—Assuming an ambiguity, it is permissible to refer, as an aid to construction, to other statutes dealing with the same matter (in pari materia), and decisions thereon, not to statutes dealing with different matters.[51] In construing a consolidating Act it is proper to look at the earlier provisions which it consolidated only if it contains an ambiguity.[52] The title,[53] and the preamble[54] (usually omitted in recent statutes) may be referred to as determining the scope of the statute, though neither can override an express provision. It seems that it is now permissible to refer to marginal notes but they must not be given equal weight with the words of the Act.[55] Where a statute is divided into parts by specific headings,

---

[44] *Fergusson* v. *Skirving* (1852) 1 Macq. 232; *Heriot's Trust* v. *Paton's Trs.*, 1912 S.C. 1123, per Lord President Dunedin at p. 1135.

[45] See Maxwell, *Interpretation of Statutes;* Craies, *Statute Law.*

[46] *Stock* v. *Frank Jones (Tipton) Ltd.* [1978] 1 W.L.R. 231.

[47] *Lord Advocate* v. *Earl of Moray's Trs.* (1905) 7 F. (H.L.) 116; *Lawrie* v. *Banknock Colliery Co.,* 1912 S.C. (H.L.) 20, per Lord Shaw; *Feeney* v. *Miller,* 1925 J.C. 65.

[48] *Cal. Ry.* v. *N.B. Ry.* (1881) 8 R. (H.L.) 23, Lord Blackburn, p. 30. See also *Inland Revenue* v. *Luke,* 1963 S.C. (H.L.) 65, per Lord Reid at p. 80.

[49] Per Lord Dunedin, *Murray* v. *Inland Revenue,* 1918 S.C. (H.L.) 111, at p. 124. In *Dumfries and Maxwelltown Co-operative Society* v. *Williamson,* 1950 J.C. 76, a statutory provision was found unworkable.

[50] *Paterson* v. *Ardrossan Harbour Co.,* 1926 S.C. 442.

[51] *Lord Advocate* v. *Sprot's Trs.* (1901) 3 F. 440; *Lord Advocate* v. *Hamilton,* 1919 S.C. (H.L.) 90.

[52] *Inland Revenue Comnrs.* v. *Hinchy* [1960] A.C. 748, per Lord Reid at p. 768; *I.R.C.* v. *Joiner* [1975] 1 W.L.R. 1701; *Reg.* v. *Curran* [1976] 1 W.L.R. 87; *Farrell* v. *Alexander* [1977] A.C. 59.

[53] *Ayr* v. *St. Andrew's Ambulance Association,* 1918 S.C. 158; *Magistrates of Buckie* v. *Dowager Countess of Seafield's Trs.,* 1928 S.C. 525.

[54] *Att-Gen.* v. *Prince Ernest Augustus of Hanover* [1957] A.C. 436.

[55] *R.* v. *Schildkamp* [1971] A.C. 1, Lord Reid at p. 10; Maxwell (12th ed.), p. 49; Craies (6th ed.), p. 195; *Alexander* v. *Mackenzie,* 1947 J.C. 155, 166; *Magistrates of Buckie,* supra, at p. 530. Cf. *Nelson* v. *McPhee* (1889) 17 R (J.) 1; *Magistrates of Buckie,* supra, opinion of Lord President Clyde.

the heading limits the application of the sections which follow.[56] If a statute contains contradictory provisions the later sections override the earlier, but nothing in a schedule can overcome a provision in an enacting clause.[57] Where a particular term had, before the statute was passed, been interpreted in one way, either in contracts or in a statute, it is presumably used in the meaning these cases have given to it.[58] Historical facts are relevant, in so far as they show the state of knowledge of the legislators at the time the statute was passed,[59] or the meaning which a word then bore.[60] It is not permissible to refer to extrinsic sources of construction, such as the debates in Parliament.[61] The report of a Royal Commission or departmental committee on which the statute followed can be examined to ascertain the mischief aimed at and the state of the law as it was then understood to be but it is not permissible to take into account the recommendations made in the report or any comments made on a draft Bill annexed to the report.[62] Where the statute has apparently been passed to implement the obligations of the United Kingdom under an international convention, there is a presumption that Parliament did not intend to act in breach of specific treaty obligations and where there is ambiguity a meaning should be attached to the legislation consonant with the obligations assumed under the convention.[63] If the convention is not referred to in the body of the statute, it can be looked at only if the statute is ambiguous and there is cogent evidence that the enactment was intended to give effect to the particular convention.[64] If the Act gives effect to the convention as set forth in English in a Schedule, it is permissible to resolve doubt or ambiguity by examining a text of the convention in another language which is stated to be the authentic text,[65] or to be an equally authentic text.[66]

13. General Rules of Interpretation.—When the sole question is the construction of the statutory words, there is a general presumption that a statute is not retrospective,[67] unless it expressly bears to be declaratory of the meaning of a prior Act, when the meaning so declared will apply to all

---

[56] *Nelson,* supra; *Inglis* v. *Robertson & Baxter* (1898) 25 R. (H.L.) 70; *Magistrates of Buckie,* supra. Cf. *R.* v. *Schildkamp,* supra.
[57] *Jacobs* v. *Hart* (1900) 2 F. (J.) 33.
[58] *North British Ry.* v. *Budhill Coal Co.,* 1910 S.C. (H.L.) 1; *Barras* v. *Aberdeen Trawling Co.,* 1933 S.C. (H.L.) 21. See, however, *Haigh* v. *Charles W. Ireland,* 1974 S.L.T. 34.
[59] *Henretty* v. *Hart* (1885) 13 R. (J.) 9; *Hall* v. *Incorporated Society* (1901) 3 F. 1059; *Ealing L.B.C.* v. *Race Relations Board* [1972] A.C. 342.
[60] *Scottish Cinema* v. *Ritchie,* 1929 S.C. 350.
[61] *The Queen* v. *Hertford College* (1878) 3 Q.B.D. 693. See, however, as to the use of *travaux préparatoires* to construe statutes giving effect to an international convention, *Fothergill* v. *Monarch Airlines* [1978] 1 Q.B. 108.
[62] *Black-Clawson* v. *Papierwerke Waldhof-Aschaffenburg A.G.* [1975] A.C. 591.
[63] *Post Office* v. *Estuary Radio* [1968] 2 Q.B. 740.
[64] *Ellerman Lines* v. *Murray* [1931] A.C. 126, where, in the absence of ambiguity in the section under construction, the House of Lords refused to refer to the draft convention mentioned in the preamble and set forth in a schedule to the Act; *Salomon* v. *Commissioners of Customs and Excise* [1967] 2 Q.B. 116.
[65] *Fothergill* v.*Monarch Airlines,* supra. In *Corocraft* v. *Pan American Airways* [1969] 1 Q.B. 616, the Court of Appeal proceeded on the ambiguous French text rather than the unambiguous English version.
[66] *James Buchanan & Co.* v. *Babco Forwarding and Shipping (U.K.)* [1978] A.C. 141.
[67] *Gardner* v. *Lucas* (1878) 5 R. (H.L.) 105; *Henshall* v. *Porter* [1923] 2 K.B. 193.

pending questions, though not to cases already decided. A partial exception is that statutes introducing new forms of procedure apply to cases already in Court.[68] And it may be a necessary inference from the language of the Act, even though there is no express enactment, that it was intended to be retrospective.[69] There is a presumption that a palpable injustice, such as enabling a party to profit by his own wrong or breach of contract, was not intended.[70] When a list of things to which the statute is to apply is given followed by words of wide general import, the normal rule of construction, known as the rule of construction ejusdem generis, is that the general words apply only to things of the same kind as those in the preceding list. So where betting was prohibited "in any house, office, room or other place" it was held, construing the term "other place" as a place of the same kind as a house, office or room, that the Act did not apply to a racecourse.[71] This rule of construction is a presumption only, and may yield to the argument that the statutory provision was intended to be general, and that the list was given merely as an illustration.[72] It does not apply unless the things mentioned have some common and dominant feature. Where it was provided that a landlord, on certain specified conditions, might resume possession of the subjects let for "building, feuing, planting or other purposes," it was held that as building, feuing and planting could not be ascribed to any one genus there was no ground for limiting the generality of the words "or other purposes."[73] It has been laid down that "an intention to take away the property of a subject without giving to him a legal right to compensation for the loss of it is not to be attributed to the legislature unless that intention is expressed in unequivocal terms."[74] If, however, the intention to take away property be clear, any claim to compensation must be founded on the terms of the statute.[75] Subordinate rules of construction are that the exclusion of the jurisdiction of the Court of Session is not to be presumed;[76] and that the Crown (including departments of State) is not bound by a statute unless mentioned expressly[77] or by necessary implication.[78]

14. Ample and Restrictive Interpretation.—The theory that certain statutes should receive a beneficial, or ample, and others a restrictive interpretation,[79]

[68] *Ballinten* v. *Connor* (1852) 14 D. 927.
[69] *Wilson* v. *Wilson,* 1939 S.C. 102.
[70] *Malins* v. *Freeman* (1838) 4 Bing. N.C. 395.
[71] *Henretty* v. *Hart* (1885) 13 R. (J.) 9; contrast *Dawson* v. *Wright,* 1924 J.C. 121; *Murray* v. *Keith* (1894) 22 R. (J.) 16; *Chernack* v. *Mill,* 1938 J.C. 39; English cases are collected in Maxwell (12th ed.), pp. 297 et seq., and Craies (7th ed.) pp. 178 et seq.
[72] *Symington* v. *Symington's Quarries* (1905) 8 F. 121; *Baird* v *Lees,* 1924 S.C. 83.
[73] *Crichton Stuart* v. *Ogilvie,* 1914 S.C. 888.
[74] Per Lord Atkinson, *Central Board* v. *Cannon Brewery Co.* [1919] A.C. 744, 752. See *Marshall* v. *Blackpool Corporation* (1932) 49 T.L.R. 148.
[75] *Hammersmith Ry.* v. *Brand* (1869) L.R. 4 H.L. 171; *Cal. Ry.* v. *Walker's Trs* (1882) 9 R. (H.L.) 19; *Scott-Plummer* v. *Board of Agriculture,* 1916 S.C. (H.L.) 94, per Lords Haldane and Parmoor.
[76] *Dunbar* v. *Scottish County Investment Co.,* 1920 S.C. 210, per Lord Salvesen.
[77] *Somerville* v. *Lord Advocate* (1893) 20 R. 1050; *Magistrates of Edinburgh* v. *Lord Advocate,* 1912 S.C. 1085. In *Bell* v. *Secretary of State for Scotland,* 1933 S.L.T. 519, interdict was given against the Secretary of State's proceeding under the Agricultural Marketing Act 1931.
[78] *Att-Gen. for Ceylon* v. *A.D. Silva* [1953] A.C. 461.
[79] Erskine, I., 1, 53.

is in modern law discredited, and it is held that the duty of the Court is to interpret a statute according to its terms, without any bias. There are still, however, certain cases in which a statute is read, in dubio, in a restrictive sense, i.e., in the narrowest sense which the words will bear. This applies to statutes extending the criminal law. Offences are not to be created by implication, unless the implication is so plain as to be equivalent to express enactment.[80] In construing revenue statutes, while considerations of hardship or apparent injustice are irrelevant if the meaning of the statute is clear,[81] it is a recognised rule that no one is to be subjected to taxation unless his case comes within the letter of the law,[82] and that no one can claim exemption from a general tax unless his case is expressly provided for.[83] A private Act of Parliament, obtained by a public body or company, is to be read as a contract between them and the public, expressed in terms which they have chosen, and therefore, subject to the rule of construction verba interpretanda sunt contra proferentes, so that no privilege or right is conferred unless the words founded on as conferring it are unambiguous.[84]

15. Permissive Words.—When the words of a statute are permissive, where, for instance, it is provided that a party "may" perform a certain act, or that "it shall be lawful" for him to perform it, the general construction is, in accordance with the maxim "cuilibet licet renunciare juri pro se introducto," that an option is conferred, and no obligation imposed.[85] But if such words are employed in a statute dealing with a matter in which the general public have an interest, permissive words may be read as imperative. So where a statute authorised road trustees to make and keep highways 20 feet in width it was held that an obligation to keep highways of that width was inferred.[86] Where a discretionary power is conferred on a Court or on a public body, the statute, however absolute its terms may be, is to be construed subject to the implied limitation that the power is to be exercised in a judicial spirit, and under the conditions observed in judicial proceedings.[87]

16. Casus Omissus.—Circumstances may arise which show that a particular case has been overlooked by the framers of a statute. It is not within the power of the Court, as interpreter, to read into the statute words which are not there.[88] But in non-contentious procedure an application to the

[80] *Barty* v. *Hill,* 1907 S.C. (J.) 36; *Remington* v. *Larchin* [1921] 3 K.B. 404.
[81] *Duncan* v. *Inland Revenue,* 1923 S.C. 388.
[82] *Coltness Iron Co.* v. *Black* (1881) 8 R. (H.L.) 67, per Lord Blackburn at p. 72; *Tennant* v. *Smith* (1892) 19 R. (H.L.) 1; *Scottish Milk Marketing Board* v. *Ferrier,* 1936 S.C. (H.L.) 39.
[83] *Gillanders* v. *Campbell* (1884) 12 R. 309.
[84] *Countess of Rothes* v. *Kirkcaldy Water Works* (1882) 9 R. (H.L.) 108; *Milligan* v. *Ayr Harbour Trustees,* 1915 S.C. 937; *North British Ry.* v. *Birrell's Trs.,* 1918 S.C. (H.L.) 33 at p. 52.
[85] *Julius* v. *Bishop of Oxford* (1880) 5 App. Cas. 214; *Fleming & Ferguson* v. *Burgh of Paisley,* 1948 S.C. 547.
[86] *Gray* v. *St. Andrew's District Committee,* 1911 S.C. 266. See Maxwell, *Interpretation of Statutes* (12th ed.), p. 234; Craies (7th ed.), p. 284.
[87] *Macbeth* v. *Ashley* (1874) 1 R. (H.L.) 14; *Goodall* v. *Bilsland,* 1909 S.C. 1152; *Sharp* v. *Wakefield* [1891] A.C. 173.
[88] *The Queen* v. *Ellis* (1844) 6 Q.B. 501, but see *M'Dermott* v. *Owners of S.S. Tintoretto* [1911] A.C. 35.

Court of Session under the nobile officium, or equitable power, may get over the difficulty caused by a casus improvisus in a statute. Thus the Court has power to dispense with a statutory formality in a case where, owing to circumstances overlooked in the statute, its observance has been found to be impossible.[89] Though there is no statutory provision for the resuscitation of a company more than two years after its dissolution it has been held to be within the power of the Court,[90] and where there was no statutory power to recall a sequestration the Court declared it at an end.[91] The limits of the power of the Court of Session in virtue of its nobile officium have not been determined, but if a statutory right is given to certain specified persons it cannot, even in a case where there is no opposition, be extended to others.[92]

17. Interpretation Clauses.—Many statutes contain an interpretation clause, giving the meaning to be assigned to expressions used in the Act. If it is declared that a particular word shall "include" something, the result is to enlarge the scope of the word, but not to exclude its ordinary meaning.[93] If the meaning of the word is defined, that meaning, though it may exclude the ordinary meaning, must be taken, unless the context plainly shows that this was not intended. "If defined expressions are used in a context which the definition will not fit, then the words may be interpreted according to their ordinary meaning."[94] Modern statutes frequently contain provisions that something is to be "deemed" to be something else. A general statute, the Interpretation Act 1978[95], gives the meaning of a number of expressions in common use, such as "person", "month," "rules of Court," "writing." The statutory meaning is to apply "unless the contrary intention appears." So it was held that although the word "person" is defined as including male and female, yet in a statute relating to the admission of law agents its meaning might be restricted, on the ground of inveterate usage, to male persons.[96]

18. Sources of Common Law.—Rules of law which are not referable to any legislative enactment constitute the common law. It is spoken of by Lord Stair as "our ancient and immemorial customs," in which he includes the law of succession,[97] and the law, in so far as not affected by statute, of feudal conveyancing.[98] The origin of these customs is not in every case ascertainable; but it is clear that the common law of Scotland is in considerable measure derived from the civil law; to a less extent, but in important particulars, from

---

[89] *Roberts* (1901) 3 F. 779; *Train & M'Intyre,* 1923 S.C. 291. In *Murray* v. *Comptroller-General of Patents,* 1932 S.C. 726, an Outer House judge took similar action.
[90] *Forth Shipbreaking Co.,* 1924 S.C. 489.
[91] *Craig & Co.,* 1946 S.C. 19.
[92] *Crichton Stuart's Tutrix,* 1921 S.C. 840. See opinions in *Gibson's Trs., Petrs.,* 1933 S.C. 190.
[93] *Ex p. Ferguson* (1871) L.R. 6 Q.B. 280.
[94] *Strathern* v. *Padden,* 1926 J.C. 9, per Lord President Clyde.
[95] c. 30 (consolidating the Interpretation Act 1889 and other enactments).
[96] *Hall* v. *Incorporated Society* (1901) 3 F. 1059. See also *Colquhoun* v. *Magistrates of Dumbarton,* 1907 S.C. (J.) 57.
[97] As to the origin of the law of succession in moveables, see *Sommervill* v. *Murray's Creditors* (1744) M. 3902.
[98] Stair, I., 1, 16.

the canon law. Though there was probably no period at which the civil law was accounted part of the law of Scotland, yet that law, as explained and in some respects amended by the Dutch and French commentators of the sixteenth and seventeenth centuries, is the basis of the Scots law of contract and of property, apart from feudal conveyancing.[99] Before the Reformation much of the judicial business of Scotland was carried on in the Ecclesiastical Courts, with an ultimate appeal to the Papal Court at Rome, and the canon law was the law there administered. By the Act 1567, cap. 31, the authority of the canon law was expressly repudiated, but its influence remained, especially in the law relating to marriage and the domestic relations.[1] For more than a century the chief external factor, apart from legislation, in the development of the law of Scotland has been the law of England.

19. Custom as Forming Law.—Custom may still be recognised as a source of law, either in the form of usage of trade;[2] of local custom affecting rights of property;[3] of usage sanctioning some particular method of a government in a burgh[4] or determining the jurisdiction of a particular Court.[5] Usage amounting to a rule of law is distinguishable from the more common case where it is appealed to as importing an unexpressed term into a contract. There, as its recognition is based on implied agreement, knowledge or notice of the usage must be brought home to the party against whom it is pleaded;[6] whereas if the usage has acquired the force of law it falls under the general rule that everyone is supposed to know the law, and knowledge or notice is immaterial.[7] It is not possible to formulate exact rules as to the cases where a custom will be recognised as part of the common law. It need not be universal throughout Scotland; a special form of land tenure, prevailing in one locality only, has been recognised.[8] It cannot prevail against the express terms of a statute,[9] though it may be of material importance when the plea is taken that a statute is in desuetude.[10] A usage of trade that the transfer of a document of title to goods gives a real right to the goods has been uniformly held to be a misunderstanding of a general principle of law, to which no effect could be given.[11] The Court refused to sanction, on the plea of customary law, a local

---

[99] See, as to contrast with English Law, *Cantiere San Rocco* v. *Clyde Shipbuilding Co.*, 1923 S.C. (H.L.) 105; *Sinclair* v. *Brougham* [1914] A.C. 398, opinion of Lord Dunedin.
[1] *Collins* v. *Collins* (1884) 11 R. (H.L.) 19; *Purves's Trs.* v. *Purves* (1895) 22 R. 513.
[2] *Bechuanaland Exploration Co.* v. *London Trading Bank* [1898] 2 Q.B. 658; *Clydesdale BankNominees* v. *Snodgrass*, 1939 S.C. 805 (Stock Exchange); *Wilkie* v. *Scottish Aviation*, 1956 S.C. 198.
[3] *Learmonth* v. *Sinclair's Trs.* (1878) 5 R. 548.
[4] *Gardner* v. *Magistrates of Kilrenny* (1828) 6 S. 693; *Magistrates of Dunbar* v. *Duchess of Roxburghe*, 1835, 1 Shaw and M'L. 134, at p. 195; Erskine, I. 1, 20.
[5] *Neilson* v. *Vallance* (1828) 7 S. 182; *Duncan* v. *Lodijinsky* (1904) 6 F. 408.
[6] Rules of Evidence, Ch. XII., infra, 18.
[7] *Learmonth* v. *Sinclair's Trs.* (1878) 5 R. 548.
[8] Kindly Tenants of Lochmaben. See Rankine, *Leases* (3rd ed.). 153; *Marquis of Queensberry* v. *Wright* (1838) 16 S. 439; *Royal Four Towns Fishing Association* v. *Dumfries Assessor*, 1956 S.C. 379. Not all local law is customary, however; the relics of udal law, esp. udal tenure in Shetland, are attributable to the ancient connection with Norway; see *Lord Advocate* v. *Univ. of Aberdeen*, 1963 S.C. 533.
[9] See *Walker Trs.* v. *Lord Advocate*. 1912 S.C. (H.L.) 12.
[10] Supra, § 9.
[11] *Anderson* v. *M'Call* (1866) 4 M. 765; *Dobell* v. *Neilson* (1904) 7 F. 281.

usage, under which a certain class of creditors, without resort to legal process, satisfied their debts by seizing the property of their debtors.[12] And a usage must be reasonably fair. So it was held that a custom, proved to exist in Shetland, by which landlords claimed a third of the proceeds of whales killed on shore, had not the force of law, in respect that it amounted to an exaction for which no return was given.[13]

20. Authorities.—The question whether a particular rule is recognised as part of the common law must be determined, except in the case where appeal is made to a custom or usage hitherto unrecognised, by consideration of the authorities. The authorities may be statements by legal writers, or reports of decided cases. A writer on law is not in any proper sense an authority during his lifetime, unless he is raised to the Bench. After his death his works acquire an authority, varying in degree according to the reputation he may have attained. The works of certain authors, usually referred to as the institutional writers, are in Scotland treated with exceptional respect. Of these the chief, in questions of general law, are Lord Stair, Lord Bankton, Erskine and Bell; in the special sphere of criminal law, Hume[14] and Alison.

The authority of decisions as establishing a rule of law is a modern development. Erskine lays it down that a decision, even of the House of Lords, is not binding when the same question is raised between different parties, though he admits that a series of decisions should be respected.[15] And there is modern sanction for the statement that a case is an authority only for what it actually decides, not for a proposition which may seem to follow logically from it.[16] In practice, however, more deference is paid to authority than these statements would suggest. The authority of a case depends upon the jurisdiction of the Court by which it was pronounced. The decision of a sheriff principal is not binding outside his sheriffdom; the decision of the Court of Session is not binding on the House of Lords, though a decision which has ruled practice for a number of years will not readily be overturned merely because it is thought to be unfounded.[17] The decision of the House of Lords in a Scots appeal is binding on all Courts in Scotland, and on the House itself, in so far as Scots law is concerned.[18] The House may, however, depart from a previous decision when it appears right to do so.[19] A decision of the House of Lords in an English appeal not turning on the interpretation of a statute applicable to both countries is not binding in Scotland, though if it

---

[12] *Brodie* v. *Watson* (1714) M. 14757.

[13] *Bruce* v. *Smith* (1890) 17 R. 1000.

[14] Hume's *Lectures,* published posthumously and not prepared for publication by him, are not regarded as books of institutional authority: *Fortington* v. *Lord Kinnaird,* 1942 S.C. 239.

[15] Erskine, I., 1, 17. And see *Sugden* v. *H.M. Advocate,* 1934 J.C. at p. 127, where Lord Murray doubts whether the modern rule of stare decisis binds the High Court of Justiciary.

[16] *Quinn* v. *Leathem* [1901] A.C. 495; opinion of Lord Chancellor Halsbury.

[17] *Kirkpatrick's Trs.* v. *Kirkpatrick* (1874) 1 R. (H.L.) 37, qualified in *Nicol's Trustees* v. *Sutherland,* 1951 S.C. (H.L.) 21.

[18] *London Street Tramways Co.* v. *London C.C.* [1898] A.C. 375. The House of Lords in an English appeal may apply Scots Law, if that is the proper law, even though the Scots law has not been proved in the Court below: *Elliot* v. *Joicey,* 1935 S.C. (H.L.) 57.

[19] Practice Statement (Judicial Precedent) [1966] 1 W.L.R. 1234. See, for example, *Dick* v. *Burgh of Falkirk,* 1976 S.C. 1.

proceeded on grounds of general jurisprudence and not on any specialty of English law, it ought to be treated with great respect.[20] An opinion by a judge on a point not necessary to the judgment (obiter dictum) has an authority varying with the reputation of the judge. A decision clearly in point may be challenged on the ground that it is inconsistent with prior authorities which were not brought to the notice of the Court[21]; that it proceeded upon views of morality, political economy, or religious observance which are no longer held in esteem[22]; that it had as its basis some theory of physical fact which modern science has shown to be baseless[23]; or that a statutory alteration of the law has altered the basis on which the previous decision rested.[24]

21. Res Judicata.—The plea of res judicata means that the question raised has been decided already in an action between the same parties,[25] or between parties in the same interest. It is a preliminary plea, which, if sustained, excludes all consideration of the merits of the case. Where the question raised is one of law, and a prior decision of the House of Lords is in point, the distinction between a plea of res judicata and the argument that the question is settled by authority is one of form rather than of substance. If, however, the prior authority is a decision, or series of decisions, in the Court of Session, then, although neither the Lord Ordinary nor the Division may consider that the question is open in their Courts, it remains open, if the parties to the action are not the same, on an appeal to the House of Lords, whereas, when the parties are the same, and the plea of res judicata is taken, the only question open in any Court is whether the prior case decided the same point which the subsequent case proposes to raise.[26]

Apart from averments of res noviter[27] a decision in favour of the pursuer, if in foro,[28] is res judicata in all cases. A defender is bound to set forth all his defences at once, and an attempt after decree has passed against him to reopen the question on new grounds is met by the plea of competent and omitted.[29] A decree in favour of a defender, if one of dismissal on the ground of irrelevancy or incompetency, is not res judicata.[30] A decree of absolvitor, though res judicata as to any grounds of action which were in question, leaves open an action based on different media concludendi[31] though an opinion of high

---

[20] *Orr Ewing's Trs.* v. *Orr Ewing* (1885) 13 R. (H.L.) 1, per Lord Chancellor Selborne at p. 3; but see *Glasgow Corporation* v. *Central Land Board,* 1956 S.C. (H.L.) 1. See *Dalgleish* v. *Glasgow Corporation* 1976 S.L.T. 157, per Lord Justice-Clerk Wheatley at p. 159.
[21] *Mitchell* v. *Mackersy* (1905) 8 F. 198.
[22] *Bowman* v. *Secular Society* [1917] A.C. 406.
[23] *Welldon* v. *Butterley Coal Co.* [1920] 1 Ch. 130.
[24] *Beith's Trs.* v. *Beith,* 1950 S.C. 66; *Douglas-Hamilton* v. *Duke & Duchess of Hamilton's Trs.,* 1961 S.C. 205, per Lord President Clyde at p. 217.
[25] *Ryan* v. *M'Burnie,* 1940 S.C. 173.
[26] *Duke of Atholl* v. *Glover Incorporation* (1899) 1 F. 658.
[27] See § 22, infra.
[28] *Mackintosh* v. *Smith* (1865) 3 M. (H.L.) 6; see also *Esso Petroleum Co.* v. *Law,* 1956 S.C. 33; *Paterson* v. *Paterson,* 1958 S.C. 141.
[29] Erskine, IV., 3, 3; *Murray* v. *Seath,* 1939 S.L.T. 348.
[30] *Wallace* v. *Braid* (1900) 2 F. 754; *Cunningham* v. *Skinner* (1902) 4 F. 1124.
[31] *Phosphate Sewage Co.* v. *Molleson* (1879) 6 R. (H.L.) 113; *Edinburgh Water Trustees* v. *Clippens Oil Co.* (1899) 1 F. 899; *Weissenbruch* v. *Weissenbruch & Anr.,* 1965 S.L.T. 139.

authority suggests that this rule is confined to actions of reduction[32]; for the purpose of the plea of res judicata, common law negligence and breach of statutory duty are not different media concludendi.[33]

It is probably the law that a decree in the Sheriff Court, if allowed to become final, is res judicata in a subsequent action raised in the Court of Session.[34] A conviction or acquittal in a criminal Court may be res judicata to bar an action or claim in a civil Court, but only where the parties are the same, the ground of action the same and the remedy sought the same,[35] circumstances which can but seldom occur. Neither res judicata nor any analogous plea will preclude an appeal against an entry in the Valuation Roll.[36] No decree can found a plea of res judicata if the Court, in pronouncing it, exceeded its jurisdiction[37]; if it is ultra petita, i.e. beyond the conclusions of the summons; or if it is founded on an error in calculation.[38]

In order to found a plea of res judicata the question in the later case must be the same as that in the earlier.[39] So a decision by a Court which had authority to determine the parties who in right of hereditary offices were entitled to perform services at a coronation was held not to be res judicata when the question of the right to an office was raised in an action of declarator, in respect that it merely determined the right to serve at the coronation immediately in question, and not the right to the office.[40] And the parties in the two actions must either be the same, or must represent the same interest. A decision as to a right of property is res judicata in a question between the heirs or singular successors of the original parties.[41] An action by a beneficiary founded on an alleged breach of trust by the trustees is res judicata in an action by any other beneficiary.[42] A declarator of right of way, which has been tried and decided in an action by a party suing merely as a member of the public, is conclusive in an action raised by any other member of the public.[43] But there is no such community between the various owners of salmon fishings in a river as to render a decision as to the legality of a particular method of fishing res judicata in an action brought against a different owner.[44]

22. Res Noviter.—The plea of res noviter veniens ad notitiam, as a replication to the plea of res judicata, or as a ground for the reduction of a decree, imports that new evidence is tendered, of which the party was not

---

[32] *Glasgow and S.-W. Ry.* v. *Boyd & Forest*, 1918 S.C. (H.L.) 14, opinion of Lord Shaw.
[33] *Matuszczyk* v. *N.C.B.*, 1955 S.C. 418.
[34] *Duke of Sutherland* v. *Reid* (1890) 18 R. 252. See, however, *Anderson* v. *Wilson,* 1972 S.C. 147 (apportionment between joint wrongdoers).
[35] *Young* v. *Mitchell* (1874) 1 R. 1011; *Wilson* v. *Murphy,* 1936 S.L.T. 564.
[36] *Lamont* v. *Assessor for Dumfriesshire* (1900) 2 F. 610.
[37] *Pollock* v. *Thomson* (1858) 21 D. 173.
[38] Erskine III., 3, 3.
[39] *Murray* v. *Seath,* 1939 S.L.T. 348; *Malcolm Muir Ltd.* v. *Jamieson,* 1947 S.C. 314.
[40] *Earl of Lauderdale* v. *Wedderburn,* 1908 S.C. 1237, revd. (on other grounds) 1910 S.C. (H.L.) 35. See also *Burton* v. *Chapel Coal Co.,* 1909 S.C. 430.
[41] Erskine, IV., 3, 3.
[42] *Allen* v. *M'Combie's Trs.,* 1909 S.C. 710.
[43] *Macfie* v. *Scottish Rights of Way Society* (1884) 11 R. 1094.
[44] *Duke of Atholl* v. *Glover Incorporation* (1899) 1 F. 658.

aware at the former trial and which he could not have discovered by the exercise of reasonable diligence.[45] Nothing can be res noviter that was within the power of the party to discover with ordinary care.[46] It would appear that it is not enough to aver that witnesses, who might have given evidence at the previous trial, have been discovered.[47] An averment that a material document, supposed to have been lost, has been discovered is a relevant averment of res noviter if no negligence in the matter can be imputed to the party.[48] It is not enough to aver that a material witness gave evidence contrary to the truth, on the theory that it is the province of the Court to decide on the credibility of the witnesses.[49] But proof of subornation of perjury, or any other preconcerted fraud on the Court, will suffice for the reduction of a decree,[50] provided that proceedings have been taken within a reasonable time after the facts have come to the pursuer's knowledge.[51]

[45] *M'Carroll* v. *M'Kinstery,* 1924 S.C. 396, revd. 1926 S.C. (H.L.) 1.
[46] Per Lord President M'Neill in *Campbell* v. *Campbell* (1865) 3 M. 501, adopted in *M'Carroll* v. *M'Kinstery.* supra.
[47] *Miller* v. *Mac Fisheries,* 1922 S.C. 157.
[48] *M'Carroll* v. *M'Kinstery,* supra.
[49] *Mackintosh's Trs.* v. *Stewart's Trs.* (1906) 8 F. 467; but see *Maltman* v. *Tarmac Civil Engineering Ltd.,* 1967 S.L.T. 141.
[50] *Shedden* v. *Patrick* (1854) 1 Macq. 535; *Mackintosh's Trs.,* supra; *Maltman,* supra.
[51] *Lockyer* v. *Ferryman* (1877) 4 R. (H.L.) 32 (delay of thirty years).

CHAPTER II

COURTS AND JURISDICTION: ARBITRATION

Mackay, *Court of Session Practice* (1879); Mackay, *Manual* (1893); Maclaren, *Court of Session Practice* (1916); Thomson and Middleton, *Manual* (1937); Hannay, *The College of Justice* (1933); Dobie, *Sheriff Court Practice* (1948); Lewis, *Sheriff Court Practice* (8th ed., 1939); Duncan and Dykes, *Jurisdiction* (1911); Gibb, *Jurisdiction* (1926); Bell, *Arbitration* (2nd ed., 1877); Irons and Melville, *Arbitration* (1903); Guild, *Arbitration* (1936); Gow, *Mercantile and Industrial Law of Scotland* (1964), ch. 13; Russell, *Arbitration and Award* (18th ed., 1970); Walker, *Scottish Legal System* (4th ed., 1976); Mitchell, *Constitutional Law* (2nd ed., 1968); Anton, *Private International Law* (1967).

1. House of Lords.—The ultimate appeal, in a civil case originating in Scotland, is to the House of Lords, which has inherited the jurisdiction exercised by the Scots Parliament prior to the Union in 1707. Until 1876 there was no definite distinction between the House of Lords as a legislative and as a judicial body. By the Appellate Jurisdiction Act 1876,[1] provision was made for the appointment of judicial officers, known as Lords of Appeal, and no appeal can be heard unless three of these are present.[2] The Act leaves untouched the right of any Peer of Parliament to sit and vote in any appeal but even before the Act was passed it had been recognised that lay peers should not sit and if they do their votes are not counted.[3] The House of Lords has no original jurisdiction. There is no appeal to it from the High Court of Justiciary.[4] Any final judgment of the Court of Session is subject to appeal, except in cases where appeal is excluded by statute,[5] or where the question is one of expenses only.[6] If the Court of Session, on an appeal from the Sheriff Court, has made findings in fact, appeal to the House of Lords is restricted to questions of law.[7] An interlocutory judgment (i.e. one which does not dispose of the whole cause) may be appealed if the judges were not unanimous, or, in any case, with the leave of the Court.[8] An appeal lies from a judgment of the Court of Session in the exercise of its criminal jurisdiction.[9] By the Standing Orders of the House of Lords no appeal can be received unless it is lodged within three months of the last interlocutor appealed from.

---

[1] 39 & 40 Vict. c. 59, as amended by Appellate Jurisdiction Acts 1913-1947.
[2] s. 5.
[3] Mitchell p. 259.
[4] Criminal Procedure (Scotland) Act 1975 (c. 21), s. 281; *Mackintosh* v. *Lord Advocate,* (1876) 3 R. (H.L.) 34.
[5] e.g., Agricultural Holdings (Scotland) Act 1949, (12, 13 & 14 Geo. VI c. 75), 6 Sched., para. 20; Small Landholders Act 1911 (1 & 2 Geo. V c. 49), s. 25.
[6] *Caledonian Ry* v. *Barrie* (1903) 5 F. (H.L.) 10.
[7] Court of Session Act 1825 (6 Geo. IV c. 120), s. 40. *Bogota* v. *Alconda,* 1924 S.C. (H.L.) 66; *Crerar* v. *Bank of Scotland,* 1922 S.C. (H.L.) 137; *Sutherland* v. *Glasgow Corporation,* 1951 S.C. (H.L.) 1.
[8] Court of Session Act 1808 (48 Geo. III c. 151), s. 15; *Ross* v. *Ross,* 1927 S.C. (H.L.) 4; *Adelphi Hotel (Glasgow)* v. *Walker & Eglinton Hotels (Scotland),* 1960 S.C. 182 (interlocutor granting interim interdict). An appeal now lies, without leave, from an interlocutor granting a motion for a new trial (Administration of Justice (Scotland) Act 1972 (c. 59), s. 2).
[9] *Carse* v. *Lord Advocate* (1784) 3 Paton 1.

2. Privy Council.—In the seventeenth century the Scots Privy Council exercised a supreme jurisdiction in all questions relating to the public peace. It was abolished by 6 Anne, c. 40, and its functions transferred to the Privy Council of Great Britain, which has no jurisdiction of this character. The Privy Council, through its Judicial Committee, exercises a supreme jurisdiction in appeals from Courts in certain Commonwealth countries but has no judicial functions in Scotland, except under particular statutes.[10]

3. Court of Session.—The Court of Session was established in 1532, superseding the jurisdiction of the Lords Auditors, a committee of Parliament, and Courts known as the Session and the Daily Council, of which little is known.[11] As originally constituted it consisted of fourteen ordinary judges, with a President. The King had power to nominate Extraordinary Lords, who might sit and vote, but this power was abolished by 10 Geo. I, c. 19. Until 1808 all the judges sat together in the Inner House as an Appellate Court, sending one of their body by rotation to hear cases as a judge of first instance, known as a Lord Ordinary, in the Outer House. In 1808 and in 1825 the Court was reorganised.[12] It was divided into the First Division, presided over by the Lord President; the Second Division, presided over by the Lord Justice-Clerk, these two divisions constituting the Inner House; and the permanent Lords Ordinary. Since 1830 four judges have sat in each Division, and the remainder (now twelve) as permanent Lords Ordinary in the Outer House. The maximum number of judges who may be appointed is now twenty-two,[13] and the retirement age is seventy-five.[14] The Court of Session, as now existing, is a combination of two Courts—the Inner House, with a jurisdiction mainly appellate, and the Outer House, a Court of first instance. For detailed information as to the jurisdiction of the Court of Session, works devoted to procedure must be consulted.[15] Speaking generally, the Inner House sits as a Court of Appeal from the judgments of the Lords Ordinary or of any inferior civil Court,[16] except in cases where the value, exclusive of interest and expenses, does not exceed £500[17] or where the inferior Court is by statute declared to be final[18]: in the Outer House actions may be brought originally, with the same exception as to cases of small value and excluding certain cases where special statutory procedure is enjoined.[19] The criminal jurisdiction of

---

[10] E.g., Medical Act 1978 (c. 12), s. 11.
[11] See *Acta Dominorum Auditorium* (1496-1501) and Neilson's Introduction, and (1501-1554). Hannay's Introduction.
[12] 48 Geo. III c. 151; 6 Geo. IV c. 120.
[13] Administration of Justice Act 1968 (c. 5), s. 1 (*c*) as amended by Maximum Number of Judges Order 1977 (S.I. 1977/602).
[14] Judicial Pensions Act 1959 (8 & 9 Eliz. II c. 9), s. 2.
[15] See Mackay, *Manual;* Maclaren, *Court of Session Practice.*
[16] Erskine, I., 3 20; *Jeffray* v. *Angus,* 1909 S.C. 400.
[17] Sheriff Courts (Scotland) Act 1971 (c. 58), s. 31; Sheriff Courts (Scotland) Act 1971 (Privative Jurisdiction etc.) Order 1976 (S.I. 1976/900). As to what is meant by "value," see *Brady* v. *Napier,* 1944 S.C. 18.
[18] *Adair* v. *Colville,* 1926 S.C. (H.L.) 51; *Arcari* v. *Dumbartonshire County Council,* 1948 S.C. 62; *Neill's Trustee* v. *Macfarlane's Trustees,* 1952 S.C. 356.
[19] Questions involving important patrimonial interests in Church matters may be outside the purview of the Court of Session: see *Ballantyne* v. *Presbytery of Wigtown,* 1936 S.C. 625.

the Court of Session, which at one time included cases of forgery, is in modern times confined to the imposition of penalties for breach of interdict or other contempt of Court. The High Court of Admiralty (1681-1830), the Court of Exchequer (1707-1854)[20] and the Jury Court (1815-1830) are now merged in the Court of Session.

In addition to its ordinary functions the Court of Session has a general power to review, by suspension or reduction, the judgments of inferior courts or persons vested with judicial or administrative authority, on the ground that they have exceeded the jurisdiction committed to them, have contravened the principles of natural justice, or have been guilty of error in procedure so fundamental as to make their decision a nullity.[21] "Wherever any inferior tribunal or any administrative body has exceeded the powers conferred upon it by statute to the prejudice of the subject, the jurisdiction of the Court to set aside such excess of power as incompetent and illegal is not open to dispute."[22] In considering whether a tribunal has contravened the principles of natural justice, the question before the Court is not whether the tribunal has arrived at a fair result, but whether it has dealt fairly and equally with the parties before it in arriving at that result.[23] Before recourse is had to the Court of Session it must be shown that any remedy provided by the statute by which the tribunal or administrative jurisdiction is founded is inapplicable.[24] The effect of clauses providing that the decision of a particular body shall be final is not free from doubt. It is conceived that a statute may confer finality on the proceedings of an inferior Court or of a statutory body in terms so wide as to exclude any interference by the Court of Session,[25] but in most cases finality clauses are read as applicable exclusively to procedure which is intra vires and regular and do not affect jurisdiction in cases of what have been termed constitutional nullities.[26]

4. High Court of Justiciary.— The High Court of Justiciary, as a supreme criminal Court, was established by the Courts Act 1672 (c. 16).[27] As now constituted, it consists of the Lord President, under the title of Lord Justice-General, the Lord Justice-Clerk and the other judges of the Court of Session.[28] Its permanent session is in Edinburgh, but provision is made for circuit Courts.[29] The High Court of Justiciary has a universal jurisdiction as a Court of first instance in all cases of crime, except where, in the case of minor offences, its original jurisdiction is excluded by statute. It possesses a

[20] See *I.R.* v. *Barrs,* 1961 S.C. (H.L.) 22.
[21] See Mitchell, *Constitutional Law,* pp. 249 et seq; *McDonald* v. *Lanarkshire Fire Brigade Joint Committee,* 1959 S.C. 141.
[22] Per Lord Kinnear, *Moss' Empires* v. *Assessor for Glasgow,* 1917 S.C. (H.L.) 1, at p. 6. See *Cheyne* v. *Architects' Registration Council,* 1943 S.C. 468.
[23] *Barrs* v. *British Wool Marketing Board,* 1957 S.C. 72, per Lord President Clyde at 82.
[24] *Crawford* v. *Lennox* (1852) 14 D 1029; *Lang* v. *Presbytery of Irvine* (1846) 2 M. 823.
[25] See *Adair* v. *Colville,* 1926 S.C. (H.L.) 51.
[26] *Manson* v. *Smith* (1871) 9 M. 492 (Small Debt Court); *Walsh* v. *Magistrates of Pollokshaws,* 1907 S.C. (H.L.) 1, and *Goodall* v. *Bilsland,* 1909 S.C. 1152 (Licensing Court); *Moss' Empires* v. *Assessor for Glasgow,* 1917 S.C. (H.L.) 1 (Valuation Court).
[27] History in Hume on *Crime,* Vol. II., p.1.
[28] Criminal Procedure (Scotland) Act 1975 (c. 21), s. 113 (1).
[29] Ibid., s. 114.

paramount and over-riding authority which has been described as similar to the nobile officium of the Court of Session.[30] When sitting in Edinburgh the Court has at common law jurisdiction to review the decision of inferior criminal Courts where the proceedings have been initiated by complaint and not by indictment.[31] This jurisdiction has been extended by statute [32] but a power which previously existed to bring proceedings on indictment in the Sheriff Court under review by bill of suspension has been abolished.[33] By the Criminal Appeal (Scotland) Act 1926[34] provision was made for an appeal to the High Court sitting as a court of appeal against a conviction obtained on indictment on any question of law or, with the leave of the Court, on a question of fact or of mixed fact and law, or against the sentence pronounced unless it was one fixed by law.[35] The relevant provisions are now in the Criminal Procedure (Scotland) Act 1975.[36] In addition, the High Court has in respect of its nobile officium the power of interfering in extraordinary circumstances, for instance where no other procedure is available for review.[37] Three judges of the High Court constitute the court of appeal.[38] There is no appeal to the House of Lords.[39]

5. Sheriff Court.—The sheriff, as a ministerial and judicial officer, appears in the records of the law of Scotland from the twelfth century. By the eighteenth century the office had in most cases become hereditary. Hereditary jurisdictions were abolished by the Heritable Jurisdictions Scotland Act 1747,[40] under which, though sheriffs could be appointed by the Crown for a period not exceeding one year,[41] their duties were to be performed by a new officer, the sheriff-depute, who must be an advocate of at least three years' standing, and was to hold office ad vitam aut culpam.[42] Sheriffs-substitute were appointed by the sheriffs-depute until 1877[43] but had been definitely recognised as judicial officers paid by the Crown in 1787. The use of the title

---

[30] *Milne* v. *M'Nicol*, 1944 J.C. 151.
[31] Proceedings initiated by complaint are triable summarily by a sheriff or district court justice sitting alone. Proceedings on indictment (solemn procedure) are, on a plea of not guilty, tried by a jury. The common law methods of review, preserved by s. 465 (1) of the 1975 Act, are advocation, suspension and suspension and liberation. Advocation is appropriate to review of a decision, disposing of the case or part of it, made in the preliminary stages of prosecution. It is not competent where a preliminary objection to competency or relevancy has been repelled (*Aldred* v. *Strathern*, 1929 J.C. 93) and so is normally of service only to the prosecutor. Suspension or suspension and liberation is appropriate where an illegal warrant, conviction or judgment is impugned. The grounds extend to lack of jurisdiction or title to prosecute, irrelevancy or incompetency of the complaint and oppression on the part of the judge including oppressive sentence (*Ferguson* v. *Brown*, 1942 S.C. 113) but not to the merits of a conviction (*Dunn* v. *Mitchell*, 1911 S.C. (J) 46; cf. *Paterson* v. *Macpherson*, 1926 J.C. 38).
[32] 1975 Act, s. 442, re-enacting Summary Jurisdiction (Scotland) Act 1954 (2 & 3 Eliz. II c. 48) s. 62 which enables inter alia a limited review of the merits of a conviction by way of stated case.
[33] 1975 Act, s. 230, re-enacting Criminal Appeal (Scotland) Act 1926, s. 13.
[34] 16 & 17 Geo. V c. 15.
[35] 1975 (c. 21), s. 228, see *Webb* v. *H.M. Advocate*, 1927 S.C. 92.
[36] 1975 (c.21).
[37] *Wylie* v. *H.M. Advocate*, 1966 S.L.T. 149.
[38] Ib., s. 245 (1).
[39] *Mackintosh* v. *Lord Advocate*, (1876) 3 R. (H.L.) 34; 1975 Act, s. 281.
[40] 20 Geo. II c. 43.
[41] Ib., s. 5.
[42] Ib., s. 29.
[43] 40 & 41 Vict. c. 50, s. 4.

sheriff was authorised for the sheriff-depute by the Sheriff Courts (Scotland) Act 1825[44] and in 1971 he was, in accordance with what had become common usage, designated sheriff principal.[45] At the same time the title of sheriff-substitute, for long a misnomer, was replaced by sheriff.[45] No one may be appointed to the office of sheriff principal or sheriff unless he is an advocate or solicitor of at least ten years' standing.[46] The word "sheriff" includes sheriff principal unless otherwise provided or the context is repugnant to the construction.[47] Sheriffs principal and sheriffs are required to retire at the age of seventy-two.[48]

The civil jurisdiction of the Sheriff Court, as extended by the Sheriff Court Acts of 1876, 1907 and 1913, extends to nearly all actions. The leading exceptions are actions involving status (divorce, declarator of marriage, questions of legitimacy),[49] reductions, petitions for the winding up of a company if the paid-up capital exceeds £120,000,[50] suspension of charges where the debt exceeds £50[51] and actions for proving the tenor of a lost document.[52] In the case of actions involving questions of heritable right or title, divisions of commonty or division of common property, where the amount in question exceeds £50 a year, or £1,000, either party may, within six days of the closing of the record, require the sheriff to remit the case to the Court of Session;[53] otherwise the Sheriff's jurisdiction over actions of debt or damages is without pecuniary limit. In cases which are competent in the Sheriff Court and where the value, exclusive of interest and expenses, does not exceed £500 the jurisdiction of the sheriff is privative, i.e., such cases can neither be brought originally in the Court of Session nor, unless otherwise provided in the Act, taken there by appeal.[54]

"Summary cause" procedure is applicable to all actions for payment of money not exceeding £500, exclusive of interest and expenses, to multiple poindings, furthcomings and sequestrations for rent where the subject matter does not exceed £500 in value and to actions ad factum praestandum and actions for the recovery of heritable or moveable property unless there is an alternative or additional crave for payment of a sum exceeding £500.[55] The sheriff also has jurisdiction to deal in a summary manner with a wide range of common law and statutory applications to which the "summary application" procedure applies.[56] This procedure is entirely distinct from and unconnected with the "summary cause".

44 6 Geo. IV c. 23.
45 Sheriff Courts (Scotland) Act 1971 (c. 58), s. 4 (1).
46 Ib., s. 5 (1).
47 Interpretation Act 1978 (c. 30), Sch. 1.
48 Sheriffs' Pensions (Scotland) Act 1961, (9 & 10 Eliz. II c. 42) s. 6.
49 Actions of declarator of death under s. 1 of the Presumption of Death (Scotland) Act 1977 (c. 27), are, however, competent in the Sheriff Court (Ibid. Sch. 1).
50 Companies Act 1948 (11 & 12 Geo. VI c. 38), s. 220 (3) as amended by Insolvency Act 1976 (c. 60), s. 1 & Sch. 1, Pt. I.
51 Sheriff Courts (Scotland) Act 1907, s. 5 (5); Pettie v. Broadbent Finance (Leeds), 1970 S.L.T. (Sh Ct.) 70.
52 Dunbar v. Scottish County Investment Co., 1920, 1 S.L.T. 136.
53 Sheriff Courts (Scotland) Act 1907, s. 5.
54 Ib., s. 7, as amended by 1971 Act, ss. 31, 35 and 41 and S.I. 1976/900.
55 1971 Act, ss. 35 (1) and 41 and S.I 1976/900.
56 1907 Act, ss. 3 (p), 50; Dobie, Sheriff Court Practice, p.101.

The judgment of a sheriff in his ordinary Court may be appealed to the sheriff principal[57] unless such appeal is excluded by statute. If the cause is not a summary cause or application the appeal may be either to the sheriff principal[57], from whom an appeal lies to the Court of Session, or directly to the Inner House of the Court of Session.[58] To render an appeal to the Court of Session competent, the judgment of the sheriff principal[57] or sheriff must either be final, or be an interlocutor granting interim decree for payment of money other than a decree for expenses, or sisting an action, or refusing a reponing note. In other cases the leave of the sheriff principal or sheriff, as the case may be, to appeal is required.[59] In summary causes appeal is competent only against a final judgment and only on a point of law. The appeal from the sheriff is to the sheriff principal from whose judgment there may be an appeal to the Court of Session only if he certifies the cause as suitable.[60] In a summary application at common law appeal to the sheriff principal and, subject to the value rule, to the Court of Session is competent but in statutory summary applications review is often restricted or excluded by the statute under which the application is brought.[61] In cases originating in the Sheriff Court, other than claims by employees against employers in respect of injury arising out of and in the course of their employment and concluding for damages where the claim is in amount or value above £500 and an order has been pronounced allowing proof, it is competent to either party, who may conceive that the case ought to be tried by jury, to require the case to be remitted to the Court of Session for jury trial.[62]

In criminal matters the sheriff principal or sheriff is a competent judge in all crimes except treason, murder, attempt to murder, and rape. The Sheriff Court and the High Court have between them an inherent universal jurisdiction which can only be restricted or excluded by the express provision or clear implication of a statute.[63] In respect that a sheriff cannot inflict a penalty exceeding two years' imprisonment it is a question of the gravity of the alleged offence whether criminal proceedings should be taken in the Sheriff Court or in the High Court of Justiciary.

6. District Courts.—By the District Courts (Scotland) Act 1975 the Justice of the Peace Courts, Burgh Courts and Police Courts (which had until then exercised a petty criminal, and, in the case of the justices of the peace, a very limited civil, jurisdiction) were abolished and replaced by District Courts.[64] There is a District Court for each local authority district or islands area[65] and

---

[57] Ib., s. 27.
[58] Appeal to the Court of Session will, however, be subject to the value rule (see supra § 3 and footnote 17). Not every action under £500 in value is a summary cause (see 1971 Act, s. 35 (1)).
[59] Sheriff Courts (Scotland) Act 1907, s. 28 as amended by Sheriff Courts Act, 1913.
[60] 1971 Act, s. 38.
[61] See Dobie, *Sheriff Court Practice*, pp. 102, 305 & 533 ff.
[62] 1907 Act, s. 30 as amended by 1971 Act, ss. 39 & 41 and S.I. 1976/900. In claims by employees the jury trial may be held before the sheriff (s. 31 as amended by 1971 Act, ss. 40 & 41 and S.I. 1976/900).
[63] See *Blythswood Taxis* v. *Adair*, 1944 J.C. at p. 140; *Wilson* v. *Hill*, 1943 J.C. 124.
[64] 1975, c. 20, s.1.
[65] Ibid., ss. 1 and 26 (1).

its jurisdiction and powers are exercisable by one or more lay justices or by a stipendiary magistrate, where appointed, who must be an advocate or solicitor of at least five years' standing.[66] The jurisdiction and powers are those possessed by the former courts[67] and are restricted to the trial of offences summarily. But s. 285 of the Criminal Procedure (Scotland) Act 1975[68] gives a list of offences, covering most common law offences of other than a very minor character, which are excluded from the competence of the District Court. And it is a general principle that statutory offences cannot be tried by courts such as the District Court, unless jurisdiction is conferred upon them by statute, either expressly or by implication.[69] The maximum sentence which can be imposed is 60 days' imprisonment and a fine not exceeding £200.[70] These restrictions, however, only apply to the Court when it is composed of lay justices. A stipendiary magistrate has the summary criminal jurisdiction and powers of a sheriff.[71]

7. Other Courts.[72]—*The Court of the Lord Lyon:* The Lord Lyon King of Arms has jurisdiction, subject to appeal to the Court of Session and the House of Lords, in questions of heraldry, and the right to bear arms.[73] He has no jurisdiction to determine rights of precedence,[74] nor to decide a disputed question of chiefship or chieftainship.[75]

The Scottish Land Court: This Court was set up in 1911 with judicial functions under the statutes which relate to agricultural land and small holdings and crofts.[76] It consists of a legally qualified chairman, who has the status of a judge of the Court of Session, and a panel of lay members who are experienced in agriculture; one of the members must be a Gaelic speaker.[77]

The Lands Valuation Appeal Court: This Court, which consists of three judges of the Court of Session, sits to dispose of appeals on rating questions from local Valuation Appeal Committees.[78] Appeals come before it on questions of law by way of a stated case, which is final on the facts stated in it.

---

[66] Ibid., ss. 2 (2) and 5 (2).
[67] Ibid., s. 3 (1). The civil jurisdiction of the former justice of the peace courts and quarter sessions is, however, excluded.
[68] 1975, c. 21.
[69] *Macpherson* v. *Boyd.* 1907 S.C. (J.) 42.
[70] 1975, c. 21, s. 284 as amended by Criminal Law Act 1977, s. 63 and Sch. 11, § 2.
[71] 1975, c. 20, s. 3 (2). The reconciliation of this subsection with s. 285 of the Criminal Procedure (Scotland) Act 1975 is not, however, free from difficulty.
[72] See Walker, *Scottish Legal System* (4th ed.) p. 221 et seq. Note also the increasing number of tribunals which have been set up to deal with administrative matters, e.g. transport licensing, industrial injuries compensation, redundancy payments.
[73] *Hunter* v. *Weston* (1882) 9 R. 492; *Mackenzie* v. *Mackenzie,* 1920 S.C. 764, affd. 1922 S.C. (H.L.) 39.
[74] *Royal College of Surgeons* v. *Royal College of Physicians,* 1911 S.C. 1054.
[75] *Maclean of Ardgour* v. *Maclean,* 1938 S.L.T. 49; and see 1941 S.C. 613.
[76] See Leases, Ch. XXXIII., infra. § 31.
[77] Small Landholders (Scotland) Act 1911 (1 & 2 Geo. V c. 49) s. 3; amended by Agriculture (Scotland) Act 1948, (11 & 12 Geo. VI c. 45) s. 70 (1).
[78] See Armour, *Valuation for Rating,* 3rd ed., pp. 44 et seq.

No appeal lies from the decisions of this Court either to the Court of Session or the House of Lords.

The Restrictive Practices Court: A special United Kingdom court was established by the Restrictive Trade Practices Act 1956, to examine restrictive agreements and prohibit those found to be contrary to the public interest.[79] Its jurisdiction was widened by the Resale Prices Act 1964, to include the determination of whether particular classes of goods should be exempted from the provisions of that Act. Jurisdiction and powers are now governed by the Restrictive Trade Practices Act 1976[80] and Resale Prices Act 1976[81] and composition and procedure by the Restrictive Practices Court Act 1976.[82] The Court consists of five judges, one being a judge of the Court of Session nominated by the Lord President, and not more than ten other, lay, members. The quorum is three, consisting of a presiding judge and at least two other members, and the Court may sit as a single court or in two or more divisions. In Scotland an appeal on any question of law lies to the Court of Session.

Church Courts:[83] Kirk Sessions, Presbyteries, and the General Assembly of the Church of Scotland are established courts of the realm. They now, however, have only a domestic jurisdiction over members of the Church on matters affecting Church discipline, membership, doctrine and ritual.

European Courts:[84] Where questions regarding the interpretation of Community treaties or the validity and interpretation of measures taken by institutions of the European Economic Community, Euratom and the European Coal and Steel Community are raised before a court or tribunal and a decision on the question is necessary to enable the court or tribunal to give judgment it may and, if there is under the national law no possibility of appeal from its judgment, must request the Court of Justice of the European Communities to give a preliminary ruling. The ruling given on such a request is binding.

Complaints may be made to the European Commission on Human Rights in respect of a violation of rights protected by the European Convention on Human Rights. After examination by the Commission and in the event of failure of attempts at a friendly settlement, the case may be referred to the European Court of Human Rights. Reference to the Court may be made at the instance of the Commission or of a state which is a party to the Convention if (1) a national of that state is alleged to be a victim, or (2) it was

[79] See Pacta Illicita, Ch. IX., infra, § 14.
[80] 1976 (c. 34).
[81] 1976 (c. 53).
[82] 1976 (c. 33).
[83] Walker; *Scottish Legal System* (4th ed.) pp. 246 and 247.
[84] European Communities Act 1972 (c. 68), s. 2: EEC Treaty, art. 177: Euratom Treaty, art. 150: ECSC Treaty art. 41; Acts of Sederunt (Rules of Court Amendment Nos. 5 and 6) 1972; Act of Adjournal (Reference to the European Court) 1973; Act of Sederunt (Sheriff Court Procedure Amendment No. 2) 1973; Jacobs & Durand, *Reference to the European Court* (1975): Brownlie, *Basic Documents on Human Rights* (1971); Jacobs. *The European Convention on Human Rights* (1975); Beddard, *Human Rights and Europe* (1973)

at the instance of that state that the case was referred to the commission, or
(3) it is against that state that the complaint is made. Although individuals
may complain to the Commission they cannot institute a reference to the
Court. Execution of the judgments of the Court is entrusted to the committee
of ministers of the Council of Europe.

8. Children's Hearings.[85]—Children's hearings were created by the Social
Work (Scotland) Act 1968. They have no power to determine disputed
questions of law or fact and are not in any proper sense courts but rather
agencies entrusted with the determination of whether children referred to them
are in need of compulsory measures of care and the application of such care
by means of supervision requirements. Such conditions may be imposed in a
supervision requirement as the hearing thinks fit, including a residential
condition, and the child may be required to reside in a school or other
institution registered with the local authority or Secretary of State for the
purposes of the Act. The hearings also have certain advisory functions in
relation to children and young persons brought before courts. A child may be
in need of compulsory measures of care if any of the grounds mentioned in
section 32 of the Act are satisfied. These grounds include the commission of an
offence by the child, as well as those which formerly fell within the care and
protection jurisdiction of juvenile courts, and the hearings have, accordingly,
very largely replaced the functions of the courts so far as the measures to be
adopted in the case of juvenile offenders are concerned. The decision on
whether to refer a child to a hearing is taken by an officer known as the
Reporter. The hearing consists of a chairman and two members selected from
the Children's Panel which must be formed under the Act for every local
authority area. If the grounds on which the child is referred are disputed or
are not understood by the child, the hearing, unless it discharges the referral,
must direct the Reporter to apply to the sheriff for a finding on whether the
grounds are established. An appeal lies to the sheriff at the instance of the
child or its parents against any decision of a Children's Hearing and from the
sheriff's decision on such an appeal, or on a finding as to whether the grounds
of referral are established, an appeal lies at the instance of the child, its
parents or the Reporter to the Court of Session by way of stated case on a
point of law.

9. Tribunals.[86]—Numerous tribunals have been set up under statutory
authority for the determination of particular disputes. For the most part, these
are concerned with the exercise of ministerial powers or the administration of
statutory or governmental schemes in a judicial or quasi-judicial manner and
as such fall outwith the scope of this book. Some, however, of which the most

---

[85] See Social Work (Scotland) Act 1968 Parts III and IV, ss. 30 to 68. *Kennedy* v. *B.*, 1973 S.L.T.
39; *H.* v. *McGregor*, 1973 S.L.T. 110; *B.* v. *Sinclair*, 1973 S.L.T. (Sh. Ct) 47; *B.* v. *Kennedy*,
1974 S.L.T. 168; *H.* v. *Mearns*, 1974 S.L.T. 184; *K.* v. *Finlayson*, 1974 S.L.T. (Sh. Ct.) 51;
McGregor v. *T.*, 1975 S.L.T. 76.
[86] Tribunals and Inquiries Act 1971 (c. 41); Walker; *Scottish Legal System* (4th ed.) pp. 223 to 236
and 238 to 241. Hepple & O'Higgins, *Employment Law* (2nd ed. 1976) Chs. 4 and 22.

notable are Industrial Tribunals, have a function which is indistinguishable from that of courts in resolving, within the area of their competence, legal disputes between citizens.

Industrial Tribunals were set up under the Industrial Training Act 1964 but now have an extensive jurisdiction, far exceeding that originally envisaged, under inter alia the Equal Pay Act 1970, Sex Discrimination Act 1975, and the Employment Protection (Consolidation) Act 1978. They consist of a legally qualified chairman who must be an advocate or solicitor of at least seven years' standing and two lay members, one of whom is chosen from a panel of persons nominated after consultation with organisations representative of employers and the other after similar consultation with organisations representative of employed persons. An appeal lies from decisions of the tribunal to the Employment Appeal Tribunal which consists of a Judge of the Court of Session and Judges of the High Court in England nominated for the purpose and of appointed members with special knowledge or experience of industrial relations either as representatives of employers or of workers. Appeals, which must be confined to questions of law, are heard by a judge with two or four appointed members. A further appeal lies on a question of law to the Court of Session and House of Lords. ˎ

The Lands Tribunal for Scotland consists partly of legally qualified persons (one of whom is President) and partly of persons with experience in the valuation of land. Its functions include the assessment of compensation for compulsory purchase of land and the variation and discharge of obligations affecting land.[87]

The working of virtually all tribunals is kept under review by the Council on Tribunals which has advisory and consultative functions in relation to them.

10. Jurisdiction over Persons.—Jurisdiction, in relation to the persons over whom it is exercised, has been defined as "a power conferred on a judge or magistrate to determine debateable questions according to law, and to carry his sentences into execution."[88] It is not, however, an absolute rule that the Scottish Courts will refuse to pronounce a decree which cannot be carried into execution[89]; and in many cases they exercise their jurisdiction where their decree can be enforced only by proceedings in the Courts of some other country.[90] The maxim "actor sequitur forum rei" imports that no action can be entertained unless the Court has jurisdiction over the defender, but there may be jurisdiction without power to enforce the decree. It is now competent to sue the Crown for damages in respect of the negligence of its servants.[91] There are now substantial exceptions to the former rule that no Scottish Court has jurisdiction to entertain a case against a foreign sovereign State, unless its

[87] Lands Tribunal Act 1949 (c. 42); Land Compensation (Scotland) Act 1963 (c. 51) Pt II; Conveyancing and Feudal Reform (Scotland) Act 1970 (c. 35) Pt I; The Lands Tribunal for Scotland Rules 1971, (S.I. 1971 No. 218).
[88] Erskine, I., 2, 2. See Duncan and Dykes, *Civil Jurisdiction.*
[89] *Sons of Temperance Friendly Society,* 1926 S.C. 418.
[90] E.g. when jurisdiction is founded on arrestments to found jurisdiction, infra, § 14.
[91] Crown Proceedings Act 1947, s. 2.

immunity is departed from.[92] The immunity of ambassadors and other members of a diplomatic mission[93] includes the chief representatives of Commonwealth countries and their staffs, and now extends to chief representatives of states or provinces of a country within the Commonwealth, to consular officers and persons in the service of Commonwealth governments or the government of the Republic of Ireland performing duties of a consular nature, and to other persons on whom it may be conferred by Order in Council.[94] It may also be conferred by Order in Council on certain international organisations and persons connected with them.[95] Under the Visiting Forces Act 1952,[96] restrictions are placed on the power of United Kingdom courts to try members of visiting forces, as defined.

11. Court of Session: Actions involving Status.—The jurisdiction of the Court of Session over persons depends on the nature of the action. In actions of divorce and of separation and in declarators of marriage, of nullity of marriage and of freedom and putting to silence the Court of Session has jurisdiction if either of the parties to the marriage is domiciled in Scotland at the date when the action is begun or has been habitually resident in Scotland throughout the preceding year.[97] In declarators of marriage and of nullity of marriage it has, in addition, jurisdiction if either of the parties to the marriage is dead and was at death domiciled in Scotland or throughout the year preceding death was habitually resident there.[98] In declarators of death there is jurisdiction if the missing person was domiciled in Scotland on the date on which he was last known to be alive or had been habitually resident there throughout the preceding year or if, in an action at the instance of his spouse, the spouse is at the date of raising the action domiciled in Scotland or has been habitually resident there throughout the preceding year.[99] The Court of Session has jurisdiction to entertain an action for reduction of a decree granted by a Scottish court in any consistorial proceedings without the necessity of any further ground of jurisdiction.[1] In an action for custody of children the Court of Session where it is the Court of the domicile has pre-eminent jurisdiction.[2] Where it has jurisdiction in an action of divorce it has

---

92 State Immunity Act 1978 (c. 33). *Govt. of the Republic of Spain* v. *National Bank of Scotland*, 1939 S.C. 413; *Grangemouth and Forth Towing Co.* v. *Netherlands E.I. Govt.*, 1942 S.L.T. 228.
93 Diplomatic Privileges Act 1964 (c. 81) which gave effect to the Vienna Convention on Diplomatic Privileges, 1961. Note that members of the administrative and technical staff are liable civilly, and members of the service staff are liable both criminally and civilly for acts performed outside the course of their duties.
94 Consular Relations Act 1968 (c. 18) as amended by Diplomatic and other Privileges Act 1971 (c. 64). Cf. Diplomatic Immunities (Conferences with Commonwealth Countries and Republic of Ireland) Act 1961 (9 & 10 Eliz. II c. 11). Reference must be made to the statutes for details of the extent of immunity, the conferral and withdrawal of which are, in some cases, subject to resolution by Order in Council.
95 International Organisations Act 1968 (c. 48).
96 15 & 16 Geo. VI and 1 Eliz. II c. 67.
97 Domicile and Matrimonial Proceedings Act 1973 (c. 45), s. 7 (1), (2) & (3) (*a*) & (*b*).
98 Ibid.. s. 7 (3) ().
99 Presumption of Death (Scotland) Act 1977, s. 1 (2).
1 1973 Act, s. 9.
2 *Kitson* v. *Kitson*, 1945 S.C. 434; *M'Lean* v. *M'Lean*, 1947 S.C. 79; *Babington* v. *Babington*, 1955 S.C. 115.

jurisdiction in questions relating to the custody of the children.[3] It may also assume jurisdiction where there is reason to apprehend immediate danger to a child in Scotland or to enforce the order for custody of a competent court.[4] Where the Scottish Courts have pre-eminent jurisdiction regarding custody they will only decline it, if ever, on very strong grounds.[5]

12. General Grounds of Jurisdiction.—In actions where no question as to the status of the parties, as married or unmarried, legitimate or illegitimate, is involved, domicile of origin in Scotland, even when combined with personal citation, is not a general ground of jurisdiction over a defender who has acquired a domicile abroad.[6] And Scottish domicile alone, without personal service in Scotland is not sufficient, even if the action relates to a contract to be performed in Scotland, or to a wrong committed there.[7]

The two general grounds upon which the Court of Session has jurisdiction over a particular individual are—(1) that he is resident in Scotland and (2) that he is the owner of heritable property in Scotland. Residence is a ground of jurisdiction over all persons ordinarily resident in Scotland, or persons who have been resident for forty days.[8] And residence means actual and not constructive residence.[9] In the case of a partnership or company the equivalent to residence is having a place of business[10] in Scotland, not merely having an agent there, if that agent has no power to bind his principal.[11] Jurisdiction is established over a friendly society if its rules are registered in Scotland.[12] Ownership of, or a leasehold interest in, heritable property in Scotland will subject the owner to the jurisdiction of the Court of Session although the action may have no relation to that property.[13]

13. Grounds of Jurisdiction in Particular Cases.—In particular cases other grounds of jurisdiction may be applicable. In actions relating to a contract to be performed in Scotland personal citation of the defender in Scotland will found jurisdiction.[14] A similar rule, with the same necessity for personal service in Scotland, applied at common law to actions of damages for a wrong committed in Scotland.[15] By the Law Reform (Jurisdiction in Delict) (Scotland) Act 1971 the need for personal service in Scotland is abolished and

---

[3] See *Battaglia* v. *Battaglia*, 1967 S.L.T. 49; 1973 Act, s. 10 and Sch. 2, Pt. I, § 4.
[4] *McShane* v. *McShane*, 1962 S.L.T. 221; *Oludimu* v. *Oludimu*, 1967 S.L.T. 105.
[5] *Babington* v. *Babington*, supra.
[6] *Tasker* v. *Grieve* (1905) 8 F. 45.
[7] *Kerr* v. *Ferguson*, 1931 S.C. 736, overruling *Corporation of Glasgow* v. *Johnston*, 1915 S.C. 555.
[8] Erskine, I., 2, 16; *Joel* v. *Gill* (1859) 21 D. 929; *Martin* v. *Szyska*, 1943 S.C. 203. The jurisdiction afforded by forty days' residence ceases immediately on the defender's ceasing to reside in Scotland; see M'Laren. *Court of Session Practice*, p. 36; *Carter* v. *Allison*, 1967 S.L.T. 17.
[9] *Findlay* v. *Donnachie*, 1944 S.C. 306; *Carter* v. *Allison*, supra.
[10] See *O'Brien* v. *Davies & Son*, 1961 S.L.T. 85.
[11] *Laidlaw Provident, etc., Insurance Co.* (1890) 17 R. 544.
[12] *Sons of Temperance Friendly Society* 1926 S.C. 418.
[13] *Ferrie* v. *Woodward* (1831) 9 S. 854; *Fraser* v. *Fraser & Hibbert* (1870) 8 M. 400; *Smith* v. *Stuart* (1894) 22 R. 130; *Thorburn* v. *Dempster* (1900) 2 F. 583.
[14] *Sinclair* v. *Smith* (1860) 22 D, 1475; *Dallas & Co.* v. *M'Ardle*, 1949 S.C. 481.
[15] *Kermich* v. *Watson* (1871) 9 M. 984; *Corporation of Glasgow* v. *Johnston*, 1915 S.C. 555. The actual decision in *Johnston* was overruled in *Kerr* v. *Ferguson*, 1931 S.C. 736.

the Court of Session has jurisdiction in any proceedings founded on delict, and not within the privative jurisdiction of the Sheriff Court, if the cause of action was committed in Scotland.[16] The Courts have moreover power to interdict the commission of any wrongful act within their territory, though there may be no other ground of jurisdiction over the party interdicted.[17] A person who has no fixed place of residence is subject to the jurisdiction of the Court of Session if he is personally cited in Scotland.[18]

14. Arrestments to Found Jurisdiction.—The mere possession of moveable property in Scotland does not afford jurisdiction. But, under the process known as arrestment to found jurisdiction, if moveable property belonging to the defender (e.g., a ship) or a debt due to him in Scotland, is arrested, under a warrant from the Court of Session or from the Sheriff Court, he is subjected to the jurisdiction of the Courts in Scotland in the action in respect of which the arrestments are used.[19] This applies only to actions with conclusions for payment of money or delivery of an article, not to actions affecting status, nor to a bare declarator or reduction.[20] Nor is it a process which will found jurisdiction in a petition for sequestration.[21] An arrestment to found jurisdiction has no effect except to found jurisdiction in the particular case; it does not give any nexus over the subject arrested, nor does it interpel the arrestee from paying the debt.[22] But the subject arrested must be one which could be arrested in execution.[23]

15. Reconvention.—Where a party raises an action in the Court of Session he thereby submits himself to its jurisdiction in any counter action relating to the same dispute, as, for instance, in the case of cross actions arising from a collision between two ships.[24] He does not subject himself to the jurisdiction in an action relating to a separate question.[25] Reconvention will apply even although the action by the foreigner may not be the first in date.[26] It is not pleadable after the actio conventionis has been finally decided, though it may technically still be in Court.[27] In order that jurisdiction may be founded on reconvention the foreigner must have sought the Scottish Courts voluntarily. Where an Englishwoman, not otherwise subject to the jurisdiction, brought a suspension of a threatened charge on a bill it was held that she had not subjected herself to the jurisdiction of the Court of Session in an action for

---

[16] 1971 (c. 55), s. 1.
[17] *Toni Tyres* v. *Palmer Tyres* (1905) 7 F. 477.
[18] *Linn* v. *Cassadinos* (1881) 8 R. 849.
[19] See form of warrants in M'Laren, *Court of Session Practice*, Ch. II. A right to expenses may be arrested to found jurisdiction: *Agnew* v. *Norwest Construction Co.*, 1935 S.C. 771.
[20] *Morley* v. *Jackson* (1888) 16 R. 78; *Williams* v. *Royal College* (1897) 5 S.L.T. 208.
[21] *Croil, Petr.* (1863) 1 M. 509.
[22] *Leggat Bros* v. *Gray*, 1908 S.C. 67; *Fraser-Johnston Engineering Co.*, v. *Jeffs*, 1920 S.C. 222.
[23] *Leggat Bros.* supra; as to arrestability, see Diligence, Ch. XLVIII, infra, § 9.
[24] *Morrison & Milne* v. *Massa* (1886) 5 M. 130. Even a sovereign State by invoking the Scottish Court exposes itself to any lawful defence: see *Government of the Republic of Spain* v. *National Bank of Scotland*, 1939 S.C. 413, and cases there cited.
[25] *Thompson* v. *Whitehead* (1862) 24 D. 331.
[26] *Morrison & Milne* v. *Massa* (1866) 5 M. 130.
[27] *Hurst, Nelson & Co.* v. *Whatley*, 1912 S.C. 1041.

payment of the amount due on the bill, in respect that her proceedings were not voluntary but taken in self-defence.[28]

16. Prorogation.—Jurisdiction may arise from prorogation. If a person submits himself to a Court, either by express prior agreement,[29] or by appearing in answer to a citation without taking the plea of no jurisdiction before the record is closed,[30] he cannot afterwards take the objection that the Court in question has no jurisdiction over him. Prorogation will not obviate the objection of want of jurisdiction in an action of divorce.[31] In any case prorogation only meets the objection that the Court has no jurisdiction over the particular defender, not the objection that the case is one which the Court, at common law or by statute, has no power to entertain. "No parties can convey to a Court jurisdiction which does not belong to it".[32] It has been held in the Outer House that the Court might decline to accept jurisdiction, founded on a clause of prorogation, in an undefended case where neither the parties nor the matter in dispute had any connection with Scotland.[33] Any provision in a contract for the sale of an article whereby any party prorogates the jurisdiction of a particular Sheriff Court is void.[34] The same result is achieved in the case of consumer credit agreements,[35] including hire purchase agreements,[36] and consumer hire agreements[37] by the Consumer Credit Act 1974 which provides that no Court other than the Sheriff Court where the debtor or hirer resides or carries on business shall have jurisdiction to enforce at the instance of the creditor or owner such an agreement or any security relating to it or to enforce against the debtor or hirer or his relative any linked transactions.[38]

17. Jurisdiction of Sheriff Court.—The law as to the jurisdiction of the Sheriff Court depends upon s. 6 of the Sheriff Courts (Scotland) Act 1907, as amended by the Sheriff Courts (Scotland) Act 1913.[39] A sheriff has jurisdiction, in actions competent in the Sheriff Court—(a) Where the defender (or where there are several defenders over each of whom a Sheriff Court has jurisdiction in terms of the Act, where one of them) resides[40] within the jurisdiction, or, having resided there for at least forty days, has ceased to reside there for less

---

[28] *Davis* v. *Cadman* (1897) 24 R. 297; see also *Macaulay* v. *Hussain*, 1967 S.L.T. 311.
[29] *Elderslie S.S. Co.* v. *Burrell* (1895) 22 R. 389; *Lawrence* v. *Taylor*, 1934 S.L.T. 76 (prorogation by agreement to arbitrate in Scotland).
[30] *Fraser-Johnston Engineering Co.* v. *Jeffs*, 1920 S.C. 222.
[31] Fraser, *Husband and Wife*, II., 1294; but see *A.B.* v. *C.D.*, 1957 S.C. 415, cross-actions of nullity and declarator of marriage.
[32] Per Lord Brougham, *Forest* v. *Harvey*, 1845, 4 Bell's App. 197.
[33] *Styring* v. *Borough of Oporovec*, 1931 S.L.T. 493.
[34] Law Reform (Miscellaneous Provisions) (Scotland) Act 1940 (3 & 4 Geo. VI c. 42), s. 4; cf. *English* v. *Donnelly*, 1958 S.C. 494.
[35] 1974 (c. 39) s. 8 (2).
[36] Ibid., ss. 8 (2) & 9 (3).
[37] Ibid., s. 15.
[38] Ibid., s. 141 (3).
[39] 7 Edw. VII c. 51; 2 & 3 Geo. V c. 28.
[40] There must be actual residence: *Findlay* v. *Donachie*, 1944 S.C. 306; *M'Cord* v. *M'Cord*, 1946 S.C. 198. The material date for determining the question of jurisdiction is the date of citation: *M'Neill* v. *M'Neill*, 1960 S.C. 30.

than forty days, and has no known residence in Scotland. (*b*) Where the defender carries on business, and has a place of business, within the jurisdiction, and is cited either personally or at such place of business.[41] (*c*) Where the defender is a person not otherwise subject to the jurisdiction of the Courts of Scotland; and a ship or vessel of which he is owner or part owner or master, or goods, debts, money or other moveable property belonging to him have been arrested within the jurisdiction.[42] (*d*) Where the defender is the owner or part owner or tenant or joint tenant whether individually or as a trustee, of heritable property within the jurisdiction, and the action relates to such property or to his interest therein. (*e*) Where the action is for interdict against an alleged wrong being committed or threatened to be committed within the jurisdiction. (*f*) Where the action relates to a contract the place of execution or performance of which is within the jurisdiction, and the defender is personally cited there. (*g*) Where in an action of furthcoming or multiplepoinding the fund or subject in medio is situated within the jurisdiction; or the arrestee or holder of the fund is subject to the jurisdiction of the Court. (*h*) Where the party sued is the pursuer in any action pending within the jurisdiction against the party suing.[43] (*i*) Where the action is founded on delict and the delict forming the cause of action was committed within the sheriffdom.[44] (*j*) Where the defender prorogates the jurisdiction of the Court.[45] A sheriff has jurisdiction in an action of separation, or separation and aliment, if the requirements of domicile or habitual residence in Scotland are satisfied and either party to the marriage was resident in the sheriffdom for forty days preceding the raising of the action or was so resident for a period of at least forty days ending within forty days of the raising of the action and has, when the action is raised, no known residence in Scotland.[46] In an action of adherence or aliment, or interim aliment, he has jurisdiction if the husband resides in England or Northern Ireland, the parties last ordinarily resided together as man and wife in Scotland and the wife resides within the jurisdiction of the sheriff.[47] He also has jurisdiction in an action of affiliation and aliment if the alleged father resides in England or Northern Ireland, the intercourse founded on took place in Scotland and the mother resides within the jurisdiction of the sheriff.[48]

18. Forum Non Conveniens.—Either the Court of Session or the Sheriff Court may decline to exercise jurisdiction in a particular case on the plea of forum non conveniens, or, as it is stated in the earlier cases, forum non competens. The proper English equivalent of either term is, it has been laid

---

[41] *Bruce* v. *British Motor Trading Co.*, 1924 S.C. 908; *Hay's Trs.* v. *London and N.W. Ry.*, 1909 S.C. 707.

[42] See supra, § 13.

[43] As to reconvention, of which this is an extension, see supra, § 14. As to the limits of this statutory provision see *Kitson* v. *Kitson*, 1945 S.C. 434.

[44] Law Reform (Jurisdiction in Delict) (Scotland) Act 1971 (c. 55), s. 1 (2).

[45] See supra, § 16.

[46] Domicile and Matrimonial Proceedings (Scotland) Act 1973 (c. 45), ss. 8 and 9 and Sch. 2, Pt. 1, § 3.

[47] Maintenance Orders Act 1950 (14 Geo. VI c. 37), s. 6; *Plant* v. *Plant*, 1963 S.L.T. (Sh. Ct.) 58.

[48] Ibid., s. 8.

down, "appropriate."[49] For the success of the plea it is necessary to show that some other Court, in a civilised country, has concurrent jurisdiction.[50] The plea is one which will be most easily sustained in cases where foreign executors are sued in a Scottish Court on the ground that as individuals they are subject to the jurisdiction,[51] but is open in any case. No rule has been laid down as to the grounds on which a Court should hold that it is not the appropriate one to try a case where it has jurisdiction except in the very general form that the Court has "to consider how best the ends of justice in the case in question and on the facts before it, so far as they can be measured in advance, can be respectively ascertained and served."[52] Elements of weight, but not necessarily conclusive, are that the question raised is one of foreign law, that the proof must be by foreign witnesses, that neither party is resident in Scotland, or that litiscontestation occurred earlier in this country.[53] It is irrelevant to consider on what grounds the jurisdiction of the Scottish Court arises.[54] Where both the parties to the action were carrying on business in France, the question involved a claim for damages for unseaworthiness of a French ship, and all the witnesses were resident either in France or in England, the plea of forum non conveniens was sustained in reference to the Sheriff Court of Dumbarton, where, with jurisdiction established by arrestments, the action had been brought.[55]

19. Declinature.—In any particular case the exercise of jurisdiction may be excluded by the declinature of the judge. This may be either on the ground of relationship to one of the parties, or of interest in the matters in the case. The rules as to relationship are provided by the Declinature Act 1681, c. 13, applicable to all Courts. Under this Act no judge can vote in the cause of his father, brother or son, by consanguinity or affinity, nor in the cause of his uncle or nephew by consanguinity.[56] The rule does not extend to other relationships.[57] Where the objection is that of interest in the cause any pecuniary interest will disqualify, such as that of holding shares in a company which is a party to the action,[58] with an exception, resting on Act of Sederunt, of the case where the judge is a shareholder (not a director) of a chartered bank in Scotland,[59] and by statute, where the judge is a partner in a life or fire insurance company, or the holder of shares in any company merely

---

[49] Per Lord Dunedin, *Société du Gaz* v *Armateurs Français,* 1926 S.C. (H.L.) 13.
[50] *Clements* v. *Macaulay* (1866) 4 M. 583.
[51] See *Orr Ewing's Trs.* v. *Orr Ewing* (1885) 13 R. (H.L.) 1; *Robinson* v. *Robinson's Trs.,* 1929 S.C. 360; *Argyllshire Weavers Ltd.* v. *A. Macaulay (Tweeds) Ltd.,* 1962 S.C. 388. In *Dalziel* v. *Coulthurst's Exors.,* 1934 S.C. 564, an action against executors, the stronger plea of "no jurisdiction" prevailed.
[52] Per Lord Sumner, *Société du Gaz* v. *Armateurs Français,* 1926 S.C. (H.L.) at p. 22.
[53] *Sim* v. *Robinown* (1892) 19 R. 665; *Société du Gaz* supra; *Woodbury* v. *Sutherland's Trs.* 1938 S.C. 689; *Argyllshire Weavers Ltd.,* supra.
[54] Per Lord Shaw, *Société du Gaz* v. *Armateurs Français,* 1926 S.C. (H.L.) at p. 18.
[55] *Société du Gaz* v. *Armateurs Français,* 1925 S.C. 332, affd. 1926 S.C. (H.L.) 13.
[56] *Highland Road Commissioners* v. *Machray* (1858) 20 D. 1165; *Campbell* v. *Campbell* (1866) 4 M. 867.
[57] *Gordon* v. *Gordon's Trs.* (1866) 4 M. at p. 509.
[58] *Sellar* v. *Highland Ry.,* 1919 S.C. (H.L.) 19.
[59] A.S., Feb. 1, 1820.

as a trustee.[60] Where the interest is not pecuniary it must be shown to be substantial, especially in cases where declinature would result in public inconvenience.[61] In practice declinature, in cases where the interest is not really substantial, is elided by consent of parties; but if no such consent is given, or if the grounds of objection are not discovered until after decree, the decree will be reducible.[62]

20. Arbitration.—The jurisdiction of the Courts may be excluded if the parties to any dispute agree to refer the matter to arbitration. Such an agreement is known as a reference or submission. It need not take the form of a probative deed, though it is doubtful whether a merely verbal submission is binding.[63] The effect is to give either party the right to object to an appeal by the other to the ordinary tribunals. Should such an appeal be made the Court will decline to consider the case on the merits, and will sist the action to await the result of the arbitration.[64] The Arbitration Act 1950 deals with arbitrations between the subjects of different States which are parties to the agreements set out in the Act.

21. Agreements to Refer.—Prior to the Arbitration (Scotland) Act 1894,[65] the general rule was that an agreement to refer to arbiters who were not named, for instance, to refer to the holder of some particular office, was not binding. By the Act it is provided that an agreement to refer shall not be invalid by reason of the reference being to a party not named, or to a person to be named by another person, or to a person merely described as the holder for the time being of any office or appointment. On failure to agree in the nomination of an arbiter, where the agreement is to refer to one, or on failure of a party to nominate an arbiter, where the agreement is to refer to two, the Court, on the application of any party to the reference, may make the appointment.[66] An agreement to refer in the manner customary in a particular trade is valid, and proof will be allowed as to what that manner is.[67] In certain cases a particular form of arbitration is prescribed by statute[68]; where no statute is applicable there is no general rule, but the practice is to refer to a single arbiter, or to two arbiters and an oversman. Where the reference is to two arbiters, and there is no provision to the contrary, they have power to appoint an oversman, and, if they fail to agree in nomination, an oversman may be appointed by the Court on the application of any party to the reference.[69] A mere agreement to refer to arbitration, without any indication of the method, will not justify an application to the Court to appoint an

---

[60] Court of Session Act 1868 (30 & 31 Vict. c. 100), s. 103.
[61] *Wildridge* v. *Anderson* (1897) 25 R. (J.) 27. See also *Rae* v. *Hamilton* (1904) 6 F. (J.) 42.
[62] *Ommanney* v. *Smith* (1851) 13 D. 678; *Sellar* v. *Highland Ry.,* 1919 S.C. (H.L.) 19.
[63] *Otto* v. *Weir* (1871) 9 M. 660.
[64] *Hamlyn* v. *Talisker Distillery* (1894) 21 R. (H.L.) 21, opinion of Lord Watson.
[65] 57 & 58 Vict. c. 13.
[66] Ibid., ss. 1-3.
[67] *Douglas* v. *Stiven* (1900) 2 F. 575; *United Creameries* v. *Boyd,* 1912 S.C. 617.
[68] E.g. Agricultural Holdings (Scotland) Act 1949; see Leases, Ch. XXXIII., infra, § 27.
[69] Arbitration (Scotland) Act 1894, s. 4.

arbiter, and it would seem doubtful by what procedure, if at all, it can be enforced.[70]

22. Powers of Arbiter.—Some statutes provide for the determination of certain questions by arbitration and contain provisions as to the powers of the arbiters, and (in some cases) for an appeal to the Courts on a question of law. In non-statutory arbitrations and those statutory arbitrations in which it is not competent, under the relevant statute, to appeal to a court or tribunal, or for a case to be stated for the court's or tribunal's opinions, provision is now made for a case to be stated for the opinion of the Court of Session on any question of law arising in the arbitration.[71] The case may be stated by the arbiter at any stage on the application of a party and must be stated if the Court on a party's application so directs.[71] It is, however, competent for parties by express agreement to exclude resort to the Court.[71] Subject to these exceptions, the decision of the arbiter, or, where the arbiters differ, of the oversman, is final both as to fact and law.[72] An arbiter has implied power to award expenses,[73] but not, without express provision, to find either party liable in damages.[74] He has no inherent power to enforce his decision; but it is usual to insert a clause of consent to registration for preservation and execution of the award, and diligence may proceed upon an extract from the register. Otherwise an action for decree conform is necessary. If no date is fixed the powers of the arbiter lapse after a year and a day from the date of the submission, unless the parties agree to prorogate the time, or express power to prorogate is conferred.[75]

23. Scope of Reference.—The scope of the reference depends upon the terms used.[76] In arbitration clauses in a contract the reference may be merely executorial or ancillary, confined to questions arising in the course of the execution of the contract, in which case it is not to be carried beyond the term for which the contract endures[77]; or it may be of a more general character, covering all questions between the parties which may arise out of the contract. An averment that the adverse party has repudiated his contract may exclude the jurisdiction of the arbiter if the agreement to refer is merely executorial; it is now settled that it has not that effect if the reference is a general one of all questions that may arise under the contract.[78]

[70] *MacMillan* v. *Rowan & Co.* (1903) 5 F. 317.
[71] Administration of Justice (Scotland) Act 1971 (c. 59), s. 3. An application after the final award is too late (*Fairlie Yacht Slip* v. *Lumsden*, 1977 S.L.T. (Notes) 41).
[72] English law differs in this respect. See speeches of Lords Finlay and Dunedin in *Sanderson* v. *Armour*, 1922 S.C. (H.L.) 117.
[73] *Ferrier* v. *Alison* (1845) 4 Bell's App. 161. But parties must be heard on the question: *Islay Estates* v. *M'Cormick*, 1937 S.N. 28.
[74] *Mackay* v. *Leven Commissioners* (1893) 20 R. 1093.
[75] Erskine, IV., 3, 29; *Lang* v. *Brown* (1855) 2 Macq. 93; *Graham* v. *Mill* (1904) 6 F. 886.
[76] *Beattie* v. *Macgregor* (1883) 10 R. 1094; *Mackay* v. *Leven Commissioners*, supra; *North British Ry.* v *Newburgh, etc., Ry.*, 1911 S.C. 710.
[77] *Pearson* v. *Oswald*, (1859) 21 D. 419; *Bellshill & Mossend Co-operative Society* v. *Dalziel Co-operative Society*, 1960 S.C. (H.L.) 64.
[78] *Sanderson* v. *Armour*, 1922 S.C. (H.L.) 117; *Scott* v. *Del Sel*, 1923 S.C. (H.L.) 37; *Charles Mauritzen Ltd.* v. *Baltic Shipping Co.*, 1948 S.C. 646; *Heyman* v. *Darwins* [1942] A.C. 356.

24. Reduction of Award.—An arbiter must be impartial; an award may be reduced if it is proved that the arbiter had an interest in the case such as would warrant the declinature of a judge, and that interest was not known to the party impugning the award at the date of the agreement to refer.[79] So where one of the parties to an arbitration was a railway company it was held to be a ground for the reduction of the award that the arbiter was a shareholder.[80] On the other hand, interest known to both parties is not a ground of disqualification. It is a common practice, in building and engineering contracts, to insert a clause referring all disputes that may arise to the employer's architect or engineer; and an agreement under which one of the parties to a contract was made sole arbiter has been sustained.[81] An appointment of an arbiter, under statute, by a government department has been held to be an administrative act, so that the choice may not be challenged.[82] If the arbiter proceeds ultra fines compromissi and makes a pronouncement on a point not submitted to him, the award as a whole is open to reduction, unless the ultra vires part is clearly severable.[83] An award may also be reduced on the ground that the arbiter has mistaken the point at issue, or that he has not exhausted the questions submitted to him, but not merely because he has not dealt with the question of expenses.[84] By the Act of Regulations 1695,[85] it is provided that no award of an arbiter may be reduced except on the ground of corruption, bribery or falsehood. These words are to be taken in their ordinary meaning, and an error in law cannot be made a ground of reduction under the name of "constructive corruption."[86] A decision on relevancy, whether or not the Court might regard it as unsound, cannot be challenged.[87] But a serious error in procedure, such as hearing one party and refusing to hear the other, may be a ground of reduction, as a violation of what has been termed the "principle of eternal justice."[88] An award signed but improbative in form may not be sued upon.[89]

25. Remuneration of Arbiter.—In the earlier theory of law arbitration was assumed to be a service performed gratuitously, and an arbiter, or oversman, had no claim to remuneration, though he might stipulate for it without incurring the charge of corruption, within the meaning of that word in the Act

[79] *Magistrates of Edinburgh* v. *Lownie* (1903) 5 F. 711 (supervening interest).
[80] *Sellar* v. *Highland Ry.*, 1919 S.C. (H.L.) 19.
[81] *Buchan* v. *Melville* (1902) 4 F. 620; *Crawford Bros.* v. *Commissioners of Northern Lighthouses*, 1925 S.C. (H.L.) 22; see also *Fleming's Trs.* v. *Henderson*, 1962 S.L.T. 401.
[82] *Ramsay* v. *M'Laren*, 1936 S.L.T. 35.
[83] *Miller* v. *Oliver & Boyd* (1903) 6 F. 77; *M'Intyre* v. *Forbes*, 1939 S.L.T. 62; *Dunlop* v. *Mundell*, 1943 S.L.T. 286. In *M'Coard* v. *Glasgow Corporation*, 1935 S.L.T. 117, interdict against the arbiter and against the other party was given.
[84] *Pollich* v. *Heatley*, 1910 S.C. 469; *Donald* v. *Shiell's Exx.*, 1937 S.C. 52.
[85] Printed in Irons. *Arbitration*, p. 376.
[86] *Adams* v. *Great North of Scotland Ry.* (1890) 18 R. (H.L.) 1. There may be appeal on a point of law in virtue of some special statutory provision. See, e.g., *L.M. & S. Ry.* v. *Glasgow Corporation*, 1940 S.C. 363.
[87] *Brown* v. *Associated Fireclay Companies*, 1937 S.C. (H.L.) 42.
[88] *Sharpe* v. *Bickerdike* (1815) 3 Dow 102; *Holmes Oil Co.* v. *Pumpherston Oil Co.* (1891) 18 R. (H.L.) 52; *Black* v. *Williams & Co.*, 1923 S.C. 510; *Islay Estates* v. *M'Cormick*, 1937 S.N. 28.
[89] *M'Laren* v. *Aikman*, 1939 S.C. 222.

of Regulations 1695.[90] On the more recent authorities the appointment of an arbiter implies an obligation to pay him a reasonable remuneration, either in statutory arbitrations,[91] or in any case where the arbiter is professional man.[92] Each party is liable for half the arbiter's fee.[93]

[90] *Fraser* v. *Wright* (1838) 16 S. 1049; *Duff* v. *Pirie* (1893) 21 R. 80.
[91] *Murray* v. *N.B.R.* (1900) 2 F. 460.
[92] *Macintyre Bros.* v. *Smith,* 1913 S.C. 129.
[93] *Macintyre Bros.,* supra.

CHAPTER III

GENERAL LAW OF OBLIGATIONS

Stair, Book I.; Erskine, *Institute*, Book III.; Bell, *Principles* (10th ed., 1899), §§ 5-85; Holland, *Jurisprudence* (13th ed., 1924); Salmond, *Jurisprudence* (12th ed., 1966); Paton, *Jurisprudence* (4th ed., 1972); Smith, *Short Commentary* (1962), Chs. 8, 9 and 26.

1. Meaning of Obligation.—The law deals with obligations and rights. The one necessarily involves the other. There can be no obligation unless the State, or some person, or body of persons, as the creditor, has the right to exact performance. An obligation has been defined as "a legal tie by which we may be necessitated or constrained to pay or perform something."[1] To which it should be added that the obligation may be of a negative character, and the obligant may be constrained to forbear from some action or course of action.

2. Obligation and Duty.—The word obligation is sometimes used very loosely, as applicable to all legal ties, including the general duty to respect the rights of others sanctioned by the law, such as the right to liberty, to security of person, reputation or property. But such so-called obligations, in which all mankind are creditors, are more properly termed duties, and it is desirable to confine the term obligation to those legal ties which can be enforced only by some specific creditor. For instance, to refrain from defamatory statements about others is a duty, to observe an agreement not to make a particular statement about an individual is an obligation, and the defence that the statement was true, and therefore not actionable, though sufficient to meet any action founded on a breach of the duty, would be irrelevant as a defence to an action founded on a breach of the obligation.[2]

3. Sources of Obligations.—Taking an obligation in the narrower sense of the word indicated, as a legal tie by which one is bound to a specific creditor, or definite body of creditors, it may arise either with or without the consent of the debtor or obligant. If it arises with his consent it is said to arise from agreement or contract; if without his consent, it may either (*a*) be imposed by some external power or (*b*) arise from some act or omission of the obligant.

4. Statute.—In the former class (*a*) are all obligations imposed by the legislature. As a general rule a statute imposes duties, and enjoins abstention from acts which would infringe the rights which it creates or protects, but certain statutes impose obligations in which either the State, as in revenue statutes, or some particular person, as under the Rent Acts, is the creditor.

5. Decree of Court.—Obligations may be imposed by the decree of a

[1] Stair, I, 3, 1.
[2] See *R.* v. *S.*, 1914 S.C. 193.

competent Court. But it is at least arguable that a decree does not impose an obligation, it merely recognises and asserts an obligation which was already incumbent on the defender, though disputed by him. Thus, when a defender is found liable the date of his obligation is not the date of the decree, but that of the act or omission which has occasioned his liability.[3] But a decree for expenses in favour of a litigant is an instance of an obligation resting solely on the decree.

6. Common Law.—Obligations may be imposed or recognised at common law. Such obligations, e.g. the obligation to aliment relatives, or to restore property which does not belong to the possessor, are variously spoken of as arising from quasi-contract, as arising ex lege, or as obediential obligations. The term obediential, it is explained by Lord Stair, means that such obligations are exigible in accordance with the will of God.[4]

7. Breach of Contract, or of Duty.—In the second class (b) are obligations which result from the act or failure of the obligant, apart from any consent of his. That act or failure may be a breach of contract, from which arises an obligation to pay damages for the breach. It may also be a breach of duty. The duty not to interfere with the rights of others gives rise, when it is not observed, to an obligation to make reparation to the particular person whose rights are infringed. When the infringement is of the nature of a deliberate act, the obligation is said to arise from delict or wrong; when it results from the failure to exercise the degree of care required by the law in the particular circumstances, it arises from quasi-delict or negligence.

8. Trust.—The obligations which arise from trust may be said to arise from agreement, and trust is treated by Stair and Erskine as a combination of the contracts of deposit and mandate. But the obligations involved in a position of trust, or in certain fiduciary relationships, extend so far beyond what the party who accepted that position may have intended, and are so often owed to parties with whom he clearly had no direct contractual relation, that it is more in accordance with modern decisions to regard trust, or fiduciary relationship, as an independent source of obligation. Thus, on a question of procedure, it was held that the liability of trustees for the loss of the trust funds was not to be considered as arising from breach of contract or from quasi-delict, but from failure in the obligations recognised by law as resulting from the fiduciary relationship.[5]

9. Rights.—A right is defined by Professor Holland as, "capacity, residing in one man, of controlling, with the assent and assistance of the State, the actions of others."[6] The definition indicates the difference between a right, as

[3] *Miller* v. *M'Intosh* (1884) 11 R. 729; as to interest on damages, see Breach of Contract, Ch. XIII infra, § 28.
[4] Stair, I., 1, 19.
[5] *Allen* v. *M'Combie's Trs.*, 1909 S.C. 710.
[6] Holland, *Jurisprudence*, Ch. VII.

recognised in law, and a right as recognised in some system of morality, or by social usage. As the law of Scotland does not enforce gaming contracts, the man who has won a bet has no right to payment; he may be able to control the action of the loser, but he has that power in virtue of the force of public opinion and not by the assent and assistance of the State. The word "right" is often used in a wider and looser sense, as indicating a freedom of acting in a particular way, without interference from the law, but without involving any control over the actions of others. Thus it is said that a man has a right to open a shop or to make a will. A right in this wider sense may be termed a liberty or a licence.

   10. Real and Personal Rights.—Under Professor Holland's definition a right may be the counterpart either of an obligation or of a duty. Thus the right to receive an article which another has agreed to transfer consists in the capacity of controlling, with the assent and assistance of the State, the actions of the party who has made the agreement; the right of property in the article, when transferred, consists in the capacity of controlling the actions of all other persons, in so far as they may be forced to abstain from actions which would interfere with the proprietor's right to the article in question. In the former case, when the right is the counterpart of an obligation, it is known as a personal right, or jus in personam, and it gives a capacity of controlling the actions of the party who has undertaken the obligation, and of him only. A personal right is known also as jus ad rem. In the latter case, when the right is the counterpart of a duty, it is known as a real right, or jus in re, and gives a capacity of controlling the actions of all mankind. The distinction is indicated in Lord Stair's definition of a right: "A right is a power given by the law, of disposing of things, or exacting from persons that which they are due."[7] In the instance given above, the real right (jus in re) was a right of property, but it may also be a subordinate right, such as the right of a lessee or pledgee. Each, as distinguished from the personal right involved in an agreement to let or pledge, gives the power of controlling the actions of all persons in so far as they would infringe the right of the lessee or pledgee. The distinction between real and personal right is well expressed by Erskine[8]: "A real right, or jus in re, whether of property or of an inferior kind—as servitude—entitles the party vested with it to possess the subject as his own; or, if it be possessed by another, to demand it from the possessor, in consequence of the right which he hath in the subject itself; whereas the creditor in a personal right or obligation has only a jus ad rem, or a right of action against the debtor or his representatives, by which they may be compelled to fulfil that obligation, but without any right in the subject which the debtor is obliged to transfer to him." The very important distinction between real and personal rights, as illustrated in the law of sale, securities and bankruptcy, will be noticed in the chapters devoted to these subjects.

[7] Stair, I., 1, 22.
[8] Erskine, III., 1, 2.

11. Personal Bar.—The capacity of controlling the rights of others, either in the exercise of a real right in property or as the creditor in an obligation, may in particular circumstances be limited or abrogated by the operation of a principle known, according to Scottish terminology, as personal bar, according to English as estoppel.[9] In many cases the assertion of a right might conflict with ordinary conceptions of justice, either owing to the method by which the right was acquired or owing to the conduct of the party vested with it, and the principle of personal bar underlies many of the established rules of law. Thus the rule that obligations induced by fraud or misrepresentation cannot be enforced, or that the informality of an obligation may be cured by acts following on it, may be said to rest on the ground that the party against whom the rules are pleaded is personally barred from asserting a right which he would otherwise have possessed. And the interpretation of all voluntary obligations must proceed on the principle that if a man expresses himself in ordinary language he is barred from asserting that his words were not intended to bear their ordinary meaning.[10] Many of the applications of the principle of personal bar have in Scots law become known by more specialised terms, such as rei interventus, homologation, adoption, acquiescence, and in the pages of this treatise dealing with these subjects illustrations of the general principle will be found.[11] For the present it may be sufficient to cite a definition of one main branch of the doctrine—personal bar by representation—and to add some annotations on it: "Where A. has by his words or conduct justified B. in believing that a certain state of facts exists, and B. has acted upon such belief to his prejudice, A. is not permitted to affirm against B. that a different state of facts existed at the same time."[12] (1) A mere statement of intention is not a representation of any fact except that the intention has for the moment been formed, and therefore a party is not personally barred from affirming that his expressed intention has been altered.[13] (2) A man who neglects to assert his rights does not, in general, represent to those affected by the corresponding duty or obligation that his rights have been discharged or given up. So failure to state a defence to a claim does not bar the assertion of that defence at any time prior to the closing of the record in an action to enforce the claim.[14] (3) In Lord Birkenhead's definition, B. must be either a person with whom A. had actual relations, or a person whom A., as a reasonable man, is bound to regard as interested, not merely a member of the general public. A man has no general

---

[9] On this subject, see Rankine, *Personal Bar;* Spencer Bower, *Estoppel* (2nd ed., 1966); Everett and Strode, *Estoppel* (3rd ed., 1923); *Greenwood* v. *Martins Bank* [1933] A.C. 51.

[10] See Law of Contract, Ch. IV., infra, § 3.

[11] See Index. The statement that a party "cannot be heard to deny" a certain fact does not, it is conceived, indicate a plea of personal bar, but means that the party, either by his prior acts or by his pleadings, has conclusively admitted the truth of the fact in question, or that his denial would conflict with the equitable rule that when a man does an act which he has a right to do he is not allowed to maintain that the act was intentionally and in fact done wrongly. See opinion of Jessel, M.R., *Re Hallett* (1880) 13 Ch.D. 696, at p. 727.

[12] Per Lord Chancellor Birkenhead, *Gatty* v. *Maclaine,* 1921 S.C. (H.L.) 1.

[13] Law of Contract, Ch. IV., § 8.

[14] *Morrison* v. *Gray,* 1932 S.C. 712. As to the effect of delay, see Prescription, Ch. XVI., infra.

duty so to regulate his conduct that third parties may not be justified in
believing, and acting on the belief, that a certain state of matters exists. "Law
does not recognise a duty in the air, so to speak, that is, a duty to undertake
that no one shall suffer from one's carelessness."[15] A. leaves his watch on a
seat in a park, it is stolen and sold by the thief to B. A.'s conduct may be said
to have justified B. in forming and acting on the belief that the thief was the
owner of the watch, but as A. had no relations with B. and is not bound to
consider the possible results of his carelessness to members of the general
public, A. is not barred from asserting the true state of facts and recovering
his watch from B.[16] This has been illustrated by cases bearing on the result of
signing obligatory documents in a form which has facilitated fraudulent
alteration. Where a man accepted a bill of exchange in a way which rendered
it easy to alter the amount, he was not liable for more than the original
amount to an indorsee, because the indorsee was merely a member of the
general public, to whom the acceptor owed no duty to be careful.[17] But where
a cheque for £2 was drawn carelessly, fraudulently altered to £200, and paid
by the bank, it was held that as a customer does owe a duty to the bank to
take reasonable care in drawing cheques, the bank was entitled to take credit
for the £200 which had been paid.[18] (4) The party who pleads personal bar
must show that in reliance on the other's words or acts he has altered his
position, and altered it to his disadvantage. So, where a frontager, called upon
by a local authority to make up a street, pleaded in defence that the local
authority was barred by acts which had led him to suppose that the demand
would not be made, it was held that as he had suffered no disadvantage by the
delay in enforcing his obligation the plea of personal bar was untenable.[19]

12. Personal Bar by Notice.—As a general rule a person who acquires
property, or to whom an obligation embodied in a negotiable instrument is
transferred, is entitled to assume that the ostensible facts are the true ones,
and that his author has an actual, as well as an apparent, right to convey or
transfer. He is not concerned with latent claims, which might be asserted in a
question with that author. But if he knew, or, as a reasonable man, should
have known, that the latent claims existed, he is barred from asserting a right
resting merely on the ostensible or apparent facts. So while a purchaser of
lands is in general entitled to rely on the title as it stands on the Register of
Sasines, if he knows that the subjects have already been sold to a third party
he will be personally barred from asserting, in a question with that third party,
his author's ostensible capacity to sell.[20] It would appear, however, that the

---

[15] Per Greer, L.J., *Bottomley* v. *Bannister* [1932] 1 K.B. 458.
[16] *Mitchell* v. *Heys* (1894) 21 R. 600; *Morrisson* v. *Robertson*, 1908 S.C. 332; *Low* v. *Bouverie*
    [1891] 3 Ch. 82; *Farquharson* v. *King* [1902] A.C. 325; *Jones* v. *Waring & Gillow* [1926] A.C.
    670.
[17] *Scholfield* v. *Lord Londesborough* [1896] A.C. 514.
[18] *London Joint Stock Bank* v. *Macmillan* [1918] A.C. 777.
[19] *Mags. of Alloa* v. *Wilson*, 1913 S.C. 6; *Bruce* v. *British Motor Trading Corporation*, 1924 S.C.
    908.
[20] *Petrie* v. *Forsyth* (1874) 2 R. 214; *Stodart* v. *Dalzell* (1876) 4 R. 236; *Rodger (Builders)* v.
    Fawdry, 1950 S.C. 483.

purchaser of heritable property is entitled to assume that the seller has a complete and sufficient title to the subjects, and is not bound to verify grounds for suspecting that the title is in fact limited.[21]

13. Obligations, Pure, Future, Contingent.—An obligation may be pure, future or contingent.[22] An obligation is pure when, as in the case of a debt instantly payable, fulfilment is due at once. The term liquid as applied to a debt, imports that it is pure, and also that it is either admitted, or constituted in such a form, as by a bill, bond or decree, that diligence can at once proceed. An obligation is termed future (as opposed to contingent) when it will become exigible either on a fixed date, or on the occurrence of some event (e.g., the death of some person) which is certain to happen. The maxim "dies statim cedit, sed non venit," means that in the case of a future debt the debt exists but cannot be enforced until the day of payment arrives. An obligation is contingent when it is subject either to a suspensive or a resolutive condition. There is a suspensive condition, also termed a condition precedent, when the obligation will arise only on the occurrence of an event which may or may not happen, or at some period (e.g., the attainment by the creditor of a certain age) which may never arrive. There is a resolutive condition in the exceptional case of an obligation which is at once exigible but which will cease to be exigible on the occurrence of an uncertain event. Thus, where interim execution was authorised of a decree for expenses while the question between the parties was under appeal to the House of Lords, it was held that the claim for expenses was a contingent debt, in respect that although immediately exigible it would cease to be exigible if the judgment of the Court of Session was reversed.[23] A resolutive condition is also exemplified by a provision, in a disposition of property, that, on the occurrence of an uncertain event, the property shall revert to the disponer, or, a provision not uncommon in entails, shall pass to some third party.

14. Conditions.—A condition is termed potestative when it may be purified by an act which one or other of the parties has the power to do; casual, when the condition depends upon chance, or the action of third parties; mixed, when the concurrence of a potestative and a casual event is required. It is a general rule in the construction of wills that if a legacy is given on a condition which is partly potestative, it is held to be purified if the legatee has done all that he could to purify it, though he has failed. Thus if a legacy is given to A. on the condition of his marriage with B. it is due if he had asked B. to marry him and been refused.[24] In spite of a dictum of Erskine, it is conceived that this rule (grounded on the presumed intention of the testator) has no application to contracts, and that a party who has undertaken a conditional liability is not

---

[21] *Mossend Theatre Co.* v. *Livingstone,* 1930 S.C. 90; see also *Campbell* v. *McCutcheon,* 1963 S.C. 505.
[22] See Stair, I, 3, 7; Erskine, III., 1, 6.
[23] *Forbes* v. *Whyte* (1890) 18 R. 182; another recent example is *Hardy* v. *Sime,* 1938 S.L.T. 18.
[24] Erskine, III., 3, 8; founding on Roman law; *Simpson* v. *Roberts,* 1931 S.C. 259.

liable unless the condition is actually purified.[25] A party who has undertaken a conditional obligation impliedly undertakes that he will do nothing to impede the occurrence of the event on which the condition would be purified. So where A. was a creditor in a bond which was not exigible by him for eight years provided that he remained the director of a particular company it was held that he did not acquire the right to immediate payment by the voluntary resignation of his directorship.[26] And if the scheme of a contract imports that something shall be done which cannot be done unless both parties concur in doing it, the construction of the contract is that each agrees to do all that is necessary to be done on his part for the carrying out of that thing, though there may be no express words to that effect.[27] So when a machine was sold on the condition that it should satisfy a certain test, to be carried out on the premises of the buyer, it was held that he had impliedly agreed to give facilities for the test.[28] An agreement to sell goods at a time to be mutually agreed upon is not defeated by the fact that one party refuses to agree; the Court will fix a reasonable time.[29] When goods were sold at a time when, to the knowledge of both parties, the sale could not be carried out unless the seller obtained a permit, it was held that the seller, though he had not guaranteed that he would obtain a permit, had impliedly undertaken to do all that he could to obtain one.[30] But questions of this kind turn on the interpretation of each contract; there is no absolute rule that because a man has undertaken a liability conditional on the performance of an act which he has the power to perform he has come under any implied obligation to perform it. When a railway company undertook to purchase lands if they constructed a certain line, it was held that the construction of the line remained a matter within their option, and that they were not in breach of their contract when they failed to construct it during the period within which they had statutory powers.[31] If a party adds to his offer or acceptance a condition which is purely in his own interest, he is entitled to waive compliance with it and insist on implement of the contract; whether a condition is purely in the interest of one party is a question of interpretation of the contract.[32]

15. Obligations by Co-Debtors.—When an obligation is undertaken by more than one person the liability of each obligant in a question with the creditor may be either in solidum, for the whole debt, or only pro rata, for his proportionate share. When the matter is regulated by contract there is no doubt that if the parties are taken bound jointly and severally, conjunctly and

---

[25] See Gloag, *Contract* (2nd ed.), 279.
[26] *Pirie* v. *Pirie*, (1873) 11 M. 941. See also *Dowling* v. *Methven*, 1921 S.C. 948; *Leith School Board* v. *Clerk-Rattray's Trs.*, 1918 S.C. 94.
[27] See speech of Lord Blackburn, *Mackay* v. *Dick & Stevenson* (1881) 8 R. (H.L.) 37; 6 App. Cas. 251.
[28] *Mackay*, supra.
[29] *Pearl Mill Co.* v. *Ivy Tannery Co.* [1919] 1 K.B. 78; *Henry* v. *Seggie*, 1922 S.L.T. 5.
[30] *Re Anglo-Russian Merchant Traders and Batt*, [1917] 2 K.B. 679.
[31] *Philip* v. *Edinburgh, etc., Ry.* (1857) 2 Macq. 514; *Maconochie Welwood* v. *Midlothian County Council* (1894) 22 R. 56; *Paterson* v. *M'Ewan's Trs.* (1881) 8 R. 646.
[32] Gloag, *Contract*, (2nd ed.), p. 42; *Dewar and Finlay* v. *Blackwood*, 1968 S.L.T. 196, (O.H.); *Ellis and Sons Second Amalgamated Properties* v. *Pringle*, 1975 S.L.T. 10. (O.H.).

severally, or as principals and full debtors, the liability of each is in solidum. An obligation undertaken jointly, or conjunctly, involves liability only pro rata.[33] When there is no express provision there is a general presumption in favour of liability pro rata.[34] This holds in bonds, cautionary obligations,[35] and as to the liability of underwriters in marine insurance.[36] But the exceptions are numerous and important. All the parties to a bill or promissory note are liable in solidum. Each partner is liable for the whole debts of the firm. When an order is given for goods or work by several persons acting in concert, though not partners, each is liable for the whole account.[37] And when the obligation is not for payment of money, but to do a particular act (ad factum præstandum), e.g., to return an article hired, the obligation is joint and several, so that, if the obligation is not fulfilled, each is liable for the whole amount awarded as damages.[38]

16. Rights of Relief.—When a contractual obligation is joint and several there is a general legal implication, without any express agreement to that effect, that if one debtor pays the whole debt, or more than his pro rata share, he has a right of relief against the others. This right may be fortified by an assignation of the debt from the creditor, but exists without it.[39] It was extended to the case where one of two cautioners for an insolvent contractor completed the contract work at his own expense. He was entitled to recover half of the expenses incurred from the other.[40] If the obligation is pro rata, and the whole debt is exacted, no one has paid more or less than his share, and there can be no right of relief. But if less than the sum in the obligation is found to be due, one who paid more than his share has a right of relief against others bound pro rata with him.[41] Where a party who has paid the whole debt claims relief, either on the general implication of law or in virtue of an assignation from the creditor, he cannot claim against any one of his co-debtors more than that co-debtor's pro rata share, but in computing the number of co-debtors those who are insolvent are not counted.[42]

Joint wrongdoers, while each is jointly and severally liable to the person wronged by them, are entitled to relief inter se in such proportions as seem good to the Court, whether both have been sued in one action or not.[43] A joint and several decree, or some equivalent instrument constituting the debt, is an essential prerequisite to an action of relief by one wrongdoer against another; an extrajudicial settlement by one wrongdoer acting on his own will

---

[33] *Coats* v. *Union Bank*, 1929 S.C. (H.L.) 114.
[34] Stair, I, 17, 20; Bell, *Prin.*, § 51.
[35] Bell, *Prin.*, § 267.
[36] Marine Insurance Act 1906, s. 67 (2).
[37] *Walker* v. *Brown* (1803) M. App. Solidum et pro rata, No. 1. As to the competency of suing one obligant without calling the other, see *Neilson* v. *Wilson* (1890) 17 R. 608.
[38] *Darlington* v. *Gray* (1836) 15 S. 197; *Rankine* v. *Logie Den Land Co.* (1902) 4 F. 1074.
[39] Stair, I, 8, 9; Erskine, III, 3, 74.
[40] *Marshall* v. *Pennycook*, 1908 S.C. 276.
[41] *Dering* v. *Lord Winchelsea* (1787) 1 Cox 318; *Ellesmere Brewery Co.* v. *Cooper* [1896] 1 Q.B. 75; Bell, *Comm.*, I., 367.
[42] *Buchanan* v. *Main* (1900) 3 F. 215.
[43] Law Reform (Miscellaneous Provisions) (Scotland) Act 1940, s. 3; *Central S.M.T. Co.* v. *Lanarkshire County Council*, 1949 S.C. 450.

not suffice for this purpose.[44] No distinction is made by the statute between deliberate and merely negligent wrongdoing, and it remains to be seen how the Court will deal with the former.

17. Signatures of all Obligants Necessary.—It is a rule largely founded on the existence of the right of relief that when an obligation bears ex facie to be by more than one obligant, each who signs it does so on the implied condition that all the others will sign, and incurs no liability unless the signatures of all are obtained. This is an established rule in cautionary obligation,[45] with a doubtful exception in the case of judicial bonds of caution.[46] So, where a party whose debt to a bank was guaranteed forged the name of one of the guarantors, it was held that the bank could not enforce the guarantee against the others.[47] The rule applies to analogous cases. When three persons had agreed to accept a lease, and one refused to sign, the other two, who had already signed, were held entitled to resile.[48]

18. Assignation by Creditor.—Where one of several co-obligants bound jointly and severally pays the whole debt he has a right to receive from the creditor an assignation of the debt, and of any securities which any of the other co-obligants may have granted for it.[49] This is a right which arises only on full payment; not where an obligant is bankrupt and the creditor has ranked for the whole debt and received a dividend.[50] But the creditor may refuse to assign if the assignation would conflict with any legitimate interest of his own. This, when an assignation merely of the debt is demanded, can be the case in exceptional circumstances only[51]; if an assignation of securities also is demanded the creditor's interest may be that he holds a prior security over the same subjects for a separate debt. He is not entitled to refuse an assignation on the ground that he has made subsequent advances on the same security.[52]

19. Effect of Discharge of One Co-Obligant.—A creditor is not entitled to do anything which would prejudice the right of relief possessed by co-obligants who are jointly and severally bound to him. He does so if he discharges one obligant without the consent of the others. The result, if the co-obligants are co-cautioners, is, by statute, that the others are discharged[53]; if they are not cautioners, the other obligants are relieved only in so far as their rights of relief are prejudiced, and therefore they remain liable for their own share of the debt.[54] But a pactum de non petendo, by which a creditor, without discharging an obligant, undertakes not to sue him, does not

---

[44] *N.C.B.* v. *Thomson*, 1959 S.C. 353.
[45] *Paterson* v. *Bonar* (1844) 6 D. 987; *Ellesmere Brewery Co.* v. *Cooper* [1896] 1 Q.B. 75.
[46] *Simpson* v. *Fleming* (1860) 22 D. 679.
[47] *Scottish Provincial Assurance Co.* v. *Pringle* (1858) 20 D. 465.
[48] *York Buildings Co.* v. *Baillie* (1724) M. 8435; *Gordon's Exrs.* v. *Gordon* (1918) 55 S.L.R. 497.
[49] Bell, *Prin.*, § 255.
[50] *Ewart* v. *Latta* (1865) 3 M. (H.L.) 36.
[51] See *Bruce* v. *Scottish Amicable*, 1907 S.C. 637.
[52] *Sligo* v. *Menzies* (1840) 2 D. 1478.
[53] Mercantile Law Amendment (Scotland) Act 1856, s. 9.
[54] *Smith* v. *Harding* (1877) 5 R. 147.

prejudice the rights of relief of the other obligants, and therefore does not affect their liability.[55] And if there is an express reservation of the creditor's right against the other co-obligants a discharge will be read as a pactum de non petendo, which neither bars the right of relief nor affects the liability of the other obligants. Thus where a creditor acceded to a trust deed granted by one of his debtors, and to a discharge following thereon, reserving his rights against the other debtor, it was held that the latter remained liable for the debt, and that his right of relief against the debtor who had been discharged was not affected.[56] It is provided by the Bankruptcy (Scotland) Act 1913,[57] that a creditor in sequestration may assent to the discharge of the bankrupt, with or without a composition, without prejudicing his rights against the bankrupt's co-obligants.

20. Creditors giving up Securities.—It is probably the general law, though the authorities have all related to the effect on a cautionary obligation of the release of securities granted by the principal debtor, that if a creditor gives up a security granted by one co-debtor he thereby releases the others in so far as their rights of relief are prejudiced.[58]

---

[55] *Muir* v. *Crawford* (1875) 2 R. (H.L.) 148.
[56] *Morton's Trs.* v. *Robertson's Judicial Factor* (1892) 20 R. 72.
[57] s. 52.
[58] *Marshall* v. *Pennycook*, 1908 S.C. 276; *Taylor* v. *New South Wales Bank* (1886) 11 App. Cas. 596.

CHAPTER IV

LAW OF CONTRACT. FORMATION OF CONTRACT

Stair, Erskine, Bell, as in Chapter III.; Bell, *Commentaries* (7th ed., 1870), I., 4, et seq.; Gloag, *Contract* (2nd ed., 1929); Anson, *Contract* (24th ed., 1975); Pollock, *Contract* (13th ed., 1950); Chitty, *Contracts* (24th ed., 1977); Smith, *Short Commentary* (1962), Ch. 33; Treitel, *Law of Contract* (4th ed., 1975).

1. Obligations from Consent: Gratuitous Promise.—The law recognises as a general principle that an obligation may arise from mere consent: that if a man undertakes to do or pay something, or to abstain from some course of action, he has incurred an obligation which may be enforced against him by some form of legal process. The undertaking may take the form of a promise, when the resulting obligation is commonly termed unilateral, or of the acceptance of an offer, when the result is a mutual contract. Differing in this respect from the law of England, Scots law holds that consent will infer an obligation although there may be no consideration. An obligation to give, or to do or abstain from doing something without asking for any return is, in so far as its enforceability by legal process is concerned, on a par with an obligation for which a return or consideration is demanded and promised.[1] The distinction in this respect between the laws of England and Scotland is most clearly brought out in the case of an offer to sell, with an undertaking to keep the offer open for a certain period. Assuming that nothing is paid for the engagement to keep the offer open, it is an undertaking without consideration, and consequently, in English law, is not binding unless made in a deed under seal.[2] In Scotland, where consideration is not necessary, it is a binding obligation, and the offeree, if he accept within the time specified, and his acceptance be rejected, will be entitled to damages.[3]

2. Gratuitous, Onerous.—While the law of Scotland has rejected consideration as an essential element in the constitution of a voluntary obligation, this does not mean that the question of consideration is in all cases irrelevant, and that a gratuitous promise and a mutual contract stand in all respects on the same footing. There is an important difference with regard to the method by which, if disputed, the fact that the obligation was incurred may be proved. The fact that two parties have agreed to enter into an onerous contract may be proved by any evidence, but the fact that a gratuitous promise has been made can be proved only by the writ of the party who made it, or by eliciting an admission from him on a reference to his oath. So when it was averred that a lady deceased had promised to leave money for the repair of a particular

---

[1] *Morton's Trs.* v. *Aged Christian Friend Society* (1899) 2 F. 82.
[2] *Dickinson* v. *Dodds* (1876) 2 Ch.D. 463.
[3] *Littlejohn* v. *Hadwen* (1882) 20 S.L.R. 5; approved by Lord Dunedin in *Paterson* v. *Highland Ry.*, 1927 S.C. (H.L.) 32, at p. 38.

church it was decided that, although the law of Scotland would enforce such a promise, the only competent proof of it, in a case when, owing to her decease, reference to oath was impossible, was a writing by the party alleged to have made it. As no such writing was available the pursuer's case failed, not because the promise he alleged was not binding, but because there was no competent evidence that such a promise had been made.[4] Again, while in the case of an onerous contract the obligations are binding although one of the obligants may have entered into the contract by reason of some error or mistake on his own part, the man who has given a gratuitous promise, and can show that he gave it under essential error, is entitled to resile, even though he does not aver or prove that his error was induced by misrepresentation.[5] A difference between onerous and gratuitous obligations is also recognised in the law of bankruptcy. Certain prior obligations of the bankrupt are reducible or unenforceable if they were entered into gratuitously, whereas onerous contracts in the same circumstances would be unaffected.[6]

3. Mutual Contracts, Agreements.—A contract involves, and is dependent on, agreement. Consensus in idem occurs when agreement has been reached upon all the essentials of the contract; what the essentials are may vary according to the particular contract under consideration.[7] Agreement means generally that the minds of the parties are at one with regard to the point at issue. In most disputed cases, however, the question is to discover the parties' apparent, rather than their real, intentions. In matters of contract a party is generally entitled to act on the assumption that the other means what he says. The question whether the parties have agreed is to be decided not by proof of what each party really intended, but by considering what conclusion a reasonable person would draw from their words or acts. It is clear that if A uses words which have an ordinary meaning, and has no reason to suppose that B will interpret them otherwise, A cannot be heard to say that he attached a different meaning to his words, or spoke with a mental reservation.[8] Even if the parties are really at cross purposes, if one uses language which to a reasonable hearer would convey the impression that he meant to agree, he will be bound, unless the difference between their mental attitude is so fundamental as to preclude any real consent.[9] "Commercial contracts cannot be arranged by what people think in their inmost minds. Commercial contracts are made according to what people say."[10]

Agreement for all legal purposes may be reached when a party has undertaken some definite obligation, though he may not be aware of the

---

[4] *Smith* v. *Oliver*, 1911 S.C. 103; *Gray* v. *Johnston's Exr.*, 1928 S.C. 659.
[5] *M'Caig* v. *University of Glasgow* (1904) 6 F. 918; *Hunter and Another* v. *Bradford Property Trust*, 1970 S.L.T. 173. See Agreement Improperly Obtained, Ch. VIII. infra, §§ 13 et seq.
[6] See Bankruptcy, Ch. XLIX. infra, § 4.
[7] See *Dempster* v. *Motherwell Bridge & Engineering Co.*, 1964 S.C. 308, per Lord President Clyde at p. 329, Lord Guthrie at p. 332.
[8] *Duran* v. *Duran* (1904) 7 F. 87, a form of marriage, with a mental reservation by one party.
[9] See *Stuart* v. *Kennedy* (1885) 13 R. 221, and Agreement Improperly Obtained, Ch. VIII., §§15 et seq.
[10] *Muirhead and Turnbull* v. *Dickson* (1905) 7 F. 686, per Lord President Dunedin.

interpretation which the law will put on his expressions or acts, or may think that the terms to which he has bound himself are other than they are ultimately determined to be. It is for the Court, not for either party, to interpret a contract, and decide upon the conditions, express or implied. So when a party had agreed to sell an entailed estate "subject to the ratification of the Court" it did not affect the validity of the contract that he had formed an erroneous impression of the process involved in ratification by the Court.[11]

4. Agreements in the Law.—It is not every agreement of which the Courts will take cognisance.[12] The agreement must be one concerned with legal relations. Social engagements cannot be enforced by legal process. There are cases, however, where the parties may have meant to incur obligations, but where the question between them is not one which lies within the province of the Courts to decide. To justify judicial interference a patrimonial interest— some material gain or loss, or chance of material gain or loss—must be involved. Thus the question whether a member of a club, averring that he has been wrongfully expelled, can find a legal remedy, depends upon whether the club possesses property in which the members have an interest. If it has none no patrimonial interest of the member expelled has been affected, and the Court will not take account of the loss of opportunities of social intercourse.[13] A like principle applies to the case of a member of a voluntary church, alleging wrongful expulsion, in contrast with the case of a minister of a similar body, who, if expelled, loses a position which gives him a chance of employment and income, and may therefore obtain legal redress.[14]

An agreement will not be binding if it appears that the parties did not intend that it should be legally enforceable. This may appear from the surrounding circumstances[15] or from the terms of the agreement.[16] A "collective agreement" is conclusively presumed not to have been intended by the parties to be a legally enforceable contract unless it is in writing and contains a provision, however expressed, that the parties intended that the agreement would be legally enforceable; an agreement which satisfies these requirements is conclusively presumed to have been intended to be legally enforceable.[17] A "collective agreement" is an agreement made by a trade union and an employer or an employers' association and relating to terms and conditions of employment.[18]

In order to be binding as a contract an agreement must be definite, and the

---

[11] *Stewart* v. *Kennedy* (1890) 17 R. (H.L.) 25. See also *Laing* v. *Provincial Homes Co.*, 1909 S.C. 812. See *Stobo, Ltd.* v. *Morrison (Gowns), Ltd.*, 1949 S.C. 184.
[12] As to pacta illicita and sponsiones ludicrae see Pacta Illicita, Ch. IX. infra.
[13] *Anderson* v. *Manson*, 1909 S.C. 838.
[14] *Skerret* v. *Oliver* (1896) 23 R. 468.
[15] *Ford Motor Co.* v. *Amalgamated Union of Engineering and Foundry Workers* [1969] 2 Q.B. 303. In England there is a presumption that an agreement between husband and wife is not intended to create a legal relationship: *Gould* v. *Gould* [1970] 1 Q.B. 275.
[16] *Rose and Frank Co.* v. *Crompton* [1925] A.C. 445; *Tannahill* v. *Glasgow Corporation*, 1935 S.C. (H.L.) 15.
[17] Trade Union and Labour Relations Act 1974, s. 18.
[18] Ibid., s. 30 (1).

test of whether it is sufficiently definite is whether it would be possible to frame a decree of specific implement.[19]

5. Definitions of Contract.—The institutional writers in Scotland treat "contract" as synonymous with agreement involving a patrimonial interest, agreement, in an English phrase, "in the law." A more limited definition of the word "contract" was given in the Indian Contract Act 1872—"An agreement enforceable by law is a contract." This would exclude from the category of contract not only agreements when no patrimonial interest is involved but also all cases where for some specific reason, e.g., want of capacity in the parties, or illegality in the subject-matter, an agreement cannot be enforced by law. The limitation is not in accordance with the ordinary, the judicial, or even the statutory use of the word contract. A preferable definition of contract is, "A contract is an agreement which creates, or is intended to create, a legal obligation between the parties to it."[20]

6. Offer and Acceptance.—A contract may be considered as consisting of an offer by one party and an acceptance by the other. The offer, or the acceptance, or both, may be in words, spoken or written, or may be inferred from the actions of the parties. So when newspapers are laid out on a bookstall and one is taken a contract of sale is completed, though nothing may have been said. The keeper of the bookstall, by laying out the newspapers, offers to sell them, the party who takes one accepts the offer and agrees to pay the price.

7. Offer and Intention.—It may often be difficult, alike in the construction of words and of conduct, to distinguish between a mere expression of readiness to do business in a particular line and an offer to enter into a contract. A man who indicates that he is willing to contract does not necessarily make an offer which can be turned into a contract by acceptance. He may only be indicating his readiness to receive and to consider offers. The question whether a party has merely indicated an intention or has made an offer must depend on the circumstances of each case; words or acts which, if used in one connection, would amount to an offer, may, if used in another, merely indicate a readiness to chaffer. So while if a trader quotes prices of the commodity in which he deals, either in response to a request or ex proprio motu, he will, in general, be held to have made an offer to sell,[21] the statement of the lowest price which would be accepted for a particular estate, made in response to an inquiry as to the owner's readiness to sell, was read merely as an indication that he was willing to consider an offer of that price.[22] A shopkeeper, by placing goods in his window, with or without prices annexed,

---

[19] *M'Arthur* v. *Lawson* (1877) 4 R. 1134; *Murray's Trs.* v. *St. Margaret's Convent Trs.*, 1907 S.C. (H.L.) 8, and cases collected at p. 12 of Gloag on *Contract*.
[20] Jenks, *Digest of English Civil Law*, Book II., Title 1.
[21] *Philp* v. *Knoblauch*, 1907 S.C. 994.
[22] *Harvey* v. *Facey* [1893] A.C. 552.

only indicates his readiness to trade,[23] but a party who is under a duty to exercise his vocation, such as a carrier or innkeeper, makes a continuous offer, subject, no doubt, to implied conditions, but which will bind him to carry or entertain any applicant who complies with these conditions.[24]

8. Expression of Intention not Binding.—It may probably be stated without qualification that if it is decided, on the particular facts, that a party has only indicated an intention, he has incurred no liability. Where railway companies intimated that a reduced rate would be charged for a certain period, it was held that they were not precluded from withdrawing the concession before the period had expired.[25] The announcement that I intend to do something does not bind me not to change my mind, and anyone who acts or incurs expense on the assumption that I will carry out my intention does so at his own risk. So when negotiations for a loan were broken off before any definite offer had been made, it was held that the party who had proposed to lend had no claim for the expenses he had incurred in investigating the other's title to subjects which were contemplated as security, nor to interest on the money which he had kept in hand in order to make the proposed advance.[26] Certain earlier cases,[27] quoted as authorities for the proposition that if A indicates an intention to contract, and knows that B is incurring expense in expectation of a contract, A, if he changes his mind, must meet the expenses B has incurred, were distinguished or overruled. But it was observed that to indicate an intention to contract when no such intention had been formed, and thereby to lead another party to incur expense, would be an actionable wrong,[28] and the most recent case would seem to leave it open to doubt whether a claim based on *Walker* v. *Milne*,[29] if supported by averments of definite loss, and not merely of deprivation of problematical gain, is or is not maintainable.[30]

9. Parties to Whom Offer Made.—An offer may be made to a particular individual, to a specified class, or to the general public, as in the case of an offer of a reward for the recovery of lost property,[31] or of insurance in timetables or diaries.[32] In such cases it is not necessary that the party who claims fulfilment of the offer shall have given any express acceptance; acceptance is implied in doing the act called for, though it is probably necessary that the act shall have been done in the knowledge that the offer has been made. Where the proprietors of a preventive for influenza offered a payment to anyone who used it in accordance with their directions and yet

---

[23] That at least is the law in England: *Pharmaceutical Society of Great Britain* v. *Boots Cash Chemists (Southern) Ltd.* [1953] 1 Q.B. 401; *Fisher* v. *Bell* [1961] 1 Q.B. 394.
[24] *Campbell* v. *Ker*, Feb. 24, 1810, F.C.; *Rothfield* v. *North British Ry.*, 1920 S.C. 805.
[25] *Paterson* v. *Highland Ry.*, 1927 S.C. (H.L.) 32.
[26] *Gilchrist* v. *Whyte*, 1907 S.C. 984. See also *Maddison* v. *Alderson* (1883) 8 App. Cas. 467.
[27] *Walker* v. *Milne* (1823) 2 S. 379; *Dobie* v. *Lauder's Trs.* (1873) 11 M. 749; *Hamilton* v. *Lochrane* (1899) 1 F. 478.
[28] Per Lord Ardwall in *Gilchrist* v. *Whyte*, 1907 S.C. 984.
[29] Supra.
[30] *Gray* v. *Johnston's Exr.*, 1928 S.C. 659.
[31] *Petrie* v. *Earl of Airlie* (1834) 13 S. 68.
[32] *Hunter* v. *General Accident Co.*, 1909 S.C. (H.L.) 30.

caught the disease, it was held that they could not refuse payment on the ground that the claimant had not expressly indicated that he accepted the offer and proposed to try the preventive.[33]

10. Express Acceptance, When Necessary.—Apart from offers to the general public, it is a question of construction in each case whether express acceptance of an offer is necessary to complete a contract. The question to be solved is whether the offer calls for an act, or for a promise to undertake a reciprocal obligation. So an order for goods does not require express acceptance; it is accepted by sending the goods.[34] On the other hand, when the directors of a company sent a circular offering to cancel the allotment of shares it was held that this offer required express acceptance, and therefore, in the ensuing liquidation of the company, that those shareholders who had accepted the offer were free from liability, while those who had done nothing were liable as contributors.[35]

11. Acts Amounting to Acceptance.—When a party who has received an offer proceeds to act in a way which is justifiable only on the assumption that he has accepted it, his acts, if unequivocal,[36] amount to acceptance. So, in sale, if the goods have been delivered and the buyer, having had a reasonable opportunity to inspect them, does any act in relation to them which is inconsistent with the ownership of the seller, he is deemed to have accepted them, and cannot afterwards reject them as disconform to contract.[37] Action of this kind may be treated as equivalent to acceptance even if in words the offer has been refused. A ship had been stranded, and the owner offered to abandon her to the underwriters as a constructive total loss. The underwriters refused to accept the notice of abandonment, but proceeded in attempts to salve the ship in a manner which caused further damage. It was held that their actions, in spite of their formal refusal, amounted to acceptance of the notice of abandonment, or, on an alternative view, were such as to bar them from maintaining that they had not accepted.[38]

Parties may agree that an offer is to be regarded as accepted if it is not refused within a specified time. And in ordinary business matters if a party receives an order for the goods in which he deals and does not promptly intimate his refusal he will be deemed to have accepted the order and will be liable in damages if he does not fulfil it.[39] In other cases a man is not entitled to force a contract merely by intimating that he will regard his offer as accepted if it is not refused. Goods sent without an order, and without a previous course of dealing from which an order may be implied, may safely be

---

[33] *Carlill* v. *Carbolic Smoke Ball Co.* [1893] 1 Q.B. 256.
[34] Bell, *Comm.,* I., 343.
[35] *Edinburgh Employees Assurance Co.* v. *Griffiths* (1892) 19 R. 550.
[36] See *Oastler* v. *Henderson* (1877) 2 Q.B.D. 575. For an implied rejection, see *Lawrence* v. *Knight,* 1972 S.C. 26.
[37] Sale of Goods Act 1893, s. 35; *Mechan* v. *Bow, M'Lachlan & Co.,* 1910 S.C. 758.
[38] *Robertson* v. *Royal Exchange Assurance Corporation,* 1925 S.C. 1.
[39] *Barry, Ostlere & Shepherd* v. *Edinburgh Cork Importing Co.,* 1909 S.C. 1113.

rejected.[40] When A, writing to B in reference to a dispute, proposed a compromise, and added that he would assume that his proposal was accepted if he did not hear to the contrary within a certain number of days, it was held that B's failure to reply did not make the compromise binding on him.[41]

12. Incorporation of Terms.—An offer may be made conditionally; the conditions (or, more accurately, terms or stipulations) may be incorporated by express reference to the rules of an association[42] or to printed conditions a copy of which is obtainable from the offerer[43]; or they may be printed in the head-note of the letter of offer[44] or set forth in a separate notice.[45] If the offer is met by general acceptance, without any express reference to the conditions, in ordinary cases this will be read as an acceptance of the offer in the terms in which it was made, and provided that the conditions were reasonably brought to his notice the acceptor is not entitled to say that he had not noticed that conditions were imposed.[46] But this does not necessarily hold in the case where a ticket is issued by a carrier, and conditions, limiting the carrier's liability for the safe carriage of the passenger or his luggage, are printed on or issued with it; such conditions may, if sufficient notice has been given to the ticket-holder, be taken as being part of the contract, and so binding upon him and his representatives.[47] The question whether they are imported into the contract depends partly on the character of the ticket, partly on the knowledge of the passenger who takes it. If the conditions are printed on the back of the ticket, and no indication of their existence is given on the front, the passenger, if he can satisfy the Court that he was not aware that there were any conditions, is not bound by them.[48] If he has actually read the conditions he is clearly bound by them. If he knew that there were conditions, but did not read them, he will be bound by them, provided that they are reasonable and of such a character as might be expected on a ticket of the particular class.[49] On the other hand, where the conditions are not issued with the ticket or otherwise expressly made part of the contract, they cannot be incorporated into it by knowledge on the part of the passenger that conditions were usually imposed without knowledge of what they were.[50] If the front of the ticket referred to conditions printed on the back, but the passenger did not notice the reference, and was in fact unaware that there were any conditions, the question depends on the adequacy of the means adopted to bring them to his notice. A reference to conditions on the back, printed on the front of a

---

[40] *Jaffrey* v. *Boag* (1824) 3 S. 375; *Gilbert* v. *Dickson*, 1803 Hume 334.
[41] *Jaffrey* v. *Boag*, supra.
[42] *Stewart Brown & Co.* v. *Grime* (1897) 24 R. 414.
[43] *Smith* v. *U.M.B. Chrysler (Scotland) and South Wales Switchgear Co.*, 1978 S.L.T. 21.
[44] *Oakbank Oil Co.* v. *Love & Stewart*, 1918 S.C. (H.L.) 54.
[45] *W. N. White & Co.* v. *Dougherty* (1891) 18 R. 972; *Wright* v. *Howard Baker & Co.* (1893) 21 R. 25; *Lewis* v. *Laird Line*, 1925 S.L.T. 316. See also *Palmer* v. *Inverness Hospitals Board*, 1963 S.C. 311 (circular).
[46] *Oakbank Oil Co.* v. *Love*, supra.
[47] E.g. *McKay* v. *Scottish Airways*, 1948 S.C. 254.
[48] *Henderson* v. *Stevenson* (1875) 2 R. (H.L.) 71; *McCafferty* v. *Western S.M.T. Co.*, 1962 S.L.T. (Sh. Ct.) 39.
[49] *Lyons* v. *Caledonian Ry.*, 1909 S.C. 1185. Cf. *L'Estrange* v. *Graucob* [1934] 2 K.B. 394.
[50] *M'Cutcheon* v. *David MacBrayne*, 1964 S.C. (H.L.) 28.

steamer ticket, was held ineffectual when it was printed in the smallest known type, and in such a way as to be easily overlooked by a passenger, even if he were exercising ordinary care.[51] But when a ticket for a transatlantic voyage was enclosed in an envelope, with a distinct reference thereon to conditions printed on the ticket, it was held that the passenger was bound by them, though his evidence was that he had not noticed the reference and was unaware that there were any conditions on the ticket.[52] The ordinary form of a railway ticket, in which reference is made on the front to conditions on the back, and the conditions there contain nothing but a further reference to the company's time tables and bills, has been approved as affording sufficient notice to the passenger.[53] But this rule will not readily be extended to other types of contract.[54]

Conditions cannot be incorporated into a contract if they are not brought to the notice of the other party before the contract is completed.[55] But if there has been a consistent course of dealing between the parties and in each of the previous transactions conditions have been sent, after the contract was completed, by one party to the other who has raised no query or objection it may be held that the conditions are incorporated in a subsequent contract.[56] Where both parties are in the same trade and of equal bargaining power the conditions habitually imposed in contracts of the particular type may be held to be incorporated on the basis of the common understanding of the parties that the usual conditions would apply.[57]

13. Withdrawal of Offer.—As a general rule, an offer may be withdrawn at any time before acceptance. But a man may promise to enter into a contract if the party to whom he makes his offer chooses to accept, and does so if he states that his offer is open for a certain time.[58] And while in the ordinary case an application for shares in a company may be withdrawn before it is accepted by allotment, an application expressly stated to be irrevocable binds the applicant to take the shares if they are allotted to him.[59] An offer is impliedly withdrawn by the death of either party or by the offerer's bankruptcy or his insanity, even although the insanity has not been made public by any legal process, and the party who has accepted the offer was not aware of it.[60]

14. Conclusion of Contract by Acceptance: Time—An offer cannot be

---

[51] *Williamson* v. *North of Scotland Navigation Co.*, 1916 S.C. 554.
[52] *Hood* v. *Anchor Line*, 1918 S.C. (H.L.) 143.
[53] *Gray* v. *L. and N.E. Ry.*, 1930 S.C. 989; *Penton* v. *Southern Ry.*, [1931] 2 K.B. 103.
[54] *Taylor* v. *Glasgow Corporation*, 1952 S.C. 440.
[55] *M'Cutcheon* v. *David MacBrayne*, supra; *Olley* v. *Marlborough Court* [1949] 1 K.B. 532; *Thornton* v. *Shoe Lane Parking* [1971] 2 Q.B. 163.
[56] *Henry Kendall & Sons* v. *William Lillico & Sons* [1969] 2 A.C. 31; *Hollier* v. *Rambler Motors (A.M.C.)* [1972] 2 Q.B. 71. The principle may not operate where the conditions themselves incorporate by reference further conditions a copy of which is not readily available to the other party: *Grayston Plant* v. *Plean Precast*, 1976 S.C. 206. Cf. *Smith* v. *U.M.B. Chrysler (Scotland) and South Wales Switchgear Co.*, 1978 S.L.T. 21.
[57] *British Crane Hire Corporation* v. *Ipswich Plant Hire* [1975] 1 Q.B. 303.
[58] Supra, § 1.
[59] *Premier Briquette Co.* v. *Gray*, 1922 S.C. 329.
[60] *Thomson* v. *James* (1855) 18 D. 1, at p. 10.

withdrawn after acceptance. The time of acceptance is easily ascertained in contracts made verbally; it is a more difficult question in contracts made by letter or telegram. The rule is that acceptance takes effect when it is made in the manner indicated by the offer. In offers made by post it will be assumed, in the absence of any provision to the contrary, that an acceptance by letter is indicated; if so, the acceptance takes effect, and the contract is complete and binding, when the letter of acceptance is posted.[61] A message of any kind withdrawing the offer is too late if it does not arrive until after the acceptance has been posted.[62] But this rule assumes that both parties are acting in matters of business in an ordinary business way; when an offer was withdrawn by telegram which would have reached the offeree in time had he been at his place of business, it was held that the offer was effectually withdrawn although the offeree, writing to accept from some other place, had posted his letter before he actually received the telegram.[63] If there is a time fixed for acceptance it is sufficient for the acceptor to show that he posted his letter in time, although, by a delay in the post, it arrived too late.[64] It has been held in England that proof that an acceptance has been posted is sufficient to complete the contract even though the letter never arrives,[65] but this has been doubted in Scotland,[66] and the question must be considered to be open.

15. Withdrawal of Acceptance.—From the theory that a contract is completed when an acceptance is dispatched it might be inferred that an acceptance cannot be withdrawn. But in the only decision on the subject it was held that an acceptance was withdrawn effectually if the notice of withdrawal reached the offerer before, or together with, the letter of acceptance.[67]

16. Reasonable Time.—Acceptance must be within the time fixed by the offer, if any; if none, within a reasonable time. The question of what is a reasonable time may be solved by proof of a custom in the particular trade,[68] or may be decided on the whole circumstances of the case. Business offers, to buy or sell commodities which fluctuate in value, are assumed to be open for acceptance only by return of post.[69] An acceptance too late is in effect a new offer, which the original offerer may ignore without incurring any liability.[70] If a man admits that he has not accepted an offer within the proper time, and alleges that in the course of negotiation the time was extended, it lies on him to prove a definite agreement to that effect.[71]

---

[61] Where methods of instantaneous communication are used, e.g. the telephone or Telex, the rule, at any rate in England, is that the contract is not complete until the acceptance has been received by the offerer: *Entores Ltd.* v. *Miles Far East Corp.* [1955] 2 Q.B. 327.
[62] *Thomson* v. *James,* supra; *Henthorn* v. *Fraser* [1892] 2 Ch. 27.
[63] *Burnley* v. *Alford,* 1919 2 S.L.T. 123.
[64] *Jacobsen* v. *Underwood* (1894) 21 R. 654.
[65] *Household Fire Insurance Co.* v. *Grant* (1879) 4 Ex. D. 216.
[66] *Mason* v. *Benhar Coal Co.* (1882) 9 R. 883.
[67] *Countess of Dunmore* v. *Alexander* (1830) 9 S. 190.
[68] *Murray* v. *Rennie* (1897) 24 R. 965.
[69] *Wylie & Lochhead* v. *M'Elroy* (1873) 1 R. 41, per Lord President Inglis.
[70] *Wylie & Lochhead* v. *M'Elroy,* supra.
[71] *Glasgow Steam Shipping Co.* v. *Watson* (1873) 1 R 189.

17. Conditional Acceptance.—An acceptance must meet the offer.[72] If what bears to be an acceptance proposes new conditions it is in effect a new offer, which the other party may accept or not as he pleases. But if the acceptance contains a meaningless condition, that condition will be ignored and the contract, if otherwise good, held to be concluded.[73] A party who accepts an offer may be bound although in his acceptance he may propose conditions as to the method in which the contract may be carried into effect.[74] This question has arisen chiefly in cases where an offer, made verbally or by letter, is met by an acceptance "subject to contract," "subject to formal contract," or other equivalent terms. Is this merely a condition as to the method in which the contract which has been completed may be carried out, or does it postpone the mutual agreement until the formal contract has been drawn up and signed? In *Erskine* v. *Glendinning*,[75] an offer to let was accepted with the qualification "subject to lease drawn out in due form." It was held that a contract was completed by this acceptance, and that the party who had accepted could not withdraw. But where an imperfectly authenticated acceptance contained the words "subject to contract" it was held, distinguishing *Erskine* v. *Glendinning*,[75] that the obligation was suspended.[76] Where parties to an action agree to a settlement, though with a provision that its terms are to be embodied in a joint minute, the agreement is completely binding.[77]

18. Locus Poenitentiae.—While the engagement is still incomplete, e.g. while the offer remains unaccepted, or the writing, where this is required by law or has been stipulated for,[78] has yet to be executed, parties have the right to withdraw from negotiations; this right is termed locus poenitentiae.[79] It may, in the case where an offer is met by a qualified acceptance, be lost if the party proposing to withdraw has allowed the other to act on the assumption that the contract is complete. Such actings are known as rei interventus.[80] The meaning of this term will be considered in dealing with verbal or improbative agreements relating to heritage.[81] In cases where full agreement has never been reached but one or other of the parties has acted on the assumption that it has, it may be shown that they mistook each other's attitude so completely that the contract supposed to be accepted was a different one from that which was offered. In that event, in spite of any action that may have followed, the conclusion must be that since there was no agreement to any contract, matters must be restored as far as possible to their original position, and that neither party is under any obligation. This was the solution in a case where, owing to

[72] *Mathieson Gee (Ayrshire) Ltd.* v. *Quigley*, 1952 S.C. (H.L.) 38.
[73] *Nicolene, Ltd.* v. *Simmonds* [1953] 1 Q.B. 543.
[74] See *Ingram-Johnson* v. *Century Insurance Co.*, 1909 S.C. 1032; *Thomson* v. *James* (1855) 18 D. 1, at pp. 14 and 23.
[75] (1871) 9 M. 656.
[76] *Stobo, Ltd.* v. *Morrisons (Gowns) Ltd.*, 1949 S.C. 184.
[77] *Dewar* v. *Ainslie* (1892) 20 R. 203; *Murphy* v. *Smith*, 1920 S.C. 104.
[78] Agreements Defective in Form, Ch. VII., infra, § 3; see *Stobo, Ltd.*, supra, per Lord President Cooper at p. 192.
[79] Bell, *Prin.*, § 25.
[80] Gloag, *Contract*, 2nd ed., pp. 46, 172.
[81] Infra, Agreements Defective in Form, Ch. VII, § 4.

a misunderstanding, a tenant had made two offers for a farm, materially different in their conditions, and had entered into possession. It was held that there had been no agreement and that the tenant must remove.[82] In the more common case where substantial agreement has been reached, but minor details are still unsettled, it will be held that the offerer, if he knows that the other is proceeding to act in reliance on the contract, and does not interfere, has waived his objection to the terms proposed.[83] Where a person is barred by his actions from founding on the informality of contract, but it eventually proves that the other party cannot offer a valid title, he is entitled to repudiate.[84]

19. Implied Terms.—There are several types of implied term; a term may be implied in a contract because the law infers the term as an incident of contracts of a particular class;[85] a term may be implied by custom of trade;[86] a term may be implied by a previous course of dealing;[87] a term may be implied because in the circumstances of the particular contract it is necessary to give the contract business efficacy. As to the last of these cases—"The Court will only hold a term or condition to be implied in a written contract if its nature is such that it must necessarily be implied to give the contract business efficacy."[88] A term cannot be implied in a contract which contradicts its expressed terms.[89]

---

[82] *Buchanan* v. *Duke of Hamilton* (1878) 5 R. (H.L.) 69.
[83] *Colquhoun* v. *Wilson's Trs.* (1860) 22 D. 1035; *Roberts & Cooper* v. *Salvesen*, 1918 S.C. 794.
[84] *Kinnear* v. *Young*, 1936 S.L.T. 574.
[85] Gloag on *Contract*, p. 286; *Sterling Engineering Co.* v. *Patchett* [1955] A.C. 534 at p. 547, per Lord Reid; *Lister* v. *Romford Ice and Cold Storage Co.* [1957] A.C. 555, per Viscount Simonds at p. 579, Lord Tucker at p. 594; *Liverpool City Council* v. *Irwin* [1977] A.C. 239, per Lord Wilberforce at p. 253, Lord Cross at p. 257.
[86] Infra, Rules of Evidence in Relation to Contract, Ch. XII, § 18.
[87] Supra, § 12.
[88] Per Lord Jamieson, *M'Whirter* v. *Longmuir*, 1948 S.C. 577, at p. 589. The oft-quoted dictum of Lord McLaren in *Wm. Morton & Co.* v. *Muir Brothers & Co.*, 1907 S.C. 1211 at p. 1224, seems to relate to other types of implication. The well-known dictum of Bowen L. J. in *The Moorcock* (1889) 14 P.D. 64, at p. 68, has been criticised (Gloag on *Contract*, p. 289). There is also the "officious bystander" test: *Shirlaw* v. *Southern Foundries* [1939] 2 K.B. 206, per MacKinnon L.J. at p. 227; see also *Spring* v. *National Amalgamated Stevedores and Dockers Society* [1956] 1 W.L.R. 585; *Microwave Systems (Scotland)* v. *Electro-Physiological Instruments*, 1971 S.C. 140.
[89] *Cummings* v. *Charles Connell & Co. (Shipbuilders)*, 1968 S.C. 305.

CHAPTER V

AGREEMENTS VOID OR VOIDABLE

1. The statement at the outset of the last chapter that an obligation may result from mere consent is to be taken as a general rule, subject to important qualifications. There are many cases where real or apparent consent may have been given and yet no obligation may arise. This may result (1) from want of capacity in the party[1]; (2) from defect of form[2]; (3) from the nature of the means by which consent was obtained[3]; (4) from error precluding real consent[4]; or (5) from the illegality of the matter involved.[5]

2. Contracts Void, Voidable or Unenforceable.—These objections to the validity of consent may, according to the circumstances, render the obligation void, voidable or unenforceable. If an agreement, or apparent agreement, is void, it is to be treated, for all legal purposes, as a mere nullity. No one can enforce it, and, if it purport to convey property, no title to that property is given, even in a question with a third party, such as a sub-purchaser, who has no notice of the grounds of nullity. An agreement which is not void but merely voidable is valid until it is set aside by the party entitled to avoid it, with the result that if property has passed on a contract merely voidable, and has been transferred for value to a party who has no notice of any invalidity, that party's title is not affected by the reduction of the original contract.[6] An agreement is termed unenforceable when, owing to some statutory or other rule, it cannot be enforced by action, but is not so forbidden as to render it void, or to exclude the creation of incidental rights.

3. Conditions of Avoidance.—The fact that an obligation is voidable does not imply that in all circumstances it may be reduced. That is doubtless the general rule; in particular cases it may find exception on the ground (a) that restitutio in integrum is impossible; (b) that the interests of third parties are involved; (c) that the validity of the obligation has been recognised; (d) that there has been undue delay.

(a) RESTITUTIO IN INTEGRUM.—It is a general principle that where a party proposes to reduce a contract, he must be able to offer restitutio in integrum; in other words, must be able to restore the other party to the position in which he was before he entered into the contract. So if contractors have erected a building on a contract which proves to be voidable, the reduction of the

[1] Capacity to Contract, Ch. VI.
[2] Agreements Defective in Form, Ch. VII.
[3] Agreement Improperly Obtained, Ch. VIII.
[4] Ch. VIII, §§ 13-23.
[5] Pacta Illicita and Unfair Terms, Ch. IX.
[6] See *Morrisson* v. *Robertson*, 1908 S.C. 332; cf. *Macleod* v. *Kerr*, 1965 S.C. 253.

contract is precluded, whatever other remedies may in the particular case be available, on the ground that the original position of matters cannot be restored.[7] When an unincorporated company was incorporated under statute, it was held that as the original shares had been so altered that they could no longer be restored, a reduction of the contract to take shares was impossible.[8] When a particular thing has been sold, and resold by the purchaser, he cannot reduce the sale because he cannot restore the thing. His title to reduce the sale is not improved by re-acquiring the thing from the sub-purchaser.[9] But when the sub-sale was also reducible on the same ground (a misrepresentation as to the condition of the thing), and was on that ground reduced by the sub-purchaser, it was held that a reduction of the original sale was competent.[10] Restitutio in integrum may be given in cases where the question depends on the possibility of restoring a particular thing, although that thing may in the meantime have diminished in value. So a contract to take shares may be reduced so long as the company is a going concern, though the shares may have become valueless.[11] The interest in a partnership could be restored though the business was openly insolvent.[12] If a particular thing has been transferred under the contract and has been accidentally destroyed, it would appear that the contract cannot be reduced.[13] But if it has perished owing to the fault of the party proposing to maintain the contract, as when a horse, warranted sound in work, ran away and was killed, that party cannot found upon his own wrong or breach of warranty, and so cannot resist the reduction of the contract (involving repayment of the price) on the plea that restitutio in integrum cannot be offered.[14] And when a person by fraud has been able to purchase something, he may not in bar of restitution rely upon dealings with the thing purchased which his fraud has enabled him to carry out.[15]

4. (b) INTERESTS OF THIRD PARTIES.—The interests of third parties do not preclude the reduction of a contract in so far as that contract involves merely a personal obligation. So if a bond is granted under circumstances which render it voidable in a question with the original creditor, it remains voidable in a question with anyone to whom it may be assigned.[16] The obligation of an insurance company on a policy of insurance, if voidable on the ground of misrepresentation by the insured, may be reduced in a question with an assignee.[17] In cases of the assignation of a debt or other personal obligation

---

[7] *Boyd & Forrest* v. *Glasgow and S.W. Ry.*, 1915 S.C. (H.L.) 20. See also *Hay* v. *Rafferty* (1899) 2 F. 302.

[8] *Western Bank* v. *Addie* (1867) 5 M. (H.L.) 80.

[9] *Edinburgh United Breweries* v. *Molleson* (1894) 21 R. (H.L.) 10.

[10] *Westville Shipping Co.* v. *Abram Shipping Co.*, 1922 S.C. 571; affd. 1923 S.C. (H.L.) 68.

[11] *Western Bank* v. *Addie* (1867) 5 M. (H.L.) 80, opinion of Lord Cranworth; *Armstrong* v. *Jackson* [1917] 2 K.B. 822.

[12] *Adam* v. *Newbigging* (1888) 13 App. Cas. 308.

[13] See opinion of Lord Atkinson, *Boyd & Forrest* v. *Glasgow and S.W. Ry.*, 1915 S.C. (H.L.) 20, 29.

[14] *Kinnear* v. *Brodie* (1902) 3 F. 540; *Rowland* v. *Divall* [1923] 2 K.B. 500.

[15] *Spence* v. *Crawford*, 1939 S.C. (H.L.) 52.

[16] *Nisbet's Creditors* v. *Robertson* (1791) M. 9554; *M'Donells* v. *Bell & Rannie* (1772) M. 4974.

[17] *Scottish Widows' Fund* v. *Buist* (1876) 3 R. 1078; *Graham Shipping Co.* v. *Merchants Marine Insurance* [1924] A.C. 294.

(not embodied in a negotiable instrument) the maxim "assignatus utitur jure auctoris" applies, and the assignee may be met by any defence which was available against the cedent.[18] But if the result of the contract was not merely to create a personal obligation but to transfer a real right in some particular property—as where land is conveyed or goods are sold on a contract induced by misrepresentation—the original seller cannot reduce the contract so as to recover the property if it has been transferred to a third party either by sale or in security. The original sale carries a title to the property, and, though that title may be voidable, it is valid until reduced, and third parties may acquire indefeasible rights under it. This rule, recognised as a general principle in the earliest authorities,[19] may be stated in the language of the Sale of Goods Act 1893, s. 23: when the seller of goods has a voidable title thereto, but his title has not been avoided at the time of the sale, the buyer acquires a good title to the goods, provided he buys them in good faith and without notice of the seller's defect in title.[20]

INTERESTS OF CREDITORS.—When third parties are interested in maintaining a contract, not as the holders of subordinate real rights, but merely as personal creditors of the original party, it is a general rule that their interests do not preclude the reduction of the contract. The distinction between the position of heritable creditors, who obtain a real right to the lands, and adjudgers, who were only personal creditors, was taken in an early and leading case.[21] And it is settled that a trustee in a sequestration cannot take advantage of the bankrupt's fraud, and therefore cannot maintain a right which the bankrupt has acquired by fraudulent means.[22] The chief exception to this rule is the case where shares are taken in reliance on misrepresentations in the prospectus. It is established law, proceeding largely on inferences derived from the terms of the Companies Acts, that the contract cannot be reduced after the company has gone into liquidation, on the ground that the real interest is then in the creditors, or, where all creditors are paid, in the other shareholders.[23] It has been observed that a partner, reducing the contract of partnership on the ground that he has been induced to enter into it by fraud, would remain liable to the creditors of the firm.[24]

5. (c) RECOGNITION OF VALIDITY.—Cases where the reduction of a contract is precluded on the ground that the party proposing to reduce it has

[18] See opinion of Lord President Inglis, *Scottish Widows' Fund* v. *Buist*, supra.
[19] Stair, IV, 40, 21.
[20] For illustrative cases, see *Bryce* v. *Ehrmann* (1905) 7 F. 5; *Morrisson* v. *Robertson*, 1908 S.C. 332 (contrast between void and voidable contract); *Price & Pierce* v. *Bank of Scotland*, 1910 S.C. 1095; affd. 1912 S.C. (H.L.) 19.
[21] *Thomson* v. *Douglas Heron & Co.* (1786) M. 10229; 3 Ross' Leading Cases, 132. See also opinion of Lord Watson, *Heritable Reversionary Co.* v. *Millar* (1892) 19 R. (H.L.) 43.
[22] *Colquhoun's Tr.* v. *Campbell's Trs.* (1902) 4 F. 739; *Gamage* v. *Charlesworth's Tr.*, 1910 S.C. 257.
[23] *Oakes* v. *Turquand* (1867) L.R. 2 H.L. 325; *Tennent* v. *City of Glasgow Bank* (1879) 6 R. (H.L.) 69; *Burgess' Case* (1880) 15 Ch.D. 507. Contrast the case where the contract to take shares is actually void, as where A., intending to apply for shares in one company, applied for shares in another; *Baillie's Case* [1898] 1 Ch. 110.
[24] Opinion of Lord Chancellor Cairns in *Tennent* v. *City of Glasgow Bank*, supra.

recognised its validity are in Scotland known as cases of homologation and of adoption. Homologation applies to a voidable contract; adoption, to a contract, or apparent contract, actually void.

HOMOLOGATION.—Homologation is implied by any acts whereby a party, in the knowledge that a particular obligation is voidable, recognises its validity. "The law of homologation proceeds on the principle of presumed consent by the party who does the acts to pass from grounds of challenge known to him, and sciens et prudens to adopt the challengeable deed as his own."[25] Such acts as the payment or receipt of rent on a voidable lease,[26] payment of interest on a bond,[27] continuance of business with a banker on a system to which the customer might have objected,[28] helping with proceedings in the Dean of Guild Court in regard to ground alleged sold,[29] amount to homologation and bar any subsequent challenge. As a rule, and in all cases of isolated acts, it is necessary to prove that the party alleged to have homologated was aware of all the material facts,[30] but in certain cases of long sustained relationship adequate means of knowledge have been held to be sufficient.[31] The effect of homologation is to validate the obligation from the date of its inception.

ADOPTION.—Adoption applies to cases where there is nothing but the semblance of an obligation. By recognising its validity the party may render himself liable on a new contract to be inferred from his acts. The most important cases have related to forged bills. If a party whose signature is forged chooses to accept liability, he has adopted the bill, and he may act in such a way as to amount to adoption and consequent liability without any express recognition of his signature.[32] But this will not be easily inferred, and it is now established that mere silence, in face of an intimation that the bill is due, does not amount to adoption and infers no liability.[33] Where a person discovers that his signature has been forged to a document, it is his duty to inform the creditor at once, but the creditor can recover against him only if he can establish that he has been prejudiced by any delay in informing him.[34] If the objection to the contract be that the body which entered into it was acting ultra vires, no acts approving of it can cure the invalidity, or have any legal effect, unless in the meantime the contractual powers of the body have been enlarged.[35]

---

[25] *Gardner* v. *Gardner* (1830) 9 S. 138. Quoted and approved by Lord President Clyde, *Danish Dairy Co.* v. *Gillespie*, 1922 S.C. 656, 664. For a discussion of the limits of homologation, see *Westville Shipping Co.* v. *Abram Shipping Co.*, 1922 S.C. 571; affd. 1923 S.C. (H.L.) 68.

[26] *Rigg* v. *Durward* (1776) M. App. Fraud, No. 2; *Lord Advocate* v. *Wemyss* (1899) 2 F. (H.L.) 1.

[27] *M'Calman* v. *M'Arthur* (1864) 2 M. 678.

[28] *Crerar* v. *Bank of Scotland*, 1921 S.C. 736; affd. 1922 S.C. (H.L.) 137.

[29] *Mitchell* v. *Stornoway Trs.*, 1936 S.C. (H.L.) 56.

[30] *Danish Dairy Co.* v. *Gillespie*, 1922 S.C. 656.

[31] *Lord Advocate* v. *Wemyss* (1899) 2 F. (H.L.) 1; *Crerar* v. *Bank of Scotland*, supra.

[32] *Greenwood* v. *Martins Bank* [1933] A.C. 51.

[33] *MacKenzie* v. *British Linen Co.* (1881) 8 R. (H.L.) 8; *British Linen Co.* v. *Cowan* (1906) 8 F. 704; *Muir's Exrs.* v. *Craig's Trs.*, 1913 S.C. 349.

[34] *Muir's Exrs.*, supra.

[35] *General Property Investment Co.* v. *Matheson's Trs.* (1888) 16 R. 282; and see Capacity to Contract, Ch. VI., infra, § 11.

6. (d) DELAY.—In certain cases delay in taking action will preclude reduction of a contract.[36] This primarily depends on the nature of the defect which renders the contract voidable. Some grounds of avoidance are not maintainable unless they are taken advantage of within a specified or a reasonable time. Thus a minor may reduce a contract, but only if he takes action before attaining the age of twenty-two.[37] The right to reject goods, and treat the contract as repudiated in the case where the goods are disconform to contract, must be exercised within a reasonable time.[38] The right to reduce a contract to take shares, on the ground of misrepresentation in the prospectus, must certainly be exercised within a reasonable time,[39] and probably must be followed by steps for the rectification of the register.[40] In other cases, for instance in the case of contracts voidable on the ground of fraud or misrepresentation, in a question between the original parties any delay, short of the negative prescription of twenty years, is not a bar to reduction.[41] But if in consequence of unnecessary delay evidence has been lost, any point which it might have elucidated will be presumed in the defender's favour.[42] Where the interests of third parties are concerned, the law is far from clear, but it would appear that unreasonable delay may preclude reduction.[43]

[36] See also Extinction of Obligations, Ch. XV., infra.
[37] Capacity to Contract, Ch. VI., infra, §§ 3 and 4.
[38] Sale of Goods Act 1893, s. 11.
[39] *Aaron's Reefs* v. *Twiss* [1896] A.C. 273.
[40] *First National Re-Insurance Co.* v. *Greenfield* [1921] 2 K.B. 260.
[41] See, e.g., *Robinson* v. *Robinson's Trs.*, 1934 S.L.T. 183.
[42] *Bain* v. *Assets Co.* (1905) 7 F. (H.L.) 104.
[43] See *Fraser* v. *Hankey* (1847) 9 D. 415; *Buckner* v. *Jopp's Trs.* (1887) 14 R. 1006. The numerous cases are collected and, so far as possible, reconciled in Rankine, *Personal Bar*, Ch. V.

CHAPTER VI

CAPACITY TO CONTRACT

1. The first case which calls for notice as rendering an agreement void or voidable is the want of capacity to contract. The contractual powers of pupils, minors, lunatics, aliens and corporate bodies are the points which have to be considered.[1]

2. Pupils.—The law of Scotland divides nonage into two periods; pupillarity, until the age of 12 in the case of girls, 14 in the case of boys; minority, from the expiry of pupillarity until the age of 18. A pupil may have a tutor, who may contract on his behalf.[2] Whether he has a tutor or not he has no power to contract. Any agreement he may make is void, cannot be enforced against him, nor can any right be founded on it. If necessaries have been sold and delivered to a pupil, he must pay a reasonable price therefor.[3] If money has been lent, it may be recovered if and in so far as it has been expended for the benefit (in rem versum) of the pupil, as in the repair of his house.[4] In neither case is the obligation contractual; it is implied by law.

3. Minors.—The contractual powers of a minor depend upon whether he has a curator or not. If he has, and contracts with the curator's consent and concurrence, he has the ordinary contractual powers, except that he cannot dispose of his heritable property gratuitously.[5] Contracts without the curator's concurrence are void, with probable exceptions in the case of contracts of service or apprenticeship,[6] and contracts in the course of a trade carried on by the minor.[7] If a minor has no curator, he has the same power to contract as a minor with the consent and concurrence of his curator.[8] In all cases, however, whether the minor has a curator or not, his contracts may be voidable during his minority and for a period of four years after he attains majority, a period known as the quadriennium utile.

4. Minority and Lesion.—The ground on which contracts by a minor may be avoided is minority and lesion. Lesion means some considerable, or "enorm," injury to the minor's estate, it being a recognised rule that a lesser injury will be regarded as enorm if the minor acted alone than if he acted with

---

[1] The common law incapacity of a married woman was abolished by the Married Women's Property (Scotland) Act 1920.
[2] As to Tutors and Curators, see Index. The doctrine of minority and lesion (infra, § 4) applies to contracts made by the tutor on behalf of the pupil: Erskine I, 7, 34.
[3] Sale of Goods Act 1893, s. 2.
[4] *Scott's Tr.* v. *Scott* (1887) 14 R. 1043.
[5] *Brown's Tr.* v. *Brown* (1897) 24 R. 962.
[6] *M'Feetridge* v. *Stewarts & Lloyds*, 1913 S.C. 773.
[7] *O'Donnell* v. *Brownieside Coal Co.*, 1934 S.C. 534.
[8] See opinion of Lord President Inglis, *Hill* v. *City of Glasgow Bank* (1879) 7 R. 68.

a curator.[9] What will be regarded as lesion depends upon the character of the contract. Lesion to the estate is obvious, and there is no defence to the minor's action, in the case of pure gifts, cautionary obligations, and discharge of debt for an inadequate sum.[10] In the case of sale by the minor, or loans to him, reduction is competent if the terms were not reasonably fair, and also if the minor has squandered the price so that his estate at majority is diminished.[11] A purchaser from a minor is entitled to insist on security for the beneficial investment of the price.[12] Under the Consumer Credit Act 1974, s. 50, it is a criminal offence to send any document to a minor inviting him to borrow money, but there is no provision that a loan to a minor shall be void, and it is probably voidable only on proof of lesion. A compromise of the minor's claims is reducible if, considering the whole consideration obtained by the minor, it was not reasonably fair.[13] An ante-nuptial marriage contract may be reduced if, looking to the husband's means at the time of marriage, the provision for the minor wife was not reasonably adequate.[14] In the case of purchases by a minor the common law recognised his contractual liability and held that lesion existed only if what was purchased was extravagant considering the minor's position in life.[15] The provisions of section 2 of the Sale of Goods Act 1893 do not seem to add in any way to the minor's liability. If what was purchased was reasonable and sold at a fair price, the fact that it has subsequently been accidentally destroyed does not amount to lesion.[16]

The plea of minority and lesion is excluded (1) if the minor held himself out as of full age, and was believed on reasonable grounds[17]; (2) if the minor was in business or trade, and the contract was connected with that business or trade[18]; (3) if after attaining majority the minor has ratified the contract, in full knowledge of the facts and of his legal rights.[19]

A reduction on the ground of minority and lesion may be brought by the trustee in the minor's sequestration,[20] or, in the event of his death before the expiry of the quadriennium utile, by his representatives.[21] Where the contract is only voidable and not void, a third party to whom property conveyed by a

---

[9] *Cooper* v. *Cooper's Trs.* (1885) 12 R. 473.
[10] Stair, I, 6, 44.
[11] *Harkness* v. *Graham* (1833) 11 S. 760.
[12] *Ferguson* v. *Yuill* (1835) 13 S. 886.
[13] *Robertson* v. *Henderson* (1905) 7 F. 776; *M'Feetridge* v. *Stewarts & Lloyds,* 1913 S.C. 773. And see *O'Donnell* v. *Brownieside Coal Co.,* 1934 S.C. 534; *Faulds* v. *British Steel Corporation,* 1977 S.L.T. (Notes) 18.
[14] *Cooper* v. *Cooper's Trs.* (1885) 12 R. 473.
[15] *Fountaine* v. *Foster,* 1808 Hume 409.
[16] *Edgar* v. *Edgar* (1614) M. 8986.
[17] *Wilkie* v. *Dunlop* (1834) 12 S. 506. This is not the law in England, *Leslie* v. *Shiell* [1914] 3 K.B. 607.
[18] *M'Feetridge* v. *Stewarts & Lloyds,* 1913 S.C. 773. In *O'Donnell* v. *Brownieside Coal Co.* supra, the Court inclined strongly against treating an industrial employee as a minor engaged in "trade." "Trade" does not include gambling on the Stock Exchange, *Dennistoun* v. *Mudie* (1850) 12 D. 613. *Hill* v. *City of Glasgow Bank* (1879) 7 R. 68 leaves open the question whether a minor investing in shares involving liability can reduce the contract within the quadriennium utile.
[19] *M'Gibbon* v. *M'Gibbon* (1852) 14 D. 605.
[20] *Harkness* v. *Graham* (1833) 11 S. 760.
[21] *Bruce* v. *Hamilton* (1854) 17 D. 265.

minor has been transferred is safe, unless, from the narrative in the title or otherwise, he had notice of the minority.[22]

5. Insanity.—An insane person has no power to contract and contracts into which he enters are void.[23] If necessaries are sold and delivered to him, he must pay a reasonable price for them.[24] Generally his contracts are void, even although the other party may not have known that he was dealing with a lunatic.[25] But continuing contracts, into which a party has entered while he was sane, are not necessarily avoided by his supervening insanity. Thus partnership is not dissolved merely by the insanity of a partner, though that is a ground on which its dissolution may be decreed by the Court.[26] In Scotland it has been decided that the mandate of a law agent to carry on an action did not fall by the supervening insanity of the client,[27] but the English Courts have arrived at the opposite conclusion.[28] Drunkenness is not a ground for the avoidance of a contract unless it reaches a stage at which the party no longer knows what he is doing and can give no true consent. An obligation undertaken in that condition is voidable, provided that the party takes steps to avoid as soon as he recovers his senses and knows what he has done.[29]

6. Alien Enemies.—The incapacity of an alien arises only in the event of war, except that he cannot be registered as the owner of a British ship. During war any contract with an alien enemy is illegal, and a criminal offence,[30] unless a licence from the Crown has been obtained. The law in this respect has regard to residence, not to nationality or allegiance.[31] So a party voluntarily residing or carrying on business in an enemy country is an alien enemy, though his nationality may be British or neutral. Conversely, a person of enemy nationality, but resident in this country, does not lose his power of contract.[32] But a company, though registered in Britain, and carrying on its business here, may be an alien enemy if it is controlled by persons who individually hold that character, not merely because the majority of the shareholders are alien enemies.[33] A person resident in enemy-occupied territory is not eo ipso an alien enemy. If there is full and established control, he will be, but not if the occupation is slighter and less thorough.[34] A British prisoner of war in enemy territory is not an alien enemy.[35]

[22] Erskine, I, 7, 40.
[23] Stair, I, 10, 3; Erskine, III, 1, 16.
[24] Sale of Goods Act 1893, s. 2.
[25] *Loudon* v. *Elder's Curator*, 1923 S.L.T. 226.
[26] Partnership Act 1890, s. 35.
[27] *Wink* v. *Mortimer* (1849) 11 D. 995.
[28] *Yonge* v. *Toynbee* [1910] 1 K.B. 215.
[29] *Pollok* v. *Burns* (1875) 2 R. 497.
[30] Trading with the Enemy Act 1939, as amended by the Emergency Laws (Miscellaneous Provisions) Act 1953, s. 2.
[31] *Janson* v. *Driefontein Mines* [1902] A.C. 484.
[32] *Schulze Gow & Co.* v. *Bank of Scotland*, 1914, 2 S.L.T. 455. And he may resort to the Scottish Courts: *Weiss* v. *Weiss*, 1940 S.L.T. 447; *Schulze*, 1917 S.C. 400.
[33] *Daimler* v. *Continental Tyre Co.* [1916] 2 A.C. 307; *Re Badische Co.* [1921] 2 Ch. 331. And cf. *Van Uden* v. *Burrell*, 1916 S.C. 391.
[34] *Sovfracht* v. *Van Uden* [1943] A.C. 203; *Re Anglo-International Bank* [1943] 1 Ch. 233.
[35] *Vandyke* v. *Adams* [1942] Ch. 155.

7. Corporate Bodies.—Apart from a few exceptional cases, corporations in Scotland owe their origin to a royal charter, to an Act of Parliament or to the machinery provided by the Companies Acts. A particular body may act both under charter and under powers conferred by statute. The limitations of the contractual powers of a corporation depend upon its origin. A body acting under royal charter has the power to enter into any contract which is not expressly forbidden by its charter.[36] Any restriction on its activities rests, not on any limitation of its contractual powers, but on the principle that certain applications of its funds may amount to a breach of trust. So where the town council of a royal burgh, acting under charter, and possessed of property known as the common good, maintained the legality of applying its funds to further the candidature of persons in other burghs professing particular views, it was held that such expenditure amounted to a breach of trust and was ultra vires. The contention that a chartered body might do anything which an individual might lawfully do was repelled.[37]

8. Law of Ultra Vires.—A corporate body created by statute, or exercising statutory powers, cannot enter into any contract, or dispose of its funds in any way which is not authorised by the statute or reasonably incidental to the powers conferred. Thus a body established for one purpose cannot lawfully engage in any enterprise substantially different, or beyond the geographical limits within which it is authorised to act.[38] The mere fact that all the persons interested in the corporate body have consented will not validate an act which is ultra vires. So when a tramway company, incorporated by a private Act of Parliament, contracted to pay a lump sum to parties who had incurred expenses in procuring the Act, it was decided that the validity of the contract must depend upon some authority given in the Act, and, as that was lacking, that it could not be enforced because all the shareholders had consented.[39]

9. Companies.—A company incorporated under the Companies Act 1948 must register with the Registrar of Companies a memorandum of association, and in it must state, inter alia, "the objects of the company."[40] There is no limit to the powers which a company may assume in its memorandum, and in modern practice these are very wide. It is an unsettled question whether a memorandum which takes power to do anything which can be done by a corporate body satisfies the statutory obligation to state "the objects of the company."[41] Any contract which is not within the powers taken in the memorandum is ultra vires and void.[42]

However, in favour of a person dealing with the company in good faith,

[36] *Conn* v. *Corporation of Renfrew* (1906) 8 F. 905.
[37] *Kemp* v. *Corporation of Glasgow*, 1920 S.C. (H.L.) 73.
[38] *Nicol* v. *Dundee Harbour Trs.*, 1915 S.C. (H.L.) 7; *Grieve* v. *Edinburgh Water Trs.*, 1918 S.C. 700.
[39] *Mann* v. *Edinburgh Northern Tramways Co.* (1892) 20 R. (H.L.) 7.
[40] Companies Act 1948, ss. 1 and 2. As to alteration of the memorandum, see Company Law, Ch. XXV., infra, § 9.
[41] *Cotman* v. *Brougham* [1918] A.C. 514.
[42] *Shiell's Trs.* v. *Scottish Property Investment Co.* (1884) 12 R. (H.L.) 14.

any transaction decided on by the directors is deemed to be within the capacity of the company to enter into, and the power of the directors to bind the company is deemed to be free of any limitation under the memorandum or articles of association; and a party to a transaction so decided on is not bound to inquire as to the company's capacity to enter into it or as to any such limitation on the powers of the directors, and is presumed to have acted in good faith unless the contrary is proved.[43]

10. Classes of Ultra Vires Acts.—In cases of bodies under statute, and more particularly in cases of companies, ultra vires acts fall into three classes. An act may be (1) ultra vires of the company; or (2) intra vires of the company but ultra vires of the directors; or (3) intra vires only on condition that certain formalities are observed. In the first case except in a situation to which s. 9 of the European Communities Act 1972 applies,[44] the ultra vires act is void, and cannot be ratified even by the consent or approval of all the shareholders.[45] Nor can a corporate body be barred from pleading that it had no power to do that which it purports to have done.[46] In the second case the contract may be ratified by a general meeting called for that purpose, or by the consent of all the shareholders, and will then be valid.[47] In the third case the company may be barred from pleading the invalidity of its contract if that invalidity be due to the fact that its procedure has not been regular. Third parties dealing with a company are entitled to assume that what has been called the indoor management of the company has been properly carried on. So when the directors of a company had power to sell heritage, if sanctioned by a general meeting, it was held that the company could not challenge the sale on the ground that the notices calling the meeting at which it was sanctioned were irregular.[48] This principle, often referred to as the rule in *Turquand's* case,[49] will not render the company liable on share certificates forged by its secretary[50] and is subject to the consideration that any proceedings out of the ordinary course of business ought to provoke inquiry.[51]

11. Title to Reduce Contracts.—A contract which is not within, or not deemed to be within, the company's capacity to enter into, and therefore a nullity, may be reduced in an action at the instance of the company itself,[52] or

[43] European Community Act 1972 (c. 68) s. 9 (1).
[44] See § 9 supra.
[45] *Mann* v. *Edinburgh Northern Tramways Co.* (1892) 20 R. (H.L.) 7.
[46] *General Property Investment Co.* v. *Matheson's Trs.* (1888) 16 R. 282.
[47] *Irvine* v. *Union Bank of Australia* (1877) 2 App. Cas. 366; *Phosphate of Lime Co.* v. *Green* (1871) L.R. 7 C.P. 43.
[48] *Heiton* v. *Waverley Hydropathic Co.* (1877) 4 R. 830. See also *British Thomson Houston Co.* v. *Federated European Bank* [1932] 2 K.B. 176, not followed in *Rama Corporation Ltd.* v. *Proved Tin and General Investments Ltd.* [1952] 2 Q.B. 147; *Freeman & Lockyer* v. *Buckhurst Park Properties (Mangal)* [1964] 2 Q.B. 480 (company holding out a person as managing director).
[49] *Royal British Bank* v. *Turquand* (1856) 6 E. & B. 327. Applied, *Gillies* v. *Craigton Garage Co.*, 1935 S.C. 423.
[50] *Ruben* v. *Great Fingall Co.* [1906] A.C. 439.
[51] *Underwood* v. *Bank of Liverpool* [1924] 1 K.B. 775; *Houghton* v. *Nothard Lowe & Co.* [1928] A.C. 1.
[52] See § 9 supra.

of any shareholder.[53] Third parties, for instance trade rivals, have probably no title, and there is no precedent for the intervention of the Lord Advocate.[54] If the contract is one which may be ratified, the title to sue rests in most cases with the company alone, in effect with the majority of voting power.[55] A minority, or an individual shareholder, may sue on relevant averments that those having the majority are using their power for the purpose of perpetrating, or condoning, a fraud upon the company.[56]

12. Liability of Directors, etc.—The parties acting on behalf of a company which has entered into an ultra vires contract are personally liable to the other party if they fraudulently misrepresented the powers possessed by the company. If their representation was innocent but mistaken, and amounts to a representation of fact, as, for instance, that the company's borrowing powers have not been exceeded, they will be liable on the principle that they, as agents, impliedly warranted that they had the authority of the company as their principal.[57] But if the representation is merely one of law, as it is when the question turns on the construction of the private Act or of the powers taken in the memorandum of association, the directors or other managing body, acting honestly but mistakenly, incur no personal liability to those who have contracted with them.[58]

13. Methods of Contracting.—Corporate bodies necessarily act through their officers, directors or managers. Particular statutes sometimes enjoin a particular form of contracting[59]; if not, no special form is required in order to make a contract binding on a corporate body. So a verbal compromise of a claim for augmentation, made between the minister of a parish and the members of the governing body of a university, was sustained.[60]

14. Trade Unions.—A trade union[61] is not, and cannot be treated as if it were, a corporate body but it is capable of making contracts and can sue and be sued in its own name in proceedings founded on contract.[62] The purposes of any trade union are not, by reason only that they are in restraint of trade, unlawful so as to make any member of the union liable to criminal proceedings for conspiracy or otherwise or so as to make any agreement or

[53] *Balfour's Trs.* v. *Edinburgh and Northern Ry.* (1848) 10 D. 1240.
[54] *Nicol* v. *Dundee Harbour Trs.,* 1915 S.C. (H.L.) 7. In *Bell Houses* v. *City Wall Properties* [1966] 1 Q.B. 207, Mocatta J. held that the plea of ultra vires could be taken as a defence to an action at the instance of the company but this was doubted by Salmon L.J. on appeal ([1966] 2 Q.B. 656 at p. 694).
[55] *Brown* v. *Stewart* (1898) 1 F. 316; *Foss* v. *Harbottle* (1842) 2 Hare 461.
[56] *Hannay* v. *Muir* (1898) 1 F. 306; *Burland* v. *Earle* [1902] A.C. 83.
[57] *Firbank's Exrs.* v. *Humphreys* (1886) 18 Q.B.D. 54.
[58] *Beattie* v. *Lord Ebury* (1874) L.R. 7 H.L. 102.
[59] See, as to companies, Companies Act 1948, s. 32; *Panorama Developments (Guildford)* v. *Fidelis Furnishing Fabrics* [1971] 2 Q.B. 711.
[60] *Park* v. *University of Glasgow* (1675) M. 2535.
[61] Defined in Trade Union and Labour Relations Act 1974 , s. 28 (1).
[62] s. 2 (1).

trust void or voidable.[63] A rule of a trade union is not unlawful or unenforceable by reason only that it is in restraint of trade.[63]

An employers' association[64] may be a corporate body or an unincorporated association. If it is unincorporated it is nevertheless capable of making contracts and can sue and be sued in its own name.[65] The purposes and rules of an unincorporated employers' association, and, in or as far as they relate to the regulation of relations between employers and workers or trade unions, the purposes and rules of an association which is a corporate body, are not unlawful so as to give rise to criminal proceedings against the members or to make any agreement void or voidable or any such rule unenforceable.[66]

Neither a trade union nor an unincorporated employers' association can apply its funds directly or indirectly in the furtherance of political objects unless the furtherance of these objects has been approved as an object by a resolution passed on a ballot of members and rules governing the expenditure are approved by the Certification Officer appointed under the Employment Protection Act 1975.[67]

[63] s. 2 (5).
[64] Defined in s. 28 (2).
[65] s. 3.
[66] s. 3 (5).
[67] Trade Union Act 1913, s. 3 as amended by 1975 c. 71, s. 125 Sch. 16, Pt. IV. The political objects affected are specified in s. 3 (3).

CHAPTER VII

AGREEMENTS DEFECTIVE IN FORM. PROVINCE OF WRITING

Walker and Walker, *Evidence* (1964), Chs. IX-XI.

1. Defect of Form.—As a general rule the law of Scotland does not insist on any particular form for the constitution of a contractual obligation. It has nothing analogous to the stipulatio of the civil law. A contract may be entered into orally, or in writing, or may be inferred from the conduct of the parties. And the fact that an obligation has been undertaken may, in general, be proved prout de jure by any competent evidence. But these are only general rules. There are certain contracts where a verbal agreement is not binding, where the contract must be entered into in writing, and, in most cases, by writing in the form recognised as a probative writ. These contracts are usually termed obligationes litteris. There are other cases where, though there is no limitation as to the method by which contractual obligation may be created, the fact that it has been created can be proved only by the writ or oath of the party interested in denying it. In these cases (which will be considered in another chapter[1]) writing is necessary, not as a solemnity or formality in the constitution of the contract, but solely as a method of proof. Its necessity is not a part of the law of contract but of the law of evidence.

2. Obligationes Litteris.—The most important contracts which are classed as obligationes litteris, that is to say, contracts where writing is necessary to the constitution of an obligation, are contracts relating to heritage, certain contracts of employment and cautionary obligations.[2]

3. Contracts Relating to Heritage.—It is a well-established rule that contracts dealing with heritable property, with the exception of leases for a period not exceeding a year (which may be entered into verbally), must be entered into by a writing or writings probative of both parties to the contract.[3] If the agreement is merely verbal, or is entered into by writings which are not probative of both, and no actings have followed, either party is entitled to resile. The right to resile is not excluded by the fact that the party who proposes to exercise it has signed and delivered the improbative document with the full intention of binding himself to the contract. He is entitled to change his mind. Thus when A wrote out an offer and acceptance for the sale of a shop to B, signed the acceptance himself, and obtained the signature of B

---

[1] Rules of Evidence, Ch. XII, infra.
[2] As to cautionary obligations, see Ch. XXI, infra.
[3] Subscription of Deeds Act 1681 (c. 5). Stair, I, 10, 9. Bell, *Prin.*, §§ 889, 1187. As to probative writs see Rules of Evidence, Ch. XII. As to the meaning of contracts relating to heritage, see *U.K. Advertising Co.* v. *Glasgow Bag-Wash Laundry,* 1926 S.C. 303; *Allan* v. *Millar,* 1932 S.C. 620. See also *Perdikou* v. *Pattison,* 1958 S.L.T. 153; *Denvir* v. *Denvir,* 1969 S.L.T. 301.

to the offer, it was held that the contract was not binding, and that A was free to resile. He had signed an acceptance which, being holograph, was probative on his side, but the contract was not complete, and was therefore not binding on either party, because the corresponding offer, being signed without witnesses, was not probative of B.[4] "It may be that the defender is taking an undue advantage of the pursuer, but the law is quite settled that where there is not a tested writ or writs constituting the contract, or, failing them, holograph missives, there is locus poenitentiae to either of the parties, the subject of the contract being heritage."[5] And as the party who resiles is merely exercising a legal right, he is not liable in damages.

4. Rei Interventus.—If on an agreement entered into in writing, though in a writing not probative of each party, action has followed, and one party has altered his position or incurred expense, either to the knowledge of the other party, or in circumstances where such action or expenditure was the normal and probable result of the agreement, the right to resile is barred; despite the improbative nature of the writing the contract is completely binding and locus poenitentiae is excluded by rei interventus.[6] The informal documents must disclose consensus in idem[7]; but although rei interventus cannot be invoked to create an agreement, it may be proved by parole evidence in order to demonstrate that agreement has been reached.[8] Rei interventus may also exclude locus poenitentiae where the agreement is purely verbal, with this difference, that the fact that there was a verbal agreement can be proved only by the writ or oath of the party interested in denying it, and therefore that as a preliminary to any proof of action amounting to rei interventus, there must be proof, and by these limited forms of evidence, that a verbal agreement had been reached. Thus when a tenant averred that he had a verbal lease for three years, and that in reliance thereon, and to the landlord's knowledge, he had erected expensive buildings on the subjects let, it was held that there were relevant averments of rei interventus, but that the fact that there was an agreement for three years, and not, as the landlord maintained, for one year only, could be proved only by the landlord's writ or oath.[9]

5. Facts Amounting to Rei Interventus.—Rei interventus may consist in alterations in the property which is the subject of the contract,[10] in payment of the price or some substantial part of it,[11] or even, in the case of leases, in

---

[4] *Goldston* v. *Young* (1868) 7 M. 188.
[5] Per Lord President Inglis in *Goldston* v. *Young,* supra. See also *Gowan's Trs.* v. *Carstairs* (1862) 24 D. 1382.
[6] The following statement in Bell's *Principles* (§ 26) has become a legal classic: "Rei interventus raises a personal exception, which excludes the plea of locus poenitentiae. It is inferred from any proceedings not unimportant on the part of the obligee, known to and permitted by the obligor to take place on the faith of the contract as if it were perfect; provided they are unequivocally referable to the agreement, and productive of alteration of circumstances, loss, or inconvenience, though not irretrievable."
[7] *East Kilbride Development Co.* v. *Pollok,* 1953 S.C. 370.
[8] *Errol* v. *Walker,* 1966 S.C. 93.
[9] *Walker* v. *Flint* (1863) 1 M. 417; *Philip* v. *Cumming's Exrs.* (1869) 7 M. 859.
[10] *Colquhoun* v. *Wilson's Trs.* (1860) 22 D. 1035.
[11] *Foggo* v. *Hill* (1840) 2 D. 1322.

abstention, on the landlord's part, from efforts to obtain another tenant,[12] on the tenant's part, from efforts to obtain other accommodation[13]; this is, however, not an exhaustive list.[14] The actions or expenditure in question must be material, but need not be irretrievable. Thus though the payment of a small sum as earnest is not sufficient, the payment of the price is, though it might be repaid.[15] The actions or expenditure must be unequivocally referable to the agreement. Therefore entering into possession of the subjects, which is sufficient rei interventus on an agreement to sell,[16] is not sufficient to establish a lease for a period of years, because it may equally well be attributed to a lease for not more than a year.[17] And expenses incurred before the informal agreement, in making inquiries as to the subjects, or as to the title, are clearly not sufficient as rei interventus, because they are not referable to a pre-existing agreement but to one which has followed them.[18]

6. Completion of Title.—Where an action on an informal agreement has been successful on proof of rei interventus, the defender may be ordained to execute a formal contract (sale or lease as the case may be) in accordance with the agreement established against him.[19] On his refusal a remit may be made to a conveyancer to draw up an appropriate instrument, and, on a continued refusal to sign, the Clerk of Court may be authorised to sign on the defender's behalf.[20]

7. Interests of Third Parties.—Before any proceedings have been taken to establish the validity of an informal sale followed by rei interventus, the land in question may be resold to a third party. If he had no notice of the prior informal sale, his title is unchallengeable. If he had notice, he is bound to inquire and is not entitled to accept blindly the seller's statement that the prior negotiations had been broken off without reaching an agreement.[21] In the case of leases where the tenant has entered into possession any lease which could in any way be enforced against the landlord may be enforced against his singular successor.[22]

8. Claims for Reimbursement.—In cases where a party avers a verbal contract relating to heritage, and expenditure on his part in reliance thereon, and the necessary proof by the writ or oath of the other party is not available,

---

[12] *Sutherland* v. *Hay* (1845) 8 D. 283, per Lord Medwyn; *Kinnear* v. *Young*, 1936 S.L.T. 574.
[13] *Danish Dairy Co.* v. *Gillespie*, 1922 S.C. 656.
[14] See the broad terms of Bell's *Principles*, § 26, note 6, supra.
[15] *M'Lean* v. *Scott* (1902) 10 S.L.T. 447.
[16] *Smith* v. *Marshall* (1860) 22 D. 1158.
[17] *Fowlie* v. *M'Lean* (1868) 6 M. 254; *Pollok* v. *Whiteford*, 1936 S.C. 402. Rankine, *Leases* (3rd ed), p. 128. But continued possession will validate an informal agreement for a new lease; *Buchanan* v. *Harris & Sheldon* (1900) 2 F. 935.
[18] *Mowat* v. *Caledonian Banking Co.* (1895) 23 R. 270; see *Pollok,* supra, per Lord President Clyde at p. 410.
[19] *Stodart* v. *Dalzell* (1876) 4 R. 236 (feu); *Wight* v. *Newton*, 1911 S.C. 762 (lease).
[20] *Whyte* v. *Whyte*, 1913 2 S.L.T. 85.
[21] *Petrie* v. *Forsyth* (1874) 2 R. 214; *Stodart* v. *Dalzell* (1976) 4 R. 236; *Rodger (Builders)* v. *Fawdry*, 1950 S.C. 483.
[22] *Wilson* v. *Mann* (1876) 3 R. 527.

recourse may sometimes be had to an action for recovery of the expenditure. To such an action the rule that proof is limited to writ or oath is not applicable, and parole evidence is competent.[23] In the case of payments in advance, of the price, on a sale, of a term's rent, on a lease, it would seem clear that repayment may be demanded on the principle of restitution or repetition.[24] If there has been expenditure on the subjects, beneficial to their owner, the party who has verbally agreed to buy or lease them has a claim for recompense to the extent to which the owner is lucratus.[25] The question whether there can be any claim for reimbursement of expenditure which has not proved beneficial seems one which is open for future decision.[26]

9. Contracts of Employment.—A contract of employment for a period of not more than a year may be entered into verbally, and proved by parole evidence.[27] If for a longer period, it is not binding unless there is writ probative of both parties.[28] The same rules apply to apprenticeship.[29] Actual service is rei interventus, and, if founded on a written but improbative agreement, makes the contract binding for the whole period agreed upon.[30] The effect of actual service on a verbal contract for more than a year is an unsettled point, as is also the question whether the fact of an agreement to that effect can be proved otherwise than by writ or oath.[31] Writing is not necessary in a contract of agency, where payment is by commission.[32]

10. Homologation.[33]—This is similar in principle to rei interventus, but it depends on the actings, not of the person seeking to enforce the contract, but of the other party. If he acts in such a way as to show that he regards the contract as binding, he homologates.[34] Both rei interventus and homologation may arise on the same transaction.[34] To admit homologation there must, as with rei interventus, be consensus in idem.[35]

---

[23] *Bell* v. *Bell* (1841) 3 D. 1201; *Newton* v. *Newton.* 1925 S.C. 715.

[24] *Oliphant* v. *Lord Monorgan* (1628) M. 8400; *Paterson* v. *Paterson* (1897) 25 R. 144, per Lord M'Laren at p. 191.

[25] *Walker* v. *Milne* (1823) 2 S. 379; (1824) 3 S. 123; *Bell* v. *Bell* and *Newton* v. *Newton,* supra; *Gray* v. *Johnston,* 1928 S.C. 659.

[26] See *Hamilton* v. *Lochrane* (1899) 1 F. 478; *Gilchrist* v. *Whyte,* 1907 S.C. 984; *Gray* v. *Johnston,* supra.

[27] But see Employment Protection (Consolidation) Act 1978, ss. 1-11; Employment, Ch. XXII, infra, § 5.

[28] *Stewart* v. *M'Call* (1869) 7 M. 544; *Nisbet* v. *Percy,* 1951 S.C. 350; *Cook* v. *Grubb,* 1961 S.L.T. 405, affd. 1963 S.C. 1. It has been suggested that the rule may apply only to contracts of domestic service and contracts of artisans: *Brown* v. *Scottish Antarctic Expedition* (1902) 10 S.L.T. 433; cf. *Walker* v. *Greenock and District Combination Hospital Board,* 1951 S.C. 464. As to a contract for an indefinite period, see *Davies* v. *City of Glasgow Friendly Society,* 1935 S.C. 224.

[29] *Grant* v. *Ramage & Ferguson* (1897) 25 R. 35.

[30] *Campbell* v. *Baird* (1827) 5 S. 335; *Pickin* v. *Hawkes* (1878) 5 R. 676.

[31] *Brown* v. *Scottish Antarctic Expedition,* supra. But see *Walker* v. *Greenock and District Combination Hospital Board,* 1951 S.L.T. 329, per Lord Sorn, at p. 332 (O.H.); *Cook* v. *Grubb,* supra.

[32] *Currie* v. *M'Lean* (1864) 2 M. 1076; *Pickin* v. *Hawkes,* supra.

[33] For homologation of voidable contracts, see Agreements Void and Voidable, Ch. V., supra, § 5.

[34] *Mitchell* v. *Stornoway Trustees,* 1936 S.C. (H.L.) 56, at p. 63. See cases cited in notes to Agreements Void or Voidable, Ch. V., § 5.

[35] *East Kilbride Development Co.* v. *Pollok,* 1953 S.C. 370.

CHAPTER VIII

AGREEMENT IMPROPERLY OBTAINED: ERROR

Gloag on *Contract*; Smith, *Short Commentary* (1962), Ch. 37; Kerr on
Fraud and Mistake (7th ed., 1952).

1. Means by which Consent Obtained.—A contract may be rendered void
or voidable because the consent of one of the parties has been obtained by
improper means, or given under error. Under this head may be considered the
effect of (1) Fraud, (2) Misrepresentation, (3) Error, and (4) Force and Fear,
with which it is convenient to group the objection that the terms of the
contract are extortionate.

I. FRAUD.

2. Fraud.—Fraud is a machination or contrivance to deceive, by words or
acts.[1] Unless the result of the fraud is to exclude any real consent, a contract
induced by fraudulent practices is not void, but only voidable.[2] To induce a
party to contract by fraud is a civil wrong, and therefore the party defrauded
may not only reduce the contract but also recover damages for any loss he
may have suffered. If, for reasons already explained,[3] the contract cannot be
reduced, a claim for damages remains competent,[4] with the exception of the
case where a party has been fraudulently induced to take shares in a company
and sues the company as responsible for the fraud of its directors or
managers. Then, unless he can reduce the contract to take shares and thus
cease to be a shareholder (which he cannot do if the company is in
liquidation), he can have no claim for damages except against the individuals
actually responsible for the fraud.[5] Where a contract has been induced by
fraudulent misrepresentation, damages may be recovered even though the
pursuer does not offer to rescind, with the same exception in company law.[6]

It is impossible to enumerate the various words or acts which the law will
regard as fraudulent, but some light may be thrown on the question from the
negative side.

3. No Legal Fraud.—There is no such thing as legal, apart from moral,
fraud. Conscious dishonesty must be proved. Thus damages cannot be

---

[1] Bell, *Prin.*, § 13. As to facility and circumvention as a separate ground for the reduction of a
contract, see Gloag, *Contract* (2nd ed.), p. 484; *Mackay* v. *Campbell*, 1966 S.L.T. 329, affd.
1967 S.L.T. 337 (H.L.). As to facility and circumvention in relation to wills, see Testate
Succession, Ch. XLIII., infra, § 1.
[2] *Morrisson* v. *Robertson*, 1908 S.C. 332; *MacLeod* v. *Kerr*, 1965 S.C. 253, and see infra, § 16.
[3] See Agreements Void or Voidable, Ch. V. supra, § 3.
[4] *Boyd & Forrest* v. *Glasgow and S.W. Ry.*, 1912 S.C. (H.L.) 93.
[5] *Houldsworth* v. *City of Glasgow Bank* (1880) 7 R. (H.L.) 53.
[6] *Smith* v. *Sim*, 1954 S.C. 357 (O.H.), an action founded on delict.

obtained when all that is proved is that the defender made an affirmative statement without taking reasonable care to discover whether it was true or not, even although the means of information were easily accessible. In the leading English case, *Derry* v. *Peek*,[7] the directors of an insolvent tramway company were sued for damages on the ground that the plaintiff had been induced to take shares by misrepresentation in the prospectus. The misrepresentation in question was that the company had obtained authority from the Board of Trade to work the tramway by steam power. This was proved to be untrue, but it was also proved that the directors honestly believed it to be true, having misapprehended the result of their negotiations with the Board of Trade. It was held, even on the assumption that the defendants had not taken reasonable care to verify their statement, that they were not liable in damages for fraud because there was no dishonesty. In *Manners* v. *Whitehead*[8] M. had been induced to enter into a partnership with W. by inaccurate statements contained in balance sheets of the business which W. was carrying on. The business failed, and M. sued for damages. He proved that the balance sheets were inaccurate; he did not succeed in proving fraud on the part of W. It was held that the action was not maintainable; a claim for damages in such circumstances must rest on proof of conscious fraud. The general rule illustrated in these cases must be taken with the qualification that if a man does not know, or has forgotten, the truth on any particular question, he has no right to make any positive assertion on the subject, and therefore that fraud may be established although there may be no proof that the speaker was aware that his statement was untrue. It is enough that the real state of his mind was that he did not know whether it was true or not. And the absence of any reasonable grounds for belief may be evidence, to be taken with the other evidence in the case, that no positive belief existed.[9]

4. Disclosure.—Mere failure to disclose material facts does not amount to fraud; nor, except in certain special contracts, or where the parties stand to each other in some confidential relationship, is it a ground for the reduction of a contract. "Whatever may be the case in a court of morals there is no legal obligation on the vendor to inform the purchaser that he is under a mistake not induced by the act of the vendor."[10] So a bank, when offered a guarantee for a customer's account, is not bound to inform the guarantor of the state of that account.[11] When A knew that B's mine contained a valuable seam of coal, and also knew that B was unaware of that fact, it was held that a lease obtained by A was unchallengeable.[12] A settlement of an action for £20 was sustained, although obtained by the defender in a private interview with the

---

[7] 14 App. Cas. 337. See also *Boyd & Forrest* v. *Glasgow and S.W. Ry.*, 1912 S.C. (H.L.) 93; *Lees* v. *Tod* (1882) 9 R. 807.
[8] (1898) 1 F. 171.
[9] See opinion of Lord President Inglis, *Lees* v. *Tod* (1882) 9 R. 807; of Lord Herschell in *Derry* v. *Peek* (1889) 14 App. Cas. 337.
[10] Per Blackburn, J., *Smith* v. *Hughes* (1871) L.R. 6 Q.B. 597.
[11] *Royal Bank* v. *Greenshields*, 1914 S.C. 259.
[12] *Gillespie* v. *Russell* (1856) 18 D. 677; (1857) 19 D. 897; (1859) 3 Macq. 757.

pursuer by concealing the fact that he had already made a tender of £50.[13] And it is probably established that the seller of goods is under no obligation to reveal latent defects.[14]

But this rule does not hold in insurance[15]; nor in guarantees for the fidelity of an official[16]; nor probably in negotiations for entering into partnership.[17] In these contracts (known as contracts uberrimae fidei) each party is bound to reveal all facts known to him which it would be material for the other to know. The circumstances which must be disclosed in a prospectus are prescribed by statute.[18] A similar duty of disclosure may arise from the fact that the parties stand to each other in some relationship. Thus concealment of material facts will serve to avoid a contract between parent and child,[19] trustee and beneficiary,[20] partners,[21] agent and principal.[22] The circumstances may however be such, and the influence exercised by the other party may be so dominant, as to deprive the other of the power of apprehending the considerations applicable to the case; if so, the transaction may be reducible through undue influence, even though the pursuer's case falls short of any proof of actual concealment.[23] On the other hand, there has been no case where a contract has been held to be voidable where the influence has been exercised in genuine devotion to the interests of the person influenced and not on behalf of the other party to the agreement.[24] A solicitor contracting with his client is under a particularly stringent obligation; he must not only reveal all material facts but show that the contract is one which he, if consulted in a case where he was not personally interested, would have advised the client to make.[25]

5. Half-Truths.—The general rule that concealment does not affect the validity of a contract applies only to a case of mere non-disclosure, when no representation has been made. It is fraudulent to tell a half-truth, that is, to make a statement true in itself, and withhold some explanation which would alter its whole bearing. A prospectus may satisfy the statutory conditions as to disclosure, and nevertheless, by the concealment of facts which would alter the impression conveyed by the facts disclosed, amount to fraud.[26] So if an agent

---

[13] *Welsh* v. *Cousin* (1899) 2 F. 277.

[14] *Ward* v. *Hobbs* (1878) 4 App. Cas. 13; *Philip's Trs.* v. *Reid* (1884) 21 S.L.R. 698. As to possible exceptions in cases of sale, see Sale of Goods, Ch. XVII infra.

[15] Insurance, Ch. XXVII, infra, § 6.

[16] *Bank of Scotland* v. *Morrison*, 1911 S.C. 593.

[17] See *Manners* v. *Whitehead* (1898) 1 F. 171. There is no definite authority. A contract of employment is not uberrimae fidei: *Walker* v. *Greenock and District Combination Hospital Board*, 1951 S.C. 464.

[18] Companies Act 1948, s. 38 and Schedule IV.

[19] *Smith Cunninghame* v. *Anstruther's Trs.* (1872) 10 M. (H.L.) 39.

[20] *Dougan* v. *Macpherson* (1902) 4 F. (H.L.) 7.

[21] *Law* v. *Law* [1905] 1 Ch. 140. See also *Cassels* v. *Stewart* (1881) 8 R. (H.L.) 1.

[22] See *M'Pherson's Trs* v. *Watt* (1877) 5 R. (H.L.) 9.

[23] *Gray* v. *Binny* (1879) 7 R. 332, and see opinion of Lord President Inglis at p. 342; Gloag, *Contract* (2nd ed.), pp. 526 et seq.; *Allan* v. *Allan*, 1961 S.C. 200. As to undue influence in wills, see Testate Succession, Ch. XLIII infra, § 1.

[24] *Forbes* v. *Forbes' Trs.*, 1957 S.C. 325 (O.H.); but see *Allan* v. *Allan*, supra, per Lord Walker at p. 204.

[25] *Aitken* v. *Campbell's Trs.*, 1909 S.C. 1217; *Gillespie* v. *Gardner*, 1909 S.C. 1053.

[26] *R.* v. *Lord Kylsant* [1932] 1 K.B. 442.

for a bank makes any statement to a party who offers to guarantee an account
he must reveal all the relevant facts.[27] Again, if a statement made is honestly
but mistakenly believed, the party who makes it is bound to reveal the actual
facts if they come to his knowledge. There is the same duty of disclosure if by
a change of circumstances the original statement ceases to be true. So when A
had honestly and truthfully stated that there was no risk that a machine,
which B proposed to buy, would be requisitioned by the Government, it was
held that A was bound to inform B of any change of attitude on the part of
the Government officials.[28] The rule that mere failure to disclose is not
fraudulent does not extend to the case of dealing with articles which ex facie
pretend to be what they are not, such as forged stamps, faked antiques. A
purchaser may reduce the contract to buy them, though the seller may have
made no representation that the articles are genuine.[29] And it is fraudulent to
exhibit unrepresentative specimens in an auction room, though the conditions
of the sale may be that intending purchasers must satisfy themselves as to the
condition of the goods in bulk.[30] Any devices to conceal defects in an article
are clearly fraudulent.

6. Verba Jactantia.—The general rule that statements known to be untrue
are fraudulent has certain qualifications. It is not to be applied too rigorously
to advertisements, though the line which separates mere extravagant
recommendation (verba jactantia) from fraudulent misstatements cannot be
exactly drawn.[31] It has been decided by the Judicial Committee that when the
manager of a company was bound by his duty to his employers not to disclose
the fact that a particular report had been received, and knew that a refusal to
make any statement would give the inquirer the information he wanted, he
was not liable in damages for fraud though he gave an answer which was
wilfully false.[32] But a good motive is no excuse for a fraudulent act.[33]

7. Attempts to Defraud.—Attempts to defraud cause no injury, and
therefore afford no remedy. Where a seller adopted fraudulent devices to
conceal the defects in a gun, and the buyer bought it without making any
examination, it was held that, as he had not been deceived, he could not
reduce the contract on the ground of fraud.[34] An action to reduce a contract
to take shares failed where the shareholder was forced to admit that the
particular statements in the prospectus which he could prove to be untrue had
not affected his mind.[35] But it is no answer to an action based on fraud that

[27] *Falconer* v. *North of Scotland Bank* (1863) 1 M. 704; *Royal Bank* v. *Greenshields*, 1914 S.C. 259.
[28] *Shankland* v. *Robinson*, 1919 S.C. 715; revd. 1920 S.C. (H.L.) 103.
[29] *Patterson* v. *Landsberg* (1905) 7 F. 675, opinion of Lord Kyllachy; *Gibson* v. *National Cash
    Register Co.*, 1925 S.C. 500.
[30] *White* v. *Dougherty* (1891) 18 R. 972.
[31] Contrast *Bile Beans Co.* v. *Davidson* (1906) 8 F. 1181; and *Plotzker* v. *Lucas* (1907) 15 S.L.T.
    186.
[32] *Tackey* v. *M'Bain* [1912] A.C. 186.
[33] *Menzies* v. *Menzies* (1893) 20 R. (H.L.) 108, per Lord Ashbourne.
[34] *Horsfall* v. *Thomas* (1862) 1 H. & C. 90.
[35] *Smith* v. *Chadwick* (1884) 9 App. Cas. 187. Cf. *Ritchie* v. *Glass*, 1936 S.L.T. 591, a case of
    innocent misrepresentation.

the party defrauded could have discovered the true facts if he had taken the trouble to investigate.[36]

II. MISREPRESENTATION.

8. Innocent Misrepresentation.—A statement honestly believed may nevertheless, if untrue, mislead the party to whom it is made, and induce him to contract under what is known as essential error.[37] This will render the contract voidable.[38] "Error becomes essential whenever it is shown that but for it one of the parties would have declined to contract."[39] This is probably a general rule, though one case suggests that it is stated too broadly, and that there may be misrepresentations regarding collateral matters which, though in fact they induced the contract, are not sufficiently material, in the absence of fraud, to render it voidable.[40] On this theory such misrepresentations are spoken of as inducing, not essential error, but error dans causam contractui. But more recent authorities hold that a contract is voidable if it has been induced by any misrepresentation, giving more weight to the consideration that a man has no right to profit by a misrepresentation he has made, no matter how innocently, and would do so if he were allowed to retain the contract thereby induced.[41] If the misrepresentation in question relates to the credit of a third party it cannot be founded on as a ground for the reduction of the contract unless it is made in writing.[42]

9. Remedy for Innocent Misrepresentation.—A misrepresentation which is not made fraudulently does not amount to a civil wrong, and therefore does not afford any foundation for an action for damages. So it was held that while, on the reduction of a contract induced by an innocent misrepresentation, the party could recover any property transferred under the contract, or any payment made in advance, he could not claim reimbursement of expenses into which he had been led, as that would amount to an award of damages under another name.[43] And if work has been done under the contract, so that it is impossible to restore the parties to their original position, the law affords no remedy for loss incurred by acting in reliance on an innocent misrepresentation. In *Boyd & Forrest* v. *Glasgow and S.W. Ry.*,[44] contractors, who had built a branch line of railway for a contract price, sued for payment for additional work on the basis of quantum meruit, founding

---

[36] *Redgrave* v. *Hurd* (1881) 20 Ch.D. 1; *Gluckstein* v. *Barnes* [1900] A.C. 240.
[37] For a comment on the use of this terminology see Smith, *Short Commentary,* pp. 809, 811.
[38] *Stewart* v. *Kennedy* (1890) 17 R. (H.L.) 25.
[39] Per Lord Watson, *Menzies* v. *Menzies* (1893) 20 R. (H.L.) 108, at p. 142.
[40] *Woods* v. *Tulloch* (1893) 20 R. 477; and see Erskine, III, 1, 16; *Edgar* v. *Hector,* 1912 S.C. 348; and *Ritchie* v. *Glass,* 1936 S.L.T. 591.
[41] *Stewart* v. *Kennedy* (1890) 17 R. (H.L.) 25; *Mair* v. *Rio Grande Rubber Co.,* 1913 S.C. (H.L.) 74; *Westville Shipping Co.* v. *Abram S.S. Co.,* 1922 S.C. 571, opinion of Lord President Clyde. (Affd. 1923 S.C. (H.L.) 68.)
[42] *Union Bank* v. *Taylor,* 1925 S.C. 835, and see Cautionary Obligations, Ch. XXI infra, § 4.
[43] *Adams* v. *Newbigging* (1888) 13 App. Cas. 308.
[44] 1914 S.C. 472, revd. 1915 S.C. (H.L.) 20. See too cases on restitutio in integrum, Agreements Void or Voidable, Ch. V. supra, § 3.

their claim on misrepresentations, not made fraudulently, in the report of borings taken on the proposed line which, before tendering, they had been allowed to see. It was held that a claim for payment in addition to the contract price must rest on an implied agreement to pay; that no agreement could be implied while the express contract between the parties stood unreduced; that the express contract could not be reduced because, after the work was done, it was impossible to restore each party to his former position; and therefore that the contractors' claim was untenable.

10. Representations and Contractual Terms.—It may often be difficult to determine whether a particular statement is to be regarded as a term of the contract, or merely as a representation. Thus the statement by a party selling an engine that it will develop a certain horse-power may be regarded as a representation to that effect, or as a guarantee of the engine's powers.[45] If it is read as a representation, the only legal result (apart from allegations of fraud) of its untruth is to render the contract voidable, and then only if the statement was material, so that the purchaser would not have given the price he did had he known the true facts. If, on the other hand, the statement is read as a guarantee, the party who gives it is liable in damages for breach of contract if it is not fulfilled, and the terms of the contract may be such as to render it voidable even if the point guaranteed was not material. The latter question has been illustrated chiefly in cases relating to policies of insurance. These are commonly preceded by a proposal form, in which certain questions are answered by the insured. If it is expressly agreed that the validity of the policy is conditional on the truth of the answers in the proposal form the policy will be avoided even if it may appear that the particular answer proved to be untrue related to a point which was not material.[46] In a case where there was no express provision that the validity of the policy should depend upon the accuracy of the answers in the proposal form, but it was provided in the policy that the proposal form should be the "basis of the contract," the House of Lords, by a narrow majority, held that the insured warranted the statements in the proposal form, and therefore that the policy was avoided by the inaccuracy of a statement therein, even though it was not material, and did not affect the amount of the premium charged.[47] Such a conclusion, however, will not be reached if there is any ambiguity in the terms of the policy.[48]

There are no voces signatae by which to distinguish between a representation and a contractual warranty. The latter is clearly excluded by an express provision that the statement in question is not guaranteed. And statements which do not relate to the res about which the parties are contracting, but to collateral matters which may affect motive, are merely representations.[45] In the case of statements which do relate to the res it is always a question of intention whether they are to be regarded as

[45] *Robey* v. *Stein* (1900) 3 F. 278.
[46] *Standard Life Assurance Co.* v. *Weems* (1884) 11 R. (H.L.) 48.
[47] *Dawson Ltd.* v. *Bonnin*, 1922 S.C. (H.L.) 156.
[48] *Provincial Assurance Co.* v. *Morgan* [1933] A.C. 240.

representations or as contractual warranties.[49] It is merely an element in the question that one party had full means of information and the other had not.[50] The fact that the statement in question was made verbally in relation to a contract in writing does not necessarily preclude the conclusion that it was intended as a warranty. So a verbal assurance that the drains of a house were in good order, a point on which the lease was silent, was held to be a warranty, breach of which subjected the landlord to damages.[51]

11. Expressions of Opinion.—A statement may be construed neither as a representation nor as a warranty, but as an expression of the speaker's opinion or of his intentions for the future. While it is fraudulent to induce a contract by expressing an opinion or an intention which is not formed,[52] an honest statement of opinion, though unfounded, leaves the contract unaffected, and a person who states his intention does not represent that he will not change his mind.[53] While it must always be a question of construction whether a man has confined himself to stating his opinion, or has made a definite assertion, the former interpretation will generally be accepted in cases where in ordinary business the other party would make independent inquiries, e.g., a statement as to the capacity of a farm to carry a certain head of stock.[54] While a misrepresentation as to the legal effect of a contract will render it voidable,[55] it is probable that a statement as to a general principle of law would be regarded merely as an expression of opinion.[56]

12. Title to Sue on Misrepresentation.—A misrepresentation, innocent or fraudulent, affords no right of action except to the person or persons to whom, expressly or impliedly, it was addressed. Thus when A fraudulently induced B to accept a transfer of shares in a company it was held that the liquidator of the company had no title to reduce the contract, in order to place A on the list of contributories.[57] If the seller of an article, by fraudulent devices, obtains more than the proper price, a sub-purchaser, though he may be the actual loser, has no title to reduce the sale.[58] The prospectus of a company is addressed solely to the parties who may apply for shares, not to transferees from them, and these latter, though the statements in the prospectus may have induced them to buy, have no claim for damages against the parties responsible for it.[59] But fraudulent statements with regard to an existing company are addressed to the general public, and may be founded on by anyone who has been induced thereby to buy the shares.[60] If the speaker,

[49] *Hyslop* v. *Shirlaw* (1905) 7 F. 875, at p. 881.
[50] *Heilbutt* v. *Buckleton* [1913] A.C. 30.
[51] *De Lasalle* v. *Guildford* [1901] 2 K.B. 215. See also *Renison* v. *Bryce,* (1898) 25 R. 521.
[52] *Edgington* v. *Fitzmaurice* (1885) 29 Ch. D. 459.
[53] General Law of Obligations, Ch. III. supra, § 11.
[54] *Hamilton* v. *Duke of Montrose* (1906) 8 F. 1026.
[55] *Stewart* v. *Kennedy* (1890) 17 R. (H.L.) 25.
[56] See *Brownlie* v. *Miller* (1880) 7 R. (H.L.) 66.
[57] *M'Lintock* v. *Campbell,* 1916 S.C. 966.
[58] *Edinburgh United Breweries Co.* v. *Molleson* (1894) 21 R. (H.L.) 10.
[59] *Peek* v. *Gurney* (1873) L.R. 6 H.L. 377.
[60] *Andrews* v. *Mockford* [1896] 1 Q.B. 372.

as a reasonable man, must be aware that others than the party he addresses will act on his statement, he will be liable to them. So a banker, answering queries from another banker as to a customer's financial standing, must be aware that customers of the latter bank may be interested and will be liable to them if his statements are fraudulent.[61]

III. ERROR.

13. Error.—One who contracts under an erroneous belief which is not due to any misrepresentation by the party with whom he contracts, but either to his own misconception or to a false statement by a third party, is said to contract under error, or error in intention.[62] Under the same head are usually classed cases of what may be called errors of expression, when, though the parties may really have agreed, the written record of their agreement is incorrectly expressed. Cases of the latter kind, presenting the more simple problems, may be considered first.

14. Error in Expression.—The most common case of error in expression arises when after a written contract is duly signed it is discovered that owing to a mistake of the amanuensis it does not represent the agreement which the parties had made. If the question is raised between the original parties proof of the fact may be by parole evidence, and the Court has always the power to correct the written record so as to bring it into accord with the proved agreement. Thus where a clerk was told to draw up an agreement between an hotel-keeper and his manager, and by an arithmetical mistake, which was not discovered until both parties had signed the agreement, gave the manager a larger share of the profits than had been agreed to, it was held that the mistake might be proved by witnesses and corrected.[63] Accounts, docqueted as correct, may be challenged on the ground of arithmetical errors.[64] Even if the interests of third parties are involved an arithmetical or clerical error may be corrected,[65] except in two cases—(1) where the third party is a holder for value of a bill or other negotiable instrument; and (2) where the document incorrectly drawn up forms part of the title to lands recorded in the Register of Sasines.[66]

Another class of case, to be considered as error in expression, is where an offer reaches the offeree in a form which was not intended, either by some slip on the part of the offerer, or through some mistake in transmission. If the offeree knows of the mistake he is not entitled to accept, and cannot maintain the contract if he does.[67] If he did not know, and accepted in good faith, the

---

[61] *Robinson* v. *National Bank,* 1916 S.C. (H.L.) 154. See also *Fortune* v. *Young,* 1918 S.C. 1.

[62] The equivalent term in England is "mistake."

[63] *Krupp* v. *Menzies,* 1907 S.C. 903; *Anderson* v. *Lambie,* 1954 S.C. (H.L.) 43 (error in disposition).

[64] *M'Laren* v. *Liddell's Trs.* (1862) 24 D. 577.

[65] *North British Ins. Co.* v. *Tunnock* (1864) 3 M. 1.

[66] *Mansfield* v. *Walker's Trs.* (1835) 1 Sh. & M'L. 203.

[67] *Steuart's Trs.* v. *Hart* (1875) 3 R. 192. *Brooker-Simpson* v. *Duncan Logan (Builders),* 1969 S.L.T. 304.

contract is binding.[68] If an offer sent by telegram is misread by the telegraph clerk, and is therefore transmitted in a form materially different from its original terms, no contract results from acceptance, because the circumstances preclude any real agreement.[69] When the parties are negotiating by telegrams in code, and one, mistakenly decoding a message, concludes a contract, the other cannot maintain it unless he can satisfy the Court that the mistake was one which no reasonable business man could have made.[70]

15. Error in Intention.— Cases where the agreement itself is entered into under error present more difficult problems. There is no doubt of the general rule that a party cannot reduce a contract on the ground that he has entered into it in error, if his contention is merely that he would not have contracted if he had known all the relevant facts. A plea to that effect has been judicially characterised as "so preposterous as to be undeserving of any attention."[71] But the question is one of degree. Cases may arise where the error is so material as to preclude any real consent, and therefore to leave a contract, or apparent contract, without that basis of agreement on which all contractual obligation must rest. In such cases the apparent contract is not voidable on the ground of error but void because there never was a contract at all. While the interpretation of contractual obligation must accept, as a fundamental rule, that a party must be taken to mean what he says, and is barred from asserting that his words or acts did not represent his intention,[72] that rule may come in conflict with one equally fundamental, namely, that the contractual obligations of the parties must rest on their consent. The attempt of the law to reconcile the conflict may be approached by considering the various forms of error by which a contract, or apparent contract, may be affected.

16. Error Affecting Motive.—Certain forms of error clearly do not preclude consent, but only affect the motive of the party who gives it. Such cases are referred to in Bell's *Principles* as cases of error concomitans, as opposed to error in substantials. Under this head fall errors as to extraneous circumstances, which may lead a party mistakenly to suppose a contract advantageous. Such errors leave the contract unaffected and have no legal result, unless the error was induced by misrepresentation.[73] So the guarantor of a bank account may be able to say that he would not have given his guarantee had he known the true state of the account, yet, in the absence of any misrepresentation by the bank, he will be liable.[74] A case equally clear is an error as to the quality of the thing to which the contract relates; there is no doubt that when a man buys or hires a specific thing the contract is not

---

[68] *Seaton Brick Co.* v. *Mitchell* (1900) 2 F. 550; *Steel's Tr.* v. *Bradley Homes (Scotland)*, 1972 S.C. 48; cf. *Sword* v. *Sinclair* (1771) M. 14241.
[69] *Verdin* v. *Robertson* (1871) 10 M. 35; *Henkel* v. *Pape* (1870) L.R. 6 Ex. 7.
[70] *Falck* v. *Williams* [1900] A.C. 176.
[71] Per Lord Fullerton, *Forth Marine Ins. Co.* v. *Burnes* (1848) 10 D. 689.
[72] Law of Contract, Ch. IV. supra, § 3.
[73] See § 8 supra. As to gratuitous obligations, see Law of Contract, Ch. IV. supra, § 2.
[74] *Royal Bank* v. *Greenshields*, 1914 S.C. 259. See also *Welsh* v. *Cousin* (1899) 2 F. 277; *Hogg* v. *Campbell* (1864) 2 M. 848.

affected by his error as to its value or suitability. Again, a contract is not rendered voidable by the fact that one of the parties mistook its legal result, or the obligations which it imposed; as already explained, these are matters for the Court to determine.[75]

17. Error in Substantials.—Other forms of error arising as to material aspects of the contract are so fundamental as to exclude any agreement between the parties, and for this reason render the contract void ab initio.[76] "Error in substantials, whether in fact or in law, invalidates consent, or rather excludes real consent, where reliance is placed on the thing mistaken."[77] The question in such a case is not whether a contract is reducible on the ground of error, but whether there is any contract to enforce. Such error in substantials may arise in relation to (1) the nature of the contract itself, (2) the identity of the person with whom the contract is supposed to have been made, (3) the subject-matter of the contract, (4) in certain cases, the quality of the subject-matter, and (5) the price.[78] The question whether the error is such as to exclude consent is one of degree in each case.

18. Error as to Contract.—If a party, without any intention to contract, should sign some document which is ex facie obligatory (e.g., a bill of exchange) it is clear that he has incurred no obligation, and that the bill cannot be enforced against him even by a bona fide holder for value.[79] And the same rule holds where a party, intending to bind himself to one contract, is fraudulently induced to sign a document binding him to another, as where a party signed a guarantee, being told and believing that he was signing a policy of insurance. It was held that the contract was not merely voidable on the ground of fraud, but void on the ground of the want of real consent, and that no liability could be founded on the fact that, had he exercised reasonable care, the party would have discovered what he was signing.[80] But in order to sustain the plea of non est factum—that the party had no intention to bind himself—there must have been a definite mistake, so that the party thought he was entering into one contract while he was really entering into another. If obligatory documents are signed in reliance on an assurance that they are mere matters of form the party who signs them will be liable.[81] If a draft contract has been revised, and the party signs the extended copy without noticing that it has been fraudulently altered, he will be bound, in a question

---

[75] Law of Contract, Ch. IV., § 3; *Stewart* v. *Kennedy*, (1890) 17 R. (H.L.) 25; see also *Manclark* v. *Thomson's Trs.*, 1958 S.C. 147.
[76] For a discussion of whether the contract might be rendered voidable rather than void, see Smith, op. cit., pp. 810, 815; but note *Macleod* v. *Kerr*, 1965 S.C. 253.
[77] Bell, *Prin.*, § 11 (10th ed.); Stair, I, 10, 13; see opinion of Lord Watson in *Stewart* v. *Kennedy*, supra, at p. 28.
[78] Gloag, *Contract*, pp. 441–448.
[79] *Ellis* v. *Lochgelly Iron Co.*, 1909 S.C. 1278, opinion of Lord Dunedin.
[80] *Carlisle Banking Co.* v. *Bragg* [1911] 1 K.B. 489; *Foster* v. *Mackinnon* (1869) L. R. 4 C.P. 704; *Buchanan* v. *Duke of Hamilton* (1878) 5 R. (H.L.) 69.
[81] *Howatson* v. *Webb* [1908] 1 Ch. 1. And see opinion of Lord Sands in *Fletcher* v. *Lord Advocate*, 1923 S.C. 27.

with anyone not involved in the fraud, unless the alteration is so material as to make it a different contract.[82]

19. Error as to Identity.—If a party believes that he was contracting with A., and in reality is contracting with B., he has given no consent and incurred no obligation, provided that, in the circumstances, the identity of the other party was material. So where A., pretending to be the son and agent of a well-known farmer, induced a dealer to sell him on credit and deliver two cows, and at once resold them, it was held that the dealer might recover them from the purchaser. He had not merely been induced to sell by A.'s fraud (which would only have rendered the sale voidable in a question with A.); he had never intended to contract with A. at all. The sale was not merely voidable, but void.[83] So again where a party obtained a consignment of goods by pretending to be a well-known retail dealer, it was held that he obtained no title, and that the firm which had sent the goods could recover them from parties to whom they had been resold.[84]

20. Error as to Subject-Matter.—If parties are contracting about a particular thing, and use language which is equally applicable to some other thing, then assuming that they differ as to the meaning of the terms they employ, they have reached no agreement, and concluded no contract. This may happen in the case of the sale of an estate by its name if there is a reasonable difference of opinion as to the extent of the lands covered by that name.[85] Where an order was given for stone coping at so much per "foot," a term equally applicable to a lineal and a superficial foot, it was held that the contract was not binding.[86] Where certain barrels, some containing tow, others hemp, were put up for auction merely by their numbers, it was decided that a party who bid for a barrel of tow under the impression that it was a barrel of hemp had come under no obligation. His bid was read not as a bid for a particular barrel, but for a barrel of hemp; it was accepted as a bid for a barrel of tow.[87] But such cases are very exceptional; as a general rule if a party offers to sell goods of a particular description, and does so in words which, reasonably construed, have only one meaning, he is bound to fulfil his contract, though he may have mistakenly thought that the goods which he tenders were of the description which he has undertaken to supply.[88]

---

[82] *Selkirk* v. *Ferguson*, 1908 S.C. 26; *Ellis* v. *Lochgelly Iron Co.*, 1909 S.C. 1278; *Hogg* v. *Campbell*, supra.
[83] *Morrisson* v. *Robertson*, 1908 S.C. 332, and see opinion of Lord President Clyde in *MacLeod* v. *Kerr*, 1965 S.C. 253. See also *Harrison* v. *Butters*, 1969 S.L.T. 183. The decision of Horridge, J., in *Phillips* v. *Brooks* [1919] 2 K.B. 243, is irreconcilable with *Morrisson* v. *Robertson*, and could not be followed in Scotland. See *Lake* v. *Simmons* [1927] A.C. 487.
[84] *Cundy* v. *Lindsay* (1878) 3 App. Cas. 459. See also *Said* v. *Butt* [1920] 3 K.B. 497; *Ingram* v. *Little* [1961] 1 Q.B. 31. Cf. *Lewis* v. *Averay* [1972] 1 Q.B. 198.
[85] *Houldsworth* v. *Gordon-Cumming*, 1910 S.C. (H.L.) 49; *Raffles* v. *Wichelhaus* (1864) 2 H. & C. 906 (two ships with the same name). *Inst.* III., 19, 23.
[86] *Stuart* v. *Kennedy* (1885) 13 R. 221.
[87] *Scriven* v. *Hindley* [1913] 3 K.B. 564.
[88] Sale of Goods Act 1893, s. 13; *Wallis* v. *Pratt* [1911] A.C. 394.

21. Error as to Price: Rent.—The mere fact that the contract does not settle the consideration to be paid does not raise a case of error. If no acts have followed it would generally be regarded as a case where negotiations had not reached the stage of contract[89]; if it has been carried into effect the Court will fix a reasonable consideration.[90] But if each party thinks that the consideration has been fixed, but they differ as to the amount, and the difference is not attributable to the misleading words or acts of either, the result must be that there is no binding contract. This was held in the case of a sale of cattle, where the seller believed that the price per head had been fixed, the buyer, that it was to depend on the quality of the cattle.[91]

22. Mutual Error.—These rules hold in mutual and onerous contracts, not in the case of a gratuitous obligation,[92] nor in the case where both parties are in error as to material facts. If both parties are in error the contract may be voidable even although consent has been given, on the principle that they contracted on the condition that the facts were as they believed them to be. So a contract relating to a particular thing will be void, or at least voidable, if both supposed the thing to be in existence, whereas in fact it had perished,[93] though it may be difficult to distinguish the case where the continued existence of the thing was known to be doubtful, and each took the risk.[94] A mutual discharge of claims may be re-opened on proof of an error common to both, whether in fact or in law, which had induced the settlement.[95] And it would appear that even in the case where a thing sold has been examined by the purchaser, the contract may be void if it proceeded on the assumption, common to both, that the thing had some specific and essential quality which it did not in fact possess.[96] But—though the point may not be settled beyond question—it is conceived that a sale will stand though the article turns out to have a value which neither seller nor purchaser suspected, as in the case of the sale of a book afterwards discovered to be valuable as a rarity.[97] It has been held that a contract under which a director received compensation for loss of office could not be reduced on the ground that it was entered into when both parties were in ignorance of the fact that the director had been guilty of conduct which would have justified his dismissal.[98] When a contract is affected by mutual error the only remedy is its reduction; neither party is entitled to

---

[89] *Macarthur* v. *Lawson* (1877) 4 R. 1134; *Hillas* v. *Arcos* (1931) 36 Com. Cas. 353; *Foley* v. *Classique Coaches* [1934] 2 K.B. 1.
[90] Sale of Goods Act 1893, s. 8 (2), "Where the price is not determined . . . the buyer must pay a reasonable price"; *Glen* v. *Roy* (1882) 10 R. 239 (rent).
[91] *Wilson* v. *Marquis of Breadalbane* (1859) 21 D. 957.
[92] Law of Contract, Ch. IV., supra, § 2.
[93] *Scott* v. *Coulson* [1903] 2 Ch. 249; *Hamilton* v. *Western Bank* (1861) 23 D. 1033; Sale of Goods Act 1893, s. 6.
[94] *Pender-Small* v. *Kinloch's Trs.*, 1917 S.C. 307.
[95] *Dickson* v. *Halbert* (1854) 16 D. 586; *Ross* v. *Mackenzie* (1842) 5 D. 151.
[96] *Edgar* v. *Hector*, 1912 S.C. 348. The report does not bring out clearly that both parties were in error as to the nature of the chairs in question.
[97] *Dawson* v. *Muir* (1851) 13 D. 843.
[98] *Bell* v. *Lever Bros.* [1932] A.C. 161.

insist on a contract such as would probably have been made if the true facts had been known.[99]

23. Condictio Indebiti.—Money paid under the mistaken belief that it was due can be recovered.[1] The law lays on the recipient an obligation of repetition, and the civil law term for the action to enforce it, condictio indebiti, is constantly used in the law of Scotland.

This is clear law in the case of a mistake of fact, e.g., ignorance or forgetfulness that a debt has already been paid; there is more doubt if the mistake was one of law. It has been held that when a mistake has been made in construing a public general statute, payments made in consequence of that mistake are not recoverable[2] but it seems in the light of subsequent English decisions that this rule may require modification.[3] In other cases of error of law, the application of the condictio is determined on equitable considerations.[4] "Law" in this connection means a general principle of law; a mistaken construction of a private commercial contract was treated as an error of fact and payments made under the error could be recovered.[5] On the other hand, where overpayments were made by trustees to beneficiaries upon an erroneous construction by them of the trust deed, it was held that the overpayments could not be recovered by the trustees.[6]

The rule does not apply to the case of money paid as a compromise, even although the compromise was offered owing to a mistake in fact[7]; nor to money paid as a charity,[8] because in these cases there is no erroneous belief that the payment is due, only that it is expedient or desirable. Money paid under a decree cannot be recovered merely on the ground that facts have come to light which would have formed a complete defence to the action, e.g., a receipt for the debt for which decree has been granted.[9] If payment has been made under threat of legal proceedings a mere protest will not justify recovery of money really paid to avoid the expense and inconvenience of a lawsuit; if, however, it has been paid under protest to avoid some immediate inconvenience, such as seizure of goods for failure to pay market dues, or threatened ejection from a conveyance, it may be recovered on its being

---

[99] *Pender-Small* v. *Kinloch's Trs.,* 1917 S.C. 307.
[1] Stair, I, 7, 9; Erskine, III, 3, 34; Bell, *Prin.*, § 531; *Dig.*, XII, 6. See as to exceptions, *Bell* v. *Thomson* (1867) 6 M. 64.
[2] *Glasgow Corporation* v. *Lord Advocate,* 1959 S.C. 203; *Taylor* v. *Wilson's Trs.,* 1974 S.L.T. 298 (overlooking statutory provision).
[3] *Kiriri Cotton Co.* v. *Ranchhoddas Keshavji Dewani* [1960] A.C. 192; Goff and Jones, *The Law of Restitution* (1966) pp. 79-94.
[4] *Taylor* v. *Wilson's Trs., supra; Unigate Food* v. *Scottish Milk Marketing Board,* 1972 S.L.T. 137.
[5] *British Hydrocarbon Chemical Co.,* 1961 S.L.T. 280.
[6] *Rowan's Trs.* v. *Rowan,* 1940 S.C. 30. This decision, however, was founded upon *Hunter's Trs.* v. *Hunter* (1894) 21 R. 949, which seems to have been argued and decided largely on the doctrine "bona fide percepta et consumpta". In *Armour* v. *Glasgow Royal Infirmary,* 1909 S.C. 916, trustees did recover payments made to beneficiaries under an error of law but the point on the condictio does not seem to have been taken.
[7] Bell, *Prin.*, § 535.
[8] *Masters and Seamen of Dundee* v. *Cockerill* (1869) 8 M. 278, but see *Re Glubb* [1900] 1 Ch. 354.
[9] *Marriott* v. *Hampton* (1797) 2 Smith, L.C. 13th ed., 286.

established, in an action raised by a third party, that the demand in question was unwarrantable.[10]

IV. FORCE AND FEAR.

24. Force and Fear.—It is probably the law that a contract induced by violence, or by threats sufficient to overcome the fortitude of a reasonable man, is void,[11] with an exception in the case of a bill of exchange, which is merely voidable, and may be enforced by a holder who can establish affirmatively that he gave value for the bill without notice of any objection.[12] Threats need not be of actual physical violence; an allegation by a workman of threatened loss of employment has been held relevant.[13] But threats of steps which the party may lawfully and warrantably take, such as proceedings in bankruptcy, or, under the former law, imprisonment for debt, do not invalidate a payment or security thereby induced,[14] though they fall under the general rule of force and fear if used to extort consent to some independent contract.[15] And an obligation granted by a party who had been imprisoned under irregular diligence was reduced.[16] When a payment or promissory note is given in order to avoid a prosecution it is valid if it is given merely as repayment of what the giver has stolen.[17] The case of a payment for the same purpose by a third party is more doubtful,[18] and it is probably settled that any payment or obligation extending beyond reimbursement of money stolen cannot be defended.[19] Threats of violence or injury to near relations have the same legal effect as threats to the party himself.[20] Obligations granted by a married woman for her husband's debt may be reduced if they were obtained by threats used by the other party or by the husband; it is not sufficient that they were granted out of affection for him, and in order to save him from proceedings in bankruptcy.[21]

25. Extortion.—Except in the case of loans of money there is no authority at common law for holding it to be a relevant ground for the reduction of a contract that its terms are extortionate, even with the addition of averments that the defender had greatly the advantage of the pursuer in respect of

---

[10] *Maskell* v. *Horner* [1915] 3 K.B. 106; *Brocklebank* v. *The King* [1925] 1 K.B. 52.
[11] Stair, I, 9, 8; Erskine, III, 1, 16. Cases in Morison, sub voce Vis et Metus.
[12] Bills of Exchange Act 1882, ss. 29, 30, 38.
[13] *Gow* v. *Henry* (1899) 2 F. 48.
[14] *Ker* v. *Edgar* (1698) M. 16503; *Rudman* v. *Jay*, 1908 S.C. 552, opinion of Lord Ardwall; *Hunter* v. *Bradford Property Trust*, 1977 S.L.T. (Notes) 33; *Hislop* v. *Dickson Motors (Forres)*, 1978 S.L.T. (Notes) 73.
[15] *Nisbet* v. *Stewart* (1708) M. 16512.
[16] *M'Intosh* v. *Chalmers* (1883) 11 R. 8.
[17] *Lamson Co.* v. *MacPhail*, 1914 S.C. 73.
[18] *Ferrier* v. *Mackenzie* (1899) 1 F. 597.
[19] *Canison* v. *Marshall* (1764) 6 Paton 759; *Kaufman* v. *Gerson* [1904] 1 K.B. 591; opinion of Lord Salvesen in *Lamson Co.* v. *MacPhail*, supra.
[20] Bell, *Prin.*, § 12.
[21] *Priestnell* v. *Hutcheson* (1857) 19 D. 495.

education or business experience.[22] In the case of loans, until 1854, when they were finally repealed, the usury laws limited the rate of interest which might lawfully be charged. It has twice been held at common law that a loan by a money lender might be challenged where the circumstances were exceptional and the borrower a person inexperienced in business.[23] The English law as to bargains with expectant heirs is not recognised in Scotland.[24]

[22] *Cal. Ry.* v. *N.B. Ry.* (1881) 8 R. (H.L.) 23, opinion of Lord Blackburn; *Wood* v. *N.B. Ry.* (1891) 18 R. (H.L.) 27; *Mathieson* v. *Hawthorne* (1899) 1 F. 468. The statutory provisions as to extortionate credit bargains are treated in Consumer Credit Transactions, Ch. XIX infra, § 25.
[23] *Young* v. *Gordon* (1896) 23 R. 419; *Gordon* v. *Stephens* (1902) 9 S.L.T. 397.
[24] *M'Kirdy* v. *Anstruther* (1839) 1 D. 855.

CHAPTER IX

PACTA ILLICITA AND UNFAIR CONTRACT TERMS

Gloag, *Contract* (2nd ed., 1929), Ch. XXXIII; Lever, *The Law of Restrictive Practices and Resale Price Maintenance* (1964); Wilberforce, Campbell and Elles, *Law of Restrictive Trade Practices and Monopolies* (2nd ed., 1966).

1. Illegality.—An agreement may fail in obligatory effect because it is illegal, or because its object was the furtherance of some illegal purpose. The main grounds of illegality in contract may be divided into three classes—(a) When the object of the parties was to secure a result which is either criminal or generally recognised as immoral; (b) When the particular contract is forbidden by some positive rule, either of common law or statute; (c) When the particular method of contracting is prohibited. The law of ultra vires, where the contract fails because it is beyond the contractual powers of one or other of the parties, rests upon different principles, and has been already considered.[1] Instances of the various forms of illegality will appear in the sequel; for the present it may be enough to mention, in the first class, an agreement to secure the commission of a crime[2]; in the second, an unqualified agreement not to exercise a particular trade[3]; in the third, a sale where the subjects sold are estimated by other than weights and measures lawful for use for trade,[4] or a transaction requiring, yet lacking a Government licence.[5]

2. Effects of Illegality.—To whichever class a particular contract may belong the contract is so far void that it cannot be directly enforced, nor can the party who refuses to carry it out be subjected in damages. It is the duty of the Court to take notice of the illegality if it appears ex facie of the contract, although neither party may plead it.[6]

3. Turpis Causa.—Further results depend upon the nature of the illegality. To cases of the first class the maxims "in turpi causa melior est conditio defendentis," and "ex turpi causa non oritur actio," apply, with the result that even if the contract has been carried out the Court will take no cognisance of the relations of the parties. The party who has happened to profit, though only by disregarding the terms to which he has agreed, may keep what he has secured; the party on whom a loss has fallen cannot enforce an agreement to share it. In a question between thief and resetter the law cannot interfere. So when a director and the manager of a company entered into a contract, held

---

[1] Capacity to Contract, Ch. VI. supra, § 9.
[2] Infra, § 11.
[3] Infra, § 13.
[4] *Cuthbertson* v. *Lowes* (1870) 8 M. 1073.
[5] See *O'Toole* v. *Whiterock Quarry Co.,* 1937 S.L.T. 521.
[6] *Hamilton* v. *M'Laughlan* (1908) 16 S.L.T. 341. See *North-Western Salt Co.* v. *Electrolytic Alkali Co.* [1914] A.C. 461; *Rawlings* v. *General Trading Co.* [1921] 1 K.B. 635.

to be a conspiracy to defraud the shareholders, by which a certain sum should be voted to the manager and he should pay a bonus to the director, the Court declined to entertain an action for the bonus.[7] When a joint adventure, definitely illegal under an Order in Council, had resulted in a loss, the party on whom the loss had happened to light had no right to insist that the other should pay his share.[8]

To the general rule that the Court will not interfere in a case involving turpis causa there are certain exceptions.

4. Parties not In Pari Delicto.—While it is no objection that the defender is pleading and taking advantage of his own illegal act, there are certain cases where the parties, though both involved in illegality, are not regarded as equally blameworthy—are not in pari delicto. If so, the one less blameworthy may enforce rights incidentally arising under the contract. This rule is illustrated in our reports only in cases of collusive agreements in bankruptcy. While any secret payment by a bankrupt to an individual creditor is a pactum illicitum,[9] yet as the creditor who exacts and the bankrupt who may really be forced to accede are not in pari delicto the trustee may recover what the bankrupt has paid, whereas the creditor cannot enforce an obligation to pay.[10]

5. Illegality in Interests of Special Class.—If it is held that the illegality of a contract is recognised or enacted for the benefit of a particular class, a member of that class may found upon it.[11] But this exception has very narrow limits; in general the illegality of a contract rests on the interests of the State, not of any particular class.[12]

6. Money Demanded Back Before Purpose Effected.—It has been decided in England that money paid in advance for an illegal purpose may be recovered if demanded before the illegal purpose has been carried out. So where money has been deposited with a stakeholder to await the result of an illegal bet it may be recovered at any time before it has actually been paid to the winner.[13] On this rule there is no decision in Scotland; and the limits of the English decisions are ill-defined. It is hardly conceivable that the man who has paid in advance for the commission of a theft could in any circumstances maintain an action for the recovery of his payment.[14]

7. Illegal Conditions Separable.—If a contract as a whole is lawful the mere fact that one clause involves an illegality does not necessarily taint the

---

[7] *Laughland* v. *Millar* (1904) 6 F. 413; *Scott* v. *Brown* [1892] 2 Q.B. 724.
[8] *Stewart* v. *Gibson* (1840) 1 Robinson 260.
[9] *Farmers' Mart* v. *Milne*, 1914 S.C. (H.L.) 84; *Munro* v. *Rothfield*, 1920 S.C. (H.L.) 165.
[10] *Macfarlane* v. *Nicoll* (1864) 3 M. 237.
[11] *Phillips* v. *Blackhurst* 1912 2 S.L.T. 254.
[12] *Mahmoud* v. *Ispahani* [1921] 2 K.B. 716.
[13] *Burge* v. *Ashley* [1900] 1 Q.B. 744; *Hermann* v. *Charlesworth* [1905] 2 K.B. 123.
[14] See *Berg* v. *Sadler & Moore* [1937] 2 K.B. 158; *Bigos* v. *Bousted* [1951] 1 All E.R. 92.

other provisions so as to affect their enforceability. The general test is whether the pursuer can maintain his case without founding on the illegal provision.[15] Thus while in a contract for the supply of goods a clause providing for the suspension of deliveries during war is contrary to public policy and illegal, the insertion of such a clause does not in any way affect the validity of the contract during peace.[16]

8. Contracts Merely Prohibited.—Contracts where the illegality does not consist in the object of the contract being to secure an illegal or immoral result, but merely in the fact that the particular contract, or method of contracting, is prohibited (i.e., cases falling within the second and third heads mentioned in section 1) are at one with contracts involving turpis causa in respect that they cannot be enforced, but differ in respect that the Court will not refuse to give effect to the rights of the parties when the contract has been carried into effect. So where there was a contract for the sale of potatoes calculated by a Scots measure, a method of contracting declared by statute to be "void and null," and the potatoes were actually delivered, it was held that although the contract could not be enforced in defiance of the statute, still, as there was "no turpitude in a man selling his potatoes by the Scots and not by the imperial acre," the buyer was bound to pay the market price[17]; but this does not hold where the contract is actually prohibited and illegal.[18] While an insurance by a party who has no insurable interest is by statute "null and void to all intents and purposes whatsoever," yet if the insurance company has chosen to pay, the Court will decide questions between competing claimants for the money.[19]

9. Rights of Third Parties.—As a general rule an illegal contract cannot be founded on even by third parties who have no notice of the illegality. Thus no one can acquire a title to stolen goods.[20] A bond for the price of goods which had been smuggled was held to be unenforceable even by a bona fide assignee.[21] There is a statutory exception to this in the case of bills and notes granted for an illegal consideration.[22]

10. Statutory Illegality.—In endeavouring to indicate what contracts are illegal a distinction may be made between contracts rendered illegal by statute and contracts illegal at common law.[23] As a general rule, where a statute limits freedom of contract it does so either by declaring a particular contract or

---

15 See opinion of Lord Dunedin, *Farmers' Mart* v. *Milne*, 1914 S.C. (H.L.) 84. Cf. *Fegan* v. *Dept. of Health*, 1935 S.C. 823, where, however, the dissenting judgment of Lord Fleming seems correct.
16 *Zinc Corporation* v. *Hirsch* [1916] 1 K.B. 541. See also *Kearney* v. *Whitehaven Colliery* [1893] 1 Q.B. 700.
17 *Cuthbertson* v. *Lowes* (1870) 8 M. 1073.
18 *Jamieson* v. *Watt's Tr.*, 1950 S.C. 265.
19 *Hadden* v. *Bryden* (1899) 1 F. 710. The contrary has been decided in England, *Re London County Re-Insurance Co.* [1922] 2 Ch. 67,
20 Bell, *Prin.*, § 527.
21 *Nisbet's Creditors* v. *Robertson* (1791) M. 9554.
22 Bills of Exchange Act 1882, ss. 30, 38.
23 Gloag, *Contract*, p. 549.

method of contracting to be void,[24] or by imposing a penalty on the persons who contract.[25] A contract declared by statute to be void can never be enforced, although, as has been explained, if the only objection is the statutory provision, the Court will give effect to rights arising when the contract is performed.[26] If without declaring a contract to be void a statute imposes a penalty on the persons who enter into it, it is always a question of the construction of the particular statute whether or not avoidance of the contract is implied.[27] It is a strong argument against avoidance in cases where the method of contracting rather than the contract is penalised, that the penalty may be incurred by mere inadvertence.[28] Where the penalty is imposed for failure to stamp a contract the presumption is that the provision is merely for revenue purposes, and that the contract may be enforced.[29] Subject to these provisos, the general rule is that where a contract is subjected to a penalty its illegality and consequent avoidance is implied,[30] except in cases where the penalty is the deprivation of an office.[31] A defender who pleads statutory illegality, e.g. in defence of an action of payment for work carried out, must however relevantly aver and prove that the work was done unlawfully.[32]

11. Illegal at Common Law.—In contracts illegal at common law there is a general, though not an exact, distinction between contracts objectionable on moral grounds and contracts contrary to public policy. In the former class are contracts for the commission of an act criminal at common law, involving a fraud on third parties,[33] or sexual immorality, with the exception of a provision made for a mistress after sexual intercourse has ceased.[34] The rule extends beyond contracts where the direct consideration is the commission of a criminal, fraudulent or immoral act, and reaches cases where the contract is, to the knowledge of the parties, intended to further criminality or immorality. So where a brougham was hired to a prostitute "as a part of her display, to attract men," the hire could not be recovered.[35] A similar decision was given with regard to the rent of a house occupied, to the landlord's knowledge, by persons living in immoral relations.[36] The doctrine of public policy, as a ground for the avoidance of contracts, was at one time very loosely and widely applied in the English Courts, reaching perhaps its culminating point in *Egerton* v. *Earl Brownlow*,[37] where it was held that a bequest to a peer,

---

[24] E.g., Unfair Contract Terms Act 1977, ss. 16, 19, 20, 21, 23. See also Sex Discrimination Act 1975, s. 77; Race Relations Act 1976, s. 72.
[25] E.g., Mock Auctions Act 1961.
[26] *Cuthbertson* v. *Lowes* (1870) 8 M. 1073.
[27] *Whiteman* v. *Sadler* [1910] A.C. 514, per Lord Dunedin.
[28] *Whiteman* v. *Sadler*, supra, per Lord Mersey.
[29] *Learoyd* v. *Bracken* [1894] 1 Q.B. 114.
[30] *Jamieson* v. *Watt's Tr.*, 1950 S.C. 265.
[31] *Drysdale* v. *Nairne* (1835) 13 S. 348; *Aberdeen Ry.* v. *Blaikie* (1851) 14 D. 66, revd. on other grounds (1854) 1 Macq. 461.
[32] *Designers & Decorators (Scotland)* v. *Ellis*, 1957 S.C. (H.L.) 69.
[33] *Laughland* v. *Millar* (1904) 6 F. 413.
[34] Bell, *Prin.*, § 37; *Webster* v. *Webster's Tr.* (1886) 14 R. 90.
[35] *Pearce* v. *Brooks* (1886) L.R. 1 Ex. 213.
[36] *Upfill* v. *Wright* [1911] 1 K.B. 506.
[37] (1853) 4 H.L.C. 1.

dependent on his obtaining a higher rank, involved a condition contrary to public policy, as tending to induce him to misuse his position as a legislator in order to obtain the higher rank. More recently, on the principle that it is a cardinal object of public policy that contracts should be observed, opinions have been expressed that the objection is open only where there is a direct precedent or plain analogy.[38] The mere fact that a direct precedent is forthcoming is not conclusive. It is open to the answer that instructed opinion may have altered on the point.[39]

12. Illustrations of Public Policy.—Among contracts which are illegal as contrary to public policy are included contracts interfering with the foreign policy of the State, such as a contract with an enemy State or with alien enemies.[40] On the same principle it is clear law in England that contracts involving the violation of the laws of a friendly State are unenforceable.[41] Contracts for smuggling[42]; for interfering with the free exercise of his duties by the holder of a public office[43] or member of a representative body[44]; for the employment of private influence to secure advantages from the Government[45]; for the evasion of legislative provisions limiting or regulating the sale of certain commodities[46]; for suppression of information which might lead to a conviction of crime,[47] are all illegal as contrary to public policy. An agreement to indemnify a person against liability for defamation is not illegal unless the person knew that the matter published was defamatory and did not reasonably believe that he had a good defence.[48]

13. Restrictive Covenants.—As a general rule contracts which involve an undue interference with personal liberty are void as being oppressive. But this rule is qualified to the extent that it may be lawful, if certain conditions are satisfied, to secure freedom from competition by contracts, usually termed restrictive covenants, by which a party undertakes not to carry on a particular trade or profession. The test which is applied to decide whether restrictive agreements of this nature can be enforced is whether the agreement is reasonable as between the parties,[49] and is consistent with the interests of the

---

[38] Per Lord Watson, *Nordenfelt* v. *Maxim Nordenfelt Gun Co.* [1894] A.C. 535; but see *M'Caig's Trs.* v. *Kirk-Session of Lismore,* 1915 S.C. 426.
[39] *Bowman* v. *Secular Society* [1917] A.C. 406.
[40] Capacity to Contract, Ch. VI. supra, § 6 and Extinction of Obligations, Ch. XV. infra, § 28.
[41] *Ralli* v. *Compania Naviera* [1920] 2 K.B. 287; *Regazzoni* v. *K. C. Sethia (1944) Ltd.* [1958] A.C. 301. On the other hand, income tax is payable on the fruits of such an adventure: see *Lindsay* v. *Inland Revenue,* 1933 S.C. 33.
[42] Bell, *Prin.,* § 42.
[43] *Henderson* v. *Mackay* (1832) 11 S. 225.
[44] *Hoggan* v. *Wardlaw* (1735) 1 Paton 148; *Amalgamated Ry. Servants* v. *Osborne* [1910] A.C. 87.
[45] *Stewart* v. *Earl of Galloway* (1752) M. 9465; *Montefiore* v. *Menday Motor Co.* [1918] 2 K.B. 241.
[46] *Trevalion* v. *Blanche,* 1919 S.C. 617; *Eisen* v. *M'Cabe,* 1920 S.C. (H.L.) 146.
[47] *Howard* v. *Odhams Press* [1938] 1 K.B. 1.
[48] Defamation Act 1952, s. 11.
[49] See *Nordenfelt* v. *Maxim Nordenfelt Gun Co.* [1894] A.C. 535; *Mason* v. *Provident Clothing Co.* [1913] A.C. 724; *Morris* v. *Saxelby* [1916] 1 A.C. 688; *Fitch* v. *Dewes* [1921] 2 A.C. 158; *Vancouver Malt & Sake Brewing Co.* v. *Vancouver Breweries Ltd.* [1934] A.C. 181. See also Gloag. *Contract,* pp. 569 et seq.

public.[50] The practical effects of the restriction, rather than its form, are to be examined.[51] Such agreements can be divided into two kinds, those by which an employee or apprentice agrees that after leaving his present employer he will not compete against him by setting up business on his own account, and those where the seller of the goodwill of a business, or someone in an analogous position,[52] agrees that in future he will not carry on a similar business in competition with the person who acquires that goodwill. As the law on this subject has developed, a distinction has been drawn between these two situations, and the law has been more ready to acknowledge freedom of contract in the latter. In all cases it is probably necessary that there should be some limit, either in point of area or in point of time. Subject to this, the only tenable objection to a restriction imposed on the seller of a business is that it is wider than is required in the interests of the business it is designed to protect. Thus while a world-wide restriction (limited as to time) was sustained in the case of a maker of cannon,[53] a restriction within the United Kingdom was held to be too wide, and consequently unenforceable, in the case of the business of a local carrier.[54] Where the restriction is imposed on a servant or apprentice the limits of freedom of contract are much narrower. The result of the decisions in the House of Lords has been judicially summarised as follows:— "While a purchaser of the goodwill of a business may properly protect himself by covenant from the competition of his vendor, it is not permissible for an employer to protect himself merely from the competition of his former servant after his service has terminated. It is permissible for the employer by covenant to protect his trade or professional secrets, and to protect himself also against his clients being enticed away by his former assistant; in other words to protect his connection."[55] So restrictions imposed on the managing clerk of a solicitor,[56] and on a party employed to sell milk, who had exceptional means of influencing customers,[57] have been sustained. When it was proved that the object of a restriction, imposed on a film actor, was not to protect a business but to obtain a hold upon the actor by rendering it difficult for him to obtain other employment, it was held that he was entitled to disregard it.[58]

The party who proposes to enforce a restrictive covenant must have an interest to enforce it, and cannot therefore do so if he has ceased to carry on, or has parted with, the business it was designed to protect.[59] He cannot enforce a restriction if he is himself in a material breach of contract, as where the servant restricted is unjustifiably dismissed.[60] A restriction imposed in a

[50] Vancouver Brewing Co., supra, per Lord Macmillan at p. 189.
[51] Stenhouse Australia v. Phillips [1974] A.C. 391.
[52] E.g., agreement by retiring partner, Trego v. Hunt [1896] A.C. 7; Whitehill v. Bradford, [1952] 1 Ch. 236. Agreement by rival to give up business, Stewart v. Stewart (1899) 1 F. 1158.
[53] Nordenfelt v. Maxim Nordenfelt Gun Co. [1894] A.C. 535.
[54] Dumbarton Steamboat Co. v. Macfarlane (1899) 1 F. 993.
[55] Per Younger, L.J., Fitch v. Dewes [1920] 2 Ch. at p. 185; [1921] 2 A.C. 158.
[56] Fitch v. Dewes, supra.
[57] Scottish Farmers' Dairy Co. v. M'Ghee, 1933 S.C. 148.
[58] Hepworth Manufacturing Co. v. Ryott [1920] 1 Ch. 1.
[59] Berlitz Schools v. Duchene (1903) 6 F. 181.
[60] General Billposting Co. v. Atkinson [1909] A.C. 118.

contract of service is not assignable.[61] If imposed on the seller of a business it may be assigned with that business, unless it appears that the restriction was undertaken solely in favour of the purchaser.[62] It is not settled whether a third party has a title to maintain that a restrictive covenant is unenforceable.[63] If the restriction imposed is too wide it falls; the Court will not enforce it within narrower limits.[64] But where there are two restrictions, one reasonable, the other oppressive, the contract may be regarded as separable, and the reasonable restriction enforced.[65]

14. Restraint of Trade.—Closely allied to the two kinds of restrictive covenant discussed above are those agreements which restrict a person's free exercise of his trade or business. Such agreements arise where manufacturers or merchants combine to regulate their trade relations, for instance by agreeing to restrict their output or to fix the selling price of a certain commodity.[66] While it was once the rule that contracts of this nature were contrary to public policy and, therefore, pacta illicita,[67] they are now regarded as a necessary part of commercial life. Such agreements are, at common law, legal and enforceable unless they involve a restriction on liberty greater than is necessary for the interest they are designed to protect, or their object is to raise wages or prices.[68] Again, the test in deciding whether any particular agreement is to be upheld, is the double standard of whether the agreement is reasonable as between the parties, and whether it is consistent with the public interest.[69] But in this case, where the parties themselves are regarded as being in an equal position of bargaining and the best judges of the fairness of the agreement, the Court will not readily allow them to escape from their obligations by claiming that the agreement was unreasonable.[70] However, where a member of a co-operative union dedicated to a non-competitive system of trading was prohibited from trading in a certain area by a ruling of its union, it was held, on its resigning from the union, that the ruling ceased to be binding on it; it was unreasonable to suppose that on joining the union and agreeing to submit to its ruling, it intended to bind itself for all time, whether or not it continued to be a member.[71] The legality at common law of price-

---

[61] *Berlitz Schools* v. *Duchene*, supra.
[62] *Rodger* v. *Herbertson*, 1909 S.C. 256.
[63] *British Motor Trade Association* v. *Gray*, 1951 S.C. 586.
[64] *Dumbarton Steamboat Co.* v. *Macfarlane*, supra.
[65] *Mulvein* v. *Murray*, 1908 S.C. 528; *Attwood* v. *Lamont* [1920] 3 K.B. 571.
[66] The categories of agreements in restraint of trade are not closed: see as to 'solus agreements', *Petrofina (G.B.)* v. *Martin* [1966] Ch. 146, per Lord Denning, M.R., at p. 169. See also *McIntyre* v. *Cleveland Petroleum Co.* 1967 S.L.T. 95 (conditions contained in a back letter); *Esso Petroleum Co.* v. *Harper's Garage (Stourport)* [1968] A.C. 269.
[67] *Barr* v. *Carr* (1766) M. 9564; *Corporation of Shoemakers* v. *Marshall* (1798) M. 9573; *Hilton* v. *Eckersley* (1855) 6 E. & B. 47; see dicta of Harman, L.J., in *Petrofina (G.B.)*, supra, at p. 175.
[68] *North-Western Salt Co.* v. *Electrolytic Alkali Co.* [1914] A.C. 461; *English Hop Growers* v. *Dering* [1928] 2 K.B. 174.
[69] *McEllistrim* v. *Ballymacelligott Co-operative Agricultural & Dairy Society*, [1919] A.C. 548, per Lord Chancellor Birkenhead at p. 562.
[70] *English Hop Growers*, supra, per Scrutton, L.J., at p. 180.
[71] *Bellshill & Mossend Co-operative Society* v. *Dalziel Co-operative Society*, 1960 S.C. (H.L.) 64.

maintenance agreements, i.e., agreements by which an agent or retailer undertakes not to sell goods below list prices, seems to be established.[72]

The common law principles on this subject are now, however, relatively unimportant. The Restrictive Trade Practices Act 1976 (c. 34), provides for the registration of a wide range of restrictive trade agreements,[73] and for their judicial examination by a Restrictive Practices Court[74]; those agreements found to be contrary to the public interest are prohibited. The statutory presumption[75] is that all such agreements are contrary to the public interest, unlike the common law where the onus of proving incompatibility with that interest lies on the party alleging it. The party seeking to justify the restrictive agreement must bring the restriction concerned within at least one of a list of circumstances, and also show that the agreement is not unreasonable having regard to those circumstances and any detriment which the agreement may cause to the public or third parties.[75] The Resale Prices Act 1976 (c. 53) prohibits individual resale price maintenance agreements,[76] except where such an agreement can be shown to be in the public interest. Where it can be shown to the satisfaction of the Restrictive Practices Court that without such an agreement in relation to a particular class of goods the public would suffer a detriment which would outweigh any detriment which would be caused by resale price maintenance, that Court has power to make an order for the exemption of that class of goods.[77] The Act also contains a general prohibition of agreements or arrangements for the collective enforcement of conditions as to resale prices.[78]

15. Betting and Gaming.—Gaming contracts cannot be enforced. The ground of the refusal of action is not that they are illegal, but that they are sponsiones ludicrae, unworthy to occupy judicial time.[79] Accordingly, while the Courts will not sustain an action for a bet, allow a proof as to the result of a race,[80] or an action for recovery of money paid for losses, even on averments that the play was unfair,[81] yet if the result of a race or other contest be admitted the stakeholder must pay the winner,[82] and the Court will entertain the question, who, according to the rules of the particular sport, is

---

[72] *Dunlop Pneumatic Tyre Co.* v. *New Garage Co.* [1915] A.C. 79; *Palmolive Co.* v. *Freedman* [1928] 1 Ch. 264.
[73] s. 1 · Parts II, III. See also Restrictive Trade Practices Act 1977 (c. 19).
[74] Restrictive Practices Court Act 1976 (c. 33); Restrictive Trade Practices Act 1976, ss. 10, 19 (1). See Courts & Jurisdiction, Ch. II., supra, § 7.
[75] Restrictive Practices Act 1976, ss. 10, 19 (1).
[76] Part II; the sanction afforded by the Act is a civil remedy, e.g. interdict or damages, for breach of statutory duty, rather than a criminal one.
[77] s. 14. See *Re Chocolate & Sugar Confectionery Reference*, [1967] 1 W.L.R. 1175; *Re Footwear Reference* (No. 2) (1967) L.R. 6 R.P. 398; *Re Medicaments Reference (No. 2)* (1970) L.R. 7 R.P. 267.
[78] Part I.
[79] *Wordsworth* v. *Pettigrew* (1799) M. 9524; *Knight* v. *Stott* (1892) 19 R. 959. The Betting, Gaming and Lotteries Act 1963 has not affected this principle: *Johnston* v. *T. W. Archibald*, 1966 S.L.T. (Sh. Ct.) 8.
[80] *O'Connell* v. *Russell* (1864) 3 M. 89; *Kelly* v. *Murphy*, 1940 S.C. 96 (football pool).
[81] *Paterson* v. *Macqueen* (1866) 4 M. 602.
[82] *Calder* v. *Stevens* (1871) 9 M. 1074; The promoter of a "football pool" is not a stakeholder: *Wilson* v. *Murphy*, 1936 S.L.T. 564; *Kelly* v. *Murphy*, supra.

entitled to receive the prize.[83] A person employed to make bets, as he is not gambling but acting as an agent, may recover payments made on behalf of his principal.[84] The rights of parties under a joint adventure for gaming purposes may be judicially considered.[85] It has been held in the Outer House that money lent to pay gambling losses may be recovered.[86] The former English rule that an agreement to give time for payment or to refrain from making public the loser's default forms a new consideration on which direct action can be founded, is not law in Scotland,[87] and has now been abandoned in England.[88]

Certain forms of gaming are expressly made illegal by statute. Under the Betting, Gaming and Lotteries Act 1963 (c. 2), it is a criminal offence to use any premises, or to cause or knowingly permit any premises to be used, as a place for the purpose of betting,[89] or to loiter in or frequent a public place for that purpose[90]; contracts in connection with such a business are doubtless illegal. The Act legalises betting in certain closely regulated places, notably in licensed betting offices.[91] Under the Gaming Act 1968 (c. 65) most forms of gaming are closely regulated and certain conditions must be complied with; if gaming subject to the Act is conducted otherwise than in accordance with these conditions, it is unlawful, the persons concerned will be committing an offence, and contracts in connection with that gaming will be unenforceable.[92] Under the Lotteries and Amusements Act 1976 (c. 32) all lotteries which do not constitute gaming are unlawful except as provided by the Act.[93] Those which are permitted under certain conditions are lotteries incidental to certain entertainments, "private" lotteries and lotteries promoted by a society registered under the Act or promoted by a local authority.[94] The Act makes a saving for Art Unions,[95] but places restrictions on prize competitions conducted in or through newspapers.[96] A competition is a lottery although some skill is exercised, where the element of chance predominates.[97]

A bill, cheque or promissory note given for money lost at play is to be taken as given for an illegal consideration.[98] It cannot therefore be enforced, except by an indorsee who can prove that he has given value for it in good faith.[99] Where a bond is granted for money lost at cards it cannot be enforced

---

[83] *Graham* v. *Pollok* (1848) 10 D. 646, 11 D. 343.

[84] *Levy* v. *Jackson* (1903) 5 F. 1170.

[85] *Mollison* v. *Noltie* (1889) 16 R. 350; *Forsyth* v. *Czartowski*, 1961 S.L.T. (Sh. Ct.) 22.

[86] *Hopkins* v. *Baird* 1920 2 S.L.T. 94. Not, on English authority, if the particular form of gaming is a criminal offence: *Moulis* v. *Owen* [1907] 1 K.B. 746. See, as to a cheque given in payment for chips in a gambling club, *Cumming* v. *Mackie*, 1973 S.L.T. 242.

[87] *Robertson* v. *Balfour*, 1938 S.C. 207.

[88] *Hill* v. *Wm. Hill (Park Lane) Ltd.* [1949] A.C. 530, a case which has no bearing on Scots Law: Lord Normand, at p. 568.

[89] s. 1 (1).

[90] s. 8.

[91] s. 9.

[92] *J. M. Allan (Merchandising) Ltd.* v. *Cloke*, [1963] 2 Q.B. 340.

[93] s. 1; a lottery was not illegal at common law: *Clayton* v. *Clayton*, 1937 S.C. 619.

[94] ss. 3-6.

[95] s. 25 (6); Art Unions Act 1846.

[96] s. 14.

[97] See *Strang* v. *Adair*, 1936 J.C. 56.

[98] Gaming Act 1835, s. 1.

[99] Bills of Exchange Act 1882, s. 30.

against the granter even by a bona fide assignee, but the latter may recover what he has paid for it from the cedent, on the principle that everyone who assigns a debt gives implied warrandice debitum subesse.[1]

In the case of dealings on the stock exchange it has been held that if the forms of the exchange are observed, so that the one party is bound to deliver, the other to accept, stock, it is immaterial that the party never intended to take delivery but merely to pay or receive differences according to the rise and fall of the market. To bring the case within the category of gambling transactions, and therefore to preclude action on the contract, it must be proved that both parties regarded the sale-notes or other documents which passed between them as a mere form, not intended to have any legal effect. It is not enough that neither contemplated the actual transfer of the stock as a probable event.[2]

16. Unfair Terms.—The Unfair Contract Terms Act 1977 makes ineffectual some types of contractual terms excluding or restricting liability for breach of contract; in some cases the Act makes the term void; in other cases, the term has no effect if it was not fair and reasonable to incorporate it in the contract. It is not possible to evade the effect of the Act by means of a secondary contract[3] or by a term applying, or purporting to apply, a foreign law to the contract.[4] The following are regarded as forms of exclusion or restriction:[5]— (a) making the liability or its enforcement subject to any restrictive or onerous conditions; (b) excluding or restricting any right or remedy in respect of the liability, or subjecting a person to any prejudice in consequence of his pursuing any such right or remedy; (c) excluding or restricting any rule of evidence or procedure; (d) excluding or restricting any liability by reference to a notice having contractual effect; (e) excluding or restricting an obligation implied by law.[6] An agreement to submit any question to arbitration is not an exclusion or restriction. The Act does not apply to international contracts for the supply of goods.[7] The Act does not affect a contractual provision which is authorised or required by the express terms or necessary implication of an enactment or which, being made with a view to compliance with an international agreement to which the United Kingdom is a party, does not operate more restrictively than is contemplated by the agreement.[8]

17. Contracts Affected.—The Act applies to any contract to the extent that it—

[1] *Ferrier* v. *Graham's Trs.* (1828) 6 S. 818.
[2] *Shaw* v. *Cal. Ry.* (1890) 17 R. 466; *Universal Stock Exchange Co.* v. *Howat* (1891) 19 R. 128. For English authorities, which give more weight to the intention of the parties, see *Richards* v. *Starck* [1911] 1 K.B. 296, and *Woodward* v. *Wolfe* (1936) 53 T.L.R. 87 (speculation in cotton futures).
[3] s. 23.
[4] s. 27 (2).
[5] s. 25 (3).
[6] s. 25 (5).
[7] s. 26.
[8] s. 29 (1).

  (a) relates to the transfer of the ownership or possession of goods from one person to another (with or without work having been done on them);
  (b) constitutes a contract of service or apprenticeship;
  (c) relates to services of whatever kind, including (without prejudice to the foregoing generality) carriage, deposit and pledge, care and custody, mandate, agency, loan and services relating to the use of land;
  (d) relates to the liability of an occupier of land to persons entering upon or using that land;
  (e) relates to a grant of any right or permission to enter upon or use land not amounting to an estate or interest in the land.[9]

Contracts of insurance and contracts relating to the formation, constitution or dissolution of any body corporate or unincorporated association or partnership are excepted.[10] It applies only to a limited extent to charter parties, and contracts of salvage or towage.[11] The Act does not affect the validity of any discharge or indemnity given by a person in consideration of the receipt by him of compensation in settlement of any claim which he has.[12]

18. Breach of Duty.—"Breach of Duty" is the breach of any obligation arising from the express or implied terms of a contract to take reasonable care or exercise reasonable skill in the performance of the contract or the breach of any common law duty to take reasonable care or exercise reasonable skill or the breach of the duty of reasonable care imposed by s. 2 (1) of the Occupier's Liability (Scotland) Act 1960.[13] A term of a contract which purports to exclude or restrict liability for breach of duty arising in the course of any business or from the occupation of any premises used for business purposes of the occupier is void in any case where such exclusion or restriction is in respect of death or personal injury; in any other case the term has no effect if it was not fair and reasonable to incorporate the term in the contract.[14]

19. Unreasonable Exemptions.—The provision of the Act which has the widest effect applies to two types of terms in "consumer contracts" and "standard form contracts". Terms in such contracts have no effect for the purpose of enabling a party to the contract—
  (a) who is in breach of a contractual obligation, to exclude or restrict any liability of his to the consumer or customer in respect of the breach;
  (b) in respect of a contractual obligation, to render no performance, or to render a performance substantially different from that which the consumer or customer reasonably expected from the contract;
if it was not fair and reasonable to incorporate the term in the contract.[15]

---

[9] s. 15 (2).
[10] s. 15 (3) (*a*).
[11] s. 15 (3) (*b*).
[12] s. 15 (1).
[13] s. 25 (1).
[14] s. 16 (1). The liability need not be that of a party to the contract.
[15] s. 17 (1). It would seem that the expectation can be based on something other than the terms of the contract.

A "consumer contract" is a contract (not being a contract of sale by auction or competitive tender) in which (a) one party to the contract deals, and the other party to the contract ("the consumer") does not deal or hold himself out as dealing, in the course of a business, and (b) in the case of contracts relating to the transfer of the ownership or possession of goods from one person to another, the goods are of a type ordinarily supplied for private use or consumption; the onus of proving that a contract is not to be regarded as a consumer contract lies on the party so contending.[16]

"Standard form contract" is not defined but light is thrown on its meaning by the definition of customer as "a party to a standard form contract who deals on the basis of written standard terms of business of the other party to the contract who himself deals in the course of a business".[17]

20. Unreasonable Indemnity Clauses.—A term of a "consumer contract" has no effect for the purpose of making the consumer indemnify another person (whether a party to the contract or not) in respect of "liability" which that other person may incur as a result of breach of duty or breach of contract, if it was not fair and reasonable to incorporate the term in the contract.[18] "Liability" means a liability arising in the course of any business or from the occupation of any premises used for business purposes of the occupier. The corresponding English section[19] makes it clear that the liability may be to the person dealing as consumer.

21. Guarantees of Consumer Goods.—A "guarantee" is a document containing or purporting to contain some promise or assurance (however worded or presented) that defects will be made good by complete or partial replacement, or by repair, monetary compensation or otherwise. Section 19 affects a guarantee which relates to goods of a type ordinarily supplied for private use or consumption and which is *not* given by one party to the other party to a contract under or in pursuance of which the ownership or possession of the goods to which the guarantee relates is transferred. A term of such a guarantee is void in so far as it purports to exclude or restrict liability for loss or damage (including death or personal injury) arising from the goods proving defective while in use otherwise than exclusively for the purposes of a business or in the possession of a person for such use and resulting from the breach of duty of a person concerned in the manufacture or distribution of the goods.

22. Supply Contracts.—The Act limits the exclusion or restriction of liability for breach of the terms as to title, description and quality implied by law in contracts of sale and hire-purchase.[20] It makes a similar provision in

[16] s. 25 (1).
[17] s. 17 (2).
[18] s. 18.
[19] s. 4.
[20] s. 20. See Sale of Goods, Ch. XVII, infra, § 31.

respect of the corresponding terms in other contracts relating to the transfer of ownership or possession of goods from one person to another (with or without work being done on them), e.g., contracts of hire or for work and materials.[21]

23. The "Reasonableness" Test.—The onus of proving that it was fair and reasonable to incorporate a term in a contract lies on the party so contending.[22] In applying the "reasonableness" test, regard is to be had only to the circumstances which were, or ought reasonably to have been, known to or in the contemplation of the parties to the contract at the time the contract was made.[23] Where a term in a contract purports to restrict liability to a specified sum of money, regard is to be had in particular to (a) the resources which the party seeking to rely on that term could expect to be available to him for the purpose of meeting the liability should it arise, and (b) how far it was open to that party to cover himself by insurance.[24] The "guidelines" for application of the "reasonableness" test provided in Schedule 2 to the Act [25] relate only to contracts of sale and hire purchase and other contracts for the supply of goods; but some of the "guidelines" may be found to be of use in applying the "reasonableness" test to other types of contract. A term is to be taken to have been fair and reasonable to incorporate if it is incorporated or approved by, or incorporated pursuant to a decision or ruling of, a "competent authority" acting in the exercise of any statutory jurisdiction or function and is not a term in a contract to which the "competent authority" is itself a party.[26] A "competent authority" is any court, arbiter, government department or public authority.[27]

[21] s. 21.
[22] s. 24 (4).
[23] s. 24 (1).
[24] s. 24 (3).
[25] See Sale of Goods, Ch. XVII, infra, § 31.
[26] s. 29 (2).
[27] s. 29 (3).

CHAPTER X

TITLE TO SUE. ASSIGNABILITY

1. Title to Sue.—In the ordinary case the only persons whose rights and liabilities are affected by a contract are the contracting parties. Strangers to the contract have no right to sue upon it and incur no liabilities under it. But this statement is subject to very wide exceptions. There are cases where others than the contracting parties have a right to sue and cases also where others may incur liabilities. One important case, contracts by agents, may be reserved for another chapter.[1] In the present we proceed to consider—(1) the possible rights and liabilities of third parties at the time when the contract was made; (2) the cases in which right or liability may subsequently be transmitted or assigned.

2. Contract Imposes no Liability on Third Parties.—It is too clear to be illustrated by any express decision that a contract cannot impose any contractual liability on a third party. Contractual liability depends on consent, and the third party has given no consent. A and B, in contracting, cannot impose any liability on C, unless C has in some way authorised them to do so.

There is more complexity in the question whether a third party may acquire a title to sue.

3. Laws of Jus Tertii.—The primary rule is that the contracting parties alone have a title to enforce a contract, and that the mere fact that a third party may have an interest does not give him a title. An obligation imposed by a contract is jus tertii to third parties, and they have no right to enforce it.

This has been illustrated in various circumstances. A creditor has no title to sue his debtor's debtor. A, incurring a debt to B, is under no liability to B's creditor, unless the debt has been assigned.[2] And the mere fact that A has undertaken to B to pay B's creditors will not give them any direct right of action against him. Thus where a company took over a trader's business and agreed with him to pay all the outstanding debts, it was held that an individual creditor of the trader acquired no title to sue the company.[3] When a manufacturer attempted to recover charges made by a railway company on the ground that they exceeded the rates fixed in a contract between that railway and another, it was decided that as the contract was made between the two railways for their own purposes it conferred no rights upon anyone else.[4] Where it was the rule of a police force that no constable should sue any member of the staff without the consent of the chief constable it was held that

---

[1] Agency, Ch. XXIII, infra.
[2] *Henderson* v. *Robb* (1889) 16 R. 341.
[3] *Henderson* v. *Stubbs, Ltd.* (1894) 22 R. 51.
[4] *Finnie* v. *Glasgow and S.W. Ry.* (1857) 3 Macq. 75.

the rule was jus tertii to a police surgeon, and that he could not plead it in bar of an action by a constable.[5] The fact that a particular enterprise by a firm is prohibited by the terms of the partnership deed, or, in the case of a company, is ultra vires, gives no right of interdict to a third party whose interests may be affected.[6] The tenants of a vassal under a feu have, in the absence of a jus quaesitum tertio in their favour, no title to sue the vassal's superior for the determination or enforcement of the rights and conditions contained in the vassal's grant from the superior.[7] In certain circumstances a third party's title, initially good, may lapse during the continuance of an action, with the result that he is no longer entitled to the remedy which he seeks.[8]

4. Jus Quaesitum Tertio.—The rule that the contracting parties alone have the right to enforce their contract suffers exception in cases where it is shown that their object was to advance the interests of a third party. That may create a jus quaesitum tertio, which will give the third party, or tertius, a title to sue.[9] In order to make this possible the tertius, or a particular class of which he is a member, must be named or referred to in the contract. A contract intended to confer advantages on the general public would not confer a title on anyone who chose to sue upon it.[10]

5. Where Express Title given to Tertius.—Whether there is a jus quaesitum tertio or not is a question of the intention of the contracting parties, which means not only that the party creditor in the contract should have intended to confer a benefit on the tertius, but that the debtor should have intended to subject himself to liability to him. That intention may be shown by an express provision in the contract that liability to a tertius is undertaken.[11] So where money is lodged on deposit receipt, payable to a third party, that third party, though a stranger to the contract, may demand payment from the bank.[12] And there would seem to be no rule of law which would deny effect to a provision in any contract whereby it is provided that a third party may sue upon it, even in cases where that third party has no personal interest involved.[13]

6. Where Sole Interest in Tertius.—Without any express provision a jus quaesitum tertio may be inferred in cases where the only party who has any substantial interest in the fulfilment of the contract is a tertius. Thus a promise to give a subscription to a charitable society may be enforced by the society,

---

[5] *A.* v. *B.,* 1907 S.C. 1154.
[6] *Nicol* v. *Dundee Harbour Trs.,* 1914 S.C. 374; 1915 S.C. (H.L.) 7.
[7] *Eagle Lodge* v. *Keir & Cawdor Estates,* 1964 S.C. 30.
[8] See *Donaghy* v. *Rollo,* 1964 S.C. 278.
[9] See Smith, *Short Commentary,* pp. 777 et seq.
[10] *Finnie* v. *Glasgow and S.W. Ry.* (1857) 3 Macq. 75, per Lords Cranworth and Wensleydale.
[11] *Braid Hills Hotel Co.* v. *Manuel,* 1909 S.C. 120; *Nicholson* v. *Glasgow Blind Asylum,* 1911 S.C. 391, per Lord President Dunedin at p. 399; *Macdonald* v. *Douglas,* 1963 S.L.T. 191, per Lord Justice-Clerk Grant at p. 200.
[12] *Dickson* v. *National Bank,* 1917 S.C. (H.L.) 50, per Lord Dunedin.
[13] See *Pagan & Osborne* v. *Haig,* 1910 S.C. 341.

though not made to the society itself nor to anyone acting as agent for it.[14] Where the rules of a trade union provided benefits to the dependants of a member who had become insane it was held that a jus quaesitum was conferred.[15]

7. Where Contracting Party Retains Interest. Building Restrictions.— Where one of the contracting parties has a substantial interest to enforce the contract, it is doubtful whether a jus quaesitum tertio can even be inferred unless there is some indication, beyond the fact that the tertius has an interest, of an intention to confer a title to sue on him. His interest is only an incidental result of a contract between two parties for their own purposes, and is not enough to give him a title to sue.[16] Thus where a superior has imposed building restrictions on a number of co-feuars the mere fact that the same restrictions are imposed on all feuars, and that each feuar has an interest to enforce compliance with the restrictions, will not give one feuar a title to sue another. He is suing to enforce an obligation imposed in a contract to which he was not a party, and which one of the contracting parties, the superior, has an interest to enforce.[17] To give a title to sue there must, in the absence of any agreement between the feuars themselves, be either a reference to a common plan, or a stipulation in each feu contract that the same restrictions are to be imposed on all the others. Either of these provisions sufficiently indicates such a similarity of conditions and mutuality of interest between the co-feuars as to show the intention of each feuar to submit to enforcement of the restrictions at the instance of the others.[18] If, however, the superior reserves to himself the right to waive the conditions or to sanction deviations from the plan, the mutuality of obligations between the co-feuars will be destroyed[19]; but where the title to sue is the subject of an express grant in the feu charter, the mere fact of such a reservation will not in itself be enough to negative the existence of a jus quaesitum tertio.[20] While the vassal, by consenting to be bound to his superior, prima facie concedes the superior's interest to enforce the conditions contained in the charter,[21] the onus is on the co-feuar, in order that he may enforce a condition as against another co-feuar, to show that he has a patrimonial interest, as well as a title, to do so.[22]

[14] *Morton's Trs.* v. *Aged Christian Friend Society* (1899) 2 F. 82. See also *Lamont* v. *Burnett* (1901) 3 F. 797; *Cambuslang West Church* v. *Bryce* (1897) 25 R. 322.
[15] *Love* v. *Amalgamated Society of Printers*, 1912 S.C. 1078.
[16] *Finnie* v. *Glasgow and S.W. Ry.* (1857) 3 Macq. 75.
[17] *Hislop* v. *M'Ritchie's Trs.* (1881) 8 R. (H.L.) 95; the consent and concurrence of the superior will not confer a title, *Girls' School Co.* v. *Buchanan*. 1958 S.L.T. (Notes) 2. See opinion of Lord Dunedin, *Nicholson* v. *Glasgow Blind Asylum*, 1911 S.C. 391, at pp. 400-401.
[18] *Johnston* v. *Walker's Trs.* (1897) 24 R. 1061. The pursuer and defender must be subject to the same or similar, restrictions; *Botanic Gardens Picture House* v. *Adamson*, 1924 S.C. 549.
[19] *Turner* v. *Hamilton*, (1890) 17 R. 494; *Red Court Hotel* v. *Burgh of Largs*, 1955 S.L.T. (Sh. Ct.) 2.
[20] *Lawrence* v. *Scott*, 1965 S.L.T. 390.
[21] *Earl of Zetland* v. *Hislop* (1882) 9 R. (H.L.) 40, per Lord Watson at p. 47; *Mactaggart* v. *Roemmele*, 1907 S.C. 1318, per Lord President Dunedin at p. 1323. For circumstances in which the superior's interest to enforce may be lost, see *Howard de Walden Estates* v. *Bowmaker*, 1965 S.C. 163, and cases cited therein.
[22] *Aberdeen Varieties* v. *James F. Donald (Aberdeen Cinemas)*, 1940 S.C. (H.L.) 52; *Macdonald* v. *Douglas*, 1963 S.L.T. 191, per Lord Justice-Clerk Grant at p. 200.

8. Actions of Damages.—It has been authoritatively stated that although a third party may have a title to enforce an obligation under a contract he can never have any contractual right to sue for damages for the defective performance of a contract.[23] Thus where a law agent, employed to buy a house, had negligently failed to notice a prior bond, it was decided that the only person who could sue him for damages was his employer, not the person to whom the employer had gifted the house and who therefore had incurred the loss.[24] If a third party can sue for the defective performance of a contractual act it must be on the ground that the act, independently of any question of contract, amounts to a wrong to him. So the patient injured by the negligent performance of a surgical operation may sue the surgeon for damages, even if he were not the surgeon's employer, in that negligent surgery constitutes a wrong to the party injured, whether there was any contract with him or not.[25]

9. Jus Quaesitum, when Irrevocable.—When A and B in contracting, make C the creditor in their contract, for instance in a bond or policy of insurance, it is clear that C has a title to sue, but it does not follow that he has a jus quaesitum in the money. In *Carmichael* v. *Carmichael's Executrix*[26] it was held that where, by contract between A and B, A was taken bound to pay to C, the mere terms of the contract were not enough to vest any irrevocable right in C. If there was nothing beyond the terms of the contract A and B were at liberty to alter their arrangement. On the other hand it was not absolutely necessary, in order to confer a jus quaesitum on C, that the document in which the contract was embodied should be delivered or formally intimated to him. It was a question of proof of the animus donandi, and of this the terms of the contract were important though not conclusive evidence. When the contract was expressed in C's favour, and he was made acquainted with the fact, the provision became irrevocable and he acquired a jus quaesitum.[27]

10. Title of Transferees of Property.—In cases where no one but the parties was originally interested in the contract third parties may acquire rights and liabilities as transferees of the subject or res to which the contract relates; as assignees of the contract; or as successors of the contracting parties. The law will be considered in this order.

11. Contracts Running with Lands: Superior and Vassal.—The cases where contractual rights and liabilities may be so attached to a particular subject that they pass with the ownership of that subject mainly relate to heritable property, and the law is commonly referred to as the law of contracts running

---

23 *Robertson* v. *Fleming* (1861) 4 Macq. 167, per Lord Chancellor Campbell; Gloag, *Contract* (2nd ed.), p. 239. But this view has been questioned: see Smith, *Short Commentary*, pp. 782 et seq.
24 *Tully* v. *Ingram* (1891) 19 R. 65.
25 *Edgar* v. *Lamont*, 1914 S.C. 277. See Ch. XXXIV., infra, § 10.
26 1919 S.C. 636; revd. 1920 S.C. (H.L.) 195. See also *Drysdale's Trs.* v. *Drysdale*, 1922 S.C. 741.
27 Gloag, *Contract* (2nd ed.), p. 230. See, however, *Allan's Trs.* v. *Lord Advocate*, 1971 S.C. (H.L.) 45, speech of Lord Reid at p. 54.

with the lands. In contracts between superior and vassal it is the general rule that they run, not strictly with the lands, but with successors of each party in the continuing contractual relationship as conditions of tenure. The obligations imposed, and the rights conferred, in a feu contract, are not read as imposed or conferred on the parties to the contract and their heirs, but on the parties and their successors as superior and vassal in the lands conveyed, and are binding on them[28] unless personal to the original parties.[29] Thus the obligation to pay feu-duty binds the feuar only so long as he retains that character; when he has parted with the lands, and the title of the disponee is completed, he is no longer liable except for arrears, and the obligation to pay the feu-duty lies on the disponee.[30] The detailed law on this subject is beyond the scope of the present work.[31]

12. Disponer and Disponee.—When there is no continuing relationship, such as that of superior and vassal, it is less easy to infer that contracts will run with the lands. A disponer of lands may create a servitude over other lands which he retains, and the right and burden thus created will run with the ownership of the dominant and the servient tenements.[32] But, with the doubtful exception of a clause of warrandice,[33] any personal obligation undertaken in a disposition of lands does not run with the lands so as to be enforceable by singular successors of the disponee, unless the right to enforce it is expressly assigned to them.[34] Nor will personal rights, which are valid against the disponer, be exerciseable against his disponee, even if the disponee has prior knowledge of them.[35] An obligation undertaken by the disponee, if it is duly constituted a real burden in the disponee's title,[36] will form a preferable burden on the lands themselves and so be binding on singular successors in the lands, where an interest to enforce it can be shown.[37] But any positive obligations, either to pay a sum of money as a ground annual,[38] or to erect buildings on the lands in question,[39] are binding only on the disponee and his heirs, and cannot be directly enforced against a singular successor. If duly

---

[28] *Hope* v. *Hope*, (1864) 2 M. 670.

[29] *Duncan* v. *Church of Scotland General Trs.*, 1941 S.C. 145; *Jolly's Exrx.* v. *Viscount Stonehaven*, 1958 S.C. 635.

[30] Bell, *Prin.*, § 700.

[31] See Gloag, *Contract* (2nd ed.), p. 226.

[32] See, as to servitudes, Rankine, *Landownership* (4th ed.).

[33] See *Christie* v. *Cameron* (1898) 25 R. 824.

[34] *Maitland* v. *Horne* (1842) 1 Bell's App. 1; *Marquis of Breadalbane* v. *Sinclair* (1846) 5 Bell's App. 353; *Speirs* v. *Morgan* (1902) 4 F. 1069. This rule does not apply to a separate obligation expressed to be in favour of a party and his successors in a particular tenement: *Magistrates of Dunbar* v. *Mackersy*, 1931 S.C. 180.

[35] *Morier* v. *Brownlie & Watson*, (1895) 23 R. 67; *Wallace* v. *Simmers*, 1960 S.C. 255.

[36] *Tailors of Aberdeen* v. *Coutts*, (1840) 1 Rob. App. 296; Menzies, *Conveyancing*, pp. 577 et seq.; *Aberdeen Varieties* v. *James F. Donald (Aberdeen Cinemas)*, 1939 S.C. 788, aff'd. 1940 S.C. (H.L.) 52.

[37] *Braid Hills Hotel Co.* v. *Manuel*, 1909 S.C. 120. Where the question arises between the original parties, it is for the disponee to show that the disponer's interest to enforce the restrictions has been lost: *S.C.W.S.* v. *Finnie*, 1937 S.C. 835; where the question arises between singular successors, however, the onus is on the dominant owner to show, as against the successor in the servient property, that he has an interest: *Aberdeen Varieties*, 1939 S.C. 788, per Lord Justice-Clerk Aitcheson, at p. 798.

[38] *Royal Bank* v. *Gardyne* (1853) 1 Macq. 358.

[39] *Marshall's Tr.* v. *M'Neill* (1888) 15 R. 762; *Anderson* v. *Dickie*, 1915 S.C. (H.L.) 79.

constituted as real burdens, obligations of this class will indirectly affect singular successors, in so far as they form preferable burdens on the lands, but in order that a direct right of action, either for payment of money or for the performance of an obligation ad factum praestandum, may run with the lands, the continuous relationship of superior and vassal is required.

13. Landlord and Tenant.—Contractual rights and liabilities may run with the relationship of landlord and tenant. This will be considered in a later chapter.[40]

14. Contracts do not Run with Moveables.—As a general rule contracts do not run with moveables. The purchaser of an article acquires no title to sue on contracts which the seller may have made in relation to that article, nor is he bound by them. So the rights under a charterparty do not pass to a purchaser of the ship.[41] When a firm of engineers had failed to carry out a contract to fit engines in a ship it was held that a purchaser of the ship had no title to sue them for damages. He was not the party with whom they had contracted, and the mere purchase of the ship conferred no title to sue on contracts relating to it.[42] Similarly, a purchaser of moveables incurs no liabilities. If he is a sub-purchaser, he is not liable for the price to the original seller. At common law if goods were sold under a condition (usually termed a price-maintenance agreement) as to the price at which they might be resold, that condition was binding only on the party who had agreed to it; it did not run with the goods so as to be binding on anyone who acquired them.[43] Whether a sub-purchaser who has notice of the price-maintenance agreement is bound by it is an unsettled question.[44]

15. Exceptions in Shipping Law.—The general rule that contracts do not run with moveables finds some exceptions in shipping law. The right to freight runs with the ownership of the ship.[45] By the Bills of Lading Act 1855, "every consignee of goods named in a bill of lading, and every indorsee of a bill of lading to whom the property in the goods therein mentioned shall pass, upon or by reason of such consignment or indorsement, shall have transferred to and vested in him all rights of suit, and be subject to the same liabilities, in

[40] Leases, Ch. XXXIII, infra.
[41] *Fratelli Sorrentino* v. *Buerger* [1915] 3 K.B. 367.
[42] *Blumer* v. *Scott* (1874) 1 R. 379; *Craig* v. *Blackater*, 1923 S.C. 472.
[43] See opinion of Lord Shaw, *National Phonograph Co.* v. *Menck* [1911] A.C. 336. In *British Motor Trade Association* v. *Gray*, 1951 S.C. 586, the petition contained such phrases as "the vehicle concerned was subject to a covenant," but this was not the ground of the judgment. Minimum resale price conditions are, now in general, void by virtue of the Resale Prices Act, 1976 (c. 53), s. 9, but s. 26 of that Act does permit the enforcement of a lawful price maintenance condition by the supplier against a person not a party to the sale who subsequently acquires the goods with notice of the condition as if that person had been a party to the sale.
[44] As to the common law, see *M'Gruther* v. *Pitcher* [1904] 2 Ch. 306; *Dunlop* v. *Selfridge* [1915] A.C. 847; *M'Cosh* v. *Crow* (1903) 5 F. 670; *Morton* v. *Muir*, 1907 S.C. 1211; *Lord Strathcona Co.* v. *Dominion Coal Co.* [1926] A.C. 108; *B.M.T.A.* v. *Salvadori*, [1949] Ch. 556 (liability in tort).
[45] *Stewart* v. *Greenock Marine Insurance Co.* (1848) 1 Macq. 328.

respect of such goods as if the contract contained in the bill of lading had been made with himself."

16. Title of Assignees.—When a contract is assigned the assignee acquires the right to sue and in some cases may be saddled with the liabilities arising under it. An assignee may sue in his own name, or may sist himself as pursuer in an action commenced by his cedent.[46] In cases where both the contracting parties consent to the assignation there is no difficulty, but it is a question of some complexity how far one party to a contract can assign without the consent of the other.

17. Assignability: Where Contract Executed.—It is an established rule that the benefit arising under a contract is assignable, in the absence of any express provision to the contrary.[47] Therefore if a contract is so far performed that nothing remains except to pay for what has been done, or to transfer a particular thing, the right to receive payment or the thing may be assigned. Such contracts are termed executed, as opposed to executory or executorial contracts. So a debt is assignable, if there be no provision to the contrary.[48] Where there was an agreement for the sale of a ship it was held that the party who had agreed to sell could not object to an assignation of the right to receive, although in the particular circumstances he had a defence in a question with the purchaser which was not pleadable against the assignee.[49]

18. Delectus Personae.—Contracts where something more than mere payment or delivery of a particular thing remains to be done are as a general rule not assignable if it is a matter of reasonable inference that one party entered into the contract in reliance on the qualities possessed by the other. The contract is then said to involve delectus personae. The most obvious case is where a party agrees to do something which involves personal skill. It is clear, as has been judicially remarked,[50] that a contract with an artist to paint a portrait cannot either be assigned as a contract, or carried out by the agency of anyone else. And the principle covers all cases of personal service.[51] The more difficult cases arise when the performance involved, such as the supply of goods by a broker, could be given by any person in the same line of business, or where the work required must necessarily be done through the instrumentality of hired labour and not by the obligant personally.

It is not generally competent for a party to a contract, whatever its nature may be, to assign it so as to get rid of the liabilities he has undertaken. He may be entitled to tender performance by a third party, but will remain liable if that third party's performance be defective. So when a page was hired in a serial circular issued by a wine-merchant, it was held that the contract could

---

[46] *Fraser* v. *Duguid* (1838) 16 S. 1130.
[47] *Aurdal* v. *Estrella*, 1916 S.C. 882; *Whiteley* v. *Hilt* [1918] 2 K.B. 808.
[48] Stair, III, 1, 3.
[49] *Aurdal* v. *Estrella, supra.*
[50] See opinion of Lord President Dunedin, *Cole* v. *Handasyde*, 1910 S.C. 68.
[51] *Hoey* v. *M'Ewan & Auld* (1867) 5 M. 814; *Berlitz Schools* v. *Duchene* (1903) 6 F. 181.

not be assigned to a company which took over the business of the wine-merchant, and which was prepared to continue the issue of the circular. The company's position was not merely that they were entitled to tender performance, but to come in the place of the wine-merchant so as to relieve him of all liability.[52] The general rule that the debtor under a contract cannot delegate his liabilities finds an exception in the case of contracts which run with lands, where the element of property bulks more largely than the element of contract.[53] And if the contract is of a duration so great that it cannot be supposed that continued personal performance was contemplated, it may be held that both parties must have intended to make it completely assignable. This was the conclusion arrived at in the case of a contract whereby a quarrymaster undertook to supply a company with all the chalk it might require. The contract was for fifty years, and it was held to be assignable to another company, although the assignee's requirements in chalk might be different from those of the cedent.[54]

19. Delegated Performance.—Though liability cannot be delegated a party may be entitled to assign his rights under the contract, or to tender performance by a third party. There is not necessarily delectus personae in all contracts, merely because the particular party has been chosen for the contract. If the contract is one which involves no special skill, and does not call for performance by the obligant personally, he may get it performed by a third party, and there would then seem to be no objection to his assigning to that third party the right to sue for the price of his work. The right to delegate performance has been sustained in the case of an upholsterer employed to beat and relay a carpet[55]; of a paviour who had contracted to lay and upkeep a street[56]; or a company which had undertaken to keep railway wagons in repair.[57] In none of these cases did it appear that the employer relied on any special skill in the party to whom he gave the order. This element was present in *Cole* v. *Handasyde*,[58] where a broker was employed to supply black grease, and selected because he was an expert in that commodity. But it was also provided that the grease might be rejected if it failed to pass a specified test, and it was held that this provision excluded delectus personae, and that the contract could be enforced by a party to whom it had been assigned, although he was not possessed of the broker's expert knowledge.

20. Contracts Involving Mutual Obligations.—In all these cases the contract was reducible to an obligation to do a particular piece of work, or get it done, on the one side, and to pay for it on the other. If the contract is of a more complex character, involving further obligations on one party or other,

---

[52] *Grierson, Oldham & Co.* v. *Forbes Maxwell & Co.* (1895) 22 R. 812.
[53] Supra, § 11.
[54] *Tolhurst* v. *Associated Portland Cement Co.* [1903] A.C. 414. See, however, *Magistrates of Arbroath* v. *Strachan's Trs.* (1842) 4 D. 538.
[55] *Stevenson* v. *Maule*, 1920 S.C. 335.
[56] *Asphaltic Limestone Co.* v. *Corporation of Glasgow*, 1907 S.C. 463.
[57] *British Waggon Co.* v. *Lea* (1880) 5 Q.B.D. 149.
[58] 1910 S.C. 68.

it would seem that it is not assignable. So where, in a contract of a year's duration for the supply of eggs, the purchaser undertook not to buy eggs from any other dealer, it was held that this provision introduced the element of delectus personae and that the contract could not be enforced by a successor of the purchaser in business, to whom it had been assigned.[59] And when A ordered a particular machine from B, undertaking to engage in a course of business which would involve ordering other machines, and B undertook to supply these machines at cost price, it was held that the contract, involving obligations on both sides other than supplying and paying for the initial machine, could not be enforced by a company to which B had assigned it.[60] Delectus personae may be involved in the fact that the party who orders goods or work is a creditor of the party to whom he gives the order, and would therefore be entitled to set off the price against his debt. The contract cannot then be assigned to a third party, so as to give him a right to fulfil the order and sue for the price.[61]

21. Title of Representatives.—On the death of one of the parties to a contract his representatives in succession may acquire a title to sue, and, in so far as they benefit in the succession, may incur liability. Debts pass to the executor of the creditor, and, in the absence of any provision to the contrary, may be recovered from the whole estate of the debtor.[62] In the case of uncompleted contracts the title of representatives to sue may depend on whether the contract involved delectus personae. Thus the death of either master or servant dissolves the contract, and the relationship does not transmit to the representatives of either party.[63] But while, if it be clear that the personal qualities of an obligant are relied on, his death terminates the contract, there are cases where a contract may transmit to representatives though it would not be assignable inter vivos. Thus the interest of a tenant in a lease passes to his heir, although from the nature or the express terms of the lease it may not be assignable without the landlord's consent.[64] And probably all commercial or engineering contracts, unless it be clear that the personal attention of the obligant was promised, pass to and are enforceable against the personal representatives of the contracting parties.[65] Thus it was observed that, while a contract of service was ended by the death of the employer, a contract operis faciendi, such as a contract to build a house, would transmit to and be enforceable against the heir of the person who had ordered the work.[66]

22. Trustee in Sequestration.—A trustee in sequestration may have the right to enforce contracts in which the bankrupt was engaged. He is never

---

[59] *Kemp* v. *Baerselman* [1906] 2 K.B. 604.
[60] *International Fibre Syndicate* v. *Dawson* (1900) 2 F. 636; affd. (1901) 3 F. (H.L.) 32.
[61] *Boulton* v. *Jones* (1857) 2 H. & N. 564.
[62] *Gardiner* v. *Stewart's Trs.*, 1908 S.C. 985.
[63] *Hoey* v. *M'Ewan & Auld* (1867) 5 M. 814.
[64] Bell, *Prin.*, § 1219; Rankine, *Leases* (3rd ed.), p. 157.
[65] See the distinction between assignability and transmissibility drawn by Lord Lindley in *Tolhurst* v. *Associated Portland Cement Co.* [1903] A.C. 414.
[66] Per Lord President Inglis, *Hoey* v. *M'Ewen & Auld,* supra.

bound to carry out the bankrupt's contracts, and a decree ad factum praestandum will not be pronounced against him. The remedy of the other party, where the trustee does not adopt a contract, is to lodge a claim for damages in the sequestration.[67] The authorities are not clear on the question how far the element of delectus personae in a contract precludes its adoption by a trustee in sequestration, or by the liquidator of a company. The trustee cannot adopt a contract when the personal services of the bankrupt are engaged.[68] It has been decided that a contract to publish a book did not pass to the trustee in the publisher's bankruptcy.[69] On the other hand the bankrupt's interest in a lease, though it may not be assignable, will pass to his trustee in bankruptcy, unless there is an express provision to the contrary.[70] The case of ordinary commercial contracts was considered in *Anderson* v. *Hamilton*.[71] The bankrupt had contracted to supply iron by instalments. The trustee intimated that he adopted the contract; the purchasers, that they regarded it as cancelled. The decision in the purchasers' favour was based on the ground that the trustee, assuming that he had a right to adopt the contract, had not intimated his decision to do so within a reasonable time, but from the opinions given, and from a later case,[72] there can be little doubt that a contract under which the bankrupt has undertaken to deliver goods, or to execute some building or engineering work, can be adopted by the trustee in his sequestration, even although its terms might be such as to preclude voluntary assignation by the bankrupt.[73]

In *Anderson* v. *Hamilton*[74] it was held that in a contract relating to goods which fluctuate in value each party was entitled to know at once whether the contract would be carried out, and that where the bankrupt failed on March 14, and the trustee did not intimate his decision to carry out the contract until April 8, his intimation was too late, and the other party was entitled to hold the contract as cancelled. It was suggested that, prior to the election of a trustee, leading creditors might decide to adopt or reject the bankrupt's contracts, but it is difficult to see on what ground their decision could be binding on the trustee. In England it was held, in the case of an agreement to sell, that the assignees in bankruptcy might postpone their decision until, under the terms of the contract, something fell to be done by them on the bankrupt's behalf. Until then the other party was bound to fulfil any obligation prestable by him.[75]

A trustee in sequestration, if he decided to adopt a contract, cannot insist on fulfilment of the provisions in his favour unless he is prepared to

---

[67] *Kirkland* v. *Cadell* (1838) 16 S. 860; *Asphaltic Limestone Co.* v. *Corporation of Glasgow*, 1907 S.C. 463.
[68] *Caldwell* v. *Hamilton*, 1919 S.C. (H.L.) 100, per Viscount Cave, at p. 104.
[69] *Gibson* v. *Carruthers* (1841) 8 M. & W. 321, opinion of Lord Abinger. See *Griffiths* v. *Tower Publishing Co.* [1897] 1 Ch. 21.
[70] Stair, II, 9, 26; Bell, *Prin.*, § 1216.
[71] (1875) 2 R. 355.
[72] *Asphaltic Limestone Co.* v. *Corporation of Glasgow*, supra.
[73] This is the law in England, see *Tolhurst* v. *Associated Portland Cement Co.* [1903] A.C. 414, opinion of Lord Lindley.
[74] (1875) 2 R. 355.
[75] *Gibson* v. *Carruthers*, supra.

implement the provisions incumbent on the bankrupt. So where A had undertaken to erect various buildings on land feued from B, and B had agreed to allocate the feu-duty on a building which was in course of erection, it was held that A's trustee in sequestration could not require fulfilment of the obligation to allocate the feu-duty unless he was prepared to adopt and implement the contract for the erection of the other buildings.[76] But if the bankrupt has two separate contracts with the same party, the trustee is entitled to adopt one and refuse to carry out the other.[77] If the bankrupt's assets include a copyright, burdened with the obligation to pay royalties to the author, the trustee cannot dispose of copies of the work, or assign the copyright, except on terms which will secure to the author the royalties which he would have been entitled to receive from the bankrupt.[78] If a trustee adopts a contract in which the bankrupt was engaged, or continues the bankrupt's business, he incurs personal liability.[79] In the case of a lease he renders himself personally liable for all the obligations incumbent on the tenant, including all arrears of rent.[80]

---

[76] *Mitchell's Tr.* v. *Galloway's Trs.* (1903) 5 F. 612.
[77] *Asphaltic Limestone Co.* v. *Corporation of Glasgow*, 1907 S.C. 463.
[78] Bankruptcy (Scotland) Act 1913, s. 102; *Re Health Promotion Co.* [1932] 1 Ch. 65.
[79] *Mackessack* v. *Malleson* (1886) 13 R. 445; *Sturrock* v. *Robertson's Trs.*, 1913 S.C. 582.
[80] *Gibson* v. *Kirkland* (1833) 6 W. & S. 340; Rankine, *Leases* (3rd ed.), p. 698.

CHAPTER XI

IMPOSSIBILITY OF PERFORMANCE

1. Contracts to Perform Impossibility.—It is generally supposed, though without any actual decision, that a contract to do something believed by all educated men to be physically impossible would be void, even although both parties believed it to be possible.[1] But impossibility which is not obvious, but depends upon intricate calculations, as in the case of a contract to build a ship on a certain model and with a specified carrying capacity, leaves the contract unaffected.[2] The plea of commercial impossibility, that is, that the value of a ship when repaired would not cover the cost of repairs ordered, has been put forward, but unhesitatingly rejected.[3] Contracts to do something legally impossible, i.e., to do an act for which the law provides no facilities, as, for instance, to execute a valid entail after the Register of Tailzies was closed by the Entail Act, are void.[4]

2. Supervening Impossibility: Frustration.—A contract may be dissolved by a change of circumstances, or of the law, which either renders performance impossible or illegal, or so alters the conditions that performance, if given, would in substance be performance of a different contract from that to which the parties agreed. To such cases the term frustration of the adventure has been applied.[5] It is a general principle that the change in circumstances in question must have occurred from some cause independent of the volition of the contracting parties. So the statutory provision that on an agreement to sell specific goods the agreement is avoided if the goods perish before the risk passes to the buyer is qualified by the proviso that the goods shall have perished without any fault on the part of the seller or buyer.[6]

3. General Result of Impossibility.—It is not an absolute rule that a contract is at an end because performance has become impossible. But the development of the law, starting with the principle that if an unqualified obligation has been undertaken its supervening impossibility may be a ground for excusing actual performance but is no answer to a claim for damages, has been in the direction of holding that obligations are rarely intended to be unqualified, but are undertaken under the implied condition that performance

---

[1] See Indian Contract Act 1872, s. 56. The illustration given is a contract to recover treasure by magic. See also Sale of Goods Act 1893, s. 6.

[2] *Gillespie* v. *Howden* (1885) 12 R. 800.

[3] *Hong-Kong, etc., Dock Co.* v. *Netherton Shipping Co.,* 1909 S.C. 34.

[4] *Caledonian Insurance Co.* v. *Matheson's Trs.* (1901) 3 F. 865; *George Packman & Sons* v. *Dunbar's Trs.,* 1977 S.L.T. 140.

[5] See §§ 14 and 15, infra.

[6] Sale of Goods Act 1893, s. 7. See *Mertens* v. *Home Freeholds Co.* [1921] 2 K.B. 526; and Gloag, *Contract* (2nd ed.), p. 344.

shall continue to be possible.[7] The result is that there are now few cases where impossibility is not an effectual plea. Still, it is probably the law that an agreement to sell a certain quantity of a particular commodity is not affected by the fact that the commodity has become unprocurable.[8] It is an established rule in shipping law that if a certain number of days (lay-days) are provided in a charterparty for loading the ship, it is no answer to a claim for damages that owing to any circumstances, not expressly provided for and not due to the fault of the shipowner, it has proved to be impossible to load within the lay-days.[9] Even where there is no provision for lay-days the charterer is absolutely bound to have the cargo ready on receiving reasonable notice of the arrival of the ship, and is liable in damages for her detention even although his failure was due to conditions over which he had no control.[10]

4. Contract with Time Limits.—The strongest case for the enforcement of a contract according to its terms is where, as in the shipping cases above mentioned, there is an obligation to perform within a specified time, with a contractual provision for the consequences of failure. But even here it is not an absolute rule that impossibility of timely performance may not be a relevant defence. Thus when a joiner undertook to finish his work on a house by a given date, with a penalty in the event of the time being exceeded, and met a demand for the penalty by the plea that his delay was due to the fact that observance of the time limit was impossible owing to the failure of other tradesmen employed on the house, the opinions of the majority of the Court were in favour of the validity of his plea.[11]

5. Rei Interitus.—The clearest case for the dissolution of a contract on the ground of impossibility is where an obligation is undertaken which cannot be performed unless some specific thing continues to exist and to be available for the contractual purposes. Then the accidental destruction of that thing (rei interitus) or, without actual destruction, some event which precludes the performance of the contract through its means, will put an end to the contract.[12] Thus if a specific thing sold has perished before the property has passed to the buyer[13]; if a subject has been accidentally destroyed,[14] or has been requisitioned by the Government,[15] or, in the case of a lease of salmon fishing, been so affected by the action of a Government department as to be incapable of possession as a fishing[16]; if a ship, though not actually lost, has been so injured as to become totally unfit for the purpose for which she was

[7] See the history of the law traced by M'Cardie, J., *Blackburn Bobbin Co.* v. *Allen* [1918] 1 K.B. 540; affd. [1918] 2 K.B. 467.
[8] *Blackburn Bobbin Co.*, supra. But see *Re Badische Co.* [1921] 2 Ch. 331.
[9] *Hansa* v. *Alexander*, 1919 S.C. (H.L.) 122.
[10] *Ardan S.S.Co.* v. *Weir* (1905) 7 F. (H.L.) 126.
[11] *Duncanson* v. *Scottish County Investment Society*, 1915 S.C. 1106. The decision turned on a specialty.
[12] Bell, *Prin.*, § 29.
[13] Sale of Goods Act 1893, s. 7; *Leitch* v. *Edinburgh Ice, etc., Co.* (1900) 2 F. 904.
[14] *Walker* v. *Bayne* (1815) 6 Paton 217; *Allan* v. *Robertson's Trs.* (1891) 18 R. 932.
[15] *Mackeson* v. *Boyd*, 1942 S.C. 56.
[16] *Tay Salmon Fisheries Co.*, v. *Speedie*, 1929 S.C. 593.

chartered[17]; if a music hall, hired for a particular day for the purpose of giving a concert, has been burned[18]; in all cases the contract is avoided or discharged, and no damages can be recovered from the party who has failed to fulfil his obligations. An analogous case is where a party has undertaken to perform some service, as, for example, to play at a concert, which is only possible if he remain in health. His illness amounts to rei interitus; he no longer exists as a concert-playing man; and the contract is dissolved.[19]

6. Building in Course of Erection.—When a building in course of construction is accidentally destroyed the question has been, not whether the contract is discharged (which would probably depend on the stage which the building had reached), but whether the builder has any claim for payment for his work or materials. In the cases in Scotland the question has been treated on the basis of property. As the property in the unfinished building has passed to the owner of the ground, on the principle of accession[20] the general maxim res perit domino applies, the loss falls on him and the builder has a claim for his work and materials.[21]

7. Recovery of Payments in Advance.—When payment in advance has been made for a contract which is ultimately avoided on the ground of impossibility our law follows the condictio causa data, causa non secuta of the civil law, and holds that where money is paid in advance in consideration of some service to be rendered in future it may be recovered if that service is not rendered, even though, as in the case of impossibility, no breach of contract may be involved. Thus in a contract for the construction of ship's engines for an Austrian firm an instalment of the price was paid on signing the contract. Before the construction of the engines had begun war with Austria was declared. It was not in dispute that this put an end to the contract.[22] It was held, on the conclusion of peace, that the Austrian firm might recover the deposit.[23]

8. Supervening Events Altering Value of Contract.—Some early cases on leases extended the principle of rei interitus to the case where the subjects let failed to produce the expected return. The lease was not avoided, but no rent was due for the period of sterility.[24] But the authority of these cases was called in question in *Gowans* v. *Christie*.[25] It was there held that a mineral lease was not avoided by the failure of the seam, and observed that in a lease for years the tenant expected to make his profit on a balance of good and bad years,

---

[17] *London and Edinburgh Shipping Co.* v. *The Admiralty*, 1920 S.C. 309.
[18] *Taylor* v. *Caldwell* (1863) 3 B. & S. 826.
[19] *Robinson* v. *Davidson* (1871) L.R. 6 Ex. 269.
[20] See Moveable Property, Corporeal, Ch. XXXVII, infra, § 6.
[21] *M'Intyre* v. *Clow* (1875) 2 R. 278; *Richardson* v. *Dumfriesshire Roads Trs.* (1890) 17 R. 805.
[22] See Extinction of Obligations, Ch. XV infra, § 28.
[23] *Cantiere San Rocco* v. *Clyde Shipbuilding Co.*, 1922 S.C. 723, revd. 1923 S.C. (H.L.) 105. The law of England has since been brought into line with Scots law: *Fibrosa Spolka Akcyjna* v. *Fairbairn & Co.* [1943] A.C. 32; Law Reform (Frustrated Contracts) Act 1943.
[24] *Foster* v. *Adamson* (1762) M. 10131.
[25] (1873) 11 M. (H.L.) 1.

and that there was no equity in refusing rent for a year which had proved unproductive. And generally, except in cases where the execution of the contract is interrupted and the plea of frustration of the adventure is available,[26] the fact that supervening events, or a change in the law, have made the contract more burdensome or less profitable is irrelevant.[27] Thus no rise or fall of prices or wages has so far been held to avoid a contract for the supply of goods or labour.[28] It is for the legislature, by emergency legislation, to provide for exceptional cases where a change in conditions would make the performance of certain contracts ruinous. There is a general statutory provision under which, when a new duty is imposed, or an existing duty increased or diminished, on any article which is the subject of a sale or an agreement to sell, an increase or diminution of the price, as the case may be, may be claimed by the seller or purchaser.[29] At common law it was held that the loss due to an alteration in duties must fall where it might happen to light.[30] It may be regarded as an exception to the general rule that if a subject let is partially destroyed the tenant is entitled to an abatement of rent.[31]

9. Object of Contract Defeated.—Events, without rendering literal performance of the contract impossible, may disappoint the object for which one of the parties contracted. If this object was known to himself alone the contract is clearly unaffected; a seller is not concerned with the motives which induce the buyer to buy. Even if the object was known to both, its disappointment will not affect the contract unless the result be to render it completely nugatory. So an agreement for the sale of jute remained binding, although the export of jute was subsequently forbidden, since the contract did not provide that the sale was for export.[32] But there may be exceptional cases where the disappointment of the only purpose which could have induced it, even although no mention may have been made of that purpose in the contract itself, will avoid the contract. A series of cases, usually referred to as the Coronation cases, arose out of the postponement of a procession which had been fixed for the Coronation of Edward VII. Rooms had been hired on the route of the procession, without any express mention of it, but on terms which clearly indicated the object for which they were rented. On the postponement of the procession it was held that the case could be treated as one where performance had been rendered impossible, and that the contracts were avoided.[33]

---

[26] Infra, § 15.
[27] *Holliday* v. *Scott* (1830) 8 S. 831.
[28] *Wilson* v. *Tennants* [1917] A.C. 495.
[29] Finance Act 1901, s. 10; scope enlarged by Finance Act 1902, s. 7. See also Finance Act 1972 (c. 41), s. 42 (value added tax).
[30] *Maclelland* v. *Adam* (1795) M. 14247.
[31] *Muir* v. *M'Intyre* (1887) 14 R. 470; *Sharp* v. *Thomson*, 1930 S.C. 1092.
[32] *McMaster & Co.* v. *Cox, M'Euen & Co.*, 1920 S.C. 566, revd. 1921 S.C. (H.L.) 24.
[33] *Krell* v. *Henry* [1903] 2 K.B. 740; *Chandler* v. *Webster* [1904] 1 K.B. 493. Contrast *Herne Bay Steamboat Co.* v. *Hutton* [1903] 2 K.B. 683. It was further held in *Krell* and *Chandler* that the money paid in advance for the seats could not be recovered, but these decisions have been overruled on this point; see note 23.

10. Violent Acts by Third Parties.—The effect of impossibility due to the violent or unwarrantable acts of third parties is not free from doubt, but it would appear that it is not a ground for the avoidance of a contract. Thus it has been held in England in cases which, though questioned, have not been overruled, that an obligation to load a cargo at a particular port is not affected by the fact that civil disturbance or the unwarrantable acts of the port authorities have rendered it impossible.[34] In *Milligan* v. *Ayr Harbour Trustees* it was decided that the obligation of a harbour trust to provide facilities for unloading a ship was not excused by reasonable apprehensions that the result would be a strike, and in the opinion of Lord Guthrie, would not have been excused even if it had been certain that compliance would have brought the business of the harbour to a standstill.[35] Where a tenant's crops were carried off by rebel forces this was held to be no ground for a refusal to pay rent.[36]

11. Change in Law: Illegality.—If a change in the law renders performance illegal the contract is dissolved, on the theory that it is not to be presumed that a man bound himself to commit an illegal act. So, for example, a partnership is dissolved by the happening of any event which makes it unlawful for the business of the firm to be carried on, or for the members of the firm to carry it on in partnership.[37] The effect of a declaration of war as dissolving contracts with the enemy is considered later.[38] It is probably established that a contract which is to be performed in a foreign country is dissolved if a change in the law of that country renders performance illegal there.[39]

12. Change in Law: Impossibility.—If a change in the law renders performance impossible, the result is to dissolve the contract. Thus a contract for the export of goods is dissolved if their export is prohibited by statutory authority.[40] Where A contracted to leave a particular piece of ground unbuilt upon, and a railway company, under statutory powers, acquired the ground and built a station on it, it was held that A was not liable in damages.[41] But if, in similar circumstances, it is within the obligant's power to secure a clause which would safeguard his obligation, he is bound to do so.[42]

13. Impossibility: When Final.—A party is not entitled to cancel his contract on the ground that events are looming in the future which will probably render performance impossible, and, if he takes that course, will be liable in damages even although his apprehensions may be justified by the

---

[34] *Jacobs* v. *Credit Lyonnais* (1884) 12 Q.B.D. 589; *Ashmore* v. *Cox* [1889] 1 Q.B. 436. See opinions in *Matthey* v. *Curling* [1922] 2 A.C. 180.
[35] 1915 S.C. 937.
[36] *Strachan* v. *Christie* (1751) M. 10129.
[37] Partnership Act 1890, s. 34.
[38] Extinction of Obligations, Ch. XV., infra, § 28.
[39] *Ralli* v. *Compania Naviera* [1920] 2 K.B. 287; *Trinidad Shipping Co.* v. *Alston* [1920] A.C. 888.
[40] *Re Anglo-Russian Merchant Traders & Batt* [1917] 2 K.B. 679, distinguished in *Ross T. Smyth & Co., Ltd.* v. *W. N. Lindsay, Ltd.* [1953] 1 W.L.R. 1280.
[41] *Baily* v. *De Crespigny* (1869) L.R. 4 Q.B. 180.
[42] *Leith School Board* v. *Rattray's Trs.*, 1918 S.C. 94.

event.[43] The question how far it may be assumed that an existing bar to performance will remain permanent is in some respects doubtful. It is an established rule that no Court can predict how long a war may last and, therefore, that contracts affected by war are dissolved at once.[44] Probably a statute which renders performance illegal or impossible may be regarded as conclusive. But this is not clear with regard to Orders in Council having statutory force, and in one case where the export of confectionery was prohibited by Order it was held that a party who had undertaken to export it was bound to wait to see whether the Order would remain in force, and was not justified in rescinding the contract at once.[45] Where administrative measures taken by a foreign government rendered performance impossible it was held that the question whether the contract could be cancelled at once depended on whether there was or was not a reasonable probability that the measures in question would be altered in time to admit of the performance.[46]

14. Frustration of the Adventure.—The object of the principle known as frustration is to find some satisfactory way whereby the Court may allocate between the parties to a contract the risk of supervening events. The general idea behind it has been judicially explained as follows[47]: "When a lawful contract has been made and there is no default, a Court of law has no power to discharge either party from the performance of it unless either the rights of someone else or some Act of Parliament give the necessary jurisdiction. But a Court can and ought to examine the contract and the circumstances in which it was made, not of course to vary, but only to explain it, in order to see whether or not from the nature of it the parties must have made their bargain on the footing that a particular thing or state of things would continue to exist . . . . no Court has an absolving power, but it can infer from the nature of the contract and the surrounding circumstances that a condition which is not expressed was a foundation on which the parties contracted." While the principle was, in the early stages of its history, developed particularly with regard to the interruption of business activities by delay, it admits of almost indefinite application, as diverse as are the possibilities of a contract being interrupted by a vital change of circumstances.[48] The application of the general principle must depend on the circumstances of each case; and it is for the Court to decide, looking to what has actually happened and its effect on the possibility of performing the contract, what is the true position between the parties.[48] Where there is frustration, a dissolution of the contract occurs automatically, independent of the choice or election of either party.[49] It is

[43] *Watts* v. *Mitsui* [1917] A.C. 227.
[44] *Horlock* v. *Beal* [1916] 1 A.C. 486; *Geipel* v. *Smith* (1872) L.R. 7 Q.B. 404. Extinction of Obligations, Ch. XV. infra, § 28.
[45] *Millar* v. *Taylor* [1916] 1 K.B. 402.
[46] *Embiricos* v. *Reid* [1914] 3 K.B. 45.
[47] By Lord Loreburn in *Tamplin Co.* v. *Anglo-Mexican Petroleum Co.* [1916] 2 A.C. 397, at p. 403, quoted by Lord Radcliffe in *Davis Contractors Ltd.* v. *Fareham U.D.C.* [1956] A.C. 696 at p. 727.
[48] Per Lord Wright in *James B. Fraser & Co.* v. *Denny Mott & Dickson,* 1944 S.C. (H.L.) 35 at pp. 42-43.
[49] *Hirji Mulji* v. *Cheong Yue S.S. Co.* [1926] A.C. 497 at p. 510.

immaterial that the possibility of the frustrating event was within the contemplation of both parties; the only thing that is essential is that the parties should have made no provision for it in their contract.[50] Where a clause can be read as providing specifically for the event which occurred, the rule can have no application.[51]

15. Theory of Principle of Frustration.—While the doctrine of frustration is itself now well established, the search for a theoretical basis for it has continued. Dicta in the House of Lords have over the years favoured a variety of theories, and, while the results have in most cases been consistent, it may be a matter of significance which theory is applied.[52] According to what may be called the "implied term" theory, which has had wide support in past decisions of the House of Lords in English appeals, the principle upon which supervening impossibility was held to dissolve a contract was that it is an implied condition in the particular contract that performance is promised only if it remains possible and legal. The Court, it was said, has no power to dissolve or vary a contract, but it has the power and duty to give effect to the intentions of the parties by interpreting the contract according to its conditions, implied as well as express.[53] The implied term theory was, however, not without its critics,[54] and seems now to have been rejected in favour of another which has had some currency in the past and seems more in line with the Scottish approach.[55] According to this view, which may be called the "material change" theory, as contractual obligation rests on consent, there can be no obligation to perform in circumstances so altered that performance, if given, would in substance be the performance not of the original contract, but of a different contract, and one to which the parties have not consented. Lord Radcliffe in *Davis Contractors Ltd.* v. *Fareham U.D.C.*[56] has formulated the theory as follows: ". . . frustration occurs whenever the law recognises that without default of either party a contractual obligation has become incapable of being performed because the circumstances in which performance is called for would render it a thing radically different from that which was undertaken by the contract. Non haec in foedera veni. It was not this that I promised to do." Lord Reid's opinion in the same case,[57] that frustration depends upon

---

[50] *Tamplin Co.,* supra; *Ocean Tramp Tankers Corporation* v. *v/o Sovfracht (The Eugenia)* [1964] 2 Q.B. 226, per Lord Denning, M.R., at p. 240.
[51] *Scott* v. *Del Sel,* 1922 S.C. 592, affd. 1923 S.C. (H.L.) 37.
[52] *Davis Contractors Ltd.,* supra, per Lord Reid at p. 719, Lord Radcliffe at p. 728.
[53] See opinion of Earl Loreburn, *Tamplin Co.* v. *Anglo-Mexican Petroleum Co.* [1916] 2 A.C. 397, 405; of Lord Dundas, *Macmaster* v. *Cox, M'Euen & Co.,* 1920 S.C. 566, revd. 1921 S.C. (H.L.) 24; of Lord Simon in *Joseph Constantine Steamship Line* v. *Imperial Smelting Corporation* [1942] A.C. 154 at p. 164; of Lord Simon and Lord Simmonds in *British Movietonews* v. *London Cinemas* [1952] A.C. 166 at pp. 183, 187.
[54] See, e.g., Lord Wright in *James B. Fraser & Co.,* supra, at p. 43; Lord Reid in *Davis Contractors Ltd.,* supra, at p. 720.
[55] See opinion of Lord Dunedin, *Metropolitan Water Board* v. *Dick, Kerr & Co.* [1918] A.C. 119. The Scottish approach has been that the Court in the exercise of its equitable jurisdiction does, upon a proper construction of the contract, what seems just in the circumstances: see "Frustration of Contract in Scots Law", by Lord Cooper (1946) 28 J. Comp. Leg. 1 at p. 5.
[56] [1956] A.C. 696 at p. 729. See also *Tsakiroglou & Co. Ltd.* v. *Noblee Thorl GmbH,* [1962] A.C. 93; *The Eugenia,* supra, per Lord Denning, M.R., at pp. 238-40.
[57] At p. 720.

the true construction[58] of terms of the contract and of the relevant surrounding circumstances when the contract was made, is really another way of saying the same thing. As he puts it, the question in each case is whether the contract which the parties did make is, on its true construction, wide enough to apply to the new situation; if not, it is at an end.

16. Illustrations.—The application of this rule will most easily be understood by examples. Where a servant is unable to attend to his duties through illness this does not form a breach of contract on his part, but if the time for which he is absent is in the circumstances material, it does bring the case within the law of frustration of the adventure, and the employer is entitled to cancel the contract.[59] In what is usually regarded as the leading case A undertook to send a ship to Cardiff to load a cargo for South America. His obligation was to arrive, with all convenient speed, unless prevented by perils of the sea. By perils of the sea the ship was injured, with the result that her voyage to Cardiff took some five months more than the normal time. Though she had arrived in time according to the terms of the contract, it was held that the delay so altered the conditions as to entitle the charterer to declare it cancelled.[60] Where a house let furnished was requisitioned by the military authorities it was held that both landlord and tenant were liberated by "constructive total destruction" of the premises.[61] And where a vessel which had been chartered to carry a cargo was so damaged by a violent explosion that she was unable to perform the charterparty, it was held that the voyage had been frustrated and that the owners were not liable in damages for non-performance.[62]

17. Limits of Principle of Frustration.—The principle does not apply to a change in economic conditions which may render the contract more onerous than had been contemplated; the fact that it has become more expensive or commercially less attractive for one party than he anticipated is not enough to bring about a frustration of the contract.[63] A policy of marine insurance is not affected by the declaration of war, however seriously that may affect the risk.[64] Further, the principle of frustration of the adventure arises only when there is no fault on either side.[65] But it operates automatically for the good or ill of both parties, and the person who relies upon it lies under no obligation to disprove fault on his part in connection with the frustrating event.[66]

---

[58] For an earlier statement of the "true construction" approach, see Lord Simon in *British Movietonews*, supra, at p. 185; Lord Wright in *James B. Fraser & Co.*, supra, at pp. 42-3.

[59] *Manson* v. *Downie* (1885) 12 R. 1103; *Poussard* v. *Spiers & Pond* (1876) 1 Q.B.D. 410. There is no need for the employer (in a proper case) to give notice of termination: *Westwood* v. *Scottish Motor Traction Co.*, 1938 S.N. 8.

[60] *Jackson* v. *Union Marine Insurance Co.* (1874) L.R. 10 C.P. 125. See also *Nelson* v. *Dundee East Shipping Co.*, 1907 S.C. 927.

[61] *Mackeson* v. *Boyd*, 1942 S.C. 56; see also *Metropolitan Board of Works* v. *Dick, Kerr & Co.* [1918] A.C. 119.

[62] *Joseph Constantine Steamship Line* v. *Imperial Smelting Corporation* [1942] A.C. 154.

[63] *Wilson* v. *Tennants* [1917] A.C. 495; *Davis Contractors Ltd.*, supra; *Tsakiroglou & Co.*, supra; *The Eugenia*, supra, per Lord Denning, M.R., at p. 239.

[64] *Brown* v. *Maxwell* (1824) 2 Sh.App. 373.

[65] *Maritime National Fish* v. *Ocean Trawlers* [1935] A.C. 524.

[66] *Joseph Constantine Steamship Line*, supra.

CHAPTER XII

RULES OF EVIDENCE IN RELATION TO CONTRACT

Dickson, *Evidence* (3rd ed., 1887); Walker and Walker. *Law of Evidence* (1964).

THOUGH the law of evidence is beyond the scope of this treatise it is proposed to consider in this chapter certain rules affecting contract. As a preliminary, some explanation of terms is necessary.

1. Proof Prout de Jure.—When a proof is allowed without qualification it is said to be proof prout de jure, proof by the evidence of witnesses (parole evidence) and by the production of any writings that may be available.

2. Proof by Writ or Oath.—In contrast to proof prout de jure is proof by writ or oath. The evidence of witnesses is then incompetent, and the proof is limited to the writ of the defender, with the alternative of referring the matter at issue to his oath. With the statutory exception[1] of the case where the defender has been examined as a witness, any matter of fact may be referred to his oath. The party who refers a question to the oath of his opponent perils his case on being able to elicit an admission, and cannot lead evidence of any kind to contradict the statement made on oath.[2]

3. Probative Writ.—When a writing is probative no further evidence is required of the obligations or rights which it purports to involve or confer. The writing is in itself obligatory, and the onus of disproving its provisions rests on the party who disputes them, and the method of proof is limited.[3] The methods of authentication which will render a document probative depend on the nature of the document. Certain writs used in ordinary business, in re mercatoria, are sufficiently authenticated by the signature of the grantor. These are known as privileged writings. In this class are included bills, promissory notes and cheques, receipts and mandates or orders used in the ordinary course of business.[4]

4. Modes of Authentication.—A writing is probative (1) if it is subscribed by the grantor, and is holograph, i.e., if its operative clauses are in the handwriting of the grantor[5]; (2) if it is subscribed by the grantor and

---

[1] Evidence (Scotland Act 1853, s. 5.
[2] Dickson, *Evidence,* § 1414; *Thomson* v. *Philp* (1867) 5 M. 679.
[3] See § 12 infra.
[4] Bell, *Prin.*, § 2232; *Comm.*, I, 342; Dickson, *Evidence,* § 793; *U.K. Advertising Co.* v. *Glasgow Bag Wash Laundry,* 1926 S.C. 303; *Beardmore* v. *Barry,* 1928 S.C. 101; affd. on a separate ground, 1928 S.C. (H.L.) 47.
[5] A statement in gremio of a holograph writing that the writing is holograph of the subscriber has no effect unless the subscription is admitted or proved to be genuine: *Harper* v. *Green,* 1938 S.C. 198. A document typewritten by the grantor, "accepted as holograph" and signed by him

docqueted, in his handwriting, with the words, "adopted as holograph", or words to a similar effect[6]; or (3) if it is an attested deed.

5. Attestation.—The forms necessary for attestation have varied at different periods in the history of the law.[7] The normal and regular method of executing a deed[8] is that the party or parties to it should subscribe on the last page[9] before two witnesses, who also sign. The witnesses must see the parties sign, or hear them acknowledge their signatures, and must have credible information as to their identity.[10] An interest in the deed is no objection to a witness.[11] A clause, known as a testing clause, is added, giving the name and designation of the writer of the deed, the names and designations of the witnesses, the number of pages, and the place and date of the signatures. The insertion in the testing clause of the names and designations of the writer and witnesses and of the number of pages is not essential, provided that where the witnesses are not so named or designed their designations are written after their signatures.[12] Section 39 of the Conveyancing (Scotland) Act 1874 provides that no deed, instrument or writing subscribed by the grantor and bearing to be attested by two subscribing witnesses, shall be deemed invalid or denied effect because of an informality of execution, but that the burden of proving that it was signed by the grantor and by the witnesses shall rest on the party upholding the deed. Proof to that effect may be led in any action in which the deed is founded on or objected to or in a special application to the Court of Session or Sheriff Court. The section will not, however, validate a deed subscribed without two witnesses, or where the witnesses, or one of them, sign after the grantor's death, or after any serious interval of time.[13]

6. Party Unable to Write.—If a party is blind or unable to write, a deed may be signed for him by a solicitor or notary public or justice of the peace or, in the case of testamentary writings, by a parish minister acting in his own parish, in the presence of two witnesses. The signature must be preceded by a docquet setting forth that the deed has been authorised by the grantor, who has declared that he is blind or unable to write, and that it has been read over to him all in his presence and in the presence of the witnesses.[14] It is a fatal

---

was sustained in *M'Beath's Trs.* v. *M'Beath*. 1935 S.C. 471, distinguished in *Chisholm* v. *Chisholm*, 1949 S.C. 434.

[6] See *Harvey* v. *Smith* (1904) 6 F. 511.

[7] For the history of the law, see Dickson, *Evidence*, § 638. See also Menzies, *Conveyancing*, (Sturrock's ed.), 129.

[8] For the case of companies registered under the Companies Acts, see Companies Act 1948, s. 32 (4).

[9] A will or other testamentary writing must be subscribed on each page: Conveyancing and Feudal Reform (Scotland) Act 1970 (c. 35), s. 44.

[10] *Brock* v. *Brock*, 1908 S.C. 964.

[11] *Simson* v. *Simson* (1883) 10 R. 1247.

[12] Conveyancing (Scotland) Act 1874, s. 38.

[13] *Walker* v. *Whitwell*, 1916 S.C. (H.L.) 75; *Baird's Trs.* v. *Baird*, 1955 S.C. 286, distinguished in *Ferguson*, 1959 S.C. 56.

[14] Conveyancing (Scotland) Act 1924, s. 18 and Sched. 1, the terms of which must be precisely complied with: *Hynd's Tr.* v. *Hynd's Trs.*, 1954 S.C. 112, affd. 1955. S.C. (H.L.) 1.

objection to the validity of the deed that the solicitor, notary or justice of the peace is an interested party.[15]

7. Onus of Proof of Authenticity.—When a deed is regularly drawn up and signed before witnesses the authenticity of the signature is presumed, and the onus of proof that it is not authentic rests upon the party disputing it. In other cases, though in other respects the writings may have the privileges of a probative deed, the genuineness of the signature, if disputed, must be proved by the party founding upon it.[16]

8. Contracts Requiring Proof by Writ.—The necessity of writing in a probative form for the constitution of an obligation in contracts relating to heritage and in certain other contracts (obligationes litteris) has been already noticed.[17] In certain other contracts, though the contractual obligation may be constituted verbally, the fact that it has been constituted can only be proved by writ or oath. Writing is not necessary to create the obligation, or as a solemnity, but only in modum probationis. In these cases the doctrines of rei interventus and homologation have no application. They are applicable to cases where writing, as a necessary means to the constitution of an obligation, is required by the law of contract, not where it is required only by the law of evidence. And it is a general rule that where a writing is founded on merely as evidence, and not as constituting an obligation, it is not necessary that it should be in probative form. All that is necessary is proof that it is the writing of the party, or of some person authorised to act on his behalf.[18]

As a general rule the fact that a contract has been entered into may be proved prout de jure. Obligationes litteris and contracts where writing is required in modum probationis, are exceptional cases. The following are the chief cases where proof is limited to writ or oath: gratuitous obligations; trust; loan; obligations of relief; innominate and unusual contracts. The first two cases are noticed in other parts of this work.[19]

9. Loan.—It has long been established that the proof of a loan of money, in an action for repayment, is limited to the writ or oath of the alleged borrower, including in that term the borrower's agent.[20] Parole proof of agency or of other circumstances showing the writ to be constructively that of the borrower is competent.[21] It was decided by the whole Court that the writ,

---

[15] *Ferrie* v. *Ferrie's Trs.* (1863) 1 M. 291; *Finlay* v. *Finlay's Trs.*, 1948 S.C. 16; *Gorrie's Tr.* v. *Stiven's Exx.*, 1952 S.C. 1; *Crawford's Trs.* v. *Glasgow Royal Infirmary*, 1955 S.C. 367. But see *Irving* v. *Snow*, 1956 S.C. 257.

[16] *M'Intyre* v. *National Bank of Scotland*, 1910 S.C. 150 (bill).

[17] Agreements Defective in Form, Ch. VII, supra, § 1.

[18] See opinion of Lord Kyllachy, *Paterson* v. *Paterson* (1897) 25 R. 144. As to discharge of a claim for solatium, see *Davies* v. *Hunter*, 1934 S.C. 10.

[19] Law of Contract, Ch. IV., supra, § 2, and Executors, etc. Ch. XLIV., infra, § 15.

[20] Stair, IV, 43, 4; Dickson, *Evidence*, § 594; *Dryburgh* v. *Macpherson*, 1944 S.L.T. 116, distinguished: *Fisher* v. *Fisher*, 1952 S.C. 347. Parole proof that a particular article has been lent is competent, *Geddes* v. *Geddes*, (1678) M. 12730.

[21] *Clark's Exx.* v. *Brown*, 1935 S.C. 110.

being necessary merely as a method of proof, need not be probative.[22] The limitation of proof does not necessarily apply where the loan is part of a series of transactions between the parties and the question is whether it ought to be taken into account in striking the balance. An endorsed cheque does not prove a loan,[23] but in *Robb* v. *Robb's Trs.*,[24] endorsed cheques were held sufficient to prove loans by a solicitor to his client which formed part of a credit and debit account between them. The real question was whether the client received the money, and the endorsed cheques established that he did. Therefore the amount was properly debited to him. In such a case the appropriate method of proof depends on the precise circumstances, and this, it is thought, is the true meaning of Lord Dunedin's dicta in *Smith's Tr.* v. *Smith*,[25] which are sometimes misapplied.[26] In bankruptcy, neither a reference to the bankrupt's oath, [27] nor a written acknowledgment by him dated after the commencement of sequestration, is admissible.[28] But an acknowledgment may be sufficient, though granted when the debtor was insolvent, or within six months of his notour bankruptcy.[29] A receipt for money expressed in unqualified terms is evidence of a loan, and its production lays upon the party who has signed it the onus of proof that it was granted for some other purpose, e.g., for payment of a debt.[30] And where a defender admitted receipt of money, which the pursuer averred that he had lent to him, but alleged that it was a gift, it was held that the onus was on the defender, in the light of his admission, to prove donation.[31]

10. Obligation of Relief.—An obligation of relief, if not inferred by law, but alleged to have been undertaken as a separate obligation, can be proved only by writ or oath. The rule was applied where it was averred that a director of a company had agreed to relieve his co-directors of their liability for a bank overdraft.[32]

11. Innominate and Unusual Contracts.—Proof of innominate and unusual contracts is limited to the defender's writ or oath. This as applied in modern decisions raises a question of degree. The dictum that the limitation applied to all obligations to pay money not incidental to one of the well-known consensual contracts,[33] has been disapproved, and it is for the Court to decide, in each case, whether the contract averred is so unusual, anomalous, and peculiar as

---

[22] *Paterson* v. *Paterson*, supra.
[23] *Haldane* v. *Speirs* (1872) 10 M. 537; *Scotland* v. *Scotland*, 1909 S.C. 505.
[24] (1884) 11 R. 881.
[25] 1911 S.C. 653.
[26] *McKie* v. *Wilson*, 1951 S.C. 15.
[27] *Adam* v. *Maclachlan* (1847) 9 D. 560.
[28] *Carmichael's Tr.* v. *Carmichael*, 1929 S.C. 265.
[29] *Williamson* v. *Allan* (1882) 9 R. 859; *Matthew's Tr.* v. *Matthew* (1867) 5 M. 957.
[30] *Thomson* v. *Geekie* (1861) 23 D. 693; *Gill* v. *Gill*, 1907 S.C. 532. As to an IOU, see *Black* v. *Gibb*, 1940 S.C. 24.
[31] *Penman* v. *White*, 1957 S.C. 338.
[32] *Devlin* v. *M'Kelvie*, 1915 S.C. 180. As to implied obligations of relief, see General Law of Obligations, Ch. III., supra, § 16.
[33] Per Lord President Dunedin, *M'Fadzean's Exr.* v. *Macalpine*, 1907 S.C. 1269.

to demand a limitation of proof.[34] The rule was applied in a case where a tenant averred that the landlord had promised, on certain conditions, to repay all money lost in the course of the lease[35]; it was held inapplicable, and parole evidence was admitted, when it was alleged that the owner of a drifter, which it was proposed to hire to the Admiralty, had promised the crew a bonus on their Admiralty pay.[36]

12. Extrinsic Evidence in Written Contracts.—It is a general rule that when a contract has been entered into in writing it is incompetent to contradict or qualify its terms by parole evidence. Proof that the intention of the parties was not as it is expressed in the written contract is not excluded, but is limited to the writ, which must be subsequent to the contract, of the party proposing to maintain it,[37] or to an admission on a reference to his oath.[38] Thus where the subjects let were specified in a lease it was incompetent to prove, by the evidence of the landlord's factor, that additional subjects were intended to be included.[39] And when a party undertook, in unqualified terms, to deliver shares, it was held that parole evidence was not admissible to prove that he was acting merely as an agent, and that no personal liability was intended or expected.[40] Nor is it competent to prove by parole an agreement that the conditions which the law would imply should not hold in the particular case.[41]

These rules hold only in a question with a party who takes his stand on the written contract. An admission by a defender that the written contract does not accurately represent the agreement between the parties leaves it open to prove by parole what the real agreement was.[42] It is competent to establish by parole evidence a prior oral agreement the subject-matter of which does not fall under the terms of the written contract.[43] And when the question is not as to the meaning of the contract, but as to its validity, parole evidence is admissible. Thus there is no restriction as to the methods of proof of averments of fraud, misrepresentation, clerical error, or illegality.[44]

13. Bills of Exchange.—The general rule that parole evidence cannot be led to contradict the terms of a written contract has been impinged upon by statute in the case of bills of exchange. Section 100 of the Bills of Exchange Act 1882 provides: "In any judicial proceeding in Scotland any fact relating to a bill of exchange, bank cheque or promissory note, which is relevant to any

[34] *Smith* v. *Reekie*, 1920 S.C. 188.
[35] *Garden* v. *Earl of Aberdeen* (1893) 20 R. 896.
[36] *Smith* v. *Reekie*, supra.
[37] *Stewart* v. *Clark* (1871) 9 M. 616.
[38] *Sinclair* v. *M'Beath* (1869) 7 M. 934.
[39] *Gregson* v. *Alsop* (1897) 24 R. 1081.
[40] *Lindsay* v. *Craig*, 1919 S.C. 139.
[41] *Johnson* v. *Edinburgh, etc., Union Canal Co.* (1835) 1 Sh. & M'L. 117; *Barclay* v. *Neilson* (1878) 5 R. 909.
[42] *Grant's Trs.* v. *Morison* (1875) 2 R. 377; *Cairns* v. *Davidson*, 1913 S.C. 1054; *M'Menemy* v. *Forster's Trustee*, 1938 S.L.T. 555; but see *Pickard* v. *Pickard*, 1963 S.C. 604.
[43] *William Masson* v. *Scottish Brewers*, 1966 S.C. 9.
[44] *Steuart's Trs.* v. *Hart* (1875) 3 R. 192; *Krupp* v. *Menzies*, 1907 S.C. 903; *Bell Bros.* v. *Aitken*, 1939 S.C. 577; *Anderson* v. *Lambie*, 1954 S.C. (H.L.) 43.

question of liability thereon, may be proved by parole evidence." The generality of this enactment has been so far limited by decision that it has been held that parole evidence of payment is incompetent,[45] and that when the alleged liability is not rested exclusively on the bill, but on the bill as a method of carrying out a prior written contract, the section is not applicable.[46] So where a business carried on in leasehold premises was sold, and promissory notes given for the price, it was held that section 100 did not authorise parole evidence of the alleged verbal agreement that payment of the notes was not to be demanded until the lease had expired.[47] But it is competent to prove that the bill was granted for the accommodation of a particular party,[48] or that it had been agreed to renew it until the occurrence of a certain event.[49] The competency of proof that the holder had agreed that one of the parties to the bill should incur no liability is not settled.[50]

14. Proof of Additional Terms.—It is probably the law that it is incompetent to prove a term in a written contract which is not expressed, and which the law would not imply.[51] But there are cases which render it difficult to make any confident statement on the point.[52] It is competent to prove that an obligatory document has been delivered subject to the condition that it is not to be put in force until the occurrence of a certain event.[53]

15. Actions of Parties.—The cases as to the competency of interpreting a written contract by evidence of the actions of the parties under it result in the unsatisfactory rule that such evidence is competent, on the principle of contemporanea expositio, in contracts of ancient date,[54] not in contracts de recenti.[55] But where there were contradictory statements in the contract as to the acreage and boundaries of the subjects conveyed, it was held that evidence of acting upon it was competent, although the contract was of recent date.[56]

16. Patent and Latent Ambiguities.—It has been said that a patent ambiguity must be solved by a construction of its terms but in practice the distinction between patent and latent ambiguity seems to have been ignored and in a number of cases extrinsic evidence has been admitted to resolve a patent ambiguity.[57] A latent ambiguity in a contract may be resolved by extrinsic evidence. An ambiguity is latent when the meaning is only rendered doubtful by a knowledge of the surrounding circumstances, e.g., when

[45] *Robertson* v. *Thomson* (1900) 3 F. 5; *Nicol's Trs.* v. *Sutherland,* 1951 S.C. (H.L.) 21.
[46] *Stagg & Robson* v. *Stirling,* 1908 S.C. 675; *M'Allister* v. *M'Gallagley,* 1911 S.C. 112.
[47] *Stagg & Robson* v. *Stirling, supra.*
[48] *Viani* v. *Gunn* (1904) 6 F. 989.
[49] *Dryburgh* v. *Roy* (1903) 5 F. 665. See also *Thomson* v. *Jolly Carters Inn,* 1972 S.C. 215.
[50] *National Bank of Australasia* v. *Turnbull* (1891) 18 R. 629.
[51] Dickson, *Evidence,* § 1020. But as to collateral agreements, see Dickson, *Evidence,* § 1033, and Walker and Walker, *Law of Evidence,* § 262; *Perdikou* v. *Pattison,* 1958 S.L.T. 153.
[52] *Renison* v. *Bryce* (1898) 25 R. 521; *De Lassalle* v. *Guildford* [1901] 2 K.B. 215.
[53] *Abrahams* v. *Miller (Denny) Ltd.,* 1933 S.C. 171.
[54] *North British Ry.* v. *Magistrates of Edinburgh,* 1920 S.C. 409.
[55] *Scott* v. *Howard* (1881) 8 R. (H.L.) 59, opinion of Lord Watson.
[56] *Watcham* v. *Att.-Gen. of East Africa* [1919] A.C. 533.
[57] See Walker and Walker, *Law of Evidence,* § 269.

property is conveyed by name, and it turns out that there are two properties to which that name would apply.[58]

17. Proof of Surrounding Circumstances.—Parole evidence is admissible to establish the state of knowledge of the parties at the time when their contract was made, in cases where, as in a sale for a particular purpose, the liabilities involved depend on that state of knowledge.[59] And there is a general and ill-defined principle that the Court is entitled to know all the circumstances surrounding the parties at the time when the contract was made. So where two ships were sold by separate bills of sale it was held competent to lead evidence, in the guise of surrounding circumstances, that it had been agreed that if the seller was unable to furnish one of the ships the purchaser was not bound to take the other.[60]

18. Usage of Trade.—The fact that a contract has been entered into in writing does not exclude proof of usage of trade, either to introduce an implied term into the contract, or to give to the words used a meaning which they would not ordinarily bear. Unless the contract is expressly made subject to the usage it cannot rule if it contradicts the actual provisions of the writing. Thus where a contractor accepted an offer for "the whole of the steel" required for a bridge "the estimated quantity to be 30,000 tons, more or less," it was held that the plain meaning of the words could not be qualified by proof of a usage in the steel trade that such an offer meant an offer to supply 30,000 tons only.[61] But there would seem no limit to the variation of meaning which may be given to any particular word. The word "thousand" has been held to mean "twelve hundred".[62] If the contract expressly refers to a usage, as where in a charterparty the provisions for loading expressly refer to the custom of the port, it is immaterial that one or both parties may be unaware of what the actual custom is.[63] And where a man authorises another to deal for him on a particular exchange he must be deemed to have consented to his contract being interpreted in accordance with the usages of that exchange.[64] In other cases usage of trade will not affect a contract unless both parties were aware of it.[65] It has been held that while in a particular trade there may be a customary rate of wages which will be binding in the absence of express agreement, this will not prevail where as between parties there is a well-established practice of paying and receiving another rate.[66] A usage to be

---

[58] *Raffles* v. *Wichelhaus* (1864) 2 H. & C. 906; *Houldsworth* v. *Gordon-Cumming*, 1909 S.C. 1198, revd. 1910 S.C. (H.L.) 49.
[59] *Jacobs* v. *Scott* (1899) 2 F. (H.L.) 70.
[60] *Claddagh Steamship Co.* v. *Steven*, 1919 S.C. 184; 1919 S.C. (H.L.) 132.
[61] *Tancred, Arrol & Co.*, v. *Steel Co. of Scotland* (1887) 15 R. 215; affd. (1890) 17 R. (H.L.) 31; *Affréteurs Réunis* v. *Walford* [1919] A.C. 801; *Arthur Duthie & Co.* v. *Merson and Gerry*, 1947 S.C. 43.
[62] *Smith* v. *Wilson* (1832) 3 B. & Ad. 728.
[63] *Strathlorne S.S. Co.* v. *Baird*, 1915 S.C. 956, revd. 1916 S.C. (H.L.) 134.
[64] *Forget* v. *Baxter* [1900] A.C. 467. See *Robinson* v. *Mollett* (1875) L.R. 7 H.L. 802.
[65] *Holman* v. *Peruvian Nitrate Co.* (1878) 5 R. 657.
[66] *Eunson* v. *Johnson & Greig*, 1940 S.C. 49.

admissible must be reasonably fair,[67] and generally, though not necessarily universally, recognised in the trade.[68] It has been observed that a usage cannot be established by proof of a series of protests against it.[69]

19. Formal Deed Excludes Prior Writing.—In the cases referred to in the preceding pages the evidence tendered has been that of witnesses. But where a contract has been drawn up in a formal and probative form not only the evidence of witnesses, but evidence of all prior communings, whether verbal or in writing, is excluded, unless it is expressly incorporated or unless there has been an error in the deed.[70] The following explanation of the principle has been constantly cited: "Where parties agree to embody, and do actually embody, their contract in a formal written deed, then in determining what the contract really was and really meant a Court must look to the formal deed and to that deed alone. This is only carrying out the will of the parties . . . The very purpose of a formal contract is to put an end to the disputes which would inevitably arise if the matter were left upon verbal negotiations or upon mixed communings, partly consisting of letters and partly of conversations."[71] But parties may competently agree to waive the ordinary rule[72] and where the contract has been partly performed before the deed is executed, parole evidence may be competent to prove the terms on which parties were acting before execution.[73]

20. Conveyance as Superseding Prior Writs.—There is high authority for the statement that a conveyance, even if it expressly bears to be in execution of a prior written contract, supersedes that contract, and becomes the sole measure of the rights and liabilities of the parties.[74] But prior writings, though excluded in a question as to the subjects conveyed, may be referred to in a question as to the conditions on which a sale took place.[75] It may be proved that two conveyances, although executed without reference to each other, were really interdependent.[76] And even with regard to the subjects conveyed the rule holds only if the subject in question was one which would normally find mention in the conveyance. So where, by missive of sale, a house was sold with fixtures and fittings, it was held that the purchaser might refer to the missives in support of his right to the fittings, though they were not mentioned

---

[67] *Bruce* v. *Smith* (1890) 17 R. 1000; *Devonald* v. *Rosser* [1906] 2 K.B. 728.
[68] *Hogarth* v. *Leith Cottonseed Oil Co.*, 1909 S.C. 955; *Dick* v. *Cochrane & Fleming*, 1935 S.L.T. 432.
[69] Per Lord Shaw, *Strathlorne S.S. Co.* v. *Baird*, 1916 S.C. (H.L.) 134.
[70] *Anderson* v. *Lambie*, 1954 S.C. (H.L.) 43.
[71] Per Lord Gifford, *Inglis* v. *Buttery* (1877) 5 R. 58, affd. (1878) 5 R. (H.L.) 87; *Norval* v. *Abbey*, 1939 S.C. 724. As to reference to words deleted, see conflicting opinions in *Taylor* v. *John Lewis Ltd.*, 1927 S.C. 891.
[72] *Young* v. *M'Kellar*, 1909 S.C. 1340; *Fraser* v. *Cox*, 1938 S.C. 506.
[73] *Korner* v. *Shennan*, 1950 S.C. 285.
[74] *Lee* v. *Alexander* (1883) 10 R. (H.L.) 91, opinion of Lord Watson. Distinguished, *Wann* v. *Grey*, 1935 S.N. 8. See also *Butter* v. *Foster*, 1912 S.C. 1218; *Anderson* v. *Lambie*, 1954 S.C. (H.L.) 43, per Lord Reid at p. 62.
[75] *Young* v. *M'Kellar*, 1909 S.C. 1340.
[76] *Claddagh Steamship Co.* v. *Steven*, 1919 S.C. (H.L.) 132.

in the disposition which had followed, on the ground that a contract as to fittings would not normally be mentioned in a conveyance of a house.[77]

21. Alteration of Written Contract.—Where parties have entered into a written contract a verbal agreement to alter its provisions is not binding, and, if no action has followed on it, either party may resile and insist on the performance of the contract in its original terms.[78] But if there has been an agreement to alter the terms of the contract, and one party, to the knowledge of and without objection from the other, has proceeded to act upon the contract as altered, such action may amount to rei interventus and bar the right to resile.[79] Mere acquiescence in acts which, assuming that the original terms of the contract remained in force, would be a breach thereof, can at the highest merely bar a claim of damages for what is past, it can confer no sanction for the future.[80] To establish an alteration in the terms of the contract for the future there must either be a writing to that effect, an admission on reference to oath, or a verbal agreement on which action has followed.[81] And the action in question must be clearly inconsistent with the original terms of the contract. Thus where A, who was liable under a decree, averred that his creditor had agreed to accept payment by weekly instalments, and that certain instalments had been paid, it was held that as the acceptance of instalments was not inconsistent with the right to demand immediate payment of the balance, there were no relevant averments of rei interventus, and the alleged verbal agreement could not be admitted to proof.[82]

[77] *Jamieson* v. *Welsh* (1900) 3 F. 176.
[78] See opinion of Lord President Inglis, *Kirkpatrick* v. *Allanshaw Coal Co.* (1880) 8 R. 327, at p. 332.
[79] *Bargaddie Coal Co.* v. *Wark* (1856) 18 D. 772, revd. (1859) 3 Macq. 467; *Kirkpatrick* v. *Allanshaw Coal Co.*, supra.
[80] *Carron Co.* v. *Henderson's Trs.* (1896) 23 R. 1042.
[81] See *Earl of Ancaster* v. *Doig*, 1960 S.C. 203, per Lord Justice-Clerk Thomson, at p. 211.
[82] *Lavan* v. *Gavin Aird & Co.*, 1919 S.C. 345.

CHAPTER XIII

BREACH OF CONTRACT

Walker, *The Law of Civil Remedies in Scotland* (1974).

1. Right to Specific Implement.—When one party to a contract refuses, or fails, to fulfil his obligations the other may generally insist on specific implement. If the obligation in question is of a positive character, it may be enforced by a decree ad factum praestandum, and if of a negative, by interdict. A person who fails to obtemper a decree ad factum praestandum may be imprisoned until he does, but for not more than six months, and only if the Court is satisfied that his refusal to comply with the decree is wilful.[1] Breach of interdict is punishable by fine or imprisonment. Subject to the discretion of the Court to refuse decree when it would cause exceptional hardship,[2] the right to demand specific implement of a contract is, in Scots law, a general rule.[3] The following are the leading exceptions:—

2. Cases where Specific Implement Refused.—(1) Where the obligation in question is the payment of money. As a rule the sole remedy of a creditor is to enforce payment by diligence; he is not entitled to a decree ad factum praestandum, which might result in the imprisonment of the debtor. Such a decree is by statute competent in the case of a contract to take up and pay for debentures of a company,[4] and may be granted in other cases where there is an order for consignation of money in Court.[5]

(2) Where the contract if fulfilled would involve an intimate relationship, where forced compliance would be worse than none. So specific implement will not be granted of a contract of service, or of a contract to enter into partnership.[6]

(3) Where compliance with the decree would be impossible. As the only sanction of a decree ad factum praestandum is imprisonment it will not be pronounced where the defender cannot possibly comply with it, even if the impossibility may be due to his own fault.[7] Thus if a man undertakes

[1] Law Reform (Miscellaneous Provisions) (Scotland) Act 1940, s. 1.
[2] *Grahame* v. *Magistrates of Kirkcaldy* (1882) 9 R. (H.L.) 91.
[3] *Stewart* v. *Kennedy* (1890) 17 R. (H.L.) 1; the English law is contrasted by Lord Watson, at p. 9. The Court cannot, however, grant decree of specific implement against the Crown: Crown Proceedings Act 1947, s. 21(1).
[4] Companies Act 1948, s. 92.
[5] *Mackenzie* v. *Balerno Paper Mill Co.* (1883) 10 R. 1147.
[6] *Macarthur* v. *Lawson* (1877) 4 R. 1134, at p. 1136; *Skerret* v. *Oliver* (1896) 23 R. 468, at p. 485. Cf. *Murray* v. *Dunbarton C.C.,* 1935 S.L.T. 239; interdict against transfer of a teacher, so as, in effect, to enforce compliance, refused. An industrial tribunal may make an order for reinstatement or re-engagement of an employee, failure to comply with which may result in an additional award of compensation: Employment Protection (Consolidation) Act 1978 (c. 44), ss. 69-71; see infra ch. XXII, § 13.
[7] *Macarthur* v. *Lawson,* supra, per Lord President Inglis; *Rudman* v. *Jay,* 1908 S.C. 552.

something which he cannot lawfully do, e.g., to execute work on land to which he has no right of access, he may be liable in damages for failure, but specific implement is not an appropriate remedy.[8]

(4) Where the Court cannot enforce the decree. Where the defender is a foreigner, subject to the jurisdiction of the Scottish Courts only on some exceptional ground, these Courts, as they have no power to enforce a decree ad factum praestandum by his imprisonment, will not pronounce a decree which would be futile. Nor will such a decree be pronounced in pursuance of an obligation which can be performed by a corporate body only as a whole, and not by its officials, and where there is no means of enforcement except by the imprisonment of all the individual members of the body.[9]

(5) Where there is no pretium affectionis. In the case of generic sales, i.e., sales of a certain quantity of a commodity which can be procured in the open market, the purchaser's remedy is to supply himself at the seller's expense, and decree of specific implement against the seller is incompetent.[10]

3. Remedies for Breach of Contract: Rescission.—Where specific enforcement of a contract is either incompetent, or not demanded, the party aggrieved by a breach is always entitled to damages, nominal or substantial. He may have other remedies. He may have the right to break off all contractual relations, to rescind the contract, or, in a phrase made familiar by the Sale of Goods Act 1893, to "treat the contract as repudiated." He may also be entitled to exercise a right of retention, whereby, without ending the contract, he may withhold performance of the obligations incumbent on him until the obligations due to him are tendered or performed. Postponing in the meantime the law of retention, we have to consider the circumstances which will justify a party in breaking off contractual relations on the ground that the other is in breach of the contract. This right will depend on two considerations—(1) the materiality of the breach in question; (2) the unity of the contract, i.e., the question whether it is to be regarded as a single whole, or as a collection of independent stipulations.

4. Materiality of Breach: Fundamental Breach.—As a general rule a party is not entitled to break off contractual relations, or treat the contract as repudiated, unless the other party is in breach of some contractual obligation which is in the circumstances material. Breach of some minor obligation may give rise to a right of retention or lien, or to a claim for damages, but not, in the absence of any provision to that effect, to a total and summary rescission. The failure treated as repudiation "must not be in some incidental or accidental particular, but it must fundamentally affect the fair carrying out of the bargain as a whole."[11]

[8] *Sinclair* v. *Caithness Flagstone Co.* (1898) 25 R. 703.
[9] *Gall* v. *Loyal Glenbogie Lodge* (1900) 2 F. 1187; contrast *Collins* v. *Barrowfield Oddfellows,* 1915 S.C. 190; *Ponder* v. *Ponder,* 1932 S.C. 233. See, as to the position of a receiver, *Macleod* v. *Alexander Sutherland,* 1977 S.L.T. (Notes) 44.
[10] *Union Electric Co.* v. *Holman,* 1913 S.C. 954.
[11] Per Lord Shaw, *Forslind* v. *Bechely-Crundall,* 1922 S.C. (H.L.) 173, at p. 190.

The question whether any particular provision in a contract is a material or fundamental term of the contract, or, to use an English term which has penetrated Scots law, is a condition precedent,[12] is one which the parties may settle for themselves. If they choose to provide that the whole contract shall be dependent on the fulfilment of one provision or condition, then, no matter how trivial it may appear to be, the Court will give effect to the expressed intention of the parties.[13] Where there is no such provision the question whether any particular condition is material is to be decided on the terms of each contract. No general rules can be laid down, but two cases may be narrated as illustrations. In *Wade* v. *Waldon*,[14] a comedian undertook to perform in a theatre on a date a year subsequent to the contract. It was a condition that he should give a fortnight's notice, with bill matter, before the date of appearance. This condition he failed to comply with, and the manager of the theatre in consequence refused to fulfil his engagement. It was held that the comedian was entitled to damages, on the ground that, although he was in breach of contract in failing to send the notice, the breach was not sufficiently material to justify the manager in breaking off the whole contract. In *Graham* v. *United Turkey Red Co.*[15] an agent for the sale of goods undertook not to sell the same goods supplied by others. This condition he broke. It was held that it was a material condition, and that the breach precluded the agent from suing for the commission to which he was entitled under the contract. Any claim he might have must rest on the ground, apart from the contract, that his employers had taken benefit from his service.

Apart from the provisions of the Unfair Contract Terms Act 1977,[16] it is open to the parties to a contract to provide by means of exclusion or exemption clauses that the failure by one of them in the performance of his obligations under the contract will not entitle the other to recover damages or to rescind the contract. It is now accepted that it is possible to frame a clause of this kind which will exclude liability for even a "total" or "fundamental breach", a "fundamental breach" being "the well known type of breach which entitles the innocent party to treat it as repudiatory and to rescind the contract".[17] But such clauses are strictly construed, and it is a question of construction in each case whether the clause is so clearly and unambiguously expressed as to be effectual where there has been a fundamental breach of

---

[12] "Precedent" refers to materiality, not to time.

[13] *Standard Life Assurance Co.* v. *Weems* (1884) 11 R. (H.L.) 48; *Dawson's* v. *Bonnin,* 1922 S.C. (H.L.) 156; *Provincial Insurance Co.* v. *Morgan* [1933] A.C. 240.

[14] 1909 S.C. 571. The following passage in the opinion of Lord President Dunedin has been frequently referred to: "It is familiar law, and quite well settled by decision, that in any contract which contains multifarious stipulations there are some which go so to the root of the contract that a breach of those stipulations entitles the party pleading the breach to declare that the contract is at an end. There are others which do not go to the root of the contract, but which are part of the contract, and which would give rise, if broken, to an action of damages." To this general rule it would appear that the contract of sale of goods by description must be treated as an exception. Sale of Goods, Ch. XVII., infra, § 26.

[15] 1922 S.C. 533.

[16] See Pacta Illicita and Unfair Terms, Ch. IX, supra.

[17] *Suisse Atlantique Société d'Armement Maritime S.A.* v. *N.V. Rotterdamsche Kolen Centrale* [1967] 1 A.C. 361, per Lord Reid at p. 397.

contract.[18] In England it has been held that if, on a fundamental breach, the innocent party rescinds the contract, the other party cannot then rely on a clause limiting liability because the contract, including the exclusion clause, has ceased to exist; and the result is the same where the fundamental breach itself brings the contract to an end.[19] Although it has been held that that is not the law of Scotland,[20] the Unfair Contract Terms Act 1977, s. 22, provides "for the avoidance of doubt" that where the Act requires that the incorporation of a term in a contract to which the Act applies must be fair and reasonable for that term to have effect—(a) if that requirement is satisfied, the term may be given effect to notwithstanding that the contract has been terminated in consequence of breach of that contract, (b) for the term to be given effect to, that requirement must be satisfied even where a party who is entitled to rescind the contract elects not to rescind it.

5. Building Contracts.—There is some difficulty in the law relating to building contracts, mainly due to the fact that a failure by a builder to observe the building conditions may not materially affect the value of the building and yet may not be remediable without inordinate expense. If the builder so far deviates from his contract as to produce a building substantially different from that ordered, the owner may reject it; if he prefers to keep it, he is not liable for the contract price, but only quantum lucratus, in so far as he is enriched by the building.[21] If the defects are of minor importance and admit of being remedied, the builder may recover the contract price under deduction of the sum necessary to bring the building into consonance with the plans.[22] If the deviation is irremediable without demolition, e.g., where the wrong kind of cement has been used, it was held in *Steel* v. *Young*,[23] that even if the difference in value was inappreciable the builder could not sue for the contract price, and that, if his action contained no conclusions for payment on the basis of quantum lucratus, it must be dismissed. But this decision has been doubted in *Forrest* v. *Scottish County Investment Co.*[24] From the opinions there given it would appear that if the contract had scheduled prices for each item (a measure and value, as distinguished from a lump-sum, contract) failure in one item would not preclude action for the amount due for the rest. The effect of an irremediable but immaterial failure in a lump-sum contract is doubtful[25]; in an English case opinions were given to the effect that the builder might sue for the contract price under deduction of any damage which the owner might have suffered.[26]

[18] *Pollock* v. *Macrae*, 1922 S.C. (H.L.) 192; *Mechans* v. *Highland Marine Charters*, 1964 S.C. 48.
[19] *Harbutt's "Plasticine"* v. *Wayne Tank and Pump Co.* [1970] 1 Q.B. 447; *Photo Production* v. *Securicor* [1978] 1 W.L.R. 856.
[20] *Alexander Stephen (Forth)* v. *J. J. Riley (U.K.)*, 1976 S.C. 151.
[21] *Ramsay* v. *Brand* (1898) 25 R. 1212.
[22] *Spiers* v. *Petersen*, 1924 S.C. 428.
[23] 1907 S.C. 360.
[24] 1916 S.C. (H.L.) 28.
[25] See comments on *Forrest* v. *Scottish County Investment Co.* in *Graham* v. *United Turkey Red Co.*, 1922 S.C. 533.
[26] *Dakin* v. *Lee* [1916] 1 K.B. 566. See also *Eshelby* v. *Federated Bank* [1932] 1 K.B. 423.

6. Materiality of Time of Performance.—The question whether time of performance is material, or, as it is sometimes put, whether time is of the essence of the contract, depends upon the nature of the obligations undertaken. Time is clearly material, and failure will justify rescission, in contracts for the supply, or carriage, of goods which vary in price from day to day.[27] In other mercantile contracts, where the element of fluctuation in price is absent, performance on the actual day is not generally material, but any lengthened delay will justify rescission.[28] In contracts for the construction of a particular article delay is not generally sufficiently material to justify the rejection of the article when ultimately tendered.[29] Failure to tender a marketable title to heritage on the day fixed will not entitle a buyer to resile,[30] but will entitle him to intimate that he will resile if the title is not tendered at some definite date in the future.[31] It is clear that time of performance is not so material in a lease as to justify the tenant in throwing up the lease in the event of the landlord failing to execute improvements or repairs within the time stipulated.[32]

7. Degrees in Materiality.—There are degrees in materiality. A failure may not be sufficiently material to justify the rescission of the contract, yet may justify the party aggrieved in withholding performance of the obligations incumbent on him. This has been illustrated chiefly in the case of leases. Failure by a landlord to place, or to uphold, the subjects in the condition required by the contract may be so material as to justify the tenant in abandoning the subjects and claiming damages; or, where less material, may justify him in withholding payment of his rent; or may be in such a subordinate point that the tenant's only remedy is a claim for damages. The questions involved depend so much on the particular circumstances, and on the reasonableness, or otherwise, of the conduct of the parties, that it is not proposed to deal with the cases here.[33] Similar rules, equally insusceptible of precise definition, prevail in the case of a contract for the supply of goods by instalments.[34]

8. Unity of Contract.—There is a general presumption that a contract is to be regarded as a whole, that the stipulations on either side are the counterparts and consideration given for each other, and therefore that failure by one party will justify the other in breaking off contractual relations, or in withholding performance of the obligations incumbent on him, according to the degree of materiality of the breach in question.[35] And it is competent to

[27] *Colvin* v. *Short* (1857) 19 D. 890; *Nelson* v. *Dundee East Coast Shipping Co.,* 1907 S.C. 927.
[28] *Carswell* v. *Collard* (1892) 19 R. 987; affd. (1893) 20 R. (H.L.) 47.
[29] *Macbride* v. *Hamilton* (1875) 2 R. 775.
[30] *Kelman* v. *Barr's Tr.* (1878) 5 R. 816.
[31] *Stickney* v. *Keeble* [1915] A.C. 386; see also *Rodger (Builders)* v. *Fawdry,* 1950 S.C. 483, per Lord Sorn (O.H.) at p. 492.
[32] *M'Kimmie's Trs.* v. *Armour* (1899) 2 F. 156.
[33] See Leases, Ch. XXXIII., infra § 7; Rankine, *Leases,* (3rd ed.), pp. 245, 326.
[34] Sale of Goods, Ch. XVII., infra, § 40.
[35] Stair, I., 10, 16, *Turnbull* v. *M'Lean & Co.* (1874) 1 R. 730; *Barclay* v. *Anderston Foundry Co.* (1856) 18 D. 1190; *Dingwall* v. *Burnett,* 1912 S.C. 1097.

prove that two contracts are so related to each other that their respective provisions are interdependent. Thus where a verbal contract for the sale of two ships was, for reasons of convenience, carried into effect by two separate bills of sale, it was held that there was really only one contract, and therefore that the seller, who was unable to supply one of the ships, could not insist on the purchaser taking the other.[36]

There is only a presumption that the provisions of a contract are dependent on each other. There is nothing to prevent two separate contracts, for instance a lease and an option to buy, being recorded in the same deed, and it is then a question of construction whether they are interdependent or not.[37] And even when there is clearly only one contract, some of its provisions may be independent covenants; for instance, a general arbitration clause may be insisted on even by a party who is in breach of the other provisions of the contract.[38]

As illustrations of the general rule that the provisions of a contract are interdependent may be cited the decisions that where a restrictive covenant is imposed on an employee the employer cannot enforce it if he has wrongfully dismissed the employee and is therefore himself in breach of contract[39]; that where a landlord undertook to take over the sheep stock on a farm at the tenant's waygoing the tenant could not enforce the obligation when he was in breach of the material conditions of the lease[40]; that provisions under which a carrier stipulates for exemption from liability for the loss of the goods cannot be enforced if the carrier, by deviating from the prescribed route, has placed himself in breach of the contract[41]; and that a custodier cannot rely on conditions limiting his liability if he has handed over the article to a third party without authority.[42] Of the exceptional case where provisions are read as independent covenants the best illustration, apart from cases as to arbitration clauses, is *Pendreigh's Tr.* v. *Dewar.*[43] There a tenant undertook to lay out £200 on repairs, to be repaid on the expiry of the lease; it was held that, although the tenant was in breach of his contract under the lease, the right to repayment of the sum which he had expended was an independent stipulation, which was not affected by the fact that the other provisions of the lease had not been implemented.

9. Anticipatory Breach of Contract.—A definite refusal by one party to perform his obligations under a contract, even if made before the time for performance has arrived, may be treated by the other as an actual breach of contract which entitles him at once to the remedies which such a breach may

---

[36] *Claddagh Steamship Co.* v. *Steven,* 1919 S.C. 184, 1919 S.C. (H.L.) 132.
[37] *Penman* v. *Mackay,* 1922 S.C. 385.
[38] *Sanderson* v. *Armour,* 1921 S.C. 18, affd. 1922 S.C. (H.L.) 117; *Heyman* v. *Darwins* [1942] A.C. 356; *Mauritzen* v. *Baltic Shipping Co.,* 1948 S.C. 646.
[39] *General Billposting Co.* v. *Atkinson* [1909] A.C. 118; *Measure Bros.* v. *Measure* [1910] 2 Ch. 248.
[40] *Marquis of Breadalbane* v. *Stewart* (1904) 6 F. (H.L.) 23.
[41] *Lord Polwarth* v. *N.B. Ry.,* 1908 S.C. 1275; *London and N.-W. Ry.* v. *Neilson* [1922] A.C. 263.
[42] *Alexander* v. *Railway Executive* [1951] 2 K.B. 882.
[43] (1871) 9 M. 1037.

entail.[44] He may accept the refusal as final; if he does so, any subsequent offer of performance comes too late.[45] He may decline to accept the refusal, and, when the time for performance arrives, sue for damages measured by the loss suffered at the date of failure, not at the date of the anticipatory refusal.[46] By adopting this attitude he puts it in the power of the other to reconsider his refusal, and also to take advantage of any intervening circumstance, such as a declaration of war, which, by rendering performance impossible or illegal, may offer a defence to a claim for damages.[47] In a case where he has the active duties under the contract, he has also the option, rather than accepting the refusal and claiming damages for breach of contract, of disregarding it so that the contract remains effectual. He may proceed to carry out the contract and then claim for the full contract price.[48] It may be, however, that, if he has no legitimate interest to do so, he will not be allowed to saddle the other party with an additional burden which will involve no benefit to himself.[49] Mere indications of doubt as to ability to perform cannot safely be regarded as an anticipatory breach[50]; but where A had attempted to evade his obligations, and had persistently failed to give any definite answer to demands for performance, it was held that his whole attitude amounted to a refusal to perform, which entitled B to treat the contract as repudiated by him.[51] If performance is due on demand, or on the occurrence of an uncertain event, any act by which the obligant puts it out of his power to perform, as when A transfers to B the article which he has agreed to sell to C, on demand or on the occurrence of some event, amounts to a repudiation of the contract.[52] C in such a case has bargained not merely for ultimate performance, but for the expectation of performance in the meantime, and to deprive him of that expectation is a material breach of the contract.[53] If, on the other hand, the date for performance is fixed the obligant fulfils his contract if he is ready to perform when that date arrives, and it is doubtful whether any intervening act of his with regard to the subject to which the contract relates can be regarded as so irremediable as to amount to a refusal of ultimate performance.[54]

10. Retention.—In cases where a contract has been so far performed that its rescission would confer no advantage, and also in certain cases where the

---

[44] *Hochester* v. *De La Tour* (1853) 2 E. & B. 678, as explained by Lords Haldane and Wrenbury in *Bradley* v. *Newsom* [1919] A.C. 16.

[45] *Gilfillan* v. *Cadell & Grant* (1893) 21 R. 269.

[46] *Howie* v. *Anderson* (1848) 10 D. 355; *Millet* v. *Van Heek* [1921] 2 K.B. 369; *Tai Hing Cotton Mill* v. *Kamsing Knitting Factory* [1978] 2 W.L.R. 62.

[47] *Avery* v. *Bowden* (1856) 6 E. & B. 953.

[48] *White & Carter (Councils)* v. *M'Gregor,* 1962 S.C. (H.L.) 1, overruling *Langford & Co.* v. *Dutch,* 1952 S.C. 15. See *Finelli* v. *Dee* (1968) 67 D.L.R. (2d) 393; *Decro-Wall International S.A.* v. *Practitioners in Marketing Ltd.* [1971] 1 W.L.R. 361; *Attica Sea Carriers Corpn.* v. *Ferrostaal Poseidon Bulk Reederei GmbH* [1976] 1 Lloyd's Rep. 250.

[49] Per Lord Reid in *White & Carter (Councils),* supra, at p. 14.

[50] *Johnstone* v. *Milling* (1886) 16 Q.B.D. 460; *Thorneloe* v. *McDonald* (1892) 29 S.L.R. 409.

[51] *Forslind* v. *Bechely-Crundall,* 1922 S.C. (H.L.) 173.

[52] *Leith School Board* v. *Rattray's Trs.,* 1918 S.C. 94; *Synge* v. *Synge* [1894] 1 Q.B. 466.

[53] See opinion of Lord President Clyde, *Sanderson* v. *Armour,* 1921 S.C. 18, affd. 1922 S.C. (H.L.) 117.

[54] *Harvey* v. *Smith* (1904) 6 F. 511; *Smith* v. *Butler* [1900] 1 Q.B. 694.

breach is not so material as to justify rescission, the party aggrieved by a breach of contract may find his remedy in withholding performance of the obligation incumbent on him. This right, when it takes the form of refusal to pay a debt, is always known as a right of retention; when it takes the form of a refusal to deliver a particular thing it is more commonly referred to as a lien. But in this connection the terms retention and lien are often used as synonymous.

11. Retention not a General Rule.—While on the principle of compensation debts which are liquid and payable may be set against each other and extinguished[55] there is no general rule that a party who is debtor in a liquid debt has any right to refuse or delay payment in respect of any illiquid claim he may have against his creditor. His obligation is to pay the liquid debt at once, his only right is to receive payment when his illiquid claim is established. So a purchaser cannot refuse to pay for goods on the ground that he has a claim of damages for the defective quality of goods previously supplied by the seller[56] or for the fraud by which he was induced to buy.[57] When a company had two contracts with the town council for the paving of streets, and, through its liquidator, executed one contract, it was held that the town council could not refuse to pay for the work done on the plea that they had a claim of damages in respect of the company's failure to carry out the other contract.[58] The provisions of Rule 55 of the First Schedule to the Sheriff Courts (Scotland) Act 1907[59] have, it has been held, made no alteration in the law.[60] But the general rule, that an action for a liquid debt cannot be met by a plea of retention based on an illiquid claim, must be stated with the qualification that it has been allowed in exceptional cases, either when the illiquid claim admitted of instant verification,[61] or where, in the opinion of the Court, it would be inequitable to reject the plea.[62]

The more definite exceptions to the rule arise—(1) when both claims arise under the same contract; (2) when the creditor in the liquid claim is bankrupt.

12. Retention where Debts Arise from the Same Contract.—When two claims, one liquid, the other in the nature of a claim for damages, arise from the same contract the creditor in the claim for damages may withhold payment of his debt until the amount due to him as damages is established. On this principle is based the rule, in leases, that if the landlord fails, to any

---

[55] As to compensation, see Extinction of Obligations, Ch. XV., infra, § 11.
[56] *Mackie* v. *Riddell* (1874) 2 R. 115.
[57] *Smart* v. *Wilkinson*, 1928 S.C. 383.
[58] *Asphaltic Limestone Co.* v. *Corporation of Glasgow*, 1907 S.C. 463.
[59] "Where a defender pleads a counter claim it shall suffice that he state the same in his defences, and the sheriff may thereafter deal with it as if it had been stated in a substantive action, and may grant decree for it in whole or in part, or for the difference between it and the claim sued on." See also Rules of Court of Session (1965), II, 84.
[60] *Christie* v. *Birrell*, 1910 S.C. 986. But it is indisputable that this is not consistent with some of the reasoning in *Armour & Melvin* v. *Mitchell*, 1934 S.C. 94; see also *Croall & Croall* v. *Sharp*, 1954 S.L.T. (Sh. Ct.) 35.
[61] *Ross* v. *Ross* (1895) 22 R. 461.
[62] *Henderson* v. *Turnbull*, 1909 S.C. 510.

material extent, to execute repairs or improvements which he has agreed to make the tenant may withhold payment of his rent.[63] A carrier's demand for freight may be met by a claim for damages for injury done to the goods.[64] A purchaser of goods may retain the price, in respect of the seller's failure to deliver within a specified or within a reasonable time.[65] But if the price is payable by instalments the buyer is not entitled to retain earlier instalments in security for damages so long as the amount of the unpaid instalments exceeds the amount of his claim.[66] A bondholder in possession under a decree of maills and duties may be met by a plea of retention based on judgments in the tenants' favour in actions previously brought to enforce their rights under their leases.[67]

13. Retention in Bankruptcy.—In bankruptcy a party who is a debtor to the bankrupt and has an illiquid claim against him is entitled to withhold payment until the amount of his illiquid claim is ascertained, and then to compensate the one debt with the other, even although the two debts do not arise out of the same contract.[68]

14. Lien: Special Lien.—In contracts of employment, if the party employed has been placed in possession of an article or property belonging to his employer he has the right to retain until his claim for payment for his work is satisfied. This right, known as a special lien, is based on the principle that one party to a contract may withhold performance of his obligation to return the article until performance of the counter-obligation, viz., payment for the work, is made or tendered.[69] The substantial result is to create a right in security.[70]

15. Provisions for Breach of Contract.—The remedies for breach of contract considered in the preceding pages may in particular cases be supplemented by a provision for an irritancy or a penalty.

16. Irritancies.—An irritancy is a right to put an end to the contractual relation. When it is conditional on a breach of contract it is a general rule of construction that, no matter how it is expressed, it can be enforced only by the party aggrieved by the breach. It gives no right to the party in default. Thus a provision, in a contract between A and B, that the contract shall be void in the event of a specified breach by B, is read as rendering it voidable at A's option,

---

[63] *McDonald* v. *Kydd* (1901) 3 F. 923; *Earl of Galloway* v. *M'Connell,* 1911 S.C. 846; *Haig* v. *Boswall-Preston,* 1915 S.C. 339. As to agreement not to withhold payment of rent, see *Skene* v. *Cameron,* 1942 S.C. 393.
[64] *Taylor* v. *Forbes* (1830) 9 S. 113. Cf. *Aries Tanker Corporation* v. *Total Transport* [1977] 1 W.L.R. 185.
[65] *British Motor Body Co.* v. *Shaw,* 1914 S.C. 922.
[66] *Dick & Stevenson* v. *Woodside Iron & Steel Co.* (1888) 16 R. 242.
[67] *Marshall's Trs.* v. *Banks,* 1934 S.C. 405.
[68] Bell, *Comm.,* II, 122.
[69] Bell, *Prin.,* §§ 1411, 1419; *Robertson* v. *Ross* (1887) 15 R. 67; *Paton's Trs.* v. *Finlayson,* 1923 S.C. 872.
[70] Rights in Security, Ch. XX, infra.

not as giving B the opportunity of getting rid of his contract by committing a breach thereof.[71]

17. Legal Irritancies.—Irritancies may be legal, imposed by law, or conventional, provided in the particular contract. The only legal irritancies known to the law relate to the non-payment of feu-duty or rent. Legal irritancies are purgeable, and an action to enforce them may be met by tender of payment at any time before decree is granted.[72]

18. Conventional Irritancies.—A conventional irritancy may be inserted in any contract, and is a matter which parties may arrange as they please. But what is in terms an irritancy may in substance amount to a penalty, and then cannot be enforced unless it can be regarded as a pre-estimate of damages.[73] So where in a contract of sale with a price payable by instalments a provision is made for the irritancy of the contract (involving forfeiture of all that has been paid) this is in substance a penalty and one which the law will not enforce.[74] A conventional irritancy cannot be purged; considerations of hardship are out of place in a question of enforcing an unambiguous provision in a contract.[75] But conventional provisions in feus, and probably in leases if they merely express the irritancy which the law would infer, may be purged.[76] And the Court has an equitable jurisdiction to allow an irritancy to be purged when its exercise could be shown to be oppressive, as where it was enforced without giving adequate notice that the debt was due.[77]

19. Irritancy as Precluding Damages.—The enforcement of an irritancy in a feu contract, by annulling the contract, not only precludes any claim for damages but bars any claim for arrears of feu-duties.[78] In leases, if the event for which the irritancy is provided is the bankruptcy of the tenant, its enforcement is a bar to any claim for damages.[79] But the charterer of a ship may take advantage of a cancelling clause in the charterparty, and also recover damages, if the non-arrival of the ship by the cancelling date is due to the fault of the shipowner.[80]

20. Penalty Clauses.—A provision in a contract for the incurring of a penalty in the event of a breach will not be enforced according to its terms unless it admits of being construed as a pre-estimate of damages. "If the

---

[71] *Bidoulac* v. *Sinclair's Tr.* (1889) 17 R. 144; *New Zealand Shipping Co.* v. *Société des Ateliers* [1919] A.C. 1.
[72] Erskine, I., 5, 27. See history of the law in *Duncanson* v. *Giffen* (1878) 15 S.L.R. 356.
[73] § 20, infra.
[74] *Steedman* v. *Drinkle* [1916] 1 A.C. 275.
[75] *Lyon* v. *Irvine* (1874) 1 R. 512; *M'Douall's Trs.* v. *MacLeod*, 1949 S.C. 593; *Anderson* v. *Valentine*, 1957 S.L.T. 57; *Dorchester Studios (Glasgow)* v. *Stone*, 1975 S.L.T. 153.
[76] *Duncanson* v. *Giffen* (1878) 15 S.L.R. 356; see *Anderson*, supra.
[77] *Stewart* v. *Watson* (1864) 2 M. 1414. *M'Douall's Trs.*, supra.
[78] *Magistrates of Edinburgh* v. *Horsburgh* (1834) 12 S. 593; *Malcolm* v. *Donald*, 1956 S.L.T. (Sh. Ct.) 101.
[79] *Buttercase and Geddie's Tr.* v. *Geddie* (1897) 24 R. 1128.
[80] *Nelson* v. *Dundee East Shipping Co.*, 1907 S.C. 927.

penalty be truly a penalty—that is, a punishment—the Court will not allow that, because the law will not let people punish each other."[81]

21. Penalty and Liquidate Damages.—The rule is general, and applies to a clause of irritancy if in substance it amounts to a penalty. It has been illustrated in cases where there is a provision for the payment of a specified sum in the event of a breach of the contract. This may be termed a penalty, or may be termed liquidate damages, but the result does not depend on the term used. It is regarded as a penalty unless it bears some intelligible relation to the loss which the breach will probably cause; as liquidate damages if it can be regarded as a fair, though not necessarily exact, pre-estimate of the amount of that loss. If the provision is sustained as liquidate damages, proof of the actual damage sustained is unnecessary,[82] and proof that damage has been sustained beyond the pre-estimate is inadmissible[83]; if regarded as a penalty, nothing can be recovered without proof of actual loss, and the amount fixed as a penalty is not a limit to the amount of damages that may be awarded.[84]

22. Penalties in Bonds and Leases.—There are two cases where clauses providing for a penalty or liquidate damages are inoperative. One is a clause in a bond, imposing a penalty on failure of punctual payment of interest. This is not enforceable according to its terms,[85] though there is no legal objection to the enforcement of a provision whereby, though interest at a lower rate than that fixed in the bond will be accepted, the full rate will be exacted on failure of punctual payment.[86] The other case is a provision in an agricultural lease for the payment of increased rent (usually termed "pactional rent") or other liquidated damages for breach of the terms of the lease. By statute such a provision is unenforceable.[87]

23. Liquidate Damages.—Apart from these two special cases the tendency of modern decisions has been to sustain clauses providing for liquidate damages, unless the amount is plainly exorbitant, or where the same sum is fixed for any breach of a contract involving various obligations, some of trivial, and some of relatively great importance. Such a provision indicates that no real pre-estimate of damages was aimed at, only a punishment of the defaulter.[88] Thus where in a lease of an hotel various obligations were laid on each party it was held that a general clause providing for a payment of £50 by

---

[81] Per Lord Young, *Robertson* v. *Driver's Trs.* (1881) 8 R. 555. An interesting case on penalties, involving the Roman-Dutch law, is *Pearl Assurance Co.* v. *Union of South Africa* [1934] A.C. 570.

[82] *Clydebank Engineering Co.* v. *Castaneda* (1904) 7 F. (H.L.) 77.

[83] *Diestal* v. *Stevenson* [1906] 2 K.B. 345; *Cellulose Acetate Silk Co.* v. *Widnes Foundry* [1933] A.C. 20.

[84] *Dingwall* v. *Burnett*, 1912 S.C. 1097.

[85] *Nasmyth* v. *Samson* (1785) 3 Paton 9; Debts Securities (Scotland) Act 1856, s. 7 (not applicable to a standard security: Conveyancing and Feudal Reform (Scotland) Act 1970, s. 32, Sch. 8, para. 1).

[86] *Gatty* v. *Maclaine*, 1921 S.C. (H.L.) 1.

[87] Agricultural Holdings (Scotland) Act 1949, s. 16.

[88] See opinion of Lord Watson, *Lord Elphinstone* v. *Monkland Iron Co.* (1886) 13 R. (H.L.) 98.

either in the event of any failure could not be regarded as a pre-estimate of damages, and, as a penalty, could not be enforced.[89] But it is not an objection that the same sum is fixed for a number of specified acts, if these acts are all of the same class, and if, from the nature of the case, the actual damage likely to result from each act is difficult or impossible to determine. So where agents for the sale of tyres agreed not to tamper with the tyre marks, to export without written consent, or to sell under list prices, a penalty of £5 per tyre was sustained.[90] In a leading case torpedo boats were ordered by the Spanish Government, with a penalty of £500 per week for late delivery. It was held that as it was impossible to prove the amount of loss which a nation might sustain owing to the want of torpedo boats any reasonable pre-estimate, whether termed a penalty or liquidate damages, would be sustained.[91] And it may perhaps be regarded as settled that in a contract for work to be done within a specified time, a penalty calculated at so much per day, week, or month will be sustained, unless plainly exorbitant.[92] In a hire-purchase case, where terms were agreed upon the basis of which the hirer had an option to return the hired article to the seller and he exercised that option, it was held that despite the use of the term "liquidate damages" as applying to the sum to be paid, the case was truly neither one of penalty nor of liquidate damages.[93] On the other hand, where a hire-purchase contract was terminated by the owner on the ground that the hirer was in breach, it was found necessary to consider whether a clause requiring the hirer to pay in that event the same amount as he would have had to pay had he exercised his option to terminate was a penalty.[94]

24. Deposits on Sale.—In sale it is a common provision that the purchaser must deposit a portion of the price, to be forfeited if he fail to carry out his contract. This, though in substance a penalty, is not so regarded, and the contract may be enforced according to its terms.[95]

25. Penalty Does Not Excuse Performance.—It is a general rule that where the consequences of a breach of contract are provided for by a penalty or by liquidate damages the provision is to be read as an addition to the remedies which the party aggrieved would otherwise possess, not as a licence to the other party to break his contract on payment of the penalty. So building restrictions, though fortified by a penalty, may be enforced by interdict,[96] and the same rule applies to the case where a party has agreed not to carry on a particular business.[97] Penalties are spoken of as "by and attour performance."

---

[89] *Dingwall* v. *Burnett*, supra.
[90] *Dunlop Tyre Co.* v. *New Garage Co.* [1915] A.C. 79; followed, *Imperial Tobacco Co.* v. *Parslay*, (1936) 52 T.L.R. 585.
[91] *Clydebank Engineering Co.* v. *Castaneda* (1904) 7 F. (H.L.) 77.
[92] *Cameron Head* v. *Cameron*, 1919 S.C. 627.
[93] *Bell Bros.* v. *Aitken*, 1939 S.C. 577. See also *Granor Finance* v. *Liquidator of Eastore*, 1974 S.L.T. 296.
[94] *Bridge* v. *Campbell Discount Co.* [1962] A.C. 600.
[95] *Commercial Bank* v. *Beal* (1890) 18 R. 80; *Roberts & Cooper* v. *Salvesen*, 1918 S.C. 794.
[96] *Dalrymple* v. *Herdman* (1878) 5 R. 847.
[97] *Curtis* v. *Sandison* (1831) 10 S. 72.

26. Damages.[98]—Where there is no conventional provision for the consequence of a breach of contract, or where that provision is found to be unenforceable, the party aggrieved is in almost all cases entitled to damages. The principal exception is where the breach consists in failure to pay money at the appointed date, when, though interest may be due, no general damages can be demanded.[99]

Damages are intended—and the rule holds in cases of wrongs as well as in cases of breach of contract[1]—as compensation to the injured party, not as a punishment of the party in breach. It is, consequently, irrelevant to consider how far a party who has broken his contract has gained by doing so[2]; or, with an exception in the case of an action for breach of promise of marriage,[3] the question whether he is rich or poor.[4] Neither point affects the loss which the pursuer has sustained, and for which he is to be compensated. It was a general rule in cases of breach of contract that the law will consider material loss or inconvenience only, not injury to feelings arising from the breach or the circumstances in which it was made[5] but in cases where one party was contracting on a non-commercial basis sums have been awarded in respect of mental distress, disappointment and frustration.[6] It is now established that, in accordance with the principle that compensation to the injured party should be limited to the true loss which he has suffered, consideration of his income tax liability is a necessary element in the calculation of the amount to be awarded as damages.[7]

Where injury is inflicted, whether by breach of contract or by a wrongful or negligent act, the damages that may be claimed are limited by the principle that the party who is aggrieved is bound to take all reasonable means to minimise his loss.[8] So a servant who has been wrongfully dismissed must endeavour to find other employment[9]; a buyer, if the seller has failed to supply the goods, must take measures to supply himself, if there is an available market in which the goods in question can be obtained.[10] Whether such efforts to minimise the loss have in fact been taken or not, the damages awarded will not exceed the loss which their adoption would not have prevented. Similarly, if reasonable care in the inspection of a defective article would have averted some item of loss, that loss will not be included in the damages recoverable

[98] See Walker, *Law of Damages in Scotland* (1955).
[99] Erskine, III, 3, 86; Bell, *Prin.*, § 32.
[1] *Black* v. *N.B. Ry.*, 1908 S.C. 444.
[2] *Teacher* v. *Calder* (1899) 1 F. (H.L.) 39.
[3] *Stroyan* v. *M'Whirter* (1901) 9 S.L.T. 242.
[4] *Black* v. *N.B. Ry.*, supra.
[5] *Addis* v. *Gramophone Co.* [1909] A.C. 488.
[6] *Jarvis* v. *Swans Tours* [1973] 1 Q.B. 233; *Jackson* v. *Horizon Holidays* [1975] 1 W.L.R. 1468; *Diesen* v. *Samson*, 1971 S.L.T. (Sh. Ct.) 49.
[7] *M'Daid* v. *Clyde Navigation Trs.*, 1946 S.C. 462; *British Transport Commission* v. *Gourley* [1956] A.C. 185. See also *Spencer* v. *Macmillan's Trs.*, 1958 S.C. 300; *Stewart* v. *Glentaggart*, 1963 S.L.T. 119.
[8] *The Admiralty* v. *Aberdeen Steam Trawling Co.*, 1910 S.C. 553.
[9] *Ross* v. *Macfarlane* (1894) 21 R. 396.
[10] *Warin & Craven* v. *Forrester* (1876) 4 R. 190; affd. 4 R. (H.L.) 75; Sale of Goods Act 1893, ss. 50, 51. It has been held in England that a disappointed buyer may even have to accept some offer by way of compromise made by the seller: see *Houndsditch Warehouse Co.* v. *Waltex* [1944] 1 K.B. 579.

from the party who supplied the article.[11] It has been laid down that "a contracting party is not entitled to proceed so as to cause unnecessary loss to the other party without any resulting benefit to himself."[12] Where, however, the pursuer can show that he has taken all reasonable means to minimise the loss, he has done enough; the defender cannot successfully avert a claim for damages by proof that some extraordinary or exceptional measures might have been adopted.[13]

27. Measure of Damages.—The formula as to the measure of damages in the case of breach of contract is often referred to as the rule of *Hadley* v. *Baxendale*,[14] but that case merely restated a principle which had long been recognised in Scotland.[15] The formula or rule is expressed in *Hadley* v. *Baxendale* in the following terms: "Where two parties have made a contract which one of them has broken, the damages which the other party ought to receive in respect of such breach of contract should be such as may fairly and reasonably be considered either arising naturally, i.e., according to the usual course of things, from such breach of contract itself, or such as may reasonably be supposed to have been in the contemplation of both parties at the time they made the contract as the probable result of the breach of it." The former alternative points to the general rule of what are known as ordinary damages: everyone, as a reasonable person, is taken to know the ordinary course of things and consequently what loss is liable to result from a breach of contract in that ordinary course.[16] The latter shows that to this knowledge, which a party in breach is assumed to possess whether he actually possesses it or not, there may have to be added in a particular case any knowledge which he does actually possess, through, e.g., prior notice or special experience, of special circumstances which would be liable, in the event of a breach, to cause more loss.[17] The measure, in short, depends upon the knowledge, actual or imputed, of the party in breach: "a party who breaks his contract is liable for those consequences which a reasonable man, possessing the knowledge which the party had at the time of contracting, would have anticipated."[18] The breach itself does not have to have been foreseeable.[19]

In computing ordinary damages, an allowance for the inconvenience and dislocation of business involved in the breach of any mercantile contract is permissible, even where no actual pecuniary loss can be established.[20] There may also be included the expenses directly incurred by the party whose

[11] *Carter* v. *Campbell* (1885) 12 R. 1075; *Wilson* v. *Carmichael* (1894) 21 R. 732.
[12] *Dunford & Elliot* v. *Macleod* (1902) 4 F. 912, per Lord M'Laren.
[13] *Gunter & Co.* v. *Lauritzen* (1894) 31 S.L.R. 359; *Clippens Oil Co.* v. *Edinburgh Water Trustees,* 1907 S.C. (H.L.) 9.
[14] (1854) 9 Exch. 341; Bell, *Prin.,* § 33; *A/B Karlshamns Oljefabriker* v. *Monarch S.S. Co.,* 1949 S.C. (H.L.) 1; *Victoria Laundry (Windsor)* v. *Newman Industries* [1949] 2 K.B. 528.
[15] Brown, *Sale,* 214 (published in 1821).
[16] See, e.g., *Waddington* v. *Buchan Poultry Products,* 1963 S.L.T. 168.
[17] *Den of Ogil Co.* v. *Cal. Ry.* (1902) 5 F. 99; *Victoria Laundry (Windsor),* supra, in which see opinion of Asquith, L.J., at p. 539.
[18] Gloag, *Contract,* 2nd ed., p. 697; *Koufos* v. *C. Czarnikow* [1969] 1 A.C. 350.
[19] *H. Parsons (Livestock)* v. *Uttley Ingham & Co.* [1978] Q.B. 791.
[20] *Webster* v. *Cramond Iron Co.* (1875) 2 R. 752.

contract had been broken, if such expenses would have been incurred by a reasonable man[21]; the cost of litigation with third parties, if traceable to the breach of contract and if reasonably incurred[22]; the loss of a sub-contract, in cases of failure to supply or carry goods, if that sub-contract contained no exceptional conditions.[23] In many cases a person who supplies an article impliedly warrants that it is fit for ordinary use, and any injury which may result from the fact that it is unsuitable or inadequate will form part of the damages.[24] Damages for injury resulting from some exceptional use of the article, on the other hand, will be due only where the party supplying it had notice that such a use of it was contemplated.[25] Among the items of loss which would not fall under ordinary damages, but might be recovered, as consequential damages, in cases where the party in breach had notice of the actual facts, are the loss incurred where goods are supplied or conveyed too late for a particular market[26]; or the loss involved by delay in the provision or carriage of an article from the want of which some larger enterprise is brought to a standstill.[27] In the latter case, e.g., where some necessary part of a mill or of a ship is delayed in transit, it is possibly the law that mere notice of the facts is not enough to render the carrier liable for the exceptional loss which his delay may cause; there must be something such as the payment of a special rate, indicating that he took the risk.[28]

28. Interest.—As already noticed, mere failure to pay at the appointed time does not give rise to any claim for damages for the loss which may have resulted. It may, however, render the party in delay liable for interest. This may be expressly provided, with or without a period of credit. Interest may also, but only in a limited class of cases, be due ex lege. It has been stated to be due when the pursuer "is deprived of an interest-bearing security or a profit-producing chattel ... or ... by virtue of a principal sum having been wrongfully withheld and not paid on the day when it ought to be paid."[29] It is due when possession is taken on the sale of land, even if the price is not settled or the title not complete.[30] It is due, after maturity, on a bill of exchange or promissory note.[31] It is also due on money lent,[32] unless the circumstances of the case were exceptional.[33] In the case of an I.O.U., interest, unless stipulated for, is due only from the date of citation.[34] It may be recovered by a solicitor

[21] *Le Blanche* v. *London & N.-W. Ry.* (1876) 1 C.D.P. 286.
[22] *Munro* v. *Bennett*, 1911 S.C. 337; *Buchanan & Carswell* v. *Eugene*, 1936 S.C. 160.
[23] *Ströms Bruks A/B* v. *Hutchison* (1905) 7 F. (H.L.) 131. Contrast *Horne* v. *Midland Ry.* (1872) L.R. 8 C.P. 131.
[24] *Dickie* v. *Amicable Property Investment Co.*, 1911 S.C. 1079.
[25] *Cory* v. *Thames Ironworks, etc., Co.* (1868) L.R. 3 Q.B. 181.
[26] *Macdonald* v. *Highland Ry.* (1873) 11 M. 614; *Anderson* v. *N.B. Ry.* (1875) 2 R. 443.
[27] *Hadley* v. *Baxendale* (1854) 9 Exch. 341; *Den of Ogil Co.* v. *Cal. Ry.* (1902) 5 F. 99; *Hydraulic Engineering Co.* v. *M'Haffie* (1878) 4 Q.B.D. 670.
[28] See *British Columbia Saw Mills Co.* v. *Nettleship* (1868) L.R. 3 C.P. 499.
[29] *Kolbin & Sons* v. *Kinnear & Co.*, 1931 S.C. (H.L.) 128, per Lord Atkin, at p. 137.
[30] *Greenock Harbour Trustees* v. *Glasgow and S.-W. Ry.*, 1909 S.C. 1438, affd. 1909 S.C. (H.L.) 49; *Prestwick Cinema Co.* v. *Gardiner*, 1951 S.C. 98.
[31] Bills of Exchange Act 1882, s. 57.
[32] *Cunninghame* v. *Boswell* (1868) 6 M. 890.
[33] *Forbes* v. *Forbes* (1869) 8 M. 85; *Smellie's Exx.* v. *Smellie*, 1933 S.C. 725.
[34] *Winestone* v. *Wolifson*, 1954 S.C. 77.

on his outlays, but not on his professional charges.[35] It is due on money paid under protest which ultimately turns out not to have been legally exigible.[36] It is not due on arrears of rent or feu-duties.[37] The general rule with regard to tradesmen's and professional accounts is that no interest is due unless there has been a judicial demand for payment, or an intimation that interest will be charged on the account if not paid on a specified date.[38] No interest is due on sums payable as demurrage.[39]

Where legal action is taken, and the debt arises directly from contract, interest will be due from the date of citation.[40] Where the action concludes for damages, either for breach of contract or on some other ground, the general rule is that no interest is due until the damages are awarded, and the decree has become enforceable.[41] The Court has, however, a discretion, to award interest on damages for the whole or any part of the period between the date when the right of action arose and the date of the decree.[42]

[35] *Blair's Trs.* v. *Payne* (1884) 12 R. 104.
[36] *Haddon's Exx.* v. *Scottish Milk Marketing Board*, 1938 S.C. 168.
[37] *Marquis of Tweeddale's Trs.* v. *Earl of Haddington* (1880) 7 R. 620; Rankine, *Leases* (3rd ed.), 460.
[38] *Somervell's Tr.* v. *Edinburgh Life Assurance Co.*, 1911 S.C. 1069.
[39] *Pollich* v. *Heatley*, 1910 S.C. 469, per Lord President Dunedin, at p. 478.
[40] Erskine, III, 3, 10.
[41] *Roger* v. *Cochrane*, 1910 S.C. 1; *M'Cormack* v. *N.C.B.*, 1957 S.C. 277.
[42] Interest on Damages (Scotland) Acts 1958 (c. 61) and 1971 (c. 31). See *Macrae* v. *Reed & Mallik*, 1961 S.C. 68; *R. & J. Dempster* v. *Motherwell Bridge & Engineering Co.*, 1964 S.C. 308; *Fraser* v. *Morton Wilson* (2), 1966 S.L.T. 22; *James Buchanan & Co.* v. *Stewart Cameron (Drymen)*, 1973 S.L.T. (Notes) 78.

CHAPTER XIV

QUASI-CONTRACT

IN a previous chapter[1] it was noted that certain obligations, implied by law, are commonly referred to as arising from quasi-contract.[2] Quasi-contractual so far resemble contractual obligations that the obligation is directly to pay or to perform, and not, as in the case of wrongs or negligence, to make reparation for something already done or omitted. They differ in respect that the obligation arises by force of law, and not from the consent of the party obliged. They are cases where obligations analogous to those of promiser are imposed, for reasons of equity or convenience, on a party who has not made any promise. So quasi-contract should be distinguished from implied contract. The latter term means that the law presumes, in particular circumstances, that a party has given his consent, whereas in cases of quasi-contract consent is neither presumed nor necessary.

The obligation to aliment relatives,[3] the obligations involved in salvage[4] and general average,[5] all of which may be classed under the head of quasi-contract, are noticed in other parts of this book, and this chapter may be confined to the law of restitution, recompense, and negotiorum gestio.

1. Restitution.—When a party is in possession of goods to which he can assert no title, as in the case of a finder, or a person to whom goods have been delivered by mistake,[6] or the purchaser from a thief, he is, under the obligation of restitution, bound to give them up to the true owner, or, in the case of goods consumed, to pay their value. The same rule holds when a limited or qualified right to possession has come to an end.[7]

2. Stolen Goods.—With an exception in the case of current coin, bank notes and negotiable instruments, theft involves a vitium reale in the goods stolen, which precludes the acquisition of a title in a question with the true owner. Good faith on the part of the possessor is no answer to a demand for restitution; and the English law of market overt, under which the purchaser of stolen goods may acquire a title if he bought them in a public market, is not recognised in the law of Scotland.[8] When a bona fide purchaser of stolen goods has re-sold them before receiving notice of the defect in his title, he is

---

[1] General Law of Obligations, Ch. III., supra, § 6.
[2] For a discussion of the principle and further references, see Smith, *Short Commentary,* pp. 623 et seq.
[3] See Index.
[4] Ch. XXXII, infra.
[5] Ibid.
[6] *Finlay* v. *Monro* (1698) M. 1767; *Pride* v. *St. Anne's Bleaching Co.* (1838) 16 S. 1376.
[7] *Scottish Central Ry.* v. *Ferguson* (1863) 1 M. 750.
[8] *Todd* v. *Armour* (1882) 9 R. 901. See as to negotiable instruments, *Walker & Watson* v. *Sturrock* (1897) 35 S.L.R. 26, and Moveable Property, Incorporeal, Ch. XXXVIII, infra, § 9.

liable only for any profit he may have made on the re-sale, and then only in the event of the goods being irrecoverable.[9] If, using other materials of his own, he has used the stolen goods to make a new thing, as when lard was made with stolen oil, the property in the new thing, on the principle of specification, vests in him, but he is liable to the owner of the stolen goods for their value.[10]

3. Repetition.—The principle of restitution may be held to include the plea of repetition, under which money paid may be recovered, either, under the condictio indebiti, because it has been paid under a mistake,[11] or, under the condictio causa data causa non secuta, because it has been paid in advance for a consideration which has not been received.[12] But if money has been paid in furtherance of a criminal purpose of the payer's it has been held in England that a person receiving it and suspecting an illegal purpose cannot be forced by the payer to restore it.[13]

4. Recompense.—The principle of recompense is defined in Bell's *Principles* in the following terms: "Where one has gained by the lawful act of another, done without any intention of donation, he is bound to recompense or indemnify that other to the extent of the gain."[14] This definition, though useful as indicating the general nature of the plea of recompense, has been criticised as too widely expressed, since it would cover cases of incidental benefits arising without loss to the party who has conferred them.[15]

5. Recompense and Implied Contract.—The principle of recompense is properly applicable either to cases where there is no contract between the parties, or to cases where work has been done under a contract in circumstances which preclude any direct contractual claim. It is not a plea which is open to a party who has done work under a contract and has the right to sue for the contract price. So a contractor cannot claim recompense on the ground that the work he has done has enriched the employer to an amount greater than the contract price.[16] And a claim for payment for extra work done under a contract must, it is conceived, be founded on an express or implied agreement to pay, not on the principle of recompense.[17] When work has been done under a contract which makes no express provision for payment, a claim for payment, though sometimes referred to as a claim for recompense,[18] is more properly a claim under an implied contract for payment, measured, on the principle of quantum meruit, by the market value

---

[9] *Scot* v. *Low* (1704) M. 9123; *International Banking Co.* v. *Ferguson, Shaw & Sons,* 1910 S.C. 182, at p. 191.
[10] *International Banking Co.* v. *Ferguson, Shaw & Sons,* 1910 S.C. 182.
[11] Agreement Improperly Obtained, Ch. VIII., supra, § 23.
[12] Impossibility of Performance, Ch. XI., supra, § 7.
[13] *Berg* v. *Sadler & Moore* [1937] 2 K.B. 158.
[14] Bell, *Prin.,* § 538.
[15] *Edinburgh Tramways Co.* v. *Courtenay,* 1909 S.C. 99; *Exchange Telegraph Co.* v. *Giulianotti,* 1959 S.C. 19. See *Stewart* v. *Steuart,* (1878) 6 R. 145, opinion of Lord President Inglis at p. 149.
[16] *Boyd & Forrest* v. *G. and S.-W. Ry.,* 1915 S.C. (H.L.) 20. See opinion of Earl Loreburn.
[17] *Wilson* v. *Wallace* (1859) 21 D. 507; *Tharsis Co.* v. *M'Elroy* (1878) 5 R. (H.L.) 171.
[18] As in Bell, *Prin.,* § 539.

of the services rendered, and maintainable whether they have proved beneficial or not, in contrast to a claim quantum lucratus, measured and limited by the advantage which the services have produced to the recipient.[19] In such cases, however, assuming that the work has proved beneficial, a claim based either on recompense or on implied contract may be open.[20]

6. Cases of Recompense.—The typical cases for a plea of recompense as contrasted with a claim for payment under an implied contract would appear to be three—(1) Where a party has expended money on property in the bona fide but ill-founded belief that it is his own and is compelled to give it up to the true owner, he has a claim for his expenditure in so far as it has proved beneficial and the true owner consequently is enriched.[21] He has no such claim if his possession was not bona fide.[22] (2) Where a party has done work under a contract, but has so far departed from the contractual terms that a claim for the contract price is excluded. Thus if a builder produces a building materially different from that ordered he may have no claim directly under his contract, but if the employer does not choose to reject the building he is at least liable quantum lucratus.[23] And where a commission agent had broken a term in his contract under which he was precluded from acting for rival traders, it was held that he could not recover commission during the period in which he was thus in breach of his contract but observed that he might have a claim for recompense on proof that his employers had benefited by the business he introduced.[24] (3) Where goods have been supplied or work done in circumstances where a direct contractual claim for the price must fail, either because the defender could plead his lack of contractual power[25] or because the contract is one which has been declared by statute to be void,[26] a claim for the value of the goods or work is generally relevant. And in certain cases it may be competent for a pursuer, who is prepared to prove a contractual right by parole evidence, but is met by the plea that the defender's writ or oath is the only evidence competent, to lead parole evidence in support of a claim for payment in so far as the defender is lucratus.[27]

7. Limits of Recompense.—The limits of the plea of recompense are indicated by the maxim on which it is founded, "nemo debet locupletari ex aliena jactura." Two elements must occur: The pursuer must have suffered loss; the defender must have been the gainer (lucratus) by that loss. The loss

[19] See *Landless* v. *Wilson* (1880) 8 R. 289.
[20] *Anderson* v. *Anderson* (1869) 8 M. 157; *Mellor* v. *Beardmore*, 1927 S.C. 597.
[21] *Magistrates of Selkirk* v. *Clapperton* (1830) 9 S. 9; *Newton* v. *Newton*, 1925 S.C. 715.
[22] *Barbour* v. *Halliday* (1840) 2 D. 1279.
[23] *Ramsay* v. *Brand* (1898) 25 R. 1212. As to the conditions excluding the builder's claim for the contract price, see Breach of Contract, Ch. XIII., supra, § 5.
[24] *Graham* v. *United Turkey Red Co.*, 1922 S.C. 533; *Abrahams* v. *Campbell*, 1911 S.C. 353.
[25] See Sale of Goods Act 1893, s. 2; *Sinclair* v. *Brougham* [1914] A.C. 398, speech of Lord Dunedin; *Stonehaven Magistrates* v. *Kincardineshire Country Council*, 1939 S.C. 760.
[26] *Cuthbertson* v. *Lowes* (1870) 8 M. 1073, distinguished in *Jamieson* v. *Watt's Trs.*, 1950 S.C. 265, where the contract was illegal. See also *Duncan* v. *Motherwell Bridge and Engineering Co.*, 1952 S.C. 131; Pacta Illicita and Unfair Terms, Ch. IX., supra, § 8.
[27] *Newton* v. *Newton*, supra; *Gray* v. *Johnston*, 1928 S.C. 659.

may consist in expenditure which has not met with the expected return, or in the work or service for which no payment has been received. But if a man has expended money for a particular purpose, and that purpose has been attained, he cannot appeal to the principle of recompense in support of a claim for payment from a party who has incidentally gained by the expenditure in question. Thus where the lessee of the advertising rights on a tramway system was the gainer by the fact that the tramway company, in order to satisfy the regulations of the Board of Trade, constructed new cars with boards on which the advertisements might be placed, it was held that the tramway company had no right to an increased rent, on the ground that the lessee was saved the expense of erecting the boards for himself. He was a gainer by the company's expenditure, but his gain was merely the incidental result of an expenditure which had secured its purpose.[28] And where a person holding property on a limited title, as in the case of a liferenter, expends money on improvements, it will generally be assumed that he did so with a view to his own advantage, and his representatives will have no claim against the fiar for the amount by which the improvements have enriched him.[29] Such a claim, however, may be established on proof that the liferenter acted on a reasonable expectation that his expenditure would be repaid.[30] And there is early authority for the statement that if a house is destroyed by fire, and rebuilt by a liferenter, his representatives have a claim against the fiar.[31] It would appear to be the law that a heritable creditor in possession and expending money on the subjects has a claim against the debtor in so far as the subjects are increased in value.[32] Any claim by a tenant for improvements must rest on express contract or statutory provision.[33] As recompense is an equitable remedy it cannot be invoked if another legal remedy is available.[34]

8. Meaning of Lucratus.—To found a claim for recompense it is not enough to prove expenditure without return unless it can also be proved that the party against whom the claim is made is lucratus. A man is not lucratus, in a question of recompense, merely because he has obtained payment of a debt.[35] Therefore in bankruptcy a creditor has no preference on the ground that the work he has done has increased the value of the bankrupt's estate. The other creditors are not lucrati merely because the dividend on their debts is larger.[36] This principle has led to narrow distinctions in cases where money has been obtained by fraudulent means. If A, by fraud, obtains money from

---

[28] *Edinburgh Tramways Co.* v. *Courtenay,* 1909 S.C. 99. See also *Exchange Telegraph Co.* v. *Giulianotti,* 1959 S.C. 19; *Microwave Systems (Scotland)* v. *Electro-Physiological Instruments,* 1971 S.C. 140.
[29] *Wallace* v. *Braid* (1900) 2 F. 754; *Rankin* v. *Wither* (1886) 13 R. 903.
[30] *Morgan* v. *Morgan's Factor,* 1922 S.L.T. 247.
[31] *Haliday* v. *Garden* (1706) M. 13419.
[32] *Nelson* v. *Gordon* (1874) 1 R. 1093. See Gloag, *Contract* (2nd ed.), 326.
[33] *Thomson* v. *Fowler* (1859) 21 D. 453; *Walker* v. *M'Knight* (1886) 13 R. 599.
[34] *Varney (Scotland)* v. *Burgh of Lanark,* 1976 S.L.T. 46.
[35] Kames, *Principles of Equity* (3rd ed.), I, 153; *Thomson* v. *Clydesdale Bank* (1893) 20 R. (H.L.) 59, opinion of Lord Chancellor Herschell.
[36] *Burns* v. *M'Lellan's Creditors* (1735) M. 13402; *Mess* v. *Sime's Tr.* (1898) 25 R. 398, affd., (1898) 1 F. (H.L.) 22.

B, and uses it to pay his debt to C, B can found no claim against C.[37] But if in similar circumstances A uses the money to meet obligations for which C is liable, C is then lucratus, and, on the principle that no one can take profit from a fraud, must account to B to the extent of the obligations of which he has been relieved.[38] This was applied in *Clydesdale Bank* v. *Paul,* to the case where an agent had fraudulently involved his principal in liabilities, and met them by money obtained from a bank by a forged cheque. The principal was liable to the bank on the ground that he was lucratus by the money which the bank had lost. Again, a party is not lucratus by the acquisition of a thing for which he has paid, or which some party other than the pursuer in the action for recompense is bound to provide. Therefore a party who has let an article on hire, with an obligation on the hirer to keep it in repair, is not liable to the artificer who has repaired it under contract with the hirer.[39] Where an accountant undertook to carry out the amalgamation of two companies for a contract price, it was held that those who employed him, and who had paid the contract price, were under no liability to a law agent who, on the accountant's instructions, had drawn up a necessary agreement.[40] There is no such doctrine in the law of Scotland as that every person who has profited by work done under a contract is to be liable for the work so done.[41]

9. Negotiorum Gestio.—A negotiorum gestor is a person who, without any regular authority, intervenes to manage the affairs of another who, temporarily or permanently, is unable to manage them himself, and in circumstances where it is reasonable to assume that authority would have been given had the circumstances rendered it possible to apply for it.[42] The position is held by one who acts on behalf of a pupil, minor,[43] or absentee,[44] of a person in prison,[45] or even of a person who has become insane.[46] A negotiorum gestor is entitled to be reimbursed for any expenditure he has incurred in the proper course of administration, even although it has not proved beneficial,[47] and to be relieved of all liabilities. He must account for his intromissions, and is liable for any loss caused by his failure to exercise the care and diligence which a prudent man would have shown in relation to his own property.[48] A person reasonably and properly employed by a negotiorum gestor, as, for example, a solicitor, has a direct right of action for his account against the party whose affairs have been managed.[49]

[37] *Gibbs* v. *British Linen Co.* (1875) 4 R. 630.
[38] *Clydesdale Bank* v. *Paul* (1877) 4 R. 626; *Traill* v. *Smith's Trs.* (1876) 3 R. 770.
[39] *Lamonby* v. *Foulds,* 1928 S.C. 89.
[40] *Robertson* v. *Beatson, M'Leod & Co.,* 1908 S.C. 921.
[41] Per Lord Kyllachy, *Cran* v. *Dodson* (1893) 1 S.L.T. 354.
[42] Stair, I, 8, 3; Erskine, III, 3, 52; Bell, *Prin.,* § 540. For the analogous principle of agency by necessity, see Agency, Ch. XXIII, infra, § 2.
[43] *Fulton* v. *Fulton* (1864) 2 M. 893.
[44] *Bannatine's Trs* v. *Cunninghame* (1872) 10 M. 317; see *S.M.T. Sales & Services Co.* v. *Motor & General Finance Co.,* 1954 S.L.T. (Sh. Ct.) 107.
[45] *Gemmell* v. *Annandale* (1899) 36 S.L.R. 658.
[46] *Dunbar* v. *Wilson & Dunlop's Tr.* (1887) 15 R. 210.
[47] Stair, I, 8, 3.
[48] *Kolbin & Son* v. *United Shipping Co.,* 1931 S.C. (H.L.) 128.
[49] *Fernie* v. *Robertson* (1871) 9 M. 437; *Dunbar* v. *Wilson & Dunlop's Tr.* (1887) 15 R. 210.

CHAPTER XV

EXTINCTION OF OBLIGATIONS

AN obligation may be extinguished by a discharge by the creditor; by performance or payment; by compensation; by novation; by confusion; or by lapse of time. The result of impossibility of performance has already been considered.[1]

1. Acceptilation and Discharge.—Acceptilation is the technical term applicable when the creditor discharges his right without payment or performance. If the contract was entered into verbally a verbal discharge is probably sufficient, and the fact that it was given is provable by parole evidence. If the contract was in writing the discharge also requires writing; an oral discharge probably leaves it open to the creditor to resile and in any event requires proof by writ or oath.[2]

It is always a question of construction what debts are covered by a discharge. If the discharge was in general terms, without reference to any particular debt, or class of debts, the normal construction is that the debtor is freed from any claim of which the creditor was then aware, e.g., from a debt in which the debtor was merely cautioner.[3] If a list of debts is given, followed by general words of discharge, no debts of a different kind from those enumerated are included.[4] If it turns out that there existed a debt of which the creditor, at the time of granting the discharge, was not aware, a general discharge may be reducible on the ground that, so far as relates to the debt in question, it was gratuitous, and granted under error.[5] Fitted accounts, i.e., accounts rendered by one party and docqueted as correct by the other, are documents in re mercatoria, and do not require to be in probative form.[6] They do not preclude proof that some item or items have been omitted or entered incorrectly, but they lay the onus of proof on the party who challenges their accuracy.[7] The rule applies to entries made by a banker in his customer's passbook; proof that the banker never received the money is competent.[8] Fitted accounts, or even a formal discharge, do not preclude a subsequent demand by a client for the taxation of his solicitor's account.[9]

2. Performance.—The question whether an obligation ad factum prae-

[1] Supra, Ch. XI.
[2] Dickson, *Evidence,* § 627; Walkers, *Evidence,* § 125; *Lavan* v. *Aird & Co.,* 1919 S.C. 345, opinion of Lord Justice-Clerk; *Edinburgh Entertainments Co.* v. *Stevenson,* 1926 S.C. 363; *Nicol's Trs.* v. *Sutherland,* 1951 S.C. (H.L.) 21.
[3] *British Linen Co.* v. *Esplin* (1849) 11 D. 1104.
[4] *Greenock Banking Co.*v. *Smith* (1844) 6 D. 1340; *M'Adam* v. *Scott* (1913) 50 S.L.R. 264.
[5] *Dickson* v. *Halbert* (1854) 16 D. 586; *Purdon* v. *Rowat's Tr.* (1856) 19 D. 206.
[6] *Fell* v. *Rattray* (1869) 41 Sc. Jurist 236.
[7] *Laing* v. *Laing* (1862) 24 D. 1362; *Struthers* v. *Smith,* 1913 S.C. 1116.
[8] *Couper's Trs.* v. *National Bank* (1889) 16 R. 412.
[9] *Macfarlane* v. *Macfarlane's Trs.* (1897) 24 R. 574.

standum has been performed is one of fact in each case. Proof may be prout de jure. The onus of proof is on the party alleging performance.[10]

3. Proof of Payment.—The law as to proof of payment in discharge of an antecedent obligation is not entirely in accordance with the general maxim, "unumquodque eodem modo solvitur quo colligatur." When the debt arises from a written contract or when there is a written voucher for it, the general rule is that the only competent proof of payment is the writ or oath of the creditor. Parole evidence is inadmissible.[11] But it has been held to be competent to prove that the party who puts forward a voucher of a debt has no right to be in possession of it,[12] and proof of a general settlement of accounts between the parties, subsequent to the constitution of the debt in question, has been allowed.[13] Debts arising on a verbal contract, such as rent or wages on a verbal lease or engagement, allow parole proof of payment if each item does not exceed £100 Scots (£8.33); above that limit, proof must be by writ or oath.[14] Proof of payment for goods sold over the counter, where payment of the price is the immediate counterpart of the delivery of the goods, may be by parole,[15] but if delivery is delayed, although the contract was verbal, only by writ or oath.[16]

4. Presumption of Payment.—In certain cases there is a legal presumption of payment. Counsel's fees are presumed to be paid. It is conceived that no action is competent against the client, but counsel may recover from the agent fees which the latter has actually received.[17] A similar common law rule with regard to fees of physicians has been limited by statute.[18] The onus of proof that a hotel bill has not been paid after the guest has left lies on the hotel-keeper.[19]

5. Apocha Trium Annorum.—The production of receipts for three consecutive instalments of any termly payment, such as rent, feu-duty, interest or wages, raises a presumption that all prior instalments have been paid.[20] It is open to the creditor to prove, and by parole evidence, that payment has not in fact been made.[21] The presumption is not raised, and the onus of proof therefore remains with the debtor, if there is only one receipt, though for

---

[10] See *Svendborg* v. *Love & Stewart*, 1916 S.C. (H.L.) 187; *Carruthers* v. *Macgregor*, 1927 S.C. 816.

[11] *Thiem's Trs.* v. *Collie* (1899) 1 F. 764; *Robertson* v. *Thomson* (1900) 3 F. 5; *Hope Brothers* v. *Morrison*, 1960 S.C. 1; see Walkers, *Evidence*, § 127.

[12] *Bishop* v. *Bryce*, 1910 S.C. 426, distinguished in *Keanie* v. *Keanie*, 1940 S.C. 549; *Mackenzie's Exrs.* v. *Morrison's Trs.*, 1930 S.C. 830.

[13] See *Chrystal* v. *Chrystal* (1900) 2 F. 373.

[14] *Brown* v. *Mason* (1856) 19 D. 137.

[15] *M'Donald* v. *Callender* (1786) M. 12366.

[16] Bell, *Prin.*, § 565; *Young* v. *Thomson*, 1909 S.C. 529; see *Hope Brothers*, supra.

[17] *Batchelor* v. *Pattison & Mackersy* (1876) 3 R. 914.

[18] Bell, *Prin.*, § 568; Medical Act 1886 (49 & 50 Vict. c. 48), s. 6. A byelaw of a college of physicians prohibiting fellows from recovering at law expenses, charges or fees may be pleaded in bar of legal proceedings by a fellow: Medical Act 1956 (4 & 5 Eliz. II c. 76), s. 27 (2).

[19] *Barnet* v. *Colvil* (1840) 2 D. 337.

[20] Erskine, III, 4, 10; Bell, *Prin.*, § 567; Walkers, *Evidence*, § 64.

[21] *Cameron* v. *Panton's Trs.* (1891) 18 R. 728.

several instalments.[22] Nor do receipts for three instalments raise any presumption that a bill, granted for prior arrears, has been paid.[23]

6. Document of Debt in Debtor's Hands.—The maxim "chirographum apud debitorem repertum praesumitur solutum" imports that the fact that a document of debt is in the possession of the debtor raises a presumption that the debt has been paid. Parole evidence is admissible to prove the contrary.[24] It is competent to prove by parole that a receipt which is in the hands of the debtor was given without payment.[25]

7. Ascription of Payments.—Where a party owing more than one debt makes payments without ascribing them to any particular debt it is open to the creditor to ascribe them so as to diminish or extinguish any debt he pleases.[26] He cannot, however, thereby preclude the challenge of the validity of any debt.[27] Where there is a continuous account, such as that between banker and customer, the rule, usually termed the rule in *Clayton's Case*,[28] is that the earliest credit item wipes out the earliest debit item. This principle, immaterial in questions solely between the debtor and creditor, is of importance where there are parties subsidiarily liable. Thus where a cautioner is liable for a fixed period, and after that period the account is allowed to go on without any settlement, any payments subsequently made by the principal debtor, being applied, on the rule in *Clayton's* case, to wipe out the earliest debit items, will extinguish pro tanto the debt for which the cautioner is liable, even although payments are made to the principal debtor which preserve the debit balance against him.[29] The rule is not applicable to a tradesman's account,[30] nor, probably, to any account except that of banker and customer, or other parties whose relationship is substantially the same.[31] Nor can the rule be applied where two separate accounts are kept with a bank.[32]

8. Mode of Payment: Legal Tender.—A creditor, in the absence of any agreement to the contrary, is entitled to insist on payment in legal tender. Gold coins are legal tender for payment of any amount. Coins of cupro-nickel or silver of denominations of more than 10 new pence, are legal tender for payment of any amount not exceeding 10 pounds; coins of cupro-nickel or silver of denominations of not more than 10 new pence for payment of any

---

[22] Dickson, *Evidence*, § 177.
[23] *Patrick* v. *Watt* (1859) 21 D. 637.
[24] Bell, *Prin.*, § 566; Walkers, *Evidence*, § 66.
[25] *Henry* v. *Miller* (1884) 11 R. 713.
[26] Bell, *Prin.*, § 563. A mere uncommunicated intention of the debtor will not suffice: *Leeson* v. *Leeson* [1936] 2 K.B. 156.
[27] *Dougall* v. *Lornie* (1899) 1 F. 1187.
[28] *Devaynes* v. *Noble (Clayton's Case)* (1816) 1 Merivale 529, 572.
[29] *Royal Bank* v. *Christie* (1841) 2 Robinson 118; *Cuthill* v. *Strachan* (1894) 21 R. 549; *Deeley* v. *Lloyds Bank* [1912] A.C. 756.
[30] *Dougall* v. *Lornie* (1899) 1 F. 1187.
[31] *Cory Bros.* v. *Owners of the Mecca* [1897] A.C. 286; *Hay* v. *Torbet*, 1908 S.C. 781; *Macdonald, Fraser & Co.* v. *Cairns' Exrs.*, 1932 S.C. 699.
[32] *Bradford Old Bank* v. *Sutcliffe* [1918] 2 K.B. 833.

amount not exceeding five pounds; coins of bronze for payment of any amount not exceeding 20 new pence.[33] By the Currency and Bank Notes Act 1954[34] the Bank of England is empowered to issue bank notes of such denominations as the Treasury may approve, and all such notes of a denomination of less than five pounds are legal tender in Scotland.[35] Bank notes issued by a bank of issue in Scotland are not legal tender.[36] A cheque, if accepted, is conditional payment. The condition is resolutive, so that the debt is extinguished but revives if the cheque be dishonoured.[37] If payment is made in any unusual or unbusinesslike way any loss by theft or fraud will fall upon the debtor.[38]

9. Duty of Debtor to Tender Payment.—It is the duty of the debtor to tender payment, at the creditor's residence or place of business,[39] on the appointed date. Once the date of payment has arrived the creditor is within his rights in taking legal proceedings or using diligence without any formal demand. He must stop his proceedings or diligence on tender of payment in full and expenses, but is not bound to accept a tender of the debt without the expenses of the legal proceedings which he has taken.[40]

10. Bona Fide Payments.—Payment to a person honestly and reasonably believed to be the creditor is good, as, for instance, payment to the original creditor after he has assigned the debt but before intimation has been made. The rule holds even if payment is made before it is due.[41] But a tenant who pre-pays his rent may have to pay again to a party to whom the subjects have been sold, though not to the trustee in the landlord's bankruptcy.[42] A banker granting a deposit receipt is bound to pay according to his contract, and incurs no liability if the payee (a trustee) should embezzle the money.[43] But where a deposit receipt was paid to a person who alleged he was the depositor's brother, and presented the deposit receipt and a letter of authority, it was held, on proof that he had stolen the documents, that the bank could not rely on the payment as a discharge.[44] Payment made to the creditor's agent is good if in fact he had authority to receive it, or if he was in a line of business such as to give ostensible authority.[45] A solicitor has ostensible

---

[33] Coinage Act 1971 (c. 24), s. 2.
[34] 2 & 3 Eliz. II c. 12, s. 1 (1) and (2).
[35] As to payment of interest on gold bonds, see *Feist* v. *Société Intercommunale Belge* [1934] A.C. 161; *New Brunswick Ry.* v. *British & French Trust Corporation* [1939] A.C. 1. As to decree for payment in a foreign currency, see *Commerzbank Aktiengesellschaft* v. *Large*, 1977 S.L.T. 219.
[36] See Smith, *Short Commentary*, p. 842.
[37] *Leggat Bros.* v. *Gray*, 1908 S.C. 67; *Bolt & Nut Co. (Tipton)* v. *Rowlands Nicholls & Co.* [1964] 2 Q.B. 10.
[38] *Robb* v. *Gow* (1905) 8 F. 90; *Mitchell Henry* v. *Norwich, etc., Assurance Co.* [1918] 2 K.B. 67.
[39] *Fowler* v. *Midland Electric Corporation* [1917] 1 Ch. 656; *Haughhead Coal Co.* v. *Gallocher* (1903) 11 S.L.T. 156.
[40] *Pollock* v. *Goodwin's Trs.* (1898) 25 R. 1051.
[41] Bell, *Prin.*, § 561.
[42] *Davidson* v. *Boyd* (1868) 7 M. 77.
[43] *Dickson* v. *National Bank*, 1917 S.C. (H.L.) 50.
[44] *Wood* v. *Clydesdale Bank*, 1914 S.C. 397.
[45] *International Sponge Importers* v. *Watt*, 1911 S.C. (H.L.) 57.

authority to receive payment of a sum sued for,[46] or of the price of shares he has been employed to sell,[47] but not to receive payment of the principal sum in a bond.[48]

11. Compensation.—The right to compensate, or set off, one debt against another, with the result that each debt is pro tanto extinguished, is in Scotland referable to statute, namely, the Compensation Act 1592 (c. 143). The terms of the Act exclude compensation after decree, and it has accordingly been decided that if A allows a decree (in foro or in absence) to pass against him he must pay his debt and recover any counter-claim by separate proceedings.[49] This rule probably holds only while both parties are solvent,[50] and does not apply unless there was an opportunity of pleading compensation before the decree. So it was held to be competent to plead compensation against a claim for a sum decerned for as expenses.[51]

12. Liquid Debts.[52]—Compensation is pleadable only between liquid debts, with an exception, largely in the discretion of the Court, of cases where an illiquid debt may be rendered liquid without delay.[53] So there is no right to compensate a debt instantly payable by a future or contingent debt,[54] or by a claim of damages arising on a separate ground. The right of retention when debts arise out of the same contract, or where bankruptcy has supervened, has been already considered.[55]

Compensation must be pleaded: cross debts are not extinguished ipso facto.[56] So a debt may prescribe although, during the years of prescription, compensation might have been pleaded against it.[57] But if compensation is ultimately sustained neither debt bears interest ex lege during the period of concourse.[58]

13. Concursus Debiti et Crediti.—To admit of compensation there must be concursus debiti et crediti. The parties must be debtor and creditor not only at the same time but in the same capacity. So an executor, when sued for his private debt, could not plead compensation in respect of a debt owed to him as executor.[59] A banker who has granted a deposit receipt payable to either of two persons cannot plead compensation in respect of a debt due by one of them,[60] and the same rule holds in all cases where there are joint creditors.[61]

---

[46] *Smith* v. *North British Ry.* (1850) 12 D. 795.
[47] *Pearson* v. *Scott* (1878) 9 Ch.D. 198.
[48] *Richardson* v. *M'Geoch's Trs.* (1898) 1 F. 145.
[49] *Cunninghame* v. *Wilson,* Jan. 17, 1809, F.C.
[50] Bell, *Comm.,* II, 121.
[51] *Fowler* v. *Brown,* 1916 S.C. 597.
[52] See General Law of Obligations, Ch. III., supra, § 13.
[53] See *Ross* v. *Ross* (1895) 22 R. 461.
[54] *Paul & Thain* v. *Royal Bank* (1869) 7 M. 361.
[55] Breach of Contract, Ch. XIII., supra, § 10.
[56] Erskine, III, 4, 12; Bell, *Comm.,* II, 124; *Cowan* v. *Gowans* (1878) 5 R. 581.
[57] *Carmichael* v. *Carmichael* (1719) M. 2677.
[58] Bell, *Comm.,* II, 124.
[59] *Stuart* v. *Stuart* (1869) 7 M. 366.
[60] *Anderson* v. *North of Scotland Bank* (1901) 4 F. 49.
[61] *Burrell* v. *Burrell's Trs.,* 1916 S.C. 729.

The death of a debtor does not raise a separation of interests so as to preclude a plea of compensation against his executor. So where A died in debt to his law agent, and the latter was employed to ingather the estate, it was held that he was entitled to satisfy his claim against the deceased out of the executry funds which he had ingathered.[62] There is no concursus debiti et crediti between a debt due to a principal and a debt due by his agent.[63] But if the agency was not disclosed and the party with whom the agent dealt was not aware of it, he may plead compensation on a debt due by the agent provided that the right to compensate had accrued before he was informed of the principal's interest in the matter.[64]

14. Compensation in Partnership.—In partnership, a debtor to the firm cannot plead compensation on a debt due to him by an individual partner. A partner, sued for his private debt, cannot plead compensation on a debt due to the firm, unless the firm, while still solvent, is dissolved, when the partner becomes the creditor in a pro rata share of the debts to the firm, and to that extent may plead compensation. A partner, suing for his private debt, may be met with a plea of compensation on a debt due by the firm. A firm may plead compensation on a debt due to an individual partner. The principle underlying these rules is that a partner, so long as the firm remains undissolved, is not a creditor in debts due to the firm, whereas he is a debtor in debts due by the firm.[65]

15. Compensation in Bankruptcy.—The bankruptcy of one of the obligants so far enlarges the right of compensation that by the exercise of the right of retention compensation may be pleaded on illiquid debts due by the bankrupt.[66] In other respects, the bankruptcy of one party effects a separation of interests, which precludes concursus debiti et crediti. So the debtor to a bankrupt estate cannot plead compensation on debts which he has acquired after the bankruptcy,[67] nor on debts subsequently incurred to him by the bankrupt.[68] If, however, A is a contingent creditor of B, and the contingency is purified after B's bankruptcy, A has the right to plead compensation, as in the case where a bill, accepted by the bankrupt, was at the date of bankruptcy held by a bank, and was subsequently paid by the drawer.[69] There is no compensation between a debt due by the bankrupt and a debt subsequently incurred to the trustee. So when a liquidator adopted and carried out a contract in which the company was engaged it was held that his action for payment could not be met by a plea of compensation or retention in respect of

[62] *Mitchell* v. *Mackersy* (1905) 8 F. 198, overruling *Gray's Trs.* v. *Royal Bank* (1895) 23 R. 199.
[63] *National Bank* v. *Dickie's Tr.* (1895) 22 R. 740; *Mathews* v. *Auld & Guild* (1874) 1 R. 1224.
[64] *Wester Moffat Colliery Co.* v. *Jeffrey*, 1911 S.C. 346; *Kaltenbach* v. *Lewis* (1885) 10 A.C. 617; *Greer* v. *Downs Supply Co.* [1927] 2 K.B. 28.
[65] See *Heggie* v. *Heggie* (1858) 21 D. 31; *Mitchell* v. *Canal Basin Co.* (1869) 7 M. 480.
[66] Breach of Contract, Ch. XIII., supra, § 13.
[67] *Cauvin* v. *Robertson* (1783) M. 2581.
[68] *Meldrum's Trs.* v. *Clark* (1826) 5 S. 122.
[69] *Hannay's Tr.* v. *Armstrong Bros* (1875) 2 R. 399; affd. (1877) 4 R. (H.L.) 43.

separate claims against the company.[70] And where a landlord took over a waygoing crop from the trustee in the tenant's sequestration it was held that there was no concursus debiti between the price and a claim for arrears of rent. The one was a debt due by the bankrupt, the other a debt subsequently incurred to the trustee.[71]

16. Specific Appropriation.—Compensation cannot be pleaded if the plea is in conflict with the express or implied terms of a contract between the parties. So if money is placed in A's hands for a specific purpose, and that purpose cannot be effected, A cannot refuse to return the money on the ground that the depositor was otherwise indebted to him.[72]

17. Novation.—Where a new document of debt is accepted with the result of extinguishing all liability on the prior document, the case is said to be one of novation; when a new obligant is accepted, with the result of freeing the original debtor, the case is more strictly one of delegation. But the term novation is often used to cover both cases.[73] Either novation or delegation has the effect of releasing a cautioner for the original debt or for the original obligant.[74] But either requires the consent of the creditor, and, although that consent may in certain circumstances be implied, there is a presumption against novation. A creditor who accepts a new voucher of his debt, or a new obligant, without any express discharge of the old, is presumed to have obtained an additional voucher or guarantor for his debt rather than to have surrendered the rights which he already held,[75] and it is only in exceptional cases, or on proof of a custom of trade,[76] that the original obligant, or a cautioner for him, can successfully maintain that he had been impliedly discharged.

The typical case of pure novation is the renewal of a bill of exchange. When a new bill is accepted, and the old one given up, the inference is that all liability on the old bill is extinguished,[77] though in one very special case it was held that the renewal of a promissory note given for a loan, at a time when the original note was on the verge of prescription, did not exclude a claim for interest on the loan during the currency of the original note, in spite of the fact that that note had been given up to the debtor.[78] If the original bill or note is retained by the creditor there would seem to be no case for novation. So where the original bill was renewed for one of a smaller amount, and the balance was not paid, it was held that there was no objection to an action for that balance against a party who had signed the original bill as a cautioner.[79]

---

[70] *Asphaltic Limestone Co.* v. *Corporation of Glasgow,* 1907 S.C. 463.
[71] *Taylor's Tr.* v. *Paul* (1888) 15 R. 313; *Sutherland* v. *Urquhart* (1895) 23 R. 284.
[72] *Middlemas* v. *Gibson,* 1910 S.C. 577; *Reid* v. *Bell* (1884) 12 R. 178.
[73] Bell, *Prin.,* § 576.
[74] *Commercial Bank of Tasmania* v. *Jones* [1893] A.C. 313. The assignation of a debt, and consequent introduction of a new creditor, does not amount to novation, so as to liberate a cautioner. *Bradford Old Bank* v. *Sutcliffe* [1918] 2 K.B. 833.
[75] See opinion of Lord President Inglis, *M'Intosh* v. *Ainslie* (1872) 10 M. 304.
[76] *North* v. *Basset* [1892] 1 Q.B. 333.
[77] *Stevenson* v. *Lord Duncan,* 1805 Hume 245.
[78] *Hope Johnstone* v. *Cornwall* (1895) 22 R. 314.
[79] *Hay & Kyd* v. *Powrie* (1886) 13 R. 777.

18. Delegation.—The general presumption is also strongly against delegation. Where a creditor accepted a promissory note from his debtor's factor the liability of the debtor was in no way affected.[80] A statutory provision under which the personal obligation in a bond and disposition in security may transmit against a purchaser of the lands was construed as giving the creditor an additional obligant, not, without his express consent, as depriving him of the obligation of his original debtor.[81] Where a partner in a firm retires and the firm continues without the introduction of any new partners, the mere fact that the creditor in an outstanding debt continues to accept interest, or ultimately ranks in the bankruptcy of the firm, does not amount to delegation so as to discharge the liability of the retiring partner.[82] But in such a case delegation may be inferred from the fact that a party from whom the firm as originally constituted had ordered goods supplied them after the change, and in full knowledge of the facts, entered the new firm as his debtor in his books.[83] Where new partners are introduced the acceptance of the obligation of the firm as newly constituted, with some change in the form of the obligation (as where a bill, or deposit receipt, is renewed) will amount to delegation in a question with a partner who has retired.[84] It is laid down in England that where two companies amalgamate very clear evidence is required to prove that a creditor of one of the original companies has accepted the obligation of the amalgamation in substitution for that of his original debtors.[85]

19. Confusion.—When the same person is creditor and debtor in an obligation it may be extinguished confusione,[86] a doctrine which will not be extended to cases not covered by the prior authorities.[87] The obligation must be for the payment of money, and therefore a permanent right, such as that involved in a lease,[88] a superiority,[89] or a ground annual,[90] is not extinguishable confusione, though while the same person is debtor and creditor the annual prestations, such as rent or feu-duty, do not come into existence.

The merger of the interests of debtor and creditor may arise either by succession, when the debtor succeeds as heir to his creditor, or vice versa; or by contract, when the creditor in a bond acquires the subjects over which it is secured, under an arrangement by which the amount of the bond is deducted from the price, or where the owner of an estate acquires bonds which affect it. In such cases the confusion of interests is absolute and the debt is extinguished

---

[80] *M'Intosh* v. *Ainslie* (1872) 10 M. 304.
[81] *University of Glasgow* v. *Yuill's Tr.* (1882) 9 R. 643.
[82] *Morton's Trs.* v. *Robertson's Judicial Factor* (1892) 20 R. 72; *Smith* v. *Patrick* (1901) 3 F. (H.L.) 14; Partnership Act 1890, s. 17 (3).
[83] *Pearston* v. *Wilson* (1856) 19 D. 197.
[84] *Buchanan* v. *Somerville* (1779) M. 3402; *Bilborough* v. *Holmes* (1876) 5 Ch. D. 255.
[85] *Re Family Endowment Society* (1870) L.R. 5 Ch. 118; Halsbury (4th ed.), vol. IX., p. 403.
[86] Stair, I, 18, 9; Erskine, III, 4, 23. The English term is "merger".
[87] *Craig* v. *Mair's Trs.,* 1914 S.C. 893, per Lord President and Lord Johnston.
[88] *Lord Blantyre* v. *Dunn* (1858) 20 D. 1188.
[89] *Motherwell* v. *Manwell* (1903) 5 F. 619. As to the effect of consolidation, see *Earl of Zetland* v. *Glover Incorporation* (1870) 8 M. (H.L.) 144.
[90] *Craig* v. *Mair's Trs.,* 1914 S.C. 893.

ipso facto, and, in the case of bonds, is not kept alive by the indication of intention involved in taking an assignation instead of a discharge. If for any reason it is desired that the bond shall still subsist it must be assigned to a trustee.[91]

20. Confusion Excluded by Separation of Interests.—Confusion does not operate where there is any separation of interests, but only where the full and absolute right of the creditor and the full and absolute right of the debtor merge in one person. Thus there is a sufficient distinction between the position of a party deceased and his executor to preclude the extinction of a debt by confusio when a debtor confirms as executor to his creditor, or a creditor as executor to his debtor.[92] Bonds affecting an entailed estate are not extinguished when the creditor becomes heir in possession, because his right is a limited and not an absolute one.[93] The same rule holds when bonds are acquired by a fiar during the subsistence of a liferent.[94] Where a prior bondholder obtained, in security of a further advance, a disposition ex facie absolute of the subjects, it was held that the prior bond was not extinguished confusione[95]; and a similar decision was pronounced where, in course of the arrangements for the assignation of a prior bond, the right of creditor and debtor had temporarily been vested in the same party.[96] And no confusion takes place where a person only subsidiarily liable for the debt, such as a cautioner, acquires the right of the creditor. It may still be enforced against the principal debtor.[97]

21. Lapse of Time: End of Fixed Period.—The effect of lapse of time primarily depends upon whether the obligation or contract has been entered into for a definite period or not. When a contract is entered into for a definite period, as a general rule the lapse of that period extinguishes the obligation on either side. But this is subject, in contracts of lease, service and partnership, to the principle of tacit relocation, under which a new contract may be implied. There is no authority for extending the principle beyond these contracts.

22. Tacit Relocation: Leases.—A lease, if neither party gives due notice of his intention to end it at the expiry of its term, is continued by tacit relocation on the old terms, except in reference to duration. In that respect, if the lease was for less than a year, continuation for the same period is inferred; if for more than a year, continuation for a year.[98] The period of notice depends on

---

[91] *Codrington* v. *Johnston's Trs.* (1824) 2 Sh. App. 118; *Balfour-Melville's Trs.* v. *Gowans* (1896) 4 S.L.T. 111.
[92] *Salaman* v. *Sinclair's Tr.*, 1916 S.C. 698.
[93] *Colville's Trs.* v. *Marindin*, 1908 S.C. 911.
[94] *Fraser* v. *Carruthers* (1875) 2 R. 595.
[95] *King* v. *Johnston*, 1908 S.C. 684.
[96] *Whiteley* v. *Delaney* [1914] A.C. 132.
[97] Stair, I, 18, 9.
[98] Stair, II, 9, 23; Rankine, *Leases* (3rd ed.), p. 598; Agricultural Holdings (Scotland) Act 1949, s. 3. See especially *Douglas* v. *Cassillis & Culzean Estates*, 1944 S.C. at p. 361, where Lord Justice-Clerk Cooper points out that in tacit relocation while the contract may be new the lease is not; *Smith* v. *Grayton Estates*, 1960 S.C. 349, per Lord President Clyde at p. 354.

the nature of the subjects let.[99] The contract under tacit relocation is binding on both parties, whether the tenant continues in possession or not. Tacit relocation rests on implied contract, and is therefore excluded by an arrangement for a new lease, though not in probative form.[1] And where the landlord intimated an increase of rent, and the tenant, though refusing to pay it, did not give notice to end the lease, and in fact stayed on after the term, it was held that tacit relocation was inapplicable, and that the tenant must be taken to have assented to the landlord's terms.[2] But where a house and shop were let together, it was held that notice to quit the shop only was ineffectual, and did not exclude tacit relocation of the whole subjects.[3] The question whether, in case of joint tenancy, all the tenants must concur in giving notice in order to avoid a renewal by tacit relocation has been considered but not decided.[4] If a landlord, after giving notice to quit, takes no further steps, and allows the tenant to remain in possession, he may be held to have passed from his notice, and a new lease by tacit relocation may be inferred.[5] If a tenant, after giving notice, refuses to leave, he is in the position of an intruder without a title, and liable for violent profits, i.e., for the largest sum for which the subjects could be let.[6]

The inference of a new lease by tacit relocation has been held to be based on universal understanding, and is therefore probably not applicable to seasonal lets of grass parks, furnished houses, shootings or fishings. In these cases the obligations on either side terminate without notice.[7] And a party who occupies a house as part of his remuneration on a contract of service must remove when his contract comes to an end.[8]

23. Service.—In certain contracts of service the law of tacit relocation applies, and if neither party gives notice a reasonable time before the expiry of the term a new contract is inferred either for the original period, or, at the longest, for a year, on the same terms. "The law of tacit relocation has reference only to specific classes of servants, agricultural, domestic, and the like."[9] So it was held not to be applicable to a contract between dressmakers and the manager of their fur department.[10] It does not apply to contracts of service on exceptional terms, such as an arrangement, made during a strike, under which a workman, usually engaged and paid by the week, was guaranteed employment for a year.[11] Nor does it apply to part-time

---

[99] See Leases, Ch. XXXIII, infra, § 20.
[1] *Buchanan* v. *Harris & Sheldon* (1900) 2 F. 935.
[2] *McFarlane* v. *Mitchell* (1900) 2 F. 901.
[3] *Gates* v. *Blair*, 1923 S.C. 430.
[4] *Graham* v. *Stirling*, 1922 S.C. 90.
[5] *Taylor* v. *Earl of Moray* (1892) 19 R. 399.
[6] *Tod* v. *Fraser* (1889) 17 R. 226. See Landownership, Ch. XXXIX, infra, § 12.
[7] *Macharg*, (1805) M. Removing App. 4.
[8] *Dunbar's Trs.* v. *Bruce* (1900) 3 F. 137; *Sinclair* v. *Tod*, 1907 S.C. 1038; *Cairns* v. *Innes*, 1942 S.C. 164.
[9] Per Lord Justice-Clerk Moncreiff in *Lennox* v. *Allan* (1880) 8 R. 38, approved by Lord President Dunedin in *Stanley* v. *Hanway* (1911) 48 S.L.R. 757. But see *Stevenson* v. *N.B. Ry.* (1905) 7 F. 1106.
[10] *Stanley* v. *Hanway*, supra.
[11] *Lennox* v. *Allan*, supra.

employments, nor, probably, to any employment for a period exceeding a year.[12]

24. Partnership.—In partnership for a fixed period no notice is required to terminate the contract at the expiry of the term.[13] But if the partnership business is continued a partnership at will is inferred, in which the rights and duties of the partners continue as they were, in so far as is consistent with a partnership at will.[14]

25. Delay in Enforcement.—In the case of obligations which have no definite period the effect of lapse of time depends upon whether the obligation in question was definitely constituted or whether it requires to be established by proof. In the former case the mere fact that the creditor in the obligation has not chosen to enforce it for any period short of the negative prescription[15] has no legal effect. "I am not aware of anything short of prescription or express discharge which can cut off a liquid debt standing on a written contract. Delay in making a claim may be fatal if the claim depends on the ascertainment of facts, and the opposite party's case on the facts is prejudiced by the delay."[16] So a bond has been held to be enforceable although no action had been taken upon it until one day before the expiry of the years of prescription.[17]

26. Mora.—In the case of obligations which require to be constituted by proof the plea of mora and taciturnity may be put forward,[18] but delay per se is no bar to an action.[19] If the obligation is in origin contractual, e.g., a claim for damages for breach of contract, or a demand for payment for work done without any definite agreement,[20] the law would appear to be, as in the case of the reduction of a contract, that mere lapse of time short of the prescriptive period does not extinguish the obligation, but increases the onus of proof which lies upon the party asserting the claim.[21] The same rule applies to belated claims on a trust or executry estate.[22] Excessive delay in intimating a claim for reparation or in instituting an action of reparation may appear from the pleadings to have affected the quantity or quality of the evidence available to such an extent as to render proof preferable to jury trial as the means of ascertaining the truth.[23] Unexplained delay may result in a pursuer being ordained to find caution for expenses.[24]

[12] *Brenan* v. *Campbell's Trs.* (1898) 25 R. 423.
[13] *Wallace* v. *Wallace's Trs.* (1906) 8 F. 558; Partnership Act 1890, s. 27.
[14] Partnership Act 1890, s. 27. See *M'Gowan* v. *Henderson,* 1914 S.C. 839.
[15] As to prescription, see infra, Ch. XVI.
[16] Per Lord Stormonth-Darling, *Alexander's Trs.* v. *Muir* (1903) 5 F. 406.
[17] *Graham* v. *Veitch* (1823) 2 S. 594; *Cunninghame* v. *Boswell* (1868) 6 M. 890.
[18] See Rankine, *Personal Bar,* p. 117.
[19] See Maclaren, *Court of Session Practice,* p. 403; also *Halley* v. *Watt,* 1956 S.C. 370.
[20] *Mackison* v. *Burgh of Dundee,* 1910 S.C. (H.L.) 27.
[21] *Bain* v. *Assets Co.* (1905) 7 F. (H.L.) 104; opinion of Lord President Dunedin in *Bishop* v. *Bryce,* 1910 S.C. 426; *M'Kenzie's Exx.* v. *Morrison's Trs.,* 1930 S.C. 830. And see Agreements Void or Voidable, Ch. V., supra, § 6.
[22] *Robson* v. *Bywater* (1870) 8 M. 757; *Miller's Exx.* v. *Miller's Trs.,* 1922 S.C. 150.
[23] See cases cited in Walker on *Delict,* vol. I., pp. 441-2; also *Conetta* v. *Central S.M.T. Co. Ltd.,* 1966 S.L.T. 302. As to limitation of actions, see Reparation, Ch. XXXIV, infra, § 33.
[24] *G.* v. *H.* (1899) 1 F. 701.

27. Acquiescence.—The plea of mora, taciturnity and acquiescence is a plea to the merits.[25] It applies to the case where the defender maintains that some act of his, involving an invasion of the pursuer's rights, unjustifiable and not easily remediable, was done with the knowledge of and without objection from the pursuer, and infers that the latter is barred from now insisting on the right invaded.[26] The vagueness of the plea makes it difficult to summarise the cases in which it is applicable.[27] It necessarily imports knowledge by the pursuer of the defender's act, and also power to intervene. So the plea of acquiescence cannot be sustained merely because the pursuer did not intervene while the defender was incurring expenditure on work which he was entitled to carry out, as, for example, alterations on a mill with a view to taking and using an increased quantity of water from a river, even although it may have been obvious that the work and expenditure would be useless unless followed by the aggression of which the pursuer complains.[28] Acquiescence is not a method by which the title to heritable property can be altered, and therefore if A builds on B's land the fact that B was aware of his proceedings and took no objection does not operate as a conveyance of the land to A.[29] But it may bar B's right to insist on the removal of the building in a case where A acted in good faith and the invasion was due to a mistake as to the boundary between his own land and that of B.[30] And acquiescence in operations involving considerable expenditure may bar the right to object to such acts as the unjustifiable withdrawal of water from a river,[31] or the heightening of a building in contravention of a servitude non altius tollendi.[32] Where the same building restrictions are imposed in all feu contracts in a particular street or locality, and a number of the feuars have been allowed to disregard them without objection, with the result that the character of the locality has changed, the superior may be barred from enforcing the restrictions on the remaining feuars.[33] In such circumstances the superior is held to have lost his interest to enforce the restrictions.[34] Non-intervention by the superior does not necessarily bar action by a neighbouring feuar.[35] The bar raised by acquiescence is, except in special circumstances, personal to the person who acquiesced and his heirs, and will not bar a singular successor in the title.[36] Apart from cases of building restrictions, if the relations of the parties are regulated by a written contract the fact that one party has been allowed to

[25] See Maclaren, cit. supra.
[26] The distinction between failure to intervene while an act is in progress and failure to take timely objection after it has been done is drawn in De Bussche v. Alt (1877) 8 Ch. D. 286.
[27] See Rankine, Personal Bar, p. 54.
[28] Earl of Kintore v. Pirie (1903) 5 F. 818, affd. (on other grounds) 8 F. (H.L.) 16.
[29] Nicol v. Hope (1663) M. 5627; Melville v. Douglas' Trs. (1830) 8 S. 841.
[30] Duke of Buccleuch v. Magistrates of Edinburgh (1865) 3 M. 528; Wilson v. Pottinger, 1908 S.C. 580.
[31] Cowan v. Lord Kinnaird (1865) 4 M. 236; Bicket v. Morris (1866) 4 M. (H.L.) 44, opinion of Lord Chelmsford.
[32] Muirhead v. Glasgow Highland Society (1864) 2 M. 420; Grahame v. Magistrates of Kirkcaldy (1882) 9 R. (H.L.) 91.
[33] Campbell v. Clydesdale Bank (1868) 6 M. 943.
[34] Howard de Walden Estates v. Bowmaker, 1965 S.C. 163; and see Gloag, Contract (2nd ed.), p. 252; Title to Sue, Ch. X, supra, § 7.
[35] Mactaggart v. Roemmele, 1907 S.C. 1318.
[36] Brown v. Baty, 1957 S.C. 351.

disregard its terms, to the knowledge of and without objection from the other, though it may bar an action of damages for what has been done in the past, will not infer any licence for the future.[37] To amount to such a licence—in effect, to alter the terms of the contract—an agreement for such alteration, though it may be merely verbal, must be proved.[38] In a case where an employee had regularly accepted his salary and given unqualified receipts he was held to have acquiesced in payment of that salary, and he was not allowed to prove, in support of his contention that he was entitled to a higher salary, that he had frequently protested against the amounts paid.[39] A creditor may be held to have acceded to a private trust deed, and therefore to be barred from using independent diligence, if he take no objection to proceedings following on it which are being done with his knowledge[40]; and a son, or the trustee in his sequestration, may be barred from claiming legitim by acquiescing in family arrangements for carrying out the provisions of his father's will.[41]

28. Outbreak of War.[42]—The general rule is that the outbreak of war between this country and another puts an end to all executory contracts which for their further performance require commercial intercourse between a British subject and an enemy alien.[43] The rule rests on the principle that it is contrary to public policy that a relationship should continue which may strengthen the enemy or facilitate communication with him. But the principle is not carried to its logical conclusion and there is no general rule that a state of war avoids all contracts between subjects and alien enemies.[44] A debt due to an enemy alien incurred before the declaration of war (including a debt arising from a contract which is itself abrogated) is not extinguished and at common law may be recovered after the war,[45] and property belonging to an enemy alien is not confiscated, though the existence of these rights may be an indirect source of strength to the enemy. But by statute enemy property, including debts, vests in the Custodian of Enemy Property and is dealt with by him on the restoration of peace.[46] In certain rare cases[47] such a contract has been held to have survived the outbreak of war, e.g., a lease,[48] a power of attorney[49] and a policy of life assurance.[50]

[37] *Carron Co.* v. *Henderson's Trs.* (1896) 23 R. 1042.
[38] *Bargaddie Coal Co.* v. *Wark* (1859) 3 Macq. 467; *Kirkpatrick* v. *Allanshaw Coal Co.* (1880) 8 R. 327. And see Rules of Evidence, Ch. XII, supra, § 21.
[39] *Davies* v. *City of Glasgow Friendly Society*, 1935 S.C. 224; *Eunson* v. *Johnson & Greig*, 1940 S.C. 49.
[40] *Marianski* v. *Wiseman* (1871) 9 M. 673.
[41] *Bell's Tr.* v. *Bell's Tr.* 1907 S.C. 872.
[42] See McNair and Watts, *Legal Effects of War* (4th ed., 1966).
[43] As to meaning of "enemy alien" see Capacity to Contract, Ch. VI, supra, § 6.
[44] See opinion of Lord Dunedin in *Ertel Bieber & Co.* v. *Rio Tinto Co. Ltd.* [1918] A.C. 260, at pp. 267-9.
[45] *Ertel Bieber & Co.*, supra; *Schering, Ltd.* v. *Stockholms Enskilda Bank Aktiebolag* [1946] A.C. 219, at p. 241; *Arab Bank* v. *Barclay's Bank* [1954] A.C. 495.
[46] Trading with the Enemy Act 1939, as amended by the Emergency Laws (Miscellaneous Provisions) Act 1953 and the Foreign Compensation Act 1969, s. 1.
[47] McNair and Watts, op. cit., at p. 134.
[48] *Halsey* v. *Lowenfeld* [1916] 2 K.B. 707, a lease now being regarded as "a concomitant of a right of property," Lord Dunedin's phrase in *Ertel Bieber*, supra, at p. 269.
[49] *Tingley* v. *Müller* [1917] 2 Ch. 144, where the circumstances were very special.
[50] *Seligman* v. *Eagle Insurance Co.* [1917] 1 Ch. 519, a doubtful decision.

CHAPTER XVI

PRESCRIPTION

Millar, *Prescription* (1893); Napier, *Prescription* (1854); Walker, *The Law of Prescription and Limitation of Actions in Scotland* (2nd ed., 1978).

1. Prescription and Limitation.—This chapter is concerned only with prescription, i.e. the establishment or definition of a right or title, or the extinction of a right or obligation, through lapse of time. Limitation does not affect the subsistence of rights or obligations, but merely renders them unenforceable by Court action after a certain time.[1]

2. Common Law and the 1973 Act.—It is doubtful whether lapse of time can at common law fortify a right or extinguish an obligation. The effect of mere delay (mora) has already been considered.[2] It would appear that if a particular exaction has been submitted to for forty years it becomes exigible at common law, though the creditor may be unable to explain the basis of his claim.[3] Most of the law relating to prescription is statutory. The Prescription and Limitation (Scotland) Act 1973[4] repeals much previous legislation and in Part I[5] enacts a comprehensive new scheme of prescription, consisting of the positive prescription, the long negative prescription and the quinquennial prescription.

3. Positive Prescription.—Positive prescription is the effect of continued possession in establishing and defining (a) title to interests in land, and (b) positive servitudes[6] and public rights of way. "Land" includes heritable property of any description, including buildings and minerals.[7] An "interest in land" is not defined, but it does not include a servitude.[7] The title to an interest in land is often, although not invariably, recorded in the General Register of Sasines.[8] The dominium directum of a superior, the dominium utile of a vassal, a liferent, a lease, and a heritable security are probably all interests in land.

4. Period.—(a) 10 years: Where possession of an interest in land is founded upon a recorded title, the period of the positive prescription is ten

---

[1] Limitation is dealt with in Reparation, Ch. XXXIV, infra, § 33. Where a right or obligation is affected by limitation rather than by prescription, alternative methods of enforcement such as security or lien, remain open to the creditor. Furthermore if payment has been made, a condictio indebiti is impossible.
[2] Extinction of Obligations, Ch. XV, supra, § 26.
[3] *Kirk Session of South Leith* v. *Scott* (1832) 11 S. 75; *Mann* v. *Brodie* (1885) 12 R. (H.L.) 52, at p. 57.
[4] (c. 52). All subsequent statutory references are to the 1973 Act, unless otherwise indicated.
[5] ss. 1-16. Part I came into force on 25th July 1976: s. 25 (2) (b).
[6] Negative servitudes can only be acquired by express grant: *Inglis* v. *Clark* (1901) 4 F. 288.
[7] s. 15 (1).
[8] See, e.g., s. 1 (2); s. 2.

years.[9] If the foundation writ is a decree of adjudication for debt, the prescriptive period does not begin to run until after the expiry of a ten-year period known as "the legal."[10]

(b) 20 years: In certain less common cases the period of the positive prescription is twenty years. Possession for twenty years is required in order to establish or define a title to an interest in foreshores and salmon fishings in any question with the Crown.[11] A period of twenty years is also necessary in certain special cases where the foundation writ does not require to be, and has not in fact been, recorded. Thus where prescriptive possession is founded upon an unrecorded lease or sub-lease or upon an unrecorded title to an interest in allodial lands,[12] or where prescriptive possession is relied upon in any other case where by virtue of pre-1973 law the foundation writ need not be recorded, a period of twenty years is required.[13] Finally, a period of twenty years is required where prescription is relied upon as establishing or fortifying a positive servitude[14] or public right of way.[15]

5. Requisites: Interests in Land.—If an interest in particular land has been possessed by any person[16] for a continuous period of ten years openly, peaceably and without any judicial interruption, and if the possession was founded on and followed the recording in the General Register of Sasines of a deed[17] which is sufficient in respect of its terms to constitute in favour of that person a title to that interest in the particular land,[18] the validity of that title is rendered unchallengeable except on the ground that the deed is ex facie invalid or was forged.[19]

6. Recorded Deed.—The deed forming the basis of prescription must be ex facie valid. Intrinsic defects, such as the lack of the proper statutory solemnities of execution, are struck at, but not extrinsic defects such as fraud

---

[9] s. 1 (1). The period of the positive prescription was originally 40 years: Prescription Act 1617 (c. 12). It was reduced (with the exception of servitudes, public rights of way and other public rights) to 20 years by the Conveyancing (Scotland) Act 1874, s. 34, as restated by the Conveyancing (Scotland) Act 1924, s. 16. It was further reduced (with the exception of servitudes, public rights of way, other public rights; and foreshores and salmon fishings in any question with the Crown) to 10 years by the Conveyancing and Feudal Reform (Scotland) Act 1970, s. 8.

[10] s. 1 (3). The debtor can redeem his land during the legal. He may also redeem his land after the expiry of the legal unless the adjudger obtains a decree of declarator of expiry of the legal without payment.

[11] s. 1 (4). 10 years suffices where a claim is made against someone other than the Crown.

[12] Allodial lands are held of no superior: for example, the Crown's paramount superiority; and the Crown's own property: Erskine, II.3.8. Many allodial titles are unrecorded.

[13] ss. 2, 15 (1). See for example, *Wallace* v. *University of St. Andrews* (1904) 6 F. 1093.

[14] s. 3 (1), (2).

[15] s. 3 (3).

[16] Or by any person and his successors: s. 1 (1) (*a*).

[17] "Deed" includes a judicial decree, and any instrument of sasine, notarial instrument or notice of title which narrates or declares that a person has a title to an interest in land: s. 5 (1).

[18] Or in land of a description habile to include the particular land: s. 1 (1) (*b*). See, e.g., *Lock* v. *Taylor & Anor.*, 1976 S.L.T. 238.

[19] s. 1 (1).

or duress.[20] Where a deed has been at any time ex facie invalid by reason of an informality of execution within the meaning of s. 39 of the Conveyancing (Scotland) Act 1874 and the appropriate Court has subsequently declared that it was subscribed by the granter or maker and the witnesses, the deed shall be deemed not to be ex facie invalid by reason of any such informality of execution[21]. The foundation deed must also be recorded in the General Register of Sasines,[22] except, as has been indicated, in certain special cases,[23] and in such cases possession for twenty years is required.[24]

It is no objection to the plea of prescription that the title proceeds from a party who had no title to the lands in question or no right to dispose of them.[25] This is indeed the very objection which it is the object of prescription to exclude: good titles stand in no need of prescription.[26] Nor is bona fides necessary: the plea of prescription may be taken by a party who has been in possession in the knowledge that his title was defective.[27]

7. Possession.—Possession is a question of fact, and may be actual or civil, through the actual possession of tenants. Possession must be continuous, and must be nec vi nec clam, nec precario, so that possession by force, by stealth, or by leave rather than as a matter of right will not suffice. Possession must be referable to the title, and a person in possession under some subordinate right (e.g. a long lease) cannot by obtaining an ex facie valid title from some party other than his landlord, and continuing to possess for the prescriptive period, maintain that his right is one of property.[28] Possession by an institute[29] under a deed which satisfies the statutory requirements, may be appealed to by any substitute[29] as excluding any extrinsic objection to the right which the deed confers upon him.[30] The requisite possession may fortify a title although the adverse right was a grant by the possessor himself, or his predecessor in title.[31]

8. Requisites: Servitudes and Public Rights of Way.—Unlike an interest in land, a positive servitude over land may be constituted or its existence proved by prescription without the necessity of a foundation deed, recorded or otherwise. Mere possession of the servitude by any person also in possession[32] of the dominant tenement for a continuous period of twenty years openly,

---

[20] cf. Bell, *Prin.*, § 610; *Cooper Scott* v. *Gill Scott*, 1924 S.C. 309; *Abbey* v. *Atholl Properties*, 1936 S.N. 97.
[21] s. 5 (2).
[22] s. 1 (1) (b); s. 15 (1).
[23] Viz., the interest in land of the lessee under a lease or sub-lease; any interest in allodial land; any other interest in land the title to which could in terms of pre-1973 law be established without the necessity of recording the foundation writ: s. 2. cf. § 4, supra.
[24] s. 2 (1) (a). If the deed has in fact been recorded, 10 years' possession suffices: s. 2 (3).
[25] Erskine, III. 7.4; *Fraser* v. *Lord Lovat* (1898) 25 R. 603.
[26] *Cooper Scott* v. *Gill Scott*, 1924 S.C. 309 at pp. 315 and 326.
[27] *Duke of Buccleuch* v. *Cunynghame* (1826) 5 S. 57; contrary to Bell, *Prin.*, § 2004.
[28] *Duke of Argyll* v. *Campbell*, 1912 S.C. 458.
[29] See Testate Succession. Ch. XLIII, infra § 20.
[30] *Cooper Scott* v. *Gill Scott*, 1924 S.C. 309.
[31] *Wallace* v. *University of St. Andrews* (1904) 6 F. 1093.
[32] s. 3. (4) The 1973 Act dispenses with the need for infeftment in the dominant tenement by the party claiming the servitude.

peaceably and without judicial interruption will render unchallengeable the existence of the servitude as so possessed.[33] Where a servitude is thus constituted, the extent of the possession affords the measure of the right acquired: tantum praescriptum quantum possessum.[34] However if there be a deed[35] sufficient in respect of its terms, whether expressly or by implication, to constitute the servitude, the deed itself is the measure of the right[36] although where its terms are unclear they may be explained or interpreted by the prescriptive possession. The deed need not be recorded.[37] If the deed is followed by the requisite possession, the validity of the servitude as so constituted is unchallengeable except on the ground that the deed is ex facie invalid or was forged.[37]

The existence of a public right of way becomes unchallengeable where it has been possessed by the public for a continuous period of twenty years openly, peaceably, and without any judicial interruption.[38] Again the extent of the possession affords the measure of the right.

Servitudes and public rights of way are dealt with in greater detail in the chapter on Landownership.[39]

9. Computation of Period.—The Act provides certain rules for computation.[40] Where the prescriptive period commences at a time other than at the beginning of the day, the period is deemed to have commenced at the beginning of the next following day.[41] If the prescriptive period ends on a holiday (as defined[42]) the period is extended to include the next succeeding day which is not a holiday.[43] Any time during which any person against whom prescription is pled was under legal disability[44] is to be reckoned as if the person were free from that disability.[45] In general, regard is to be had to the principles formerly applicable in computing the prescriptive periods for the purposes of the Prescription Act 1617.[46]

Thus positive prescriptions will in most cases run from the midnight following upon the recording of the deed,[47] or from the midnight following

---

[33] s. 3 (2).
[34] s. 3 (2) and cf. *Kerr* v. *Brown*, 1939 S.C. 140.
[35] See note 17, supra.
[36] s.3 (1).
[37] s. 3 (1) (b). cf. Bell, *Prin.*, § 994; *Cowan* v. *Stewart* (1872) 10 M. 735.
[38] s. 3 (3).
[39] Ch. XXXIX, infra.
[40] s. 14.
[41] s. 14 (1) (c).
[42] s. 14 (2). "Holiday" means a Saturday, a Sunday, and a Scottish bank holiday.
[43] s. 14 (1) (d).
[44] Legal disability is defined in s. 15 (1) as meaning legal disability by reason of nonage or unsoundness of mind.
[45] s. 14 (1) (b). It is not clear to what extent the 1973 Act affects the equitable common law plea of non valens agere cum effectu. There may be grounds other than nonage or unsoundness of mind which could form the basis of the plea: cf. *Campbell's Trs* v. *Campbell's Trs.*, 1950 S.C. 48, per Lord President Cooper at p. 57. However it has been said that the plea should not be extended beyond the decided cases: *Pettigrew* v. *Harton*, 1956 S.C. 67, per Lord Justice-Clerk Thomson at p. 73.
[46] s. 14 (1) (c).
[47] s. 1 (1); s. 14 (1) (c); and cf. *Simpson* v. *Marshall* (1900) 2 F. 447.

upon possession if possession is subsequent to recording or if recording is unnecessary.

10. Effect.—The positive prescription excludes all inquiry into the previous titles and rights to the lands.[48] It may also define the extent of an interest in land, positive servitude or public right of way either where there is no foundation writ or where the extent of the right is not precisely set forth in the title.[49]

11. Interruption.—Only the interruption of possession or "judicial" interruption will stop the running of the positive prescription.[50] Judicial interruption is defined[51] as the making in appropriate proceedings [52] by any person having a proper interest to do so of a claim which challenges the possession in question. The date of interruption is normally the date when the claim was made.[53] In arbitration proceedings where the nature of the claim has been stated in a preliminary notice the date of interruption is the date on which the preliminary notice is served by one party on the other requiring him to appoint an arbiter or to agree to the appointment of an arbiter or to submit the dispute to the arbiter previously designated.[54] Interruption may take place on the last day of the prescriptive period.[55] After interruption the prescriptive period starts to run afresh.

12. Negative Prescription: Long and Quinquennial.—While lapse of time in the positive prescription has the effect of establishing or defining a right or title to heritable property, lapse of time in the negative prescription extinguishes rights and obligations relating to both heritable and moveable property. The creditor is deemed by his non-enforcement thereof to have abandoned his claim.[56]

Before the coming into force [57] of Part I of the Prescription and Limitation (Scotland) Act 1973 there were several negative prescriptions of differing periods which fell into two groups: (a) prescriptions which extinguished rights and obligations after certain periods of time;[58] and (b) prescriptions which did not extinguish rights and obligations but which merely affected the onus and

---

[48] s. 1 (1); and cf. *Fraser* v. *Lord Lovat* (1898) 25 R. 603.
[49] See, e.g., s. 3 (3), (4), and the long title to the Act. Cf. *Lord Advocate* v. *Cathcart* (1871) 9 M. 744; *Auld* v. *Hay* (1880) 7 R. 663, per Lord President Inglis at p. 681.
[50] s. 1 (1).
[51] s. 4.
[52] Appropriate proceedings are any proceedings in a Court of competent jurisdiction and any arbitration proceedings provided that the arbitration award would be enforceable in Scotland: s. 4 (2). The definition does not include proceedings initiated in the Court of Session by a summons which is not subsequently called: s. 4 (2) (*a*).
[53] s. 4 (3) (*b*).
[54] s. 4 (3) (*a*) and s. 4 (4).
[55] *Simpson* v. *Marshall* (1900) 2 F. 447.
[56] *Macdonald* v. *North of Scotland Bank*, 1942 S.C. 369, per Lord Justice-Clerk Cooper at p. 373.
[57] See note 5, supra.
[58] The septennial prescription of cautionary obligations (Cautioners Act 1695 (c. 7)); the long negative prescription (Prescription Acts 1469 (c. 4); 1474 (c. 9); 1617 (c. 12)), although *quaere* whether the latter prescription was truly extinctive: see *Stirling's Trs.* v. *Legal and General Assurance Society*, 1957 S.L.T. 73; Anton, *Private International Law*, p. 225.

method of proof.[59] Part I and Schedule 5 of the 1973 Act abolished these prescriptions and replaced them with two extinctive prescriptions, one of five years (the quinquennial) and one of twenty years (the long). It is impossible to contract out of the statutory provisions relating to negative prescription.[60]

13. Long Negative Prescription (Twenty Years).—If an obligation[61] becomes enforceable and thereafter subsists for a continuous period of twenty years[62] without any relevant claim being made in relation to the obligation and without the subsistence of the obligation being relevantly acknowledged, then as from the expiration of that period the obligation is extinguished.[63] Similarly if a right[64] relating to property (heritable or moveable) becomes exercisable or enforceable and thereafter subsists for a continuous period of twenty years without being exercised or enforced, and without any relevant claim being made in relation to the right, then as from the expiration of that period the right is extinguished.[65]

14. To what Rights and Obligations Applicable.—The long negative prescription applies to all rights and obligations which have become enforceable including those obligations affected by the quinquennial prescription[66] but excluding those rights and obligations designated as imprescriptible.[67] In pre-1973 law the long negative prescription has been held to apply to all ordinary debts;[68] reparation claims;[69] rights to land if merely personal;[70] the right to object to the use of property as a nuisance;[71] the right to reduce a contract on any extrinsic ground such as fraud;[72] the right to

---

[59] The triennial prescription (Prescription Act 1579 (c. 21)); the quinquennial prescription (Prescription Acts 1669 (c. 14) and 1685 (c. 14)); the sexennial prescription (Bills of Exchange (Scotland) Act 1772 (c. 72)); and the vicennial prescription of holograph writings (Prescription Act 1669 (c. 14)).

[60] s. 13.

[61] Any reference to an obligation includes a reference to the right correlative thereto: s. 15 (2).

[62] The period of the long negative prescription was originally 40 years: Prescription Acts 1469 (c. 4); 1474 (c. 9); 1617 (c. 12). It was reduced (with the exception of servitudes, public rights of way and other public rights) to 20 years by the Conveyancing (Scotland) Act 1924, s. 17, as amended by the Conveyancing Amendment (Scotland) Act 1938, s. 4.

[63] s. 7 (1).

[64] Any reference to a right includes a reference to the obligation (if any) correlative thereto: s. 15 (2).

[65] s. 8. This section applies to any right relating to property (heritable or moveable) not being a right designated as imprescriptible (see § 15, infra) nor a right falling within ss. 6 or 7 as being a right correlative to an obligation to which either of those sections applies: s. 8 (2). It is thought that s. 8 was necessary, despite s. 7 and the provision for correlative rights in s. 15 (2), for the reason that while every obligation must have a correlative right, the correlative of a right need not be an obligation. For example, a person may have a right to raise an action of reduction (cf. *Paul* v. *Reid,* 8 February 1814, F.C.; *Pettigrew* v. *Harton,* 1956 S.C. 67) but it would seem that no corresponding obligation (as distinct from, say, a liability to be disadvantaged) can arise unless and until decree of reduction is pronounced.

[66] s. 7 (2). Because of the special rules applying to the quinquennial prescription (see § 25, infra) it is possible that an enforceable obligation might subsist for twenty years without being extinguished by the quinquennial prescription. Hence the need for s. 7 (2).

[67] See § 15, infra.

[68] Bell, *Prin.,* § 608.

[69] *Cooke* v. *Falconer* (1850) 13 D. 157; but see §§ 28 et seq., infra.

[70] *Paterson* v. *Wilson* (1859) 21 D. 322; *Pettigrew* v. *Harton,* 1956 S.C. 67. Real rights of ownership in land are imprescriptible: Sched. 3, para. (*a*). See § 15, infra.

[71] *Harvie* v. *Robertson* (1903) 5 F. 338.

[72] *Cubbison* v. *Hyslop* (1837) 16 S. 112, at p. 119.

recover things which have been lost or lent;[73] the right of a bank customer to recover a sum placed on current account with the bank;[74] and a right of servitude.[75]

15. Imprescriptible Rights and Obligations: Schedule 3.—The rights and obligations specified in Schedule 3 can never prescribe.[76] These are, any real right of ownership in land; the right in land of the lessee under a recorded lease; any right to recover property extra commercium; the obligation of a trustee[77] to account, make reparation in respect of any fraudulent breach of trust, or make trust property furthcoming; any obligation of a mala fide recipient of trust property to make it furthcoming; any right to recover stolen property from the thief or anyone privy to the theft; any right to be served as heir to an ancestor or to take any steps necessary for making up or completing title to any interest in land; and any right exercisable as a res merae facultatis, i.e. a right which the creditor may assert or not as he pleases, without losing the right by failure to assert it for the prescriptive period.[78]

Any right to challenge a deed on the ground that it is ex facie invalid or was forged is also imprescriptible.[79]

16. Computation of Period.—The rules set out in s. 14 apply equally to the long negative as they do to the positive prescription.[80] Thus the prescriptive period runs from the midnight after an obligation has become enforceable[81] (or a right exercisable or enforceable[82]). In the case of a debt, prescription runs from the midnight following upon the date when the debt became payable;[83] in the case of legitim and jus relictae, as a general rule, from the midnight following upon the date of death;[84] in the case of a positive servitude, from the midnight following upon the date of the last exercise of the servitude.

17. Effect.—The long negative prescription extinguishes rights and obligations which have not been enforced. When the prescriptive period

---

[73] *Kirk Session of Aberscherder* v. *Kirk Session of Gemrie* (1633) M. 10972.
[74] *Macdonald* v. *North of Scotland Bank*, 1942 S.C. 369.
[75] *Bell*, Prin., § 999; and see s. 3 (5). See too Landownership, Ch. XXXIX, infra, § 30. Prior to the 1973 Act the period of the long negative prescription in relation to servitudes and public rights of way was 40 years. Cf. note 62, supra.
[76] ss. 7 (2), 8 (2).
[77] "Trustee" is widely defined in s. 15 (1) and includes not only executors, tutors, curators, and judicial factors, but anyone who could be said to be holding property in a fiduciary capacity for another.
[78] Rights exercisable as res merae facultatis include the right to exercise the ordinary uses of property: *Inglis* v. *Clark* (1901) 4 F. 288; a contractual right to open a door onto a common stair: *Gellatly* v. *Arrol* (1863) 1 M. 592; and the right of a superior to exact feuduties, although individual payments will be affected by the quinquennial prescription: see § 24, infra, and cf. *Duke of Buccleuch* v. *Officers of State* (1770) M. 10751. A right of servitude is not exercisable as a res merae facultatis and may therefore prescribe: see § 14, supra.
[79] s. 12 (2).
[80] s. 14. See § 9, supra.
[81] s. 7 (1); s. 14 (1) (c).
[82] s. 8 (1); s. 14 (1) (c).
[83] cf. Erskine, III, 7, 36.
[84] cf. *Sanderson* v. *Lockhart-Mure*, 1946 S.C. 298, *Campbell's Trs.* v. *Campbell's Trs.*, 1950 S.C. 48; but see *Mill's Trs.* v. *Mill's Exrs.*, 1965 S.C. 384.

expires, the right or obligation is gone. So, in the case of a debt, it is of no consequence that the debtor may admit that he never paid, and a reference to his oath is incompetent.[85]

18. Interruption: Obligations: Section 7.—To interrupt the running of the long negative prescription, a relevant claim in relation to the obligation must be made,[86] or the subsistence of the obligation must be relevantly acknowledged.[86] However in the case of an obligation arising from a bill of exchange or a promissory note, only a relevant claim will suffice to interrupt prescription.[87] The prescriptive period starts anew from the date of the interruption.

19. Relevant Claim: Obligations.—A relevant claim in relation to s. 7 is defined in s. 9 (1) as a claim made by or on behalf of the creditor for implement or part-implement of the obligation, being a claim made in appropriate proceedings[88] or by the procedure mentioned in s. 105 of the Bankruptcy (Scotland) Act 1913 including that section as applied by s. 318 of the Companies Act 1948.[89] Prior to the 1973 Act it was held that a summons, although not in proper form and therefore incompetent, could nevertheless interrupt prescription.[90]

Where a claim is made in an arbitration, and the nature of the claim has been stated in a preliminary notice, the date of interruption is the date on which the preliminary notice is served.[91] If diligence is executed against a debtor in an attempt to enforce an obligation, the diligence is deemed to be a relevant claim.[92]

20. Relevant Acknowledgment: Obligations.—Relevant acknowledgment is defined in s. 10 (1) as such performance by or on behalf of the debtor towards implement of the obligation as clearly indicates that the obligation still subsists,[93] or an unequivocal written admission by or on behalf of the debtor to the creditor or his agent clearly acknowledging that the obligation still subsists. If the nature of the obligation requires the debtor to refrain from doing something or to permit or suffer something to be done or maintained, he will be regarded as acknowledging the obligation if he so refrains, permits or suffers.[94] If an obligation is relevantly acknowledged by the performance

---

85 ss. 7 and 8; cf. *Napier* v. *Campbell* (1703) M. 10656.
86 s. 7 (1); and see §§ 19 and 20, infra.
87 Proviso to s. 7 (1).
88 See note 52, supra.
89 i.e. the presenting of or concurring in a petition for sequestration or winding up, or the lodging a claim in the hands of the trustee, or liquidator, or the Court, or the preses at any meeting of creditors.
90 *Bank of Scotland* v. *Fergusson* (1898) 1 F. 96.
91 s. 9 (3), (4); s. 4 (4); cf. § 11, supra.
92 s. 9 (1).
93 For example, the payment of interest on a debt: cf. *Kermack* v. *Kermack* (1874) 2 R. 156. However it has been held that the payment of interest under a principal bond does not interrupt the running of prescription against the obligation in a bond of corroboration: *Yuill's Trs.* v. *Maclachlan's Trs.*, 1939 S.C. (H.L.) 40.
94 s. 10 (4).

of, or on behalf of, one joint obligant, the running of prescription is interrupted as respects each joint obligant.[95] If on the other hand a written admission is made by or on behalf of one joint obligant, the running of prescription is only interrupted as respects that joint obligant.[96] Where, however, an obligation affects a trust estate, it matters not whether one trustee acknowledges by performance or by written admission: the running of prescription is interrupted as respects the liability of the trust estate and any liability of each of the trustees.[97]

21. Interruption: Rights: Section 8.[98]—To interrupt the running of the long negative prescription, the right must be exercised or enforced, or a relevant claim in relation to the right must be made.[99]

22. Relevant Claim: Rights.—A relevant claim in relation to section 8 is a claim made in appropriate proceedings[1] by or on behalf of the creditor to establish the right or to contest any claim to a right inconsistent therewith.[2]

Where a claim is made in an arbitration, and the nature of the claim has been stated in a preliminary notice, the date of interruption is the date on which the preliminary notice is served.[3]

23. The Quinquennial Prescription (Five Years).—If after the "appropriate date"[4] an obligation[5] to which s. 6 applies subsists for a continuous period of five years without any relevant claim being made in relation to the obligation and without the subsistence of the obligation being relevantly acknowledged then as from the expiration of that period the obligation is extinguished.[6]

24. To what Obligations Applicable: Schedule 1.—Unlike the long negative prescription, the quinquennial prescription applies only to a limited but important group of obligations[7], viz. any obligation (a) to pay a sum of money due in respect of a particular period;[8] (b) based on redress of unjustified enrichment;[9] (c) arising from negotiorum gestio; (d) arising from liability to make reparation, other than reparation in respect of personal injuries or death;[10] (e) under a bill of exchange or promissory note;[11] (f) of

---

[95] s. 10 (2) (a).
[96] s. 10 (2) (b).
[97] s. 10 (3).
[98] For the ambit of s. 8, see s. 8 (2) and note 65, supra.
[99] s. 8 (1).
[1] See note 52, supra.
[2] s. 9 (2).
[3] s. 9 (3), (4); s. 4 (4); s. 4 (4); cf. § 11, supra.
[4] See § 25, infra.
[5] See s. 15 (2) and note 61, supra.
[6] s. 6 (1).
[7] s. 6 (2); Sched. 1, para. 1.
[8] i.e. interest, an annuity instalment, feuduty, ground annual, rent or other periodical payment in respect of the occupancy or use of land or a periodical payment under a land obligation: Sched. 1, para. 1 (a).
[9] Restitution, repetition, or recompense.
[10] Sched. 1, para. 2 (g); and see § 28 et seq, infra.
[11] Cheques are therefore affected by the quinquennial prescription: Bills of Exchange Act 1882, s. 73. Bank notes are not: Sched. 1, para. 2 (b) of the 1973 Act.

accounting;[12] and (g) arising from, or by reason of any breach of, a contract or promise.

The Act specifically provides[13] that the quinquennial prescription is not to apply to any obligation to recognise or obtemper a Court decree, arbitration award, or an order of any tribunal or authority exercising jurisdiction under any enactment;[14] any obligation arising from the issue of a bank note; any obligation constituted or evidenced by a probative writ;[15] any obligation under a contract of partnership or of agency, not being an obligation remaining or becoming prestable on or after the termination of the relationship between the parties under the contract; any obligation relating to land including an obligation to recognise a servitude;[16] any obligation to satisfy any claim to terce, courtesy, legitim, jus relicti or jus relictae, or to any prior right of a surviving spouse under ss. 8 or 9 of the Succession (Scotland) Act 1964; any obligation to make reparation in respect of personal injuries[17] or in respect of the death of any person as a result of such injuries; and any obligation specified in Sched. 3 as imprescriptible.[18]

25. Computation of Period.—The rules set out in section 14 apply equally to the quinquennial prescription as they do to the positive and the long negative prescriptions.[19] However while the long negative prescription invariably commences when the obligation has become enforceable,[20] the quinquennial prescription begins to run after "the appropriate date", which is usually but not always the date when the obligation became enforceable.[21] Thus, for example, the prescription begins to run from the midnight of the date of a bill of exchange or cheque payable on demand;[22] or from the midnight after the expiry of the period of notice, where payment is due only after a certain period after demand.[23]

"The appropriate date" is defined for certain special purposes in Schedule 2:—

(a) Series of transactions: sale, hire or services rendered: where goods are

---

[12] Other than accounting for trust funds, which is imprescriptible: Sched. 3, para. (e).

[13] Sched. 1, para. 2.

[14] "Enactment" is defined in s. 15 (1).

[15] However cautionary obligations (and see Sched. 1, para. 3) and obligations to make periodical payments in terms of Sched. 1, para. 1 (a), are affected by the quinquennial prescription whether or not incorporated in a probative writ: Sched. 1, para. 2 (c). "Probative writ" means a writ which is authenticated by attestation or in any such other manner as may be provided by an enactment (as defined by s. 15 (1)) as having an effect equivalent to attestation: Sched. 1, para. 4 (b). Holograph writs and writs adopted as holograph are therefore affected by the quinquennial prescription, as they are not equivalent to attested writs by virtue of any enactment. Missives relating to heritage are usually adopted as holograph but are probably excluded from the quinquennial prescription as being obligations "relating to land".

[16] But excluding those obligations to make periodical payments in terms of Sched. 1, para. 1 (a) to which the quinquennial prescription does apply.

[17] "Personal injuries" includes any disease and any impairment of a person's physical or mental condition: Sched. 1, para. 2 (g) and s. 22 (1). See §§ 28 et seq infra.

[18] See § 15, supra.

[19] s. 14.

[20] See § 16, supra.

[21] s. 6 (3).

[22] cf. *Stephenson* v. *Stephenson's Trs.* 1807 M. App. Bill No. 20.

[23] cf. *Brodelius* v. *Grischotti* (1887) 14 R. 536.

supplied on sale[24] or hire, or where services are rendered, in the form of a series of transactions between the same parties charged on a continuing account, the appropriate date in respect of any obligation to pay for the goods or services is the date on which payment for the goods last supplied or the services last rendered became due.[25] Prescription cannot be elided by inserting a charge for keeping the account in question.[26] If an account has been definitely closed, the prescriptive period will begin to run on the appropriate date although trading between the parties may continue.[27] The death of the debtor is equivalent to the closing of the account.[28]

(b) Money lent to or deposited with the debtor: the appropriate date is the date stipulated in the contract as the repayment date; or if no such date is stipulated, the date when a written demand for payment is first made.[29]

(c) Termination of partnership or agency: where an obligation arises under a contract of partnership or of agency, being an obligation remaining or becoming prestable on or after the termination of the relationship between the parties under the contract, the appropriate date is the date stipulated in the contract as the date on or before which performance of the obligation is due; and if no such date is stipulated, the date when the relationship terminated.[30]

(d) Payment or work by instalments: where there is an obligation to pay an instalment of a sum of money or to execute an instalment of work, the appropriate date is the date on which the last of the instalments is due to be paid or executed.[31]

In computing the five-year period, no account is to be taken of time during which the creditor was induced to refrain from making a relevant claim by reason of fraud on the part of the debtor or his agent, or error on the creditor's part induced by the debtor or his agent.[32] However once the creditor could with reasonable diligence have discovered the fraud or error, any time elapsing thereafter is to be included in the prescriptive period.[33] Unlike the positive and long negative prescriptions, the quinquennial prescription can be affected by the legal disability of the creditor. Any period during which the

[24] Sale includes hire-purchase, credit-sale, or conditional sale: Sched. 2, para. 1 (2) (*a*).
[25] Sched. 2, para. 1. See special provision for the termination of a series of transactions on the bankruptcy of a partnership or partner: para. 1 (3).
[26] Sched. 2, para. 1 (2) (*b*).
[27] cf. *Christison* v. *Knowles* (1901) 3 F. 480.
[28] cf. Bell, *Comm.*, I, 349.
[29] Sched. 2, para. 2. In the sphere of banking, the Scottish Law Commission recommended (in para. 74 of their Report No. 15 on Reform of the Law Relating to Prescription and Limitation of Actions) that the quinquennial prescription should run from the date when the creditor demands repayment, but that the long negative prescription should run (as before) from the date of deposit in accounts where the bank is debtor, and from the date of advance in accounts where the bank is creditor: *Macdonald* v. *North of Scotland Bank*, 1942 S.C. 369. This recommendation appears to have been implemented in the Act.
[30] Sched. 2, para. 3.
[31] Sched. 2, para. 4.
[32] s. 6 (4)(*a*); cf. *Caledonian Railway* v. *Chisholm* (1886) 13 R. 773; *Inglis* v. *Smith*, 1916 S.C. 581.
[33] Proviso to s. 6 (4).

original creditor (while he is the creditor) was under legal disability[34] is not to be included in the computation.[35] The fact that any time is to be discounted on the ground of fraud, error or disability is not to be regarded as separating the periods before and after that time.[36]

26. Effect.—Unlike most of the former short prescriptions, which did not extinguish rights or obligations but merely affected the onus and method of proof, the quinquennial prescription extinguishes obligations (and rights correlative thereto) which have not been enforced. When the prescriptive period expires, the obligation ceases to exist.

27. Interruption.—To interrupt the running of the quinquennial prescription, a relevant claim in relation to the obligation must be made,[37] or the subsistence of the obligation must be relevantly acknowledged.[38] However in the case of an obligation arising from a bill of exchange or a promissory note, only a relevant claim will suffice to interrupt prescription.[39] The prescriptive period starts anew from the date of the interruption.

28. Reparation.[40]—For the purposes of prescription the 1973 Act in effect divides reparation into two categories: (a) reparation in respect of personal injuries or death;[41] and (b) reparation in respect of any other loss, injury or damage, arising from, for example, negligent actings in relation to property, breach of contract or promise, or defamation.

29. Personal Injuries or Death.—An obligation to make reparation in respect of personal injuries or death cannot be extinguished by the quinquennial prescription, but only by the long negative prescription.[42] The obligation is regarded as having become enforceable when the loss, injury or damage occurred,[43] or in the case of loss, injury or damage arising as a result of a continuing act, neglect or default, on the date when the latter ceased.[44] The long negative prescription would appear to run whether or not the creditor is aware of any loss, injury or damage.[45]

---

[34] Legal disability is defined in s. 15 (1) as meaning legal disability by reason of nonage or unsoundness of mind.

[35] s. 6 (4) (b).

[36] s. 6 (5). Thus a creditor who for example becomes temporarily insane two years after an obligation has become enforceable will have a further three years after regaining his sanity within which to claim.

[37] s. 6 (1); s. 9; and see § 19, supra.

[38] s. 6 (1); s. 10; and see § 20, supra.

[39] Proviso to s. 6 (1).

[40] Reparation is not defined in the Act, but appears to have been used in its widest sense, viz., the making good of any civil wrong usually by an award of damages. See, e.g. the terms of s. 11.

[41] "Personal injuries" includes any disease or any impairment of a person's physical or mental condition: s. 22 (1).

[42] Sched. 1, para. 2 (g). However limitation may prevent enforcement by court action after three years: See Reparation, Ch. XXXIV, infra, § 33.

[43] s. 11 (1) and (4).

[44] s. 11 (1); (2); (4).

[45] s. 11 (4); contrast with limitation: see Reparation, Ch. XXXIV, § 33; and contrast with the quinquennial prescription: § 30, infra.

30. Other Loss, Injury or Damage.—Any other obligation to make reparation is extinguished by the quinquennial prescription.[46] Thus the quinquennial prescription applies to claims for breach of contract, property damage and so on. In computing the prescriptive period, the obligation is regarded as having become enforceable on the date when the loss, injury or damage occurred;[47] or in the case of loss, injury or damage arising as a result of a continuing act, neglect or default, on the date when the latter ceased;[48] or where the creditor is unaware of any damage, on the date when the creditor first became aware or could with reasonable diligence have become aware that the loss, injury or damage had occurred.[49]

31. Transitional.—Part I of the Act did not come into force until 25th July 1976, i.e. three years after the passing of the Act on 25th July 1973[50]. The purpose of the three-year delay was to enable people to readjust to the new prescriptive periods, and to avoid penalising anyone by the unexpectedly early extinction of a right or obligation.[51] The fact that the Act is to some extent retroactive [52] also made the three-year delay necessary. Thus if an obligation subject to the quinquennial prescription had become enforceable more than five years before the commencement of Part I, the obligation could not be extinguished before 25th July 1976.[53]

Where the subsistence of an obligation was by virtue of a former prescription provable only by writ or oath as at 25th July 1976, its subsistence was thereafter provable prout de jure.[54]

Rights and obligations affected by specific statutory limitations created before the passing of the 1973 Act are not to be extinguished by either of the new negative prescriptions until the end of the relevant statutory limitation period.[55]

Any proceedings brought before 25th July 1976 are not affected by the Act.[56]

32. The Crown.—The Act binds the Crown.[57] Prescription may therefore be pleaded against the Crown.[58]

[46] s. 6 (2); Sched. 1, para. 1 (d).
[47] s. 11 (1); and see *Dunlop* v. *McGowans*, 1979 S.L.T. 34, (O.H. 1978 S.L.T. 103). unreported. (O.H. 1978 S.L.T. 103).
[48] s. 11 (2).
[49] s. 11 (3).
[50] s. 25 (2) (b).
[51] For example, some rights and obligations formerly extinguishable only by the long negative prescription became extinguishable after five years: see *Dunlop* v. *McGowans,* supra.
[52] In terms of s. 14 (1) (a) time occurring before the commencement of Part I is reckonable towards the prescriptive period in like manner as time occurring thereafter, so long as any time reckoned in terms of s. 14 (1) (a) is less that the prescriptive period.
[53] *Dunlop* v. *McGowans,* supra. Such an obligation might not be extinguished until after 25th July 1976 if (say) a period of legal disability were to delay the expiry of the prescriptive period.
[54] s. 16 (3).
[55] s. 12. If at the end of the limitation period any claim to establish the right or enforce the obligation has not been finally disposed of, the right or obligation is deemed to be extinguished on the date when the claim is so disposed of.
[56] s. 25 (3).
[57] s. 24.
[58] cf. *Lord Advocate* v. *Graham* (1844) 7 D. 183. See § 4, supra.

CHAPTER XVII

SALE OF GOODS

Brown, *Sale of Goods Act* (2nd ed., 1911); Benjamin, *Sale of Goods* (1974); Chalmers, *Sale of Goods Act* (17th ed., 1975); J. J. Gow, *Mercantile and Industrial Law of Scotland* (1964), Ch. 2.

1. Sale of Goods Act.—Apart from the sale of heritable property, and of rights such as debts, or shares in a company, the law of sale is now regulated by the Sale of Goods Act 1893. This statute, in its main provisions applicable both to Scotland and England, is with regard to the law of England in substance a codification of the pre-existing law; in regard to the law of Scotland it made changes which may be called revolutionary. It has been amended in important respects by the Supply of Goods (Implied Terms) Act 1973 (c. 13) and the Consumer Credit Act 1974 (c. 39).

2. Meaning of "Goods."—Goods are defined as including, in Scotland, "all corporeal moveables except money." "The term includes emblements, industrial growing crops and things attached to or forming part of the land which are agreed to be severed before sale or under the contract of sale."[1] The provisions of the Act have been held applicable to the sale of ships,[2] standing trees,[3] and growing crops,[4] but not to a mineral lease.[5]

3. Sale as Contract and as Transfer of Property.—The effect of the alterations in the common law of Scotland introduced by the Act may be apprehended by considering that the law of sale has two main aspects.[6] It deals with sale as a contract, and indicates the contractual obligations on either side which will be implied in the absence of any express provision. In this aspect the alterations due to the Act are of minor importance, and may be indicated in summarising the statutory provisions. But it also deals with sale as a method of transferring the property (jus in re) of the thing sold, and in this aspect the law has been altered so fundamentally that it is desirable to insert, before dealing with the Act, a statement of the common law and of the modifications introduced by prior legislation.

4. Transfer of Goods Sold: Common Law.—By the common law of Scotland a contract to sell goods had no effect on the property of the goods in

---

[1] Sale of Goods Act, 1893, s. 62 (1).
[2] *Behnke* v. *Bede Shipping Co.* [1927] 1 K.B. 649.
[3] *Morison* v. *Lockhart*, 1912 S.C. 1017; *Munro* v. *Liquidator of Balnagown Estates Co.*, 1949 S.C. 49. See note 35, infra.
[4] *Kennedy's Tr.* v. *Hamilton* (1897) 25 R. 252; *Paton's Trs.* v. *Finlayson*, 1923 S.C. 872; *Allan* v. *Millar*, 1932 S.C. 620.
[5] *Morgan* v. *Russell* [1909] 1 K.B. 357.
[6] See also §§ 9 and 11, infra, and General Law of Obligations, Ch. III, § 10, supra.

question. The property, and the real right, jus in re, remained with the seller (whether the price had been paid or not) until the goods were delivered to the buyer. Until delivery a purchaser had no right higher than that of a creditor in a personal obligation to deliver the goods. Sale was an example of the general rule, expressed in the maxim "traditionibus, non nudis pactis, dominia rerum transferuntur," that a contract for the transfer of a thing merely created a jus in personam, or personal claim against the transferor. It did not carry the real right in the thing. This was a rule of law, independent of the volition of the parties. It was, it is true, open to the parties, by selling under a suspensive condition, to reserve to the seller the property in the thing even after it had been delivered[7]; it was not within their power to transfer the property before delivery.[8] But the risk of accidental destruction or damage passed to the buyer before delivery: in the sale of specific goods, when the contract was concluded: in the sale of unascertained goods, when the seller appropriated particular goods to the contract for delivery to the buyer.[9]

5. Results of Rules of Common Law.—The most important practical results of the general rule that the property in the goods sold could not pass until they were delivered were the following:—(a) In the event of the bankruptcy of the seller before delivery the buyer, though he might have paid the price, could not obtain the article sold. It was still the property of the seller, and passed, with the rest of his property, to the trustee in his sequestration. The buyer had merely a claim for damages for the non-fulfilment of the contract, his right being to rank for a dividend on that claim with the other personal creditors of the seller.[10] (b) The seller, being still undivested owner, could, in a question with the purchaser or in his bankruptcy, retain the thing sold in security of any debt which might be due to him by the purchaser.[11] (c) The seller had a similar right in a question with a sub-purchaser. He was still the owner of the goods, the sub-purchaser had merely a personal right to delivery, and that personal right was postponed to the seller's right to retain his position as owner, and therefore to withhold delivery of the goods, until he had received payment, not only of the price,[12] but of any general balance which might be due to him by the original purchaser.[13]

6. Mercantile Law Amendment Act.—The general principle that the property in goods sold did not pass until delivery ruled until the Sale of Goods Act 1893 came into operation (Jan. 1, 1894), but certain of its practical results were affected by the Mercantile Law Amendment (Scotland) Act 1856, sections 1-5. As these sections are repealed by the Schedule to the Sale of Goods Act, it

[7] *Macartney* v. *Macredie's Creditors* (1799) M. App. Sale No. 1; *Murdoch* v. *Greig* (1889) 16 R. 396.
[8] As to the common law, see Bell, *Comm.,* I, 181, and General Law of Obligations, Ch. III, § 10, supra.
[9] See the discussion of the common law in *Widenmeyer* v. *Burn Stewart & Co.,* 1967 S.C. 85.
[10] *Mathison* v. *Alison* (1854) 17 D. 274.
[11] *Wyper* v. *Harveys* (1861) 23 D. 606.
[12] *M'Ewan* v. *Smith* (1849) 6 Bell's App. 340.
[13] *Melrose* v. *Hastie* (1851) 13 D. 880.

is unnecessary to deal with their provisions in detail. Their general result was to entitle the purchaser of specific goods in a deliverable state to delivery in a question with the trustee in the bankruptcy of the seller,[14] and to abolish the right of an undivested seller to retain goods, in a question with a sub-purchaser, for any general balance due by the original purchaser.[15]

7. General Effect of Sale of Goods Act.—The provisions of the Sale of Goods Act with regard to the passing of the property in goods sold are detailed later,[16] but it may be stated generally that they introduce the English law on the subject, under which the passing of the property does not depend upon the delivery of the goods but on the force of the contract. The property passes at the time when the parties intend it to pass, whether the goods are delivered or not.

8. Sale of Goods Act: Construction and Scope.—With these preliminary explanations we pass to the consideration of the Act. It has been laid down as a general canon of construction that the fair meaning of the words used in the Act must be taken, although that meaning may be inconsistent with the result of prior decisions, and although there may be no apparent reason for supposing that a change in the law was intended.[17] The Act does not deal with such questions as the effects of error, misrepresentation or fraud, which fall to be decided according to the general law of contract. Section 61 provides that the rules of the common law, including the law merchant, save in so far as they are inconsistent with the express provisions of the Act, shall continue to apply to the contract of sale of goods. In the following pages the figures in square brackets refer to the sections of the Act, which should in all cases be read.

9. Definition of Contract of Sale.—The contract of sale of goods is defined [1] as a contract whereby the seller transfers or agrees to transfer[18] the property in goods for a money consideration, called the price. Capacity to buy and sell is regulated by the general law as to capacity to contract, but where necessaries are sold and delivered to a minor or a person who, by reason of mental incapacity or drunkenness, is incompetent to contract, he must pay a reasonable price therefor [2]. The contract may be entered into verbally, and proved by parole evidence. So a verbal sale of a ship is binding.[19] Such subjects as growing crops or standing trees, though included in the definition of "goods," are heritable, and probably a contract for their sale would require to be in writing.[20]

---

[14] *M'Meekin* v. *Ross* (1876) 4 R. 154.
[15] See as to the result of the Mercantile Law Amendment Act, *Wyper* v. *Harveys* (1861) 23 D. 606; *Distillers' Co.* v. *Russell's Tr.* (1889) 16 R. 479.
[16] § 14 et seq.
[17] *Bristol Tramway Co.* v. *Fiat Motors* [1910] 2 K.B. 831.
[18] These are the alternatives referred to in § 3, supra, and § 11, infra.
[19] *M'Connachie* v. *Geddes*, 1918 S.C. 391.
[20] *Morison* v. *Lockhart*, 1912 S.C. 1017.

10. Sale and Other Contracts.—The definition serves to distinguish sale from such contracts as pledge, where there is no agreement to transfer the property in goods; donation, where there is no price; barter, where the consideration is not in money.[21] And where in a contract for building a ship, it was provided that the ship, as she was constructed, and all materials intended for her, should become the property of the purchasers, it was decided that there was only a contract for the sale of a complete ship, and that the provision as to the unfinished ship and the materials was not a sale but an attempt to create a right in security, which required delivery in order to make it effectual.[22]

11. Sale and Agreement to Sell.—The Act draws a distinction between a sale and an agreement to sell. It depends on the transfer of the property in the goods. When the property is transferred under the contract it is a sale; where the transfer of the property is to take place at a future time or subject to some condition thereafter to be fulfilled, it is an agreement to sell. An agreement to sell becomes a sale when the time elapses or the conditions are fulfilled subject to which the property in the goods is to be transferred[23] [1]. A "sale," under the Act, is both a contract and a transference of the property in goods; an "agreement to sell" is merely a contract.

12. Sale and Security.—By section 61 (4) it is provided that "the provisions of this Act relating to contracts of sale do not apply to any transaction in the form of a contract of sale which is intended to operate by way of mortgage, pledge, charge or other security." In the case of such transactions the common law as to passing of the property in goods is still applicable, and, therefore, the property in the goods which are nominally sold does not pass without delivery. The mere contract does not confer on the nominal purchaser any real right in the goods, and he has no claim to them which he can vindicate in the bankruptcy of the nominal seller. So where £40 was advanced to a dealer in bicycles, and he granted a promissory note for that amount, and also a document in the form of a receipt for certain bicycles sold to the lender, it was decided that the sale of the bicycles was a transaction intended to operate by way of security; that the provisions of the Sale of Goods Act did not apply; and that the nominal purchaser had no real right in the bicycles until they were delivered.[24] The transaction was not really a sale, but an attempt to give a security in a method which the law of Scotland does not recognise. But it may be stipulated, without bringing the transaction within the purview of section 61 (4), that the seller shall have a right to repurchase the goods at the same price,[25] or that the purchaser, if he make

---

21 For a modern case on barter, see *Widenmeyer* v. *Burn Stewart & Co.,* 1967 S.C. 85.
22 *Reid* v. *Macbeth & Gray* (1904) 6 F. (H.L.) 25.
23 *A.K. Stoddart* v. *Scott,* 1971 J.C. 18.
24 *Jones & Co.'s Tr.* v. *Allan* (1901) 4 F. 374; see also *Hepburn* v. *Law,* 1914 S.C. 918; *Scottish Transit Trust* v. *Scottish Land Cultivators,* 1955 S.C. 254; *G. & C. Finance Corporation* v. *Brown,* 1961 S.L.T. 408.
25 *Gavin's Tr.* v. *Fraser,* 1920 S.C. 674; *Newbigging* v. *Morton,* 1930 S.C. 273.

any profit by a resale of the goods, shall be bound to account for that profit to the seller.[26] And probably if the legal relations of buyer and seller are created the transaction is to be regarded as a sale to which the Act will apply, although it may be proved that the object of the parties in entering into the transaction was to give security for money borrowed. It is inconsistent with the legal relationship of buyer and seller that the nominal seller should be bound by some separate obligation (e.g., a promissory note) to repay the price; it is not inconsistent with that relationship that the seller should have an option to repay, and a right, on repayment, to recover the goods.[27]

13. Price.—The Act provides [8] that the price of goods sold may be fixed by the contract, left to be fixed in some manner agreed to, or determined by the course of dealing between the parties. If not so determined, the buyer must pay a reasonable price. If it is agreed that the price shall be fixed by a third party, and that third party cannot or does not act, an agreement to sell is avoided, but if any part of the goods has been delivered to and appropriated by the buyer he must pay a reasonable price therefor. If the third party is prevented from fixing the price by the fault of buyer or seller, the party in fault is liable in damages [9]. It is no objection to the validity of a contract of sale that the buyer is left to fix his own price.[28] Proof of a definite misunderstanding as to price will preclude the enforcement of the contract if no part of the goods has been delivered.[29]

14. Transfer of Property: Unascertained Goods.—In dealing with sale as a method of transferring the property in goods it must be noted that the contract may either relate to particular and existing things, identified at the time the contract is made, and referred to in the Act as specific or ascertained goods (venditio rei specificae); or to future goods, goods to be manufactured or obtained by the seller after the contract is made; or to generic goods, so much of some particular commodity (venditio generis); or to an unserved portion of some particular quantity of goods.[30] In the last three cases the goods are unascertained, and the property does not pass to the purchaser until they are ascertained [16]. They are ascertained when goods of that description and in a deliverable state[31] are unconditionally appropriated to the contract either by the seller with the consent of the buyer or by the buyer with the consent of the seller[32] [18, Rule 5 (1)]. Notification of such appropriation is not essential if the necessary consent can be implied from the terms of the contract.[33] If the seller delivers the goods to a carrier for transmission to the

[26] *M'Bain* v. *Wallace* (1881) 8 R. (H.L.) 106.
[27] *Gavin's Tr.* v. *Fraser*, 1920 S.C. 674; see opinion of Lord President Clyde; *Newbigging* v. *Morton*, supra.
[28] *Lavaggi* v. *Pirie* (1872) 10 M. 312.
[29] *Wilson* v. *Marquis of Breadalbane* (1859) 21 D. 957. See Agreement Improperly Obtained, Ch. VIII, supra, § 21.
[30] See *Hayman* v. *M'Lintock*, 1907 S.C. 936.
[31] *Philip Head & Sons* v. *Showfronts* (1970) 113 Sol. Jo. 978.
[32] The appropriation may be by a third party: *Wardar's (Import & Export) Co.* v. *W. Norwood & Sons* [1968] 2 Q.B. 663.
[33] See *Widenmeyer* v. *Burn Stewart & Co., Ltd.*, 1967 S.C.85, per Lord President Clyde, at p. 101.

buyer, and does not reserve the right of disposal, he is deemed to have unconditionally appropriated them to the contract [18, Rule 5 (2)].

15. Specific Goods: General Rules.—The general rule as to the transfer of the property in specific goods is given in section 17: "Where there is a contract for the sale of specific or ascertained goods the property in them is transferred to the buyer at such time as the parties to the contract intend it to be transferred. For the purpose of ascertaining the intention of the parties regard shall be had to the terms of the contract, the conduct of the parties, and the circumstances of the case." In contrast with the common law, which demanded delivery in order to pass the property, this section places it in the power of the parties to the contract to decide when the property is to pass. It depends on their intention. In some cases that intention may be clear, either from the express terms of the contract or from the circumstances of the case. But in many cases buyer and seller do not consider the question of the property in the goods, and have really no intention in the matter. It is a question which rises into importance if the creditors of the seller, or his trustee in bankruptcy, assert a right to the goods, or if the goods are accidentally injured or destroyed. Where no actual intention can be ascertained the presumed intention is to be gathered from rules given in section 18. It must be remembered that these rules are not applicable if there is proof of intention to the contrary.[34]

Rule 1.—"Where there is an unconditional contract for the sale of specific goods,[35] in a deliverable state, the property in the goods passes to the buyer when the contract is made, and it is immaterial whether the time of payment or the time of delivery, or both, be postponed." It may be presumed that in this, the general rule for the ordinary case of sale of specific articles, the term "unconditional" means without any condition relating to the passing of the property, and that the property in an article which is sold in a deliverable state will pass at once to the purchaser, although the contract may involve conditions as to the quality of the article. Goods are in a deliverable state when they are in such a state that the buyer would under the contract be bound to take delivery of them [62 (4)].

Rule 2.—"Where there is a contract for the sale of specific goods and the seller is bound to do something to the goods, for the purpose of putting them into a deliverable state, the property does not pass until such thing be done, and the buyer has notice thereof." From the opinions in an English case it would appear that the rule does not apply, and that the passing of the property is not postponed, merely because the seller has undertaken to pack the goods, or because, as in the case of a billiard-table, the article sold must be

---

[34] As examples see *Re Anchor Line* [1937] 1 Ch. 1; *Lacis* v. *Cashmarts* [1969] 2 Q.B. 400; *Aluminium Industrie Vaassen B.V.* v. *Romalpa Aluminium* [1976] 1 W.L.R. 676.

[35] Specific goods are "goods identified and agreed upon at the time a contract of sale is made," [62]. Standing trees sold for felling and removal cannot become the property of the buyer until they are severed from the ground; *Morison* v. *Lockhart*, 1912 S.C. 1017; *Munro* v. *Liquidator of Balnagown Estates Co.*, 1949 S.C. 49.

taken to pieces before it can be removed. But where the article sold was at the date of the contract affixed to a building the property did not pass until it was severed.[36] And there may be a narrow distinction between putting goods in a deliverable state and initiating the process of delivery. When growing potatoes were sold, and the seller undertook to lift and put them in pits at maturity, and to cart them to the station, it was decided that the potatoes had reached a deliverable state, and that the property passed to the purchaser, when they were put into pits; the subsequent obligation of the seller, to cart the potatoes to the station, relating not to deliverable state but to actual delivery.[37]

Rule 3.—"Where there is a contract for the sale of specific goods in a deliverable state, but the seller is bound to weigh, measure, test or do some other act or thing with reference to the goods for the purpose of ascertaining the price, the property does not pass until such act or thing be done, and the buyer has notice thereof." This rule is applicable only where the seller has undertaken to weigh, measure or test the goods, not to the case where there is no agreement on the point, though the price cannot as a matter of fact be ascertained until such operation has been performed. So in the sale of "my crop of hay" the property was held to pass at once, though the sale was at so much per ton, and the price consequently could not be ascertained until the hay was weighed.[38] Similarly, when it was agreed that the goods should be weighed at the station and the result accepted by both parties as determining the price, it was held that Rule 3 was inapplicable because there was no obligation on the seller to weigh the goods.[39]

(Rule 4, relating to the contract of sale and return, will be considered subsequently, section 49.)

16. Risk: Generic Sales.—The question of risk, i.e., the question on whom the loss is to fall if goods sold are accidentally injured or destroyed, is, in general, raised only in the case of the sale of specific articles. If a man agrees to supply a certain quantity of a particular commodity there is nothing under the contract at risk. "Genus nunquam perit," the particular commodity does not cease to exist, although the seller's whole stock may be accidentally destroyed. In all ordinary cases he remains liable under his contract.[40] Even if the particular commodity has ceased to exist, or has become unprocurable, the contract is not affected, if the buyer has no notice of the seller's sources of supply. So where A agreed to supply a certain quantity of Finnish birch, he was held liable in damages for failure to fulfil his contract, in spite of the fact that owing to war conditions it had become impossible to procure that particular commodity.[41] But where the subject of sale was a particular chemical, and both parties were aware that it was to be imported from

[36] *Underwood* v. *Burgh Castle Syndicate* [1922] 1 K.B. 343.
[37] *Cockburn's Tr.* v. *Bowe*, 1910, 2 S.L.T. 17. See also *Woodburn* v. *Motherwell*, 1917 S.C. 533; *Paton's Trs.* v. *Finlayson*, 1923 S.C. 872.
[38] *Kennedy's Tr.* v. *Hamilton* (1897) 25 R. 252.
[39] *Woodburn* v. *Motherwell*, 1917 S.C. 533.
[40] *Anderson and Crompton* v. *Walls* (1870) 9 M. 122.
[41] *Blackburn Bobbin Co.* v. *Allen* [1918] 2 K.B. 467.

Germany, and therefore during the war could not be obtained without trading with the enemy, it was held that the contract was avoided.[42]

17. Risk: Specific Goods.—Where the contract relates to specific goods, or to goods which have been unconditionally appropriated to the contract by one party with the consent of the other, the result of their accidental destruction depends upon the date of that occurrence. If, without the knowledge of the seller, they have perished at the date when the contract was made, the contract is void [6]. This has been held to apply to a case of partial destruction by theft.[43] Unless otherwise agreed, they are at the seller's risk until the property has passed to the buyer, thereafter at the buyer's risk whether they have been delivered or not [20].[44] If they are accidentally destroyed before the risk has passed to the buyer the contract is avoided, and neither party is under any liability [7]. Otherwise the maxim "res perit domino" applies, and if the risk has passed to the buyer he must pay the price.[45] It is, however, open to the parties to agree that the risk shall not pass with the property, and such agreement may be express or implied. If the seller has undertaken to deliver the goods the general rule is that both property and risk pass to the buyer when they are delivered to a carrier, and, by the transfer of the bill of lading or otherwise, they are placed at the buyer's disposal [18, Rule 5 (2); 32] but if the contract is read as an obligation to deliver the goods at a particular place the risk is with the seller until they arrive there.[46] It is possible that the risk may be divided; the risk of total destruction being on one party, the risk of deterioration on the other. So where herrings were sold, and, owing to delay on the voyage, arrived in a state unfit for consumption, it was held that the buyer might reject them, even on the assumption that the property in the herrings, and with it the risk of their accidental destruction, had passed to him.[47]

18. Risk: Where One Party is in Fault.—In the case of specific goods the risk may be affected by the fact that one or other party was in fault. If the destruction of the goods is due to the fault of one or other party, he will be liable in damages. If delivery be delayed through the fault of buyer or seller, the risk is on the party in fault as regards any loss which might not have occurred but for that fault [20]. If goods are sent to the buyer by a route involving sea transit in circumstances where it is usual to insure, and the seller fails to give such notice to the buyer as may enable him to insure, the goods are at the seller's risk during the sea transit [32 (3)].

---

[42] *Badische Co.* [1921] 2 Ch. 331.
[43] *Barrow Lane & Ballard* v. *Phillips* [1929] 1 K.B. 574.
[44] Cf. the common law rule that risk passed when the contract was completed, not when property in the goods passed: see *Widenmeyer* v. *Burn Stewart & Co., Ltd.,* 1967 S.C. 85.
[45] *Woodburn* v. *Andrew Motherwell,* 1917 S.C. 533; *Wardar's (Import & Export) Co.* v. *W. Norwood & Sons* [1968] 2 Q.B. 663.
[46] *Henckell Du Buisson* v. *Swan* (1889) 17 R. 252.
[47] *Pommer* v. *Mowat* (1906) 14 S.L.T. 373. In such cases the buyer takes the risk of deterioration necessarily incident to the transit (s. 33). See also *Sterns* v. *Vickers* [1923] 1 K.B. 78.

19. Title of Buyer.—As a general rule the purchaser of goods obtains no better title to them than the seller possessed.[48] So if the seller be a thief, or a person who has no right to be in possession of the goods or to dispose of them, the purchaser obtains no title in a question with the true owner. It is immaterial, in Scots law, that the sale may have taken place in a public market or market overt.[49] The general rule is qualified by the proviso to section 21 (1)[50] and by other statutory provisions which give effect to the ostensible authority to dispose of goods which is involved in possession of the goods or of the documents of title to them.

20. Sales by Ostensible Owner.—By the Factors Act 1889 (extended to Scotland by the Factors (Scotland) Act 1890, s. 2), it is provided: "Where a mercantile agent is, with the consent of the owner, in possession of goods or of the documents of title to goods, any sale, pledge, or other disposition of the goods, made by him when acting in the ordinary course of business of a mercantile agent, shall, subject to the provisions of this Act, be as valid as if he were expressly authorised by the owner of the goods to make the same: provided that the person taking under the disposition acts in good faith, and has not at the time of the disposition notice that the person making the disposition has not authority to make the same." By the Sale of Goods Act [25] (re-enacting ss. 8 and 9 of the Factors Act) similar provisions are made for the case of an unauthorised disposition of goods to a party who takes in good faith either (a) by a person who has sold goods but continues in possession[51] of the goods or of the documents of title to them; or (b) by a person who has bought or agreed to buy goods and has obtained, with the consent of the seller, possession of the goods or of the documents of title to them. If the seller in fact consents, it is immaterial that his consent has been obtained by fraud.[52] For purposes of s. 9 of the Factors Act and s. 25 (2) of the Sale of Goods Act a buyer under a conditional sale agreement (as defined in the Consumer Credit Act 1974) is deemed not to be a person who has bought or agreed to buy goods.[53] A private purchaser of a motor vehicle which is the subject of a prior conditional sale agreement may, however, acquire a good title to it if he purchases in good faith and without notice of the prior agreement.[54]

21. Meaning of Good Faith.—A person who takes goods or documents of title in the circumstances covered by these statutory provisions takes in good

---

[48] Section 21. As to the distinction between void and voidable agreements, see Agreements Void or Voidable, Ch. V, supra.

[49] *Todd* v. *Armour* (1882) 9 R. 901.

[50] *Central Newbury Car Auctions* v. *Unity Finance* [1957] 1 Q.B. 371.

[51] The test is continuity of physical possession regardless of any alteration of the legal title under which the possession is held; *Pacific Motor Auctions Pty.* v. *Motor Credits (Hire Finance)* [1965] A.C. 867; *Worcester Works Finance* v. *Cooden* [1972] 1 Q.B. 210.

[52] *Du Jardin* v. *Beadman Bros., Ltd.* [1952] 2 Q.B. 712.

[53] Both Acts are amended by the Consumer Credit Act 1974, Sch. 4, paras. 2, 4.

[54] Hire Purchase Act 1964 (c. 53), ss. 27-29, as substituted by Consumer Credit Act 1974, Sch. 4, para. 22.

faith if he in fact takes honestly, whether he takes negligently or not [62]. But absence of inquiry, or an inadequate price, may be evidence of want of good faith.[55] Where bills of lading were taken by A in the ordinary course of business, in the knowledge that the person from whom he took them (B) was in financial difficulties and had not paid for the goods, but without any notice that B had obtained the bills of lading fraudulently, it was held that A's title was unchallengeable.[56]

22. Mere Possession Confers no Power to Dispose of Goods.—There may be exceptional cases in which a party who is in possession of goods, or of documents to title, but who neither is a mercantile agent, seller left in possession, nor a buyer intrusted with possession, is able to confer a good title by a fraudulent sale of the goods, on the ground that the party who allowed him to be in possession is personally barred from disputing his authority to sell.[57] But there is no general rule that mere possession of goods, as for instance by a hirer,[58] or a carrier or forwarding agent,[59] gives the possessor any ostensible right to dispose of them, or is any ground for a plea of personal bar put forward by a party who has bought the goods from the person in possession, and whose right is challenged by their true owner.[60]

23. Warranties.—Warranties by a seller of goods may be either express, imposed by statute, implied, i.e., implied by the Sale of Goods Act, or annexed by custom of trade. The question whether a particular statement is to be read as a warranty, or merely as a representation, has been already considered.[61] An example of a warranty imposed by statute is the Agriculture Act 1970 (c. 40), s. 72, by which, in a sale of any material for use as a feeding stuff for animals, there is implied a warranty by the seller that the material is suitable to be used as such. The term has effect notwithstanding any contract or notice to the contrary.

24. Implied Warranties.—The warranties implied in sale are dealt with by sections 12-15. An express warranty does not negative an implied warranty or condition unless inconsistent with it.[62] Implied warranties are of three classes:—warranties as to title, as to description, and as to quality. Apart from certain provisions as to title (infra, § 25), the Act refers to "conditions," instead of "warranties." But probably the distinction, though of importance in

---

55 See *Jones* v. *Gordon* (1877) 2 App. Cas. 616; *Hayman* v. *American Cotton Oil Co.* (1907) 45 S.L.R. 207; 15 S.L.T. 606.
56 *Price & Pierce* v. *Bank of Scotland,* 1910 S.C. 1095; 1912 S.C. (H.L.) 19.
57 See *London Joint Stock Bank* v. *Simmons* [1892] A.C. 201, opinion of Lord Herschell; *Commonwealth Trust* v. *Akotey* [1926] A.C. 72, on which see opinion of Lord Sumner in *Jones* v. *Waring & Gillow* [1926] A.C. 670.
58 *Mitchell* v. *Heys* (1894) 21 R. 600; *Lamonby* v. *Foulds,* 1928 S.C. 89; *George Hopkinson Ltd.* v. *Napier & Son,* 1953 S.C. 139 (diligence).
59 *Martinez y Gomez* v. *Allison* (1890) 17 R. 332.
60 *Mitchell* v. *Heys,* supra; *Farquharson* v. *King* [1902] A.C. 325.
61 Agreement Improperly Obtained, Ch. VIII, supra, § 10.
62 Section 55 (2); *Douglas* v. *Milne* (1895) 23 R. 163.

English law,[63] may in Scotland be disregarded. The result of a failure to fulfil a condition, and of failure to fulfil a warranty, is, according to the law of Scotland, the same.[64]

   25. Warranties of Title.—There is (a) an implied condition on the part of the seller that, in the case of a sale, he has a right to sell the goods, and, in the case of an agreement to sell, he will have a right to sell the goods at the time when the property is to pass; and (b) an implied warranty that the goods are free, and will remain free until the time when the property is to pass, from any charge or encumbrance not disclosed or known to the buyer before the contract is made and that the buyer will enjoy quiet possession of the goods except so far as it may be disturbed by the owner or other person entitled to the benefit of any charge or encumbrance so disclosed or known. These provisions do not apply in the case in which there appears from the contract or is to be inferred from the circumstances of the contract an intention that the seller should transfer only such title as he or a third person may have; in such a case there is—(a) an implied warranty that all charges or encumbrances known to the seller and not known to the buyer have been disclosed to the buyer before the contract is made; and (b) an implied warranty that neither— (i) the seller, nor (ii) in a case where the parties to the contract intend that the seller should transfer only such title as a third person may have, that person, nor (iii) anyone claiming through or under the seller or that third person otherwise than under a charge or encumbrance disclosed or known to the buyer before the contract is made, will disturb the buyer's quiet possession of the goods [12]. Any term of a contract which purports to exclude or restrict liability for breach of the obligations arising from any of these implied undertakings as to title or to exclude or restrict the undertakings themselves is void.[65] With regard to these provisions it may be noted that if the buyer knows that the seller has only a limited right he cannot insist on an implied warranty of an absolute one.[66] It has been held that a seller did not fulfil the warranty of his right to sell when he supplied goods with a label which constituted an infringement of a third party's trade mark, and which the buyer could not deal with without risk of a law suit.[67] The warranty of "quiet possession" does not import a warranty against unfounded claims by third parties, and therefore the buyer cannot recover from the seller the expenses he has incurred in resisting these.[68]

   26. Warranty of Description.—"Where there is a contract for the sale of

---

[63] See, as to conditions and warranties in English law, s. 11 (1); opinion of Fletcher Moulton, L.J., in *Wallis* v. *Pratt* [1910] 2 K.B. 1003; *Baldry* v. *Marshall* [1925] 1 K.B. 260.
[64] See opinion of Lord Kinnear, *Nelson* v. *Chalmers,* 1913 S.C. 441, 450, and definition of "warranty" as regards England and Ireland, and "breach of warranty" as regards Scotland, in s. 62.
[65] Unfair Contract Terms Act 1977 (c. 50), ss. 20 (1) (*a*), 25 (5).
[66] *Leith Heritages Co.* v. *Edinburgh Glass Co.* (1876) 3 R. 789.
[67] *Niblett* v. *Confectioners' Materials* [1921] 3 K.B. 387. See also *Microbeads A. G.* v. *Vinhurst Road Markings* [1975] 1 W.L.R. 218.
[68] *Stephen* v. *Lord Advocate* (1878) 6 R. 282; *Dougall* v. *Magistrates of Dunfermline,* 1908 S.C. 151.

goods by description there is an implied condition that the goods shall correspond with the description" [13]. A sale of goods is not prevented from being a sale by description by reason only that, being exposed for sale or hire, the goods are selected by the buyer [13 (2)]. The word "description", which is not defined in the Act, may be synonymous with "kind."[69] Thus it has been observed "If a man offer to buy peas of another, and he sends him beans, he does not perform his contract, but that is not a warranty, there is no warranty that he should sell him peas; the contract is to sell peas, and if he sends him anything else in their stead, it is a non-performance of it."[70] In this meaning of the word "description," there is no difficulty in holding that the party who orders goods of a particular description, and gets either different goods or a consignment in part of the goods ordered, and in part of goods of a different description, is entitled to reject them.[71] But the word "description" may refer to any statement as to the origin or history of the goods,[72] as, for instance, that they form part of a particular stock,[73] that they have been shipped in a particular month,[74] that they have been carried,[75] or packed,[76] in a specified way. In such cases failure to answer the description may make no difference to the value of the goods. It would appear, nevertheless, that, according to English law, the buyer, in respect that the seller has failed in a "condition," may reject,[77] with an exception in the case of a failure so trivial as to fall within the rule "de minimis non curat lex."[78] It would seem doubtful if this result, proceeding largely on the technical meaning given by English law to the word "condition," is applicable to Scotland. It seems difficult to reconcile it with the provision in section 11 (2) as to the results of failure ·by a seller to perform any material part of a contract of sale,[79] or with the general principle of the law of contract that rescission is open only where the breach is material, and that for minor breaches the remedy must be sought in damages.[80]

27. Warranties as to Quality.—At common law the rule was expressed in the statement that a fair price demanded a fair article, and therefore it was held that, in the absence of any provision to the contrary, the seller undertook to supply goods of reasonably good quality.[81] The English law on the subject, generally referred to by the phrase "caveat emptor," was applied to Scotland

---

[69] *Rutherford & Son* v. *Miln & Co.,* 1941 S.C. 125, at p. 135. In *Christopher Hill Ltd.* v. *Ashington Piggeries Ltd.* [1972] A.C. 441, it was said that description went to the identification of the goods.
[70] Per Lord Abinger, *Chanter* v. *Hopkins* (1838) 4 M. & W. 399.
[71] *Jaffe* v. *Ritchie* (1860) 23 D. 242; *Carter* v. *Campbell* (1885) 12 R. 1075; *Rutherford & Son* v. *Miln,* 1941 S.C. 125; see also *Christopher Hill* v. *Ashington Piggeries,* supra, and the opinions in *M'Callum* v. *Mason,* 1956 S.C. 50, as to effects of mixed ingredients.
[72] *Varley* v. *Whipp* [1900] 1 Q.B. 513.
[73] *Thomson Bros.* v. *Thomson* (1885) 13 R. 88.
[74] *Bowes* v. *Shand* (1877) 2 App. Cas. 455.
[75] *Meyer* v. *Travaru* (1930) 46 T.L.R. 553; contrast *Meyer* v. *Kivisto* (1929) 142 L.T. 480.
[76] *Moore & Landauer* [1921] 2 K.B. 519.
[77] *Moore & Landauer,* supra.
[78] *Shipton, Anderson & Co.* v. *Weil Bros.* [1912] 1 K.B. 574.
[79] Infra, § 35.
[80] Breach of Contract, Ch. XIII, supra, § 4. See the doubts expressed in *Millars of Falkirk* v. *Turpie,* 1976 S.L.T. (Notes) 66.
[81] *Whealler* v. *Methuen* (1843) 5 D. 402.

by section 5 of the Mercantile Law Amendment (Scotland) Act 1856, but that section is now repealed, and the law as to implied warranties of quality now rests on the following provision [14][82]: "(1) Except as provided by this section, and section 15 of this Act and subject to the provisions of any other enactment, there is no implied condition or warranty as to the quality or fitness for any particular purpose of goods supplied under a contract of sale.

(2) Where the seller sells goods in the course of a business, there is an implied condition that the goods supplied under the contract are of merchantable quality, except that there is no such condition—

     (a) as regards defects specifically drawn to the buyer's attention before the contract is made; or

     (b) if the buyer examines the goods before the contract is made, as regards defects which that examination ought to reveal.

(3) Where the seller sells goods in the course of a business and the buyer, expressly or by implication, makes known—

     (a) to the seller, or

     (b) where the purchase price or part of it is payable by instalments and the goods were previously sold by a credit-broker to the seller, to that credit-broker,

any particular purpose for which the goods are being bought, there is an implied condition that the goods supplied under the contract are reasonably fit for that purpose, whether or not that is a purpose for which such goods are commonly supplied, except where the circumstances show that the buyer does not rely, or that it is unreasonable for him to rely, on the skill or judgment of the seller or credit-broker.[83]

In this subsection 'credit-broker' means a person acting in the course of a business of credit brokerage carried on by him, that is a business of effecting introductions of individuals desiring to obtain credit—

     (i) to persons carrying on any business so far as it relates to the provision of credit, or

     (ii) to other persons engaged in credit brokerage.

(4) An implied condition or warranty as to quality or fitness for a particular purpose may be annexed to a contract of sale by usage."

A "business" includes a profession and the activities of any government department (including a department of the Government of Northern Ireland) or local or public authority. The provisions apply to a sale by a person who in the course of a business is acting as agent for another as they apply to a sale by a principal in the course of a business, except where that other is not selling

---

[82] Subsections 1, 2 and 4 are as substituted by the Supply of Goods (Implied Terms) Act 1973 (c. 13) s. 3. Subsection 3 is as substituted by the Consumer Credit Act 1974, (c. 39) Sch. 4, para. 3 (which is assumed to be in force). On English authority, a warranty no less stringent applies in the case of work done and material supplied than in the case of sale; *Myers* v. *Brent Cross Service Co.* [1934] 1 K.B. 46; *Stewart* v. *Reavell's Garage* [1952] 2 Q.B. 545; *Young & Marten* v. *McManus Childs* [1969] A.C. 454.

[83] See, as to reliance on the skill or judgment of the seller, *Cammell Laird* v. *Manganese Bronze & Brass Co.* [1934] A.C. 402; *Grant* v. *Australian Knitting Mills* [1936] A.C. 85; *Godley* v. *Perry* [1960] 1 W.L.R. 9. For reliance by a corporation, see *Ashford Shire Council* v. *Dependable Motors* [1961] A.C. 336.

in the course of a business and either the buyer knows that fact or reasonable steps are taken to bring it to the notice of the buyer before the contract is made.[84]

28. Merchantable Quality.—Goods of any kind are of merchantable quality if they are as fit for the purpose or purposes for which goods of that kind are commonly bought as it is reasonable to expect having regard to any description applied to them, the price (if relevant) and all the other relevant circumstances [62 (1A)].[85] It has been held that the implied condition is not applicable where goods are supplied which do not correspond with the description given, e.g. sodium chlorate weedkiller instead of magnesium sulphate fertiliser.[86]

29. Fitness for Particular Purpose.—The general application of the implied condition that the goods must be fit for a particular purpose may be illustrated by a case where hay was sold as "good, sound, timothy hay." The buyer's purpose, resale in a particular market, the conditions of which were known to the seller, was disclosed. The hay, though not of bad quality, did not satisfy the market conditions. It was held that the buyer was entitled to reject the hay, and recover damages, in respect that the seller had impliedly warranted that it was fit for the particular purpose for which, to his knowledge, the buyer required it. It was also decided that the circumstances involving the implied warranty could be proved by parole evidence although the contract was in writing.[87] There is a strong body of authority to the effect that in the case of articles which are commonly used for one purpose only, e.g., milk,[88] articles of food,[89] a hot-water bottle,[90] coals,[91] the buyer's purpose is sufficiently made known to the seller merely by asking for the article, without any express statement as to the object for which he requires it. The condition can be implied in the sale of second-hand goods.[92]

30. Warranties on Sale by Sample.—In the case of a sale by sample the seller impliedly warrants (a) that the bulk shall correspond with the sample; (b) that the buyer shall have a reasonable opportunity of comparing the bulk with the sample; (c) that the goods shall be free from any defect rendering them unmerchantable, which would not be apparent on reasonable examination of the sample [15].[93] If the sale is also by description the bulk must

---

[84] s. 14 (5).
[85] Added by the Supply of Goods (Implied Terms) Act 1973, s. 7 (2).
[86] *McCallum* v. *Mason*, 1956 S.C. 50.
[87] *Jacobs* v. *Scott* (1899) 2 F. (H.L.) 70. See also *Manchester Liners* v. *Rea* [1922] 2 A.C. 74; *Buchanan & Carswell* v. *Eugene*, 1936 S.C. 160.
[88] *Frost* v. *Aylesbury Dairy Co.* [1905] 1 K.B. 608.
[89] *Wallis* v. *Russell* [1902] 2 Ir. R. 585, "two nice fresh crabs for tea."
[90] *Priest* v. *Last* [1903] 2 K.B. 148.
[91] *Duke* v. *Jackson*, 1921 S.C. 362.
[92] *Bartlett* v. *Sidney Marcus* [1965] 1 W.L.R. 1013; *Crowther* v. *Shannon Motor Co.* [1975] 1 W.L.R. 30.
[93] *Drummond* v. *Van Ingen* (1887) 12 App. Cas. 284; *F. E. Hookway Co.* v. *Alfred Isaacs & Son* [1954] 1 Lloyd's Rep. 491, per Devlin J., at p. 511; *Godley* v. *Perry* [1960] 1 W.L.R. 9.

correspond not only with the sample but with the description [13]. A sale is a sale by sample when there is a term in the contract, express or implied, to that effect [15]. So where the conditions of a sale by auction provided that intending purchasers must satisfy themselves of the condition of the goods in bulk, it was held that the sale was not by sample, in spite of the fact that a sample was open to inspection in the auction room.[94]

31. Exclusion of Warranties.—A right, duty or obligation arising by implication under a contract of sale may be negatived or varied by express agreement, or by the course of dealing between the parties or by usage if the usage is such as to bind both parties to the contract[95] but the extent to which this can be done effectually in respect of the implied warranties discussed in the five preceding sections is severely limited by the provisions of the Unfair Contract Terms Act 1977.[96]

Any term of a contract which purports to exclude or restrict[97] liability for breach of any obligation arising from the seller's implied undertakings as to description, quality, fitness for purpose or conformity with samples or to exclude or restrict the obligation itself,[98] is, in the case of a consumer contract, void against the consumer; in the case of other contracts, such a term has no effect if it was not fair and reasonable to incorporate the term in the contract.[99]

A consumer contract of sale is a contract of sale (not being a contract of sale by auction or competitive tender) in which one party to the contract deals, and the other party to the contract (the consumer) does not deal or hold himself out as dealing, in the course of a business, and the goods are of a type ordinarily supplied for private use or consumption.[1] The onus of proving that a contract is not to be regarded as a consumer contract lies on the party so contending.

In determining whether it was fair and reasonable to incorporate a term in a contract which is not a consumer contract, regard is to be had only to the circumstances which were, or ought reasonably to have been, known to or in the contemplation of the parties to the contract at the time the contract was made.[2] Regard is to be had in particular to:[3]

  (a) the strength of the bargaining positions of the parties relative to each other, taking into account (among other things) alternative means by which the customer's requirements could have been met;

  (b) whether the customer received an inducement to agree to the term, or in

---

[94] *White* v. *Dougherty* (1891) 18 R. 972.
[95] s. 55 (1). Such terms are strictly construed: *Wallis* v. *Pratt* [1911] A.C. 394; *Baldry* v. *Marshall* [1925] 1 K.B. 260.
[96] See Pacta Illicita and Unfair Terms, Ch. IX, supra, § 16. As to exclusion of the warranty of title, see § 25, supra.
[97] Unfair Contract Terms Act 1977 (c. 50), s. 25 (3). The references to sections in the succeeding part of this section are to sections of that Act.
[98] s. 25 (5).
[99] s. 20.
[1] s. 25 (1).
[2] s. 24 (1).
[3] s. 24 (2); Sch. 2. See *Rasbora* v. *J. C. L. Marine* [1977] 1 Lloyd's Rep. 645.

accepting it had an opportunity of entering into a similar contract with other persons, but without having to accept a similar term;

(c) whether the customer knew or ought reasonably to have known of the existence and extent of the term (having regard, among other things, to any custom of the trade and any previous course of dealing between the parties);

(d) where the term excludes or restricts any relevant liability if some condition is not complied with, whether it was reasonable at the time of the contract to expect that compliance with that condition would be practicable;

(e) whether the goods were manufactured, processed or adapted to the special order of the customer.

Where the term purports to restrict liability to a specified sum of money regard should be had to—(a) the resources which the party seeking to rely on that term could expect to be available to him for the purpose of meeting the liability should it arise; (b) how far it was open to that party to cover himself by insurance.[4] The onus of proving that it was fair and reasonable to incorporate a term lies on the party so contending.[5]

32. Rules as to Delivery.—It is the obligation of the seller to deliver the goods, of the buyer to accept and pay for them, in accordance with the terms of the contract [27]. Unless otherwise agreed, delivery and payment of the price are concurrent conditions, so that the seller is not bound to deliver the goods unless the price is paid or tendered, the buyer is not bound to pay the price unless the goods are delivered [28]. The case of a sale on credit is an obvious example of an agreement to the contrary. But in the absence of any express provision on the subject, inference from a previous course of dealing between the parties, or proof of custom of trade, a sale is presumably for cash, and the seller, if he chooses to stand on his strict rights, may refuse delivery unless the price is tendered.[6] Even where the sale is on credit, or a term is fixed for delivery before the term of payment, the seller is not bound to deliver the goods if the buyer is insolvent. He may retain them in the exercise of his right of lien, or, if they have been dispatched and are in course of transit, recover them by the exercise of his right of stoppage in transitu.[7]

The time for delivery may be fixed; if not, the law will infer a time reasonable in the whole circumstances of the case [29 (2)]. Late delivery will give the buyer the right to retain the price in security of his claim for damages.[8] Whether it will entitle him to rescind the contract, and refuse to accept the goods, depends upon whether, in the particular case, the delay amounts to a material failure on the part of the seller.[9]

Whether the seller is to send the goods to the purchaser, or the purchaser

[4] s. 24 (3).
[5] s. 24 (4).
[6] *Hall* v. *Scott* (1860) 22 D. 413.
[7] See infra, §§ 44, 45.
[8] *British Motor Body Co.* v. *Shaw*, 1914 S.C. 922. See Breach of Contract, Ch. XIII, supra, § 12.
[9] Infra, § 35.

to send for them, depends upon the agreement, express or implied, in each case. If the seller is to send by carrier he must make a reasonable contract of carriage.[10] In the absence of any agreement to the contrary the expense of putting the goods in a deliverable state falls on the seller [29 (5)]. Prima facie the place of delivery is the seller's place of business, if he has one; if not, his residence. But if the contract is for specific goods, which, to the knowledge of the parties when the contract is made, are in some other place, then that place is the place of delivery [29].

33. Remedies of Buyer: Failure to Deliver.—The remedies of the buyer depend upon the nature of the seller's failure. If he fails to supply the goods, he is liable in damages. Where there is an available market for the goods,[11] the measure of damages is prima facie to be ascertained by the difference between the contract price and the market price at the time when they ought to have been delivered; if no time was fixed, then at the time of refusal to deliver [51]. The buyer may also demand specific implement of the contract [52], but this remedy is available only when the sale is of some specific article, and the buyer can show a pretium affectionis, some reason for preferring the thing he contracted for to other things of the same kind; it is not competent when the sale is merely of a certain quality of some particular commodity.[12] If the seller delivers less than he contracted to sell, the buyer may reject the goods, but if he accepts them must pay for them at the contract rate. If the seller delivers goods in excess of what he contracted to sell, the buyer may accept the amount he contracted for and reject the rest, or he may reject the whole. If he accepts the whole of the goods delivered, he must pay for them at the contract rate [30]. If the seller delivers the goods contracted for mixed with goods of a different description, the buyer may accept the goods which are in accordance with the contract, and reject the rest, or he may reject the whole [30 (3)]. But neither under the Act nor at common law has the buyer the right, when part of the consignment is of contract quality and the rest, though of the same description, of inferior quality, to keep what is of contract quality and reject the rest.[13] The question as to the remedy of the buyer where the goods do not correspond with the description has been noticed already.[14]

34. Defective Quality: Common Law.—The law as to the remedies of the buyer where the goods delivered are not of the quality demanded by the contract, is a subject on which the Act has made an important alteration in the law of Scotland. At common law the sole remedy of a buyer, if the goods tendered were disconform to contract, was to reject them, and, on doing so, to recover damages for breach of contract. If, however, he chose to accept the

---

[10] *Young* v. *Hobson* (1949) 65 T.L.R. 365.
[11] *Marshall & Co.* v. *Nicoll & Son,* 1919 S.C. 244, affd. 1919 S.C. (H.L.) 129, on meaning of "available market." See also *Thompson* v. *Robinson* [1955] Ch. 177; *Charter* v. *Sullivan* [1957] 2 Q.B. 117.
[12] *Union Electric Co.* v. *Holman,* 1913 S.C. 954, 958.
[13] *Aitken, Campbell & Co.* v. *Boullen,* 1908 S.C. 490.
[14] Supra, § 26.

goods—and in certain cases the exigencies of his business might make acceptance unavoidable—then (except in the case of latent defects) he was held to have condoned their defects, and could not recover damages for their defective quality. The actio quanti minoris, which involves the right to retain goods and claim from the seller the difference between their value and the value they would have possessed had they fulfilled the contractual conditions, was not recognised by the law of Scotland.[15]

35. Remedies Provided by Act.—The law now depends on section 11, which, it may be noted, has separate provisions for England and Scotland. "In Scotland, failure by the seller to perform any material part of a contract of sale is a breach of contract, which entitles the buyer either within a reasonable time after delivery to reject the goods and treat the contract as repudiated,[16] or to retain the goods and treat the failure to perform such material part as a breach which may give rise to a claim for compensation or damages."[17] Under this provision, as interpreted by decisions, the buyer has alternative remedies, in the case where the seller's failure is material, i.e., (a) he may reject the goods, treat the contract as repudiated by the seller, and claim damages; (b) he may keep the goods and claim damages for their defective state, in substance the actio quanti minoris of the civil law.[18]

36. Rejection Excluded by Acceptance.—The right to reject is excluded if the buyer has accepted the goods,[19] even though after acceptance the goods reveal latent defects.[20] If he has not previously examined them, he is not deemed to have accepted them unless and until he has had a reasonable opportunity of examining them for the purpose of ascertaining whether they are in conformity with the contract [34 (1)]. He is deemed to have accepted them when he intimates to the seller that he has accepted them[21] or when the goods have been delivered to him, he has had a reasonable opportunity of examining them[22] and he does any act in relation to them which is inconsistent with the ownership of the seller, or when, after the lapse of a reasonable time, he retains the goods without intimating to the seller that he has rejected them

---

[15] M'Cormick v. Rittmeyer (1869) 7 M. 854, opinion of Lord President Inglis.
[16] As to the construction of clauses whereby the buyer undertakes not to reject goods tendered, with provision for arbitration as to their defects, see Leary v. Briggs (1904) 6 F. 857; Munro v. Meyer [1930] 2 K.B. 312.
[17] See also ss. 53 and 59 of the Act, and George Cohen Sons & Co. v. Jamieson & Peterson, 1963 S.C. 289.
[18] It is conceived that there is nothing in the Act to affect the common law distinction between the laws of England and Scotland, to the effect that, according to Scots law, any material failure in the quality of the goods will entitle the buyer to reject them, whilst according to English law, rejection is incompetent for a failure in quality not amounting to a difference in kind, unless there is an express provision for it. See opinion of Lord Chelmsford in Couston, Thomson & Co. v. Chapman (1872) 10 M. (H.L.) 74, at p. 81; referred to, as applicable to the existing law, by Lord Dunedin, Pollock v. M'Crae, 1922 S.C. (H.L.) 192, at pp. 202-3.
[19] Mechan v. Bow, M'Lachlan & Co., 1910 S.C. 758; Woodburn v. Motherwell, 1917 S.C. 533; Hardy v. Hillerns [1923] 2 K.B. 490 (re-sale); Gloag, Contract (2nd ed.), at p. 611.
[20] Morrison & Mason v. Clarkson Bros. (1898) 25 R. 427; Mechans v. Highland Marine Charters, 1964 S.C. 48.
[21] Mechans v. Highland Marine Charters, supra (unqualified acceptance).
[22] Misrepresentation Act 1967, s. 4 (2). This alters the law as stated in Hardy v. Hillerns, supra.

[35]. Thus where it was a condition of a contract for the supply of a boiler for a tank which was being built for the Navy that it should have passed Admiralty tests, it was held that the buyer, by fitting the boiler in the tank, had done an act inconsistent with the ownership of the seller, and could not reject it on the ground that the tests had not been passed.[23] But the fact that the property of a thing in course of construction may have passed to the buyer does not preclude his ultimate rejection of it. So where there was a contract to build a yacht, with provisions under which the property passed to the buyer as the various instalments of the price were paid, it was held that the buyer was still entitled to reject when, on completion, the yacht proved disconform to contract.[24] It has been held that it is not necessarily too late to reject after the lapse of two years when the goods had been stored and the defect only discovered when they were taken out.[25]

Conditions of Rejection.—Rejection is inconsistent with any further use of the goods. So it is established that if the buyer merely intimates rejection and, on the seller refusing to take the goods back, continues to use them, he cannot insist on his right to reject.[26] In one case it was decided that in these circumstances the buyer, having by his notice of rejection elected one of two alternative remedies, was bound by that election, and could not fall back on the alternative of keeping the goods and claiming damages for their defective condition.[27] But this decision has been authoritatively disapproved.[28] Where the buyer has lost or foregone his right of rejection and is confined to a claim for damages, a clause which purports to exclude liability may not be operative if there has been a fundamental breach of contract on the part of the seller.[29] But it has been emphasised that the applicability of such an exceptions clause in that situation depends upon the true construction of the particular contract.[30] Continued use after intimation of rejection will still, it is conceived, bar rejection, but will not bar a claim of damages on the principle of the *actio quanti minoris.*

37. Duty When Goods Rejected.—When the buyer rejects the goods he has no right to retain them in security of his claim of damages.[31] In the absence of any express provision, he is not bound to return them to the seller [36]. But where a horse was rejected as unsound, and the seller refused to take it back, opinions were expressed that it was the duty of the buyer either to have it placed in neutral custody or to obtain judicial authority for its re-sale.[32] If the

---

23 *Mechan* v. *Bow, M'Lachlan & Co.*, supra. See also *Morrison & Mason* v. *Clarkson Bros.*, supra.
24 *Nelson* v. *Chalmers*, 1913 S.C. 441.
25 *Burrell* v. *Harding's Exrs.*, 1931 S.L.T. 76 (a decision on relevancy).
26 *Electric Construction Co.* v. *Hurry & Young* (1897) 24 R. 312; *Croom & Arthur* v. *Stewart* (1905) 7 F. 563.
27 *Electric Construction Co.* v. *Hurry & Young,* supra.
28 *Pollock* v. *M'Crae*, 1922 S.C. (H.L.) 192.
29 *Pollock* v. *M'Crae,* supra.
30 *Suisse Atlantique* v. *N.V. Rotterdamsche* [1967] 1 A.C. 361; and see Breach of Contract, Ch. XIII, § 4, supra.
31 *Lupton* v. *Schulze* (1900) 2 F. 1118.
32 *Malcolm* v. *Cross* (1898) 25 R. 1089.

goods rejected are perishable the buyer is entitled, and probably bound, to re-sell them at once.[33]

38. Examination of Goods.—In a question of rejection, the buyer is bound to examine the goods within a reasonable time. What is a reasonable time is a question of the circumstances of each particular case.[34] But two general points are established—(a) When, as in the case of machinery, the defect is apparently remediable, and the seller, on being appealed to, attempts to remedy the defect, no lapse of time or continued use of the article while his attempts are still in progress will bar ultimate rejection by the buyer.[35] (b) Where goods are ordered for export, the buyer, unless he can prove that the circumstances rendered it impossible, is bound to examine the goods before forwarding them, and failure to do so will preclude rejection on the ground of any defect which a prompt examination would have revealed, on the principle that a seller is entitled to have an opportunity to remedy the goods.[36]

39. Failure in Minor Respects.—The Act has no provision for the case of failure by the seller in some respect which is not material. The rule at common law is that the buyer is not then entitled to reject the goods, but may recover damages for the defect.[37] What is a material failure is a question of the circumstances of each case, and of degree. Any serious defect in quality is undoubtedly material. But at least in cases of machinery the buyer is not within his rights in instant rejection on the ground of some remediable defect.[38] Failure in respect of time of delivery is as a rule material in the case of mercantile contracts for the supply of goods where time is usually of the essence of the contract,[39] but not in the case of a contract for the supply of an article to be built or manufactured by the seller.[40]

40. Instalment Contracts.—Contracts for the supply of goods by instal-ments, with provisions for intermediate payments, have raised the question whether the delivery of defective goods, or failure of delivery, in respect of one instalment, and, conversely, whether delay in payment of one instalment of the price, will justify the party aggrieved in rescinding the contract as repudiated by the other. By section 31 it is stated that it is a question of the circumstances of each case. That question, it would appear, is whether the conduct of the party in default is such as to justify the other in inferring that he does not intend to fulfil his contract, or is unable to do so. That inference may more easily be drawn in the case of failure in early than in later instalments. The law has been judicially stated as follows: "If on one occasion

[33] *Pommer* v. *Mowat* (1906) 14 S.L.T. 373.
[34] See *Hyslop* v. *Shirlaw* (1905) 7 F. 875.
[35] *Munro* v. *Bennett*, 1911 S.C. 337; *Aird & Coghill* v. *Pullan* (1904) 7 F. 258.
[36] *Pini* v. *Smith* (1895) 22 R. 699; *Magistrates of Glasgow* v. *Ireland* (1895) 22 R. 818; *Dick* v. *Cochrane & Fleming*, 1935 S.L.T. 432.
[37] *Webster* v. *Cramond Iron Co.* (1875) 2 R. 752; *Bradley* v. *Dollar* (1886) 13 R. 893.
[38] *Morrison & Mason* v. *Clarkson* (1898) 25 R. 427.
[39] *Shaw, Macfarlane & Co.* v. *Waddell* (1900) 2 F. 1070.
[40] *Macbride* v. *Hamilton* (1875) 2 R. 775.

the seller should tender goods inferior to contract quality, the purchaser would not in ordinary circumstances be justified in rescinding the whole contract, though he would be entitled to return the particular lot of goods which were objectionable. But if a seller systematically send goods which are not conformable to contract, and the contract is for successive deliveries, I do not doubt that, where such conduct is persisted in, so as to make it evident that the seller does not intend to fulfil his contract, the purchaser may rescind the contract and refuse to take further deliveries."[41] Only in exceptional circumstances would delay in payment justify the seller in rescinding the contract.[42]

41. Rights of Seller: Refusal of Acceptance.—Questions as to the rights of the seller arise where the buyer wrongfully refuses to accept the goods, or when he fails to pay the price. In the case of refusal to accept and pay for the goods the seller may maintain an action of damages for non-acceptance, the measure of damages being, if there is an available market for the goods,[43] the difference between the contract price and the market price ruling at the date when the goods ought to have been accepted [50]. He is also entitled to a reasonable charge for the care and custody of the goods [37]. Refusal by the buyer, either to accept the goods or to pay the price, would seem to amount to a repudiation of the contract by him, which would justify the seller in an immediate re-sale, preferably under a warrant from the sheriff.[44]

42. Failure in Payment.—Where the buyer fails to pay the price we have to consider (a) the seller's right of action; and (b) his rights over the goods.

If the property in the goods has passed to the buyer, i.e., if the contract was a sale, as contrasted with an agreement to sell, the seller may maintain an action for the price [49 (1)]. He may also do so if the price was payable on a day certain,[45] irrespective of delivery, although the property in the goods has not passed, and the goods have not been appropriated to the contract [49 (2)]. In other cases his action is for damages for non-acceptance [50]. Mere failure to pay the price does not entitle the seller to rescind the contract and demand re-delivery of the goods after the property has passed to the buyer.[46] But, if the contract was induced by fraud, the seller may reduce it and recover the goods in a question either with the buyer himself or with the trustee in his sequestration, and it is sufficient proof of fraud if it be established that the buyer bought the goods without any intention to pay for them.[47]

---

[41] *Govan Rope Co.* v. *Weir* (1897) 24 R. 368, per Lord M'Laren. See *Dunford & Elliot* v. *Macleod & Co.* (1902) 4 F. 912; *Mersey Steel Co.* v. *Naylor Benzon & Co.* (1884) 9 App. Cas. 434; *Maple Flock Co.* v. *Universal Furniture Products* [1934] 1 K.B. 148.

[42] s. 10 (1); *Barclay* v. *Anderston Foundry Co.* (1856) 18 D. 1190; *Linn* v. *Shields* (1863) 2 M. 88.

[43] *Thompson* v. *Robinson* [1955] Ch. 177 (where there was no available market); *Charter* v. *Sullivan* [1957] 2 Q.B. 117. Cf. *Lazenby Garages* v. *Wright* [1976] 1 W.L.R. 459.

[44] Bell, *Prin.*, § 128.

[45] On meaning of "a day certain", see *Henderson & Keay Ltd.* v. *A.M. Carmichael Ltd.*, 1956 S.L.T. (Notes) 58.

[46] *Muirhead & Turnbull* v. *Dickson* (1905) 7 F. 686.

[47] *Gamage* v. *Charlesworth's Tr.*, 1910 S.C. 257.

43. Rights of Unpaid Seller over Goods.—The rights of a seller over the goods are dealt with in Part IV of the Act, under the heading "Rights of Unpaid Seller against the Goods."[48] A seller is deemed to be unpaid (a) when the whole of the price has not been paid or tendered; (b) when a bill of exchange or other negotiable instrument has been received as conditional payment, and the condition on which it was received has not been fulfilled by reason of the dishonour of the instrument or otherwise[49] [38]. The unpaid seller may have one or more of the following rights:— Lien; stoppage in transitu; re-sale; attachment of the goods by arrestment or poinding.

44. Lien.—Lien is the right of the seller while still in possession of the goods (whether the property has passed or not) to retain them until payment or tender of the price, in the following cases:—(a) Where the goods have been sold without any stipulation as to credit; (b) when the period of credit has expired; (c) when the buyer becomes insolvent [41]. A buyer is deemed to be insolvent if he either has ceased to pay his debts in the ordinary course of business or cannot pay his debts as they become due, whether he has become a notour bankrupt or not [62 (3)]. A right of lien is lost (a) when the seller delivers the goods to a carrier for the purpose of transmission to the buyer without reserving the right of disposal; (b) when the buyer or his agent lawfully obtains possession of the goods[50]; (c) by waiver [43]. A right of lien is not affected by the fact that the buyer may have re-sold or pledged[51] the goods to a third party [47]. But in a case before the Act it was held that where A had sold to B on a month's credit and B re-sold to C, who intimated the sub-sale to A within the month, A had waived his right of lien in a question with C and must deliver to him, although B was bankrupt and could not pay A.[52] And if the buyer has obtained a document of title to the goods, and that document has been transferred to a person who takes it in good faith,[53] and for valuable consideration, then if that transfer was by way of sale the original seller's right of lien is defeated; if by way of pledge, the right of lien can only be exercised subject to the rights of the pledgee [47]. Delivery of part of the goods does not preclude the exercise of lien over the remainder [42].

45. Stoppage in Transitu.—Stoppage in transitu is a principle which was introduced into the law of Scotland by the decision of the House of Lords in *Jaffrey* v. *Allan, Stewart & Co.,*[54] in place of a doctrine, which was then disapproved, that if a buyer took delivery of goods within three days of

---

[48] See Gow, pp. 186 et seq.
[49] *M'Dowall & Neilson's Tr.* v. *Snowball Co.* (1904) 7 F. 35.
[50] But where a seller retakes possession from the buyer, he does not retain his right of lien: *London Scottish Transport* v. *Tyres (Scotland),* 1957 S.L.T. (Sh. Ct.) 48.
[51] Since ex hypothesi the seller is still in possession and pledge requires delivery (Rights in Security, Ch. XX, infra, § 18), the circumstances in which the buyer can pledge must be exceptional.
[52] *Fleming* v. *Smith* (1881) 8 R. 548.
[53] As to the meaning of "good faith," see supra, § 21.
[54] (1790) 3 Paton 191.

stopping payment (intra triduum) he was presumed to have taken them fraudulently, and the seller could recover them in a question with his trustee in bankruptcy.

The right of stoppage in transitu, as now regulated by the Act, is the right of an unpaid seller, in the case where the property has passed to the buyer, and the goods are in course of transit to him, to resume possession, and to retain the goods until payment or tender of the price [44]. Where the property has not passed to the buyer the seller has a right of withholding delivery similar to and co-extensive with the right of stoppage in transitu [39 (2)]. The right of stoppage can be exercised only when the buyer becomes insolvent.[55] If the seller stops the goods and is unable to prove that the buyer is insolvent he is liable in damages.

Stoppage in transitu may be effected either by taking actual possession of the goods, or by giving notice to the carrier requiring him to re-deliver the goods to the seller, at the latter's expense [46 (2)]. Notice may be given either to the actual custodier, or to his principal, e.g., to the British Railways Board or shipping company. In the latter case it must be given in time to allow of communication with the actual custodier [46 (1)]. Where the contract of carriage has been made by the buyer, the seller, by giving notice to stop, incurs personal liability for the freight.[56] If the carrier disregards the notice, and delivers the goods to the buyer, the stoppage is defeated, and the goods fall to be treated as part of the assets in the buyer's bankruptcy, but the carrier is liable in damages to the seller.[57]

Stoppage in transitu is competent only while the goods are in transit. The Act deals with the duration of the transit in seven rules [45]. These should be referred to, but it may be convenient to state the general law. The transit may end either at the actual place of delivery or when the buyer or his agent obtains possession at some intermediate place. Actual delivery is not necessary to end the transit, if the carrier acknowledges to the buyer that he holds the goods for him after their arrival at the place of destination. So where goods were sent by rail to a particular station, and the consignee there signed a receipt for them but did not take them away, it was held that the transit had ended, and that a subsequent notice to stop came too late.[58] There is no room for stoppage in transitu if the buyer sends for the goods. If he charters a ship the goods are in his custody, and cannot therefore be stopped, as soon as they are put on board.[59] But the duration of the transit is not affected by the fact that the contract of carriage with the shipowner is made by the buyer, if the ship is not chartered by him in such a way as to make the captain of the ship his servant.[60]

If part of the goods is delivered to the buyer, the remainder may be stopped, unless the part delivery has been made in such circumstances as to

---

[55] As to the meaning of insolvency, see supra, § 44.
[56] *Booth Co.* v. *Cargo Fleet Iran Co.* [1916] 2 K.B. 570.
[57] *Mechan* v. *N.-E. Ry.* 1911 S.C. 1348.
[58] *Muir* v. *Rankin* (1905) 13 S.L.T. 60.
[59] *Rosevear China Clay Co.* (1879) 11 Ch.D. 560.
[60] *Booth Co.* v. *Cargo Fleet Iron Co.* [1916] 2 K.B. 570.

show an agreement to give up possession of the whole [45 (7)]. When two boats arrived at Sunderland station, and one of them was delivered to a carter who had general instructions to take all goods arriving for the consignee, and the other would have been delivered to the carter if he had had room for it, it was held that the circumstances did not show an agreement by the railway company to give up possession of the second boat, and that it might still be stopped in transitu.[61] Rules, similar to those applicable to lien,[62] apply where a document of title has been transferred to a third party either as a sub-purchaser or as a pledgee.

46. Re-Sale.—The unpaid seller, if in possession of the goods, either under lien or after he has stopped them in transitu, is entitled to re-sell them either if they are perishable or if he has given notice to the buyer of his intention to re-sell, and the buyer does not within a reasonable time pay or tender the price. The contract of sale is not rescinded by the exercise of a right of lien or of stoppage in transitu [48 (1)] but, if the seller then re-sells, the contract is rescinded, whether the resale is of the whole of the goods or part of them, and the property in them reverts to the seller who may then recover from the original buyer damages for non-acceptance[63] [48 (3)]. If the seller expressly reserves the right of re-sale in case the buyer should make default, and, on the buyer making default, re-sells, the original contract of sale is rescinded, without prejudice to any claim the seller may have for damages [48 (4)]. In all cases of re-sale the buyer obtains a good title to the goods as against the original buyer [48 (2)].

47. Arrestment or Poinding.—The Act provides [40]: "In Scotland a seller of goods may attach the same while in his own hands or possession by arrestment or poinding; and such arrestment or poinding shall have the same operation and effect in a competition or otherwise as an arrestment or poinding by a third party." There is no analogous process in England. In a case under the Mercantile Law Amendment (Scotland) Act 1856 (which contained a similar provision), it was held that arrestment was the appropriate diligence.[64] It would seem unnecessary for the seller of goods to use this diligence merely to secure the price, already covered by lien, though it might possibly enable him to obtain a right over the goods in security of other debts due to him by the buyer.

48. Auction Sales.—The law of sale by auction is regulated by section 58. Prima facie each lot is to be regarded as a separate contract of sale. So it was held that where wine was sold in lots the purchaser was entitled to reject certain lots which were defective and to keep the rest.[65]

---

[61] *Mechan* v. *North-Eastern Ry.*, 1911 S.C. 1348.
[62] s. 47, and see supra, § 44.
[63] *R. V. Ward* v. *Bignall* [1967] 1 Q.B. 534.
[64] *Wyper* v. *Harveys* (1861) 23 D. 606.
[65] *Couston, Thomson & Co.* v. *Chapman* (1872) 10 M. (H.L.) 74.

A sale by auction is complete when the auctioneer announces its completion by the fall of the hammer. Until such announcement is made any bidder may retract his bid [58 (2)]. The common law, which will still rule in sales to which the Act does not apply, e.g., sales of heritage, was not settled, but probably was that a bid could not be retracted, unless it were refused, or a higher bid made.[66] It has been held to follow from the statutory provision that as each bidder may retract his bid the exposer has a corresponding right to withdraw the article even after the bidding has commenced.[67]

A reserve price is lawful [58 (4)], but unless the right of the seller to bid is expressly reserved, it is unlawful and may be treated as fraudulent for him to bid or to employ anyone else, commonly spoken of as a white-bonnet, to bid for him [58 (3)]. Should it transpire that fraudulent bids of this kind have been made the highest bona fide bidder is entitled to the article at the last bid he made before the fraudulent bidding commenced.[68] If, however, the objection to the sale is merely that a person has made bids who was not entitled to do so, and there is no proof of fraud, the bidder to whom the article is ultimately adjudged must pay the full price he has offered.[69] But if the party disqualified proves to be the highest bidder the sale is open to reduction by other bidders or by anyone who can show an interest in obtaining the highest possible price.[70] It is a general rule that a party directly interested in the sale is not entitled to bid. So a beneficiary may not bid in a sale by a trustee,[71] and one of several part owners is equally disqualified.[72] It is doubtful whether the creditor in a bond and disposition in security, exposing the subjects for sale under the powers in his bond, is entitled to bid; in any event the disqualification does not apply where there are several creditors, and bids are made by one.[73] In a sale by a trustee in bankruptcy a creditor holding a security over the subject sold is entitled to bid, but the trustee himself, the law agent employed by him, a partner of such law agent, and the commissioners in the sequestration, are not.[74]

It has twice been held in Scotland that when an intending bidder bribed others not to compete with him his conduct amounted to fraud on the exposer, which entitled the latter to reduce the sale and recover the expenses of it from the party implicated.[75] It was decided in England that such an agreement was not a pactum illicitum, and that its conditions could be enforced by the parties to it inter se.[76] Now, by the Auctions (Bidding Agreements) Act 1927 (17 & 18 Geo. V., c. 12), if any dealer[77] agrees to give,

---

[66] Cree v. Durie, 1st December, 1810, F.C.
[67] Fenwick v. Macdonald, Fraser & Co. (1904) 6 F. 850.
[68] Faulds v. Corbet (1859) 21 D. 587.
[69] Wishart v. Howatson (1897) 5 S.L.T. 84.
[70] Shiell v. Guthrie's Trs. (1874) 1 R. 1083.
[71] Shiell, supra.
[72] Morrice v. Craig (1902) 39 S.L.R. 609.
[73] Wright v. Buchanan, 1917 S.C. 73.
[74] Bankruptcy (Scotland) Act 1913, s. 116.
[75] Murray v. M'Whan (1783) M. 9567; Aitchison (1783) M. 9567.
[76] Rawlings v. General Trading Co. [1921] 1 K.B. 635.
[77] Defined as "a person who in the normal course of his business attends sales by auction for the purpose of purchasing goods with a view to reselling them."

or gives, or offers to give, any gift or consideration to any other person as a reward for abstaining, or for having abstained, from bidding at a sale by auction, he and any person who agrees to accept, or accepts, or attempts to obtain, any such gift commits a criminal offence. Where goods are purchased at an auction by a person who has entered into an agreement with another or others that the other or others (or some of them) will abstain from bidding for the goods (not being an agreement to purchase the goods bona fide on joint account) and he or the other party, or one of the other parties, to the agreement is a dealer, the seller may avoid the contract under which the goods were purchased; if restitution of the goods is not made the parties to the bidding agreement are jointly and severally liable to make good to the seller the loss (if any) he sustained by reason of the operation of the agreement.[78] It is also an offence to permit or conduct an auction where (a) any person bidding has an article in a lot sold to him for less than his highest bid for that lot; or (b) part of the price at which it was sold is repaid or credited to him; or (c) the right to bid for any lot is restricted to persons who have bought or agreed to buy one or more articles; or (d) any articles are given away or offered as gifts.[79]

An auctioneer is entitled to give notice that he will not receive bids from particular parties, or from parties representing a particular interest, and his refusal of their bids does not constitute an actionable wrong.[80]

49. Sale or Return: Sale on Approval.—The contract of sale or return is usually entered into when goods are supplied by a wholesaler to a retail dealer on the condition, variously expressed, that the latter may sell them to his customers, but has the option to return them. A sale on approval implies that possession of an article is given, with an unqualified option to buy it or to return it within a specified period. When a horse was sold with a warranty, and delivered on a week's trial, it was held that the contract was not a sale on approval. The buyer's option to return the horse within the week was not unqualified, he could do so only if it failed to fulfil the warranty.[81]

In the question of the passing of the property in the goods the contracts of sale or return and sale on approval are dealt with in the same subsection of the Act [18, Rule 4]: "When goods are delivered to the buyer on approval or 'on sale or return' or other similar terms the property therein passes to the buyer—(a) When he signifies his approval or acceptance to the seller or does any other act adopting the transaction; (b) If he does not signify his approval or acceptance to the seller but retains the goods without giving notice of rejection, then, if a time has been fixed for the return of the goods, on the expiration of such time, and, if no time has been fixed, on the expiration of a reasonable time. What is a reasonable time is a question of fact."[82] In certain cases the retail dealer, having obtained goods on sale or return, has pawned

[78] Auctions (Bidding Agreements) Act 1969 (c. 56), s.3.
[79] Mock Auctions Act 1961 (9 & 10 Eliz. II, c. 47). See *Allen* v. *Simmons* [1978] 1 W.L.R. 879.
[80] *Scottish Co-operative Society* v. *Glasgow Fleshers* (1898) 35 S.L.R. 645.
[81] *Cranston* v. *Mallow,* 1912 S.C. 112.
[82] See *Poole* v. *Smith's Car Sales* [1962] 1 W.L.R. 744.

them, and the question of the title of the pawnbroker in a question with the wholesale dealer has been raised. If the contract merely provides that the retail dealer may sell the goods or may return them it is probably established that by pawning them (although fraudulently) he does an act adopting the transaction, the property passes to him, and the pawnbroker obtains a good title.[83] The wholesale dealer may seek to protect himself by stipulating that, before disposing of any article, the retail dealer must have it invoiced by him. In *Bryce* v. *Ehrmann*[83] opinions were expressed that in spite of such a clause a pawnbroker would obtain a good title, but, in view of a contrary English decision,[84] the law cannot be regarded as settled. Goods on sale or return do not pass to the trustee in the sequestration of the retail dealer,[85] nor, it is conceived, could they be attached by his creditors by poinding. But as invecta et illata they are possibly covered by the landlord's hypothec, and could be attached by him by sequestration.[86]

50. Sale: f.o.b.; c.i.f.—In sale f.o.b. (free on board) or, in inland carriage, f.o.r. (free on rail) the seller undertakes to ship the goods at the port of shipment, or to load them at the station named, the expense of the carriage, and of insurance, falling upon the buyer, to whom the property of the goods is transferred, and on whom the risk falls. Any charge necessarily payable before the goods are put on board, such as an export duty newly imposed, falls upon the seller.[87]

A sale c.i.f. (cost, insurance, freight) imports that the price includes the freight of the goods to their destination, and their insurance during transit. If, as is usual, the arrangement with the shipowner is that the freight is to be paid by the buyer or consignee on delivery of the goods, the amount is deducted from the invoice price. The obligation of the seller, in a contract c.i.f., is to ship the goods and transmit to the buyer the shipping documents, these being an invoice, a bill of lading and a policy of insurance. When these are sent to the buyer the property and risk pass to him.[88] On tender of the shipping documents the buyer is bound to pay the price, and is not entitled to withhold payment until the goods arrive and he has had an opportunity of examining them.[89] But payment of the price does not imply acceptance of the goods, and if they arrive and are disconform to contract, the buyer may still reject them, and recover the price or damages.[90] If the goods are lost in transit the buyer cannot recover the price; his remedy lies in the policy of insurance.[91] When timber in New Brunswick was sold "c.i.f. Glasgow" it was decided, in a question of stoppage in transitu, that it was in course of transit until it reached

[83] *Bryce* v. *Ehrmann* (1904) 7 F. 5; *Kirkham* v. *Attenborough* [1897] 1 Q.B. 201.
[84] *Weiner* v. *Gill* [1906] 2 K.B. 574.
[85] *Macdonald* v. *Westren* (1888) 15 R. 988.
[86] See Leases, Ch. XXXIII, infra, § 10.
[87] *Bowhill Coal Co.* v. *Tobias* (1902) 5 F. 262.
[88] *Delaurier* v. *Wylie* (1889) 17 R. 167.
[89] *Horst* v. *Biddel* [1912] A.C. 18.
[90] *Pommer* v. *Mowat* (1906) 14 S.L.T. 373; *Harrower, Welsh & Co.* v. *M'William*, 1928 S.C. 326.
[91] *Delaurier* v. *Wylie* (1889) 17 R. 167; *Manbre Saccharine Co.* v. *Corn Products Co.* [1919] 1 K.B. 198.

Glasgow, in spite of the fact that in the contract it was stated to be "deliverable" at a New Brunswick port.[92]

A development of the c.i.f. contract is that the buyer agrees to open in favour of the seller a confirmed banker's credit on which the seller may draw on presentation of the shipping documents, possibly with other documents.[93] The buyer is bound to keep the credit open during the whole period allowed for shipping.[93]

51. Hire-Purchase.—The term "hire-purchase" is commonly used to describe a variety of different types of agreement. Strictly, however, a contract of hire-purchase is one under which articles are taken on hire and the hirer is granted an option to purchase them on his fulfilling certain conditions of the contract.[94] This type of contract is to be contrasted with a contract of sale under which the buyer and seller are under binding obligations to each other respectively to buy and to sell.[95] Accordingly, if the terms of the hire-purchase agreement in any way bind the hirer to purchase the article hired, the contract is one of sale, not of hire-purchase.[96] This distinction is of importance in considering whether a hirer has conferred a good title upon an innocent third party to whom he has purported to sell the article hired. If the contract is only one of hire-purchase, the third party does not obtain a good title.[97] If on the other hand, it is one of sale, the hirer is a person who has bought or agreed to buy goods and is in possession of them with the consent of the owner; and under the provisions of section 25 (2) of the Sale of Goods Act[98] he has the power to give a good title to the third party.[99] But where the contract is truly one of hire-purchase, the hirer has the right to acquire the article by completing the payments and this right he may assign to a third party. If he sells the article, at least if there is no proof that in doing so he acted fraudulently, it will be assumed that he transferred all the right he possessed, and the purchaser from him, though he will not get a complete title to the article, will be entitled to retain it and complete his right by payment of the remaining instalments of the hire-purchase, provided that there is no term in the agreement forbidding assignation.[1] Articles on hire-purchase do not pass to the trustee in the hirer's sequestration,[2] but presumably he has the power to

---

[92] M'Dowall & Neilson's Tr. v. Snowball Co. (1904) 7 F. 35.
[93] Pavia & Co., S.P.A. v. Thurmann-Neilsen [1952] 2 Q.B. 84; Trans Trust S.P.R.L. v. Danubian Trading Co. [1952] 2 Q.B. 297.
[94] Compare, however, the definition of "hire-purchase agreement" in the Consumer Credit Act 1974, s. 189.
[95] Murdoch v. Greig (1889) 16 R. 396, especially per Lord President Inglis at p. 400, and per Lord Shand at p. 402.
[96] The Court will examine the substance of each agreement carefully to see whether it is one of hire-purchase or sale, whatever its terms: Murdoch v. Greig, supra; Scottish Transit Trust v. Scottish Land Cultivators, 1955 S.C. 254.
[97] Helby v. Matthews [1895] A.C. 471. Motor vehicles are now a statutory exception where sold to a private purchaser by the hirer: Hire-Purchase Act 1964 (c. 53), Part III; see infra.
[98] See supra, § 20.
[99] Lee v. Butler [1893] 2 Q.B. 318. But see § 20, supra as to conditional sales which are subject to the Consumer Credit Act 1974.
[1] Whiteley v. Hilt [1918] 2 K.B. 808.
[2] Stewart, Diligence, pp. 341-3.

adopt the contract and acquire them by completing the payments. They fall under the landlord's hypothec.[3]

Part III of the Hire-Purchase Act 1964 provides that where the hirer of a motor vehicle under a hire-purchase agreement or the buyer of such a vehicle under a conditional sale agreement disposes of the vehicle to a private purchaser[4] who purchases in good faith and without notice[5] of the said agreement, the disposition has effect as if the title of the owner or seller to the vehicle had been vested in the hirer or buyer, immediately before that disposition.[6]

The Supply of Goods (Implied Terms) Act 1973 (as amended by the Consumer Credit Act 1974, Sch. 4, para. 35), ss. 8-11, imposes implied stipulations as to the title, description, quality and fitness of goods let on hire-purchase, corresponding to those implied in the sale of goods. Section 20 of the Unfair Contract Terms Act 1977 applies to these terms.[7]

---

[3] *Rudman* v. *Jay*, 1908 S.C. 552.

[4] To be contrasted with a "trade or finance purchaser": s. 27 (3). A person who carries on a part-time business of buying and selling motor-vehicles is a "trade or finance purchaser" even in relation to a vehicle he acquires for his own private use: *Stevenson* v. *Beverley Bentinck* [1976] 1 W.L.R. 483.

[5] Notice of a prior hire-purchase agreement which has been paid off does not affect the private purchaser's title: *Barker* v. *Bell* [1971] 1 W.L.R. 983.

[6] It is doubtful whether, in Scotland, the person who let the vehicle on hire has any remedy against a trade purchaser, who, having acquired the vehicle in good faith from the hirer, re-sells it to a private purchaser who thus may acquire a good title: *North-West Securities* v. *Barrhead Coachworks*, 1976 S.C. 68. Cf. *F. C. Finance* v. *Langtry Investment Co.* 1973 S.L.T. (Sh. Ct.) 11, where the doctrine of specificatio was applied. For the English position, see *Moorgate Mercantile Co.*, v. *Twitchings* [1977] A.C. 890,

[7] See § 31, supra.

CHAPTER XVIII

CONSUMER PROTECTION

O'Keefe, *The Law Relating to Trade Descriptions* (1971); Cunningham, *The Fair Trading Act 1973* (1974); Harvey, *Law of Consumer Protection and Fair Trading* (1978).

The most important measures for the protection of the consumer—the Supply of Goods (Implied Terms) Act 1973 and the Unfair Contract Terms Act 1977—have already been discussed. In this chapter some miscellaneous statutory provisions are collected. No attempt is made to deal with the Food and Drugs Acts or the Weights and Measures Acts.

    1. Unsolicited Goods and Services.—A person who receives unsolicited goods may as between himself and the sender treat them as if they were an unconditional gift to him and any right of the sender to the goods is extinguished if the following conditions are satisfied:— (i) the goods were sent to the recipient with a view to his acquiring them, (ii) the recipient has no reasonable cause to believe that they were sent with a view to their being acquired for the purposes of a trade or business and has neither agreed to acquire nor agreed to return them, (iii) the sender has not taken possession of the goods and the recipient did not unreasonably refuse to permit the sender to do so in the period of six months beginning with the day of receipt, (iv) not less than thirty days before the expiration of the six months the recipient gave written notice to the sender of the location of the goods and of the fact that they are unsolicited and the sender has not within the thirty days following the notice taken or tried to take possession of the goods.[1] It is an offence to demand payment or to assert a right to payment or to attempt to enforce payment for goods which are known to be unsolicited.[2] A person is not liable to make payment for inclusion of an entry relating to him in a directory unless an order or note satisfying specified requirements has been signed by him.[3] It is an offence to send or cause to be sent to another person, in the knowledge that it is unsolicited, a book, magazine or leaflet which describes or illustrates human sexual techniques or advertising material for such a publication.[4] An invoice or similar document stating the amount of any payment is regarded as asserting a right to payment unless it complies with the Unsolicited Goods and Services (Invoices, etc.) Regulations 1975.[5]

[1] Unsolicited Goods and Services Act 1971(c. 30), s. 1.
[2] s. 2; *Readers Digest Association* v. *Pirie,* 1973 S.L.T. 170.
[3] An attempt to recover payment is again an offence.
[4] s. 4; *Director of Public Prosecutions* v. *Beate Uhse (U.K.)* [1974] Q.B. 158.
[5] S.I. 1975 No. 732; ss. 3A, 6 (2) as added by Unsolicited Goods and Services (Amendment) Act 1975 (c. 13).

2. Trade Descriptions Act 1968.[6]—The Act makes it an offence to misdescribe goods or services or to give false indications as to the price of goods. A contract for the supply of any goods is not void or unenforceable by reason only of a contravention of the Act.[7]

It is an offence for a person in the course of a trade or business[8] to apply a false trade description to any goods or to supply or offer to supply any goods to which a false trade description is applied at the time of supply or has been so applied in the course of negotiations leading to such supply.[9] A person exposing goods for supply or having goods in his possession for supply is deemed to offer to supply them. The offence of applying a false trade description may be committed by a buyer if he is acting in the course of a trade or business[10] but the offence is not committed by a description given incidentally in the course of performance of the service of advising in regard to some matter affecting the goods.[11] A statement made after the sale or supply cannot give rise to an offence.[12]

A trade description is an indication, direct or indirect, and by whatever means given, of the quantity, composition,[13] fitness for purpose or other specified characteristics of the goods.[14] The mileage recorded on the mileometer of a car may be a trade description.[15] "Extra value" on the wrapper of a bar of chocolate is not a trade description.[16]

3. False Description.—A false trade description is a trade description which is false to a material degree.[17] A trade description which, though not false, is misleading, i.e., likely to be taken for such an indication of the specified matters as would be false to a material degree, is deemed to be a false trade description.[18] Anything which, though not a trade description, is likely to be taken for an indication of any of the specified matters, and, as such an indication, would be false to a material degree, is deemed to be a false trade description.[19] An indication which appears to be a false trade description may be shown not to be by a disclaimer which is about as precise and compelling as the indication itself, and which is effectively brought to the notice of any person to whom the goods may be supplied.[20]

---

[6] c. 29.
[7] 1968 Act, s. 35.
[8] See *Havering London Borough Council* v. *Stevenson* [1970] 1 W.L.R. 1375.
[9] s. 1 (1); *Norman* v. *Bennett* [1974] 1 W.L.R. 1229.
[10] *Fletcher* v. *Budgen* [1974] 1 W.L.R. 1056.
[11] *Wycombe Marsh Garages* v. *Fowler* [1972] 1 W.L.R. 1156.
[12] *Hall* v. *Wickens Motors (Gloucester)* [1972] 1 W.L.R. 1418. Cf. *Fletcher* v. *Sledmore* [1973] R.T.R. 371.
[13] See *British Gas Corporation* v. *Lubbock* [1974] 1 W.L.R. 37.
[14] s. 2 (1).
[15] *McNab* v. *Alexanders of Greenock* 1971 S.L.T. 121; *Tarleton Engineering Co.* v. *Nattrass* [1973] 1 W.L.R. 1261.
[16] *Cadbury* v. *Halliday* [1975] 1 W.L.R. 649. Cf. *Robertson* v. *Dicicco* [1972] R.T.R. 431 ("beautiful car").
[17] s. 3 (1).
[18] s. 3 (2).
[19] s. 3 (3).
[20] *Norman* v. *Bennett*, supra; *R.* v. *Hammertons Cars* [1976] 1 W.L.R. 1243. See also *Doble* v. *David Greig* [1972] 1 W.L.R. 703; *Zawadski* v. *Sleigh* [1975] R.T.R. 113.

4. Applying Description.—A person applies a trade description to goods if he—

"(a) affixes or annexes it to or in any manner marks it on or incorporates it with—

    (i) the goods themselves, or

    (ii) anything in, on or with which the goods are supplied; or

(b) places the goods in, on or with anything which the trade description has been affixed or annexed to, marked on or incorporated with, or places any such thing with the goods; or

(c) uses the trade description in any manner likely to be taken as referring to the goods"[21] [4(1)]. An oral statement may amount to the use of a trade description.[22] Where goods are supplied in pursuance of a request in which a trade description is used and the circumstances are such as to make it reasonable to infer that the goods are supplied as goods corresponding to that description, the supplier is deemed to have applied that description to the goods.[23] Where a trade description is used in relation to any class of goods in an advertisement, it is taken as referring to all goods of the class, whether or not in existence at the time the advertisement is published.[24] Repairs carried out in such a way as to conceal a defect in the goods may result in a false trade description but it is not "applied" by someone who did not carry out the repairs and who was unaware of the defect.[25]

5. Prices.—It is an offence for a person offering to supply goods to give, by whatever means, any false indication to the effect that the price at which the goods are offered is equal to or less than a recommended price or the price at which the goods or goods of the same description were previously offered by him, or is less than such a price by a specified amount.[26] An indication as to a recommended price is treated, unless the contrary is expressed, as an indication that it is a price recommended by the manufacturer or producer generally for supply by retail in the area where the goods are offered.[27] An indication that goods were previously offered at a higher price or at a particular price is treated as an indication that they were so offered by the person giving the indication unless it is expressly stated that they were so offered by others and it is not expressed or implied that they were, or might have been, so offered also by that person.[28] An indication as to that previous price is treated, unless the contrary is expressed, as an indication that they were so offered within the preceding six months for a continuous period of not

[21] See *Rees* v. *Munday* [1974] 1 W.L.R. 1284.
[22] s. 4 (2).
[23] s. 4 (3).
[24] s. 5.
[25] *Cottee* v. *Douglas Seaton (Used Cars)* [1972] 1 W.L.R. 1408. See also *Donnelly* v. *Rowlands* [1970] 1 W.L.R. 1600.
[26] s. 11; anything likely to be taken as an indication as to a recommended price or as to the previous price shall be treated as such an indication. The section does not apply to a transaction within a private members' club: *John* v. *Matthews* [1970] 2 Q.B. 443.
[27] s. 11 (3) (b).
[28] s. 11 (3) (a). See *House of Holland* v. *Brent London Borough Council* [1971] 2 Q.B. 304.

less than 28 days.[28] It is an offence if a person offering to supply any goods, gives, by whatever means, any indication likely to be taken as an indication that the goods are being offered at a price less than that at which they are in fact being offered.[29] A person advertising goods as available for supply shall be taken as offering to supply them.[30]

6. Services.—It is an offence for a person in the course of a trade or business to make a statement which he knows to be false or recklessly to make a statement which is false as to the provision, nature, time of provision, or evaluation of any services,[31] accommodation or facilities provided in the course of any trade or business[32] or as to the location or amenities of any accommodation so provided.[33] Anything likely to be taken for such a statement as would be false is deemed to be a false statement;[34] "false" means false to a material degree.[35] Where services involve the application of any treatment or process or the carrying out of any repair, statements as to the effect thereof are covered by the section.[36] A statement made regardless of whether it is true or false is deemed to be made recklessly, whether or not the person making it had reasons for believing that it might be false.[37] The statement need not be one inducing entry to the contract and can be one made after the contract is concluded.[38] A promise, forecast or warranty cannot be a false statement[39] but a statement of present intention can be false and such a statement may be implied in a promise or forecast.[40] Where the false statement is in a brochure as many offences are committed as there are readers.[41]

7. Defences.—In any proceedings under the Act it is a defence that the commission of the offence was due to a mistake or to reliance on information supplied or to the act or default of another person, an accident or some other cause beyond the control of the person charged and that he took all reasonable precautions and exercised all due diligence to avoid the commission of such an offence by himself or any person under his control.[42] The mistake must be that of the person charged.[43] The act or default relied on

---

[29] s. 11 (2); *Raskin* v. *Herron,* 1971 S.L.T. (Notes) 33; *Doble* v. *David Greig,* supra; *Richards* v. *Westminster Motors* (1975) 61 Cr. App. R. 228 (failure to include value added tax).

[30] s. 11 (3) (*d*).

[31] A statement as to the qualifications of the person providing services is a statement as to the provision of the services; *R.* v. *Breeze* [1973] 1 W.L.R. 994.

[32] The statement may be about services to be provided by someone other than the person making the statement: *Bambury* v. *Hounslow London Borough Council* [1978] R.T.R. 1.

[33] s. 14 (1).

[34] s. 14 (2) (*a*); *R.* v. *Clarksons Holidays* (1972) 57 Cr. App. R. 38.

[35] s. 14 (4).

[36] s. 14 (3).

[37] s. 14 (2) (*b*). See *M.F.I. Warehouses* v. *Nattrass* [1973] 1 W.L.R. 307.

[38] *Breed* v. *Cluett* [1970] 2 Q.B. 459.

[39] *Beckett* v. *Cohen* [1972] 1 W.L.R. 1593.

[40] *British Airways Board* v. *Taylor* [1976] 1 W.L.R. 13; *R.* v. *Sunair Holidays* [1973] 1 W.L.R. 1105.

[41] *R.* v. *Thomson Holidays* [1974] Q.B. 592.

[42] s. 24 (1); *Aitchison* v. *Reith and Anderson (Dingwall and Tain)* 1974 S.L.T. 282.

[43] *Birkenhead and District Co-operative Society* v. *Roberts* [1970] 1 W.L.R. 1497.

may be that of a manager or servant; but where the accused is a body corporate the other person cannot be a director, manager, secretary or similar officer.[44] It is a defence to a charge of supplying or offering to supply goods to which a false trade description is applied that the person charged did not know, and could not with reasonable diligence have ascertained, that the goods did not conform to the description or that the description had been applied to the goods.[45]

8. Orders.—There are powers to make orders assigning definite meanings to expressions used in relation to goods, services, accommodation or facilities and an expression thus defined is deemed to have the assigned meaning for purposes of the Act when used in a trade description or in a statement about services, accommodation or facilities.[46] Orders may be made requiring that goods should be marked with or accompanied by information or instructions relating to the goods; contravention of such an order is an offence.[47] Orders may also be made requiring specified information to be included in advertisements relating to goods.[48] For purposes of the Act, goods are deemed to have been manufactured or produced in the country in which they last underwent a treatment or process resulting in a substantial change; orders may be made specifying what treatment or process is to be regarded as resulting in a substantial change and specifying what is to be regarded as the country of origin where different parts of goods are manufactured or produced in different countries.[49]

9. Price Marking.—Orders may require that the price or charge is indicated on or in relation to goods which a person indicates are or may be for sale by retail and for services which a person indicates may be provided except those provided only for purposes of businesses carried on by other persons.[50] The price or charge to be indicated may be a price expressed by reference to a specified unit of measurement. Thus, cheese which is not pre-packed must have the price per pound weight indicated.[51] Where goods are subject to value added tax, the order may make provision as to the indication to be given of the tax included in, or payable in addition to, the price. Thus, in the case of petrol, a price including taxes and duties must be marked on the pump.[52] Orders may also be made requiring retailers to display information with respect to the range of prices at which certain goods are commonly sold by

[44] *Tesco Supermarkets* v. *Nattrass* [1972] A.C. 153.
[45] s. 24 (3).
[46] ss. 7, 15.
[47] s. 8. The Eggs (Marketing Standards) Regulations 1973 (S.I. 1973 No. 15) and similar orders have been made under the European Communities Act 1972, s. 2.
[48] s. 9.
[49] s. 36. The Trade Descriptions Act 1972 (c. 34) requires a conspicuous indication of the country of origin of goods produced outside the U.K. if a name or mark associated with the U.K. has been applied to them.
[50] Prices Act 1974, s. 4 (as amended by Price Commission Act 1977 (c. 17)).
[51] Price Marking (Cheese) Order 1977 (S.I. 1977 No. 1334).
[52] Petrol Prices (Display) Order 1978 (S.I. 1978 No. 1389).

retail in the United Kingdom, or in a particular part thereof, at a particular date or during a particular period.[53]

10. Fair Trading Act 1973.—The Director General of Fair Trading has a general duty to keep under review the carrying on of commercial activities which relate to goods or services supplied to consumers.[54] Under Part II of the Act the Director can initiate a procedure by which "consumer trade practices"[55] can be regulated by an order made by the Secretary of State for Prices and Consumer Protection, a contravention of the order being a criminal offence. Several orders have been made. A person must not, in the course of a business, in a notice, advertisement, or document furnished to a consumer include a statement purporting to apply to consumer transactions a term which would be void by virtue of sections 6 or 20 of the Unfair Contract Terms Act 1977 or section 4(1) (c) of the Trading Stamps Act 1964.[56]

A seller in the course of a business must not supply to a consumer pursuant to a consumer transaction a statement about the rights which the consumer has against him if the goods are defective unless in close proximity to the statement there is another conspicuous statement to the effect that the first mentioned statement does not affect the rights of the consumer under the Sale of Goods Act, the Supply of Goods (Implied Terms) Act 1973 and the Trading Stamps Act 1964.[57] Similarly, a manufacturer or distributor must not furnish a guarantee, unless it includes a conspicuous statement that the statement of obligations accepted by him in relation to the goods does not affect the consumer's rights against the retailer under these statutes.[58] A mail order advertisement or catalogue must contain in legible characters the true name or registered business name of the person carrying on the mail order business and the address at which that business is managed.[59]

A person who is seeking to sell goods that are being sold in the course of a business must not publish an advertisement which indicates that the goods are for sale and which is likely to induce consumers to buy the goods unless it is reasonably clear from the contents of the advertisement, its format or size, the place or manner of its publication or otherwise that the goods are to be sold in the course of a business; this does not apply to sales by auction or competitive tender or to sales of horticultural and farm produce produced by the seller.[60]

11. Unfair Conduct.—If it appears to the Director General that a person in the course of carrying on a business has persisted in a course of conduct which is detrimental to the interests of, and unfair to, consumers, he may attempt to

---

[53] 1974 Act, s. 5.
[54] Fair Trading Act 1973 (c. 41), s. 1.
[55] As defined in s. 13.
[56] Consumer Transactions (Restrictions on Statements) Orders 1976 (S.I. 1976 No. 1813) as amended by Consumer Transactions (Restrictions on Statements) (Amendment) Order 1978 (S.I. 1978 No. 127) art. 3.
[57] art. 4.
[58] art. 5.
[59] Mail Order Transactions (Information) Order 1976 (S.I. 1976 No. 1812).
[60] Business Advertisements (Disclosure) Order 1977 (S.I. 1977 No. 1918).

obtain from the person a satisfactory written assurance that he will refrain from continuing that course of conduct and from carrying on any similar course of conduct in the course of that business.[61] A course of conduct is unfair if it consists of criminal offences, or breaches of contract or breaches of duties enforceable by civil proceedings.[62] If the person fails to give an assurance, or fails to observe an assurance he has given, the Director General may bring proceedings against him before the Restrictive Practices Court (or, in certain circumstances, the sheriff court[63]) which may, if no appropriate undertaking is given, make an order directing the person to refrain from continuing that, or a similar, course of conduct.[64] Where the person is a body corporate an order may be made against an officer of it, or a person controlling it, directing him to refrain from consenting to or conniving at the course of conduct in question or from carrying on any similar course of conduct in the course of any business carried on by him or from the carrying on of any such course of conduct by any other body corporate of which he is an officer or which he controls.[65]

12. Pyramid Selling.—Part XI of the Fair Trading Act empowers the Secretary of State to make regulations as to the practice known as "pyramid selling".[66]

13. Safety.—The Consumer Safety Act 1978 (c. 38) empowers the Secretary of State to make safety regulations to secure that goods are safe or that appropriate information is provided and inappropriate information is not provided in respect of goods.[67] Contravention of certain types of regulation is an offence. The Secretary of State may also make "prohibition orders" prohibiting persons from supplying specified goods or serve "prohibition notices" prohibiting a person from supplying specified goods except with the consent of the Secretary of State and in accordance with the conditions on which consent was given.[68] A "notice to warn" requires a person to publish a warning about specified goods. Contravention of a prohibition order, a prohibition notice or a warning notice is an offence. A contravention of a safety regulation, a prohibition order or a prohibition notice is actionable as a breach of statutory duty owed to any person who may be affected by the failure to perform the obligation imposed.[69] An agreement to exclude or restrict the obligation or liability for breach thereof is void.[70] The

---

[61] s. 34 (1).
[62] s. 34 (2).
[63] s. 41. See Gamble, 1977 S.L.T. (News) 113; *Director General of Fair Trading* v. *Boswell,* 1978 S.L.T. (Sh. Ct.) 9.
[64] s. 37.
[65] ss. 38, 39.
[66] See Pyramid Selling Schemes Regulations 1973 (S.I. 1973 No. 1740).
[67] s. 1. Regulations made under the repealed Consumer Protection Act 1961 (c. 40) continue in force. See, for example, the Toys (Safety) Regulations 1974 (S.I. 1974 No. 1367).
[68] s. 3.
[69] s. 6 (1).
[70] s. 6 (2).

contravention and the commission of an offence does not affect the validity of any contract except so far as the contract provides otherwise.[71]

14. Trading Stamps.—An exchange of goods for stamps is not a sale. A "trading stamp" is "a stamp which is, or is intended to be, delivered to any person on or in connection with either (i) the purchase of any goods, or (ii)... the hiring of any goods under a hire-purchase agreement, (other than the purchase of a newspaper or other periodical of which the stamp forms part or in which it is contained) and is, or is intended to be, redeemable (whether singly or together with other such stamps) by that or some other person".[72] Only a company or an industrial and provident society can carry on business as the promoter of a trading stamp scheme.[73] A stamp must bear on its face in clear and legible characters a value expressed in or by reference to current coin of the realm and the name of the promoter of the scheme.[74] If the holder of stamps having an aggregate value of not less that 25p so requests, the promoter must redeem them by paying over their aggregate cash value.[75] In the redemption of stamps there are implied stipulations as to the promoter's title to the goods, quiet possession, and merchantable quality similar to those contained in sections 12 and 14 of the Sale of Goods Act 1893;[76] it is not possible to exclude these implied stipulations.[77] A shop in which a trading stamp scheme is operated must display a notice stating the cash value of stamps issued under the scheme and giving such particulars as will enable customers readily to ascertain the number of trading stamps, if any, to which they are entitled on any purchase.[78] If a catalogue has been published for the scheme, it must contain a statement of the name of the promoter and the address of its registered office and a copy must be kept in the shop.[79] Any stamp book must contain the promoter's name and the address of its registered office.[80] It is an offence for the promoter to advertise in terms which convey the cash value of stamps by means of a statement which associates the worth of any trading stamps with what the holder pays or may pay to obtain them or in terms which are misleading or deceptive.[81]

[71] s. 6 (4).
[72] Trading Stamps Act 1964 (c. 71), s. 10.
[73] s. 1 (1). (Consumer Credit Act 1974, Sch. 4, para. 26).
[74] s. 2.
[75] s. 3.
[76] s. 4. (As substituted by Supply of Goods (Implied Terms) Act 1973, s. 16).
[77] s. 4 (1).
[78] s. 7.
[79] ss. 5, 7 (1) (b).
[80] s. 5 (1).
[81] s. 6.

CHAPTER XIX

CONSUMER CREDIT TRANSACTIONS

Goode, *Introduction to the Consumer Credit Act 1974* (1974); Bennion, *Consumer Credit Control* (1977); Guest and Lomnicka, *An Introduction to the Law of Credit and Security* (1978).

1. Scope of the Legislation.—The Consumer Credit Act 1974[1] establishes a system of licensing of persons concerned with the provision of credit and regulates consumer credit transactions of all kinds. It replaces the Pawn-brokers Acts, the Moneylenders Acts and the Hire-Purchase (Scotland) Act 1965. The mode of operation of ancillary credit business[2] and, in particular, of credit reference agencies,[3] is controlled.

The Director General of Fair Trading ("the Director") has the duty of generally superintending the working and enforcement of the Act, of administering the licensing system set up by the Act and of exercising various adjudicatory functions under the Act.[4]

2. Licensing.—A licence is required to carry on a consumer credit or consumer hire business or an ancillary credit business.[5] A regulated agreement (other than a non-commercial agreement) made when the trader or credit-broker was unlicensed is enforceable against the debtor only where the Director has made an order applying to the agreement.[6] A person is not to be treated as carrying on a particular type of business merely because occasionally he enters into transactions belonging to a business of that type.[7] A local authority and a body corporate empowered by a public general Act naming it to carry on a business do not need a licence.[8]

A "standard licence" is issued to a person, a partnership or an unincorporated body of persons. A standard licence is granted to a person

---

[1] c. 39. This chapter has been written on the assumption that the Act is completely in force. For the previous legislation on money-lending and hire-purchase, reference can be made to the last edition of this work. The Act should in all cases be read.

[2] Pt. X.

[3] ss. 157-160; Consumer Credit (Credit Reference Agency) Regulations 1977 (S.I. 1977 No. 329); Consumer Credit (Conduct of Business) (Credit References) Regulations 1977 (S.I. 1977 No. 330).

[4] s. 1.

[5] ss. 21, 147. Certain exemptions are made in commencement orders, e.g., the Consumer Credit Act 1974 (Commencement No. 2) Order 1977 (S.I. 1977 No. 325 (c. 11)) exempts consumer credit businesses carried on by an individual in the course of which only consumer credit agreements for sums not exceeding £30 are made. Ancillary credit business is credit brokerage, debt-adjusting, debt-counselling, debt-collecting or the operation of a credit reference agency (s. 145). An advocate acting in that capacity and a solicitor engaging in business done in or for the purposes of proceedings before a court or an arbiter are not engaged in ancillary credit business (s. 146).

[6] ss. 40, 149. See s. 148 as to the agreement between the customer and the unlicensed person carrying on an ancillary credit business.

[7] s. 189 (2).

[8] s. 21.

who satisfies the Director that he is a fit person to engage in activities covered by the licence and that the name under which he applies is not misleading or otherwise undesirable.[9] A "group licence" covers such persons and such activities as are described in the licence and may be issued only where it appears to the Director that the public interest is better served by doing so than by obliging the persons concerned to apply separately for standard licences.[10] The Director has powers to vary, suspend or revoke a licence.[11] Decisions on these matters are subject to appeal to the Secretary of State[12] and from him on a question of law to the Court of Session.[13]

3. Definitions.—A "personal credit agreement" is "an agreement between an individual ('the debtor') and any other person ('the creditor') by which the creditor provides the debtor with credit of any amount."[14] An "individual" includes a partnership or other unincorporated body of persons not consisting entirely of bodies corporate.[15] "Credit" includes a cash loan and any other form of financial accommodation.[16] An item entering into the total charge for credit is not treated as credit even though time is allowed for its payment.[17] A "hire-purchase agreement" is regarded as a provision of a fixed-sum credit to finance the transaction of an amount equal to the total price of the goods less the aggregate of the deposit (if any) and the total charge for credit.[18] A hire-purchase agreement is an agreement, other than a conditional sale agreement, under which goods are hired in return for periodical payments and the property will pass to the hirer if the terms of the agreement are complied with and the hirer exercises an option to purchase, or any party to the agreement does another specified act or another specified event occurs.[19]

A "consumer credit agreement" is a personal credit agreement by which the creditor provides the debtor with credit not exceeding £5,000.[20] A consumer credit agreement is a "regulated agreement" if it is not an "exempt agreement".[21]

---

[9] s. 25. A standard licence is valid for three years: Consumer Credit (Period of Standard Licence) Regulations 1975 (S.I. 1975 No. 2124). On the death, sequestration or incapacity of the licensee the business may be carried on under the licence by some other person: s. 37; Consumer Credit (Termination of Licences) Regulations 1976 (S.I. 1976 No. 1002).

[10] s. 22. A group licence issued to the Law Society of Scotland covers all solicitors holding practising certificates in respect of consumer credit, credit brokerage, debt-adjusting and debt-counselling and debt-collecting in activities arising in the course of practice as a solicitor: see 1976 J.L.S. 212. A group licence has been issued to cover persons appointed to be a liquidator, receiver, executor, judicial factor, trustee in sequestration, curator bonis, or trustee under a deed of arrangement or trust deed: 1976 J.L.S. 261.

[11] ss. 29-34.

[12] s. 41; Consumer Credit Licensing (Representations) Order 1976 (S.I. 1976 No. 191); Consumer Credit Licensing (Appeals) Regulations 1976 (S.I. 1976 No. 837).

[13] Tribunals and Inquiries Act 1971 (c. 62) s. 13 (6) (a). See A. S. (Rules of Court Amendment No. 6) (Appeals under Consumer Credit Act 1974) 1976.

[14] s. 8 (1).

[15] s. 189 (1).

[16] s. 9 (1).

[17] s. 9 (4). Items included in the total charge for credit are specified in the Consumer Credit (Total Charge for Credit) Regulations 1977 (S.I. 1977 No. 327).

[18] s. 9 (3).

[19] s. 189 (1).

[20] s. 8 (2). There is power to alter the limit by statutory instrument (s. 181 (1)).

[21] s. 8 (3).

There is, however, another class of regulated agreements—a consumer hire agreement is a regulated agreement if it is not an exempt agreement.[22] A "consumer hire agreement" is an agreement for the hiring of goods to an individual, which is not a hire-purchase agreement, which is capable of subsisting for more than 3 months and which does not require the hirer to make payments exceeding £5,000.[23]

A "running-account credit" is a facility under a personal credit agreement whereby the debtor can receive cash, goods and services to a value such that, taking repayments by the debtor into account, the credit limit is not exceeded, the credit limit being in any period the maximum debit balance permissible in the period, disregarding any term of the agreement which allows the maximum to be exceeded merely temporarily.[24] For purposes of the £5,000 limit in the definition of a consumer credit agreement, the running-account credit is taken not to exceed £5,000 if the credit limit does not exceed £5,000; but even if there is no credit limit or there is a limit exceeding £5,000, the credit may be taken not to exceed £5,000 if the debtor cannot draw more than £5,000 at one time *or* if the credit charge increases or the agreement otherwise becomes more onerous when the debit balance rises above a given amount not exceeding £5,000 *or* if "at the time the agreement is made it is probable, having regard to the terms of the agreement and any other relevant considerations, that the debit balance will not at any time rise above" £5,000.[25] A "fixed-sum credit" is any facility other than a running-account credit under a personal credit agreement whereby the debtor is enabled to receive credit in one amount or by instalments.[26]

4. Exempt Agreements.—The following are "exempt agreements":—
(1) certain debtor-creditor-supplier and debtor-creditor agreements[27] secured over land where the creditor is a local authority, a building society, or a body specified in an order made by the Secretary of State;[28]
(2) debtor-creditor-supplier agreements for a fixed-sum credit where the number of payments to be made by the debtor does not exceed four with the exception of (a) agreements financing the purchase of land; (b) conditional sale agreements and hire-purchase agreements; and (c) agreements secured by a pledge (other than a pledge of documents of title);[29]

---

[22] s. 15 (2).
[23] s. 15 (1).
[24] s. 10 (1), (2). A bank overdraft is a running-account credit (Sch. 2, Exs. 18, 23).
[25] s. 10 (3). If the agreement contains a term signifying that in the opinion of the parties the last of these conditions is not satisfied it should be taken not to be satisfied unless the contrary is proved (s. 171 (1)).
[26] s. 10 (1) (*b*); e.g., a loan granted in instalments or a hire-purchase agreement (Sch. 2, Exs. 9, 10).
[27] These terms are defined in § 7, infra. There is a circularity in the definitions; regulated agreements are consumer credit agreements which are not exempt agreements; exempt agreements include debtor-creditor-supplier and debtor-creditor agreements which are defined as including some regulated agreements.
[28] s. 16 (1); Consumer Credit (Exempt Agreements) Order 1977 (S.I. 1977 No. 326), art. 2; Consumer Credit (Exempt Agreements) (Amendment) Order 1977 (S.I. 1977 No. 1493).
[29] Consumer Credit (Exempt Agreements) Order 1977 (S.I. 1977 No. 326), art. 3 (1) (*a*) (i).

(3) debtor-creditor-supplier agreements for running-account credit providing for payments by the debtor in relation to specified periods and requiring that the number of payments to be made in repayment of the whole amount of the credit provided in each such period shall not exceed one (there are the same exceptions as in (2));[30]

(4) debtor-creditor-supplier agreements financing the purchase of land where the number of payments to be made by the debtor does not exceed four;[31]

(5) debtor-creditor agreements (other than those in which repayments may vary according to a formula) where the total charge for credit does not exceed a prescribed rate;[32]

(6) agreements made in connection with trade in goods or services between the U.K. and other countries or within a country or between countries outside the U.K., being agreements under which credit is provided to the debtor in the course of a business carried on by him;[33]

(7) consumer hire agreements for telecommunications apparatus or for meters or metering equipment owned by electricity, gas or water suppliers.[34]

   5. Restricted-Use Agreements.—A "restricted-use agreement" is a regulated consumer credit agreement of one of three types:— (a) financing a transaction between the debtor and the creditor; (b) financing a transaction between the debtor and someone other than the creditor (the "supplier") whose identity need not be known when the agreement is made; (c) refinancing any existing indebtedness to the creditor or another person.[35] It is important to note that an agreement is not a restricted-use one if credit is in fact provided in such a way as to leave the debtor free to use it as he chooses, even though certain uses would contravene that or any other agreement.[36] An "unrestricted-use agreement" is a regulated consumer credit agreement which is not a restricted-use one.[37]

   6. Creditor-Supplier "Arrangements".—A consumer credit agreement is made under pre-existing arrangements between a creditor and a supplier if it is entered into in accordance with, or in furtherance of, arrangements previously made between the creditor or his associate and the supplier or his associate.[38] "Associates" are, broadly, relatives, partners and controlled bodies corporate.[39] A consumer credit agreement is entered into in contemplation of

[30] art. 3 (1) (a) (ii).
[31] art. 3 (1) (b).
[32] art. 3 (1) (c). The prescribed rate is the higher of (i) the sum of one per cent and the minimum lending rate determined by the Bank of England, being the latest rate in operation on the date 28 days before the date on which the agreement is made, and, (ii) 13 per cent. The method of calculating the rate is prescribed by the Consumer Credit (Total Charge for Credit) Regulations 1977 (S.I. 1977 No. 327).
[33] art. 3 (1) (d).
[34] art. 4.
[35] s. 11 (1).
[36] s. 11 (3).
[37] s. 11 (2).
[38] s. 187 (1).
[39] s. 184.

future arrangements if it is entered into in the expectation that arrangements will subsequently be made between the creditor or his associate and the supplier or his associate for the supply of cash, goods or services to be financed by the agreement.[40] If the creditor is an associate of the supplier's, the agreement is treated as entered into under pre-existing arrangements unless the contrary is proved.[41] Arrangements are disregarded if they are merely arrangements for the making, in specified circumstances, of payments to the supplier by the creditor and the creditor holds himself out as willing to make, in such circumstances, payments of the kind to suppliers generally.[42]

7. Debtor-Creditor-Supplier Agreements.—A "debtor-creditor-supplier agreement" is a regulated consumer credit agreement being:—
(a) one financing a transaction between the debtor and the creditor, or
(b) one financing a transaction between the debtor and the supplier with "arrangements", pre-existing or contemplated, or
(c) an unrestricted-use agreement with pre-existing "arrangements" and knowledge on the part of the creditor that the credit is to be used to finance a transaction between the debtor and the supplier.[43]

A "debtor-creditor agreement" is a regulated consumer credit agreement being:—
(a) one financing a transaction between the debtor and the supplier without "arrangements", or
(b) one refinancing any existing indebtedness to the creditor or another person, or
(c) an unrestricted-use agreement without "arrangements" and without knowledge on the part of the creditor that the credit is to be used to finance a transaction between the debtor and the supplier.[44]

8. Other Definitions.—A "multiple agreement" is an agreement part of which falls within one category of agreement and part in another or an agreement which, or part of which, falls within two or more categories of agreement mentioned in the Act.[45] A part of a multiple agreement is to be treated as a separate agreement.[46] A transaction, other than one for the provision of security, is a "linked transaction" in relation to an actual or prospective regulated agreement (the "principal agreement") if it is entered into by the debtor or his relative in compliance with a term of the principal agreement or if it is financed by a principal debtor-creditor-supplier agreement or if the other party to the transaction is a person of a specified class and the transaction is suggested by a person of a specified class and it is entered into to induce the creditor to enter into the principal agreement or for another

[40] s. 187 (2).
[41] s. 187 (5).
[42] s. 187 (3).
[43] s. 12; e.g., a bank credit-card agreement so far as it relates to goods: Sch. 2, Ex. 16.
[44] s. 13; e.g., an agreement for a bank overdraft: Sch. 2, Ex. 18.
[45] s. 18 (1).
[46] s. 18 (2).

purpose related to the principal agreement, or, where the principal agreement is a restricted-use credit agreement, for a purpose related to a transaction financed, or to be financed, by the principal agreement; the specified classes of persons are the creditor, his associate, a person who knows that the principal agreement has been made or who contemplated that it might be made and a person who, in the negotiation of the transaction, is represented by a credit-broker who is also a negotiator in antecedent negotiations for the principal agreement.[47]

A "small agreement" is (a) a regulated consumer credit agreement for credit not exceeding £30 other than a hire-purchase or conditional sale agreement or (b) a regulated consumer hire agreement which does not require the hirer to make payments exceeding £30, being, in either case, an agreement which is unsecured or secured only by a guarantee or indemnity.[48]

A "non-commercial agreement" is a consumer credit or hire agreement not made by the creditor or owner in the course of a business carried on by him.[49]

9. Regulated Agreements.—The provisions of the Act which affect regulated agreements generally are summarised in this section;[50] thereafter provisions affecting special kinds of regulated agreement will be noticed. Specified information must be disclosed to the debtor in a specified manner before the agreement is made.[51] In the antecedent negotiations, the negotiator is deemed to be the creditor's agent and he cannot validly be made the debtor's agent.[52] Regulated agreements must be in the prescribed form and have the prescribed content.[53] The document must be readily legible, must be signed by the debtor and the creditor and must embody all the terms of the agreement other than implied terms.[54] The debtor must be given a copy of the executed agreement and, if the agreement does not become executed when he signs it, a copy of the unexecuted agreement.[55] An agreement which does not conform to the foregoing requirements is "improperly-executed" and is enforceable only on the order of the court.[56] An agreement may be cancelled by the debtor within a specified period if the antecedent negotiations included

---

[47] s. 19. The "negotiator" is defined by s. 56 (1).

[48] s. 17 (1). There are provisions to prevent evasion by the splitting of an agreement into several small agreements: s. 17 (3), (4).

[49] s. 189 (1). The following do not apply to a non-commercial agreement: ss. 55; 57-73; 75; 77-80; 82; 83; 103; 107-110; 112; 114-123.

[50] References to the "debtor" include references to the hirer. There are important exceptions to some of the following provisions. Part V (ss. 55-74), dealing with entry into agreements, does not, except for s. 56, apply to non-commercial agreements or to certain current account overdraft agreements or to certain debtor-creditor agreements to finance certain payments arising on death: s. 74 (1); and does not, except for ss. 55 and 56, apply to a small debtor-creditor-supplier agreement for restricted-use credit: s. 74 (2). There are exceptions to the exception where a term of the agreement is expressed in writing: s. 74 (4).

[51] s. 55. The seeking of business is governed by ss. 43–54. Discrimination in providing credit facilities is unlawful: Sex Discrimination Act 1975 (c. 65), s. 29 (2) (c); Race Relations Act 1976 (c. 74), s. 20 (2) (c).

[52] s. 56.

[53] s. 60.

[54] s. 61.

[55] ss. 62, 63.

[56] s. 65.

oral representations made by the negotiator in the presence of the debtor unless the agreement is secured on land or is for the purchase of land or the debtor signed the agreement at the premises of the creditor or the negotiator or any party to a linked transaction.[57] Notice of his cancellation rights must be given to the debtor.[58] There are provisions for the recovery of sums paid by the debtor,[59] the return of goods and the repayment of any credit extended on cancellation;[60] these provisions also operate, so far as applicable, where the debtor has withdrawn from a prospective regulated agreement.[61]

Restrictions are placed on the creditor's liberty to do any of the following acts whether he is acting under the terms of the agreement or by reason of a breach of the agreement by the debtor:—

 (i) demanding earlier payment of any sum;
 (ii) recovering possession of any goods or land;
 (iii) treating any right of the debtor (other than a right to draw credit) as terminated, restricted or deferred;
 (iv) terminating the agreement;
 (v) enforcing any security.

In general, he cannot do any of these acts without giving notice to the debtor and the debtor, on receipt of the notice, can apply to the court for relief. The creditor cannot enforce a term of an agreement by doing any of (i), (ii) or (iii) during the specified period of duration of the agreement without giving not less than seven days' notice to the debtor unless the right to enforce arises from the debtor's breach of the agreement.[62] Similarly, the creditor cannot terminate the agreement for reasons other than the debtor's breach during the specified period of duration of the agreement without giving not less than seven days' notice to the debtor.[63]

If, under a power contained in the agreement, the creditor varies the agreement, the variation does not take effect before notice of it is given to the debtor in the prescribed manner.[64] The creditor is obliged to give the debtor, on request and payment of a fee, information as to the state of the debt[65] and the debtor is under a similar duty to inform the creditor as to the whereabouts of any goods to which the agreement relates and which are required by the agreement to be kept in the debtor's possession or control.[66] There are rules as to the appropriation of payments where there are two or more agreements.[67]

A credit-broker, a supplier or a negotiator is deemed to be the creditor's agent for the purpose of receiving any notice rescinding the agreement.[68]

[57] ss. 67-69.
[58] s. 64.
[59] s. 70.
[60] ss. 71-72.
[61] s. 57.
[62] s. 76. A right of enforcement arising by reason of breach of the agreement is not affected: s. 76 (6); nor is the creditor's right to restrict or defer the drawing on any credit: s. 76 (4).
[63] s. 98.
[64] s. 82; Consumer Credit (Notice of Variation of Agreements) Regulations 1977 (S.I. 1977 No. 328).
[65] ss. 77-79.
[66] s. 80.
[67] s. 81.
[68] s. 102.

It is an offence for a trader to fail to give a customer who serves an appropriate notice on him a counter-notice stating either that the customer's indebtedness is discharged or his grounds for alleging that the indebtedness is not discharged.[69]

10. Debtor's Death.—On the debtor's death, the creditor in an agreement which has a specified period of duration which has not ended cannot do any of the acts (i)-(v) specified in the preceding section if the agreement is fully secured.[70] If the agreement is only partly secured or is unsecured he can do them only on an order of the court which will be made only if the creditor proves that he has been unable to satisfy himself that the debtor's present and future obligations under the agreement are likely to be discharged.[71]

11. Default.—Where there is a breach of the agreement by the debtor the creditor cannot by reason of the breach do any of the acts (i)-(v) specified in section 9 unless he has served on the debtor a default notice in the prescribed form.[72] This notice must specify inter alia what action is required to remedy the breach, or, if the breach is not capable of remedy, the compensation required to be paid therefor;[73] and if the action is taken or the compensation paid within a period of not less than seven days specified in the notice, the breach shall be treated as not having occurred.[74]

12. Time Orders.—There are three ways in which the agreement can come before the court: (a) when the creditor applies for an enforcement order, (b) on an application by the debtor, after service of a default notice, a notice of termination, or a notice of intention to do the acts (i), (ii) or (iii) specified in section 9, supra, under the agreement, and (c) when the creditor brings an action to enforce the agreement, or a security, or recover possession of any goods or land.

In any of these circumstances the court may make a "time order" providing for payment by instalments of any sum due under the agreement or for the remedying of any breach other than non-payment of money by the debtor within a specified time.[75] In any order made in relation to an agreement the court may make the operation of a term conditional on the doing of certain acts by any party or suspend the operation of any term.[76] The court may also include in the order such provision as it considers just for

[69] s. 103.
[70] s. 86. The creditor may, however, restrict or defer the drawing on any credit: s. 86 (4); and the section does not affect the operation of an agreement that sums will be paid out of the proceeds of a policy of assurance on the debtor's life: s. 86 (5).
[71] s. 128.
[72] s. 87.
[73] s. 88.
[74] s. 89.
[75] s. 129. An action to enforce a regulated agreement, a security or a linked transaction can be brought only in the sheriff court for the district in which the debtor resides or carries on business: s. 141 (3).
[76] s. 135.

amending the agreement or security in consequence of a term of the order.[77] On the application of the creditor or owner, the court may make such order as it thinks just for the protection of his property or of property subject to a security pending the determination of the proceedings.[78]

13. Enforcement Orders.—Where an application is made for an enforcement order, there are some situations in which the court cannot make the order, e.g., where the agreement was a cancellable one and the debtor was not given a notice of his right to cancel.[79] In other situations, e.g., in the case of some improperly executed agreements, the court is to dismiss the application if it considers it just to do so having regard to the prejudice caused to any person by the contravention in question and the degree of culpability for it and having regard also to the court's powers, already mentioned, to make conditional or suspended orders or to vary the terms of the agreement.[80] In an enforcement order the court may reduce or discharge any sum payable by the debtor or by a surety to compensate him for any loss suffered as a result of the contravention.[81] Where the agreement is not in the correct form but the debtor did sign a document containing all the prescribed terms, the order may direct that the agreement is to have effect as if it did not include a term omitted from that document.[82]

14. Securities.—Documents embodying regulated agreements have to embody any security[83] provided in relation to the agreement by the debtor.[84] If the person by whom a security is provided (the "surety") is not the debtor, the security must be expressed in writing in the prescribed form, the document containing all the terms of the security other than implied terms must be signed by or on behalf of the surety and a copy of the document and the principal agreement given to him.[85] If these requirements are not satisfied, the security is enforceable against the surety only on an order of the court and if an application for such an order is dismissed (except on technical grounds) the security is treated as never having effect, property lodged with the creditor for purposes of the security must be returned, any entry relating to the security in any register must be cancelled and any amount received by the creditor on realisation of the security must be repaid to the surety;[86] there is a partial exemption for heritable securities.[87] The creditor is obliged to give the surety

---

[77] s. 136.
[78] s. 131.
[79] s. 127 (4).
[80] s. 127 (1).
[81] s. 127 (2).
[82] s. 127 (5).
[83] A "security" means a mortgage (including a heritable security), charge, pledge, bond, debenture, indemnity, guarantee, bill, note or other right provided by the debtor or at his request to secure the carrying out of his obligations: s. 189.
[84] s. 105 (9).
[85] s. 105.
[86] s. 106.
[87] s. 177 (5).

on request a copy of the principal agreement and of the security instrument and information about the present state of the debtor's indebtedness.[88]

A copy of any default notice served on the debtor must be served on the surety.[89] The realisation of securities is subject to regulation.[90] A security cannot be enforced so as to benefit the creditor to an extent greater than would be the case if there were no security and the obligations of the debtor were carried out to the extent (if any) to which they would be enforced under the Act.[91] Accordingly, if a regulated agreement is enforceable only on a court order, or on an order of the Director, the security is enforceable only where an order has been made[92] and, generally, if the agreement is cancelled or becomes unenforceable, the security becomes ineffective.[93]

15. Pledges.[94]—It is an offence to take an article "in pawn" from a minor.[95] It is also an offence for the "pawnee" to fail to give the "pawnor" a copy of the agreement, notice of his cancellation rights and a pawn-receipt.[96] The pawn is redeemable during the "redemption period", i.e., six months after it was taken or the period fixed for the duration of the credit, if longer, or such longer period as the parties may agree; the pawn remains redeemable after the expiry of the redemption period until it is realised or the property in it passes to the pawnee.[97] No special charges or higher charges for safe-keeping of the pawn can be made on redemption after the expiry of the redemption period.[98]

The pawnee must deliver the pawn on surrender of the receipt and payment of the amount owing unless he knows or suspects that the bearer of the receipt is not the owner of the pawn.[99] If the owner claiming the pawn does not have the receipt he may make a statutory declaration (or, where the loan is not over £15, a written statement in prescribed form) which is treated as the receipt.[1] It is an offence to fail without reasonable cause to allow redemption of a pawn.[2] Where a pawn is an article which has been stolen or obtained by fraud the court which has convicted a person of the offence may order delivery of the pawn to the owner subject to such conditions as to payment of the debt as it thinks fit.[3]

If the credit does not exceed £15, and the pawn has not been redeemed at the end of a redemption period of six months, the property in the pawn passes to the pawnee. In other cases, the pawn becomes realisable if it has not been

[88] ss. 107-110.
[89] s. 111.
[90] s. 112.
[91] s. 113 (1).
[92] s. 113 (2).
[93] s. 113 (3).
[94] The provisions as to pledges do not apply to pledges of documents of title or to non-commercial agreements: s. 114 (3).
[95] s. 114 (2).
[96] s. 115.
[97] s. 116.
[98] s. 116 (4).
[99] s. 117.
[1] s. 118.
[2] s. 119.
[3] s. 122.

redeemed at the end of the redemption period.[4] The pawnor must be given notice of the pawnee's intention to sell and, after the sale, information as to the sale, its proceeds and expenses. If the net proceeds are not less than the debt, the debt is discharged and any surplus is payable to the pawnor; otherwise the debt is reduced pro tanto. On challenge, it is for the pawnee to prove that he used reasonable care to ensure that the true market value was obtained and that the expenses of sale were reasonable.[5]

16. Negotiable Instruments.—Except in the case of a non-commercial agreement, a negotiable instrument cannot be taken as a security for discharge of a sum due under a regulated agreement and a negotiable instrument other than a bank note or cheque cannot be taken from a debtor or surety in discharge of a sum payable.[6] The person who takes the negotiable instrument is not a holder in due course and is not entitled to enforce it.[7] A cheque taken in discharge cannot be negotiated except to a banker[8] and negotiation to a non-banker is a defect in the negotiator's title.[9] Contravention of these provisions makes the agreement or security enforceable on order of the court only.[10] The rights of a holder in due course of a negotiable instrument are not affected but where the debtor or surety becomes liable to a holder in due course as a result of a contravention of these provisions the creditor must indemnify him.[11]

17. Consumer Credit Agreements.—The debtor under a regulated consumer credit agreement is not liable to the creditor for any loss arising from use of the credit facility by another person not acting, or to be treated as acting, as the debtor's agent.[12] The debtor is entitled to discharge his indebtedness under the agreement at any time by notice to the creditor and payment of all amounts due to the creditor; the debtor may be entitled to a rebate for early payment.[13]

There is a restriction on the rate of interest which can be charged on sums which the debtor, in breach of the agreement, has not paid.[14]

18. Agreements about Goods.—The creditor under a regulated hire-purchase, conditional sale or consumer hire agreement cannot enter premises to take possession of the goods except under an order of the court.[15]

[4] s. 120.
[5] s. 121.
[6] s. 123.
[7] s. 125 (1).
[8] s. 123 (2).
[9] s. 125 (2).
[10] s. 124.
[11] s. 125 (3), (4).
[12] s. 83. This does not apply to any loss arising from misuse of an instrument to which the Cheques Act 1957, s. 4, applies.
[13] ss. 94-95.
[14] s. 93.
[15] s. 92. It seems that in Scotland an owner is never entitled to retake goods at his own hand from a person who possesses them under a contract: Gow, *Law of Hire-Purchase* (2nd ed. 1968), p. 210. Section 134 dealing with "adverse possession" purports to apply to Scotland but is incomprehensible.

Contravention is actionable as a breach of statutory duty. Where, after the making of a time order in relation to such an agreement the debtor is in possession of the goods, he shall be treated as the custodier of the goods notwithstanding that the agreement has been terminated.[16]

19. Hire-Purchase and Conditional Sale Agreements.[17]—If the debtor is in breach of a hire-purchase or conditional sale agreement relating to goods but has paid one-third or more of the total price, the goods, even although they are the creditor's property, are "protected goods" and the creditor cannot recover possession of them without a court order.[18] If he does recover them without an order, the agreement is terminated and the debtor is released from all liability and can recover all that he has paid under the agreement.[19]

The debtor is entitled to terminate the agreement by giving notice at any time before the final payment.[20] He must, however, pay the creditor the amount (if any) by which one-half of the total price exceeds the aggregate of the sums paid and the sums due immediately before termination unless (a) the agreement provides for a smaller payment or does not provide for any payment, or (b) the court makes an order for payment of a lesser sum which it is satisfied is equal to the loss sustained by the creditor in consequence of the termination of the agreement.[21] In addition, the debtor must recompense the creditor if he has contravened an obligation to take reasonable care of the goods.

Goods comprised in a hire-purchase or conditional sale agreement which have not become vested in the debtor are not subject to the landlord's hypothec in the period between service of a default notice and the date on which the notice expires or is earlier complied with, or, if the agreement is enforceable on an order of the court only, in the period between the commencement and the termination of the creditor's action.[22]

A time order in relation to a hire-purchase or conditional sale agreement may deal with sums which, although not payable at the time the order is made, would if the agreement continued in force become payable under it subsequently.[23]

In an application for an enforcement order or a time order in relation to a hire-purchase or conditional sale agreement or in an action brought by the

---

[16] s. 130 (4).
[17] A conditional sale agreement is an agreement for the sale of goods or land under which the purchase price or part of it is payable by instalments and the property in the goods or land is to remain in the seller (notwithstanding that the buyer is to be in possession of the goods or land) until such conditions as to the payment of instalments or otherwise as may be specified in the agreement are fulfilled: s. 189. The buyer under such an agreement which is a consumer credit agreement is deemed for purposes of s. 25 of the Sale of Goods Act 1893 not to be a person who has bought or agreed to buy goods: Sch. 4, para. 4. See Sale of Goods, Ch. XVII, supra, §. 20
[18] s. 90.
[19] s. 91.
[20] s. 99.
[21] s. 100.
[22] s. 104.
[23] s. 130 (2).

creditor to recover the goods, the court may make a "return order" or a "transfer order".[24] A "return order" is an order for return of the goods to the creditor; a "transfer order" is an order for transfer to the debtor of the creditor's title to such of the goods as the court thinks just and the return to the creditor of the remainder of the goods. A transfer order can be made only where the amount of the total price which has been paid exceeds the part of the total price referable to the transferred goods by at least one-third of the unpaid balance of the total price. Notwithstanding the making of a return order or a transfer order, the debtor may, before the goods enter the creditor's possession, on payment of the balance of the total price and on fulfilment of any other necessary conditions, "claim" the goods ordered to be returned.[25] When, under that provision, or under a time order, the total price is paid and any other necessary conditions are fulfilled, the creditor's title to the goods vests in the debtor. If goods are not returned under a return order or transfer order the court may revoke so much of the order as relates to those goods and order the debtor to pay the unpaid portion of so much of the total price as is referable to those goods.

20. Conditional Sale Agreements Relating to Land.—When the debtor is in breach of a conditional sale agreement relating to land, the creditor can recover possession of the land on an order of the court only.[26] A conditional sale agreement relating to land cannot be terminated after the title has passed to the debtor.[27]

21. "Land Mortgages".—A "land mortgage" is any security charged on land, "land" being defined to include heritable subjects of whatever description.[28]

Before sending to the debtor for signature an unexecuted agreement where the prospective regulated agreement is to be secured on land, the creditor must give the debtor a copy of the unexecuted agreement containing a notice indicating the debtor's right to withdraw from the prospective agreement and how and when the right is exercisable.[29] This does not apply to a restricted-use credit agreement to finance the purchase of the land or to an agreement for a bridging loan in connection with the purchase of the "mortgaged land" or other land.

A land mortgage is not properly executed unless in addition to the requirements applying to regulated agreements generally (a) the copy agreement and notice of the withdrawal right is sent to the debtor, (b) the unexecuted agreement is sent by post to the debtor for his signature not less than seven days after the copy was given to him, (c) in the period between the giving of that copy and the expiry of seven days after the sending of the

---

[24] s. 133.
[25] The words "... may ... claim ..." are presumably used to mean "is entitled to retain".
[26] s. 92 (2).
[27] s. 99 (3).
[28] s. 189.
[29] s. 58.

unexecuted agreement for his signature (or its return signed if earlier) the creditor refrained from approaching the debtor, in person, by telephone or letter or otherwise except in response to a specific request made by the debtor, (d) no notice of withdrawal by the debtor was received by the creditor before the sending of the unexecuted agreement.[30]

A land mortgage securing a regulated agreement is enforceable (so far as provided in relation to the agreement) on order of the court only.[31] Nothing in the Act is to affect the rights of a creditor in a heritable security, other than one carrying on the business of debt-collecting, who became the creditor for value and without notice of any defect in title arising by virtue of the other provisions of the Act or who derived title from such a creditor.[32]

22. Consumer Hire Agreements.—The hirer is entitled to terminate a regulated consumer hire agreement by giving to the person entitled to receive the sums payable thereunder notice which is not to expire earlier than 18 months after the making of the agreement.[33] A minimum period of notice is prescribed according to the intervals at which payment is made. This power to terminate is not available where the hire payments exceed £300 in any year or where the goods are hired for purposes of a business carried on by the hirer.

If the owner recovers possession of the goods otherwise than by action, the court, on the hirer's application, may, if it appears just to do so, having regard to the extent of the hirer's enjoyment of the goods, order that any sums already paid by the hirer shall be repaid and that the hirer's obligation to pay any sums owed to the owner shall cease.[34] Similar provisions may be made by the court in an order for delivery of the goods to the owner.

23. Connected Lender Liability.—A substantial liability is imposed upon the creditor in a debtor-creditor-supplier agreement in which there are "arrangements" between the creditor and the supplier.[35] If the debtor has, in relation to a transaction financed by such an agreement, any claim against the supplier in respect of a misrepresentation or breach of contract, he has a like claim against the creditor who is jointly and severally liable with the supplier but has a right to be indemnified by the supplier. The provision does not apply to a non-commercial agreement nor where the claim relates to any single item to which the supplier has attached a cash price not exceeding £30 or more than £10,000.

24. Credit-Token Agreements.—A credit-token is "a card, check, voucher, coupon, stamp, form, booklet or other document or thing" given to an individual by a person carrying on a consumer credit business who undertakes

[30] s. 61.
[31] s. 126.
[32] s. 177.
[33] s. 101.
[34] s. 132.
[35] s. 75. See A. S. (Sheriff Court Procedure, Consumer Credit) 1977 (S.I. 1977 No. 1180). The section applies only to agreements made on or after 1st July 1977: Consumer Credit Act 1974 (Commencement No. 3) Order 1977 (S.I. 1977 No. 802).

that he will supply, or reimburse a third party who supplies, cash, goods and services on credit on production of the token. A credit-token agreement is a regulated agreement for the provision of credit in connection with the use of a credit-token.[36]

It is an offence to give a person a credit-token if he has not asked for it.[37] In the case of credit-token agreements there are relaxations of the requirements to send the debtor a copy of the executed agreement and to send a notice of cancellation rights.[38] The debtor is not liable under a credit-token agreement for use made of the token by any person unless the use constituted an acceptance of it by him or he had previously accepted it by signing it or a receipt for it or first using it.[39] The debtor may be liable to the extent of £30 (or the credit limit if lower) for loss to the creditor caused by use of the token when it is outwith the possession of the debtor or of a person authorised by him to use it, the use being before the creditor has been given notice that the token is lost or stolen or for other reason liable to misuse.[40] The debtor may be liable to any extent for loss to the creditor from use (before similar notice) of the token by a person who got possession of it with the debtor's consent.[41] When, in connection with a credit-token agreement (other than a small agreement) a token (other than the first) is given to the debtor, the creditor must give him a copy of the executed agreement and of any other document referred to in it; if he fails to do this he cannot enforce the agreement and, if the default continues for one month, he commits an offence.[42]

The onus is on the creditor to prove that the token was lawfully supplied to the debtor and accepted by him. If the debtor alleges that any use of the token was not authorised by him, it is for the creditor to prove either that the use was so authorised, or that the use occurred before the creditor was given notice of the loss or theft of the token.[43]

25. Extortionate Credit Bargains.—A "credit agreement" is an agreement between an individual and any other person by which that person provides credit of any amount. A "credit bargain" is the credit agreement if no other transactions are to be taken into account in computing the total charge for credit; otherwise it means the credit agreement and those other transactions taken together.[44] The court is given power, if it finds a credit bargain extortionate, to reopen the credit agreement so as to do justice between the parties. It is important to notice that this provision is not restricted to consumer credit agreements and is thus not subject to a financial limit.

A credit bargain is extortionate if it requires the debtor or a relative of his

[36] s. 14. Examples of credit-tokens are a bank credit-card (Sch. 2, Ex. 3) and a trading check (Ex. 14).
[37] s. 51.
[38] ss. 63 (4), 64 (2).
[39] s. 66.
[40] s. 84 (1).
[41] s. 84 (2).
[42] s. 85.
[43] s. 171 (4).
[44] s. 137. As to the transactions to be taken into account, see § 3 supra, note 17.

to make payments (whether unconditionally, or on certain contingencies) which are grossly exorbitant or if it otherwise grossly contravenes ordinary principles of fair dealing. In considering the question of extortion, regard shall be had to such evidence as is adduced concerning:— interest rates prevailing when the bargain was made; the debtor's age, experience, business capacity and state of health; the degree to which, at the time of making the bargain, he was under financial pressure, and the nature of that pressure; the degree of risk accepted by the creditor, having regard to the value of any security provided; the creditor's relationship to the debtor; whether or not a colourable cash price was quoted for any goods or services included in the credit bargain; in relation to a linked transaction, how far the transaction was reasonably required for the protection of the debtor or creditor or was in the interest of the debtor; any other relevant considerations.[45]

If the debtor or surety alleges that the bargain is extortionate it is for the creditor to prove the contrary.[46]

The credit agreement may be reopened on an application for that purpose made by the debtor or surety or in any proceedings to enforce the agreement or a security or any linked transaction or in other proceedings in any court where the amount paid or payable under the agreement is relevant.[47] In reopening the agreement the court may, to relieve the debtor or surety from payment of any sum in excess of that fairly due and reasonable, direct an accounting to be made, set aside obligations, require the creditor to make repayments, direct the return of property to the surety or alter the terms of the credit agreement or of any security instrument.[48] These orders may be made notwithstanding that the effect is to place a burden on the creditor in respect of an advantage unfairly enjoyed by another person who is a party to a linked transaction.[49]

[45] s. 138.
[46] s. 171 (7).
[47] s. 139 (1).
[48] s. 139 (2).
[49] s. 139 (3).

CHAPTER XX

RIGHTS IN SECURITY

Gloag and Irvine, *Rights in Security* (1897); J. J. Gow, *Mercantile and Industrial Law of Scotland* (1964), Ch. 4

1. Nature of Right in Security.—The term "right in security" may be read as denoting any right which a creditor may possess for the recovery of his debt in the event of the bankruptcy of his debtor, distinct from, and in addition to, the right which he possesses in common with all other creditors of claiming a ranking in the sequestration. The right may be a nexus over some particular property, acquired either by express contract, by implication of law, or by the use of diligence, or it may be the corroborative obligation of some party other than the bankrupt. The latter case is considered in the chapter on cautionary obligations. Taking "right in security" in this meaning it is clear that it does not include such documents as a promissory note granted by the debtor, which is evidence of the debt but no security for it.[1] And a mere undertaking by the debtor to set aside some particular fund in order to meet the debt, unless it can be treated as a completed assignation of that fund, leaves the party who has received it to rank as an ordinary creditor, and is not a right in security.[2]

2. Sequestration as a Test of Security.—Sequestration (or, in the case of a company, liquidation) is the ultimate test by which it may be determined whether a security has been created, in contrast with an attempt or obligation to give one. The holder of a security can, in some way or other, and to a greater or less extent, satisfy his debt from the subjects impledged or hypothecated, whereas an undertaking or attempt to give a security, while it may have reached the stage at which it would found an action against the debtor while solvent, leaves the creditor in the same position as the other creditors who have relied on the personal credit of the debtor. And the theory that an obligation to transfer some specific thing in security made the obligant a trustee, with the corollary that the creditor might vindicate that thing, in the capacity of beneficiary, in the debtor's bankruptcy, was finally rejected in *Bank of Scotland* v. *Hutchison, Main & Co.*[3] There a company (H., M. & Co.) had undertaken to procure a certain debenture and assign it to a bank in security of a debt. H., M. & Co. went into liquidation after they had procured the debenture but before they had executed an assignation. It was held that H., M. & Co. did not hold the debenture in trust for the bank and accordingly that the bank had no security over it, but ranked as ordinary creditors.

[1] *Bowe* v. *Spankie,* June 1, 1811, F.C. See *George Shaw* v. *Duffy,* 1943 S.C. 350.
[2] *Graham* v. *Raeburn & Verel* (1895) 23 R. 84; *Brown* v. *Port Seton Harbour Commissioners* (1898) 1 F. 373.
[3] 1914 S.C. (H.L.) 1.

3. Necessity of Delivery.—It is a general principle in the law of Scotland that a security, in the sense indicated in the preceding paragraphs, cannot be created by mere contract. The security holder must have a real right in the subject, and this involves some form of delivery, actual, symbolical or constructive. Nor will the law infer any right in security over property in favour of anyone who is not in possession thereof. To this general rule there are certain exceptions, known as hypothecs, where a security may be created by mere contract, or may be implied by law without possession. But such cases are exceptional; the general trend of the law is against any latent charges on property without any overt change in its possession.[4] There is nothing in the law of Scotland analogous to the English bill of sale in the case of corporeal moveables such as furniture.

4. Securities under Statute.—These statements assume that no statute, public or private, applies to the particular case. A statute may provide that a particular body shall have the power to create a security over its assets by some method which does not involve any form of delivery, or which is not in accordance with the general rules of Scottish conveyancing.[5] The validity of the security must be determined by considering whether it complies with the statutory conditions, and not by asking whether, if no statute were applicable, it would have been effectual at common law.[6]

5. Hypothecs.—Hypothec is the general term used to denote a security without possession. Hypothecs are either conventional, i.e. created by express contract, or legal, implied by law in particular circumstances.

6. Bottomry and Respondentia.—The only conventional hypothecs which are recognised in the law of Scotland are bonds of bottomry and of respondentia. These, now nearly obsolete, are bonds, covering in the case of bottomry, a ship; in the case of respondentia, a cargo, granted by the owner or master of a ship, and constituting a floating charge without possession or any entry on the ship's register. Bottomry bonds by the owner are now unknown. The master of a ship has an implied power to grant a bond of bottomry when the ship is in a foreign port, unable to proceed on its voyage without an advance of money, and when no money is procurable on the personal credit of the owner.[7] Before granting a bottomry bond in these circumstances the master must communicate with the owner, if in the circumstances such communication is practicable; if not, he may grant the bond on his own authority.[8] The lender on bottomry has no claim unless he can show that the condition as to communication with the owner was fulfilled;

---

[4] Stair, I, 13, 14; Bell, *Prin.,* § 1385.
[5] See especially the Companies (Floating Charges and Receivers) (Scotland) Act 1972 (c. 67); Conveyancing and Feudal Reform (Scotland) Act 1970 (c. 35); §§ 12 and 14 infra, and Company Law. Ch. XXV., § 26 infra.
[6] *Lord Advocate* v. *Earl of Moray's Trs.* (1905) 7 F. (H.L.) 116.
[7] Bell, *Prin.,* § 452.
[8] *Kleinwort, Cohen & Co.* v. *Cassa Marittima* (1877) L.R. 2 App.Cas. 156.

that the circumstances justified the bond; and that the ship has arrived at her port of destination. As the bond depends on the safe arrival of the ship, in a competition between two bottomry bonds that last in date, as presumably the means by which the ship ultimately arrived, is preferable.[9] While there is no established form of bottomry bond it must indicate the risk, the voyage and the event on which it will become exigible. If it fails in these particulars it is not a bond of bottomry, and is not in any way binding on the owner.[10] Assuming the validity of the bond the lender may arrest the ship and insist on a judicial sale.[11] He is preferable to any ordinary creditor or to a mortgagee, although not to the maritime lien of the seamen or master.[12]

A bond of respondentia covers the cargo. Communication with the cargo owner, if possible, is essential. If communication is not possible, it may be granted by the master, if there is no other means of raising money necessary for the prosecution of the voyage.[13] The bond is effectual if the cargo arrive at the port of destination, though the ship may not.[14] Where the cargo is attached and sold under a bond of respondentia the shipowner is liable to the cargo owner for its value.[15]

7. Legal Hypothecs.—The recognised legal hypothecs are those of a landlord, of a superior, of a solicitor, and certain maritime hypothecs.

8. Landlord: Superior.—The hypothec of a landlord will be considered in the chapter on Leases.[16] A superior has a hypothec analogous to that of a landlord, which he may exercise by sequestration for the recovery of his feu-duty. Like the hypothec of a landlord it covers the invecta et illata and is not affected by the mercantile sequestration of the debtor or the liquidation of a company.[17] As it is not mentioned in the Hypothec Abolition Act 1880,[18] it probably exists in rural as well as in urban subjects.

9. Hypothec of Solicitor.—A solicitor who has defrayed the costs of an action has at common law a right in the nature of a hypothec over any expenses to which his client may be found entitled. This he may make effectual by moving for decree in his own name as agent-disburser. He thereby acquires a right preferable to that of any creditor of the client, and may obtain decree even after the client is sequestrated.[19] The party liable in expenses cannot oppose decree in the solicitor's name merely on the ground that he has a claim against the client on which he could plead compensation. But if cross awards of expenses are made in the course of an action, or in two actions arising out

---

9 Bell, *Prin.*, § 456.
10 *Miller* v. *Potter, Wilson & Co.* (1875) 3 R. 105; *The Elwell* [1921] P. 351.
11 *Lucovich, Petr.* (1885) 12 R. 1090.
12 *The Daring* (1868) L.R. 2 Adm. 260.
13 *Dymond* v. *Scott* (1877) 5 R. 196.
14 Bell, *Comm.*, I., 584.
15 *Anderston Foundry Co.* v. *Law* (1869) 7 M. 836.
16 Infra, Ch. XXXIII.
17 *Anderson's Trs.* v. *Donaldson,* 1908 S.C. 38.
18 See Leases, Ch. XXXIII., infra, and Erskine, II, 6, 63.
19 *Hunter* v. *Pearson* (1835) 13 S. 495.

of the same matter (ex eodem negotio), the right of compensation thereon arising is preferable to the solicitor's claim under hypothec. So when A made an unsuccessful claim for damages against his employer, and was found liable in expenses, and was subsequently found entitled to expenses in a claim under the Workmen's Compensation Act, decree in the name of A's solicitor was refused on the ground that the employer was entitled to set off the expenses to which he had been found entitled against those in which he had been found liable.[20] This does not hold if the decree in the first action has been extracted before the second action came into Court,[21] and is an exception to the solicitor's right which will not be extended.[22]

Should the solicitor allow decree to be pronounced in favour of his client he has still a right in security over the expenses, and by intimating his claim to the other party, will acquire a right preferable to that of the trustee in the client's sequestration.[23] But his claim will be excluded if the sum due for expenses is arrested,[24] or transferred by a duly intimated assignation.[25] And the party liable in the expenses may plead compensation on any debt due by the client.[26]

In certain cases a solicitor is entitled to be sisted as a party to the action in order to make his hypothec over expenses effectual. This may protect him where the client, without his consent, has settled or abandoned the action. This right is recognised in three cases:—(1) where decree for expenses has been actually pronounced; (2) where an interlocutor has been pronounced of which decree for expenses is the legitimate sequel; (3) where the action has been settled in the knowledge that the client was insolvent and with the object of defeating the solicitor's right.[27]

10. Solicitor's Charge over Subject of Action.—At common law a solicitor's hypothec was confined to expenses; he had no preferable right over property which might be recovered in the action. By section 43 of the Solicitors (Scotland) Act 1933,[28] the Court in any action may declare the solicitor entitled to "a charge upon and against, and a right to payment out of, the property, of whatsoever nature, tenure or kind the same may be, which shall have been recovered or preserved on behalf of his client by such solicitor in such action or proceeding for the taxed expenses." The effect of such a declaration, it is provided, is that acts or deeds granted by the client after it, except acts or deeds in favour of a bona fide purchaser or lender, shall be void and of no effect as against the solicitor's right. On the construction of the corresponding section of the Law Agents (Scotland) Act 1891[29] (which was in

---

20 *Lochgelly Iron Co.* v. *Sinclair*, 1907 S.C. 442; *Fine* v. *Edinburgh Life Assurance Co.*, 1909 S.C. 636; *Byrne* v. *Baird*, 1929 S.C. 624.
21 *Baird* v. *Campbell*, 1928 S.C. 487.
22 *Jack* v. *Laing*, 1929 S.C. 426.
23 *M'Tavish* v. *Peddie* (1828) 6 S. 593.
24 *Stephen* v. *Smith* (1830) 8 S. 847.
25 *Fleeming* v. *Love* (1839) 1 D. 1097, per Lord Mackenzie.
26 *Fleeming* v. *Love*, supra.
27 *Ammon* v. *Tod*, 1912 S.C. 306; *Peek* v. *Peek*, 1926 S.C. 565.
28 23 & 24 Geo. V, c. 21.
29 54 & 55 Vict., c. 30.

similar terms, but is now repealed), it has been decided that a declaration under it is precluded by the sequestration of the client;[30] that it is not precluded by a prior arrestment;[31] that a declaration in favour of the country solicitor, in Court of Session proceedings, is competent;[32] that the Court has a general discretion to grant or refuse a declaration;[33] that the solicitor cannot obtain a charge to the prejudice of a counter-claim for expenses by the other party to the action.[34] A solicitor acting for a person on the Poor's Roll has been held entitled to an order.[35]

11. Maritime Hypothecs or Liens.—Maritime hypothecs, more commonly termed maritime liens, give certain creditors a right in security over a ship, without possession, and with the power of enforcing the right by a judicial sale. Such creditors are preferable to any mortgagee.[36] On this subject it has been laid down that the laws of England and of Scotland are the same.[37] Seamen have a maritime lien for wages, of which they cannot deprive themselves by contract;[38] the master, for his wages and disbursements;[39] a salvor, for any sum found due for salvage.[40] There is a maritime lien for repairs executed or necessaries supplied in a foreign port; no such right, unless the ship is actually detained, for similar services in a home port.[41] There is a maritime lien for damages for a collision, provided that the ship was physically the agent of the injury; not, therefore, where the captain and crew of one ship had, without any actual collision, caused injury to another.[42] A party who pays seamen's wages is entitled, without written assignation, to the preference accorded to seamen, unless it is proved that he made the payment in reliance on the personal credit of the owner, when he is only an ordinary creditor, and postponed to a mortgagee.[43] In the same case it was decided that questions of maritime liens depend on the law of the place where the action is raised (lex fori).

12. Floating Charges.—Security may be given to the creditor of an incorporated company or society registered under the Industrial and Provident Societies Acts 1965 and 1967, by creating in favour of the creditor a floating charge over the company's heritable and moveable property.[44] The floating charge crystallises or attaches only upon the commencement of the winding up of the company or upon the appointment of a receiver by the

[30] *Tait* v. *Wallace* (1894) 2 S.L.T. 252; but see *Philip* v. *Wilson,* 1911 S.C. 1203 (liquidation).
[31] *Automobile Syndicate* v. *Cal. Ry.,* 1909 1 S.L.T. 499.
[32] *Bannatyne,* 1907 S.C. 705.
[33] *Carruthers' Tr.* v. *Finlay & Watson* (1897) 24 R. 363.
[34] *O'Keefe* v. *Grieve's Trs.,* 1917 1 S.L.T. 305.
[35] *Cameron* v. *M'Donald,* 1935 S.N. 25.
[36] *Harmer* v. *Bell* (1851) 7 Moore P.C. 267.
[37] *Currie* v. *M'Knight* (1896) 24 R. (H.L.) 1.
[38] Merchant Shipping Act 1970 (c. 36), s. 16.
[39] Ibid., s. 18.
[40] *Harmer* v. *Bell,* supra.
[41] *Clydesdale Bank* v. *Walker & Bain,* 1926 S.C. 72.
[42] *Currie* v. *M'Knight* (1896) 24 R. (H.L.) 1.
[43] *Clark* v. *Bowring,* 1908 S.C. 1168; doubted in *Clydesdale Bank* v. *Walker & Bain,* supra.
[44] Companies (Floating Charges and Receivers) (Scotland) Act 1972 (c. 67).

creditor; until then it "floats" over the property in the sense that it is not attached to any specific item. In this respect at least it is analogous to the landlord's hypothec.[45] When the charge has been registered with the registrar of companies a valid security is conferred without the transference of possession, the giving of intimation, or, in the case of heritage, of registration in the Register of Sasines.[46] A fuller discussion of floating charges will be found below in the chapter on Company Law.[47]

13. Securities Founded on Possession.—In securities founded on possession a general distinction may be drawn between rights due to express contract between the parties and rights implied by law in particular circumstances. The latter class includes rights of retention and lien.

14. Forms of Constituting Security.—The constitution of a security by express contract may take one or other of two general forms. It may be effected by transferring the subject to the creditor expressly in security—a proceeding of which a bond and disposition in security, in dealing with heritable property, or a pledge, in the case of moveables, may be taken as types. Alternatively, the subject of the security may be transferred by an ex facie absolute conveyance, subject to an obligation to reconvey on repayment of the debt. In the former case the possession of the subject, in the other the property, is, actually or symbolically, transferred. The authorities seem to lead to the conclusion that where documents of title to goods are transferred with the intention to give a security, the result is to vest in the security holder a right of property in the goods represented and not merely a right of pledge.[48] The best known example of a security by conveyance of property was, in the case of heritage, an ex facie absolute disposition with back bond. Since the coming into force of the Conveyancing and Feudal Reform (Scotland) Act 1970 (29 November 1970)[49] the only permissible way of creating a *heritable* security for a debt, subject to one minor exception,[50] is by a standard security.[51] This form of security therefore supersedes the bond and disposition in security, cash credit bond and disposition in security and the ex facie absolute disposition with back bond or letter. It is a more flexible type of security which gives security for a debt contracted after the recording of the deed,[52] and no specific sum of money need be stated as the sum secured by the deed.[52] It is regulated by standard conditions which may be varied by the parties with the broad exceptions of the conditions relating to powers of sale, redemption and foreclosure.[53] The Act provides statutory codes of procedure

---

[45] See § 8, supra; and Leases, Ch. XXXIII, infra.
[46] See s. 3 of the Act.
[47] Ch. XXV.
[48] *Hamilton* v. *Western Bank* (1856) 19 D. 152; *Hayman* v. *McLintock*, 1907 S.C. 936.
[49] 1970 c. 35.
[50] See s. 9 (7) of the Act.
[51] s. 9 (3).
[52] s. 9 (6).
[53] ss. 11 (2), 11 (3), and Sched. 3, as amended by the Redemption of Standard Securities (Scotland) Act 1971 (c. 45), s. 1.

for redemption of a standard security,[54] as well as the enforcement of the security,[55] which are too detailed to note here.

15. Power to Realise.—The form in which the security is constituted may have important effects on the rights which are conferred. One of these is with regard to the creditor's power to realise the subjects. A pledgee, or any person to whom subjects are transferred expressly in security, has no implied power to sell. His right is limited by his title. In order to realise the subject of his security he must either have an express power of sale or obtain that power by application to the Court.[56] If, on the other hand, an absolute title is given, qualified only by a separate obligation to reconvey, the creditor is invested with a power of sale which he can exercise without notice to the debtor.[57] Should he sell in violation of an agreement not to do so, or by some method involving disregard of the debtor's interests, he may be liable in damages, but the title of the purchaser is not affected.[58]

16. Scope of Security.—The form in which the security is given may also affect its scope. If ex facie an express security, or pledge, it covers only the debt for which it was granted, and gives the holder no preferential right in the bankruptcy of the debtor for any debts subsequently contracted.[59] If the title of the creditor is in form absolute, his security, unless limited by some express contract,[60] involves a right of retention, which will cover any debt incurred in the future.[61] This right may be limited by notice that the reversion is no longer in the hands of the party who granted the security. Thus if he is sequestrated the creditor cannot retain his security for advances made after the date of the sequestration.[62] And notice that the reversionary right, or right to demand a reconveyance, has been assigned to a third party, will preclude any further advances on the faith of the security. Thus property was conveyed by A to the National Bank by an ex facie absolute conveyance. In a back letter it was provided that the property was to be held in security of a present advance and of all advances to be made in future. Subsequently, A assigned his reversionary right to the Union Bank, and the assignation was duly intimated to the National Bank. On A's bankruptcy it was held that the National Bank could not claim any preference over the subjects for any advances after they had been made aware, by intimation from the Union Bank, that the right to demand a reconveyance was no longer vested in their debtor.[63] Similarly, there

---

[54] See s. 18, Scheds. 3 and 5, as amended by the 1971 Act above.
[55] See ss. 19 to 29, as amended by the 1971 Act above.
[56] Bell, *Prin.,* § 207.
[57] *Baillie* v. *Drew* (1884) 12 R. 199; *Aberdeen Trades Council* v. *Shipconstructors, etc., Association,* 1949 S.C. (H.L.) 45.
[58] *Duncan* v. *Mitchell* (1893) 21 R. 37; *Davidson* v. *Scott,* 1915 S.C. 924; *Aberdeen Trades Council* v. *Shipconstructors, etc. Association,* supra.
[59] *National Bank* v. *Forbes* (1858) 21 D. 79; *Colquhoun's Tr.* v. *Diack* (1901) 4 F. 358.
[60] *Anderson's Tr.* v. *Somerville* (1899) 36 S.L.R. 833.
[61] *Hamilton* v. *Western Bank* (1856) 19 D. 152; *National Bank* v. *Union Bank* (1886) 14 R. (H.L.) 1.
[62] *Callum* v. *Goldie* (1885) 12 R. 1137.
[63] *National Bank* v. *Union Bank* (1886) 14 R. (H.L.) 1. See also *Deeley* v. *Lloyds Bank* [1912] A.C. 756.

is no preference for interest falling due after intimation.[64] The trustee in the sequestration of a security holder who holds upon an ex facie absolute title, if called upon to fulfil the obligation to reconvey, is bound to do so.[65]

17. Subjects of Security.—Subject to the distinction between express securities and conveyances ex facie absolute, the law with regard to securities arising by express contract turns on the nature of the subject over which the security is given. As already indicated, the rules with regard to heritable securities are not within the scope of this work.

18. Security over Moveables.—The ordinary methods by which corporeal moveables are used as a security is by the contract of pledge. Pledge requires the delivery of the article, and it is a well established rule that an agreement to pledge, not followed by actual delivery, confers no preference in bankruptcy, and is in no sense a right in security. The maxim "traditionibus, non nudis pactis, dominia rerum transferuntur" applies. This has led to many attempts to create some form of security over subjects, such as furniture or stock-in-trade, which it would be inconvenient to deliver in pledge. How far the general rule that a security cannot be created over corporeal moveables without delivery can be evaded by a contract in the form of a sale has been already considered.[66] Attempts to evade it by placing a label on the goods,[67] by a fictitious lease,[68] or by an imitation of the process, appropriate only in the case of heritage, of giving sasine,[69] have failed. If, however, the object of a proposed loan is to enable the borrower to acquire some particular property, for instance, the furniture required for a new hotel, what is in effect a security for the loan may be obtained if the lender purchases the articles, and places them in the possession of the borrower on a contract of hire. In the event of the borrower's bankruptcy his trustee cannot assert a right to the articles preferable to that of the lender to remove them.[70] It is probably the law that if subjects are so situated that any form of delivery is impossible, as in the case of pipes sunk in the ground,[71] of subjects already in the lender's possession[72] or (it may be suggested) of goods in course of transit without any document of title, an assignation in writing would be effectual in the event of the borrower's bankruptcy.

19. Forms of Delivery.—Delivery does not in every case involve the

---

[64] *Campbell's Judicial Factor* v. *National Bank,* 1944 S.C. 495.
[65] *Heritable Reversionary Co.* v. *Millar* (1892) 19 R. (H.L.) 43; *Forbes's Trs.* v. *Macleod* (1898) 25 R. 1012.
[66] Sale of Goods, Ch. XVII., supra. A power to create securities without delivery, in special statutory cases, in favour of a bank, is provided by the Agricultural Credits (Scotland) Act 1929 (19 & 20 Geo. V, c. 13); as to aircraft, see the Mortgaging of Aircraft Order 1972 (S.I. 1972 No. 1268).
[67] *Orr's Tr.* v. *Tullis* (1870) 8 M. 936.
[68] *Heritable Securities Investment Association* v. *Wingate's Tr.* (1880) 7 R. 1094.
[69] *Stiven* v. *Cowan* (1878) 15 S.L.R. 422.
[70] *Union Bank* v. *Mackenzie* (1865) 3 M. 765; *Duncanson* v. *Jefferis' Tr.* (1881) 8 R. 563.
[71] *Darling* v. *Wilson's Tr.* (1887) 15 R. 180.
[72] *Blundell Leigh* v. *Attenborough* [1921] 3 K.B. 235.

physical transfer of the article. It may be actual, symbolical, or constructive. Actual delivery takes place when goods are physically transferred from one party to another. Also if the goods are in any confined space, and the complete command of that space is transferred, the goods are delivered. So where barrels in the yard of a company were enclosed by a fence, and the key of its gate was given to a party who had advanced money on the security of the barrels it was held that the security was completed by delivery.[73] The question whether goods can be held as delivered if they are set aside in the premises of the party who transfers them is not settled.[74]

20. Symbolical Delivery.—The main instance of symbolical delivery arises in the case where goods are shipped and a bill of lading is taken for them. The bill of lading is recognised as a symbol of the goods, and its transfer, either in pursuance of a sale or of a pledge of the goods to which it refers, has the same legal effect as the physical delivery of the goods themselves.[75] It has been suggested, though not decided, that this rule holds even where the goods are not ascertained, e.g. in the case where several bills of lading are taken for a parcel of goods, and there are no means of identifying the ipsa corpora to which each bill relates.[76] But this dictum seems inconsistent with the provisions of section 16 of the Sale of Goods Act.

Apart from the case of bills of lading, attempts to evade the necessity of actual delivery by some symbolical form have not usually proved successful, either in the case of sales before the Sale of Goods Act 1893, or in the case of securities. A sale of standing trees was followed by cutting and removing a few of them, with a written minute declaring that the purchaser had thereby "entered into his bargain." It was held that the trees were not delivered, and passed to the trustee in the seller's sequestration.[77] When it was attempted to complete a right in security over the moveable machinery in a mill by stopping the mill and going through a form of taking sasine both of the mill and the machinery, it was decided that delivery of the machinery had not been effected, and therefore that no effectual right in security had been created.[78]

21. Constructive Delivery.—Constructive, as distinguished from symbolical, delivery is the term applied when goods are in a store, and their delivery is attempted either by a delivery order addressed to the storekeeper, or by the indorsation of the storekeeper's warrant. This is effectual to transfer a real right in the goods, i.e. is equivalent to actual delivery, under the following conditions:—(1) Intimation of the transfer must be made to the keeper of the store. A delivery order, or storekeeper's warrant, is not regarded as a symbol of the goods in the sense that a bill of lading is. While the mere transfer of the bill of lading carries the real right in the goods without any intimation to the

---

[73] *West Lothian Oil Co.* v. *Mair* (1892) 20 R. 64; contrast *Pattison's Tr.* v. *Liston* (1893) 20 R. 806.
[74] *Gibson* v. *Forbes* (1833) 11 S. 916; *Boak* v. *Megget* (1844) 6 D. 662.
[75] Bell, *Prin.*, § 417.
[76] *Hayman* v. *McLintock*, 1907 S.C. 936, 952 (Lord McLaren).
[77] *Paul* v. *Cuthbertson* (1840) 2 D. 1286.
[78] *Stiven* v. *Cowan* (1878) 15 S.L.R. 422.

captain of the ship in which they are situated, the issue or transfer of a delivery order or warrant leaves the right of the transferee merely personal until it is completed by intimation to the custodier of the goods. The theory of the law is that the storekeeper, on intimation of the transfer being made to him, ceases to hold the goods as custodier for the transferor, and holds them subsequently as custodier for the transferee. The latter has acquired civil possession, through the actual possession of the custodier holding for him, and that civil possession is not acquired until intimation is made.[79] (2) Intimation must be made to the actual custodier, the keeper of the store in which the goods are. It is not sufficient to intimate to a party, for instance, an excise officer in a bonded store, who may have the control of the goods, but is not the keeper of the store.[80] A custom of trade to regard such intimation as sufficient is a misunderstanding of the law, to which no effect can be given.[81] (3) The custodier must be an independent third party, not the servant of the owner of the goods. The law does not recognise constructive delivery by the medium of orders addressed by the owner of goods to the keeper of his own store, and it is immaterial that the store may be used also for keeping goods belonging to third parties.[82] (4) The goods must be ascertained, so that in some way those referred to and transferred by the delivery order may be distinguished from the general mass of goods kept by the transferor in the particular store. So where there were a number of bags of flour in a store, with no marks whereby one bag could be distinguished from another, it was held that a delivery order for a certain number of bags, though intimated to the storekeeper and entered by him in the store books, did not effect constructive delivery, because there were no means of determining which bags were transferred and which were not.[83] In such a case, however, if the goods are subsequently ascertained, by being physically separated from the general mass, they are constructively delivered as at the date when they are so ascertained.[84]

22. Securities over Ships.—The Merchant Shipping Act 1894, repeating prior legislation, makes provision for the constitution and registration of mortgages over a ship or shares thereof.[85] It is probably the law that a bill of sale or other conveyance in writing even although it did not follow the provisions of the Act, and was not registered, would form a security effectual in the bankruptcy of the owner, provided that it was followed by actual possession or by possession inferred from the receipt of the earnings of the ship.[86] Under the Act the ship may be mortgaged in a statutory form (Schedule B) and on the production of such an instrument the registrar is

[79] *Inglis* v. *Robertson & Baxter* (1898) 25 R. (H.L.) 70.
[80] *Rhind's Tr.* v. *Robertson & Baxter* (1891) 18 R. 623. See also *Dobell* v. *Neilson* (1904) 7 F. 281.
[81] *Dobell* v. *Neilson*, supra.
[82] *Anderson* v. *McCall* (1866) 4 M. 765; *Pochin* v. *Robinow* (1869) 7 M. 622, per Lord President Inglis at pp. 628-9.
[83] *Hayman* v. *McLintock*, 1907 S.C. 936; contrast *Price & Pierce* v. *Bank of Scotland*, 1910 S.C. 1095; 1912 S.C. (H.L.) 19.
[84] *Black* v. *Incorporation of Bakers* (1867) 6 M. 136; *Pochin* v. *Robinow*, supra.
[85] 57 & 58 Vict., c. 60, ss. 32-46.
[86] *Watson* v. *Duncan* (1879) 6 R. 1247.

directed to enter it in the ship's register. Preference depends on the order in which the mortgages appear on the register. It is provided that the mortgagee shall not be affected by any "act of bankruptcy" by the mortgagor subsequent to registration,[87] but a similar enactment was held not to preclude the reduction of the mortgage, under the Bankruptcy Act 1696, c. 5, if registered within 60 days of the notour bankruptcy of the mortgagor, and granted in security for a prior debt.[88] And, as already noted, a mortgagee's right may be defeated by the holder of a bond of bottomry or of a maritime lien.[89] It may also be affected by a lien acquired by a shipwright for repairs instructed by the mortgagor.[90] While the ship is on a voyage securities may be granted by means of a certificate of mortgage and sale, issued by the registrar, and entered on the register.[91] Mortgages so effected are preferable from the date when the certificate was registered; inter se according to the date when they were indorsed on the certificate. Provision is made for the assignation, and for the discharge, of mortgages in statutory forms.

23. Powers of Mortgagee of Ship.—A mortgagee has a statutory power of sale. He is entitled to interdict any act of the owner which may imperil his security, e.g. a voyage uninsured.[92] Though the Act has no express provision on the subject, it has long been established that the statutory power of sale implies the right to take possession of the ship.[93] A mortgagee, if he enters into possession, not otherwise, is liable for furnishings supplied to the ship on the order of the master.[94]

24. Securities over Incorporeal Property.—A debt of any kind, for instance, a policy of insurance, may be transferred in security by a written assignation, followed by intimation to the debtor. The law of Scotland does not recognise any security (known in England as an equitable mortgage) by the mere deposit of title deeds,[95] and therefore the mere transfer of the voucher of a debt (unless it is a negotiable instrument[96]) or a mere assignation not followed by intimation to the debtor, creates no effectual security. So no preferential right is created by the transfer of a policy of insurance without intimation to the insurance company.[97] The same principles were applied to an assignation of the uncalled capital of a company, which was held to be ineffectual as a security unless it was completed by intimation to each shareholder.[98]

---

87 Merchant Shipping Act 1894, s. 36.
88 *Anderson* v. *Western Bank* (1859) 21 D. 230.
89 Supra, §§ 6, 11.
90 *Tyne Dock Engineering Co.* v. *Royal Bank of Scotland,* 1974 S.L.T. 57.
91 Merchant Shipping Act, 1894, s. 39.
92 *Laming* v. *Seater* (1889) 16 R. 828.
93 Bell, *Prin.,* § 1382A.
94 *Havilland, Routh & Co.* v. *Thomson* (1864) 3 M. 313.
95 *Christie* v. *Ruxton* (1862) 24 D. 1182.
96 See Moveable Property—Incorporeal, Ch. XXXVIII, infra.
97 *Strachan* v. *McDougle* (1835) 13 S. 954; *Wylie's Executrix* v. *McJannet* (1901) 4 F. 195.
98 *Liquidators of Union Club* v. *Edinburgh Life Assurance Co.* (1906) 8 F. 1143.

25. Shares in Company.—Shares in a company may be used as a security by transferring them to the creditor, subject to an obligation by him to retransfer. As this involves expense, publicity, and in certain cases, liability on the shares, other methods have been attempted. No security is effected by a mere deposit of share certificates, and when this was followed by a transfer registered within 60 days of the debtor's bankruptcy it was held that the transfer was reducible under the Bankruptcy Act 1696, c. 5, as a security for prior debts.[99] If, however, a duly executed transfer of the shares is given to the creditor with the certificates he is placed in a position in which he can complete his security by sending in the transfer for registration. It was held that it was no objection to his title that he did so within 60 days of the debtor's sequestration,[1] and in one case it was held that the transfer might be registered even after a petition for the sequestration of the debtor had been presented, and at any time before the trustee in the sequestration had taken steps to have himself registered as owner of the shares.[2] The deposit of share certificates, with transfers duly executed, may therefore be regarded as forming a security over the shares, though it is a security which, so long as the creditor is not actually registered, is liable to be defeated by arrestments used by some other creditor, or by a subsequent and fraudulent transfer by the debtor.[3] It is a practice, more common in England than in Scotland,[4] to deposit the share certificate with blank transfers, i.e. transfers executed by the transferor, but without the name of the transferee. The advantage is that it enables the creditor to transfer his right without any further procedure. The validity of a security by means of blank transfers is established in England; in Scotland it may be doubtful, and has not been decided, whether they are open to challenge under the Blank Bonds and Trusts Act 1696, c. 25, which declares that instruments delivered blank in the name of the creditor shall be void.[5]

26. Obligations of Security Holder.[6]—The obligation of a party who holds any property in security is to exercise reasonable care. Thus when a company offered new shares to its shareholders on advantageous terms it was decided that a party who was registered as owner of certain shares but really held them in security was bound either to take the new shares or to intimate the offer to the debtor, for whom he held.[7] But a creditor is not liable for the accidental loss or destruction of the subject he holds in security, nor is his right to recover his debt affected,[8] unless tender of payment has been made and the return of the security subjects wrongfully refused.[9] If, however, the creditor is

---

[99] *Gourlay* v. *Mackie* (1887) 14 R. 403.
[1] *Guild* v. *Young* (1884) 22 S.L.R. 520. The period under the 1696 Act is now six months.
[2] *Morrison* v. *Harrison* (1876) 3 R. 406.
[3] *Rainford* v. *Keith* [1905] 1 Ch. 296.
[4] See *Crerar* v. *Bank of Scotland*, 1921 S.C. 736, affd. 1922 S.C. (H.L.) 137.
[5] *Colonial Bank* v. *Cady* (1890) 15 App.Cas. 267; see *Shaw* v. *Caledonian Ry.* (1890) 17 R. 466, at p. 478.
[6] As to the regulation of the pledge by the Consumer Credit Act 1974, see Consumer Credit Transactions, Ch. XIX, *supra*. § 15.
[7] *Waddell* v. *Hutton*, 1911 S.C. 575.
[8] *Syred* v. *Carruthers* (1858) E.B. & E. 469.
[9] *Fraser* v. *Smith* (1899) 1 F. 487.

unable to return the security, from some cause attributable to his own fault, he cannot demand payment of the debt.[10] As a general rule where a security, such as a pledge, is constituted by delivery, the creditor cannot restore the possession of the subjects pledged to the debtor without abandoning his right in security;[11] but it has been held, in the case of a bill of lading, and on grounds which are applicable generally, that a creditor, desirous of realising his security, might employ the debtor as his agent to effect a sale, and on that footing restore the subjects to the debtor's possession, without losing his preferable right to the proceeds of the sale.[12] On payment of the debt it is the duty of the creditor to restore the exact subject given in security, and hence it was held that a bank, to which shares had been transferred in security, was not justified in tendering in return equivalent shares of the same company unless in virtue of an agreement under which this method of dealing was sanctioned by the debtor.[13]

In realising his security the creditor must proceed exactly in the terms, express, or in the case of heritable securities statutory, of his power of sale, and failure in this respect may entitle a purchaser to resile,[14] or afford ground for a reduction of the sale at the instance of the debtor.[15] He must also have regard to the interests of the debtor, and of postponed bondholders.[16] A sale without such regard may be interdicted, or may lead to a claim of damages but not, it is conceived, to a reduction of a sale to a bona fide purchaser.[17] A creditor proposing to realise his security is bound to assign the debt, and the security held for it, to anyone who tenders payment, and can show a reasonable interest[18] though he may refuse an assignation of the security if he can show that his own interests would be prejudiced thereby,[19] or that he would be exposed to any liability.[20] A creditor, in selling the subject of his security, is not entitled to purchase,[21] except under the provisions, applicable to heritable securities only, of the Heritable Securities (Scotland) Act 1894 or the Conveyancing and Feudal Reform (Scotland) Act 1970.[22] But a creditor may purchase at a sale by the trustee in the debtor's sequestration,[23] by another bondholder,[24] or by one of several creditors in the bond.[25]

27. Lien.—A lien is a right to retain property until some debt or other

[10] *Ellis & Co.'s Tr.* v. *Dixon-Johnston* [1925] A.C. 489.
[11] *Hunter* v. *Slack* (1860) 22 D. 1166.
[12] *North-Western Bank* v. *Poynter* (1894) 22 R. (H.L.) 1. See also *Moore* v. *Gledden* (1869) 7 M. 1016.
[13] *Crerar* v. *Bank of Scotland,* 1921 S.C. 736, affd. 1922 S.C. (H.L.) 137. See also *M'Kirdy* v. *Webster's Trs.* (1895) 22 R. 643.
[14] *Ferguson* v. *Rodger* (1895) 22 R. 340.
[15] *Stewart* v. *Brown* (1882) 10 R. 192.
[16] Bell, *Comm.,* II, 271.
[17] *Beveridge* v. *Wilson* (1829) 7 S. 279; *Kerr* v. *McArthur's Trs.* (1848) 11 D. 301.
[18] *Adair's Tr.* v. *Rankin* (1895) 22 R. 975.
[19] *Smith* v. *Gentle* (1844) 6 D. 1164.
[20] *Bruce* v. *Scottish Amicable Insurance Co.,* 1907 S.C. 637.
[21] *Stirling's Trs.* (1865) 3 M. 851.
[22] 57 & 58 Vict., c. 44, 1970 c. 35.
[23] Bankruptcy (Scotland) Act 1913, s. 116.
[24] *Begbie* v. *Boyd* (1837) 16 S. 232.
[25] *Wright* v. *Buchanan,* 1917 S.C. 73.

obligation is satisfied. If constituted by express contract it is a pledge under another name, and it is only liens implied by law which need be considered here.

"Lien" and "right of retention" are sometimes used as synonymous terms. Thus in the interpretation clause (s. 62) of the Sale of Goods Act 1893, it is provided that "lien in Scotland includes right of retention." But, more strictly, a lien is a right founded on mere possession, retention a right founded on property. A lien is a right to remain in possession of a subject held on a limited title; a right of retention the right of a party, whose title is one of ownership subject to an obligation to convey, to refuse to implement his obligation until some counter-obligation due by the party entitled to demand conveyance has been fulfilled. The effect and limits of a right of retention have been considered in dealing with securities constituted by ex facie absolute conveyance qualified by a backbond.[26] In what follows lien is taken in its more restricted sense as a right founded on possession of property belonging to another.

28. Special and General Liens.—Liens are classed as special and general. A special lien is a right implied by law to retain an article until some specific debt is paid. A general lien is a right to retain until some balance, arising on a contract of employment, is discharged. The law of Scotland does not recognise as a corollary from mere possession, as distinguished from ownership, any right in the possessor to continue in possession until all debts due to him by the owner are paid.[27] A lien is in all cases a limited right, and its extent depends either on the contract under which possession was obtained, or on usage of trade. The chief instances are in sale and in contracts of employment. The lien of an unpaid seller has been already considered.[28]

29. Special Lien: In Contracts of Employment.—In contracts of employment it is a general rule, based, according to the Scottish authorities, on principles of mutual contract, that if the party employed has been placed in possession of an article belonging to his employer he has a right to retain it until he is paid for his work under that contract. The mutual obligations of the parties are on the one hand to pay for the work done; on the other to return the article, and the party employed is not bound to fulfil his obligation until the obligation due to him, and arising out of the same contract, is fulfilled. On this footing the assertion of a special lien does not require proof of custom of trade; it is an implied condition in all contracts of employment.[29] So it is immaterial that no work has actually been done on the article over which the lien is claimed, and an accountant, who had been placed in possession of business books in order to collect debts, was held to be entitled to a lien over the books, and the defence that he had done no work on the

---

[26] Supra, § 16; and as no retention of debts, Breach of Contract, Ch. XIII, supra, § 10.
[27] *Harper* v. *Faulds* (1791) Bell's Octavo Cases, 440; *Anderson's Tr.* v. *Fleming* (1871) 9 M. 718.
[28] Sale of Goods, Ch. XVII, supra.
[29] Bell, *Comm.*, II., 92; *Miller* v. *Hutcheson* (1881) 8 R. 489; *Robertson* v. *Ross* (1887) 15 R. 67.

books themselves was rejected.[30] But to found a special lien the party employed must be placed in possession of the article; a servant, who has merely the custody, and not the possession, of his master's property, has no lien.[31]

30. General Lien.—A general lien is recognised by the custom of certain professions and trades. Its range depends on the usage of the particular trade, and varies from a right covering all debts arising from prior employment, as in the case of a solicitor,[32] to a right covering merely the balance due on the working of a particular year, as in the case of a bleacher.[33] In a case not covered by decision the question whether a general lien existed is to be determined on the evidence of parties engaged in the trade that their dealings were on the footing of a lien. The fact that a general lien is recognised in a particular trade in England is evidence, though not necessarily conclusive evidence, that it is also recognised in that trade in Scotland.[34]

Among cases of general lien particular notice may be taken of the lien of a factor, a banker, a solicitor and an innkeeper.

31. Lien of Factor.—A factor or mercantile agent has a general lien over all goods, bills, money or documents belonging to his employer which have come into his possession in the course of his employment.[35] It covers all advances made to the principal, the factor's salary or commission, and any liabilities incurred on the principal's behalf.[36] It will not cover, in the principal's bankruptcy, debts due to the factor, but arising on some separate account.[37] A mercantile agent is defined, for the purposes of the Factors Act 1889, as an agent "having in the customary course of his business as such agent authority either to sell goods, or to consign goods for the purpose of sale, or to buy goods, or to raise money on the security of goods."[38] In questions of lien the term is used somewhat more widely, and the factor's or mercantile agent's lien has been held to belong to an auctioneer,[39] and to a stockbroker.[40]

32. Lien of Banker.—A banker has a general lien over all bills, notes and negotiable securities. It covers any balance due by the customer.[41] There is no case in Scotland extending the lien to any instrument not negotiable, for instance, to share certificates. In order that negotiable securities may be subject to the lien they must have been lodged with the banker in his capacity

---

[30] *Meikle & Wilson* v. *Pollard* (1880) 8 R. 69.
[31] *Barnton Hotel Co.* v. *Cook* (1899) 1 F. 1190; contrast *Findlay* v. *Waddell*, 1910 S.C. 670.
[32] *Anderson's Tr.* v. *Fleming* (1871) 9 M. 718.
[33] Infra, § 34.
[34] *Strong* v. *Philipps* (1878) 5 R. 770 (packer).
[35] Bell, *Prin.*, § 1445.
[36] *Sibbald* v. *Gibson* (1852) 15 D. 217; *Glendinning* v. *Hope*, 1911 S.C. (H.L.) 73.
[37] *Miller* v. *McNair* (1852) 14 D. 955.
[38] 52 & 53 Vict., c. 45, s. 1.
[39] *Miller* v. *Hutcheson* (1881) 8 R. 489.
[40] *Glendinning* v. *Hope*, 1911 S.C. (H.L.) 73.
[41] Bell, *Prin.*, § 1451.

as monetary agent, not merely for safe keeping. Thus when exchequer bills were sent to a bank in a locked box, of which the bank had no key, it was held that there was no lien over them, although the bills were periodically taken from the box and given to the banker in order that he might collect the interest.[42] But the terms of a receipt given by the bank and indicating that the documents were held for safe keeping does not necessarily exclude lien, in a case where there is proof that the bank, relying on lien, had made advances to the customer.[43] Where negotiable securities are lodged with a banker by a stockbroker, the banker, in the absence of notice to the contrary, may be entitled to assume that they are the stockbroker's own property, and claim a lien over them, in the stockbroker's bankruptcy, in a question with the clients to whom they really belong. But where the banker has notice, either express, or from his knowledge of the usual course of business, that the securities are the property of the stockbroker's clients, there is a difference between a right founded on express pledge and on the lien implied by law. Where securities are expressly pledged for a specific advance the banker is entitled to assume that the stockbroker has the authority of his clients so to pledge them, and may therefore, on the stockbroker's failure, retain them to meet the amount advanced. But a claim to retain them to meet the general balance due by the stockbroker, founded on lien and not on any specific pledge, is in a different position, because the banker has no right to assume that the stockbroker has any authority to subject his client's securities to a lien for his own general balance.[44] It would appear that a banker's right in the exercise of lien is merely to retain the securities, not to realise them.[45]

33. Lien of Solicitor.—A solicitor has a general lien over all papers placed in his hands by his client. It extends over title deeds of any description, and miscellaneous documents, such as the client's will.[46] It does not entitle the solicitor to obstruct the course of justice by refusing to produce papers entrusted to him for the purposes of an action.[47] Nor can it be exercised over the register of shareholders of a company, which, by statute, cannot be subjected to any form of security.[48] It covers the solicitor's business accounts, and advances usually made in the ordinary course of business, such as to counsel or witnesses.[49] It does not cover cash advances to the client;[50] nor, it would appear, the account of an Edinburgh solicitor in Court of Session proceedings, if paid by the country solicitor;[51] nor the account of an English solicitor, unless a Scottish solicitor has paid it, or is liable for it.[52] The solicitor's lien, so far as it is a general lien, rests on professional usage, and is

[42] *Brandao* v. *Barnett* (1846) 12 Cl. & F. 787.
[43] *Robertson's Tr.* v. *Royal Bank* (1890) 18 R. 12.
[44] *National Bank* v. *Dickie's Tr.* (1895) 22 R. 740.
[45] *Robertson's Tr.* v. *Royal Bank* (1890) 18 R. 12.
[46] *Paul* v. *Meikle* (1868) 7 M. 235. See also *McIntosh* v. *Chalmers* (1883) 11 R. 8.
[47] *Callman* v. *Bell*, (1793) M. 6255.
[48] *Garpel Haematite Co.* v. *Andrew* (1866) 4 M. 617.
[49] *Richardson* v. *Merry* (1863) 1 M. 940, at p. 946.
[50] *Christie* v. *Ruxton* (1862) 24 D. 1182; *Wylie's Executrix* v. *McJannet* (1901) 4 F. 195.
[51] *Largue* v. *Urquhart* (1883) 10 R. 1229.
[52] *Liquidator of Grand Empire Theatre* v. *Snodgrass*, 1932 S.C. (H.L.) 73.

not enjoyed by unprofessional persons similarly employed. Thus an accountant has a lien over papers entrusted to him only for his charge for work done in connection with those papers, not a general lien for his whole professional account,[53] and the scope of the lien of the factor or land agent on an estate has been held to depend upon whether he is a qualified solicitor.[54]

34. Lien in Questions with Third Parties.—The lien of a solicitor may be exercised against the client, and also, in certain cases, against parties deriving right from him. Thus the solicitor of a seller may retain title deeds against the purchaser, the solicitor of a borrower against the lender on heritable security. In neither case can he exercise this right if he acts for both parties (i.e. for seller and purchaser, or for borrower and lender) unless he has intimated to the purchaser or lender that he holds the title deeds and proposes to claim a lien over them.[55] A rule established by early decision— that the solicitor might exercise his lien even if he obtained the papers after a lender's security was recorded[56]—has been altered by statute, and now no lien can be acquired, in a question with a heritable creditor, after the date of recording the security.[57] Where the lien is exercised the solicitor's right cannot be evaded by raising an action, obtaining a diligence for the recovery of documents, and calling on the solicitor to produce the title deeds as a haver.[58]

35. Solicitor's Lien in Sequestration.—A trustee in sequestration, or the liquidator of a company, is entitled to insist on the production of all papers relating to the estate under his charge, and the solicitor must give them up.[59] He does so under implied reservation of his lien: express reservation is unnecessary.[60] The result is not to give him any claim against the trustee or liquidator,[61] but to entitle him to be ranked for his account as a preferred creditor.[62] It is not decided how he ranks in competition with other preferred creditors, but he is postponed to the expenses of the liquidation or sequestration.[63]

The solicitor's lien does not give him the right to dispose of the papers, only to retain them.[64] Accordingly, his lien is worthless in a case where there is nothing in the bankrupt's estate over which he can be given a preference. In that case he ranks as an ordinary creditor.[65] The fact that papers were held under lien did not preclude the triennial prescription of the account.[66]

[53] *Findlay* v. *Waddell*, 1910 S.C. 670; *Morrison* v. *Fulwell's Tr.* (1901) 9 S.L.T. 34.
[54] *Macrae* v. *Leith*, 1913 S.C. 901.
[55] *Gray* v. *Graham* (1855) 2 Macq. 435; *Drummond* v. *Muirhead & Guthrie Smith* (1900) 2 F. 585
[56] *Provenhall's Creditors*, (1781) M. 6253.
[57] Conveyancing (Scotland) Act 1924, s. 27.
[58] *Dalrymple* v. *Earl of Selkirk* (1751) Elch, Hypothec, No. 17.
[59] Bankruptcy (Scotland) Act 1913, s. 76; *Train & McIntyre* v. *Forbes*, 1925 S.L.T. 286; *Garden, Haig Scott & Wallace* v. *Stevenson's Tr.*, 1962 S.C. 51.
[60] Bankruptcy Act 1913, ss. 76 and 97; *Adam & Winchester* v. *White's Tr.* (1884) 11 R. 863, per Lord President Inglis at p. 865; *Garden, Haig Scott & Wallace* v. *Stevenson's Tr.*, supra.
[61] *Adam & Winchester* v. *White's Tr.*, supra; *Lochee Sawmills Co.* v. *Stevenson*, 1908 S.C. 559.
[62] *Skinner* v. *Henderson* (1865) 3 M. 867.
[63] *Miln's Factor* v. *Spence's Trs.*, 1927 S.L.T. 425.
[64] *Ferguson* v. *Grant* (1856) 18 D. 536, at p. 538.
[65] *Garden, Haig Scott & Wallace* v. *Stevenson's Tr.*, supra.
[66] Bell, *Prin.*, § 1441.

36. Lien of Innkeeper.—An innkeeper has a lien over his guest's luggage for the amount of his bill.[67] He cannot detain the guest or the clothes he is wearing.[68] The lien covers articles not of the nature of ordinary luggage, such as a solicitor's letter book.[69] It does not cover articles not brought as luggage, but hired by the guest during his stay at the inn,[70] or articles, not luggage, handed to the innkeeper as security for the bill.[71] By statute it also does not cover "any vehicle or any property left therein, or any horse or other live animal or its harness or other equipment."[72] It may be exercised even if the articles brought as luggage do not belong to the guest, and the innkeeper is aware of the fact.[73] Under the Innkeepers Act 1878,[74] an innkeeper is entitled, after advertisement, to sell by auction goods brought to or left in his inn, provided that a debt for board and lodging, or for the keep of any horse, shall have been six weeks outstanding. He must account to the guest for any surplus.

37. Limit of Rights under Liens.—It has been laid down that lien is a right over which the Court may exercise an equitable control, and therefore, that, in particular circumstances, a ship might be released from a lien for repairs on terms to be fixed by the Court.[75] And no lien founded on possession can be asserted if it would conflict with the express or implied terms of the contract under which possession was obtained. Thus if a bill is sent to a banker for discount, and he refuses to discount it, he cannot retain it under lien.[76] Where money was deposited with a solicitor in order to effect a composition with the depositor's creditors, and this proved impracticable, it was held that the solicitor could not retain the money to meet a general balance on his business account in a question with the trustee in the depositor's sequestration.[77] And it is a general principle that when a security is constituted by express pledge it cannot be extended, on the plea of lien, to cover other debts or a general balance.[78] The primary purpose of a lien is to constitute a security for payment of charges incurred in connection with the object over which the lien exists.[79] But this is a right of limited value unless, where the debtor proves recalcitrant, the object in question can be sold.

38. Extinction of Lien.—As a lien is founded on possession it is lost if

---

67 Bell. *Prin.*, § 1428. This lien can be regarded as a special lien: see Gloag & Irvine, p. 397, and Walker, *Principles* (2nd ed.), p. 1585.
68 *Sunbolf* v. *Alford* (1838) 3 M. & W. 248.
69 *Snead* v. *Watkins* (1856) 1 C.B. (N.S.) 267.
70 *Broadwood* v. *Granara* (1854) 10 Ex. 417.
71 *Marsh* v. *Commissioner of Police* (1943) 60 T.L.R. 96.
72 Hotel Proprietors Act 1956 (4 & 5 Eliz. II, c. 62), s. 2 (2).
73 *Robins* v. *Gray* [1895] 2 Q.B. 78, 501.
74 41 & 42 Vict., c. 38.
75 *Garscadden* v. *Ardrossan Dry Dock Co.*, 1910 S.C. 178.
76 *Borthwick* v. *Bremner* (1833) 12 S. 121.
77 *Middlemas* v. *Gibson*, 1910 S.C. 577.
78 Supra, § 18.
79 But in the case of a depositary to whom goods have been handed over for repairs etc., the depositary cannot exercise his lien over the goods to secure payment of garaging or other storage costs unless that is a matter of separate agreement with the depositor; *Stephen* v. *Swayne* (1861) 25 D. 158; *Carntyne Motors* v. *Curran*, 1958 S.L.T. (Sh. Ct.) 6.

possession is relinquished, with a probable exception, as in the case of a pledge, where an article is restored to its owner on a contract whereby he is constituted the agent of the holder of the lien for the purpose of selling the article.[80] Some of the articles held under lien may be restored without affecting the lien over the rest.[81] Where a bill is taken for the debt, and subsequently dishonoured, the presumption is that the bill has been taken as an additional security, and the lien is not affected, unless the currency of the bill is unusually long, when the lien will be held to have been relinquished unless it was expressly reserved.[82]

39. Equitable Restrictions on Contracts with Debtors.—Freedom of contract, in cases between debtor and creditor, is in some respects limited on equitable grounds. Thus a creditor cannot enforce a provision for a penalty in the event of failure in punctual payment,[83] though he may secure the same result by a provision under which if the interest is punctually paid a lower rate is to be accepted than that stipulated in the bond.[84] The rule "once a mortgage, always a mortgage" means that if a conveyance was in origin a security, although, it may be, expressed as an ex facie absolute transfer, a provision that the right of redemption shall expire after a certain period will not receive effect. A declarator that the right to redeem has expired is necessary, and may at any time be met by an offer of payment.[85] So where a party, borrowing money from an insurance company on the security of a contingent interest, took out a policy on his life, and assigned it and his contingent interest to the company, with a provision that if the contingent interest should lapse by his predecease the policy should become the property of the company, it was held, on his predecease, that the company must pay the policy to his executors, under deduction of the amount of the debt, on the ground that the policy was originally transferred in security and that a contract that the subject of a security should become the property of the creditor on the occurrence of a certain event was one to which the law would not give effect.[86] It is competent to provide that a creditor shall have the right to exact immediate payment, but that the right of redemption shall be postponed.[87] But the period of redemption cannot be so postponed as to preclude the return of any subject given in security on payment being made; it must not therefore, where the subject of the security is of a wasting character (e.g. a lease), be fixed at a period when that subject would have ceased to exist.[88] It is somewhat doubtful how far a creditor can enforce agreements for advantages other than the payment of his debt and interest. In Scotland an

---

[80] Supra, § 26. See also *Wolifson* v. *Harrison* 1974 S.L.T. (Notes) 55; 1978 S.L.T. 95.
[81] *Gray* v. *Graham* (1855) 2 Macq. 435.
[82] *Palmer* v. *Lee* (1880) 7 R. 651; approving Bell, *Comm.*, II., 109.
[83] *Nasmyth* v. *Samson* (1785) 3 Paton 9.
[84] *Gatty* v. *Maclaine*, 1921 S.C. (H.L.) 1.
[85] *Smith* v. *Smith* (1879) 6 R. 794. As to the power of the creditor in a bond and disposition in security to acquire the subjects, see Heritable Securities (Scotland) Act 1894, s. 8. As to a standard security see Conveyancing and Feudal Reform (Scotland) Act 1970, s. 28.
[86] *Marquis of Northampton* v. *Salt* [1892] A.C. 1.
[87] *Ashburton* v. *Escombe* (1892) 20 R. 187.
[88] *Fairclough* v. *Swan Brewery Co.* [1912] A.C. 565.

agreement that a borrower should not start a rival business was sustained.[89] In England a bargain for some collateral advantage, if it does not amount to an obstacle, or clog, on the borrower's right of redemption, is an admissible contract, and may be enforced, according to its terms, even after the loan has been repaid.[90]

40. Catholic and Secondary Securities.—When A has a prior bond or other security over two subjects belonging to the debtor, and B has a postponed bond over one of these subjects, A is termed the catholic and B the secondary creditor. If in these circumstances A chooses to realise the subjects over which B's security extends, and thereby obtains payment of his debt, he is bound to assign to B his security over the other subject.[91] And if both subjects are realised, and the debtor is bankrupt, it will be assumed that the catholic creditor exhausted first the subject over which the secondary bond did not extend, and therefore that the secondary creditor has a preferable right to the balance of the sum realised from both subjects, in a question with the general creditors of the debtor represented by his trustee in bankruptcy.[92] But the secondary creditor has no direct control over the acts of the catholic creditor, and cannot object to a discharge of the bond over the subjects not covered by his own security.[93] And the catholic creditor may disregard the interests of the secondary creditor in pursuance of any legitimate interest of his own. So if he holds a bond for another debt over the subjects not covered by the secondary creditor's bond, he is entitled, in realising, to exhaust first the subjects covered by the secondary bond, so as to leave the largest possible surplus to meet his own postponed bond.[94]

If there are secondary bonds on each estate the burden of the catholic bond is, in a question between the secondary bondholders, to be apportioned rateably, according to the value of each estate, and irrespective of the question which secondary bond was prior to date.[95] The same principles apply in analogous cases. So, when a catholic bond covered two estates, and one of them was burdened with a secondary bond and the other sold, it was held that the burden of the catholic bond was, on the debtor's bankruptcy, to be apportioned rateably between the secondary creditor on the one estate and the purchaser of the other.[96]

---

[89] *Stewart* v. *Stewart* (1899) 1 F. 1158.
[90] *Kreglinger* v. *New Patagonia Syndicate* [1914] A.C. 25.
[91] Bell, *Comm.*, II, 417.
[92] *Littlejohn* v. *Black* (1855) 18 D. 207; *Nicol's Tr.* v. *Hill* (1889) 16 R. 416.
[93] *Morton (Liddell's Curator)* (1871) 10 M. 292.
[94] *Preston* v. *Erskine*, (1715) M. 3376.
[95] *Ferrier* v. *Cowan* (1896) 23 R. 703.
[96] *Earl of Moray* v. *Mansfield* (1836) 14 S. 886.

CHAPTER XXI

CAUTIONARY OBLIGATIONS

Gloag and Irvine, *Rights in Security* (1897); Bell, *Principles* (10th ed., 1899); Gow, *Mercantile and Industrial Law of Scotland* (1964), Ch. 5.

1. Nature of the Contract.—A cautionary obligation is defined by Bell as "an accessory engagement, as surety for another, that the principal obligant shall pay the debt or perform the act for which he has engaged, otherwise the cautioner shall pay the debt or fulfil the obligation."[1] The obligation may be for the payment of a debt already incurred; for debts to be incurred, or furnishings to be supplied, in the future; for the faithful performance of an office or contract of service; for the due execution of any contract; or, as in the case where a party accused of crime is allowed bail, for the performance of some particular act. The person undertaking the obligation is called indifferently cautioner, guarantor, or surety; the party to whose debt or acts the obligation applies is known as the principal debtor; the party entitled to exact performance is the creditor.

2. Cautionry as an Accessory Obligation.—As an accessory obligation, cautionry requires the existence of a principal debt. If the apparent principal debt be unenforceable, as granted by a party with no power to contract, or in its nature a pactum illicitum, the cautioner is not liable.[2] A guarantee, however, for some debt or other obligation to be contracted in the future is binding.[3] And there is some, though doubtful, authority to the effect that if the principal debtor, though a person (e.g., a pupil, or, under the older law, a married woman) unable to contract, has actually entered into an engagement morally binding, the obligation of the cautioner is enforceable.[4] If the party interposing as cautioner was aware that the principal obligation was invalid, as where directors guaranteed an undertaking of the company which they knew to be ultra vires, the doctrine of personal bar may be invoked so as to preclude the defence of invalidity.[5]

3. Constitution of Cautionary Obligation.—A cautionary obligation may arise from an offer, addressed to a particular creditor, and offering to guarantee a particular debt, or the conduct of a third party. It is then a

---

[1] *Prin.,* § 245. Cautionary obligations may be affected by the Consumer Credit Act 1974 (c. 39); see Consumer Credit Transactions, Ch. XIX, supra.
[2] The cautioner may be liable if the illegality is merely technical, e.g., the inability of a company to purchase its own shares, and the parties contracted on the assumption of legality; *Garrard* v. *James* [1925] 1 Ch. 616.
[3] *Fortune* v. *Young,* 1918 S.C. 1.
[4] See Bell, *Prin.,* § 251.
[5] *Yorkshire Railway Waggon Co.* v. *M'Clure* (1881) 19 Ch.D. 478; *Stevenson* v. *Adair* (1872) 10 M. 919.

question of construction, on which no definite rule can be given, whether an express acceptance is required, or whether the cautioner's liability is clinched when credit is given to the third party whose actings or dealings he has offered to guarantee.[6] A cautionary obligation may also arise from an undertaking to guarantee the debt or dealings of another, given to the party who is to be guaranteed, and not addressed to any particular creditor. In that case anyone who has given credit on the faith of the guarantee is entitled to enforce it, unless from its terms it appears that it was limited to some particular class of prospective creditors.[7]

4. Necessity of Writing.—By the Mercantile Law Amendment (Scotland) Act 1856, it is provided (in general, though not exact, accordance with English statutory rules) that all guarantees, securities and cautionary obligations made or granted by any person for any other person shall be in writing, and shall be subscribed by the person undertaking, or by some person duly authorised by him, otherwise the same shall have no effect.[8] A written undertaking to give a guarantee when required satisfies the conditions imposed by the Act.[9] It is not decided whether the writing by which a cautionary obligation is undertaken must be a probative writ.[10] But such writing need not be probative if the obligation is in re mercatoria,[11] or if in reliance on it advances have been made to the debtor, or there have been other actings amounting to rei interventus.[12] A signature in the firm name is sufficient to bind the partner who so signs.[13]

5. Representations as to Credit.—Section 6 of the Mercantile Law Amendment Act also requires writing in the case of "representations and assurances as to the character, conduct, credit, ability,[14] trade or dealings of any person, made or granted to the effect or for the purpose of enabling such person to obtain credit, money, goods or postponement of payment of debt, or of any other obligation demandable from him." Under this section no action can be founded on any oral statement of the character referred to, and it is irrelevant to aver that the statement was made fraudulently,[15] nor can such verbal statement be founded on as a defence to an action on an obligation which has been induced by it.[16]

6. Representations and Guarantees.—It is a question of construction whether a particular writing amounts to a guarantee or is merely a

[6] See *Wallace* v. *Gibson* (1895) 22 R. (H.L.) 56.
[7] *Fortune* v. *Young*, 1918 S.C. 1.
[8] 19 & 20 Vict. c. 60, s. 6.
[9] *Wallace* v. *Gibson* (1895) 22 R. (H.L.) 56.
[10] See the divergent judicial opinions in *Snaddon* v. *London, Edinburgh and Glasgow Assurance Co.* (1902) 5 F. 182; *Hylander's Exr.* v. *H. & K. Modes*, 1957 S.L.T. (Sh. Ct.) 69 at p. 71.
[11] *Johnston* v. *Grant* (1844) 6 D. 875.
[12] *National Bank* v. *Campbell* (1892) 19 R. 885.
[13] *Fortune* v. *Young*, 1918 S.C. 1.
[14] Construed as meaning "ability to pay," *Irving* v. *Burns*, 1915 S.C. 260.
[15] *Clydesdale Bank* v. *Paton* (1896) 23 R. (H.L.) 22 ; *Irving* v. *Burns*, supra.
[16] *Union Bank* v. *Taylor*, 1925 S.C. 835; *Muir* v. *Burnside*, 1935 S.N. 13.

representation as to the character or credit of another.[17] If the former construction be adopted, the writer is liable directly on his contractual obligation; if the latter, no contractual obligation has been undertaken, but the writer may be liable ex delicto if his statement was fraudulent, or the statement may be a ground for the reduction of a contract or obligation induced by it.[18] An honest, though mistaken, opinion as to the credit of another infers no liability even if made negligently,[19] unless the relations of the writer and the person he addresses are of such a fiduciary or other special character as to involve a duty to take reasonable care, as for example, where their relationship is that of solicitor and client.[20] In such a case it has been held in England that as the ground of action is failure in the duty involved in the relationship, action may lie although the representation was verbal.[21] A positive statement of fact, not of opinion, if acted on by the party to whom it is made, may possibly involve liability on the ground that the party making it is personally barred from showing that it is untrue.[22]

7. Cautionary or Independent Obligation.—There are many cases where it is difficult to say whether an independent or a cautionary obligation has been undertaken. If A orders goods to be supplied to B, and undertakes to be responsible for payment, this may, according to the circumstances, be an independent obligation by A, and proveable by parole evidence, or a cautionary obligation for a debt primarily undertaken by B, and, if so, invalid if not constituted in writing.[23]

It has been decided in England that agency del credere, when the agent guarantees the solvency of the party with whom he deals on his principal's behalf, is not to be regarded, in a question as to the necessity of writing, as a contract of guarantee.[24] And a guarantee against loss from a contract, which does not involve any obligation of performance by any principal debtor, e.g., an obligation to take over shares if they do not reach a certain price, is not a cautionary obligation.[25] Contracts which do involve performance by a principal debtor, but are framed as policies of insurance, may really be cautionary obligations. So far as any rule can be stated in such cases, the incidents of the contract depend on the law of insurance if the guarantee is obtained by the creditor, on the law of cautionary obligations if it is obtained by the debtor.[26]

8. Cautionry, Proper and Improper.—In form, a cautionary obligation may

[17] *Park* v. *Gould* (1851) 13 D. 1049; *Fortune* v. *Young*, 1918 S.C. 1.
[18] *Union Bank* v. *Taylor*, supra.
[19] *Robinson* v. *National Bank*, 1916 S.C. (H.L.) 154.
[20] *Nocton* v. *Lord Ashburton* [1914] A.C. 923; *Banbury* v. *Bank of Montreal* [1918] A.C. 626; *Hedley Byrne & Co.* v. *Heller* [1964] A.C. 465.
[21] *Banbury* v. *Bank of Montreal*, supra; *Hedley Byrne & Co.* v. *Heller*, supra.
[22] *Park* v. *Gould* (1851) 13 D. 1049.
[23] *Stevenson's Tr.* v. *Campbell* (1895) 23 R. 711.
[24] *Sutton* v. *Grey* [1894] 1 Q.B. 285.
[25] *Milne* v. *Kidd* (1869) 8 M. 250.
[26] *Laird* v. *Securities Insurance Co.* (1895) 22 R. 452; *Seaton* v. *Burnand* [1899] 1 Q.B. 782, revd. on other grounds [1900] A.C. 135; *Re Law Guarantee Society* [1914] 2 Ch. 617.

be proper or improper: proper, when the fact that the parties are principal debtor and cautioner appears in the instrument by which they are bound; improper, where, ex facie of the instrument, they appear as co-obligants, though inter se they are principal and cautioner.

9. Benefit of Discussion.—In proper cautionry the cautioner had at common law, unless otherwise agreed, the benefit of discussion (beneficium ordinis). That is to say, he was entitled to insist that before he was called upon, diligence should be used against the principal debtor. No such right was implied in the case of improper cautionry. The implied benefit of discussion was abolished by section 8 of the Mercantile Law Amendment Act 1856, and, since that Act, requires express stipulation. Without it there may now be direct action against the cautioner, and it is no longer necessary to establish the failure of the principal debtor before suing the cautioner and using diligence against him on the dependence of the action.[27]

10. Benefit of Division.—On the distinction between proper and improper cautionry, again, depends the right of division (beneficium divisionis). Where more than one cautioner is expressly bound as such for an obligation in its nature divisible, such as a debt, none can be sued for more than his pro rata share, unless the others are insolvent.[28] In improper cautionry, when all the obligants are bound jointly and severally and ex facie as full debtors, anyone may be sued for the whole debt.[29]

11. Obligations by More than One Cautioner.—Where a cautionary obligation is to be undertaken by more than one cautioner it is as a general rule the duty of the creditor to secure that all become bound. Each cautioner who signs does so on the implied condition that the others are to be bound with him, and is not liable if this condition is not fulfilled. This rule holds even although the form of the obligation is joint and several, provided that the creditor was aware that some of the obligants were really cautioners. So where an insurance company agreed to lend money to A on condition that four other persons should become jointly and severally liable with him in a bond, and three of the four signed and A forged the signature of the fourth, it was held that the bond could not be enforced against any of the cautioners.[30] The general rule finds exception in judicial cautionry, where a bond is lodged in obedience to the orders of the Court. No duty is then cast on the creditor to see that the signatures of all the obligants are obtained, and therefore an obligant who signed was held liable although the signature of the other obligant was forged.[31]

---

[27] *Johannesburg Municipal Council* v. *Stewart*, 1909 S.C. (H.L.) 53.
[28] Bell, *Prin.*, § 267.
[29] *Richmond* v. *Grahame* (1847) 9 D. 633.
[30] *Scottish Provincial Assurance Co.* v. *Pringle* (1858) 20 D. 465. See also *Ellesmere Brewery Co.* v. *Cooper* [1896] 1 Q.B. 75.
[31] *Simpson* v. *Fleming* (1860) 22 D. 679.

12. Effect of Fraud: Concealment.—On general principles of contract a cautionary obligation is not binding if obtained by fraud or misrepresentation on the part of the creditor. But the debtor, whose obligation is guaranteed, is not the creditor's agent, and fraud or misrepresentation by him will not liberate the cautioner.[32] In cautionary obligations for a debt there is no obligation on the creditor to disclose all the material facts. So a bank, accepting a guarantee for a customer's account, is not bound to inform the guarantor that the account is overdrawn, and may enforce the guarantee, although the guarantor may have been induced to intervene by fraudulent statements made by the customer.[33] A different rule applies in the case of guarantees for the fidelity of a servant or official, when the employer is bound to disclose all prior irregularities or other facts calculated to influence the mind of the guarantor.[34] The ground of the distinction between the two classes of cautionry is that in the latter class, fidelity guarantees, the contract is in substance one of insurance, and falls within the rule that in insurance all material facts must be disclosed.[35]

13. Extent of Cautioner's Liability.—The obligation undertaken by a cautioner may or may not be limited to a certain amount. It is a general rule that his undertaking is to be construed in the narrowest sense which the words will reasonably bear.[36] If there is no limitation in amount, the cautioner is liable for all loss resulting from the failure in fulfilment of the obligation guaranteed, e.g., for interest, or for expenses reasonably incurred in attempting to enforce the debt against the principal debtor.[37] As cautionry is an accessory obligation, the cautioner's liability can never exceed that of the principal debtor. So where the cautionary obligation took the form of a blank promissory note, and the cautioner was bankrupt, it was held that the creditor could not rank in the sequestration for a greater amount than he had advanced to the principal debtor, by filling up the note for a larger sum in order to draw his actual advance as a dividend.[38]

Where a cautionary obligation contains no limit of time, but does contain a limit of the amount for which the cautioner undertakes liability, it is a question of construction whether it is to be read as a continuing guarantee, such as a cash credit with a bank, or as a guarantee which is ended when the limit of liability is reached. In the former case the cautioner is liable for the balance due when his obligation is ultimately enforced; in the latter, any payments made by the principal debtor, after the maximum of liability has been reached, go to diminish the amount for which the cautioner is responsible, and he is not liable for advances subsequently made.[39] Where the obligation is not incurred for any definite period, the cautioner may safeguard

---

[32] *Young* v. *Clydesdale Bank* (1889) 17 R. 231. See also *Sutherland* v. *Low* (1901) 3 F. 972.
[33] *Royal Bank* v. *Greenshields*, 1914 S.C. 259.
[34] *French* v. *Cameron* (1893) 20 R. 966; *Bank of Scotland* v. *Morrison*, 1911 S.C. 593.
[35] *Wallace's Factor* v. *M'Kissock* (1898) 25 R. 642, per Lord M'Laren at p. 653.
[36] *Harmer* v. *Gibb*, 1911 S.C. 1341; *Veitch* v. *National Bank*, 1907 S.C. 554.
[37] *Struthers* v. *Dykes* (1847) 9 D. 1437.
[38] *Jackson* v. *M'Iver* (1875) 2 R. 882.
[39] *Scott* v. *Mitchell* (1866) 4 M. 551.

himself for any liability in the future by giving notice to the creditor that his
guarantee is withdrawn. And a cautioner is entitled, on giving reasonable
notice, to call upon the principal debtor to relieve him of all liabilities which
he may have incurred. The principal debtor will be ordained to procure and
deliver to the cautioner a discharge from the creditor.[40]

14. Relief.—A cautioner, on payment of the debt, is entitled to recover
what he has paid from the principal debtor. In the case where all are ex facie
co-obligants parole evidence as to their real relationship is competent, because
the written instrument by which the debt is constituted is intended to regulate
the contract between the creditor and the obligants, not the rights of the
obligants inter se.[41] It is also a general rule, which will yield only to an express
contract to the contrary, that where more than one cautioner is engaged,
anyone who has paid more than his share may claim relief from the others. On
this principle, where A and B were cautioners for a contractor, and A, on the
contractor's failure, carried out the contract at his own expense, he was held
entitled to recover half his outlay from B.[42] In determining the amount of
relief, those cautioners who are insolvent are not counted, e.g., if A, B and C
are cautioners, and C is insolvent, A, who has paid the whole debt, is entitled
to recover half of what he has paid from B.[43] Where each cautioner is liable
for a specified sum, and the whole debt is exacted, no one has paid more than
his share, and there can be no claim of relief. But if less than the whole debt is
due, anyone who has paid more than his proportionate share may claim relief
if the cautioners are bound in the same instrument; if, in separate contracts,
each cautioner engages for a specific sum, there is no right of relief.[44]

15. Right to Assignation of Debt.—On payment a cautioner is entitled to
demand from the creditor an assignation of the debt, any security held for it,
and any diligence done upon it, so as to enable him to enforce his right of
relief against the principal debtor, or against co-cautioners.[45] It has been
decided that no such right exists except upon full payment, so that where a
cautioner was bankrupt, and a dividend was paid on the debt, his trustee
could not demand an assignation.[46] In exceptional cases the creditor may
refuse an assignation of the debt on the ground that to grant it would conflict
with some legitimate interest of his own.[47] Where the demand is for the
assignation of securities held for the debt, it cannot be refused on the ground
that the creditor proposes to retain the securities to meet some other debt
subsequently incurred.[48] It is a general principle that an assignation from the
creditor, though it may afford a convenient means of enforcing a right of

[40] *Doig* v. *Lawrie* (1903) 5 F. 295.
[41] *Hamilton* v. *Freeth* (1889) 16 R. 1022; *Crosbie* v. *Brown* (1900) 3 F. 83.
[42] *Marshall* v. *Pennycook*, 1908 S.C. 276.
[43] *Buchanan* v. *Main* (1900) 3 F. 215.
[44] *Morgan* v. *Smart* (1872) 10 M. 610.
[45] Bell, *Prin.*, § 255; *Sligo* v. *Menzies* (1840) 2 D. 1478.
[46] *Ewart* v. *Latta* (1865) 3 M. (H.L.) 36.
[47] *Graham* v. *Gordon* (1842) 4 D. 903.
[48] *Fleming* v. *Burgess* (1867) 5 M. 856.

relief, does not in any way enlarge that right.[49] And it has been laid down that a cautioner, with or without an assignation, can enforce only securities over the estate of the debtor, not securities granted by third parties.[50]

16. Right to Share in Securities.—A cautioner is entitled to share in the benefit of any securities which any of his co-cautioners may have obtained over the estate of the principal debtor.[51] The rule applies, although the cautioner claiming the right to share had already engaged without any security.[52] But it yields to any express agreement to the contrary. And if one cautioner engages under a contract with the principal debtor whereby he obtains a security of which he is to have the whole benefit, the fact that the other cautioners have agreed to this may be proved by parole evidence.[53] The theory underlying the rule is that the estate of the principal debtor is to be regarded as a fund in which all the cautioners have an equal right to share, and therefore it was held that it did not extend to the case where one cautioner had obtained a security from a third party.[54]

17. Ranking in Bankruptcy.—On the bankruptcy of the principal debtor, if the creditor ranks for the debt, receives a dividend, and obtains payment of the balance from the cautioner, the latter is not entitled to a ranking for what he was paid, because, to allow it, would conflict with the principle that no debt can be ranked twice on a sequestrated estate.[55] Where the cautioner is liable for the whole debt, it is open to him to pay it, obtain an assignation and rank in place of the creditor. To this the creditor has no legitimate interest to object. If the cautioner's liability is limited to a fixed sum, and the principal debt exceeds this, the bond may be read as a guarantee of part of the debt. If so, the cautioner is entitled, on payment of the amount he has guaranteed, to rank in place of the creditor for that amount, or, if the creditor ranks, the cautioner's liability is limited to the balance of the guaranteed amount remaining after payment of the dividend.[56] On the other hand, if the bond is read as a guarantee of the whole debt, with a limit of the amount for which the cautioner is liable, the general construction of the obligation is that the creditor is entitled to rank for his whole debt, and recover from the cautioner any balance remaining, in so far as that balance does not exceed the limit for which the cautioner has engaged.[57] But if, before the sequestration of the principal debtor, the cautioner has paid any part of the debt, the creditor is bound to deduct what has been paid and rank for no more than the balance, whether the cautioner makes a claim for a ranking or not.[58]

[49] *Thow's Tr.* v. *Young*, 1910 S.C. 588.
[50] *Thow's Tr.*, supra, per Lord President Dunedin.
[51] Bell, *Comm.*, I, 367.
[52] *Steel* v. *Dixon* (1881) 17 Ch.D. 825.
[53] *Hamilton* v. *Freeth* (1889) 16 R. 1022.
[54] *Scott* v. *Young*, 1909, 1 S.L.T. 47.
[55] *Anderson* v. *Mackinnon* (1876) 3 R. 608; *Mackinnon* v. *Monkhouse* (1881) 9 R. 393.
[56] *Veitch* v. *National Bank*, 1907 S.C. 554.
[57] *Harvie's Trs.* v. *Bank of Scotland* (1885) 12 R. 1141.
[58] *Mackinnon's Tr.* v. *Bank of Scotland*, 1915 S.C. 411.

18. Discharge of Cautionary Obligations.—In addition to the methods applicable in general to the discharge of obligations the following require notice:—(1) prescription; (2) extinction of the principal obligation; (3) death of principal debtor, cautioner or creditor; (4) discharge of co-cautioner; (5) giving time to principal debtor; (6) release of securities; (7) alteration of the contract; (8) change in a partnership.

19. Prescription.—The septennial prescription of cautionary obligations, which was introduced by the Cautioners Act 1695, c. 5,[59] was abolished by the Prescription and Limitation (Scotland) Act 1973[60] with effect from 25th July 1976. The prescriptive period now applicable is five years. Thus, if a cautionary obligation, being an obligation arising from a contract, has subsisted for a continuous period of five years without any relevant claims having been made in relation to it and without the subsistence of the obligation having been relevantly acknowledged in terms of the Act, it will be extinguished.[61]

20. Extinction of Principal Obligation.—As cautionry is an accessory obligation, the absolute discharge of the principal debtor implies the discharge of the cautioner. There is a statutory exception to this in the case of the discharge of the bankrupt in sequestration.[62] And a distinction is recognised between a discharge, which extinguishes the principal debt and also frees the cautioner, and a pactum de non petendo, whereby the creditor gives up his right to sue the principal debtor, but reserves his claim against the cautioner. In the latter case the cautioner is not discharged, and, on payment, may demand an assignation of the debt and sue the principal debtor thereon.[63] Apart from a discharge the cautioner may be liberated by the extinction of the principal debt by other methods, as where it is allowed to prescribe.[64] Novation of the principal debt, in the case where the principal debt is discharged and a new one substituted, will liberate the cautioner.[65] The assignation of the debt, merely substituting a new creditor, has no such effect.[66] The fact that at some period in the history of the transaction compensation might have been pleaded in respect of a debt due by the creditor to the principal debtor does not extinguish the debt and therefore does not liberate the cautioner, but the latter is entitled, on a claim being made against him, to insist on any ground of compensation then available to the principal debtor.[67] The debt for which the cautioner is liable, and consequently his own liability, may be extinguished by the application of the rule that where

[59] See, on the effect of this Act, Millar, *Prescription,* p. 178.
[60] (c. 52), Sched. 5. See Prescription, Ch. XVI, supra.
[61] s. 6, and Sched. 1, paras. 1 (*g*) and 2 (*c*). A cautionary obligation may also be affected by the long negative prescription of 20 years: see Prescription, Ch. XVI, supra, § 13
[62] Bankruptcy Act 1913, s. 52. This does not cover private trust deeds for creditors.
[63] *Muir* v. *Crawford* (1875) 2 R. (H.L.) 148.
[64] Erskine, III., 3, 66.
[65] *Commercial Bank of Tasmania* v. *Jones* [1893] A.C. 313. See also *Hay & Kyd* v. *Powrie* (1886) 13 R. 777.
[66] *Bradford Old Bank* v. *Sutcliffe* [1918] 2 K.B. 833.
[67] *Bechervaise* v. *Lewis* (1872) L.R. 7 C.P. 372.

indefinite payments are made, the earliest credit item goes to wipe out the earliest debit item. This may happen if, when the cautioner's obligation for a continuous account, such as a cash credit with a bank, is in any way withdrawn or terminated, the account is continued with the principal debtor without any definite break. Then, though there may be a continuous adverse balance against the debtor, any payments made by him, if ascribed to meet the earliest debt in the account, will in time extinguish the balance due when the cautionary obligation was withdrawn, and, by thus extinguishing the principal debt, will liberate the cautioner.[68] But probably this rule is limited to the case of accounts between banker and customer, when, in regular banking practice, a new account would be opened when the cautionary obligation ceased to be operative.[69]

21. Death of One of the Parties.—The death of a cautioner has no effect on his existing liability, which may be enforced against his representatives. And if the cautionary obligation is of the nature of a continuing guarantee— as in the case of a cash credit with a bank— the representatives of a deceased cautioner will remain liable for debts subsequently incurred, unless they intimate that the guarantee is withdrawn. It is immaterial that the cautioner's representatives were not aware of the obligation, and no duty is cast upon the creditor to intimate to them.[70] The death of the principal debtor will, as a general rule, exclude the liability of the cautioner for any debt not then due.[71] But where caution for expenses was the statutory condition of an appeal from the Sheriff Court, it was held that the cautioner was liable for expenses incurred after the death of the appellant, when his representatives were sisted as parties and carried on the appeal.[72] The death of the creditor does not affect the liability of a cautioner for an existing debt. In guarantees for the fidelity of an employee the death of the employer terminates the guarantee, even although the party employed is kept on by his representatives.[73]

22. Discharge of Co-Cautioners.—Where there are several cautioners, the discharge of one without the consent of the others has, by statute, the effect of liberating them.[74] The section by which this rule is established expressly excepts the case of the creditor's consent to the discharge of a co-cautioner who has become bankrupt. It has been held in England that the co-cautioners are not liberated if the creditor's rights are expressly reserved.[75] And, by a decision in Scotland, the section applies only where the cautioners are bound jointly and severally for the whole debt, not to the case where each has engaged for a specific sum.[76]

[68] *Royal Bank* v. *Christie* (1841) 2 Rob. 118; *Cuthill* v. *Strachan* (1894) 21 R. 549.
[69] *Hay & Co.* v. *Torbet*, 1908 S.C. 781; Extinction of Obligations, Ch. XV., § 7, supra.
[70] *British Linen Co.* v. *Monteith* (1858) 20 D. 557.
[71] *Woodfield Finance Trust (Glasgow)* v. *Morgan*, 1958 S.L.T. (Sh. Ct.) 14.
[72] *Wilson* v. *Ewing* (1836) 14 S. 262.
[73] *Stewart* v. *Scot* (1834) 7 W. & S. 211.
[74] Mercantile Law Amendment (Scotland) Act 1856, s. 9.
[75] *Bateson* v. *Gosling* (1871) L.R. 7 C.P. 9.
[76] *Morgan* v. *Smart* (1872) 10 M. 610.

23. Giving Time.—It is a general and in some respects very technical rule that a cautioner is liberated if the creditor has given time to the principal debtor. By giving time is not meant failure to press the principal debtor for payment or to rank in his bankruptcy. For such failure the cautioner has his remedy by paying the debt, obtaining an assignation of it and exercising the rights of the creditor.[77] By giving time is meant any act by which the creditor deprives himself of the right to sue for immediate payment, and thus alters the contract for which the cautioner undertook liability. This may be by an express agreement not to sue, or by taking a bill payable at some future date,[78] or by an arrangement for payment by instalments.[79] By such agreements the cautioner is, or may be, prejudiced, since, as he can only stand in the place of the creditor, he loses the power to enforce immediate payment from the debtor. On this footing it is an established rule that he is liberated, and it is immaterial that he is unable to show that he has suffered any actual prejudice,[80] or that, before time was given, he has repudiated his liability on other grounds.[81] If the cautionary obligation is for a debt already incurred, the giving of time for any period, however short, precludes recourse against the cautioner; if the obligation is to guarantee payment of furnishings to be supplied in the future, the creditor is not held to have given time by allowing any ordinary period of credit, or taking a bill for the price. But the cautioner may have a valid defence if he can prove that the amount of credit given, or the currency of the bill, was unreasonably long; it is not sufficient to prove that the credit given was more than was usual in the particular trade.[82]

The rule that a cautioner is liberated if time be given to the principal debtor does not apply if in the contract whereby time is given the rights of the cautioner are expressly reserved. The cautioner may then, by paying the debt and obtaining an assignation, enforce immediate payment and therefore, as he has suffered no injury, his liability is unaffected.[83] And if the creditor has obtained decree against the cautioner, the fact that he has subsequently given time to the principal debtor does not affect the cautioner's liability.[84]

24. Giving up Securities.—As a cautioner has the right, on payment of the debt, to an assignation of any security the creditor may hold for it,[85] his position is prejudiced if, without his consent, any security is given up, and therefore the release of securities, if a voluntary act on the part of the creditor, will operate as a release to the cautioner.[86] Unless there is an express agreement that the creditor shall avail himself of a particular security before calling on

[77] *Hay & Kyd* v. *Powrie* (1886) 13 R. 777, per Lord Rutherfurd Clark; *Hamilton's Exr.* v. *Bank of Scotland*, 1913 S.C. 743, where the effect of a clause entitling the creditor to give time is considered.
[78] *Johnstone* v. *Duthie* (1892) 19 R. 624; *Goldfarb* v. *Bartlett* [1920] 1 K.B. 639.
[79] *Wilson* v. *Lloyd* (1873) L.R. 16 Eq. 60.
[80] *Johnstone* v. *Duthie*, supra; *Polak* v. *Everett* (1876) 1 Q.B.D. 669.
[81] *Johnstone* v. *Duthie*, supra.
[82] *Calder* v. *Cruikshank's Tr.* (1889) 17 R. 74.
[83] *Crawford* v. *Muir* (1875) 2 R. (H.L.) 148.
[84] *Aikman* v. *Fisher* (1835) 14 S. 56.
[85] Supra, § 15.
[86] *Sligo* v. *Menzies* (1840) 2 D. 1478.

the cautioner (when the release of that security operates as an absolute discharge),[87] the cautioner is released only in so far as he is prejudiced, i.e., to the extent of the value of the security which has been given up.[88] The same rules apply to the case where the creditor, without giving up a security, fails to take the steps necessary to make it effectual, as where the holder of a bond and disposition in security failed to complete his title, with the result that the trustee in the debtor's sequestration acquired a preferable right to the subjects.[89]

25. Alteration of the Contract.—A cautioner is discharged if his position is adversely affected by an alteration of the contract between the creditor and the principal debtor without the consent of the cautioner.[90] Thus where the creditors in a composition contract took a trust deed from the debtor, it was held that they had liberated the cautioner.[91] The mere fact that the creditor failed to disclose to the cautioner that he had grounds for suspecting forgery by the principal debtor was held to be no ground on which the cautioner could dispute his liability, though it was observed that the creditor, in the case of a cash credit bond, would not be justified in making further advances without disclosing to the cautioner any circumstances materially affecting the honesty of the debtor.[92]

In the case of fidelity guarantees, if in the original contract certain checks on the behaviour of the party guaranteed are provided for, the cautioner is discharged if they are not observed, and it is no defence to the creditor to prove that the checks would have been useless or that equivalent methods of supervision were instituted.[93] In the absence of any provision there is no implied obligation on the part of the creditor to exercise any special precautions, and therefore the cautioner will not escape liability by proof that more careful supervision would have precluded the failure in respect of which he is sued.[94] There is probably an exception to this in the case of a guarantee for the acts of a bank official, when the cautioner is entitled to rely on the checks, such as periodical audits, which are usual in banking business.[95] A change in the duties to be performed by the party guaranteed will release the cautioner if the terms of that party's appointment were made known to him at the time when he undertook the cautionary obligation, even when the change had no bearing on the loss for which the cautioner is sued.[96] This has been held even where the change in duties was due not to the act of the creditor but to the provisions of a statute.[97] The cautioner has engaged for a party

[87] *Drummond* v. *Rannie* (1836) 14 S. 437.
[88] *Wright's Trs.* v. *Hamilton* (1835) 13 S. 380.
[89] *Fleming* v. *Thomson* (1826) 2 W. & S. 277.
[90] See Bell, *Prin.,* § 259; *N. G. Napier* v. *Crosbie,* 1964 S.C. 129.
[91] *Allan, Allan & Milne* v. *Pattison* (1893) 21 R. 195.
[92] *Bank of Scotland* v. *Morrison,* 1911 S.C. 593.
[93] *Haworth* v. *Sickness, etc., Insurance Co.* (1891) 18 R. 563; *Clydebank Water Trs.* v. *Fidelity Co.,* 1916 S.C. (H.L.) 69.
[94] *Mayor of Kingston* v. *Harding* [1892] 2 Q.B. 494; *Mactaggart* v. *Watson* (1835) 1 S. & M'L. 553.
[95] *Falconer* v. *Lothian* (1843) 5 D. 866, at p. 870.
[96] *Bonar* v. *Macdonald* (1850) 7 Bell's App. 379.
[97] *Pybus* v. *Gibb* (1856) 6 E. & B. 902.

performing particular duties, and he is not, without his consent, to be rendered liable for a party performing duties of a different kind. If, however, the particular nature of the duties to be performed was not known to the cautioner, and he gave a general guarantee, he will remain liable unless he can prove that the alteration in the contract of employment was material.[98] It has been held that if an employer discovers an act of dishonesty on the part of an official whose acts have been guaranteed, he is bound to give immediate notice to the cautioner, and failure to do so will justify the cautioner in repudiating his obligation even if he can offer no proof that the notice which was withheld would have been of any advantage to him.[99]

26. Change in a Firm.—It is provided by section 18 of the Partnership Act 1890, re-enacting section 7 of the Mercantile Law Amendment (Scotland) Act 1856, and in substance reproducing the common law,[1] that a continuing guarantee or cautionary obligation given either to a firm or to a third person in respect of the transactions of a firm is, in the absence of agreement to the contrary, revoked as to future transactions by any change in the constitution of the firm to which, or of the firm in respect of the transactions of which, the guarantee or obligation was given. The change in the firm may be effected either by the admission of a new partner,[2] or by the retirement of an existing partner,[3] or, without any change in the persons composing the firm, by its registration as a company under the Companies Acts.[4]

[98] *Nicolson* v. *Burt* (1882) 10 R. 121.
[99] *Snaddon* v. *London, Edinburgh, etc., Insurance Co.* (1902) 5 F. 182.
[1] *Royal Bank* v. *Christie* (1841) 2 Rob. 118.
[2] *Spiers* v. *Houston's Exrs.* (1829) 3 W. & S. 392.
[3] *Royal Bank* v. *Christie,* supra.
[4] *Hay & Co.* v. *Torbet,* 1908 S.C. 781.

CHAPTER XXII

EMPLOYMENT

Fraser, *Master and Servant* (3rd ed., 1882); Umpherston, *Master and Servant* (1904); Miller, *Industrial Law in Scotland* (1970); Fridman, *The Modern Law of Employment* (1963 and supplements 1964, 1967 & 1972) Munkman, *Employer's Liability at Common Law* (9th ed., 1979); Hepple and O'Higgins, *Employment Law* (2nd ed., 1976); *Encyclopedia of Labour Relations Law* (continuously revised); Rideout, *Principles of Labour Law* (2nd ed., 1976).

1. Definition of Employment.—Previous editions of this book, which discussed employment in terms of the relationship of master and servant,[1] offered the following definition of a servant: "A servant is one who is employed to render personal service to his employer otherwise than in pursuit of an independent calling, and who in such service remains entirely under the control or direction of the other, who is called the master."[2] The stress on control, as the distinguishing feature of the contract of employment, represents the classical view, and close control, where it exists, is still a sure indication that the person subject to control is an employee. In modern sophisticated classes of employment the control exercised by an employer may, however, often not extend to the manner in which the work is to be done[3] and may be so remote as to be scarcely distinguishable from that appropriate to other contractual relationships.[4] Accordingly it has been suggested that the true test of employment is whether the work is done as an integral part of the business or organisation in question,[5] and a multiple or mixed test has also been suggested.[6] In cases of difficulty, whether a relationship is one of employment is a question of facts and circumstances to be answered by an examination of a number of factors, among which control and integration are prominent but not exhaustive.

There is in Scotland no rule against a gratuitous obligation to work as an employee. In an onerous contract the advantage accruing to the person employed need not take the form of wages; it may consist in an opportunity of earning, e.g., by tips, or by instruction in a trade or profession. A person who attends in the hope of employment, even although, if no employment be

---

[1] The terminology had advantages in avoiding the ambiguities which sometimes attach to the use of "employment". It had, however, become increasingly archaic, was apt to cause confusion by perpetuating obsolete views of the relationship between employer and employee and, except for secondary purposes of definition, had been abandoned in the language of statute. In accordance with the statutory example, employer, employee and employment are the terms used in this edition unless the context renders the earlier terminology more appropriate.

[2] See, e.g. 6th ed., p. 233.

[3] E.g., a surgeon *(Macdonald* v. *Glasgow Western Hospitals Board,* 1954 S.C. 453, a trapeze artiste *(Whittaker* v. *Ministry of Pensions and National Insurance* [1967] 1 Q.B. 156), a professional footballer *(Walker* v. *Crystal Palace Football Club* [1910] 1 K.B. 87). See also *Morren* v. *Swinton and Pendlebarry Council* [1965] 2 All E.R. 349 per Lord Parker C.J. at 351.

[4] E.g., agency and a contract to perform services (see infra §§ 2 to 4).

[5] *Macdonald* v. *Glasgow Western Hospitals Board,* supra, per Lord President Cooper at 478; *Bank voor Handel en Scheepuaart* v. *Slatford* [1953] 1 Q.B. 248, per Denning L.J. at 295.

[6] *Ready Mixed Concrete (South East)* v. *Ministry of Pensions and National Insurance* [1968] 2 Q.B. 497, per McKenna J. at 512.

available, he may receive payment for his attendance, is not an employee.[7] Often, however, the method of remuneration is crucial to the distinction between a contract of employment and a joint adventure.[8] The question whether a partner can be an employee of his own firm has been raised but not settled.[9] It has been decided that a partner does not by his negligence render the firm liable to another partner who has been injured as a result of that negligence.[10]

2. Employment and Agency.—The distinction between employment and agency may be merely verbal, and the same person may act as an employee and as an agent. The term "agent" is, however, more properly applicable to the case where the duties of the person employed are to bring his employer into contractual relations with third parties.[11]

3. Employee or Independent Contractor.—The question whether a person is engaged as an employee or as an independent contractor, in some cases a narrow one, especially if the work is to be done on the employer's property, is often capable of being solved by considering whether the employer has a contractual right to direct how the work is to be done, as distinguished from the right to decide what is to be done, and to object, after the work is done, that it is not in accordance with the conditions of the contract.[12] In the latter event the contract is not one of employment but is a contract to perform services. This basis of distinction is not, however, applicable to cases such as those noted in the following paragraph where there is neither a right to direct how the work is to be done nor a specification or stipulated result with which it must conform.

4. Contract to Perform Services.—A contract of employment may require to be distinguished from a contract to perform services, either in the case where the party who renders the services (e.g., a solicitor) has a separate and independent occupation, or in the case, such as that of a surgeon at a hospital, where, though there may be no separate occupation, and the power to appoint and dismiss may be vested in a particular body, yet that body has no right of interference or direction as to the way in which the work is to be done. In the former case, the contract will normally be for the performance of services[13] and clear contrary indications will be necessary for the constitution of a contract of employment. In the latter case, authorities in which it was held that a person so employed was not an employee, either in a question as to the employer's liability for his negligence,[14] or in the construction of statutes

---

[7] *Conlon* v. *Glasgow Corporation* (1899) 1 F. 869.
[8] See *Parker* v. *Walker*, 1961 S.L.T. 252.
[9] See *Fife County Council* v. *Minister of National Insurance*, 1947 S.C. 629 at p. 636.
[10] *Mair* v. *Wood*, 1948 S.C. 83.
[11] Agency, Ch. XXIII., infra.
[12] *Stephen* v. *Thurso Police Commissioners* (1876) 3 R. 535; *Sweeney* v. *Duncan* (1892) 19 R. 870.
[13] See, e.g., *Renfrewshire and Port Glasgow Joint Committee* v. *Minister of National Insurance*, 1946 S.C. 83.
[14] *Foote* v. *Greenock Hospital*, 1912 S.C. 69; *Lavelle* v. *Glasgow Royal Infirmary*, 1932 S.C. 245; *Reidford* v. *Magistrates of Aberdeen*, 1933 S.C. 276.

dealing with the incidents of service,[15] must now be regarded as obsolete.[16] Thus it has been held that a hospital board is liable for the negligence of resident medical staff,[17] and similar principles will apply in analogous cases with possible exceptions for visiting consultants and for certain classes of work done for charitable bodies.[18]

5. Constitution of Contract.—A contract of employment for more than a year requires to be constituted by writing which is probative of both parties or by improbative writing upon which rei interventus has followed.[19] If for less, it may be entered into orally, or implied from the relationship of the parties. But in nearly every contract of employment the employer must now within thirteen weeks after the beginning of an employee's period of employment give the employee a written statement identifying the parties, specifying the date when the employment began, and giving certain statutory particulars of the terms of employment.[20] Where services are rendered without any express agreement, there is a general presumption (except in cases of near relatives) in favour of an implied contract of service and consequent right to payment.[21] The presumption is displaced by proof of a professional custom to render similar services gratuitously.[22] A belated claim, or one made by executors when no claim has been made by the deceased, is regarded unfavourably.[23] Where the parties are nearly related, there is probably a presumption in favour of the pursuer in the case of a claim by a son who has assisted his father in his work or business;[24] in favour of the defender, in the case of a daughter or niece who claims payment for domestic services or for nursing.[25]

6. Obligations of Employee.—The varieties of types of employment preclude any but a very general statement of the obligations of an employee. He is bound to obey orders; not to absent himself without leave during working hours; to refrain from such misconduct or immorality as may be incompatible with the reasonable performance of the particular service;[26] to do nothing to injure the employer's interests. Refusal to obey orders may be justified if the demand, not excused by an emergency, is to do work other than

---

[15] *Scottish Insurance Commissioners* v. *Edinburgh Infirmary,* 1913 S.C. 751.
[16] *Macdonald* v. *Glasgow Western Hospitals Board,* supra; cf. *Stagecraft Ltd.* v. *Minister of Pensions and National Insurance,* 1952 S.C. 288.
[17] *Macdonald,* supra; cf. *Kilboy* v. *South Eastern Fire Area Joint Committee,* 1952 S.C. 280.
[18] *Macdonald,* supra, per Lord President Cooper at 478.
[19] Agreements Defective in Form, Ch. VII., supra, § 9; *Cook* v. *Grubb,* 1963 S.C. 1.
[20] Employment Protection (Consolidation) Act 1978 (c. 44), s. 1. Employments in which the hours of employment are normally less than sixteen hours weekly are excluded, as are certain cases where the contract of employment is in writing (ss. 3, 5).
[21] *Thomson* v. *Thomson's Tr.* (1889) 16 R. 333.
[22] *Corbin* v. *Stewart* (1911) 28 T.L.R. 99 (doctor attending widow of deceased colleague).
[23] *Mackersy's Exrs.* v. *St. Giles Managing Board* (1904) 12 S.L.T. 391; see *Mackison* v. *Burgh of Dundee,* 1910 S.C. (H.L.) 27.
[24] *Thomson* v. *Thomson's Tr.,* supra; *Miller* v. *Miller* (1898) 25 R. 995; *Urquhart* v. *Urquhart's Tr.* (1905) 8 F. 42.
[25] *Russell* v. *M'Clymont* (1906) 8 F. 821.
[26] See Fraser, *Master and Servant,* p. 84. And see, as to fiduciary position of an employee or agent, Agency, Ch. XXIII., infra.

that which the employee engaged for;[27] if it is illegal;[28] or if compliance would expose the employee to some danger not contemplated at the time of engagement. So the crew of a ship were held to be justified in refusing to continue a voyage when the emergence of war had rendered that ship liable to seizure as carrying contraband.[29] It has been held that an ordinary contract of employment does not involve any fiduciary relationship, and therefore that an employee is not bound to reveal the fact that he has been guilty of a breach of contract.[30]

7. Standard of Care and Skill.—An employee, if he does not hold himself out as belonging to any particular trade or profession, does enough if he performs his duties with reasonable care.[31] One engaged as a member of some trade or profession spondet peritiam artis, and is liable in damages if he fails to exhibit the degree of skill reasonably to be expected from an ordinary member of his craft.[32] This rule has been applied in the case of a plumber,[33] and of a solicitor. The latter does not guarantee the accuracy of his advice on law[34] or on investments,[35] but he is liable for omissions or blunders in conveyancing[36] or Court procedure,[37] and has been held responsible for ignorance or forgetfulness of a statute under which his client's action had to be commenced within a certain period.[38] No liability for professional negligence attaches to counsel, and a solicitor is protected when acting on the advice of counsel.[39] A party, such as an unregistered dentist, who is not a member of a profession, but undertakes professional work and is not known by his employer to be unqualified, must exhibit average professional skill.[40]

8. Remedies of Employer.—Where an employer is held vicariously liable for the fault or negligence of his employee, he is entitled to claim an indemnity from the employee for the damages and expenses he has had to pay.[41] The remedy of an employer for an employee's breach of contract is dismissal, and a claim for damages. Where an employee is justifiably dismissed, no wages are due for the part of the term which he has served.[42] A decree ad factum

---

27 *Thomson* v. *Douglas*, 1807 Hume 392; *Moffat* v. *Boothby* (1884) 11 R. 501.
28 As to the illegality of Sunday labour, see *Middleton* v. *Trough*, 1908 S.C. (J.) 32; *Smith* v. *Beardmore*, 1922 S.C. 131; Factories Act 1961, s. 93.
29 *Lang* v. *St. Enoch Shipping Co.*, 1908 S.C. 103.
30 *Bell* v. *Lever Bros.* [1932] A.C. 161.
31 See *Gunn* v. *Ramsay*, 1801 Hume 38; *Lister* v. *Romford Ice & Cold Storage Co.* [1957] A.C. 555.
32 In the case of a doctor, see, e.g., *Hunter* v. *Hanley*, 1955 S.C. 200.
33 *McIntyre* v. *Gallacher* (1883) 11 R. 64.
34 See *Free Church* v. *M'Knight's Trs.*, 1916 S.C. 349 (knowledge of English decisions) in contrast to *Hart* v. *Frame* (1839) M'L. & R. 595 (mistake in criminal procedure).
35 *Johnstone* v. *Thorburn* (1901) 3 F. 497; *Stewart* v. *M'Lean, Baird & Neilson*, 1915 S.C. 13; *Wernham* v. *M'Lean, Baird & Neilson*, 1925 S.C. 407.
36 *Stevenson* v. *Rowand* (1830) 4 W. & S. 177; *Fearn* v. *Gordon and Craig* (1893) 20 R. 352; *M'Connachie* v. *M'Queen's Trs.*, 1913, 1 S.L.T. 41.
37 *Anderson* v. *Torrie* (1856) 19 D. 356; *Urquhart* v. *Grigor* (1857) 19 D. 853.
38 *Simpson* v. *Kidston*, 1913, 1 S.L.T. 74.
39 *Batchelor* v. *Pattison* (1876) 3 R. 914. As to English barristers, see *Rondel* v. *Worsley* [1967] 3 W.L.R. 1666 (H.L.).
40 *Dickson* v. *Hygienic Institute*, 1910 S.C. 352.
41 *Lister* v. *Romford Ice & Cold Storage Co.* [1957] A.C. 555.
42 Fraser, *Master and Servant*, pp. 113, 119.

praestandum, ordaining the employee to remain at his work, will not be pronounced.[43] On English authority an employee cannot be forced to stay in his employment by interdict against his obtaining employment elsewhere, unless he has expressly covenanted not to do so.[44] To harbour an employee, i.e., to give him employment in the knowledge that he is in desertion, is an actionable wrong to his employer.[45] It is also a wrong to induce him to break his contract.[46] The common law rule that workmen deserting their employment could be imprisoned would not be followed in a modern case,[47] and it is thought that a similar rule affecting apprentices[48] is also now obsolete.[49] Under the Conspiracy and Protection of Property Act 1875, an employee commits a criminal offence if he wilfully and maliciously breaks a contract of service in the knowledge that by the breach, whether done alone or in combination, serious injury to life or property will probably be entailed.[50] Seamen are under special legislation.[51]

9. Obligations of Employer.[52]—The obligations of an employer, like those of an employee, can be indicated only in general terms. He is bound to pay wages if, expressly or impliedly, wages are due. Suspension without pay is, unless it can be justified in terms of the contract, a breach of contract for which damages may be recovered.[53] Where remuneration is to be by piecework, and the engagement is for a fixed period, work must be provided.[54] In domestic service the employer is bound not only to pay wages but to supply board and lodging, and to exhibit a reasonable amount of care for the servants' welfare. So, though he is probably not bound to supply medical attendance, it was held that an employer in the case of illness, was bound to intimate to the panel doctor, and was liable in damages where, without doing so, he sent the servant home in a state when it was dangerous for her to travel.[55] It is settled that an employer is not bound to give an employee a character[56] or to answer inquiries, and doubtful whether a custom of trade can lay upon him the obligation to give a certificate of the fact of employment.[57] Seamen, on discharge, have a statutory right to such a

---

[43] Fraser, *Master and Servant*, p. 37; *Rose Street Foundry Co.* v. *Lewis*, 1917 S.C. 341, per Lord Salvesen, p. 351.
[44] *Mortimer* v. *Beckett* [1920] 1 Ch. 571.
[45] *Rose Street Foundry Co.* v. *Lewis*, 1917 S.C. 341.
[46] *Lumley* v. *Gye* (1853) 2 E. & B. 216; *Couper* v. *Macfarlane* (1879) 6 R. 683. See Reparation, Ch. XXXIV., § 8, infra.
[47] See Umpherston, *Master and Servant*, p. 134.
[48] *McDermott* v. *Ramsay* (1876) 4 R. 217.
[49] The statutory provisions for imprisonment of certain deserting apprentices laid down in the Employers and Workmen Act 1875 (38 & 39 Vict. c. 90, ss. 6 and 12) have been repealed (Family Law Reform Act 1969 (c. 46), ss. 11 (b) and 28 (4) (e); Statute Law Repeals Act 1973 (c. 39), Sched. 1, Pt. XIII).
[50] 38 & 39 Vict. c. 86, s.5.
[51] Merchant Shipping Act 1970, c. 36, ss. 27 to 42 as amended by Merchant Shipping Act 1974 (c. 43), s. 19 and Trade Union and Labour Relations Act 1974 (c. 52), s. 25 (1) & Sch. 3, § 14.
[52] See also §§ 28 to 32, infra.
[53] *McArdle* v. *Scotbeef*, 1974 S.L.T. (Notes) 78.
[54] *Devonald* v. *Rosser* [1906] 2 K.B. 728. See, as to Agency, infra, Ch. XXIII.
[55] *McKeating* v. *Frame*, 1921 S.C. 382.
[56] *Fell* v. *Lord Ashburton*, December 12, 1809, F.C.; Fraser, *Master and Servant*, p. 127.
[57] *Grant* v. *Ramage & Ferguson* (1897) 25 R. 35; *Royce* v. *Greig*, 1909, 2 S.L.T. 298.

certificate.[58] In giving a character an employer enjoys a qualified privilege, and averments of malice are necessary to the relevancy of an action of damages against him for defamation.[59] A character reference unduly laudatory may render him liable to a party who engages the employee in reliance on it and suffers loss.[60]

10. Wages: Truck Acts.—Payment of wages is in certain employments regulated by the Truck Acts of 1831, 1887, 1896 and 1940, as amended by the Payment of Wages Act 1960.[61] The Acts apply to persons engaged in manual labour, other than domestic servants.[62] They probably do not apply to contracts for payment of wages exclusively in a foreign country.[63] They enact that wages must be paid in current coin, and not in goods, or orders for goods. Any contract to the contrary is illegal and void, allows the workman to recover what has not been paid,[64] and is an offence for which the employer may be prosecuted. But if an employee makes a written request for this and the employer agrees, payment of wages may be made by payment into a bank account, by postal order, money order or cheque.[65] The entire wages must be paid. Accordingly deductions from wages are also illegal and void, give rise to a right of recovery and attract criminal sanctions.[66] Certain exceptions, including rent and the price of food to be consumed on the employer's premises, are, however, allowed, provided that they are sanctioned by a written agreement signed by the workman.[67] Deductions may also be made, at the workman's request, for payment to a third party who is independent of the employer.[68] Where deductions which would have been lawful under a written agreement have been made in the absence of one, no wage or penalty is recoverable in respect of any period before 10th July 1940.[69] Without a written agreement it is lawful to contract with a "servant in husbandry" for the provision of food, drink (not intoxicating), a cottage or other allowance in addition to money wages.[70] It is illegal to provide that a workman shall expend his wages in any particular shop whether the employer is interested

---

[58] Merchant Shipping (Crew Agreements etc.) Regulations 1972 (S. I. 1972 No. 918) § 26 (4).
[59] Bell, *Prin.*, § 188. Defamation, Ch. XXXV., infra, § 12.
[60] *Anderson* v. *Wishart* (1818) 1 Murray 429.
[61] 1 & 2 William IV. c. 37; 50 & 51 Vict. c. 46; 59 & 60 Vict. c. 44; 3 & 4 Geo. VI. c. 38; 8 & 9 Eliz. II. c. 37. The amount of remuneration and holidays are in many cases controlled by Wages Councils; see Wages Councils Act 1959 (7 & 8 Eliz. II. c. 69) and Payment of Wages Act 1960, s. 6 (4). See *Penman* v. *Fife Coal Co.,* 1935 S.C. (H.L.) 39; *Duncan* v. *Motherwell Bridge & Engineering Co.,* 1952 S.C. 131.
[62] Truck Act 1887, s. 2, incorporating Employers and Workmen Act 1875, s. 10.
[63] *Duncan* v. *Motherwell Bridge & Engineering Co.,* supra.
[64] *McLucas* v. *Campbell* (1892) 30 S.L.R. 226.
[65] Payment of Wages Act 1960, s. 1.
[66] 1831 Act, s. 3; *Williams* v. *North's Navigation Collieries* [1906] A.C. 136.
[67] Truck Act 1831, s. 23; *Pratt* v. *Cook, Son & Co. (St. Paul's)* [1904] A.C. 437. See, as to pay-tickets, *Hynd* v. *Spowart* (1884) 22 S.L.R. 702.
[68] *Hewlett* v. *Allen* [1894] A.C. 383. It is on this basis that deductions for trade union dues may be made. If there is an agreed procedure for terminating such deductions no offence is committed if the employer continues to make the deductions, after the employee has intimated his withdrawal of agreement, until the procedure for termination is invoked (*Williams* v. *Butlers* [1975] 2 All E.R. 889).
[69] Truck Act 1940 (3 & 4 Geo. VI. c. 38), s. 1.
[70] Truck Act 1887, s. 4.

therein or not, or to dismiss him on account of the manner in which his wages are expended.[71] No deduction from wages can be made for the price of goods in a shop in which the employer has an interest.[72] Deductions for fines, payments for injury to the employer's property, or for the use of materials, machinery, light or heating, are permitted by the Truck Act 1896, provided they are just and reasonable, and either assented to by the workman in writing, or provided in a notice kept constantly posted in such a position that it may be easily read and copied. Any such agreement or notice must on demand be produced to an inspector of mines or factories. Shop assistants who, according to an English decision,[73] were not affected by the earlier statutes, are expressly included in the Act of 1896. The general construction of the Truck Acts has been that they prohibit any deductions from wages which they do not authorise, and so it is a contravention to deduct a debt separately incurred to the employer,[74] or to provide for the deduction of sums due by the workman on refusing to quit a house after his employment is ended.[75]

11. Wages: Other Statutory Provisions.—Statute now provides for guarantee payments to be made in respect of any whole day in which an employee, who has been continuously employed for at least four weeks, is not provided with work because of diminution in the requirements of the employer's business or other occurrence affecting its normal working.[75A] The payment is not available in event of a trade dispute involving employees of the employer or an associated employer or of unreasonable refusal by the employee of suitable alternative work.[76] Payments are at the guaranteed hourly rate, subject to a maximum of £7.25 per day, and cannot exceed five days in each quarterly period.[77]

An employee who has been continuously employed for at least two years is entitled to maternity pay for a period of six weeks during which she is absent from work because of pregnancy or confinement.[78] Payment of maternity pay cannot commence until the beginning of the eleventh week before the expected week of confinement.[79] It accrues from day to day, is payable whether or not the employee intends to return to work, and amounts to nine-tenths of a week's pay for each week's absence, less any maternity allowance payable under the Social Security Acts.[80]

An employee who has been continuously employed for at least four weeks is entitled to a week's pay during each week up to twenty-six weeks during which he is suspended because of a requirement imposed by statute or a

---

[71] Ibid., s. 6. See *Finlayson* v. *Braidbar Quarry Co.* (1864) 2 M. 1297.
[72] Truck Act 1831, s. 6.
[73] *Bound* v. *Laurence* [1892] 1 Q.B. 226.
[74] *Williams* v. *North's Navigation Collieries*, supra.
[75] *McFarlane* v. *Birrell* (1888) 16 R. (J.) 28; *Summerlee Iron Co.* v. *Thomson*, 1913 S.C. (J.) 34.
[75a] Employment Protection (Consolidation) Act 1978, (c. 44), s. 12 (1).
[76] s. 13 (1).
[77] ss. 14, 15.
[78] ss. 33 (1) (*a*), (3) (*b*), 34 (1).
[79] s. 34 (2).
[80] s. 35 (1), (2).

recommendation made under a Code of Practice authorised by the Health and Safety at Work Act 1974.[81] Employees who are incapable of work because of illness or injury, who unreasonably refuse alternative work or who do not make themselves available for work, are excepted.[82]

Unpaid wages up to a total of £800 owed by a bankrupt employer and accruing during the four months preceding bankruptcy constitute a preferential debt.[83] In addition, certain amounts owed by an insolvent employer, up to a total of £800 in respect of arrears of pay,[84] may be recovered from the Redundancy Fund.[85] Every employee is now entitled to an itemised pay statement on each occasion that payment of wages or salary is made.[86]

12. Employee's Remedies: Common Law.—At common law the remedy of an employee, in the event of a material breach of contract on the employer's part, or unjustifiable dismissal, is an action of damages. In certain cases it may be possible to reduce the employer's resolution to dismiss.[87] He has no right to insist on remaining in a post from which he has been dismissed, even although the dismissal was not justified.[88] In special circumstances, however, the Court may, where damages would not afford an adequate remedy, restrain the implementation of an invalid notice of dismissal.[89] The measure of damages in the case of unjustifiable dismissal is normally the amount which the employee would have earned had the contract been duly fulfilled, not to be increased by proof that the dismissal had caused third parties to form unfavourable opinions of his character.[90] But certain parties, e.g., an actor to whom publicity is of value, may recover damages for the loss of opportunity for gain through enhanced reputation arising from wrongful dismissal[91] and although damages are not recoverable for hurt feelings as such, they may be awarded in respect of mental stress where that is within the contemplation of the parties as a likely consequence of the employer's breach.[92] Moreover an apprenticeship agreement is regarded as being of a special character and in the event of its wrongful termination by the employer damages may be awarded not only for loss of earnings during the remainder of the apprenticeship but for loss of training and loss of future prospects.[93] Where dismissal was justified, an action of damages by the employee is not rendered relevant by averments that

---

[81] s. 19 (1).
[82] s. 20.
[83] Companies Act 1948, s. 319; Bankruptcy (Scotland) Act 1913, s. 118; both as amended by Insolvency Act 1976, Sch. 1.
[84] 1978, c. 44, s. 122 (3) (a) and (5). Other maxima apply to other debts.
[85] s. 122.
[86] s. 8.
[87] *Palmer* v. *Inverness Hospitals Board of Management*, 1963 S.C. 311; see § 22, infra.
[88] *First Edinburgh Building Society* v. *Munro* (1884) 21 S.L.R. 291; *Chappell* v. *Times Newspapers* [1975] 1 W.L.R. 482.
[89] *Hill* v. *C. A. Parsons & Co* [1972] 1 Ch. 305.
[90] *Addis* v. *Gramophone Co.* [1909] A.C. 488.
[91] *Clayton & Waller* v. *Oliver* [1930] A.C. 209.
[92] *Cox* v. *Philips Industries* [1976] 1 W.L.R. 638.
[93] *Dunk* v. *Geo. Waller & Son* [1970] 2 Q.B. 163.

the motives of the employer were malicious.[94] An employee dismissed is bound to minimise the loss by endeavouring to obtain other employment, and his claim for damages will be subject to deduction of what he has actually earned or, with reasonable effort, would have been able to earn.[95] The question whether a breach of contract will enable the employee to leave, and claim damages, depends generally, as in other contracts, on the materiality of the breach in question.[96] But a domestic servant, if ill-treated, must leave, and by staying on will be held to have abandoned any claim for damages.[97]

13. Employee's Remedies: Statutory Provision.—Although the common law remedies noticed in the preceding paragraph remain in force, their practical significance is now largely overshadowed by statutory remedies. These include the various remedies discussed in the following paragraphs as well as the remedies for unfair dismissal with which this paragraph is concerned. Where an employee is unfairly dismissed an industrial tribunal may, if the employee wishes it to do so, make an order for his reinstatement or re-engagement.[98] If reinstated, he is to be treated in all respects as if he had not been dismissed;[99] if the order is for re-engagement, its effect is that he is to be engaged in employment comparable to that from which he was dismissed, or other suitable employment, on terms specified in the order.[1] In exercising its discretion, the tribunal must first consider reinstatement, and take into account the dismissed employee's wishes, the practicability of reinstatement or re-engagement, and the justice of making an order where the employee caused or contributed to his dismissal.[2] If the employee does not wish reinstatement or re-engagement, or if the tribunal does not make an order, or in the event of non-compliance by the employer with the order, the employee is entitled to an award of compensation consisting of a basic award calculated on the same basis as a redundancy payment, with a minimum of two weeks' pay, and a compensatory award of such an amount as is just and equitable having regard to the loss sustained in consequence of dismissal, in so far as that is attributable to the employer's action.[3] The loss so sustained is to be taken to include any expense reasonably incurred in consequence of dismissal and any benefit which the employee might reasonably be expected to have had but for dismissal.[4] Where there has been non-compliance by the employer with an order for reinstatement or re-engagement the employee is entitled to an additional compensatory award of from 13 to 26 weeks' pay or, in certain

[94] *Brown* v. *Magistrates of Edinburgh*, 1907 S.C. 256.
[95] *Ross* v. *Macfarlane* (1894) 21 R. 396.
[96] Breach of Contract, Ch. XIII, supra, § 4.
[97] *Fraser* v. *Laing* (1878) 5 R. 596.
[98] Employment Protection (Consolidation) Act 1978 (c. 33) ss. 68 (1) and 69. On what constitutes unfair dismissal, see para. 23 infra.
[99] s. 69 (2).
[1] s. 69 (4).
[2] s. 69 (5) and (6). In relation to re-engagement the employee's contribution to his dismissal is a factor which bears on what the terms of any re-engagement order should be, as well as on whether such an order should be made.
[3] ss. 68 (2), 71 (1), 73 and 74.
[4] s. 74 (2).

cases, from 26 to 52 weeks' pay, unless the employer satisfies the tribunal that it was not practicable for him to comply with the order.[5] Both the basic award and the compensatory award may be reduced in respect of the employee's contribution to his dismissal,[6] but no such reduction may take the basic award below the minimum of two weeks' pay.[7]

14. Trade Union Membership.—Dismissal on the ground of trade union membership or activities is unfair in the statutory sense, and gives rise to the remedies noticed in the previous paragraph.[8] An employee is, however, also entitled to be protected against action by his employer, short of dismissal, taken for the purpose of preventing or deterring him from being, or seeking to become, a member of an independent trade union, or from taking part in its activities at any appropriate time, and also against penalising him on these grounds.[9] Where, however, a union membership agreement is in force, in accordance with which it is the practice for employees of a particular class, grade or category, to belong to a specified union, the protection applies, in relation to such employees, only to membership of, or participation in, the activities of that union.[10] There is, on the other hand, no general protection against action by an employer for the purpose of compelling an employee to belong to a trade union, but such protection is accorded against compulsion to join a trade union which is not independent, and also to an employee who genuinely objects on grounds of religious belief to being a member of any trade union whatsoever.[11] In the event of infringement of any of these rights, a complaint may be made to an industrial tribunal which, if it finds the complaint well-founded, may make a declaration to that effect and award such compensation as it considers just and equitable, having regard to the infringement of the complainant's right and any loss sustained by him (including expenses reasonably incurred, and loss of any benefit which he might reasonably be expected to have had but for his employer's action).[12]

15. Time Off.—An employer has a statutory obligation to permit an employee in any of the following categories to take time off during working hours for certain purposes:
(1) An official of an independent trade union recognised by the employer— if the time off is taken for the purpose of enabling him to carry out his official duties concerned with industrial relations between his employer and any associated employer and their employees, or to undergo approved training in aspects of industrial relations relevant to the carrying out of these duties;[13]

[5] s. 71 (2) and (3).
[6] ss. 73 (7) and 74 (6).
[7] s. 73 (8).
[8] s. 58.
[9] s. 23 (1).
[10] s. 23 (3), (4) and (5).
[11] s. 23 (1) (c) and (6).
[12] ss. 24 and 26.
[13] s. 27 (1).

(2) A member of an independent trade union recognised by the employer—
if the time off is taken for the purpose of taking part in activities of that
trade union or in other trade union activities in relation to which the
employee is acting as a representative of his trade union, excluding
activities consisting of industrial action;[14]

(3) A Justice of the Peace or a member of a local authority, statutory
tribunal or certain other public bodies—if the time off is taken for the
purpose of performing his public duties;[15] and

(4) An employee who is given notice of dismissal by reason of redundancy
and has been continuously employed for at least two years—if the time
off is taken in order to look for new employment or make arrangements
for training for future employment.[16]

The amount of time off which an employer is bound to permit and the
conditions to which it may be subject are such as may be reasonable in all the
circumstances.[17] In determining what is reasonable in the case of a trade union
official or member, regard is to be had to any relevant provision of a code of
practice[18] and, in the case of time off for public duties, to how much time is
required for the performance of the duties, to how much time the employee
has already been permitted, and to the circumstances of the employer's
business and the effect of the employee's absence on its running.[19] Time off in
the case of trade union officials and redundant employees is to be paid, but
there is no such requirement in the other categories.[20] A complaint may be
made to an industrial tribunal in the event of the employer's failure to permit
time off as required by the Act.[21] On such a complaint by a trade union
official or redundant employee, the tribunal may order the employer to pay to
the employee the amount due to him,[22] and in all cases, except that of the
redundant employee, may award compensation having regard both to the
employer's default and to any loss sustained by the employee.[23]

16. Maternity.—An employee who is absent from work on account of
pregnancy or confinement has, subject to certain qualifications, and in
addition to her entitlement to maternity pay,[24] a right to return to work.[25]
The qualifications are that: (1) she has continued to be employed until
immediately before the beginning of the eleventh week before the expected
week of confinement; (2) at that time she has been continuously employed by
the same employer for at least two years; and (3) she has informed her

---

[14] s. 28 (1) and (2).
[15] s. 29 (1), (2) and (3).
[16] s. 31 (1) and (2).
[17] ss. 27 (2), 28 (3), 29 (4) and 31 (1). The words "in all the circumstances" do not occur in s. 31
(1).
[18] ss. 27 (2) and 28 (3).
[19] s. 29 (4).
[20] ss. 27 (3) to (6) and 31 (3) to (5).
[21] ss. 27 (7), 28 (4), 29 (6) and 31 (6).
[22] ss. 30 (3) and 31 (8).
[23] s. 30 (2).
[24] See para. 11 supra.
[25] s. 33 (1).

employer at least twenty-one days before her absence begins or, if that is not reasonably practicable, as soon as reasonably practicable, that she will be absent from work because of pregnancy or confinement and that she intends to return to work.[26] In order to avail herself of this right she must, if so requested, give the required information to her employer in writing and supply for his inspection a medical certificate stating her expected date of confinement.[27] An employee who is dismissed before the beginning of the eleventh week, by reason of her incapacity because of pregnancy adequately to do her work, or her inability on that ground to continue doing it without contravention of a statutory duty or restriction, is, provided she informs her employer as soon as reasonably practicable after dismissal of her intention to return to work, deemed, for the purposes of her right to return, to have continued to work until the beginning of the eleventh week.[28] The right is exigible at any time before the end of twenty-nine weeks from the beginning of the week of confinement,[29] and is a right to be reinstated in the job in which she was employed under her original contract of employment, and on terms and conditions no less favourable than if she had not been absent.[30] Failure by the employer to permit return constitutes dismissal with effect from the notified day of return, and the dismissal is deemed to be for the reason for which she was not permitted to return.[31] Unless there is a supervening reason unconnected with her pregnancy which justifies dismissal, the remedies for unfair dismissal will ensue.[32]

17. Racial Discrimination.—A dismissal wholly, or mainly, on the ground of the employee's racial identity will almost always be unfair. The Race Relations Act 1976 provides, however, additional protection for employees against racial discrimination,[33] and extends that protection to workers engaged under contracts for the provision of services.[34] There is discrimination for the purposes of the Act if, on racial grounds, A treats B less favourably than he treats, or would treat, other persons, or if he applies to B a requirement or condition which (1) is such that the proportion of persons of B's racial group who can comply with it is considerably smaller than the proportion of persons not of that group who can so comply, (2) he cannot show to be justifiable on other than racial grounds, and (3) is to B's detriment because he cannot comply with it.[35] To segregate a person from others on racial grounds is to treat him less favourably,[36] and the definition of racial grounds and racial group covers considerations of colour, nationality or

---

[26] s. 33 (3).
[27] s. 33 (3) (c) and (5).
[28] s. 33 (4).
[29] s. 45 (1).
[30] Ibid.
[31] s. 56.
[32] See para. 13 supra. Redundancy (on which see s. 45 (3) and (4)) may be a supervening reason.
[33] 1976 c. 74, Parts I and II.
[34] s. 7.
[35] s. 1 (1).
[36] s. 1 (2).

ethnic or national origins as well as race.[37] Victimisation in connection with proceedings brought or steps taken under the Act, or in connection with allegations of contravention of the Act, is treated as discrimination.[38]

It is unlawful to discriminate on racial grounds against an employee in the terms of employment afforded to him, or the access afforded to opportunities for promotion, transfer or training, or, with certain exceptions, to any other benefits, facilities or services, or by dismissing him or subjecting him to any other detriment; and it is unlawful to discriminate against a prospective employee in the arrangements made for the purpose of determining who should be offered employment, or in the terms offered, or by refusing or deliberately omitting to offer employment.[39] The provisions relating to the making of arrangements for offering employment, to refusal or deliberate omission to offer employment, and to access afforded to opportunities for promotion, transfer or training, are excluded where membership of a particular racial group is a genuine occupational qualification.[40] It is such a qualification where it is required for reasons of authenticity in a dramatic performance or other entertainment, or in work as an artist's or photographic model, or in the provision of food or drink to the public in a particular setting, or where personal services promoting the welfare of the group can most effectively be provided by a member of that group.[41] There are also exceptions for employment outside Great Britain;[42] for employment for the purpose of providing training and skills intended to be exercised outside Great Britain;[43] for seamen recruited abroad;[44] for the provision of education or training for persons not ordinarily resident in Great Britain;[45] for provision by an employer of access to facilities for training to members of a particular racial group or encouraging such members to take advantage of opportunities for work where the group is under-represented among persons doing the work in question;[46] for discrimination, on the basis of nationality, place of birth or length of residence, in relation to selection to represent a country, place or area, or to eligibility for competition in any sport or game;[47] and for acts done under statutory authority[48] or for the purpose of safeguarding national security.[49]

The provisions so far noticed relate to discrimination by, or on behalf of, employers, but similar provisions relate to discrimination by partnerships of more than six partners in relation to a position as a partner in the firm[50] and

[37] s. 3 (1).
[38] s. 2.
[39] s. 4 (1).
[40] s. 5 (1).
[41] s. 5 (2).
[42] ss. 4 (1) and (2) and 8.
[43] s. 6.
[44] s. 9.
[45] s. 36.
[46] ss. 37 and 38.
[47] s. 39.
[48] s. 42.
[49] s. 42.
[50] s. 10.

to discrimination by trade unions,[51] by bodies which confer an authorisation or qualification for a profession or trade,[52] by vocational training bodies,[53] by employment agencies[54] and by certain government agencies concerned with employment.[55] In the case of trade unions, there is an exception to facilitate the training for posts within the union and to encourage the holding of such posts by members of under-represented racial groups,[56] and in the case of vocational training bodies there is a similar exception in relation to training and encouragement to participate in particular classes of work.[57] Employers are liable not only for their own discriminatory acts but also (except for the purposes of criminal liability) for such acts done in the course of their employment by their employees, even if done without the employer's knowledge or approval, unless the employer can prove that he took such steps as were reasonably practicable to prevent the employee from doing the act in question, or from doing acts of that description in the course of his employment.[58] A person aggrieved by racial discrimination in respect of employment may complain to an industrial tribunal, which, if it finds the complaint well founded, may grant such of the following remedies as it considers just and equitable:

(1) an order declaring the rights of the complainant and the respondent;
(2) an order for compensation for any damages sustained by the complainant, including injury to feelings (but an order for compensation cannot be made if the discrimination consists in the application to the complainant of a requirement or a condition applied equally to persons not of the same racial group, but with discriminatory results, and the respondent proves that the requirement or condition was not applied with the intention of treating the claimant unfavourably on racial grounds); and
(3) a recommendation that the respondent take, within a specified period, action appearing to the tribunal to be practicable for the purpose of obviating or reducing the adverse effect on the complainant of any act of discrimination. (If the respondent fails, without reasonable justification, to comply with a recommendation of the tribunal, the tribunal may, if it thinks it just and equitable to do so, increase the amount of compensation which the respondent was required to pay or, if an order for compensation has not been made, may make such an order.)[59]

In addition to the remedies available to the individual, compliance with the Act, in relation to employment as well as other matters, may be secured at the instance of the Commission for Racial Equality by means of non-discrimination notices and consequent procedure.[60]

[51] s. 11.
[52] s. 12.
[53] s. 13.
[54] s. 14.
[55] s. 15.
[56] s. 38 (3) to (6).
[57] s. 37.
[58] s. 32.
[59] ss. 54 and 56.
[60] ss. 58 to 69.

18. Sex Discrimination.—Under the Equal Pay Act 1970 an equality clause is, unless already expressed, deemed to be included in every contract under which anyone is employed at an establishment in Great Britain.[61] The effect of an equality clause is that for men and women employed on like work, or employed on work rated as equivalent, the terms and conditions of employment for one sex are not less favourable in any relevant respect than the terms and conditions applicable to the other sex.[62] By like work is meant work of the same or a broadly similar nature in which any differences between the things done are not of practical importance in relation to terms and conditions of employment, and by work rated as equivalent, is meant a job which has been given an equal value to another job in terms of the demand made on a worker or which would have been given an equal value but for the evaluation being made on a system setting different values for men and women.[63] Any claim in respect of the contravention of a contractual term arising out of the operation of an equality clause may be presented to an industrial tribunal or, where it appears to the Secretary of State that an employer may have contravened such a term but that it is not reasonable to expect the employees to take steps to have the question determined, the question may be referred to an industrial tribunal by him.[64] In either case, the tribunal may determine the claim, including any question of arrears of remuneration or damages in respect of the contravention, and where there is a dispute about the effect of an equality clause it may, on the application of an employer, make an order declaring the rights of parties.[65] A remedy for failure to comply with an equality clause may, however, also be pursued as a breach of contract through the courts, subject, however, to the court's power where it considers that the claim can more conveniently be disposed of by an industrial tribunal to direct that the claim be struck out and, if it thinks fit, referred to an industrial tribunal.[66] No claim in respect of the operation of an equality clause may be referred to an industrial tribunal, otherwise than on a reference directed or made by a court, unless the employee, in respect of whom the claim is made, has been in the relevant employment within the six months preceding the date of the reference and no payments may be awarded in any proceedings, whether before a court or tribunal, by way of arrears of remuneration or damages, in respect of a time earlier than two years before the date on which the proceedings were instituted.[67] The Act also contains provisions for securing equality of treatment in collective agreements and pay structures, wages regulation orders, and agricultural wages orders.[68] The equal treatment requirement is excluded in so far as the terms and conditions of a woman's employment are affected by the law regulating the employment of women and in so far as any special treatment is accorded to women in

[61] 1970 c. 41, as amended by the Sex Discrimination Act 1975 (c. 65), s. 8 and Sch. 1.
[62] s. 1 (2).
[63] s. 1 (4) and (5).
[64] s. 2 (1) and (2).
[65] s. 2 (1A).
[66] s. 2 (3).
[67] s. 2 (4) and (5).
[68] ss. 3, 4 and 5.

connection with pregnancy or the birth of a child.[69] There is moreover, no requirement of equal treatment as regards terms and conditions related to retirement or death, or to any provision made in connection therewith, except that equal access must now be afforded to occupational pensions schemes.[70]

Further protection is afforded by the Sex Discrimination Act 1975,[71] which contains provisions on discrimination on the ground of sex or, in relation to employment, on the ground of marital status, corresponding mutatis mutandis to those already noticed as laid down by the Race Relations Act 1976 for discrimination on the ground of race. The following special features should, however, be noted. A genuine occupational qualification means, in terms of the Sex Discrimination Act, (a) that the job calls for a person of one sex rather than the other for reasons of physiology (excluding physical strength or stamina), or, in dramatic performances or other entertainment, for reasons of authenticity, so that the essential nature of the job would be materially different if carried out by a person of the other sex, or (b) that the job needs to be held by a person of one sex rather than the other to preserve decency or privacy, or (c) that it is impracticable for the employee to live elsewhere than in premises provided by the employer which are normally lived in by, and equipped with accommodation for, persons of one sex and it is not reasonable to expect the employer either to equip these premises with accommodation for the other sex or to provide other premises, or (d) that the premises within which the work is to be done are part of a hospital, prison or other establishment for persons requiring special care, supervision or attention and these persons are all of one sex and it is reasonable, having regard to the essential character of the establishment, that the job should not be held by a person of the other sex, or (e) that the holder of the job provides individuals with personal services, promoting their welfare or education or the like, and these services can most effectively be provided by a person of one sex rather than the other, or (f) that the job needs to be held by a man because of restrictions imposed by the laws regulating the employment of women, or (g) that the job needs to be held by a person of one sex rather than the other because it is likely to involve the performance of duties outside the United Kingdom in a country whose laws or customs are such that the duties could not effectively be performed by a person of the other sex, or (h) that the job is one of two to be held by a married couple.[72] Discrimination in employment outside Great Britain,[73] or in acts done under statutory authority,[74] or for the purpose of safeguarding national security,[75] is excluded, as it is under the Race Relations Act, and the provisions for discriminatory training are similar. In other respects the exclusionary provisions are, however, different. Regulations under sections 26 and 27 of the Police (Scotland) Act 1967 may

[69] s. 6 (1).
[70] s. 6 (1A) and (2).
[71] 1975 c. 61.
[72] s. 7.
[73] ss. 6 (1) and 10.
[74] s. 51.
[75] s. 52.

discriminate in requirements relating to height, uniform or equipment or allowances in lieu thereof, in according special treatment to women in connection with pregnancy or childbirth, and in pensions of special constables or police cadets;[76] and discrimination as to requirements relating to height is also lawful in the recruitment and employment of prison officers.[77] Employment for the purposes of an organised religion is excluded where the employment is limited to one sex so as to comply with the doctrines of the religion or avoid offending the religious susceptibilities of a significant number of its followers, but not otherwise.[78] Men are no longer excluded from the midwifery profession, but it is lawful to discriminate on the grounds of sex in the recruitment, employment, promotion, transfer or training of midwives, subject only to the qualification that dismissal of a midwife, or subjection to any other detriment, may not be on grounds of sex discrimination.[79] The former absolute prohibition against the employment of women underground at a mine is replaced by a provision that no female shall be employed in a job, the duties of which ordinarily require the employee to spend a significant proportion of time below ground at a mine which is being worked.[80] As provisions for conferring benefits on persons of one sex only are lawful if contained in a charitable instrument,[81] discrimination between one sex and the other in a purely charitable provision for any class of employees is lawful, as is discrimination in relation to the participation of anyone as a competitor in any sport, game, or other activity of a competitive nature, where the physical strength, stamina or physique of the average woman puts her at a disadvantage to the average man.[82] In employment, as in other contexts, discrimination in respect of insurance is lawful if it is reasonable, having regard to actuarial or similar data,[83] and discrimination in respect of admission to communal accommodation, or in the provision of benefits, facilities or services which cannot properly and effectively be provided except for those using communal accommodation, is lawful, provided the accommodation is managed in a way which comes, in the given exigencies of the situation, as near as may be to fair and equitable treatment of men and women.[84]

In questions of sex discrimination, the Equal Opportunities Commission plays a role similar to that played by the Commission for Racial Equality in matters of racial discrimination.[85]

19. Duration of Contract: Notice at Common Law.—Most contracts of employment are now subject to a statutory minimum period of notice,[86] but

[76] s. 17.
[77] s. 18.
[78] s. 19.
[79] s. 20.
[80] s. 21.
[81] s. 43.
[82] s. 44.
[83] s. 45.
[84] s. 46.
[85] ss. 53 to 61, 67 to 76.
[86] Employment Protection (Consolidation) Act 1978 (c. 44) s. 49; see § 17, supra.

there are some to which the common law still applies,[87] and the common law rules as to duration are not affected by statute. The duration of a contract of employment, when not expressly fixed,[88] may depend on various considerations. In certain cases there is an established rule. Thus domestic servants, when their employment was common, were presumably engaged for a term ending at Whitsunday or Martinmas, out-door servants for a year.[89] An inference may be drawn from the terms of payment, an annual salary affording a presumption of an engagement for a year.[90] A tenure ad vitam aut culpam is not to be inferred except in established cases, such as those of judges, sheriffs, ministers of the established church, or professors in a university, who hold a munus publicum, an office involving duties to the public.[91] Where none of these considerations is applicable, the general presumption at common law is that the employment is terminable at the pleasure of either party, with or without notice. Notice, or payment of the amount that would have been earned during the period of notice, is usually necessary in engagements which take up the whole time of the party employed, e.g., that of a schoolmaster,[92] not in part-time employments, such as that of a solicitor,[93] or in commercial agency.[94] The term of notice required is that deemed reasonable in the particular case, of which the practice of other employers is evidence.[95] Even where the period of endurance is fixed, notice as a rule is necessary to bring the contractual relationship to an end.[96] In the case of domestic and agricultural servants forty days' notice before the term is the established rule,[97] in other cases notice must be for a reasonable time. If a servant is hired for the year or half-year ending at Whitsunday or Martinmas, he must remove on May 28 or November 28 in the absence of special agreement,[98] and forty days' notice before these dates is sufficient.[99] Where no notice is given the contract will be, in certain cases, renewed by tacit relocation;[1] where that principle is inapplicable, the employer's failure to give notice will entitle the servant to a payment in lieu thereof.[2] Servants of the Crown, civil or military, though they may be appointed for a fixed period, remain, as a general rule, subject to dismissal at any time and without notice.[3]

---

[87] Ibid., ss. 141 (1), 143 (3) & (4), 144 (1) & (2), 145 (1).
[88] But see ibid., s. 4 (3).
[89] Bell, *Prin.*, § 174; *Groom* v. *Clark* (1859) 21 D. 831; *Cameron* v. *Fletcher* (1872) 10 M. 301.
[90] *Campbell* v. *Fyfe* (1851) 13 D. 1041; *Dowling* v. *Henderson* (1890) 17 R. 921; *Stevenson* v. *North British Ry.* (1905) 7 F. 1106; but see *Robson* v. *Overend* (1878) 6 R. 213.
[91] *Hastie* v. *M'Murtrie* (1889) 16 R. 715.
[92] *Morrison* v. *Abernethy School Board* (1876) 3 R. 945.
[93] *Cormack* v. *Keith & Murray* (1893) 20 R. 977; *Brenan* v. *Campbell's Trs.* (1898) 25 R. 423.
[94] *London, etc., Shipping Co.* v. *Ferguson* (1850) 13 D. 51; *Stewart* v. *Rendall* (1899) 1 F. 1002.
[95] *Forsyth* v. *Heathery Knowe Coal Co.* (1880) 7 R. 887. As to the suggested effect of custom on the operation of the 1963 Act, see D. Knight Dix, *Contracts of Employment* (1966), pp. 24 and 41.
[96] *Morrison* v. *Abernethy School Board* (1876) 3 R. 945, opinion of Lord Deas; Bell, *Prin.*, § 187; and see § 20, infra.
[97] *Cameron* v. *Scott* (1870) 9 M. 233.
[98] Removal Terms (Scotland) Amendment Act 1890 (53 & 54 Vict., c. 6), ss. 2, 3.
[99] *Stewart* v. *Robertson*, 1937 S.C. 701.
[1] As to tacit relocation, see Extinction of Obligations, Ch. XV., supra, § 22.
[2] *Lennox* v. *Allan* (1880) 8 R. 38.
[3] *Dunn* v. *The Queen* [1896] 1 Q.B. 116; *Mulvenna* v. *Admiralty*, 1926 S.C. 842 (doubtful in view of *Cameron* v. *Lord Advocate*, 1952 S.C. 165). But see *Riordan* v. *War Office* [1961] 1 W.L.R.

Special rules apply to the holders of judicial office; a judge can be removed only by Act of Parliament; a sheriff principal or sheriff or procurator fiscal, by the Secretary of State for Scotland, on the ground of inability, neglect of duty or misbehaviour and on a report from the Lord President and Lord Justice-Clerk.[4]

20. Statutory Notice.—Part IV of the Employment Protection (Consolidation) Act 1978[4a] provides a statutory code relating to the minimum periods of notice which must be given by employers and employees when contracts of employment affected by the Act are terminated.[5] The Act defines an employee as an individual who has entered into or works under a contract of employment whether the contract be expressed or implied, oral or in writing, and whether it be a contract of service or of apprenticeship.[6] With the exception of certain specified contracts[7] the Act therefore applies to all contracts of employment in which the employee has been continuously employed for at least four weeks.[8] Where an employer terminates the employment of those who have been continuously employed (a) for four weeks or more but less that two years, he must give not less than one week's notice; (b) for two years or more but less than twelve years, he must give not less than one week's notice for each year of continuous employment; (c) for twelve years or more, he must give not less than twelve weeks' notice.[8] On the other hand, if an employee who has been continuously employed for at least four weeks wishes to terminate his contract of employment, he must give at least one week's notice.[9] These periods of notice are the minimum prescribed by statute. They cannot be reduced by conventional provisions, but either party can agree to waive his right to notice, or to accept payment in lieu of notice.[10] The Act preserves the contractual or common law right of an employee to receive longer notice that the statutory minimum,[11] and retains the common law right of either party to treat the contract as terminable without notice by reason of such conduct as would have justified such termination before the Act.[12] The liability of an employer to an employee during a period of notice is set out in Schedule 3 to the Act.

21. Termination of Contract.—The termination of a contract of employ-

---

210). Civil servants, but not members of the naval, military or air forces of the Crown, are however, in general protected against unfair dismissal (1978 c. 44, s. 138).
[4] Sheriff Courts (Scotland) Act 1971 (c. 58), s. 12. The removal can be effected only by statutory instrument which is subject to annulment by a resolution of either House of Parliament.
[4a] 1978 c. 44, ss. 49 to 53.
[5] Similar provisions were first enacted in the Contracts of Employment Act 1963, which was repealed and replaced by the Contracts of Employment Act 1972, also now repealed.
[6] Ibid., s. 153 (1).
[7] See ss. 141 (1), 143 (3) and (4), 144 (1) & (2), and 145 (1). Members of the Armed Forces and civil servants are also excluded (s. 138 (1)).
[8] s. 49 (1).
[9] s. 49 (2).
[10] ss. 49 (3) and 140 (1).
[11] s. 49 (1) and (3).
[12] s. 49 (5).

ment depends upon the general rules applicable to other contracts,[13] and only a few special cases require to be considered.

22. Dismissal: Common Law.—It is an established rule at common law that an employer is entitled to dismiss an employee at any time on paying wages, and, in certain employments, board wages, for the remainder of the term, and that such dismissal does not involve a breach of contract.[14] There is no analogous rule in favour of the employee.[15] A right of appeal against dismissal may, however, be incorporated in a contract of employment in terms which constitute an appellate committee as a quasi-judicial tribunal. In that event any material departure in the appeal procedure from the principles of natural justice may nullify the dismissal.[16]

23. Dismissal: Statutory Provisions.—The employer's common law right to dismiss has been modified by statute. Under legislation originating in the Industrial Relations Act 1971[17] and now embodied in the Employment Protection (Consolidation) Act 1978 an employee has a right not to be unfairly dismissed.[18] There is a dismissal for the purposes of the Act—

(1) if the contract is terminated by the employer with or without notice,

(2) where a fixed term contract expires without renewal, and

(3) where the employee terminates the contract with or without notice in circumstances such that he is entitled to terminate it without notice by reason of the employer's conduct.[19]

There is dismissal in the last of these senses only if the employer's conduct is a significant breach going to the root of the contract or shows that he no longer intends to be bound by one of its essential terms.[20] There is no dismissal and so no infringement of the employee's rights where a contract of employment is frustrated, as may happen after a long period of absence through illness.[21] There is, however, a dismissal if an employee who has a right to return to work after an absence because of pregnancy is not permitted to return.[22]

A dismissal is to be regarded as unfair if it was by reason of trade union membership or activities or, with certain exceptions, by reason of pregnancy.[23] It is to be regarded as fair if a closed shop has been established in accordance with a union membership agreement and the dismissal was because the

[13] E.g. it may be repudiated by fundamental breach on the part of either party (cf. *Donovan* v. *Invicta Airways* [1970] 1 Lloyd's Rep. 486; *Pepper* v. *Webb* [1969] 1 W.L.R. 516; *Carvill* v. *Irish Industrial Bank* [1968] I.R. 325).

[14] *Graham* v. *Thomson* (1822) 1 S. 309; *Mollison* v. *Baillie* (1885) 22 S.L.R. 595.

[15] *Wallace* v. *Wishart*, 1800 Hume 383.

[16] *Palmer* v. *Inverness Hospitals Board of Management*, 1963 S.C. 311.

[17] 1971 c. 72.

[18] 1978 c. 44, s. 54.

[19] s. 55.

[20] *Western Excavating (E.C.C.)* v. *Sharp*, (1978) I.R.L.R. 27, (1978) 13 I.T.R. 132.

[21] *Jones* v. *Wagon Repairs* (1968) 3 I.T.R. 168; *Pritchard* v. *Dinorwie Slate Quarries* (1971) 6 I.T.R. 102; *Marshall* v. *Harland & Wolff (No. 2)* (1972) 7 I.T.R. 150; *Egg Stores (Stamford)* v. *Leibovici* (1976) I.R.L.R. 376; cf. *Watts, Watts & Co.* v. *Steeley* (1968) 3 I.T.R. 363; *Farmer* v. *Willow Dye Works* (1972) 7 I.T.R. 226; *Hebden* v. *Forsey & Son* (1973) 8 I.T.R. 656.

[22] s. 56.

[23] ss. 58 (1) and 60.

employee was not a member of a union specified in the agreement unless the employee genuinely objects on grounds of religious belief to being a member of any trade union whatsoever.[24] In the latter event[25] the dismissal is to be regarded as unfair. A dismissal by reason of redundancy is to be regarded as unfair if selection was by reason of trade union membership or activity or genuine objection on grounds of religious belief to such membership or activity or was, without special reasons to justify it, in contravention of a customary arrangement or agreed procedure.[26] In all other cases the dismissal is regarded as unfair unless the employer can show—

(1) that the reason for dismissal related to the employee's capability, qualifications or conduct or was that the employee was redundant or that his continued employment would involve contravention of a statutory obligation or restriction or was some other substantial reason of a kind such as to justify dismissal, and

(2) that, having regard to the reason shown, he acted reasonably in the circumstances in treating that reason as a sufficient reason for dismissal.[27]

If on engaging an employee an employer informs him in writing that his employment will be terminated on the return to work of an employee absent because of pregnancy or of a suspension on medical grounds in accordance with a statutory requirement or recommendation, dismissal of that employee on the return of the employee whom he was replacing is to be regarded as having been for a substantial reason of a kind such as to justify dismissal.[28] That is, however, without prejudice to the onus which remains on the employer of showing that he acted reasonably in the circumstances. The reasonableness of the employer's actings is to be assessed in the light of the adequacy of the procedures which he followed and the facts which were known, or might, on a reasonable investigation, have been known to him at the time the decision to dismiss was taken.[29] Accordingly, if an employer acted unreasonably at that time the dismissal will be regarded as unfair even if facts subsequently emerge on which it could have been justified. On the other hand if an employer follows fair procedures and, in appropriate cases, makes such investigations as may reasonably be required in the circumstances, it is immaterial that on facts which subsequently emerge he can be shown to have been mistaken. Where a dismissal takes place in the course of a lock-out, strike, or other industrial action, proceedings for unfair dismissal cannot be entertained unless it is shown that there has been discrimination between the dismissed employee and other relevant employees.[30]

[24] s. 58 (3).
[25] Ibid.
[26] s. 59.
[27] s. 57.
[28] s. 61.
[29] *Earl* v. *Slater & Wheeler (Airlyne) Ltd.* (1973) 8 I.T.R. 33; *A. J. Dunning & Sons (Shopfitters) Ltd.* v. *Jacomb* (1973) 8 I.T.R. 453; *St. Anne's Board Mill Co.* v. *Brien* (1973) 8 I.T.R. 453; *Merseyside & North Wales Electricity Board* v. *Taylor* (1975) 10 I.T.R. 52; *W. Devis & Sons* v. *Atkins* [1977] 3 W.L.R. 214.
[30] s. 62.

Part VI of the Employment Protection (Consolidation) Act 1978, which substantially re-enacts provisions of the Redundancy Payments Act 1965,[31] imposes upon employers the obligation to make a "redundancy payment" to any employee who, after continuous employment for 104 weeks,[32] is (a) dismissed by reason of redundancy, or (b) laid off or kept on short time for specified periods, provided that in the latter event he gives written notice of his claim.[33] An employee is dismissed by reason of "redundancy" if his dismissal is due wholly or mainly to the cessation of the employer's business, or to the cessation or diminution of demands for particular work.[34]

24. Death of Either Party.—The death of either employer or employee terminates the contract. An engagement to serve a firm is dissolved by the death of a partner,[35] but not by a mere change in the constitution of the firm.[36]

25. Illness or Imprisonment of Employee.—Absence from illness or accident is not a breach of contract on the employee's part. But where the accident was due to the employee's own fault it was held that the employer was justified in dismissal, and that no further wages were due.[37] And prolonged absence from illness, though no fault may be attributed to the employee, may justify the employer in treating the contract as frustrated, and therefore at an end.[38] Where an employee is sentenced to a term of imprisonment which makes it impossible for him to perform his part of the contract, his employment is automatically terminated at the date of the sentence.[39]

26. Bankruptcy of Employer.—The bankruptcy of an employer amounts to a breach of contract on his part. The employee is entitled to leave, and to claim the amount which he would have earned as wages. But his claim is for damages, not for wages, and is therefore not entitled to the preferential ranking accorded to wages.[40]

27. Apprenticeship.—A contract of apprenticeship differs from other contracts of employment in respect that it must in all cases be entered into in writing, usually known as an indenture.[41] An informal writing may be validated by part performance,[42] but a merely verbal agreement is not in any case binding.[43] There must be an obligation, express or implied, on the

[31] 1965, c. 62, s. 1.
[32] s. 81.
[33] Ibid.
[34] Ibid.
[35] Bell, *Prin.*, § 179.
[36] *Hoey* v. *M'Ewen & Auld* (1867) 5 M. 814.
[37] *M'Ewan* v. *Malcolm* (1867) 5 S.L.R. 62.
[38] *Manson* v. *Downie* (1885) 12 R. 1103; *Poussard* v. *Spiers & Pond* (1876) 1 Q.B.D. 410; *Westwood* v. *S.M.T. Co.*, 1938 S.N. 8.
[39] *Hare* v. *Murphy Bros* [1974] 3 All E.R. 940.
[40] *Day* v. *Tait* (1900) 8 S.L.T. 40.
[41] *Grant* v. *Ramage & Ferguson* (1897) 25 R. 35.
[42] *Neil* v. *Vashon*, 1807 Hume 20.
[43] *Murray* v. *M'Gilchrist* (1863) 4 Irv. 461.

employer to teach his profession or trade; without it the contract is merely one of service.[44] In apprenticeship the employer is bound to instruct the apprentice in his business, either personally or through the agency of his other employees.[45] Where an apprentice baker was able to prove that instruction in part of his trade had not been given, and that in consequence he earned lower wages, he was found entitled to damages.[46] An apprentice cannot be assigned to another employer without his own consent.[47] On the death of the employer during the term of the apprenticeship the apprentice may recover a portion of the premium paid,[48] but no such repayment is due on the death of the apprentice.[49] The competency of imprisonment of a deserting apprentice has already been mentioned.[50]

28. Injury to Employee.—Although the relationship between an employer and his employee is regulated by contract, the liability of an employer to make reparation to an employee injured in the course of his employment is regarded as delictual.[51] An employer at common law owes a duty to his employee to take reasonable care for his safety throughout the course of his employment. This may extend, where the employer has relevant and special knowledge, to advice calculated to minimise the consequences of injury sustained by an employee in the course of his employment, even if the injury was not attributable to the employer's fault. Thus, where an employer becomes aware of past circumstances connected with the employment which make it desirable for present employees to have a medical examination, he has a duty to advise them of that.[52]

Whether or not an employer is in breach of duty depends upon the facts and circumstances of each case.[53] This duty is personal to the employer, and while he may delegate performance of the duty to a third party, he cannot escape liability in the event of negligent performance by that party.[54] However, the employer is not in the position of an insurer of the safety of his employee. Thus under a rule of the common law now abrogated by statute an employer was held not to be liable for an injury to an employee arising from a latent defect in a tool obtained from a reputable supplier.[55] Since the abolition

[44] *Royce* v. *Greig*, 1909 2 S.L.T. 298.
[45] *Gardner* v. *Smith*, 1775 M. 593.
[46] *Lyle* v. *Service* (1863) 2 M. 115.
[47] *Edinburgh Glasshouse Co.* v. *Shaw*, 1789 M. 597.
[48] *Cutler* v. *Littleton*, 1711 M. 583.
[49] *Shephard* v. *Innes*, 1760 M. 589.
[50] Supra, § 9.
[51] *MacKinnon* v. *Iberia Shipping Co.*, 1955 S.C. 20.
[52] *Wright* v. *Dunlop Rubber Co.* [1971] 11 K.I.R. 311; cf *Stokes* v. *Guest, Keen & Nettlefold (Bolts and Nuts)* [1968] 1 W.L.R. 1776.
[53] See Reparation, Ch. XXXIV, infra, Negligence, §§ 10-14; Contributory Negligence, § 15; Exclusions of Liability and volenti non fit injuria, § 16. As to the general nature of the employer's duty, see *English* v. *Wilsons and Clyde Coal Co.* 1937 S.C. (H.L.) 46; *Paris* v. *Stepney Borough Council* [1951] A.C. 367; *Qualcast (Wolverhampton) Ltd.* v. *Haynes* [1959] A.C. 743; *Cavanagh* v. *Ulster Weaving Co.* [1960] A.C. 145, per Lord Keith at pp. 164-6; and see *Smith* v. *Austin Lifts* [1959] 1 W.L.R. 100 (H.L.), where employee working on the premises of a third party.
[54] *English* v. *Wilsons and Clyde Coal Co.*, supra, per Lord Thankerton, at p. 57; per Lord Wright, at p. 64.
[55] *Davie* v. *New Merton Board Mills* [1959] A.C. 604; see infra, § 30.

of the defence of common employment,[56] an employer is now vicariously liable for the negligence of one employee who causes injury to another.[57] The tendency of the Courts to classify the nature of the employer's personal duty to exercise reasonable care for the safety of his employees into three categories of provision of competent staff, adequate plant and machinery, and a proper system of work,[58] serves to illustrate the scope of the duty, but the categories are neither conclusive nor exhaustive.[59]

29. Competent Staff. —The vicarious liability of an employer for the negligence of a fellow employee has largely overridden this aspect of the personal duty of the employer. However, the employer remains personally liable when it is shown that he has failed to exercise reasonable care to select competent staff for the task in question, as where a skilled employee lacks the necessary experience to meet a situation which the employer ought to have foreseen,[60] or where an employer fails to discharge an employee who has shown himself through his habitual conduct to be a source of danger to his fellow employees.[61]

30. Plant and Machinery.—The employer is bound to exercise reasonable care in the provision and maintenance of adequate plant and materials for the job. Liability arises when the employer has not provided any plant,[62] or where the plant supplied is insufficient,[63] defective[64] or dangerous.[65] The extent of the duty is only to exercise reasonable care, and there is no liability for injury caused by a latent defect which reasonable inspection would not have revealed.[66] That formulation of the duty must now, however, be read subject to the statutory gloss that liability attaches to the employer where the defect is attributable wholly or partly to the fault of a third party such as a manufacturer or supplier.[67] An employer may therefore be liable for a defect which is latent to him if it is attributable to the fault of someone else. The obligation does not extend to the provision of the latest improvements, but is only to take such steps as are reasonable in the circumstances, in respect of both provision and maintenance of the plant.[68]

---

[56] By the Law Reform (Personal Injuries) Act 1948 (11 & 12 Geo. VI, c. 41), s. 1 (1). See *Lindsay* v. *Connell*, 1951 S.C. 281.
[57] *Staveley Iron and Chemical Co.* v. *Jones* [1956] A.C. 62. Note that the defence of volenti non fit injuria is only valid when the employer is sued vicariously: *I.C.I.* v. *Shatwell* [1965] A.C. 656. See Reparation, Ch. XXXIV., infra, § 16.
[58] *English* v. *Wilsons and Clyde Coal Co.*, supra.
[59] See note 53, supra. Other examples are safe place of work and safe means of access.
[60] *Black* v. *Fife Coal Co.*, 1912 S.C. (H.L.) 33.
[61] *Hudson* v. *Ridge Manufacturing Co.* [1957] 2 Q.B. 348.
[62] *Williams* v. *Birmingham Battery & Metal Co.* [1899] 2 Q.B. 338; *Lovell* v. *Blundells & Crompton & Co.* [1944] 1 K.B. 502.
[63] *Machray* v. *Stewarts & Lloyds* [1965] 1 W.L.R. 602.
[64] *Henderson* v. *Carron Co.* (1889) 16 R. 633.
[65] *Robertson* v. *Thomas's* (1907) 15 S.L.T. 32 (vicious horse).
[66] *Gavin* v. *Rogers* (1889) 17 R. 206; *Milne* v. *Townsend* (1892) 19 R. 830; *M'Millan* v. *B.P. Refinery (Grangemouth)*, 1961 S.L.T. (Notes) 79.
[67] Employer's Liability (Defective Equipment) Act 1969, s.1.
[68] *Toronto Power Co. Ltd.* v. *Paskwan* [1915] A.C. 734.

31. Proper System.—The employer is bound to take reasonable care to institute and maintain a safe and proper system of work.[69] It is his duty to give such general safety instructions as a reasonably careful employer who has considered the problem presented by the work would give to his employees.[70] Each case, therefore, turns on its own facts and circumstances,[71] and even where facts closely correspond to a previous decision, no necessary inference as to the decision of the instant case arises.[72] Evidence of trade practice is not conclusive[73] but may be an indication of what reasonable care requires. If it is evident that a practice is dangerous, and a precaution which would avoid the risk could reasonably be adopted, it is no defence that accidents rarely occurred or that the practice was widespread.[73a] Physical disability of the employee may render the performance of the duty by the employer more onerous, since the employer owes the duty to each of his employees as individuals.[74] The decided cases merely serve as illustrations of this aspect of the personal duty of the employer.[75]

32. Statutory Provisions.—Many industries are closely regulated by statute.[76] In most cases the observance of the statutory regulations is protected by the sanction of a fine, but civil liability is inferred if the person injured by their non-observance was one whose interests the regulation was designed to protect.[77] The harm which the pursuer sustains must be harm of a type which the statute envisages,[78] although it is not generally essential that the harm must be sustained in a particular manner.[79] As with liability at common law the pursuer must establish on a balance of probabilities that a breach of the statutory provisions caused him injury.[80] It depends upon the facts in each case whether the breach leads to a legitimate inference that the injury resulted from it.[81] Thus an employer will escape liability if he can show that, even if he had provided the safety equipment enjoined by the statute, the

---

[69] *English* v. *Wilsons and Clyde Coal Co.*, 1937 S.C. (H.L.) 47.
[70] *General Cleaning Contractors* v. *Christmas* [1953] A.C. 180, per Lord Oaksey, at p. 189.
[71] *Grace* v. *Alexander Stephen & Son*, 1952 S.C. 61.
[72] *Qualcast* v. *Haynes* [1959] A.C. 743.
[73] *Morris* v. *West Hartlepool Steam Navigation Co.* [1956] A.C. 552; *Cavanagh* v. *Ulster Weaving Co.* [1960] A.C. 145, applying *Morton* v. *Dixon*, 1909 S.C. 807, per Lord Dunedin, at p. 809; *Brown* v. *Rolls Royce*, 1960 S.C. (H.L.) 22; *Riddick* v. *Weir Housing Corporation*, 1970 S.L.T. (Notes) 71; *Macdonald* v. *Scottish Stamping & Engineering Co.*, 1972 S.L.T. (Notes) 73.
[73a] *Brown* v. *John Mills & Co. (Llanidloes)*, (1970) 8 K.I.R. 702.
[74] *Paris* v. *Stepney Borough Council* [1951] A.C. 367.
[75] See Walker on *Delict*, Vol. II., pp. 568–579; Munkman, *Employer's Liability* (6th ed.), pp. 127 et seq.
[76] See in general Factories Act 1961 (9 & 10 Eliz. II c. 34) and regulations made thereunder; Mines and Quarries Act 1954 (2 & 3 Eliz. II c. 70); Agriculture (Safety, Health and Welfare Provisions) Act 1956 (4 & 5 Eliz. II c. 49); Offices, Shops and Railway Premises Act 1963, c. 41; Health and Safety at Work etc. Act 1974 (c. 37); and Redgrave, *Health and Safety in Factories* (1976).
[77] *Groves* v. *Lord Wimborne* [1898] 2 Q.B. 402; *Bett* v. *Dalmeny Oil Co.* (1905) 7 F. 787; *Macmillan* v. *Lochgelly Iron, etc., Co.* 1933 S.C. (H.L.) 64; see also *Marshall & Son* v. *Russian Oil Products*, 1938 S.C. 773, and Reparation, Ch. XXXIV., § 3, infra.
[78] *Gorris* v. *Scott* (1874) L.R. 9 Ex. 125.
[79] *Grant* v. *N.C.B.*, 1956 S.C. (H.L.) 48.
[80] *Wardlaw* v. *Bonnington Castings*, 1956 S.C. (H.L.) 26.
[81] *Gardiner* v. *Motherwell Machinery and Scrap Co.* 1961 S.C. (H.L.) 1.

injured workman would not have used it.[82] If the statutory duties are laid upon the employer, they involve liability for injury caused by failure to observe them, though the immediate cause of failure may have been the fault of a fellow employee or sub-contractor.[83] And it will not be easy for a defender to prove that statutory regulations supersede the common law duty of care.[84] If an absolute duty is placed upon an employer, his only defences in case of failure are such statutory defences as may be provided,[85] but this does not include defences provided against a criminal charge.[86] If they are laid upon a particular official, the employer is not necessarily liable for his negligence, but the onus of proof that the official was competent is laid upon him.[87] In a case based on failure to fence machinery in compliance with the Factories Act 1937 it was held that the duty related to the plant used in manufacturing and not to the machine being manufactured.[88] Contributory negligence may lead to apportionment of damages;[89] but the degree of care required of a man in a factory or mine may be lower that that required of an ordinary man not exposed to the noise, strains and risks of a factory or mine.[90] An employer who is in breach of statutory duty may avoid liability altogether if it is established that the conduct of the employee was the sole cause of the breach.[91]

[82] *Qualcast* v. *Haynes* [1959] A.C. 743; *M'Williams* v. *Sir William Arrol & Co.*, 1962 S.C. (H.L.) 70; and see Note 91, below.

[83] *Bett* v. *Dalmeny Oil Co.*, supra; *Rodger* v. *Fife Coal Co.*, 1923 S.C. 108; *Alford* v. *National Coal Board*, 1952 S.C. (H.L.) 17; and see Reparation, Ch. XXXIV., infra, Liability of Employer of Independent Contractor, § 26, note 94.

[84] *Matuszczyk* v. *National Coal Board*, 1953 S.C. 8; *Bux* v. *Slough Metals* [1973] 1 W.L.R. 1358.

[85] *Bain* v. *Fife Coal Co.*, 1935 S.C. 681; *Reilly* v. *Beardmore & Co.*, 1947 S.C. 275; *Millar* v. *Galashiels Gas Co.*, 1949 S.C. (H.L.) 31; *Taylor* v. *National Coal Board*, 1953 S.C. 349.

[86] *Riddell* v. *Reid*, 1942 S.C. (H.L.) 51.

[87] *Black* v. *Fife Coal Co.*, 1912 S.C. (H.L.) 33; *Connell* v. *Nimmo*, 1924 S.C. (H.L.) 84.

[88] *Parvin* v. *Morton Machine Co.*, 1952 S.C. (H.L.) 9.

[89] See Reparation, Ch. XXXIV., infra, Contributory Negligence, § 15.

[90] *Caswell* v. *Powell Duffryn Associated Collieries Ltd.* [1940] A.C. 152; *Hunter* v. *Glenfield & Kennedy*, 1947 S.C. 536; *Barnes* v. *Southhook Potteries*, 1946 S.L.T. 259; *John Summers & Sons Ltd.* v. *Frost* [1955] A.C. 740.

[91] See *Ross* v. *Associated Portland Cement Manufacturers* [1964] 1 W.L.R. 768 (H.L.), and cases cited therein, where employee disobeyed instructions; also *Crowe* v. *James Scott & Sons*, 1965 S.L.T. 54, and *Horne* v. *Lec Refrigeration* [1965] 2 All E.R. 898; cf. *Quinn* v. *J. W. Green (Painters)* [1966] 1 Q.B. 509.

CHAPTER XXIII

AGENCY

Bowstead, *Agency* (14th ed., 1976); Story, *Agency* (9th ed., 1882); Powell, *Agency* (2nd ed., 1961); Fridman, *The Law of Agency* (4th ed., 1976).

1. Meaning of Agency.—Agency has been defined as "the relationship that exists between two persons one of whom expressly or impliedly consents that the other should represent him or act on his behalf, and the other of whom similarly consents to represent the former or so to act."[1] The express or implied power which the agent has to bring the principal into contractual relations with third parties is known as his "authority." Under the head of agency will be considered the branch of the law of employer and employed where the employment consists in bringing the employer into contractual relations with third parties. An agent has been defined as "a person having express or implied authority to act on behalf of another party, who is called the principal."[1] There are many cases included where the terms agent and principal are not commonly used; directors are the agents of the company; a partner, in dealing with partnership affairs, is the agent of the firm and of the other partners; a wife, in ordering goods for the household, is an agent for her husband. If the contract is gratuitous it is usually termed mandate instead of agency, and the terms mandant and mandatory are used instead of principal and agent.

2. Constitution of the Contract.—The authority of an agent or mandatory may arise from express contract, which, even although the engagement is entered into for more than a year, may be entered into orally[2]; may be inferred from the prior conduct of the parties; or may be assumed because an emergency has made action in the character of an agent reasonable or even necessary. The last case—termed in England agency of necessity—arises when A is in possession of B's goods; where some action by A with regard to the goods is necessary; and where communication with B is impossible. Thus a carrier, or seller, of perishable goods, when, owing to circumstances not due to his fault, delivery is delayed or rendered impossible, may assume authority to dispose of the goods, and his act will be binding on their owner.[3] The rule seems indistinguishable from the principle of negotiorum gestio.[4]

3. Ratification.—Where one party acts for another without any prior authority—express, inferred, or arising from necessity—the relationship of agent and principal may be constituted if the act of the ostensible agent is

---

[1] Bowstead, *Agency*, p. 1.
[2] *Pickin* v. *Hawkes* (1878) 5 R. 676.
[3] *Sims* v. *Midland Ry.* [1913] 1 K.B. 103; *Prager* v. *Blatspiel* [1924] 1 K.B. 566.
[4] See Quasi-Contract, Ch. XIV, supra, § 9. But in England it is limited in its application.

ratified or homologated by the party for whom he professed to act. Ratification need not be in express words, it may be inferred from conduct.[5] All the material facts must be known, unless the words or conduct of the party ratifying can be construed as a ratification of whatever the agent may have done.[6] To admit of the ratification of a contract made without authority so as to make the ratifier a party to the contract as a principal, the agent must have contracted ostensibly as agent; if he contracted ostensibly as principal, though in the expectation that his contract would be ratified by another, that other cannot ratify so as to acquire the right to sue or subject himself to liability to be sued.[7] And to make ratification possible the principal must have been in existence at the time when the agent acted, and therefore a company cannot ratify contracts made ostensibly on its behalf before it came into existence.[8] If the acts of the agent could not competently have been performed by the principal, the principal cannot ratify these acts.[9] Where the validity of an act depends on its being done within a certain time or before a certain event, and it is done timeously but without authority, subsequent ratification will not make the act valid.[10] It is an anomalous exception to this that in marine insurance a principal may ratify a contract of insurance made on his behalf and without his authority, even after he is aware of a loss.[11] And when ratification has to be inferred from conduct without any express statement, it has been held that that inference cannot be drawn unless the party ratifying had a choice in the matter. So where an agent had ordered repairs on a ship without authority, the shipowner did not ratify his act, and thereby incur liability to pay for the repairs, merely because he received and used the ship.[12]

4. Principal and Agent Inter Se.—In many respects the rights and liabilities of principal and agent, in questions solely inter se, and where no third party is affected, are the same as those of master and servant.[13]

5. Del Credere Agency.—In the normal case an agent in entering into a contract on behalf of his principal does not guarantee that the party with whom he contracts will fulfil his contract. If, by arrangement with his principal, he does so guarantee, he is said to act del credere. An agent del credere is substantially a cautioner, though the rule that cautionary obligations must be entered into in writing does not apply.[14] He is not, if he discloses the name of his principal, a party to the contract, and cannot be sued

5 *Ballantine* v. *Stevenson* (1881) 8 R. 959; *Barnetson* v. *Petersen* (1902) 5 F. 86.
6 *Fitzmaurice* v. *Bayley* (1856) 6 E. & B. 868.
7 *Keighley, Maxted & Co.* v. *Durant* [1901] A.C. 240.
8 *Tinnevelly Sugar Refining Co.* v. *Mirrlees* (1894) 21 R. 1009; *Kelner* v. *Baxter* (1886) L.R. 2 C.P. 174.
9 *Boston Deep Sea Fishing Co.* v. *Farnham* [1957] 1 W.L.R. 1051.
10 *Goodall* v. *Bilsland*, 1909 S.C. 1152.
11 Marine Insurance Act 1906, s. 86. This does not hold in fire insurance; *Grove* v. *Mathews* [1910] 2 K.B. 401.
12 *Forman* v. *The Liddlesdale* [1900] A.C. 190. The Scots courts might hold that the shipowner was liable, on the principle of recompense, in so far as he was lucratus; see Quasi-Contract, Ch. XIV, supra, and also § 24, infra.
13 Employment, Ch. XXII, supra.
14 *Sutton* v. *Grey* [1894] 1 Q.B. 285.

by the other party to it. It may often be a narrow question whether the contract is one of del credere agency or of sale and return.[15]

6. Relief.—An agent is entitled to be relieved by the principal of all liabilities which he may incur in the due performance of his contract as agent. Thus if, acting in accordance with his instructions, the agent so contracts as to render himself liable on the contract, the principal is bound to relieve him of this liability.[16] Where an agent was employed to make a report and a third party brought an unsuccessful action for damages for statements in the report which reflected on him, it was held that the principal was liable to the agent in the expenses—which the unsuccessful plaintiff was unable to pay—incurred in defending the action.[17]

7. Remuneration of Agent.—It is a question depending on circumstances whether an agent, in the absence of any express provision on the point, is entitled to remuneration. Where the services rendered are of the nature of supplying an introduction, or introducing business, and the party who has rendered the service is a broker or commission agent, he will be entitled to payment, in cases where a private individual would have been assumed to have acted gratuitously,[17A] if his claim can be shown to be sanctioned by a custom of trade.[17B] Though the actual business done may not be directly due to the broker, he may be entitled to commission if he was the means of bringing the parties into relations with each other;[18] not where the parties were already acquainted and the broker's claim is founded on a suggestion which was declined.[18A] The general principle that a mercantile agent is entitled to remuneration in some form may be excluded by proof of a custom in a particular trade that agents rely exclusively on the proceeds of the sale of goods placed in their hands.[19] If the agent is to receive commission on completion of the contract, he is entitled to damages if his principal refuses to complete.[19A]

8. Lien.—In security of his wages or commission, or of any debt incurred by the principal in the course of the agent's employment, a commercial agent has a general lien over any property of the principal which has been placed in his hands.[20] It has been laid down that "every agent who is required to

---

[15] *Michelin Tyre Co.* v. *Macfarlane*, 1917 2 S.L.T. 205 (H.L.).
[16] *Robinson* v. *Middleton* (1859) 21 D. 1089. See Lord McLaren's note to Bell, *Comm.*, I., 534.
[17] *Famatina Development Corporation* [1914] 2 Ch. 271; distinguished in *Tomlinson* v. *Liquidators of Scottish Amalgamated Silks*, 1935 S.C. (H.L.) 1.
[17A] See opinion of Lord Justice-Clerk Moncreiff in *White* v. *Munro* (1876) 3 R. 1011.
[17B] *Walker, Donald & Co.* v. *Birrell* (1883) 11 R. 369; *Kennedy* v. *Glass* (1890) 17 R.1085; *Dawson* v. *Fisher* (1900) 2 F. 941; *Howard* v. *Manx Line Co.* [1923] 1 K.B. 110.
[18] *Walker, Donald & Co.*, supra; *Walker, Fraser & Steele* v. *Fraser's Trs.*, 1910 S.C. 222.
[18A] *Van Laun* v. *Neilson* (1904) 6 F. 644.
[19] *Dinesmann* v. *Mair*, 1912, S.L.T. 217.
[19A] *Dudley Bros.* v. *Barnet*, 1937 S.C. 632. The House of Lords in an English case seems to have taken another view, but the Scottish decision seems preferable. See *Luxor (Eastbourne)* v. *Cooper* [1941] A.C. 108.
[20] Bell, *Prin.*, § 1445; and see, as to lien, Rights in Security, Ch. XX., § 28, et seq.

undertake liabilities or make payments for his principal, and who in the course
of his employment comes into possession of property belonging to his
principal over which he has power of control and disposal, is entitled, in the
first place, to be indemnified for the moneys he has expended or the loss he
has incurred, and, in the second place, to retain such properties as come into
his hands in his character of agent."[21] Proof that a general lien is recognised in
the particular branch of agency is not required.[22] But the factor on an estate
has no general lien, unless he happens to be a solicitor;[23] and it is doubtful
whether an accountant could assert anything more than a special lien on the
plea that the particular work on which his claim was based was of the nature
of agency.[24]

9. Fiduciary Character of Agency.—Agency is a contract involving a
fiduciary relationship, and therefore an agent is bound to account to his
principal for any incidental advantage which, without the knowledge of the
principal, he has obtained from his position as agent. So a director must
account to the company for any benefit which he has received from a
promoter, even although it cannot be shown that the company has suffered
any loss.[25] Where an agent employed to sell a ship but unable to find a seller
on the cash terms the principal demanded, purchased it himself, having
received an offer of a higher price although on less advantageous cash terms
which he did not disclose to the principal, it was held that he must account to
the principal for the profit he made on the transaction.[26] The rule so far rests
on principles of trust that the agent's liability is measured by the gain he has
made, and not by the loss, if any, which the principal has sustained[27]; but it
has been held in England, in the case of a secret commission, that the legal
position of the principal was that of a creditor, and not that of a beneficiary.
So in the bankruptcy of the agent the principal could rank only as a creditor,
not as a beneficiary for whom the agent held money in trust.[28] There is no
implied condition of contract between agent and principal, at least where the
contract is constituted in writing, that the agent shall not without the
permission of his principal act, even in an outside matter, in such a way as to
bring his interests into conflict with those of his principal.[28A]

10. Secret Commissions.—An agent employed to introduce business is not
entitled, without the knowledge and consent of his principal, to take any
commission from the party with whom he deals. The principal's consent may
be presumed if the principal gave no payment, and if the agent's work was of

---

[21] *Glendinning* v. *Hope*, 1911 S.C. (H.L.) 73, per Lord Kinnear at p. 78.
[22] *Glendinning*, supra (stockbroker).
[23] *Macrae* v. *Leith*, 1913 S.C. 901. As to the lien of a solicitor, see Rights in Security, Ch. XX,
supra, § 33.
[24] See *Findlay* v. *Waddell*, 1910 S.C. 670.
[25] *Henderson* v. *Huntingdon Copper Co.* (1877) 5 R. (H.L.) 1; *Boston Deep Fishing Co.* v. *Ansell*
(1888) 39 Ch. D. 339; *Jubilee Cotton Mills* v. *Lewis* [1924] A.C. 958.
[26] *De Bussche* v. *Alt* (1878) 8 Ch. D. 286. See also *Graham* v. *Paton*, 1917 S.C. 203.
[27] *Ronaldson* v. *Drummond & Reid* (1881) 8 R. 956.
[28] *Lister* v. *Stubbs* (1890) 45 Ch.D. 1.
[28A] *Lothian* v. *Jenolite*, 1969 S.C. 111.

a character not generally done gratuitously.[29] But a custom of trade, not known to the principal, is no defence for a secret commission.[30] Where an agent is proved to have received a secret commission the following civil consequences ensue:—The principal may dismiss the agent from his employment, and, as a creditor, recover the amount of the commission from him.[31] He may also, whether he has settled with the agent or not, recover damages from the party who gave the secret commission, on the ground that such an act amounts to a civil wrong.[32] The agent forfeits all claim to a commission (which the principal, if he has already paid it, may recover) for the particular transaction in question,[33] but not the right to his commission on other transactions in which he acted honestly.[34] The principal, on discovering that his agent has been bribed, may refuse to carry out the contract, and if, in the case of sale, he has made a deposit, he may recover it.[35] As the agent and the party who offers a secret commission are engaged in an illegal transaction, the agent, whether the promise of the bribe has influenced his conduct or not, cannot recover it by action.[36]

11. Prevention of Corruption Acts.—By the Prevention of Corruption Act 1906[37] it is a criminal offence for an agent corruptly to accept or obtain, or to agree to accept or attempt to obtain, any gift or consideration as an inducement or reward for doing or forbearing to do, or for having done or forborne to do, any act in relation to his principal's affairs or business, or for showing favour or disfavour to any person in relation to his principal's affairs or business. Conversely, any person who corruptly gives or offers any gift or consideration to an agent is guilty of an offence under the Act. Increased penalties are provided by the Prevention of Corruption Act 1916[38] where the corruption involves a Government contract or a contract with a public body. In these cases if a gift has been made to a person in the employment of a Government department or public body by one who holds or is seeking a contract, it is held to have been given corruptly unless the contrary is proved. For the purposes of the Prevention of Corruption Acts, the term "agent" is defined as including any person employed or acting for another, and this has been held to include a policeman.[39] But members of a Licensing Court are not "agents" of the Court.[39A]

12. Sale or Purchase between Agent and Principal.—An agent, employed to buy, is not entitled, without the principal's knowledge, to supply his own

[29] *Great Western Insurance Co.* v. *Cunliffe* (1874) L.R. 9 Ch. 525.
[30] *Ronaldson* v. *Drummond & Reid* (1881) 8 R. 956.
[31] *Ronaldson,* supra; *Powell & Thomas* v. *Jones* [1905] 1 K.B. 11.
[32] *Mayor of Salford* v. *Lever* [1891] 1 Q.B. 168.
[33] *Andrews* v. *Ramsay* [1903] 2 K.B. 635.
[34] *Graham* v. *United Turkey Red Co.,* 1922 S.C. 533.
[35] *Shipway* v. *Broadwood* [1899] 1 Q.B. 369; *Alexander* v. *Webber* [1922] 1 K.B. 642.
[36] *Harrington* v. *Victoria Graving Dock Co.* (1878) 3 Q.B.D. 549.
[37] 6 Edw. VII, c. 34.
[38] 6 & 7 Geo. V, c. 64.
[39] *Graham* v. *Hart,* 1908 S.C. (J.) 26.
[39A] *Copeland* v. *Johnston,* 1967 S.L.T. (Sh.Ct.) 28.

goods. A custom of a particular trade, not known to the principal, will afford no justification.[40] Thus if an agent, employed by several persons to buy goods, or shares, purchases a sufficient quantity to meet all his orders, and allocates to each principal the amount he has ordered at an average price, he is selling his own property instead of buying for his principal, and the latter is not bound by the contract.[41]

It is not necessarily illegal for an agent to purchase property belonging to his principal, even without disclosing the fact that he is the purchaser.[42] But such a transaction cannot stand if the agent were employed to sell the property in question; and a law agent must disclose to his client that he is the purchaser.[43]

13. Delegation.—It is a question depending on the nature of the employment in each particular case whether an agent has any implied power to delegate his work. The maxim "delegatus non potest delegare" is only a general presumption.[44] If the circumstances are such that delegation was permissible the sub-agent and the principal are brought into contractual relations, both in respect of the liability of the principal to pay for the services rendered, and in the application of the rule that no one in the position of an agent can obtain any secret advantage or commission.[45] Failure on the part of the sub-agent to carry out his duties in the proper way will infer the liability of the original agent.[46]

14. Termination of the Contract.—In most respects the rules applicable to the termination of the contract of agency are the same as in other contracts of employment.[47]

15. Mandate in Interest of Mandatory.—If a mandate is given to do something in the mandatory's own interest it is known as a procuratory in rem suam (or, in English law, as an authority coupled with an interest), and differs from other mandates in being irrevocable without the mandatory's consent. So it was held that a cheque, when granted for value, was a mandate to the payee to draw the money in his own interest and therefore, when presented at the bank, constituted a completed assignation of any funds standing at the drawer's credit.[48] And if an application for shares in a company is given to one who has an interest in the shares being allotted the applicant is not entitled to withdraw his application.[49]

[40] *Robinson* v. *Mollett* (1874) L.R. 7 (H.L.) 802.
[41] *Maffett* v. *Stewart* (1887) 14 R. 506.
[42] See Gloag, *Contract* (2nd ed.), pp. 522-3.
[43] *McPherson's Trs.* v. *Watt* (1877) 5 R. (H.L.) 9.
[44] *Robertson* v. *Beatson*, 1908 S.C. 921; *Black* v. *Cornelius* (1879) 6 R. 581; *Knox & Robb* v. *Scottish Garden Suburb Co.*, 1913 S.C. 872.
[45] *De Bussche* v. *Alt* (1878) 8 Ch.D. 286.
[46] *Mackersy* v. *Ramsay, Bonar & Co.* (1843) 2 Bell's App. 30.
[47] Employment, Ch. XXII, § 21, supra.
[48] *British Linen Co.* v. *Carruthers* (1883) 10 R. 923.
[49] *Premier Briquette Co.* v. *Gray*, 1922 S.C. 329; *Carmichael's Case* [1896] 2 Ch. 643.

16. Obligation to Furnish Agent with Work.—Some difficult questions are raised when an agent is appointed for a definite period, and his remuneration is to be by commission. Does the appointment imply an obligation on the part of the principal to continue his business in order that the agent may have an opportunity of earning a commission? If the agency has been in any way paid for, as where the agent subscribes for shares in a company by which he is engaged, there is a strong though not conclusive presumption that an obligation not to discontinue business voluntarily is implied.[50] If no payment has been made for the agency the general rule of construction is that the agent takes his chance of getting employment, and cannot complain if his employer discontinues or transfers his business.[51] If, however, the contract contains an obligation to employ the agent,[52] or to execute any orders which he may be able to obtain,[53] an obligation not to discontinue the business voluntarily may be implied. An appointment as sole selling agent does not preclude a sale by the principal himself, unless the terms of the contract amount to sale and not agency.[54]

17. Contracts with Third Parties.—When an agent, in pursuance of his authority, enters into a contract with a third party, the question as to the rights and liabilities thence arising depends materially on the method by which the agent has contracted. He may contract (1) as agent for a particular principal; (2) as an agent, but without disclosing for whom he is acting; (3) ostensibly as a principal, without disclosing the fact of agency.

18. Contracts where Principal Disclosed.—In the first case, where the agent names his principal, the general rule is that the principal alone is the contracting party, and that the agent is under no liability and has no title to sue on the contract.[55] The other party to the contract cannot, in respect of a debt arising out of it, plead compensation on a debt due to him by the agent— a rule which holds even if the name of the principal has not been disclosed,[56] but yields to proof of a custom of trade known to all the parties.[57] Payment to the agent is valid if the agent had authority to receive it, or if the nature of the agency was such as to involve ostensible authority to receive payment. So far as a general rule can be stated, it would appear that if an agent is in possession of goods the buyer may assume that he has authority to receive payment of the price; if he is merely a broker or traveller employed to take orders,

---

[50] *Galbraith* v. *Arethusa Shipping Co.* (1896) 23 R. 1011; *Ogden* v. *Nelson* [1905] A.C. 109.
[51] *Patmore* v. *Cannon* (1892) 19 R. 1004; *State of California Co.* v. *Moore* (1895) 22 R. 562; *Rhodes* v. *Forwood* (1876) 1 App.Cas. 256; *French* v. *Leeston Shipping Co.* [1922] 1 A.C. 451. Gloag, *Contract* (2nd ed.), 294.
[52] *Turner* v. *Goldsmith* [1891] 1 Q.B. 544.
[53] *Reigate* v. *Union Manufacturing Co.* [1918] 1 K.B. 592.
[54] *Bentall* v. *Vicary* [1931] 1 K.B. 253; *Lamb* v. *Goring Brick Co.* [1932] 1 K.B. 710.
[55] See Bell, *Comm.*, I., 540, Lord McLaren's note. See, as illustration, *McIvor* v. *Roy*, 1970 S.L.T. (Sh.Ct.) 58.
[56] *Matthews* v. *Auld & Guild* (1874) 1 R. 1224.
[57] *Sweeting* v. *Pearce* (1861) 9 C.B. (N.S.) 534.

without possession of the goods, a payment to the agent, if by him misapplied, leaves the buyer liable to the principal.[58]

19. Liability of Agent.—While the general rule is that an agent who is acting within his authority and who names his principal incurs no liability, there are exceptional cases in which that rule does not hold.

If the contract is in writing, and the obligations under it are ex facie undertaken by the agent, he incurs personal liability even although the other party may have known that he was dealing with an agent, and may have known who the principal was.[59] So where A undertook to send a transfer of shares for signature it was held that it was incompetent to prove by parole evidence that he was merely an agent, and that this was known to the party with whom he dealt.[60] And where heritage was sold on behalf of a named client by a firm of solicitors who gave a letter of obligation to the purchaser's solicitors, undertaking to produce certain writs relating to the heritage within a specified period, the seller's solicitors were held personally liable when they failed to produce the writs.[61] Any qualification of the liability the agent has apparently undertaken must appear from the terms of the writing.[62] Apart from cases of bills of exchange or promissory notes,[63] a signature "as agent" or "on behalf of" a principal, named or unnamed, will be sufficient to negative personal liability.[64]

With the exception of the case where an agent acts on behalf of a British Government department,[65] or a foreign Government[66] (where, though there may be no action against the principal, the agent is not personally liable) an agent incurs personal liability if the principal from whom he has received his authority, and on whose behalf he ostensibly contracts, is an unincorporated body which cannot be sued, such as a congregation,[67] or a club.[68] The same rule holds where an agent contracts on behalf of a company not yet formed.[69] An auctioneer acting for a disclosed principal may, since he is a mercantile agent having a lien for his charges, himself sue a bidder for the price of goods sold.[70]

20. Agent for Foreign Principal.—If an agent names as his principal a person not subject to the jurisdiction of the British Courts he may be held to

58 *International Sponge Importers* v. *Watt,* 1911 S.C. (H.L.) 57.
59 *Stewart* v. *Shannessy* (1900) 2 F. 1288; *Lindsay* v. *Craig,* 1919 S.C. 139; *Johnston* v. *Little,* 1960 S.L.T. 129.
60 *Lindsay* v. *Craig,* supra.
61 *Johnston* v. *Little,* supra.
62 See *Armour* v. *Duff,* 1912 S.C. 120.
63 See Bills of Exchange, Ch. XXVI, infra, § 7.
64 *Universal Steam Navigation Co.* v. *McKelvie* [1923] A.C. 492; *Stone & Rolfe* v. *Kimber Coal Co.,* 1926 S.C. (H.L.) 45; *McLean* v. *Stuart,* 1970 S.L.T. (Notes) 77.
65 *Dunn* v. *Macdonald* [1897] 1 Q.B. 555.
66 *Twycross* v. *Dreyfus* (1877) 5 Ch.D. 605.
67 *McMeekin* v. *Easton* (1889) 16 R. 363.
68 *Thomson* v. *Victoria Eighty Club* (1905) 43 S.L.R. 628.
69 *Tinnevelly Sugar Refining Co.* v. *Mirrlees* (1894) 21 R. 1009; *Kelner* v. *Baxter* (1866) L.R. 2 C.P. 174; European Communities Act 1972 (c. 68), s. 9 (2).
70 *MacKenzie* v. *Cormack,* 1950 S.C. 183.

have incurred personal liability. In every case it is a question of fact for the Court to determine what is the intention of the parties to the particular contract. But there is a presumption of fact that the agent himself intends to be bound by the contract, which is stronger in the case where the agent buys for a foreign principal—especially if the payment is stipulated to be immediate, or the credit given is short—and correspondingly weaker where the agent is selling goods to be supplied by a foreign house.[71]

21. Contracts as Agent but Principal Undisclosed.—The legal results of a contract entered into as agent, but without disclosing the name of the principal, is a question on which there is little authority in Scotland. It may often be settled by a custom in a particular market or exchange that brokers deal with others as principals. Where there is no such custom in question it would appear on English authority that as a general rule an agent who does not disclose his principal is to be treated as a party to the contract, but that the general rule may be displaced by the circumstances of the case, and is displaced if the agent purports to sell a specific article. If he acts as buyer he is liable for the price; if he sells unascertained goods he is bound to furnish them.[72] An auctioneer who gives a warranty does not bind himself personally if he discloses the name of the exposer, and was authorised by him;[73] he incurs personal liability if the name of the exposer is not given.[74] In the case of goods in the auction room he impliedly undertakes to deliver them, but not that the purchaser will obtain a good title.[75]

22. Contracts Ostensibly as Principal.—Where an agent contracts ostensibly as principal the result generally is that both principal and agent are liable on the contract, and are entitled to sue upon it.[76] But it has been suggested that for the principal to be entitled to sue, the contract must be assignable.[77] It is no answer to an action or counter-claim by the agent for damages for breach of the contract that he personally has suffered no loss; he may sue on behalf of his principal.[78] Similarly, if the principal discloses himself and sues on the agent's contract he is subject to all the pleas which could have been maintained against the agent.[79] The other party to the contract may plead compensation on a debt due by the agent, if that debt were incurred before he had notice of the existence of the principal.[80] And, on discovering the identity

---

[71] *Millar* v. *Mitchell* (1860) 22 D. 833 (opinion of majority of Whole Court); see also *Bennett* v. *Inveresk Paper Co.* (1891) 18 R. 975; and *Girvin Roper & Co.* v. *Monteith* (1895) 23 R. 129 (both cases in which the foreign principal was undisclosed); cf. *Miller, Gibb & Co.* v. *Smith & Tyrer* [1917] 2 K.B. 141; *Teheran-Europe Co.* v. *S. T. Belton (Tractors)* [1968] 2 Q.B. 545.
[72] See Chitty on *Contracts* (24th ed.), Vol. II., para. 2077, doubting the extent of *Benton* v. *Campbell, Parker & Co.* [1925] 2 K.B. 410.
[73] *Fenwick* v. *Macdonald, Fraser & Co.* (1904) 6 F. 850.
[74] *Ferrier* v. *Dods* (1865) 3 M. 561.
[75] *Benton* v. *Campbell, Parker & Co.* [1925] 2 K.B. 410.
[76] Bell, *Comm.*, I, 540, Lord McLaren's note.
[77] Gloag, *Contract* (2nd ed.), pp. 128-9.
[78] *Craig* v. *Blackater*, 1923 S.C. 472; *James Laidlaw & Sons* v. *Griffin*, 1968 S.L.T. 278.
[79] *Bennett* v. *Inveresk Paper Co.* (1891) 18 R. 975.
[80] *Wester Moffat Colliery Co.* v. *Jeffrey*, 1911 S.C. 346; *Greer* v. *Downs Supply Co.* [1927] 2 K.B. 28.

of the principal, he may sue him, and is not adequately met by the defence
that the principal has already made payment to the agent.[81]

23. Election between Agent and Principal.—The liability of principal or
agent, in the case where an agent has contracted ostensibly as principal, is
alternative, and not joint and several. The other party to the contract must at
some time elect whether he will hold the principal or the agent as his debtor,
and his election when once made is final. Election implies knowledge of the
right to elect, and therefore nothing done before the existence of the principal
is discovered can amount to election of the agent as debtor. It does not
necessarily amount to election that the agent has been debited,[82] or even that
an action for payment has been raised against him,[83] after the principal has
been disclosed. But a decree against either party even although it be a decree
in absence and nothing may be recoverable under it, amounts to election and
precludes a claim against the other.[84] The same rule holds in the case of a
ranking in the bankruptcy of either principal or agent,[85] unless perhaps the
claim against the other is expressly reserved.[86] But it will probably not amount
to election if only a claim in bankruptcy has been lodged.[87] Apart from any
definite claim, a party's conduct under a contract may amount to election,[88] a
question largely circumstantial. Where a horse was sold at auction, under
circumstances which made both the auctioneer and the owner responsible for
a warranty which had been given, it was held that the return of the horse to
the owner was a conclusive election to treat him as the party responsible, and
precluded a claim against the auctioneer for repetition of the price.[89]

24. Agent Acting without Authority.—If an agent enters into a contract
without the authority of a principal the latter is generally not bound, whether
the contract is expressly made on his behalf or not.[90] The principal may
become a party to the contract by ratifying the agent's unauthorised act.[91] He
may also incur liability under the contract if the agent's act was within his
ostensible, though not within his actual, authority. Liability on the ground of
ostensible authority cannot arise unless there was some prior contractual
relationship between the agent and the party sued as principal, or in
circumstances where it can be established that the agent has been held out as
possessing authority. If A, wholly unconnected with B, professes to contract
on B's behalf, ratification of A's act is the only ground on which B can be held

---

81 *Irvine* v. *Watson* (1880) 5 Q.B.D. 414.
82 *Stevenson* v. *Campbell* (1836) 14 S. 562.
83 *Meier* v. *Kuchenmeister* (1881) 8 R. 642; *Clarkson Booker* v. *Andjel* [1964] 2 Q.B. 775.
84 *Craig* v. *Blackater*, 1923 S.C. 472; *Morel* v. *Earl of Westmoreland* [1904] A.C. 11; *Moore* v.
   Flanagan [1920] 1 K.B. 919.
85 *Scarf* v. *Jardine* (1882) 7 App.Cas. 345. Contrast a case of joint and several liability, *Morton's
   Trs.* v. *Robertson's Judicial Factor* (1892) 20 R. 72.
86 *Black* v. *Girdwood* (1885) 13 R. 243.
87 See opinions in *Black* v. *Girdwood*, supra.
88 *Ferrier* v. *Dods* (1865) 3 M. 561; *Lamont, Nisbet & Co.* v. *Hamilton*, 1907 S.C. 628.
89 *Ferrier* v. *Dods* (1865), supra.
90 As to the agent's liability, see § 30.
91 Supra, § 3.

to be liable under the contract. Even if the agent's act was wholly without authority, actual or ostensible, the principal might nevertheless be liable to the third party on the principle of recompense, i.e. to the extent of the principal's enrichment.[92]

25. Ostensible Authority.—If one party so behaves that the reasonable inference is that he has authorised another to act for him he may incur liability, though in a question between them there may be no contract, or a contract of a different kind.[93] Thus liability for debts may be incurred by a party who allows himself to be held out as a partner in a firm, though in a question with the other member or members of that firm he would be under no liability.[94]

The usual cases of ostensible authority arise—(1) where authority has been conferred, but has been withdrawn; (2) where limited authority has been given and has been exceeded.

26. Original Authority Withdrawn.—Where a party has authorised another to act as his agent and has withdrawn his authority he is bound to give notice of the fact of withdrawal, and if he fails to do so, he will be liable on contracts which the agent may make with parties who deal with him in the belief that the authority is still in force. Notice by advertisement is sufficient in a question with parties who had no prior dealings with the agent; with those who had, some specific notice is required.[95] The general rule is well established, and, in the case of a partner retiring from a firm, is now statutory.[96] It has been illustrated in cases where it has been held that if a wife or housekeeper has been allowed to deal with tradesmen, the husband or employer remains liable until the revocation of authority is made known.[97]

27. Authority Exceeded.—In the case of an agent who has some authority, but has exceeded it, a distinction is recognised between general and special agents. The former are persons who are employed either, as in the case of a factory and commission, to transact all the business of the principal, or, in the case of the master of a ship or a solicitor, to transact all the business of some particular kind. The latter are persons who are authorised for some special occasion or act. In the former case third parties are entitled to assume in the absence of notice to the contrary, that the agent possesses the powers which are usually conferred in agency of the particular kind; in the latter case there is no presumption of any authority beyond that which has been actually given.[98] But it may often be difficult to determine to which class a particular

---

[92] *Commercial Bank of Scotland* v. *Biggar,* 1958 S.L.T. (Notes) 46. See also generally Quasi-Contract, Ch. XIV, supra, §§ 4–8.
[93] See *Hayman* v. *American Cotton Oil Co.* (1907) 45 S.L.R. 207.
[94] *Brember* v. *Rutherford* (1901) 4 F. 62.
[95] Bell, *Prin.,* § 228; *North of Scotland Bank* v. *Behn Möller & Co.* (1881) 8 R. 423.
[96] Partnership Act 1890, s. 36.
[97] *Dewar* v. *Nairne,* 1804 Hume 340; *Ferguson & Lillie* v. *Stephen* (1864) 2 M. 804.
[98] Bell, *Prin.,* § 219.

case belongs. The law may be illustrated by reference to the ostensible authority of a solicitor, and of a mercantile agent.

28. Ostensible Authority of Solicitor.—A solicitor has ostensible authority to receive payment of a sum decerned for in an action which he has been employed to conduct,[99] or to receive payments for shares which he has been employed to sell.[1] He has no such authority to receive payment of the principal sum due under a bond,[2] nor to discharge a bond, or place it in the custody of the debtor.[3] There is no ostensible authority to bind the client to any contract, e.g. a lease,[4] or a bank overdraft.[5] The solicitor of a trust has no authority to have a trustee or executor registered as a shareholder in a company.[6] Employed to purchase lands or to arrange a heritable security, a solicitor has implied authority to authorise a search of the records for incumbrances, and has been held liable to his client for failure to do so.[7] In the conduct of litigation counsel have a very wide authority to bind their client to any step in process, and the solicitor has an implied authority to follow counsel's directions.[8] Where counsel is not employed, a solicitor has ostensible authority to take any ordinary step in procedure, but not to appeal to a higher Court,[9] nor to grant delay in the execution of diligence,[10] nor to compromise an action, [11] nor to refer a question to the oath of the opposite party.[12]

29. Ostensible Authority in Commercial Agency: Factors Acts.—In commercial agency there is a general distinction between a factor and a broker, the former being a party entrusted with the possession of goods or documents of title to goods, the latter being a mere intermediary, without possession.[13] The ostensible authority of a broker depends largely on the rules of the particular market or exchange in which he deals, though it would seem that no usage will justify a broker, employed to buy, in supplying commodities or shares belonging to himself.[14] The ostensible powers of a factor, or mercantile agent, have, since 1834, been extended and defined by a series of statutes known as the Factors Acts. By the existing Act (Factors Act 1889, extended to Scotland by the Factors (Scotland) Act 1890) a mercantile agent, who is in possession of goods or of documents of title with the consent of the owner, has ostensible authority to sell or pledge them, and any sale, pledge or other disposition

---

[99] *Smith* v. *North British Ry.* (1850) 12 D. 795.
[1] *Pearson & Scott* (1878) 9 Ch.D. 198.
[2] *Peden* v. *Graham* (1907) 15 S.L.T. 143.
[3] *Bowie's Trs.* v. *Watson*, 1913 S.C. 326.
[4] *Danish Dairy Co.* v. *Gillespie*, 1922 S.C. 656.
[5] *Commercial Bank of Scotland* v. *Biggar*, 1958 S.L.T. (Notes) 46.
[6] *Smith* v. *City of Glasgow Bank* (1879) 6 R. 1017.
[7] *Fearn* v. *Gordon & Craig* (1893) 20 R. 352.
[8] *Batchelor* v. *Pattison & Mackersy* (1876) 3 R. 914; *Duncan* v. *Salmond* (1874) 1 R. 329; Begg, *Law Agents* (2nd ed.), p. 95.
[9] *Goodall* v. *Bilsland*, 1909 S.C. 1152.
[10] *Cameron* v. *Mortimer* (1872) 10 M. 817.
[11] *Cormie* v. *Grigor* (1862) 24 D. 985; (1863) 1 M. 357.
[12] *Hardie* v. *Allen*, 1709 M. 12248.
[13] See Bell, *Comm.*, I, 505.
[14] *Robinson* v. *Mollett* (1875) L.R. 7 (H.L.) 802; *Maffett* v. *Stewart* (1887) 14 R. 506.

(provided, in the case of pledge, that it is not for an antecedent debt of the mercantile agent[15]) to anyone who takes in good faith and for value, is as valid as if the mercantile agent had the express authority of his principal.[16] It has been held in England that in the case of a sale or pledge under these conditions the purchaser takes a statutory title, although there may be a custom in the particular trade that agents have no authority to sell or pledge.[17] A pledge of the documents of title to goods (e.g. a bill of lading, dock warrant or delivery order) is, if made by a mercantile agent, deemed to be a pledge of the goods, and, probably, gives an instant right which does not require completion by intimation to the custodier of the goods or any form of delivery.[18] In the case of property other than goods or documents of title an agent in possession of negotiable securities has ostensible authority to pledge them. So a bank, taking securities from a stockbroker, is entitled to assume, in the absence of information to the contrary, that he has the authority of his clients to pledge them, though not that he has any authority to subject them to a lien for his own debit balance.[19] In the exceptional case of indicia of title other than documents of title to goods or negotiable instruments, it has been held in England that mere possession gives no ostensible title to dispose of them, but that if an agent has actual authority to pledge them the pledge is good though the authority be exceeded.[20]

30. Liability of Agent Exceeding his Authority.—Where a party contracts ostensibly as agent but in excess of his actual or ostensible authority, and with the result that no principal is bound by the contract, he will as a rule, incur personal liability, but the nature and extent of that liability will depend on the circumstances of the case. If the contract is made professedly on behalf of a non-existent principal, as where contracts are made on behalf of a company which is not yet formed, the actual contracting party is liable to carry out the contract and is treated as a party to it.[21] The same rule holds where the nominal principal is a body unable to bind itself by contract, with the exception of the case of a contract on behalf of a government.[22] Where the principal, though in existence and able to give authority, has in fact not done so, the agent is not a party to the contract. If his conduct was fraudulent he will be liable in damages for fraud. If he honestly thought he had the principal's authority, as where an auctioneer, by mere mistake, sold a horse which was not for sale,[23] he will incur liability on the theory that an agent impliedly warrants that he has the authority of the principal whom he names, and is liable in damages for breach of that warranty if it turns out that he has

[15] s. 4.
[16] See also Sale of Goods, Ch. XVII, supra, § 20. As illustration, see *Astley Industrial Trust* v. *Miller* [1968] 2 All E.R. 36.
[17] *Oppenheimer* v. *Attenborough* [1908] 1 K.B. 221.
[18] Factors Act 1890, s. 3. See *Inglis* v. *Robertson & Baxter* (1898) 25 R. (H.L.) 70.
[19] *National Bank* v. *Dickie's Tr.* (1895) 22 R. 740; *London Joint Stock Bank* v. *Simmons* [1892] A.C. 201.
[20] *Fry* v. *Smellie* [1912] 3 K.B. 282 (share certificates with blank transfers).
[21] *Kelner* v. *Baxter* (1866) L.R. 2 C.P. 174; European Communities Act 1979 (c. 68), s. 9 (2).
[22] Supra, § 19.
[23] *Anderson* v. *Croall* (1903) 6 F. 153.

no authority.[24] The damages are measured by the loss the other party has sustained in not having the obligation of the principal. Thus where an agent sells, without authority, he is liable for the difference between the price paid and the actual value of the article.[25] But where a joiner had done work on the instructions of an agent who, as it turned out, had no authority, but the principal named was a company which was insolvent and had no assets, it was held that as the obligation of the company was valueless, the joiner had lost nothing by the want of it, and therefore could recover no damages from the agent for breach of his implied warranty.[26]

The rule as to the implied warranty given by an agent does not apply where the question of the agent's authority is one of law, and the other party has the means of judging for himself what that authority is. So directors of a company which had no power to borrow were not liable on debentures which they honestly but mistakenly issued, the question as to the power to borrow being one of law. But they did incur liability where the debentures were in excess of a borrowing limit, the question whether that limit had been reached being one of fact.[27]

---

[24] *Collen* v. *Wright* (1857) 8 E. & B. 647; *Firbank's Exrs.* v. *Humphreys* (1886) 18 Q.B.D. 54.
[25] *Anderson* v. *Croall,* supra. See also *Salvesen* v. *Rederi Nordstjernan* (1905) 7 F. (H.L.) 101.
[26] *Irving* v. *Burns,* 1915 S.C. 260.
[27] *Beattie* v. *Lord Ebury* (1874) L.R. 7 H.L. 102; *Firbank's Exrs.* v. *Humphreys* (1886) 18 Q.B.D. 54. See now, however, European Communities Act 1972 (c. 68), s. 9 (1).

CHAPTER XXIV

PARTNERSHIP

Lindley, *Partnership* (13th ed., 1971); Pollock, *Partnership* (15th ed., 1952); Underhill, *Partnership* (10th ed., 1975); Miller, *The Law of Partnership in Scotland* (1973).

1. Statutory Law.—The general law of partnership has been codified by the Partnership Act 1890 (53 & 54 Vict., c. 39). Except in minor details it made no change in the existing law. It has no provisions with regard to bankruptcy or goodwill.[1] There is a general provision that the rules of common law prevail except so far as they are inconsistent with the express provisions of the Act (s. 46). Further legislative provisions on the subject have been made by the Limited Partnerships Act 1907, and the Registration of Business Names Act 1916.

2. Joint-Adventure.—It would appear that under the provisions of the Act there is no general distinction between an ordinary partnership and a partnership for one particular transaction (known as a joint-adventure[2]) except that in the latter case the implied authority of each partner is more limited, and further that, in the absence of any provision to the contrary, the partnership is dissolved by the completion of the transaction in question.[3] A joint adventure is simply a species of the genus partnership, differentiated by its limited purpose and duration (which necessarily affect the extent of the rights and liabilities flowing from the relationship), but in all other essential respects indistinguishable from partnership.[4]

3. Definition.—Partnership is defined (s. 1) as, "the relation which subsists between persons carrying on a business in common with a view of profit." "Business" includes every trade, occupation or profession.[5] The relationship of the members of a company registered under the Companies Acts, or incorporated under a private Act, royal charter or letters patent, is expressly excluded. From the definition it is clear that there must be at least two persons to form a partnership. A business carried on by one person alone, though in a name indicating a firm, is not a partnership, though it is probably included under the term "firm" in certain sections of the Act.[6] Associations formed for purposes other than profit (e.g. clubs) do not fall within the Act.[7]

[1] See, as to Goodwill, Moveable Property—Incorporeal, Ch. XXXVIII, infra, § 27.
[2] See, as to joint adventure, Bell, *Prin.,* § 392; *Comm.,* II, 538; and, as distinct from a contract of service, *Parker* v. *Walker,* 1961 S.L.T. 252.
[3] s. 32. See § 27, infra.
[4] *Mair* v. *Wood,* 1948 S.C. per Lord President Cooper, at p. 86.
[5] s. 45.
[6] E.g. ss. 14, 17, 18.
[7] As to such associations, see Law of Associations, Ch. XLV., infra, §§ 2-4.

4. Limitation of Number of Partners.—By sections 429 and 434 of the Companies Act 1948 no partnership consisting of more than ten persons, if for the purpose of carrying on the business of banking, or of more than twenty persons, if for the purpose of carrying on any other business which has for its object the acquisition of gain, can be formed unless it is registered as a company or incorporated by royal charter, letters patent, or Act of Parliament. By sections 119 and 120 of the Companies Act 1967 partnerships formed for the purpose of banking may now consist of a maximum of 20 persons, and all limits to the number of partners are removed in respect of partnerships of practising solicitors, accountants, and members of a recognised stock exchange. In addition, the Department of Trade now has power to remove the limit in relation to any other form of partnership so specified. These, broadly, now include surveyors, auctioneers, valuers, estate agents, land agents, estate managers, actuaries, consulting engineers and architects.[8] An unincorporated partnership which exceeds these limits is an illegal association. It cannot sue, and each member, as a partner, is responsible for all its debts.[9] A partnership originally within the statutory limits becomes illegal when, by the admission of new partners, they are exceeded.[10]

5. Constitution of Partnership.—A partnership may be constituted orally, or in writing, or may be inferred from the relationship of the parties. It is a question of their intention, to be gathered from the whole circumstances of the case.[11] But, in questions of liability for the debts of a business, a man may be held to be a partner, and therefore liable, if he be judged to have intended to assume the position, in relation to that business, from which the law infers partnership, although he may not have regarded himself as a partner, or may have expressly disclaimed that position.[12] So a partnership may be held to have been created when the question is with creditors, although, on the same facts, it would be held that there was no partnership in a question between the alleged partners themselves.[13] The question whether the relationship of parties involves partnership, and consequent liability for debts, where there is no express agreement for partnership, has generally arisen in relation to agreements to share profits. The tendency of the earlier authorities to hold, on very inadequate reasoning, that every one who in any way shared in the profits of a business must be liable for all its debts,[14] was checked by the decision in *Cox* v. *Hickman*,[15] where it was held that a committee of creditors, who had appointed a manager to carry on their debtor's business, with a provision that all profits should go to meet their debts, were not liable as partners in the

---

[8] See the Partnerships (Unrestricted Size) No. 1 Regulations 1968, and Nos 2, 3 and 4 Regulations all in 1970.
[9] *Shaw* v. *Benson* (1883) 11 Q.B.D. 563; *Greenberg* v. *Cooperstein* [1926] 1 Ch. 657.
[10] *Shaw* v. *Simmons* (1883) 12 Q.B.D. 117.
[11] See *Morrison* v. *Service* (1879) 6 R. 1158.
[12] *McCosh* v. *Brown's Tr.* (1899) 1 F. (H.L.) 86; *Adam* v. *Newbigging* (1888) 13 App. Cas. 308, per Lord Halsbury L.C. at p. 315; *Charlton* v. *Highet*, 1923 S.L.T. 493.
[13] Bell, *Comm.*, II, 511; *Clippens Co.* v. *Scott* (1876) 3 R. 651; *Walker* v. *Hirsch* (1884) 27 Ch.D. 460.
[14] See Bell, *Comm.*, II, 511.
[15] 1860. 8 H.L.C. 268.

business. A statute of 1865 (28 & 29 Vict., c. 86), commonly known as Bovill's Act, dealing with the inference of partnership to be drawn from certain specified relationships, was repealed by the Partnership Act, but was substantially re-enacted by section 2. The section is printed below.[16] In the last two cases (d and e) the lender or seller of goodwill is, in the event of bankruptcy, postponed to all other creditors, whether the contract was in writing or not.[17]

The statutory rules, and the decisions, seem to justify the following statements:—(1) An agreement may create a partnership in a question between the parties themselves.[18] (2) An agreement to share both profits and losses necessarily involves partnership.[19] (3) A lender who stipulates for nothing more than a share in the profits is not a partner.[20] (4) A right to a share in profits, and in addition a right, absolute or conditional, to receive or dispose of the partnership assets, involves partnership.[21] (5) Where a right to a share in the profits is coupled with a power to control the method by which the business is carried on, it is a question depending upon the degree of control whether partnership is involved or not.[22] (6) Creditors appointing a manager to carry on their debtor's business, under an arrangement by which the profits are to go to meet their debts, are not partners in the business.[23] (7)

[16] 2. RULES FOR DETERMINING EXISTENCE OF PARTNERSHIP.—In determining whether a partnership does or does not exist, regard shall be had to the following rules:

(1) Joint tenancy, tenancy in common, joint property, common property, or part ownership does not of itself create a partnership as to anything so held or owned, whether the tenants or owners do or do not share any profits made by the use thereof.

(2) The sharing of gross returns does not of itself create a partnership, whether the persons sharing such returns have or have not a joint or common right or interest in any property from which or from the use of which the returns are derived.

(3) The receipt by a person of a share of the profits of a business is prima facie evidence that he is a partner in the business, but the receipt of such a share, or of a payment contingent on or varying with the profits of a business, does not of itself make him a partner in the business; and in particular—

   (a) The receipt by a person of a debt or other liquidated amount by instalments or otherwise out of the accruing profits of a business does not of itself make him a partner in the business or liable as such;

   (b) A contract for the remuneration of a servant or agent of a person engaged in a business by a share of the profits of the business does not of itself make the servant or agent a partner in the business or liable as such;

   (c) A person being the widow or child of a deceased partner, and receiving by way of annuity a portion of the profits made in the business in which the deceased person was a partner, is not by reason only of such receipt a partner in the business or liable as such;

   (d) The advance of money by way of loan to a person engaged or about to engage in any business on a contract with that person that the lender shall receive a rate of interest varying with the profits, or shall receive a share of the profits arising from carrying on the business, does not of itself make the lender a partner with the person or persons carrying on the business or liable as such. Provided that the contract is in writing and signed by or on behalf of all the parties thereto;

   (e) A person receiving by way of annuity or otherwise a portion of the profits of a business in consideration of the sale by him of the goodwill of the business is not by reason only of such receipt a partner in the business or liable as such.

[17] s. 3; *Re Fort* [1897] 2 Q.B. 495.
[18] See note 13, supra.
[19] Lindley, *Partnership* (13th ed.), p. 80.
[20] *Laing Bros. Tr.* v. *Low* (1896) 23 R. 1105. This may be doubtful if the agreement was not in writing.
[21] *McCosh* v. *Brown's Tr.* (1899) 1 F. (H.L.) 86; *Charlton* v. *Highet*, 1923 S.L.T. 493.
[22] *Stewart* v. *Buchanan* (1903) 6 F. 15; *Re Young* [1896] 2 Q.B. 484.
[23] *Cox* v. *Hickman* (1860) 8 H.L.C. 268; *Gosling* v. *Gaskell* [1897] A.C. 575; *Stott* v. *Fender* (1878) 5 R. 1104; *Alna Press* v. *Trends of Edinburgh*, 1969 S.L.T. (Notes) 91.

Persons registered as owners of shares in a ship,[24] or employed on board and remunerated by a share in the earnings,[25] are not, merely from their ownership or their method of remuneration, to be deemed partners.

It is unlawful for a firm consisting of six or more partners (or six or more persons proposing to form themselves into a partnership) to discriminate against a person on the ground of sex or race, in the arrangements they make for offering a position as a partner, or in the terms on which the position is offered, or by refusing to offer the position.[26]

6. Holding Out.—A person who is not a partner may be liable for the debts of a business on the ground that he has, by words or conduct, held himself out as a partner, or knowingly suffered himself to be so held out.[27] A retiring partner does not knowingly suffer himself to be held out merely because the remaining partner uses notepaper belonging to the partnership which, contrary to an arrangement between the partners, has not been destroyed upon the dissolution of the partnership.[28] The liability involved in holding out rests on the principle of personal bar, and is not incurred to persons who have notice of the actual facts. So a trustee in the sequestration of a firm has no title to sue a party alleged to have held himself out as a partner, because he represents all the creditors, some of whom may have had notice.[29] A man may incur liability by holding out either when, having been a partner and known as such, he has retired from the firm without giving notice,[30] or by allowing his name to appear in a business of which he is not a partner.[31] A party whose name is so used without his consent has a title to interdict.[32]

7. Limited Partnerships Act 1907.—This Act[33] makes provision for a partnership with limited liability. Little advantage has been taken of it, as it has been found that its object can be better secured by incorporation as a private company.[34] A limited partnership requires the existence of one or more partners, called general partners, responsible for all debts, and one or more limited partners (who may be corporate bodies), who are liable only to the extent of the amount they have contributed to the firm.[35] To secure this limitation of liability registration with the Registrar of Companies is essential, and an ad valorem duty on the amount contributed by the limited partners

[24] *Sharpe* v. *Carswell,* 1910 S.C. 391.
[25] *Clark* v. *Jamieson,* 1909 S.C. 132; contrast *Scottish Insurance Commissioners* v. *McNaughton,* 1914 S.C. 826.
[26] Sex Discrimination Act 1975 (c. 65), s. 11; Race Relations Act 1976 (c. 74), s. 10.
[27] s. 14 (1).
[28] *Tower Cabinet Co.* v. *Ingram* [1949] 2 K.B. 397.
[29] *Mann* v. *Sinclair* (1879) 6 R. 1078.
[30] Infra, § 15.
[31] See *Brember* v. *Rutherford* (1901) 4 F. 62.
[32] *Walter* v. *Ashton* [1902] 2 Ch. 282.
[33] 7 Edw. VII, c. 24. See, as to the nature of a limited partnership, *Re Barnard* [1932] 1 Ch. 269. See also, generally, Miller, *Partnership,* Ch. XIV.
[34] See Company Law, Ch. XXV., infra § 4.
[35] s. 4

must be paid.[36] An application for registration must state the firm name, the general nature and principal place of business, the full name of each partner, the terms, if any, of the partnership, and the date of commencement, a statement that the partnership is limited, and which are the limited partners.[37] Any change in these particulars must, under penalties exigible from the general partners, also be registered.[38] The limitation in the number of partners applicable to ordinary partnerships applies.[39]

A limited partner has no right to withdraw any portion of the capital he has contributed, and if he does so remains liable for the full amount of the original sum. He may inspect the books but cannot bind the firm, and is not entitled to take part in the management of the business. Should he do so he incurs liability for all debts incurred during the period while he intervened.[40]

The main distinctions between a limited and an ordinary partnership are as follows:—the death or bankruptcy of a limited partner does not dissolve the firm; his insanity is not a ground for an application to the Court for dissolution; only the general partner can wind up the affairs of the firm on its dissolution, unless the Court orders otherwise.[41] But there may be circumstances in which a limited partner will have to apply to the Court to wind up the affairs of the firm, as for instance where the only general partner in the firm dies.[42] In the absence of any agreement to the contrary, the death or bankruptcy of a general partner will dissolve the partnership as to all the partners.[43] Applications for winding up should be made either under the provisions of the Companies Acts,[44] at least where the members of the firm are not fewer than eight,[45] or by the appointment of a judicial factor where, for instance, the assets are so small as to make the more elaborate procedure of a winding-up under the Companies Acts inexpedient.[46]

The relationship between general and limited partners may be settled by their contract, express or implied. In the absence of any such contract the general partners may decide all ordinary matters of business, and may introduce a new partner without the limited partner's consent. A limited partner is not entitled to dissolve the firm by notice.[47]

A limited partner may, with the consent of the general partners, assign his share, when the assignee becomes a limited partner with all the rights of the assigner. Notice of the assignation must be made in the *Gazette*.[48]

8. Registration of Business Names Act 1916.—Before this Act[49] there was

[36] ss. 5, 11.
[37] s. 8.
[38] s. 8.
[39] s. 4, and see supra, § 4.
[40] s. 6 (1).
[41] s. 6 (2) and (3).
[42] See Lindley, *Partnership*, sup. cit., at pp. 813–814.
[43] Miller, p. 602.
[44] Companies Act 1948, s. 398.
[45] When the members are fewer than eight the position is not clear. See Miller at pp. 605–606.
[46] *Muirhead* v. *Borland*, 1925 S.C. 474.
[47] s. 6 (5).
[48] ss. 6 (5), 10.
[49] 6 & 7 Geo. V, c. 58.

no provision, except in the case of limited partnerships, for any public disclosure of the names of persons who carried on business either alone or in partnership. The Act provides for the registration of persons carrying on a business (including a profession), and for the publication of their names in their documents and correspondence. The Companies Act 1947 extended the requirement to limited companies carrying on business under a business name which does not consist of its corporate name without any addition[50] and the Companies Act 1976[51] extended the requirement to every corporation incorporated outside Great Britain having a place of business in Great Britain, and carrying on business under a business name which does not consist of its corporate name without any addition.

Neither registration nor publication is required in the case of a business carried on in a business name which consists of the name of the individual or corporation which is solely concerned, or of all the partners, individual or corporate, or with an addition merely indicating that the business is carried on in succession to a former owner.[52]

In other cases the following particulars must be registered—The business name, one or more; the general nature and principal place of the business; in the case of an individual, his Christian names and surname, any former names, his nationality, his usual residence, and any other business occupation; in the case of a firm, similar particulars as to all the partners; in the case of a corporation, its corporate name and registered office; the date of the commencement of the business, if commenced subsequent to the Act.[53] Any alteration in these particulars must be registered within fourteen days.[54]

Failure in registration involves penalties,[55] and a disability to enforce any contract, either in the business names or otherwise,[56] unless the Court, on application by the defaulters, grants relief on the ground that the failure was accidental or inadvertent, or that, on other grounds, it is just and equitable to grant relief. Ignorance of the Act has been accepted as a ground for relief.[57] Relief may be granted by allowing an amendment of the instance.[58]

Publication is required in all trade catalogues, circulars, show cards and business letters sent to any person within the Commonwealth. In the case of an individual these must set forth his present Christian name (or initials) and surname, any former Christian name or surname, and his nationality if not British. In the case of a firm similar particulars with regard to all partners is required.[59] Failure in publication involves penalties, but it is not provided and would not, it is conceived, be held, that it involves any disability to enforce contracts.

[50] 10 & 11 Geo. VI, c. 47, s. 58. Amended, Companies Act 1948. See s. 456.
[51] c. 69, s. 32.
[52] s. 1.
[53] s. 3.
[54] s. 6.
[55] s. 7.
[56] s. 8; *Daniel* v. *Rogers* [1918] 2 K.B. 228.
[57] *Clydesdale Motor Transport Co., Petrs.*, 1922 S.C. 18; *McLachlan, Petr.*, 1929 S.C. 357.
[58] *John and Francis Anderson* v. *Balnagown Estates Co.*, 1939 S.C. 168.
[59] s. 18.

The fact that the name of any person is or is not registered as a partner in a firm, is not, unless the registration was effected by himself, evidence in any question of his liability for its debts. On application to the Court of Session by any person who conceives that his name should or should not be registered, the register may be amended.[60]

9. Firm: Firm Name.—The Act of 1890 provides (s. 4): "Persons who have entered into partnership with one another are for the purposes of this Act called collectively a firm, and the name under which their business is carried on is called the firm name." The section expressly preserves the rule of the law of Scotland that a firm is a legal personality distinct from the persons who compose it; a principle which is not recognised in the law of England.[61] The recognition of the firm as a separate legal personality, important in many questions, bulks most largely in the rules as to actions and diligence; as to ranking in bankruptcy[62]; and in questions of compensation between debts of the firm and debts of partners.[63]

10. Actions by Firm.—As the firm is a separate legal personality an individual partner has no title to sue for the enforcement of firm obligations. An action by all the partners is good, provided that there is an indication that they are suing for a firm debt.[64] A firm cannot sue for loss of profit arising out of personal injury to a partner caused by the negligence of an outsider.[65] If the firm name be descriptive, e.g. the Antermony Coal Co., it is not a sufficient instance without the addition of the names of three partners, or of all the partners, if less than three.[66] If the firm name consists of the names of individuals, action in the firm name alone is competent, although the names may not be those of the existing partners.[67]

The same rules hold with regard to the method by which a firm may be sued; it is not competent to sue an individual partner, even though the firm be dissolved.[68]

11. Diligence.—When decree has been obtained against a firm, diligence may proceed against any individual partner, without any further judicial procedure, whether he is named in the decree or not.[69] A party who is charged for payment, and is prepared to maintain that he is not a partner, has his remedy by suspension, and may claim damages. A charge against a party who is not a partner is not justified by proof that he is liable for the firm's debts on

---

[60] s. 4.
[61] It is recognised in bankruptcy, *Re Dutton* [1924] 2 Ch. 199.
[62] Infra, § 19.
[63] Extinction of Obligations, Ch. XV, supra, § 14.
[64] *Plotzker* v. *Lucas*, 1907 S.C. 315.
[65] *Gibson* v. *Glasgow Corporation*, 1963 S.L.T. (Notes) 16.
[66] *Antermony Coal Co.* v. *Wingate* (1866) 4 M. 1017. By the Sheriff Courts (Scotland) Act 1907, Rule 11, as amended by the 1913 Act, a firm may sue and be sued in the Sheriff Court by its descriptive name alone.
[67] *Forsyth* v. *Hare* (1834) 13 S. 42; *Brims & Mackay* v. *Pattullo*, 1907 S.C. 1106.
[68] *McNaught* v. *Milligan* (1885) 13 R. 366.
[69] s. 4 (2); *Ewing* v. *McClelland* (1860) 22 D. 1347.

the ground that he has held himself out as a partner.[70] A protested bill, signed by all the partners, and followed by a charge against each of them, is a warrant for poinding the assets of the firm.[71]

12. Authority of Partners.—In matters of contract the authority of any partner to bind the firm may, in a question between the partners themselves, be regulated by the partnership deed. In questions with third parties every partner is an agent of the firm and of the other partners, and his acts in carrying on in the usual way the business of the partnership,[72] and his signature in the firm name to obligatory documents, bind the firm, unless he had in fact no authority and the person with whom he deals knows this or does not know or believe that he is a partner.[73] A partner's admission is evidence against the firm,[74] and notice to any partner who habitually acts in the firm's affairs is notice to the firm, except in the case of a fraud on the firm committed by or with the consent of that partner.[75] The extent of the implied authority of a partner as an agent for the firm depends upon the nature of the business.[76] The firm is not bound by an undertaking in the firm name which is known to be granted in the private interests of the partner. Thus while an obligation to clear the record of burdens on a subject disponed in security is within the implied authority of a partner in a firm of law agents, the firm was not bound by such an obligation when granted by a partner in connection with a loan to himself.[77] And where there are exceptional terms the other party should inquire whether the partner has in fact authority, as where a partner in a firm of builders signed the firm name to a promissory note in terms involving interest at 40 per cent.[78] An obligation in the firm name which is beyond the real or ostensible authority of a partner and is therefore not binding on the firm is binding on the partner as an individual.[79]

13. Liability of Firm for Wrongs.—The firm is liable for any wrongful act or omission of any partner acting in the ordinary course of its business, or with the authority of his co-partners, to the same extent as the partner himself,[80] except that it is not liable to one partner for an injury negligently

---

[70] *Brember* v. *Rutherford* (1901) 4 F. 62.
[71] *Rosslund Cycle Co.* v. *McCreadie,* 1907 S.C. 1208.
[72] *Mann* v. *D'Arcy* [1968] 1 W.L.R. 893; *Mercantile Credit Co.* v. *Garrod* [1962] 3 All E.R. 1103 (sale of car by partner of firm mainly concerned with lock-up garages and repairs held valid, although excluded by term of partnership).
[73] ss. 5, 6.
[74] s. 15.
[75] s. 16. See Miller on *Partnership,* p. 220; *Campbell* v. *McCreath,* 1975 S.L.T. (Notes) 5. As to notice by one partner, in a case of joint tenancy, see *Graham* v. *Stirling,* 1922 S.C. 90; *Walker* v. *Hendry,* 1925 S.C. 855.
[76] Illustrative cases are *Bryan* v. *Butters* (1892) 19 R. 490; *Mains & McGlashan* v. *Black* (1895) 22 R. 329; *Ciceri* v. *Hunter* (1904) 12 S.L.T. 293; *Cooke's Circus* v. *Welding* (1894) 21 R. 339.
[77] *Walker* v. *Smith* (1906) 8 F. 619.
[78] *Paterson Bros.* v. *Gladstone* (1891) 18 R. 403.
[79] *Fortune* v. *Young* 1918 S.C. 1.
[80] s. 10. To act as the secretary of a company is not part of the ordinary business of a firm of law agents, even although the partnership deed provides that any salary thence derived is part of the firm's assets, and therefore the firm is not liable for the fraudulent act of a partner in his capacity as secretary: *New Mining Syndicate* v. *Chalmers,* 1912 S.C. 126. Cf. *Kirkintilloch Equitable Co-op Society* v. *Livingstone,* 1972 S.L.T. 154.

done to him by another partner acting on the firm's behalf.[81] The question whether a partner can act as a servant of his firm has been raised but not decided.[82] Each partner is liable jointly and severally.[83] The firm is also liable when one partner, acting within his apparent authority, receives the money or property of a third party and misapplies it, or when a firm, in the course of its business, receives the money or property of a third party, and it is misapplied by a partner.[84] The firm may also be liable on the ground that it has gratuitously profited by the wrongful act of a partner, as when a partner, obtaining money by fraud, applies it in meeting debts due by the firm.[85] Where a partner who is a trustee improperly employs trust property in the business or on the account of the partnership, the other partners are not liable unless they had notice of the breach of trust, but the trust money can be followed and recovered from the firm if still in its possession or control.[86]

14. Liability of Partners.—Every partner is liable jointly and severally for all the debts of the firm, and the estate of a deceased partner is also liable.[87] As between themselves, a partner who has paid the firm debts is entitled to pro rata relief from the other partners.[88] A partner who has retired does not cease to be liable for all debts or obligations incurred while he was a partner,[89] and no arrangement between him and the other partners is of any avail against creditors. He may avoid liability by an arrangement between himself and the firm as newly constituted, and the creditor.[90] Such an arrangement may be inferred from a course of dealing between the firm as newly constituted and the creditor,[91] but the decisions establish that the inference is not easy, and that acceptance of interest or part-payment from a new firm, or ranking in their bankruptcy, is not sufficient.[92] The acceptance of a bill from the new firm has been held sufficient to discharge a partner who has retired, on the principle that he is a cautioner for the firm, and is discharged by the creditor giving time to the principal debtor.[93]

15. Liability of Retired Partner: Notice.—A partner who has retired and has failed to give adequate notice of the fact may be liable on obligations incurred subsequent to his retirement.[94] A partner who has become bankrupt, or the representatives of one who has died, are not in any event liable for obligations subsequently incurred by the firm, and in these cases no notice is

[81] *Mair* v. *Wood*, 1948 S.C. 83.
[82] *Fife County Council* v. *Minister of National Insurance*, 1947 S.C. 629.
[83] s. 12.
[84] s. 11.
[85] *New Mining Syndicate* v. *Chalmers*, 1912 S.C. 126.
[86] s. 13.
[87] s. 9.
[88] s. 4.
[89] s. 17 (2). See *Welsh* v. *Knarston*, 1973 S.L.T. 66.
[90] s. 17 (3).
[91] s. 17 (3).
[92] *Morton's Trs.* v. *Robertson's Judicial Factor* (1892) 20 R. 72; *Smith* v. *Patrick* (1901) 3 F. (H.L.) 14.
[93] *Goldfarb* v. *Bartlett* [1920] 1 K.B. 639; see also *Rouse* v. *Bradford Banking Co.* [1894] A.C. 586.
[94] s. 36.

required.[95] Similarly, a retired partner who was not known to the person dealing with the firm to be a partner, is not liable for partnership debts contracted after his retirement, and does not have to give notice.[96] This provision includes apparent as well as dormant partners, and operates from the date of the dissolution of the partnership.[97] In other cases the Act provides that a *Gazette* advertisement is notice to all persons who had no prior dealings with the firm.[98] With regard to persons who have had dealings, a mere *Gazette* or newspaper advertisement is not sufficient, unless knowledge of it can be brought home to the particular creditor. Intimation by circular, or by an obvious change in the firm name, is required.[99]

Liability of a partner who has retired but failed to give notice, for obligations subsequently incurred by the firm as re-constituted after his retirement, rests on the principle of holding out or personal bar. It would appear that in Scotland at least it is a joint and several, not an alternative, liability.[1] This proceeds on the principle that as the retired partner by his failure to give notice has held himself out to be a member of the new firm so far as the creditor is concerned, he must be regarded as if he were such a member.[2] But he has a right of relief against the actual members of the new firm.[3]

16. Liability of New Partner.—The Act provides (s. 17 (1)): "A person who is admitted as a partner into an existing firm does not thereby become liable to the creditors of the firm for anything done before he became a partner." Where the whole assets of a going concern are handed over to a new partnership and the business is continued on the same footing as before, the presumption is that the liabilities are taken over with the stock but the presumption may be rebutted if the new partner pays in a large sum as capital and the other partners contribute merely their shares of the going business.[4]

17. Effect of Change in Firm on Contracts.—The Act does not decide the question whether a change in the personnel of a firm has any effect on continuing contracts which involve the element of delectus personae. It is expressly provided that a continuing guarantee or cautionary obligation given either to a firm or to a third person in respect of the transactions of a firm is, in the absence of agreement to the contrary, revoked as to future transactions by any change in the constitution of the firm to which, or of the firm in respect of the transactions of which, the guarantee or obligation was given.[5]

[95] s. 36 (3).
[96] s. 36 (3).
[97] *Tower Cabinet Co.* v. *Ingram* [1942] 2 K.B. 397. See also s. 4, and § 6, *supra*.
[98] s. 36 (2).
[99] Bell, *Prin.*, § 384; *Comm.*, II., 530.
[1] *Black* v. *Girdwood* (1885) 13 R. 243 (in which an English decision to the opposite effect was discussed and disapproved by a majority of the Second Division: but the question was obiter).
[2] *Black* v. *Girdwood*, supra, per Lord Young at p. 249.
[3] *Mann* v. *Sinclair* (1879) 6 R. 1078; *Black* v. *Girdwood*, supra, per Lord Young at p. 249.
[4] *Thomson & Balfour* v. *Boag & Son*, 1936 S.C. 2; See also *Miller* v. *John Finlay MacLeod & Parker*, 1974 S.L.T. 99.
[5] s. 18, re-enacting s. 7 of the Mercantile Law Amendment (Scotland) Act 1856.

Otherwise, the general rule is the same as for the assignability of contracts as a whole.[6] Contracts of service are not dissolved by a mere change in the constitution of the firm of employers,[7] except where by the death of one of the partners the partnership necessarily comes to an end.[8] It has been pointed out that while the conversion of a partnership into a limited company releases all servants from their engagements, the retirement of one of the partners, or the adoption of a new partner, would have no such effect.[9] Where a testator authorised his trustees to invest money in a partnership business, it was held that the authority given did not justify a continuance of the investment after one partner had retired. The decision, however, proceeded on the presumed intention of the testator.[10]

18. Partnership Property.—Money or property originally brought into the partnership stock or acquired on account of the firm, or for the purposes and in the course of the partnership business, becomes partnership property, and must be held exclusively for the purposes of the partnership and in accordance with the partnership agreement.[11] Unless the contrary intention appears, property bought with money belonging to the firm is deemed to have been bought on account of the firm.[12] The interest of each partner is a right to a pro indiviso share of the firm's assets, with the results—(1) that his interest is moveable in his succession, though the property actually held may be heritable;[13] (2) that the proper diligence to attach a partner's interest is arrestment in the hands of the firm, and not adjudication or poinding of the particular assets.[14] The mere contract under which a partner agrees to contribute property to the firm does not complete the firm's title, or remove the property, as a separate asset, from the diligence of the partner's creditors; a conveyance, in the manner appropriate to the particular property in question, is required.[15] Partnership property, with the exception of land held by feudal tenure,[16] may be held in the name of the firm, or in the name of a partner. In the latter case proof that the property is really held for the firm is, under the provisions of the Trusts Act 1696 (Act 1696, c. 25), limited to the writ or oath of the partner.[17] The question of what property was brought into the partnership at the time of its constitution may be decided on parole evidence.[18]

[6] Bell, *Comm.*, II, 525–6; *Alexander* v. *Lowson's Trs.* (1890) 17 R. 571, per Lord Kinnear at p. 575; and Title to Sue, Ch. X., supra, § 18.
[7] *Campbell* v. *Baird* (1827) 5 S. 335.
[8] *Hoey* v. *McEwan & Auld* (1867) 5 M. 814.
[9] *Berlitz School* v. *Duchene* (1903) 6 F. 181, per Lord McLaren at p. 186. See, however, *Garden, Haig Scott & Wallace* v. *Prudential Society,* 1927 S.L.T. 393.
[10] *Smith* v. *Patrick* (1901) 3 F. (H.L.) 14.
[11] s. 20.
[12] s. 21.
[13] s. 22; Bell, *Comm.*, II., 501; *Minto* v. *Kirkpatrick* (1833) 11 S. 632 (legitim).
[14] Erskine, III., 3, 24; *Parnell* v. *Walter* (1889) 16 R. 917.
[15] Bell, *Comm.*, II, 501.
[16] Bell, *Prin.*, § 357 (in which case it should be taken in the name of the partners as trustees for the firm).
[17] *Laird* v. *Laird & Rutherfurd* (1884) 12 R. 294; *Adam* v. *Adam*, 1962 S.L.T. 332. See also Executors, etc. Ch. XLIV., infra, § 15.
[18] *Munro* v. *Stein*, 1961 S.C. 362.

19. Ranking in Bankruptcy.—In bankruptcy the creditors of the firm rank on the firm's estate to the exclusion of the creditors of an individual partner.[19] Contrary to the rule in England, creditors of the firm may also rank on the estate of each individual partner. But where a claim is made on the estate of a partner the trustee in sequestration must put a value on the claim against the firm's estate, deduct it from the amount claimed, and rank the creditor only for the balance.[20]

20. Fiduciary Element in Partnership.—Partnership is a contract which involves fiduciary duties. It has been held in England that if a partner supplies goods to the firm without disclosing that they are his he can make no profit on the transaction.[21] The Act provides that if a partner, without the consent of the others, carries on any business of the same nature as, and competing with, that of the firm he must account for and pay over to the firm all profits made in that business.[22] Each partner must also account to the firm for any benefit derived by him without the consent of the others from any transaction concerning the partnership, or from any use by him of the firm property, name or business connections.[23] This rule applies also, in the case of a firm dissolved by the death of a partner, to any transactions either by the surviving partners, or by the representatives of the deceased partner, before the affairs of the partnership are completely wound up.[24] Though it is not expressly stated in the Act the rule also applies to the case where a partner, having the right to do so, dissolves the partnership in order to secure for his private advantage some contract which the firm was about to obtain.[25] The phrase, "transaction concerning the partnership" does not include the purchase, by one of three partners, of the interest of another in the partnership assets, without the knowledge or consent of the third. He is under no obligation to account for his profit to the firm.[26] And where one partner owed a directorship to his connection with the firm, but the business in which he was a director did not compete with that of the firm, it was held that there were no grounds on which the other could claim a share of the director's fees.[27] The rights of a person who is not a partner, but has lent money on profit-sharing terms, are purely contractual, and no fiduciary duties are owed to him.[28]

21. Assignation.—As partnership is a contract involving delectus personae no partner, without the consent of the others, can assign his interest so as to make the assignee a partner in the firm,[29] except under the provisions of the

---

[19] Goudy, *Bankruptcy* (4th ed.), pp. 578–9.
[20] Bankruptcy (Scotland) Act 1913, s. 62.
[21] *Kuklitz* v. *Lambert Bros.*, 17 Com. Cas. 217 (Scrutton J.).
[22] s. 30.; see as illustrations of this section, *Stewart* v. *North* (1893) 20 R. 260; *Pillans Bros.* v. *Pillans* (1908) 16 S.L.T. 611; *Trimble* v. *Goldberg* [1906] A.C. 494.
[23] s. 29.
[24] s. 29.
[25] *Inst.*, III, 25, 4; Bell, *Comm.*, II, 522; *Featherstonhaugh* v. *Fenwick* (1810) 17 Vesey 298; *McNiven* v. *Peffers* (1868) 7 M. 181—both cases of leases.
[26] *Cassels* v. *Stewart* (1881) 8 R. (H.L.) 1.
[27] *Aas* v. *Benham* [1891] 2 Ch. 244.
[28] *Teacher* v. *Calder* (1899) 1 F. (H.L.) 39.
[29] s. 31.

Limited Partnerships Act 1907.[30] The interest of a partner is, however, assignable, absolutely or in security. The assignee has no right to interfere in the administration of the firm, to require any accounts, or to inspect the partnership books. He had therefore, it was held, no right to object to a resolution by which the partners arranged that they should receive salaries for attending to the partnership business.[31] He is only entitled while the firm is a going concern, to the share of the profits to which the cedent has right, and must accept the account of profits to which the partners have agreed.[32] An assignee has no power to dissolve the firm, but on its dissolution is entitled to receive the share of the partnership assets to which the cedent is entitled as between himself and the other partners, and, for the purpose of ascertaining that share, to an account as from the date of the dissolution.[33]

22. Rights of Partners Inter Se.—The interests and rights of partners may be regulated by an agreement, express or implied. The Act provides (s. 19): "The mutual rights and duties of partners, whether ascertained by agreement or defined by this Act, may be varied by the consent of all the partners, and such consent may be either express or inferred from a course of dealing." But it is conceived that if the partnership agreement were in writing, a merely oral consent to alter its terms would not be binding, unless it had been acted upon.[34] In the absence of any agreement to the contrary, the undernoted rules are provided by section 24 as regulating the relations of partners.[35]

23. Expulsion of Partner.—No majority can expel a partner, unless power to do so is conferred by express agreement.[36] Clauses in a deed of partnership

---

[30] Supra, § 7.
[31] *Re Garwood's Trusts* [1901] 1 Ch. 236.
[32] s. 31 (1).
[33] s. 31 (2).
[34] *Barr's Trs.* v. *Barr & Shearer* (1886) 13 R. 1055; *Starrett* v. *Pia*, 1968 S.L.T. (Notes) 28.
[35] (1) All the partners are entitled to share equally in the capital and profits of the business, and must contribute equally towards the losses, whether of capital or otherwise, sustained by the firm (*Garner* v. *Murray* [1904] 1 Ch. 57).
    (2) The firm must indemnify every partner in respect of payments made and personal liabilities incurred by him—
      (a) In the ordinary and proper conduct of the business of the firm; or
      (b) In or about anything necessarily done for the preservation of the business or property of the firm (*Stroyan* v. *Milroy*, 1910 S.C. 174).
    (3) A partner making, for the purpose of the partnership, any actual payment or advance beyond the amount of capital which he has agreed to subscribe, is entitled to interest at the rate of 5 per cent. per annum from the date of the payment or advance.
    (4) A partner is not entitled, before the ascertainment of profits, to interest on the capital subscribed by him.
    (5) Every partner may take part in the management of the partnership business.
    (6) No partner shall be entitled to remuneration for acting in the partnership business (*Pender* v. *Henderson* (1864) 2 M. 1428).
    (7) No person may be introduced as a partner without the consent of all existing partners.
    (8) Any difference arising as to ordinary matters connected with the partnership business may be decided by a majority of the partners, but no change may be made in the nature of the partnership business without the consent of all existing partners.
    (9) The partnership books are to be kept at the place of business of the partnership (or the principal place, if there is more than one), and every partner may, when he thinks fit, have access to and inspect and copy any of them. (As to inspection by accountant or solicitor, see *Cameron* v. *McMurray* (1855) 17 D. 1142; *Bevan* v. *Webb* [1901] 1 Ch. 724.).
[36] s. 25.

giving power to expel a partner are construed strictly, and the Court has power, on English authority, to refuse to give effect to them if satisfied that the expulsion is not in the interests of the firm but for some private reasons.[37] It is unlawful for a firm consisting of six or more persons to discriminate against a person on grounds of sex or race by expelling him from the partnership.[38]

24. Retirement of Partner.—Where the partnership is at will, i.e. not for any fixed term, any partner may determine the partnership by giving notice to all the other partners of his intention to do so.[39] In the absence of agreement to the contrary the notice may take immediate effect. There is nothing in the Act to preclude a partner from retiring without dissolving the firm, and its competency is recognised at common law, subject to the condition that a provision to that effect has been made in the partnership deed, or that all the partners consent.[40]

25. Tacit Relocation.—Where a partnership is for a fixed term, which has expired, and the business is carried on without any express agreement by such of the partners as habitually acted in the affairs of the firm, the law will infer continuance of the relationship as a partnership at will. The terms of the partnership which has expired will prevail, in so far as is consistent with a partnership at will.[41] In order that a partnership may be continued by tacit relocation there must be at least two partners surviving at the expiry of the fixed date. It is not enough that one surviving partner continues the business.[42] From the same case it appears that the business must be carried on for some period long enough to justify the inference that continuance was intended; no inference can be drawn from acts done on a single day. A right of pre-emption conferred on one of the partners and exercisable at the expiry of a fixed period, has been held to survive as a condition of a subsequent partnership by tacit relocation[43]; but a clause under which certain rights depended on notice being given three months before the expiry of the partnership was held inconsistent with a partnership at will, in respect that there was no time from which the three months could be computed.[44]

26. Rescission for Fraud: Misrepresentation.—Like other contracts, partnership may be rescinded on the ground that it was induced by fraud or misrepresentation. As it is a contract uberrimae fidei, proof of the concealment of material facts will justify rescission,[45] but will not, in the

---

[37] *Blisset* v. *Daniel* (1853) 10 Hare 493; *Green* v. *Howell* [1901] 1 Ch. 495.
[38] Sex Discrimination Act 1975 (c. 65), s. 11 (1) (*d*); Race Relations Act 1976 (c. 74), s. 10 (1) (*d*).
[39] s. 26.
[40] Bell, *Comm.*, II, 522; and see s. 32.
[41] s. 27.
[42] *Wallace* v. *Wallace's Trustees* (1906) 8 F. 558.
[43] *Macgowan* v. *Henderson*, 1914 S.C. 839.
[44] *Neilson* v. *Mossend Iron Co.* (1886) 13 R. (H.L.) 50.
[45] *Ferguson* v. *Wilson* (1904) 6 F. 779; and see Agreement Improperly Obtained, Ch. VIII, supra,
     § 4.

absence of fraud, found a claim for damages.[46] While no general claim of damages can be founded on an innocent misrepresentation, the Act provides (s. 41) that the party entitled to rescind shall have the following rights, whether fraud be proved or not:—(a) to a lien on, or right of retention of, the surplus of the partnership assets, after satisfying the partnership liabilities, for any sum of money paid for the purchase of a share in the partnership and for any capital contributed; (b) to stand in the place of the creditors of the firm for any payments made by him in respect of the partnership liabilities; (c) to be indemnified by the person guilty of the fraud or making the representation against all the debts and liabilities of the firm.[47]

27. Dissolution of Partnership.—The Act provides (s. 32): "Subject to any agreement between the partners, a partnership is dissolved—(a) if entered into for a fixed term, by the expiration of that term[48]; (b) if entered into for a single adventure or undertaking, by the termination of that adventure or undertaking[49]; (c) if entered into for an undefined time, by any partner giving notice to the other or others of his intention to dissolve the partnership. In the last mentioned case the partnership is dissolved as from the date mentioned in the notice as the date of dissolution, or, if no date is so mentioned, as from the date of the communication of the notice." A partnership is also dissolved, in the absence of any agreement to the contrary, by the death or bankruptcy of any partner[50] and, irrespective of agreement, by the happening of any event which makes it unlawful for the business of the firm to be carried on or for the members of the firm to carry it on in partnership.[51] So where, on the declaration of war, one of the partners became an alien enemy, it was held that as partnership with an alien enemy was illegal, the result was necessarily the instant dissolution of the firm.[52]

28. Dissolution by Court.—A partnership may be dissolved by the Court, on application by a partner, on the following grounds (s. 35):— (a) That a partner is of permanently unsound mind; (b) that he is permanently incapable of performing his part under the partnership contract; (c) that a partner, other than the partner suing, has been guilty of such conduct as, regard being had to the nature of the business, is calculated prejudicially to affect the carrying on of the business[53]; (d) where a partner, other than the partner suing, wilfully or persistently commits a breach of the partnership agreement, or otherwise so conducts himself in matters relating to the partnership business that it is not reasonably practicable for the other partners to carry on the business in partnership with him; (e) when the business of the partnership can only be

---

[46] *Manners* v. *Whitehead* (1898) 1 F. 171.
[47] The section is mainly founded on *Adam* v. *Newbigging* (1888) 13 App. Cas. 308.
[48] See, as to continuance by tacit relocation, supra, § 25.
[49] See *Gracie* v. *Prentice* (1904) 42 S.L.R. 9.
[50] s. 33.
[51] s. 34.
[52] *Stevenson* v. *Cartonnagen-Industrie* [1918] A.C. 239.
[53] E.g., a conviction for dishonesty, though not a matter affecting the firm, *Carmichael* v. *Evans* [1904] 1 Ch. 486.

carried on at a loss; (f) whenever, in any case, circumstances have arisen which render it just and equitable that the partnership be dissolved.[54]

29. Effects of Dissolution.—On dissolution the general authority of each partner to bind the firm is determined. But each partner (unless he is bankrupt) retains authority to bind the firm, in so far as may be necessary to wind up the affairs of the partnership, and to complete transactions begun but unfinished at the date of dissolution.[55] So where trust money was lodged with a bank on consignation receipt, payable to a firm of law agents, it was held that the bank was justified in accepting the signature of the firm name by one of the partners, some years after the firm had been dissolved, on the ground that the uplifting of the money was the completion of a transaction left unfinished at the date of the dissolution of the partnership.[56]

On dissolution, the winding up of the partnership affairs is primarily with the surviving partner or partners. Any partner may apply to the Court to wind up the business and affairs of the firm,[57] but the Court will not readily, or merely on averments that differences have arisen between the partners, accede to the application by one partner for the appointment of a judicial factor.[58]

If a premium has been paid for entering into a partnership for a fixed term, and the partnership has been dissolved before the expiration of that term otherwise than by the death of a partner (e.g. by supervening illegality) the Court may order repayment of the whole or part of the premium. This does not apply to the case where the dissolution is due wholly or chiefly to the misconduct of the partner who paid the premium, or where the firm is dissolved by agreement containing no provision for the return of the premium.[59]

30. Carrying on Business after Dissolution.—When any member of a firm has died or ceased to be a partner, and the other partners carry on the business of the firm with its capital or assets without any final settlement of accounts, then, unless there is an agreement to the contrary, or an option to purchase the share of the deceased or outgoing partner has been exercised, he or his estate has the option of claiming such share of the profits made after the dissolution as the Court may find to be attributable to the use of his share of the partnership assets, or 5 per cent. on the amount of his share of the partnership assets.[60] So where a partnership was dissolved on the declaration

[54] As to the construction of "just and equitable," in company cases, see *Elder* v. *Elder & Watson*, 1952 S.C. 49; and Company Law, Ch. XXV, *infra*, § [42].
[55] § 38. See *Welsh* v. *Knarston* 1973 S.L.T. 66. See also, as to contracts with the "house," *Inland Revenue* v. *Graham's Trs.*, 1971 S.C. (H.L.) 1; *Jardine-Paterson* v. *Fraser*, 1974 S.L.T. 93.
[56] *Dickson* v. *National Bank*, 1917 S.C. (H.L.) 50.
[57] See s. 39; but only to the Court of Session, not to the Sheriff Court: *Pollock* v. *Campbell*, 1962 S.L.T. (Sh. Ct.) 89.
[58] *Schulze* v. *Gow* (1877) 4 R. 928; *Elliot* v. *Cassils* (1907) 15 S.L.T. 190; *Allan* v. *Gronmayer* (1891) 18 R. 784. A judicial factor was appointed in *Carabine* v. *Carabine*, 1949 S.C. 521, and in *McCulloch* v. *McCulloch*, 1953 S.C. 189, where observations were made on the duties of the factor.
[59] s. 40.
[60] s. 42.

of war on the ground that one partner had become an alien enemy, and the other partners had carried on the business, it was held that a share of the profits, so far as attributable to the use of the enemy partner's share of the assets, must be set aside for him, and would become payable on the conclusion of peace.[61]

31. Settling Accounts.—In the absence of any agreement to the contrary the following rules[62] hold in settling accounts on the dissolution of a partnership:—

(a) Losses, including losses and deficiencies of capital, shall be paid first out of profits, next out of capital, and lastly, if necessary, by the partners individually in the proportion in which they were entitled to share profits;

(b) The assets[63] of the firm, including the sums, if any, contributed by the partners to make up losses or deficiencies of capital, shall be applied in the following manner and order:

   1. In paying the debts and liabilities of the firm to persons who are not partners therein;

   2. In paying to each partner rateably what is due from the firm to him for advances as distinguished from capital;

   3. In paying to each partner rateably what is due from the firm to him in respect of capital;[64]

   4. The ultimate residue, if any, shall be divided among the partners in the proportion in which profits are divisible.

[61] *Stevenson* v. *Cartonnagen-Industrie* [1918] A.C. 239.
[62] s. 44.
[63] As to the valuation of assets, see *Shaw* v. *Shaw*, 1968 S.L.T. (Notes) 94.
[64] *Garner* v. *Murray* [1904] 1 Ch. 57.

CHAPTER XXV

COMPANY LAW

Buckley, *Companies Acts* (13th ed., 1957; supplement 1964); Palmer, *Company Precedents* (17th ed., 1956); *Company Law* (22nd ed., 1976); Gower, *Modern Company Law* (3rd ed., 1969); Gow, *Mercantile Law* (1964), Ch. 11.

1. Methods of Incorporation.—Parties who desire to carry on any business or enterprise together, otherwise than as partners, may be incorporated by charter or letters patent from the Crown; by a private Act of Parliament; or under the provisions of the Companies Acts. A private Act of Parliament is still necessary in the case of any enterprise where power to take land compulsorily is required. The provisions of such private Acts, so far as not altered by the particular Act, are set forth by the Companies Clauses Acts, 1845, 1863 and 1869.

The existing provisions for the establishment, management and winding up of a company incorporated by registration, and without charter, letters patent or private Act, are contained in the Companies Act 1948 (11 & 12 Geo. VI, c. 38).[1] This chapter deals only with companies formed by registration under that Act. Important provisions relating to the control of companies, their conduct of affairs and the duties of their officers are contained in the Companies Act 1967 (c. 81), while further provisions relating to accounts, accounting records and auditors are contained in the Companies Act 1976 (c. 69). Other provisions of importance are contained in the Companies (Floating Charges and Receivers) (Scotland) Act 1972 (c. 67) and section 9 of the European Communities Act 1972 (c. 68). A detailed examination of these provisions and of the principles of modern company law is beyond the scope of this work. For this reference must be made to the specialist text books.

It is not essential to the formation of a company that its objects should be commercial or the making of profit. Any persons associated for any lawful purpose may, by complying with the provisions of the principal Act as to registration, form an incorporated company, with or without limited liability.[2] A trade union, however, cannot be registered under the Companies Acts.[3]

2. Company Distinct from Members.—A company, once incorporated,[4] is a legal personality distinct from its shareholders.[5] So though all the shareholders may, in the event of war, become alien enemies, the company does not

---

[1] See also the Rules of Court (1965), IV, 202 et seq.; A.S. The Companies (Winding-up) Forms 1949 (S.I. 1949 No. 1065), A.S. March 20, 1930, and A.S. (Sheriff Court Liquidations) 1948 (S.I. 1948 No. 2293).
[2] 1948 Act, s. 1.
[3] Capacity to Contract, Ch. VI, *supra*, § 14.
[4] Prior to incorporation a company has no legal existence: see *F. J. Neale (Glasgow)* v. *Vickery*, 1973 S.L.T. (Sh. Ct.) 88.
[5] For a discussion of this principle, see Palmer, *Company Law*, paras. 18-01 et seq.

necessarily become so, and may retain its title to sue.[6] And the fact that all the interest in the company's profits is in the hands of one individual does not make him liable for its debts to any extent beyond the amount unpaid on the shares which he has agreed to take. So where the memorandum was signed by A and six members of his family, all the shares except six were held by A, and he held debentures giving him a preferable right to all the company's assets, it was held, in liquidation, that there were no grounds on which he could be rendered personally liable for trade debts.[7] So also the fact that an individual was controlling shareholder and governing director of a company did not preclude the contractual relationship of master and servant between himself and the company: it was a logical consequence of *Salomon's* case that one person might function in the dual capacities of agent and servant of the company.[8] Similarly, where a firm of solicitors had advised the liquidator of a company, it was the liquidator as agent for the company and not its individual members who had a right to challenge their account for professional fees.[9] And it is probably established that when a wrong such as injury to neighbouring property,[10] or infringement of a patent,[11] is committed in the course of company management, the fact that two persons are the only directors and the only shareholders does not involve them in any personal liability. On the same principle no shareholder has an insurable interest in any asset belonging to the company.[12] Although undecided in Scotland, it is probable that a company can be guilty of an offence involving mens rea.[13]

While the principle of separate legal personality must normally receive full effect, the Courts may be prepared in certain special circumstances to "lift the veil" and look behind the company as a legal person.[14] This occurs in matters where the control of a company is in issue, such as in connection with the taxation of companies[15] and the law relating to trading with the enemy[16], where the device of incorporation has been used for some illegal or improper purpose[17] or where the company is a mere façade concealing the true facts.[18]

3. Kinds of Company.—A company may be registered with unlimited liability, with or without share capital; with liability limited by shares; with

---

[6] *Continental Tyre Co.* v. *Daimler* [1916] 2 A.C. 307.
[7] *Salomon* v. *Salomon & Co.* [1897] A.C. 22.
[8] *Lee* v. *Lee's Air Farming* [1961] A.C. 12; see also *Woolfson* v. *Strathclyde Regional Council*. 1978 S.L.T. 159.
[9] *Davidson & Syme, W.S.* v. *Kaye*, 1970 S.L.T. (Notes) 65.
[10] *Rainham Chemical Works* v. *Belvedere Co.* [1921] 2 A.C. 465.
[11] *British Thomson Houston Co.* v. *Crowther* [1924] 2 Ch. 33.
[12] *Macaura* v. *Northern Insurance Co.* [1925] A.C. 619.
[13] *Director of Public Prosecutions* v. *Kent and Sussex Contractors* [1944] K.B. 146. The point is expressly left open in *Galbraith's Stores* v. *McIntyre* (1912) 6 Adam 661 (cf. *Brander* v. *Buttercup Dairy Co.*, 1921 J.C. 19). See Gordon's *Criminal Law* (2nd ed.), pp. 322-3. As to proceedings on indictment against a company see Criminal Procedure (Scotland) Act 1975, s. 74.
[14] For a discussion of this principle, see Gower, pp. 189 et seq.
[15] *S. Berendsen* v. *I.R.C.* [1958] Ch. 1.
[16] *Continental Tyre Co.* v. *Daimler*, supra.
[17] *Merchandise Transport* v. *British Transport Commission* [1962] 2 Q.B. 173.
[18] *Jones* v. *Lipman* [1962] 1 W.L.R. 823; *Tunstall* v. *Steigmann* [1962] 2 Q.B. 593, per Ormerod L.J. at p. 601.

liability limited by guarantee, with or without share capital; or with limited liability as to the shareholders, but unlimited as to the directors.[19] Associations for the purpose of promoting art, science, religion, charity or any other useful object whose rules prohibit any payment of dividend to the members may, on obtaining a licence from the Department of Trade, be registered without the word "limited", and are then exempt from the obligation of sending lists of members to the Registrar of Companies.[20] They are however obliged to mention the fact that the company is a limited company on all business letters and order forms of the company.[21] A company which is registered as limited may be re-registered as unlimited, and vice versa.[22] In a unlimited company (now almost unknown) each shareholder is liable for all the debts of the company. In a company limited by guarantee, the liability of each member is limited to the amount he undertakes to contribute in the event of the company being wound up.[23] In a company limited by shares each member is liable only for the amount of the shares which he has agreed to take, the time for payment depending on the regulations of the particular company. If, however, a company carries on business for more than six months after the number of members has fallen below the legal minimum (seven, in the case of a public company; two, in the case of a private), every person who is a member of the company during the time that it so carries on business after those six months and who is cognisant of the fact is liable for all debts contracted by the company during that time[24].

4. Public and Private Companies.—The principal Act makes provision for private and for public companies. Its provisions apply to public and private companies alike unless otherwise stated, and a company is a public company unless it is clear from its constitution that it is a private company. In general any member of the public who is willing to pay the price may become a member of a public company, although a public company may have several classes of shares, some of which may be subject to restrictions on their issue or transfer. The minimum number of members of a public company is seven, and it must have at least two directors (ss. 1, 31, 176). It requires to obtain a trading certificate before it commences business, and must hold a statutory meeting and make a statutory report to its members (ss. 109, 130).

A private company on the other hand is one which by its articles (a) restricts the right of its members to transfer their shares; (b) limits the number of its members (exclusive of persons who are or were in the employment of the company) to fifty; (c) prohibits any invitation to the public to subscribe for any shares or debentures.[25] If a private company alters its articles so that they no longer include these restrictions, it ceases to be a

[19] 1948 Act, ss. 1, 11, 202.
[20] s. 19.
[21] European Communities Act 1972, s. 9(7).
[22] 1967 Act, ss. 43, 44.
[23] See, as to companies limited by guarantee, ss. 2, 21, 212; *Robertson* v. *British Linen Bank* (1891) 18 R. 1225.
[24] 1948 Act, s. 31.
[25] s. 28.

private company, and must, under penalties, within fourteen days deliver to the registrar a prospectus or statement in lieu of prospectus.[26] If without altering its articles it in fact disregards these restrictions, e.g. if its membership comes to exceed fifty, it retains its character as a private company but loses certain of the exemptions and privileges which follow.[27] A private company also loses its characteristic privileges under the Act if it advertises for deposits.[28] A private company requires only a minimum of two members (ss. 1, 31) and need have only one director (s. 176); it is not bound by the condition that shares cannot be allotted unless a certain proportion have been subscribed (ss. 47, 48); and it may commence business on the grant of a certificate of incorporation since it does not require a trading certificate before business is commenced or any borrowing powers exercised (s. 109). It is not required to hold a statutory meeting or make a statutory report (s. 130 (10)). Certain restrictions as to the appointment of directors are not applicable.[29]

5. Registration of Company.—A company, whether public or private, is brought into existence as a corporation by the registration with the registrar of its memorandum of association and its articles of association if there are to be any. The memorandum must be signed, in the case of a public company, by seven persons, in the case of a private company, by two. On the registration of the memorandum the registrar issues a certificate that the company is incorporated. The certificate of incorporation is conclusive evidence of the existence of the company from the date therein fixed.[30] Each signatory to the memorandum must subscribe for at least one share,[31] and his signature must be attested by at least one witness.[32]

6. Statutory Requisites of Memorandum.—The memorandum of association must in the case of a company limited by shares or by guarantee state (1) the name of the company, with Limited as its last word[33]; (2) whether the registered office is situated in England or Wales or Scotland; (3) the objects of the company; (4) that the liability of the members is limited; and, in the case of a company having a share capital, (5) the amount of share capital with which the company proposes to be registered and the division thereof into shares of a fixed amount.[34] A statement of the first directors and secretary of the company and of the intended situation of the company's registered office on incorporation requires to be delivered with the memorandum on application for registration of the company.[35]

[26] s. 30. Park v. *Royalties Syndicate* [1912] 1 K.B. 330.
[27] s. 29.
[28] Protection of Depositors Act 1963, s. 4.
[29] 1948 Act, s. 181; see infra, § 31.
[30] ss. 12, 13, 15. *Cotman* v. *Brougham* [1918] A.C. 514.
[31] s. 2.
[32] s. 3.
[33] The omission of the word "limited" in a legal document is not necessarily fatal: see *Whittam* v. *Daniel & Co.* [1962] 1 Q.B. 271; cf. *Wolfe* v. *Robertson* (1906) 8 F. 829.
[34] s. 2; Companies Act 1976, c. 69, s. 30.
[35] 1976 Act, ss. 21, 23(2). Notice of any change of the situation of the registered office must also be given to the Registrar of Companies: 1976 Act, s. 23(3); see also *Ross* v. *Invergordon Distilleries*, 1961 S.C. 286.

7. Name.—No company may be registered by a name which in the opinion of the Department of Trade is undesirable.[36] A company may, by special resolution and with the consent in writing of the Department of Trade, change its name[37]. Where the Department of Trade consider that the name by which a company is registered gives so misleading an indication of its activities as to be likely to cause harm to the public, they have power to direct the company to change its name.[38] Every company is required,[39] subject to certain penalties,[40] to display its name in legible characters outside every office or place in which its business is carried on, on its seal and on all business letters, official publications, bills of exchange, invoices, etc., of the company. It is also required to mention in legible characters on all business letters and order forms of the company the place of registration and the number with which it is registered, and the address of its registered office.[41]

8. Objects Clause.—The statement of the objects of the company in the memorandum defines the powers of the company and sets a limit to the acts which it may lawfully do. As a creature of statute, the company cannot enter into any contract or dispose of its funds in any way which is outside the purposes defined in the objects clause.[42] It has, however, power to do whatever it is necessary to do with a view to the attainment of the stated objects or whatever else may fairly be regarded as incidental thereto or consequential on them.[43] A transaction which is outside the powers taken in the objects clause is ultra vires of the company.[44] Under the old law such a transaction was void even when entered into with third parties,[45] and could not be ratified by the shareholders.[46] This doctrine has been considerably restricted by section 9(1) of the European Communities Act 1972, which provides in favour of a person dealing with the company in good faith that any transaction decided on by the directors shall be deemed to have been one which it is within the capacity of the company to enter into, and that a party to a transaction so decided on shall be presumed to have acted in good faith unless the contrary is proved. The doctrine of ultra vires still applies, however, to transactions which are internal to the company and to transactions which have not been approved by the directors or where the company can prove that the third party has not acted in good faith, and it may still be invoked by a third party against the company. It is a question of construction whether a particular transaction is or is not within the powers given to the company by

[36] s. 17.
[37] s. 18.
[38] 1967 Act, s. 46.
[39] 1948 Act, s. 108.
[40] See *Scottish & Newcastle Breweries* v. *Blair*, 1967 S.L.T. 72; contrast *Durham Fancy Goods* v. *Michael Jackson (Fancy Goods)* [1968] 2 Q.B. 839.
[41] European Communities Act 1972, s. 9(7).
[42] *Ashbury Railway Carriage Co.* v. *Riche* (1875) L.R. 7 H.L. 653; *Trevor* v. *Whitworth* (1887) 12 App. Cas. 409.
[43] *Att.-Gen.* v. *Great Eastern Railway* (1880) 5 App. Cas. 473.
[44] See Capacity to Contract, Ch. VI, supra, § 9; Palmer, 9-06 et seq.
[45] e.g. *Re Jon Beauforte (London)* [1953] Ch. 131.
[46] *Re Birkbeck Building Society* [1912] 2 Ch. 183.

its objects clause. General words may be regarded as restricted by what appears to be the main or dominant object of the company. A power which enables a company to carry out administrative acts, even if it is stated to be an independent object, must nevertheless be exercised for the purposes of the company as shown by other parts of its objects clause.[47]

9. Alteration of Objects.—The objects of the company may be altered or enlarged, by special resolution of the company, which requires no approval by the Court unless dissentient members apply for cancellation of the alteration, for the following purposes[48]:—(a) To carry on the business more economically or more efficiently; (b) to attain its main purpose by new or improved means; (c) to enlarge or change the local area of its operation; (d) to carry on some business which under existing conditions may conveniently or advantageously be combined with the business of the company[49]; (e) to restrict or abandon any of the objects specified[50]; (f) to sell or dispose of the whole or any part of the undertaking; (g) to amalgamate with any other company or body of persons. The statutory power to alter the objects of the company is not confined to the objects stated in the objects clause, but enables the company to alter any provision in its memorandum which relates to the objects of the company.[51] Where a resolution altering its objects is passed the company is required to deliver to the Registrar a copy of its memorandum as altered. If no application to the Court for cancellation is made within twenty-one days, the validity of the alteration cannot be questioned on the ground that it was not authorised by the statutory power.[52]

10. Provisions as to Shares: Alteration and Reduction of Capital.—The provisions of the memorandum with regard to the share capital of the company may be altered, if power to do so is given in the articles of association[53], in the following respects:—(1) The increase of its share capital by the issue of new shares; (2) consolidation and division of its share capital into shares of larger amount; (3) conversion of shares into stock; (4) subdivision of shares into shares of smaller amount; (5) cancellation of shares which have not been taken with resultant diminution of capital. These powers must be exercised by the company in general meeting,[54] and notice of their exercise must be given to the Registrar of Companies.[55] If the capital is divided into different classes of shares and the memorandum or the articles

---

[47] *Introductions* v. *National Provincial Bank* [1970] Ch. 199; *Thompson* v. *J. Barke & Co. (Caterers)*, 1975 S.L.T. 67.
[48] 1948 Act, s. 5(1).
[49] *Dundee Aerated Water Manufacturing Co.*, 1932 S.C. 473; *Hugh Baird & Sons*, 1932 S.C. 455.
[50] *Strathspey Public Assembly* v. *Anderson's Trs.*, 1934 S.C. 385.
[51] *Incorporated Glasgow Dental Hospital* v. *Lord Advocate*, 1927 S.C. 400.
[52] European Communities Act 1972, s. 9(4), (5); 1948 Act, s. 5(9).
[53] *Metropolitan Cemetery Co.*, 1934 S.C. 65.
[54] s. 61. Where, however, all the shareholders who have a right to attend and vote at a general meeting assent to a matter which the general meeting could carry into effect, that assent is as binding as assent in general meeting would be (*Re Duomatic* [1969] 2 W.L.R. 114, per Buckley J. at p. 120; cf. *Parker & Cooper* v. *Reading* [1926] Ch. 975).
[55] s. 62.

authorise the variation of the rights of any class, and such variation is made, objectors may apply to the Court for its cancellation.[56] The expression "variation" in relation to the rights of a class includes their abrogation.[57]

A company having a share capital may, if so authorised by its articles, reduce its share capital by special resolution, subject to confirmation by the Court. The Court may order that this company must add to its name the words "and reduced".[58] There is no limit to the power of a company to reduce its capital, but the Court must be satisfied that the terms are just and equitable as between the various classes of shareholders,[59] and as respects creditors.[60] A company desiring to reduce its capital must follow the statutory procedure; it is illegal, even though powers are taken in the memorandum or in the articles, for a company to effect a reduction by the purchase of its own shares.[61] The holders of the shares purchased remain liable for calls in liquidation.[62] A company however may exercise the right to forfeit the shares of a shareholder who has failed to pay calls, or may accept a surrender from one who is solvent.[63]

Except as above indicated, a company has no power to alter its memorandum.[64] This rule applies not only to the particulars required by the Act, but to any provision in fact inserted in the memorandum, unless power to alter it is expressly provided.[65]

11. Articles of Association.—Together with the memorandum, articles of association may be registered. This is compulsory in the case of an unlimited company, or a company limited by guarantee, but is optional in the case of a company limited by shares. If no articles are registered, articles in a statutory form, known as Table A, apply to the company.[66] If articles are registered, Table A applies so far as not modified or excluded.

The articles regulate the management of the company. When registered, they form a contract between the individual shareholders,[67] and between each shareholder and the company,[68] but not between the company and outsiders. So a solicitor could not enforce a clause in the articles providing that he should be employed.[69] If a provision contained in the articles is contrary to

[56] s. 72. *Re Sound City Films* [1947] Ch. 169.
[57] s. 72 (6); and see also *Frazer Bros., Petrs.,* 1963 S.C. 139.
[58] ss. 66-70.
[59] *Balmenach Glenlivet Distillery* v. *Croall* (1906) 8 F. 1135; *Caldwell* v. *Caldwell,* 1916 S.C. (H.L.) 120; *Wilsons and Clyde Coal Co.* v. *Scottish Insurance Corporation,* 1949 S.C. (H.L.) 90.
[60] *Westburn Sugar Refineries,* 1951 S.C. (H.L.) 57; see also *Anderson, Brown & Co.,* 1965 S.C. 81: *Lawrie & Symington,* 1969 S.L.T. 221.
[61] *Trevor* v. *Whitworth* (1887) 12 App.Cas. 409. See, as to shares fully paid up, *Gill* v. *Arizona Copper Co.* (1900) 2 F. 843, at p. 860.
[62] *General Property Investment Co.* v. *Matheson's Trs.* (1888) 16 R. 282.
[63] *General Property Investment Co.* v. *Craig* (1891) 18 R. 389, and see Table A. arts. 33-39.
[64] s. 4.
[65] *Welsbach Incandescent Co.* [1904] 1 Ch. 87.
[66] ss. 6-9. For model form of Articles, in cases where Table A is not adopted, see Palmer, *Company Precedents* (17th ed.), I, 473.
[67] *Welton* v. *Saffery* [1897] A.C. 299
[68] s. 20. *Hickman* v. *Kent Sheepbreeders' Association* [1915] 1 Ch. 881.
[69] *Eley* v. *Positive Life Assurance Co.* (1874) 1 Ex.D. 88; *Alexander Ward & Co.* v. *Samyang Navigation Co.,* 1975 S.L.T. 50, per Lord Fraser at p. 55.

public policy it does not bind the members and will not be enforced by the Court.[70]

12. Alteration of Articles.—A company has power, by special resolution, but without requiring confirmation by the Court, to alter or add to its articles.[71] The power cannot be excluded by any provision in the articles themselves;[72] nor can it be excluded by contract with a third party,[73] although an action of damages may lie for the breach. There are no statutory limits to the power to alter the articles, but, by the decisions, a resolution to alter is reducible if it is made in the interests of individual shareholders or classes of shareholders and not bona fide for the benefit of the company as a whole.[74] Nor can accrued rights, such as the right to have a transfer registered, be affected.[75] By section 22 no member of a company, unless he agrees in writing, is bound by an alteration of the memorandum or articles made after he became a member, if it in any way increases his liability to subscribe for shares, to contribute to the share capital or to pay money to the company. Where the articles are altered the company is required to send a copy of the articles as altered to the Registrar.[76]

13. Contracts by Company.—Although it has a separate legal personality a company can only act by agents. By section 32 it may enter into contracts, through its directors, managers or authorised agents, in the same way as an individual, i.e. verbally or in writing according to the character of the contract.[77] It is also provided that, in Scotland, a deed is validly executed if sealed with the common seal of the company, and signed by two directors or by a director and the secretary of the company, whether the signatures are witnessed or not. A bill of exchange or promissory note is deemed to have been made, accepted or indorsed on behalf of a company if made, accepted or indorsed in the name of, or by or on behalf or on account of, the company by any person acting under its authority.[78]

14. Resolutions.—Certain acts are required, either by statute or under the articles, to be done not by the directors or others to whom the management of the business of the company may have been delegated, but only by the company. The company acts by resolutions of its members passed at a general meeting. Resolutions are of three kinds, viz. ordinary, extraordinary and special. An ordinary resolution is one passed by a majority at a meeting[79]

[70] *St. Johnstone F.C.* v. *Scottish Football Association,* 1965 S.L.T. 171.
[71] s. 10.
[72] *Malleson* v. *National Insurance Corporation* [1894] 1 Ch. 200.
[73] *Southern Foundries (1926)* v. *Shirlaw* [1940] A.C. 701.
[74] *Sidebottom* v. *Kershaw* [1920] 1 Ch. 154; *Greenhalgh* v. *Arderne Cinemas* [1951] 1 Ch. 286, esp. per Lord Evershed M.R. at p. 291.
[75] *McArthur* v. *Gulf Line,* 1909 S.C. 732.
[76] European Communities Act 1972, s. 9(4), (5).
[77] For a translation of the provisions of s. 32 into the Scottish idiom, see Gow, *Mercantile Law,* pp. 579-80.
[78] s. 33; *Brebner* v. *Henderson,* 1925 S.C. 643.
[79] See s. 134.

called in accordance with the articles or Table A, if applicable. Certain ordinary resolutions, such as for the removal of a director, require special notice to have been given to the company.[80] An extraordinary resolution is one passed by a majority of not less than three-fourths of those who being entitled to do so vote at a general meeting of which notice specifying the intention to propose the resolution as an extraordinary resolution has been duly given.[81] A special resolution is one passed by the same majority, and at a general meeting of which not less than twenty-one days' notice, specifying the intention to propose the resolution as a special resolution, has been duly given.[82] A resolution can only be passed at a meeting which has been duly convened and is duly constituted. A declaration by the chairman that the resolution has been carried is conclusive evidence of the fact, unless a poll be demanded, when reference must be had to the number of votes to which each shareholder is entitled.[83] Voting by proxy is usually sanctioned by the articles.[84] A printed copy of every special resolution, extraordinary resolution and of certain other resolutions and agreements must be forwarded to the Registrar of Companies within fifteen days and recorded by him.[85]

15. Prospectus.—Except as specially provided by section 39 or in the case of an issue of shares or debentures which were not offered to the public such as rights issues or bonus issues to existing members,[86] no application form for shares or debentures may be issued unless accompanied by a prospectus containing the statutory requirements.[87] Special provisions apply to companies which advertise for loans of money at interest or repayable at a premium where no debentures or other securities are issued.[88] Before the prospectus is issued a copy must be delivered to the Registrar,[89] and if it contains a statement purporting to be made by an expert, his written consent must be obtained.[90] If no prospectus has been issued, no shares or debentures may be issued unless a statement in lieu of prospectus has first been delivered to the Registrar.[91] This rule does not apply to a private company. It is not settled whether shares (or debentures) issued when the rule has not been complied with are void.[92] The general legal principle that an invitation to take

[80] ss. 160(1); 184(2), (5).
[81] s. 141 (1).
[82] s. 141 (2). As to computation of period of notice and quorum, see *Neil McLeod & Sons,* 1967 S.C. 16. As to procedure at a meeting, see Table A, arts. 52 et seq.
[83] s. 141 (3), (4). *Graham's Morocco Co.,* 1932 S.C. 269. Usually the articles provide that on a poll a shareholder shall have one vote for each share. See Table A, art. 462.
[84] Table A, art 67. A shareholder who has given a proxy may, though he had not recalled it, attend the meeting and vote: *Cousins* v. *International Brick Co.* [1931] 2 Ch. 90.
[85] s. 143.
[86] s. 38(3). proviso.
[87] s. 38. A prospectus is defined (s. 455) as "any prospectus, notice, circular, advertisement, or other invitation, offering to the public for subscription or purchase any shares or debentures of a company," See also s. 45 and comments on the definition in Buckley, *Companies Acts* (13th ed., p. 116) and *Sleigh* v. *Glasgow Options* (1904) 6 F. 420.
[88] Protection of Depositors Act 1963. For definition of "advertisement" see s. 26 (3) of that Act.
[89] s. 41.
[90] s. 40.
[91] s. 48.
[92] *Jubilee Cotton Mills* v. *Lewis* [1924] A.C. 958, in which the Court of Appeal held that the issue

shares in a company involves uberrima fides and a full disclosure of all material facts, though expressly preserved,[93] has in effect been superseded by the detailed provisions of section 38 and Schedule IV. The obligation of disclosure cannot be evaded by a waiver clause,[94] and, if shares are issued to an intermediary, and by him offered to the public, the offer is, for all purposes, to be deemed a prospectus issued by the company.[95] It has been held that a mere omission to disclose any of the required particulars does not give an allottee the right to reduce the contract to take shares, but does give him an action of damages against the parties responsible for the prospectus.[96]

16. Liability for Untrue Statements.—A party who can prove that he has taken shares in reliance on a statement in the prospectus which is untrue may, while the company is a going concern, reduce the contract, whether the statement in question was fraudulent or not.[97] But the remedy of reduction, or any equivalent procedure, must be exercised without delay, and is not competent after the commencement of the winding up of the company.[98] Nor can a shareholder, while he remains a member, sue the company for damages for the fraud inducing his membership.[99] But he may have a remedy against the directors or other parties responsible for the prospectus. In *Derry* v. *Peek*,[1] it was held that while directors were liable in damages for fraudulent statements in a prospectus they incurred no liability for statements which were made honestly but without reasonable care. This decision led to the passing of the Directors' Liability Act 1890, which is repealed but in substance reproduced by section 43 of the 1948 Act. Every director, or person who authorised the naming of himself, and is named in the prospectus, as a director, every promoter and every other person who has authorised the issue of a prospectus offering shares or debentures is liable to make compensation for any loss[2] sustained by reason of any untrue[3] statement therein, unless he proves (a) with respect to an untrue statement not purporting to be made on the authority of an expert, or of a public official document or statement, that he had reasonable ground[4] to believe, and did, up to the time of allotment, believe, that the statement was true; (b) with respect to copies or extracts from

---

was void, a decision reversed by the House of Lords on another point. See also *Re James Burton & Sons* [1927] 2 Ch. 132.

[93] s. 38 (6).
[94] s. 38 (2).
[95] s. 45.
[96] *Re South of England Gas Co.* [1911] 1 Ch. 573.
[97] *Mair* v. *Rio Grande Estates Co.,* 1913 S.C. 183; revd. 1913 S.C. (H.L.) 74.
[98] *Addie* v. *Western Bank* (1867) 5 M. (H.L.) 80; as to commencement of winding up, see § 43 infra.
[99] *Houldsworth* v. *City of Glasgow Bank* (1880) 7 R. (H.L.) 53. Gow, *Mercantile Law,* at p. 584 suggests that the authority of this case is doubtful because the City of Glasgow Bank was a common law company, i.e. a partnership.
[1] (1889) 14 App. Cas. 337; see also Agreement Improperly Obtained. Ch. VIII, supra, § 3, and, as to the question of title to sue, Ch. VIII, § 12.
[2] As to the measure of damages, see *Clark* v. *Urquhart* [1930] A.C. 28.
[3] Defined in s. 46.
[4] As to "reasonable ground," see *Adams* v. *Thrift* [1915] 2 Ch. 21; *Cairns* v. *Dickson* (1898) 35 S.L.R. 533.

a report or valuation by an expert, that they fairly represented the report, unless it is proved that the party sued had no reasonable ground to believe that the party making the report or valuation was qualified to make it; (c) with respect to statements purporting to be made by an official person, or contained in what purports to be a copy or extract from a public official document, that it was a correct and fair representation or extract. It is a sufficient defence that a party who had consented to become a director withdrew his consent before the issue of the prospectus, and that it was issued without his consent: or that the prospectus was issued without the party's knowledge or consent and that on becoming aware of its issue he gave reasonable public notice that it was issued without his knowledge or consent; or that after the issue of the prospectus, and on becoming aware of any untrue statement therein, he withdrew his consent and gave reasonable public notice of his withdrawal and the reasons therefor. A person (other than a promoter) made liable under this section may recover contribution from other persons similarly liable, unless he was, and the other persons were not, guilty of fraudulent misrepresentation.

It is a criminal offence for a person to authorise the issue of a prospectus which includes any untrue[5] statement unless he proves that the statement was immaterial or that he had reasonable ground to believe it to be true.[6]

17. Shares: Shareholders.—The shares or other interest of any member in a company are moveable estate.[7] Unless all the issued shares, or all the issued shares of a particular class, are fully paid and rank pari passu, each share must be distinguished by its appropriate number.[8] Shares may be all of the same class, or of different classes, such as founders', ordinary and preference shares—a matter to be regulated by the articles. The creation of preference shares requires a provision in the articles, but such a provision may be added by special resolution.[9] The terms of the articles under which preference shares are issued are exhaustive of the rights of holders of these shares, and, unless otherwise provided, they have no right to any surplus assets which may remain, in liquidation, after all capital has been repaid.[10] In the absence of any provision to the contrary, preference shares are cumulative; if the full dividend has not been paid in any one year the arrears must be paid before any dividend is declared on the ordinary shares.[11]

Each of the subscribers of the memorandum is deemed to have agreed to become a member of the company, and is a shareholder for the number of shares (usually one) which he thereby agrees to take. Other persons are members of the company if they have agreed to be so, and if their names are entered in its register of members.[12] The general rules of contract as to offer

[5] See definition in s. 46.
[6] s. 44.
[7] s. 73.
[8] s. 74.
[9] *Andrews* v. *Gas Meter Co.* [1897] 1 Ch. 361.
[10] *Wilsons and Clyde Coal Co.* v. *Scottish Insurance Corporation*, 1949 S.C. (H.L.) 90.
[11] *Partick Gas Co.* v. *Taylor* (1888) 15 R. 711; *Ferguson & Forester* v. *Buchanan*, 1920 S.C. 154.
[12] s. 26.

and acceptance apply.[13] A statement of willingness to take shares will not readily be construed as an application.[14] In the ordinary case an application for shares, where there is no prior obligation on either party, is merely an offer, which must be accepted by the company, and may be withdrawn by the applicant.[15] But an application is in substance the acceptance of an offer and cannot be withdrawn, if it is made in response to an undertaking by the company to allot a certain number of shares if applied for,[16] or in pursuance of a prior agreement to underwrite the shares.[17] No shares of any company offering shares to the public can be allotted unless the whole issue has been subscribed,[18] or an amount on which allotment may proceed has been fixed and intimated in the prospectus and has been subscribed (referred to as "the minimum subscription"); and (in either case) the amount payable on application has been paid. This rule applies only to the first issue of shares, and not to an issue of debentures. Any condition binding an applicant to waive compliance with it is void.[19] An allotment made in contravention is voidable, at the instance of the applicant, within one month of the first statutory meeting, not later, and it is voidable whether or not the company is in liquidation.[20] The amount payable on application must not be less than five per cent. of the nominal value of the shares.[21]

No one may carry on the business of dealing in securities without a licence, but this restriction does not apply to members of a recognised stock exchange, managers or trustees under an authorised unit trust scheme or to certain institutions.[22] It is an offence by fraudulent or reckless[23] statements to induce persons to invest money, or to distribute any document inviting investment, except a prospectus conforming with the Companies Act, or a similar document.[24]

18. Liability on Shares.—A shareholder is liable to pay the amount for the time being unpaid on his shares up to the nominal amount of his shares as calls may be made by the company, or ultimately in its liquidation, and the company has a lien over its shares for debts due to it by the holder.[25] Shares may be issued as fully or partly paid up otherwise than in cash in return for goods, services or other consideration, but the company must in that case, within one month, lodge with the Registrar the written contract (if any) under

---

[13] Law of Contract, Ch. IV, supra.
[14] *Mason*, infra; *Millen & Sommerville* v. *Millen*, 1910 S.C. 868.
[15] *Mason* v. *Benhar Coal Co.* (1882) 9 R. 883; *Chapman* v. *Sulphite Paper Co.* (1892) 19 R. 837.
[16] *Millen & Sommerville* v. *Millen*, 1910 S.C. 868.
[17] *Premier Briquette Co.* v. *Gray*, 1922 S.C. 329.
[18] *Glasgow Pavilion* v. *Motherwell* (1903) 6 F. 116.
[19] s. 47.
[20] s. 49.
[21] s. 47 (3).
[22] Prevention of Fraud (Investments) Act 1958 (6 & 7 Eliz. 11, c. 45), ss. 1 and 2.
[23] "Reckless" means "dishonestly or otherwise": 1958 Act, s. 13 as amended by the Protection of Depositors Act 1963 (c. 16), s. 21 (1); see also *R.* v. *Russell* [1953] 1 W.L.R. 77; *R.* v. *Grunwald* [1963] 1 Q.B. 935.
[24] 1958 Act, ss. 13 and 14, as amended by the Protection of Depositors Act 1963, s. 21. See also s. 1 of the Act of 1963, which contains provisions similar to s. 13 of the 1958 Act, where the inducement is to invest money on deposit.
[25] *Bell's Tr.* v. *Coatbridge Tinplate Co.* (1886) 14 R. 246.

which the shares were allotted, or, if there were no written contract, a note specifying the consideration given for the shares.[26] The rule applies to bonus shares.[27] Failure renders the officers of the company liable to penalties, but does not affect the validity of the allotment, nor, as was the case under an earlier statute, render the allottee liable for the nominal amount of the shares. He may be so liable if the consideration is proved to be non-existent.[28] Under conditions specified in section 57, including the sanction of the Court, shares may be issued at a discount.[29] Subject to power contained in the articles and notice in the prospectus, a commission may be paid by the company to any person in consideration of his subscribing for shares or procuring subscriptions.[30] And payment of a brokerage is legal.[31]

19. Register of Shareholders and of Individual Interests.—A company is bound, under penalties, to keep a register of members at its registered office, in which the shares held by each shareholder are distinguished by numbers, so long as they have numbers.[32] Any member without, and anyone else on, payment of a fee is entitled to inspect the register.[33] It cannot be subjected to a lien.[34] By section 117 no notice of any trust may appear on the register of a company in England, but this section does not apply to Scotland, where the usual practice is to register trustees as such. But a person registered as a holder of shares in trust incurs the same liability as a person holding them for his own behoof.[35] Any person whose name is, without sufficient cause, entered in or omitted from the register may apply to the Court for its rectification. The same remedy is open when unnecessary delay occurs in entering on the register the fact that a person has ceased to be a member. The application may be made by the person aggrieved, by any member of the company, or by the company.[36]

Provision is made in the Acts of 1967 and 1976 for the disclosure to and registration by the company of substantial individual interests in share capital carrying unrestricted voting rights. These provisions apply only to a company which, as respects the whole or any proportion of its share capital, has been granted a listing on a recognised stock exchange. A person who is interested in shares comprised in such share capital of such a company of a nominal value equal to one fifth or more of the nominal value of that share capital must disclose to the company the number of shares of that class in which he is interested or acquires an interest.[37] He is also required to notify the company

---

[26] s. 52.
[27] *Scottish Heritages Co.* (1898) 5 S.L.T. 336.
[28] *Innes & Co.* [1903] 2 Ch. 254.
[29] s. 57. See *Klenck* v. *East India Mining Co.* (1886) 16 R. 271; *Ooregum Gold Mining Co.* v. *Roper* [1892] A.C. 125.
[30] s. 53. See *Australian Investment Trust* v. *Strand Properties* [1932] A.C. 735.
[31] s. 53 (3).
[32] s. 110.
[33] s. 113.
[34] *Garpel Haematite Co.* v. *Andrew* (1866) 4 M. 617.
[35] *Muir* v. *City of Glasgow Bank* (1879) 6 R. (H.L.) 21.
[36] s. 116.
[37] 1967 Act, s. 33, as amended by 1976 Act, s. 26(1); the prescribed percentage may be varied by statutory instrument.

of any changes in the amounts or disposal of such shares in which he has an interest. The company must keep a register of the information furnished to it under section 33, which is to be open to inspection by any person.[38] A company which is obliged to keep such a register may require any members of the company to disclose who has the beneficial interests in its voting shares.[39]

20. Transfer of Shares.—Shares in a company may be transferred in the manner prescribed in the articles,[40] which may, or may not, provide that the directors shall have a power to decline transfers of which they do not approve,[41] or, as is common in the case of private companies, that the shares shall not be transferred to an outsider before first being offered to the other members.[42] If not, the shareholder has an absolute right to transfer his shares to anyone he pleases, and thereby to escape liability for calls,[43] unless the transfer is presented on the eve of liquidation, when the directors are entitled to refuse registration.[44] The fact that the transferee was induced by fraud to accept the shares cannot be founded on by the company or by its liquidator.[45] If directors have a right to refuse a transfer they must exercise the power for the benefit of the company, and the transferee may insist on registration on proof that they acted arbitrarily or capriciously. The directors are not bound to give reasons for refusal.[46] The result of a valid refusal is that the transferor may avoid the contract on repaying the price; if he does not choose to do so he must regard himself as a trustee for the transferee, bound to receive dividends and hand them on.[47]

21. Share Certificates.—A company, under the sanction of penalties exigible from the company, its directors and officers, must issue a share certificate within two months after allotment, and within two months of the registration of any transfer, unless the conditions of the issue of shares otherwise provide. Similar rules apply to debentures.[48] By section 81 a certificate under the common seal of the company is prima facie evidence of the title to the shares. If regularly issued it is conclusive against the company, and therefore if a company, deceived by a forged transfer, issues a certificate, it is barred from denying the title of a bona fide transferee, and is liable to him in the value of the shares.[49] And where a company, either owing to a mistake

[38] 1967 Act, s. 34.
[39] 1976 Act, s. 27.
[40] 1948 Act, s. 73. See Table A, arts. 22 et seq. *Lyle & Scott Ltd.* v. *Scott's Trs.*, 1959 S.C. (H.L.) 64.
[41] For the form of transfers, see Stock Transfer Act 1963 (c. 18), as amended by Stock Exchange (Completion of Bargains) Act 1976, c. 47.
[42] cf. *Borland's Tr.* v. *Steel Bros. & Co.* [1901] 1 Ch. 279; *Rayfield* v. *Hands* [1960] Ch. 1.
[43] *Re Discoverer's Finance Corporation (Lindlar's case)* [1910] 1 Ch. 312; cf. *Re Swaledale Cleaners* [1968] 1 W.L.R. 1710.
[44] *Dodds* v. *Cosmopolitan Insurance Co.*, 1915 S.C. 992; cf. *Lindlar's case*, supra, per Buckley L.J., at p. 318.
[45] *McLintock* v. *Campbell*, 1916 S.C. 966.
[46] *Bede Shipping Co.* [1917] 1 Ch. 123; *Stewart* v. *Keiller* (1902) 4 F. 657; *Weinburger* v. *Inglis* [1919] A.C. 606, per Lord Atkinson at p. 626.
[47] *Stevenson* v. *Wilson*, 1907 S.C. 445.
[48] 1948 Act, s. 80.
[49] *Balkis Co.* v. *Tomkinson* [1893] A.C. 396.

or to fraud on the part of its officials, issues certificates stating, untruly, that the shares are fully paid up, they will be liable to a party who is induced to advance money on the faith of the certificates.[50] But the company is not bound by the issue of share certificates fraudulently issued by the secretary to which the names of directors have been forged.[51] Anyone who sends a transfer for registration impliedly contracts that he will relieve the company of any liability. So where a banker sent for registration a transfer of corporation stock to which the name of A, the holder, had been forged, and the corporation registered the transfer and issued new certificates to transferees, with the result that they were bound to recognise the right both of A and of the transferees, it was held that they had a right of relief from the banker.[52] The stereotyped statement that no transfer will be registered without the production of the share certificate is a mere statement of intention and does not bind the company, nor make them liable to a party who has advanced money on a deposit of share certificates, and whose right is defeated by a registered transfer of the shares.[53]

22. Majority and Minority Rights.—By his contract with the company, each individual member undertakes to accept as binding upon him the decision of the majority of the shareholders, provided that it is arrived at in accordance with the law and the articles. This principle is often referred to as the rule in *Foss* v. *Harbottle*.[54] In that case a minority of the shareholders alleged that the company had a claim of damages against certain of its directors, but at a general meeting the majority resolved that no action should be taken against them. An action against the directors by the minority was dismissed, on the ground that the acts of the directors were capable of confirmation by a majority of the members, and that it was not for the Court to interfere with their decision as to what was for the benefit of the company. The rule does not, however, apply where the act in question is ultra vires of the company, or illegal, or constitutes a fraud on the minority,[55] nor will a resolution passed by a simple majority be binding when a qualified majority is required, as in the case of special or extraordinary resolutions. A resolution constitutes a fraud on the minority if its effect is to discriminate against the minority in favour of the majority shareholders and it was not made bona fide for the benefit of the company as a whole.[56]

If the majority of the shareholders acts in oppression of the minority, the minority may apply to the Court for the winding up of the company, on the ground that it is just and equitable to do so,[57] or, in exceptional cases, for the appointment of a judicial factor.[58] The Court cannot make a winding up order

[50] *Clavering* v. *Goodwin, Jardine & Co.* (1891) 18 R. 652; *Penang Co.* v. *Gardiner*, 1913 S.C. 1203.
[51] *Ruben* v. *Great Fingall Consolidated Co.* [1906] A.C. 439.
[52] *Sheffield Corporation* v. *Barclay* [1905] A.C. 392.
[53] *Rainford* v. *Keith* [1905] 2 Ch. 147; *Guy* v. *Waterlow* (1909) 25 T.L.R. 515.
[54] (1843) 2 Hare 461; see Palmer, paras. 56-09 et seq.
[55] *North-West Transportation Co.* v. *Beatty* (1887) 12 App.Cas. 589.
[56] See *Greenhalgh* v. *Arderne Cinemas* [1951] 1 Ch. 286, per Lord Evershed M.R. at p. 291.
[57] 1948 Act, s. 222 (*f*); see § 42, infra; *Lewis* v. *Haas*, 1971 S.L.T. 57.
[58] See *Fraser, Petr.*, 1971 S.L.T. 146.

on the ground that it is just and equitable to do so, if it is of opinion that some other remedy is available to the petitioners, and that the petitioners are acting unreasonably in seeking to have the company wound up instead of pursuing that other remedy.[59]

An alternative remedy to the winding up of the company, which may in any event not be in the best interests of the oppressed minority, is provided by section 210. Any member of a company who complains that the affairs of the company are being conducted in a manner oppressive to some part of the members may apply for an order under that section. Oppressive conduct for this purpose involves a lack of probity and fair dealing in the affairs of the company to the prejudice of some portion of its members.[60] The matters complained of must affect the petitioner in his capacity as a member of the company, and relate to oppression of his rights as a member because of the manner in which the affairs of the company are being conducted.[61] An employee who is being treated oppressively has no remedy under this section, and a member who is also an employee or director, or holds some other office in the company, has no recourse to the section merely because of the treatment which he has suffered in that other capacity.[62] If the court is of opinion that the affairs of the company are being so conducted that to wind up the company would unfairly prejudice that part of the members, but that otherwise the facts would justify the making of a winding up order on the ground that it was just and equitable to do so, it may make such order as it thinks fit for ending the matters complained of. The order may regulate the company's conduct of its affairs in the future, such as by providing for the appointment of further directors or the restriction of their powers,[63] or provide for the purchase of the shares of any member of the company by other members of the company or by the company itself.[64]

The remedies referred to in the previous paragraph may be exercised by an individual member of the company. Certain other rights are conferred by the Act on a minority of the members, and may be exercised despite the wishes of the majority. These include the right of the minority of not less than one-tenth of the paid-up capital to requisition the holding of an extraordinary general meeting,[65] of a specified minority to demand a poll,[66] and of 15 per cent of the holders of special classes of shares to object to a variation of the rights attached to that class.[67]

23. Commencing Business: Meetings.—A company other than a private company is not entitled to commence business or exercise any borrowing

---

[59] s. 225(2).
[60] *Meyer* v. *Scottish Co-operative Wholesale Society,* 1958 S.C. (H.L.) 40, per Lord Keith of Avonholm at p. 65; *Re Jermyn Street Turkish Baths* [1971] 1 W.L.R. 1042.
[61] E.g. *Meyer* v. *Scottish Co-operative Wholesale Society,* supra.
[62] *Elder* v. *Elder & Watson,* 1952 S.C. 49; *Re Lundie Bros.* [1965] 1 W.L.R. 1051; *Re Jermyn Street Turkish Baths,* supra.
[63] See *Re H. R. Harmer* [1959] 1 W.L.R. 62.
[64] See *Meyer* v. *Scottish Co-operative Wholesale Society,* supra.
[65] s. 132.
[66] s. 137(1) (b).
[67] s. 72.

powers until it has obtained a certificate from the Registrar, issued on a declaration that shares have been allotted to an amount not less than the minimum subscription (see supra, § 17), that every director has paid to the company, on each of the shares taken by him, an amount equal to the proportion payable on application and allotment on the shares offered for public subscription and that no money is or may be liable to be repaid to applicants through failure to obtain permission to deal in the shares or debentures.[68] It is bound, within three months of the date at which it is entitled to commence business, to hold a general meeting of the shareholders, termed in the Act the "statutory meeting."[69] Fourteen days before this meeting every public company must file with the registrar and forward to each shareholder a report, known as the "statutory report," stating—(1) the number of shares allotted, how far paid up, and the consideration received; (2) the amount received for the shares; (3) an abstract of the receipts and payments made, and an estimate of preliminary expenses; (4) the names of the directors and officials; (5) particulars of any contract which is to be submitted for modification at the statutory meeting, and the modification proposed.[70]

Thereafter a general meeting of every company must be held once at least in every year, and not more than fifteen months from the date of the previous meeting.[71] Failure to hold such a meeting may result in the directors being held to have ceased to hold office.[72] The business of the annual general meeting depends upon the articles, but it normally includes consideration of the accounts and reports of the auditor and of the directors, declaration of a dividend, the appointment of an auditor and the election of directors in place of those who retire. A company having a share capital must complete each year, within forty-two days of the annual general meeting, a return giving the information specified in the Sixth Schedule,[73] relating to its registered office, members and debenture holders, shares and debentures, indebtedness and directors and secretary, and send it forthwith to the Registrar.[74] General meetings other than the statutory meeting and annual general meetings are called extraordinary general meetings. The articles usually provide that the directors may call an extraordinary general meeting at any time they think fit. The directors are bound to convene an extraordinary general meeting on the requisition (which must state the object of the meeting) of the holders of not less than one-tenth of the issued share capital. Should the directors fail to do so within twenty-one days of the receipt of the requisition the requisitionists, or a majority of them in value, may convene the meeting themselves.[75] Meetings of separate classes of shareholders may be required where it is proposed to alter, vary or affect the rights of a particular class.[76]

[68] s. 109.
[69] s. 130.
[70] s. 130.
[71] s. 131.
[72] *Alexander Ward & Co.* v. *Samyang Navigation Co.*, 1973 S.L.T. (Notes) 80.
[73] As amended by 1967 Act, Sched. 8.
[74] ss. 124 and 126.
[75] s. 132. See *Ball* v. *Metal Industries*, 1957 S.C. 315.
[76] See s. 23(2).

24. Accounts and Balance Sheet: Directors' Report.—Every company must keep accounting records sufficient to show and explain its transactions.[77] These require to be such as to disclose with reasonable accuracy at any time the financial position of the company, and to enable the directors to ensure that any balance sheet or profit and loss account prepared by them complies with the requirements of section 149 of the 1948 Act, namely that they give a true and fair view of the company's state of affairs at the end of its financial year and of the profit or loss of the company for that year.[78] The accounting records are to be kept at the registered office of the company or such other place as the directors think fit, and are to be at all times open to inspection by the officers of the company.[79] Every officer of the company who is in default as to the keeping of accounting records is guilty of an offence, unless he acted honestly and his default is reasonable in the circumstances.[80]

The directors of every company are required[81] to prepare accounts in respect of each accounting reference period of the company,[82] to lay these accounts before the company in general meeting, and to deliver a copy to the Registrar of Companies within a specified time. The accounts are required to comprise[83] a profit and loss account for the period, a balance sheet as at the date to which the profit and loss account is made up, the report of the auditor[84] and the report of the directors.[85] If the requirements for laying and delivering accounts are not complied with within the period allowed, every person who is a director of the company immediately before the end of the period is guilty of an offence, but it is a defence for him to prove that he took all reasonable steps for securing that the requirements would be complied with.[86] Apart from the general requirements that every balance sheet of the company shall give a true and fair view of the state of affairs of the company as at the end of its financial year, and that the profit and loss account shall give a true and fair view of its profit or loss for the financial year, these documents must also comply with the detailed requirements set out in the Eighth Schedule to the principal Act.[87] The accounts must also show separately the aggregate amounts and certain other particulars of the directors' emoluments, of their pensions and of compensation paid for loss of office,[88] and they must show certain particulars of the salaries of employees of the company receiving more than £10,000 a year.[89] They must also show any loans to its officers[90] made or guaranteed by the company.[91] The accounts

---

[77] 1976 Act, s. 12(1), (2); as to what they must contain, see subss. (4) and (5).
[78] 1976 Act, s. 12(3).
[79] 1976 Act, s. 12(6).
[80] 1976 Act, s. 12(10).
[81] 1976 Act, s. 1.
[82] See 1976 Act, s. 2.
[83] 1976 Act, s. 1(5).
[84] 1948 Act, s. 156(1); See § 38, infra.
[85] s. 157(1).
[86] 1976 Act, s. 4.
[87] Sch. 8, as amended by 1967 Act, Sch. 1, is set out in Sch. 2 to that Act.
[88] s. 196, and ss. 6, 7 of 1967 Act.
[89] 1967 Act, s. 8.
[90] Defined in s. 455 (1).
[91] s. 197.

must also disclose the identities and places of incorporation of (a) the company's subsidiaries and particulars of the company's shareholdings therein, (b) companies, not being its subsidiaries, in which the company holds shares of any class exceeding in nominal value one-tenth of the nominal value of the issued shares of that class, and (c) the company's ultimate holding company.[92] Section 157 (1) requires there to be attached to every balance sheet laid before the company in general meeting a report by the directors with respect to the state of the company's affairs, the amount, if any, which they recommend should be paid by way of dividend, and the amount, if any, which they propose to carry to reserves. In addition information must be given in the directors' report on certain general matters, and certain particulars must be given of the average number of employees and the amount of contributions for political and charitable purposes and, in the case of certain companies, of exports.[93] A copy of the balance sheet, and the documents required by law to be annexed thereto, including the directors' and auditor's reports, must be sent to every member twenty-one days before the meeting at which they are to be considered.[94] Special provision is made for the preparation of group accounts by companies with subsidiaries.[95]

25. Borrowing Powers.—Trading companies have implied power to borrow, and to grant securities over any of their assets.[96] Non-trading companies have no such implied power, but it may be expressly adopted, with or without a limit in amount, in the memorandum of association. It was formerly the law that if money was borrowed by a company which had no power to borrow, or in excess of its borrowing powers, the transaction was ultra vires and void, and the lender could not recover his money,[97] except in so far as it could be proved to have been expended in meeting obligations for which the company was liable.[98] Any such transaction decided on by the directors is, however, now deemed to be intra vires both of the company and the directors; a party thereto is not bound to inquire as to the capacity and powers of the company or directors, and is presumed to have acted in good faith unless the contrary is proved.[99]

26. Floating Charges: Registration of Charges.—Part III of the principal Act, under which a company can subject its whole assets to a floating charge, applies only to companies registered in England. Prior to the Companies (Floating Charges) (Scotland) Act 1961,[1] a company registered in Scotland not only could not create a floating charge over its assets in Scotland, but

92 1967 Act, ss. 3-5.
93 1967 Act, ss. 16-20.
94 s. 158 as amended by 1967 Act, s. 24.
95 ss. 150-154.
96 *General Auction Co.* v. *Smith* [1891] 3 Ch. 432.
97 *Brooks* v. *Blackburn Building Society* (1884) 9 App.Cas. 857; *Wenlock* v. *River Dee Co.* (1885) 10 App.Cas. 354.
98 *Reversion, etc., Co.* v. *Maison Cosway* [1913] 1 K.B. 364; *Sinclair* v. *Brougham* [1914] A.C. 398.
99 European Communities Act 1972, c. 68, s. 9(1).
1 9 & 10 Eliz. II. c. 46.

could not do so even over its assets in England, nor would a floating charge created by an English company with assets in Scotland receive recognition in Scotland.[2] To be effective any security given by the company required to be a fixed security by which a real right in the property was constituted in favour of the creditor. Under the Act of 1961, however, it became competent under the law of Scotland for an incorporated company, whether it is an English or a Scottish company, to secure any existing or future debts, including any balance on cash account, by creating in favour of a creditor a floating charge over the whole or any part of the property, heritable and moveable, which may from time to time be comprised in its property and undertaking. That Act was repealed and re-enacted with modifications by the Companies (Floating Charges and Receivers) (Scotland) Act 1972,[3] which also made it competent for the first time for receivers to be appointed in respect of Scottish companies.[4]

The essence of a floating charge is that it gives the creditor of a company security[5] over the property which is subject to the charge, without the need for delivery, intimation or, in the case of heritage, registration in the Register of Sasines.[6] The charge lies dormant until the company is wound up or a receiver is appointed, leaving the company free in the meantime to dispose of the property over which it extends; if it acquires new property that also may become subject to the charge. On the commencement of the winding up, however, or on the appointment of a receiver, the charge attaches to the property then comprised in the company's property and undertaking or such part of it as is subject to the charge.[7] It does so as if it were a fixed security over the property to which it has attached,[8] but subject to the rights of any person who has effectually executed diligence[9] on the property or any part of it, or who holds a fixed security or another floating charge over the property or any part of it which has priority of ranking.[10] A floating charge created within twelve months of the commencement of a winding up is invalid unless it is proved that the company was solvent immediately after the creation of the charge, except to the amount of any cash paid to the company at the time of or after the creation of, and in consideration for, the charge.[11] A floating charge is capable of being assigned.[11a] As regards ranking, a fixed security arising by operation of law, such as a repairer's lien, ranks in priority over a floating

---

[2] *Carse* v. *Coppen*, 1951 S.C. 233; see also *Ballachulish Slate Quarries* v. *Menzies* (1908) 45 S.L.R. 667.

[3] c. 67.

[4] 1972 Act, Pt. II; see § 28, infra.

[5] See Rights in Security, Ch. XX, supra, § 12, for a discussion of the floating charge as a right in security.

[6] 1972 Act, s. 3.

[7] ss. 1(2), 13(7), 14(7).

[8] *National Commercial Bank of Scotland* v. *Liqrs. of Telford Grier Mackay & Co.*, 1969 S.C. 181, per Lord President Clyde at p. 194. The appointment of a receiver of an English company has the same effect with regard to its property situated in Scotland: *Gordon Anderson (Plant)* v. *Campsie Construction*, 1977 S.L.T. 7.

[9] As to the meaning of "effectually executed diligence", see *Lord Advocate* v. *Royal Bank of Scotland*, 1978 S.L.T. 38; Diligence, Ch. XLVIII, infra.

[10] ss. 1(2), 15(2).

[11] 1948 Act, s. 322. See *Libertas-Kommerz*, 1978 S.L.T. 222; Palmer, para. 43–09.

[11a] *Libertas-Kommerz*, supra.

COMPANY LAW

charge.[12] Subject to that rule, the instrument creating the floating charge or any instrument of alteration may contain provisions restricting or prohibiting the creation of fixed or floating charges ranking prior to or pari passu with the charge, or regulating the order in which the floating charge shall rank with any other subsisting or future fixed and floating charges.[13] If no such provisions are contained in the instrument, a fixed security the right to which has been constituted as a real right before the crystallisation of a floating charge has priority over the floating charge, while floating charges rank inter se according to the time of registration with the Registrar of Companies, charges received by the same postal delivery ranking equally.[14] The holder of a floating charge having a postponed ranking may restrict the preference of a floating charge which has priority of ranking by giving written intimation of the registration of his charge.[15] In the event of a winding up, the provisions of the 1948 Act relating to winding up have effect as if the floating charge were a fixed security in respect of the principal of the debt or obligation to which it relates and any interest due or to become due thereon.[16] In the event of a receivership, special provisions apply in order to regulate the distribution of monies received by the receiver.[17] The instrument creating a floating charge may be altered by the execution of an instrument of alteration by the company, the holder of the charge and by the holder of any other charge which would be adversely affected by the alteration.[18]

The machinery for the registration of charges in Scotland is provided in the Schedule to the Act of 1972, which adds to the 1948 Act a new Part IIIA comprised of sections 106A to 106K. The leading provision of this Part is contained in section 106A (1), which provides that every charge created by a company, being a charge to which the section applies, shall so far as any security on the company's property is conferred thereby be void against the liquidator and any creditor of the company unless the prescribed particulars[19] of the charge together with a copy of the instrument by which it is created are delivered to or received by the Registrar within twenty-one days after the date of its creation.[20] The section applies to a charge on land, a security over uncalled share capital, a security over certain categories of incorporeal moveable property and a security over a ship as well as to floating charges.[21] The requirement for registration with the Registrar of Companies in Scotland applies to charges over heritable property situated in England as well as Scotland, where the company which created the charge is registered in Scotland.[22] The register of charges is kept by the Registrar of Companies, whose certificate of registration is conclusive evidence that the requirements of

[12] s. 5(2).
[13] s. 5(1).
[14] s. 5(3), (4).
[15] s. 5(5).
[16] s. 1(2); *National Commercial Bank of Scotland* v. *Liqrs. of Telford Grier Mackay & Co.*, supra.
[17] s. 20.
[18] s. 7. For requirements for creation by Scottish companies, see s. 2.
[19] For these particulars, see s. 106D(1).
[20] For the meaning of the date of creation of a charge, see s. 106A(10).
[21] s. 106A(2).
[22] *Amalgamated Securities*, 1967 S.C. 56.

the Act as to registration have been complied with.[23] Provision is made for the entry on the register of a memorandum of satisfaction where the debt for which the charge was given has been paid or satisfied in whole or part or the property has been released from the charge.[24] If the charge does not fall within the list of charges detailed in the definition, registration with the Registrar of Companies is not required,[25] but every company must keep at its registered office a register of all fixed and floating charges affecting its property, whether registerable under section 106A or not.[26] English companies are no longer required to register in Scotland charges affecting Scottish property, whether registrable under section 106A or not.[26] English companies created by, or on property in Scotland which is acquired by, a company incorporated outside Great Britain which has a place of business in Scotland.[28] The Court has power in a suitable case to extend the time for registration or to rectify the register where there has been an omission or mis-statement of any particular.[29]

27. Debentures.—Public companies frequently borrow by the issue of debentures. The term is defined as including debenture stock, bonds and any other securities of a company whether constituting a charge on the assets of the company or not.[30] This definition would seem to include any form of bond or mortgage which imports an obligation to pay.[31] A debenture may be merely a personal obligation of the company, but it is usual for security to be provided in the hands of trustees for the debenture-holders in the form of a fixed security or a floating charge. They may be irredeemable or redeemable only on the happening of a remote contingency or until expiry of a period however long.[32] Debentures are to be construed according to their terms, so that if the repayment of the capital sum is made optional it cannot be demanded until the company chooses to pay.[33] Provision is made for the reissue of debentures which have been paid off and at common law would be extinguished on the principle of confusio.[34] Debentures may be issued payable to bearer, and in that form are negotiable instruments.[35] Debentures payable to bearer and issued in Scotland are valid and binding according to their terms notwithstanding anything contained in the Blank Bonds and Trusts Act 1696 (c. 25).[36]

28. Receivers.—The holder of a charge or of a debenture created by a

[23] ss. 106D-E.
[24] s. 106F.
[25] *Scottish Homes Investment Co.*, 1968 S.C. 244.
[26] s. 106I.
[27] As they were by 1961 Act, s. 106K, now repealed.
[28] s. 106K, as substituted by 1972 Act.
[29] See s. 106G.
[30] s. 455(1).
[31] See *Lemon* v. *Austin Friars Co.* [1926] 1 Ch. 1.
[32] s. 89; see also Redemption of Standard Securities (Scotland) Act 1971, c. 45, s. 2.
[33] *Wylie* v. *Carlyon* [1922] 1 Ch. 51.
[34] s. 90.
[35] s. 93; *Bechuanaland Exploration Co.* v. *London Trading Bank* [1898] 2 Q.B. 658.
[36] s. 93. As to the 1696 Act, see Gloag, *Contract* (2nd ed.), p. 5.

Scottish company has the ordinary remedies available to a creditor. He may raise an action for payment of his debt or petition for the winding up of the company. The 1972 Act, however, introduced an additional remedy which may be exercised only by the holder of a floating charge, namely the power to appoint or to apply to the Court for the appointment of a receiver.[37] This remedy is available to the holders of all floating charges including those of subsisting floating charges created under the 1961 Act, and it need not be provided for in the instrument creating the charge. It remains competent for a holder of a floating charge who has secured the appointment of a receiver to apply for an order for a winding up. A receiver may be appointed on the occurrence of any event which is provided for in the instrument creating the charge as entitling the holder to make the appointment; and, in so far as the instrument does not otherwise provide, on the expiry of a period of twenty-one days after the making of a demand for payment of the whole or any part of the principal sum secured by the charge without payment being made, on the expiry of a period of two months during the whole of which interest due and payable under the charge has been in arrears, on the making of an order or the passing of a resolution for the winding up of the company, or on the appointment of a receiver by virtue of any other floating charge created by the company.[38] The receiver may be appointed either by an instrument in writing executed by or on behalf of the holder of the charge,[39] or by the Court to whom the holder requires to apply by petition served on the company.[40] The appointment of a receiver requires to be intimated to the Registrar of Companies.[41] On his appointment, the floating charge attaches to the property then subject to the charge as if it were a fixed security,[42] in the same way as on the commencement of a winding up.

The powers which the receiver is to have in relation to the property attached by the floating charge may be defined in the instrument creating the charge, but he has a wide range of statutory powers for ingathering the property and doing other acts, which may be exercised so far as not inconsistent with any provision contained in that instrument.[43] In the exercise of these powers he is not subject to the control of the directors of the company. Accordingly where a receiver is appointed of the whole assets of the company the directors are not entitled to deal in any way with the property of the company.[44] His powers are, however, subject to the rights of every person who has effectually executed diligence on all or any part of the property prior to his appointment, and to the rights of the holder of a charge ranking prior to or pari passu with the floating charge by virtue of which he was appointed.[45] The receiver is deemed to be the agent of the company in relation

[37] s. 11(1), (2).
[38] s. 12.
[39] s. 13.
[40] s. 14.
[41] ss. 13(1), 14(3).
[42] ss. 13(7), 14(7).
[43] s. 15.
[44] *Imperial Hotel* (*Aberdeen*) v. *Vaux Breweries*, 1978 S.L.T. 113.
[45] s. 15(2); see also note 9, supra.

to its property, but he is personally liable on any contracts entered into by him in the performance of his functions.[46] If the company is not at the time being wound up, he must pay out of any assets in his hands in priority to the claims of the holder of the floating charge claims which would have ranked as preferential debts in a winding up, provided they came to his notice by the end of a period of six months after he has advertised for claims.[47] In the distribution of monies received by him, he is required to give preference to the holders of fixed securities which rank prior to or pari passu with the floating charge, persons who have effectually executed diligence over the property, and to creditors in respect of liabilities incurred by him. Thereafter, subject to his own remuneration and expenses, all monies received by him are to be paid to the holder on account of the debt secured.[48] Any surplus is to be paid in accordance with their respective rights and interests to any other receiver, holder of a fixed security or the company or its liquidator.[49] The Act contains detailed provisions as to the provision of information to the receiver and the provision of information by him to the Registrar of Companies and other interested parties.[50]

29. Dividends.[51]—Although the Act contains no specific rules on the matter, dividends are payable only out of profits. It is established by the decisions, and usually provided in the articles,[52] that it is ultra vires to pay dividends out of capital, e.g. if a ship be lost it is illegal to distribute the amount recovered as insurance as a dividend.[53] But the question what sums should be ascribed to capital and what to income does not admit of any general answer. "The mode and manner in which a business is carried on, and what is usual or the reverse, may have a considerable influence in determining the question what may be treated as profits and what as capital."[54] Neither the Act, nor the general law, makes it illegal for a company to distribute the profits of its trading in any year, although its paid-up capital has been wholly or partially lost, or until it has made up trading losses incurred in previous years.[55] So the mere fact that the company possesses a wasting asset, e.g. a mine, does not render it necessary to set up a sinking fund before dividends can be paid.[56] An investment company may pay dividends on its ordinary shares although the depreciation in the value of the shares may be so great as to show that the capital represented by the shares has been lost.[57] Where

---

[46] s. 17; see *Macleod* v. *Alexander Sutherland,* 1977 S.L.T. (Notes) 44.
[47] s. 19.
[48] s. 20(1).
[49] s. 20(2).
[50] ss. 25, 26.
[51] See s. 65 for conditions relating to payment of interest out of capital.
[52] See Table A, art. 116.
[53] *Moxham* v. *Grant* [1900] 1 Q.B. 88.
[54] Per Lord Halsbury, *Dovey* v. *Cory* [1901] A.C. 477. See Palmer, *Company Law,* para. 72-05 et seq. for general rules for the determination of "divisible profits."
[55] *Ammonium Soda Co.* v. *Chamberlain* [1918] 1 Ch. 266.
[56] *Lee* v. *Neuchatel Co.* (1889) 41 Ch.D. 1; *Bond* v. *Barrow Haematite Co.* [1902] 1 Ch. 353.
[57] *City Property Investment Co.* v. *Thorburn* (1897) 25 R. 361; *Verner* v. *General Trust* [1894] 2 Ch. 239.

interest on a debt was unpaid but credited to income, on which dividends were calculated, it was held that this course was justified if there was a reasonable prospect of ultimate payment.[58] It would appear that in Scotland an unrealised profit resulting from a revaluation of the company's fixed assets cannot be treated as profit for dividend purposes.[59] Where dividends have been paid out of capital the directors are jointly and severally liable to the company or to its liquidator, with a right to recover from the shareholders what they have received, provided that they received the dividend in knowledge of its origin.[60] When the articles provide for payment of dividends in a certain event—provided it does not amount to payment out of capital—a shareholder, or one class of shareholder, may enforce compliance by action.[61]

30. Promoters.—A promoter is defined in the Act, though only for the purposes of the section which imposes liability for untruthful statements in the prospectus, as "a promoter who was a party to the preparation of the prospectus, or of the portion thereof containing the untrue statement, but does not include any person by reason of his acting in a professional capacity for persons engaged in procuring the formation of the company."[62] It has been judicially referred to as "a term not of law but of business usefully summing up in a single word a number of business operations familiar to the commercial world by which a company is generally brought into existence."[63] The term is probably too vague to admit of an exact definition.[64]

A promoter is not a trustee for the company which he brings into existence. Thus—subject to the necessity of full disclosure of the facts—a sale by a promoter to the company is valid.[65] And where a private Act gave power to a company to pay the expenses of its formation it was no objection to the charges of the law agent and the engineer that they were promoters of the company.[66] A promoter cannot be an agent for a company which is not yet in existence. So a company is neither bound by, nor entitled to sue on, contracts made ostensibly on its behalf by a promoter before its incorporation.[67] But it has been held that a promoter "must put himself in the position of an agent for the company which he has promoted, and must regulate his relations to the company according to the duty of an agent."[68] He stands in a fiduciary position to the company and must disclose all material facts.[69] The principle is not that it is illegal for a promoter to make a profit, but that the nature and source of his profit must be disclosed; and they must be disclosed to the

[58] *City of Glasgow Bank* v. *Mackinnon* (1882) 9 R. 535.
[59] *Westburn Sugar Refineries* v. *I.R.C.*, 1960 S.L.T. 297. This is not the case in England: see *Dimbula Valley (Ceylon) Tea Co.* v. *Laurie* [1961] Ch. 353; Palmer, para. 72-13.
[60] *Flitcroft's Case* (1882) 21 Ch. D. 519; *Moxham* v. *Grant* [1900] 1 Q.B. 88.
[61] *City Property Inv. Co.* v. *Thorburn* (1897) 25 R. 361; *Paterson* v. *Paterson*, 1917 S.C. (H.L.) 13.
[62] s. 43 (5). See supra, § 16.
[63] *Whaley Bridge Co.* v. *Green* (1879) 5 Q.B.D. 109, per Bowen L.J., at p. 111.
[64] See *Lydney Co.* v. *Bird* (1886) 33 Ch. D. 85; *Jubilee Cotton Mills* v. *Lewis* [1924] A.C. 958.
[65] *Lagunas Nitrate Co.* v. *Lagunas Syndicate* [1899] 2 Ch. 392.
[66] *Edinburgh Northern Tramways* v. *Mann* (1896) 23 R. 1056.
[67] *Tinnevelley Sugar Refining Co.* v. *Mirrlees* (1894) 21 R. 1009.
[68] per Lord McLaren, in *Edinburgh Northern Tramways*, supra, at p. 1066.
[69] *Erlanger* v. *New Sombrero Phosphate Co.* (1878) 2 App.Cas. 1218.

shareholders, not merely to the directors who may be his nominees.[70] So while a man may purchase a property for £10,000 and sell it next day for £20,000, he cannot do so without disclosure of the facts, if he is a promoter and the company the purchaser.[71] The company has in such cases the right, resting on general principles of law and not on any express provision of the Companies Act, either to avoid the contract or to recover from the promoter any benefit he, or a firm of which he is a partner, may have gained.[72] To justify such a claim it is not necessary that the promoter has obtained something from the company, or at its expense. Where what he obtained were debentures, irregularly issued, and really valueless, it was held that the company could recover from him the price at which he had fraudulently sold them to a third party.[73]

31. Directors: Appointment.—Every company, except a private company, registered after November 1, 1929, must have at least two directors; and every company registered before that date and every private company must have at least one director.[74] Every company must also have a secretary, and a sole director cannot also be secretary.[75] There is no general rule that a director must be a shareholder. But it is generally provided in the articles that every director must hold one or more shares, commonly referred to as qualification shares.[76] By section 181, which does not apply to private companies, no person can be a director unless he has filed with the registrar a consent in writing to be a director, and either signed the memorandum for a number of shares not less than his qualification (if any), or signed and filed a contract to take from the company and pay for his qualification shares. By section 182 a director vacates his office if he does not obtain his qualification shares within two months of his appointment.[77] Other grounds of disqualification may be provided by the articles.[78] An undischarged bankrupt is disqualified from acting as a director or being concerned in the management of any company without the leave of the Court by which his estates were sequestrated, and he commits a criminal offence if he does so without leave.[79] The Court has power to order that a person who is or has been a director of an insolvent company shall not be a director or be concerned in the management of a company for a period of up to five years without leave of the Court.[80] The Court also has power to disqualify a person from being a director for a period of up to five years in cases of fraud or breach of duty.[81] It is provided however that the acts

[70] *Mann* v. *Edinburgh Northern Tramways* (1891) 18 R. 1140; affd. 20 R. (H.L.) 7; *Erlanger* v. *New Sombrero Phosphate Co.*, supra; *Re Lady Forrest Mine* [1901] 1 Ch. 582.
[71] See opinion of Lord Blackburn in *Erlanger*, supra.
[72] *Henderson* v. *Huntingdon Copper Co.* (1877) 4 R. 294, affd. 5 R. (H.L.) 1; *Scottish Pacific Coast Mining Co.* v. *Falkner* (1888) 15 R. 290; *Mann* v. *Edinburgh Northern Tramways Co.*, supra.
[73] *Jubilee Cotton Mills* v. *Lewis* [1924] A.C. 958.
[74] s. 176.
[75] s. 177.
[76] s. 182; Table A, art. 77.
[77] See *Holmes* v. *Keyes* [1959] Ch. 199; *Pollock* v. *Garnett*, 1957 S.L.T. (Notes) 8.
[78] See Table A, art. 88.
[79] s. 187.
[80] Insolvency Act 1976, (c. 60), s. 9.
[81] 1948 Act, s. 188.

of a director or manager are to be valid notwithstanding any defect that may afterwards be discovered in his appointment or qualification.[82]

Under the provisions of Table A the first directors are appointed by the signatories to the memorandum.[83] They vacate office, subject to re-election, at the first general meeting of the company. Thereafter a third of their number retire annually, but may be re-elected.[84] Failure to hold an annual general meeting may result, depending upon the terms of the articles, in the company ceasing to have directors.[85] The company may increase or reduce the number of directors.[86] A director may be removed by the company during his term of office.[87] Where a director has been removed from office or has resigned and no official notification of that event has been given, and he continues to act as director, or if he does so within fifteen days even if official notification has been given, his acts will bind the company unless the company can prove that the third party knew of the irregularity.[88] Subject to certain exceptions no person aged over seventy may be appointed director in a public company or a private company which is a subsidiary of a public company.[89] A company must keep a register of its directors showing, inter alia, other directorships held by them,[90] and must keep and make available for inspection by members of the company a record of the terms of the contract of service of each director.[91] A company registered after November 23, 1916, must show on its catalogues, letters, etc., the names of its directors and their nationality, if not British.[92] The directors are normally given power to appoint one of their number as managing director, and to fill up casual vacancies on the board.[93]

The remuneration of the directors may be provided for in the articles, or by the company in general meeting,[94] or in the case of a managing director by the directors themselves.[95] Although they are the persons by whom the company normally acts and by whom its business is carried on as its agents,[96] they are not as such employees of the company. A director may nevertheless be a salaried employee of the company.[97] As a director, though not in all respects a trustee for the company, holds a fiduciary position, he is not entitled to remuneration without contract merely because he has done extra work for the company.[98] And the directors have no power to vote themselves additional

[82] s. 180; Table A, art. 105; *Morris* v. *Kanssen* [1946] A.C. 459; see *Freeman & Lockyer* v. *Buckhurst Park Properties* [1964] 2 Q.B. 480; and Capacity to Contract, Ch. VI., supra, § 10.
[83] Table A, art. 75.
[84] Ibid., art. 89.
[85] *Alexander Ward & Co.* v. *Samyang Navigation Co.*, 1973 S.L.T. (Notes) 80.
[86] Table A, art. 94.
[87] s. 184.
[88] European Communities Act 1972, s. 9(4).
[89] ss. 185, 186.
[90] s. 200.
[91] 1967 Act, s. 26.
[92] s. 201.
[93] Table A, arts 95, 107.
[94] Table A, art. 76.
[95] Table A, art. 107; see also *Richmond Gate Property Co.* [1965] 1 W.L.R. 335.
[96] *Ferguson* v. *Wilson* (1866) L.R. 2. Ch. 77.
[97] See *Anderson* v. *James Sutherland (Peterhead)*, 1941 S.C. 203.
[98] *McNaughton* v. *Brunton* (1882) 10 R. 111.

remuneration which is not authorised by the articles, e.g. travelling expenses to board meetings.[99]

32. Powers of Directors.—The powers delegated by the company to its directors are set out in its articles.[1] While these powers are frequently expressed in general terms, they are limited by certain principles. First, since in exercising these powers the directors are merely the agents of the company, they cannot act beyond the powers which have been taken by the company in its memorandum of association. Secondly, even when acting within the powers of the company, the directors are limited to the powers which the company has delegated to them either by the articles or in general meeting. In questions with third parties however who deal with the company in good faith any transaction decided on by the directors is deemed to be one which it is within the capacity of the company to enter into and the power of the directors to bind the company is deemed to be free of any limitation under the memorandum or articles of association.[2] A party to a transaction decided on by the directors is not bound to inquire as to the capacity of the company to enter into it or as to whether there is any limitation on the powers of the directors, and he is presumed to have acted in good faith unless the contrary is proved.[3] Where there is a general clause in the articles vesting the management of the company in the directors, the directors have full powers of management and so long as the articles remain unaltered are not subject to the control of the members of the company by ordinary resolution in general meeting.[4] The members retain however a measure of control in that they have power to alter the articles[5] or to remove a director at any time,[6] and they may also be entitled to an order under section 210.[7] Furthermore the directors are required to exercise their powers bona fide for the benefit of the company, and an abuse of their powers may be restrained by the Court.[8] A transaction which is voidable on the ground that it is outside the powers of the directors may be ratified by the company in general meeting, unless it is ultra vires of the company or involves a fraud on the minority.[9]

33. Contracts Between Director and Company.—At common law a director, or a firm of which he is a partner, cannot enforce any contract made with the company.[10] Such a contract may be ratified by a general meeting,[11]

---

[99] *Marmor* v. *Alexander*, 1908 S.C. 78.
[1] See Table A, arts. 80-87.
[2] European Communities Act 1972, s. 9(1).
[3] Do.
[4] *Quin & Axtens* v. *Salmon* [1909] A.C. 442; *Alexander Ward & Co.* v. *Samyang Navigation Co.*, 1975 S.L.T. 50, per Lord Fraser at p. 56; affd., 1975 S.L.T. 126 (H.L.).
[5] s. 10.
[6] s. 184.
[7] § 22, supra.
[8] E.g. *Hogg* v. *Cramphorn* [1967] Ch. 254; *Pergamon Press* v. *Maxwell* [1970] 1 W.L.R. 1167.
[9] *Bamford* v. *Bamford* [1970] Ch. 212; also *Alexander Ward & Co.* v. *Samyang Navigation Co.*, 1975 S.L.T. 50, per Lord Fraser at p. 55; affd., 1975 S.L.T. 126 (H.L.).
[10] *Aberdeen Railway* v. *Blaikie* (1854) 1 Macq. 461
[11] *North-Western Transportation Co.* v. *Beatty* (1887) 12 App.Cas. 589.

and the objection may be obviated by a provision in the articles.[12] Even with such a provision a contract between a director and the company is one involving uberrima fides, and reducible unless all material facts have been disclosed.[13] A director having any interest in a contract or proposed contract is bound, under penalties, to disclose it at a directors' meeting.[14] Material interests in contracts of significance with the company must be disclosed in the directors' report, as must particulars of their emoluments.[15] Loans by a company to any person who is its director or a director of its holding company are, with certain exceptions, prohibited.[16]

34. Secret Profits.—A director is so far in the position of a trustee that he is not entitled to make any undisclosed or secret profit from his position.[17] So a payment by a promoter or vendor to a director may be recovered by the company.[18] When one company takes over the business of another an undisclosed payment to the directors of the latter cannot be justified.[19] As a company is entitled to the unbiased services of its directors any payment by a promoter to a director for acting, or even a guarantee against loss, will entitle the company to recover from the director what he has gained thereby.[20]

35. Director's Shares.—A director owes no fiduciary duty to the company with regard to his own shares, qualification or other. He has the same right to transfer them as any other shareholder. In *McLintock* v. *Campbell*,[21] a director, at a time when the board knew the position of the company to be hopeless, transferred his shares, on which there was a large liability, to his housekeeper, using fraudulent devices to induce her to accept them. It was held that there were no grounds on which the liquidator could rectify the register and replace the director's name. Only the party defrauded, not the liquidator, could found on the fraud; apart from fraud the director was within his rights.

A director is required to notify the company of his interests and those of his spouse and children in the shares and debentures of the company, and of the occurrence of certain events in connection with such interests.[22] The company must keep a register for the recording of that information, and of certain other related particulars.[23] It has power to require the disclosure of beneficial interests in its voting shares.[24] A director and his spouse and

---

12 *Liqr. of West Lothian Oil Co.* v. *Mair* (1892) 20 R. 64. And see Table A, art. 84.
13 *Imperial Credit Association* v. *Coleman* (1873) L.R. 6 H.L. 189.
14 s. 199; *Hely-Hutchison* v. *Brayhead* [1968] 1 Q.B. 549.
15 1967 Act, ss. 16(1) (c), 6.
16 1948 Act, s. 190; see *Thompson* v. *J. Barke & Co.* (*Caterers*), 1975 S.L.T. 67.
17 See *Cook* v. *Deeks* [1916] A.C. 544; *Phipps* v. *Boardman* [1967] 2 A.C. 46; Palmer, paras. 58-05 et seq.; *Regal Hastings* v. *Gulliver* [1967] 2 A.C. 134.
18 *Henderson* v. *Huntingdon Copper Co.* (1877) 5 R. (H.L.) 1.
19 *Clarkson* v. *Davies* [1923] A.C. 100.
20 *Archer's Case* [1892] 1 Ch. 322.
21 *McLintock* v. *Campbell*, 1916 S.C. 966. The directors had no discretionary power to refuse a transfer.
22 1967 Act, ss. 27, 28, 31; as amended by 1976 Act, s. 24.
23 1967 Act, s. 29.
24 1976 Act, s. 27.

children are prohibited from purchasing options to buy or sell shares in or debentures of the company and certain associated companies.[25]

36. Liabilities of Directors.[26]—Apart from cases turning on his fiduciary position, a director may incur liability either to third parties or to the company.[27] In entering into contracts on behalf of the company, a director acts as agent for a disclosed principal, the company, and so incurs no personal liability merely because the company may be unable to fulfil the contract.[28] But this applies only to contracts which are within the director's powers, and where, therefore, the company is bound. If he exceeds his powers, with the result that the company is not bound, he will incur liability on the principle, already explained, that as an agent he impliedly warrants that he has the authority of his principal.[29]

37. Liabilities to Company.—A director is liable to the company if he pays dividends out of capital[30] or if he acts beyond his powers and the money of the company is lost.[31] In a winding up he may be ordered to repay or restore to the company any money or property which he has misapplied or retained, or to make compensation in respect of any misapplication of funds or breach of trust.[32] A director who signs a cheque for ultra vires expenditure is personally liable, though he may have signed it as a mere matter of form.[33] He is clearly liable for any fraudulent act, and also for his failure to exercise reasonable care in the administration of the company's affairs, though it is doubtful on what standard his actions are to be judged.[34] He is entitled to place reliance on the statements of the manager or of the auditor of the company, if he has no reason to doubt their honesty.[35] The question what amounts to negligence on the part of a director which will render him liable for loss caused by the fraud of his co-directors or of the manager of the company depends so much on the nature of the particular company as to preclude any definite statement.[36] By section 205 any provision, whether contained in the articles or in any contract, for exempting any officer[37] of a company from, or indemnifying him against, any liability which would

---

[25] 1967 Act, ss. 25, 30. Note the Department of Trade's power to investigate share dealings in s. 32 of that Act.

[26] See for a general statement, *Re City Equitable Fire Ins. Co.* [1925] 1 Ch. 407, per Romer J. at pp. 426-30; Palmer, paras. 62-07 et seq.

[27] As to liability for untruthful statements in the prospectus, see supra, § 16.

[28] *Ferguson* v. *Wilson* (1866) L.R. 2 Ch. App. 77, per Lord Cairns L.C. at p. 89; *McLean* v. *Stuart*, 1977 S.L.T. (Notes) 77.

[29] Agency, Ch. XXIII supra, § 30.

[30] Supra, § 29.

[31] *Maxton* v. *Brown* (1839) 1 D. 367.

[32] s. 333.

[33] *Joint Discount Co.* v. *Brown* (1869) L.R. 8 Eq. 381.

[34] *City of Glasgow Bank* v. *Mackinnon* (1882) 9 R. 535; *Re City Equitable Insurance Co.* [1925] 1 Ch. 407.

[35] *Dovey* v. *Cory* [1901] A.C. 477.

[36] *Caledonian Heritable Securities Co.* v. *Curror's Tr.* (1882) 9 R. 1115; *City Equitable Insurance Co.*, supra.

[37] Defined in s. 455 (1).

otherwise attach to him for negligence, default, breach of duty or breach of trust is declared to be void.

38. Auditor.—Every company must at each general meeting before which accounts are laid appoint an auditor or auditors to hold office until the next such general meeting.[38] If no appointment is made, the Secretary of State may appoint a person to fill the vacancy.[39] A person is qualified to act as auditor only if he is a member of a recognised body of accountants or he is for the time being authorised by the Department of Trade to be so appointed.[40] The following persons are disqualified: (a) an officer or servant[41] of the company; (b) a person who is a partner of or in the employment of an officer or servant of the company; (c) a body corporate.[42] A Scottish firm is qualified as auditor of a company only if all the partners are qualified for appointment as auditors.[43]

The auditor is bound to make a report to the members on the accounts examined by him, and on every balance sheet laid before the company in general meeting. The report must state (1) whether in the auditor's opinion the company's balance sheet and profit and loss account and (if it is a holding company submitting group accounts) the group accounts have been properly prepared and kept in accordance with the provisions of the Acts; and, with an exception for special classes of company, (2) whether in his opinion a true and fair view is given, in the case of the balance sheet, of the company's affairs at the end of its financial year; in the case of the profit and loss account, of the profit or loss for the year; and in the case of group accounts submitted by a holding company, of the state of affairs and profit or loss of the company and its subsidiaries thereby, so far as concerns members of the company. It is the duty of the auditor in preparing his report to carry out such investigations as will enable him to form an opinion as to whether proper books of account have been kept by the company and proper returns adequate for their audit have been received from branches not visited by him, and whether the company's balance sheet and profit and loss account are in agreement with the books of account and returns. If the auditor is of the opinion that proper books of account have not been kept, or that proper returns have not been received, if the balance sheet and profit and loss account are not in agreement with the books of account and returns, or if he fails to obtain all the information and explanations which to the best of his knowledge and belief are necessary for the purposes of his audit, he must state that fact in his report.[44] The auditor has a right of access at all times to the company's books

---

[38] 1976 Act, s. 14(1); for detailed provisions regarding the appointment, rights and duties of auditors, see 1948 Act, s. 161; 1967 Act, ss. 13 and 14; 1976 Act, ss. 13-19.
[39] 1976 Act, s. 14(2).
[40] 1948 Act, s. 161; see also 1967 Act, s. 13, and 1976 Act, s. 13.
[41] Defined in 1948 Act, s. 455(1).
[42] 1948 Act, s. 161(2).
[43] 1948 Act, s. 161(4).
[44] 1967 Act, s. 14, amended by 1976 Act, Sched. 2. For comment on the general duties of an auditor, see *Re City Equitable Insurance Co.* [1925] 1 Ch. 407, per Romer J. at pp. 480-2, 497-9. For liability of an auditor for negligence, see *Re Thomas Gerrard & Son* [1968] Ch. 455.

and vouchers and is entitled to require from the officers of the company and from subsidiary companies and their auditors such information and explanations as he thinks necessary.[45] He has the right to attend any general meeting of the company and to be heard on any part of the business of the meeting which concerns him as auditor.[46]

39. Investigation.—The Department of Trade may on the application of a proportion of a company's members, or, if the Department suspect fraud or the withholding of information from members, on their own initiative, appoint inspectors to investigate the affairs of a company; they are bound to do so if the company by special resolution, or the Court, declares that the company's affairs ought to be investigated.[47] Under the 1967 Act the Department may require a company to produce any of its books or papers at any time if they think there is a good reason so to do.[48] Failing production by a company when so required, its premises may be entered and searched, and there are penalties for the destruction, mutilation or falsification of a document affecting or relating to the property or affairs of a company.[49] The Department have power, in the light of the inspectors' report or of any information or document obtained by them under these provisions, to bring civil proceedings for fraud, the recovery of property or otherwise on behalf of any body corporate or to present an application to the Court for the winding up of the company.[50]

40. Arrangements and Reconstructions.—A compromise or arrangement between a company and its creditors, or any class of them, or between the company and its members,[51] or any class of them, is binding if approved by a majority of three-fourths in value of the creditors or members concerned present at a meeting called by order of the Court.[52] Before the meeting the creditors or members concerned must be given an explanation of the effect of the compromise or arrangement and of the material interests of the directors.[53] Where the compromise or arrangement is proposed in connection with the reconstruction of a company or the amalgamation of companies and under the scheme property is to be transferred from one company to another the Court may provide for, inter alia, the transfer or allotment of shares.[54] The transferee company may acquire the shares of dissenting shareholders,[55]

---

[45] 1967 Act, s. 14(5); 1976 Act, s. 18.
[46] 1967 Act, s. 14(7).
[47] ss. 164-165, as amended by 1967 Act, s. 38. For powers of inspectors see ss. 166-167, as amended by 1967 Act, s. 39, and 1967 Act, s. 41.
[48] 1967 Act, s. 109; see also Protection of Depositors Act 1963, ss. 18 and 19; Insurance Companies Act 1974, s. 36.
[49] 1967 Act, ss. 110, 113.
[50] 1967 Act, ss. 35, 37.
[51] See *Singer Manufacturing Co.* v. *Robinow*, 1971 S.C. 11.
[52] s. 206.
[53] s. 207, see *Coltness Iron Co.*, 1951 S.C. 476; *City Property Investment Trust Corporation*, 1951 S.C. 570; *Second Scottish Investment Trust Co., Petrs.*, 1962 S.L.T. 392; *Scottish Eastern Investment Trust, Petrs.*, 1966 S.L.T. 285.
[54] s. 208.
[55] s. 209.

but the Court has power to order otherwise on the application of a dissenting shareholder.[56]

41. Winding Up.[57]—A company, though it may be made notour bankrupt, with the statutory effects on diligence and securities for prior debts,[58] cannot be sequestrated under the Bankruptcy Acts.[59] It may be wound up—a proceeding commonly known in Scotland as liquidation. Provision is made for three forms of winding up—(a) by the Court (also termed compulsory or judicial); (b) voluntary; (c) subject to the supervision of the Court.[60] A sub-division, introduced by the 1929 Act, distinguishes between a members' and a creditors' voluntary winding up.[61] Where the amount of the share capital paid up or credited as paid up does not exceed £120,000 the Sheriff Court of the Sheriffdom where the registered office of the company is situated has concurrent jurisdiction with the Court of Session.[62] The Court of Session may remit any petition, if within this limit, to the Sheriff Court.[63]

42. Winding Up by the Court.—A company registered in Scotland may be wound up by the Court by petition presented to the Outer House[64] of the Court of Session, in vacation, to the Vacation Judge,[65] or, as above stated, to the Sheriff. An unregistered company which is dissolved or has ceased to carry on business may also be wound up by the Court in Scotland if there are or may be assets in this country belonging to the company and at least one person in Scotland is interested in the distribution of the assets of the company.[66] The title to petition rests with the company, with any creditor, absolute or contingent, or with any contributory who is either an original allottee or has held shares for six out of the preceding eighteen months,[67] or, in certain situations, with the Department of Trade.[68]

A company may be wound up by the Court on any one or more of the following grounds:[69]—(a) That the company has by special resolution resolved to be wound up by the Court; (b) that default has been made in delivering the statutory report to the Registrar or in holding the statutory meeting; (c) that the company has not commenced business within a year

---

[56] s. 209 (1); *Nidditch* v. *Calico Printers' Association,* 1961 S.L.T. 28; *Standard Property Investment Co.* v. *Dunblane Hydropathic* (1884) 12 R. 328.

[57] For a detailed discussion of the process of winding up in Scotland, see Palmer, paras. 83-01 et seq.

[58] *Clarke* v. *Hinde* (1884) 12 R. 347. As to notour bankruptcy, see Law of Bankruptcy, Ch. XLIX, infra.

[59] *Standard Property Investment Co.* v. *Dunblane Hydropathic* (1884) 12 R. 328.

[60] s. 211.

[61] See infra, § 45.

[62] s. 220 (2), amended by Insolvency Act 1976, Sched. 1.

[63] See *Chaney & Bull,* 1930 S.C. 759.

[64] Rules of Court (1965) 202, 203; For an account of liquidation procedure in the Court of Session, see article by Dr W. W. McBryde in 1977 S.L.T. (News) 237.

[65] Rules of Court, 1.

[66] *Inland Revenue* v. *Highland Engineering,* 1975 S.L.T. 203.

[67] s. 224.

[68] s. 224 (1) (*d*); 1967 Act, s. 35. See also Protection of Depositors Act 1963, s. 16.

[69] s. 222 (*a*) - (*f*); ground (*g*) was added by the Companies (Floating Charges and Receivers) (Scotland) Act 1972, s. 4.

from its incorporation, or has suspended business for a year; (d) that the number of members is reduced, in a private company, below two, in any other company, below seven; (e) that the company is unable to pay its debts; (f) that the Court is of opinion that it is just and equitable that the company should be wound up; and (g) that the security of a creditor of the company entitled to the benefit of a floating charge is in jeopardy. The construction of the term "just and equitable" in paragraph (f)[70] has been that it is not confined to cases ejusdem generis with the grounds of petition which precede, but covers such cases as the loss of the substantial part of the company's business or abandonment of its objects or impossibility of carrying them out, i.e., what is referred to as the disappearance of the "substratum of the company,"[71] persistent disregard by the directors of the provisions of the Acts or other circumstances sufficient to warrant the inference that there has been an unfair abuse of power and an impairment of confidence in the probity with which the affairs of the company are being conducted;[72] or, in a private company which is in substance a partnership, a division between the directors which brings the affairs of the company to a deadlock[73] or the unjustified exclusion of one of the parties from its affairs.[74] The usual ground for a petition for winding up is however that afforded by paragraph (e), namely inability to pay debts. By section 223[75] a company is deemed unable to pay its debts when (1) a creditor, to whom a debt exceeding £200 is due, has served on the company a demand to pay, and the company has for three weeks neglected to pay, or to compound or secure the debt to the satisfaction of the creditor; (2) the induciae of a charge for payment on an extract decree, or an extract registered bond, or an extract registered protest, has expired without payment, even although the debt be less than £200[76]; (3) when it is proved to the satisfaction of the Court that the company is unable to pay its debts.[77]

The Court has a discretion to grant or refuse a petition for winding up, but will not readily refuse the application of a creditor,[78] and is directed not to refuse it merely on the ground that the company has no assets.[79] Where the application is made by members of the company as contributories[80] on the ground that it is just and equitable that the company should be wound up, the Court is not entitled to make a winding up order if it is of the opinion that some other remedy is available to the petitioners and that they are acting unreasonably in seeking to have the company wound up instead of pursuing

---

[70] See Palmer, para. 81-08; *Re Westbourne Galleries* [1973] A.C. 360.
[71] Palmer, para. 81-08: *Galbraith* v. *Merito Shipping Co.*, 1947 S.C. 446; *Levy* v. *Napier*, 1962 S.C. 468.
[72] *Elder* v. *Elder & Watson*, 1952 S.C. 49, per Lord President Cooper at p. 55.
[73] *Baird* v. *Lees*, 1924 S.C. 83; *Lewis* v. *Haas*, 1971 S.L.T. 57.
[74] *Re Lundie Bros.* [1965] 1 W.L.R. 1051; *Re Fildes Bros.* [1970] 1 W.L.R. 592.
[75] As amended by Insolvency Act 1976, Sched. 1.
[76] *Spiers* v. *Central Building Co.*, 1911 S.C. 330.
[77] See *Re Bryant Investment Co.* [1974] 1 W.L.R. 826.
[78] *Gardner* v. *Link* (1894) 21 R. 969; cf. *Foxhall* v. *Gyle Nurseries*, 1978 S.L.T. (Notes) 29.
[79] s. 225; *Spiers* v. *Central Building Co.*, supra.
[80] As to the meaning of this expression, see s. 213.

that other remedy. An alternative remedy to wind up in cases of oppression is provided by section 210.[81]

43. Consequences of Winding up.—If the Court grants an order for the winding up of the company, the winding up is deemed to have commenced at the time of the presentation of the petition.[82] Thereafter no action or proceeding against the company can be commenced or proceeded with without leave of the Court,[83] and any disposition of the company's property, or transfer of shares, is void, unless the Court otherwise directs.[84] The winding up is equivalent to an act of bankruptcy with regard to transactions which would in bankruptcy be deemed fraudulent preferences.[85] It has the same effect as a sequestration with regard to the equalisation of diligences,[86] and it is equivalent to a decree of adjudication of the heritable estates of the company for the payment of its debts.[87] The property of a company in liquidation does not vest in the liquidator, as the estates of a bankrupt vest in the trustee. A liquidator is merely an administrator, taking the place of the directors, for the special purpose of dividing the company's assets among the creditors and any balance among the contributories.[88] But the Court may direct that all or any part of the company's property shall vest in the liquidator.[89] And the compulsory liquidation of a company has been treated, in questions as to the completion of securities, as equivalent to the sequestration of an individual.[90] The Court has also power to appoint a provisional liquidator.[91]

44. Liquidators.—When an order for winding up is pronounced, a liquidator, styled "the official liquidator,"[92] is appointed by the Court.[93] There are no statutory provisions as to the qualifications for the post of liquidator. He will usually be required to find caution, and is entitled to remuneration. A committee of shareholders and creditors, known as a committee of inspection,[94] may be appointed to assist the liquidator, but its members have no claim to remuneration.[95] He may ratify acts or proceedings done or started

---

[81] See § 22, supra. On the relationship between s. 210 and s. 222, see *Elder* v. *Elder & Watson*, supra, especially per Lord Keith at p. 60; and *Re Lundie Bros.*, supra.
[82] s. 229. See also *Haig* v. *Lord Advocate*, 1976 S.L.T. (Notes) 16. Where the company has already passed a resolution for voluntary winding up, tne date of commencement is the date of the passing of the resolution.
[83] s. 231.
[84] s. 227; but see *United Dominions Trust*, 1977 S.L.T. (Notes) 56, where the property was subject to a standard security and a warrant to sell the subjects had been granted by the sheriff.
[85] s. 320; see Law of Bankruptcy, Ch. XLIX, infra, §§ 4, 5 and 6.
[86] s. 327; see Law of Bankruptcy, Ch. XLIX, infra § 7.
[87] s. 327(1) (b); *Gibson* v. *Hunter Home Designs*, 1976 S.C. 23.
[88] *Clark* v. *West Calder Oil Co.* (1882) 9 R. 1017, per Lord President Inglis at p. 1025.
[89] s. 244.
[90] *Clark* v. *West Calder Oil Co.*, supra; *Bank of Scotland* v. *Hutchison*, 1914 S.C. (H.L.) 1.
[91] s. 238 (3); see *Levy* v. *Napier*, 1962 S.C. 468.
[92] s. 237.
[93] ss. 237, 241.
[94] s. 252.
[95] *Liquidator of Pattisons* (1902) 4 F. 1010.

in the name of the company without proper authority.[96] The general powers of a liquidator are detailed in section 245.

45. Voluntary Winding Up.—Voluntary liquidation is a step often taken when it is proposed to reconstitute the company with wider powers, when two companies propose to amalgamate, or where for any reason it is desired to bring a company to an end. It is competent in the following cases:—(1) when the period (if any) fixed for the duration of the company by its articles has expired, or the event (if any) occurs, on the occurrence of which the articles provide that the company is to be dissolved, and the company in general meeting has passed a resolution requiring the company to be wound up voluntarily; (2) if the company resolves by special resolution that it be wound up voluntarily; (3) if the company resolves by extraordinary resolution to the effect that it cannot, by reason of its liabilities, continue its business, and that it is advisable to wind up.[97] The date of the liquidation is the date of the resolution to wind up.[98] The company is bound to give notice of the resolution by advertisement in the *Gazette*.[99]

When a company is wound up voluntarily it must cease to carry on business, except in so far as may be required for the beneficial winding up.[1] Any subsequent transfer of shares, without the sanction of the liquidator, is void.[2] The resolution does not bar an action being commenced or proceeded with against the company.[3] It is no bar to an application for winding up by the Court,[4] but where a majority of the creditors favour a voluntary winding up, the Court as a rule has regard to their views.[5]

A voluntary winding up may be either a members' or a creditors' voluntary winding up. It is the former if the directors, at a meeting held before the notices for the meeting at which the resolution to wind up is to be proposed are sent out, make, and deliver to the registrar of companies, a declaration, termed a declaration of solvency, to the effect that they have made a full inquiry into the affairs of the company, and that, having so done, they have formed the opinion that the company will be able to pay its debts in full within a period, not exceeding twelve months, from the commencement of the winding up. If no such declaration is made and delivered to the registrar, it is a creditors' voluntary winding up.[6] In a members' winding up the liquidator is appointed by the company in general meeting.[7] Provisions are made for the sale, or transfer to another company, of the company's business,[8] and for its

---

[96] *Alexander Ward & Co.* v. *Samyang Navigation Co.*, 1975 S.L.T. 50, per Lord Fraser at p. 55; aff'd., 1975 S.L.T. 126 (H.L.).
[97] s. 278. As to special and extraordinary resolutions, see supra, § 14.
[98] s. 280
[99] s. 279.
[1] s. 281.
[2] s. 282.
[3] *Sdeuard* v. *Gardner* (1876) 3 R. 577; but see s. 308.
[4] s. 310
[5] *Bouboulis* v. *Mann, Macneal & Co.*, 1926 S.C. 637; *Re Home Remedies* [1943] Ch. 1.
[6] s. 283.
[7] s. 285.
[8] s. 287.

dissolution.[9] In a creditors' voluntary winding up the company must call a meeting of its creditors for the day, or the day next following the day, on which there is to be held the meeting at which the resolution for voluntary winding up is to be proposed.[10] One of the directors must be appointed to preside at the meeting. The company and the creditors may at their respective meetings appoint a liquidator; if different persons are nominated the one nominated by the creditors becomes (subject to a right of appeal to the Court) the liquidator.[11] A committee of inspection may be appointed by the creditors, with a right to the company to appoint members to act upon it.[12] On the appointment of a liquidator, all the powers of the directors cease, except so far as the committee of inspection, or, if none, the creditors, sanction their continuance.[13] A member of a committee of inspection is in a position of trust; accordingly, if it is proposed that he should purchase some of the assets of the company, the liquidator ought to have the sanction of the Court before the sale is made.[14]

46. Supervision Order.—When a company has resolved to wind up voluntarily the Court may make an order that the winding up shall continue, but subject to such supervision of the Court, and with such liberty for creditors, contributories and others to apply to the Court, and generally on such terms and conditions as the Court thinks just.[15] A supervision order has in general, and in particular with regard to the equalisation of diligence and the rights of creditors holding securities, the same effect as an order for winding up by the Court.[16] The principal difference is that in a winding up under supervision, the liquidator may exercise his powers without the sanction of the Court, unless it is otherwise directed in the order,[17] and with an exception in the case of companies with creditors or contributories.[18]

A single creditor is not entitled to insist on a supervision order as a matter of right, and without allegations that other creditors are in course of completing preferable rights or that the management of the company has been improper.[19] A majority of creditors will prevail as against a minority advocating compulsory liquidation,[20] or in opposition to the shareholders.[21] Where no creditors intervene, one shareholder may obtain an order, on allegations of a proposed sale of the company's assets at an inadequate price to persons in the interest of the other shareholders.[22]

[9] s. 290.
[10] s. 293.
[11] s. 294.
[12] s. 295.
[13] s. 296 (2).
[14] Notwithstanding ss. 303 (1) (b) and 245 (2) (a); see *Dowling* v. *Lord Advocate*, 1963 S.C. 272.
[15] s. 311.
[16] s. 315 (2).
[17] *Pattison's Ltd.* v. *Kinnear* (1899) 1 F. 551.
[18] s. 315 (1).
[19] *Crawford* v. *Cowper* (1902) 4 F. 849; *Bouboulis* v. *Mann, Macneal & Co.*, 1926 S.C. 637.
[20] *Pattison's Ltd.* v. *Kinnear* (1899) 1 F. 551.
[21] *McQuisten* v. *Adams* (1896) 23 R. 910.
[22] *Donald* v. *Eglinton Chemical Co.* (1900) 2 F. 402.

47. Ranking of Creditors.—In a winding up by the Court or under a supervision order, but not in a members' voluntary liquidation,[23] creditors claiming to vote at meetings or to rank for dividends are bound to value and deduct their securities according to the rules in sequestration,[24] and rank as preferred or ordinary creditors as they would in bankruptcy.[25] The rules as to preferential debts are given in section 319, and are approximately those that apply in sequestration.[26]

48. Contributories.—Should the assets of the company in liquidation be insufficient to meet its liabilities, calls may be made on the shareholders as contributories in so far (in a limited company) as the shares are not fully paid up.[27] The primary liability rests on the existing holders of the shares, but, should it appear to the Court that they are unable to meet their liabilities, calls may be made on those prior shareholders who have held the shares during the twelve months preceding the liquidation. Two lists of contributories may be drawn up, known as the A and the B list, the former containing the names of existing, the latter those of prior, shareholders.[28]

A contributory on the B list is not liable for debts incurred after he has ceased to be a member,[29] and it has been decided that the B list contributories, by paying off the earlier debts, escape liability altogether.[30] When, however, calls are made on the B list the proceeds go to meet the general liabilities of the company, and are not earmarked to meet prior debts.[31] In no case is a B contributory liable for more than the balance unpaid on the particular shares which he formerly held.[32]

49. Dissolution of Company.—A company is dissolved, in the case of a liquidation either compulsorily or under supervision, when an order to that effect has been pronounced by the Court[33]; in the case of a voluntary liquidation, three months after the registration by the registrar of a notice by the liquidator that a final meeting of the company has been held.[34] At any time within two years of the dissolution of a company, the Court, on the application of the liquidator or of any person interested, may make an order declaring the dissolution to have been void, and thereafter such proceedings may be taken as might have been taken if the company had not been

---

[23] *Collin's Trs.* v. *Borland,* 1907 S.C. 1287.
[24] s. 318, which applies the provisions of the Bankruptcy (Scotland) Act 1913, ss. 45-62 and 96-105.
[25] Ibid.
[26] See Law of Bankruptcy, Ch. XLIX, infra; for an up to date version of s. 319 incorporating the amendments, see *Parliament House Book,* Division I.
[27] s. 212.
[28] See *Liqs. of Caledonian Heritable Security Co.* (1882) 9 R. 1130; *Re City of London Insurance Co.* [1932] 1 Ch. 226.
[29] s. 212 (*b*).
[30] *Brett's Case* (1871) L.R. 6 Ch. 800; (1873) L.R. 8 Ch. 800.
[31] *Webb* v. *Whiffin* (1872) L.R. 5 H.L. 711.
[32] *Liqr. of Caledonian Heritable Security Co.* (1882) 9 R. 1130.
[33] ss. 274, 315.
[34] ss. 290 (4), 300 (4).

dissolved.[35] If the application is made within two years the actual order may be made after the two years have expired.[36] The Act has no provision for the resuscitation of a company more than two years after its dissolution. The Court has power, under its nobile officium, to declare the dissolution to have been void in a case where the company has failed or omitted to grant a conveyance of property sold,[37] but will not exercise this power if there are other means of completing the title.[38]

While a winding up is the normal process by which a company is dissolved, the registrar of companies may take steps which will result in striking a company off the register if he has reasonable cause to believe that it is not carrying on business or in operation. In that case the company may be restored to the register at any time within twenty years if the Court is satisfied that the company was carrying on business or that it is just that it should be restored.[39]

When a company is dissolved, and not resuscitated, all property and rights vested in, or held in trust for the company immediately before its dissolution, are deemed to be bona vacantia, and belong to the Crown.[40]

[35] s. 352.
[36] *Re Scald* [1941] Ch. 386; *Dowling, Petr.*, 1960 S.L.T. (Notes) 76.
[37] *Collins Bros., Petrs.*, 1916 S.C. 620.
[38] *Lord Macdonald's Curator*, 1924 S.C. 163; *Forth Shipbreaking Co.*, 1924 S.C. 489.
[39] s. 353 (6); *Healy, Petr.* (1903) 5 F. 644; *Tyman's Ltd.* v. *Craven* [1952] 2 Q.B. 100.
[40] s. 354; and see *Healy, Petr.*, supra.

CHAPTER XXVI

BILLS OF EXCHANGE

Bell, *Comm.*, I., 411; Hamilton, *Bills of Exchange Act* (1903); Byles, *Bills of Exchange* (22nd ed., 1965); Chalmers, *Bills of Exchange* (13th ed., 1964); Gow, *Mercantile and Industrial Law of Scotland* (1964), Ch. 7.

THE law of bills of exchange, cheques and promissory notes was codified by the Bills of Exchange Act 1882 (45 & 46 Vict., c. 61). In its main provisions the Act applies both to Scotland and England.

1. Origin and Use of Bills.—In origin a bill of exchange was a method whereby a merchant in one country might pay a debt due in another without the actual transmission of money. If A in London owed money to B in Paris, and was himself the creditor of C in Paris, a bill of exchange was the means by which the debt owed by C could be used to meet the debt due to B. A, known as the drawer, gave an order to C (the drawee) to pay to B (the payee). If C was willing to accede to this order he indicated the fact by signing his name on the bill, and thereby became the acceptor and incurred a direct liability to the payee. It was at an early period established that a bill of exchange in this, its ordinary form, was negotiable; that B, in the case supposed, by signing his name on the back of the bill (known as indorsement), could transfer his right as payee either to the bearer of the bill or to some named party. And in the case of ordinary mercantile bills an indorsee, who paid for the bill and took it regularly and honestly, acquired, by law originally resting on the recognition of mercantile custom, an independent title, and was not affected by any imperfection or qualification of the title of the person from whom he took it. Such an indorsee is termed in the Act a holder in due course.

2. Normal Relations of Parties.—The ensuing sketch of the main provisions of the Bills of Exchange Act will be more easily understood if it is borne in mind that while the holder of a bill is entitled to demand payment from anyone whose name appears on it, drawer, acceptor or indorser, the relations of these parties inter se are regulated by the character in which they became parties to the bill. Before the bill is accepted, the principal debtor is the drawer, and any indorsers may recover from him and are liable among themselves in the order in which their names appear on the bill. After acceptance, the acceptor becomes the principal debtor; the drawer, and after him any indorsers in their order, are subsidiarily liable. In many respects the position of a person who became a party to a bill is that of a cautioner for those who are already parties to it, but, if forced to pay, he is entitled to recover the whole, and not merely a contribution, from anyone who, in the order of liability on the bill, ranks before him.

These rules as to the order of liability on a bill hold only in the absence of proof to the contrary. It is competent to prove in any particular case, that the true relationship of the parties is not that which would appear on the face of the bill. It may be proved that the principal debtor is not the acceptor, but the drawer, or an indorser. Such cases generally arise when a bill is used, not for its original purpose of transferring a debt, but as a means whereby money is borrowed by one party, and a guarantee for its payment is given by another. Bills of this character are known as accommodation bills.[1]

In what follows it is proposed to deal first with the course of a normal bill of exchange, afterwards with exceptional cases, and with the law applicable to cheques and promissory notes.

3. Definitions.—The following statutory definitions should be noted:—

A bill of exchange is an unconditional order in writing, addressed by one person to another, signed by the person giving it, requiring the person to whom it is addressed to pay on demand or at a fixed or determinable future time a sum certain in money to or to the order of a specified person, or to bearer.[2]

"Holder" means the payee or indorsee of a bill who is in possession of it, or the bearer thereof.[3] This definition is extended to include a collecting bank which takes delivery from a customer of an unindorsed cheque.[4]

A holder in due course is a holder who has taken a bill, complete and regular on the face of it,[5] under the following conditions, namely (a) that he became the holder of it before it was overdue, and without notice that it had been previously dishonoured, if such was the fact; (b) that he took the bill in good faith and for value, and that at the time the bill was negotiated to him he had no notice of any defect in the title of the person who negotiated it.[6]

In particular the title of a person who negotiates a bill is defective within the meaning of the Act when he obtained the bill, or the acceptance thereof, by fraud, duress, or force and fear, or other unlawful means, or for an illegal consideration, or when he negotiates it in breach of faith, or under such circumstances as amount to a fraud.[7]

A holder (whether for value or not) who derives his title to a bill through a holder in due course, and who is not himself a party to any fraud or illegality

---

[1] See *Macdonald* v. *Whitfield* (1889) 8 App.Cas. 733, and infra, § 31.
[2] s. 3. See Cheques Act 1957 (5 & 6 Eliz. II., c. 36), s. 5. As to the meaning of an "unconditional" order, see *Guaranty Trust* v. *Hannay* [1918] 2 K.B. 623. The sum may be expressed, and judgment given, in foreign currency; ss. 57 (2) and 72 (4) of the 1882 Act have ceased to have effect: Administration of Justice Act 1977 (c. 38), s. 4.
[3] s. 2.
[4] Cheques Act 1957, s. 2; *Midland Bank* v. *Harris* [1963] 1 W.L.R. 1021.
[5] See *Macdonald* v. *Nash* [1924] A.C. 625; *Arab Bank* v. *Ross* [1952] 2 Q.B. 216. As to cheques, see *Westminster Bank* v. *Zang* [1966] A.C. 182.
[6] A person who takes a negotiable instrument in contravention of s. 123 (1) or (3) of the Consumer Credit Act 1974 is not a holder in due course and cannot enforce the instrument: Consumer Credit Act 1974 (c. 39), s. 125 (1); see Consumer Credit Transactions, Ch. XIX, supra, § 16.
[7] Where a person negotiates a cheque in contravention of s. 123 (2) of the Consumer Credit Act 1974, his doing so constitutes a defect in his title: Consumer Credit Act 1974, s. 125 (2); see Consumer Credit Transactions, Ch. XIX, supra, § 16.

affecting it, has all the rights of that holder in due course as regards the acceptor and all parties to the bill prior to that holder.[8]

4. Stamp.—A bill of exchange does not now require to be stamped.[9] A bill is not invalid by reason only that it is not stamped in accordance with the law of the place of issue.[10]

5. Inland and Foreign Bills.—A bill may be an inland or a foreign bill. It is an inland bill if it is or on the face of it purports to be (a) both drawn and payable within the British Islands, or (b) drawn within the British Islands on some person resident therein. Unless the contrary appears on the face of the bill the holder may treat it as an inland bill.[11] The chief difference between inland and foreign bills is that the latter, and not the former, when dishonoured by non-acceptance or non-payment, must be protested in order to preserve recourse against the drawer and indorsers.[12]

6. Methods of Signing Bills.—A person may become a party to a bill either when he signs it or when it is signed for him by a person to whom he has given authority. The latter case is termed a signature by procuration. A bill may be signed by initials or by a mark, and will then form a ground of action on proof that this was the party's usual method of signature.[13] The Act provides (s. 23) that where a person signs a bill in a trade or assumed name he is liable thereon as if he had signed in his own name, and that the signature of the name of a firm is equivalent to the signature by the person so signing of the names of all the persons liable as partners of that firm. A bill of exchange is deemed to have been made, accepted or indorsed on behalf of a company if made, accepted or indorsed in the name of, or by or on behalf or on account of, the company by any person acting under its authority.[14] A signature by procuration operates as notice that the party has but a limited authority to sign, and the principal is only bound by such signature if the agent in so signing was acting within the actual limits of his authority.[15] But if the agent has authority the principal will be liable though the agent has misused his authority for his own purposes.[16]

---

[8] s. 29. The payee of a cheque is not, under any circumstances, a holder in due course: *Jones* v. *Waring & Gillow* [1926] A.C. 670. The drawer may become a holder in due course if the bill is renegotiated to him by a party who was a holder in due course: *Jade International Steel Stahl und Eisen G.m.b.H. & Co. KG* v. *Robert Nicholas (Steels)* [1978] Q.B. 917.
[9] Finance Act 1970 (c. 24), Sched. 7, para. 2 (2).
[10] Bills of Exchange Act 1882, s. 72.
[11] Bills of Exchange Act 1882, s. 4.
[12] Bills of Exchange Act 1882, s. 51.
[13] Bell's *Prin.*, § 323.
[14] Companies Act 1948, s. 33.
[15] Act, s. 25. *Midland Bank* v. *Reckitt* [1933] A.C. 1.
[16] *North of Scotland Banking Co.* v. *Behn* (1881) 8 R. 423; *Bryant Powis & Co.* v. *La Banque du Peuple* [1893] A.C. 170.

7. Signature as Agent.—Where a person signs a bill and adds words to his signature, indicating that he signs for or on behalf of a principal, or in a representative capacity, he is not personally liable thereon; but the mere addition to his signature of words describing him as an agent, or as filling a representative character, does not exempt him from personal liability.[17] In determining whether a signature on a bill is that of the principal or that of the agent by whose hand it is written the construction most favourable to the validity of the instrument must be adopted.[18] So if a bill is signed on behalf of an unincorporated body, such as a club, or a congregation, which has no power to incur liability by bill, the persons who sign, although they may do so expressly on behalf of the body, incur personal liability.[19] But it is always open to any drawer or indorser to insert an express stipulation negativing his own liability to the holder.[20]

8. Form of Bill.—A bill of exchange is usually expressed as an order by one person, known as the drawer, addressed to another, known as the drawee, requiring the drawee to pay a sum of money either to the drawer himself, to his order, to a named payee, or to the bearer. But a man may draw a bill on himself; if so, any holder may, in his option, treat it as a bill or as a promissory note. The same rule applies where the drawee is a fictitious person or a person who has no capacity to contract.[21] To form a bill of exchange the order must be solely for payment of money, and must be, on the face of it, unconditional. It is not unconditional if it is an order to pay out of some particular fund, but it may indicate the fund from which the drawee is to be indemnified, or the account which is to be debited.[22] An instrument which is expressed as a conditional order may, if transferred to a third party, be used by him as proof of a debt, but it is not a bill of exchange.[23]

9. Liabilities of Drawer.—The drawer of a bill incurs a conditional liability to subsequent holders. He is liable if the drawee refuses to accept the bill, or fails to pay it, provided that the requisite proceedings for notice on dishonour are duly taken.[24] He may exclude this liability by appropriate terms, the usual phrase being "without recourse."[25] He is precluded from denying to a holder in due course the existence of the payee and his then capacity to indorse.[26]

10. Negotiation of Bill.—Unless otherwise expressed a bill is negotiable. If payable to bearer, it may be negotiated by mere delivery; if payable to a

---

[17] s. 26. See illustrative cases collected in Chalmers, *Bills of Exchange,* p. 83; *Brebner* v. *Henderson,* 1925 S.C. 643.
[18] s. 26 (2).
[19] *McMeekin* v. *Easton* (1889) 16 R. 363.
[20] s. 16.
[21] Bills of Exchange Act 1882, s. 5.
[22] Act, s. 3.
[23] See *Lawson's Exrs.* v. *Watson,* 1907 S.C. 1353.
[24] Act, s. 55.
[25] Act, s. 16.
[26] Act, s. 55.

particular payee, it may be negotiated by that party indorsing the bill, i.e., writing his name on the back of it, followed by delivery.[27] If a bill contains words prohibiting transfer, or indicating an intention that it should not be transferred, it is valid as between the parties to it, but is not negotiable.[28] Ambiguous expressions, such as the words "against cheque" will not readily be construed as indicating that a bill should not be negotiable.[29]

11. Term of Payment.—A bill of exchange may be payable on demand, and is assumed to be so if no term of payment is mentioned. A bill may be payable on, or at a fixed period after, the occurrence of an event which is certain to happen, though the date of the occurrence is uncertain, but a document payable on the occurrence of an event which may or may not happen is not in any event a bill of exchange.[30] Bills are usually made payable either after a certain period from the date at which they are drawn, or at a certain period after sight or presentation. The bill is due and payable on the last day of the time of payment as fixed by the bill or, if that is a non-business day, on the succeeding business day; there are now no days of grace.[31] Non-business days are Saturdays, Sundays, Good Friday, Christmas Day, bank holidays, days appointed by Royal proclamation as public fast or thanks-giving days, and days declared by order to be non-business days.[32]

12. Presentment for Acceptance.—If a bill is payable at a certain period after sight or presentation, presentment for acceptance to the drawee is necessary in order to fix its maturity. In other cases presentment for acceptance is not necessary to render any party liable on the bill, unless it is expressly stated that it is required, or the bill is payable elsewhere than at the residence or place of business of the drawee.[33] The following rules as to presentment for acceptance are provided by section 41:—It must be made by or on behalf of the holder or his agent to the drawee or his agent at a reasonable hour on a business day and before the bill is overdue; if there are two or more drawees, who are not partners, presentment must be made to all, unless one has authority to accept for the rest; if the drawee is dead, presentment may be made to his personal representative, if bankrupt, to him or to his trustee; if authorised by agreement or usage, presentment may be made through the post office. The usual time allowed for acceptance is twenty-four hours, excluding non-business days. If after the lapse of that period the bill is not accepted it may be treated as dishonoured by non-acceptance. Presentment is excused where the drawee is dead or bankrupt, a fictitious person, or a person not having power to contract by bill, where it cannot be effected by reasonable diligence, or where though the presentment has been

[27] Act, s. 31.
[28] Act, s. 8.
[29] Glen v. Semple (1901) 3 F. 1134.
[30] Act, s. 11.
[31] Act, s. 14 (1) as substituted by Banking and Financial Dealings Act 1971 (c. 80), s. 3 (2).
[32] Act, s. 92 as amended by Banking and Financial Dealings Act 1971, ss. 3 (1), 4(4).
[33] Act, s. 39.

irregular, acceptance is refused on some other ground. But reason to believe that the bill will be dishonoured is not an excuse for failure to present it. Where presentment for acceptance is necessary the holder of the bill is bound to present or negotiate it within a reasonable time, and his failure discharges the drawer and all prior indorsers.[34]

13. Acceptance by Other than Drawee.—No one but the drawee, or an agent authorised by him, can accept a bill, except in two cases. (1) Where the drawer or an indorser has inserted the name of a party to whom the holder may resort in case of need, that is in case the bill is dishonoured by non-acceptance (or non-payment), it is in the option of the holder to resort to a referee in case of need or not.[35] (2) Where a bill has been protested for non-acceptance any person, not already a party to it, may sign the bill in the capacity of an acceptor for honour. In the absence of any statement to the contrary such a party is presumed to engage for the honour of the drawer. He incurs liability to the holder and to all parties to the bill subsequent to the party for whose honour he has accepted.[36] Except in these cases any party who becomes a party to a bill, other than the drawer or drawee, incurs the liabilities of an indorser to a holder in due course.[37]

14. Acceptance by Drawee: Qualified Acceptance.—An acceptance must be in writing on the bill. The mere signature of the drawee is sufficient.[38] The acceptance may be general or qualified. It is qualified if it is conditional; partial, for part only of the amount of the bill; payable only at a particular place; qualified as to time; the acceptance of one or more drawees, but not of all.[39] It is in the option of the holder to take a qualified acceptance, or to treat the bill as dishonoured by non-acceptance. If he takes it without the express or implied authority of the drawer or of a prior indorser, or their subsequent assent, their liability is discharged. This rule does not apply to the case of a partial acceptance.[40]

15. Liabilities of Acceptor.—An acceptor engages that he will pay the bill according to the tenor of his acceptance. He is precluded from denying to a holder in due course (a) the existence of the drawer, the genuineness of his signature, and his capacity and authority to draw the bill; (b) if the bill is payable to the drawer's order, the then capacity of the drawer to indorse but not the genuineness or validity of his indorsement; (c) if payable to the order of a third party, the existence of the payee and his then capacity to indorse, but not the genuineness or validity of his indorsement.[41]

---

[34] Act, s. 40.
[35] Act, s. 15.
[36] Act, ss. 65, 66.
[37] Act, s. 56.
[38] Act, s. 17.
[39] Act, s. 19.
[40] Act, s. 44.
[41] Act, s. 54.

16. Indorsement.—The holder of a bill may at any stage transfer it by indorsement and delivery. Where there are several indorsers their liability inter se is, in the absence of proof to the contrary, regulated by the order in which they appear on the bill. The indorser by indorsing a bill engages that it shall be accepted and paid according to its tenor, and that if it be dishonoured he will compensate the holder or a subsequent indorser who is compelled to pay it, provided that the requisite proceedings on dishonour are duly taken. He is precluded from denying to a holder in due course the genuineness and regularity of the drawer's signature and of all previous indorsements; and from denying to any subsequent indorsee, whether a holder in due course or not, that the bill was at the time of his indorsement a valid and subsisting bill, and that he had then a good title thereto.[42]

17. Holder in Due Course.—Every holder of a bill is prima facie deemed to be a holder in due course; but if in an action on a bill it is admitted or proved that the acceptance, issue or subsequent negotiation of the bill is affected with fraud, duress, force and fear, or illegality, the burden of proof is shifted, unless and until the holder proves that, subsequent to the alleged fraud or illegality, value has in good faith been given for the bill.[43]

18. Rights of Holder.—The rights of a holder in due course are (s. 38)— (1) he may sue on the bill in his own name; (2) he holds the bill free from any defect of title of prior parties, as well as from mere personal defences available to prior parties among themselves, and may enforce payment against all parties liable on the bill. Thus a holder who takes under the conditions which make him a holder in due course gets a valid title to the bill although the person from whom he took it may be a thief, or may have obtained the bill by fraud. But a party who has been fraudulently induced to sign a bill under the impression that it was a document of a different character is not liable even to a holder in due course.[44] A holder of a bill who is not a holder in due course, even although he has given value for the bill, takes no higher right than that of the indorser, and is subject to all equities affecting him. Such is the case of a party who takes the bill when it is overdue or has been dishonoured[45]; when it is not complete and regular on the face of it; with notice, or with good reason to suppose, that the title of the party from whom he takes is defective[46]; or that it was delivered conditionally.[47]

19. Payee.—A bill may be drawn payable to a named payee; or two or more payees, or their order; to the holder of an office; or to bearer. It becomes payable to bearer if indorsed by the payee in blank, that is, without

---

[42] Act, s. 55 (2).
[43] s. 30 (2). For definition of holder in due course, see supra, § 3.
[44] *Foster* v. *Mackinnon* (1869) L.R. 4 C.P. 704; *Lewis* v. *Clay* (1897) 67 L.J.Q.B. 224. As to forgery, see infra, § 33.
[45] *Semple* v. *Kyle* (1902) 4 F. 421.
[46] *Jones* v. *Gordon* (1877) 2 App.Cas. 616.
[47] *Martini* v. *Steel & Craig* (1878) 6 R. 342.

specifying a particular indorsee.[48] When a bill has been indorsed in blank any holder may convert the blank indorsement into a special indorsement by writing above the indorser's signature a direction to pay the bill to or to the order of himself or some other person.[49] When the payee is a fictitious or non-existing person the bill may be treated as payable to bearer.[50] In the construction of this rule it has been held that it includes the case where the payee is actually non-existent and also the case where the name of an existing party is inserted by the drawer without any intention that that party should receive the money or have any connection with the bill,[51] but not the case where the drawer intended the payee (an existing person) to receive the money, though he may have been induced to form that intention by fraud and the payee may be unaware that his name has been used.[52] These authorities show that if the bill may be treated as payable to bearer anyone who takes with the name of the payee indorsed upon it (though that indorsement be a forgery) may enforce it against prior parties, whereas if the bill cannot be so treated no one can acquire a valid title except on a genuine signature by the nominal payee.

20. Presentment for Payment.—A bill payable on demand must be presented for payment within a reasonable time after its issue, in a question as to the liability of the drawer, or within a reasonable time after indorsement, in a question as to the liability of the indorser.[53] But the drawer of a cheque is not discharged by delay in presentment except in so far as he has suffered damage thereby.[54] When a bill is payable at a fixed date it must be presented for payment at that date.[55] Failure in presentment does not affect the liability of the acceptor.[56]

21. Excuses for Delay in Presentment.—Delay in presentment is excused where caused by circumstances beyond the control of the holder, and not attributable to any default of his.[57] Presentment is dispensed with when it cannot be effected by the exercise of reasonable diligence, by waiver, express or implied, where the drawee is a fictitious party, but not merely because the holder has reason to believe that the bill if presented will be dishonoured.[58]

The rules as to the method of presentment for payment are similar to those applicable to presentment for acceptance.[59]

---

[48] Act, s. 34.
[49] Ibid.
[50] Act, s. 7 (3).
[51] *Bank of England* v. *Vagliano* [1891] A.C. 107; *Clutton* v. *Attenborough* [1897] A.C. 90.
[52] *North and South Wales Bank* v. *Macbeth* [1908] A.C. 137.
[53] Act, s. 45.
[54] Act, s. 74.
[55] Act, s. 45.
[56] Act, s. 52. *McNeill* v. *Innes Chambers & Co.,* 1917 S.C. 540 (summary diligence).
[57] Act, s. 46 (1). *Bank of Scotland* v. *Lamont* (1889) 16 R. 769.
[58] Act, s. 46 (2). As to circumstances amounting to waiver, see *McTavish's Factor* v. *Michael's Trs.,* 1912 S.C. 425.
[59] Act, s. 45; and see supra, § 12.

22. Notice of Dishonour.—Where a bill has been dishonoured either by non-acceptance or non-payment, notice of dishonour must be given to the drawer and each indorser, and any of these to whom notice is not given is discharged.[60] The notice must be given within a reasonable time, and as a general rule it is not given within a reasonable time unless, if the parties reside in the same place, it is dispatched in time to reach the party on the day after the bill was dishonoured; if the parties reside in different places, it is posted on that day.[61] It is sufficient if the holder can prove that he posted the notice in time though it may be delayed in transit, or may never arrive.[62] The notice is bad if it was received before the bill itself was dishonoured.[63] Notice may be oral or in writing, and no special form of notice is specified by the Act. The return of the dishonoured bill to the drawer or to an indorser is sufficient notice.[64] For the specific rules as to giving notice reference must be made to the Act (s. 49).

23. Protest: When Necessary.—Besides giving notice the holder of a bill which on the face of it bears to be a foreign bill must, in order to preserve recourse against the drawer or prior indorsers, protest it either in the case of non-acceptance or non-payment. Protest is not necessary in the case of an inland bill merely to preserve recourse, but is necessary if it is desired to enforce the bill by summary diligence.[65]

24. Form of Protest: Noting.—For the purpose of protest the bill must be noted by a notary public not later than the succeeding business day after it has been dishonoured.[66] Noting is effected by the notary public marking on the bill the date of dishonour, his initials and the letters N.P.[67] The protest may be subsequently extended as of the date of the noting.[68] It must contain a copy of the bill, must be signed by the notary making it and must specify the person at whose request the bill is protested, the place and date of protest, the cause or reason for protesting, the demand made and the answer given, or the fact that the drawee or acceptor could not be found.[69] If the bill has been lost or destroyed, or is wrongly detained from the person entitled to hold it, protest may be made on a copy or written particulars thereof. In a question of recourse protest is dispensed with by any circumstances which would dispense with notice of dishonour.[70]

Where the services of a notary public cannot be obtained at the place where the bill was dishonoured, any householder of the place may, in the

---

60 Act, s. 48. See *Lombard Banking* v. *Central Garage and Engineering Co.* [1963] 1 Q.B. 220.
61 s. 49, Rule 12.
62 *Dunlop* v. *Higgins* (1848) 6 Bell's App. 195.
63 *Eaglehill* v. *J. Needham* [1973] A.C. 992.
64 Act, s. 49, Rules 5, 6.
65 Act, s. 51.
66 Bills of Exchange (Time of Noting) Act 1917 (7 & 8 Geo. V., c. 48), s. 1.
67 See Hamilton, *Bills of Exchange Act*, p. 110.
68 Act, s. 51 (4).
69 Ibid.
70 Ibid.

presence of two witnesses, give a certificate, signed by the witnesses, attesting the dishonour of the bill, and the certificate shall in all respects operate as if it were a formal protest of the bill.[71] It is doubtful whether a householder's certificate will form a warrant for summary diligence.[72]

25. Summary Diligence.—Summary diligence is the method by which payment of a bill or promissory note may be enforced without the necessity of an action to constitute the debt. It has been held in the Outer House that it is incompetent on a dishonoured cheque.[73] The Bills of Exchange Act provides (s. 98) that nothing in the Act or in any repeal effected thereby shall extend or restrict or in any way alter or affect the law and practice in Scotland on the subject. The statutes in force are the Bills of Exchange Act 1681 (c. 20), the Inland Bills Act 1696 (c. 36), and 12 Geo. III, c. 72, ss. 42, 43. Summary diligence is competent when a bill (or note) is dishonoured either by non-acceptance or non-payment. In the latter case it is competent against any party to the bill, including the acceptor; in the former against any actual party to the bill, but not against the drawee who has refused acceptance. For summary diligence a regular protest is required, and therefore while presentment for payment is not necessary to render the acceptor liable, it is necessary, and must be regularly made, in order to justify summary diligence against him.[74] But the practice under which six months is allowed for presentment to the acceptor, without prejudice to summary diligence against him, has been sustained.[75] The protest of the bill or note must be registered not more than six months after dishonour (by non-acceptance or non-payment as the case may be) in the Books of Council and Session or the books of a Sheriff Court to whose jurisdiction the party is subject.[76] The process cannot be used against a party who is not subject to the jurisdiction of the Scottish Courts, even although the bill may be payable in Scotland.[77] When registered, an extract may be obtained, which is a warrant for arrestment, or for a charge for payment to be followed by poinding or by a petition for sequestration. The induciae of the charge are six days.[78]

26. When Summary Diligence Competent.—Summary diligence is competent only for the amount of the bill or note, with interest. Damages or expenses must be recovered by action.[79] It is generally competent only when the liability of the party appears on the face of the bill without extrinsic proof, and hence is not competent against a party who has signed the bill merely by initials, or against an acceptor who has accepted conditionally,[80] or on a bill

---

[71] s. 94. See *Somerville* v. *Aaronson* (1898) 25 R. 524.
[72] See Hamilton, *Bills of Exchange Act*, p. 210.
[73] *Glickman* v. *Linda*, 1950 S.C. 18.
[74] *Neill* v. *Dobson* (1902) 4 F. 625.
[75] *McNeill* v. *Innes Chambers & Co.*, 1917 S.C. 540.
[76] Bills of Exchange Act 1681, c. 20.
[77] *Charteris* v. *Clydesdale Bank* (1882) 19 S.L.R. 602; *Davis* v. *Cadman* (1897) 24 R. 297.
[78] Graham Stewart, *Diligence*, p.313.
[79] Erskine, III, 2, 36.
[80] *Summers* v. *Marianski* (1843) 6 D. 286; Hamilton, *Bills of Exchange Act*, p. 208.

which has been cancelled by mistake.[81] But it was held competent against a firm carrying on business under a descriptive name, in the case where the bill was signed by all the partners.[82]

27. Bill as Assignation.—The Act provides (s. 53 (2)), "In Scotland, where the drawee of a bill has in his hands funds available for the payment thereof, the bill operates as an assignment of the sum for which it is drawn in favour of the holder, from the time when the bill is presented to the drawee." This rule applies, in the case of bills, where the bill has been presented for acceptance, and acceptance has been refused. The holder acquires a completed right to any funds in the hands of the drawee which are available to meet the bill, in a question either with the drawee himself, or with other parties having competing assignations.[83] As the principle is that presentment operates as intimation of the assignation of the debt due by the drawee to the drawer, it is no objection that it may have been irregular in form.[84] In the case of cheques, presentment for payment, though payment may be refused on the ground of insufficient funds to meet the cheque, operates as a completed assignation of any balance there may be to the drawer's credit, and, in the event of the drawer's bankruptcy, will give the holder a preferential right to that balance.[85] But in order that presentment may operate as an assignation of the balance standing at the credit of the drawer of a cheque there must be a debt due by the bank to him. In *Kirkwood* v. *Clydesdale Bank*,[86] A had several accounts with a bank, including a current account, in which there was a balance standing to his credit. He drew a cheque on this account. It was presented and payment was refused on the ground that notice of A's death had been received. On the various accounts A was in debt to the bank, though the debt was covered by securities. In a question between the payee of the cheque and the bank it was held that presentment did not operate as an assignation of the balance due on the current account, because, although there was a credit balance on that account, there was no debt due by the bank to A.

28. Discharge of Bill.—A bill is discharged by payment in due course, when made by or on behalf of the drawee or acceptor.[87] Payment in due course means payment at or after the maturity of the bill to the holder thereof in good faith and without notice that his title is defective. In the case of an accommodation bill payment in due course by the person accommodated discharges the bill. Payment by the drawer or by an indorser does not discharge the bill; it remains available as a document of debt against the acceptor or other antecedent party.[88] When the acceptor of a bill is or

---

[81] *Dominion Bank* v. *Bank of Scotland* (1889) 16 R. 1081; affd. (1891) 18 R. (H.L.) 21.
[82] *Rosslund Cycle Co*. v. *McCreadie*, 1907 S.C. 1208.
[83] *Watt's Trs*. v. *Pinkney* (1853) 16 D. 279.
[84] Ibid., opinion of Lord Ivory, 16 D., at p. 287.
[85] *British Linen Co*. v. *Carruthers* (1883) 10 R. 923.
[86] 1908 S.C. 20.
[87] s. 59 (1). *Coats* v. *Union Bank*, 1929 S.C. (H.L.) 114. Proof of payment must be by writ or oath: *Nicol's Trs*. v. *Sutherland*, 1951 S.C. (H.L.) 21.
[88] s. 59 (2).

becomes the holder of it at or after its maturity, in his own right, the bill is discharged.[89] The mere fact that a party liable in a bill is in possession of it raises a presumption of payment, but does not necessarily discharge the bill.[90] Where a promissory note was given up, and a new one granted, it was held that the fact that the debtor was in possession of the original note did not infer abandonment of any claim for interest on it.[91] A bill may also be discharged by a renunciation by the holder of his rights against the acceptor, or any other party to the bill. The renunciation, unless the bill is given up to the party discharged, must be in writing, and is not effectual in a question with a holder in due course.[92] A bill is discharged by its cancellation by the holder, and the liability of any party on the bill is discharged by the intentional cancellation of his signature by the holder or his agent, this carrying with it the discharge of any indorser who would have had a right of recourse against the party whose signature is cancelled. Cancellation which is unintentional, without the authority of the holder, or done under a mistake, is inoperable, but the onus of proof is laid upon the party founding on the cancelled bill.[93]

29. Alteration of Bill.—Where a bill or acceptance is materially altered without the assent of all parties liable in it, the bill is avoided, except as against a party who has himself made, authorised or assented to the alteration, and subsequent indorsers, unless the alteration is not apparent, and the bill is in the hands of a holder in due course.[94] It is immaterial that the party founding on the alteration as involving avoidance has suffered no prejudice.[95] The drawee of a bill of exchange owes no duty to those into whose hands the bill may come to exercise any care in accepting it, and therefore where a bill was accepted with a blank space which rendered it possible to alter the amount, and the amount was altered, it was held that the acceptor was not liable to a holder in due course for any more than the original sum in the bill.[96] But this rule does not apply in a case between banker and customer.[97]

30. Inchoate Bills.—The Act provides (s. 20), "Where a simple signature on a blank paper is delivered by the signer in order that it may be converted into a bill, it operates as a prima facie authority to fill it up as a complete bill for any amount using the signature for that of the drawer, or the acceptor, or an indorser; and in like manner, when a bill is wanting in any material particular, the person in possession of it has a prima facie authority to fill up the omission in any way he thinks fit." Once the bill has been filled up and transferred, complete and regular on the face of it, to a holder in due course, it

---

[89] s. 61; and see *Nash* v. *De Freville* [1900] 2 Q.B. 72.
[90] Erskine, III, 4, 5.
[91] *Hope Johnstone* v. *Cornwall* (1895) 22 R. 314.
[92] s. 62.
[93] s. 63. See *Dominion Bank* v. *Anderson* (1888) 15 R. 408.
[94] s. 64. *Slingsby* v. *District Bank* [1932] 1 K.B. 544.
[95] *Koch* v. *Dicks* [1933] 1 K.B. 307.
[96] *Scholfield* v. *Lord Londesborough* [1896] A.C. 514.
[97] See infra, § 36.

may be enforced by him according to its tenor,[98] although it has not been filled up according to the authority given, as where a larger sum than that agreed upon was inserted,[99] or after material delay, as where a blank acceptance was kept and filled up after the giver had become bankrupt and obtained a discharge.[1] In a question between the original parties it must be filled up "within a reasonable time, and strictly in accordance with the authority given."[2] Thus the party receiving the blank acceptance at least if, as is usual, it was given for his accommodation, cannot fill it up after the giver has been sequestrated.[3] The onus of proof that the bill has not been filled up in accordance with the authority given rests on the party who signed and delivered it.[4] In the absence of any contract to the contrary there is implied authority to fill in the name of a third party as drawer,[5] or, in the case of a bill payable to the drawer's order, to the drawer to insert his own name as payee.[6] Where an acceptance addressed to A was found after his death still uncompleted, it was doubted whether his executor had any right to complete it as a bill of exchange, but held that he might sue upon it as a document of debt, which laid on the party who signed the onus of proof that it was not delivered as an acknowledgment of debt, or that the debt had afterwards been paid.[7]

31. Accommodation Bills.—According to Scots law the fact that no consideration has been given for a bill, as where it was, for instance, a donation, is no objection to its enforcement, either by the drawer in a question with the acceptor, or by any holder.[8] Every party whose signature appears on a bill is prima facie deemed to have become a party thereto for value.[9] If, however, it is admitted or proved that the true relations of the parties are not as they appear on the face of the bill, and that one or more of the parties have received no value for the liability they have incurred, the bill may be regarded as an accommodation bill, and differs in certain of its incidents from a bill granted for value. The normal case of an accommodation bill is where, as between themselves, the drawer is the true debtor, and the acceptor a party who has interposed as cautioner for him. The Act provides (s. 28), "An accommodation party to a bill is a person who has signed a bill as drawer, acceptor or indorser, without receiving value therefor, and for the purpose of lending his name to some other person."[10] In a question with any holder who has given value for the bill, an accommodation party is liable, and it is immaterial whether the holder did or did not know that the bill was an

[98] s. 20 (2).
[99] Lloyds Bank v. Cooke [1907] 1 K.B. 794.
[1] McMeekin v. Russell (1881) 8 R. 587.
[2] s. 20 (2).
[3] McMeekin v. Russell, supra.
[4] Anderson v. Somerville (1898) 1 F. 90.
[5] Russell v. Banknock Coal Co. (1897) 24 R. 1009.
[6] Macdonald v. Nash [1924] A.C. 625.
[7] Lawson's Exrs. v. Watson, 1907 S.C. 1353.
[8] Law v. Humphrey (1876) 3 R. 1192.
[9] Act, 30 (1).
[10] "Value" is defined by s. 27.

accommodation bill.[11] "Holder" in this case includes a transferee of the bill, who has taken it for value, but without indorsement.[12] But in questions between the original parties their rights are regulated by the true relations between them which may be proved by parole evidence.[13] So where several directors had indorsed a promissory note it was held, on proof that they had done so as guarantors for the company, that the general rule that a prior was liable to a later indorser was displaced, and that the director who had been compelled to pay could recover a proportionate share from each of the others.[14] The holder of an accommodation bill, when the acceptor is the person lending his name, and the claim is made against the drawer as the person accommodated, is not barred by failure to present the bill for payment,[15] failure to give notice of dishonour,[16] or failure to protest the bill for non-acceptance or non-payment.[17]

32. Accommodation Bills in Bankruptcy.—Where an accommodation bill is discounted and the parties are sequestrated the bank as holder may rank on each estate for the whole amount of the bill. As no debt can be ranked twice on the same estate the trustee on the estate of the party who has lent his name cannot rank on the estate of the party accommodated for the dividend paid by the estate under his charge on the bill. Nor can he secure the same result by claiming a right of retention over property in his hands belonging to the estate of the party accommodated, in the case where that property was not expressly pledged, to meet the liability arising on the bill.[18] If it was so pledged, the rule in Scotland is that it may be applied to relieve the estate of the party who has lent his name for any dividend paid on the bill, and that any surplus is an asset in the estate of the party accommodated; the English rule is that property so pledged may be taken by the holder of the bill, who deducts its value from the sum due on the bill, and ranks on the estates of the parties to it only for the balance.[19].

33. Forged Bills.—As a general rule no liability is incurred by a person whose name is forged as a party to a bill, or used without his authority.[20] He cannot ratify but may adopt the bill, and will then be liable upon it.[21] Short of adoption he may be personally barred from disputing the validity of his signature if his conduct has caused loss to the holder. But such cases are very exceptional; and mere failure to repudiate the bill at once will not infer liability.[22]

[11] 28 (2).
[12] *Hood* v. *Stewart* (1890) 17 R. 749.
[13] Act, s. 100.
[14] *Macdonald* v. *Whitfield* (1883) 8 App.Cas. 733.
[15] Act, s. 46 (2) (*c*).
[16] Act, s. 50 (2) (*c*) (*d*).
[17] Act, s. 51 (9).
[18] *Anderson* v. *Mackinnon* (1876) 3 R. 608. See also *Mackinnon* v. *Monkhouse* (1881) 9 R. 393.
[19] *Royal Bank* v. *Saunders' Trs.* (1882) 9 R. (H.L.) 67.
[20] Act, s. 24.
[21] *Mackenzie* v. *British Linen Co.* (1881) 8 R. (H.L.) 8, as explained in *Greenwood* v. *Martins Bank* [1933] A.C. 51.
[22] *British Linen Co.* v. *Cowan* (1906) 8 F. 704.

The Act provides (s. 24), "Subject to the provisions of this Act, where a signature on a bill is forged or placed thereon without the authority of the person whose signature it purports to be, the forged or unauthorised signature is wholly inoperative, and no right to retain the bill or to give a discharge therefor, or to enforce payment thereof against any party thereto can be acquired through or under that signature, unless the party against whom it is sought to retain or enforce payment of the bill is precluded from setting up the forgery or want of authority." The provisions of the Act forming exceptions to this rule are (1) the clauses safeguarding a banker who pays a cheque on a forged indorsement[23]; (2) the right to treat the bill as payable to bearer when the payee is a fictitious or non-existent person[24]; (3) the rule that, in a question with a holder in due course, the acceptor is precluded from denying the genuineness of the signature of the drawer,[25] and an indorser from denying the genuineness of the signature of the drawer or of prior indorsers[26]; or, in a question with his immediate or a subsequent indorsee, that the bill was at the time of his indorsement a valid and subsisting bill, and that he had then a good title thereto.[27] Thus the acceptor of a bill, who pays on a forged indorsement, cannot charge the drawer, and a bank which pays on behalf of the acceptor cannot charge its customer.[28] A person who has paid on a bill vitiated by forgery or after a material and unauthorised alteration may recover from the holder, unless by delay he has prejudiced the holder's right of recourse against other parties to the bill.[29]

34. Evidence.—The construction of section 100, which allows parole evidence of any facts relevant to any question of liability on a bill, has been already considered.[30]

35. Cheques.—The statutory definition of a cheque is, "A bill of exchange drawn on a banker payable on demand." It is enacted that except where otherwise provided in Part III of the Act the statutory provisions applicable to a bill of exchange payable on demand apply to a cheque.[31] So the holder of a cheque, if in circumstances which satisfy the provisions of section 29,[32] has all the rights of the holder in due course of a bill of exchange.[33] The chief difference is that delay in presentment of a cheque does not give the drawer any remedy except in so far as he has suffered prejudice, which he can only do in the event of the bankruptcy of the banker.[34]

---

[23] See now Cheques Act 1957, s. 1; infra, § 37.
[24] Act, s. 7 (3); supra, § 19.
[25] Act, s. 54 (2).
[26] Act, s. 55 (2) (b).
[27] Act, s. 55 (2) (c).
[28] Bank of England v. Vagliano [1891] A.C. 107, opinion of Lord Watson.
[29] Imperial Bank of Canada v. Bank of Hamilton [1903] A.C. 49.
[30] Rules of Evidence, Ch. XII., supra, § 13.
[31] s. 73; see Chalmers, Bills of Exchange, pp. 247 et seq.
[32] § 3, supra.
[33] McLean v. Clydesdale Bank (1883) 11 R. (H.L.) 1.
[34] s. 74.

36. Contract between Banker and Customer.[35]—A banker undertakes to pay cheques drawn by his customer so long as he has funds in his hands. He may determine the contract at any time by giving notice, but, provided that he has funds to meet them, must pay cheques drawn before the notice was received.[36] He is under no obligation to allow an overdraft, and no such obligation can be inferred for the future merely from the fact that the customer has been allowed to overdraw in the past.[37] Even where a banker holds a cash credit bond there is no obligation, in the absence of express agreement, to allow the customer to overdraw to the extent of the cash credit, though a refusal to honour a cheque without prior notice to the customer would probably be wrongful.[38] Where a customer keeps several accounts, e.g., a current and loan account, with a banker, the latter is not entitled, without notice, to mass the accounts together and to refuse to honour a cheque in respect of a debit balance thence arising.[39] But it has been held that where a customer had current accounts with two branches of a bank, the bank was entitled, without notice, to refuse to honour a cheque on the ground that, taking the two accounts together, the customer was overdrawn.[40] A bank is not bound to pay at a branch other than that where the account is kept.[41] Dishonour of a cheque, without adequate grounds, is a breach of contract, and one for which the customer has been found entitled to damages; but damages will usually be nominal unless the customer is a trader, whose credit may be injured,[42] or can show that he has sustained actual loss.[43] Entries in a bank pass-book or counterfoil are prima facie evidence of the receipt of that amount of money against a bank which disputes their accuracy, and the onus of displacing the presumption of accuracy lies upon the bank.[44]

The customer owes a duty to his banker to take reasonable care in drawing cheques, and if he draws them in a manner which facilitates alteration, and the banker pays an altered cheque in good faith and without negligence, he may debit the customer with the full amount he has paid.[45] The customer is also under a duty to disclose forgeries when he becomes aware of them, and he will be barred from raising the matter at a later stage if he remains silent and allows the banker to pay.[46]

37. Indorsement.—The object of the Cheques Act 1957 was to restrict the

[35] See Chalmers, op. cit., p. 257.
[36] *King* v. *British Linen Co.* (1899) 1 F. 928.
[37] *Ritchie* v. *Clydesdale Bank* (1886) 13 R. 866.
[38] *Johnston* v. *Commercial Bank* (1858) 20 D. 790.
[39] *Kirkwood* v. *Clydesdale Bank*, 1908 S.C. 20, at p. 25.
[40] *Garnett* v. *McKewan* (1872) L.R. 8 Ex. 10.
[41] *Clare* v. *Dresdner Bank* [1915] 2 K.B. 576; *Richardson* v. *Richardson* [1927] P. 228.
[42] *King* v. *British Linen Co.* (1899) 1 F. 928.
[43] *Gibbons* v. *Westminster Bank* [1939] 2 K.B. 882. Note that these rules relate to dealings with a customer's current account, and that they may not be applicable where the dealings are with a deposit account: *Gibb* v. *Lombank*, 1962 S.L.T. 288.
[44] *Couper's Trs.* v. *National Bank* (1889) 16 R. 412; *Docherty* v. *Royal Bank of Scotland*, 1963 S.L.T. (Notes) 43.
[45] *London Joint Stock Bank* v. *Macmillan* [1918] A.C. 777; *Slingsby* v. *District Bank* [1932] 1 K.B. 544.
[46] *Greenwood* v. *Martins Bank* [1933] A.C. 51.

circumstances in which indorsement of cheques is required. To that end it is provided that when a cheque (or bill of exchange drawn on a banker and payable on demand) is paid by the banker in good faith and in the ordinary course of business, he is deemed to have paid the cheque in due course, although there is no indorsement or the indorsement of the name of the payee may be forged.[47] He may therefore charge his customer with the amount so paid, and incurs no liability by reason only of the absence of, or irregularity in, indorsement. Consequently the banker may in practice ignore indorsements. But the protection thus given to a banker does not apply where the cheque, before payment, has obviously been altered in a material particular,[48] nor where the cheque is crossed and the banker pays in disregard of the crossing.[49] In such circumstances the banker pays the cheque at his own risk. And the section applies only to the banker on whom the cheque is drawn, and does not protect any third party who may pay on a forged indorsement.[50]

To allow the collecting banker to sue on a cheque which has not been indorsed, it is provided that a banker who gives value for, or has a lien on, a cheque payable to order which the holder delivers to him for collection without indorsing it, has such (if any) rights as he would have had if, upon delivery, the holder had indorsed it in blank.[51] This is so even where the holder lodges the cheque for collection for an account other than his own.[52]

An unindorsed cheque which appears to have been paid by the banker on whom it is drawn is evidence of the receipt by the payee of the sum payable by the cheque.[53]

The practical effect is that the payee is not now required to indorse the cheque when he lodges it with his bank for collection. As a matter of banking practice, an indorsee is required to indorse the cheque when he lodges it for collection. It is still, of course, necessary for the payee to indorse the cheque if he is negotiating it to a third party.

38. Determination of Authority to Pay.—The Act provides (s. 75) that the duty and authority of a banker to pay a cheque are determined by countermand of payment and notice of his customer's death. In the latter case the cheque (if duly presented) will operate as an assignation in favour of the payee of any funds in the banker's hands available to meet the cheque, but in determining whether any funds are available, the balance on all the accounts kept by the customer must be considered.[54] Countermand of payment does not affect the liability of the drawer to any indorsee of the cheque who is in the position of a holder in due course, for instance, to the bank to whom the

---

[47] Cheques Act 1957, s. 1.
[48] *Slingsby* v. *District Bank,* supra.
[49] *Smith* v. *Union Bank* (1875) 1 Q.B.D. 31.
[50] *Ogden* v. *Benas* (1874) 9 C.P. 513; but for statutory protection of collecting banker, see § 41, infra, and 1957 Act, s. 4.
[51] 1957 Act, s. 2; see *Midland Bank* v. *Harris* [1963] 1 W.L.R. 1021.
[52] *Westminster Bank* v. *Zang* [1966] A.C. 182.
[53] 1957 Act, s. 3; see as to the effect of this, *Westminster Bank* v. *Zang,* supra.
[54] *Kirkwood* v. *Clydesdale Bank,* 1908 S.C. 20; and see supra, § 27.

payee may have paid the cheque.[55] The authority of a banker to pay a cheque is also determined by notice of the customer's sequestration,[56] of the appointment of a curator bonis on his estate,[57] or by arrestment.[58] A banker is under no obligation to inquire into the motives of the payee in taking payment.[59]

39. Crossed Cheques.—A cheque is crossed generally when it bears across its face two parallel lines, with or without the words "& Co.," and with or without the words "not negotiable." It is crossed specially, and to the banker named, when it bears across its face the name of a banker, with or without the words "not negotiable."[60] A cheque may be crossed by the drawer, or by any holder. Where a cheque is crossed generally the holder may cross it specially, and may add the words "not negotiable." Where a cheque is crossed specially the banker to whom it is crossed may again cross it specially to another banker for collection. Where an uncrossed cheque, or a cheque crossed generally, is sent to a banker for collection, he may cross it specially to himself.[61] Except in these respects it is not lawful for any person to add to, or alter the crossing. The crossing is a material part of the cheque, and any unauthorised alteration avoids it.[62] But when the obliteration or alteration of the crossing is not apparent on the face of the cheque a banker who pays in good faith and without negligence may charge his customer with the amount so paid.[63]

40. Effect of Crossing.—The effect of a general crossing is that if the banker on whom it is drawn pays to anyone except a banker he is liable to the customer for any loss sustained owing to the cheque being so paid; of a special crossing, that the same liability is incurred by payment to anyone except the banker to whom the cheque is crossed, or his agent for collection being a banker.[64] If it is paid in good faith and without negligence in accordance with the crossing the banker is placed in the same position and has the same rights as if payment had been made to the true owner of the cheque, i.e., the banker may debit his customer although the cheque has been stolen or paid on a forged indorsement.[65]

41. Protection of Collecting Bank.—Section 4 of the Cheques Act 1957 extended to a banker collecting on uncrossed cheques and other instruments

[55] *McLean* v. *Clydesdale Bank* (1883) 11 R. (H.L.) 1.
[56] Bankruptcy (Scotland) Act 1913, s. 107.
[57] *Mitchell & Baxter* v. *Cheyne* (1891) 19 R. 324.
[58] See *Graham* v. *Macfarlane* (1869) 7 M. 640.
[59] *Dickson* v. *National Bank*, 1917 S.C. (H.L.) 50.
[60] s. 76.
[61] s. 77.
[62] s. 78; see as to alteration of a material part, supra, § 29.
[63] s. 79 (2).
[64] s. 79.
[65] s. 80. The section does not apply to the case where a cheque has been materially altered: *Slingsby* v. *District Bank* [1932] 1 K.B. 544.

the protection which was formerly provided by section 82 of the 1882 Act to a banker collecting upon a crossed cheque. Where in good faith and without negligence he receives payment for a customer of a cheque, bank draft, customer's payment order or certain other instruments,[66] or, having credited a customer's account with the amount of such an instrument, receives payment thereof for himself, and the customer has no title or a defective title thereto, the banker will not incur any liability to the true owner by reason only of having received such payment. To render a person a "customer" within the meaning of the section he must have had some form of account with the bank before the cheque in question was presented; it is not enough that the bank had on previous occasions cashed cheques for him.[67] A banker is not to be treated as having been negligent[68] for this purpose by reason only of his failure to concern himself with the absence of or irregularity in indorsement of the instrument[69]; but the onus is on the banker to show that he acted in good faith and without negligence.[70]

42. Cheques marked "Not Negotiable."—When a crossed cheque bears on it the words "not negotiable" it is not imported that the cheque cannot be transferred but that the transferee gets no better title than his author had, and no better title can be obtained by an indorsee from him.[71] It is probably the law that no other words on a cheque can make it not negotiable.[72]

43. Certified Cheques.—When a bank certifies a cheque it undertakes that the customer has funds to meet it, and therefore will be liable on his failure.[73] Where, after certification, the cheque was fraudulently altered in amount, and, as altered, was paid to the holder by the certifying bank, it was held that the bank was entitled to recover from the holder.[74]

44. Promissory Notes.[75]—Promissory notes are dealt with by sections 83-89 of the Act. The statutory definition is (s. 83), "A promissory note is an unconditional promise in writing made by one person to another signed by the maker, engaging to pay, on demand, or at a fixed or determinable future time, a sum certain in money to, or to the order of, a specified person or to bearer." The section provides that an instrument payable to maker's order is not a note

---

[66] See s. 4 (2).
[67] *Great Western Ry* v. *London and County Bank* [1901] A.C. 414; *Commissioners of Taxation* v. *English, Scottish and Australian Bank* [1920] A.C. 683; *Woods* v. *Martins Bank* [1959] 1 Q.B. 55.
[68] As to facts amounting to negligence, see *Underwood* v. *Bank of Liverpool* [1924] 1 K.B. 775; *Midland Bank* v. *Reckitt* [1933] A.C. 1; *Marfani & Co.* v. *Midland Bank* [1968] 1 W.L.R. 956; *Lumsden & Co.* v. *London Trustee Savings Bank* [1971] 1 Lloyd's Rep. 114. Negligence is not necessarily excluded by proof that an established banking practice has been followed: *Lloyds Bank* v. *Savory* [1932] 2 K.B. 122; affd. [1933] A.C. 201.
[69] s. 4 (3).
[70] Chalmers, *Bills of Exchange,* p. 313.
[71] s. 81.
[72] *Glen* v. *Semple* (1901) 3 F. 1134 (against cheque); *Importers Co.* v. *Westminster Bank* [1927] 2 K.B. 297.
[73] *Gaden* v. *Newfoundland Bank* [1899] A.C. 281.
[74] *Imperial Bank of Canada* v. *Bank of Hamilton* [1903] A.C. 49.
[75] See Gow, *Mercantile Law,* pp. 455-6.

within the section until it has been indorsed by the maker, and that a note is not invalid because it contains a pledge of collateral security with a power to dispose thereof. An instrument may be a promissory note though the words "agree to pay," and not "promise to pay," are used,[76] but not if it reserves an option to pay at an earlier date than the fixed date and so creates an uncertainty or contingency as to the time of payment.[77] A document which contained, in addition to a promise to pay, further and separate contractual stipulations was held not to be a promissory note.[78] In questions of stamp law it has been held that documents expressed as an obligation to pay a debt of unspecified amount,[79] or as a written obligation of indebtedness,[80] or as a mere receipt,[81] or as a promise to pay a certain sum with interest at an unspecified rate,[82] were not promissory notes, and therefore admitted either of being after-stamped as bonds or as agreements or of being used in evidence unstamped as proof of a debt. A mere obligation to pay, not addressed to anyone, and not bearing to be payable to bearer, was held not to be a promissory note, and to be invalid as a "blank bond" under the Blank Bonds and Trusts Act 1695 (c. 25).[83] It is no objection to the validity of a note that it contains provisions safeguarding the holder in the event of time being given to one or other of the joint makers.[84]

The provisions of the Act as to bills apply also to promissory notes. In applying them the maker of a note corresponds with the acceptor of a bill, the first indorser with the drawer of an accepted bill payable to drawer's order. The following provisions are not applicable to promissory notes: (a) presentment for acceptance; (b) acceptance; (c) acceptance supra protest; (d) bills in a set. A further difference is that where a foreign note is dishonoured protest is unnecessary.[85]

Presentment for payment is necessary in order to make an indorser liable, but is not necessary in order to make the maker liable, unless it is in the body of it made payable at a particular place.[86] It must then be presented at that place, but not necessarily at the date of payment of the principal sum or of any instalment.[87] If a note payable on demand is not presented for payment within a reasonable time the indorser is discharged.[88] But it is not deemed to be overdue, so as to affect a holder with defects of title of which he had no notice, because it appears that a reasonable time for presenting it for payment had elapsed.[89]

---

[76] *Macfarlane* v. *Johnston* (1864) 2 M. 1210; *Vallance* v. *Forbes* (1879) 6 R. 1099; *McTaggart* v. *McEachern's J.F.*, 1949 S.C. 503.
[77] *Williamson* v. *Rider* [1963] 1 Q.B. 89.
[78] *Dickie* v. *Singh*, 1974 S.L.T. 129.
[79] *Henderson* v. *Dawson* (1895) 22 R. 895.
[80] *Todd* v. *Wood* (1897) 24 R. 1104.
[81] *Welsh's Trs.* v. *Forbes* (1885) 12 R. 851.
[82] *Lamberton* v. *Aiken* (1899) 2 F. 189.
[83] *Duncan's Trs.* v. *Shand* (1872) 10 M. 984.
[84] *Kirkwood* v. *Carroll* [1903] 1 K.B. 531.
[85] s. 89.
[86] s. 87.
[87] *Gordon* v. *Kerr* (1898) 25 R. 570.
[88] s. 86 (11).
[89] s. 86 (2).

The maker of a note, by making and delivering it, engages that he will pay it according to its tenor, and is precluded from denying to a holder in due course the existence of the payee and his then capacity to indorse.[90]

[90] s. 88; as to delivery, see s. 84.

CHAPTER XXVII

INSURANCE

Macgillivray, *Insurance* (6th ed., 1975); Colinvaux, *Insurance* (3rd ed., 1970); Arnould, *Marine Insurance* (15th ed., 1961), *British Shipping Laws,* vols. 9 and 10; Gow, *Mercantile Law* (1964), Ch. 6; Ivamy, *Principles of Insurance Law* (3rd ed., 1975); Ivamy, *Fire and Motor Insurance* (2nd ed., 1973); Ivamy, *Marine Insurance* (2nd ed., 1974); Ivamy, *Personal, Accident, Life and Other Insurance* (1973).

1. Nature of Contract.—Insurance may be a contract to indemnify against possible loss or to make a payment on the occurrence of a certain event.[1] The contract need not necessarily provide for payment of a sum of money.[2] The continued existence or safety of anything, or the occurrence or non-occurrence of any event, may be made the subject of a policy of insurance, and there has been no case where, apart from questions of insurable interest, a policy has been held void as in substance a bet or sponsio ludicra.[3] The main distinction between contracts classed under the general name of insurance is between those cases where the contract is one of indemnity, and the insured recovers, and can only recover, the amount of his loss, except in the case of a valued policy,[4] and those which are merely contracts to pay on a certain condition being fulfilled. In the former class are fire and marine and third party accident insurance, in the latter, life and endowment insurance. Marine insurance law, which has many specialities, has been codified by the Marine Insurance Act 1906. Before dealing with particular forms it may be well to consider certain principles which are generally applicable.

2. Terminology.—The party effecting the insurance is termed the insured or the assured; the party insuring, the insurer, office or (in marine insurance) underwriter; the consideration is known as the premium.

3. Restrictions upon Insurance Companies.—The right to act as insurer, in various forms of insurance, including life, fire, and accident, industrial and employers' liability, motor vehicle, marine, aviation and transit,[5] is limited by legislation. The Insurance Companies Act 1974[6] regulates the entry of new

---

[1] Insurance contracts are unaffected by the Unfair Contract Terms Act 1977 (c. 50): 1977 Act, s. 15 (3) (*a*).
[2] *Department of Trade and Industry* v. *St. Christopher Motorists' Association* [1974] 1 W.L.R. 99.
[3] See *Carlill* v. *Carbolic Smoke Ball Co.* [1893] 1 Q.B. 256; *Re London County, etc., Re-insurance Co.* [1922] 2 Ch. 67. However public policy may render a contract unenforceable: *Gray* v. *Barr* [1971] 2 Q.B. 554.
[4] See §§ 24, 38, infra.
[5] Insurance Companies Act 1974 (c. 49) ss. 1, 2, 83, as amended by the Insurance Companies (Classes of General Business) Regulations 1977 (S.I. 1977 No. 1552).
[6] c. 49, consolidating, with certain omissions and alterations, the provisions of the Insurance Companies Act 1958, the Companies Act 1967, Part II, and the Insurance Companies (Amendment) Act 1973.

companies into the insurance business[7] and the conduct of insurance business generally[8]. The fundamental requirement[9] is that a person must have authorisation from the Secretary of State for the Department of Trade in order to carry on an insurance business of one of the specified classes.[10] Companies which were carrying on insurance businesses immediately before 3 November 1966 are authorised to carry on those businesses by s. 3 (1) (a) of the Act.[11] Such companies nevertheless require authorisation should they wish to extend their business to additional classes of insurance.[12] With minor exceptions, the Secretary of State may not issue an authorisation unless he is satisfied that the insurer has a sufficiency of assets,[13] and if it is a company limited by shares, that its paid up share capital is not less than £100,000.[14] The Secretary of State must also be satisfied that adequate reinsurance arrangements have been or will be made, or that the lack of such arrangements is justifiable.[15] He must withhold authorisation if it appears to him that any director, controller or manager of the insurance company is not a fit and proper person to hold that office.[16] Once in business, an insurance company to which the Act applies[17] must inter alia produce annual accounts, obey rules as to advertising and the conduct of insurance agents,[18] and maintain a margin of solvency.[19] The powers of the Secretary of State under the 1974 Act are far-reaching. He may communicate with an insurance company concerning inaccuracies or deficiencies in its accounts.[20] He may object to the appointment of a director or chief executive in the company.[21] He may in certain circumstances[22] actively intervene by imposing requirements and restrictions on the company, or ordering that an actuarial investigation be carried out.[23] He may also in certain circumstances petition for the winding up of the company.[24]

[7] 1974 Act, Part I.
[8] 1974 Act, Parts II and III.
[9] A requirement introduced by the Companies Act 1967.
[10] 1974 Act, ss. 1-3, as amended by S.I. 1977 No. 1552. Exceptions include Lloyd's, friendly societies, trade unions making provisions for strike benefits, and bankers.
[11] Provided that the companies were not carrying on business in contravention of the Insurance Companies Act 1958: 1974 Act, s. 3 (1) (a). The 1958 Act provided inter alia that subject to certain exceptions (including existing companies, Lloyd's and other associations of under-writers, and companies registered under the Acts relating to friendly societies or to trade unions) only a company with a paid-up capital of £50,000 might carry on the business of insurance.
[12] 1974 Act, s. 3 (1) (b).
[13] As defined in s. 4.
[14] 1974 Act, s. 5.
[15] 1974 Act, s. 6.
[16] 1974 Act, s. 7.
[17] As to Part II of the 1974 Act, see s. 12.
[18] 1974 Act, ss. 13, 16, 62-64. Contraventions may result in penalties. See for example R. v. Clegg [1977] 4 C.L. § 69.
[19] 1974 Act, s. 44. See too the Insurance Companies (Solvency: General Business) Regulations 1977 (S.I. 1977 No. 1533).
[20] 1974 Act, s. 18 (5).
[21] 1974 Act, s. 52.
[22] For example, where there is a risk that a company may be unable to meet its liabilities, or where it has furnished the Secretary with misleading information: 1974 Act, s. 28.
[23] 1974 Act, ss. 29-37. He may also demand that information be supplied, or that the company take such action as he thinks appropriate.
[24] For example, where a company is in breach of its duties under the 1974 Act: 1974 Act, s. 46.

4. Formation of Contract: Writing.—It would seem that at common law insurance is a contract which must be entered into in writing, and that a verbal agreement to insure, so long as no premium was paid, would leave each party free to resile.[25] In contracts of life assurance, revenue statutes impose the necessity of a stamped policy, and provide that any unstamped contract shall be void.[26] This may affect the validity of any preliminary contract to insure. In fire and accident insurance, where there is no statutory avoidance, the policy is often preceded by a covering note, under which the applicant is insured for a period during which the company may decide whether they will take the risk. This forms a binding contract, and the company will be liable even although the risk is ultimately declined.[27] In the ordinary practice of marine insurance the policy is preceded by a document known as a slip, by which the underwriters indicate that they accept the risk and settle the amount which each will contribute on a loss. But a slip, though its observance is secured by professional usage, is not a contract and does not bind those who sign it to issue a policy, nor does it subject them to any claim of damages if they do not.[28] It may be used as evidence of the date when the proposal for insurance was accepted, or, for any purpose, when there is a policy, duly stamped if necessary.[29] Contracts of insurance affected by the Insurance Companies Act 1974 (c. 49) may be void if the sum assured is unlimited in amount.[30]

5. Insurable Interest Generally.—It is a general statutory rule that no one may insure unless he has an insurable interest in the subject of the policy. Apart from marine insurance this is provided by the Life Assurance Act 1774.[31] This Act, primarily dealing with life insurance, provides that no insurance shall be made on the life of any person, "or on other event or events whatsoever," wherein the person for whose use the insurance is made shall have no interest, or by way of gaming or wagering. Every such policy is declared void.[32] Marine insurance is expressly excluded from the Act.[33] The general words "other event" have been held to cover accident insurance,[34] and probably any other form of insurance except marine.[35] The result of want of insurable interest is that the policy is void, and cannot be enforced, or be the

---

[25] *McElroy* v. *London Assurance Corporation* (1897) 24 R. 287; but see *Parker* v. *Western Assurance Co.*, 1925 S.L.T. 131, and Gloag on *Contract* (2nd ed.), p. 181. Probably a verbal contract is enough if there has been rei interventus, e.g. payment of a premium.

[26] All policies of insurance other than life insurances are currently exempt from stamp duty: Stamp Act 1891, s. 1; Sch. 1; Finance Act 1959, s. 30 (1); Finance Act 1970, s. 32 (*a*); Sch. 7, para. 1 (2) (*b*).

[27] *Bhugwandass* v. *Netherlands Insurance Co.* (1888) 14 App.Cas. 83; *Neil* v. *S.E. Lancashire Insurance Co.*, 1932 S.C. 35; *Cunningham* v. *Anglian Ins. Co.*, 1934 S.L.T. 273.

[28] Marine Insurance Act 1906, s. 22; Finance Act 1959 (c. 58) s. 30 (6); s. 37 (5); Sch. 8, Pt. II; cf. *Clyde Marine Insurance Co.* v. *Renwick*, 1924 S.C. 113.

[29] Marine Insurance Act 1906, ss. 21, 89; Finance Act 1959 (c. 58), Sch. 8, Pt. II; Arnould, *Marine Insurance*, para. 47.

[30] 1974 Act, s. 27.

[31] 14 Geo. III., c. 48. As to marine insurance, see § 28, infra.

[32] Ibid., s. 1.

[33] Ibid., s. 4.

[34] *Shilling* v. *Accidental Death Co.* (1857) 2 H. & N. 42.

[35] Cf. Macgillivray, *Insurance*, Ch. 1; Ivamy, *Fire and Motor Insurance*, p. 176; but see "Insurable Interest," J. N. Quar, 1971 S.L.T. (News) 141. Marine insurance is dealt with at § 28, infra.

foundation of any claim.[36] It is pars judicis to take the objection.[37] But it has been held that if the insurer chooses to pay, the Court will decide who has the right to the money.[38] If A, without B's authority, and with no insurable interest, insures B's property against fire, and the insurance company pay on a loss without objection, it would appear that B has no claim to the money.[39] The return of the premiums paid may be claimed if the insurance was induced by the fraudulent representations of the insurance agent,[40] but not merely because the insured was unaware of the law.[41] The question what amounts to an insurable interest depends upon the particular form of insurance involved.

6. Duty of Disclosure.—All forms of insurance are contracts "uberrimae fidei," in which each party is bound to reveal all material facts known to him. Failure in this respect, a fortiori any misrepresentation in any material point, whether fraudulent or not, renders the policy voidable.[42] Though most cases have related to concealment by the insured, the same rules apply to the insurer.[43] A general definition of materiality in insurance may be taken from the Marine Insurance Act 1906, s. 18 (2): "Every circumstance is material which would influence the judgment of a prudent insurer in fixing the premium, or determining whether he will take the risk."[44] The evidence of persons engaged in the particular branch of insurance is admissible, but may be disregarded if it merely amounts to proof of a custom to take gambling risks.[45] Circumstances may make any fact material, so, though the name of the party having interest in a ship is not usually material, when the party having the main interest was a Greek, and ships belonging to Greeks were at the time uninsurable, it was held that concealment of his identity was sufficient to render a policy voidable.[46] Where the policy is preceded by a proposal form and one of the queries therein is left unanswered without objection, it will be assumed that the insurers accept the point as not material,[47] but the fact that the queries are all answered does not justify the concealment of a material point regarding which there is no query.[48] In the case of certain policies, amongst which are fire and accident policies, where the insurers may decline to renew the policy at the expiry of the original period, each renewal is made on the understanding that the original representations remain true and that no

---

[36] *Cheshire* v. *Vaughan* [1920] 3 K.B. 240, no claim against broker for negligence.

[37] *Gedge* v. *Royal Exchange* [1900] 2 Q.B. 214; *Cheshire* v. *Vaughan*, supra.

[38] *Hadden* v. *Bryden* (1899) 1 F. 710. The contrary has been decided in England: *London County Re-insurance Co.* [1922] 2 Ch. 67.

[39] *Ferguson* v. *Aberdeen P.C.*, 1916 S.C. 715

[40] *Hughes* v. *Liverpool Friendly Society* [1916] 2 K.B. 482.

[41] *Harse* v. *Pearl Life Co.* [1904] 1 K.B. 558; see also *London, etc., Re-insurance Co.* [1922] 2 Ch. 67; *Came* v. *City of Glasgow Friendly Society*, 1933 S.C. 69, a decision under the Industrial Insurance Act 1923, which provides expressly for repayment of premiums.

[42] Bell, *Prin.*, §§ 474, 522; *Comm.*, I, 665.

[43] Marine Insurance Act 1906, s. 17.

[44] See for example *Lambert* v. *Co-operative Insurance Society* [1975] 2 Lloyd's Rep. 485.

[45] *Zurich General Accident, etc., Co.* v. *Leven*, 1940 S.C. 406; *Gunford Ship Co.* v. *Thames, etc., Insurance Co.*, 1911 S.C. (H.L.) 84, 90.

[46] *The Spathari*, 1925 S.C. (H.L.) 6.

[47] *Joel* v. *Law Union Co.* [1908] 2 K.B. 863.

[48] *Life Association* v. *Foster* (1873) 11 M. 351.

new fact has emerged which ought to be disclosed.[49] The points on which disclosure is not required are, in marine insurance and probably also in other forms, the following[50]:—(a) Any circumstance which diminishes the risk; (b) any circumstance which is known or presumed to be known to the insurer. The insurer is presumed to know matters of common notoriety or knowledge, and matters which an insurer in the ordinary course of his business, as such, ought to know[51]; (c) any circumstance as to which information is waived by the insurer[52]; (d) any circumstance which it is superfluous to disclose by reason of any express or implied warranty.[53]

7. Disclosure in Questions with Agents.—An insured person is presumed to know, and is therefore bound to disclose, every material fact known to his mercantile agent, which the agent, with reasonable diligence, could have communicated.[54] But the knowledge possessed by an agent who is employed merely for the purpose of insuring, e.g. an insurance broker, is not necessarily attributed to the insured. So if a broker fails to disclose a material fact, this, while it will render voidable any policy negotiated by that broker, will not invalidate other policies on the same risk effected through other brokers.[55] An agent to insure is assumed to know, and bound to disclose, every circumstance which in the ordinary course of business ought to be known by, or to have been communicated to, him, and every material circumstance which the insured is bound to disclose, unless it came to his knowledge too late to be communicated to the agent.[56] On the other hand, if an insurance is effected with the agent of the insurance company it is a sufficient answer to any objection based on the common law obligation of disclosure that the fact in question was known to the agent.[57]

8. Warranties.—Where reduction of a policy is attempted on the ground of failure in disclosure, or of misrepresentation, the fact in question must be material to the risk. But certain facts may be warranted by the insured, either (in marine insurance) impliedly,[58] or expressly; and if a particular fact or statement is warranted the validity of the policy depends on the warranty being fulfilled, and it does not matter whether the fact or statement be material or not. Thus if the policy is preceded by a proposal form, and is

[49] *Law Accident Ins. Society* v. *Boyd.* 1942 S.C. 384.
[50] Marine Insurance Act 1906, s. 18 (3).
[51] See *London General Insurance Co.* v. *Guarantee, etc., Association* [1921] 1 K.B. 104.
[52] *Mann, Macneal & Steeves* v. *Capital, etc., Insurance Co.* [1921] 2 K.B. 300.
[53] See opinion of Lord President Dunedin, *Gunford Ship Co.* v. *Thames, etc., Insurance Co.,* 1910 S.C. 1072, revd. 1911 S.C. (H.L.) 84.
[54] *Blackburn* v. *Vigors* (1887) 12 App.Cas. 531.
[55] *Blackburn* v. *Haslam* (1888) 21 Q.B.D. 144. As to a broker's duties and liabilities generally, see the Insurance Brokers (Registration) Act 1977 (c. 46); *Claude R. Ogden & Co.* v. *Reliance Sprinkler Co.* [1975] 1 Lloyd's Rep. 52; *Warren* v. *Henry Sutton & Co.* [1976] 2 Lloyd's Rep. 276; *Beattie* v. *Furness Houlder Insurance,* 1976 S.L.T. (Notes) 60; *Cherry* v. *Allied Insurance Brokers* [1978] 1 Lloyd's Rep. 274; *Woolcott* v. *Excess Insurance Co.* [1978] 1 Lloyd's Rep. 633.
[56] Marine Insurance Act, 1906, s. 19.
[57] *Cruikshank* v. *Northern Insurance Co.* (1895) 23 R. 147; *Joel* v. *Law Union Co.* [1908] 2 K.B. 863.
[58] Infra, § 31.

issued expressly on the condition that the answers to the queries in the proposal form are true, any untruth, even on a minor point, will vitiate the policy.[59] The same rule was applied where it was provided that the proposal form "shall be the basis of the contract and be held as incorporated herein." A mis-statement as to the place where a motor car, which was the subject of the policy, was garaged, was held to render the policy voidable, though it was not material to the risk, and in spite of an express provision that material mis-statements should avoid.[60] And in such cases where the accuracy of the answers in the proposal form is contractually the test of the validity of the policy, it is no answer to the company that the true facts were within the knowledge of their agent, or that the proposal form was actually filled up by him, and the inaccuracy due to his misunderstanding of the information furnished by the insured.[61] Nor will it necessarily save the policy that the statement was one (e.g. as to freedom from latent disease) of which the insured could have no actual knowledge; although, in doubtful cases, such statements will be read as assertions of opinion and not of fact.[62]

9. Assignation.—A policy of insurance is assignable unless there is a provision to the contrary.[63] The transfer of the subject at risk does not amount to an assignation of the policy.[64] The assignation of a policy requires writing; the mere physical transfer of the policy does not give the transferee any right to sue the insurance company, and is not a completed gift in a question with the executors of the insured.[65] When the question is one of donation no special words are necessary to constitute an assignation; in doubtful cases the construction of the writing may be assisted by parole evidence of the circumstances under which it was prepared, executed and delivered.[66] Where the question is with other creditors of the insured or with the trustee in his sequestration, a mere assignation, with or without the transfer of the policy, is not sufficient to give the assignee a real right in the policy or in its proceeds. The assignation must be followed by intimation to the insurance company.[67] Both at common law and by statute[68] an assignee of a policy may sue in his own name. But he is subject to any defence which the insurer could state in a question with the original insured.[69] Thus, in life insurance, the company may refuse payment to an assignee on the ground of

59 *Standard Life Assurance Co.* v. *Weems* (1884) 11 R. (H.L.) 48.
60 *Dawsons* v. *Bonnin*, 1922 S.C. (H.L.) 156; *Provincial Ins. Co.* v. *Morgan* [1932] 2 K.B. 70, affd. [1933] A.C. 240, where answers in the proposal form were held to be merely descriptive of the risk.
61 *McMillan* v. *Accident Insurance Co.*, 1907 S.C. 484; *National Farmers, etc. Society* v. *Tully*, 1935 S.L.T. 574.
62 *Standard Life Assurance Co.* v. *Weems*, supra, opinion of Lord Blackburn.
63 Bell, *Prin.*, § 516; Marine Insurance Act 1906, s. 50.
64 *Rayner* v. *Preston* (1881) 18 Ch.D. 1 (fire); Marine Insurance Act 1906, s. 15.
65 *Scottish Provident* v. *Cohen* (1888) 16 R. 112; *Brownlee* v. *Robb*, 1907 S.C. 1302; *United Kingdom Co.* v. *Dixon* (1838) 16 S. 1277.
66 *Brownlee* v. *Robb*, supra; *Carmichael* v. *Carmichael's Exx.*, 1920 S.C. (H.L.) 195.
67 *Strachan* v. *McDougle* (1835) 13 S. 954; *Wylie's Exx.* v. *McJannet* (1901) 4 F. 195.
68 Policies of Insurance Act 1867 (30 & 31 Vict., c. 144), s. 1.
69 See § 10 infra as to statutory assignations.

mis-statements by the insured in the proposal form. The brocard "assignatus utitur jure auctoris" applies.[70] In marine insurance, when a ship is lost by the fault of the owner, a claim by a mortgagee will fail if he is merely the assignee of the policy[71]; but may succeed if his interest, as well as that of the owner, was originally insured, and where therefore he has an independent and not merely a derivative right.[72]

10. Rights under Policy in Bankruptcy.—In the ordinary case, if the policy is not assigned, and is not made payable to any third party, any sum becoming due under it passes to the trustee in the sequestration of the insured. At common law, there was no exception to this rule in the case of insurance against liability arising from injury to third parties.[73] Under the Third Parties (Rights against Insurers) Act 1930,[74] "where any party is insured against liabilities to third parties which he may incur," and is bankrupt, or has made a composition with his creditors (or, in the case of a company, is being wound up), his rights under the policy are transferred to, and vest in, the party to whom the liability has been incurred, whether the injury to him occurred before or after the bankruptcy. The party to whom the claim under the policy is transferred takes no higher right, in a question with the insurance company, than the insured possessed.[75] It has been decided in England that, where the insolvent insured's liability is unascertained, the third party should obtain the Court's leave to sue the insured and so fix his liability.[76] The insurer is not entitled to set off against the claim of a judgment creditor the amount of premiums due from a judgment debtor.[77] An insurer sued directly by an employee can set up any defence which he could have set up against the employer.[78] He may rely on exclusion clauses.[79]

11. Protection for Policyholders.—Provision has been made for the protection of policyholders whose insurance companies are unable to meet their liabilities.[80] Only holders of United Kingdom policies issued by authorised insurance companies are protected.[81] A body known as the Policyholders Protection Board is empowered, subject to guidance from the Secretary of State for Trade,[82] to indemnify or otherwise assist policyholders who have been or may be prejudiced by an insurance company's inability to meet its liabilities, and also to impose levies on insurers in order to finance

---

[70] *Scottish Equitable* v. *Buist* (1877) 4 R. 1076, affd. (1878) 5 R. (H.L.) 64.
[71] *Graham Shipping Co.* v. *Merchants' Marine Insurance Co.* [1924] A.C. 294.
[72] *Samuel* v. *Dumas* [1924] A.C. 431.
[73] *Hood's Trs.* v. *Southern Union Insurance Co.* [1928] 1 Ch. 793.
[74] 20 & 21 Geo. V, c. 25.
[75] *Greenlees* v. *Port of Manchester Ins. Co.*, 1933 S.C. 383. But see § 12, infra.
[76] *Post Office* v. *Norwich Union Fire Insurance Society* [1967] 2 Q.B. 263.
[77] *Murray* v. *Legal & General Assurance Society* [1970] 2 Q.B. 495.
[78] *Farrell* v. *Federated Employers Assurance Association* [1970] 1 W.L.R. 1400.
[79] *Kearney* v. *General Accident* [1968] 2 Lloyd's Rep. 240.
[80] Policyholders Protection Act 1975 (c. 75).
[81] 1975 Act, ss. 3, 4.
[82] 1975 Act, s. 2.

these protective measures.[83] In certain cases, a policyholder will be indemnified in full[84]; in other cases, only in part.[85] The Board has no duty to assist a policyholder who is insured with two or more companies, one of which is an authorised insurance company not in liquidation.[86] Protection may be given although no policy has been issued.[87]

Some protection is also extended to insured persons by the European Communities Act 1972[88] which allows an insured to enforce a policy issued ultra vires of the company, provided that the issue of the policy was decided on by the directors, and provided that the insured acted in good faith.

12. Motor Vehicle Insurance.—By the Road Traffic Act 1972,[89] it is provided that it is unlawful for any person to use, or to cause or permit any other person to use,[90] a motor vehicle on a road unless there is in force in relation to the use of the vehicle by that person or that other person a policy of insurance covering third party risks which complies with the requirements of that Act.[91] This provision does not, however, render the owner of a motor vehicle personally liable in a case where he has permitted a third party, covered by his insurance, to drive it, and the third party's negligence has caused injury.[92] But the owner of a car who allows another person to use it, when there is no adequate policy in regard to third party risks, is liable for any loss caused by the fault of the driver which the driver cannot meet.[93]

The Road Traffic Act 1934,[94] enhanced the rights of persons injured as a result of the negligent driving of insured persons. An injured person who has obtained judgment against a wrongdoer, to whom a policy has been issued in accordance with the statutory requirements, may recover direct from the insurer such sum as is payable under the policy.[95] And the right avails even although the insurer is entitled to avoid, or has already avoided the policy. This drastic provision admits of one partial modification. By section 149 (3) it is open to insurers to take proceedings, within certain limits of time, for declarator that they are entitled to avoid the policy on the ground of material

---

[83] 1975 Act, ss. 1, 5-16, 18 et seq., as amended by S.I. 1977 No. 1552. See for example *Policyholders Protection Board* v. *Official Receiver* [1976] 1 W.L.R. 447.
[84] For example, compulsory insurance under Part VI of the Road Traffic Act 1972; 1975 Act, ss. 6, 7.
[85] 1975 Act, ss. 8, 10 (as amended by S.I. 1977 No. 1552).
[86] 1975 Act, s. 9.
[87] 1975 Act, s. 23.
[88] c. 68, s. 9 (1).
[89] c. 20, s. 143.
[90] See *Houston* v. *Buchanan*, 1940 S.C. (H.L.) 17; also *Kelly* v. *Cornhill Insurance Co.*, 1964 S.C. (H.L.) 46.
[91] ss. 145-150, as amended by the Motor Vehicles (Compulsory Insurance) (No. 2) Regulations 1973 (No. 2143) and the 1974 Regulations (S.I. 1974 No. 791). The policy must be issued by an authorised insurer who is a member of the Motor Insurers Bureau; Road Traffic Act 1974 (c. 50), s. 20.
[92] *Lindsay* v. *Robertson*, 1933 S.C. 158. As to the liability of an employee under a contract of service, see *Lister* v. *Romford Ice & Cold Storage Co.*, [1957] A.C. 555.
[93] *Houston* v. *Buchanan*, supra; *Fleming* v. *McGillivray*, 1946 S.C. 1.
[94] See now 1972 Act, s. 149 (previously the 1960 Act, s. 207).
[95] As to the right of insurers to enter a defence in an action at the instance of an injured person against the assured, see *Windsor* v. *Chalcraft* [1939] 1 K.B. 279.

non-disclosure or material misrepresentation. In these proceedings the claimants on the insured person, the defender, are entitled to come in and be heard.[96] The section, of course, does not apply in a case where the policy does not cover the risk at all.[97] Section 148 further helps the injured third party by invalidating certain restrictions on the liability of insurers. The third party's right, it should also be noted, was substantially underwritten by an agreement made in June 1946 between the Minister of Transport and the Motor Insurers Bureau.[97a] Under the 1971 agreement the Bureau undertook to satisfy any unsatisfied decree arising from any liability required by the Act[98] to be covered by a policy of insurance. It is a condition for recovery from the Bureau of whole or part of the damages and expenses awarded against an uninsured person that notice of the action is given to the Bureau within seven days of its commencement.

FIRE INSURANCE

13. Nature of Contract.—Fire insurance is a contract of indemnity, in which the insured must prove the amount of his loss and can recover no more.[99] A policy under which the subjects insured are valued beforehand may nevertheless be valid, unless there appears to be fraudulent intent.[1] Unless otherwise provided[2] a policy of fire insurance is a specific policy, in which the whole amount of the insurance may be recovered on a partial loss, provided that damage to that amount has been suffered, as opposed to an average policy, usual in marine insurance, when the insured is entitled, on a partial loss, to no more than a proportional part of the sum insured.[3]

14. Insurable Interest.—Fire insurance is one of the forms of insurance to which the Life Assurance Act 1774 (14 Geo. III, c. 48), applies, and the insured must probably have an interest at the time when the insurance is effected and certainly at the time when the loss occurs. That interest may consist in the ownership of the subjects insured, or in some subordinate right, such as that of a lessee or the holder of a security.[4] A mere expectancy, such as that of an heir, does not furnish an insurable interest.[5] A shareholder, even though he holds all the shares, has no insurable interest in the property of the

---

[96] *Zurich, etc. Ins. Co.* v. *Livingston*, 1938 S.C. 582. For sequel, see *Zurich, etc., Ins. Co.* v. *Leven*, 1940 S.C. 406.

[97] See *Robb* v. *McKechnie*, 1936 J.C. 25.

[97a] Now replaced by an agreement between the Secretary of State for the Environment and the M.I.B. dated 1st February 1971.

[98] See *Lees* v. *Motor Insurers Bureau* [1952] 2 All E.R. 511.

[99] Bell, *Prin.*, § 511.

[1] See Bunyon, *Fire Insurance* (7th ed.), p. 200; Macgillivray, *Insurance*, para. 2141; Gow, *Mercantile Law*, p. 343. Overvaluation of the property may be evidence of fraud: cf. *Hercules Insurance* v. *Hunter* (1835) 14 S. 1137.

[2] *Buchanan* v. *Liverpool, London and Globe* (1884) 11 R. 1032.

[3] See Bunyon, *Fire Insurance* (7th ed.), 19.

[4] Bell, *Prin.*, § 509.

[5] *Lucena* v. *Craufurd* (1806) 2 Bos. & P. (N.R.) 325.

company.[6] Neither has a creditor in the property of his debtor.[7] Where property which is insured is sold and the risk has passed to the purchaser before the price is paid the right under the policy does not pass to the purchaser unless the policy is assigned to him.[8] Should a fire then occur the seller has still an interest which will entitle him to recover from the insurance company, in respect that the buyer may fail to pay the price, but if the price is met, the company may recover what they have paid.[9]

15. Subrogation.—From the principle that fire insurance is a contract of indemnity, in which the insured is not entitled to recover more than he has lost, spring the rights of subrogation and of contribution. The right of subrogation arises when some third party is liable for the loss covered by the policy, either by contract, or because the loss arose from his wrongful or negligent act. The insurance company is not entitled to refuse payment of the sum due on the policy merely on the ground that a third party is liable for the loss,[10] nor, conversely, is that third party entitled to plead the insurance as a defence.[11] But the company, on payment, and without any assignation, is subrogated to the rights of the insured, and may recover from any third party who would have been liable in a question with the insured.[12] Another aspect of the principle of subrogation is that if the insured, after payment on the policy, recovers anything from a third party who is liable for the loss, he must account to the insurance company for what he has recovered.[13] The insured cannot, after a loss has occurred, defeat the insurer's right of subrogation by any gratuitous discharge of his claims against third parties. Should he do so he must give credit to the insurance company for the value of the claim which he has abandoned.[14]

16. Contribution.—The right of contribution arises where property is insured in more than one office, and a fire causes loss less than the combined amount of the policies. Then prima facie the insured may recover from any one office the whole amount insured by it[15]; but there is usually a clause in the policy providing that each shall be liable to contribute rateably only.[16] Any

---

[6] *Macaura* v. *Northern Assurance Co.* [1925] A.C. 619.

[7] *Macaura*, supra.

[8] *Rayner* v. *Preston* (1881) 18 Ch.D. 1.

[9] *Castellain* v. *Preston* (1883) 11 Q.B.D. 380.

[10] *Castellain* v. *Preston* (1883) 11 Q.B.D. 380; Marine Insurance Act 1906, s. 14 (3).

[11] *Port-Glasgow Sailcloth Co.* v. *Cal. Ry.* (1892) 19 R. 608.

[12] *Castellain* v. *Preston*, supra; *King* v. *Victoria Ins. Co.* [1896] A.C. 250. As to interest on damages, see *H. Cousins & Co.* v. *D. & S. Carriers* [1971] 2 Q.B. 230.

[13] *Darrell* v. *Tibbits* (1880) 5 Q.B.D. 560; *Castellain* v. *Preston*, supra. But the insurer probably cannot recover from the insured a greater sum than he has paid the insured: cf. *Yorkshire Insurance Co.* v. *Nisbet Shipping Co.* [1962] 2 Q.B. 330 (Shipping). Also the insurer must have indemnified the insured: cf. *Scottish Union National Insurance Co.* v. *Davis* [1970] 1 Lloyd's Rep. 1 (Motor Vehicle).

[14] *West of England Fire Co.* v. *Isaacs* [1897] 1 Q.B. 226; *Phoenix Assurance Co.* v. *Spooner* [1905] 2 K.B. 753.

[15] *Glasgow Provident Society* v. *Westminster Fire Office* (1887) 14 R. 947, affd. (1888) 15 R. (H.L.) 89, per consulted judges, 14 R. 965; Marine Insurance Act 1906, s. 32.

[16] As to rateable proportion clauses, see *Commercial Union Assurance Co.* v. *Hayden* [1977] Q.B. 804.

company which has paid more than its rateable share of the total loss has, by implication of law and without any assignation from the insured, a right of contribution, i.e. a right to recover from the other companies their rateable shares.[17] To admit of the right of contribution the insurances must not only be over the same physical subject, but over the same interest in that subject. If parties having separate interests insure, there is no right of contribution. Thus where a wharfinger, who was liable for corn stored with him in the event of fire, insured it, and the owners also insured, it was held that the company with which the wharfinger had insured had no right of contribution against the company with which the owners had insured.[18] The same principle was applied, and the right of contribution was negatived, where separate policies were effected covering the interest of prior and of postponed bondholders over a building which was destroyed by fire.[19] If, as is usual in such cases, the policies are taken out by the debtor to cover his own interest and that of the respective bondholders, there is the apparent objection to the recovery on both policies that the owner, by the extinction or reduction of the sum due on the bonds, will gain more than he has lost by the fire. But this is met by holding that the company, paying on its policy to the postponed bondholder, is entitled to an assignation of the bond.[20]

17. Reinstatement.—Fire policies invariably contain a provision entitling the company, at their option, to reinstate or replace the property which has been injured, instead of paying the amount of the loss.[21] It would appear that if the company indicate which course they propose to take, by entering into negotiations as to the amount of the damage, they have conclusively elected to pay and not to reinstate.[22] The Act, 14 Geo. III., c. 78, under which parties interested in a house destroyed by fire may insist on reinstatement, does not apply to Scotland.[23]

18. Notice of Loss.—In fire, as also in accident insurance policies, there are generally provisions whereby the claim on the policy is made contingent on notice of a loss being given within a certain period. Such conditions are effectual, and failure to comply with them is not excused on the ground that it was due to circumstances beyond the insured's control.[24] But the company may be barred from taking the objection, as in a case where they had intimated rejection of the claim upon another and untenable ground.[25]

[17] *Sickness, etc. Association* v. *General Accident Co.* (1892) 19 R. 977.
[18] *North British and Mercantile Co.* v. *London Liverpool and Globe* (1876) 5 Ch.D. 569.
[19] *Scottish Amicable etc. Association* v. *Northern Assurance Co.* (1883) 11 R. 287.
[20] *Glasgow Provident Society* v. *Westminster Fire Office,* supra.
[21] See, e.g. *Carrick Furniture House* v. *General Accident,* 1978 S.L.T. 65.
[22] *Scottish Amicable, etc., Association* v. *Northern Assurance Co.,* supra.
[23] *Glasgow Provident Society* v. *Westminster Fire Office,* supra.
[24] *Worsley* v. *Wood* (1976) 6 T.R. 710; *London Guarantee Co.* v. *Fearnley* (1880) 5 App.Cas. 911, Lord Blackburn.
[25] *Shiells* v. *Scottish Assurance Corporation* (1889) 16 R. 1014; *Donnison* v. *Employers Accident Co.* (1897) 24 R. 681.

19. Indirect Loss.—In the absence of any special provision a fire policy covers only loss directly resulting from the destruction or injury of the subject insured, not indirect loss, such as injury to business or the loss of rent.[26]

LIFE INSURANCE

20. Nature of Contract.—As the value of a man's life to himself cannot be estimated in money it has never been doubted that the ordinary policy on the life of the insured is not a contract of indemnity, but a contract to pay on the occurrence of a certain event. And after some conflicting decisions it is now settled that the same rule applies to all contracts of life insurance. So where a policy on the life of his debtor was taken out by a creditor it was held that the sum in the policy might be recovered on the death of the debtor, although the debt had in the meantime been discharged, and the creditor consequently had suffered no loss.[27]

21. Insurable Interest.—Under the Life Assurance Act 1774, the party who takes out a policy of life insurance must have an insurable interest.[28] A man has always an interest in his own life. But if he merely takes the policy, and assigns it without paying any premium, it may be held void as an evasion of the Act.[29] In order to support a policy on the life of another the interest in the life must be of a pecuniary nature, not mere relationship. The pecuniary interest may be contractual, or may consist in a right to aliment. On the former ground a creditor has an interest, limited to the amount of his debt, in the life of his debtor[30]; a cautioner, in the life of the principal debtor[31]; an employee, if engaged for a specific term, in the life of his employer[32]; an employer in the life of an agent through whose endeavour he obtains business.[33] On the latter ground, an obligation to aliment, husband and wife have an interest in each other's lives[34]; and, probably, a child in the life of its parent, parents in the lives of their children.[35] Where a person maintains a foster-child for reward, he is deemed to have no insurable interest in the child's life.[36] If there was an insurable interest at the time when the policy was taken, it may be kept up after the interest has lapsed,[37] and assigned to an assignee who has no interest.[38]

[26] *Menzies* v. *North British Insurance Co.* (1847) 9 D. 694.
[27] *Dalby* v. *Indian, etc. Co.* (1854) 15 C.B. 365; Bell, *Prin.,* § 519.
[28] Supra, § 5, where questions as to return of premium are considered.
[29] *Macdonald* v. *National Association* (1906) 14 S.L.T. 173, 249.
[30] *Lindsay* v. *Barmcotte* (1851) 13 D. 718; *Simcock* v. *Imperial Insurance Co.* (1902) 10 S.L.T. 286.
[31] *Stevenson* v. *Cotton* (1846) 8 D. 872.
[32] *Hebdon* v. *West* (1863) 3 B. & S. 579.
[33] *Turnbull* v. *Scottish Provident* (1896) 34 S.L.R. 146.
[34] *Wight* v. *Brown* (1849) 11 D. 459.
[35] *Carmichael* v. *Carmichael's Exr.,* 1919 S.C. 636, per Lords Dundas and Guthrie, revd. 1920 S.C. (H.L.) 195.
[36] Children Act 1958 (c. 65), s. 9 as amended.
[37] *Turnbull* v. *Scottish Provident* (1896) 34 S.L.R. 146.
[38] Bell, *Prin.,* § 520.

22. No Insurance until Premium Paid.—Proposals for life insurance are commonly accepted subject to the condition that there is no insurance until the premium is paid. The result of this condition is that the company may refuse to accept the premium, and to issue a policy, if there has been any intervening and material change, e.g. a change in the health of the applicant.[39]

MARINE INSURANCE

23. Generally.—The law of marine insurance,[40] which developed largely from recognition of the customs of those engaged in the trade,[41] presents so many special features that only the leading points can be considered here. For other aspects of the law, in so far as not dealt with in the preceding pages, reference must be made to the Marine Insurance Act 1906, or to the leading textbook.[42] The Act expressly bears to be a codifying statute, but in certain respects it has been held to alter the law.[43] By section 91 the rules of the common law, including the law merchant, save in so far as they are inconsistent with the express provisions of the Act, are preserved.

24. How Far Contract of Indemnity.—Marine insurance is described in the Act (s. 1) as a contract of indemnity. But it is a recognised and common practice that the value of the subject-matter insured may be agreed on beforehand and specified in the policy, and that in such a policy, known as a valued policy, the amount agreed upon is, in the absence of averments of fraud, conclusive as between the parties, except for the purpose of ascertaining whether there has been a constructive total loss.[44] Thus where the rules of a mutual insurance society provide that a certain proportion of the ship must remain uninsured, it is a proportion of the agreed-on, and not the actual, value, that has to be considered.[45]

25. Policy.—The contract must be embodied in a policy of insurance which may be issued at the time the contract is concluded or afterwards.[46] The policy must specify the name of the assured, or of his agent, and must be signed by him or on his behalf.[47] The subject-matter insured must be designated with reasonable certainty.[48] The policy need not be stamped.[49]

---

[39] *Canning* v. *Farquhar* (1886) 16 Q.B.D. 727; *Sickness, etc. Assurance* v. *General Accident*, (1892) 19 R. 977.
[40] See Gow, *Mercantile Law*, p. 353.
[41] *Moore* v. *Evans* [1918] A.C. 185.
[42] Arnould, *Marine Insurance*.
[43] *Polurrian S.S. Co.* v. *Young* [1915] 1 K.B. 922.
[44] Act, s. 27. Policies generally provide that the agreed-on value is to be conclusive in a question of a constructive total loss: Arnould, *Marine Insurance*, §§ 405, 1085, 1125. As to the business reasons for valued policies, see *Gunford Ship Co.* v. *Thames, etc., Insurance Co.*, 1911 S.C. (H.L.) 84.
[45] *Muirhead* v. *Forth, etc. Association* (1894) 21 R. (H.L.) 1.
[46] Act, s. 22. As to a "slip," see supra, § 4.
[47] Act, ss. 23 (1), 24 (1).
[48] Act, s. 26 (1); see Gow, pp. 356-7.
[49] Only life assurance policies currently attract stamp duty: see § 4, supra, n. 26.

26. Subjects of Marine Adventure.—A policy of marine insurance must relate to a marine adventure. It may cover a ship in course of building, or being launched, or actually exposed to maritime perils. It may also cover goods so exposed, freight, profit, the security for any advance, loan or disbursements, or liability to third parties by reason of maritime perils.[50] But a time policy on specific goods is not a marine policy, or subject to the provisions of the Act, merely because the goods are sent to a destination involving sea transit.[51]

27. Floating Policy.—A floating policy is one effected by a merchant to cover goods which he intends to ship, usually specifying the particular kind of goods, the ports of loading and discharge, and a limit of time, but not the ship in which the goods are to be sent. It is expressed to be "by ship or ships to be declared."[52] The effect is that the policy vests at once, and the goods are covered as soon as they are shipped.[53] The insured is bound to declare each shipment (usually by indorsement on the policy) as soon as he is aware of it. He is bound to declare all shipments falling within the terms of the policy in their order, and therefore is not entitled to leave some shipments uninsured, or insured with third parties.[54] If he fails to declare any shipment the underwriter may treat it as declared, and, if in this way the sum fixed in the policy is exhausted, may refuse to pay for a loss on a subsequent shipment.[55] If by inadvertence a shipment is not declared, it is the duty of the insured to rectify the omission, and he may do so even after a loss has occurred.[56] But where the policy provided for a declaration within a time limit it was held that the declaration was a condition precedent to any claim, and therefore that the insured could not recover for a loss on a shipment which had been declared too late.[57] As the underwriter in a floating policy has undertaken liability for any shipments made he cannot refuse payment on the ground of failure in disclosure or innocent misrepresentation regarding the character of the ship actually selected. So where, on a particular shipment, a declaration on a floating policy was made, and also a new and independent policy was taken out, it was held that the latter, but not the former, was rendered voidable by a material but not fraudulent mis-statement as to the age of the ship.[58]

28. Insurable Interest.—The insured must have an insurable interest at the time of a loss under the policy; not necessarily at the time when the policy is

---

[50] Act, ss. 2, 3. As to the possible twofold insurance in the case of goods, viz., in respect of the goods themselves and of the adventure, see *Rickards* v. *Forestal Land, Timber and Ry.* [1942] A.C. 50.

[51] *Moore* v. *Evans* [1918] A.C. 185.

[52] Act, s. 29.

[53] Arnould, *Marine Insurance*, § 242; *Stephens* v. *Australasian Insurance Co.* (1872) L.R. 8 C.P. 18 (customs of trade proved and accepted as law).

[54] Act, s. 29; *Stephens,* supra.

[55] *Dunlop Bros.* v. *Townend* [1919] 2 K.B. 127.

[56] Act, s. 29 (3).

[57] *Union Insurance Society of Canton* v. *Wills* [1916] 1 A.C. 281.

[58] *Ionides* v. *Pacific, etc., Co.* (1871) L.R. 6 Q.B. 674.

effected.[59] He cannot acquire an interest after he is aware of a loss.[60] If, in the usual form, the subject-matter is insured "lost or not lost," the insured may recover though he may not have acquired his interest until after the loss, unless at the time of effecting the contract the assured was aware of the loss, and the insurer was not.[61] The Act, reproducing earlier legislation,[62] provides (s. 4): "(1) Every contract of marine insurance by way of gaming or wagering is void. (2) A contract of marine insurance is deemed to be a gaming or wagering contract—(a) Where the assured has not an insurable interest as defined by this Act, and the contract is entered into with no expectation of acquiring such an interest; or (b) Where the policy is made 'interest or no interest' or 'without further proof of interest than the policy itself' or 'without benefit of salvage to the insurer,' or subject to any other like term; Provided that, where there is no possibility of salvage, a policy may be effected without benefit of salvage to the insurer."[63] It has been held that where a policy is effected in such terms (usually known as p.p.i., policy proof of interest; or f.i.a., full interest admitted) it is void, even although the insured had in fact an insurable interest.[64] By the Marine Insurance (Gambling Policies) Act 1909 (9 Edw. VII., c. 12), the issue of a marine policy without interest is a criminal offence on the part of the insurer, insured or broker. In spite of these statutory regulations p.p.i. policies are still in common use and their existence is a material fact which the insured must disclose to subsequent underwriters.[65]

29. Nature of Interest.—Insurable interest is thus defined (s. 5): "Subject to the provisions of this Act, every person has an insurable interest who is interested in a marine adventure. In particular a person is interested in a marine adventure where he stands in any legal or equitable relation to the adventure or to any insurable property at risk therein, in consequence of which he may benefit by the safety or due arrival of insurable property, or may be prejudiced by its loss, or by damage thereto, or by the detention thereof, or may incur liability in respect thereof." The interest may be defeasible, contingent or partial. The insurer has an interest to reinsure. A mortgagor or lender on bottomry, to the extent of the amount due, the master and seamen in respect of wages, a party who has paid freight in advance have all insurable interests.[66] The owner of property has an insurable interest in respect of the full value thereof though some third party may have agreed, or be liable, to indemnify him in case of loss.[67]

30. Insurable Value.—Except in the case of a valued policy the insurable interest is limited to the insurable value of the subject matter at risk. Reference

---

[59] Act, s. 6 (1).
[60] Act, s. 6 (2).
[61] Act, s. 6 (1) and Sched. I, Rule 1.
[62] Geo. II, c. 37.
[63] See *Re London County Re-insurance Co.* [1922] 2 Ch. 67.
[64] *Cheshire* v. *Vaughan* [1920] 3 K.B. 240.
[65] *Gunford Ship Co.* v. *Thames, etc., Insurance Co.*, 1911 S.C. (H.L.) 84.
[66] Act, ss. 7-14.
[67] Act, s. 14 (3).

must be made to the Act for a definition of the insurable value of a ship, of freight and of goods.[68]

31. Warranties: Seaworthiness.—The rules with regard to disclosure of material facts, innocent misrepresentation, and express warranties are in their main aspects the same as those applicable to other forms of insurance.[69] They are set forth in the Act in sections 17-21 and 33-35. The principal implied warranty is that of seaworthiness. It is warranted, in the absence of any provision to the contrary, in a voyage policy, i.e., in a policy from one port to another, not in time policies, when the insurance is for a definite period of time. In the latter case if the ship is, with the privity of the insured, sent to sea in an unseaworthy state, the insurer is not liable for any loss attributable to unseaworthiness.[70] In voyage policies the warranty is that the ship is seaworthy at the commencement of the voyage; in voyages performed in different stages, during which the ship requires different kinds of or further preparation or equipment, the warranty is that at the commencement of each stage the ship is seaworthy in respect of such preparation or equipment for the purposes of that stage.[71] There is no implied warranty, in a policy on goods, that they are seaworthy, but in a voyage policy on goods there is an implied warranty that at the commencement of the voyage the ship is not only seaworthy as a ship but also that she is reasonably fit to carry the goods to the destination contemplated by the policy.[72]

32. Deviation.—An insurer may be discharged from liability by a change in the voyage, or by deviation. A change in the voyage occurs when the destination of the ship is voluntarily changed from the destination contemplated by the policy. In the absence of any provision to the contrary the insurer is discharged from the time when determination to change was manifested, although the loss may have occurred before the ship has actually left her course.[73] An insurer is also discharged from liability by deviation from the course contemplated by the policy. In general the rules as to deviation in questions of affreightment apply in questions of marine insurance,[74] but the provision, in the Carriage of Goods by Sea Act 1971, by which deviation in attempting to save property at sea, or any reasonable deviation, is excused,[75] is not applicable to policies of insurance. In the Marine Insurance Act the following excuses for deviation (also for delay) are enumerated: (a) when authorised by any special term in the policy; (b) where caused by

---

[68] Act, s. 16; *Williams* v. *Atlantic Assurance Co.* [1933] 1 K.B. 81; *Berger and Light Diffusers* v. *Pollock* [1973] 2 Lloyd's Rep. 442.
[69] Supra, §§ 6-8.
[70] Act, s. 39. *Compania Maritima* v. *The Oceanus Mutual* [1977] Q.B. 49; *The Eurysthenes* [1976] C.L.Y. 2571. As to the meaning of seaworthiness, see Carriage by Sea, Ch. XXX, infra, § 4.
[71] Act, s. 39. So, in a voyage in stages, the ship must have sufficient fuel for each stage, not necessarily for the whole voyage: *Greenock Co.* v. *Maritime Insurance Co.* [1903] 2 K.B. 657.
[72] Act, s. 40. See *Elder, Dempster & Co.* v. *Paterson* [1924] A.C. 522.
[73] s. 45.
[74] Infra, Ch. XXX, § 19.
[75] 1971 Act, (c. 19), Sched., art. IV, Rule 4.

circumstances beyond the control of the master and his employer; (c) where reasonably necessary in order to comply with an express or implied warranty; (d) where reasonably necessary for the safety of the ship or subject-matter insured; (e) for the purpose of saving human life or aiding a ship in distress where human life may be in danger; (f) where reasonably necessary for the purpose of obtaining medical or surgical aid for any person on board the ship; (g) where caused by barratrous conduct of the master or crew, if barratry be one of the perils insured against.[76] There is often a clause in the policy authorising a change of voyage or deviation, at an increase of premium to be mutually agreed upon, provided that notice of the change be given.[77]

33. Perils Insured Against.—The sum due under a policy becomes payable when there has been a loss, total or partial, of the subject-matter of the insurance, and that loss has been occasioned by one of the perils insured against. What these perils are may depend on the terms of the particular policy; the following are enumerated in the statutory form[78]:—"Touching the adventures and perils which we the assurers are contented to bear and do take upon us in this voyage; they are of the seas, men of war, fire, enemies, pirates, rovers, thieves, jettisons, letters of mart and countermart, surprisals, takings at sea, arrests, restraints and detainments of all kings, princes, and people, of what nation, condition, or quality soever, barratry of the master and mariners, and of all other perils, losses and misfortunes, that have or shall come to the hurt, detriment or damage of the said goods and merchandise, and ship, etc., or any part thereof." The general words with which this enumeration ends include only perils similar in kind to the perils specifically mentioned,[79] and "perils" refers only to fortuitous accidents or casualties of the seas, and does not include the ordinary action of the winds and waves.[80]

34. Causa Proxima.—The general rule has been long recognised that in considering whether a particular loss was due to one of the perils insured against the maxim "causa proxima non remota spectatur" applies. The rule is expressed in the Act as follows (s. 55): "Subject to the provisions of this Act and unless the policy otherwise provides, the insurer is liable for any loss proximately caused by a peril insured against, but, subject as aforesaid, he is not liable for any loss which is not proximately caused by a peril insured against." In recent cases it has been explained that the term proximate cause does not necessarily mean the cause latest in time.[81] In considering the question, not infrequently raised, whether a stranding or collision has been caused by a warlike operation or a marine risk, the House of Lords has reiterated the rule that the proximate cause of the loss of a ship is not

---

[76] Act, s. 49.
[77] See *Maritime Assurance Co.* v. *Stearns* [1901] 2 K.B. 912, at p. 917.
[78] Act, Sched. I. In the rules given in the schedule the meaning of the terms used in the policy is explained.
[79] Act, Sched. I., Rule 12.
[80] Ibid., Rule 7; *Samuel* v. *Dumas* [1924] A.C. 431.
[81] See, e.g. *Wayne Tank and Pump Co.* v. *Employers' Liability Assurance Corporation* [1974] Q.B. 49.

necessarily that which operates last, but is the effective and predominant cause, selected from among co-operating causes.[82] Thus where a ship was torpedoed, and necessarily towed to a harbour where she was stranded and wrecked, it was held that the war risk involved in the torpedo, and not the subsequent stranding, was the cause of her loss. It was observed that the term causa proxima might be rendered "dominant cause" or "cause proximate in efficiency."[83] A distinction is recognised between loss due to a peril insured against and loss resulting from measures due to apprehension of that peril. Thus where, in 1914, a German ship, not actually pursued by Allied ships, put into a neutral port, with resultant loss, it was held that the loss was not due to "restraint of princes," but to measures adopted to avoid that restraint.[84] But restraint of princes was held to apply where, on hearing of the declaration of war, and without any actual compulsion, a British ship abandoned a voyage to a German port.[85] Other questions have led to equally fine distinctions. Thus if a particular peril is encountered owing to negligent navigation, the peril in question, and not the preceding negligence, is the proximate cause of the loss,[86] whereas if the peril is incurred owing to an act deliberately wrongful, with the intent to wreck the ship, the wrongful act, and not the subsequent peril, is the proximate cause.[87] The distinction has been explained on the ground that in the former case, and not in the latter, there is the element of the fortuitous or unexpected in the mishap.[88]

35. Total and Partial Loss.—A loss may be total or partial. A partial loss may in certain cases, and at the option of the insured, be treated as a constructive total loss. In the absence of any provision to the contrary an insurance against total loss includes a constructive, as well as an actual, total loss.[89] The Act provides that there is an actual total loss when the subject-matter is destroyed, or so damaged as to cease to be a thing of the kind insured, or where the assured is irretrievably deprived thereof, or where a ship is missing, and after a reasonable time no news of her has been received.[90] Thus, for example, if goods insured arrive in an unmarketable state,[91] or if they are sold at an intermediate port on the ground that symptoms of decay show that they cannot be safely carried to their destination,[92] there is an actual total loss. Where a ship is sunk the question whether she is an actual total loss depends on the possibility of raising her.[93] Where a ship is

[82] *Yorkshire Dale S.S. Co.* v. *Minister of War Transport* [1942] A.C. 691.
[83] *Leyland Shipping Co.* v. *Norwich Union* [1918] A.C. 350. See also *Britain S.S. Co.* v. *The King* [1921] 1 A.C. 99; *Canada Rice Mills* v. *Union Marine & General Ins. Co.* [1941] A.C. 55; *Wayne Tank and Pump Co.* v. *Employers' Liability Assurance Corporation* [1973] 3 W.L.R. 483.
[84] *Becker, Gray & Co.* v. *London Assurance* [1918] A.C. 101.
[85] *British and Foreign Insurance Co.* v. *Sanday* [1916] A.C. 101.
[86] Act, s. 55 (2); *Trinder, Anderson & Co.* v. *Thames, etc., Assurance Co.* [1898] 2 Q.B. 114.
[87] *Samuel* v. *Dumas* [1924] A.C. 431.
[88] *Trinder, Anderson & Co.*, supra.
[89] Act, s. 56 (3).
[90] Act, ss. 57, 58.
[91] *Asfar* v. *Blundell* [1896] 1 Q.B. 123.
[92] *Roux* v. *Salvador* (1836) 2 Bing N.C. 266.
[93] *Blairmore Co.* v. *Macredie* (1898) 25 R. (H.L.) 57.

abandoned by her crew and taken possession of by salvors, the loss is only partial, but if she is sold by a decree of a competent court at the instance of the salvors, there is an actual total loss.[94] There is no total loss of freight if, by the arrival of the cargo, it is earned, though it may never be paid, or though, owing to the abandonment of the ship to the underwriters, they, and not the insured, are entitled to payment.[95] But there is a total loss of freight where the cost of temporary repairs to a vessel would exceed the repaired value.[96] In the event of an actual total loss the insured is entitled to recover under the policy without giving notice of abandonment.[97]

36. Constructive Total Loss.—Where the loss is not an actual total loss, it may amount to a constructive total loss. In that event the insured may either treat the loss as a partial loss or abandon the subject-matter insured to the insurer and treat the loss as if it were an actual total loss.[98] There is a constructive total loss where the subject-matter insured is reasonably abandoned on account of an actual total loss appearing to be unavoidable, or because it could not be preserved from actual total loss without an expenditure which would exceed its value when the expenditure has been incurred.[99] In the case of loss of possession, e.g. by enemy capture, there is a constructive total loss if the cost of recovery would exceed the value when recovered, or if it is unlikely that the subject can be recovered.[1] Under this provision it is no longer, as it was before the Act, sufficient to prove that the recovery of a captured ship was uncertain; the proof must establish that it was unlikely.[2] Where a ship is damaged the Act provides that she is a constructive total loss if the cost of repairing her would exceed her value when repaired.[3] It is doubtful whether this provision, which leaves out of account the break-up value of the wreck, excludes the test established by the prior authorities, which was whether a prudent owner, if uninsured, would repair the ship or not.[4] In the case of damage to goods there is a constructive total loss when the cost of repairing the damage and forwarding the goods to their destination would exceed their value on arrival.[5] Also if the voyage is frustrated, though the goods are not damaged, as where, on the declaration of war, it became illegal to proceed to the enemy port of destination and the goods were landed intact at a British port.[6]

37. Notice of Abandonment.—Where the insured proposes to claim as on a

---

[94] *Cossman* v. *West* (1887) 13 App.Cas. 160.
[95] *Scottish Marine Ins. Co.* v. *Turner* (1853) 1 Macq. 334.
[96] *Kulukundis* v. *Norwich Union* [1937] 1 K.B. 1.
[97] Act, s. 57 (2).
[98] Act, s. 61.
[99] Act, s. 60. The definition in the section is exhaustive: *Irvin* v. *Hine* [1950] 1 K.B. 555.
[1] Act, s. 60 (2).
[2] *Polurrian S.S. Co.* v. *Young* [1915] 1 K.B. 922; as to barratry, see *Marstrand Fishing Co.* v. *Beer* (1936) 53 T.L.R. 287.
[3] Act, s. 60 (2).
[4] See *Macbeth* v. *Maritime Ass. Co.* [1908] A.C. 144.
[5] Act, s. 60 (2).
[6] *British and Foreign, etc., Co.* v. *Sanday* [1916] 1 A.C. 650.

constructive total loss he must give notice of abandonment to the underwriter,[7] unless there is nothing to abandon, and no possibility of benefit to the underwriter,[8] as in the case of a policy on freight when the ship is wrecked,[9] or a policy on a ship which is captured by an enemy.[10] Notice may be given verbally or in writing.[11] It must be given with reasonable diligence after the receipt of reliable information of the loss.[12] On receiving notice the underwriter may accept it, expressly or by implication.[13] His mere silence is not acceptance.[14] If, without express acceptance, he takes measures for the safety or recovery of a wreck, it is a question of circumstances whether he thereby indicates acceptance of the notice, or whether he is acting as a salvor of property which has been abandoned and become res nullius.[15] It would appear that notice of abandonment or acceptance of notice given under a material mistake of fact is a nullity.[16]

38. Measure of Indemnity.—On an actual or constructive total loss, in a valued policy, the sum fixed by the policy may be recovered; in an unvalued policy, the insurable value of the subject-matter.[17] This is termed in the Act the measure of indemnity.[18]

39. Subrogation.—On payment as for a total loss, actual or constructive, the insurer is entitled, on the principle of subrogation, to exercise the rights of the insured in the subject-matter of the policy.[19] He may recover the damages due from a third party from whose wrongful or negligent act the loss has resulted[20]; but where the insured himself recovers damages from the third party, the insurer may not recover from the insured a greater sum than he himself has already paid over to the insured.[21] If a ship has reached her port of destination, and earned freight, but has arrived so damaged as to be abandoned to the underwriters, they are entitled to the freight.[22] They are also entitled, where a ship has been abandoned as a constructive total loss, to a transfer which will enable them to be registered as her owners.[23] But the insurers, in virtue of their right of subrogation, stand in the same position as

---

[7] Act, s. 62; *Watt's Tr.* v. *Scottish Boatowners Mutual Insurance Association*, 1968 S.L.T. (Sh. Ct.) 79.
[8] Ibid., subs. (7).
[9] *Rankin* v. *Potter* (1872) L.R. 6 H.L. 83.
[10] *Roura, etc.* v. *Townend* [1919] 1 K.B. 189; *Nomikos* v. *Robertson* [1938] 2 K.B. 603.
[11] Act, s. 62.
[12] Ibid., subs. (3). See *Fleming* v. *Smith* (1848) 6 Bell's App. 278; *Kaltenbach* v. *Mackenzie* (1878) 3 C.P.D. 467.
[13] *Watt's Tr.* v. *Scottish Boatowners Mutual Insurance Association*, supra.
[14] Ibid., subss. (5), (6).
[15] *Shepherd* v. *Henderson* (1881) 9 R. (H.L.) 1; *Robertson* v. *Royal Exchange Corporation*, 1925 S.C. 1.
[16] *Norwich Union* v. *Price* [1934] A.C. 455.
[17] Act, s. 68.
[18] s. 67.
[19] Act, s. 79; see *Boag* v. *Standard Marine Insurance Co.* [1937] 2 K.B. 113.
[20] *North of England Assurance Co.* v. *Armstrong* (1870) L.R. 5 Q.B. 244.
[21] *Yorkshire Insurance Co.* v. *Nisbet Shipping Co.* [1962] 2 Q.B. 330.
[22] *Stewart* v. *Greenock Insurance Co.* (1848) 1 Macq. 328.
[23] *Whitworth* v. *Shepherd* (1884) 12 R. 204.

the insured, and may be met by any defence which would have been available against him. So where two ships belonging to the same owner came into collision, and the underwriters of the ship which was not in fault, and which was wrecked, paid the insurance, it was held that they had no right to a ranking on the amount paid into court to meet claims against the offending ship. They could make no claim which the insured could not have made, and he could not have claimed against himself.[24]

40. Liabilities in Case of Abandonment.—Abandonment when accepted divests the insured of the property in the subject-matter, and also frees him from any liabilities subsequently effeiring to it, such as the liability to meet the expenses of local authorities having statutory powers to remove wrecks.[25] It would seem to be a doubtful point whether the insurer, if on abandonment he merely pays for a total loss and takes no active steps to invest himself with the subject-matter, comes under any liability.[26]

41. Partial Loss: Particular Average.—Where damage occurs through a peril insured against which is not of sufficient gravity to amount to a constructive total loss, or which the insured does not choose to treat as such, there is a partial loss. The partial loss may result from a sacrifice which amounts to a general average act, and is then known as a general average loss.[27] Where there is not a general average loss, a partial loss is known as a particular average, or sometimes as an average, loss.[28] Where, in a policy covering ship and cargo, certain kinds of goods are "warranted free from average," the insurer is not liable for a partial loss of the goods in question, unless the contract be apportionable. The contract may be apportionable either expressly, e.g., by the insertion of such words as "to pay average on each package as if separately insured," or impliedly, e.g., where the insurance is general, but on separate articles wholly distinct in their nature.[29] In such cases the underwriter is liable for a total loss of any separate package or article. Where goods are warranted free from average under a certain percentage of their value, he is not liable unless the damage exceeds that percentage.[30] Such conditions are inserted in a clause, known as the memorandum, appended to the policy. In the statutory form of policy the words are "free from average, unless general, or the ship be stranded." Under a policy in these terms the insurer is liable if the ship be stranded, although the stranding may not be the cause of the injury to the goods.[31] To stranding is added, in some policies, sinking, burning and collision.[32]

---

[24] *Simpson* v. *Thomson* (1877) 5 R. (H.L.) 40. See also *Société du Gaz* v. *Armateurs Français,* 1925 S.C. 332.
[25] *Barraclough* v. *Brown* [1897] A.C. 615.
[26] Arnould, *Marine Insurance,* §§ 1204, 1214.
[27] As to general average, see Ch. XXXII, infra.
[28] Act, s. 64.
[29] Arnould, §§ 1074, 1075.
[30] Act, s. 76.
[31] *The Alsace Lorraine* [1893] P. 209; Arnould, *Marine Insurance,* §§ 882-5.
[32] See *The Glenlivet* [1894] P. 48 (burning).

42. Measure of Indemnity.—The amount which may be recovered as a partial loss, termed in the Act the "measure of indemnity,"[33] is, in the case of injury to a ship which has been repaired, the reasonable cost of the repairs, "less the customary deductions, but not exceeding the sum insured in respect of any one casualty."[34] The principal customary deduction, recognised before the Act as a custom of trade, is a deduction of one-third of the cost of the repairs in respect of the advantage gained by the insured in having new material instead of old.[35] If the ship is partially repaired the insured is entitled to the cost of the repairs, under like deduction, and also to the depreciation resulting from the unrepaired damage. When the ship has not been repaired, and has not been sold in her damaged state during the risk, the insured is entitled to the depreciation in value, provided that does not exceed the reasonable cost of repair.[36] If she is sold unrepaired, the measure of indemnity is the difference between her value, if undamaged, at the place of sale, and the actual price obtained.[37] When there is a partial loss of freight the measure of indemnity is such proportion of the sum fixed by the policy, in the case of a valued policy, or of the insurable value in the case of an unvalued policy, as the proportion of freight lost by the assured bears to the whole freight at the risk of the assured under the policy.[38] For the complicated rules with regard to the measure of indemnity in the case of a partial loss of goods reference must be made to the Act, and to the exposition in Arnould on *Marine Insurance*.[39]

43. Successive Losses.—Unless the policy otherwise provides the insurer is liable for successive losses, even although the total amount of such losses may exceed the sum insured.[40] But when a partial loss has not been repaired and is followed by a total loss, whether from a peril insured against or not, the underwriter is not liable for the partial loss, and it is immaterial that under another policy by which the cause of the total loss is covered a deduction may be made for the loss in value caused by the partial loss.[41]

44. Suing and Labouring Clause.—In certain cases, under a clause in the policy known as the suing and labouring clause, a sum in excess of that fixed in the policy may be recovered. This clause, in its usual form, provides that in case of any loss or misfortune, it shall be lawful to the assured "to sue, labour and travel in and about the defence safeguard and recovery" of the ship or goods, and that the insurers will contribute to the charges thereof.[42] This clause is read as supplementary to the contract of insurance, and entitles the insured to recover from the underwriters any sums reasonably expended in

33 s. 67.
34 s. 69 (1).
35 *Aitchison* v. *Lohre* (1879) 4 App.Cas. 755.
36 s. 69 (2), (3); *Irvin* v. *Hine* [1950] 1 K.B. 555.
37 *Pitman* v. *Universal Marine Insurance Co.* (1882) 9 Q.B.D. 192.
38 s. 70.
39 s. 71; Arnould, § 1009.
40 s. 77.
41 *British and Foreign Insurance Co.* v. *Wilson Shipping Co.* [1921] 1 A.C. 188.
42 Arnould, § 32.

endeavour to prevent or minimise a loss, provided that it was a loss insured against under the policy.[43] A claim of this nature may be made although the underwriters have paid for a total loss,[44] or, in the case of a partial loss, though the policy was free of particular average.[45] The clause does not cover anything paid for salvage, although services of a similar kind, if rendered under contract and not as salvage, fall within it.[46] Nor does it include general average losses and contribution.[47] The Act provides that "it is the duty of the assured and his agent, in all cases, to take such measures as may be reasonable for the purpose of averting or minimising a loss."[48] It is not stated, and has not been decided, what is the result of a failure in this duty.[49]

---

[43] Act, s. 78 (3); *Kidston* v. *Empire Marine Insurance Co.* (1867) L.R. 2 C.P. 357; *Wilson's Bobbin Co.* v. *Green* [1917] 1 K.B. 860; *Nishina Trading Co.* v. *Chiyoda Fire and Marine Insurance Co.* [1969] 2 Q.B. 449.
[44] s. 78 (1); *Aitchison* v. *Lohre* (1879) 4 App.Cas. 755.
[45] s. 78 (1); *Kidston*, supra.
[46] *Aitchison* v. *Lohre*, supra.
[47] s. 78 (2).
[48] s. 78 (4).
[49] See Arnould, *Marine Insurance*, § 788.

CHAPTER XXVIII

HIRING, LOAN AND DEPOSIT

Bell, *Prin.*, § 133, seq.; Paton on *Bailment* (1952); Gow, *Mercantile Law* (1964), Ch. 3.

1. Forms of Location.—Location is a general term for contracts whereby the owner of an article places it in the possession of another or a person hires out his services to another.[1] There may be distinguished—(1) locatio conductio rei, the letting to hire of a thing; (2) locatio custodiae, or deposit; (3) locatio operis faciendi, or contract to do work on an article; and (4) locatio conductio operarum, the letting to hire of services. The letting to hire of services is dealt with in the chapters on Employment and on Agency; the contract of location, where the subject let is heritable property, in the chapter on Leases; the law as to hire-purchase in the chapter on Sale.

2. Hiring: Terms.—Hiring is the location of moveable property. The party who takes the thing, and agrees to pay the hire, is the hirer (conductor); for the other party the most convenient term, in spite of its connection with heritable property, is lessor (locator).

3. Obligations of Lessor.—The lessor undertakes to supply either a specific thing, or a thing of a particular kind, according to the terms of the contract. He is bound to take care that the article he supplies is reasonably fit for the purpose (if any) disclosed by the hirer, and is liable for loss due to failure in that duty,[2] but he does not give any implied warranty of its fitness.[3] Should the thing cause injury to the hirer the lessor is clearly liable if he was aware of its dangerous character and failed to give warning.[4] A mere lender on gratuitous terms has no further duty, and is not liable merely because he has failed to examine the thing he lends.[5] Should the thing hired occasion some exceptional expense to the hirer—where, for instance, a horse falls lame, and has to be left at a livery stable—the lessor will be liable for the expense, provided that it was necessary and not due to any fault of the hirer, and that notice was given by the hirer to the lessor as soon as the circumstances permitted.[6]

---

[1] For the contracts considered in this and the three succeeding chapters there is no general term established in Scots law. Bell (*Prin.*, § 84) describes them as "contracts in the course and existence of which the property of one is necessarily entrusted to the care or custody of another." The English term "bailments" is sometimes met with in Scotland. For its meaning, see Beven, *Negligence* (4th ed.), 903.

[2] *Reed* v. *Dean* [1949] 1 K.B. 188; *Oliver* v. *Saddler*, 1929 S.C. (H.L.) 94.

[3] *Wood* v. *Mackay* (1906) 8 F. 625, Lord McLaren.

[4] *Coughlin* v. *Gillison* [1899] 1 Q.B. 145. See *Clarke* v. *Army and Navy Stores* [1903] 1 K.B. 155.

[5] *Oliver* v. *Saddler*, supra, Lord Atkin at p. 101.

[6] Bell, *Comm.*, I, 482; *Johnston* v. *Rankin* (1687) M. 10080.

4. Obligations of Hirer.—The hirer is bound to pay the hire agreed upon or, in the absence of any express agreement, a reasonable hire. The accidental destruction of the thing terminates the contract, and with it the obligation to pay hire; an accidental injury gives the hirer the option of terminating the contract or claiming a proportionate reduction of the hire.[7]

5. Degrees of Care.—The hirer is bound to take reasonable care for the safety of the article hired. The care required is such as a diligent and prudent man takes of his own property. In estimating it the value of the article is obviously a relevant consideration. The civilian distinction between culpa lata, culpa levis and culpa levissima, though possibly still recognised in the law of Scotland,[8] is difficult to apply in any concrete case. If the distinction is still maintainable at all, the liability of a hirer, as the contract of hire is one beneficial to both parties, is for culpa levis[9]: liability for culpa levissima would be appropriate, in commodate, where the contract is beneficial only to the party in fault, and liability for culpa lata would be applicable in contracts like gratuitous mandate or deposit where the party alleged to be in fault is acting solely in the interests of the other. It has been suggested, though not decided, that a party who hires an article, or undertakes the care of it for reward, is liable for loss or injury due to the fault of his servant, even though acting outwith the scope of his employment, whereas no such liability would rest on a gratuitous depositary.[10]

6. Facts Indicating Fault.—Fault, or want of reasonable care, on the part of a hirer, may consist in overloading or overworking the article hired (as in the case of a horse[11]), or using it in some way, involving an extra risk, which was not contemplated at the time of the contract.[12] Probably if the article is injured by use in the way contemplated by the contract, the onus of proof that he was not in fault lies on the hirer.[13] It may also consist in the want of reasonable precautions against loss or theft, a question necessarily of circumstances[14]; or in failure to take the proper steps after an injury or loss has occurred, as where an agister of cattle failed to give notice, either to the owner or the police, that the cattle had been stolen, and was held to be liable unless he could prove that the notice would have been useless.[15] It is cogent evidence of negligence that the hirer took less care of the article hired than he

---

[7] Bell, *Prin.*, § 141; *Muir* v. *McIntyre* (1887) 14 R. 470.
[8] *Wernham* v. *McLean, Baird & Neilson,* 1925 S.C. 407. See, however, opinion of Lord Atkin, *Kolbin* v. *Kinnear,* 1931 S.C. (H.L.) 128, at p. 139. In *Giblin* v. *McMullen* (1868) L.R. 2 P.C. 317, Lord Chelmsford said: "though degrees of care are not definable, they are with some approach to certainty distinguishable."
[9] Bell, *Comm.,* I, 483.
[10] *Central Motors Co.* v. *Cessnock Garage Co.,* 1925 S.C. 796; *Coupé Co.* v. *Maddick* [1891] 2 Q.B. 413.
[11] *Pullars* v. *Walker* (1858) 20 D. 1238.
[12] *Seton* v. *Paterson* (1880) 8 R. 236; *Gardner* v. *McDonald,* 1792 Hume 299.
[13] *Hinshaw* v. *Adam* (1870) 8 M. 933.
[14] See *Davidson* (1749) M. 10081; *McLean* v. *Warnock* (1883) 10 R. 1052; *Giblin* v. *McMullen* (1868) L.R. 2 P.C. 317.
[15] *Coldman* v. *Hill* [1919] 1 K.B. 443.

did of his own property.[16] It is no defence that he treated his own property with the same lack of care.[17]

7. Exclusion Clauses in Hire Contracts.—The Unfair Contract Terms Act 1977[18] applies to contracts of hire.[19] Thus contractual terms purporting to restrict or exclude liability for breach of duty may be void or unenforceable[20] as may terms purporting to exclude implied terms as to description, quality, fitness for purpose or title.[21]

8. Obligation to Restore Article: Unauthorised Disposal.—The hirer is bound to restore the article on the expiry of the time agreed upon, or, if no time was fixed, on demand. Failure in this respect involves liability ˙for accidental loss.[22] Otherwise he is not liable for deterioration by ordinary wear and tear, nor for the accidental destruction of the article. But it would appear, from analogous cases, that the onus of proof of accidental loss lies on the hirer.[23] A hirer, or, it is conceived, a borrower or depositary, has no ostensible authority to dispose of the article, nor to subject it to a lien, and third parties acquire no right against its owner.[24]

9. Claim by Third Party.—Where an article hired is claimed by a third party the hirer should have recourse to an action of multiplepoinding. A refusal to return the article to the lessor, based merely on the ground of notice of an adverse claim, is a breach of contract unless the hirer can prove that the adverse claim was well founded.[25]

10. Regulated Consumer Hire Agreements.—Certain hire agreements (a) involving the supply of credit to an individual, (b) capable of subsisting for more than three months, and (c) not requiring the hirer to make payments exceeding £5000, are regulated consumer hire agreements.[26] A person entering into such an agreement may require to be licensed.[27] The Act restricts advertising and canvassing in relation to such agreements, and regulates entry

---

16 *Campbell* v. *Kennedy* (1828) 6 S. 806.
17 *Re United Service Co., Johnston's Claim* (1871) L.R. 6 Ch. 212; *Raes* v. *Meek* (1889) 16 R. (H.L.) 31, at p. 33 (trust).
18 c.50. See Pacta Illicita and Unfair Terms, Ch. IX, supra.
19 s.15 (2) (*a*) et seq.
20 s. 16.
21 s. 21.
22 *Shaw* v. *Symmons* [1917] 1 K.B. 799.
23 *Wilson* v. *Orr* (1879) 7 R. 266; *Copland* v. *Brogan*, 1916 S.C. 277. See also conflicting opinions in *Moes Moliere & Co.* v. *Leith, etc., Shipping Co.* (1867) 5 M. 988; *Mustard* v. *Paterson*, 1923 S.C. 142.
24 *Murdoch* v. *Greig* (1889) 16 R. 396, and see, as to hire-purchase, Sale of Goods, Ch. XVII., supra, § 52; *Mitchell* v. *Heyes* (1894) 21 R. 600; *Lamonby* v. *Foulds*, 1928 S.C. 89. See, however, *Albemarle Supply Co.* v. *Hind* [1928] 1 K.B. 307.
25 *Ex p. Davies* (1881) 19 Ch.D. 86.
26 Consumer Credit Act 1974 (c.39), s. 15. See Ch. XIX. The Act was passed on 31 July 1974, but is being brought into effect in stages by means of regulations and orders made by the Secretary of State for Prices and Consumer Protection. The monetary limit is alterable by the Secretary of State: s. 181.
27 s. 21.

into, matters arising during, and the termination of, such agreements.[28] It is impossible to contract out of the Act.[29]

11. Loan.—Loan[30] is a contract under which the owner of a thing gives, for the temporary accommodation of another, the use or services derivable from it.[31] If the obligation is to return the particular thing the contract is known as commodate, or proper loan; if it is to return an equivalent amount, as in the case of money, or goods which are consumed by use, it is known as mutuum, or improper loan. In commodate the property in the thing does not pass to the borrower, and, on his bankruptcy, it may be recovered by the lender; in mutuum the property passes and the lender is merely a personal creditor.[32] In mutuum the borrower takes the risk of accidental destruction[33]; in commodate, while the standard of care required is a high one, proof of accidental loss, or accidental injury, the onus of proof being on the borrower, will excuse him. But the borrower is bound not to put the article to a use other than that (if any) indicated, and will be liable for any loss due to his failure in this respect.[34]

12. Deposit.—Similar rules apply to the contract of deposit, locatio custodiae. The obligations of a depositary are to provide a secure place of custody, and to exercise due care to prevent damage or loss in connection with the property.[35] A contractual term purporting to exclude or restrict liability for breach of duty may be void or unenforceable.[36] The fact that the contract was gratuitous, might, in narrow and doubtful cases, be of weight in determining whether sufficient care had been taken to exclude liability for the loss of the article.[37] So the degree of care required from bankers taking articles for safe custody has been held to depend on whether they make any charge.[38] But where a carrier undertook, gratuitously, to carry a parcel, and lost it, it was held that he was liable for its value unless he could explain the loss or prove that he had exercised reasonable care.[39] Where the deposit is for reward the standard of care, unless the depositary is an innkeeper or livery stable

---

[28] Parts IV, V, VI and VII.
[29] s. 173.
[30] See Gow, *Mercantile Law,* p. 261 et seq.; as to proof of loan, see Rules of Evidence, Ch. XII., supra, § 9.
[31] Bell, *Prin.,* § 194.
[32] Bell, *Prin.,* § 1315. As to following trust money, see Executors, Ch. XLIV., infra, § 22.
[33] *Anderson & Crompton* v. *Walls* (1870) 9 M. 122, opinion of Lord Neaves.
[34] *Bain* v. *Strang* (1888) 16 R. 186.
[35] Bell, *Prin.,* § 155, adopted in *Ballingall* v. *Dundee Ice etc., Co.,* 1924 S.C. 238. See as to motor parking place, *Ashby* v. *Tolhurst* [1937] 2 K.B. 242; *Drynan* v. *Scottish Ice Rink Co.,* 1971 S.L.T. (Sh.Ct.) 59; see as to garage, *Tognini Bros.* v. *Dick Bros.,* 1968 S.L.T. (Sh.Ct.) 87; *B.G. Transport Service* v. *Marston Motor Co.,* [1970] 1 Ll. Rep. 371; see as to bonded warehouse, *Brooks Wharf* v. *Goodman* [1937] 1 K.B. 534. Many of these cases must now be read in the light of the Unfair Contract Terms Act 1977.
[36] Unfair Contract Terms Act 1977, s. 15 (2) (c) et seq. See Ch. IX.
[37] Stair, I, 13, 2; *Coggs* v. *Bernard* (1703) 1 Smith L.C. (13th ed.), 125; *Houghland* v. *R. R. Low (Luxury Coaches)* [1962] 1 Q.B. 694; *Walker* v. *Scottish & Newcastle Breweries,* 1970 S.L.T. (Sh.Ct.) 21.
[38] *Giblin* v. *McMullen* (1868) L.R. 2 P.C. 317.
[39] *Copland* v. *Brogan,* 1916 S.C. 277.

keeper, is that required from a hirer.[40] If a person undertakes to repair, or do other work on, an article for the owner (locatio operis faciendi) and has the article in his possession for that purpose, the contract normally includes an element of locatio custodiae, with the consequent obligations.[41]

13. Innkeepers and Livery Stable Keepers.—An innkeeper and a livery stable keeper may in certain cases incur a higher degree of liability than other depositaries. They, like common carriers,[42] fall under the provisions of the Praetorian Edict.[43] Under the head of stabularii are included all livery stable keepers, whether attached to an inn or not,[44] but probably not the keeper of a motor garage.[45] In England, the exceptional liability of an innkeeper is held to depend on the custom of the realm and not on the Praetorian Edict.[46]

14. Liability under Edict.—An innkeeper or livery stable keeper is at common law liable for the loss of, or injury to, property brought to the inn or stable, unless he can prove that the loss or injury arose from the negligence of the owner[47] or is attributable to the Queen's enemies or to the act of God.[48] This latter term excludes liability for fire caused by pure accident, but the onus is on the depositary to prove the cause of the fire, or at least to exclude his own negligence.[49] Act of God has been defined generally as an accident due to natural causes, directly and exclusively, without human intervention, which could not have been prevented by any amount of foresight and pains and care reasonably to be expected.[50] As it is clear that a depositary for reward is in any event liable for loss due to the negligence of his servants, and is probably also liable for any loss or injury from unexplained causes, the practical difference between one who is, and one who is not, subject to the edict, would seem to be that the former alone is liable for loss by theft or by the wrongful act of third parties.[51]

15. Hotel Proprietors Act.—The liability of hotel proprietors is regulated by the Hotel Proprietors Act 1956,[52] which repealed the Innkeepers' Liability Act 1863. An establishment, but only such an establishment, which is a hotel

---

[40] *Central Motors* v. *Cessnock Garage Co.,* 1925 S.C. 796.
[41] *Sinclair* v. *Juner,* 1952 S.C. 35; *Macrae* v. *K. & I.,* 1962 S.L.T. (Notes) 90; *Forbes* v. *Aberdeen Motors,* 1965 S.L.T. 333; *Miller* v. *Howden,* 1968 S.L.T. (Sh.Ct.) 82.
[42] As to carrier, see Carriage by Land, Ch. XXIX, infra.
[43] Dig., IV, 9, 1. "Nautae, caupones, stabularii, quod cujusque salvum fore receperint, nisi restituant, in eos judicium dabo."
[44] *Mustard* v. *Paterson,* 1923 S.C. 142.
[45] *Central Motors* v. *Cessnock Garage Co.,* 1925 S.C. 796.
[46] *Calye's Case,* 1 Smith L.C. (13th ed.), 130.
[47] *Medawar* v. *Grand Hotel Co.* [1891] 2 Q.B. 11.
[48] Bell, *Prin.,* § 237.
[49] *Sinclair* v. *Juner,* 1952 S.C. 35; *Burns* v. *Royal Hotel* (*St Andrews*), 1958 S.C. 354.
[50] James L.J. in *Nugent* v. *Smith* (1876) 1 C.P.D. 423, adopted by Lord Hunter in *Mustard* v. *Paterson,* 1923 S.C. 142.
[51] *Mustard* v. *Paterson,* supra; *Macpherson* v. *Christie* (1841) 3 D. 930; *Whitehouse* v. *Pickett,* 1908 S.C. (H.L.) 31; *Winkworth* v. *Raven* [1931] 1 K.B. 652.
[52] 4 & 5 Eliz. II, c. 62.

within the meaning of the Act,[53] is deemed to be an inn; and its proprietor, as an innkeeper, has the same duties, liabilities and rights which before the commencement of the Act attached to an innkeeper as such, in particular under the Edict. The proprietor's liability under the Edict extends to the making good to any guest of any damage to property brought to the hotel, as well as the loss of such property.[54] On the other hand he is not subject to the liability of an innkeeper under the Edict, whatever may be his liability under contract or for negligence, in respect of any loss of or damage to any vehicle or property left therein, or any horse or other live animal or its harness or equipment, nor does his lien extend to these articles.[55]

Without prejudice to any other ground of liability, the proprietor is only liable as an innkeeper to make good loss or damage to the property of a traveller for whom at the time of the loss or damage sleeping accommodation had been engaged, and where the loss or damage occurred during the period commencing with the midnight immediately preceding, and ending with the midnight immediately following, a period for which the traveller was a guest at the hotel and entitled to use such accommodation.[56] The proprietor may also limit his liability as an innkeeper to £50 for any one article or £100 in the aggregate, provided that at the time when the property in question was brought to the hotel a notice in statutory form[57] was conspicuously displayed in a place where it could conveniently be read by his guests at or near the reception desk or, if none, at or near the main entrance. But this limit will not apply where (a) the property was stolen, lost or damaged through the default, neglect or wilful act of the proprietor or his servant,[58] (b) the property was deposited expressly for safe custody, or (c) if not so deposited, it had been offered for deposit and refused, or if not so offered, where the guest wishing to offer it for deposit was unable to do so through the default of the proprietor or his servant.[59] It has been held under the 1863 Act that in order to satisfy the condition that the property has been "deposited expressly" the fact of the deposit must be definitely brought to the innkeeper's notice, and that where there is no such express deposit the onus of proof of fault or neglect on the part of the innkeeper lies on the guest.[60]

---

[53] "Hotel" is defined (s. 1 (3)) as "an establishment held out by the proprietor as offering food, drink and, if so required, sleeping accommodation, without special contract, to any traveller presenting himself who appears able and willing to pay a reasonable sum for the services and facilities provided and who is in a fit state to be received."
[54] s. 1 (2).
[55] s. 2 (2).
[56] s. 2 (1).
[57] See Schedule.
[58] *Kott & Kott* v. *Gordon Hotels* [1968] 2 Ll. Rep. 228.
[59] s. 2 (3).
[60] *Whitehouse* v. *Pickett*, 1908 S.C. (H.L.) 31.

CHAPTER XXIX

CARRIAGE BY LAND

Kahn-Freund, *Law of Inland Transport* (4th ed., 1965); Chitty, *Contracts* (24th ed., 1977), Vol. 2.

1. Common Carriers.—A carrier may or may not be a common carrier. A common carrier is one who undertakes for hire[1] to transport the goods of all who choose to employ him in the business which he professes to ply. He may be a common carrier though he limits the class of goods which he is willing to carry, or though he indicates that certain goods will be carried only on special conditions, but it is essential that he should profess to be willing to carry for all those who choose to employ him.[2] If he makes no such profession he is a private carrier. Until 1st September 1962 the railways, although nationalised by the Transport Act 1947,[3] were common carriers. The Transport Act 1962[4] altered this and the Railways Board has freedom to impose such terms in its contracts of carriage as it wishes,[5] which results in its being a private carrier. The old law relating to the Standard Terms and Conditions[6] now no longer applies. Cabmen[7] and removal contractors[8] are private carriers. Bus companies and road hauliers are common carriers but in most cases their liability as such for loss or damage to goods is modified by contract.[9] The Post Office is not a common carrier.[10]

2. Obligation to Carry.—The distinction between common and private carriers is of importance in two respects—(1) in the obligation to accept employment; (2) in the degree of liability for loss or injury to goods. A private carrier may accept any offer of employment or refuse it. A common carrier makes a continuous offer to carry[11] provided, in the case of goods, that they are of the class he professes to carry; that they are not dangerous or insufficiently packed; that they arrive in time; that he has room in his conveyance; that his charges are paid or tendered; in the case of passengers also that they are in a reasonably fit state to be carried.[12] An unjustifiable

---

[1] See *Barr* v. *Caledonian Ry.* (1890) 18 R. 139.
[2] *Great Northern Ry.* v. *L.E.P.* [1922] 2 K.B. 742.
[3] 10 & 11 Geo. VI, c. 49.
[4] 10 & 11 Eliz. II, c. 46.
[5] s. 43 (3).
[6] As settled by the Railway Rates Tribunal under the Railways Act 1921; see § 12, infra.
[7] *Ord* v. *Gemmell* (1898) 1 F. 17.
[8] *Pearcey* v. *Player* (1883) 10 R. 564. As to wharfingers, see *Consolidated Tea Co.* v. *Oliver's Wharf* [1910] 2 K.B. 395.
[9] To the extent permitted by the Unfair Contract Terms Act 1977 (c. 50). See § 8 infra.
[10] See *Harold Stephen & Co.* v. *Post Office* [1977] 1 W.L.R. 1172 at p. 1177; ss. 29 and 30 of the Post Office Act 1969 (c. 48).
[11] See, e.g. *A. Siohn & Co. and Academy Garments (Wigan)* v. *R. H. Hagland & Son (Transport)* [1976] 2 Lloyd's Rep. 428.
[12] Bell, *Prin.*, § 159; *Clarke* v. *West Ham Corporation* [1909] 2 K.B. 858. Compare the analogous obligation of an innkeeper: *Rothfield* v. *N.B.R.*, 1920 S.C. 805.

refusal is a ground for an action for damages.[13] A common carrier is bound by a list of fares publicly advertised,[14] and in any case is not entitled to charge more than a reasonable fare.[15]

3. Strict Liability of Common Carrier.—The exceptional liability for the loss of goods which rests on a common carrier is in Scotland based on the Praetorian Edict; in England, on the custom of the realm.[16] The common carrier is in the position of an insurer, and is liable for loss of or damage to goods without affirmative proof of negligence. Proof that the goods were stolen is no defence.[17] For loss by accidental fire, which was an exception to the carrier's liability at common law,[18] a common carrier by land, though not by sea, is liable by statute.[19] It is a valid defence to the carrier that the goods have been lost by the fault of the sender, as where they are insufficiently addressed;[20] by the act of God; by the Queen's enemies, including the case of a rebellion, not of a mere riot;[21] or by their inherent vice, as where a horse struggled through an opening left as a feeding window.[22] These defences are available only if the carrier has not deviated from the route agreed upon, or can show that the particular event would have happened even if he had not deviated.[23] In addition he must show that neither he nor his servants contributed to the casualty through their negligence.[24] In the absence of express agreement to the contrary, a carrier who issues a ticket or consignment note is responsible for the whole journey, though it is known that he carries only for part of it.[25]

4. Passenger's Luggage.—A common carrier is liable for the loss of passenger's luggage.[26] The relevant rules were largely formulated in cases relating to luggage accompanying rail passengers. Although the Transport Act 1962 has removed the railways from the class of common carriers, these rules are probably still applicable to operators of public service vehicles. There is liability for loss even if the luggage is inside the vehicle with the passenger unless the carrier can show that its loss was due to lack of reasonable care on

[13] Bell, *Prin.*, § 159.
[14] *Campbell* v. *Ker*, Feb. 24, 1810, F.C.
[15] *Great Western Ry.* v. *Sutton* (1868) L.R. 4 H.L. 226, at p. 237.
[16] Dig., IV., 9, 1; Stair, I, 13, 3; Bell, *Prin.*, § 235; and see supra, Hiring, Loan and Deposit, Ch. XXVIII, § 13; and *Burns* v. *Royal Hotel* (*St. Andrews*), 1958 S.C. 354, as to onus of proof. A private carrier is liable only for fault or negligence: Stair I, 13, 3; Bell, *Prin.*, § 235; *Copland* v. *Brogan*, 1916 S.C. 277 (gratuitous carriage).
[17] Bell, *Prin.*, § 238.
[18] See Hiring, Loan and Deposit, Ch. XXVIII, § 14; and *Burns* v. *Royal Hotel* (*St. Andrews*) as to onus of proof.
[19] Mercantile Law Amendment (Scotland) Act 1856, s. 17. A private carrier is also liable under s. 17; *James Kemp* (*Leslie*) v. *Robertson* 1967 S.L.T. 213.
[20] *Caledonian Ry.* v. *Hunter* (1858) 20 D. 1097.
[21] See *Curtis* v. *Matthews* [1919] 1 K.B. 425.
[22] *Ralston* v. *Caledonian Ry.* (1878) 5 R. 671.
[23] *Morrison* v. *Shaw Savill, etc., Co.* [1916] 2 K.B. 783.
[24] *Burns* v. *Royal Hotel* (*St. Andrews*) supra.
[25] *Logan* v. *Highland Ry.* (1899) 2 F. 292. Referred to, *Aberdeen Grit Co.* v. *Ellerman's Wilson Line*, 1933 S.C. 9.
[26] *Parker* v. *L.M.S. Ry.*, 1930 S.C. 822; *Campbell* v. *Cal. Ry. Co.* (1852) 14 D. 806.

the part of the passenger.[27] The liability ends when the luggage is delivered at the end of the journey, though it may then be left with the carrier as a depositary or custodier,[28] in which case he is only liable for negligence.[29] A carrier is not bound to carry, as passenger's luggage, anything the passenger may choose to bring with him. The following general definition of passenger's luggage has been given: "Whatever a passenger takes with him for his personal use or convenience, according to the habits and wants of the particular class to which he belongs, either with reference to the immediate necessities or to the ultimate purpose of the journey".[30] The carrier is also entitled to refuse to carry, without additional charge, articles requiring special care in carriage, such as a bicycle, gun or fishing-rod, not so packed as to be readily carried without special precautions.[31] Where, without notice to the carrier, articles are taken which are not properly passenger's luggage he is not liable for their loss.[32]

5. Delay in Transit.—The obligation of a common carrier does not amount to insurance against loss or injury caused by delay in transit. It is an obligation to carry within a time reasonable in the circumstances. So where goods were injured by delay due to a general strike of railwaymen,[33] or to a block on the line caused by an accident not due to the company's negligence,[34] it was held that there was no liability. The carrier, if aware of circumstances likely to cause delay, is bound to warn the passenger or sender of goods.[35] Should delay threaten injury to perishable goods the carrier, as an agent by necessity, is entitled to sell them, but before doing so is bound to communicate with the owner, if reasonably practicable.[36] An obligation to carry within a particular time may be expressly undertaken, or may be inferred from advertisement, as where a railway advertises trains to meet a particular market.[37] Proof that a railway company regularly gave preference in transit to goods marked perishable was held to render them liable for injury on an occasion when they had failed to do so.[38]

6. Delay in Carriage of Passengers.—With regard to passengers the general obligation is merely to carry within a time reasonable in all the circumstances of the case. It has never been held that the publication of a time-table indicating times of departure and connections amounts to an undertaking that

---

[27] *Jenkyns* v. *Southampton Steam Packet Co.* [1919] 2 K.B. 135; *Vosper* v. *G.W.Ry.* [1928] 1 K.B. 340; *Parker* v. *L.M. and S.Ry.* 1930 S.C. 822.
[28] *Parker* v. *L.M.S. Ry.*, 1930 S.C. 822.
[29] *Lyons* v. *Caledonian Ry.*, 1909 S.C. 1185.
[30] *Jenkyns* v. *Southampton Steam Packet Co.* [1919] 2 K.B. 135; *Buckland* v. *The King* [1933] 1 K.B. 329.
[31] *Britten* v. *Great Northern Ry.* [1899] 1 Q.B. 243.
[32] *Macrow* v. *Great Western Ry.* (1871) L.R. 6 Q.B. 612.
[33] *Sims* v. *Midland Ry.* [1913] 1 K.B. 103.
[34] *Anderson* v. *N.B.R.* (1875) 2 R. 443.
[35] *McConnachie* v. *Great North of Scotland Ry.* (1875) 3 R. 79; *Jarvie* v. *Cal. Ry.* (1875) 2 R. 623.
[36] *Springer* v. *Great Western Ry.* [1921] 1 K.B. 257.
[37] *Finlay* v. *N.B.R.* (1870) 8 M. 959.
[38] *Macdonald* v. *Highland Ry.* (1873) 11 M. 614.

these times will be observed,[39] but it may amount to an undertaking that the trains indicated will be run.[40] It has been held that where a connection was missed owing to want of reasonable care on the part of the company the question whether the passenger could recover, as damages, the expense of a special train which he had ordered depended upon whether he would probably have done the same if he had had no recourse.[41] As has been seen the Railways Board will only incur liability arising from a breach of the terms of its private contract, but these rules still apply in substance to the liability of a common carrier who has not made special contractual arrangements with his customer.

7. Liability for Negligence.—Quite apart from the strict liability of common carriers, all carriers, whether common or private, are subject to the ordinary principles of the law of reparation.[42] Thus a carrier is liable for his own or his servants' negligence, whether it constitutes a breach of the implied conditions of the contract or a breach of the carrier's duty to take reasonable care for the safety of persons or property lawfully placed in his charge.[43] Negligence involves failure in a duty, and therefore in cases where the responsibility of a common carrier does not attach, there is no liability for injury by pure accident, by the criminal or wrongful acts of parties, such as fellow-passengers, for whom the carrier is not responsible,[44] or from a breakdown in the carriage which could not have been prevented by a reasonable system of inspection.[45] If goods are delivered to a private carrier in good condition, and tendered by him in a damaged state, that is prima facie evidence of fault.[46] Similarly anything in the nature of a railway accident is prima facie evidence of negligence, and it rests with the Railways Board to prove that the accident was due to some cause, for example a latent and undiscoverable flaw, for which they were not responsible.[47] It would appear that the carrier's duty of care does not extend to persons who travel surreptitiously, or in violation of the carrier's regulations.[48] But his responsibility does extend to persons carried gratuitously.[49]

8. Exclusion of or Limitation of Liability by Contract.—The Carriers Act 1830 leaves it open to a common carrier to make special arrangements with individuals excluding or restricting liability for loss of or damage to goods, and private carriers were always free to contract on their own terms. However

---

[39] See Deas on *Railways* (2nd ed.), p. 724.
[40] *Denton* v. *Great Northern Ry.* (1856) 5 E. & B. 800.
[41] *Le Blanche* v. *L. and N.-W. Ry.* (1876) 1 C.P.D. 286.
[42] See Ch. XXXIV.
[43] *Meux* v. *Great Eastern Ry.* [1895] 2 Q.B. 387.
[44] *East Indian Ry.* v. *Mukerjee* [1901] A.C. 396.
[45] *Readhead* v. *Midland Ry.* (1869) L.R. 4 Q.B. 379; *Reynolds* v. *Lancashire Tramways Co.* (1908) 16 S.L.T. 230.
[46] *Sutton & Co.* v. *Ciceri & Co.* (1890) 17 R. (H.L.) 40.
[47] *Ballard* v. *N.B.R.*, 1923 S.C. (H.L.) 43.
[48] *Thompson* v. *N.B.R.* (1882) 9 R. 1101; *Grand Trunk Ry.* v. *Barnett* [1911] A.C. 361.
[49] *Austin* v. *Great Western Ry.* (1867) L.R. 2 Q.B. 442.

the Unfair Contract Terms Act 1977 now applies to all contracts of carriage.[50] A contractual[51] term purporting to exclude or restrict liability for breach of duty[52] arising in the course of the carrier's business or from the occupation of the carrier's business premises is void if it excludes or restricts liability in respect of death or personal injury, and may be unenforceable if it was not fair and reasonable to incorporate the term in the contract.[53] The fact that a passenger agreed to, or was aware of, the term is not in itself sufficient evidence that he knowingly and voluntarily assumed the risk.[54] "Breach of duty" does not extend to duties higher than the duty to use reasonable care and skill, and thus the Act does not cover any clause avoiding the strict liability of the common carrier.[55] But neither a private nor a common carrier may exclude liability for death or injury caused by their negligence.[56] A clause purporting to exclude or restrict liability for breach of contract or for unsatisfactory performance may be unenforceable if the contract of carriage is either a consumer contract[57] or a standard form contract.[58]

Any valid exclusion or restriction clause must be shown to have been incorporated in the contract.[59] It has been held that if a carrier deviates from the agreed route, he loses the benefit of any valid conditions in his favour, and is liable for damage however caused.[60] The right of the carrier to found on a valid limitation clause may be lost by actings which amount to repudiation of the contract.[61]

9. Statutory Limitation of Liability.—The Carriers Act 1830, section 1, provides that the liability of a common carrier by land for loss or injury to goods (including passengers' luggage[62]) is excluded, in the case of certain specified goods, unless their nature and value have been declared when they are placed in the carrier's hands, and an increased charge, if demanded, has been paid. Thirty-six classes of goods are specified, having the common characteristic of great value relative to their bulk, and including the precious metals, bank notes or securities, jewellery, pictures, furs and lace. Such goods must be declared if their value exceeds £10. If an increased charge is to be made it must be posted in the office or receiving-house of the carrier, but

---

[50] 1977 Act, s. 15 (2) (c).
[51] It would appear that, in Scotland, non-contractual statements or disclaimers are outwith the Act's control: see Rogers & Clarke, *The Unfair Contract Terms Act, 1977*.
[52] "Breach of Duty" is defined in s. 25 (1).
[53] 1977 Act, s. 16 (1). As to reasonableness, see Pacta Illicita and Unfair Terms, Ch. IX, supra.
[54] 1977 Act, s. 16 (3).
[55] See Rogers and Clarke, op. cit.
[56] 1977 Act, s. 16. See too the Road Traffic Act 1960, s. 151, in relation to operators of public service vehicles.
[57] "Consumer contract" is defined in s. 25 (1).
[58] 1977 Act, ss. 15 (2) (c); 17; 25 (1). As to purported indemnity clauses in consumer contracts, see s. 18. See generally, Pacta Illicita and Unfair Terms, Ch. IX, supra.
[59] See Law of Contract, Ch. IV, supra; cf. *McCutcheon v. Macbrayne*, 1964 S.C. (H.L.) 28.
[60] *Lord Polwarth v. N.B.R.*, 1908 S.C. 1275; *L. and N,-W.Ry. v. Neilson* [1922] 2 A.C. 263; *Hain S.S. Co. v. Tate & Lyle* [1936] 2 All E.R. 597.
[61] *John Carter (Fine Worsteds) v. Hanson Haulage (Leeds) Ltd.* [1965] 2 Q.B. 495. Contrast with actings amounting to material breach entitling the other party to rescind: see 1977 Act, s. 22, and Pacta Illicita and Unfair Terms, Ch. IX, supra.
[62] *Casswell v. Cheshire Lines Committee* [1907] 2 K.B. 499.

failure in this respect does not deprive the carrier of the statutory immunity.[63] The nature and value of the goods must be declared; it is not sufficient to make a general statement that they are valuable.[64] The Act does not protect the carrier from loss due to any theft, embezzlement or forgery of his servants, but the sender of the goods must prove circumstances, beyond the mere fact of opportunity, which render it more likely that the goods have been stolen by the carrier's servants than by some other thief.[65]

10. Ejection from Conveyance.—There is some authority for the view that any carrier has at common law the right to eject from his conveyance a passenger who refuses to pay the fare.[66] The Railways Board has express statutory power to arrest and detain any person who travels, or attempts to travel, without paying his fare, and with the intent to avoid payment[67]; and this has been held to justify summary expulsion of a passenger who had a ticket which was not available on a particular day, though there was no averment that he had any intention to travel without paying his fare.[68] In England, it was held not to cover the case of a passenger who had lost his ticket, and refused to comply with a demand that he should pay the fare from the place from which the train started.[69] Any unnecessary violence in ejecting a passenger will found an action for damages.[70]

11. Lien of Carrier.—A carrier has at common law a special lien over goods for his charges for their carriage, but no lien for a general balance.[71] He is not entitled to detain a passenger, or any part of his clothing, for the fare.[72] A contract between a carrier and a trader whereby the former obtains a general lien is effectual in a question with the trustee in the sequestration of the trader.[73] A provision in a contract whereby goods were carried at owner's risk, under which the goods were subjected to a general lien for all charges due by the "owners", was held not to preclude the senders of the goods, as unpaid sellers, from exercising their right of stoppage in transitu, and thereby acquiring a right to delivery preferable to a claim by the railway company for a general balance due by the consignee.[74]

12. Carriage of Goods by Rail.—The railways are now under the general control of the Railways Board and have ceased to be common carriers.[75]

---

[63] *Rusk* v. *N.B.R.*, 1920, 2 S.L.T. 139.
[64] *Rusk*, supra.
[65] Carriers Act 1830, s. 8 as amended by the Criminal Law Act 1967 (c. 58); *Campbell* v. *N.B.R.* (1875) 2 R. 433.
[66] *North-Eastern Ry.* v. *Mathews* (1866) 5 Irvine 237; but see opinions in *Harris* v. *N.B.R.* (1891) 18 R. 1009.
[67] Railway Clauses Act 1845, ss. 96, 97. *Gerber* v. *British Railways Board*, 1969 J.C. 7.
[68] *Highland Ry.* v. *Menzies* (1878) 5 R. 887.
[69] *Butler* v. *Manchester, etc., Ry.* (1888) 21 Q.B.D. 207.
[70] *Maxwell* v. *Cal. Ry.* (1898) 25 R. 550.
[71] *Peebles* v. *Cal. Ry.* (1875) 2 R. 346.
[72] *Wolf* v. *Summers* (1811) 2 Camp. 631.
[73] *Great Eastern Ry.* v. *Lord's Tr.* [1909] A.C. 109.
[74] *U.S. Steel Products Co.* v. *G.W. Ry.* [1916] 1 A.C. 189.
[75] See § 1, supra.

Accordingly the Standard Terms and Conditions in force prior to 1962 have ceased to have any effect.[76] While the General Conditions of Carriage issued by the Railways Board bear some resemblance to the old standard conditions, these conditions are no more than the framework for each ad hoc contract made by the Board. The Board is not now an insurer of the goods it carries but can only be liable for negligence, subject to any valid condition in the contract in question limiting or excluding that liability.[77] Similarly the Carriers Act 1830 no longer applies to carriage of goods by rail.

13. Passengers.—Any person who holds himself out as willing to carry members of the public is a common carrier of passengers inasmuch as he is bound to carry persons willing to pay the fare unless there is some good reason for not doing so.[78] However, there is no edictal liability imposed for the safety of the passengers carried.[79]

14. Road Haulage.—With certain exceptions[80] no haulier may use a goods vehicle for the carriage of goods for hire or reward or in connection with his trade or business without an operator's licence.[81] An operator's licence may be standard or restricted, national or international.[82] All hauliers are subject to the common law, as modified by the Carriers Act 1830,[83] and any conditions contained in licences. A road haulier may, and usually does, limit his liability by special conditions.[84] The modern practice is for road hauliers to limit their profession to that of private carriers.

15. Public Service Vehicles.—Any motor vehicle is a public service vehicle if it carries passengers for hire at separate fares or if it carries passengers for hire and is adapted to carry at least eight passengers.[85] Public service vehicles fall into three classes, stage carriages (carrying persons at separate fares, not being an express carriage), express carriages (on which the minimum fare is twenty-one pence[86] or over) and contract carriages (which are hired by a person or a group of persons for a lump sum)[87]; but a vehicle carrying passengers for separate fares may in certain circumstances be treated as a contract carriage.[88] Each vehicle requires its appropriate public service vehicle

---

[76] For a statement of the position prior to September 1, 1962, see Gow, *Mercantile and Industrial Law of Scotland*, pp. 480-1.

[77] See Transport Act 1962, s. 43 (3) and § 8, supra.

[78] *Clarke* v. *West Ham Corporation* [1909] 2 K.B. 858.

[79] As to liability for negligence, see § 7 supra.

[80] See for example Schedule 1 of the Goods Vehicles (Operators' Licences) Regulations 1977 (No. 1737).

[81] Transport Act 1968 (c. 73), ss. 59-61; *Alderton* v. *Richard Burgon Associates* (*Manpower*) [1974] R.T.R. 422.

[82] See the Goods Vehicle Operators (Qualifications) Regulations 1977 (No. 1462); the Goods Vehicles (Operators' Licences) Regulations 1977 (No. 1737). See, too, the International Road Haulage Permits Act 1975 (c. 46).

[83] s. 6.

[84] § 8, supra; e.g. the Conditions issued by the Road Haulage Association.

[85] cf. *Traffic Commissioners for the South Wales Traffic Area* v. *Snape* [1977] R.T.R. 367.

[86] Public Service Vehicles (Definition of Express Carriage) Regulations 1977 (No. 1496).

[87] Road Traffic Act 1960, ss. 117 et seq., and Schedule 12; Transport Act 1968 (c. 73), s. 145 (1).

[88] Ibid., s. 118 (2); see *MacLeod* v. *Penman*, 1962 J.C. 31.

licence, and stage and express carriages also require road service licences, which are issued by the Traffic Commissioners for the traffic district, if they are satisfied as to the need for the service.[89] Someone suspected of contravening public service vehicle regulations may be arrested without warrant.[90]

The liabilities of the owner of a public service vehicle in respect of injury to passengers or their luggage are those of common carriers,[91] although in most cases his liability is modified or restricted by contract.[92]

16. International Carriage.—International carriage by land has been the subject of several international conventions.[93] The Unfair Contract Terms Act 1977 does not strike at any restriction or exclusion clause authorised by such conventions if the United Kingdom is a party thereto.[94]

17. International Carriage by Road: Goods.—The Carriage of Goods by Road Act 1965[95] applies to every contract for the carriage of goods by road[96] in vehicles[97] for reward, when the place of taking over of the goods and the place designated for delivery, as specified in the contract, are situated in two different countries, at least one being a contracting country.[98] The residence or nationality of the contracting parties is irrelevant.[98] With certain limited exceptions,[99] it is impossible to contract out of the statutory provisions.[1] Carriage should be effected under a consignment note, containing certain particulars.[2] The note is prima facie evidence of the contract, and gives rise to certain presumptions.[2] The sender's rights and obligations are set out in detail, as are the carrier's.[3] The carrier is liable for loss of or damage to goods, and for delay in delivery.[4] However in certain circumstances,[5] his liability is

---

[89] Road Traffic Act 1960, ss. 134, 135 et seq.

[90] Public Service Vehicles (Arrest of Offenders) Act 1975 (c. 53).

[91] The Courts are reluctant to hold that a carrier is a common carrier; see *Belfast Ropeworks* v. *Bushell* [1918] 1 K.B. 210.

[92] See § 8, supra.

[93] See infra. The texts of the conventions are detailed, and should be referred to in any particular case.

[94] 1977 Act, s. 29.

[95] (c. 37). The 1965 Act implements the Geneva Convention on the Contract for the International Carriage of Goods by Road 1956, the terms of which are set out in the Schedule to the Act.

[96] As to carriage partly by road and partly by other modes of transport, see 1965 Act, Sched., art. 2.

[97] "Vehicles" are defined in art. 1 (2) of the Schedule.

[98] 1965 Act, Sched., art. 1 (1). See e.g. the Carriage of Goods by Road (Parties to Convention) Orders, S. I. 1967/1683; 1969/385; 1973/596. The Act does not apply to carriage performed under the terms of any international postal convention; to funeral consignments; or to furniture removals: ibid., art. 1 (4). The Act does apply to carriage by states and governmental institutions: art. 1 (3).

[99] Ibid., art. 40.

[1] 1965 Act, Sched., art. 41.

[2] Ibid., arts. 4-9. *S.G.S.-Ates Componenti Elettronici S.P.A.* v. *Grappo* [1977] R.T.R. 442.

[3] Ibid., arts. 7-16. The sender may inter alia stop the goods in transit, or change the cosignee. The carrier may inter alia sell perishable goods.

[4] Ibid., art. 17.

[5] Ibid., arts. 17-18; for example, where the loss or damage was caused by the claimant's wrongful act; or by the claimant's instructions; or by inevitable accident; or by inherent vice. *Ulster-Swift and Pig Marketing Board (Northern Ireland)* v. *Taunton Meat Haulage* [1975] 2 Lloyd's Rep. 502.

excluded and if not excluded, is limited.[6] However he cannot benefit from the Act's protection where he has been guilty of wilful misconduct or default.[7] Where several carriers are liable, damages will be apportioned.[8] Any action under the 1965 Act must be raised within certain time limits.[9] Where a right of action is time-barred, it may not be exercised by way of set-off.[9]

18. International Carriage by Road: Passengers and Luggage.—The Carriage of Passengers by Road Act 1974 (c. 35), when brought into force,[10] will regulate every contract for the carriage[11] of passengers[12] and their luggage in vehicles[12] by road[13] when the contract provides that the carriage shall take place in the territory of more than one state, and that either or both the place of departure or place of destination is situated in a contracting state's territory.[14] It will be impossible to contract out of the Act.[15]

19. International Carriage by Rail.—Three conventions regulate international carriage by rail.[16] The Additional Convention has been expressly implemented by United Kingdom legislation,[17] and the remaining two conventions (CIM and CIV) have been impliedly incorporated into United Kingdom law.[18]

20. International Carriage by Rail: Goods (CIM).—The CIM applies to the carriage of goods[19] by rail[20] under a consignment note providing for carriage over the territories of at least two contracting states.[21] The sender has the right in certain circumstances to stop the goods in transit, or to change the consignee or destination.[22] The railway is liable for loss of or damage to

---

[6] Ibid., arts. 23-26, as amended by the Carriage by Air and Road Act 1979 (c. 28), s. 4 (2); *William Tatton & Co.* v. *Ferrymasters* [1974] 1 Lloyd's Rep. 203; *James Buchanan & Co.* v. *Babco Forwarding & Shipping (U.K.)* [1977] 3 W.L.R. 907.

[7] Ibid., art. 29.

[8] Ibid., arts. 34-39. But see art. 40.

[9] Ibid., art. 32. *Muller Batavier* v. *Laurent Transport Co.* [1977] R.T.R. 499.

[10] The 1974 Act is to be brought into force on a date to be appointed: s. 14 (5). It will implement the Convention on the Contract for the International Carriage of Passengers and Luggage by Road (Geneva, 1973) with amendments made by the Carriage by Air and Road Act 1979 (c. 28), s. 4 (3). However the United Kingdom is not as yet a contracting party to the Convention.

[11] The carrier must be acting in the course of a trade or business: 1974 Act, Sched., art. 1 (2). Taxis and hired cars with drivers are excluded.

[12] "Passengers" and "Vehicles" are defined in art. 1 (2) of the Schedule to the 1974 Act.

[13] As to carriage partly by road and partly by other modes of transport, see arts. 2, 3.

[14] 1974 Act, Sched., art. 1 (1). Parties' residences and nationalities are irrelevant.

[15] Ibid., art. 23.

[16] The revised International Convention concerning the Carriage of Goods by Rail (Convention internationale concernant le transport des marchandises par chemins de fer—or CIM), (Berne, 1970); the revised International Convention concerning the Carriage of Passengers and Luggage by Rail (Convention internationale concernant le transport des voyageurs et des bagages par chemins de fer—or CIV), (Berne, 1970); and the Additional Convention to the CIV (Berne, 1966) (originally supplementary to an earlier CIV of 1961).

[17] Carriage by Railway Act 1972 (c. 33).

[18] The 1972 Act specifically refers to the Railway Freight Convention (CIM) and the Railway Passenger Convention (CIV).

[19] As to unacceptable goods and special categories of goods, see CIM, arts. 3, 4.

[20] As to carriage partly by rail and partly by another mode of transport, see CIM, art. 2 (1).

[21] CIM, art. 1 (1).

[22] CIM, arts. 21, 23.

goods, and for delay.[23] It is relieved of liability in circumstances similar to those giving rise to relief in international carriage of goods by road.[24] In any event the railway's liability is limited[25]; but the limits are doubled where loss or damage arose from the railway's gross negligence, and do not apply at all if the railway's wilful misconduct caused the loss.[26] There are provisions limiting the periods within which actions may be raised, and also provisions extinguishing rights of action after certain time limits.[27]

21. International Carriage by Rail: Passengers and Luggage (CIV; Carriage by Railway Act 1972).—The CIV[28] and the Carriage by Railway Act 1972 apply to the carriage by rail of passengers and luggage over the territories of at least two contracting states,[29] provided that the carriage is exclusively over lines listed in the Convention.[30] The CIV regulates inter alia loss of or damage to luggage, or delay in delivery; the 1972 Act regulates liability in respect of death or personal injury, or loss of or damage to hand-luggage. Carriage of luggage other than hand-luggage is effected under a luggage registration voucher.[31] The railway is liable for loss of or damage to registered luggage, or for delay in delivery.[32] Liability is limited, although the limits are doubled where the railway was guilty of gross negligence and do not apply at all where the railway's wilful misconduct caused the loss.[33] Actions must be raised within certain time limits, and in certain cases delay results in the extinction of a right of action.[34] Where passengers are carried under a passenger ticket,[35] the railway is liable for death or personal injury caused by an accident arising out of the operation of the railway and happening while the passenger is in, entering, or alighting from a train.[36] The railway is also liable for loss of or damage to hand-luggage.[36] The railway is relieved of liability in certain circumstances, and its liability is limited unless there has been wilful misconduct or gross negligence.[37] Any contractual provision not complying with the 1972 Act is void.[38] Claims under the 1972 Act may become time-barred, and rights of action may in certain circumstances be extinguished.[39]

[23] CIM, art. 27.
[24] CIM, arts. 27, 28. And cf. § 17 supra.
[25] CIM, arts. 31-34.
[26] CIM, art. 37.
[27] CIM, arts. 46-47.
[28] The revised International Convention concerning the Carriage of Passengers and Luggage by Rail (Berne, 1970). See note 16, supra.
[29] For current contracting states, see Carriage by Railway (Parties to Convention) Order 1972 (No. 1580) as amended by S.I. 1973/2088 and S.I. 1975/1035.
[30] CIV, art, 1 (1).
[31] CIV, arts. 19-20.
[32] CIV, arts. 27 et seq.
[33] CIV, arts. 31-33.
[34] CIV, arts. 42-43.
[35] CIV, arts. 4, 5.
[36] Carriage by Railway Act 1972 (c. 33), as amended by S.I. 1974/1250, Schedule, arts. 2-5.
[37] Ibid., arts. 2, 6-8.
[38] Ibid., art. 10.
[39] Ibid., arts. 16-17.

CHAPTER XXX

CARRIAGE BY SEA

Carver, *Carriage by Sea* (12th ed., 1971); *British Shipping Laws*, Vols. 1 and 2; Payne and Ivamy, *Carriage of Goods by Sea* (10th ed., 1976); Scrutton, *Charterparties* (18th ed., 1974).

1. Constitution of the Contract.—A contract for the carriage of goods by sea, or affreightment, may be entered into verbally,[1] and its terms are then to be gathered from proof of the words or actions of the parties, from advertisements, or from their prior business relations.[2] More commonly the contract of affreightment is entered into in writing. Then the relationship of the parties may depend upon a charterparty; on the combined effect of a charterparty and a bill of lading; on a bill of lading alone; or on a document known as a receipt.[3] The edict nautae, caupones, stabularii, although applying to carriage by sea, has largely been superseded by legislation.[4]

2. Charterparty.—A charterparty is a contract whereby a ship, or some portion thereof, is hired either for a definite time (time charter) or for a particular voyage (voyage charter) in return for a payment known as freight. It may either take the form of the hire of the ship or merely of the accommodation in the ship. In the first form, usually termed a demise of the ship, the charterer takes for the time being the position of an owner, and the responsibility to third parties, e.g. in the case of a collision, rests solely with him.[5] The master of the ship, in signing a bill of lading, binds the charterer, and not the owner.[6] Where merely the accommodation in the ship is hired these responsibilities remain with the owner. Where not only the ship but its master and crew are hired, the contract will not be read as a demise of the ship merely because it is stated that the crew are to be in the service of the charterer, unless the power of appointment and dismissal is also vested in him.[7]

3. Normal Form of Charterparty.—A charterparty, a term derived from the ancient custom of executing the document in duplicate and cutting it

---

[1] *Nordstjernan* v. *Salvesen* (1903) 6 F. 64, at p. 75; Bell, *Comm.*, I., 586.

[2] *Hill* v. *Scott* [1895] 2 Q.B. 371, 713.

[3] The receipt was introduced by the Carriage of Goods by Sea Act 1924. See now the Carriage of Goods by Sea Act 1971 (c. 19), Sched., art. VI; and § 17 infra. The 1971 Act came into force on 23rd June 1977 (S.I. 1977 No. 981) when it repealed the 1924 Act. However the unamended Hague Rules as set out in the 1924 Act may still have relevance: see 1977 Lloyd's M.C.L.Q. 512.

[4] For example, the Merchant Shipping Act 1894, the Carriage of Goods by Sea Act 1971. The Carriers Act 1830 does not apply to carriage by sea.

[5] *Clark* v. *Scott* (1896) 23 R. 442; *The Briton* [1975] 1 Lloyd's Rep. 356; *Attica Sea Carriers Corporation* v. *Ferrostaal Poseidon Bulk Reederei G.M.b.H.* [1976] 1 Lloyd's Rep. 250.

[6] *Baumwoll Manufacturer* v. *Furness* [1893] A.C. 8.

[7] *Manchester Trust* v. *Furness* [1895] 2 Q.B. 539. See also *Wills* v. *Burrell* (1894) 21 R. 527.

across, is a contract usually entered into by a printed form, with or without additional clauses, typed or in manuscript. In its normal form, in voyage charters, it describes the ship, the voyage proposed, and contains an undertaking to deliver the cargo to the charterer or his assignee on payment of freight. Provisions as to time for loading or unloading are added, and responsibility for loss occasioned by certain specified causes excluded.[8]

4. Seaworthiness.—In a charterparty it is open to the contracting parties to exclude the liability of the shipowner for any cause of loss to the cargo.[8] But in the absence of any express stipulation to the contrary the law implies a warranty of seaworthiness, which is not excluded by any general exception of loss due to the negligence of the officers or crew and is a guarantee that the ship is seaworthy, not merely that the owner has taken all reasonable steps to make her so.[9] Seaworthiness has been defined as "that degree of fitness which an ordinary careful and prudent owner would require his vessel to have at the commencement of her voyage, having regard to all the probable circumstances of it."[10] The warranty is that the ship is fit to encounter the normal dangers of the voyage and to carry the cargo contracted for, that her refrigerating machinery, for instance, is in good order.[11] It involves the provision of a qualified master and competent crew.[12] It is a warranty that the ship is ready to receive the cargo at the time of loading, e.g. that a cattle ship has been properly disinfected,[13] and is fit to sail at the time of sailing. But for defects occurring during the voyage, and not due to initial unseaworthiness, the shipowner's obligation is only to execute and pay for repairs, not a warranty that repairs will not be necessary, and therefore he is not liable for delay due to a breakdown of machinery.[14] The question whether a temporary defect, e.g. a porthole left open or failure to case a pipe, is unseaworthiness, or a defect attributable to the negligence of the crew, depends upon whether, in the particular circumstances, it could be remedied during the voyage.[15] The onus of proving unseaworthiness primarily rests with the charterer who asserts it, but is displaced by proof that the ship broke down in the initial stage of her voyage.[16] The warranty of seaworthiness formerly applied in cases arising under bills of lading as well as under charterparties, but the law in this respect was altered by the Carriage of Goods by Sea Act 1924, section 2.

---

[8] But see § 17 infra; Unfair Contract Terms Act 1977.
[9] *Steel & Craig* v. *State Line Co.* (1877) 4 R. (H.L.) 103; *A/B Karlshamns Oljefabriker* v. *Monarch S.S. Co.,* 1949 S.C. (H.L.) 1.
[10] Carver, *Carriage by Sea,* p. 95, approved, *McFadden* v. *Blue Star Line* [1905] 1 K.B. 697.
[11] *Maori King* v. *Hughes* [1895] 2 Q.B. 550. As to the distinction between unfitness to receive the cargo, and bad stowage, see *Elder-Dempster* v. *Paterson* [1924] A.C. 522.
[12] *Gunford Ship Co.* v. *Thomas, etc., Insurance Co.,* 1911 S.C. (H.L.) 84; *Standard Oil Co.* v. *Clan Line,* 1924 S.C. (H.L.) 1; *Hong Kong Fir Shipping Co.* v. *Kawasaki Kisen Kaisha* [1962] 2 Q.B. 27. As a result of their decision there would not appear to be any disagreement between English and Scots law as to the effect of a breach of this warranty on the charterparty as a whole. Cf. *Universal Cargo Carriers Corp.* v. *Citari* [1957] 2 Q.B. 401 for a breach by the charterers.
[13] *Tattersall* v. *National S.S. Co.* (1884) 12 Q.B.D. 297.
[14] *Giertsen* v. *Turnbull,* 1908 S.C. 1101.
[15] *Steel & Craig* v. *State Line Co.,* supra; *Gilroy* v. *Price* (1892) 20 R. (H.L.) 1.
[16] *Klein* v. *Lindsay,* 1911 S.C. (H.L.) 9.

5. Lay-Days and Demurrage.—It is a common though not an invariable provision in charterparties that a certain number of days, known as lay-days, are allowed for loading and unloading, with a further provision for the payment of a fixed sum for a certain number of days after the lay-days have expired. The fixed sum is known as demurrage. Should the period of demurrage be exceeded damages for detention are due by the charterer, but where demurrage is not restricted to a certain fixed period of time any damages claimed by the shipowners for delay owing to the detention of the vessel in circumstances where the demurrage provisions apply must be restricted to the sum fixed by those provisions.[17] A provision for loading or unloading at a fixed rate per day is equivalent to a provision for lay-days, and has the same legal results.[18] Where the provision is for "days" or "running days" the period is calculated without considering whether the days are working days or not; the term "working days" excludes Sundays and holidays at the port.[19] The obligation to load or unload the ship within the lay-days is an absolute one, and demurrage will be due although the delay is due to causes beyond the control of the charterer. His only relevant defences are either that the delay was occasioned by the fault of the shipowner, or was due to some cause excepted in the charterparty.[20] But there can be no claim where the ship is totally destroyed.[21] It has been held in England that the charterer is in breach of contract if he fails to load within the lay-days,[22] disapproving the suggestion of Lord Trayner that days on demurrage are really lay-days which have to be paid for.[23] The lay-days do not begin to run until the ship has arrived, and is ready to load or discharge, as the case may be.[24] Where the charterparty contains no provisions for lay-days and demurrage the obligation of the charterer is merely to load within a time reasonable in the circumstances and in determining this any special causes of delay, such as a shortage of labour at the port, are to be taken into account.[25] He is, however, bound to have the cargo ready, and, in the absence of any express provisions in the charterparty, will be liable in damages for failure to do so, even although caused by circumstances beyond his control.[26]

---

[17] *Suisse Atlantique Société d'Armement Maritime S.A.* v. *N.V. Rotterdamsche Kolen Centrale* [1967] 1 A.C. 361, where the House of Lords regarded the demurrage clause as an agreed damages clause.
[18] *Hansa* v. *Alexander,* 1919 S.C. (H.L.) 122.
[19] *Holman* v. *Peruvian Nitrate Co.* (1878) 5 R. 657.
[20] *Hansa* v. *Alexander,* supra; *Reardon Smith Line* v. *Ministry of Agriculture, Food and Fisheries* [1963] A.C. 691, where the whole question is extensively reviewed; *Tramp Shipping Corp.* v. *Greenwich Marine Incorp.* [1975] 1 W.L.R. 1042. A contractual provision that time spent treating the ship's holds shall not count cannot be relied upon where such treatment takes place after the permitted lay-days: *Dias Compania Naviera S.A.* v. *Louis Dreyfus Corp.* [1978] 1 W.L.R. 261.
[21] *A/S Gulnes* v. *I.C.I.* [1938] 1 All E.R. 24.
[22] *Aktieselskabet Reidar* v. *Arcos* [1927] 1 K.B. 352.
[23] *Lilly* v. *Stevenson* (1895) 22 R. 278.
[24] For decisions as to when a ship has arrived, see Scrutton, *Charterparties* (18th ed.), pp. 133–141; *E.L. Oldendorff & Co. G.m.b.H.* v. *Tradax Export S.A.* [1974] A.C. 479; *Federal Commerce and Navigation Co. Ltd.* v. *Tradax Export S.A.* [1978] A.C. 1.
[25] *Rickinson* v. *Scottish Co-operative Society,* 1918 S.C. 440.
[26] *Ardan S.S. Co.* v. *Weir* (1905) 7 F. (H.L.) 126.

6. Obligations of Shipowner.—The obligation of the shipowner is to have the ship ready to load at the time fixed by the charterparty, or, if no time be fixed, within a reasonable time, unless prevented by causes specified in the contract. If delay is caused by an excepted cause, as for example by the perils of the sea, the shipowner has not committed a breach of contract, yet the delay may be so great as to amount to frustration of the adventure, and to entitle the charterer to declare the contract at an end.[27] As this is a question of degree it is common to provide a clause, known as a cancelling clause, giving the charterer the option to declare the contract at an end if the ship is not ready to load by a certain date.[28] If the failure of the ship to arrive is due to the fault of the shipowner he is liable in damages.[29]

7. Dead Freight.—A charterer is usually taken bound to provide a full and complete cargo. Failure to do so, or in any case to provide the amount and kind[30] of cargo agreed upon, involves liability for dead freight, which is a payment in compensation for the stow-room left empty. If not fixed in amount by the charterparty it is, in the case where the whole cargo is loaded by one charterer, the difference between the freight actually earned and the freight that would have been earned had the whole cargo been provided; in a general ship it has to be calculated under deduction of any expense saved to the shipowner, and of any sums he has received, or might have received, from carrying the goods of third parties.[31]

8. Cesser Clause.—A clause, known as the cesser clause, is commonly inserted in charterparties, whereby the charterer's liability under the contract ceases when the goods are put on board, and the shipowner's lien over the goods, which at common law only covers the freight, is extended to cover claims for dead freight and demurrage. This clause, unless expressed so as plainly to cover all grounds of liability, will not exempt the charterer from claims where his exemption would leave the shipowner without any remedy, as in the case of detention at the port of loading beyond the days allowed on demurrage.[32]

9. Freight Pro Rata Itineris.—As a general rule no freight is due unless and until the goods arrive at their destination. But if the voyage be interrupted by causes beyond the control of the shipowner, and the party entitled to the goods chooses to take delivery at some intermediate place, having the option to have the goods forwarded to their destination, he comes under an implied obligation to make a payment, estimated as a proportionate part of the freight

---

[27] *Jackson* v. *Union Marine Insurance Co.* (1874) L.R. 10 C.P. 125.
[28] See, e.g. *The Mihalis Angelos* [1971] 1 Q.B. 164.
[29] *Nelson* v. *Dundee East Coast Shipping Co.,* 1907 S.C. 927; *Monroe* v. *Ryan* [1935] 2 K.B. 28.
[30] *Angfartygs A/B* v. *Price & Pierce* [1939] 3 All E.R. 672.
[31] *McLean & Hope* v. *Fleming* (1871) 9 M. (H.L.) 38; *Henderson* v. *Turnbull,* 1909 S.C. 510.
[32] *Gardiner* v. *Macfarlane* (1889) 16 R. 658; *Salvesen* v. *Guy* (1885) 13 R. 85; and see *Hill S.S. Co.* v. *Hugo Stinnes,* 1941 S.C. 324 (charterparty with cesser clause; charterer named as shipper in bill of lading); *Overseas Transportation Co.* v. *Mineralimportexport: The Sinoe* [1972] 1 Lloyd's Rep. 201.

and known as freight pro rata itineris.[33] To found a claim of this character there must be circumstances from which it may be inferred that the cargo owner dispenses with further carriage; the mere fact that he has accepted the goods at an intermediate port, when he had no option in the matter, is not enough to infer any liability.[34]

10. Advance Freight.—It is sometimes provided in a charterparty that the freight, or an instalment thereof, shall be paid in advance. The Scottish Courts, disagreeing with the English rule, but agreeing with the commercial law of other countries, have held that if the voyage cannot be accomplished the amount paid as advance freight may be recovered.[35]

11. Primage: Petty Average.—In addition to freight the usual form of a charterparty or bill of lading contains an obligation to pay primage and petty average, fixed as a certain percentage on the freight. Primage was originally a payment made to the master of the ship for his care of the goods.[36] Petty average, to be distinguished from particular and general average,[37] is a percentage on the freight in place of certain customary charges for towage and beaconage.[38]

12. Charterparty followed by Bill of Lading.—A contract of charterparty may be, and usually is, followed by a bill of lading when the goods are put on board. If there is any discrepancy between the terms of the charterparty and the bill of lading, and the question raised is between shipowner and charterer, the charterparty is the ruling instrument and the bill of lading is regarded as a mere receipt.[39] Thus where the charterparty contained a provision exempting the shipowner from loss resulting from the negligence of master or crew, and no such provision appeared in the bill of lading, it was held that the shipowner was entitled to found on the negligence clause in a question with the charterer or with a party for whom he was acting as agent.[40] But this, which is the general rule, will yield to proof (which may be by parole evidence) that the parties intended to vary their contract by the bill of lading.[41] From the definition of "contract of carriage" in the Carriage of Goods by Sea Act 1971,[42] it would appear that the rules relating to bills of lading and contracts thereunder which are provided by that Act do not apply to cases where the

---

[33] Bell, *Prin.*, § 425. *The Soblomsten* (1886) L.R. 1 Ad. & Ecc. 293.
[34] *The Iolo* [1916] P. 206.
[35] *Watson* v. *Shankland* (1871) 10 M. 142; affd. (1873) 11 M. (H.L.) 51. See also *Cantiere San Rocco* v. *Clyde Shipbuilding Co.*, 1923 S.C. (H.L.) 105.
[36] See *Howitt* v. *Paul, Sword & Co.* (1877) 5 R. 321.
[37] See General Average, Ch. XXXII, infra.
[38] Bell, *Comm.*, I, 614.
[39] *President of India* v. *Metcalfe Shipping Co.* [1970] 1 Q.B. 289. Where the question (as to the operation of a cesser clause) was between the owner and the charterer, qua shipper, it was held that the bill of lading ruled; *Hill S.S. Co.* v. *Hugo Stinnes*, 1941 S.C. 324.
[40] *Delaurier* v. *Wyllie* (1889) 17 R. 167; *Rodocanachi* v. *Milburn* (1886) 18 Q.B.D. 67. The rule is questioned in Scrutton, *Charterparties* (18th ed.), p. 59 et seq.
[41] *Davidson* v. *Bisset* (1878) 5 R. 706.
[42] See § 15, infra.

charterparty is the ruling contract but the charterparty may contain a clause paramount embodying these rules.[43] Where the bill of lading has been indorsed and the question is between the shipowner and the indorsee the contract is that contained in the bill of lading and not that contained in the charterparty.[44] And a mere reference to the charterparty, e.g. "other conditions as per charter," is construed as importing only conditions affecting the consignee at the port of discharge, not as introducing into the bill of lading an exemption from the consequences of negligence which is to be found in the charterparty.[45] It lies on the charterer to see that bills of lading are not signed in terms inconsistent with the charterparty, and he will be liable to relieve the shipowner should the latter in consequence incur liability to an indorsee.[46]

13. Bill of Lading.—A bill of lading is the normal document under which goods are carried in a general ship. It may be considered here in its aspects as a receipt for the goods and as a contract of carriage, its remaining aspect, as a symbol of the goods, being considered elsewhere.[47]

14. Bill of Lading as Receipt.—In its ordinary form a bill of lading is signed by the master of a ship, acknowledges receipt of the goods, and contains an undertaking to deliver them to the shipper, or his assigns by indorsement. When in the hands of an indorsee for valuable consideration the bill of lading is conclusive evidence that the goods have been shipped in a question with the master or other person who has signed it, unless the holder had notice when he received the bill of lading that the goods were not in fact shipped, or unless the master can prove that the mis-statement in the bill of lading was due to the fraud of the shipper.[48] But as the master has no authority to sign for goods not in fact shipped the statement in the bill of lading is not conclusive against the shipowner,[49] though it lays the onus of proof of non-shipment on him.[50] The Carriage of Goods by Sea Act 1971 provides that the carrier[51] must, on the demand of the shipper, furnish a bill of lading stating (a) the leading marks for identification of the goods; (b) either the number of packages, or the quantity, or weight, as furnished in writing by the shipper; (c) the apparent order and condition of the goods, with the proviso that there is no obligation to state any marks, number, quantity or weight which the master has reasonable ground for believing not to be

[43] *Adamastos Shipping Co.* v. *Anglo-Saxon Petroleum Co.* [1959] A.C. 133.
[44] But see *President of India* v. *Metcalfe Shipping Co.,* supra.
[45] *Delaurier* v. *Wyllie,* supra; cf. *The Annefield* [1971] P. 168.
[46] *Kruger* v. *Moel Tryvan Co.* [1907] A.C. 272.
[47] See Rights in Security, Ch. XX: § 19.
[48] Bills of Lading Act 1855 (18 & 19 Vict., c. 111), s. 3.
[49] *McLean & Hope* v. *Fleming* (1871) 9 M. (H.L.) 38; *Immanuel (Owners of)* v. *Denholm* (1887) 15 R. 152.
[50] *Smith* v. *Bedouin Steam Navigation Co.* (1895) 23 R. (H.L.) 1.
[51] "Carrier" is defined in article I of the Schedule as including the owner or the charterer who enters into a contract of carriage with the shipper.

accurate, or which he has no reasonable means of checking.[52] The shipper is deemed to have guaranteed the accuracy of the information furnished by him, and is bound to indemnify the carrier for any loss, damages or expenses resulting from its inaccuracy.[53] The bill of lading is prima facie evidence of the receipt by the carrier of the goods as therein described, but, if the bill is transferred to a third party acting in good faith, proof to the contrary is not admissible.[54]

15. Bill of Lading as Contract.—The incidents of a bill of lading as a contract of carriage are now largely regulated by the provisions of the Carriage of Goods by Sea Act 1971. It supplies rules, which are to have effect in relation to and in connection with the carriage of goods by sea in ships where the port of shipment is a port in the United Kingdom,[55] or where goods[56] are carried between ports in two different states and either the bill of lading is issued in a contracting state, or the carriage is from a port in a contracting state, or the bill of lading provides that the rules or legislation of any state giving effect to them are to govern the contract.[57] A "contract of carriage" is defined as applying only "to contracts of carriage covered by a bill of lading or any similar document of title, in so far as such document relates to the carriage of goods by sea, including any bill of lading or any similar document as aforesaid, issued under or pursuant to a charterparty from the moment at which such bill of lading or similar document of title regulates the relations between a carrier and a holder of the same."[58] In a contract of carriage, as thus defined, there is no warranty that the ship is seaworthy, though the carrier is bound to exercise due diligence (a) to make the ship seaworthy; (b) properly to man, equip and supply the ship; (c) to make the holds, refrigerating and cool chambers, and all other parts in which goods are carried fit and safe.[59] When loss or damage has resulted from unseaworthiness the burden of proving the exercise of due diligence lies on the carrier.[60] The carrier does not discharge this obligation merely by showing that he exercised reasonable care in the selection of an independent contractor to render the ship seaworthy.[61]

16. Claims for Injury to Goods.—The 1971 Act makes provision as to the effect of the receipt and removal of the goods. Unless notice in writing of loss or damage is given by the person entitled to receive the goods at the port of

---

[52] 1971 Act, Sched., art. III, rule 3.
[53] Carriage of Goods by Sea Act 1971 (c. 19), Sched., article III. See *Attorney-General of Ceylon* v. *Scindia Steam Navigation Co.* [1962] A.C. 60.
[54] Article III, rule 4.
[55] As to live animals and deck cargo, see 1971 Act, s. 1 (7); Sched., art. I (c).
[56] 1971 Act, s. 1 (3).
[57] 1971 Act, s. 1 (6) (a); Sched., art. X. For current contracting states, see the Carriage of Goods by Sea (Parties to Convention) Order 1978 (S.I. 1978 No. 1885).
[58] Schedule, Article I.; *Harland & Wolff* v. *Burns and Laird Lines,* 1931 S.C. 722.
[59] Carriage of Goods by Sea Act 1971, s. 3, Sched., Article III; cf. *Riverstone Meat Co. Pty.* v. *Lancashire Shipping Co.* [1961] A.C. 807.
[60] Ibid., Sched., article IV.
[61] *Riverstone Meat,* supra.

discharge prior to their removal, or, if the damage be not apparent, within three days, their removal is prima facie evidence of their delivery in the state described in the bill of lading. Such notice need not be given if the state of the goods has been at the time of their receipt the subject of joint survey or inspection. In any event the carrier is discharged from all liability in respect of loss or damage unless suit is brought within one year after delivery of the goods or the date when the goods should have been delivered.[62] However the parties may agree to extend the period after the cause of action has arisen. An action for indemnity against a third person may be brought even after the expiry of the year, provided that the action is not time-barred by the lex fori.[63]

17. Exemption from and Exclusion of Liability.—Where carriage is effected under a bill of lading,[64] the Carriage of Goods by Sea Act 1971 provides that neither the carrier[65] nor the ship shall be liable for injury resulting from the undernoted causes,[66] nor in certain circumstances for loss of or damage to goods which were dangerous.[67] Nor is the carrier liable for loss of or damage to goods if the shipper knowingly mis-stated the nature or value of the goods in the bill of lading.[68] Other exemptions from liability under the 1971 Act have already been mentioned.[69] The Merchant Shipping Act 1894,[70] s. 502, as amended by the Merchant Shipping (Liability of Shipowners and Others) Act 1958,[71] provides that a shipowner[72] is not responsible for damage by fire

---

[62] Carriage of Goods by Sea Act 1971 (c. 19), Sched., article III, rule 6. See *Aries Tanker Corp.* v. *Total Transport* [1977] 1 W.L.R. 185.

[63] 1971 Act, Sched., Art. III, rule 6 bis. The lex fori must allow at least three months from the date when the pursuer settled the claim or was served with process in the action against him.

[64] Or possibly a receipt: Carriage of Goods by Sea Act 1971 (c. 19), s. 1 (6) (*b*).

[65] As to his servants or agents, see 1971 Act, Sched., Art IV bis.

[66] 1971 Act, Sched., art. IV, rule 2; "(a) Act, neglect or default of the master, mariner, pilot or the servants of the carrier in the navigation or in the management of the ship. (b) Fire, unless caused by the actual fault or privity of the carrier. (c) Perils, dangers and accidents of the sea or other navigable waters. (d) Act of God. (e) Act of war. (f) Act of public enemies. (g) Arrest or restraint of princes, rulers or people, or seizure under legal process. (h) Quarantine restrictions. (i) Act or omission of the shipper or owner of the goods, his agent or representative. (j) Strikes or lock-outs or stoppage or restraint of labour from whatever cause, whether partial or general. (k) Riots and civil commotions. (l) Saving or attempting to save life or property at sea. (m) Wastage in bulk or weight or any other loss or damage arising from inherent defect, quality or vice of the goods. (n) Insufficiency of packing. (o) Insufficiency or inadequacy of marks. (p) Latent defects not discoverable by due diligence. (q) Any other cause arising without the actual fault or privity of the carrier, or without the fault or neglect of the agents or servants of the carrier, but the burden of proof shall be on the person claiming the benefit of this exception to show that neither the actual fault or privity of the carrier nor the fault or neglect of the agents or servants of the carrier contributed to the loss or damage." The term "in the navigation or in the management of the ship" in (a) supra has been construed in England as limited to navigation, as distinguished from care of the cargo. Thus it does not cover defective stowage, *Gosse Millard* v. *Canadian Marine, etc. Co.* [1929] A.C. 223 but see *Ismail* v. *Polish Ocean Lines* [1976] Q.B. 893; nor failure in refrigerating machinery, *Foreman & Ellams* v. *Federal Steam Navigation Co.* [1928] 2 K.B. 424. See *Albacora S.R.L.* v. *Westcott and Laurence Line*, 1966 S.C. (H.L.) 19 (note the doubt cast upon *Gosse Millard*, supra) and *Leesh River Tea Co.* v. *British India S.N. Co.* [1967] 2 Q.B. 250.

[67] 1971 Act, Sched., art. IV, rule 6.

[68] Ibid., rule 5 (*h*).

[69] §§ 15, 16, supra.

[70] (57 & 58 Vict., c. 60). The provision is to be replaced by Merchant Shipping Act 1979 (c. 39), s. 18.

[71] (6 & 7 Eliz. II., c. 62).

[72] Or charterer or any person interested in or in possession of the ship, and in particular any manager or operator of her: 1958 Act, s. 3.

occurring without his actual fault or privity,[73] nor for theft of gold, silver, watches or precious stones, unless the owner or shipper has, at the time of shipping, inserted in the bill of lading, or declared in writing, the nature and value of the article.[74]

A clause in a bill of lading excluding liability in any manner other than that permitted by the Carriage of Goods by Sea Act 1971 is void.[75] Where carriage is effected under a receipt,[76] the parties may agree on any terms which are not contrary to public policy.[77] A clause in a charterparty or in a contract for the carriage of goods by ship may be void if it excludes liability for death or personal injury, or may be unenforceable if one contracting party is a consumer and it was unfair and unreasonable to incorporate the clause in the contract.[78] In a contract for the carriage by sea of passengers, a carrier cannot exclude liability for death or personal injury or loss of or damage to passengers' luggage occurring during the course of carriage and due to his own or his servants' or agents' fault or neglect.[79]

Non-contracting parties, such as stevedores, may benefit from a valid exclusion clause.[80]

18. Limitation of Liability.—Where a carrier is neither exempted nor excluded from liability, his liability may nevertheless be limited. The Carriage of Goods by Sea Act 1971 provides that, in the case of loss of, or damage to, goods carried under a bill of lading,[81] a carrier[82] shall not be liable beyond 10,000 gold francs[83] per package or unit,[84] or 30 gold francs per kilo of gross weight, whichever is the higher, unless the nature and value of the goods were declared by the shipper before shipment, and were inserted in the bill of lading.[85] A higher limit may be fixed by agreement.[86] Where a carrier and his servants or agents are sued, the aggregate amount recoverable cannot exceed

[73] See, e.g. *Dreyfus* v. *Tempus Shipping Co.* [1931] A.C. 726.
[74] s. 502 is unaltered by the Carriage of Goods by Sea Act 1971. See 1971 Act, s. 6 (4); Sched., art. VIII.
[75] 1971 Act, Sched., art. III, rule 8. However, the carrier may validly contract to surrender his own rights and immunities under the 1971 Act: Sched., art. V.
[76] A non-negotiable instrument, marked as such, used in cases where shipments are not of an ordinary commercial character made in the ordinary course of trade: 1971 Act, Sched., art. VI.
[77] Ibid.: subject, however, to the Unfair Contract Terms Act 1977.
[78] Unfair Contract Terms Act 1977 (c. 50), ss. 15 (3), 16, 25.
[79] 1977 Act, s. 28.: cf. article 3 of the Athens Convention relating to the Carriage of Passengers and their Luggage by Sea, 1974.
[80] *New Zealand Shipping Company* v. *A. M. Satterthwaite & Co.; The Eurymedon* [1975] A.C. 154.
[81] Or possibly a receipt: 1971 Act, s. 1 (6) (*b*).
[82] As to his servants or agents, see 1971 Act, Sched., Art. IV bis.
[83] "Franc" is defined in the 1971 Act, Sched., art. IV, rule 5 (*d*). The latest sterling equivalents order is the Merchant Shipping (Sterling Equivalents) (Various Enactments) Order 1978 (No. 1468). It is the exchange rate at the date of decree which is relevant: *The Abadesa (No. 2)* [1968] P. 656; *West* v. *Ritchie* [1969] 1 Lloyd's Rep. 511. The total amount recoverable is calculated by reference to the value of the goods at the place and time where in terms of the contract the goods were or should have been discharged: 1971 Act, Sched., art. IV, rule 5 (*b*) and (*c*).
[84] If the number of packages or units packed in a container, pallet or similar article is stated in the bill of lading, that number is deemed the number of packages or units for purposes of limitation; otherwise the article of transport is considered the package or unit: art. IV, rule 5 (*c*).
[85] 1971 Act, Sched., art. IV, rule 5 (*a*).
[86] Ibid., rule 5 (*g*). But any restriction clause not permitted by the Act is void: art. III, rule 8.

the specified limits.[87] However, the carrier cannot benefit from the limitation provisions where it is proved that the loss or damage resulted from an act or omission of the carrier, done with intent to cause damage, or recklessly with knowledge that damage would probably result.[88] The Merchant Shipping Act 1894, s. 503[89] as amended, provides that a shipowner's liability for loss of life or personal injury[90] is limited to 3,100 gold francs[91] per ton of the ship's tonnage, and his liability for any other loss or damage[90] is limited to 1,000 gold francs per ton, provided that the loss, injury or damage occurred without the owner's actual fault or privity.[92]

In a contract for the carriage by sea of passengers and their luggage, a carrier may limit his liability for death or personal injury to passengers to 700,000 gold francs[93] per passenger, and from 12,500 to 50,000 gold francs in respect of loss of or damage to luggage. The carrier may not rely on a limitation clause where the loss, injury or damage resulted from an act or omission done with intent to cause damage, or recklessly with knowledge that damage would probably result.[94]

19. Deviation.—At common law a contract of carriage by sea implied a warranty that the carrier would not deviate from the prescribed course, or, where no course was prescribed, from that usual and customary.[95] Deviation was excused in order to save life, not in order to save property.[96] It was also excused if necessary for the repair of ship or cargo,[97] or if due to the unseaworthiness of the ship,[98] or to credible information of some imminent danger on the proper course.[99] The result of deviation if not so justified, was to displace the contract, and, consequently, to render the shipowner liable for any injury to the cargo, though arising from a cause excepted in the charterparty, and although the loss occurred after the proper course had been resumed.[1] The shipowner could plead in defence, when the loss occurred from

---

87 1971 Act, Sched., art. IV bis, rule 3.
88 1971 Act, Sched., art. IV, rule 5 (e).
89 To be replaced by Merchant Shipping Act 1979 (c. 39), s. 17, Sched. 4.
90 i.e. any loss, injury or damage occurring on board ship; or if not on board ship, arising as a result of improper navigation or management of the ship, or as a result of an act or omission of any person on board ship, or arising from the loading, carriage or discharge of cargo, or the embarkation, carriage or disembarkation of passengers: s. 503. See for example *The Tojo Maru* [1972] A.C. 242.
91 "Franc" is defined in s. 1 (2) of the 1958 Act; cf. note 83 supra and S.I. 1978 No. 1468.
92 s. 503 is unaltered by the Carriage of Goods by Sea Act 1971: see 1971 Act, Sched., art. VIII. The question of actual fault or privity arose in *Dreyfus* v. *Tempus Shipping Co.,* supra; *The Norman* [1960] 1 Lloyd's Rep. 1; *The Lady Gwendolen* [1965] P. 294; *Groen* v. *The England (Owners)* [1973] 1 Lloyd's Rep. 373. See also *The Annie Hay* [1968] P. 341 (owner/master).
93 See S.I. 1978 No. 1468.
94 Unfair Contract Terms Act 1977 (c. 50), s. 28; cf. arts. 7 and 8 of the Athens Convention, 1974. The Convention will have the force of law when the Merchant Shipping Act 1979 (c. 39), s. 14 and Sched. 3 come into force. The sums expressed in francs will be expressed in terms of the Special Drawing Right defined by the International Monetary Fund.
95 Bell, *Prin.,* § 408; Scrutton, *Charterparties* (18th ed.), p. 257.
96 *Scaramanga* v. *Stamp* (1880) 5 C.D.P. 295.
97 *Phelps* v. *Hill* [1891] 1 Q.B. 605.
98 *Kish* v. *Taylor* [1912] A.C. 604.
99 *The Teutonia* (1872) L.R. 4 C.P. 171.
1 *Thorley* v. *Orchis Co.* [1907] 1 K.B. 660; *Hain S.S. Co.* v. *Tate & Lyle* (1936) 41 Com. Cas. 350. See *Lord Polwarth* v. *N.B.R.,* 1908 S.C. 1275 (land carriage).

the Act of God, of the Queen's enemies, or from the inherent vice of the goods carried, that the loss would have occurred even if no deviation had taken place.[2] The law is so far modified by the Carriage of Goods by Sea Act 1971,[3] that, in cases to which the Rules under that Act apply, deviation in saving or attempting to save property at sea, or any reasonable deviation,[4] shall not be deemed an infringement of those Rules or of the contract of carriage, and the carrier shall not be liable for any loss or damage resulting therefrom. In circumstances where the contract of carriage has been held to be displaced by the deviation of the ship, the question arises of the freight that may be claimed by the shipowner on completion of the voyage, when no damage has been caused to the cargo. A claim for freight on the principle of quantum meruit appears possible.[5]

20. Delivery of Goods.—At the conclusion of the voyage the carrier is bound to deliver the goods to the holder of the bill of lading. In the absence of any provision to the contrary the actual work of unloading falls to be done by the carrier or at his expense.[6] In any question as to injury to the goods they are to be regarded as delivered as soon as they pass over the ship's side and are received by porters employed by the consignee.[7] As bills of lading are commonly made out in sets of three, with a provision that on one being accomplished the others are to stand void, it is possible for the shipper fraudulently to indorse copies of the bill of lading to different indorsees, and thus to raise competing titles. The shipmaster, if he has no notice of any competing right, is entitled to deliver the goods to the first party presenting a bill of lading; if he has notice, he must select the true owner at his peril, or refuse delivery.[8] Delivery in these circumstances does not affect the ownership of the goods, which vests in the first indorsee of the bill of lading.[9] Should a party alleging right to the goods be unable to produce the bill of lading, as in cases where it has been lost or has not reached the consignee at the time when the ship arrives, the master's duty is either to deliver the goods on receiving a guarantee against any possible liability, or else to unload them and place them in a warehouse. Should he unreasonably refuse to take either course nothing can be recovered for the consequent detention of the ship.[10]

21. Warehousing.—If the goods are not claimed on arrival, or if the holder of the bill of lading fails to pay the freight, the shipmaster is at common law entitled, after waiting for a reasonable time, to warehouse the goods under

---

[2] *Morrison* v. *Shaw Savill, etc., Co.* [1916] 2 K.B. 783.
[3] Sched., article IV., rule 4.
[4] *Stag Line* v. *Foscolo Mango & Co.* [1932] A.C. 328.
[5] See *Hain, supra.*
[6] *Ballantyne* v. *Paton*, 1912 S.C. 246.
[7] *Knight S.S. Co.* v. *Fleming Douglas & Co.* (1898) 25 R. 1010.
[8] *Glyn Mills & Co.* v. *East & West India Dock Co.* (1882) 7 App.Cas. 591; delivery will not decide ownership: *Pirie* v. *Warden* (1871) 9 M. 523.
[9] *Barber* v. *Meyerstein* (1870) L.R. 4 H.L. 317; *Pirie* v. *Warden, supra.*
[10] *Carlberg* v. *Wemyss Co.*, 1915 S.C. 616.

reservation of his lien for freight.[11] This right is commonly expressly conferred in the bill of lading. Statutory provisions apply to the case of ships arriving from a foreign port.[12] In that case if the owner of the goods fails to make entry[13] thereof, or to take delivery at the time fixed in the charterparty, bill of lading or agreement, or, if no time has been fixed, within seventy-two hours (exclusive of Sundays and holidays) after the ship is reported, the shipowner may place the goods in a warehouse under lien for the freight. They may then be detained both for freight and for warehouse rent. Ninety days afterwards, in the event of no payment being made, the warehouse-keeper on the demand of the shipowner is bound to sell the goods by auction, after advertisement and notice to the owner of the goods, if his address be known. He has also a discretionary power to sell perishable goods at any time. The proceeds, after payment of the warehouse rent and the shipowner's charges in respect of the goods, are to be paid to their owner.

   22. Liability for Freight.—A charterer, or the shipper of goods under a bill of lading, is liable for the freight, unless his liability is excluded by a cesser clause. The Bills of Lading Act 1855 provides (s. 1): "Every consignee of goods named in a bill of lading and every endorsee of a bill of lading to whom the property in the goods therein mentioned shall pass, upon or by reason of such consignment or endorsement, shall . . . be subject to the same liabilities in respect of such goods as if the contract contained in the bill of lading had been made with himself."[14] In the construction of this section it has been held in England that where the bill of lading was indorsed with the intention to create a security, and the indorsee had not taken possession of the goods, he had incurred no liability for freight, on the ground that he had obtained only a special property in the goods, and not the property in them as referred to in the Act.[15] But as the distinction between "special property" and "property" is not recognised in the law of Scotland, the application of this decision seems doubtful.[16] Any holder of the bill of lading, whether the property has passed to him or not, incurs liability for freight if he takes possession of the goods, on the principle that the shipowner must be presumed to have relinquished his lien in return for the obligation of the party to whom he delivers the goods.[17] A seller who stops in transitu, even although he does not take possession of the goods, becomes liable for the freight though the contract of carriage has been made by the buyer.[18] Should the full cargo, as stated in the bill of lading, not be forthcoming at the port of discharge, the shipowner is entitled to freight only for what he has actually carried, but if the full freight has been

---

[11] Bell, *Comm.*, I, 605.
[12] Merchant Shipping Act 1894, ss. 492-501. See *Smailes* v. *Dessen* (1906) 12 Com. Cas. 117.
[13] i.e., the entry required by the customs laws to be made for the landing or discharge of goods from an importing ship (s. 492).
[14] 18 & 19 Vict., c. 111.
[15] *Sewell* v. *Burdick* (1884) 10 App.Cas. 74.
[16] See *Hayman* v. *McLintock*, 1970 S.C. 936, 949.
[17] *White* v. *Furness* [1895] A.C. 40.
[18] *Booth Co.* v. *Cargo Fleet Iron Co.* [1916] 2 K.B. 570.

paid he may set off a claim for dead freight in an action for repetition of the balance.[19]

23. Lien.—At common law a shipowner has a lien over the goods for freight, unless this is excluded by the terms of the contract, as where the freight was payable at a certain time after delivery,[20] or bills given for it were still current at the time when delivery was demanded.[21] Apart from express contract there is no lien for dead freight or demurrage.[22] Nor is there any lien for a general balance due to the shipowner on another account.[23]

24. Cargoes of Oil.—Ships carrying cargoes of oil in bulk are subject to special legislation.[24]

25. Hovercraft.—A hovercraft is a vehicle which is designed to be supported when in motion wholly or partly by air expelled from the vehicle to form a cushion of which the boundaries include the ground, water or other surface beneath the vehicle.[25] Many principles of maritime law have been made applicable to hovercraft.[26]

---

[19] *Henderson* v. *Turnbull*, 1909 S.C. 510.
[20] *Foster* v. *Colby* (1858) 3 H. & N. 705.
[21] *Tamvaco* v. *Simpson* (1866) L.R. 1 C.P. 363.
[22] *McLean & Hope* v. *Fleming* (1871) 9 M. (H.L.) 38.
[23] *Stevenson* v. *Likly* (1824) 3 S. 291.
[24] See, e.g. the Merchant Shipping (Oil Pollution) Act 1971 (c. 59); Prevention of Oil Pollution Act 1971 (c. 60); Merchant Shipping Act 1974 (c. 43); and relevant subordinate legislation.
[25] Hovercraft Act 1968 (c. 59), s. 4 (1).
[26] See, e.g. the Hovercraft (Civil Liability) Order 1971 (No. 720), applying, with modifications, principles of maritime law to the carriage of goods by hovercraft. The Hovercraft (Application of Enactments) Order 1972 (No. 971) also applies to hovercraft a number of enactments relating to ships.

CHAPTER XXXI

CARRIAGE BY AIR

McNair, *Law of the Air* (3rd ed., 1964); Shawcross and Beaumont, *Air Law* (4th ed. 1977)

1. General.—As will be seen in the chapter on Landownership, property in land extends "a coelo usque and centrum," so that in strictness the passage of aircraft over a man's land is a trespass. Since, however, the maintenance of such a rule would largely defeat travel by air, the owner's rights have been restricted by a statutory provision to the effect that no action shall lie in respect of trespass or nuisance by reason only of the passage of aircraft at a reasonable height above the ground, provided that the statutory requirements have been complied with.[1]

The law relating to the use of the air has developed rapidly.[2] While largely statutory, some common law principles apply. Thus the ordinary principles of reparation have been resorted to.[3] Similarly an air carrier might in some circumstances be held to be a common carrier, although as indicated below the possibility seems remote.[4] This Chapter outlines some of the more important rules specifically relating to carriage by air.

2. The Aircraft and the Outsider.—The concession already noted as having been made by section 40 (1) of the Civil Aviation Act 1949 is in respect of the bare fact of flight over another's property and that only at a reasonable height. But where actual damage is done by an aircraft, or anyone in it, to person or property on land or water, the owner is liable without proof of fault except in the case of contributory negligence.[5] An owner who has paid damages on account of the wrongful act of someone in the aircraft may recover from him the amount which he has paid.[6] In the case of a demise of the aircraft for more than fourteen days the person to whom the demise is made bears the responsibility in place of the owner.[7] Dangerous flying is discouraged by heavy penalties.[8] The potentialities of injury to others possessed by aircraft are obviously great and the legislature has made provisions for lessening them. Thus, for example, an aircraft is bound to be registered, to bear the proper marks, to hold a certificate of "airworthiness,"

---

[1] Civil Aviation Act 1949, s. 40 (1). See *Cubitt* v. *Gower* (1973) 47 Ll. L. Rep. 65; *Bernstein* v. *Skyviews and General* [1977] 3 W.L.R. 136.
[2] Shawcross and Beaumont, *Air Law* (4th ed.) provides in Vol. 2 a useful noter-up.
[3] See for example *Fosbroke-Hobbes* v. *Airwork* [1937] 1 All E.R. 108, where the doctrine of res ipsa loquitur was applied to the negligent handling of an aeroplane; Shawcross and Beaumont, op cit. paras. 87 et seq.
[4] *Aslan* v. *Imperial Airways* (1933) 49 T.L.R. 415; Shawcross and Beaumont, op. cit., paras, 380 et seq.; McNair, *Law of the Air* (3rd ed.), pp. 138–144.
[5] Civil Aviation Act 1949, s. 40 (2).
[6] Ibid.
[7] s. 49 (2).
[8] s. 11.

to have a certified and licensed crew, and to carry certain papers.[9] Similarly an air transport licence is required where an aircraft is used for the carriage for reward of passengers or cargo.[10] However the law imposes no statutory obligation upon the owner of aircraft to insure against third party risks.[11] Noise, vibration, and other pollution from aircraft is regulated by statute.[12]

The analogy of the law of sea-transport has been and will probably continue to be influential in the development of the law of the air. Examples are the law relating to wreck, the salvage of life or property, and in particular allowing to the owner of aircraft a reasonable reward for salvage services.[13] The Act gives power to make rules prescribing signals of distress and urgency in the case of seaplanes on the surface of the water and for the prevention of collisions between seaplanes on the water and vessels and seaplanes on the water.[14] The general regulations applying to lights, signals and the rule of the air generally will be found in the Schedule to the Rules of the Air and Air Traffic Control Regulations 1976.[15]

3. Aircraft as Carrier.—At common law the liability of the carrier of goods depends on whether he is a common carrier or not.[16] If he is, he is liable for loss of or damage to the goods without proof of fault; if he is not, fault must be proved. In either case he has no liability for injury to passengers except on proof of fault.[17] It has been held that there is no common law obligation to supply an "airworthy" aircraft.[18] However the common law has been superseded in both international and non-international carriage by the provisions of the Convention of Warsaw, as applied by the Carriage by Air Act 1961,[19] the Carriage by Air (Supplementary Provisions) Act 1962,[20] and the Carriage by Air Acts (Application of Provisions) Order 1967.[21] Moreover each airline has detailed conditions of contract.[22] The result is that the

[9] Air Navigation Order 1976 (S.I. 1976 No. 1783), as amended (the latest amendment being S.I. 1978 No. 284), and Air Navigation (General) Regulations 1976 (S.I. 1976 No. 1982), as amended (the latest amendment being S.I. 1978 No. 873).
[10] Civil Aviation Act 1971 (c. 75), s. 21 et seq; see too the Civil Aviation Authority Regulations 1972 (S.I. 1972 No. 178); *Corner* v. *Clayton* [1976] 1 W.L.R. 800.
[11] Compulsory third party insurance in relation to aircraft was the subject of two conventions at Rome, one in 1933 and one in 1952. The United Kingdom intended to give effect to the 1933 Convention but never did so, and the enabling legislation has been repealed. (Ss. 43–46, 49 (1) and Schedule 6 of the Civil Aviation Act 1949 were repealed by the Companies Act 1967, s. 128; and ss. 42, 48, and 50, and Schedule 5 of the 1949 Act were repealed by the Civil Aviation Act 1968, s. 26).
[12] See for example s. 19 of the Civil Aviation Act 1968 (c. 61), s. 29 of the Civil Aviation Act 1971 (c.75) as amended.
[13] s. 51.
[14] s. 52.
[15] S.I. 1976 No. 1983 (the latest amendment being S.I. 1978 No. 877); cf. *Dickson* v. *Miln*, 1969 J. C. 75.
[16] See Carriage by Land, Ch. XXIX., § 1.
[17] See Carriage by Land, Ch. XXIX., § 3. *Chisholm* v. *British European Airways* [1963] 1 Lloyd's Rep. 626.
[18] *Aslan* v. *Imperial Airways* (1933) 49 T.L.R. 415. See Carriage by Sea, Ch. XXX, § 4.
[19] c. 27, as amended by the Prescription and Limitation (Scotland) Act 1973 (c. 52), Sched. 4.
[20] c. 43.
[21] S.I. 1967 No. 480, as amended by S.I. 1969 No. 1083.
[22] See for example the passenger ticket conditions and the air waybills conditions to be used by airlines who are members of the International Air Transport Association; Shawcross and Beaumont, op cit, paras. 373–375.

likelihood of an airline or aircraft operator ever being regarded as a common carrier must be considered very remote.

4. International Carriage.—The Convention of Warsaw[23] applies only to "international carriage," which is defined as "any carriage in which according to the contract made by the parties the place of departure and the place of destination... are situated either within the territories of two High Contracting Parties or within the territory of a single High Contracting Party, if there is an agreed stopping place within" the territory of another state,[24] even if that state is not a High Contracting Party.[25] Carriage between two points within the territory of a single High Contracting Party without an agreed stopping place in another state is not international carriage. The carrier must hand over the appropriate document, i.e., passenger ticket, luggage ticket or air consignment note, and if he fails to do so cannot rely on the provisions which exclude or limit his liability.[26] He is liable in damages for death of or injury to a passenger by accident on board or in embarking or disembarking,[27] for loss of or damage to registered luggage or goods while in his charge on board or in an aerodrome,[28] and for any delay in the carriage of passengers, luggage or goods.[29] But he avoids liability if he proves that he and his agents[30] or servants have taken all "necessary measures"[31] to avoid the damage or that it was impossible for him or them to take such measures. This applies equally to passengers, luggage and cargo.[32] If there was contributory negligence the court may, according to its own law, exonerate him wholly or partly.[33] Unless by special contract a higher sum is agreed, liability for injury to a passenger is limited to 16,600 special drawing rights, for registered luggage and goods to 17 special drawing rights per kilogram and for hand luggage to 332 special drawing rights per passenger.[34] Any condition relieving the carrier of liability or fixing a lower limit is null.[35] The carrier cannot rely on provisions excluding or limiting his liability if the damage is caused by his own act or omission[36] or

---

[23] All references are to the 1961 Act and Schedule 1, setting out the amended Warsaw Convention. The 1967 Order sets out the unamended Warsaw Convention.

[24] art. 1. *Grein v. Imperial Airways Ltd.* [1937] 1 K.B. 50.

[25] For a list of the High Contracting Parties, see Carriage by Air (Parties to Convention) Order 1977 (S.I. 1977 No. 240); Carriage by Air (Parties to Convention) (Supplementary) Order 1977 (S.I. 1977 No. 1631); and Carriage by Air (Parties to Convention) (Supplementary) Order 1978 (S.I. 1978 No. 1058).

[26] art. 3–16; *Lisi* v. *Alitalia-Linee Aeree Italiane, S.P.A.* [1967] 1 Lloyd's Rep. 140; *Corocraft* v. *Pan American Airways* [1969] 1 Q.B. 616; *Ludecke* v. *Canadian Pacific Airlines* [1975] 2 Lloyd's Rep. 87; *Canadian Pacific Airlines* v. *Montreal Trust Co.* [1975] 2 Lloyd's Rep. 90.

[27] art. 17; 1961 Act, s. 3.

[28] art. 18; *Fothergill* v. *Monarch Airlines* [1978] Q.B. 108.

[29] art. 19.

[30] art. 20.

[31] This must mean "proper" or "reasonable." If he took all necessary measures, there would be no damage. See also *Rustenberg Platinum Mines* v. *Pan American World Airways* [1979] 1 Lloyd's Rep. 19.

[32] art. 20.

[33] art. 21.

[34] art. 22 as amended by Carriage by Air and Road Act 1979 (c. 28), s. 4. See *Samuel Montagu & Co.* v. *Swiss Air Transport Co.* [1966] 2 Q.B. 306.

[35] art. 23.

[36] Replacing the phrase "wilful misconduct" contained in the 1932 Act. See *Bastable* v. *N.B.R.*, 1912 S.C. 555.

that of any agent or servant acting within the scope of his employment, done with intent to cause harm or recklessly and with knowledge that damage would result.[37] The Unfair Contract Terms Act 1977,[38] while applying to contracts of carriage by air,[39] does not affect exclusion or limitation clauses authorised by an enactment such as the Carriage by Air Act 1961.[40] Complaint of damage to luggage must be made within seven days of delivery, of damage to cargo within fourteen and of delay within twenty-one of receipt by the carrier.[41] Any right to damages is lost if the action is not brought within two years.[42] Where carriage is performed by various successive carriers, each is subject to the Convention.[43] Where a carrier delegates performance of a contract to another[44] both are subject to the Convention, the former for the whole of the carriage contemplated in the agreement, the latter solely for the carriage which he performs.[45] The delegating carrier is vicariously liable for the acts and omissions of the actual carrier and of his servants and agents acting within the scope of their employment.[45]

5. Non-International Carriage.—The Warsaw Convention does not extend to internal carriage.[46] However, the Convention has been applied with modifications[47] to "non-international" carriage, by the Carriage by Air Acts (Application of Provisions) Order 1967.[48]

6. Protection for Air Passengers.—Air travel organisers (i.e. persons who make available or who hold themselves out as persons who may make available accommodation for the carriage of persons on aircraft) must be licensed.[49] An Air Travel Reserve Fund has been established to meet customers' losses when air travel organisers cannot meet their financial commitments.[50]

7. The Civil Aviation Authority.—The Civil Aviation Authority[51] is responsible for the licensing of air transport.[52] It has other important functions, including the registration of aircraft, air safety, the control of air traffic, the certification of aircraft operators and the licensing of air crews.[52] The Authority's objectives are to provide a safe but economic air transport service, to promote the United Kingdom air industry, to ensure that at least

[37] art. 25.
[38] c. 50.
[39] 1977 Act, s. 15 (2) (c).
[40] 1977 Act, s. 29.
[41] art. 26; *Fothergill* v. *Monarch Airlines* [1978] Q.B. 108.
[42] art. 29.
[43] art. 30.
[44] The "actual carrier".
[45] Carriage by Air (Supplementary Provisions) Act 1962 (c. 43), Schedule.
[46] See § 4, supra.
[47] For example arts. 3–16 (Ch. II) of the Convention do not apply to internal carriage. Also liability for injury to a passenger is limited to 875,000 francs: art. 22.
[48] S.I. 1967 No. 480 as amended by S.I. 1969 No. 1083; art. 4 and Schedule 1.
[49] Civil Aviation Act 1971 (c. 75) s. 26; Civil Aviation (Air Travel Organisers' Licensing) Regulations 1972 (S.I. 1972 No. 223), as amended by S.I. 1974 No. 1802, S.I. 1975 No. 1049.
[50] Air Travel Reserve Fund Act 1975 (c. 36).
[51] The Authority consists of 6 to 12 persons appointed by the Secretary of State for Trade: Civil Aviation Act 1971 (c. 75), s. 1.
[52] 1971 Act, s. 2.

one major British airline not controlled by British Airways participates in the air industry, and to further the reasonable interests of users of air transport services.[53] The Secretary of State may give the Authority written guidance with respect to the performance of its functions[54] although the Authority is neither a servant nor agent of the Crown.[55] The Secretary may also give the Authority directions.[56]

8. The Air Corporations.—On 1st April 1974 the British Overseas Airways Corporation and the British European Airways Corporation were dissolved and their property rights and liabilities vested in the British Airways Board.[57] The functions of the British Airways Board include the provision of air transport services and the promotion of related undertakings.[58] British Airways, although neither a servant nor agent of the Crown[59] is a nationalised industry dependent on the Department of Trade.[60] There are many independent airlines.[61]

As international carriage is regulated by the Warsaw Convention, little freedom of contract is conferred upon the airlines. Only when the statutory provisions are silent does the question of individual conditions arise, and even then the conditions may have been drafted to comply with standards, recommended practices, or standard conditions laid down by the International Civil Aviation Organisation or the International Air Transport Association.[62]

9. Prevention of Crime and Terrorism.—Legislation has been passed to combat increasing crime and terrorism relating to aircraft.[63] An Aviation Security Fund has been established to meet expenses incurred in carrying out preventative measures.[64]

10. Hovercraft.—A hovercraft is part aircraft, part ship.[65] Its hybrid nature is reflected in the relevant subordinate legislation.[66] The Unfair Contract Terms Act 1977 applies to hovercraft, to a limited extent.[67]

[53] 1971 Act, s. 3; *Laker Airways* v. *Department of Trade* [1977] Q.B. 643.
[54] 1971 Act, s. 3. (2); but see *Laker Airways,* supra.
[55] 1971 Act, s. 1 (4).
[56] 1971 Act, s. 4, as amended by Sched. 1 of the Civil Aviation Act 1978 (c. 8).
[57] Air Corporations (Dissolution) Order 1973 (S.I. 1973 No. 2174); British Airways Board Act 1977 (c. 13), as amended by the Civil Aviation Act 1978 (c. 8). The 1977 Act consolidated inter alia Pt. III and Sched. 8 of the Civil Aviation Act 1971 (c. 75). The Board consists of 8 to 15 persons appointed by the Secretary of State for Trade: 1977 Act, s. 1 (2).
[58] 1977 Act, s. 2. "Air transport services" means services for the carriage by air of passengers or cargo, including mail; 1977 Act, s. 2 (3).
[59] 1977 Act, s. 1 (4).
[60] See for example ss. 2 (2), 3, 4, 6, 7, 16 and 17 of the 1977 Act.
[61] For example British Caledonian, Dan-Air Services, Loganair.
[62] See Shawcross and Beaumont, op cit, paras. 140, 206, 373–375, and vol. 2, Appendix D.
[63] Tokyo Convention Act 1967 (c. 52); Hijacking Act 1971 (c. 70); Protection of Aircraft Act 1973 (c. 47); Policing of Airports Act 1974 (c. 41); Airports Authority Act 1975 (c. 78) s. 12; Civil Aviation Act 1978 (c. 8).
[64] Civil Aviation Act 1978 (c. 8), s. 2; see too s. 23 of the Protection of Aircraft Act 1973 and s. 7 of the Policing of Airports Act 1974.
[65] Hovercraft Act 1968 (c. 59).
[66] Hovercraft (Civil Liability) Order 1971 (S.I. 1971 No. 720); Hovercraft (General) Order 1972 (S.I. 1972 No. 674); Hovercraft (Application of Enactments) Order 1972 (S.I. 1972 No. 971) as amended by S.I. 1977 No. 1257.
[67] (c. 50), s. 15 (3), (4).

CHAPTER XXXII

GENERAL AVERAGE. SALVAGE

Lowndes and Rudolf *General Average* (10th ed., 1975) (*British Shipping Laws,* vol. 7); Carver, *Carriage by Sea* (12th ed., 1971); (*British Shipping Laws*, vols. 2 & 3); Arnould, *Marine Insurance* (15th ed., 1961) (*British Shipping Laws,* vols. 9 & 10); Kennedy, *Civil Salvage* (4th ed., 1958); Maclachlan, *Shipping* (7th ed., 1932).

1. Particular and General Average.—Average is the term used in shipping law for any loss or injury to ship or cargo during a voyage. Such a loss may be a particular or a general average loss. Under the head of particular average falls any loss which is not due to a voluntary act, as, for instance, injury to a ship by striking a rock, or cargo being washed overboard. It also includes losses which, though they are voluntarily incurred, do not satisfy the conditions of general average. In relation to marine insurance it is enacted that "a particular average loss is a partial loss of the subject-matter insured, caused by a peril insured against, and which is not a general average loss."[1] A particular average loss must be borne by the party whose property is injured.[2]

2. History of General Average.—The law of general average was recognised in civil law as derived from the maritime law of Rhodes, the lex Rhodia de jactu,[3] and has been adopted, though with differences in detail, in all mercantile countries. In Scotland the law of England on the subject has been recognised. As the result of international conferences, rules, known as the York-Antwerp Rules, have been drawn up on the subject, and were last revised in 1974.[4] They have no statutory authority, but are commonly incorporated in bills of lading. They differ, in certain minor respects, from the common law, which holds where the Rules have not been expressly incorporated.

3. Nature of General Average Act.—The theory of general average is that when one of the three main interests at stake during a voyage, the ship, the cargo and the freight, is voluntarily sacrificed for the safety of all, the loss must be borne rateably by all interested. Such a voluntary sacrifice, known as a general average act, has been defined as follows: "There is a general average act when, and only when, any extraordinary sacrifice or expenditure is intentionally and reasonably made or incurred for the common safety for the purpose of preserving from peril the property involved in a common maritime adventure."[5]

[1] Marine Insurance Act 1906, s. 64. See Insurance, Ch. XXVII., supra, § 41.
[2] See Bell, *Prin.,* § 437; *Comm.,* I, 630.
[3] *Digest,* XIV, 2, 1: "Si levandae navis gratia jactus mercium factus est, omnium contributione sarciatur quod pro omnibus datum est." See *Goulandris* v. *Goldman* [1958] 1 Q.B. 74 at 93.
[4] See Lowndes and Rudolf, *General Average* (10th ed., 1975), Appx. 1.
[5] York-Antwerp Rules, 1974, Rule A. For a statutory definition, see Marine Insurance Act 1906, s. 66.

4. Instances of General Average.—A general average act may cause loss to the cargo, to the ship, or to the freight. There is a general average loss to the cargo, when it is jettisoned for the safety of the ship; when, with the same object, it is landed at some place other than its destination[6]; or when, though the cargo may not be actually touched, its value is affected by measures, other than mere delay, taken for the common safety.[7] There is a general average loss to the ship when some portion, e.g. the mast or sails, is sacrificed, or where, without any actual sacrifice, the appurtenants of the ship are used in some abnormal way, with consequent injury, as where the engines were used to move a ship which had been stranded, and were damaged in the process.[8] Voluntary stranding to avoid a threatened wreck is probably general average at common law, and is recognised with a modification in the York-Antwerp Rules.[9] Where a ship, to avoid being wrecked or stranded, entered a harbour, knowing that in entering she would probably strike the pier, it was held that both the injury to the ship and the damages fixed for injury to the pier were general average.[10] The freight is affected when cargo is sacrificed, and the freight for it consequently lost.[11] Mere delay, resulting in a loss of market for the cargo, or a partial loss of freight in a time charter, is not a general average loss.[12] A payment made under an indemnity in a towage contract may be a general average loss.[13]

5. Contribution.—Those who have to contribute to meet a general average loss are the owners of the ship, the various owners of the cargo, and the parties entitled to the freight. A party whose fault gave rise to the peril in question is not entitled to recover contribution in general average.[14] The owner of the property sacrificed contributes rateably according to its value.[15] There is no claim on passengers, their luggage or their effects carried without a bill of lading.[16] The owner of deck cargo, unless it is carried under a custom of trade or with the consent of the other cargo owners, has no claim if his property is jettisoned,[17] but is bound to contribute to another general average loss.[18] The party in right of the respective interests at the completion of the voyage, not the party in such right at the time when the sacrifice was made, is liable.[19]

6. Lien.—The owner of cargo which has been jettisoned has a lien over the

---

[6] *Royal Mail Steam Packet Co.* v. *English Bank* (1887) 19 Q.B.D. 362.
[7] *Anglo-Argentine Live Stock Co.* v. *Temperley Shipping Co.* [1899] 2 Q.B. 403.
[8] *The Bona* [1895] P. 125.
[9] See *The Seapool* [1934] P. 53.
[10] *Austin Friars Co.* v. *Spillers & Bakers* [1915] 1 K.B. 586.
[11] *Iredale* v. *China Traders' Insurance Co.* [1900] 2 Q.B. 515.
[12] *The Leitrim* [1902] P. 256.
[13] *Australian Coastal Shipping Commission* v. *Green* [1971] 1 Q.B. 456.
[14] *Goulandris* v. *Goldman* [1958] 1 Q.B. 74; *Diestelkamp* v. *Baynes (Reading): The Aga* [1968] 1 Lloyd's Rep. 431; *E. B. Aaby's Rederi A/S* v. *Union of India: The Evje (No. 2)* [1976] 2 Lloyd's Rep. 714; York-Antwerp Rules, 1974; Rule D.
[15] *Strang, Steel & Co.* v. *Scott* (1889) 14 App.Cas. 601.
[16] *Bell, Comm.*, I., 636; York-Antwerp Rules, 1974, Rule XVII.
[17] *Strang, Steel & Co.* v. *Scott, supra.*
[18] *Bell, Comm.*, I., 636.
[19] *Ranking* v. *Tod* (1870) 8 M. 914.

rest of the cargo for a general average contribution. The captain is impliedly his agent in this respect, and is entitled to enforce the lien, and liable in damages if when called upon he refuses or fails to do so.[20]

7. Conditions of Right to Contribution.—The right to a general average contribution depends upon an act which has caused loss and which has been done for the safety of all. So a claim was rejected for damage caused by turning on steam into the hold under the mistaken impression that the ship was on fire.[21] It is a question in the circumstances of each case whether a general average act was done reasonably. Only those whose interests were actually in peril can be called upon to contribute. Thus where gold was landed to ensure its safety, and not for the purpose of lightening the ship, its owner, as his property was not in peril, was not liable to contribute in respect of cargo that was afterwards jettisoned.[22] The party to whose fault the peril is due, e.g., the shipowner, when the peril is due to the negligence of the captain, has no claim to a general average contribution,[23] with an exception in the case of fire.[24]

8. General Average Expenditure.—Certain expenditure by the shipowner, known as general average expenditure, may be the subject of contribution if it was incurred for the safety of all.[25] As a shipowner is bound under his contract to take measures for the safety of the ship he has no claim to an average contribution unless the circumstances were exceptional or abnormal.[26] So on the ground that risk from submarines was a normal incident during war a shipowner was refused contribution for the expenses of a tug hired to lessen that risk.[27] When a ship is forced to put in to a port of refuge the expense of unloading the cargo with a view to repairs is in all cases allowed as a general average charge; but the expense of reloading, though allowed by the York-Antwerp Rules,[28] is at common law admissible only if the reason why the port of refuge was necessary was a general average act, e.g., the deliberate sacrifice of some part of the ship's equipment as contrasted with accidentally springing a leak.[29]

9. General Average in Marine Insurance.—In questions of insurance, an underwriter, in the absence of any provision to the contrary, is liable to the assured for any general average contribution which may be payable in respect

[20] *Strang, Steel & Co.,* v. *Scott, supra.*
[21] *Watson* v. *Firemen's Fund Insurance Co.* [1922] 2 K.B. 355.
[22] *Royal Mail Packet Co.* v. *English Bank* (1887) 19 Q.B.D. 362.
[23] *Strang, Steel & Co.* v. *Scott* (1889) 14 App.Cas. 601; cf. *Diestelkamp* v. *Baynes (Reading): The Aga* [1968] 1 Lloyd's Rep. 431; *E. B. Aaby's Rederi A/S* v. *Union of India: The Evje (No. 2)* [1976] 2 Lloyd's Rep. 714.
[24] *Dreyfus* v. *Tempus Shipping Co.* [1931] A.C. 726, decided on the construction of s. 502 of the Merchant Shipping Act 1894.
[25] See for example *Australian Coastal Shipping Commission* v. *Green* [1971] 1 Q.B. 456.
[26] *Ocean Co.* v. *Anderson Tritton & Co.* (1883) 13 Q.B.D. 651.
[27] *Société Nouvelle d'Armement* v. *Spillers & Bakers* [1917] 1 K.B. 865.
[28] Rule X. (a).
[29] *Atwood* v. *Sellar* (1880) 5 Q.B.D. 286; *Svendson* v. *Wallace* (1885) 10 App.Cas. 404.

of the interest covered by the policy.[30] He is liable for the whole amount if the interest in question is insured to its full contributory value; to a proportional amount if the insurance was only partial.[31] The assured may recover from the underwriters the proportion of any general average expenditure which falls upon him, and, in the case of a general average sacrifice, the whole loss, without having enforced his right of contribution from the other parties liable to contribute.[32] Though all the interest in the ship, the cargo and the freight may be vested in one person, the insurer of any one of these interests is liable in a general average contribution in the same way as if they had been vested in different persons.[33]

SALVAGE

10. Nature of Salvage.—A claim for salvage, like a claim for general average, is one not resting on any contract but on an obligation implied by law. At common law salvage has been defined as "a reward or recompense given to those by means of whose labour, intrepidity or perseverance a ship, or goods, have been saved from shipwreck, fire or capture."[34] It is settled in England, and there is no authority in Scotland to the contrary, that salvage is applicable only to the rescue of a ship, her cargo and equipment[35]; and that a person who saves the property of others on land has no analogous claim.[36] At common law saving life at sea gave no direct right to salvage; by statute it is allowed for saving life on a British ship, or on a foreign ship in British waters. Such a claim is preferable to a claim for salvage of ship or cargo, but is not exigible unless some property also has been saved.[37] To justify a claim for salvage, the subjects salved must have been in a position of danger, or at least believed by those in charge of them to be so. Assistance to a ship which is disabled, but in no danger, is merely towage, a service which founds a claim for payment, but not for payment at salvage rates.[38] When a vessel is injured on going to the rescue of a ship run down by a third, she is not exposed to the plea that she assumed the risk. She goes in pursuance of a duty.[39]

11. Parties Entitled to Salvage.—The persons entitled to salvage are the owners of the ship, or ships, which have rendered assistance, their masters and

---

[30] Marine Insurance Act 1906, s. 66 (5).
[31] Ibid., s. 73.
[32] Ibid., s. 66 (4).
[33] Ibid., s. 66 (7); *Montgomery* v. *Indemnity Insurance Co.* [1902] 1 K.B. 734.
[34] Bell, *Prin.,* § 443; *Comm.,* I, 638. A statutory definition is given in s. 158 (1) of the Road Traffic Act 1972 (c. 20).
[35] *Wells* v. *The Whitton* [1897] A.C. 337. But see Civil Aviation Act 1949 (c. 67) s. 51; Hovercraft (Application of Enactments) Order 1972 (S.I. 1972 No. 971), para. 8.
[36] *Falcke* v. *Scottish Imperial Assurance Co.* (1886) 34 Ch.D. 234.
[37] Merchant Shipping Act 1894 (57 & 58 Vict. c. 60), s. 544; *Jorgensen* v. *Neptune, etc., Co.* (1902) 4 F. 992.
[38] *Robinson* v. *Thoms* (1851) 13 D. 592; *Lawson* v. *Grangemouth Dockyard Co.* (1888) 15 R. 753; *The Kangaroo* [1918] P. 327; *The Troilus* [1951] A.C. 820; *Aberdeen Harbour Board* v. *Marz H. F.,* 1971 S.L.T. (Notes) 34.
[39] *The Gusty* v. *The Daniel* [1940] P. 159.

crew.[40] The claimant must be a person who was not under any obligation to render services prior to the emergency which rendered them necessary.[41] This excludes any claim by the master and crew of the ship salved; they are bound by their contract to do everything in their power for the safety of the ship.[42] Passengers, though not contractually bound, are under an obligation to assist in their own rescue and that of others, and a claim by them is not maintainable except in the case where, having an opportunity of leaving the ship, they voluntarily remained and assisted in saving her.[43] Similar rules apply to a pilot.[44] Where the rules of a mutual assurance society provided that each assured should render assistance to every other, it was held that as such assistance was given under a contractual obligation, it afforded no ground for salvage.[45] An agent for the shipowner may recover salvage, but any bargain he may make will be unfavourably regarded.[46] A ship which has been injured by a collision, though under a statutory obligation to render assistance to the other ship involved, is, if not in fault, entitled to salvage,[47] and possibly even if she was in fault.[48] When salvage services are rendered by a King's ship, any claim by the officers and crew requires the consent of the Admiralty, and must be supported by proof of services of an exceptional kind.[49] The position of the Admiralty in relation to salvage claims by or against the Crown is now the same as that of any other shipowner.[50] A salvor may require a licence if carrying out operations at or near a wreck of historical, archaeological or artistic importance.[51]

12. Conditions of Salvage Claim.—Except in cases where an express bargain to pay for attempts to salve is proved, success is a condition of a claim for salvage. Such a bargain, it has been held, is a true salvage agreement.[52] If nothing is saved, nothing is due.[53] If the ship is ultimately saved, those who were invited to assist her, though their efforts proved unsuccessful, have a claim.[54] The efforts of a voluntary salvor, if unsuccessful, go unrewarded.[55] Where a salvor removed the ship from a position of danger, but left her in a

---

[40] See *Bennet* v. *Henderson* (1887) 24 S.L.R. 625. Agreements by which seamen give up their claim to salvage are, in general, void: Merchant Shipping Act 1970 (c. 36), s. 16; *Nicholson* v. *Leith Salvage, etc., Co.*, 1923 S.C. 409.

[41] cf. *The Gregerso* [1973] Q.B. 274. However a salvage contract may be and often is entered into after the emergency has arisen. Lloyd's has a standard form of salvage agreement. The Unfair Contract Terms Act 1977 (c. 50) applies to salvage contracts, to a limited extent: 1977 Act, s. 15(3) (*b*); see Pacta Illicita and Unfair Terms, Ch. IX, supra.

[42] Bell, *Prin.*, § 444. See *The Albionic* [1942] P. 81.

[43] Kennedy, *Civil Salvage*, p. 241; *Newman* v. *Walters* (1804) 3 B. & P. 612.

[44] *Akerblom* v. *Price* (1881) 7 Q.B.D. 129; *The Hudson Light* [1970] 1 Lloyd's Rep, 166.

[45] *Clan Steam Trawling Co.* v. *Aberdeen Trawling Co.*, 1908 S.C. 651.

[46] *The Crusader* [1907] P. 196.

[47] Merchant Shipping Act 1894, s. 422; *Melanie, Owners of* v. *Owners of San Onofre* [1925] A.C. 246.

[48] *The Beaverford* v. *The Kafiristan* [1938] A.C. 136.

[49] Merchant Shipping Act 1894, s. 557; *The Ulysses* (1888) 13 P.D. 205; *Swanney* v. *Citos*, 1925 S.L.T. 491: *The Valverda* [1938] A.C. 173.

[50] Crown Proceedings Act 1947 (10 & 11 Geo. VI, c. 44), s. 8.

[51] Protection of Wrecks Act 1973 (c. 33), s. 1.

[52] *The Valverda*, supra.

[53] See Carver, *Carriage by Sea*, § 799.

[54] *Ross & Marshall* v. *Owners of Davaar* (1907) 15 S.L.T. 29.

[55] *Steel & Bennie* v. *Hutchison*, 1909, 2 S.L.T. 110.

position no more favourable, it was held, although the ship was ultimately saved, that no salvage was due because the efforts to salve had met with no success.[56] Misconduct on the part of salvors, for instance looting, may bar any right to salvage on the part of those implicated.[57] A successful salvor may be liable for negligence on his part.[58]

13. Parties Liable.—The parties liable for salvage are those who have a beneficial interest in the property which is saved, generally the owners of the ship and cargo, and the persons entitled to the freight. They may be sued personally.[59] As a general rule, all who are liable to contribute must be called as defenders, but where the peril of the ship was due to the fault of the shipowner, and he, had she been lost, would have been liable to the owners of the cargo, it was held that an action against him alone was competent; and opinions were expressed that in the case of a general ship, where the owners of the cargo are numerous, the action may be directed against the shipowner.[60] A claim for salvage may also be enforced by the retention of the property salved, if in the salvor's possession, or in that of the Receiver of Wreck for the district.[61] And the salvor has a maritime lien or hypothec, in virtue of which the ship may be arrested.[62] The salvor's lien takes priority over all other maritime liens.[63]

14. Amount of Salvage Award.—The amount payable as salvage may be settled by agreement between the parties. But such an agreement, if made at the time when the ship was in peril, is not necessarily binding, and may be reduced if in the circumstances it was grossly exorbitant.[64] Where there has been no agreement, and the amount has to be settled by the Court, it has constantly been laid down that the award should be on a generous scale, in order to induce efforts to salve, and that the assessment by a Court of first instance will not readily be disturbed.[65] The following circumstances may be considered in estimating the amount: the enterprise by the salvors and the risk they ran, and, as entering into the question of risk, the value of the salving ship; the labour, loss of time and risk of loss of insurance involved; the degree of peril of the ship salved; the value of the property saved.[66] The last is a controlling element; in no modern case has the award of salvage exceeded half

---

[56] *Melanie, Owners of* v. *Owners of San Onofre* [1925] A.C. 246.
[57] *The Clan Sutherland* [1918] P. 332.
[58] *The Tojo Maru* [1972] A.C. 242; obiter dicta in *The St. Blane* [1974] 1 Lloyd's Rep. 557.
[59] *Duncan* v. *Dundee, etc., Shipping Co.* (1878) 5 R. 742.
[60] *Duncan*, supra.
[61] Merchant Shipping Act 1894, s. 552; *Walker, etc., Co.* v. *Mitre Co.*, 1913, 1 S.L.T. 67.
[62] *Hatton* v. *Durban Hansen*, 1919 S.C. 154; *The Lyrma (No. 2)* [1978] 2 Lloyd's Rep. 30.
[63] *The Lyrma (No. 2)*, supra.
[64] *The Silesia* (1880) 5 P.D. 177; *The Crusader* [1907] P. 196. As previously indicated, the Unfair Contract Terms Act 1977 (c. 50) applies to salvage contracts: s. 15(3) (*b*).
[65] But see *The Evaine* [1966] 2 Lloyd's Rep. 413.
[66] *Vulcan, Owners of* v. *Owners of Berlin* (1882) 9 R. 1057; see also *Ld. Adv.* v. *Owners of Graziella*, 1962 S.L.T. (Notes) 4; and *Watt* v. *Campbell*, 1950 S.L.T. (Notes) 56; lifeboat new; *Aberdeen Harbour Board* v. *Marz H.F.* 1971 S.L.T. (Notes) 34; *Bruce's Stores (Aberdeen)* v. *Richard Irvin & Sons*, 1978 S.L.T. (Notes) 85.

the value of the property saved, except in the case of a derelict, where there is no claim put forward by the owners.[67]

15. Procedure.—A dispute as to the amount of salvage, whether of life or property, must, if the value of the property salved does not exceed £1,000, or the amount claimed does not exceed £300, be determined in the Sheriff Court.[68] When these limits are exceeded the action, unless the parties otherwise agree, must be brought in the Court of Session.[69] In the case of an action in the Court of Session, if the amount awarded does not exceed £300, the pursuer is not entitled to expenses, unless the Court certifies the case as one fit to be tried otherwise than in the Sheriff Court. Proceedings should be commenced within two years of the rendering of salvage services.[70] However the period may be and has been extended.[71]

[67] See Kennedy, *Civil Salvage,* p. 180.
[68] See Merchant Shipping Act 1894, s. 547; Dobie, *Sheriff Court Practice,* pp. 619-621; *Swanson* v. *Craig,* 1939 S.L.T. 297.
[69] Merchant Shipping Act 1894, s. 547.
[70] Maritime Conventions Act 1911 (1 & 2 Geo. V, c. 5), s. 8.
[71] *Brown* v. *Devanha Fishing Co.,* 1968 S.L.T. (Notes) 4.

CHAPTER XXXIII

LEASES

Hunter, *Landlord and Tenant* (4th ed., 1876); Rankine, *Leases* (3rd ed., 1916); Connell, *Agricultural Holdings (Scotland) Acts* (6th ed., 1970); Scott, *Law of Smallholdings* (1933); Fraser, *Rent Acts in Scotland* (2nd ed., 1952); Megarry, *Rent Acts* (10th ed., 1967); Paton and Cameron, *Landlord and Tenant* (1967).

The common law of leases, for social and economic reasons, has for many years been substantially eclipsed by statute, especially with regard to the security of the tenant's tenure and the amount of rent which he can be required to pay. Few lettings in town or country are now unaffected by statutory codes and those of residential property and agricultural land are particularly closely controlled. The common law is still, nevertheless, of importance, and it and those statutory provisions of general application are dealt with first in this chapter. Thereafter the codes dealing with agricultural holdings, landholders and crofters, and dwelling-houses and shops will be summarised.

I. GENERAL LAW

1. Nature of Contract.—The contract of lease is one whereby certain uses, or the entire possession and control of lands, houses or other heritable subjects are given to the tenant for a return, known as rent or lordship, in money or goods. The analogous contract in the case of moveables is that of hire. A mineral lease, since it involves a conveyance of part of the subjects and not merely of their fruits, is in substance a sale; but it has been uniformly treated, in questions as to the incidents implied in the contract, as falling under the law of leases.[1] A right to the use of a heritable subject, where no possession of any specific part is given, e.g., a right to exhibit advertisements on the walls of a building, is a contract which does not fall under the law of leases.[2] The right to possession conferred by the contract must be exclusive.[3] Where a servant is given the occupancy of a house the contract, unless the provisions are exceptional,[4] will be regarded as a contract of service and not as a lease,[5] and the servant a "service occupier" and not a tenant; but for this to be so the servant's residence in the house must be ancillary and necessary to

[1] A power to grant leases does not generally import a power to grant leases of minerals which have not previously been let: *Campbell* v. *Wardlaw* (1883) 10 R. (H.L.) 65; *Nugent's Trs.* v. *Nugent* (1898) 25 R. 475.
[2] *U.K. Advertising Co.* v. *Glasgow Bag-Wash Co.*, 1926 S.C. 303. The question whether a bargain about the use of land is a lease or not has been discussed in land valuation cases: e.g., *Magistrates of Perth* v. *Assessor for Perth*, 1937 S.C. 549; *L.N.E.R. Ry.* v. *Assessor for Glasgow*, 1937 S.C. 309.
[3] *Chaplin* v. *Assessor for Perth*, 1947 S.C. 373.
[4] See *Dunbar's Trs.* v. *Bruce* (1900) 3 F. 137; *Carron Co.* v. *Francis*, 1915 S.C. 872.
[5] *Sinclair* v. *Tod*, 1907 S.C. 1038. As a service occupier he is not entitled to security of tenure or rent protection under the Rent Acts: see *Marquis of Bute* v. *Prenderleith*, 1921 S.C. 281.

the performance of his duties.[6] Where a person is permitted to occupy premises as an act of grace or friendship, and the intention to create a tenancy is not present, the right conferred on him may be construed as a mere licence to occupy, and not a lease.[7] There are four cardinal elements in a lease, the parties, the subjects, the rent and the duration; in the absence of consensus in idem as to these elements, or at least the first three, there will be no lease.[8] The occupant of a house or other subject belonging to another is however presumed to occupy as tenant and though no direct obligation to pay rent is proved is bound to pay the annual value of the subject to the proprietor.[9] There is probably no limit of the time for which subjects may be let, but if no term be expressed the contract will be treated as a lease for a year only, and not in perpetuity.[10] The necessity of writing in the case of leases for more than a year has already been considered.[11]

2. Lease as a Real Right.—At common law a lease was merely a personal contract, binding on the lessor and his representatives, not upon his singular successors as purchasers or creditors; the tenant thus had no security of tenure against the lessor's singular successor, who could repudiate the lease. This was altered by the Leases Act 1449 (c. 17), whereby, when its provisions, as interpreted by decisions, are complied with, a real right in the subjects let is obtained by the tenant. The Act is applicable to leases of lands, houses, mines, and salmon fishings, but not to leases of shootings, which are not capable of being created separate tenements; such lettings, consequently, are not binding in a question with a singular successor.[12] By the Freshwater and Salmon Fisheries (Scotland) Act 1976 (c. 22), s. 4, it has been extended to any contract in writing for a consideration and for a period of not less than a year whereby an owner of land to which a right of fishing for freshwater fish in any inland waters pertains or the occupier of such a right authorises another person so to fish. The conditions required to bring a lease within the purview of the Leases Act, and so make it binding on singular successors, are (1) that the lease (if for more than a year) must be in writing; (2) that there must be a specific continuing rent[13]; (3) that there must be an ish, or term of expiry; and (4) that the tenant must have entered into possession, possession being the equivalent of sasine in the feudal system.[14] Leases in perpetuity, therefore, though valid

---

[6] *Cairns* v. *Innes,* 1942 S.C. 164; *MacGregor* v. *Dunnett,* 1949 S.C. 510, per Lord President Cooper at p. 514; *Cargill* v. *Phillips,* 1951 S.C. 67.

[7] *Commissioners of H. M. Works* v. *Hutchison,* 1922 S.L.T. (Sh. Ct.) 127; Paton & Cameron, *Landlord and Tenant,* p.12; cf. *Heslop* v. *Burns* [1974] 1 W.L.R. 1241. See also *Stirrat* v. *Whyte,* 1967 S.C. 265, where fields were let for a rotation of cropping on condition that the let should terminate in the event of the sale of the farm at any time.

[8] *Gray* v. *Edinburgh University,* 1962 S.C. 157; *Erskine* v. *Glendinning* (1871) 9 M. 656.

[9] *Glen* v. *Roy* (1882) 10 R. 239.

[10] *Dunlop* v. *Steel Co. of Scotland* (1879) 7 R. 283; *Gray* v. *Edinburgh University,* supra.

[11] Agreements Defective in Form, Ch. VII, supra, § 3.

[12] *Birkbeck* v. *Ross* (1865) 4 M. 272. A lease of, e.g., a deer forest, where the tenant has the exclusive occupation of the lands themselves, is not a lease of shootings: *Farquharson* (1870) 9 M. 66.

[13] *Mann* v. *Houston,* 1957 S.L.T. 89.

[14] Bell, *Prin.,* § 1190. An incoming tenant who in advance of the term is allowed to perform certain acts on the ground may not have possession for the purpose of the Act: *Millar* v. *M'Robbie,* 1949 S.C. 1.

in a question with the lessor, are not binding on his singular successors. There is probably no limit to the number of years for which a lease, valid against singular successors, may be granted, but where the lease is for a definite period, with a continual option to the tenant to demand a new lease on the expiry of the old, the arrangement is binding on a singular successor only for the period current at the commencement of his interest.[15] The rent must not be illusory, a term never more exactly interpreted, but it is no objection, providing there is a continuing rent, that a capital sum, known as a grassum, has been taken at the beginning of the lease.[16]

3. Real and Personal Conditions.—When a lease falls within the provisions of the Leases Act 1449, all its ordinary conditions are binding on singular successors. But there may be conditions which are not inter naturalia of the lease, that is, provisions which have reference to the private relations of the contracting parties, and not to their general relations as landlord and tenant. By such provisions a singular successor of the landlord is not bound. Examples are a provision under which the rent is to be ascribed to payment of a prior debt,[17] or a provision that a deduction from the rent is to be made for services to be rendered by the tenant,[18] or a provision, in a lease for 999 years, under which the landlord undertook to grant a feu on demand.[19]

Obligations which would be binding on a singular successor of the landlord are not necessarily binding on a succeeding heir of entail. They may fail, not because they are exceptional or personal obligations not inter naturalia of the lease, but because if they were allowed to transmit they would by burdening the succession contravene the fetters of the entail. Thus although an obligation to pay for improvements executed by the tenant,[20] or to take over the sheep stock at valuation, transmits against singular successors,[21] neither was held to be binding on a succeeding heir of entail.[22] Under the Entail (Scotland) Act 1914, however, an obligation to take over sheep stock contained in a lease granted by an heir of entail in possession is now binding on succeeding heirs of entail.[23]

4. Long Leases.—In the case of leases of lands and heritages in Scotland for a period ⬥ exceeding twenty years, an equivalent to possession as a means of obtaining a real right is afforded by the Registration of Leases (Scotland) Act 1857.[24] Such leases may be recorded in the Register of Sasines,

---

[15] See *Bisset* v. *Magistrates of Aberdeen* (1898) 1 F. 87.
[16] Bell, *Prin.*, § 1201; see *Mann* v. *Houston*, supra.
[17] Bell, *Prin.*, § 1202.
[18] *Ross* v. *Duchess of Sutherland* (1838) 16 S. 1179. See also *Montgomery* v. *Carrick* (1848) 10 D. 1387.
[19] *Bisset* v. *Magistrates of Aberdeen* (1898) 1 F. 87.
[20] *Stewart* v. *M'Ra* (1834) 13 S. 4.
[21] *Panton* v. *Mackintosh* (1903) 10 S.L.R. 763.
[22] *Moncreiff* v. *Tod & Skene* (1825) 1 W. & S. 217 (improvements); *Gillespie* v. *Riddell*, 1908 S.C. 628, affd. 1909 S.C. (H.L.) 3 (sheep stock). Compare *Jolly's Exix.* v. *Viscount Stonehaven*, 1958 S.C. 635.
[23] 4 & 5 Geo. V. c. 43, s. 5.
[24] 20 & 21 Vict. c. 26, as amended by the Conveyancing (Scotland) Act 1924, s. 24, by the Long Leases (Scotland) Act 1954, s. 26, and by the Land Tenure Reform (Scotland) Act 1974, Sched. 6.

and, when recorded, will be effectual against the singular successors of the lessor, even though the lessee has not entered into possession. The Act in effect provided an alternative to feuing, where that for technical reasons, e.g. an entail or a prohibition of sub-feuing, was impossible, which could afford similar security to the person in enjoyment of the right or his assignee. The requirements for a valid recording of a lease under the 1857 Act, as amended by the Land Tenure Reform (Scotland) Act 1974 (c. 38), are (1) that the lease must be executed in a probative writing and (2) that the period of the lease must exceed twenty years, failing which there must be an obligation to renew the lease so as to endure for a period exceeding that number of years. Prior to the amendments made by the 1974 Act the period of the lease required to be at least thirty-one years, and the subjects let, except in the case of a lease of mines and minerals, required not to exceed fifty acres in extent. On the other hand, no rent is necessary, and no definite ish is required. The particular value of the Act is that it enables the lessee of a registered lease to borrow on the security of the lease by conferring an effectual real right on his assignee in security without relinquishing possession to him. Such leases may be assigned absolutely or in security. The Act provides forms of deeds for executing such assignations,[25] but the grant of a right under a lease by way of a heritable security requires now to take the form of a standard security.[26] Obligations created in registered leases may be varied or discharged by the Lands Tribunal under the Conveyancing and Feudal Reform (Scotland) Act 1970.[27]

Prior to 1st September 1974 it was permissible to provide in leases of long duration for the payment of a casualty on events such as the assignation of the lease to a singular successor,[28] but it is now no longer lawful to stipulate for the payment of any casualty.[29] It remains permissible however to stipulate for review of rent or a periodical variation of rent on terms prescribed in the lease.

5. Limitation on Residential Use of Property Let under Long Leases.—The Land Tenure Reform (Scotland) Act 1974[30] provides for the prohibition of the imposition in deeds executed after the commencement of that Act of any feuduty, ground annual or other periodical payment and for the right to redeem, and in certain circumstances redemption by law of, such payments in deeds executed before that date. This reform is likely to result in more extensive use of long leases. Accordingly, while long leases of industrial or commercial property are not affected, the Act has introduced limitations upon the residential use of property let under long leases. It is a condition of every long lease executed after 1st September 1974 that no part of the property which is subject to the lease shall be used as or as part of a private dwelling house.[31] An exception is made in the case of use as a private dwelling house

---

[25] Schedules; and see 1924 Act, s. 24; *Crawford* v. *Campbell*, 1937 S.C. 596.
[26] Conveyancing and Feudal Reform (Scotland) Act 1970 (c. 35), ss. 9 (3), 32, Sched. 8.
[27] 1970 (c. 35), ss. 1, 2 (6); *McQuisan* v. *Eagle Star Insurance Company*, 1972 S.L.T. (Lands Tr.) 39.
[28] E.g. *Crawford* v. *Campbell*, supra.
[29] Land Tenure Reform (Scotland) Act 1974, s. 16.
[30] 1974 (c. 38), Part I.
[31] s. 8; see, as to the meaning of this expression, *Brown* v. *Crum Ewing's Trs.*, 1918, 1 S.L.T. 340.

which is ancillary to the use of the remainder of the subjects let for other purposes, where it would be detrimental to the efficient use of the remainder of the subjects if the ancillary use did not occur on that property.[32] Caravan sites, agricultural holdings, small landholdings and crofts are also exempted from the prohibition.[33] "Long lease" for this purpose is defined as meaning any grant of a lease or a liferent or other right of occupancy granted for payment subject to a duration which could extend for more than twenty years, or if there is to be liability to make some payment or perform some other obligation if renewal so as to extend the period for more than twenty years is not effected.[34] If a breach of the statutory prohibition occurs, the lessor may give notice to the lessee to terminate the use which constitutes the breach within twenty eight days.[35] If the lessee does not do so within that period the lessor may raise an action of removing to terminate the lease, but the lessee may avoid the consequences by ceasing the use at any time before decree is extracted.[36] If it is proved that the lessor has either expressly or by his actings approved of the use which contravenes the statutory prohibition the lessee is not subject to immediate removal, but the remaining duration of the lease is restricted so as not to continue for more than twenty years.[37] This defence is available only to a lessee who is actually occupying the subjects, but provision is made to enable a sub-lessee to be sisted in the action and to plead the defence if the use has been approved by the lessor in his sub-lease.[38] Provision is also made for the intimation of the action to heritable creditors, who may seek to be sisted in the action and plead any defence which could be pleaded by the defender.[39]

6. Rights of Tenant.—The tenant's principal right is to be placed in full possession of the subjects let, and to be allowed to remain there for the duration of the lease. In agricultural and urban leases alike, although not in the case of leases of minerals, there is an implied warranty that the subjects are reasonably fit for for the purpose for which they are let.[40] There is however no general implication of fitness for any particular business which the tenant may desire to carry on there, the presumption being that the tenant has satisfied himself of the suitability of the subjects for his own purposes.[41] In agricultural leases the landlord is under an implied obligation to put the houses, offices and fences into "tenantable repair," in other words into such a condition that they will last, with reasonable care, for the period of the lease.[42] During the

---

[32] s. 8 (3).
[33] s. 8 (5).
[34] s. 8 (4).
[35] s. 9 (1).
[36] s. 9 (3), (6).
[37] s. 9 (4).
[38] s. 10 (3)-(5).
[39] s. 10 (2).
[40] Erskine, II., 6, 39; Rankine, *Leases*, (3rd ed.), 241, 249.
[41] *Glebe Sugar Refining Co.* v. *Paterson* (1900) 2 F. 615; *Paton* v. *MacDonald*, 1973 S.L.T. (Sh. Ct.) 85.
[42] *Davidson* v. *Logan*, 1908 S.C. 350; *Christie* v. *Wilson*, 1915 S.C. 645 (water supply). As to houses, see *Reid* v. *Baird* (1876) 4 R. 234; *Wolfson* v. *Forrester*, 1910 S.C. 675.

lease the obligation lies on the tenant to keep up and repair the buildings and fences on the farm so that they are in the same tenantable condition at the ish; but he is not liable for extraordinary repairs rendered necessary by damnum fatale or natural wear and tear.[43] In the case of urban subjects, however, the obligation to repair lies at common law, in default of stipulations to the contrary, upon the landlord.[44] The obligation is to uphold the subjects during the currency of the lease in a wind- and water-tight condition so that they will be proof against the ordinary attacks of the elements,[45] but he is not liable for defects due to damnum fatale or which arise out of failures by third parties to perform their obligations. His obligation is not a warranty to the tenant that no disrepair will occur, nor is there an absolute duty to keep the subjects free from defects; it amounts to an undertaking to put matters right on receiving notice of their existence, and there is no breach until a particular defect is brought to his notice and he fails to remedy it. Landlords have accordingly been held not to be liable in damages for injury sustained by the tenant owing to a chance defect arising during the currency of the lease.[46] The obligation is confined to the maintenance of the subjects let, and the landlord is not in breach of it if damage occurs within them caused by defects in property which lies beyond the curtilage of the subjects.[47]

The Housing (Scotland) Act 1966[48] provides that in the case of houses let at a rent not exceeding £26 there shall be implied an undertaking that the house will be kept by the landlord during the tenancy in all respects reasonably fit for human habitation. In the case of leases of houses for a period of less than seven years the landlord is required by that Act[49] to keep in repair the structure and exterior of the house, including drains, gutters and external pipes, and in repair and proper working order the installations in the house for the supply of water, gas, electricity and sanitation, and for space heating or heating water; contracting out of this statutory obligation may only be done with the concurrence of the sheriff.[50] The landlord's obligations, conventional, statutory or at common law, carry with them a liability to any persons who or whose property may be on the premises for any injury or damage arising to them as a result of any failure on his part to perform them.[51]

The obligation of upkeep is subject to the law of rei interitus, and therefore the accidental destruction of a house puts an end to the obligation on either

---

[43] *Johnstone* v. *Hughan* (1894) 21 R. 777.
[44] Rankine, *Leases*, p. 241.
[45] *Wolfson* v. *Forrester*, 1910 S.C. 675; per Lord President Dunedin at p. 680; see also *Reid* v. *Baird* (1876) 4 R. 234; *McGonigal* v. *Pickard*, 1954 S.L.T. (Notes) 62.
[46] *Hampton* v. *Galloway* (1899) 1 F. 501; *Dickie* v. *Amicable Property Investment Co.*, 1911 S.C. 1079; *North British Storage Co.* v. *Steele's Trs.*, 1920 S.C. 194.
[47] *Golden Casket (Greenock)* v. *B.R.S. (Pickfords)*, 1972 S.L.T. 146.
[48] 1966 (c. 49), s. 6 (1); this has been construed in a decision upon the same provision in an English Act, as involving the necessity of notice to the landlord of any defect: *Morgan* v. *Liverpool Corporation* [1927] 2 K.B. 131.
[49] ss. 8-9.
[50] s. 10.
[51] Occupier's Liability (Scotland) Act 1960, s. 3; see also *Haggarty* v. *Glasgow Corporation*, 1964 S.L.T. (Notes) 54.

side.[52] Total destruction of the subjects of lease, without fault, has the effect of putting an end to the contract and liberating both landlord and tenant from its obligations.[53] In the case of partial injury it is a question of degree whether the tenant is entitled to abandon the lease.[54] If not, or if he does not choose to do so, he is entitled to claim a proportionate deduction, or abatement, from the rent.[55] A landlord is under no implied obligation to abstain from using other property in competition with the business carried on by the tenant.[56] If by alterations or repairs on other property he interferes with the tenant's interests, he will be liable, even although there is no proof that the work in question was not carried out with reasonable care, for any structural damage, and for injury to the tenant's effects or interference with his business, but not for injury resulting merely from noise, vibration or temporary interference with access.[57] A tenant, as the occupier, normally pays the rates, but in the case of a furnished letting, in a question between himself and the landlord, the landlord is by custom bound to relieve the tenant of this liability in the absence of express stipulation to the contrary.[58]

The tenant, as a residential occupier, is protected by the Rent Act 1965,[59] against harassment by any person, including his landlord, which is intended to induce him to give up the occupation of the premises or any part of them, or to refrain from exercising any right or pursuing any remedy to which he is entitled in respect of the premises. Where the tenancy has come to an end and the occupier continues to reside in the premises he has the right not to be ejected without a Court order[60]; the landlord's proper course is to apply to the Court for a warrant for his ejection, and if he attempts to eject the occupier at his own hand he may be liable in damages for wrongous ejection[61] as well as to the criminal penalty provided by the 1965 Act.[62]

The Sex Discrimination Act 1975 (c. 65), s. 30, and the Race Relations Act 1976 (c. 74), s. 21, make discrimination unlawful in the letting of premises, in affording access to facilities in premises let, and in evicting tenants.

7. Tenant's Remedies.—If the subjects are at the outset to a material extent unfit for their purpose, the tenant may refuse to enter into possession and claim damages.[63] He has the same remedy where the subjects are advertised as possessing certain qualities or advantages which they do not

---

[52] *Cameron* v. *Young,* 1908 S.C. (H.L.) 7. See, too, Impossibility of Performance, Ch. XI, supra, § 5. As to the case where a house is rendered unfit to live in by reason of war damage, see the War Damage to Land (Scotland) Act 1941.
[53] Stair, I., 15, 2; *Duff* v. *Fleming* (1870) 8 M. 769; *Cantors Properties (Scotland)* v. *Swears & Wells,* 1977 S.L.T. (Notes) 30.
[54] *Allan* v. *Markland* (1882) 10 R. 383.
[55] *Muir* v. *M'Intyre* (1887) 14 R. 470; *Sharp* v. *Thomson,* 1930 S.C. 1092.
[56] *Craig* v. *Millar* (1888) 15 R. 1005.
[57] *Huber* v. *Ross,* 1912 S.C. 898.
[58] *Macome* v. *Dickson* (1868) 6 M. 898; *Sturrock* v. *Murray,* 1952 S.C. 454.
[59] 1965 (c. 75), s. 30 (2).
[60] ss. 30, 32; cf. *N.C.B.* v. *McInnes,* 1968 S.C. 321.
[61] See Rankine, *Leases,* p. 592; *Cairns* v. *Innes,* 1942 S.C. 164.
[62] s. 30 (3).
[63] *Critchley* v. *Campbell* (1884) 11 R. 475.

possess.[64] If, during the currency of the lease, the landlord should fail to execute repairs, with the result that the subjects become unfit for their purpose, the tenant may abandon the lease. If he proposes also to claim damages he is probably bound to give immediate notice; if not, and the landlord accepts his renunciation, a compromise between the parties, involving an abandonment of the tenant's claim for damages, will be inferred.[65] The question whether a tenant may abandon the lease depends upon the materiality of the defects, which admits of no rule more definite than that both parties must behave reasonably in the matter.[66] Short of abandoning the lease, the tenant may find a remedy in damages,[67] or in the retention of his rent. This right has been rested on the principle that payment of rent, and furnishing a subject in the condition agreed upon, expressly or impliedly, are the correlative obligations in a mutual contract, and therefore that any material failure on the part of the landlord justifies the tenant in the exercise of a right of retention.[68] A defect will more readily be held to be material, especially in the case of failure to carry out improvements, in the later than in the earlier years of the lease.[69] An offer to consign the rent is an element in favour of the tenant's case, but is not per se a good answer to a demand for payment.[70] The fact that the tenant has paid certain instalments of the rent while the defects of which he complains were obvious does not bar an ultimate plea of retention.[71] It is a question of circumstances whether the payment of rent without objection will bar an ultimate claim for damages for defects existing during the period for which the rent was paid.[72] It is open to the parties to agree that the tenant shall not withhold payment of the rent.[73]

8. Obligations of Tenant.—A tenant is bound to enter into possession, to occupy and use the subjects. The tenant of an hotel, who had shut it up in the interests of a rival house of which he had obtained a lease, was found liable in damages for breach of a material condition.[74] A landlord was held entitled to terminate a lease on the same ground when the tenant who had undertaken to reside on the farm leased was sent to prison for a substantial period.[75] In his occupation and use he is bound to exercise reasonable care. Thus damages

[64] *Brodie* v. *M'Lachlan* (1900) 8 S.L.T. 145.
[65] *Lyons* v. *Anderson* (1886) 13 R. 1020.
[66] *M'Kimmie's Trs.* v. *Armour* (1899) 2 F. 156 (house had become insanitary).
[67] Continued occupation in the knowledge that a house is in a dangerous state may, on the principle of volenti non fit injuria, bar a claim for damages: *Dickie* v. *Amicable Property Investment Co.*, 1911 S.C. 1079; *Mullen* v. *C. C. of Dunbarton*, 1933 S.L.T. 185; *Proctor* v. *Cowlairs Co-operative Society*, 1961 S.L.T. 434.
[68] *Christie* v. *Birrells*, 1910 S.C. 986; *Earl of Galloway* v. *M'Connell*, 1911 S.C. 846; *Haig* v. *Boswall-Preston*, 1915 S.C. 339; *Fingland & Mitchell* v. *Howie*, 1926 S.C. 319; for a discussion of the principle of mutuality in relation to leases, see Paton & Cameron, *Landlord and Tenant*, p. 90; *Edmonstone* v. *Lamont*, 1975 S.L.T. (Sh. Ct.) 57.
[69] *Bowie* v. *Duncan*, 1807, Hume 839.
[70] *Earl of Galloway* v. *M'Connell*, supra.
[71] *Haig* v. *Boswall-Preston*, supra.
[72] *Ramsay* v. *Howison*, 1908 S.C. 697. Opinion of Lord Salvesen in *Haig* v. *Boswall-Preston*, supra.
[73] *Skene* v. *Cameron*, 1942 S.C. 393.
[74] *Graham* v. *Stevenson*, 1792, Hume 781. See *Smith* v. *Henderson* (1897) 24 R. 1102.
[75] *Blair Trust Co.* v. *Gilbert*, 1940 S.L.T. 322; affd., 1941 S.N. 2.

were held to be due for injury caused by burst pipes, in a case where a tenant had left the house in winter without turning off the water or giving notice to the landlord.[76] In the cases where the landlord has a right of hypothec the tenant is bound to plenish or stock the subjects, and the obligation may be enforced by a replenishing order in the Sheriff Court.[77] The tenant may not invert the possession, by utilising the subjects for some purpose other than that for which they were let. So the tenant of a farm is not entitled to use it as a posting station[78]; a priest may not erect, in premises let as his residence, wooden huts for the accommodation of evicted tenants.[79] On the other hand the tenant of a furnished house may alter the position of the furniture or pictures[80]; the tenant of a shop may sell his stock by auction.[81] The tenant is also bound to pay rent when it becomes due.

9. Rent: Hypothec.—A landlord has the ordinary remedies of a creditor for the recovery of his rent. In certain subjects he has in addition a right in security known as hypothec, which he may put in force by the process known as landlord's sequestration. At common law a general incident of the contract of lease, the landlord's hypothec was abolished, in 1880, as to all subjects let for agriculture or pasture, and exceeding two acres in extent.[82] It was also excluded, by the House Letting and Rating Act 1911, in all lets to which that Act applied, from all bedding material and all implements of trade used by the occupier or a member of his family, and also from all such furniture as the occupier might select, to the value of £10, according to the sheriff-officer's valuation.[83] That Act has however now been repealed,[84] and these exclusions no longer apply. In a case where the hypothec has been abolished a landlord has no preference over any other creditor.[85]

10. Invecta et Illata.—In cases where hypothec still exists, mainly in leases of houses, shops, mines and market gardens, the hypothec covers the ordinary equipment, the furniture in a house, the stock-in-trade in a shop. The subjects covered are known as the invecta et illata. Money, bonds, bills and the tenant's clothes are not included.[86] Probably, on the analogy of the law as to other forms of diligence, tools of trade are also exempt.[87] The hypothec may cover goods brought to the premises, though they do not belong to the tenant, as in the case of hired furniture.[88] It, then, applies whether the whole of the

---

[76] *Mickel* v. *M'Coard,* 1913 S.C. 896.
[77] *Whitelaw* v. *Fulton* (1871) 10 M. 27; *Wright* v. *Wightman* (1875) 3 R. 68.
[78] *Baillie* v. *Mackay* (1842) 4 D. 1520.
[79] *Kehoe* v. *Marquis of Lansdowne* [1893] A.C. 451.
[80] *Miller* v. *Stewart* (1899) 2 F. 309.
[81] *Keith* v. *Reid* (1870) 8 M. (H.L.) 110; *Morrison* v. *Forsyth,* 1909 S.C. 329 (clearance sale).
[82] Hypothec Abolition (Scotland) Act 1880 (43 Vict., c. 12). See Rankine, *Leases,* pp. 371–2.
[83] 1 & 2 Geo. V, c. 53, s. 10.
[84] Local Government (Scotland) Act 1973 (c. 65), Sched. 29.
[85] *M'Gavin* v. *Sturrock's Tr.* (1891) 18 R. 576.
[86] Bell, *Prin.,* § 1276.
[87] *Macpherson* v. *Macpherson's Tr.* (1905) 8 F. 191. See Sheriff Court cases in Rankine, *Leases,* 3rd ed., p. 374.
[88] *M'Intosh* v. *Potts* (1905) 7 F. 765; *Nelmes* v. *Ewing* (1883) 11 R. 193.

tenant's plenishing, or merely a single article,[89] is obtained on hire or hire-purchase, though not where the subjects are let furnished and an additional article is obtained on hire.[90] It is doubtful whether the right of hypothec over hired furniture is affected by notice given to the landlord before it is placed in the house.[91] Goods in a shop on sale or return present another doubtful case.[92] An agreement between the owner of the article and the tenant to exclude the article from the landlord's hypothec will not be effective against the landlord unless he has been informed of the agreement.[93] Hypothec does not cover goods belonging to the tenant which are on the premises for a purpose merely temporary, such as goods sent to be repaired, or for exhibition.[94] Nor does it cover goods which are the property of a member of the tenant's family, or of a lodger.[95] Goods of a sub-tenant, however, may be sequestrated for the rent due by the principal tenant, and also for the rent due by the sub-tenant himself.[96] If no steps are taken to enforce the hypothec it does not preclude the sale and removal of articles forming part of the invecta et illata, but if sequestration is used before an article sold has been removed the landlord's right is preferable to that of the purchaser, even although the property in the thing sold may have passed at the time of the sale.[97] In a sale under sequestration the owner of property attached as invecta et illata may insist that the tenant's goods shall be sold first.[98]

11. Hypothec: Rents Covered.—Hypothec secures one year's rent, not prior arrears.[99] It falls if not put in force by sequestration within three months of the last term of payment. It is the usual practice to sequestrate for the rent actually due and in security of that to become due at the next term.

The right of a landlord to sequestrate for rent is not affected by the bankruptcy of the tenant.[1] He is, however, subject to certain preferable claims, which must be met as far as the proceeds of the invecta et illata, when ultimately sold, suffice. The claims preferable are those which form preferred debts in bankruptcy.[2]

12. Sequestration.—Sequestration for rent is exclusively a Sheriff Court process.[3] The ordinary course of procedure is that a warrant to sequestrate is granted on an ex parte statement, the goods are inventoried and valued by a sheriff-officer, and ultimately sold, under a separate warrant from the sheriff,

---

[89] *Dundee Corporation* v. *Marr*, 1971 S.C. 96.
[90] *Edinburgh Albert Building Co.* v. *General Guarantee Corporation*, 1917 S.C. 239.
[91] See Rankine, *Leases*, p. 375.
[92] Stewart, *Diligence*, 470; Rankine, *Leases*, 377.
[93] *Jaffray* v. *Carrick* (1836) 15 S. 43; *Dundee Corporation* v. *Marr*, supra.
[94] *Pulsometer Co.* v. *Gracie* (1887) 14 R. 316.
[95] *Bell* v. *Andrews* (1885) 12 R. 961.
[96] *Steuart* v. *Stables* (1878) 5 R. 1024.
[97] *Ryan* v. *Little*, 1910 S.C. 219.
[98] *M'Intosh* v. *Potts* (1905) 7 F. 765.
[99] *Young* v. *Welsh* (1833) 12 S. 233.
[1] Bankruptcy (Scotland) Act, 1913, s. 115.
[2] See Bankruptcy, Ch. XLIX, infra, § 27; 1913 Act, s. 118, as amended.
[3] *Duncan* v. *Lodijinsky* (1904) 6 F. 408.

by auction. After they have been inventoried the goods are in manibus curiae, and anyone who removes them, be he the tenant, a purchaser, or another creditor, must, if in good faith, account for their value, and, if in bad faith, is liable for the rent.[4]

13. Right of Retention under Hypothec.—Without applying for sequestration a landlord may interdict the removal of the invecta et illata, and, if they have been removed, may obtain a warrant to have them brought back. It has been held that such a warrant should not be pronounced without intimation to the tenant, except for some exceptional reason specified in the judgment.[5] Interdict and recovery of goods constitute exceptional remedies, and the landlord will be liable in damages, either if the statement on which he obtains authority proves untrue,[6] or if there is a genuine dispute as to the rent, and the circumstances render extreme measures unnecessary.[7]

14. Rent: Legal and Conventional Terms.—The term of payment of rent is usually expressly agreed as between landlord and tenant in the lease. But in a question in the succession of the landlord or, if the landlord sells the subjects let, between him and the purchaser, the allocation of the rents may depend, in agricultural or pastoral leases,[8] on the legal and not on the conventional terms. The legal terms, in farms primarily arable, and where the tenant's entry is at Martinmas, are the Whitsunday and Martinmas following the term of entry. In a pastoral farm, with entry at Whitsunday, the first half-year's rent is legally due at entry, the second at the following Martinmas.[9] The underlying theory is that rent is not due legally (though it may be conventionally) until the tenant has had the benefit of the crop. Rents conventionally payable before the legal term are known as forehand, payable later, as backhand. The legal terms rule in allocating rents between the heir of a landlord and his executor, and also between a fiar and the representatives of the liferenter, except when the rent is forehand, when the conventional terms rule. The executor is entitled to all backhand rents which were legally due for the term preceding the landlord's death, and also, under the Apportionment Act 1870, to a share of the next term's rent corresponding to the number of days by which the deceased survived that term.[10] In the case of a sale, in the absence of any express provision, the purchaser is entitled to the rents to become due for the possession following his term of entry, according to the legal and not the conventional terms, except in the case of forehand rents, in which case he is entitled to the rents payable at the conventional terms following the term of entry.[11]

---

[4] Bell, *Prin.,* § 1244.
[5] *Johnston* v. *Young* (1890) 18 R. (J.C.) 6; *Jack* v. *Black,* 1911 S.C. 691.
[6] *Jack* v. *Black,* supra; *Shearer* v. *Nicoll,* 1935 S.L.T. 313.
[7] *Gray* v. *Weir* (1891) 19 R. 25.
[8] These rules do not apply to the rents of residential property, which accrue de die in diem: *Butter* v. *Foster,* 1912 S.C. 1218.
[9] See opinion of Lord Johnston in *Butter,* supra, at p. 1224; *Baillie* v. *Fletcher,* 1915 S.C. 677.
[10] *Campbell* v. *Campbell* (1849) 11 D. 1426; *Balfour-Kinnear* v. *Inland Revenue,* 1909 S.C. 619.
[11] Titles to Land Consolidation Act 1868, s. 8; *Baillie* v. *Fletcher,* 1915 S.C. 677.

15. Assignability: Subletting.—A lease may or may not be assignable. Where there is no express provision in the lease an exclusion of the power to assign or sublet will be implied at common law in accordance with the principle of delectus personae, subject to certain exceptions. Judicial or legal assignees are not excluded. Leases of unfurnished urban subjects, in town or country, may be assigned, for here the element of delectus personae is less strong.[12] Leases of rural subjects may also be assigned where they are for an extraordinary duration, on the basis that such a lease amounts in effect to a right of property.[13] Rural leases of ordinary duration, however, i.e., farm leases whether arable or pastoral, leases of shootings and fishings, are, according to the general rule, not assignable.[14] Subletting follows the same rules.[15] A provision (once common in mining leases) that the tenant shall not assign without the landlord's consent gives the landlord an absolute right to refuse, or to impose conditions.[16] Prior to the Land Tenure Reform (Scotland) Act 1974 a proprietor who had granted a lease to a tenant could not interpose another party as tenant so as to degrade the first lessee into the position of a sub-tenant.[17] It is however now competent, and deemed always to have been competent, to a lessor during the subsistence of the lease to grant a lease of or including his interest in the whole or part of the land already let, whether for a longer or shorter period or for the same duration as the lease already granted.[18] Such a grant is now effectual for all purposes as a lease of land.

16. Effects of Assignation.—The assignation of a lease is completed, in questions between the landlord, the tenant and the assignee, by intimation to the landlord.[19] While a sublease involves no change of tenant so far as the landlord is concerned and the original tenant continues bound to implement the obligations of the lease, an assignation involves the substitution of the assignee as the sole tenant. The result is that the cedent disappears and has no further rights or obligations after the date of entry, while the assignee incurs liability to the landlord for all future rents, and also probably for arrears.[20] There is no rule to preclude the assignation of an unprofitable lease, if assignable, to a person of no means. A sublet, on the other hand, does not bring the sub-tenant into any contractual relations with the landlord, does not involve him in any liability for rent, or affect the liability of the tenant.[21] In questions in the bankruptcy of a tenant an assignation, though followed by intimation to the landlord, does not complete the right of the assignee in a

---

[12] *Robb* v. *Brearton* (1895) 22 R. 885; Rankine, *Leases*, p. 175.
[13] Rankine, *Leases*, p. 173; *Bain* v. *Mackenzie* (1896) 23 R. 528 at 532, per Lord Kinnear.
[14] Bell, *Prin.*, § 1214; *Mackintosh* v. *May* (1895) 22 R. 345.
[15] Bell, *Prin.*, § 1216.
[16] *Marquis of Breadalbane* v. *Whitehead* (1893) 21 R. 138. See, however, as to discrimination by withholding consent on grounds of sex or race, Sex Discrimination Act 1975 (c. 65), ss. 31-32; Race Relations Act 1976 (c. 74), s. 24.
[17] *Wilson* v. *Wilson* (1859) 21 D. 309, per Lord Justice-Clerk Inglis at p. 312.
[18] 1974 Act (c. 38), s. 17.
[19] *Inglis* v. *Paul* (1829) 7 S. 469.
[20] *Skene* v. *Greenhill* (1825) 4 S. 25; *Burns* v. *Martin* (1887) 14 R. (H.L.) 20, opinion of Lord Watson.
[21] Bell, *Prin.*, § 1252.

question with the trustee in the sequestration. For that actual possession is required,[22] unless the lease is registered under the Registration of Leases (Scotland) Act 1857, in which case the assignation may be effectually completed by registration in the forms provided by the Act.[23]

17. Sale by Landlord.—When lands subject to a lease are sold, the original landlord, and his executors after his death, remain liable on all obligations which do not transmit against the purchaser.[24] Whether he remains liable on obligations which do transmit is not fully settled, but the law probably is that he remains liable on all obligations to pay money, such as an obligation to pay for improvements executed by the tenant, but that the purchaser alone is liable for upkeep and repairs.[25]

18. Bankruptcy of Tenant.—Except under an express provision, bankruptcy of the tenant does not put an end to the lease.[26] Whether a lease is assignable voluntarily or not it will pass, in the absence of an express provision to the contrary, to the trustee in bankruptcy of the tenant.[27] The trustee is never bound to adopt the lease. If he does, he incurs personal liability not only for the rent, but for arrears.[28] He is entitled to a reasonable time to consider the question, and temporary intromissions with the subjects, for the purpose of realising the bankrupt's effects, will not readily be construed as precluding ultimate rejection.[29] A conventional exclusion of the right of a trustee in sequestration is construed as giving the landlord an option to refuse, and cannot be founded on by the bankrupt.[30]

19. Succession to Tenant.—Prior to the assimilation of heritable and moveable succession by the Succession (Scotland) Act 1964,[31] a lease was heritable in the succession to a deceased tenant, and vested on his intestacy in his heir at law. It now vests in the tenant's executor,[32] and the right to succeed, unless carried by a destination in the lease or by a valid testamentary bequest, passes to his heirs in intestacy. To avoid cases where, because the deceased tenant has made no valid bequest of the lease or it has not been accepted by the legatee, a lease might otherwise require to be divided among several of the heirs in intestacy, the Act extended to the executor a limited power to assign the lease; this power may be exercised notwithstanding a prohibition of assignation in the lease, whether this be express or implied.[33]

---

[22] *Ramsay* v. *Commercial Bank* (1842) 4 D. 405.
[23] 20 & 21 Vict., c. 26, ss. 2, 16; See § 4, supra.
[24] *Gardiner* v. *Stewart's Trs.*, 1908 S.C. 985; *Riddell's Exrs.* v. *Milligan's Exrs.*, 1909 S.C. 1137.
[25] *Walker* v. *Masson* (1857) 19 D. 1099.
[26] *Dobie* v. *Marquis of Lothian* (1864) 2 M. 788; Rankine, *Leases*, p. 693.
[27] Bell, *Prin.*, § 1216. As to the trustee's right to dispose of growing crops, see *M'Kinley* v. *Hutchison's Tr.*, 1935 S.L.T. 62.
[28] *Dundas* v. *Morison* (1857) 20 D. 225.
[29] *M'Gavin* v. *Sturrock's Tr.* (1891) 18 R. 576.
[30] *Dobie* v. *Marquis of Lothian* (1864) 2 M. 788.
[31] 1964, c. 41, s. 1.
[32] ss. 14, 36 (2); see *Cormack* v. *McIldowie's Exrs.*, 1975 S.L.T. 214.
[33] s. 16 (1), (2).

He may transfer the lease under this statutory power to any one of the deceased's heirs in intestacy, or in or towards the satisfaction of a claim by a person entitled to legal or prior rights out of the deceased's estate; but, where he has to rely on this power, he may not transfer the lease to anyone else without the consent of the landlord.

Unless the lease could be assigned inter vivos the tenant had no power at common law to bequeath his lease so as to compel the landlord to accept his legatee,[34] although if the landlord accepts the legatee as tenant the bequest will be effective.[35] The 1964 Act, however, conferred on the tenant a limited right of bequest in cases where a prohibition of assignation was merely implied. Provided there is no express prohibition, the tenant may validly bequeath the lease to any one of the persons who would have been entitled to succeed to it as his intestate heirs.[36] A slightly wider right of bequest was afforded by the Agricultural Holdings and Crofters Acts, which is unaffected by this provision of the 1964 Act.[37] In the case of dwelling-houses which are subject to the Rent Acts certain persons are entitled to succeed to the lease to the extent of remaining in the house by virtue of the Acts on the death of the tenant, independently of any rights at common law. Two transmissions of the right to remain in occupation may occur; thereafter, in the case of a contractual tenancy, the normal law of succession will operate.[38]

20. Termination: Notice.—A lease comes to an end if either party gives notice within a certain period before the term fixed for its expiry. Such notice is necessary because in its absence the relationship of landlord and tenant is continued by tacit relocation.[39] The lease is then renewed, not for the original term but for a year, and from year to year thereafter. The legal effect of tacit relocation is that all the stipulations and conditions of the original contract remain in force, so far as these are consistent with a lease from year to year; an option to renew a lease for a longer period will not be exercisable during tacit relocation.[40] In the case of an urban lease, verbal notice within the necessary period by either party of his intention to terminate the contract is sufficient to prevent the setting in of tacit relocation.[41] Where there are joint tenants, to exclude tacit relocation, a notice of removal by one of them will be enough.[42] If, having served notice to quit, the landlord continues regularly and without reservation to accept rent from the tenant he may be held to have departed from the notice or to be barred from insisting on it, so that a new lease will arise by tacit relocation.[43] If on the expiry of the contractual term the tenant remains in possession after notice to quit, he is in the position of an

[34] See Hunter, *Landlord and Tenant*, i., p. 237; *Bain* v. *Mackenzie* (1896) 23 R. 528; *Reid's Trs.* v. *Macpherson*, 1975 S.L.T. 101.
[35] *Kennedy* v. *Johnstone*, 1956 S.C. 39, per Lord Sorn at p. 47.
[36] s. 29 (1).
[37] s. 29 (2).
[38] See infra, § 45.
[39] See Extinction of Obligations, Ch. XV, supra, § 22.
[40] *Commercial Union Assurance Co.*, 1964 S.L.T. 62.
[41] See Rankine, *Leases*, p. 574; *Craighall Cast Stone Co.* v. *Wood Bros.*, 1931 S.C. 66.
[42] *Smith* v. *Grayton Estates*, 1960 S.C. 349.
[43] See Gloag, *Contract*, p. 735; *Milner's C.B.* v. *Mason*, 1965 S.L.T. (Sh. Ct.) 56.

intruder without title, and may be liable for violent profits.[44] The landlord's remedy in order to recover possession from the tenant is to raise an action of removing against him.[45]

In order to be effective, the landlord's notice to quit, or the tenant's notice of removal, must be served so as to give due notice to the other party. The period of notice required is laid down by statute and varies according to the type of lease. The leading provisions may be summarised as follows[46]:

(a) in the case of lands exceeding two acres in extent, written notice must be given, failing an agreement to the contrary, not less than one or more than two years before the ish[47]; where the lease is from year to year, however, or for any other period less than three years, the minimum period is six months.[48] Where the lease is one of agricultural or pastoral land and falls within the Agricultural Holdings Act the period of notice, of not less than one or more than two years, is fixed by law and cannot be varied by agreement; this period applies in all cases, including leases from year to year, except where the lease is for a period of less than year to year.[49]

(b) in the case of houses or land not exceeding two acres in extent, fishings and shootings, the period of notice prescribed, unless otherwise agreed, is a minimum of 40 days before 15th May or 11th November according to the term at which the tenancy is to end[50]; where the subjects are let for a period not exceeding four months the period of notice must be one third of the full duration of the lease.[51] These requirements are reinforced by a general provision with regard to dwelling-houses now contained in the Rent (Scotland) Act 1971,[52] which cannot be varied by agreement, that a minimum of four weeks' notice must be given in all cases where a notice to quit is required.

In the case of leased premises in respect of which a closing order or the like has been made, either the landlord or the tenant may apply to the Sheriff for an order determining the lease.[53] If an executor, to whom a lease has devolved in intestacy, is satisfied that he cannot dispose of the lease according to law or has in fact not done so within a certain period, normally one year from the date of the deceased tenant's death, he or the landlord may, by giving due notice, terminate the lease altogether.[54]

[44] See Extinction of Obligations, Ch. XV, supra, § 22.
[45] For procedure in actions of removing, see Sheriff Courts (Scotland) Act 1907, Sched. 1, rules 110-122; such actions are subject to the summary cause procedure: Sheriff Courts (Scotland) Act 1971, s. 35.
[46] See, for a full statement, Paton and Cameron, *Landlord and Tenant,* pp. 262 et seq.
[47] 1907 Act, s. 34 (*a*).
[48] 1907 Act, s. 34 (*b*).
[49] Agricultural Holdings (Scotland) Act 1949, s. 24.
[50] Sheriff Courts (Scotland) Act 1907, s. 37; note that, under s. 38, notice to quit is obligatory, where the lease is for a period less than one year, only in the absence of express stipulation. See also Removal Terms (Scotland) Act 1886, s. 4.
[51] 1907 Act, s. 38, and 1886 Act, s. 5, both as amended by Rent (Scotland) Act 1971, Sched. 18, Pt. II.
[52] 1971 (c. 28), s. 131; see *Schnabel* v. *Allard* [1967] 1 Q.B. 627.
[53] Housing (Scotland) Act 1966, s. 187.
[54] Succession (Scotland) Act 1964, s. 16 (3), (4).

21. Termination: Irritancies.—Although a lease is normally terminated by a notice to quit or of removal, it may also be brought to an end before the date of its natural expiration by the destruction of the subjects,[55] or their acquisition in whole or part by a third party acting under compulsory powers,[56] or because there is no-one left who can claim to be a tenant, as where a lease was granted in favour of a partnership and the partnership has been dissolved by death.[57] The lease itself may contain provisions for its premature termination, known as breaks, in favour of either party or both, that in the option of the tenant being a power to renounce and that in favour of the landlord being a power to resume.[58] A power in favour of the landlord to resume for planting woodlands is common in agricultural leases.[59] The landlord may also consent to a renunciation of the subjects by the tenant before the ish.

A lease may also be terminated before the date of its natural expiration by the enforcement of an irritancy,[60] legal or conventional, in which case the tenant's right to occupy the subjects will be forfeited or annulled. The legal irritancies relate solely to non-payment of rent. An irritancy is recognised at common law, and enforceable only by an extraordinary action of removing in the Court of Session, in all cases where two years' rent is unpaid.[61] There is no other legal irritancy in urban subjects. In subjects falling under the Agricultural Holdings Act 1949, where six months' rent is due and unpaid, the landlord may raise an action in the Sheriff Court concluding for the removal of the tenant at the next term of Whitsunday or Martinmas.[62] Conventional irritancies[63] are unlimited in number and may be used to underwrite a variety of obligations; usually they cover non-payment of rent and the various forms of insolvency. Legal irritancies may be purged at any time before decree is granted. Conventional irritancies cannot be purged, unless they merely express the irritancy which the law would infer. Once incurred they will be strictly enforced,[64] subject however to the power which is reserved to the Court to prevent oppressive use or abuse of the irritancy.[65] A landlord who enforces an irritancy cannot also claim damages for the premature determination of the lease.[66] Whatever may be the terms in which a conventional irritancy is expressed, it is construed as giving the landlord an option to avoid the lease, not as giving the defaulting tenant a right to abandon it.[67]

---

[55] *Duff* v. *Fleming* (1870) 8 M. 769.
[56] *Mackeson* v. *Boyd*, 1942 S.C. 56.
[57] *Inland Revenue* v. *Graham's Trs.*, 1971 S.C. (H.L.) 1; *Jardine-Paterson* v. *Fraser*, 1974 S.L.T. 93.
[58] Rankine, *Leases*, p. 527; Paton & Cameron, *Landlord and Tenant*, p. 242.
[59] *Sykes and Edgar*, 1974 S.L.T. (Land Ct.) 4.
[60] The word "irritancy" means forfeiture: see *Dorchester Studios (Glasgow)* v. *Stone*, 1975 S.L.T. 153 (H.L.) per Lord Fraser of Tullybelton at p. 160.
[61] Erskine, II., 6, 44. As to the construction of irritancies, see Breach of Contract, Ch. XIII, supra, § 16.
[62] 1949 Act, s. 19.
[63] As to purging of conventional irritancies, see *McDouall's Trs.* v. *MacLeod*, 1949 S.C. 593; *Dorchester Studios (Glasgow)* v. *Stone*, 1975 S.L.T. 153 (H.L.).
[64] Note however the limited protection where the lease is vested in an executor: Succession (Scotland) Act 1964, s. 16 (7).
[65] See *Lucas's Exrs.* v. *Demarco*, 1968 S.L.T. 89; *Dorchester Studios (Glasgow)* v. *Stone*, supra.
[66] *Buttercase* v. *Geddie* (1897) 24 R. 1128.
[67] *Bidoulac* v. *Sinclair's Tr.* (1889) 17 R. 144.

22. Ground Game.—An agricultural tenant, if there is no stipulation to the contrary in his lease, may kill rabbits, and may authorise anyone else to do so.[68] Under the Ground Game Act 1880,[69] an occupier of land has the right, declared to be "incident to and inseparable from his occupation of the land," and of which he cannot deprive himself by any contract,[70] to kill hares and rabbits. This right may be exercised by the occupier himself, or, with his authority in writing, by members of his household resident on the land, persons in his ordinary employment, and one other person bona fide employed for reward[71]; the occupier and the owner or any other person having the right to kill or take game on the land may make an agreement for the joint execution, or the execution for their joint benefit, of that right otherwise than by the use of firearms.[72] Only the occupier and one other person authorised in writing may use firearms,[73] except where authorisation of additional persons is sanctioned by the Secretary of State.[74] There are limitations as to the period of the year during which the occupier's right to kill ground game with firearms may be exercised.[75] It is a criminal offence for anyone to use firearms for the purpose of killing ground game between the expiration of the first hour after sunset, and the commencement of the last hour before sunrise, or to employ poison.[76] The use of spring traps is closely regulated, and it is an offence to use traps other than those approved, or to use them in an unapproved manner, or, except under licence, to use them elsewhere than in a rabbit hole.[77]

II. AGRICULTURAL HOLDINGS[78]

23. Agricultural Holdings Acts.—At common law a tenant who made improvements on the subjects let had no claim for compensation against the landlord, the legal presumption being that he made the improvements in the hope of recouping himself during the remaining years of the lease.[79] While this remains the law in urban leases, a series of statutes have introduced a right to compensation in the case of agricultural holdings with the object of encouraging the tenant to farm well and to make the necessary improvements to his holding. The code relating to agricultural holdings is contained principally in the Agricultural Holdings (Scotland) Act 1949,[80] as amended by

---

[68] *Crawshay* v. *Duncan,* 1915 S.C. (J.) 64.
[69] 43 & 44 Vict., c. 47.
[70] 1880 Act, s. 3. *Sherrard* v. *Gascoigne* [1900] 2 Q.B. 279.
[71] s. 1. *Stuart* v. *Murray* (1884) 12 R. (J.) 9; *Niven* v. *Renton* (1888) 15 R. (J.) 42.
[72] Agriculture (Scotland) Act 1948, s. 48 (4).
[73] 1880 Act, s. 1 (1) (a).
[74] See 1948 Act, s. 48 (2); Pests Act 1954.
[75] 1800 Act, s. 1 (3), as amended by 1948 Act, s. 48 (1).
[76] Hares (Scotland) Act 1848, s. 4; 1880 Act, s. 6, as amended by Pests Act 1954.
[77] 1948 Act, s. 50, as amended by Pests Act 1954, s. 10.
[78] See Connell, *Agricultural Holdings Acts,* (6th ed., 1970). For a convenient statement of the current legislation, see *Parliament House Book,* Division L.
[79] *Walker* v. *M'Knight* (1886) 13 R. 599.
[80] 12 & 13 Geo. VI, c. 75.

the Agricultural Act 1958,[81] and the Agriculture (Miscellaneous Provisions) Acts 1968 and 1976.[82] The 1949 Act was a consolidating measure, and decisions under earlier enactments[83] remain of importance. Besides conferring on the tenant important compensation rights, these Acts have afforded him substantial security of tenure and regulate closely the rights and obligations of each party under the lease. The Acts recognise only one type of tenant, that is, the tenant entitled to claim the benefit of the statutory provisions in favour of agricultural tenants[84]; and contracting out of the statutory provisions is widely prohibited.[85]

24. Agricultural Holding: Meaning.—The 1949 Act defines the term "agricultural holding" as "the aggregate of the agricultural land comprised in a lease, not being a lease under which the said land is let to the tenant during his continuance in any office, appointment or employment held under the landlord."[86] "Agricultural land" is itself defined[87] as meaning "land used for agriculture which is so used for the purposes of a trade or business" including any other land which may be designated as agricultural land by the Secretary of State under the 1948 Act.[88] The definition of the word "agriculture" in the 1949 Act is comprehensive and covers every kind of horticultural and farming activity.[89] "Lease" is defined as meaning "a letting of land for a term of years, or for lives, or for lives and years, or from year to year."[90]

25. Incidents of Lease.—*Minimum Term.*—The Act contains a general restriction on letting agricultural land for less than from year to year; unless the lease was entered into for grazing or mowing only for a specified period of the year, or was granted by a person who is himself a tenant for a shorter period than from year to year, such a lease, in the absence of the prior approval of the Secretary of State, will be treated, with the necessary modifications, as if it were a lease from year to year.[91] When the ish is reached the lease is held to be continued in force from year to year by tacit relocation until notice to terminate is given by either party.[92]

Written Lease.—Where there is no written lease[93] embodying the terms of a tenancy, either party may require the other to enter into a written agreement for this purpose.[94] Where a written lease has been entered into but it does not

---

[81] 6 & 7 Eliz. II, c. 71.
[82] 1968 (c. 34); 1976 (c. 55).
[83] Esp. Agricultural Holdings (Scotland) Act 1923; Smallholders and Agricultural Holdings (Scotland) Act 1931; and Agriculture (Scotland) Act 1948.
[84] *Dalgety's Trs.* v. *Drummond,* 1938 S.C. 709.
[85] e.g., ss. 3, 15, 16, 24 (1), 64 of the 1949 Act.
[86] s. 1 (1); see further, Connell, op. cit., p. 105.
[87] s. 1 (2).
[88] Under s. 86 (1) of the 1948 Act.
[89] s. 93 (1) of the 1949 Act.
[90] s. 93 (1); see *Stirrat* v. *Whyte,* 1967 S.C. 265, for an example of a let which was held not to be a lease within the meaning of this definition.
[91] s. 2; see *Gairneybridge Farm and King,* 1974 S.L.T. (Land Ct.) 8.
[92] s. 3; see *Smith* v. *Grayton Estates,* 1960 S.C. 349.
[93] As to meaning of "lease in writing," see *Grieve* v. *Barr,* 1954 S.C. 414.
[94] 1949 Act, s. 4 (1) (a).

contain any one or more of the matters specified in Schedule 5[95] to the 1949 Act or is inconsistent with it or with the provisions of section 5 as to the liability for the maintenance of fixed equipment, a similar request may be made.[96] If parties are unable to agree the matter may be referred to arbitration.

Liability for Maintenance.—The Act deems[97] the incorporation in every lease of an undertaking by the landlord to put the fixed equipment on the holding into a thorough state of repair, and to provide the necessary buildings and other equipment. The landlord is also bound to make such replacement or renewal as may be rendered necessary by natural decay or by fair wear and tear. The tenant's liability is limited to an undertaking to maintain the equipment in a state of good repair, fair wear and tear excepted.

Variation of Rent.—The Act enables either party to seek a variation of the contractual rent; he may serve a written demand on the other party for a reference of the matter to arbitration.[98] A criterion for the arbiter in determining what figure represents the rent properly payable in respect of the lease was introduced by the 1958 Act[99]; shortly stated, he is required to decide having regard to the terms of the lease, but not to the personal circumstances of the particular parties making the reference,[1] what is an open market rent for the holding. The landlord, where he has carried out certain specific improvements, has an absolute right to increase the rent by an amount equal to the increase in the rental value of the holding attributable to the carrying out of the improvements[2]; the increase operates from the date of completion and the landlord must serve notice in writing on the tenant.

Pactional Rent.—A provision in a lease for penal or pactional rent, i.e. for payment of a fixed sum as damages for any breach of its conditions, is not binding. The landlord, in spite of the existence of such a clause in the lease, must prove the actual damage which he has sustained in consequence of the tenant's breach of the conditions of the lease.[3]

Freedom of Cropping.—A tenant may practise any system of cropping arable lands, and may dispose of the produce of the farm other than manure produced on it as he pleases, notwithstanding any provision of the lease or local custom which may bind him to some particular method of cultivation.[4]

---

[95] These matters are: (i) the names of the parties, (ii) particulars of the holding, with reference to a map or plan, (iii) the terms of the lease, (iv) the rent and the dates on which payable, (v) certain undertakings by the parties relating to damage to buildings and the destruction of harvested crops.

[96] 1949 Act, s. 4 (1) (*b*).

[97] Ibid., s. 5.

[98] Ibid., s. 7.

[99] 1958 Act, s. 2, amending 1949 Act, s. 7 (1); see *Kilmarnock Estates* v. *Barr*, 1969 S.L.T. (Land Ct.) 10.

[1] The decision in *Guthe* v. *Broatch*, 1956 S.C. 132, is thus superseded.

[2] 1949 Act, s. 8.

[3] Ibid., s. 16.

[4] Ibid., s. 12 (1).

This provision does not apply to the last year of the lease, nor, in leases from year to year, to the year before the tenant leaves; and it does not apply to land in grass which is to be retained in that condition throughout the tenancy.[5] On the other hand, the tenant must make provision against the deterioration of the holding; and, in the case of crops sold contrary to the provisions of the lease or to local custom, must return to the holding the full equivalent manurial value thereof. The landlord is entitled to obtain an interdict to restrain the exercise of the tenant's freedom of cropping if he allows the holding to deteriorate, and to damages for his failure in these duties. After notice to terminate has been given, the tenant may not remove any manure or compost unless and until he has given the landlord or the incoming tenant a reasonable opportunity to purchase it at its fair market value.[6]

Fixtures.—It is provided that any engine, machinery, fencing or other fixture affixed to a holding by a tenant, and any building erected by him for which he is not entitled to compensation, and which is not affixed or erected in pursuance of some obligation, or in substitution for some fixture or building belonging to the landlord, shall be the property of the tenant and removable by him before, or within six months after, the termination of the lease. The right of removal is conditional on the tenant having paid all rent owing by him, and satisfied his other obligations in respect of the holding. In removal no avoidable damage to other buildings must be done, and all damage done must be made good. The tenant must give one month's notice in writing of his intention to remove a fixture or building, and the landlord may elect to purchase it at a price which is the equivalent of the fair value to an incoming tenant.[7]

Record of Holding.—Either landlord or tenant may at any time require the making of a record of the condition of the fixed equipment on and of the cultivation of the holding[8]; the tenant may also require the making of a record of the existing improvements carried out by him or for which he, with the consent in writing of his landlord, has paid compensation to an outgoing tenant, and of any fixtures or buildings which he is entitled to remove. Such record will, where required, be made by a person appointed by the Secretary of State, and the cost, unless otherwise agreed, will be borne equally by the parties. In leases entered into after the Act of 1949, however, a record of the condition of the fixed equipment must be made forthwith.[9] The existence of such a record is a pre-requisite to any claim by the tenant for compensation for continuous good farming, and to any claim by the landlord for compensation for deterioration.[10]

[5] s. 12 (5).
[6] s. 13.
[7] s. 14.
[8] s. 17.
[9] s. 5.
[10] ss. 56-58.

26. Notice to Quit and Removal.—Where a tenant is six months in arrear with his rent, the landlord may raise an action in the Sheriff Court for his removal at the next term of Martinmas or Whitsunday.[11] Decree of removal and ejection of the tenant may follow, unless the tenant pays the arrears due by him or finds caution for them to the Sheriff's satisfaction. A lease terminated in this way is treated[12] as if it had expired naturally at that term, and the tenant will be entitled to the usual away-going rights, except compensation for disturbance.

Where a tenancy is to be terminated otherwise than of consent at the expiry of the stipulated period for the endurance of the lease, notice to quit or of removal must be given.[13] In order to be effective, such notice[14] must be given not less than one or more than two years before the expiry of the lease, notwithstanding any contractual provision to the contrary[15]; failing such notice, the lease is renewed by tacit relocation from year to year. Where notice is served on the tenant, he may within one month serve a counter-notice on the landlord.[16] This has the effect of restricting the operation of the notice to quit to cases where the landlord can obtain the consent of the Land Court, except in certain special circumstances,[17] e.g., where the notice is given by reason of the tenant's bankruptcy,[18] or on the issue within the last nine months by the Land Court of a certificate of bad husbandry,[19] or because the tenant has failed to comply with a demand in writing to remedy a breach of any term or condition of his tenancy,[20] or where the tenant has acquired right to the lease by succession or as a legatee, and in each case it is stated in the notice to quit that it is given by reason of these circumstances.[21] The Land Court may only give their consent, where it is required, to the operation of a notice to quit if they are satisfied as to one or more of the following reasons, which the landlord must specify in his application[22]:

(a) that the carrying out of the purpose for which the landlord seeks to terminate the tenancy is desirable in the interests of good husbandry;

---

[11] s. 19 (1).
[12] s. 19 (2).
[13] s. 24 (1); the landlord's right to remove a tenant whose estate has been sequestrated, or who has incurred an irritancy under the lease, remains unaffected: s. 24 (5).
[14] See Removal Terms (Scotland) Act 1886, s. 6; Sheriff Courts (Scotland) Act 1907, ss. 36, 37 and Form H. As to the effect of deviation from the requirements of Form H, see *Rae* v. *Davidson*, 1954 S.C. 361; *Callander* v. *Watherston*, 1970 S.L.T. (Land Ct.) 14; *Mackie* v. *Gardner*, 1973 S.L.T. (Land Ct.) 11; *Gemmell* v. *Andrew*, 1975 S.L.T. (Land Ct.) 5. The tenant's notice of removal may be informal.
[15] *Duguid* v. *Muirhead*, 1926 S.C. 1078.
[16] Under s. 25, as amended by 1958 Act, Sched. I, para. 35.
[17] s. 25 (2); the tenant may take any question arising under this subsection to arbitration: s. 27, as substituted by 1958 Act, Sched. I., para. 37.
[18] s. 25 (2) (g).
[19] s. 25 (2) (d).
[20] s. 25 (2) (e), subject however in the case of a breach relating to fixed equipment to Agriculture (Miscellaneous Provisions) Act 1976, s. 14. Note that the rights afforded by sub-heads (d) and (e) are mutually exclusive: *Macnabb* v. *Anderson*, 1955 S.C. 38.
[21] 1958 Act, s. 6 (3), as amended by Succession (Scotland) Act 1964, Sched. 2, para. 23; an exception is made in the case of near relatives: see Agriculture (Miscellaneous Provisions) Act 1968, s. 18.
[22] s. 26 (1) and see proviso; *Altyre Estate Trs.* v. *McLay*, 1975 S.L.T. (Land Ct.) 12.

(b) that its carrying out is desirable in the interests of sound management of the estates of which it forms part;[23]

(c) that its carrying out is desirable for the purposes of agricultural research, experiment, etc.;

(d) that greater hardship would be caused by withholding than by giving consent to the operation of the notice;[24] or

(e) that the landlord's purpose is to employ the land for use other than for agriculture.

Further protection is afforded to the tenant by the general proviso that the Land Court may withhold their consent, even if they are satisfied as to one or more of these reasons, if it appears to them that a fair and reasonable landlord would not insist on possession.[25]

27. Compensation to Tenant for Improvements: Arbitration.—A tenant is entitled, on quitting the holding, to compensation for certain improvements.[26] The rules relating to the improvements for which compensation may be claimed are set out in sections 36-56 of the 1949 Act and Schedules of some complexity. Schedules I to IV, to which reference must be made, enumerate the improvements and they are classified (a) according to the dates when they were begun, and (b) according as they call or do not call for the consent of or notice to the landlord. It should be noted that a landlord, if the holding has deteriorated through the failure of the tenant to cultivate according to the rules of good husbandry, may claim compensation in his turn.[27] In the cases of leases entered into after certain dates no claim is good unless a record of the condition of the holding has been made. The amount of compensation will be ascertained, in default of agreement, by arbitration.[28] In fixing compensation for improvements the arbiter is to give such sum as fairly represents the value of the improvement to an incoming tenant[29] and is bound in certain cases to take into account any benefit which the landlord has given or allowed in consideration of the tenant executing the improvement.[30] It was held[31] that no compensation was due if the tenant was expressly bound to execute the improvement in question, but this is no longer the law except as to leases before January 1, 1921.[32] In general, contracting out of the compensation provisions of the Act is not allowed.[33]

Arbitration is the method by which all claims of whatever nature by the tenant or the landlord[34] arising under the Act or on or out of the termination

[23] See *Gemmell* v. *Andrew, supra.*
[24] See *Graham* v. *Lamont,* 1970 S.L.T. (Land Ct.) 10.
[25] s. 26 (1) and see proviso; *Altyre Estate Trs.* v. *McLay,* 1975 S.L.T. (Land Ct.) 12.
[26] s. 38; see also s. 86 (3).
[27] ss. 57-59.
[28] See Sched. VI of the 1949 Act for provisions regulating arbitration.
[29] ss. 38, 49.
[30] See s. 49 (2).
[31] *Earl of Galloway* v. *M'Clelland,* 1915 S.C. 1062.
[32] s. 37 (1).
[33] s. 64 (1); *Young* v. *Oswald,* 1949 S.C. 412 was decided on the very different wording of the Act of 1923 and is of doubtful application.
[34] As to meaning of landlord, see *Cunningham* v. *Fife County Council,* 1948 S.C. 439.

of the holding are to be settled.[35] A general reference to arbitration, as to "any question or difference of any kind" except a question or difference as to liability for rent, is made by the Act to cover cases for which no express provision is made.[36] Where the question or difference relates to a demand in writing served on the tenant by the landlord requiring the tenant to remedy a breach of any term or condition of the tenancy by the doing of any work of provision, repair, maintenance or replacement of fixed equipment, the arbiter has power to modify that demand.[37] An arbiter acting under the Act may at any stage in the proceedings ex proprio motu state a case on a question of law for the opinion of the Sheriff, and either party may apply to the Sheriff to direct the arbiter to do so.[38] The Sheriff's opinion, once given, is binding upon the arbiter,[39] but there is a final right of appeal to the Court of Session.[40]

28. Compensation to Tenant for Disturbance.—When a landlord gives notice to quit (or the tenant gives a counter-notice under section 33) and the tenant leaves the holding, he is entitled to compensation for disturbance,[41] unless the proviso to section 35 (1) applies. The minimum amount is one year's rent; the maximum, on proof of additional loss directly attributable to his removal, two years' rent.[42] Particulars of any claim must be given to the landlord within two months of the termination of the tenancy even where the claim is restricted to the minimum.[43] And the particulars must give fair notice of the basis of the demand made against the landlord.[44]

Where he is entitled to compensation for disturbance, the tenant is in certain cases entitled under section 9 of the 1968 Act[45] to payment in addition of a sum to assist in the reorganisation of his affairs, being a sum equal to four times the annual rent or an appropriate proportion in the case of part of a holding. No such sum is payable however if the tenancy is terminated by virtue of a notice to quit which contains a statement,[46] and, if an application is made to the Land Court for consent to the operation of the notice, the Court is satisfied that the carrying out of the purpose for which the landlord proposes to terminate the tenancy is desirable on one or other of a number of grounds set out in section 11 of the Act. These grounds relate to good husbandry, sound management of the estates of which the holding forms part, agricultural research, and to the fact that the landlord will suffer hardship

---

[35] s. 68. As to appointment of arbiter, see *Chalmers Property Investment Co.* v. *MacColl*, 1951 S.C. 24. Note that, if both parties agree, recourse may be made to the Land Court instead of to arbitration: s. 78.
[36] s. 74. See *Brodie* v. *Ker*, 1952 S.C. 216.
[37] Agriculture (Miscellaneous Provisions) Act 1976 (c. 55), s. 13.
[38] 1949 Act, Sched. 6, para. 19.
[39] *Mitchell-Gill* v. *Buchan*, 1921 S.C. 390.
[40] 1949 Act, Sched. 6, para. 20.
[41] s. 35 (1).
[42] s. 35 (2).
[43] *M'Laren* v. *Turnbull*, 1942 S.C. 179.
[44] *Simpson* v. *Henderson*, 1944 S.C. 365; *Edinburgh Corporation* v. *Gray*, 1948 S.C. 538.
[45] Agriculture (Miscellaneous Provisions) Act 1968 (c. 34). This is a fixed payment, regardless of actual loss: *Copeland* v. *McQuaker*, 1973 S.L.T. 186.
[46] As to this requirement, see *Barnes-Graham* v. *Lamont*, 1971 S.C. 170; *Copeland* v. *McQuaker*, supra.

unless the notice to quit has effect.[47] The right to an additional payment is also excluded in cases where the tenancy is terminated by notice to quit served on a tenant who has acquired right to the lease by succession or as a legatee.[48]

29. Compensation for Damage by Game.—A tenant is entitled to compensation for damage by game (i.e. deer, pheasants, partridges, grouse, black game) provided that the amount of damage done exceeds 12 pence per hectare of the area affected, and that the tenant has not permission in writing to kill the game in question.[49] Provision is made for timely notice to the landlord of a claim under this head.[50] A shooting tenant is bound to indemnify the landlord against claims for such compensation.[51] It has been held to be no objection to a claim that the damage was done by black game coming from another property and at a season of the year when it was unlawful to kill them.[52] When a tenant has permission from the landlord to kill any of the enumerated kinds of game, no claim for compensation in respect of damage by game of that kind is competent.[53]

30. Bequest of Lease: Succession.—The tenant of a holding may, unless his power to do so is expressly excluded by the lease,[54] bequeath his lease to his son-in-law or daughter-in-law or to any one of the persons who would be, or would in any circumstances have been, entitled to succeed to the estate on his intestacy.[55] The legatee must, unless unavoidably prevented, intimate the bequest to the landlord within 21 days of the tenant's death. By so doing he accepts the lease, which then becomes binding upon both as from the date of the deceased's death unless the landlord, within one month of intimation being made, gives a counter-notice to the legatee that he objects to receiving him as tenant. If such objection is made, the legatee may apply to the Land Court for an order declaring him to be tenant under the lease, which the Land Court must grant unless a reasonable ground of objection is established by the landlord.[56] If the legatee refuses the bequest or is rejected, the right to the lease will be treated as intestate estate of the deceased tenant, and will pass accordingly.[57] The acquirer of such a lease, that is to say any person to whom the lease is transferred under section 16 of the Succession (Scotland) Act

---

[47] 1968 Act, s. 11 (1). Note however that the sub-section does not apply if the reasons given by the Land Court for consent to the operation of the notice include or would have included the reason that the landlord's purpose is to employ the land for use other than agriculture: see s. 11 (2).
[48] 1968 Act, s. 11 (1) (c).
[49] 1949 Act, s. 15 (1), as amended by Agriculture (Adaptation of Enactments) (Scotland) Regulations 1977 (S.I. 1977 No. 2007).
[50] s. 15 (1) (a), (b) and see *Earl of Morton's Trs.* v. *Macdougall,* 1944 S.C. 410.
[51] s. 15 (3).
[52] *Thomson* v. *Earl of Galloway,* 1919 S.C. 611.
[53] *Ross* v. *Watson,* 1943 S.C. 406.
[54] *Kennedy* v. *Johnstone,* 1956 S.C. 39.
[55] s. 20 (1), as substituted by Succession (Scotland) Act 1964, Sched. 2, para. 19.
[56] s. 20 (4). Such a ground must be personal to the heir; e.g., *Reid* v. *Duffus Estate,* 1955 S.L.C.R. 13.
[57] s. 20 (7), as substituted by Succession (Scotland) Act 1964, Sched. 2, para. 21.

1964,[58] must also within 21 days notify the landlord, who may again give a counter-notice, remitting the matter to the Land Court.[59]

III. LANDHOLDERS AND CROFTERS

31. Small Landholders Acts.—A substantial proportion of the agricultural and pastoral land in Scotland does not fall under the Agricultural Holdings Acts, but is dealt with, as landholders' holdings or as crofts, by separate statutory provisions. These holdings are lettings of agricultural land which do not exceed 20 hectares whatever the rent, or do not exceed £50 in rent, whatever the area; in the case of crofts the maximum area, whatever the rent, is 30 hectares. These lettings were originally brought under statutory control by the Crofters Holdings (Scotland) Act 1886,[60] which applied only in the crofting counties.[61] That Act was amended by the Small Landholders (Scotland) Act 1911,[62] which extended the statutory protection to similar holdings throughout the country; the 1911 Act was itself amended by the Land Settlement (Scotland) Act 1919,[63] and the Small Landholders and Agricultural Holdings (Scotland) Act 1931.[64] In 1955 the separate category of crofters was reinstituted in the crofting counties only by the Crofters (Scotland) Act 1955.[65]

The 1911 Act established the Scottish Land Court,[66] which superseded the Crofters Commission operating under the 1886 Act. A new Crofters Commission was set up by the 1955 Act for administrative purposes, but the Land Court continues to have jurisdiction over crofters as well as landholders in judicial matters, and it has important functions with regard to agricultural holdings.[67] The Land Court is final on all questions of fact, but may ex proprio motu, and must, on the application of either party, state a case on a question of law to either Division of the Court of Session. There is no appeal to the House of Lords.[68] The powers and jurisdiction of the Land Court lie solely within the limits which statute has laid down, and questions which it has no jurisdiction to decide require to be determined in the ordinary Courts.[69] An order or determination of the Land Court may be enforced as if it were a decree of the Sheriff having jurisdiction in the area in which the order or determination is to be enforced.[70]

[58] See § 19, supra.
[59] s. 21, as substituted do., para. 22; as to the notice to be given by the acquirer to the landlord, see Garvie's Trs. v. Garvie's Tutors, 1975 S.L.T. 94.
[60] 49 & 50 Vict., c. 29.
[61] Argyll, Caithness, Inverness, Orkney, Ross and Cromarty, Sutherland, and Zetland.
[62] 1 & 2 Geo. V, c. 49.
[63] 9 & 10 Geo. V, c. 97.
[64] 21 & 22 Geo. V, c. 44.
[65] 3 & 4 Eliz. II, c. 21; see infra, § 35.
[66] s. 24; see Courts & Jurisdiction, Ch. II, supra, § 8.
[67] See supra, §§ 26, 28, 30.
[68] Small Landholders Act 1911, s. 25. As to members' tenure of office, see Mackay and Esslemont v. Lord Advocate, 1937 S.C. 860.
[69] Garvie's Trs. v. Still, 1972 S.L.T. 29.
[70] Crofting Reform (Scotland) Act 1976, s. 17.

32. Landholders: Meaning.—The Small Landholders Acts apply to agricultural holdings,[71] other than market gardens,[72] outside the crofting counties,[73] which are holdings under the 1911 Act, that is were, in April 1912, let at a rent not exceeding £50 or did not, exclusive of common grazings, exceed 20 hectares in extent.[74] The provisions of the 1911 Act extended to existing holdings held under the 1886 Act, new holdings registered under the 1911 Act,[75] and holdings held by tenants under an existing lease from year to year.[76] The tenants in the last category, existing yearly tenants, are required, in order to qualify under the Act, to reside on or within three kilometres of the holding, and to cultivate the holding themselves or with members of their family, with or without hired labour.[77] It is also necessary, in order to qualify as a "landholder" and so benefit fully under the Acts, that the tenant or his predecessor in the same family should have provided or paid for the whole or greater part of the buildings and permanent improvements without receiving payment for them from the landlord or his predecessor in title[78]; if the existing yearly tenant did not fulfil this latter requirement, he became a "statutory small tenant".[79] Tenants under an existing lease for more than a year who qualified under the 1911 Act became landholders or statutory small tenants on the expiry of the period of the contractual lease.[80]

Grass parks, let for the purposes of a business not primarily agricultural, are excluded[81]; so are subjects let "to any innkeeper or tradesman placed in the district by the landlord for the benefit of the neighbourhood."[82] It has been held where the subjects would have been a holding under the Acts but for the existence of a second house, which was not used for the purpose of the holding but for letting in summer, that this house might be excised and the statutory provisions applied to the rest of the holding.[83] Occupants of land for less than a year, and persons who did not satisfy the conditions as to residence and cultivation, are not within the Act. If, however, a tenant became either a landholder or a statutory small tenant on the Act of 1911 coming into operation, he does not lose his rights as such by a subsequent agreement with the landlord under which he accepts a lease for less than a year.[84]

33. Tenure of Landholder.—The following are the main provisions

---

[71] See § 24, supra.
[72] See *Grewar* v. *Moncur's C.B.,* 1916 S.C. 764.
[73] Holdings in these counties (see n. 61, supra) are regulated by the Crofters Acts 1955 and 1961; see infra, § 35.
[74] 1911 Act, s. 26, as amended by Agriculture (Adaptation of Enactments) (Scotland) Regulations 1977 (S.I. 1977 No. 2007). See *Malcolm* v. *M'Dougall,* 1916 S.C. 283.
[75] s. 7, as amended by Land Settlement Act 1919, s. 9.
[76] s. 2 (1).
[77] s. 2 (1) (ii), as amended by Agriculture (Adaptation of Enactments) (Scotland) Regulations 1977.
[78] s. 2 (1) (iii), proviso a.
[79] See infra, § 34.
[80] s. 2 (1) (iii).
[81] 1911 Act, s. 26 (3) (g).
[82] 1886 Act, s. 33. See *Stormonth-Darling* v. *Young,* 1915 S.C. 44; *Taylor* v. *Fordyce,* 1918 S.C. 824.
[83] *M'Neil* v. *Duke of Hamilton's Trs.,* 1918 S.C. 221.
[84] *Clelland* v. *Baird,* 1923 S.C. 370.

regulating the tenure of a landholder, and these are not affected by any agreement to the contrary:—

Fair Rent.—While the Acts fixed the rent at its existing level, parties were left free to negotiate a new rent by agreement. Failing agreement, application may be made by either party to the Land Court to fix a fair rent. The Land Court may cancel arrears of rent, in whole or part, where it considers it reasonable to do so.[85] Once the rent has been fixed it cannot be altered, except by agreement, for the next seven years. The Land Court is directed, in fixing a fair rent, to consider all the circumstances of the case, holding and district.[85] It has been held that they should take into consideration any special circumstances affecting the holding, e.g., on the one hand, its suitability for summer letting,[86] on the other, its liability to damage from game or deer.[87] But they may not take into consideration the fact that the tenant has incurred the burden of a loan from his landlord to enable him to build a house on the holding.[88]

Security of Tenure.—The landholder cannot be removed from his tenancy except on certain clear grounds specified in the Acts, termed statutory conditions. These include non-payment of rent for a year or more; failure to cultivate the holding; execution of a deed purporting to assign the holding; subletting; notour bankruptcy or execution of a trust deed for the benefit of his creditors; opening a public-house without the landlord's consent.[89]

Resumption by Landlord: Renunciation.—The landlord has the right, on making application to the Land Court, and on making such compensation as that Court may determine, to resume possession of the holding, "for some reasonable purpose, having relation to the good of the holding or of the estate."[90] Building, feuing, and planting are among the grounds expressly specified. The landlord's intention to reside on the holding is not a ground of resumption of possession.[91] A landholder may renounce his holding on giving one year's notice to the landlord.[92]

Compensation for Improvements.—On renunciation, or on being removed from the holding, the tenant is entitled, in addition to his rights under the Agricultural Holdings Acts,[93] to compensation for any permanent improvements, if suitable to the holding, executed or paid for by himself or a predecessor in the same family, and not made in obedience to a specific

---

[85] 1886 Act, s. 6.
[86] *M'Neil* v. *Duke of Hamilton's Trs.*, 1918 S.C. 221.
[87] *M'Kelvie* v. *Duke of Hamilton's Trs.*, 1918 S.C. 301.
[88] *Dept. of Agriculture* v. *Burnett*, 1937 S.L.T. 292.
[89] 1886 Act, ss. 1 and 3; 1911 Act, s. 10.
[90] 1886 Act, s. 2; 1911 Act, s. 19, and, as to statutory small tenant, s. 32 (15). See *Whyte* v. *Stewart*, 1914 S.C. 675.
[91] Small Landholders, etc., Act 1931, s. 8.
[92] 1886 Act, s. 7; 1911 Act, s. 18.
[93] Supra, § 27.

obligation in writing.[94] The compensation is fixed, failing agreement, by the Land Court; this forms an important part of the Court's work.

Assignation: Subletting.—A landholder has in general no power to assign his holding. But if he is unable to work the holding through age or infirmity, he may apply to the Land Court for power to assign it to his son-in-law or to any person who would succeed him on intestacy.[95] He has no power, without the landlord's consent, to subdivide the holding or to sublet it, except to "holiday visitors"[96] or, probably, for a period less than a year.[97] Unless he is a new holder established by the Board of Agriculture, now the Secretary of State for Scotland, he is not entitled to erect a new house on his holding, except in substitution for one already existing; a new holder may do so with the consent of the landlord and the Secretary of State.[98]

Succession.—The landholder may bequeath his holding to his son-in-law or to any one of the persons who would be, or would in any circumstances have been, entitled to succeed to his estate on his intestacy; otherwise a holding passes to the tenant's executor on his death, according to the law of intestate succession.[99]

Provisions are made for the compulsory enlargement of holdings,[1] for the rights of a landlord in the event of a vacancy in a holding,[2] for the regulation of common grazing,[3] and for a record, by the Land Court, as to the state of the holding.[4]

34. Statutory Small Tenants.—A statutory small tenant is a person who would have been a landholder but for the fact that the whole or greater part of the buildings and permanent improvements were not provided by him nor by any predecessor in the same family.[5] Save as provided by section 32 of the Act of 1911, the provisions of the Acts do not apply to him. Under that section he is entitled, notwithstanding any agreement to the contrary,[6] to obtain, on application to the Land Court, a renewal of his tenancy at the expiry of the lease, unless the landlord can satisfy the Court that there is a reasonable objection to him. Either he or the landlord may apply to the Court to fix an "equitable" rent. An equitable rent is one which would be equitable as between a willing lessor and a willing lessee, but allowing no rent in respect of improvements made by the tenant or his predecessors in title and for which no

---

[94] 1886 Act, s. 8.
[95] 1911 Act, s. 21, as amended by Succession (Scotland) Act 1964, Sched. 2, para. 15.
[96] 1886 Act, s. 1 (4); 1911 Act, s. 10.
[97] *M'Neil* v. *Duke of Hamilton's Trs.*, 1918 S.C. 221.
[98] 1886 Act, s. 1 (4); 1911 Act, s. 10 (2).
[99] 1886 Act, s. 16 (*h*) and 1911 Act, s. 21, as amended by Succession (Scotland) Act 1964, Sched. 2, paras. 9 and 15.
[1] 1886 Act, s. 11; 1911 Act, s. 16, as amended by 1919 Act, s. 11, and 1931 Act, s. 7.
[2] 1911 Act, s. 17.
[3] 1911 Act, s. 24.
[4] Small Landholders, etc., Act 1931, s. 10.
[5] See 1911 Act, s. 2 (1) (iii), proviso b.
[6] See *Clelland* v. *Baird*, 1923 S.C. 370.

payment has been received. Unless the lease permits, he has no power to assign his lease.[7] The landlord has power to resume the subjects under the same conditions as those specified for resumption in the case of a landholder,[8] and the statutory small tenant is entitled in the event of a resumption to the like compensation as would be payable under the Agricultural Holdings Acts to a tenant to whom a notice to quit has been served.[9] The 1931 Act gave the statutory small tenant the option, on giving notice to the landlord, of converting his tenure into that of a landholder, and becoming entitled to all the consequent rights and privileges.[10]

35. The Crofters Acts.—The category of crofters, and with it the Crofters Commission, were reintroduced to the crofting counties by the Crofters (Scotland) Act 1955.[11] The effect of the Act was to substitute in these counties[12] a fresh code of law for that which had applied to landholders and statutory small tenants; the distinction between landholders and statutory small tenants was abolished. The statutory rights to a fair rent, security of tenure and compensation for permanent improvements, first introduced by the Crofters Holdings (Scotland) Act 1886, remain the basis of crofting tenure.

A croft is defined[13] as a holding in the crofting counties which was a landholder's or a statutory small tenant's holding immediately before the 1955 Act came into operation, or which was before the 1961 Act came into operation constituted a croft by the registration of an order of the Land Court authorising the registration of the tenant as a crofter under that Act,[14] or which the Secretary of State has directed shall be a croft.[15] A croft may be enlarged by the addition of non-crofting land by agreement of the owner and the crofter so long as the enlarged area, exclusive of any common pasture or grazing held therewith, does not exceed 30 hectares and the combined rent does not exceed £100.[16] The Crofters Commission may in certain circumstances authorise the enlargement of a holding which exceeds these limits.[17]

The function of the Crofters Commission is to reorganise, develop and regulate crofting in the crofting counties and to promote the welfare and interests of the crofting communities.[18] The Commission's sphere of action is primarily administrative, and jurisdiction over legal matters, which may be referred to them by the parties themselves or by the Commission, remains with the Land Court.[19]

7 1911 Act, s. 32 (1).
8 s. 32 (15).
9 1931 Act, s. 13: Agriculture (Miscellaneous Provisions) Act 1968, s. 16 and Sched. 5.
10 1931 Act, s. 14; see also 1911 Act, s. 32 (11).
11 3 & 4 Eliz. II, c. 21; amended by Crofters (Scotland) Act 1961 (9 & 10 Eliz. II, c. 58), and Crofting Reform (Scotland) Act 1976 (c. 21).
12 See note 61, supra.
13 1955 Act, s. 3, as amended by 1961 Act, Sched. 1, para. 9; as to whether rights in pasture or grazing land held by the tenant form part of the croft, see 1955 Act, s. 3 (5) and (6), substituted by Crofting Reform (Scotland) Act 1976, s. 14. See also *Ross* v. *Graesser*, 1962 S.C. 66.
14 Under 1955 Act, s. 4, repealed by 1961 Act, Sched. 3.
15 Under 1961 Act, s. 2 (1), which has now ceased to have effect: see 1976 Act, Sched. 2, para. 17.
16 1961 Act, s. 2 (2), as amended by 1976 Act, Sched. 2, para. 17.
17 1961 Act, s. 2 (2A), added by 1976 Act, Sched. 2, para. 17.
18 1955 Act, s. 1 (1).
19 See 1961 Act, s. 4.

36. Crofting Tenure.—Generally speaking, the 1955 Act re-enacted the existing law as to the tenure of holdings; there are, however, differences in detail, for which reference must be made to the Act itself. Applications for the fixing of a fair rent for the croft are made to the Land Court, and the fair rent is determined on the same principles as under the Small Landholders Acts.[20] Similar provisions regulate the resumption of a croft by the landlord[21]; but the 1955 and 1961 Acts substantially altered the existing law as to compensation, in the event of resumption or renunciation, to the crofter for permanent improvements and to the landlord for deterioration or damage to any fixed equipment provided by him.[22] The crofter has security of tenure, but he may be removed by the Land Court on the landlord's application where one year's rent remains unpaid or one of the statutory conditions of tenure[23] has been broken.[24] The crofter may not sub-let his croft except to holiday visitors,[25] nor may he assign it unless to a member of his family except where the Commission has given its written consent,[26] nor may he subdivide it without the consent of the Commission and the landlord.[27] The crofter may bequeath the croft to any member of his family,[28] but a bequest of it to anyone else without the Commission's approval will be invalid.[29] In a case of intestacy, or the failure of a bequest, the right to the croft is treated as intestate estate of the deceased crofter in accordance with Part I of the Succession (Scotland) Act 1964.[30] If the executor fails within three months to furnish to the landlord particulars of the transferee under section 16 (2) of the 1964 Act, the Commission may nominate a person as successor to the tenancy of the croft, or may declare the croft vacant.[31] The landlord is obliged to accept the transferee or the person nominated by the Commission as successor to the tenancy of the croft.[32]

37. Cottars.—A cottar is defined as being the occupier of a dwelling-house situate in the crofting counties with or without land who pays no rent, or the tenant from year to year of a dwelling-house situate in those counties who resides therein and pays an annual rent not exceeding £6 whether with or without garden ground but without arable or pasture land.[33] Under the 1955 Act a cottar who if not paying rent is removed from his dwelling and any land

[20] 1955 Act, s. 5.
[21] s. 12; see *Portman Trs.* v. *Macrae,* 1971 S.L.T. (Land Ct.) 6.
[22] See 1955 Act, s. 14, as amended by 1961 Act, s. 6 and by Law Reform (Miscellaneous Provisions) (Scotland) Act 1968, Sched. 2; *Balfour* v. *Couper,* 1963 S.L.C.R. 13.
[23] See list in Schedule 2, as amended by 1961 Act, Sched. 1, para. 20.
[24] s. 13.
[25] Sched, 2, para. 5, as amended by 1961 Act, s. 11 and Sched. 1.
[26] s. 8, as amended by 1976 Act, s. 15 and Sched. 2, para. 6.
[27] s. 9.
[28] s. 10 (1) and 10 (7).
[29] s. 10 (1).
[30] ss. 10 (5), 11 (1), as amended by Law Reform (Miscellaneous Provisions) (Scotland) Act 1968, s. 8 and Sched. 2 with reference to the estates of persons dying on or after 25th November 1968. Note that the Succession (Scotland) Act originally did not apply to crofts: 1964 Act, s. 37 (1) (*b*).
[31] s. 11 (4) and 11 (5), as amended by 1968 Act, Sched. 2.
[32] s. 11 (1) and 11 (4B), as amended by 1968 Act, Sched. 2.
[33] 1955 Act, s. 28 (4).

or buildings occupied by him in connection therewith, or if paying rent renounces his tenancy or is removed, is entitled to compensation for permanent improvements.[34] Failing agreement the amount of compensation payable is fixed by the Land Court in the same manner as for crofters.[35]

38. Rights of Acquisition.—The Crofting Reform (Scotland) Act 1976[36] introduced important new rights in favour of crofters and cottars. A crofter now has the right, failing agreement with the landlord, to apply to the Land Court to acquire croft land tenanted by him.[37] He has an absolute right subject to such terms and conditions as the Land Court may determine to a conveyance of the site of the dwelling house on or pertaining to his croft including the building thereon and garden ground, and a cottar has the same right to a conveyance of the site of the dwelling house occupied by him.[38] It is in the discretion of the Land Court whether or not to make an order authorising the crofter to acquire croft land, but they are directed not to make such an order where they are satisfied that to do so would cause a substantial degree of hardship to the landlord or that the acquisition would be substantially detrimental to the sound management of the estate.[39] Failing agreement, the consideration payable in respect of the acquisition of croft land and the conveyance of the site of the dwelling house, and the terms and conditions to be imposed, are to be determined by the Land Court.[40] Provision is made for the repayment to the landlord or his representatives of part of the consideration if the former crofter or a member of his family disposes of the croft land or any part of it other than by lease for crofting or agricultural purposes at any time within five years.[41] Finally a crofter now has, in addition to his right to any compensation, the right to a share in the value of any part of his croft which is resumed by the landlord or is acquired by an authority possessing compulsory powers.[42]

39. Administration of Crofting.—The Crofters Commission is given wide powers to enable it to perform its function of promoting the welfare and development of the crofting communities. It has the duty of compiling a Register of Crofts,[43] and of exercising a general supervision over common grazings.[44] Where a croft becomes vacant, the landlord must give notice of the fact to the Commission, and may only re-let it with the Commission's consent.[45] If the landlord fails to take steps to re-let it, the Commission may

[34] s. 28 (1).
[35] s. 28 (2).
[36] 1976 (c. 21).
[37] s. 1 (1).
[38] s. 1 (2) and 1 (4); see *Campbell* v. *Duke of Argyll's Trs.*, 1977 S.L.T. (Land Ct.) 22.
[39] s. 2.
[40] ss. 3, 4; *Fraser* v. *Noble*, 1977 S.L.T. (Land Ct.) 8; *Ferguson* v. *Ross Estates*, 1977 S.L.T. (Land Ct.) 19.
[41] s. 3 (3).
[42] ss. 9, 10.
[43] 1961 Act, s. 3.
[44] 1955 Act, ss. 24-27; 1976 Act, s. 16.
[45] s. 16 (1)-(3).

step in and re-let it themselves on his behalf[46]; in certain cases where the croft
has become vacant the Commission has power to direct that it cease to be a
croft.[47] Where the crofter is an absentee, that is, is not resident on or within
ten miles of the croft, the Commission may, where this is in the general
interests of the community, terminate his tenancy; if however, he has provided
or paid for the whole or the greater part of the dwelling-house, he may be able
to obtain a feu of it on the termination of his tenancy.[48] Provision is made for
a crofter who, through illness, old age, or infirmity, is unable to work the croft
properly; he may renounce the croft, but at the same time may obtain a feu of
the dwelling-house if he wishes to do so.[49]

IV. THE RENT ACTS

40. General.—The statutory code relating to tenancies of dwelling-houses
is now contained in the Rent (Scotland) Acts 1971 to 1974. The Rent
(Scotland) Act 1971[50] consolidated a considerable number of enactments
commonly known as the Rent Acts[51] in their application to Scotland, together
with a number of ancillary provisions which were formerly contained in the
Housing Acts. The 1971 Act has since been the subject of numerous
amendments,[52] and its principal provisions have been extended by the Rent
Act 1974.[53] The main purposes of the Acts are to provide for the security of
tenure of tenants of certain dwelling-houses by restricting the landlord's right
to remove them at the end of the lease, and to control or regulate the amount
of rent which the tenant can be required to pay. The Acts also contain
provisions prohibiting the charging of premiums by a landlord, and giving
power to the Court in certain cases to mitigate hardship to a landlord who is
the debtor in a heritable security.

The Rent Acts are notoriously complicated, and have been said to bristle
with difficulties.[54] For political and economic reasons the extent and pattern
of control have fluctuated considerably since legislation on this subject was
first introduced. The Act of 1920 consolidated a series of earlier Acts which
had been passed between 1915 and 1919. It provided for a system of control of
rents, security of tenure and control of heritable securities and it applied to the
majority of dwelling-houses which were let unfurnished to tenants. The Acts
of 1923, 1933 and 1938, while taking many of the more valuable dwelling-

[46] s. 16 (4).
[47] s. 16 (7) as amended by 1976 Act, s. 13 and Sched. 2, para. 8.
[48] s. 17, as amended by 1961 Act, s. 7 (1).
[49] s. 18.
[50] 1971 (c. 28).
[51] The principal Acts were those of 1920 (10 & 11 Geo. 5, c. 17), 1923 (13 & 14 Geo. 5, c. 32), 1933
    (23 & 24 Geo. 5, c. 32), 1938 (1 & 2 Geo. 6, c. 26), 1939 (2 & 3 Geo. 6, c. 71), 1954 (2 & 3 Eliz.
    2, c. 50), 1957 (5 & 6 Eliz. 2, c. 25) and 1965 (1965, c. 75). The principal Acts relating to
    furnished lettings were those of 1943 (6 & 7 Geo. 6, c. 44) and 1949 (12 & 13 Geo. 6, c. 40).
[52] Notably by the Fire Precautions Act 1971 (c. 40), Housing (Financial Provisions) (Scotland)
    Act 1972 (c. 46), Housing Act 1974 (c. 44), and the Housing Rents and Subsidies (Scotland) Act
    1975 (c. 28).
[53] 1974 (c. 51).
[54] See the collection of epithets in the preface to Megarry, *The Rent Acts* (10th ed).

houses out of control, extended and amended the provisions of the 1920 Act relating to security of tenure. The Act of 1939 reimposed control over a wide range of dwelling-houses let unfurnished, and introduced in relation to those houses which had been newly controlled by it a separate system to be applied in order to assess the limit of recoverable rent. The Act of 1957 decontrolled many dwelling-houses which were at the time subject to control, but the situation was again reversed by the Act of 1965 which not only brought into protection most of the houses which had been decontrolled by the 1957 Act but also introduced a new form of rent regulation and made a number of amendments to the system of security of tenure. The protection of tenants of dwelling-houses let furnished originated from the Act of 1943, which introduced a system whereby reasonable rents for the dwelling-houses might be assessed by a Rent Tribunal and registered. The Act of 1949 introduced a measure of security of tenure to tenants who chose to take advantage of the provisions of the 1943 Act as to rent. The Act of 1971 preserved the distinction which then existed between dwelling-houses let unfurnished on the one hand and those let furnished on the other, but this distinction was removed by the Act of 1974.

The provisions of the Rent (Scotland) Acts 1971 and 1974 are too complicated to state here in detail, and reference must be made to the specialist text books and to the relevant legislation.[55] What follows is merely a statement in outline of the main features of the current legislation. Because there is not yet a uniform pattern of control the main essential is to understand what tenancies are and what are not protected by the Acts, and the categories into which protected tenancies have been divided.

41. Application of the Acts: Protected Tenancies.—The definition of the expression "protected tenancy" in the 1971 Act[56] takes the form of providing that every tenancy under which a dwelling-house is let as a separate dwelling is a protected tenancy, and then excepting certain specific tenancies from this description. These exceptions are as follows—

(a) Where the rateable value of the dwelling-house exceeded £200 on 23rd March 1965 or exceeded that figure when a rateable value was first shown on the Valuation Roll[57];

(b) Where either no rent is payable under the tenancy or the rent payable is less than two-thirds of the rateable value on 23rd March 1965 or when first shown on the Valuation Roll[58];

(c) Where the dwelling-house is *bona fide* let at a rent which includes payments in respect of board or attendance,[59] provided in the case of

---

[55] Esp. Megarry, *The Rent Acts,* 10th ed. (1967); Fraser, *The Rent Acts in Scotland,* 2nd ed., (1952) is now substantially out of date. For a convenient statement of the current legislation and references to the relevant statutory instruments, see *Parliament House Book*, Division L.
[56] s. 1 (1).
[57] ss. 1 (1) (*a*), 6.
[58] s. 2 (1) (*a*); but as regards existing controlled tenancies see s. 7 (3); see also *Thomson* v. *Lann,* 1967 S.L.T. (Sh. Ct.) 76; *Fennel* v. *Cameron,* 1968 S.L.T. (Sh. Ct.) 30.
[59] s. 2 (1) (*b*), as amended by 1974 Act, s. 1 (4).

attendance that the amount of the rent attributable to it forms a substantial part of the whole rent[60];

(*d*) Where the tenancy is granted by an educational institution to a person who is pursuing or intends to pursue a course of study provided by that institution[61];

(*e*) Where the purpose of the tenancy is to let the house for a holiday[62];

(*f*) Where the dwelling-house is let together with land other than the site of the dwelling-house[63];

(*g*) Where the tenancy has been granted by the Crown, a local authority, a housing corporation, a housing association or certain other public bodies[64];

(*h*) Premises which consist of or comprise premises licensed for the sale of exciseable liquor[65]; and

(*i*) Where the landlord's interest belongs to a resident landlord, i.e. if the dwelling-house forms part only of a building, the tenancy was granted by a person who occupied as his residence another dwelling-house which also forms part of that building, and the landlord has at all times since it was granted continued to occupy another dwelling-house there as his residence.[66]

Furnished tenancies, where the amount of rent attributable to the use of furniture was substantial, were previously excluded from the Rent Acts, although furnished tenants could apply to the Rent Tribunal to fix a reasonable rent and were afforded a limited security of tenure in the event of service of a notice to quit.[67] The full protection of the Rent Acts was however extended to these tenancies by the 1974 Act,[68] and they now fall within the definition of protected tenancy unless excluded from it by one or other of the exceptions listed above.

The expression "tenancy" is defined[69] as including a sub-tenancy, but the right to possession conferred upon the tenant must be exclusive and a right which amounts merely to a licence to occupy will be excluded from protection under the Acts.[70] Similarly a service occupier, whose occupancy of the dwelling-house is attributable not to a lease but to his contract of service, is not protected.[71] The term dwelling-house for this purpose covers as well as self-contained dwelling-houses part of a house if let as a separate dwelling, even if it amounts only to a single room[72]; but it does not cover the lease of a house which contains a number of units of habitation within it.[73] Premises do

[60] s. 2 (3); as to the meaning of "substantial", see *Marchant* v. *Charters* [1977] 1 W.L.R. 1181.
[61] s. 2 (1) (*bb*), added by 1974 Act, s. 2 (1).
[62] s. 2 (1) (*bbb*), added by 1974 Act, s. 2 (1).
[63] s. 2 (1) (*c*); see also s. 1 (2).
[64] ss. 1 (1) (*c*), 4, 5.
[65] s. 9 (2).
[66] ss. 1 (1) (*d*), and 5A added by 1974 Act, Sched. 2, para. 2; as regards such tenancies granted before 14th August 1974, see Sched. 3, para. 2.
[67] 1943 Act, s. 2 (1) and 1949 Act, ss. 11 and 17; see infra, § 47.
[68] 1974 c. 51, s. 1.
[69] s. 133 (1).
[70] *Commissioners of H. M. Works* v. *Hutchison*, 1922 S.L.T. (Sh. Ct.) 127; *Heslop* v. *Burns* [1974] 1 W.L.R. 1241; *Marchant* v. *Charters*, supra.
[71] *Cairns* v. *Innes*, 1942 S.C. 164; *MacGregor* v. *Dunnett*, 1949 S.C. 510; *Cargill* v. *Phillips*, 1951 S.C. 67.
[72] s. 1 (1); *Neale* v. *Del Soto* [1945] K.B. 144; *Cole* v. *Harris* [1945] K.B. 474.
[73] *Horford Investments* v. *Lambert* [1976] Ch. 39.

not lose their character as a dwelling-house merely because part of the house is used for business purposes, provided that the main use can be said to be residential occupation.[74] The premises must however be such as would within accepted principles be held to be a dwelling-house for the purposes of the Acts.[75] Where any retail trade or business is carried on from the house so as to bring the premises within the definition of "shop" for the purposes of the Tenancy of Shops (Scotland) Act 1949, the tenancy will not be a regulated tenancy.[76] Unless he retains possession of the dwelling-house as his residence the tenant will not be entitled to the protection of the Acts.[77] Since the whole policy of the Acts is to protect the home, a tenant who ceases to reside in the premises to any substantial extent loses protection even though he may continue to use the premises for other purposes.[78]

42. Classification: Controlled and Regulated Tenancies.—Since the 1965 Act, which introduced a new pattern of rent regulation, it has been necessary to distinguish between the categories of controlled and regulated tenancies, as follows:

(a) *Controlled Tenancies.*[79]—These are tenancies which are still covered by the system of rent control which was contained in the Acts prior to 1965. In 1939 the limit of control was set at £90. The 1954 Act excluded from control lettings of houses produced by erection or conversion after 30th August 1954, and the 1957 Act decontrolled all lettings where the 1956 rateable value of the house was more than £40, or which were let by an agreement coming into operation after 6th July 1957. Accordingly this category now consists only of lettings of dwellings, whose 1956 rateable value did not exceed £40, which were let before 6th July 1957 to the sitting tenant or a tenant whose successor[80] continues to occupy the house as a statutory tenant.

(b) *Regulated Tenancies.*—This category, which was introduced by the 1965 Act,[81] comprises all other tenancies of dwellings whose rateable value on 23rd March 1965 did not exceed £200.[82] Thus a house falls into this category as it becomes decontrolled on being re-let to a new tenant.[83] Similarly, where a house is released from control on a second transmission from a controlled tenant,[84] it becomes a regulated tenancy.

The distinction between the tenant who occupies under a contract or a relocated contract and the tenant who remains in occupation after the expiry

---

74 s. 9; *Cargill* v. *Phillips*, supra; *Cowan & Sons* v. *Acton*, 1952 S.C. 73. This provision does not apply to regulated tenancies.
75 *Maunsell* v. *Olins* [1975] A.C. 373.
76 s. 9 (3); see infra, § 48.
77 s. 3 (1); *Menzies* v. *Mackay*, 1938 S.C. 74; *Cowan & Sons* v. *Acton*, supra; *Langford Property Co.* v. *Tureman* [1949] 1 K.B. 29.
78 *Stewart* v. *Mackay*, 1947 S.C. 287, per Lord President Cooper at p. 293.
79 See 1971 Act, Sched. 2, Part I, for provisions for determining whether a tenancy is a controlled tenancy.
80 See infra, § 45.
81 1965 Act, s. 1 (4).
82 1971 Act, s. 7 (2).
83 1971 Act, Sched. 2, paras. 1 (c), 4.
84 Sched. 2, para. 5; see infra, § 45.

of the lease by virtue of the Rent Acts—the statutory tenant[84a]—is also of importance. The transition from a protected tenancy to a statutory tenancy takes place where the tenant has invoked the protection of the Acts in answer to a notice to quit and his contractual right to occupancy has otherwise ceased.

43. Recoverable Rent. —Where the Acts apply, the rent that can be recovered from the tenant is limited by what is called, in the case of controlled tenancies, the standard rent,[85] in the case of regulated tenancies, the contractual rent limit.[86] Where the rent is payable weekly, the landlord is required to provide a rent book.[86a] Increases in the rent may only be made in certain limited circumstances.

(a) *Controlled Tenancies.*[87]—The basis for the standard rent is the figure at which the rent for the dwelling-house stood when the Acts were applied to it. In the case of "old control" houses, that is those controlled immediately before 2nd September 1939, it is the rent payable under the lease on 3rd August 1914. For "new control" houses, that is those which were controlled or recontrolled by the 1939 Act as from 2nd September 1939, the key figure is the rent payable on 1st September 1939, subject to the right of either party to apply to the rent tribunal to determine a reasonable rent.[88] If the dwelling-house was not let on the appropriate date, the standard rent is the rent at which it was last let before that date, or, if it was first let after that date, the rent at which it was first let. Thereafter the basic rent remained frozen, and the current maximum recoverable rent is calculated by adding to it any of the increases permitted by the Acts for the tenancy in question.

Increases in rent are permitted in the following circumstances: (1) Where the landlord has incurred expenditure on the improvement or structural alteration of the dwelling-house, at the rate of $12\frac{1}{2}$ per cent. of his expenditure.[89] Improvements for this purpose include the provision of new fixtures and fittings, but not decoration or repairs. The tenant can apply to the sheriff for a suspension or reduction of the increase on the ground that the expenditure was unnecessary. (2) Where there is an increase in the amount of the rates for the payment of which the landlord is responsible, by the full amount of the increase.[90] (3) In addition, to such amounts not exceeding 15 per cent. and a further amount not exceeding 25 per cent. of the rent where the landlord is responsible for the repairs, with a proportionate reduction in the latter if he is responsible for part only of the repairs.[91] (4) Except in the case of houses first let after 1st September 1939, a repairs increase, introduced

[84a] Defined in s. 3 (1).
[85] Sched. 8, para. 6.
[86] ss. 19, 21.
[86a] s. 132.
[87] See s. 48 and Sched. 8.
[88] s. 59.
[89] Sched. 8, para. 1 (3) (a).
[90] Sched. 8, para. 1 (3) (b).
[91] Sched. 8, para. 1 (3) (c), (d).

by the 1954 Act, where the landlord is responsible in whole or part for the repair of the house and has satisfied an expenditure test by carrying out work during the preceding twelve months to the value of not less than three-fifths of the 1954 rent, of one half of the rent payable immediately before 30th August 1954, or proportionately less where his responsibility is for part only of the repairs.[92] Alternatively, an increase of a quarter of the rent is permitted where the landlord is responsible in whole or in part for repair, without proof that repairs have been carried out.[93]

(b) *Regulated Tenancies.*—The 1965 Act introduced machinery for the determination of fair rents for tenancies by local rent officers and rent assessment committees, and for their registration.[94] Until the rent payable in respect of a regulated tenancy has been registered under these provisions, it remains frozen at that payable at December 8, 1965, with limited opportunities for increase, similar to those applied to controlled tenancies, referable in the event of dispute to the Sheriff.[95] Where the system of registration of rents is in force, however, either party or both may apply to the rent officer to fix a fair rent for the dwelling-house. When fixed, the fair rent forms the basis for the figure which is registered by the rent officer for the house; the registered rent becomes the rent limit, an amount in excess of which will be irrecoverable from the tenant.[96] The term "fair rent" is not defined, but certain guide lines are set,[97] for instance, that regard should be had to all the circumstances other than circumstances personal to the parties themselves, that improvements carried out by the tenant should be disregarded[98] and that it should be assumed that there is no substantial shortage of accommodation for letting in the locality. Regard must be had to market rents, making such adjustment as may be necessary to take account of scarcity.[99] Since a fair rent should be fair to the landlord as well as to the tenant, a fair return to the landlord on the capital value of the property is also a relevant and necessary consideration to be taken into account.[1] In considering the capital value of the house the fact that there is a sitting tenant with a right to possess the house is a personal circumstance to which regard must not be had.[2] Subject to these considerations the appropriate method or methods of valuation will depend on the circumstances.[3]

The fair rent may, in the first place, be agreed between the parties. themselves, and a joint application made on that basis to the rent officer.[4] Alternatively, applications for registration may be made by one party only,

[92] s. 49.
[93] s. 50.
[94] See now 1971 Act, Part IV, ss. 37-47.
[95] 1971 Act, Part III, ss. 19-36.
[96] ss. 19, 21, 43.
[97] See s. 42, as amended by 1974 Act, Sched. 1, para. 18.
[98] See *Stewart's J. F.* v. *Gallacher*, 1967 S.C. 59.
[99] *Learmonth Property Investment Co.* v. *Aitken*, 1970 S.C. 223.
[1] *Learmonth Property Investment Co.* v. *Aitken*, supra; *Skilling* v. *Arcari's Exrx.*, 1974 S.L.T. 46.
[2] *Skilling* v. *Arcari's Exrx.*, supra.
[3] *Albyn Properties* v. *Knox*, 1977 S.L.T. 41.
[4] For procedure in applications to rent officers, see s. 40 and Sched. 6.

and the other may or may not lodge objections as he pleases. In either case the rent officer has an overriding discretion as to the amount which is fair in the circumstances; where objections are raised, or he is not satisfied as to the figure applied for, he may himself determine the appropriate figure, after consultation with the parties. Either party then has the right to appeal against his decision to the rent assessment committee, whose decisions are final in fact but not on points of law. The committee are bound to observe the rules of natural justice,[5] and it is their duty not merely to inform the parties of the result of their deliberations but also to give reasons for their decision.[6] A certificate of fair rent may be sought in advance by a person intending to provide a dwelling-house by the erection or conversion of premises, or to make improvements in a dwelling-house, or to let a house as a regulated tenancy which is not subject to such a tenancy at the time.[7] The certificate, obtainable on application to the rent officer, specifies the rent which would in the rent officer's opinion be a fair rent under a regulated tenancy of the dwelling-house, or if the contemplated work were carried out, and thus provides a valuable indication of the return which the prospective landlord can expect on his expenditure.

The opportunities for variation of the registered rent are stated more broadly than in earlier Acts. Entries may be made in the register which will enable the landlord to vary the rent in respect of variations in the rates paid by him or other naturally fluctuating expenditure incurred by him in connection with the tenancy, such as in relation to the use of furniture or the provision of services, without further recourse to the rent officer.[8] Otherwise the registered rent remains fixed for three years. An application for variation of the figure by either party within that period will only be entertained on the ground that owing to some change of circumstance the registered rent no longer represents a fair rent for the dwelling-house,[9] except that a landlord alone may make an application within the last three months of the three year period. After three years an application for variation can be made by either party alone for a new consideration of the fair rent, when once again the whole circumstances, including any improvements made in the meantime, will be taken into account.

44. Security of Tenure.—While the contract of tenancy exists and the tenant continues to occupy the premises as a contractual tenant he has security of tenure under his contract; he cannot be ejected by his landlord except for a breach of the conditions of the lease, and he does not need the protection of the Acts. But, when the contractual tenancy is terminated, the Rent Acts will enable the tenant to retain possession of the dwelling-house, whatever contractual undertaking he may have made to remove as a statutory tenant, provided he continues personally to occupy the house as his

[5] *Learmonth Property Investment Co.* v. *Aitken,* supra.
[6] *Albyn Properties* v. *Knox,* supra.
[7] s. 41 and Sched. 7.
[8] s. 43.
[9] s. 40 (3) and (3A) as amended by 1974 Act, s. 4 (3).

residence.[10] Unless he voluntarily gives up possession of the house, he may only be removed by decree of removal granted by the Court. The Court[11] may not make an order for possession of a house which is let on a protected tenancy or is subject to a statutory tenancy except on certain conditions.[12] These are (1) that it considers it reasonable to make such an order[13] and (2) either that suitable alternative accommodation[14] is available for the tenant or will be available for him when the order in question takes effect, or that the landlord can establish that his application falls within any of the Cases set out in Part I of Schedule 3 to the 1971 Act. In the case of regulated tenancies only however there are a number of additional Cases, set out in Part II of Schedule 3, in which if the landlord can establish his right to possession at common law the Court must order possession.[15]

The Cases listed in Part I of the Schedule, being the grounds on which the Court has a discretion whether or not to make an order for possession, are in summary as follows: (1) non-payment of rent, or breach of an obligation of the tenancy; (2) conduct on the part of the occupiers of the dwelling-house which is a nuisance to adjoining occupiers, or its use for an illegal or immoral purpose; (3) deterioration of the condition of the dwelling-house owing to neglect or default on the part of the tenant or any person residing with him; (3A) deterioration of the condition of any furniture provided for use under the tenancy owing to ill treatment by the tenant or any person residing with him[16]; (4) steps taken by the landlord in consequence of a notice to quit given by the tenant; (5) unauthorised assignation or sub-letting by the tenant; (6) controlled tenancies consisting of or including licensed premises, in the case of default or non-renewal of the licence; (7) requirement of the dwelling-house by the landlord for occupation as a residence for his employee; (8) requirement[17] of the dwelling-house by the landlord for occupation as a residence for himself or certain members of his family, provided the landlord did not become landlord of the dwelling-house by purchase after certain dates[18]; (9) rent charged by the tenant for sub-letting of any part of the dwelling-house in excess of the rent recoverable under the Act; and (10) overcrowding, where the tenant has failed to take reasonable steps to alleviate the situation. The Court has a general discretion to adjourn the application, sist the action, suspend execution of the order for possession or postpone the date of possession for such periods and on such terms as it thinks fit.[19]

The Cases listed in Part II of the Schedule which apply to regulated tenancies only and are the Cases in which the Court is directed to make an

---

[10] See § 41, supra.
[11] Normally the Sheriff: see s. 122.
[12] s. 10 (1).
[13] See *Smith* v. *Poulter* [1947] K.B. 339; *Barclay* v. *Hannah*, 1947 S.C. 245.
[14] *Turner* v. *Keiller*, 1950 S.C. 43; see also Sched. 3, Part IV.
[15] s. 10 (2).
[16] Added by 1974 Act, Sched. 1, para. 1.
[17] As to requirement, see *Kennealy* v. *Dunne* [1977] Q.B. 837.
[18] Note however that the Court is directed not to make the order if greater hardship would be caused by granting it than by refusing to do so: s. 10 (3) and Sched. 3, Part III; see also *Kerr* v. *Gordon*, 1977 S.L.T. (Sh. Ct.) 53.
[19] s. 11.

order for possession if the circumstances of the Case are established,[20] are in summary as follows: (11) requirement of the dwelling-house by the owner-occupier for occupation as a residence for himself or a member of his family; (11A) requirement of the dwelling-house for occupation by himself or by a member of his family by a person who acquired the house with a view to occupying it as his residence after his retirement[21]; (11B) where the dwelling-house has been the subject of a holiday letting and is let out of season for a specified period not exceeding eight months[21]; (11C) where the dwelling-house has been the subject of a student letting and is let out on another tenancy for a specific period not exceeding twelve months[21]; (12) requirement of the dwelling-house for occupation by a minister or full-time lay missionary; (13) requirement of the dwelling-house by the landlord for occupation by a person employed by him in agriculture; (14) as Case 13, where an amalgamation has been carried out under the provisions of the Agriculture Act 1967; and (15) requirement of the dwelling-house by the landlord for occupation by a person responsible for the control of the farming of any part of the land or by a person employed by him in agriculture, in certain situations where neither Case 13 nor Case 14 would apply. In all of these Cases the tenant must be warned in writing at the outset that the relevant provisions of the 1971 Act may be invoked by the landlord,[22] although in some of them the Court has a discretion to dispense with this requirement if it is of opinion that it is just and equitable to make an order for possession.[23]

45. Transmission on Death.—The persons who are protected by the Rent Acts are spoken of in the Acts as tenants. The expression "tenant" is defined[24] as including a statutory tenant, and this expression in turn includes statutory tenants by succession.[25] If the original tenant was a man who died leaving a widow who was residing with him at his death, then after his death the widow is statutory tenant by succession so long as she retains possession of the dwelling-house without being entitled to do so under a contractual tenancy.[26] If the tenant leaves no widow or is a woman, the statutory tenant by succession will be such member of the tenant's family as may be decided by agreement between the parties, or in default of agreement by the Sheriff,[27] provided that member was residing with the tenant for not less than six months immediately before his death. The effect of these provisions is to confer a right on the tenant's successor to remain in occupation of the dwelling-house after the tenant's death; this is the case whether the deceased was a contractual or a statutory tenant,[28] and no formal claim is required.

Prior to the 1965 Act it was the rule that only one statutory transmission

[20] ss. 10 (2), 11 (5).
[21] Added by 1974 Act, s. 3 (2).
[22] See also 1971 Act, Sched. 3, Part III, para. 2.
[23] Cases 11, 11A.
[24] s. 133 (1).
[25] See s. 3 (1) (b); Sched. 1.
[26] Sched. 1, para. 2.
[27] Sched. 1, para. 3; see Williams v. Williams [1970] 1 W.L.R. 1530.
[28] s. 3 (1) (b); Moodie v. Hosegood [1952] A.C. 61; Walker v. M'Ardle, 1952 S.L.T. (Sh. Ct.) 60.

could take place,[29] and then only in favour of one person.[30] The Acts now provide for a further transmission to a second successor, similarly qualified, who is entitled to remain in occupation on the first successor's death. Where the deceased tenant occupied under a controlled tenancy, it is provided that the tenancy will become a regulated tenancy on its transmission to a second successor.[31] The same rules apply to the second transmission as to the first, and on the termination of the second successor's occupancy the right to possession will pass, if it is a subsisting contractual tenancy, to the heir, if it is a statutory tenancy, to the landlord. In a clear case a fresh contractual tenancy may be inferred from the parties' actings in favour of a person remaining in occupation after the death of the second successor.[32]

A statutory tenancy is regarded as a purely personal right, which cannot be assigned; a statutory tenant cannot bequeath his right to occupancy by will, nor will it transmit on his intestacy to his executor.[33] Where the contractual tenancy still subsists at his death, however, the right to occupy the house under the lease may pass under the deceased's will or to his executor; in such a case, in view of the provisions for statutory transmission, complicated situations can arise. Where the heir and the person who would be entitled to occupy the house as a successor are one and the same person, he will be presumed to occupy the house as a successor and not as a contractual tenant, unless he intimates to the landlord the fact that he has inherited the lease.[34] The mere payment and acceptance of rent from a contractual tenant's widow will not of itself constitute a fresh contractual tenancy in her favour where her occupancy can be attributed to a succession under the Acts.[35] If the person to whom the lease would pass by testate or intestate succession is not the same as the successor, the heir's rights and obligations are suspended while the successor continues to occupy the house.[36] While the contractual tenancy is suspended, however, the landlord still has the right to terminate the lease at the ish, and it is recommended that this be done to prevent an eventual succession by the deceased tenant's heir.[37]

46. Termination of Statutory Tenancy: Release from Control.—Generally speaking, so long as the statutory tenant continues to occupy the dwelling-house he will continue to be protected by the Acts. He will, however, lose the right to protection if he voluntarily surrenders possession of the house,[38] or fails to use the house as his residence, or if the house ceases to exist. His tenancy will come to an end if he accepts a new contractual tenancy from the landlord, or, it is thought, agrees to a rent which is less than two-thirds of the

29 *Joint Properties* v. *Williamson*, 1945 S.C. 68; *Campbell* v. *Wright*, 1952 S.C. 240.
30 *Dealex Properties* v. *Brooks* [1966] 1 Q.B. 542.
31 1971 Act, Sched. 1, paras. 5-7.
32 E.g. *Isherwood* v. *Currie*, 1954 S.L.T. (Sh. Ct.) 61.
33 *Lovibond & Sons* v. *Vincent* [1929] 1 K.B. 687.
34 *Grant's Trs.* v. *Arrol*, 1954 S.C. 306.
35 *Campbell* v. *Wright*, 1952 S.C. 240.
36 *Moodie* v. *Hosegood*, supra.
37 See Fraser, op. cit., pp. 8-9.
38 Note, however, protection against harassment, 1965 Act, s. 30 (2) (a).

relevant rateable value of the house. It will also be terminated where decree of removal is granted by the Sheriff,[39] or where, by reason of a change in the law or the scope of the Acts, the statutory protection ceases to apply to the dwelling-house. Under current legislation, the 1971 Act provides[40] for the release of houses exceeding a specified rateable value or of any class or description of house on the making of an order to that effect by the Secretary of State. Where such an order is made, transitional provisions may be included to avoid or mitigate hardship to existing tenants.[41] The provisions formerly contained in the 1957 Act for the release from contract of houses re-let to a new tenant[42] remain in force, but since the effect of the release of houses from control is that they become regulated tenancies there is no loss of protection.

47. Lettings within Jurisdiction of Rent Tribunals.—Under the Rent of Furnished Houses Control (Scotland) Act 1943,[43] rent tribunals were set up to fix, on application, reasonable rents for furnished lettings; and the Landlord and Tenant (Rent Control) Act 1949[44] extended the 1943 Act by introducing provisions which were designed to afford a measure of security of tenure to tenants of furnished houses. The provisions of these Acts, as amended by subsequent legislation, were re-enacted in Part VII of the Rent (Scotland) Act 1971.[45] They apply to what are described in the 1971 Act as Part VII Contracts, that is to say contracts whereby one person grants to another the right to occupy as a residence a house or part of a house in consideration of a rent which includes payment for the use of furniture or for services.[46] Where however the house is subject to a regulated tenancy Part VII of the Act is expressly excluded.[47] There are certain other express exclusions: a letting is not subject to the 1943 Act if the contractual rent includes a substantial element attributable to board[48]; a right to occupy a house or part of a house for a holiday is not to be treated as a right to occupy it as a residence[49]; and an owner-occupier who grants to another person a right to occupy his house which is a Part VII contract and gives the requisite written notice to that person may recover possession when he requires the house again as his residence without the intervention of the Rent Tribunal.[50] Part VII of the 1971 Act applies within the same limits of rateable value as are set for protected tenancies,[51] that is where the rateable value of the house in question on 23rd March 1965 or when a rateable value was first shown for it on the Valuation

[39] See § 44, supra.
[40] s. 117; cf. re furnished lettings, s. 86 (2).
[41] s. 117 (2); cf 1957 Act, Sched. 4, for transitional provisions applicable to de-control under that Act.
[42] 1971 Act, Sched. 2, para. 4.
[43] 6 & 7 Geo. 6, c. 44.
[44] 12, 13 & 14 Geo. 6, c. 40.
[45] 1971 Act, ss. 83-100.
[46] s. 85 (1).
[47] s. 85 (3) (c).
[48] s. 85 (3) (b).
[49] s. 85 (4).
[50] s. 94.
[51] cf. s. 1 (1).

Roll did not exceed £200.[52] Since furnished tenancies have now been brought within the full protection of the Rent Acts and where appropriate fall within the definition of regulated tenancy,[53] they no longer as a general rule fall within Part VII of the 1971 Act except where there is a resident landlord.[54] On the other hand a tenancy which is precluded from being a protected tenancy by virtue only of the fact that there is a resident landlord is now to be treated as a Part VII contract even although the rent may not include payment for the use of furniture or for services.[55] The effect of the amendments introduced by the 1974 Act therefore is that resident landlord lettings have replaced furnished lettings as the main concern of Rent Tribunals. The jurisdiction of Rent Tribunals also extends to other cases where the protection of the Rent Acts is not available, e.g. where the tenant shares accommodation with his landlord,[56] where the right to occupy in consideration of a rent which includes payment for the use of furniture is a licence and not a tenancy,[57] where there is substantial attendance,[58] where the rent includes any payment in respect of board,[59] where there is a furnished tenancy but at a rent too low for it to be a protected tenancy,[60] or where there is a student letting which includes payment for furniture or services.[61]

Rent control is effected by a reference of the contract by either party to the Rent Tribunal.[62] The tribunal may, on consideration of the case, approve the rent payable under the contract, or reduce it to such sum as they may in all the circumstances think reasonable, or dismiss the application.[63] Once fixed, the rent is entered on a register kept by the tribunal, and becomes the limit beyond which any payment in excess is irrecoverable[64]; it may be varied on the application of either party on proof of change of circumstance.[65] The rent fixed by the tribunal must not be lower than any amount which has been registered for the house as the rent recoverable under a regulated tenancy under Part IV of the 1971 Act.[66]

Security of tenure of a temporary nature is available to the lessee under a Part VII contract on the service on him of a notice to quit.[67] Where an application has been made to the tribunal to fix or reconsider the rent, a subsequent notice to quit will not have effect before the expiry of six months after the tribunal's decision, unless the tribunal sees fit in the circumstances to substitute a shorter period; an application made after the service of the notice

[52] s. 86 (1).
[53] See § 41, supra.
[54] 1974 Act, s. 1; 1971 Act, s. 5A, added by 1974 Act, Sched. 2, para. 2.
[55] 1971 Act, s. 119A, added by 1974 Act, Sched. 2, para. 6.
[56] 1971 Act, s. 118.
[57] cf. *Luganda* v. *Service Hotels* [1969] 2 Ch. 209.
[58] 1971 Act, s. 2 (1) (*b*), (3).
[59] s. 2 (1) (*b*).
[60] s. 2 (1) (*a*).
[61] s. 2 (1) (*bb*).
[62] As to jurisdiction of the Rent Tribunal, see *R.* v. *Croydon & South West London Rent Tribunal* [1977] Q.B. 876.
[63] 1971 Act, ss. 87, 88.
[64] ss. 89, 91.
[65] s. 88 (4).
[66] s. 88 (2).
[67] ss. 92–95.

will also entitle the lessee to this extension of notice.[68] Thereafter, unless the tribunal has substituted a shorter period, further extensions of not more than six months at a time may be granted.[69] Because this mechanism for protecting the lessee in occupation after the expiry of the lease operates only by means of extensions of periods of notice on a reference to the tribunal, it has been held not to apply where the contract is terminated by the expiration of a fixed period.[70]

48. Tenancy of Shops.—Security of tenure for the tenant of a shop is afforded by the Tenancy of Shops (Scotland) Act 1949.[71] The expression "shop" is defined in that Act as including any shop within the meaning of the Shops Acts,[72] that is, any premises where any retail trade or business is carried on.[73] The Act has been held not to apply to subtenants of a shop[74]; and a tenant who occupies premises which fall within the 1949 Act cannot claim the protection of the Rent Acts as the tenant of a regulated tenancy.[75]

Where the tenant has been given notice of the termination of his tenancy and he is unable to obtain a renewal of it on terms which are satisfactory to him, he may apply to the Sheriff for a renewal of the tenancy, provided that he does so within 21 days after the service of the notice and before it takes effect.[76] Where such an application is made, the Sheriff may grant a renewal for such period not exceeding one year, at such rent and on such conditions as he thinks reasonable.[77] Thereafter a new lease is deemed to take effect, and the landlord's notice to quit is treated as having lapsed.[78] The tenant may apply for further renewals, having the same right to do so as if the tenancy had been renewed by agreement between the parties.[79] Applications are conducted and disposed of under the summary cause procedure, and the Sheriff's decision is final.[80]

Where he thinks it reasonable to do so, the Sheriff has power to dismiss the tenant's application. He may in any event not renew the tenancy if he is satisfied as to certain grounds for a termination specified in the Act.[81] For instance, a tenant will not be able to obtain a renewal where he is in breach of a material condition of the lease, where he has refused an offer by the landlord

---

[68] s. 92 (1).
[69] s. 93.
[70] *Langford Property Co.* v. *Goodman* [1954] 163 Estates Gazette 324 (Q.B.); see also *Schnabel* v. *Allard* [1967] 1 Q.B. 627, per Lord Denning, M.R., at p. 1298. Note, however, that under the Sheriff Courts (Scotland) Act 1907, ss. 37 and 38, a notice to quit is mandatory where a house is let for a period of a year or more.
[71] 12, 13 & 14 Geo. VI, c. 25.
[72] s. 3 (2); see Shops Act 1950, s. 74 (1).
[73] See *Golder* v. *Thos. Johnstons (Bakers)*, 1950 S.L.T. (Sh. Ct.) 50; *Thom* v. *B.T.C.*, 1954 S.L.T. (Sh. Ct.) 21; *Wright* v. *St. Mungo Property Co.* (1955) 71 Sh. Ct. Rep. 152; *King* v. *Cross Fisher Properties*, 1956 S.L.T. (Sh. Ct.) 79.
[74] *Ashley Wallpaper Co.* v. *Morrisons Associated Cos.*, 1952 S.L.T. (Sh. Ct.) 25.
[75] 1971 Act, s. 9 (3).
[76] 1949 Act, s. 1 (1).
[77] Ibid., s. 1 (2).
[78] *Scottish Gas Board* v. *Kerr's Trs.*, 1956 S.L.T. (Sh. Ct.) 69.
[79] 1949 Act, s. 1 (4).
[80] Ibid., s. 1 (7), as amended by Sheriff Courts (Scotland) Act 1971, Sched. 1.
[81] Ibid., s. 1 (3).

of reasonable alternative accommodation on terms and conditions which the Sheriff thinks reasonable, or if it can be shown by the landlord that greater hardship would be caused by renewing the tenancy than by refusing to do so.[82]

[82] See *Craig* v. *Saunders & Connor*, 1962 S.L.T. (Sh. Ct.) 85.

CHAPTER XXXIV

REPARATION

Glegg, *Reparation* (4th ed., 1955); Smith, *Short Commentary* (1962); Walker, *Damages* (1955); Walker, *Delict* (1966); Charlesworth on *Negligence* (6th ed., 1977); Clerk and Lindsell, *Torts* (14th ed., 1975); Salmond, *Torts* (17th ed., 1977), Winfield and Jolowicz on *Tort* (10th ed., 1975); Street, on *Torts* (6th ed., 1976).

1. Terminology.—Reparation is the term used in Scots law for making good, so far as possible in terms of money, loss (damnum) caused (datum) by a legal wrong (injuria), provided that the loss is not too remote from the wrong. The maxim applicable is "damnum injuria datum" and all three elements of the maxim must be present before liability to make reparation arises.[1] A legal wrong may be defined as an invasion of the legal rights of another without lawful justification or excuse. The wrong may be done by an act or omission. It is not necessary for the act to be conscious and deliberate. Accordingly, it is immaterial whether or not it constitutes a criminal offence; the law of reparation is concerned only with its civil consequences. The term "delict" is now often used for those wrongs in which intention must be proved, all other being known as "quasi-delicts," but an alternative, and better, terminology is to apply "delict" to all legal wrongs other than those of strict liability and to apply "quasi-delict" to the latter.[2] "Negligence" has numerous meanings. It may be used broadly in the sense of neglect of (i.e., failure to fulfil) a legal duty, whether that failure is intentional or unintentional.[3] It may also be used to denote unintentional wrongs only, as distinct from intentional wrongs. But nowadays it is most often used in the narrow sense of failure to exercise such care as is reasonable in all the circumstances to avoid damage to others and to their property.[4] Culpa or fault has been used as synonymous with negligence in all its meanings. There is a question as to whether culpa should not be restricted to denote only breach of the common law duty of taking reasonable care.[5] Discussion of this question is beyond the scope of this book but, as the English phrase "strict liability" is to be found in recent text-books on Scots law,[6] for the sake of uniformity liability to make reparation for invasion of legal rights which is neither intentional nor due to breach of a duty to exercise reasonable care is treated in this edition under the head of "strict liability."[7] The basis of liability in such cases is clear whether or not it is labelled as culpa.

---

[1] See Causation, § 12, infra, and Remoteness of Damage, § 13, infra.
[2] See Smith, *Short Commentary*, p. 633.
[3] See *Bastable* v. *N.B. Ry.*, 1912 S.C. 555, per Lord President Dunedin, at pp. 565-6; and *Hester* v. *Macdonald*, 1961 S.C. 370, per Lord Guthrie, at p. 390.
[4] See Glegg, pp. 8-22; also §§ 10 and 11, infra.
[5] Ibid.; Smith, op. cit., 639-641, 663-672; Walker, *Delict*, pp. 47-50; cf. Lord Hunter in *Henderson* v. *John Stuart* (*Farms*) *Ltd.*, 1963 S.C. 245, at p. 248.
[6] Smith, supra; Walker, supra; cf. Glegg.
[7] See §§ 19-24, infra.

2. Invasion of Rights: Classification.—It is not proposed to attempt any enumeration of actionable wrongs, but some indication may be given by considering the rights or liberties which the policy of the State will protect. A man is clearly entitled to personal security, and therefore violence, or threats of violence, are actionable. Personal liberty is also safeguarded, and therefore an invasion of it, by unjustifiable restraint, amounts to a wrong. A man has a right to be safeguarded from unfounded aspersions on his character, and therefore slander amounts to a wrong.[8] Fraud may be described as an invasion of a right not to be deceived, or as an invasion of a right of property. In that latter category may be included all aggressions on property, corporeal or incorporeal, either directly, or by acts which amount to a nuisance,[9] and also cases such as irregular diligence, abuse of legal process,[10] or efforts at redress brevi manu,[11] where property which a party may be entitled to claim is taken by improper means.

3. Crimes: Breach of Statutory Duty.—The fact that a particular act which is done wilfully and which causes injury is a criminal offence at common law may, it is conceived, be regarded as a sufficient indication that it also constitutes a civil wrong. With regard to acts penalised by statute, there is no inflexible rule. So although sexual intercourse with a girl under 16 is by statute a criminal offence, even if she consents, it was held that the statute had not altered the common law rule that it did not constitute an actionable wrong unless accomplished by fraud or circumvention.[12] When failure to observe some statutory regulation has caused injury to an individual, it is a question of the construction of the statute whether civil liability as well as criminal responsibility was intended.[13] The mere fact that a duty has been created by a statute does not entitle a person injured by the breach to claim damages therefor.[14] There must be a clear intention to confer a right to civil damages for breach of the statutory duty and a definite class of persons upon whom the right is conferred.[15] If the statute is aimed only at preventing a certain kind of injury, then civil liability results only if that kind of injury is caused by a breach.[16] So where sheep in course of transit were not penned in accordance with statutory regulations, and were washed overboard, it was held that the statute was irrelevant in the question of the carrier's liability in respect that the regulations were designed for the prevention of infection and not for the safety of the animals during transit.[17] But a statutory provision designed to prevent

[8] Defamation, Ch. XXXV, infra.
[9] As to nuisance, see Landownership, Ch. XXXIX, infra, § 24.
[10] Defamation, Ch. XXXV, infra, §§ 23-25.
[11] *Brash* v. *Munro* (1903) 5 F. 1102; and see infra, § 29.
[12] *Murray* v. *Fraser*, 1916 S.C. 623.
[13] *Atkinson* v. *Newcastle Water Works* (1877) 2 Ex.D. 441; *Cutler* v. *Wandsworth Stadium* [1949] A.C. 398; *Pullar* v. *Window Clean*, 1956 S.C. 13; see also Walker, *Delict*, pp. 313-320.
[14] *Atkinson* v. *Newcastle Water Works*, supra, per Lord Chancellor Cairns, at p. 448.
[15] *Pullar* v. *Window Clean*, supra, per Lord President Clyde, at p. 22.
[16] *Grant* v. *N.C.B.*, 1956 S.C. (H.L.) 48, per Lord Reid, at p. 57.
[17] *Gorris* v. *Scott* (1874) L.R. 9 Ex. 125. See also *O'Brien* v. *Arbib*, 1907 S.C. 975; *Balmer* v. *Hayes*, 1950 S.C. 477 (failure by motor-driver to disclose physical unfitness when applying for a licence).

accidents will not be narrowly construed.[18] The question in each case is whether the legislature intended to impose public duties only[19] or, in addition, duties enforceable by any individuals injured by breach.[20] In determining this question the scope and purpose of the statute as a whole, as well as the state of the pre-existing law, must be considered.[21] Thus the purpose of section 143 of the Road Traffic Act 1972, in making it an offence to allow a car to be used without insurance against third party risks, being to provide third parties with better protection, involves a party in breach thereof in civil liability to injured third parties.[22]

The remedy of assythement,[23] which was formerly available when death or injury had been caused by a criminal act of which the defender had been convicted, has been abolished.[24]

4. Damnum Absque Injuria.—The invasion of a mere liberty, or advantage enjoyed on sufferance, is known as "damnum absque injuria" (loss without legal wrong) and infers no liability. So competition in trade, whatever injury it may inflict, is not per se a legal wrong, because a trader, though he may in fact have enjoyed it, has no legal right to a monopoly in his trade. But the law protects an injured trader (1) if the interference with his trade is carried out by an unlawful means,[25] and (2) if the act causing the interference is done by a combination of persons and their predominant purpose is to injure the party with whom they interfere.[26] Competition does not, however, become a wrong giving rise to a right to reparation for delict merely on the ground that the newcomer may be acting in breach of his contract with a third party, or, in the case of a corporate body, ultra vires. So a shipowner, catering for excursion parties on a navigable river, had no title, merely as a shipowner, to interdict a statutory body which proposed to use a ship for the same purpose, although such use was prohibited by statute.[27] Parties interested in a river cannot claim damages for loss of water caused by a diversion of the underground springs, on the theory that the continuance of the springs is merely an advantage enjoyed on sufferance, not a right which can be vindicated by legal action.[28]

5. Elements in Wrong: Intention and Motive.—Intention to invade the rights of others is clearly immaterial in the case of an invasion resulting from negligence. In the domain of wilful wrongs intention to deceive is the element

[18] *Grant* v. *N.C.B.,* supra.
[19] *West* v. *David Lawson,* 1949 S.C. 430 (Road Transport Lighting Act 1927, s. 1).
[20] *Byrne* v. *Tindal's Exrx.,* 1950 S.C. 216 (duty under Burgh Police (Scotland) Act 1892 to maintain lighting in common stair).
[21] *Cutler* v. *Wandsworth Stadium,* supra, per Lord Normand at p. 413; *Pullar* v. *Window Clean,* supra, per Lord President Clyde at p. 21; *Phillips* v. *Britannia Hygienic Laundry Co.* [1923] 2 K.B. 832; *Byrne* v. *Tindal's Exrx.,* supra.
[22] *Monk* v. *Warbey* [1935] 1 K.B. 75; *Houston* v. *Buchanan,* 1940 S.C. (H.L.) 17; cf. *Balmer* v. *Hayes,* supra.
[23] *McKendrick* v. *Sinclair,* 1972 S.L.T. 110.
[24] Damages (Scotland) Act 1976, (c. 13), s. 8.
[25] Infra, § 7.
[26] Infra, § 6.
[27] *Nicol* v. *Dundee Harbour Trustees,* 1915 S.C. (H.L.) 7.
[28] *Chasemore* v. *Richards* (1859) 7 H.L.C. 349; *Mayor of Bradford* v. *Pickles* [1895] A.C. 587.

which distinguishes fraud, involving a wrong and consequent liability in damages, from innocent misrepresentation, which may be a ground for the reduction of a contract, but which does not generally give rise to delictual liability.[29] But the English rule, founded on historical considerations peculiar to English law,[30] that any invasion of a legal right, however innocent, amounts to a legal wrong, is no part of the law of Scotland.[31] Thus a party who, without negligence, has purchased and re-sold stolen goods is in England liable for their value in respect of a wrongful conversion[32]; in Scotland his liability depends upon the obligation of restitution, and not of reparation, and is limited to any profit he may have made on the re-sale.[33] And an unintentional trespass on land belonging to another, where there is no ground to suppose that the trespass will be repeated, will afford in Scots law no remedy, either by an action for nominal damages or by an application for interdict.[34]

Intention must be distinguished from motive or purpose, which is the actor's reason for doing the intentional act. "The words 'motive,' 'object,' 'purpose,' are in application to practical matters difficult strictly to define or distinguish. Sometimes mere animus, such as spite or ill will, malevolence or a wanton desire to harm without any view to personal benefit is meant. But motive is often used as meaning purpose, something objective and external, as contrasted with a mere mental state."[35] When the sole reason for an act is to harm someone, the motive is said to be malicious. But a man may have more than one reason for doing something and one purpose may predominate over others. His motive, object or purpose is in most cases irrelevant as will be seen from the following propositions which are illustrated in the next three paragraphs.

Proposition 1: If an intentional act is plainly lawful, the actor's motive for or purpose in doing it is irrelevant. There is liability to make reparation only if the act is unlawful.

Proposition 2: If an intentional act is plainly unlawful, motive or purpose is again irrelevant.[36] The act is not excused, for purposes of delictual liability, by the fact that the actor was not moved by desire to injure but acted in order to call attention to a defect in the law or in order to forward what he conceived to be the true interest of the party injured. So too, if A causes loss to B through interference with B's rights by unlawful means,[37] it is no defence that A's motive, object or purpose was to protect his own interests.

Proposition 3: Motive, although generally irrelevant, may exceptionally be relevant to whether an act is lawful or unlawful. The exceptions are noticed in

---

[29] Agreement Improperly Obtained, Ch. VIII, supra, § 9; and see Defamation, Ch. XXXV, infra, 32, where malicious intent is presumed.
[30] See Pollock, *Torts*, (15th ed.), pp. 8 et seq.
[31] See *Leitch* v. *Leydon*, 1931 S.C. (H.L.) 1, per Lords Dunedin and Blanesburgh, as to the application to Scotland of the English law of conversion and trespass.
[32] *Hollins* v. *Fowler* (1872) L.R. 7 H.L. 757.
[33] *Scot* v. *Low* (1704) M. 9123.
[34] *Hay's Trs.* v. *Young* (1877) 4 R. 398.
[35] *Crofter Hand Woven Harris Tweed Co.* v. *Veitch*, 1942 S.C. (H.L.) 1, per Lord Wright, at p. 29.
[36] But see Inducing Breach of Contract, § 8 infra.
[37] See §§ 7 and 8 infra.

Proposition 4. Otherwise, the considerations determining the lawfulness of an act are various but do not include motive.

Proposition 4: As the law stands there are only three clearly recognised exceptions to the general irrelevance of motive: (1) actings in concert with the predominant purpose of harming another[38] (2) operations on land *in aemulationem vicini*[39] and (3) inducement of breach of contract.[40]

The above propositions are illustrated in the next three paragraphs but without mention of operations in aemulationem vicini which are discussed elsewhere.[41] The view that there is room in Scots law for a wider doctrine of abuse of rights has been canvassed[42] but remains unsettled.

6. Malice: Trade Competition.—It follows from the general irrelevance of motive that, where a party acts in the exercise of his own right, the fact that his motive in acting is a desire to injure another, usually stigmatised as malice, is generally insufficient to convert an otherwise lawful act into an actionable wrong. But interference with opportunities of trade or work is regarded as an exceptional case. If A, by inducements in themselves lawful, induces B not to deal with C, or not to employ C, the law will have regard exclusively to A's act as one lawful or unlawful, and if A has a legitimate interest to act as he did, his motive is irrelevant.[43] But if the same thing be done by a combination of persons acting in concert, the character of their act—as lawful or unlawful— will depend upon whether their predominant purpose or object was to advance their own material interests or to injure C.[44] The former and more usual result followed where a combination of shipowners, by offering rebates to those exporters who agreed to deal with them alone, injured the trade of a shipowner who was not in the combine, and were held not to have inflicted upon him any actionable wrong;[45] where a combination of butchers intimated that they would refuse to bid at auction sales of imported meat unless bids from co-operative stores were refused;[46] where an association of owners of newspapers cut off a newsagent's sources of supply[47]; and where trade union officials directed their members not to handle the goods of a company whose trade practices were supposed to be detrimental to the concerns for which the defenders' members worked.[48] In these cases it was decided that the members

---

[38] i.e. if A interferes with B's right by means not otherwise unlawful B may nonetheless have a remedy if A is acting in concert with others and their predominant purpose is to harm B: *Crofter etc. Co.* v. *Veitch,* supra, per Lord Simon, L.C., at p. 10; and see § 6, infra.

[39] i.e. if A is conducting operations on his land, for the sole purpose of annoying B, B may have a remedy although the operations, had their purpose been otherwise, would have been lawful. See Landownership, Ch. XXXIX., infra, § 13; and Smith, *Short Commentary,* on "abuse of rights," at pp. 662-3.

[40] i.e. acts inducing breach of contract, which are normally unlawful, may in some circumstances be justified on grounds of motive. See § 8 infra.

[41] See footnote 39, supra.

[42] Smith, *Short Commentary,* supra.

[43] *Mackenzie* v. *Iron Trades Association,* 1910 S.C. 79; *Allen* v. *Flood* [1898] A.C. 1.

[44] *Sorrell* v. *Smith* [1925] A.C. 700.

[45] *Mogul S.S. Co.* v. *Macgregor* [1892] A.C. 25.

[46] *Scottish Co-operative Society* v. *Glasgow Fleshers* (1898) 35 S.L.R. 645.

[47] *Sorrell* v. *Smith,* supra.

[48] *Crofter Hand Woven Harris Tweed Co.* v. *Veitch,* 1942 S.C. (H.L.) 1; see per Lord Simon L.C., at p. 10. On p. 28 Lord Wright comments that the distinction between conduct by one man and conduct by two or more may be difficult to justify.

of the combination were acting legitimately in pursuance of their own business interests. In the exceptional case of *Quinn* v. *Leathem*,[49] on the other hand, the officials of a trade union, acting in concert, had intimated to one of L's customers that his men would be called upon to strike if he continued to deal with L., who had employed non-union labour. L. in consequence suffered loss. In the circumstances of the case the Court arrived at the conclusion that the dominant purpose of the union officials was to injure L., and held that they were liable in damages. The trade union officials would probably not be protected by the Trade Union and Labour Relations Acts 1974 and 1976 since they were not pursuing a "trade dispute" but rather a spite or grudge against L.[50]

7. Interference with Rights: Illegal Means.—Interference with trade or employment is actionable if the means employed are illegal.[51] The service of a strike notice of proper length is not illegal.[52] Nor is it illegal to offer advantages to B if he will refrain from dealing with C, or to influence B by intimating that the speaker, or others with whom he is acting, will refuse to work if C is employed.[53] But any violence or threats addressed to B in order to induce him to abstain from dealing with or employing C, with resulting loss to C, will amount to a wrong (intimidation) for which he can claim damages.[54] In this connection a mere intimation that a party proposes to do some lawful act (e.g., to abstain from working) is not to be construed as a threat merely because the speaker's attitude was menacing.[55] And to induce B by fraud to act in a way detrimental to C's business interests is a wrong to C. So where a manufacturer placed certain dealers on a stop list, and directed his agents not to supply them with goods, and one of these dealers obtained supplies by fraudulently concealing his identity, it was held that he was liable in damages even on the assumption that the agent who supplied him could not be regarded as in breach of contract.[56]

8. Inducing Breach of Contract.—Knowingly to induce a man to break a contract is in general a wrong for which the party whose contractual anticipations are disappointed may claim damages.[57] He may, on principles of contract, claim redress from the breaker of the contract; on principles of reparation, redress from the party who induced the breach.[58] The breach may

---

49 [1901] A.C. 495, as explained in *Sorrell* v. *Smith,* supra; see also *Hewit* v. *Edinburgh & District Lathsplitters Assn.* (1906) 14 S.L.T. 489.

50 See Trade Union and Labour Relations Acts, § 9, infra, and note 71, infra.

51 But see Trade Union and Labour Relations Acts, § 9 infra.

52 *Morgan* v. *Fry* [1968] 2 Q.B. 710.

53 *Mogul S.S. Co.* v. *Macgregor,* supra.

54 *Conway* v. *Wade* [1909] A.C. 506. *Rookes* v. *Barnard* [1964] A.C. 1129. See Walker, *Delict,* pp. 932-4; 1964 S.L.T. (News) 81.

55 *Ware etc.* v. *Motor Trades Manufacturing Co.* [1921] 3 K.B. 40; *Sorrell* v. *Smith* [1925] A.C. 700.

56 *National Phonograph Co.* v. *Edison Bell & Co.* [1908] 1 Ch. 335.

57 But see Trade Union and Labour Relations Acts, § 9 infra.

58 *Couper* v. *Macfarlane* (1879) 6 R. 683; *Lumley* v. *Gye* (1853) 2 E. & B. 216; *B.M.T.A.* v. *Gray,* 1951 S.C. 586; *Exchange Telegraph Co.* v. *Guilianotti,* 1959 S.C. 19. See also *D. C. Thomson* v. *Deakin* [1952] Ch. 646; *J. T. Stratford & Son* v. *Lindley* [1965] A.C. 269; Walker, op. cit., pp. 920-22.

be of implied conditions of the contract, as where a clerk or workman is induced to betray his employer's secrets.[59] But in cases of inducing breach of contract motive may be a determining element. It is recognised throughout the cases that a party incurs no liability merely because the advantageous terms he offers in fact lead to a breach of contract, that is, of a contract of which he was not aware.[60] Even where he is aware of it, his inducements to breach are not actionable if his conduct was justifiable, as, for instance, where he was acting in pursuance of a social or professional duty.[61] So a doctor advising a patient to leave a service prejudicial to his health would incur no liability; and the same rule was applied where a society induced the owner of a theatre to break his contract with a touring company on the ground that the wages paid were in the nature of a public scandal.[62] A father who induces his minor son to break off an engagement to marry is presumed to have done so in the proper exercise of parental control and an action founded on that act will not be sustained without relevant averments of malice or other oblique motive.[63]

It is an actionable wrong to employ a servant in the knowledge that he is in breach of an unexpired contract with another employer, although there may have been no inducement to break the contract.[64] But the first employer cannot recover damages from the second employer if it is established that in no circumstances would the servant have returned to his former employment.[65]

9. Trade Union and Labour Relations Acts.—In the case where an act alleged to be wrongful has been done by the officials of a trade union or employers' association action may be excluded under the provisions of the Trade Union and Labour Relations Acts 1974 and 1976.[66] These provisions replace earlier legislation contained in the Trade Disputes Acts 1906 and 1965[67] and the Industrial Relations Act 1971.[68] The Act of 1906 foilowed a decision that a trade union might be sued in an action directed against its office-bearers without calling each individual member of the union as a defender, and that the union as a body was, like other employers, liable for the wrongful acts of its servants or agents.[69] Section 4 of the Act had provided that "an action against a trade union, or against any members or officials thereof on behalf of themselves and all other members of the trade union in respect of any tortious act committed by or on behalf of the trade union, shall not be entertained by any court."[70] Thus in the case of slander in a publication authorised by a union, neither damages nor interdict against the

---

[59] Roxburgh v. Macarthur (1841) 3 D. 556.
[60] D. C. Thomson v. Deakin, supra; cf. J. T. Stratford & Son v. Lindley, supra.
[61] Glamorgan Coal Co. v. South Wales Federation [1905] A.C. 239; B.M.T.A. v. Gray, supra, per Lord President Cooper at p. 600.
[62] Brimelow v. Casson [1924] 1 Ch. 302.
[63] Findlay v. Blaylock, 1937 S.C. 21.
[64] Rose Street Foundry Co. v. Lewis, 1917 S.C. 341.
[65] Jones Bros. (Hunstanton) Ltd. v. Stevens [1955] 1 Q.B. 275.
[66] 1974, (c. 52); 1976, (c. 7).
[67] Edw. VII, c. 47; 1965, (c. 48).
[68] 1971, (c. 72).
[69] Taff Vale Ry. v. Amalgamated Ry. Servants [1901] A.C. 426.
[70] 1906 Act, s. 4.

repetition of the slander could be obtained against the union or its officers in their official capacity.[71] This general immunity from liability in delict was abolished by the 1971 Act[72] but the substance of it was re-enacted, with some modifications, by the 1974 Act which also extended to employers' associations the protection hitherto enjoyed only by trade unions.[73] The principal modification is that a trade union may now be sued, as may an employers' association, in respect of any negligence, nuisance or breach of duty resulting in personal injury or any breach of duty in connection with the ownership, occupation, possession, control or use of property provided always that the cause of action does not arise from an act done in contemplation or furtherance of a trade dispute.[74] The immunity is confined, as it was under the 1906 Act, to delictual liability and there is nothing to preclude actions based on breaches of contract per se. Where the immunity applies, it strikes, however, at interdict as well as at actions of damages.[75]

The Trade Union and Labour Relations Acts do not confer immunity on the officials of a trade union. They remain personally liable for any wrong they may commit.[76] But, provided that the act be done "in contemplation or furtherance of a trade dispute," it is not actionable if done in combination unless it would be actionable if done without it,[77] and is not actionable on the ground only that it induces some other person to break a contract or interferes or induces any other person to interfere with its performance, or that it consists in threatening such breach of contract or inducement,[78] or that it is an interference with the trade, business or employment of some other person, or with the right of some other person to dispose of his capital or his labour as he wills.[79] A trade dispute is widely defined and extends to disputes between workers and workers as well as between employers and workers.[80]

In *Rookes* v. *Barnard*[81] it was held (1) that, if the wrong could have been committed by a single person and was actionable when done without agreement or combination, as in the case of intimidation,[82] section 1 of the 1906 Act (which protected acts done in combination if they would not have been actionable if done without it) would not apply; and (2) that section 3 of the Act (which provided that an act in contemplation or furtherance of a trade dispute was not actionable on the ground only that it induced some other person to break a contract of employment) did not apply where the

---

[71] *Vacher* v. *Society of Compositors* [1913] A.C. 107; *Shinwell* v. *National Sailors' Union*, 1913 2 S.L.T. 83.
[72] Sched. 9.
[73] s. 14.
[74] s. 14 (2).
[75] s. 14 (1) (c).
[76] See *Shinwell* v. *N.S.U.*, supra.
[77] 1974 Act s. 13 (4).
[78] 1974 Act s. 13 (1) as amended by 1976 Act s. 7 (2).
[79] 1974 Act s. 13 (2); *Brimelow* v. *Casson* [1924] 1 Ch. 302; *Square Grip Reinforcement Co.* v. *Macdonald*, 1966 S.L.T. 232, 1968 S.L.T. 65; *Morgan* v. *Fry* [1968] 2 Q.B. 710.
[80] 1974 Act, s. 29. See *Conway* v. *Wade* [1909] A.C. 506; *Larkin* v. *Long* [1915] A.C. 814; *Milligan* v. *Ayr Harbour Trs.*, 1915 S.C. 937; *Square Grip Reinforcement Co.*, supra; *Camden Exhibition & Display*, supra; *J. T. Stratford & Son* v. *Lindley* [1965] A.C. 269. *Torquay Hotel* v. *Cousins* [1969] 2 Ch. 106.
[81] [1964] A.C. 1129. cf. *Morgan* v. *Fry*, supra at pp. 728, 733 & 734.
[82] See § 7, supra.

inducement to break the contract of employment was brought about by intimidation or other unlawful means.[82] So the defendants, who were a trade union official and two fellow employees of the plaintiff, were found liable to indemnify the plaintiff whose contract of employment had been terminated by his employers in response to threats by the defendants to withdraw labour from the employers unless the plaintiff's contract was terminated. The effect of *Rookes* v. *Barnard*[81] has, however, been expressly limited by the protection given by the Trade Union and Labour Relations Act 1974 to acts done in contemplation or furtherance of a trade dispute and consisting in threats relating to breach of a contract or interference with its performance.[83]

10. Negligence: Duty of Care.—Liability for negligence in its narrowest sense[84] depends upon proof of three things, viz., (1) that the defender owed to the pursuer the duty to take reasonable care for the safety of the pursuer's person or property; (2) that the defender was in breach of that duty; and (3) that the breach caused damage to the pursuer's person or property.[85]

The duty to take care is the duty to avoid an act or omission which may have as its reasonable and probable consequence injury to others, and the duty is owed to those to whom injury may reasonably and probably be anticipated if the duty is not observed.[86] Thus the duty is not owed to the world at large. "Legal liability is limited to those consequences of our acts which a reasonable man of ordinary intelligence and experience so acting would have in contemplation."[87] "The standard of foresight of the reasonable man...eliminates the personal equation and is independent of the idiosyncrasies of the particular person whose conduct is in question."[87] Negligence is not, therefore, synonymous with carelessness.[88] It involves a failure to exercise the duty of care[89] and the existence of this duty depends upon injury to the pursuer's person or property being a reasonable and probable consequence of that failure.[90] It follows that not every party who sustains injury as a direct result of a negligent act or omission has a relevant claim for damages. The duty is owed by a motorist to A, with whom he collides, but not to B who has observed the accident from a point outwith the area of potential danger, although sustaining nervous shock.[91] The duty is probably owed to a child in utero at the time of an accident in respect of injuries attributable to that

---

[83] See footnote 78 supra; cf Trade Disputes Act 1965 (c. 68), s. 1.

[84] See Terminology, § 1, supra.

[85] Note that a defender is not necessarily liable for all the consequences of his negligence, those heads of loss which are "too remote" from the negligence being excluded: see Remoteness of Damage, § 13, infra.

[86] See *Muir* v. *Glasgow Corporation*, 1943 S.C. (H.L.) 3, per Lord Macmillan, at p. 10. The risk of injury must be real and substantial, not a remote possibility: see *Bolton* v. *Stone* [1951] A.C. 850 (the cricket ball case) and Lord Reid's comments thereon in *Carmarthenshire C.C.* v. *Lewis* [1955] A.C. 549, at p. 565, and in *Overseas Tankship (U.K.)* v. *Miller Steamship Co.* [1966] 3 W.L.R. 498 (P.C.), at pp. 510-2.

[87] Per Lord Macmillan, supra.

[88] See *Donoghue* v. *Stevenson*, 1932 S.C. (H.L.) 31, per Lord Macmillan, at p. 70.

[89] See *Clelland* v. *Robb*, 1911 S.C. 253, per Lord President Dunedin, at p. 256.

[90] *Bourhill* v. *Young*, 1942 S.C. (H.L.) 78; as to damage to property, see *Weller* v. *Foot & Mouth Disease Research Institute* [1966] 1 Q.B. 569.

[91] *Bourhill* v. *Young*, supra.

accident which persist after birth.[92] The test of "reasonable foreseeability" of injury thus defines the class of persons to whom the duty of care is owed; but, even if a pursuer is a member of that class and there is a breach of duty which results in injury to him, the foreseeability test is again applicable to determine whether or not the defender is liable in damages for the immediate physical consequences of his negligence.[93] To attract liability it is necessary that the kind of injury sustained[94] and the manner in which it was sustained[95] should be reasonably foreseeable, but not the precise chain of events leading up to the particular accident.[96] If the pursuer is within the area of potential danger (i.e., of reasonably foreseeable physical injury) created by a careless act, the duty of care exists and the defender will be liable to make reparation for nervous shock caused by fear of bodily harm, although the pursuer may escape physical injury.[97] The question of whether nervous shock, sustained by a person outwith the area of potential physical danger as a result only of seeing or hearing an accident to a third party may in some cases be a reasonable and probable consequence of the defender's carelessness and, therefore, actionable, is not settled.[98] In England close relatives and others have been held entitled to sue if they were in the immediate vicinity of the accident at the time,[99] but the dividing line may have to be drawn "where in the particular case the good sense of the jury or judge decides."[1] It seems that a bystander has no cause of action unless he is in some way connected with the person injured or with the occurrence.

The appropriate question to be posed in every case of negligence is—"Was what happened to the pursuer in this case a reasonably foreseeable consequence of the defender's carelessness?"[2]—because the answer to it determines (a) whether or not the duty of care was owed to the pursuer, and (b) if so, whether or not the defender is liable for the type of accident or injury sustained by the pursuer. This test may result in liability for negligence to parties who are injured in preventing or attempting to prevent injury to other

---

[92] *Watt* v. *Rama* [1972] V.R. 353 following *Donoghue* v. *Stevenson* 1932 S.C. (H.L.) 31 and *Grant* v. *Australian Knitting Mills* [1936] A.C. 85; *Duval* v. *Seguin* (1972) 26 D.L.R. (3d) 418. cf. *Williams* v. *Luff, The Times*, 14 Feb. 1978 in which liability was admitted.

[93] Note that this is a different question from that of the defender's liability for all the consequences of his negligence: see Remoteness of Damage, § 13, infra; and *McKillen* v. *Barclay Curle*, 1967 S.L.T. 41.

[94] *Hughes* v. *Lord Advocate*, 1963 S.C. (H.L.) 31; *Blaikie* v. *B.T.C.*, 1961 S.C. 44.

[95] *Hughes*, supra; *Malcolm* v. *Dickson*, 1951 S.C. 542; see also *Doughty* v. *Turner Mfg. Co.* [1964] 1 Q.B. 518.

[96] *Harvey* v. *Singer Mfg. Co.*, 1960 S.C. 155; and see *Carmarthenshire C.C.* v. *Lewis* [1955] A.C. 549, per Lord Reid, at p. 564.

[97] *Brown* v. *Glasgow Corporation*, 1922 S.C. 527; and see Walker, at p. 678.

[98] See *Currie* v. *Wardrop*, 1927 S.C. 538; *Bourhill* v. *Young*, 1942 S.C. (H.L.) 78; and see Walker, pp. 679-84.

[99] *Hambrook* v. *Stokes* [1925] 1 K.B. 141, where negligence admitted; *Boardman* v. *Sanderson* [1964] 1 W.L.R. 1317; cf. *King* v. *Phillips* [1954] 1 Q.B. 429; see also *M'Linden* v. *Richardson*, 1962 S.L.T. (Notes) 104 (proof before answer allowed where mother suffered shock from seeing van reversing with child injured beneath it.) cf. *Dooley* v. *Cammell Laird and Co* [1951] 1 Lloyd's Rep. 271; *Chadwick* v. *British Transport Commission* [1967] 2 All E.R. 945.

[1] *Bourhill* v. *Young*, supra, per Lord Wright, at p. 93; *King* v. *Phillips*, supra, per Singleton, L.J., at p. 437.

[2] See *Miller* v. *S.S.E.B.*, 1958 S.C. (H.L.) 20, per Lord Keith, at p. 34.

persons[3] or damage to property[4] imperilled by the defender's acts. It also brings trespassers within the class of persons to whom an occupier of or operator on land owes the duty of care, if the presence of the trespasser at the material time was reasonably foreseeable.[5] Similarly a manufacturer of goods owes a duty of care to the ultimate consumer if it is reasonably foreseeable that lack of reasonable care in the preparation of goods may cause injury to the consumer.[6] This principle applies to all kinds of dangerous defects in goods, structures and installations created by careless workmanship or permitted to exist in circumstances in which they ought to have been detected before they caused injury.[7] It also applies where, through lack of control, damage is caused to the property of third parties by persons under the control of officers to whose custody they have been committed.[8] One of the qualifications imposed by Lord Atkin in the manufacturer's case of *Donoghue* v. *Stevenson*[9] was that there should be "no reasonable possibility of intermediate examination"; but, as a result of the consideration of this phrase in later cases in England, it must probably be construed in a more restricted sense as meaning that there was "no reasonable possibility of the dangerous defect being discovered by a third party before it caused injury to the consumer or user."[10] It is not the possibility of subsequent inspection which breaks the chain of foreseeable consequences but the possibility of detection before the defect causes damage.[11]

The test of reasonable foreseeability in the form suggested above is of general application to cases of personal injury and damage to property only.[12] There is no duty to take care to avoid causing financial loss to individuals who suffer such loss as a direct result of negligence which kills or injures other persons with whom they had some form of relationship by contract or otherwise. Thus a master cannot claim reparation for the loss caused to him by the death or injury of a servant through the fault of a third party, even if the master has been injured in the same accident.[13] Similarly, no duty is owed to individuals who sustain financial loss when deprived of services through damage, negligently caused, to the property of another. Thus when, on the

---

[3] *Haynes* v. *Harwood* [1935] 1 K.B. 146; *Baker* v. *Hopkins* [1959] 1 W.L.R. 966; *Videan* v. *B.T.C.* [1963] 2 Q.B. 650; see also *Carmarthenshire C.C.* v. *Lewis* [1955] A.C. 549.

[4] *Steel* v. *Glasgow Iron & Steel Co.*, 1944 S.C. 237. But note that the deceased had responsibilities for the safety of his employer's property: see Lord Justice-Clerk Cooper, at p. 250.

[5] *M'Glone* v. *B.R.B.*, 1966 S.L.T. 2 (H.L.), per Lord Reid, at p. 9; and see Occupiers' Liability, § 17, infra; Walker, p. 598; and *Videan* v. *B.T.C.*, supra, where English trespass cases are considered.

[6] *Donoghue* v. *Stevenson*, 1932 S.C. (H.L.) 31; followed in *Lockhart* v. *Barr*, 1943 S.C. (H.L.) 1; and see *Grant* v. *Australian Knitting Mills* [1936] A.C. 85.

[7] See cases cited in Walker, *Delict*, pp. 617-30.

[8] *Home Office* v. *Dorset Yacht Co.* [1970] A.C. 1004.

[9] 1932 S.C. (H.L.) 31, at p. 57.

[10] See *Clay* v. *A. J. Crump* [1964] 1 Q.B. 533, and cases referred to therein.

[11] The chain of foreseeable consequences must be distinguished from the chain of causation: see Causation, § 12, infra; and see Lord Denning's justifiable criticism of the decision on relevancy in *Eccles* v. *Cross & M'Ilwham*, 1938 S.C. 697, in *Miller* v. *S.S.E.B.*, 1958 S.C. (H.L.) 20, at p. 39; also Lord Keith, at p. 34.

[12] *Allan* v. *Barclay* (1864) 2 M. 873, per Lord Kinloch, at p. 874.

[13] *Reavis* v. *Clan Line Steamers*, 1925 S.C. 725. Note that in *M'Bay* v. *Hamlett*, 1963 S.C. 282, the Lord Ordinary (Cameron) seems to suggest that the husband and wife relationship forms an exception to this rule, but the decision may be explained by the fact that the damages claimed were included as outlays in a claim which the husband had in his own right: see Walker, p. 721.

pursuers' averments, contractors negligently damaged an electricity supply cable belonging to the Electricity Board so that the supply of electricity to the pursuers' factory was cut off and loss of production with consequent financial loss ensued, the action was dismissed.[14]

When the alleged negligence relates to statements, verbal or written, and not to deeds, different considerations apply.[15] It has long been recognised that a duty to take reasonable care that such statements are accurate may arise from special relationships in special circumstances.[16] In *Hedley Byrne & Co.* v. *Heller and Partners* the House of Lords considered the circumstances in which a party sustaining financial loss as a direct result of acting upon an incorrect statement, given by another with whom there was no contractual relationship, might sue for damages on the ground of negligence.[17] The "special relationships" contemplated by the House of Lords were independent of contract and extended beyond fiduciary relationship. Lord Reid could see "no logical stopping place short of all those relationships where it is plain that the party seeking information or advice was trusting the other to exercise such a degree of care as the circumstances required, where it was reasonable for him to do that, and where the other gave the information or advice when he knew or ought to have known that the inquirer was relying on him."[18] As their Lordships unanimously overruled *Candler* v. *Crane, Christmas & Co.*,[19] the facts of that case illustrate circumstances in which their Lordships found such a relationship and corresponding duty of care. In that case the accountants of a company carelessly, but honestly, prepared accounts, which gave a wholly misleading picture of the state of the company, at the request of the managing director in the knowledge that he required them to show to the plaintiff with a view to investment in the company. On the faith of the accounts the plaintiff invested money in the company and lost it when the company was wound up soon afterwards. The duty, therefore, is not confined to the party who receives the information at first hand but is owed to the party whom the informant knows or ought to know is likely to act upon the faith of the information. It is owed to future owners and occupiers by a local authority which, in exercise of statutory powers, approves building plans.[20] But, where the misleading character of such approval arises from failure to make an inspection or the inadequacy of an inspection, there is liability only if the discretion not to make

In *McCallum* v. *Patterson* 1968 S.L.T. (Notes) 98 and *Sleigh* v. *Aberdeen Corporation* (30th May 1969, unreported) opinions were expressed obiter in agreement with the decisions in *M'Bay* v. *Hamlett* which was not however, followed by the Lord Ordinary (Keith) in *Jacks* v. *Alex. MacDougall & Co (Engnrs.)*, 1973 S.L.T. 88.

[14] *Dynamco* v. *Holland and Hannen and Cubitts (Scotland)*, 1972 S.L.T. 38; cf. *S.C.M. (United Kingdom)* v. *W. G Whittall and Sons* [1971] 1 Q.B. 137; *Spartan Steel Alloys* v. *Martins and Co. (Contractors)* [1973] Q.B. 27.

[15] "Words are more volatile than deeds": per Lord Pearce in *Hedley Byrne & Co.* v. *Heller & Partners* [1964] A.C. 465, at p. 534; see also Lord Reid, at p. 483.

[16] *Robinson* v. *National Bank of Scotland*, 1916 S.C. (H.L.) 154.

[17] [1964] A.C. 465.

[18] Ibid., at p. 486. There is, however, no liability if the person making the statement does not hold himself out as having skill in the subject matter of the statement (*Mutual Life and Citizens Assurance Company* v. *Evatt* [1971] A.C. 793).

[19] [1951] 2 K.B. 164. In his dissenting judgment Denning, L.J., at pp. 179-84, suggested circumstances in which the duty of care would be incumbent upon specified professional and skilled men; approved in *Hedley Byrne*, supra, per Lord Devlin, at p. 530, and per Lord Pearce, at p. 539. cf. *Central B.C. Planers* v. *Hocker* (1970) 9 D.L.R. (3d) 689.

[20] *Dutton* v. *Bognor Regis Urban District Council* [1972] 1 Q.B. 373.

an inspection or as to the manner in which the inspection was to be carried out was not properly exercised.[21] It may be excluded, in circumstances in which it would otherwise arise, by an express disclaimer of responsibility.[21a] But a banker is probably under no such duty when answering the enquiry of another banker (who stands in no special relationship to him) about the credit-worthiness of a customer.[22]

11. Negligence: Standard of Care.—The duty is to take care to avoid an act or omission which may have as its reasonable and probable consequence injury to others.[23] The standard of care required is that of the reasonably careful, the ordinary prudent, man in all the circumstances of the case.[24] "The reasonable man is presumed to be free both from over-apprehension and from over-confidence."[23] What amounts to reasonable care depends upon the facts of the particular case.[25] Whether or not there has been a breach of that duty is a question of fact.[26] While there is only one standard of care, "the degree of care for the safety of others which the law requires human beings to observe in the conduct of their affairs varies according to circumstances."[24] The degree of care varies directly with the risk involved.[24] Thus a higher degree of care is required in activities which are obviously highly dangerous.[27] At the other end of the scale the risk may be so small that a reasonable man would feel justified in disregarding it.[28] The appropriate degree of care is not determined by reference solely to the actual knowledge of the defender but also to the sources of knowledge open to him and to the actual knowledge of kindred persons.[29] The pursuer's own knowledge and experience are also relevant to the question of what precautions were reasonable in the circumstances.[30] A greater degree of care is due to parties with abnormal susceptibilities or infirmities.[31] The magnitude of the risk must be weighed against the difficulty and expense of taking precautions and the importance of the particular operation.[32] An

[21] *Anns* v. *Merton London Borough Council* [1977] 2 W.L.R. 1024.
[21a] *Hedley Byrne*, supra.
[22] *Robinson* v. *National Bank,* supra, per Viscount Haldane, at p. 157, and see opinions in *Hedley Byrne,* supra, in particular per Lord Reid, at p. 498. Aliter if a banker undertakes to advise an individual as to investment: *Woods* v. *Martins Bank,* [1959] 1 Q.B. 55.
[23] *Muir* v. *Glasgow Corporation,* 1943 S.C. (H.L.) 3, per Lord Macmillan, at p. 10.
[24] ibid.; *Mackintosh* v. *Mackintosh* (1864) 2 M. 1357, per Lord Neaves, at pp. 1362-3.
[25] ibid.; *Miller* v. *S.S.E.B.,* 1958 S.C. (H.L.) 20, per Lord Keith, at p. 33; *Donoghue* v. *Stevenson,* 1932 S.C. (H.L.) 31, per Lord Atkin, at p. 44; *Cavanagh* v. *Ulster Weaving Co.* [1960] A.C. 145; *Brown* v. *Rolls Royce,* 1960 S.C. (H.L.) 22.
[26] *Qualcast* v. *Haynes* [1959] A.C. 743.
[27] *Dominion Natural Gas Co.* v. *Collins* [1909] A.C. 640, per Lord Dunedin, at p. 646; *Read* v. *Lyons & Co.* [1947] A.C. 156, per Lord Macmillan, at p. 171—"an exacting standard of care is incumbent on manufacturers of explosive shells."
[28] See *Carmarthenshire C.C.* v. *Lewis* [1955] A.C. 549, per Lord Reid, at p. 565; also *Overseas Tankship (U.K.)* v. *Miller Steamship Co.* [1967] 1 A.C. 617 (P.C.) at pp. 641-44.
[29] See *Balfour* v. *Beardmore & Co.,* 1956 S.L.T. 205; cf. *Quinn* v. *Cameron & Roberton,* 1956 S.C. 224, per Lord President Clyde, at p. 232 (reversed on another ground, 1957 S.C. (H.L.) 22); *Cramb* v. *Caledonian Ry.* (1892) 19 R. 1054; *Roe* v. *Minister of Health* [1954] 2 Q.B. 66.
[30] *Qualcast* v. *Haynes* [1959] A.C. 743, per Lord Radcliffe, at p. 754; *Ross* v. *A.P.C.* [1964] 1 W.L.R. 768 (H.L.).
[31] *M'Kibbin* v. *Glasgow Corporation,* 1920 S.C. 590, and *Haley* v. *London Elec. Board* [1965] A.C. 778 (blind persons); *Paris* v. *Stepney B.C.* [1951] A.C. 367 (man known to have only one eye); as to children, see *Taylor* v. *Glasgow Corp.,* 1922 S.C. (H.L.) 1; *Miller* v. *S.S.E.B.,* 1958 S.C. (H.L.) 20; *Hughes* v. *L.A.,* 1963 S.C. (H.L.) 31; also Occupiers' Liability, § 17, infra.
[32] *Morris* v. *West Hartlepool Steam Navig. Co.* [1956] A.C. 552, per Lord Reid, at p. 574; per Lord Cohen, at p. 579; *Daborn* v. *Bath Tramways Co.* [1946] 2 All E.R. 333, per Asquith, L.J., at p. 336.

emergency may justify the taking of a risk which in other circumstances might be negligent.[33] And a professional man is not negligent unless he has adopted a course of action which no professional man of ordinary skill would have taken, if he had been acting with ordinary care.[34]

12. Negligence: Causation.—Once negligence is established, liability depends upon proof that it caused the damage in issue. Where the alleged negligence was failure to provide a workman with a safety belt, it was suggested that there were four steps of causation: (1) a duty to supply a safety belt; (2) a breach; (3) that, if there had been a safety belt, the workman would have used it; and (4) that, if the workman had been using a safety belt, he would not have been killed, and the failure to prove the third step rendered the first two steps inoperative.[35] The first two steps, however, are not truly links in the chain of causation, the tracing of which does not begin until the question is posed—"Did the proven breach of duty cause this event?"[36] To increase the risk of harm, by more than a negligible degree, is, for this purpose, the equivalent of causing that harm should it ensue.[37]

Where a number of factors contribute to an event, any one which makes a material contribution thereto is held to be a real or efficient cause.[38] "This choice of the real or efficient cause from out of the whole complex of the facts must be made by applying commonsense standards. Causation is to be understood as the man in the street, and not as either the scientist or the metaphysician would understand it."[39] The phrase "causa causans" covers all causes which contribute materially to the end result[40]; a "causa sine qua non" is one which is not efficient or material but is a collateral or concomitant cause.[41] Where two or more causes combine concurrently to cause an accident, each is an efficient cause.[42] But difficulty may arise when a number of factors operate consecutively to produce a result. Then the factors which are efficient and material causes must be separated from those which are not. The mere fact that a subsequent act of negligence has been the immediate cause of the disaster does not exonerate the original wrongdoer if there is no sufficient separation of time, place and circumstances to justify the exclusion of the original negligence as an efficient cause.[43] This principle now applies

---

[33] See, e.g., *Watt* v. *Hertfordshire C.C.* [1954] 1 W.L.R. 835; also *Latimer* v. *A.E.C. Ltd.* [1953] A.C. 643, where it was held that failure to close a factory to prevent employees slipping on a flooded floor was not negligent.

[34] *Hunter* v. *Hanley*, 1955 S.C. 200, per Lord President Clyde, at p. 206; see also *Roe* v. *Minister of Health* [1954] 2 Q.B. 66; and *Stewart* v. *H. A. Brechin & Co.*, 1959 S.C. 306, as to the degree of care expected from property surveyors.

[35] *M'Williams* v. *Wm Arrol & Co.*, 1962 S.C. (H.L.) 70, per Lord Chancellor Kilmuir, at p. 77.

[36] See Duty of Care, § 10, supra.

[37] *McGhee* v. *National Coal Board*, 1973 S.L.T. 14.

[38] *Wardlaw* v. *Bonnington Castings*, 1956 S.C. (H.L.) 26.

[39] *Yorkshire Dale S.S. Co.* v. *M.O.W.T.* [1942] A.C. 691, per Lord Wright at p. 706; see also Lord Macmillan, at pp. 702-3; and *Brown* v. *M.O.P.*, 1946 S.C. 471, per Lord Justice-Clerk Cooper, at p. 475.

[40] See Lord Wright, supra; *Leyland Shipping Co.* v. *Norwich Union Fire Insce. Co.* [1918] A.C. 350, per Lords Dunedin, at p. 363, and Shaw, at pp. 368-70.

[41] For an example of the latter, see *Weld-Blundell* v. *Stephens* [1920] A.C. 956.

[42] *Boy Andrew* v. *St. Rognvald*, 1947 S.C. (H.L.) 79.

[43] *The Volute* v. *Admiralty Commissioners* [1922] A.C. 129, per Lord Chancellor Birkenhead, at pp. 144-5; see also *Grant* v. *Sun Shipping Co.*, 1948 S.C. (H.L.) 73, per Lord du Parcq at p. 94; *Stapley* v. *Gypsum Mines* [1953] A.C. 663, per Lord Reid, at pp. 681-2; and *Drew* v. *Western S.M.T.*, 1947 S.C. 222.

even if the final act of negligence is that of the pursuer himself,[44] unless the final act is held to be the sole efficient cause of the accident.[45] But the chain of causation between the original negligent act and the ultimate consequences may be broken by "a new cause which disturbs the sequence of events, something which can be described as either unreasonable or extraneous or extrinsic, outside the exigencies of the emergency."[46] That new cause may be some act by the injured party himself or by a third party. If it is held to break the chain of causation, it is known as a novus actus interveniens; and, in determining whether or not such an act is sufficient to break the chain, the test of reasonable foreseeability may be applied.

The pursuer's own act will break the chain of causation if the effect of it is to render useless the precaution desiderated by him,[47] or if he has acted in wilful defiance of orders,[48] but probably not if he has merely been careless (which results in apportionment of blame), and certainly not if he has acted reasonably in the circumstances.[49] An error of judgment made by the pursuer when acting in an emergency created by the defender's negligence will not break the chain.[50] While the deliberate unwarranted intervention of a third party will break the chain[51] if it is thought to be the proximate cause or not reasonably foreseeable,[51] an act which is reasonable in the circumstances will not. So a man who threw a lighted squib into a crowded market place was found liable in damages to the person injured when it exploded, notwithstanding the fact that it had only reached the injured party through the intervention of two other people who, acting in the interests of their own safety, had picked it up and thrown it onwards.[52] There is liability for all the natural and probable consequences of the negligent act[53]; and the fact that the last link in the chain is a wrongful[54] or negligent[55] or voluntary act[56] of a third party will not exclude liability if that act is a reasonably foreseeable consequence of the defender's original negligence.

13. Negligence: Remoteness of Damage.—"A wrongdoer is not held responsible for all the results which flow from his negligent act. Practical

[44] Blame is then apportioned under the Law Reform (Contributory Negligence) Act 1945; and see *Ross* v. *A.P.C.* [1964] 1 W.L.R. 768 (H.L.).
[45] See cases of deliberate disobedience of instructions referred to by Lord Reid in *Ross* v. *A.P.C.*, supra, at pp. 776-7; and Contributory Negligence, § 15, infra.
[46] Per Lord Wright in *The Oropesa* [1943] P. 32, at p. 39.
[47] E.g., by refusing to wear a safety belt: see *M'Williams* v. *Wm. Arrol & Co.*, 1962 S.C. (H.L.) 70.
[48] See *Stapley* v. *Gypsum Mines Ltd.* [1953] A.C. 663; *Ginty* v. *Belmont Building Supplies* [1959] 1 All E.R. 414; *Horne* v. *Lec Refrigeration* [1965] 2 All E.R. 898; also *Crowe* v. *James Scott & Sons*, 1965 S.L.T. 54.
[49] *Steel* v. *Glasgow Iron & Steel Co.*, 1944 S.C. 237, in particular, Lord Jamieson at p. 268; cf. *Malcolm* v. *Dickson*, 1951 S.C. 542; *Macdonald* v. *MacBrayne*, 1915 S.C. 716.
[50] See *S.S. Baron Vernon* v. *S.S. Metagama*, 1928 S.C. (H.L.) 21, per Viscount Dunedin, at pp. 26-27.
[51] See *Weld-Blundell* v. *Stephens* [1920] A.C. 956; cf. *Marshall* v. *Caledonian Ry.* (1899) 1 F. 1060.
[52] *Scott* v. *Shepherd* (1773) 2 W. Bl. 892; see also *Clark* v. *Chambers* (1878) 3 Q.B.D. 327; *The Oropesa* [1943] P. 32; and *Haynes* v. *Harwood* [1935] 1 K.B. 146.
[53] *Scott's Trs.* v. *Moss* (1887) 17 R. 32; *Miller* v. *S.S.E.B.*, 1958 S.C. (H.L.) 20; *Steel* v. *Glasgow Iron & Steel Co.*, 1944 S.C. 237, per Lord Jamieson, at p. 268.
[54] *Marshall* v. *Caley. Ry.*, supra.
[55] *Miller* v. *S.S.E.B.*, supra; cf. *S.S. Singleton Abbey* v. *S.S. Paludina* [1927] A.C. 16.
[56] See *Haynes* v. *Harwood* [1935] 1 K.B. 146 (where boys caused horses to bolt), *Baker* v. *Hopkins* [1959] 1 W.L.R. 966 and *Hosie* v. *Arbroath Football Club*, 1978 S.L.T. 122.

considerations dictate, and the law accepts, that there comes a point in the sequence of events when liability can no longer be enforced. This rule of convenience and commonsense is enshrined in the maxim 'causa proxima non remota spectatur'."[57] Liability for injury to a person or damage to property through negligence extends to all the natural and direct consequences of that injury or damage.[58] There must be an unbroken causal connection between the original damage and every item of loss claimed to flow therefrom.[59] "The grand rule on the subject of damages is, that none can be claimed except such as naturally and directly arise out of the wrong done, and such, therefore, as may reasonably be supposed to have been in the view of the wrongdoer."[60] Although this statement was made obiter by Lord Kinloch, it is an accurate statement of the rule in Scotland governing liability for both the immediate and subsequent consequences of negligence.[61] It is, however, open to construction. "Naturally" means "according to the ordinary, usual or normal course of things" and this includes reasonable human conduct.[62] "Directly" means "without any break in the chain of causation."[63] Everything which arises in the ordinary course of things from the negligence without the intervention of any extraneous act or factor is in law deemed to have been in the view of the wrongdoer.[64] Damages which flow directly and naturally (i.e., in the ordinary course of things) from the wrongful act cannot be regarded as too remote.[65] While the foreseeability test may be of assistance in certain cases in determining whether the loss claimed has arisen from the negligent act "in the ordinary course of things" and is, therefore, a natural, ordinary or normal result as opposed to an unnatural, extraordinary and abnormal result,[66] our law does not permit that test to be pressed to the length of excluding liability for any item of loss which has arisen naturally and directly (in the sense beforementioned) from the negligence. For example, there is liability for all medical expenses reasonably incurred as a natural and direct consequence of

---

[57] *Malcolm* v. *Dickson,* 1951 S.C. 542, per Lord Justice-Clerk Thomson, at p. 547; see also *Liesbosch* v. *S.S. Edison* [1933] A.C. 449, per Lord Wright, at p. 460.

[58] Liability having been established by the reasonable foreseeability of the kind of damage sustained and the manner in which it was sustained: see Duty of Care, § 10, supra. See also *Adm. Commrs.* v. *S.S. Susquehanna* [1926] A.C. 655, per Lord Dunedin, at p. 661; approved in *Hutchison* v. *Davidson,* 1945 S.C. 395, by Lord Russell, at p. 404, and by Lord Moncrieff, at p. 410, and by Lords Mackay and Patrick in *Pomphrey* v. *Cuthbertson,* 1951 S.C. 147, at pp. 157 and 162.

[59] See *The Vitruvia,* 1925 S.C. (H.L.) 1; *The Cameronia* v. *The Hauk,* 1928 S.L.T. 71; and *Carslogie S.S. Co.* v. *Royal Norwegian Govt.* [1952] A.C. 292.

[60] *Allan* v. *Barclay* (1864) 2 M. 873, per Lord Kinloch, at p. 874.

[61] For immediate consequences, see Causation, § 12, supra.

[62] See *S.S. Baron Vernon* v. *S.S. Metagama,* 1928 S.C. (H.L.) 21, per Lord Haldane, at p. 25; *The Oropesa* [1943] P. 32, per Lord Wright, at pp. 37-8, and *Steel* v. *Glasgow Iron & Steel Co.,* 1944 S.C. 237, at pp. 248 and 268.

[63] See Causation, § 12, supra.

[64] Note. If "naturally" is construed in the broader sense above mentioned instead of the narrow sense of "in the ordinary course of nature," the difficulties created in England by the *Polemis* case ([1921] 3 K.B. 560) do not arise in respect that liability for the fire damage in both the *Polemis* case and *The Wagon Mound* ([1961] A.C. 388) must be excluded as being an unnatural (i.e., extraordinary or abnormal) consequence and such, therefore, as cannot reasonably be supposed to have been in the view of the wrongdoer.

[65] See *Clyde Navigation Trs.* v. *Bowring S.S. Co.,* 1929 S.C. 715, per Lord Hunter at p. 723, quoting Lord Herschell.

[66] See *Steel* v. *Glasgow Iron & Steel Co.,* 1944 S.C. 237, per Lord Justice-Clerk Cooper, at p. 248, and per Lord Jamieson, at p. 268.

physical injury and this liability extends to the expense of unnecessary treatment wrongly, but not negligently, prescribed by doctors.[67] The foreseeability test cannot be applied first and in isolation exclude liability for such expenses.[68]

"The personal injuries of the individual himself will be properly held (i.e., deemed) to have been in the contemplation of the wrongdoer."[69] In other words, the negligent party "must take his victim as he finds him" and is liable for all the natural and direct effects of the original injury on the particular pursuer.[70] These include the consequences of inappropriate medical treatment if that was not negligent.[71] But death by suicide is neither a natural nor a direct result of a moderate eye injury.[72] The same rules apply to patrimonial loss. Probable loss due to prospects of promotion being prejudiced is relevant, but the loss of hypothetical gain is too remote.[73] It has been held that an injured company director and principal shareholder could not claim for a share of the profits lost by the company due to his absence from business because the company itself had no right of action and his loss was, therefore, too remote.[74] Where a pursuer had placed in his own stable a horse which, unknown to him, had become infected through the fault of the defender while in the latter's custody, with the result that two other horses belonging to the pursuer also became infected, the Court held that he was entitled to recover his whole loss as a natural and direct result of the defender's misconduct.[75] Lastly, in assessing the measure of damages applicable to the loss of working plant through negligence, extraordinary or abnormal loss, sustained by the owners as a result of their inability through impecuniosity to purchase a replacement, is too remote, the financial embarrassment of the owners being an extrinsic and unusual factor which was the effective cause of the said loss.[76]

Where the wrongful act of a third party is not a consequence of the defender's negligence and so operates that the physical effects of that negligence are brought to an end and replaced by other and more serious injuries, the extent of the defender's liability in damages is unaffected. Thus where a plaintiff sustained leg injuries caused by the fault of the defendant and

---

[67] *Rubens* v. *Walker*, 1946 S.C. 215. If the treatment had been negligently perscribed, that negligence might be held on the facts to be a novus actus interveniens excluding the defender's liability for such expenses but exposing the doctors to a claim against them.

[68] See also *H.M.S. London* [1914] P. 72, where a claim for loss of use of a vessel in dock for collision repairs was allowed to cover the period of a shipyard strike as natural and direct loss.

[69] *Allan* v. *Barclay* (1864) 2 M. 873, per Lord Kinloch, at p. 874.

[70] *M'Killen* v. *Barclay Curle & Co.*, 1967 S.L.T. 41. This also appears to be the law of England: see *Smith* v. *Leech Brain & Co.* [1962] 2 Q.B. 405.

[71] cf. *Robinson* v. *Post Office* [1974] 1 W.L.R. 1176 where although there was negligence in the medical treatment that negligence was not a cause of the condition which resulted from the treatment and so did not constitute novus actus interveniens.

[72] *Cowan* v. *N.C.B.*, 1958 S.L.T. (Notes) 19. It may however, be possible to establish death by suicide as a natural and direct consequence of a severe head injury.

[73] See *M'Call* v. *Foulis*, 1966 S.L.T. 47, and cases cited therein.

[74] *Young* v. *Ormiston*, 1936 S.L.T. 79; cf. *Lee* v. *Sheard* [1956] 1 Q.B. 192, where the Court of Appeal held that the pursuer could recover his share of lost profits *because* the company could not.

[75] *Robertson* v. *Connolly* (1851) 13 D. 779. Note that the action was laid on contract but it is thought that the result would have been the same if based on negligence.

[76] See *Liesbosch* v. *S.S. Edison* [1933] A.C. 449, in particular Lord Wright, at pp. 460 and 465-6.

was susequently shot in the same leg by criminals with the result that the leg had to be amputated, it was held that the defendant was liable not only for the consequences of his negligent act up to the time of amputation but also for the damages prospectively attributable to his act if the shooting had not taken place.[77]

14. Proof of Negligence: Res Ipsa Loquitur.—The burden of proving negligence generally rests upon the pursuer and it must be established on "the balance of probabilities."[78] Although the onus of proof may shift to and fro according to the state of the evidence as the case proceeds, the decision may ultimately turn upon the question of whether or not the pursuer has discharged the burden of proving negligence.[79] In some cases the pursuer may establish a prima facie case of negligence which transfers to the defender the onus of proving that he was not negligent.[80] In other cases the admitted or proved fact that an accident occurred may per se yield an inference of negligence which must be negatived by the defender.[81] It is to the latter type of case "where the thing is shown to be under the management of the defendant or his servants, and the accident is such as in the ordinary case does not happen if those who have the management use proper care,"[82] that the maxim "res ipsa loquitur" ("the thing itself speaks") applies. It is a presumption of law to which, therefore, if the conditions for its operation are satisfied, effect must be given.[83] In this as in other similar cases "it is the policy of the law that intervenes to relax the logical stringency of proof and so invert the normal onus in order to avoid denial of justice to those whose rights depend on facts incapable of proof by them, and often exclusively within the knowledge and control of their opponent."[84] Thus where shop owners were sued as a result of an accident due to spillage on the floor of the shop it was held that there was an onus on them to show that the accident did not occur through want of care on their part.[85] Once the onus is inverted, the defender can only exclude liability by proof that he was not negligent. It has been said, however, that it is essential to the application of res ipsa loquitur that the pursuer cannot reasonably be expected to know the exact cause of the accident and that, if he does, he must aver the cause and prove negligence.[86] If the res

---

[77] *Baker* v. *Willoughby* [1970] A.C. 467.

[78] *Hendry* v. *Clan Line Steamers,* 1949 S.C. 320. Corroboration is no longer essential in actions of damages where the damages claimed include damages or solatium for personal injuries (Law Reform (Miscellaneous Provisions) (Scotland) Act 1968, (c. 70), s. 9).

[79] Ibid., per Lord Justice-Clerk Thomson at p. 322; see also *Brown* v. *Rolls Royce Ltd.,* 1960 S.C. (H.L.) 22, per Lord Denning, as to the difference between the legal and provisional burden of proof.

[80] See, e.g., *Gunn* v. *M'Adam,* 1949 S.C. 31.

[81] See, e.g., *Ballard* v. *N.B. Ry. Co.,* 1923 S.C. (H.L.) 43.

[82] Per Erle, C.J., in *Scott* v. *London, etc., Docks Co.* (1865) 3 H. & C. 596, adopted by the House of Lords in *Ballard* v. *N.B. Ry. Co.,* supra.

[83] *Henderson* v. *Henry E. Jenkins and Sons* [1970] A.C. 282.

[84] *Elliot* v. *Young's Bus Service,* 1945 S.C. 445. per Lord Justice-Clerk Cooper. at p. 456: see also p. 454, where the Lord Justice-Clerk points out that it is "unsafe to generalise upon the question of who must prove what without due regard to the precise legal relationship between the parties."

[85] *Ward* v. *Tesco Stores* [1976] 1 W.L.R. 810.

[86] See note 90, infra.

does not per se exclude the possibility of the event having been caused by the pursuer or a third party for whom the defender is not responsible,[87] the pursuer, in order to establish a prima facie case, must adduce evidence which, if accepted, excludes interference by the pursuer and third parties.[88] If the pursuer fails to establish a prima facie case by his evidence, the legal burden of proving negligence remains on the pursuer throughout.[89]

If the cause of an accident is averred by the pursuer to have been a defect in the defender's plant, the onus of proving that the defect was patent (i.e., discoverable by reasonable inspection) and that the defender was at fault in failing to discover it is on the pursuer.[90] If the pursuer does not aver the exact nature of the defect and cannot reasonably be expected to do so, proof by the pursuer that the plant collapsed brings the maxim res ipsa loquitur into play so that the defender must exculpate himself.[91] If the defender pleads that the defect was latent and, therefore, not ascertainable by reasonable examination, the defender must prove that defence [92] But the defender will not exculpate himself by proving only that the defect was latent if it is a reasonable inference from the whole evidence that careless handling of the plant was an effective cause of the breakage.[93] If the exact cause of the accident is unknown to either party, proof or admission of the accident throws upon the defender the burden of proving that it happened without negligence on his part (i.e., that he had taken reasonable care in the circumstances of the case).[94] In the case of defective plant the defender may achieve this by proving that the plant was regularly and properly inspected and no defect found.[95]

Where the accident is of a kind which may occur without fault on the part of the person having control of the object causing the accident (e.g. a vehicle) "res ipsa non loquitur". In such cases the pursuer must first establish a prima facie case of negligence by proving that the vehicle stopped or swerved suddenly for no apparent reason; thereafter, the defender can only exculpate himself by proving a reason for the driver's emergency action which negatives negligence on his part.[96] If, however, the pursuer avers that the sudden stop or swerve was made in order to avoid a collision with some person or thing on

---

[87] See *Macfarlane* v. *Thompson* (1884) 12 R. 232.
[88] *Inglis* v. *L.M.S. Ry. Co.*, 1941 S.C. 551; cf. *Easson* v. *L. & N.E.R.* [1944] K.B. 421; *Lloyds* v. *West Midlands Gas Board* [1971] 1. W.L.R. 749.
[89] *Connelly* v. *L.M.S. Ry. Co.*, 1940 S.C. 477; see also *Moore* v. *R. Fox & Sons* [1956] 1 Q.B. 596 (alternative ground).
[90] *Gavin* v. *Rogers* (1889) 17 R. 206; *Milne* v. *Townsend* (1892) 19 R. 830.
[91] *Macaulay* v. *Buist & Co.* (1846) 9 D. 245; *Fraser* v. *Fraser* (1882) 9 R. 896; *Walker* v. *Olsen* (1882) 9 R. 946.
[92] *Elliot* v. *Young's Bus Service*, 1945 S.C. 445, per Lord Justice-Clerk Cooper, at p. 456; *Gibson* v. *Concrete*, 1954 S.L.T. (Notes) 7; see also *Moore* v. *R. Fox*, supra, per Evershed, M.R., at pp. 611-2.
[93] *Ballard* v. *N.B. Ry. Co.*, 1923 S.C. (H.L.) 43.
[94] *Elliot* v. *Young's Bus Service*, supra; *Marshall & Son* v. *Russian Oil Products*, 1938 S.C. 773, per Lord Justice-Clerk Aitchison, at p. 791; *Devine* v. *Colvilles*, 1969 S.C. (H.L.) 67. see also *Woods* v. *Duncan* (*The Thetis*) [1946] A.C. 401.
[95] *Devine* v. *Colvilles*, supra; *Elliot* v. *Young's Bus Service*, supra, per Lord Justice-Clerk Cooper, at pp. 454-5.
[96] *Mars* v. *Glasgow Corp.*, 1940 S.C. 202; *O'Hara* v. *Central S.M.T. Co.*, 1941 S.C. 363; *Doonan* v. *S,M.T.*, 1950 S.C. 136. See also *Roberts* v. *Matthew Logan*, 1966 S.L.T. 77. *Ludgate* v. *Lovett* [1969] 1 W.L.R. 1016.

the roadway, the onus of proving negligence remains on the pursuer throughout.[97]

In Scotland, therefore, once the onus is transferred to the defender, whether by application of the maxim res ipsa loquitur or by the pursuer establishing by evidence a prima facie case, the Court will find for the pursuer unless the defender has cleared himself of negligence by "full legal proof."[98] But the pursuer is tied to his pleadings.[99] If it appears from the evidence that the accident was probably due to some cause not founded on by the pursuer as a ground of negligence, the pursuer fails to prove the only relevant negligence, i.e., the grounds founded on.[1]

15. Contributory Negligence.—"The technical meaning of 'contributory negligence' is negligence on the part of the pursuer which is itself jointly causative of the accident along with the negligence of the defender,"[2] but in ordinary usage it means fault on the part of a pursuer either wholly causing or materially contributing to an accident. In this context "fault" connotes breach of a legal duty only in the sense that the law requires a man in his own interest to take reasonable care of himself[3] and the scope of the accident must be taken to extend to the whole involvement of the pursuer in the occurrence.[4] The burden of proving that the pursuer's fault was at least one of the effective causes of an accident is on the defender.[5] Up to 1945,[6] if the pursuer was held to any extent to blame for his injury, his claim failed and he could recover nothing. To mitigate the harshness of this doctrine the Courts developed the so-called "last opportunity" rule,[7] under which he who had the last opportunity of avoiding the accident was held liable. The fault of the first party was regarded as a "causa sine qua non"; that of the second and later party was regarded as the "causa causans" of the accident. This "was a fallacious test because the efficiency of the causes did not depend on their proximity in point of time."[8]

---

[97] *Ballingall* v. *Glasgow Corp.*, 1948 S.C. 160; see also *M'Gregor* v. *Dundee Corp.*, 1962 S.C. 15, where the Court inferred that a skid was caused by excessive speed.

[98] *O'Hara* v. *Central S.M.T.*, supra, and see Lord President Normand at p. 379 on "sufficient legal corroboration"; *Spindlow* v. *Glasgow Corporation*, 1933 S.C. 580; but corroboration is now no longer essential in personal injury actions, see Note 78 supra.

[99] On the significance to be attached to pleadings see, however, *Gibson* v. *British Insulated Callender's Construction Co.*, 1973 S.L.T. 2.

[1] *Connelly* v. *L.M.S. Ry. Co.*, 1940 S.C. 477; see also *Esso Petroleum Co.* v. *Southport Corp.* [1956] 2 W.L.R. 81 (H.L.) but see *Gibson* v. *British Insulated Callender's Construction Co.*, supra.

[2] *Robinson* v. *Hamilton (Motors)*, 1923 S.C. 838, per Lord President Clyde, at p. 841.

[3] *Nance* v. *British Columbia Electric Ry. Co.* [1951] A.C. 601, per Viscount Simon, at p. 611; *Davies* v. *Swan Motor Co.* [1949] 2 K.B. 291, per Bucknill, L.J., at p. 308: per Denning, L.J., at p. 324.

[4] e.g. a pursuer may in a case arising out of a motor accident be guilty of contributory negligence although he did nothing to cause the collision if his conduct contributed to the injuries he sustained. See footnote 15, infra.

[5] See Causation, § 12, supra.

[6] Law Reform (Contributory Negligence) Act 1945 (8 & 9 Geo. VI, c. 28).

[7] *Davies* v. *Mann* (1842) 10 M. & W. 546; *Carse* v. *North British Steam Packet Co.* (1895) 22 R. 475; *British Columbia Electric Co.* v. *Loach* [1916] 1 A.C. 719; *Ward* v. *Revie*, 1944 S.C. 325, per Lord Moncreiff, at p. 335.

[8] Per Denning, L.J., in *Davies* v. *Swan Motor Co.* [1949] 2 K.B. 291, at p. 321; and see *Boy Andrew* v. *St. Rognvald*, 1947 S.C. (H.L.) 70; Causation, § 12, supra.

The common law rule as to contributory negligence did not, however, apply to collisions between ships. By the Maritime Conventions Act 1911 (1 & 2 Geo. V, c. 57), it is provided that when, by the fault of two or more vessels, damage or loss is caused to one or more of these vessels, to their cargoes or freights, or to any property on board, the liability to make good the damage or loss shall be in proportion to the degree in which each vessel was in fault, with the proviso that if, having regard to all the circumstances of the case, it is not possible to establish different degrees of fault, the liability shall be apportioned equally.[9]

The principle of the Maritime Conventions Act 1911 was made generally applicable by the Law Reform (Contributory Negligence) Act 1945,[10] which provides (s. 1 (1)) that "where any person suffers damage as the result partly of his own fault and partly of the fault of any other person or persons, a claim in respect of that damage shall not be defeated by reason of the fault of the person suffering the damage, but the damages recoverable in respect thereof shall be reduced to such extent as the Court thinks just and equitable having regard to the claimant's share in the responsibility for the damage." This subsection is not to operate to defeat any defence arising under a contract (s. 1 (1) (a)). The judge or jury must determine the total damages recoverable by the claimant had he not been in fault (s. 1 (2) and (6)). The jury can also determine the extent to which these damages are to be reduced (s. 1 (6)) in the same way as the Court under s. 1 (1). Where any person dies as the result partly of his own fault and partly of the fault of any other person, the damages or loss of society award recoverable by any dependant of the deceased may be reduced according to the share of the deceased in the responsibility for his death (s. 1 (4)).[11]

Under the Act the Court assesses the measure of contribution made by all the causes to the end result and apportions liability accordingly.[12] The question is "whose act caused the damage?" This should "be dealt with somewhat broadly and upon common sense principles as a jury would probably deal with it."[13] Regard must be had both to the relative importance of the pursuer's act in causing the damage and also to his relative blameworthiness.[14] Consideration is not restricted to causation of the accident in a narrow sense but extends to all the factors, in respect of which fault can be imputed, contributing to the damage.[15]

The standard of care required of a pursuer is such care for his own safety as is reasonable in the circumstances. He will be guilty of contributory

---

[9] See Marsden, *Collisions at Sea* (*British Shipping Laws* (1961), vol. 4), § 27. As an example see *Boy Andrew* v. *St. Rognvald, supra.*
[10] 8 & 9 Geo. VI, c. 28.
[11] See, e.g., *Kelly* v. *Glasgow Corporation,* 1951 S.C. (H.L.) 15.
[12] See per Denning. L.J., in *Davies* v. *Swan Motor Co.,* supra, at p. 322.
[13] *The Volute* [1922] 1 A.C. 19, per Lord Chancellor Birkenhead, at p. 136; see also Causation, § 12, supra.
[14] *Stapley* v. *Gypsum Mines* [1953] A.C. 663, per Lord Reid at p. 682; *Kilgour* v. *N.C.B.,* 1958 S.L.T. (Notes) 48.
[15] *Davies* v. *Swan Motor Co.,* supra; *Froom* v. *Butcher* [1976] Q.B. 286. The onus is, however, on the defender to show that the injuries sustained were, in part at least, caused by failure to adopt the precaution desired (e.g. wearing a seat-belt) (*Barker* v. *Murdoch,* 1977 S.L.T. 75).

negligence if he ought reasonably to have foreseen that, if he did not act as a reasonable, prudent man, he might hurt himself, and he ought to take into account the possibility of others being careless.[16] What amounts to reasonable care depends upon the circumstances of each case.[17] Allowance must be made for inadvertence due to necessary haste, fatigue or familiarity,[18] and also for emergency action necessitated by the negligence of the defender.[19] In the case of children it is always a question of circumstances whether they are guilty of contributory negligence. Relevant factors are their age and whether or not they appreciated or should have appreciated the danger.[20] A child should only be found guilty of contributory negligence if he or she is of such an age as to be expected to take precautions for his or her own safety; even then the child is only to be found guilty if blame should be attached.[21] It may be contributory negligence for a person to allow himself to be driven in a car in the knowledge that overcrowding made steering difficult and that the driver is so drunk as to be unable to drive safely.[22] A servant or employee may be held to be negligent although his claim is based upon breach of statutory duty on the part of his master or employer[23]; but his erroneous assumption that the duty has been performed may not amount to negligence.[24]

16. Exclusion of Liability and Volenti Non Fit Injuria.—Under the Unfair Contract Terms Act 1977 a term of a contract which purports to exclude or restrict liability for breach of duty arising in the course of any business, or from the occupation of any premises used for business purposes, is void where the exclusion or restriction is in respect of personal injury or death and in any other case is of no effect if it is not fair and reasonable.[24a] Where the Act does not apply delictual liability may generally be excluded by a contractual term to that effect agreed between the wrongdoer and the person injured. The Scottish provisions of the Act, in contrast with the English,[24b] do not control extra-contractual attempts to exclude liability by notice. Notice of exclusion of liability, other than in contractual terms, may therefore be founded on as a basis for a plea of volenti non fit injuria unaffected by the Act.

The phrase "volenti non fit injuria" means that in certain circumstances a pursuer will be held to have accepted the risk of the injury which has befallen him, and on that ground to be precluded from claiming damages from the party who has caused the injury.[25] It is to be observed that injuria means,

---

[16] *Jones* v. *Livox Quarries* [1952] 2 Q.B. 608, per Denning, L.J., at p. 615.
[17] See *Caswell* v. *Powell Duffryn Assoc. Collieries* [1940] A.C. 152, per Lord Wright, at p. 176.
[18] Ibid., at pp. 178-9; and see *John Summers & Sons* v. *Frost* [1955] A.C. 740.
[19] *Laird Line* v. *U.S. Shipping Board*, 1924 S.C. (H.L.) 37.
[20] *Fraser* v. *Edinburgh Tramways Co.* (1882) 10 R. 264; *Yachuk* v. *Oliver Blais & Co.* [1949] A.C. 386; see also *Hughes* v. *Lord Advocate*, 1961 S.C. 310, per Lord Wheatley, at p. 323.
[21] *Gough* v. *Thorne* [1966] 1 W.L.R. 1387, per Lord Denning, M.R., at p. 1390.
[22] *M'Caig* v. *Langan*, 1964 S.L.T. 121; it may also amount to volenti non fit injuria: see § 16, infra.
[23] *Caswell* v. *Powell Duffryn Assoc. Collieries*, supra; *Cakebread* v. *Hopping Bros. Ltd.* [1947] K.B. 641.
[24] *Grant* v. *Sun Shipping Co. Ltd.*, 1948 S.C. (H.L.) 73, per Lord du Parcq, at p. 97.
[24a] 1977 (c. 50), s. 16 (1).
[24b] s. 2.
[25] See Walker, *Delict*, pp. 350-7.

strictly, an unlawful act, not an injury. Where a term of a contract is void or of no effect under the Unfair Contract Terms Act 1977 agreement to or knowledge of that term is not of itself sufficient evidence that a risk was knowingly and voluntarily assumed so as to found a plea of volenti non fit injuria.[25a] "The question raised by a plea of volenti non fit injuria is not whether the injured party consented to run the risk of being hurt, but whether the injured party consented to run that risk at his own expense so that he and not the party alleged to be negligent should bear the loss in the event of injury. In other words, the consent that is relevant is not consent to the risk of injury but consent to the lack of reasonable care that may produce that risk."[26] The consent must be free and voluntary and so the plea may not be open to a defender in a question with an employee of a third party who incurred the risk in the course of his employment.[27] Where, however, the risk has been accepted it is immaterial that it was done on a false premise.[28] The principle clearly applies to injuries sustained in any lawful game or sport, provided the rules be observed. It has also been applied to spectators at games and sports who take the risk of physical damage caused to them by any act of a participant of adequate skill and competence unless the participant's conduct is such as to evince a reckless disregard of the spectators' safety.[29] But the maxim is only required if harm has been caused by a wrongful act or omission; if there is no legal wrong, there is no need for this defence. It was the foundation of the former rule that an employer was not liable for injuries due to the fault of a fellow-servant.[30]

In cases between employer and workman, when the ground of the action is an injury sustained through faulty organisation, the plea of volenti non fit injuria cannot be sustained merely by showing that the workman knew of the risk and continued to work in spite of it. The word in the maxim is volenti, not scienti.[30a] Accordingly, the defence of volenti is rarely applicable in master and servant cases,[31] and, since the abolition of contributory negligence as a complete defence, there has been increasing reluctance to find volenti as a defence.[32] It has been held in England that volenti is not a defence to a breach of the employer's own statutory duty[33]; but it does afford a complete defence to the employer's vicarious liability for the acts of a fellow-servant when the pursuer invited or freely aided and abetted his fellow-servant's disobedience of an order.[34]

The maxim has been applied in cases between landlord and tenant. The proper course for a tenant, on discovering that the subjects let are in a

[25a] 1977 (c. 50); s. 16 (3).
[26] *M'Caig* v. *Langan,* 1964 S.L.T. 121, per Lord Kilbrandon at p. 124; cf. *Bankhead* v. *M'Carthy,* 1963 S.C. 263, per Lord Walker, at p. 265; Smith, *Short Commentary,* p. 704.
[27] *Burnett* v. *British Waterways Board* [1973] 1 W.L.R. 700.
[28] *Bennett* v. *Tugwell* [1971] 2 Q.B. 267.
[29] *Wooldridge* v. *Sumner* [1963] 2 Q.B. 43; *Hall* v. *Brooklands Auto Racing Co.* [1933] 1 K.B. 205.
[30] *Bartonshill Coal Co.* v. *Reid* (1858) 3 Macq. 266.
[30a] *Smith* v. *Baker* [1891] A.C. 325; *Wallace* v. *Culter Paper Co.* (1892) 19 R. 915.
[31] But see *Keenan* v. *City Line,* 1953 S.L.T. 128.
[32] *I.C.I.* v. *Shatwell* [1965] A.C. 656, per Lord Pearce, at p. 686.
[33] *Wheeler* v. *New Merton Board Mills* [1933] 2 K.B. 669.
[34] *I.C.I.* v. *Shatwell,* supra; *Hugh* v. *National Coal Board,* 1972 S.C. 252.

dangerous condition, is to give notice to the landlord, and, if the defect is not remedied within a reasonable time, to abandon the lease.[35] If he stays on without giving notice, or if, having given notice, he remains in face of the danger for more than a reasonable time, he may be held to have taken the risk.[36] The plea is open to an occupier of property who is sued for damages by a person injured thereon.[37]

The plea of volenti will not avail a person whose fault creates a situation of peril which he ought reasonably to have foreseen would invite rescue by another person who voluntarily exposes himself to danger in attempting rescue.[38] And the right of a servant to interfere in circumstances of danger for the safeguarding of an employer's property is also recognised.[39]

17. Occupiers' Liability (Scotland) Act 1960 (c. 30).[40]—The effect of this Act is to abolish the categories of invitee, licensee and trespasser which were introduced to the law of Scotland in 1929 by the House of Lords' decision in *Dumbreck* v. *Addie & Sons*.[41] Section 2 of the Act provides: "The care which an occupier of premises is required, by reason of his occupation or control of the premises, to show towards a person entering thereon in respect of dangers which are due to the state of the premises or to anything done or omitted to be done on them and for which the occupier is in law responsible shall, except in so far as he is entitled to and does extend, restrict, modify or exclude by agreement his obligations towards that person, be such care as in all the circumstances of the case is reasonable to see that that person will not suffer injury or damage by reason of any such danger." "Occupier of premises" is defined in section 1 (1) as "a person occupying or having control of land or other premises." This includes "any fixed or moveable structure, including any vessel, vehicle or aircraft," and the duty extends towards all persons and property on such premises.[42] The Act substantially restores the pre-1929 common law relating to the duties of occupiers of land[43] and the "category" decisions between 1929 and 1959 are no longer relevant except on the question of "control."

The statutory concept of occupation or control is the same as the common law basis of liability, namely, possession and control.[44] The duty of care rests upon the person who has the right and means in the circumstances of taking

---

[35] *Dickie* v. *Amicable Investment Co.*, 1911 S.C. 1079.
[36] *Smith* v. *Maryculter School Board* (1898) 1 F. 5; *Hardie* v. *Sneddon*, 1917 S.C. 1; *Mullen* v. *C.C. of Dunbartonshire*, 1933 S.C. 380.
[37] See Occupiers' Liability (Scotland) Act 1960 (8 & 9 Eliz. II. c. 30), s. 2 (3); and § 17, infra.
[38] *Haynes* v. *Harwood* [1935] 1 K.B. 146; *Baker* v. *Hopkins* [1959] 3 All E.R. 225 (C.A.); *Videan* v. *B.T.C.* [1963] 2 Q.B. 650, per Lord Denning, M.R., at p. 669.
[39] *Steel* v. *Glasgow Iron & Steel Co.*, 1944 S.C. 237.
[40] See Walker, *Delict*, Vol. II, pp. 586-607. There is a similar, but not identical, Act for England: Occupiers' Liability Act 1957 (5 & 6 Eliz. II, c. 31).
[41] 1929 S.C. (H.L.) 51; now disapproved even as a statement of the duty owed to a trespasser (*British Railways Board* v. *Herrington* [1972] A.C. 877).
[42] 1960 Act, c. 30, s. 1 (3). see *A.M.F. International* v. *Magnet Bowling* [1968] 1 W.L.R. 1028.
[43] See *Shillinglaw* v. *Turner*, 1925 S.C. 807, per Lord President Clyde, at p. 816; per Lord Sands, at p. 820; and Walker, Vol. II, pp. 595-6.
[44] See *Laurie* v. *Mags of Aberdeen*, 1911 S.C. 1226; and *Laing* v. *Paull and Williamsons*, 1912 S.C. 196; *Kennedy* v. *Shotts Iron Co., Ltd.*, 1913 S.C. 1143; *M'Ilwaine* v. *Stewart's Trs.*, 1914 S.C. 934.

effective steps to protect the visitor from the particular danger whether by removal, notice, fencing or forbidding entry to the premises.[45] Thus physical occupation per se will not impose the duty on a resident. The duty is owed by the occupier only if he is in control of the premises; if he is not, the obligation rests upon the party in control,[46] who may be the owner or tenant or a contractor conducting operations on the premises.[47]

The Act does not differentiate between public and private property, and the degree of care required from any occupier to any individual is deducible from and referable to the particular facts of the case.[48] Accordingly, there is no general rule as to the liability of an occupier for damage caused by the faulty work of an independent contractor employed by him.[49] The dangers which section 2 of the Act requires the occupier to guard against are those which are (a) due to the state of the premises: (b) due to anything done on the premises: and (c) due to anything omitted to be done on the premises. "The state of the premises" certainly covers all dangers due to structural defects[50] and poisonous shrubs,[51] and probably also to unfenced shafts or excavations,[52] although the latter may be alternatively classified as a danger due to omission (i.e., to fence). Machinery which is not in use, such as an unlocked turntable upon which children were known to play,[53] must also come under this head. "Anything done on the premises" covers all dangers created by operations thereon[54] and is probably wide enough to cover keeping a vicious dog[55] and placing a savage horse in a field used by the public.[56] While the failure to fence or light holes and keep doors leading to cellars locked[57] may be classified under "state" or "omission," some dangers created by operations carried on may be due to omissions, e.g., the failure of a railway company's employees to close carriage doors before a train started.[58]

While the standard of care required of the occupier is that of the reasonable, prudent man, the degree of care required is "such care as in all the circumstances of the case is reasonable." Accordingly, the range of care will vary from the maximum, in the case of a very young child on the premises for

---

[45] *Murdoch* v. *A. & R. Scott,* 1956 S.C. 309; *Devlin* v. *Jeffray's Trs.* (1902) 5 F. 130, where owner had no right of entry.

[46] *Kennedy* v. *Shotts Iron Co.,* supra; *M'Phail* v. *Lanarkshire C.C.,* 1951 S.C. 301; *Wheat* v. *Lacon & Co.* [1966] A.C. 552, where the House of Lords held that the owners were occupiers of premises although their manager resided there under a service agreement.

[47] See *Murdoch* v. *A. & R. Scott,* supra; also *Hartwell* v. *Grayson, etc., Docks* [1947] K.B. 901; *Telfer* v. *Glasgow Corpn.,* 1976 S.L.T. (Notes) 71.

[48] See *M'Kinley* v. *Darngarvil Coal Co.,* 1923 S.C. (H.L.) 34, per Lord Dunedin, at p. 37; cf. *M'Murray* v. *Glasgow School Board,* 1916 S.C. 9, where there was no averment that the occupiers knew that the gate was being used as a swing.

[49] See Liability of Employer of Independent Contractor, § 26, infra, last para.

[50] See Glegg, pp. 295-307.

[51] See *Taylor* v. *Glasgow Corp.,* 1922 S.C. (H.L.) 1.

[52] See Glegg, pp. 274-9, 281-2.

[53] *Cooke* v. *M.G.W. Ry., of Ireland* [1909] A.C. 229.

[54] E.g., *Messer* v. *Cranston* (1897) 25 R. 7 (defective stow); *Ross* v. *M'Callum's Trs.,* 1922 S.C. 322 (petrol in water pail); *Excelsior Wire Rope Co.* v. *Callan* [1930] A.C. 404 and *Murdoch* v. *A. & R. Scott,* supra (moving machinery).

[55] *Smillies* v. *Boyd* (1886) 14 R. 150.

[56] *Lowery* v. *Walker* [1911] A.C. 10.

[57] *Cairns* v. *Boyd* (1879) 6 R. 1004.

[58] *Tough* v. *N.B. Ry. Co.,* 1914 S.C. 291. For additional examples of dangers on land and premises, see cases cited in Glegg, pp. 60-72, and in Walker, Vol II, pp. 597 and 599.

the first time by invitation of the occupier and known to him to be unaccompanied by an adult, to the minimum in the case of a trespasser whose presence is unknown to the occupier. "The section applies both to trespassers and to persons entering property by invitation or licence express or implied. But that does not mean that the occupier must always show equal care for the safety of all such persons.... In deciding what degree of care is required, ... regard must be had both to the position of the occupier and to the position of the person entering his premises and it may often be reasonable to hold that an occupier must do more to protect a person whom he permits to be on his property than he need do to protect a person who enters the property without permission."[59] An occupier may not be required to fence a quarry or other dangerous place which is so far from a public road that it is not reasonably foreseeable that members of the public will come near it,[60] but secure fencing will be necessary if injury to the particular victim is reasonably foreseeable through proximity of the danger to a public road[61] or otherwise.[62] While the pre-1929 law relating to trespassers was far from clear,[63] the Act now imposes upon an occupier the duty of taking such care as is reasonable in the circumstances to protect from reasonably foreseeable injury a trespasser whose presence is reasonably foreseeable. In the case of a boy injured while climbing an electric transformer, that duty was held to be discharged by the erection of a barrier which could only be overcome by a deliberate act intended to defeat its obvious function.[64] The age and capacity of persons entering premises are relevant considerations along with the likelihood of them being there. "A measure of care appropriate to the inability or disability of those who are immature or feeble in mind or body is due from others who know of, or ought to anticipate, the presence of such persons within the scope and hazard of their own operations."[65] The Act probably does not alter the law that the owner of a public park is not required to fence obvious dangers, such as a pond[66] or a river bank,[67] against which it is the duty of parents to protect their children; but parents are entitled to rely on such proprietors taking reasonable care to protect their children from injury from anything in the nature of a hidden danger or trap, whether natural or artificial.[68] And a

[59] M'Glone v. B.R.B., 1966 S.L.T. 2 (H.L.), per Lord Reid, at p. 9.
[60] Prentices v. Assets Co. (1890) 17 R. 484; Holland v. Lanarkshire D.C., 1909 S.C. 1142, per Lord President Dunedin, at p. 1149; Melville v. Renfrewshire C.C., 1920 S.C. 61.
[61] Black v. Cadell (1804) Mor. 13905; Gibson v. Glasgow Police Commrs. (1893) 20 R. 466 (a public highway case, but the ratio is relevant to s. 2 of the Act).
[62] Hislop v. Durham (1842) 4 D. 1168; M'Feat v. Rankin's Trs. (1879) 6 R. 1043. British Railways Board v. Herrington [1972] A.C. 877.
[63] See M'Glone v. B.R.B., supra, per Lord Reid, at p. 9.
[64] M'Glone v. B.R.B., supra. "The liability of an occupier cannot fairly be made to depend on the outcome of a conflict between his precautions to exclude entry and the ingenuity and agility of a youthful and determined trespasser": per Lord Guthrie, at p. 8.
[65] Per Lord Sumner, Taylor v. Glasgow Corp., 1922 S.C. (H.L.) 1, at p. 15; see also Johnstone v. Mags. of Lochgelly, 1913 S.C. 1078, per Lord Kinnear, at p. 1089, Cooke v. M.G.W. Ry. of Ireland [1909] A.C. 229, per Lord Atkinson, at p. 238: "The duty ... must ... be measured by his [the occupier's] knowledge, actual or imputed, of the habits, capacities and propensities of those persons," and Southern Portland Cement v. Cooper [1974] A.C. 623.
[66] Hastie v. Mags. of Edinburgh, 1907 S.C. 1102.
[67] Stevenson v. Glasgow Corp., 1908 S.C. 1034.
[68] Taylor v. Glasgow Corp., 1922 S.C. (H.L.) 1 (poisonous berries); and see Lord Shaw, at pp. 10-12.

very high degree of care is incumbent upon local authorities who provide children's playgrounds and thus invite parents to send their children there unaccompanied.[69]

Section 2 (1) of the Act permits an occupier, in so far as he is entitled to do so,[70] to extend, restrict, modify or exclude his obligations to any person by agreement, i.e., by contract, written or verbal.[71] The English Act[72] adds "or otherwise" which seems to permit this to be done by the mere posting of a restricting or exempting notice,[73] whereas the Scottish Act does not. But the existence of such a notice in relation to a particular danger would be a relevant factor in determining whether or not the injured party had agreed to run the risk of injury through the occupier's lack of care, since the defence of volenti non fit injuria is expressly retained by the Act.[74] Where the premises are used for the business purposes of the occupier these rules on exclusion of liability have now to be read subject to the provisions of the Unfair Contract Terms Act 1977.[74a]

Where premises are occupied or used by virtue of a tenancy or subtenancy under which the landlord is responsible for maintenance or repair of the premises, section 3 of the Act imposes on the landlord the same duty of care towards persons or property as section 2 (1) imposes on the occupier, but only in respect of dangers arising from faulty maintenance or repair.[75] "Tenancy" includes a statutory tenancy which does not in law amount to a tenancy[76] and includes also any contract conferring a right of occupation.[77] This section alters the law laid down in *Cameron* v. *Young,*[78] and anyone in the house, be he tenant, member of the tenant's family, lodger or visitor, now has a title to sue the landlord for injury caused through breach of his duty. Under the Housing (Scotland) Act 1966,[79] where the rent does not exceed £26 per annum, the landlord's obligation is to keep the house "in all respects reasonably fit for human habitation."[80] Section 3 is silent as to the right of a landlord to vary his statutory liability by agreement but it is thought that this must either be presumed as an inherent right or implied from the reference in section 3 to "the foregoing provisions of this Act." He has certainly not been deprived of his common law right to plead volenti non fit injuria.[81] The Act applies to the Crown.[82]

---

[69] *Plank* v. *Stirling Mags.,* 1956 S.C. 92. See Lord Justice-Clerk Thomson, at pp. 105, 107; Lord Patrick, at p. 115; and Lord Mackintosh, at p. 118.
[70] E.g., the operator of a public service vehicle is not entitled to do so: see Road Traffic Act 1960, c. 16, s. 151.
[71] E.g., by notice on ticket of such conditions: see Formation of Contract, Ch. IV, supra, Ticket Cases, § 12.
[72] 1957, c. 31, s. 2 (1).
[73] See *Ashdown* v. *Williams* [1957] 1 Q.B. 409, decided before the English Act was passed.
[74] s. 2 (3). See § 16, supra, and *M'Glone* v. *B.R.B.,* supra, per Lord Pearce at p. 12.
[74a] 1977 (c. 50), s. 16. See § 16 supra.
[75] For illustrations of the extent of his liability, see Walker, Vol. II, pp. 603-7.
[76] I.e., under the Rent Acts: see Leases, Ch, XXXIII, supra, §§ 39, 41.
[77] E.g., under a service agreement.
[78] 1908 S.C. (H.L.) 7.
[79] c. 49, s. 6 (2); see Leases, Ch. XXXIII, supra, § 6.
[80] See *Haggarty* v. *Glasgow Corp.,* 1964 S.L.T. (Notes) 95.
[81] See § 16, supra.
[82] See s. 4.

18. Public Roads and Streets.[83]—The Occupiers' Liability Act does not apply to public roads, streets or footpaths which at common law or by public or private Acts are the responsibility of public bodies. Public authorities responsible for the management and maintenance of public roads, streets and footpaths are bound to take reasonable care to maintain them in a condition safe for use by all members of the public.[84] They are liable to individuals injured by any type of danger of which they knew or ought to have known if regular inspections had been made.[85] As the basis of liability is "possession and control," the owner of the solum of a footpath is not liable for defects therein unless he also has control of it[86]; but he may be jointly liable with the local authority for failure to fence off a dangerous subsidence.[87] And a local authority may assume by private Act a joint responsibility with the owner for the safety of a private footpath.[88]

19. Strict Liability: General.—In certain cases it is not necessary for an injured party to aver and prove that the defender was negligent in the sense of failing to exercise reasonable care. In such cases it is no defence that the defender was legitimately exercising his lawful rights or that all reasonable care was taken to prevent damage; if damage results naturally and directly from the act in question,[89] the defender is liable in reparation. Such cases require separate consideration as examples of strict liability. They fall under the following heads:—(1) Edictal liability[90]: (2) Nuisance[91]: (3) Unintentional slander[92]: (4) Liability for flooding damage caused by interference with the natural flow of water[93]: (5) Liability for animals[94]: (6) Statutory liability[95]: and (7) Vicarious liability.[96]

20. Strict Liability: Interference with Natural Flow of Water.—Anyone who erects a novum opus in a stream on his own property for the purpose of collecting water in a dam is liable for damage to adjacent property caused by flooding which would not have occurred if the stream had been left unaltered.[97] An unprecedented fall of rain is not a damnum fatale which exempts the proprietor from liability.[97] The Lord Ordinary (Ardmillan)

---

[83] See Glegg, pp. 104-5, 301-3; and Walker, Vol. II, pp. 607-17. As to liability for hazardous work, see § 26, infra.
[84] Including blind persons; see *M'Kibbin* v. *Glasgow Corp.*, 1920 S.C. 590; *Haley* v. *L.E.B.* [1965] A.C. 778; and see Standard of Care, § 11, supra.
[85] The English distinction between liability for misfeasance and no liability for nonfeasance is no part of the law of Scotland.
[86] *Laing* v. *Paull & Williamsons*, 1912 S.C. 196.
[87] *Laurie* v. *Mags. of Aberdeen*, 1911 S.C. 1226.
[88] *Rush* v. *Glasgow Corp.*, 1947 S.C. 580; *Kinnell* v. *Glasgow Corp.*, 1950 S.C. 573; *Black* v. *Glasgow Corp.*, 1958 S.C. 260.
[89] See Causation, § 12, supra.
[90] See Hiring, Loan and Deposit, Ch. XXVIII, supra, §§ 11-13; Carriage by Land, Ch. XXVIII, supra, §§ 3-6.
[91] See Landownership, Ch. XXXIX, infra, § 24.
[92] See Defamation, Ch. XXXV, infra, § 9.
[93] See § 20, infra.
[94] See § 21, infra.
[95] See § 22, infra.
[96] See §§ 23, 24, infra.
[97] *Kerr* v. *Earl of Orkney* (1857) 20 D. 298.

decided this case on the ground that the failure of the defender's dam raised a presumption of fault which he had not rebutted, but the Lord Justice-Clerk (Hope) at one point required the defender to "secure" his works against danger.[98] This decision was approved by the House of Lords on the basis of strict liability in *Caledonian Railway Co.* v. *Greenock Corporation.*[99]

In the early editions of this book the learned authors and editors treated as applicable to Scotland the general rule of *Rylands* v. *Fletcher*,[1] namely, "that a man who brings anything to land which, if it escapes, is likely to cause injury, does so at his peril." It is doubtful if they were justified in so doing without substantial qualification. It has been said that this "extreme form of the rule of absolute liability is simply a modern revival or survival of the medieval principle of English common law that a man acts at his peril,"[2] which has never been part of Scots law. While support for the application of the broad *Rylands* v. *Fletcher* principle can be found in the opinions delivered in *Chalmers* v. *Dixon*,[3] all the judges considered the defenders to have been at fault in accumulating on their land a huge bing of combustible materials, presumably on the ground that they knew or ought to have known that they were liable to ignite and emit noxious fumes to the harm of neighbouring properties and their crops. In *Miller* v. *Robert Addie & Sons' Collieries*[4] Lord Justice-Clerk Aitchison pointed out that "in those cases in which the doctrine of *Rylands* v. *Fletcher* has been held to apply the obligation to take adequate precautions has been of so onerous and imperative a kind that the mere occurrence of damage and injury has of itself been sufficient to justify an inference of negligence. In *Rylands* v. *Fletcher* negligence on the part of the engineer who had constructed the reservoir was expressly found to be established." Accordingly, it has been argued that cases such as *Kerr* v. *Earl of Orkney* and *Caledonian Railway Co.* v. *Greenock Corporation* could now be decided on the ground that the facts raised an almost irrebuttable presumption of negligence, flood damage being a reasonably foreseeable consequence of the work done.[5] They were not, however, so decided. The extent of the doctrine of strict liability for which they are authority is uncertain but extends at least to interference by a novum opus with the natural flow of water on land. In general, however, culpa is the established Scottish basis of liability in the exceptional cases in which a thing or operation inherently dangerous in itself causes damage to persons or property, whether

[98] Ibid., at pp. 301 and 302.
[99] 1917 S.C. (H.L.) 56.
[1] (1866) L.R. 1 Ex. 265; (1868) L.R. 3 H.L. 330.
[2] Per Lord President Cooper in *M'Laughlan* v. *Craig,* 1948 S.C. 599, at p. 610; see also Bell, *Prin.,* § 970; the Reparation section in Green's *Encyclopaedia of the Law of Scotland,* Vol. 12, contributed by the late Hector M'Kechnie, Q.C., especially at pp. 488-496; Glegg, pp. 18-21; Smith, *Short Commentary,* pp. 642-7; and Walker, Vol. II, pp. 973-985.
[3] (1876) 3 R. 461; see also *Gemmill's Trs.* v. *Cross* (1906) 14 S.L.T. 576; *Reynolds* v. *Lanarkshire Tramways Co.* (1908) 16 S.L.T. 230; and *Western Silver Fox Ranch* v. *Ross & Cromarty C.C.,* 1940 S.C. 601 (as to which, see criticism in Walker, supra, at pp. 984-5).
[4] 1934 S.C. 150, at p. 155.
[5] See 7th edition of this book where it is also suggested that *Rylands* v. *Fletcher* could have been decided on the vicarious liability of the proprietor for the negligence of his agent.

inside or outside the defender's premises, as it is in the ordinary case.[6] There is no liability for the escape of domestic gas[7] or water[8] without proof of negligence, but the greater the risk, the greater the degree of care required.[9]

21. Strict Liability: Liability for Animals.[10]—It is the duty of the owner or custodier of all animals to take reasonable care to prevent them from injuring third parties or their property[11] and there will be liability for accidents caused by negligently allowing animals to stray on to the highway, even sheep and cattle if injury to a road user is a natural and probable consequence of their presence at the locus.[12] But for damage caused by the vicious or savage propensities of an animal, liability is strict and need not be based on negligence.[13] Strict liability is founded on the owner's or custodier's knowledge of the dangerous propensities of the animal. In that event the duty is to confine or control the animal so as to prevent it from doing damage and liability stems from breach of that duty.[14] While this is culpa and may be called negligence in the broad sense of neglect of a duty, it is not negligence in the narrow sense, in which that word is now commonly understood, as connoting neglect or failure to exercise such care as is reasonable in all the circumstances of the situation.[15] Where, however, scientia is negatived there is nonetheless liability if negligence in the latter sense is proved.[16]

A distinction is drawn between animals which, according to the experience of mankind, are not dangerous to man (mansuetae naturae) and those which are (ferae naturae). The first category includes all domestic animals such as dogs, cats, fowls, cattle, horses, pigs, etc., and the second, lions, tigers, bears, boars,[17] monkeys,[18] elephants[19] and the like. The reason for the distinction is that the owner or custodier of an animal in the second category is presumed to know that the animal is dangerous by nature, whereas in the case of domesticated animals liability depends upon proof that the owner or custodier knew that the animal had previously shown savage tendencies. The principle is that a man who keeps an animal known to him to be dangerous keeps it at his

---

6 *Mackintosh* v. *Mackintosh* (1864) 2 M. 1357 (escape of muir-burning fire to neighbour's land); *Gray* v. *Caley Ry. Co.*, 1912 S.C. 339 (hot cinders from railway engine); *Gilmour* v. *Simpson*, 1958 S.C. 477 (fire caused by painter's blow-lamp).

7 *M'Laughlan* v. *Craig*, 1948 S.C. 599.

8 *Moffat* v. *Park* (1877) 5 R. 13; *Miller* v. *Addie & Sons' Collieries*, 1934 S.C. 150; *R. Wylie Hill & Co.* v. *Glasgow Corp.*, 1951 S.L.T. (Notes) 3.

9 *Muir* v. *Glasgow Corp.*, 1943 S.C. (H.L.) 3, per Lord Macmillan, at p. 10; *Gilmour* v. *Simpson*, supra, per Lord Wheatley, at p. 479.

10 For comprehensive treatment of this subject, see Glegg, pp. 354-363, and Walker, Vol. II, pp. 641-51.

11 See *Henderson* v. *John Stuart* (*Farms*), 1963 S.C. 245, where Lord Hunter reviews the authorities; Glegg, p. 357.

12 *Gardiner* v. *Miller* (O.H.) 1967 S.L.T. 29. Note Lord Thomson's reference to the probable difference of the law of England on this point. For illustrations of liability for damage done by animals on the basis of negligence, see Walker, Vol. II, pp. 630-2.

13 See Glegg, pp. 354-5; Walker, p. 649.

14 *Burton* v. *Moorhead* (1881) 8 R. 892, per Lord Justice-Clerk Moncreiff, at p. 895.

15 Contra, Glegg, p. 356, where failure to control is termed negligence.

16 *Draper* v. *Hodder* [1972] 2 Q.B. 556.

17 *Hennigan* v. *M'Vey* (1881) 9 R. 411.

18 *May* v. *Burdett* (1846) 9 Q.B. 101.

19 *Behrens* v. *Bertram Mills Circus* [1957] 2 Q.B. 1.

own risk.[20] Proof that a member of the owner's household knew that the animal was dangerous may yield the inference that the owner also knew.[21] Bulls are treated in the same way as cows and liability for injury by a bull depends upon proof either of negligence or scientia.[22] The risk principle necessarily involves the owner in liability even if the animal has been incited to attack the pursuer by a third party,[23] but not if the pursuer caused his own injury[24] or voluntarily accepted the risk created by the existence of the animal.[25]

There is strict (in this case, absolute) liability under the Dogs Act 1906,[26] which renders the owner of a dog liable in damages for injury done to cattle (which includes (s. 7) horses, mules, asses, sheep, goats, swine and poultry[27]) without proof of negligence or scientia. The owners of two or more dogs which have worried sheep are jointly and severally liable for the loss caused.[28] Under the Winter Herding Act 1686 (c. 11), the owner of "horses, nolt, sheep, swine or goats" straying on another's land is made liable, in addition to his liability for any damage done, in a penalty of half a mark for each beast, and the beasts may be detained until this and the expenses of keeping them are paid.[29]

22. Strict Liability: Statutory Liability.—Breach of statutory provisions or regulations which prescribe the degree of care to be exercised in particular circumstances may reasonably be described as "statutory negligence,"[30] notwithstanding the fact that the degree prescribed is higher than that required by the common law. But in some cases on grounds of policy there is imposed an absolute duty, which amounts to insurance and is not related to care.[31] In such cases, while a plea of contributory negligence may competently be taken, neither inevitable accident nor volenti non fit injuria[32] may be pled in defence.

23. Strict Liability: Vicarious Liability.[33]—A person may involve himself as a joint delinquent in a wrong which he did not personally commit by

---

[20] *Burton* v. *Moorhead,* supra; *M'Donald* v. *Smellie* (1903) 5 F. 955; *Gordon* v. *Mackenzie,* 1913 S.C. 109, per Lord Dundas, at p. 109.

[21] See Glegg, p. 363; Walker, vol II, p. 647; *Flockhart* v. *Ferrier,* 1959 S.L.T. (Sh. Ct.) 2.

[22] See Glegg, p. 358; *Clark* v. *Armstrong* (1862) 24 D. 1315; *Henderson* v. *John Stuart (Farms),* 1963 S.C. 245.

[23] *Baker* v. *Snell* [1908] 2 K.B. 825; applied in *Behrens* v. *Bertram Mills Circus,* supra; Aliter, if no scientia, *Fleeming* v. *Orr* (1855) 18 D. (H.L.) 21.

[24] *Daly* v. *Arrol Bros.* (1886) 14 R. 154.

[25] See Volenti Non Fit Injuria, § 16, supra, and *Behrens* v. *Bertram Mills Circus,* supra, per Devlin, J., at pp. 20-1.

[26] 6 Edw. VII, c. 32.

[27] "Poultry" added by 18 & 19 Geo. V, c. 21.

[28] *Arneil* v. *Paterson,* 1931 S.C. (H.L.) 117.

[29] See Rankine on *Landownership,* pp. 611-2. *Farquharson* v. *Walker,* 1977 S.L.T. (Sh. Ct.) 22.

[30] Per Lord President Cooper in *Hamilton & Co.* v. *Anderson & Co.,* 1953 S.C. 129, at p. 137; and see Smith, *Short Commentary,* pp. 639-641.

[31] E.g., see Factories Act 1961 (c. 34), s. 22 (1): "Every power or lift shall be... properly maintained," i.e. in efficient working order (s. 176 (1); *Millar* v. *Galashiels Gas Co.,* 1949 S.C. (H.L.) 31. See also Liability of Employer of Independent Contractor, § 26, infra.

[32] See *I.C.I.* v. *Shatwell* [1965] A.C. 656.

[33] See Glegg, Ch. 17, pp. 409 et seq.; Walker, *Delict,* Vol. I, pp. 130-61.

expressly authorising or subsequently ratifying the wrongful act, but his liability is then direct, not vicarious. In certain cases, however, the maxim "qui facit per alium facit per se" is applied to produce vicarious liability for the act of another. It applies only to certain contractual relationships, namely, those of partnership, principal and agent, master and servant, and exceptionally to employer and independent contractor.[34] On principles of agency vicarious liability for the negligence of the driver of a vehicle may attach to the owner of the vehicle if the driver was using it for the owner's purposes under delegation of a task or duty, but, where a car is owned by one spouse, vicarious liability for the negligent driving of the other spouse or someone driving on his behalf does not attach to the owner on the ground merely that the car is treated as a family car.[35] A parent who, for the purpose of his child being conveyed as a passenger, lends his car to another may be liable for the driver's negligence if the proposal for use of the car originated from the parent but not if it originated from the child.[36] It has been suggested, obiter, that the vicarious liability of a principal for an agent may be less extensive than that of a master for a servant in that "it has never been laid down as a general proposition that all principals (as distinguished from masters) are liable for the negligence of their agents (as distinguished from servants) in the execution of their mandate."[37] It is thought, however, that the only material distinction between the two is that the right of a master at all times to direct his servant how his work is to be done[38] may extend the net of his vicarious liability wider than that of a principal for an agent, who is normally free of his principal's control as regards the manner in which he executes his mandate. In agency the test is whether the act causing the damage was within the scope of the agent's authority, express or implied; in contracts of service the same test is applied, although "scope of authority" is usually termed "scope of employment." As the same principles apply to vicarious liability both in agency and locatio operarum, it is proposed to treat both under the general head of master and servant. The law in cases of partnership has already been considered.[39]

24. Vicarious Liability: Master and Servant.—It has long been established law that a master is vicariously liable for the wrongful or negligent acts of his servant committed within the general scope of his employment.[40] Without attempting to lay down an exhaustive definition of the phrase, "scope of employment" limits liability to those acts which the servant is required or entitled to do under his contract of service and to acts incidental thereto[41]—in other words, to acts related to the employer's business which he can only perform through an agent.[42] Where the phrase "course of employment" is

---

[34] See Liability of Employer of Independent Contractor, § 26, infra.
[35] *Morgan* v. *Launchbury* [1973] A.C. 127; *Nottingham* v. *Aldridge* [1971] 2 Q.B. 739.
[36] *Carberry* v. *Davies* [1968] 1 W.L.R. 1103.
[37] Per Lord President Cooper, in *Mair* v. *Wood,* 1948 S.C. 83, at p. 87.
[38] See Employment, Ch. XXII, supra, § 1.
[39] Partnership, Ch. XXIV, supra, § 13.
[40] Bell, *Prin.,* § 547.
[41] See *Bell* v. *Blackwood Morton & Sons,* 1960 S.C. 11, per Lord Sorn, at p. 26.
[42] See *Neville* v. *C. & A. Modes,* 1945 S.C. 175.

used, it must be construed in this context in the same sense as "scope of employment," because the emphasis is upon the scope of the authority expressly or impliedly delegated to the servant or other agent by his employer. A principal is liable in damages to third parties "for the frauds, deceits, concealments, misrepresentations, torts, negligences, and other malfeasances, or misfeasances, and omissions of duty, of his agent, in the course of his employment, although the principal did not authorise, or justify, or participate in, or indeed know of such misconduct, or even if he forbade the acts, or disapproved of them."[43] "But although the principal is thus liable for the torts and negligences of his agent, yet we are to understand the doctrine with its just limitations, that the tort or negligence occurs in the course of the agency, for the principal is not liable for the torts or negligences of his agent beyond the scope of his agency, unless he has expressly authorised them to be done, or he has subsequently adopted them for his own use and benefit."[44] Whether the agent is acting within the scope of his authority[45] or the servant acting within the scope of his employment is largely a question of fact.[46] A master who entrusts the general management of his business to a servant is liable for the fraud of his servant on a client, although the master obtained no benefit from it.[47] Conversely, benefit to the master from the fraud of his servant will not render the master liable if the servant had no authority to perform honestly the act which he performed dishonestly.[48] Although the particular act which gives the cause of action may not be authorised, still if the act is done in the course of employment which is authorised, then the master is liable for the act of the servant.[49] The general rule, which is often difficult to apply, is that a master is liable for authorised acts done in an unauthorised way but not for acts of a kind altogether unauthorised.[50] Thus a general mandate of management involves the master in liability for all acts, including criminal acts, of his manager done in that capacity.[51] But in more restricted fields of employment, the master is not liable for acts which the servant was not employed to do.[52] "The criterion is whether the act which is unauthorised is so connected with acts which have been authorised that it may be regarded as a mode—although an improper mode—of doing the authorised act, as distinct from constituting an independent act for which the master would not

[43] Story on *Agency* (9th ed.), s. 452.
[44] Ibid., s. 456, quoted by Viscount Haldane in *Percy* v. *Glasgow Corp.*, 1922 S.C. (H.L.) 144, at p. 151, as applicable to a master and servant relationship.
[45] See *Laing* v. *Provincial Homes Investment Co.*, 1909 S.C. 812.
[46] *Kirby* v. *N.C.B.*, 1958 S.C. 514, per Lord President Clyde, at p. 532; *Bell* v. *Blackwood Morton & Sons*, 1960 S.C. 11.
[47] *Lloyd* v. *Grace, Smith & Co.* [1912] A.C. 716.
[48] *Sinclair Moorhead & Co.* v. *Wallace & Co.* (1880) 7 R. 874 (borrowing money).
[49] Per Lord Lindley in *Citizen's Life Assurance Co.* v. *Brown* [1904] A.C. 423, at pp. 427-8; quoted by Lord Justice-Clerk Macdonald in *Mackenzie* v. *Cluny Hill Hydropathic*, 1908 S.C. 200, at p. 205.
[50] *Kirby* v. *N.C.B.*, supra.
[51] *Lloyd* v. *Grace Smith & Co.*, supra; *Central Motors (Glasgow)* v. *Cessnock Garage, etc., Co.*, 1925 S.C. 796 (garage night watchman borrowing car); *Mackenzie* v. *Cluny Hill Hydropathic*, supra; *Dyre* v. *Munday* [1895] 1 Q.B. 742.
[52] *Martin* v. *Wards* (1887) 14 R. 814; *Beard* v. *London General Omnibus Co.* [1900] 2 Q.B. 530 (conductor driving bus); cf. *Ricketts* v. *Tilling* [1915] 1 K.B. 644 (where driver negligent in permitting conductor to drive); *O'Brien* v. *Arbib*, 1907 S.C. 975; and see Glegg, pp. 421-5.

be liable."[53] Examples of the former are as follows:—smoking while working with inflammable materials[54]; use by servant of own uninsured motor car on master's business[55]; garage attendant driving a car when instructed to move cars by hand[56]; blacksmith's apprentice without a driving licence voluntarily driving a car which was impeding his work[57]; and a substantial deviation from the direct route by a driver implementing his master's contract to convey passengers from A to B.[58] An independent journey, undertaken for the servant's private purposes, is not within the scope of his employment.[59] But an act may fall within the scope of employment although prohibited.[60] The relevant connection of service between master and servant commences, in the ordinary case, when the employee enters his employer's premises for the purpose of going to work[61] and continues while the servant is leaving a factory by an inside stairway after finishing work[62]; but a servant who goes to an unauthorised place for the sole purpose of performing a prohibited act, namely, smoking during a work break, has temporarily broken that connection.[63] It is not enough to create vicarious liability that the act is done for the benefit of or at the request of the employer if it is outwith the scope of employment and is not part of a delegated task or duty.[64] Firemen, and others, called out by their employer are, however, acting within the scope of their employment while travelling to work.[65]

A master is not liable for the act of a servant which the master himself had no power to do,[66] but he is liable for the use of excessive force or wrongous detention by a servant to whom he has delegated, expressly or impliedly, the power to use force against persons or to detain them,[67] unless the servant was

---

[53] *Kirby* v. *N.C.B.*, 1958 S.C. 514, per Lord President Clyde at p. 533. Another test suggested is "whether the activity was reasonably incidental to the performance of his duties": see Lord Pearce in *Williams* v. *A. & W. Hemphill* 1966 S.L.T. 259, p. 260 (H.L.).
[54] *Jefferson* v. *Derbyshire Farms Ltd.* [1921] 2 K.B. 281; *Century Insurance Co.* v. *N.I.R.T.B.* [1942] A.C. 509.
[55] *C.P.R. Co.* v. *Lockhart* [1942] A.C. 591.
[56] *L.C.C.* v. *Cattermoles (Garages) Ltd.* [1953] 1 W.L.R. 997.
[57] *Mulholland* v. *Reid & Leys,* 1958 S.C. 290.
[58] *Williams* v. *A. & W. Hemphill,* 1966 S.L.T. 259 (H.L.). "It is a question of fact and degree in each case whether the deviation is sufficiently detached from the master's business to constitute a frolic of the servant unconnected with the enterprise for which he was employed": per Lord Pearce, at p. 260. cf. *Angus* v. *Glasgow Corporation,* 1977 S.L.T. 206 (deviating driver is outside the scope of his employment only when he departs altogether from his employer's business).
[59] See cases in Glegg, pp. 422-3; cf. *Central Motors* v. *Cessnock Garage Co.,* 1925 S.C. 796, where delegation to a servant of the care of customers' cars brought "a frolic" of the servant within the scope of employment.
[60] *C.P.R. Co.* v. *Lockhart,* supra; *L.C.C.* v. *Cattermoles (Garages),* supra; *Limpus* v. *London General Omnibus Co.* (1862) 1 H. & C. 526 (bus driver racing another bus driver). For examples of prohibited acts which the servant was not employed to do, see *Alford* v. *N.C.B.,* 1951 S.C. 248 (shot-firing); *Twine* v. *Bean's Express* (1946) 62 T.L.R. 458 (C.A.), and *Conway* v. *George Wimpey & Co.* [1951] 2 K.B. 266 (drivers giving prohibited lifts); see also *Roberts* v. *Matthew Logan* (O.H.) 1966 S.L.T. 77. *Rose* v. *Plenty* [1976] 1 W.L.R. 141.
[61] *Compton* v. *McClure* [1975] I.C.R. 378.
[62] *Bell* v. *Blackwood Morton & Sons Ltd.,* 1960 S.C. 11.
[63] *Kirby* v. *N.C.B.,* 1958 S.C. 514.
[64] *Nottingham* v. *Aldridge* [1971] 2 Q.B. 739.
[65] *Stitt* v. *Woolley* (1971) 115 S.J. 708. (The act of a passenger in grabbing hold of the steering wheel of the vehicle in which he is travelling is however, in these circumstances, outwith the scope of his employment).
[66] *Poulton* v. *L. & S.W. Ry. Co.* (1867) L.R. 2 Q.B. 534 (wrongous detention).
[67] See cases in Glegg, pp. 426-9 *Percy* v. *Glasgow Corp.,* 1922 S.C. (H.L.) 144.

actuated by personal motives, such as hatred or spite.[68] Vicarious liability for defamation rests upon the same principles as other wrongs.[69] The only specialty arises when the employer is entitled to plead "qualified privilege." In that event express malice may be inferred from the reckless and extreme nature of charges made by the servant within the scope of his employment and the employer will be liable[70]; but the personal malice of the servant due to ill-will and in no way connected with the master's business excludes his liability.[71]

A distinction was formerly drawn between employees engaged to exercise professional skill and others, but this distinction is no longer valid and an employer is now vicariously liable for the negligence of full-time salaried employees in the exercise of their professions.[72] The existence of a contract of service is not, however, the factor which determines vicarious liability, because A may have a contract of service with B and yet be acting as agent or servant pro hac vice of C. Thus if C borrows a car and appoints A to drive it on C's business, C will be liable for A's negligent driving jointly with A.[73] But difficulty may arise when the servant of A is lent or hired to B and the question is whether A or B is vicariously liable for the servant's act. There is on the injured party a heavy onus of proving that the servant was transferred pro hac vice to the service of B.[74] In the case of a negligent act regard must be had to all the circumstances of the case to determine whether A or B had the right to control the way in which that act was done.[75] Where a ship is let out on hire with its master to a charterer, or a vehicle let out with a driver,[76] or plant with an operator, the owner remains vicariously liable for the negligent control of the operator unless he has divested himself of all possession and control of his property in favour of another. "The reason is that he has delegated to the driver the task of driving his vehicle and he must be responsible for the way in which his delegate does his work."[77] The case of the owner of a vehicle hiring the servant of another to drive the hirer's vehicle

[68] See Power v. Central S.M.T. Co., 1949 S.C. 376.
[69] See Ellis v. National Free Labour Association (1905) 7 F. 629; Finburgh v. Moss Empires, 1908 S.C. 928; Nevile v. C. & A, Modes, 1945 S.C. 175; and cf. Riddell v. Glasgow Corporation, 1911 S.C. (H.L.) 35 (where the House of Lords held that the servant had no authority to make any statement on the point); Eprile v. Cal. Ry. (1898) 6 S.L.T. 65 (O.H.); and Mandelston v. N.B. Ry. Co., 1917 S.C. 442.
[70] Finburgh v. Moss Empires, supra: see Lord Ardwall's opinion, at p. 940.
[71] Aitken v. Cal. Ry. Co., 1913 S.C. 66.
[72] Macdonald v. Glasgow Western Hospitals, 1954 S.C. 453 (resident physicians and surgeons); Fox v. G. & S.W. Hospital Board, 1955 S.L.T. 337 (nurse).
[73] Elliot v. Beattie 1926 S.L.T. 588 (O.H.); and see Smith v. Moss [1940] 1 K.B. 424 (son driving mother's car on mother's business); cf., Hewitt v. Bonvin [1940] 1 K.B. 188 (son driving father's car on son's business).
[74] Malley v. L.M.S. Ry., 1944 S.C. 129, per Lord Justice-Clerk Cooper, at pp. 136-8; Mersey Docks & Harbour Board v. Coggins & Griffith Ltd. [1947] A.C. 1, per Viscount Simon, at p. 10; M'Gregor v. J. S. Duthie & Sons, 1966 S.L.T. 133 (where the onus was held to be discharged— but the driver was driving a vehicle belonging to the temporary employer on that employer's business at the material time).
[75] See Malley and Mersey Docks etc., supra.
[76] See Anderson v. Glasgow Tramways Co. (1893) 21 R. 318.
[77] John Young & Co. Ltd. v. O'Donnell, 1958 S.L.T. (Notes) 46, per Lord Denning. Note that a term in such a hiring contract that the driver or operator is to be the servant of the hirer will not exclude the owner's liability for injury to a third party: see Mersey Docks etc., supra, at pp. 2 and 10. An indemnity clause provides the only effective protection.

presents no difficulty because the real interest in the method of driving is in the owner and the car is being driven on his business.[78]

Pilotage authorities are not liable for the fault of their licensed pilots while so acting, because pilots are servants of the public.[79] By statute the owners of the vessel are vicariously liable for such fault.[80] The Crown is vicariously liable for delicts committed by its servants or agents, including independent contractors[81]; and firemen are the servants of the fire area committees set up under the Fire Services Act 1947.[82]

25. Culpa Tenet Suos Auctores.—The vicarious liability of an employer does not affect the servant's personal liability, as everyone is responsible for the consequences of his own wrongful or negligent acts. It is no defence that he was acting in accordance with instructions from a party whom he was contractually bound to obey,[83] or even, as in the case of a soldier obeying an unjustifiable order to fire, one to whom his obedience was due by statute.[84] An independent contractor is personally liable for his own acts or omissions (and for acts of his servants within the scope of their employment), whether or not his employer is also liable to the injured party.[85]

26. Liability of Employer of Independent Contractor.—In *Stephen* v. *Thurso Police Commrs.*[86] Lord Justice-Clerk Inglis said:—"The law is well established. In the first place, a master is liable for the injurious act of his servant. In the second place, if the wrongdoer be a contractor who is subject to the control of his employer, the latter is responsible; and, in the third place, if the contractor be independent, and may do as he pleases as regards the execution of the work, he is to be viewed as the principal, and alone is liable." There are no exceptions to the first two propositions. Although the contract in the first is a locatio operarum (a letting of his services by the servant) and in the second a locatio operis faciendi (a letting out of a job or piece of work to be done by a contractor), the maxims "qui facit per alium facit per se" and "respondeat superior" apply to both. If the employer of an independent contractor retains control of the work, he has the right to direct the contractor and his servants as to how the work is to be done, with the result that the contractor and his servants are deemed to be the servants pro hac vice of the employer.[87] The third proposition, supra, lays down the general rule that the contractor alone is liable, and this is true provided that the employer is not personally at fault.

[78] *Bowie* v. *Shenkin*, 1934 S.C. 459.
[79] *Holman* v. *Irvine Harbour Trs.* (1877) 4 R. 406, per Lord Ormidale, at p. 416; and see Walker, Vol. II, p. 1017.
[80] Pilotage Act, 1913 (2 & 3 Geo. V, c. 31), s. 15 (1); *Thom* v. *J. & P. Hutchison*, 1925 S.C. 386.
[81] Crown Proceedings Act 1947 (10 & 11 Geo. VI, c. 44), ss. 2 and 38 (2). Note that s. 2 (6) excludes, inter alia, police; vicarious liability was imposed on chief constables: Police (Scotland) Act 1967 (c. 77), s. 39.
[82] *Kilboy* v. *S.E. Fire Area Joint Committee*, 1952 S.C. 280.
[83] *Miller* v. *Renton* (1885) 13 R. 309.
[84] *Rogers* v. *Rajendro Dutt* (1860) 13 Moore P.C. 209.
[85] *Grieve* v. *Brown*, 1926 S.C. 787.
[86] (1876) 3 R. 535, at p. 540.
[87] *Nisbett* v. *Dixon & Co.* (1852) 14 D. 973; *Stephen* v. *Thurso Police Commrs.*, supra; *Gregory* v. *Hill* (1869) 8 M. 282.

Thus, when normal building operations were being carried out on private land, neither the owner nor the principal contractor were liable to a third party injured by colliding with a heap of lime left on the public street by servants of the plastering sub-contractor.[88] But an employer may himself be negligent, e.g., by careless selection of an incompetent contractor, by ordering dangerous work,[89] or by failing to take steps to remove or guard an obstacle placed on the highway by the contractor's men if the employer knew or ought to have known it was there,[90] in which case he will be liable for damage caused by his own negligence, whether or not the contractor has been negligent. But, in addition to breach of this duty, certain other duties have been held to be personal to the employer so that, if they are not performed, he is liable, however careful he may have been in the selection of a competent contractor to perform them on his behalf. The exceptions now recognised to the general rule that an employer is not liable for damages caused by work done by an independent contractor are as follows:—

(1) When the employer has no legal right to do the work ordered by him, he will be liable not only for the infringement of the rights of others caused by the work per se but also for any other injuries which third parties may suffer as a result of negligence of the contractor or his servants. For example, a gas company, which had no authority to make excavations in the street but employed a contractor for that purpose, was held liable for injury to a member of the public caused by a heap of stones negligently left on the roadway by the contractor's servants.[91] The same principle would apply to the case of an employer instructing or authorising a contractor to execute lawful work in an unlawful manner to the injury of neighbouring proprietors.[92]

(2) Certain statutory duties are personal to the incumbent, so that he cannot escape liability for breach by delegating the performance to competent parties or by any other means. Examples of these are as follows:—(a) absolute duties[93]; (b) duties laid on contractors and employers of workmen undertaking operations and works to which the various Construction Regulations apply[94]; (c) statutory provisions requiring or empowering some specific act to be done[95]; and (d) the obligation imposed by the Carriage of

[88] *MacLean* v. *Russell* (1850) 12 D. 887; *Blake* v. *Woolf* [1898] 2 Q.B. 426 (owner not liable for overflow from cistern after repair by competent plumber).
[89] *Boyle* v. *Glasgow Corp.,* 1949 S.C. 254.
[90] See *Stephen* v. *Thurso Police Commrs.,* supra, per Lord Justice-Clerk Inglis, at p. 538, and *Burgess* v. *Gray* (1845) 1 C.B. 578.
[91] *Ellis* v. *Sheffield Gas Co.* (1853) 2 E. & B. 767.
[92] See *Cameron* v. *Fraser* (1881) 9 R. 26 and *Miller* v. *Renton* (1885) 13 R. 309, although no question of incidental negligence arose in these cases.
[93] See, e.g., Factories Act 1961, ss. 12, 13 and 14 (certain machinery "shall be securely fenced"); *Millar* v. *Galashiels Gas Co.,* 1949 S.C. (H.L.) 31: "Every hoist...shall be properly maintained". etc.; and *Wolfson* v. *Forrester,* 1910 S.C. 675, per Lord President Dunedin, at p. 680.
[94] See S.I. 1961, No. 1580, Reg. 3 (1); S.I. 1966, No. 94, Reg. 3 (1); S.I. 1966, No 95, Reg. 4 (1), but note Reg. 4 (2); see also *Mulready* v. *Bell* [1953] 2 Q.B. 117 (C.A.), and *Donaghey* v. *O'Brien* [1966] 1 W.L.R. 1170 (C.A.), at p. 1177.
[95] *Stephen* v. *Thurso Police Commrs.* (1876) 3 R. 535, 538 (cleansing streets); *Robinson* v. *Beaconsfield* R.D.C. [1911] 2 Ch. 188 (disposal of sewage); *Hole* v. *Sittingbourne Ry.* (1861) 6 H. & N. 448 (erection of bridge suitable for river traffic): referred to in *Hardaker* v. *Idle D. C.,* [1896] 1 Q.B. 335, at pp. 340 and 345.

Goods by Sea Act 1924 on a shipowner in the work of repair of using "due diligence" to make the ship seaworthy.[96]

(3) In certain cases, where damage is the natural and probable consequence of negligent execution of the work, the employer has the personal obligation of seeing that the work is carefully and properly done. These cases fall broadly into two classes. The first covers excavations and other hazardous work on public roads and streets[97]; the second relates to hazardous work on private property, such as building operations which expose adjacent property to risk of damage,[98] work involving the risk of fire spreading to adjacent property[99] or injuring persons present[1] or any work involving an obvious inherent risk of serious injury.[2] The case of *Tarry* v. *Ashton*[3] may be fitted under this head, where a lamp projecting over a public street was an obvious danger to the public if not secure. The owner was held liable to a passer-by, upon whom it fell, for the negligent execution of repair work by an independent contractor shortly before the accident. The perplexing case of *Cleghorn* v. *Taylor*,[4] where a chimney-can fell and damaged adjacent property shortly after its repair by a master slater, could also have been decided under this head, although it is not the stated ratio decidendi.

There is no general rule that a master is liable for breach of his personal duties to a servant injured through the negligent work of an independent contractor employed by the master, nor is there any general rule that an occupier of premises is not liable for damage to persons or property on the premises caused by such faulty work. The question of whether or not the master has discharged his duty of taking reasonable care for the safety of his servant, or an occupier for the person who or whose property is injured on the premises, by selecting a skilled contractor of established reputation to carry out any work on plant or premises, including the inspection thereof, is a question of fact and degree in all the circumstances of the particular case and every decision on this subject should be treated as turning on its own facts.[5]

---

[96] *Riverstone Meat Co. Pty. Ltd.* v. *Lancashire Shipping Co. Ltd.* [1961] A.C. 807.

[97] *Gray* v. *Pullen* (1864) 5 B. & S. 970 (subsidence of pavement after construction of drain); *Hardaker* v. *Idle D. C.*, supra (gas main broken during construction of sewer); *Penny* v. *Wimbledon U.D.C.* [1899] 2 Q.B. 72 (heap of soil on road after dark); *Holliday* v. *Nat. Tel. Co.* [1899] 2 Q.B. 392 (risk of explosion during work on highway).

[98] *Bower* v. *Peate* (1876) 1 Q.B.D. 321 (excavation of foundations); *Dalton* v. *Angus* (1881) 6 App.Cas. 740 (interference with right of support); *Hughes* v. *Percival* (1883) 8 App.Cas. 443; and see *Cameron* v. *Fraser* (1881) 9 R. 26, per Lord Young, at p. 29 (truly a nuisance case).

[99] *Black* v. *Christchurch Finance Co.* [1894] A.C. 48; *Balfour* v. *Barty-King* [1956] 1 W.L.R. 779. *Emanuel (H. & N.)* v. *Greater London Council* [1971] 2 All E.R. 835.

[1] *Honeywill & Stein* v. *Larkin Bros.* [1934] 1 K.B. 191, in which the words "absolute obligation" were used in lieu of "strict liability": see *Pass of Ballater* [1942] P. 112, per Langton, J., at pp. 115-6.

[2] *Stewart* v. *Adams*, 1920 S.C. 129 (contract for removal of poisonous paint scrapings on pasture land: employer liable for death of cow).

[3] (1876) 1 Q.B.D. 314.

[4] (1856) 18 D. 664. See comment of Lord Justice-Clerk Inglis in *Campbell* v. *Kennedy* (1864) 3 M. 121, at p. 126; and Rankine on *Landownership* (4th ed.), p. 375. Note: it is unnecessary to classify it under the actio de positis vel suspensis of Roman law as Professor Walker does: *Delict*, Vol. I, p. 292.

[5] See opinions in *Davie* v. *New Merton Board Mills* [1959] A.C. 604; *Sumner* v. *Henderson & Sons* [1964] 1 A.B. 450; [1963] 2 W.L.R. 330, where Phillimore, J., purported to lay down a general

27. Landlord and Tenant.—While the mere relationship of landlord and tenant does not involve the landlord in vicarious liability analogous to that of a master, there are cases in which a landlord may be held liable for damage caused by his tenant's operations. This may come about because the lease expressly or impliedly authorises the tenant to commit a wrongful act, such as the working of minerals which the lessor has no right to work[6] or the use of a mill which necessarily involves the pollution of a river.[7] Moreover, if damage is a reasonably foreseeable result of the tenant's occupation, the landlord will be liable for it.[8]

28. Damages and Title to Sue.—As we have seen,[9] a wrongdoer is liable to make good all loss caused naturally and directly by his wrongful act. This covers wages lost by the injured party,[10] but not those of a spouse who voluntarily stops working to nurse the injured party[11]: all medical expenses reasonably incurred[12] and other outlays[13]: repair of a damaged article plus the cost of hiring a replacement pending repair[14] and, in the case of destruction, the market value of that article less its scrap value plus the cost of hire for a reasonable period pending the acquisition of a replacement.[14] If there is no market for the article destroyed, the actual cost of replacement may be allowed.[15] Where the pursuer's expectation of life has, as a result of personal injuries to him, been reduced, that reduction is, for the purposes of assessing patrimonial loss, ignored; and the court may, for those purposes, have regard to any amount by way of benefits in money or money's worth, other than benefits from his own estate, which, in its opinion, he would have received in the period up to the date when he would have been been expected to die if he had not sustained the injuries in question, less expenses which might reasonably have been incurred in that period.[15a] The pursuer's right to damages by way of solatium for shortened expectation of life is unaffected. When heritable property is totally destroyed, reinstatement value will only be

---

rule and was reversed by the Court of Appeal, [1963] 1 W.L.R. 823. For property cases, see *MacDonald* v. *Reid's Trs.* (O.H.) 1947 S.C. 726, and cases cited therein; also *Green* v. *Fibreglass* [1958] 2 Q.B. 245, per Salmon, J., at p. 253 (and note s. 2 (4) (*b*) of the English Occupiers' Liability Act 1957, (c. 31), the terms of which are implied in s. 2 (1) of the Occupiers' Liability (Scotland) Act 1960, (c. 30)).

[6] *N.B. Ry. Co.* v. *Budhill Coal Co.,* 1911 1 S.L.T. 249; 1910 S.C. (H.L.) 1.

[7] *Robertson* v. *Stewart* (1872) 11 M. 189; *Cal. Ry.* v. *Baird* (1876) 3 R. 839 (sewage from workmen's houses).

[8] See opinion of Lord President Dunedin in *Fleming* v. *Gemmill,* 1908 S.C. 340, at p. 349.

[9] See Remoteness of Damage, § 13, supra.

[10] *Doonan* v. *S.M.T.,* 1950 S.C. 136.

[11] *Edgar* v. *P.M.G.,* 1965 S.L.T. 158, *Collins* v. *South of Scotland Electricity Board,* 1977 S.L.T. 58.

[12] *Rubens* v. *Walker,* 1946 S.C. 215; and see s. 2 (4) of the Law Reform (Personal Injuries) Act 1948 (c. 41).

[13] It appears that a parent may recover outlays made in visiting an injured child, although the parent has no other right of action: *Higgins* v. *Burton,* 1967 S.L.T. (Notes) 61 (O.H.); see also *M'Bay* v. *Hamlett,* 1963 S.C. 282 (O.H.), where a husband was held entitled to claim the cost of domestic help in the absence of his injured wife, but note that he was suing for damages for inter alia personal injury.

[14] *Pomphrey* v. *Cuthbertson,* 1951 S.C. 147.

[15] *Clyde Navigation Trs.* v. *Bowring S.S. Co.,* 1929 S.C. 715.

[15a] Damages (Scotland) Act 1976, (c. 13), s. 9.

allowed in exceptional cases.[16] In the ordinary case interest will run from the date of decree but may now be awarded in special circumstances from the date of citation.[17]

In awarding damages the Court should take into account the decline in the value of money,[18] and must deduct the appropriate income tax from a sum given for loss of earnings.[19] Under the Law Reform (Personal Injuries) Act 1948 it is enacted[20] that in an action of damages for personal injuries there is to be taken into account against loss of earnings or profit, one-half of the value of rights accruing in respect of industrial injury benefit and industrial disablement or sickness benefit for the five years beginning with the time when the cause of action accrued. In cases in which the injured person has become redundant no deduction is made in respect of statutory redundancy payments or of payments under a non-statutory redundancy scheme.[21] Proceeds of insurance policies are normally to be regarded as collateral and non-deductible but in some circumstances a discretionary payment made by an employer to an employee in respect of an accident may be deductible.[21] In an action in respect of a person's death no account is to be taken of any gain or advantage accruing by way of succession or settlement, or any insurance money, benefit under the Social Security Act 1975, any payment by a friendly society or trade union for the relief or maintenance of a member's dependants, or any pension or gratuity payable as a result of the deceased's death.[22] A widow's private means are not a relevant factor.[23]

A person who is injured through the fault of another is entitled to claim solatium as pecuniary reparation for the pain and suffering inflicted upon him.[24] Such a claim covers wounded feelings, physical injuries or nervous shock. It may be considered under three heads: (1) pain and suffering (2) loss of faculties and amenities and (3) shortened expectation of life.[25]

The title to sue for damages in respect of a wrongful or negligent act rests with the party injured. Insurance against the particular injury is no objection to title.[26] If death has resulted from the injury, certain near relatives have a title to sue, but third parties, who may have suffered loss from the want of the

---

[16] *Hutchison* v. *Davidson,* 1945 S.C. 395; *Fraser* v. *Morton Wilson,* 1965 S.L.T. (Notes) 81 (O.H.). The Lord Ordinary also allowed interest from the date of citation; ibid., 1965 S.L.T. (Notes) 85.
[17] Interest on Damages (Scotland) Act 1958 (c. 61), s. 1; see *Macrae* v. *Reed & Mallik,* 1961 S.C. 68; *Killah* v. *Aberdeen Milk Marketing Board,* 1961 S.L.T. 232 (O.H.); *R. & J. Dempster* v. *Motherwell Bridge, etc., Co.,* 1964 S.C. 308, per Lord President Clyde, at pp. 333-4.
[18] *Kelly* v. *Glasgow Corporation,* 1951 S.C. (H.L.) 15.
[19] *British Transport Commission* v. *Gourley* [1956] A.C. 185; *Stewart* v. *Glentaggart,* 1963 S.C. 300; see also *Cockburn & Co.* v. *Scottish Motor Omnibus Co.,* 1964 S.L.T. (Notes) 7.
[20] 11 & 12 Geo. VI, c. 41, s. 2 (1).
[21] *Wilson* v. *National Coal Board,* 1978 S.L.T. 129.
[22] Damages (Scotland) Act 1976, (c. 13), s. 1 (5).
[23] *Cruickshank* v. *Shiels,* 1953 S.C. (H.L.) 1.
[24] See Bell, *Prin.,* § 2032; *Traynor's Exx.* v. *Bairds & Scottish Steel,* 1957 S.C. 311 (O.H.), per Lord Guthrie, at p. 314.
[25] *Rose* v. *Ford* [1937] A.C. 826; *Balfour* v. *Beardmore & Co.,* 1956 S.L.T. 205, at p. 215; and see *Yorkshire Electricity Board* v. *Naylor* [1968] A.C. 529; *Dalgleish* v. *Glasgow Corporation,* 1976 S.L.T. 157.
[26] *Port-Glasgow Sailcloth Co.* v. *Cal. Ry.* (1892) 19 R. 608.

injured person's services, have no such title.[27] Where injury to the health of X resulted in loss to a limited company, of which X was the manager, secretary and principal shareholder, it was held that he could not recover in respect of loss of dividends.[28]

The law formerly refused an action of reparation by one spouse against another on the ground of the intimate relationship obtaining between them.[29] Since the Law Reform (Husband and Wife) Act 1962[30] however, each spouse has had the right to bring an action against the other in respect of a wrongful or negligent act or omission,[31] but the Court has power to dismiss proceedings if it appears that no substantial benefit would accrue to either party from the continuation of the action.[32] An action of reparation has always been competent at the instance of a minor against his parent,[33] and at the instance of a parent against his child.[34]

If the injury causes patrimonial loss, the right to sue therefor passes, on the death of the injured party, to his executor; on his bankruptcy, to his trustee.[35] The right to sue may be assigned, but does not pass, without express assignation, with the transfer of a damaged thing.[36]

If an action of damages is raised by an injured party during his lifetime and he thereafter dies, the common law is that his executor may sist himself as pursuer in lieu of the deceased and recover damages for solatium and patrimonial loss[37]; on bankruptcy the trustee is in a similar position.[38] But neither the executor nor the trustee in bankruptcy can initiate an action claiming solatium on behalf of the deceased or bankrupt, even if he has intimated a claim before death or sequestration.[39] If no action has been raised before death or sequestration, the title of the executor or trustee is restricted to suing for patrimonial loss to the estate,[40] unless the right to claim solatium has been assigned to them by the injured party.[41] The common law has, however, been altered in the case of actions by an executor, by the Damages (Scotland) Act 1976.[42] These changes do not affect actions by a trustee in bankruptcy. The rights to damages in respect of personal injuries sustained by a deceased person which transmit to his executor are now the like rights as were vested in the deceased immediately before his death except that damages by way of

---

[27] *Reavis* v. *Clan Line Steamers,* 1925 S.C. 725; *Gibson* v. *Glasgow Corporation,* 1963 S.L.T. (Notes) 16.
[28] *Young* v. *Ormiston,* 1936 S.L.T. 79; cf. *Lee* v. *Sheard* [1956] 1 Q.B. 192.
[29] *Harper* v. *Harper,* 1929 S.C. 220; and see *Cameron* v. *Glasgow Corporation,* 1936 S.C. (H.L.) 26.
[30] 10 & 11 Eliz. II, c. 48.
[31] s. 2 (1). Section 2 applies to Scotland only.
[32] s. 2 (2).
[33] *Young* v. *Rankin,* 1934 S.C. 499.
[34] *Wood* v. *Wood,* 1935 S.L.T. 431.
[35] *Muir's Tr.* v. *Braidwood,* 1958 S.C. 169, at p. 173; *Smith* v. *Duncan Stewart & Co. (No. 2),* 1961 S.C. 91; *Russell* v. *B.R.B.,* 1965 S.L.T. 413.
[36] *Symington* v. *Campbell* (1894) 21 R. 434.
[37] *Neilson* v. *Rodger* (1853) 16 D. 315; *Smith* v. *Duncan Stewart & Co. (No. 1),* 1960 S.C. 329.
[38] *Thom* v. *Bridges* (1857) 19 D. 721.
[39] *Smith* v. *Duncan Stewart & Co. (No. 1),* supra; *Muir's Tr.* v. *Braidwood,* supra.
[40] *Smith* v. *Duncan Stewart & Co. (No. 2),* 1961 S.C. 91.
[41] *Traill* v. *Dalbeattie* (1904) 6 F. 798; *Cole-Hamilton* v. *Boyd,* 1963 S.C. (H.L.) 1; cf. *Muir's Tr.* v. *Braidwood,* supra.
[42] 1976, (c. 13).

solatium or by way of compensation for patrimonial loss attributable to any period after the deceased's death are excluded.[43] The effect is that the executor's rights are restricted to recovery of patrimonial loss attributable to the period before death. He may enforce recovery of that loss by action whether or not the deceased had raised an action in his lifetime.[44] As the executor's right to sue for patrimonial loss was at common law also limited by reference to the duration of the deceased's survivance the effective change is that the right to solatium is now never transmissible. Similarly, any right which the deceased had to solatium or a loss of society award in respect of the death of another does not transmit to his executor.[45]

The right of a relative to damages for an injury which has resulted in death was admitted at common law in favour of husband or wife, and ascendants or descendants, of the deceased, but not in the case of brother or sister.[46] Adopted children, adoptive parents,[47] illegitimate children and natural, as distinct from lawful, parents[48] of the deceased were by statute included among the relatives to whom this right attached. Rules which precluded an action by a mother in respect of the death of her child, or of a child in respect of the death of his mother, during the lifetime of the father were abolished in 1962.[49] The common law and the statutory modifications of it hitherto in force have, however, been superseded by the Damages (Scotland) Act 1976 which now governs the right of relatives of a deceased person to recover damages attributable to his death where that has been caused by the wrongful act of another.[50] The class of relatives who may sue has been enlarged and the principles regulating the award of damages redefined. A spouse, a parent or child (including adopted and illegitimate children or their parents, as the case may be) and anyone accepted by the deceased as a child of his family may sue for damages in respect both of loss of support and loss of the deceased's society.[51] Any ascendant or descendant (other than a parent or child), a brother, sister, uncle, aunt, or any of their issue and, where the deceased had been divorced, an ex-spouse, may sue in respect of loss of support only.[52] Loss of support is to be measured by the extent to which the deceased, if he had not died, would have been likely to provide or contribute to support, and a legally enforceable alimentary obligation, although relevant to the question of likelihood, is not essential.[53] Funeral expenses, if incurred, may also be claimed.[54] The loss of society award, which replaces and broadly corresponds

---

[43] 1976, (c. 13), s. 2, (1) & (3).
[44] ibid, s. 2 (1).
[45] ibid, s. 3.
[46] *Eisten* v. *N.B. Ry.* (1870) 8 M. 980.
[47] Law Reform (Miscellaneous Provisions) (Scotland) Act 1940, s. 2 (1).
[48] Law Reform (Damages and Solatium) (Scotland) Act 1962 (c. 42), s. 2; Law Reform (Miscellaneous Provisions) (Scotland) Act 1960, (3 & 4 Geo. VI. c. 42), s. 2 (1).
[49] Law Reform (Damages and Solatium) (Scotland) Act 1962 (c. 42), s. 1, superseding *Laidlaw* v. *N.C.B.*, 1957 S.C. 49.
[50] 1976, (c. 13), s. 1.
[51] ibid. ss. 1 (1), (3) & (4), & 10, (2), & Sched. 1, § 1.
[52] ibid. s.1, (1) & (3) & Sched, 1, § 2.
[53] ibid, s. 1 (3) & (6).
[54] ibid. s. 1 (3).

to an award of solatium under the previous law, is to be such sum as the court thinks just by way of compensation for the loss of such non-patrimonial benefit as the relative might have been expected to derive from the deceased's society and guidance if he had not died.[55] In assessing damages payable to a widow in respect of the death of her husband, whether for loss of support or loss of society, no account is taken of her remarriage or prospects of remarriage.[56] An action commenced by the injured party is not a bar to subsequent action by relatives,[57] and whether or not the deceased has raised an action in his lifetime, it is competent for his widow qua relict to claim loss of support and loss of society for herself and qua executrix to claim for patrimonial loss to his estate.[57]

If the executor of a deceased person is pursuing an action for damages in respect of the injuries from which the deceased died any relative with a title to sue in respect of the deceased's death is entitled to be sisted as a pursuer in that action.[58] Similarly if a relative is pursuing an action in respect of the deceased's death any other relative with a title to sue and the executors are entitled to be sisted as pursuers.[58] Failure to apply to be sisted bars the executor or relative concerned from pursuing a subsequent independent action against the same defender unless he satisfies the court that by reason of lack of knowledge of the earlier action, or for any other reasonable cause, he was unable to apply to be sisted.[58] Action at the instance of the executor or relatives is also barred if liability has been excluded or discharged by the deceased during his lifetime.[59]

An award of solatium under the previous law was made in respect of grief felt on account of the death[60] as well as for loss of society. The former element is not represented in the new loss of society award. It may therefore no longer be relevant to prove the sufferings inflicted on the deceased as tending to increase the injury to the feelings of the relative.[61] The degree of fault attributable to the defender[61] and injury to health by reason of bereavement[62] will, on the other hand, remain irrelevant as, probably, will a widow's cohabitation with a man after her husband's[63] death. Failure to consider entitlement to a loss of society award may, as in the case of a right to solatium, be ground for a new trial.[64] The right to redress for a wrongful or negligent act depends in part on the lex loci delicti, and therefore, in respect that English law does not recognise any claim for solatium, it was held, in an action by a father for damages for the death of his son in a railway accident

---

[55] ibid. s. 1 (4).
[56] Law Reform (Miscellaneous Provisions) Act 1971, (c. 43), s. 4.
[57] Damages (Scotland) Act 1976, (c. 13), s. 4. For the previous law see *McGhie* v. *B.T.C.*, 1964 S.L.T. 25 and *Dick* v. *Burgh of Falkirk*, 1976 S.L.T. 21.
[58] ibid. s. 5. Provisions requiring a pursuer to serve notice of the action (section 5 (6)) restrict the circumstances in which lack of knowledge will be pleadable.
[59] ibid. ss. 1 (2), and 2 (1).
[60] They had to prove grief; mere proof of relationship is not enough; *Rankin* v. *Waddell*, 1949 S.C. 555.
[61] *Black* v. *N.B. Ry.*, 1908 S.C. 444.
[62] *Kirkpatrick* v. *Anderson*, 1948 S.C. 251; *Nicolson* v. *Cursiter*, 1959 S.C. 350.
[63] *Donnelly* v. *Glasgow Corporation*, 1949 S.L.T. 362.
[64] *Gibson* v. *Kyle*, 1933 S.C. 30.

which had occurred in England, that no damages on that ground could be given by the Court in Scotland in which the action was raised.[65] The same would, in principle, be true of a claim for loss of society, but this question may require reconsideration.[66]

29. Self-Defence.—Self-defence, or defence of those whom one has a duty to protect, is an excuse for injury inflicted on the aggressor, unless the injury was unreasonably greater than the occasion warranted.[67] Even if it was, the attack or provocation may be proved in mitigation of damages.[67a] Because it is a matter which depends essentially on the circumstances of each case, limits of the right to defend property, or to resort to self-help, cannot be clearly defined. Probably a thief could not claim damages for injury inflicted in an attempt to recover the stolen property. And a mere squatter, or a person whose title to possess has expired, and who refuses to remove, may be removed by force, without any liability except on the ground that the measures taken involved more injury than was reasonably necessary.[68] But if a title to possess can be shown, even though that title may be voidable, measures of self-help are not justifiable, and will found an action for damages for any injury that may have resulted.[69] A carrier has a very wide discretion in the use of force to remove passengers who refuse to pay the fare or to submit to reasonable regulations.[70] A similar discretion is accorded to the managers of a place of entertainment or of a public meeting.[71] The limits of the right to use force against trespassers have never been definitely settled.[72]

30. Statutory Authority.—What would otherwise amount to a wrong may be excused if it is done under the authority of a statute. "No action can be maintained for anything which is done under the authority of the legislature, though the act is one which, if unauthorised by the legislature, would be injurious and actionable."[73] Any right to compensation must be founded on some provision in the statute in question.[74] But the defence of statutory authority is available only where the statutory operation is carried out without negligence, and negligence may consist either in carrying out work without reasonable care, or in neglecting precautions to avoid injury to third parties where such precautions are within the statutory powers.[75] It has been held

---

[65] *Naftalin* v. *L.M.S. Ry.*, 1933 S.C. 259. Followed in *McElroy* v. *M'Allister*, 1949 S.C. 110.
[66] See the views expressed on choice of law in *Chaplin* v. *Boys* [1971] A.C. 356.
[67] Glegg, *Reparation*, (4th ed.), p. 131.
[67a] *Falconer* v. *Cochran* (1837) 15 S. 891.
[68] *Macdonald* v. *Watson* (1883) 10 R. 1079; *Sinclair* v. *Tod*, 1907 S.C. 1038; *Hemmings* v. *Stoke Poges Golf Club* [1920] 1 K.B. 720.
[69] *Brash* v. *Munro* (1903) 5 F. 1102.
[70] *Highland Ry.* v. *Menzies* (1878) 5 R. 887; *Whittaker* v. *London* C.C. [1915] 2 K.B. 676.
[71] *Wallace* v. *Mooney* (1885) 12 R. 710; *Doyle* v. *Falconer* (1866) L.R. 1 P.C. 328. The Public Meetings Act 1908 (8 Edw. VII, c. 66) penalises disorderly conduct at a meeting, but does not give authority to eject. See, further, Public Order Act 1936, s. 6.
[72] See *Wood* v. *N.B. Ry.* (1899) 2 F. 1.
[73] Per Lord Blackburn, *Cal. Ry.* v. *Walker's Trs.* (1882) 9 R. (H.L.) 19, 32.
[74] As to the construction of the phrase "injuriously affected" in private Acts incorporating the Companies Clauses or Railway Clauses Acts, see *Cal. Ry.* v. *Walker's Trs.*, supra.
[75] *Edinburgh Water Trs.* v. *Somerville* (1906) 8 F. (H.L.) 25; *Farnworth* v. *Manchester Corporation* [1930] A.C. 171.

that if work authorised by statute can be done in two ways, one injurious to a third party, the other innocuous, the body exercising the statutory powers is bound to choose the latter method, even though it be the more expensive.[76] In private Acts the plea of statutory authority is often in substance elided by a clause providing that nothing in the Act shall excuse those acting under it from liability for the commission of a nuisance.[77]

When the legislature authorises a particular thing to be done, it impliedly legalises all results which necessarily flow from its being done. So, as railway companies, as they then were, ran their trains under statutory powers, it was held that their duty was merely to use the best type of spark arrester, and that they were not liable for fires caused by sparks which the spark arrester failed to prevent.[78]

31. Proceedings Against the Crown.[79]—Before 1947 the Crown, in modern times at least,[80] was not vicariously liable for the wrongful acts of its servants or agents.[81] The effect of the Crown Proceedings Act 1947,[82] however, is to render the Crown liable for wrongs committed by its servants or agents, provided that, apart from the provisions of the Act, the act or omission complained of would have rendered the servant or agent liable.[83] The Crown is also made liable in respect of any breach of those duties which a person owes to his servants and agents as their employer, and in respect of any breach of the duties attaching at common law to the ownership, occupation, possession or control of property.[84] Where the Crown is bound, whether expressly or by necessary implication, by a statutory duty which is binding also upon persons other than the Crown and its officers, it is liable for breach of such a duty in the same way as if it were a private person.[85] No proceedings, however, will lie against the Crown in respect of acts or omissions by judicial persons[86] or by public servants, such as policemen,[87] not directly or indirectly appointed by the Crown and paid out of the Consolidated Fund or certain other national sources[88]; and the Post Office is no longer regarded as an agent of the Crown or as enjoying Crown immunity.[89] The generality of the Crown's liability is further limited by

[76] *West* v. *Briston Tramways* [1908] 2 K.B. 14; see also *Metropolitan Asylums District Board* v. *Hill* (1881) 6 App.Cas. 193.
[77] *Farnworth* v. *Manchester Corporation,* supra.
[78] *Port-Glasgow, etc., Sailcloth Co.* v. *Cal. Ry.* (1893) 20 R. (H.L.) 35. The rule was modified by statute (see Railway Fires Acts 1905 & 1923, (5 Edw. VII. c. 11 and 13 & 14 Geo. V. c. 27)).
[79] See generally Mitchell, *Constitutional Law* (2nd ed.), pp. 304-312.
[80] At one stage it seems that an action of reparation against the Crown was competent; see Mitchell, p. 304.
[81] *Macgregor* v. *Lord Advocate,* 1921 S.C. 847.
[82] 10 & 11 Geo. VI, c. 44.
[83] s. 2 (1) (*a*). This proviso prevents the Crown from being sued where the defence of act of state would protect the individual; see note 85 infra. "Agent"is defined as including an independent contractor employed by the Crown (s. 38).
[84] s. 2 (1) (*b*) and (*c*). The Occupiers' Liability (Scotland) Act 1960, s. 4, binds the Crown.
[85] s. 2 (2).
[86] s. 2 (5).
[87] But see Police (Scotland) Act 1967 (c. 77), s. 39.
[88] s. 2 (6).
[89] Post Office Act 1969, (c. 48), s. 6 (5).

section 11 of the Act, which specifically preserves all powers and authorities of a prerogative nature or conferred on the Crown by any statute, particularly those connected with defence. An executive officer of the Crown may incur personal liability in respect of his own wrongful or negligent act.[90]

The Sheriff Court has jurisdiction in actions against the Crown, subject to the power of the Lord Advocate to have cases which are important remitted to the Court of Session.[91] In Scotland actions against the Crown or any public department may be raised against the Lord Advocate, who before representing the Crown or the public department must have their authority to do so.[92]

32. Judicial Immunity.—Judges of the Court of Session, the High Court of Justiciary and probably the Sheriff Court[93] enjoy absolute immunity at common law from civil action for anything done by them in their judicial capacity.[94] At common law judges of an inferior court, such as magistrates or justices of the peace, probably could be sued for damages in respect of acts done in excess of their jurisdiction apart altogether from malice,[95] but their position is now regulated by statute. Under the Criminal Procedure (Scotland) Act 1975[96] no judge, clerk of court or prosecutor in the public interest may be found liable in damages in respect of any proceedings taken, act done or judgment, decree or sentence pronounced under that Act unless (1) the person claiming damages was imprisoned in consequence thereof, (2) the proceeding complained of has been quashed, (3) malice and want of probable cause are specifically averred and proved and (4) the action is begun within two months of the proceeding complained of. Where a judge acts in an administrative capacity,[97] he will be liable only on averment and proof that he acted maliciously and without probable cause.[98]

The Lord Advocate is protected by absolute privilege in respect of matters in connection with criminal proceedings on indictment.[99] Since all prosecutions on indictment must have the authority of the Lord Advocate either in person or through his deputes,[1] that privilege extends to procurators fiscal and depute procurators fiscal acting on his authority and instructions.[2] In summary proceedings procurators fiscal are protected by the Criminal Procedure (Scotland) Act 1975.[96]

---

[90] *MacGregor* v. *Lord Advocate,* 1921 S.C. 847; *Bainbridge* v. *Postmaster General* [1906] 1 K.B. 178. For the defence of act of state, see *Poll* v. *Lord Advocate* (1899) 1 F. 823; *Johnstone* v. *Pedlar* [1921] 2 A.C. 262; and Mitchell, op. cit., at p. 180.
[91] s. 44.
[92] Crown Suits (Scotland) Act 1857.
[93] *Harvey* v. *Dyce* (1876) 4 R. 264; but see Mitchell, p. 262.
[94] *Haggart's Trs.* v. *Hope* (1824) 2 Shaw's App. 125; *M'Creadie* v. *Thomson,* 1907 S.C. 1176, per Lord Justice-Clerk Macdonald, at p. 1182.
[95] *M'Phee* v. *Macfarlane's Exr.,* 1933 S.C. 163, per Lord President Clyde, at p. 169.
[96] 1975, (c. 21), s. 456; cf. Summary Jurisdiction (Scotland) Acts 1908 and 1954, ss. 59 and 75 respectively.
[97] On the distinction between "administrative" and "judicial" acts, see Walker, *Delict,* Vol. I, pp. 110-11 and 114-5.
[98] *Beaton* v. *Ivory* (1887) 14 R. 1057; *M'Pherson* v. *M'Lennan* (1887) 14 R. 1063.
[99] *Henderson* v. *Robertson* (1853) 15 D. 292; *Hester* v. *Macdonald,* 1961 S.C. 370.
[1] See Criminal Procedure (Scotland) Act 1887, s. 2.
[2] *Hester* v. *Macdonald, supra.*

33. Prescription and Limitation.—Negative prescription is to be distinguished from limitation of actions. By negative prescription an obligation and its correlative right are extinguished. By limitation it is merely the right to sue that is cut off; substantive rights and obligations, although no longer directly enforceable, remain in force and may be pleaded by way of exception. Prescription is therefore substantive while limitation is procedural. Until the Prescription and Limitation (Scotland) Act 1973[3] obligations to make reparation, in common with other obligations, had from ancient times[4] been subject to the long negative prescription originally of forty but latterly of twenty years.[5] Short of that they were affected by the running of time only in so far as they came within the purview of certain modern statutes on limitation or in that the pursuer might face difficulties of proof on account of his mora, taciturnity and acquiescence. An obligation to make reparation, other than in respect of personal injuries or death, now prescribes in a period of five years[6] which runs from the date when the damage occurred or, when damage has occurred before the cessation of a continuing act, neglect or default, from the date of cessation.[7] Where, however, the claimant was not and could not, with reasonable diligence, have been aware that damage had occurred, the prescriptive period runs from the date when he first became, or could have become, so aware.[8] Subject to the rules on limitation of actions noticed below, an obligation to make reparation in respect of personal injuries or death prescribes in twenty years[9] as does any other reparative obligation which has not within that time been extinguished by the running of the five year prescription.[10]

Limitation of actions is a creature of English law which has been introduced into the law of Scotland by a number of statutes dealing mainly with damages for personal injury or death.[11] Historically the most notable of these was the Public Authorities Protection Act 1893,[12] which hampered pursuers by enacting that action against public authorities must be taken within six months. This statute along with some others was, however, repealed by the Law Reform (Limitation of Actions) Act 1954,[13] which made the Crown and other public bodies liable to be sued within the same limits of time as other persons or bodies. The relevant law is now contained in the Prescription and Limitation (Scotland) Act 1973 which provides that no actions of damages, where the damages claimed consist of or include damages or solatium in respect of personal injuries shall be brought unless

---

[3] 1973, (c. 52).
[4] The Acts 1469 (c. 28), 1474 (c. 54) and 1617 (c. 12); *Cooke* v. *Falconer* (1850) 13 D 157.
[5] Conveyancing (Scotland) Act 1924, (14 & 15 Geo. V, c. 27), s. 17.
[6] 1973 Act, s. 6 & Sched. 1, paras. 1 (*d*) and 2 (*g*).
[7] ibid. s. 11 (1) & (2).
[8] ibid. s. 11 (3).
[9] ibid. s. 7.
[10] As may happen where the running of the five year period is prevented or interrupted by reason of fraud on the part of or error induced by the debtor or by the legal incapacity of the claimant [s. 6 (4)] or because the claimant was throughout unaware that damage had occurred (see s. 11 (4)).
[11] For a detailed list, see Walker, Vol. I, pp. 445-53.
[12] 56 & 57 Vict., c. 61.
[13] 2 & 3 Eliz. II, c. 36, s. 1.

commenced[14] within three years of the date when the injuries were sustained or, where there has been a continuing act, neglect or default, within three years of the date on which the act, neglect or default ceased, whichever is the later.[15] Where the action is brought by one person to whom a right of action has accrued on the death of another person, it must be brought within three years of that death.[16] Actions by relatives for loss of support or loss of society as well as actions by executors are included in this limitation.[17] In the case of persons under legal disability by reason of pupillarity or minority or of unsoundness of mind who are not in the custody of the parent,[18] the action must be brought within three years of the cessation of that disability.[19] It has been held that the limitation period does not apply where a pursuer seeks compensation for a wrong consisting of allowing his right of action against his employer or other person as a result of whose act he has suffered personal injury to lapse without having been exercised, as where a trade union official or a solicitor fails to raise the action within the statutory period; such an action is not one relating to damages for personal injuries.[20]

The three-year limitation does not apply where it is proved that the material facts[21] relating to the right of action (other than a right of action accruing on death) included those of a decisive character which were at all times outside the actual or constructive knowledge[22] of the pursuer until a date not earlier than three years before the date on which the action is brought.[23] In the case of a right of action which accrues on the death of another person the period does not apply if (1) the deceased lacked the necessary knowledge until (a) his death or (b) a date less than three years before his death or (c), where the deceased brought an action which was still pending at his death, a date not earlier than three years before the commencement of that action, *and* (2) either the action is brought not later than three years after the deceased's death or no one who was an executor or a relative entitled to sue, as the case may be, had the necessary knowledge until a date not earlier than three years before the date on which the action is brought.[24] Relaxation of the limitation period affords relief to persons who have contracted, for instance, pneumoconiosis but who do not become aware

[14] As to the meaning of "commenced," see *M'Graddie* v. *Clark*, 1966 S.L.T. (Sh. Ct.) 36; see also *Miller* v. *N.C.B.*, 1960 S.C. 376, per Lord President Clyde, at p. 382.
[15] s. 17 (1) (*a*).
[16] s. 17 (1) (*b*).
[17] *Gray* v. *North British Steel Foundry Ltd.*, 1969 S.L.T. 273.
[18] See definition in s. 17 (2).
[19] s. 17 (2).
[20] *Robertson* v. *Bannigan*, 1965 S.C. 20; *M'Gahie* v. *Union of Shop Distributive & Allied Workers*, 1966 S.L.T. 74.
[21] See s. 22 (3); *Avinou* v. *Scottish Insulation Co.*, 1970 S.L.T. 146; *Clark* v. *Forbes Stuart (Thames Street)* [1964] 1 W.L.R. 836; *Goodchild* v. *Greatness Timber Company* [1968] 2 Q.B. 372; *Pickles* v. *N.C.B.* [1968] 1 W.L.R. 997; *Drinkwater* v. *Joseph Lucas (Electrical)* [1970] 3 All E.R. 769; *Central Asbestos Co.* v. *Dodd* [1972] 3 W.L.R. 333; *Knipe* v. *British Railways Board* [1972] 1 Q.B. 361; *Howell* v. *West Midlands Passenger Transport Executive* [1973] 1 Lloyd's Rep. 199; *Hunter* v. *Glasgow Corporation*, 1971 S.C. 220; *Kerr* v. *J. A. Stewart (Plant)*, 1976 S.L.T. 255; *McIntyre* v. *Armitage Shanks*, 1978 S.L.T. 53.
[22] See s. 22 (4).
[23] s. 18.
[24] s. 19. If the material facts of a decisive character were within the knowledge of one relative but not of another there are provisions obscurely expressed which seem to be intended to provide

of their condition for several years after the cessation of the act, neglect or default which gave rise to the disease.[25]

The Court will not in general allow a pursuer by amendment to change the basis of his case or cure a radical incompetence in his action,[26] to substitute or call in another defender[27] or to amend his conclusion so as to enable the Court to grant decree against a third party,[28] if he seeks to make such amendments or adjustments outwith the period of the statutory limitation.

---

relief for the latter (s. 19 (4) (*b*) proviso). On material facts of a decisive character see cases cited supra, *Newton* v. *Cammell Laird* [1969] 1 W.L.R. 415; and *Provan* v. *Glynwed*, 1975 S.L.T. 192.

[25] See *Cartledge* v. *E. Jopling & Sons Ltd.* [1963] A.C. 758. The Limitation Act 1963, (c. 47) (now repealed) was passed to remedy this situation.

[26] See *Pompa's Trs.* v. *Edinburgh Mags.*, 1942 S.C. 119, per Lord Justice-Clerk Cooper, at p. 125; *Dryburgh* v. *N.C.B.*, 1962 S.C. 485; *O'Hare* v. *Western Heritable Investment Co., Ltd.*, 1965 S.L.T. 182. For cases in which amendments have been allowed on the view that they did not alter the basis of the pursuer's case see *Emslie* v. *Toguarelli's Exrs.*, 1969 S.L.T. 20 and *Mazs* v. *The Dairy Supply Co.*, 1978 S.L.T. 208.

[27] *Miller* v. *N.C.B.*, 1960 S.C. 376; *Maclean* v. *B.R.B.*, 1966 S.L.T. 39 (an attempt to include further pursuers); but see *Pompa's Trs.* v. *Edinburgh Mags.*, supra.

[28] *Aitken* v. *Norrie*, 1967 S.L.T. 4; *Travers* v. *Neilson*, 1967 S.L.T. 64.

CHAPTER XXXV

DEFAMATION: ABUSE OF LEGAL PROCESS

Glegg on *Reparation* (4th ed., 1955); Walker, *Delict* (1966), Vol. II., Chapters 23 and 24; Cooper, *Defamation* (2nd ed., 1906) Gatley, *Libel and Slander* (7th ed., 1974); Duncan and Neill, *Defamation* (1978).

1. Defamation.—Defamation in its widest sense covers all imputations which are injurious. The Courts, however, have drawn a distinction between slander, which has been confined to injurious imputations against character, credit or reputation, and other types of verbal injury, e.g., (a) statements exposing a person to public hatred and contempt[1]; (b) slander of title[2]; (c) slander of property[2]; and (d) slander of goods or business.[3] In this chapter the words "slander," "defamation" and "defamatory" are used in the narrow sense and are not related to those other aspects of verbal injury.

2. Requisites of Defamation.—Defamation consists of the communication of a false statement or idea which is defamatory of the pursuer.[4] If the statement is untrue and defamatory, malice is irrelevant unless privilege is pleaded or there has, because of the defender's malice, been greater injury to the pursuer's reputation than would otherwise have occurred.[5] The statement may be oral, in writing, or, in exceptional cases, inferred from acts, as where the waxwork figure of the pursuer was placed in the department of an exhibition devoted to the effigies of notorious criminals.[6] Technically, written defamation is known as libel, oral as slander, but the distinction is not of importance in the law of Scotland.

3. Statement must be Untrue: Veritas.[7]—To be actionable the statement must be untrue, as is indicated in the maxim "veritas convicii excusat."[8] In the case of statements which are defamatory there is a presumption of their untruth, and the defender, if he relies on veritas, must affirm the truth of his statement in his defences, and, in Court of Session procedure, table a definite counter-issue. Without such a counter-issue evidence of the truthfulness of the statement is not admissible.[9] Where there are two separate charges, it is

---

[1] See § 17, infra.
[2] See § 18, infra.
[3] See Walker, Vol. II, p. 908.
[4] See § 6 and § 7, infra.
[5] *Stein* v. *Beaverbrook Newspapers,* 1968 S.C. 272; cf. Privilege, § 10, infra.
[6] *Monson* v. *Tussauds* [1894] 1 Q.B. 671; *Adamson* v. *Martin,* 1916 S.C. 319; *Tolley* v. *Fry* [1931] A.C. 333: and see Defamation Act 1952, s. 16 (1). For limits of slander by acts, see *Drysdale* v. *Lord Rosebery,* 1909 S.C. 1121. A representation in a "talking film" is libel and not slander: *Youssoupoff* v. *Metro-Goldwyn-Mayer,* (1934) 50 T.L.R. 581.
[7] See Walker, Vol. II, pp. 798-802; also Fair Comment, § 16, infra.
[8] *McKellar* v. *Duke of Sutherland* (1859) 21 D. 222.
[9] *Craig* v. *Jex-Blake* (1871) 9 M. 973; *Browne* v. *Macfarlane* (1889) 16 R. 368.

536

competent to take a counter-issue with regard to one of them.[10] By the Defamation Act 1952,[11] where a statement sued on contains two or more charges against a pursuer, a defence of veritas is not to fail by reason only that the truth of every charge is not proved, provided that the words not proved to be true do not materially injure the pursuer's reputation in view of the proven truth of the remaining charges.

4. Publication.—In Scotland it is not necessary that the statement be communicated to a third party. It is sufficient if it was made or sent to the injured party because damages are recoverable for injured feelings.[12] The dictation of a defamatory letter to a clerk is not publication and no action would lie if the letter was not despatched.[13]

5. Defamation: When Criminal.—Defamation in general is not a criminal offence. It is a civil wrong, which grounds an action for damages, or an interdict against publication or repetition.[14] But it is a criminal offence, under the Representation of the People Act 1949,[15] for any person, or the directors of any association, before or during a parliamentary election, to make or publish, for the purpose of affecting the return of any candidate, any false statement of fact in relation to the personal character or conduct of such candidate. In a prosecution under the Act it is a sufficient defence that the accused had reasonable grounds for believing, and did believe, the statement made by him to be true.

6. What Amounts to Defamation.—Whether or not the words complained of are reasonably capable of bearing a defamatory meaning, either per se or by innuendo,[16] is a question of law for the Court.[17] In determining this question the whole statement must be read.[18] Thus the contents of a newspaper report, when read together with the heading, may negative the defamatory meaning of the heading alone.[19] If the Court holds that the language may be construed in a defamatory sense, it is then a question for the jury to decide whether or not the proper construction in all the circumstances of the case is defamatory or innocent.[17]

Imputations against a man's moral character are defamatory.[20] Imputations of guilt of crime or of attempt to commit a crime or of criminal intent are clearly defamatory, as also are allegations of dishonesty, immorality and

---

[10] *O'Callaghan* v. *Thomson & Co.,* 1928 S.C. 532.
[11] 15 & 16 Geo. VI & 1 Eliz. II, c. 66, s. 5. The last six words of this sentence are substituted for those of the section.
[12] *Mackay* v. *McCankie* (1883) 10 R. 537; *Ramsay* v. *Maclay* (1890) 18 R. 130.
[13] See *Evans* v. *Stein* (1904) 7 F. 65.
[14] *British Legal Life Co.* v. *Pearl Insurance Co.* (1887) 14 R. 818.
[15] 12 & 13 Geo. VI, c. 68, s. 91 (1). The Act does not in Scotland apply to an election of councillors: s. 91 (3).
[16] See § 7 infra.
[17] *Russell* v. *Stubbs,* 1913 S.C. (H.L.) 14, per Lord Kinnear, at p. 20.
[18] *Campbell* v. *Ritchie & Co.,* 1907 S.C. 1097.
[19] *Leon* v. *Edinburgh Evening News,* 1909 S.C. 1014.
[20] *Brownlie* v. *Thomson* (1859) 21 D. 480, per Lord Justice-Clerk Inglis, at p. 485. See Cooper, op. cit., and Walker, Vol. II, pp. 777-85, for examples of defamatory imputations.

drunkenness, if seriously made. Words which are prima facie defamatory may be held to have been used in their slang sense[21] or in the heat of a quarrel (in rixa)[22] as words of mere abuse, but not if a definite charge is made.[23] While the law affords no remedy for a reflection on manners, a definite charge of conduct usually regarded as dishonourable, either in general society,[24] or in a particular class to which the pursuer belongs,[25] is actionable. To say of a man that he is an informer may be actionable.[26]

Any imputation on solvency is actionable.[27] In the case of "black lists," i.e., lists of persons against whom decrees in absence have been pronounced, the publication of such a list, compiled from official sources, and accurate, cannot be made the subject of an action on the ground merely that it may be read as an imputation on the solvency of the parties whose names are included.[28] But it becomes actionable if prefaced by a caution against giving credit,[29] or if it is averred that the publication is generally read as inferring insolvency.[30] A party whose name is entered by mistake may claim damages. A prefatory statement, to the effect that the publication of a name does not import any inability to pay, will preclude an innuendo, by a party whose name has been inserted by mistake, that the insertion involves a charge of insolvency,[31] but not an innuendo that it involves a statement that he is a party to whom credit should not be given.[32]

False statements which disparage a man's professional or business capacity or fitness for his office or vocation may be defamatory,[33] but they must be distinguished from those which, while injurious, do not impugn his character or business reputation. The latter are not defamatory. While they are actionable under the general head of verbal injury, malice must be specifically averred and proved by the pursuer.[34] There is also a material distinction between private individuals and public figures, critics of the latter being allowed a wide latitude in the public interest.[35]

7. Innuendo.[36]—In some cases it may be necessary to explain technical, ironical or ambiguous language or to supply a stigma which may, but does not necessarily, lurk in the words used. This is done by setting forth on record and putting in issue an innuendo, i.e., the precise defamatory meaning which the

---

[21] *Murdison* v. *Scottish Football Union* (1896) 23 R. 449; *Agnew* v. *British Legal Assce. Co.* (1906) 8 F. 422.
[22] *Watson* v. *Duncan* (1890) 17 R. 404.
[23] *Christie* v. *Robertson* (1899) 1 F. 1155, per Lord M'Laren, at p. 1157; and see Walker, Vol. II, pp. 797-8.
[24] *Menzies* v. *Goodlet* (1835) 13 S. 1136 (anonymous letter).
[25] *Griffen* v. *Divers*, 1922 S.C. 605; *Tolley* v. *Fry* [1931] A.C. 333; *Cuthbert* v. *Linklater*, 1936 S.L.T. 94; *Lloyd* v. *Hickley*, 1967 S.L.T. 225.
[26] *Winn* v. *Quillan* (1899) 37 S.L.R. 38. Aliter in England: see *Byrne* v. *Dean* [1937] 1 K.B. 818.
[27] *A.B.* v. *C.D.* (1904) 7 F. 22; see cases in Walker, pp. 780-3.
[28] *Taylor* v. *Rutherford* (1888) 15 R. 608; *M'Lintock* v. *Stubbs* (1902) 5 F. 1.
[29] *Andrews* v. *Drummond* (1887) 14 R. 568.
[30] *Barr* v. *Musselburgh Merchants*, 1912 S.C. 174.
[31] *Russell* v. *Stubbs*, 1913 S.C. (H.L.) 14.
[32] *Mazure* v. *Stubbs*, 1919 S.C. (H.L.) 112.
[33] See cases cited in Walker, Vol. II, pp. 782-4, and Glegg on *Reparation*, p. 150.
[34] See Verbal Injury, § 17, infra.
[35] See Glegg, pp. 183-4, and Fair Comment, § 16, infra.
[36] See Walker, Vol. II, pp. 770-6; Glegg, pp. 146-53.

pursuer attaches to the words.[37] The language itself may support the innuendo, but the pursuer may also aver facts extrinsic to the libel which tend to show that the language may reasonably be construed in the sense of the innuendo.[38] It is for the Court to determine whether the innuendo is one which the words actually used may reasonably bear and for the jury to decide as matter of fact whether the language ought to be construed in the sense of the innuendo.[39] "The innuendo must represent what is a reasonable, natural, or necessary inference from the words used, regard being had to the occasion and the circumstances of their publication."[40] An innuendo is also used when the slander is in a foreign language and may be used to extract the substance of the charge from a series of letters or articles, although the words used therein are themselves defamatory.

8. Defences.—The following defences are open in an action for defamation:—

(1) That the words founded on were not used by the defender.[41]

(2) That the statement did not refer to the pursuer and could not reasonably be construed as referring to him.[42]

(3) That the words used were not reasonably capable of bearing the alleged defamatory meaning.[43]

(4) That the words used could not in all the circumstances bear the meaning ascribed to them.[43]

(5) That the slander was unintentional, coupled with an offer of amends.[44]

(6) That the pursuer expressly or impliedly assented to the statement being made.

(7) That the statement was true (veritas).[45]

(8) Absolute privilege.[46]

(9) Qualified privilege.[47]

(10) Fair retort.[48]

(11) Fair comment.[49]

[37] *Murdison* v. *S.F.U.* (1896) 23 R. 449, per Lord Kinnear, at p. 463; *James* v. *Baird* 1915 S.C. 23.

[38] *James* v. *Baird*, 1916 S.C. (H.L.) 158, per Lord Kinnear, at p. 165; *Smith* v. *Walker*, 1912 S.C. 224; *Gordon* v. *Leng,* 1919 S.C. 415; *Gollan* v. *Thompson Wyles,* 1930 S.C. 599, per Lord President Clyde, at pp. 603-4. Note that as a result of the terms of a procedural rule in England the House of Lords has been forced to hold that any meaning that does not require the support of extrinsic fact must be treated as part of the ordinary meaning of the words and not as a "legal" innuendo: *Lewis* v. *Daily Telegraph* [1964] A.C. 234. This is NOT the law of Scotland.

[39] *Langlands* v. *Leng,* 1916 S.C. (H.L.) 102

[40] Per Lord Shaw, *Russell* v. *Stubbs,* 1913 S.C. (H.L.) 14, at p. 24; *Lord Hamilton* v. *Glasgow Dairy Co.,* 1931 S.C. (H.L.) 67. See *Fullam* v. *Newcastle Chronicle and Journal* [1977] 1 W.L.R. 651, on requirements of pleading where innuendo would be drawn only by those with special knowledge.

[41] The plea of veritas may be taken as an alternative defence.

[42] See § 9, infra.

[43] See § 6, infra.

[44] See § 9, infra.

[45] See § 3, supra. If the truth of the statement is evident from the pursuer's pleadings, the action is irrelevant: *Carson* v. *White,* 1919 2 S.L.T. 215.

[46] See §§ 10 and 11, infra.

[47] See §§ 10 and 12, infra.

[48] See § 15.

[49] See § 16.

9. Unintentional Slander.—The pursuer in an action of defamation does not require to prove that the defender intended to disparage him or that he even knew of his existence. His obligation is to satisfy the Court, as matter of relevancy, that the words used might reasonably be read as referring to him, and to satisfy the jury that they were in fact so read. In *Jones* v. *Hulton*[50] a newspaper article was defamatory of "Artemus Jones," the name given by the author to a fictitious character. A person of that name, who was unknown to the author of the article and to the editor of the paper, proved that the article had been read as referring to him and was found entitled to damages from the publishers. An action of damages lies for publication of a statement which is ex facie innocent but which is reasonably read in a sense defamatory of the pursuer by persons with knowledge of facts unknown to the defender. It is no defence that the author or publisher was unaware of these extrinsic factors.[51] So, in the case of a newspaper notice inserted by an unknown party, it has been held that malice may be inferred from the failure of the publishers to make sufficient enquiry into the genuineness of the notice and that the circumstances surrounding the publication of the notice are relevant only to quantum of damages.[52]

Liability for unintentional slander has been modified by the Defamation Act 1952,[53] which entitles a person claiming innocent publication[54] to offer "amends" by way of published correction and apology and by notifying persons known to have received copies of the slanderous statement.[55] The offer must be accompanied by a signed declaration specifying the facts relied upon to demonstrate innocent publication.[56] If this offer is accepted and fulfilled, no proceedings for libel or slander can be taken or continued against the offeror.[57] Rejection of the offer enables the offeror to set up as a complete defence on the merits of an action the fact of innocent publication coupled with a timeous offer of amends.[58]

10. Privilege.[59]—In cases of defamation privilege may be absolute or qualified. Where privilege is absolute no action can be based on defamatory words. Averments of malice are irrelevant. Where privilege is not absolute, but qualified, action is not excluded, but malice on the part of the defender must be averred and proved.[60]

11. Absolute Privilege.[61]—The following are the leading cases of absolute privilege:—Any statement made in Parliament, in a petition to Parliament, in

---

[50] [1910] A.C. 20, followed in *Wragg* v. *Thomson*, 1909 2 S.L.T. 409.
[51] *Morrison* v. *Ritchie* (1902) 4 F. 645; *Cassidy* v. *Daily Mirror* [1929] 2 K.B. 331.
[52] *Morrison* v. *Ritchie*, supra; but note opinions of Lords Salvesen and Kinnear in *Wood* v. *Edinburgh Evening News*, 1910 S.C. 895. See Walker, pp. 788-9.
[53] 15 & 16 Geo. VI, & 1 Eliz. II, c. 66, s. 4.
[54] Ibid., s. 4 (5).
[55] s. 4 (3).
[56] ss. 4 (2) and 14 (c).
[57] ss. 4 (1) (a) and (4) and 14 (d).
[58] s. 4 (1) (b).
[59] See Glegg on *Reparation*, Ch. 9, pp. 160 et seq.
[60] *Langlands* v. *Leng*, 1916 S.C. (H.L.) 102, per Lord Shaw, at p. 109.
[61] See Walker, pp. 803-10.

a report authorised by Parliament,[62] including reports broadcast by wireless telegraphy,[63] official reports to any department of State, or to a colonial government[64]: any statement by a judge, of any Court, while acting in his judicial capacity[65]: any statement by an advocate, i.e., by any person professionally addressing a Court[66]: a witness, both in respect to his statements in Court and in precognition.[67] But the privilege of a litigant, in statements made on record, or in statements which he instructs his counsel or solicitor to make in Court, is not absolute.[68]

Absolute privilege extends to a fair report of what took place on any privileged occasion, such as the proceedings in Parliament, or in any Court. The report need not be verbatim, and it is for the jury to decide whether any omission deprives it of the character of a fair report.[69] The privilege covers the publication of any decree, or official record.[70] While it is doubtful whether privilege covers a report of statements made in the closed record of an action, it is clear that it does not extend to statements before the record is closed.[71] The publication of such statements amounts to contempt of Court, and may be visited by penalties.[72]

12. Qualified Privilege.[73]—Qualified privilege does not relate to persons or to the nature of statements but to occasions, and it is for the Court to decide whether or not the occasion is privileged, although it may not be possible to do so until the relevant facts have been ascertained.[74] "The proper meaning of a privileged communication is only this; that the occasion on which the communication was made rebuts the inference [of malice] *prima facie* arising from a statement prejudicial to the character of the plaintiff, and puts it upon him to prove that there was malice in fact—that the defendant was actuated by motives of personal spite or ill-will, independent of the occasion on which the communication was made."[75]

Qualified privilege exists where the statement is "made by a person in the discharge of some public or private duty, whether legal or moral, or in the conduct of his own affairs, in matters where his interest is concerned."[76] As is

---

[62] *Dillon* v. *Balfour*, 20 L.R.Ir., 600; Parliamentary Papers Act 1840 (3 & 4 Vict., c. 9); *Mangena* v. *Wright* [1909] 2 K.B. 958; *Dingle* v. *Associated Newspapers* [1960] 2 Q.B. 405; [1961] 2 Q.B. 162.

[63] Defamation Act 1952, s. 9 (1).

[64] *Dawkins* v. *Lord Paulet* (1869) L.R. 5 Q.B. 94; *Isaacs* v. *Cook* [1925] 2 K.B. 391.

[65] *Primrose* v. *Waterson* (1902) 4 F. 783.

[66] *Williamson* v. *Umphray* (1890) 17 R. 905; *Rome* v. *Watson* (1898) 25 R. 733.

[67] *Watson* v. *M'Ewan* (1905) 7 F. (H.L.) 109; cf. *Trapp* v. *Mackie*, 1977 S.L.T. 194 (witness at inquiry under Education (Scotland) Act 1946, s. 81 (3) absolutely privileged).

[68] *Williamson* v. *Umphray, supra; M.* v. *H.,* 1908 S.C. 1130; and see § 12, infra.

[69] *Wright & Greig* v. *Outram* (1890) 17 R. 596; *Duncan* v. *Associated Newspapers,* 1929 S.C. 14; *Harper* v. *Provincial Newspapers,* 1937 S.L.T. 462; see Walker, Vol II, pp. 839-40.

[70] *Buchan* v. *N.B. Ry.* (1894) 21 R. 379.

[71] *Macleod* v. *J.P. of Lewis* (1892) 20 R. 218.

[72] *Young* v. *Armour,* 1921, 1 S.L.T. 211.

[73] See Walker, pp. 810-41.

[74] *Adam* v. *Ward* [1917] A.C. 309; *Mintner* v. *Priest* [1930] A.C. 558, per Viscount Dunedin, at pp. 571-2.

[75] *Wright* v. *Woodgate* [1835] 2 C.M. & R. 573, per Parke B., at p. 577, quoted by Lord Hunter in *Cochrane* v. *Young,* 1922 S.C. 696, at p. 701.

[76] Per Parke, B., in *Toogood* v. *Spyring* (1834) 1 C.M. & R. 181, adopted in *M'Intosh* v. *Dun* [1908] A.C. 390; *A.B.* v. *X.Y.,* 1917 S.C. 15; *Hines* v. *Davidson,* 1935 S.C. 30, per Lord Anderson, at p. 38.

added later in the same judgment, the communication must be to some person legitimately interested in the matter.[77] One established case is criticism by a master of his servant,[78] either to himself, in giving him a character, or in speaking to some party who has an interest to inquire, but not in repeating his criticism unnecessarily to third parties.[79] A master is also privileged in speaking to his servants of the character of their associates.[80] Charitable intention has been held to afford privilege to a statement regarding the treatment of pauper patients by a doctor.[81] An elector has qualified privilege in speaking of a candidate in his own constituency,[82] not in another.[83] A Member of Parliament has a qualified privilege in passing on to the appropriate body a complaint received from a constituent about the conduct of a professional man.[83a] A defamatory statement published by or for a candidate at a local or Parliamentary election is not privileged on the ground that it is material to a question at issue in the election.[84] The members of a public body or board are privileged in discussing any matter pertinent to the business.[85] The Public Bodies (Admission to Meetings) Act 1960 (c. 67), s. 1(5)) confers qualified privilege on the agenda of any meeting required by the Act to be open to the public, a copy of which is supplied to a member of the public attending the meeting or supplied for the benefit of a newspaper. A trade protection society, established for profit, and issuing lists of persons to whom it is dangerous to give credit, has no privilege,[86] but privilege is allowed where similar lists are issued by a private body of traders, as the list may be regarded as the communication by one trader to another of facts in which he has a legitimate business interest.[87] And it would seem that an answer to a specific inquiry regarding the credit of a particular party is privileged.[88] A statement made by one litigant to another that the latter's manager had tampered with a juryman is privileged in an action for libel brought by the manager.[89]

No special privilege is enjoyed at common law by a newspaper,[90] but the Defamation Act 1952[91] has conferred privilege in a number of cases. Thus the

[77] See *Watt* v. *Longsdon* [1930] 1 K.B. 130.
[78] A comparable case is chairman and employee of a company; see *M'Gillivray* v. *Davidson*, 1934 S.L.T. 45.
[79] *Bryant* v. *Edgar*, 1909 S.C. 1080.
[80] *Hunt* v. *Great Northern Ry.* [1891] 2 Q.B. 189; *A.B.* v. *X.Y.*, 1917 S.C. 15; but see *Milne* v. *Smith* (1892) 20 R. 95.
[81] *James* v. *Baird*, 1916 S.C. (H.L.) 158.
[82] *Bruce* v. *Leisk* (1892) 19 R. 482.
[83] *Anderson* v. *Hunter* (1891) 18 R. 467.
[83a] *Beach* v. *Freesan* [1972] 1 Q.B. 14.
[84] Defamation Act 1952, s. 10; and see *Plummer* v. *Charman* [1962] 1 W.L.R. 1469.
[85] *Shaw* v. *Morgan* (1888) 15 R. 865; *Griffen* v. *Divers*, 1922 S.C. 605.
[86] *Mackintosh* v. *Dun* [1908] A.C. 390.
[87] *Barr* v. *Musselburgh Merchants*, 1912 S.C. 174; *Keith* v. *Lauder* (1905) 8 F. 356.
[88] *Bayne & Thomson* v. *Stubbs* (1901) 3 F. 408.
[89] *Hines* v. *Davidson*, 1935 S.C. 30.
[90] *Wright & Greig* v. *Outram* (1890) 17 R. 597; *Langlands* v. *Leng*, 1916 S.C. (H.L.) 102, per Lord Shaw at p. 110. See also *Brims* v. *Reid* (1885) 12 R. 1016 and *M'Kerchar* v. *Cameron* (1892) 19 R. 383, in which pleas of privilege were repelled in relation to publication of anonymous letters. It is thought that "privilege" was not an appropriate plea as the subject-matter was of public interest. See *Merivale* v. *Carson* (1887) 20 Q.B.D. 275, per Lord Esher, M.R., at p. 280; also Fair Comment, § 16, infra, fn. 47.
[91] 15 & 16 Geo. VI & Eliz. II, c. 66, s. 1 and Sched.

publication in a newspaper of a "fair and accurate" report of the following matters is privileged unless proved to be made maliciously: public proceedings of a Dominion legislature outside Great Britain: public proceedings of an international organisation or conference: public proceedings of an international court: proceedings before a court with jurisdiction in H.M. Dominions outside Britain or court-martial proceedings outside Britain: public proceedings at an inquiry instituted by a Government in H.M. Dominions outside Britain. Similarly privileged is a fair and accurate copy or extract from a public register kept in pursuance of an Act of Parliament and a notice or advertisement published by or on the authority of a United Kingdom Court. Then s. 7 (2) confers privilege in the following cases, but subject to the defender publishing at the request of the pursuer a reasonable explanation or contradiction in the newspaper in which the original publication was made: a fair and accurate report of the findings of associations formed for various purposes such as the encouragement of art, science, religion or learning, the promoting or safeguarding of trade, business or profession, and the promoting of the interests of games, sports or pastimes played or viewed by the public. The privilege is extended also to fair and accurate reports of the proceedings of public meetings in the United Kingdom, the proceedings at meetings of Local Authorities, Justices of the Peace, Commissions, Tribunals, etc., appointed for the purposes of inquiry and other like purposes, the proceedings at the general meeting of companies incorporated by Royal Charter or under the Companies Act 1948, and to a notice issued for public information by Government Department, Officer of State, Local Authority or Chief of Police. It should be observed that by s. 9 the protection given to newspapers is substantially extended to cover statements made by broadcasting. The latitude thus given to newspapers is not to protect the publication of any matter whose publication is prohibited by law, or any matter which is not of public concern and the publication of which is not for the public benefit.[92]

The term "judicial slander" includes oral statements made in Court and written statements in pleadings. Both occasions are absolutely privileged quoad the advocate or solicitor,[93] but the litigant himself enjoys only a qualified privilege in relation to oral statements made in Court by himself,[94] or by the pleader on his instructions,[95] and to statements inserted in his pleadings. If the latter are defamatory and not pertinent to the question at issue, the litigant is not entitled to plead privilege,[96] but, if the defamatory statements are relevant, the litigant is protected by a qualified privilege.[97] The

---

[92] Ibid., s. 7 (3).
[93] See § 11, supra; *Williamson* v. *Umphray* (1890) 17 R. 905; *Rome* v. *Watson* (1898) 25 R. 733.
[94] *Neill* v. *Henderson* (1901) 3 F. 387.
[95] *Williamson* v. *Umphray*, supra; see also *Bayne* v. *Macgregor* (1862) 24 D. 1126, where the solicitor was sued on the ground that he had maliciously instructed counsel to make the statement.
[96] *Mackellar* v. *Duke of Sutherland* (1859) 21 D. 222, where the averments were treated as pertinent, although irrelevant—see Lord Ordinary, at p. 225, and *Scott* v. *Turnbull* (1884) 11 R. 1131, per Lord President Inglis, at p. 1134. For an example of irrelevance and impertinence, see *Brodie* v. *Blair* (1834) 12 S. 941.
[97] *Scott* v. *Turnbull*, supra.

party who sues upon them is not bound to aver want of probable cause, but is bound to aver malice and facts from which malice may reasonably be inferred.[98] It is not enough to aver that the statements were made without belief in their truth.[99] Statements by a party, verbal or written, in answer to a threat of legal action are also subject to qualified privilege.[1]

The question of whether communications passing between solicitor and client on a subject upon which the client has retained the solicitor are protected by absolute or qualified privilege has not been decided in Scotland.[2] While it is thought that qualified, not absolute, privilege applies to all statements made by solicitors to third parties in their clients' interests,[3] it may be impossible to decide as a matter of relevancy whether or not the particular statement has gone beyond what is necessary to protect the client's interest. In such a case the whole circumstances in which it was made must be ascertained before the judge can decide that the occasion is privileged and direct the jury to decide whether or not malice is proved.[4] If the statement made by the solicitor is expressed in terms which may reasonably be read as an expression of his own opinion and not that of his client, malice must be proved.[5] In the ordinary case an agent's liability for publishing defamatory matter on the instructions of his principal stands or falls with that of his principal,[6] but a solicitor who publishes defamatory matter which is prima facie in his client's interests, upon his client's instructions, is entitled to plead at least qualified privilege in his own right whether or not the occasion is privileged quoad his client.[7]

13. Averments of Malice.[8]—While it is recognised that there may be exceptional cases where a statement is so violent as to afford evidence that it could not have been fairly and honestly made,[9] in most cases of qualified privilege a mere general averment that the defender acted maliciously is not sufficient. Facts and circumstances from which malice may be inferred must be set forth, and it is for the Court to decide whether they are relevantly stated.[10]

---

[98] Ibid.; *M.* v. *H.*, 1908 S.C. 1130; *Webster* v. *Paterson*, 1910 S.C. 459; *Mitchell* v. *Smith*, 1919 S.C. 664.

[99] *Mitchell* v. *Smith*, supra.

[1] *Campbell* v. *Cochrane* (1905) 8 F. 205.

[2] Note. The answer may differ according to circumstances, but it is thought that the English decision of *More* v. *Weaver* [1928] 2 K.B. 520 is consistent on its facts with public policy in respect that the communications seem to have been made in confidential circumstances in which it was not reasonably foreseeable that they would be disclosed by the solicitor to any third party; but see *Mintner* v. *Priest* [1930] A.C. 558, where opinions on this point were reserved.

[3] *Baker* v. *Carrick* [1894] 1 Q.B. 838; cf. opinions in *Crawford* v. *Adams* (1900) 2 F. 987.

[4] See opinions in *Adam* v. *Ward* [1917] A.C. 309 and *Wilson* v. *Purvis* (1890) 18 R. 72. Note: *Ramsay* v. *Nairne* (1833) 11 S. 1033 should be treated as a case in which the judge left it to the jury to decide whether or not malice was proved.

[5] *Crawford* v. *Adams* (1900) 2 F. 987.

[6] Gatley, pp. 168-169. *Adam* v. *Ward*, supra, per Lord Finlay, L.C., at p. 320.

[7] But see opinions of Lords Young, Trayner and Moncreiff in *Crawford* v. *Adams*, supra, which suggest that statements made by a solicitor to third parties in strict accordance with his client's instructions are absolutely privileged.

[8] See Glegg on *Reparation*, pp. 154-6; Walker, Vol. II, pp. 813 et seq.

[9] *Lyal* v. *Henderson*, 1916 S.C. (H.L.) 167.

[10] *Suzor* v. *M'Lachlan*, 1914 S.C. 306; *Rogers* v. *Orr*, 1939 S.C. 121.

Averments of a prior quarrel or ill-feeling are sufficient,[11] or, possibly, a definite averment that the defender, at the time when he spoke, knew that the charge was unfounded.[12] It is not enough to say that the charge was made without due inquiry,[13] or, short of recklessness, that it was the result of unreasonable prejudice[13a] or that the defender refused to listen to the pursuer's explanation of his conduct,[14] or refused to withdraw the charge after it had been held unfounded in an official inquiry.[15]

In a rare type of case it has been held competent to aver and prove malice on the part of the defender in order, not to defeat a plea of privilege, but to strengthen an inference that the defender was the author of a particular libel, namely, an anonymous letter.[16]

14. No Probable Cause.—Want of probable cause, as well as malice, must be averred and proved (1) where the statement complained of is made in reporting an alleged crime to the criminal authorities,[17] and (2) where it is made by a public officer in the discharge of his duty. Such statements receive the additional protection on the ground of public interest.[18] In an ordinary action of defamation the words "without probable cause" have no place at all.[19]

15. Fair Retort.—The fact that a party has been slandered is no justification for a slander by him.[20] But in repelling a charge made publicly, as by publication in a newspaper, the party who has been attacked is entitled to the privilege of fair retort, to the extent that his repudiation of the charge is not actionable on the ground that it involves, or states, an imputation against the party by whom the charge was made.[21] "If A should charge B with theft, a denial by B of the charge would not warrant an action of damages by A however vigorous or gross the language might be in which B's denial was couched. But if B should go on to charge A with theft, that would be actionable, and would not be protected or privileged to any extent on account of A's previous attack."[22]

16. Fair Comment.[23]—Anyone is entitled to comment on matters of public interest, such as the policy and administration of a government

---

[11] *Dinnie* v. *Hengler*, 1910 S.C. 4.

[12] *Couper* v. *Lord Balfour*, 1913 S.C. 492; but see *Mitchell* v. *Smith*, 1919 S.C. 664; and *M'Gillivray* v. *Davidson*, 1934 S.L.T. 45.

[13] *A.B.* v. *X.Y.*, 1917 S.C. 15; *Hayford* v. *Forrester-Paton*, 1927 S.C. 740.

[13a] *Horrocks* v. *Lowe* [1975] A.C. 135 (privileged if there was honest and positive belief coupled with absence of abuse of privileged position).

[14] *A.B.* v. *X.Y.*, supra.

[15] *Couper* v. *Lord Balfour*, 1913 S.C. 492.

[16] *MacTaggart* V. *MacKillop*, 1938 S.C. 847; and see *Swan* v. *Bowie*, 1948 S.C. 46.

[17] Infra, § 23.

[18] *Macdonald* v. *Martin*, 1935 S.C. 621; *Notman* v. *Commercial Bank of Scotland*, 1938 S.C. 522.

[19] *Webster* v. *Paterson & Sons*, 1910 S.C. 459, per Lord Dunedin, at p. 468.

[20] *Milne* v. *Walker* (1893) 21 R. 155.

[21] *Gray* v. *Society for Prevention of Cruelty to Animals* (1890) 17 R. 1185.

[22] Per Lord Kincairney, Lord Ordinary, in *Milne* v. *Walker*, supra, 21 R., at p. 157.

[23] See Walker, pp. 841-50, and *Burton* v. *Board* [1928] 1 K.B. 301, per Sankey, L.J., at p. 306.

department or local authority, the administration of justice, the conduct of the holder of any public office or aspirant thereto, literary or artistic productions, public exhibitions and entertainments, and indeed any published matter which invites comment from the general public. This liberty is the basis of the defence of "fair comment," which requires proof of the following: (1) that the facts stated are true: (2) that the comment on or criticism of those facts was fairly and honestly made: (3) on a matter of public interest. "Fair comment" differs from the defence of qualified privilege in respect that the latter arises out of the special relationship of the pursuer and defender as individuals,[24] whereas the former is based upon the interests of the public and is the prerogative of all members of the public.[25] The distinction between "fair comment" and "veritas" is that "to succeed upon the plea of justification the defendant must prove not only that the facts were truly stated, but also that the innuendo is true. Upon fair comment, however, if it be established that the facts stated are true, the defence of fair comment will succeed even if the imputation or innuendo be not justified as true, but be fair and bona fide comment upon a matter of public interest."[26]

A comment is a statement of opinion or inference drawn from facts.[27] It may be expressed in the form of a statement of fact[28] and it may often be difficult to distinguish between fact and comment.[29] The respective scope of the pleas of veritas and fair comment may be considered in the following circumstances:—(1) If all the alleged defamatory matter is contained in statements of fact, the plea of fair comment is inept.[30] (2) If the only matter alleged to be defamatory arises from a statement which appears at the end of a factual narrative, it may be obvious that it is merely an expression of the writer's opinion based upon the facts stated.[31] In that event the plea of fair comment is appropriate and the plea of veritas unnecessary, although competent. (3) The imputation may stem from a statement of opinion only without any express statement of facts upon which the opinion is based.[32] If a sufficient substratum of fact may be implied by the public from that statement in its context, the plea of fair comment is competent and may be supported by averments of particular facts which, although not published, are alleged to be true, to have been known to the writer at the time of publication, and to have formed the basis of the comment.[33] If the Court holds that a sufficient

[24] See § 12, supra.
[25] See *Merivale* v. *Carson* (1887) 20 Q.B.D. 275, per Lord Esher, M.R., at p. 280.
[26] Per Lord Anderson in *Wheatley* v. *Anderson*, 1927 S.C. 133, at p. 147; see also *Broadway Approvals* v. *Odhams Press* [1965] 1 W.L.R. 805, per Sellers, L.J., at p. 817.
[27] See *Sutherland* v. *Stopes* [1925] A.C. 47, at p. 83: "He has murdered his father, and therefore is a disgrace to human nature."
[28] E.g., "he is a disgrace to human nature."
[29] "Comment . . . is often to be recognized and distinguished from allegations of fact by the use of metaphor": *Grech* v. *Odhams Press* [1958] 2 Q.B. 275, at p. 282.
[30] "Fair comment is a defence to comment only and not to defamatory statements of fact": see *Broadway Approvals* v. *Odhams Press* [1964] 2 Q.B. 683, and [1965] 1 W.L.R. 805 (C.A.), at p. 818.
[31] See, e.g., *Gray* v. *S.P.C.A.* (1890) 17 R. 1185.
[32] *Kemsley* v. *Foot* [1952] A.C. 345—"Lower than Kemsley."
[33] Ibid.; see also *Wheatley* v. *Anderson*, 1927 S.C. 133, per Lord Justice-Clerk Alness, at p. 143, and per Lord Anderson, at p. 147; cf. Lord Hunter, at pp. 145-6.

substratum of fact cannot reasonably be implied from the words published, they must be construed as an allegation of fact, thus excluding the defence of fair comment. (4) Fact and comment may be so bound up together that it is difficult to distinguish the one from the other. In that situation both pleas may be taken and the jury has to decide into which category, fact or comment, the statements respectively fall, under direction from the judge as to the legal effect of their classification.[34] (5) It is for the Court to decide as matter of law whether the statements founded on by the defender as comment may reasonably be classified in their context as such.[35] (6) If comment is so much mixed up with fact that they cannot reasonably be separated, the whole publication may have to be treated as containing allegations of fact only. The plea of fair comment would then fall to be repelled.[36] (7) If the defender establishes the substantial truth of the imputation, whether arising from fact or comment or both, the plea of veritas will be sustained, thereby rendering redundant a plea of fair comment.[37]

As has already been pointed out, the first requisite of a plea of fair comment is that the facts upon which the comment is based are proved or admitted to be true, and the defender may in his defences expand and elucidate facts which the libel clearly adumbrates.[38] It is no longer necessary to prove the truth of every such fact provided that sufficient is proved to enable the judge or jury to hold the comment to be fair.[39] Honest belief in the truth of such facts will not found the plea of fair comment but may mitigate damages.[40]

The second requisite is that the comment on or criticism of these facts must have been fairly and honestly made. In cases where the comment follows logically from a preceding narrative of facts, which are proved or admitted to be true, it may be possible for the Court to hold as matter of law that the criticism does not exceed the bounds of fair comment.[41] Normally it is for the jury to decide whether the comment was fairly and honestly made. There are two elements here. The first is that the comment must be warranted by true

---

[34] *Hunt* v. *Star Newspaper* [1908] 2 K.B. 309; *Aga Khan* v. *Times Publishing Co.* [1924] 1 K.B. 675, per Bankes, L.J., at pp. 680-1; *Jones* v. *Skelton* [1963] 1 W.L.R. 1362 (P.C.), at pp. 1379-80. Note that in *Sutherland* v. *Stopes* [1925] A.C. 47, the "rolled-up" plea was held to be a plea of fair comment only. See Gatley, pp. 437-438, and Walker, p. 844, fn. 7, for form of plea. See also *London Artists* v. *Littler* [1969] 2 Q.B. 375, where it was held that the defence of fair comment could not apply to an allegation of a plot as that was an allegation of fact.

[35] *Aga Khan* v. *Times Publishing Co.*, supra; *Jones* v. *Skelton*, supra.

[36] *Hunt* v. *Star Newspaper*, supra, per Fletcher Moulton, L.J., at pp. 319-20; approved by Lord Anderson in *Wheatley* v. *Anderson*, 1927 S.C. 133, at p. 147.

[37] See *Sutherland* v. *Stopes*, supra, per Viscount Cave, L.C., at p. 55; also Defamation Act 1952, (c. 66), s. 5.

[38] *Wheatley* v. *Anderson*, 1927 S.C. 133, per Lord Justice-Clerk Alness, at p. 143, and per Lord Anderson, at pp. 747-8: "The jury are entitled to know what was in the defender's mind when he made the comment." See also Gatley, pp. 300-305, and cases cited therein.

[39] See Defamation Act 1952, s. 6. Note that this section does not apply if any of the allegations of fact is defamatory: *Broadway Approvals* v. *Odhams Press* [1964] 2 Q.B. 683, and [1965] 1 W.L.R. 805 (C.A.), at p. 818.

[40] See Gatley, p. 294.

[41] See *Gray* v. *S.P.C.A.* (1890) 17 R. 1185 (in which the plea of fair comment could have been taken), per Lord M'Laren, at p. 1200; *Dakhyl* v. *Labouchère* [1908] 2 K.B., 325n., per Lord Atkinson, at p. 329; *M'Quire* v. *Western Morning News Co.* [1903] 2 K.B. 100, per Collins, M.R., at pp. 110-1.

facts, stated or implied, in the sense that upon those facts a fair-minded man might reasonably hold that opinion.[42] This is an objective test and the jury are not entitled to substitute their own opinion for that of the defender.[43] Moreover, every latitude must be given to opinion and to prejudice.[44] The test for a theatrical review has been stated to be:—"Would any fair man, however prejudiced he may be, however exaggerated or obstinate his views, have said that which this criticism has said of the work which is criticised?"[45] But criticism cannot be used as a cloak for mere invective or for personal imputations not arising out of the subject matter.[46] Accordingly, if a personal attack on the character of a public man or the author of a published work or a public entertainer is mounted upon facts which, although true, do not warrant such an attack, the defence of fair comment will fail. The second element is that the comment must be honestly made. The right of comment is exercisable in the public interest, not for the gratification of the writer's personal spite. Therefore, as in the case of qualified privilege, the motives of the critic are relevant and his honest belief in the opinions expressed is an ingredient to be considered by the jury in determining whether that which has been written or said exceeds the limits of fair comment.[47] Proof of malice may take a criticism prima facie fair outside the limits of fair comment by demonstrating that the predominant purpose of the critic was not to criticise for the benefit of the public but to injure the pursuer.[48]

The third requisite of the defence of fair comment is that the comment must be upon a matter of public interest. This covers a wide field.[49] It is in the public interest that the conduct of public officials should be open to criticism,[50] but the right does not extend to criticism of their character or private conduct[51] unless their fitness for office is being questioned.

17. Verbal Injury.[52]—The basic distinction which the Courts have drawn between statements which are per se or by innuendo defamatory in the narrow

[42] *Wheatley* v. *Anderson,* supra; *Peter Walker & Son Ltd.* v. *Hodgson* [1909] 1 K.B. 239, per Buckley, L.J., at p. 253.
[43] *M'Quire* v. *Western Morning News,* supra, per Collins, M.R., at p. 109.
[44] *Merivale* v. *Carson* (1887) 20 Q.B.D. 275, per Lord Esher, M.R., at p. 280. "The basis of our public life is that the crank, the enthusiast, may say what he honestly thinks just as much as the reasonable man or woman who sits on a jury": per Diplock, J., in *Silkin* v. *Beaverbrook Newspapers* [1958] 1 W.L.R. 743, at p. 747.
[45] *Merivale* v. *Carson,* supra, per Lord Esher, M.R., at p. 281; and see *Crotty* v. *Macfarlane,* referred to in Glegg at p. 178.
[46] *M'Quire* v. *Western Morning News,* supra, per Collins, M.R., at p. 109.
[47] For this reason alone it is submitted that the plea of fair comment is not open to a newspaper which has published a letter by an unknown writer: see *Brims* v. *Reid* (1885) 12 R. 1016, and *M'Kerchar* v. *Cameron* (1892) 19 R. 383, referred to in § 12, supra, fn. 90.
[48] *Thomas* v. *Bradbury Agnew & Co.* [1906] 2 K.B. 627; *Silkin* v. *Beaverbrook Newspapers* [1958] 1 W.L.R. 743, per Diplock J., at p. 747; *Broadway Approvals* v. *Odhams Press* [1965] 1 W.L.R. 805 (C.A.); cf. the comment at p. 178 of Glegg on *Reparation* on Lord Stormonth-Darling's opinion in *Crotty* v. *Macfarlane.*
[49] See Walker, pp. 846-50.
[50] *Langlands* v. *Leng,* 1916 S.C. (H.L.) 102, per Viscount Haldane, at pp. 106-7.
[51] *Gray* v. *S.P.C.A.* (1890) 17 R. 1185, per Lord M'Laren, at p. 1200.
[52] See Walker, Vol. II, at pp. 736-46, where he divides verbal injury into three categories, namely, defamation, convicium and malicious falsehood. For a different, and cogent, view of the nature of verbal injury and the characteristics which distinguish it from slander see T. B. Smith: *Short Commentary,* pp. 724-732. That view still awaits, however, recognition in modern judicial authority.

sense of the word[53] and other false injurious statements is that, whereas, in the case of the former, malice is irrelevant and once the defamatory statements are proved to have been made, they are presumed to be false, a pursuer who founds on statements of the latter type must not only prove that they have been made by the defender but must also aver and prove that they were untrue and were made with deliberate intent to injure him or at least with such reckless disregard of injury as to yield the inference of such intent.[54] Certain statements which are not defamatory, in respect that they do not impugn the morality, solvency or business capacity of the person regarding whom they are made, may be actionable as "verbal injury." One case is where the pursuer maintains that a statement holds him up to public hatred and contempt, as by ascribing to him the expression of unpopular opinions.[55] Mere ridicule, where the element of public hatred is absent, is not actionable.[56] Where a pursuer takes an issue of public hatred and contempt, the onus of proving the untruth of the statement, i.e., of proving that he had not expressed the opinion ascribed to him, lies upon him. Moreover, at common law he had to prove some specific injury which had resulted. But now by the Defamation Act 1952[57] it is provided that special damage need not be proved if the words on which the action is based "are calculated to cause pecuniary damage."

18. Slander of Title: of Property.[58]—Other forms of verbal injury are known as slander of title and slander of property, in which the pursuer must also aver and prove that the statements were untrue and were made maliciously. Slander of title is an assertion that the pursuer has no right to an article, or no right to dispose of it, as where a patentee said that the article the pursuer proposed to sell was an infringement of his patent.[59] Slander of property imports a statement reflecting on the pursuer's property. On this basis an issue was allowed on an allegation that a row of houses was built on an insecure foundation,[60] and that typhoid fever had broken out in a dairy.[61] But it does not amount to verbal injury for a dealer to state that his article is better than that of his rival, and to give reasons for his statement, even although his reasons involve disparagement of the rival commodity.[62]

19 Title to Sue.—Anyone who is defamed has a title to sue.[63] A

[53] See § 1, supra.
[54] *Paterson* v. *Welch* (1893) 20 R. 744, per Lord President Robertson, at p. 749; *Lamond* v. *Daily Record*, 1923 S.L.T. 512; *Steele* v. *Scottish Daily Record*, 1970 S.L.T. 53. See comments in Walker, supra, p. 740.
[55] *Paterson* v. *Welch*, supra; *Waddell* v. *Roxburgh* (1894) 21 R. 883; *Lamond* v. *Daily Record*, supra.
[56] *M'Laughlin* v. *Orr* (1894) 22 R. 38.
[57] s. 14 (*b*).
[58] See Walker, pp. 904-9, where additional categories of slander of goods and business are included.
[59] *Harpers* v. *Greenwood* (1896) 4 S.L.T. 116; *Philip* v. *Morton* (1816) Hume 865. There is a statutory remedy for such statements (Patents Act 1949 (12, 13 & 14 Geo. VI, c. 87), s. 65; Patents Act 1977 (c. 37), s. 70).
[60] *Bruce* v. *Smith* (1898) 1 F. 327.
[61] *M'Lean* v. *Adam* (1888) 16 R. 175.
[62] *White* v. *Mellin* [1895] A.C. 154; *Hubbuck* v. *Wilkinson* [1899] 1 Q.B. 86.
[63] Note that one spouse may now sue the other but that the Court has power to dismiss such an

defamatory statement about a person deceased does not afford any action to his representatives, unless, possibly, it can be read as amounting to a reflection on them.[64] When the injurious statement is made of a class of persons, it is a question of degree whether that class is sufficiently limited in numbers to make an imputation on the class an imputation on the individual.[65] A member of an association cannot sue if the statements are comments upon the society and not upon individual action.[66] A company or corporate body or voluntary association cannot bring an action on a statement merely reflecting on its moral character,[67] but has the same right as an individual in respect of its business interests.[68] Two or more persons may sue together in one action in respect of one defamatory statement alleged to refer to one or other or all of them provided that each concludes separately for damages.[69]

20. Parties Liable.[70] — The person who originates, and the person who repeats, a defamatory statement, are equally liable in damages. A common report may be proved in mitigation of damages, though not as a complete defence to the action.[71] A printer or publisher may be sued.[72] Persons, such as newsagents or librarians, who circulate a publication alleged to be defamatory, may escape liability by proving that they did not know that the publication contained a libel and that their ignorance was not due to negligence on their part.[73] The liability of an agent who publishes defamatory matter on the instructions of his principal follows that of his principal unless the agent is entitled to plead privilege in his own right.[74] The principles of vicarious liability for slander by an agent are the same as for master and servant.[75] It is incompetent to conclude for damages jointly and severally against two or more defenders in respect of separate slanders without averments of conspiracy.[76]

21. Damages.[77] — A pursuer who proves that he has been defamed is eo

action if it appears that no substantial benefit would accrue to either party: see Law Reform (Husband and Wife) Act 1962 (10 & 11 Eliz. II, c. 48), s. 2.

[64] *Broom* v. *Ritchie* (1904) 6 F. 942; and see Walker, pp. 757-8.

[65] *Campbell* v. *Ritchie,* 1907 S.C. 1097; *Browne* v. *Thomson,* 1912 S.C. 359; *Knupfer* v. *London Express Newspaper* [1944] A.C. 116; and see Walker, pp. 752-4.

[66] *Campbell* v. *Wilson,* 1934 S.L.T. 249.

[67] *Manchester Corporation* v. *Williams* [1891] 1 Q.B. 94; *Highland Dancing Board* v. *Alloa Publishing Co.,* 1971 S.L.T. (Sh.Ct.) 50; but see *Bognor Regis Urban District Council* v. *Campion* [1972] 2 Q.B. 169.

[68] *North of Scotland Bank* v. *Duncan* (1857) 19 D. 881; *Highland Dancing Board* v. *Alloa Publishing Co., supra.* and see cases in Walker, pp. 754-5.

[69] *Mitchell* v. *Grierson* (1894) 21 R. 367. Compare *Golden* v. *Jeffers,* 1936 S.L.T. 388 (truly a case of a conspiracy to slander) with *Turnbull* v. *Frame,* 1966 S.L.T. 24.

[70] As to the legality of an indemnity, see Defamation Act 1952, c, 66, s. 11.

[71] *Macculloch* v. *Litt* (1851) 13 D. 960.

[72] *A.B.* v. *Blackwood* (1902) 5 F. 25.

[73] *Emmens* v. *Pottle* (1885) 16 Q.B.D. 354; *Vizetelly* v. *Mudie* [1900] 2 Q.B. 170; and see *Morrison* v. *Ritchie* (1902) 4 F. 645, per Lord Moncreiff, at p. 651.

[74] See Gatley, p. 373; *Adam* v. *Ward* [1917] A.C. 309, per Lord Finlay, L.C., at p. 320; and fn. 7, supra, re solicitors.

[75] See Reparation, Ch. XXXIV, § 24, fn. 70; also Walker, p. 818.

[76] *Hook* v. *M'Callum* (1905) 7 F. 528; *Turnbull* v. *Frame,* 1966 S.L.T. 24; *Golden* v. *Jeffers,* 1936 S.L.T. 388.

[77] See Walker, pp. 790-2; also Walker on *Damages,* Ch. 25.

ipso entitled to an award of damages, which may be nominal.[78] In addition he may recover special damages on proof that he has suffered or is likely to suffer financial loss. Evidence of the circumstances of publication may aggravate the damages, e.g., proof of deliberate intention, recklessness or persistent repetition.[79] Ground for mitigation, on the other hand, has been found in the fact that there was provocation to make the statement, that there was probably cause for making it, that it was common talk and that the pursuer had a bad character.[80] By the Defamation Act 1952[81] it is competent to mitigate by proving that damages have been recovered or action has been brought in respect of publication of words similar to those on which the action is based, or that the pursuer has settled or agreed to settle in respect of such a publication. A tender in a defamation action must offer not only a sum of money but also a withdrawal and apology.[82]

22. Expenses.—A pursuer who, in Court of Session proceedings, obtains a verdict in his favour with damages less than £5 cannot recover expenses unless the presiding judge certifies that the action was brought for the vindication of character, and was in his opinion fit to be tried in the Court of Session.[83] Where a tender is lodged, and the damages ultimately awarded are less than the amount tendered, the tender has not its normal effect of entitling the defender to expenses after its date unless it is accompanied by a retraction and apology. But it is sufficient to offer an apology without any admission that the statement complained of was made.[84] The Defamation Act 1952 makes provision for awards of expenses when an offer of amends is made.[85]

ABUSE OF LEGAL PROCESS

23. Criminal Charge.[86]—To give information to the police or criminal authorities, to institute a prosecution, or, in the case of a party entitled to arrest, to arrest on suspicion of a crime, are acts which are not actionable on the ground that they were founded on a mistake, only on averments and proof of malice and want of probable cause.[87] Facts and circumstances from which malice may be inferred must be stated. A conviction on the charge made is fatal to the action, since it proves that probable cause existed[88]; an acquittal standing by itself is not enough to establish that there was no probable

[78] *Bradley* v. *Menley and James,* 1913 S.C. 923, per Lord Justice-Clerk Macdonald, at p. 926.
[79] See Cooper, *Law of Defamation,* (2nd ed.), p. 250; *Cunningham* v. *Duncan* (1889) 16 R. 383.
[80] Cooper, op. cit., p. 254; *C.* v. *M.,* 1923 S.C. 1; *Bryson* v. *Inglis* (1844) 6 D. 363; *Hobbs* v. *Tinling* [1929] 2 K.B.1.
[81] c. 66, s. 12.
[82] See Walker, p. 792, for cases.
[83] Court of Session Act 1868 (31 & 32 Vict., c. 100), s. 40. *Bonnar* v. *Roden* (1887) 14 R. 761.
[84] *Malcolm* v. *Moore* (1901) 4 F. 23.
[85] s. 4 (4) (*b*).
[86] See Walker, pp. 874-9.
[87] *Hill* v. *Campbell* (1905) 8 F. 220; *Mills* v. *Kelvin & White,* 1913 S.C. 521; *Notman* v. *Commercial Bank of Scotland,* 1938 S.C. 522. And see § 14, supra.
[88] *Hill* v. *Campbell,* supra.

cause.[89] Procurators-fiscal and deputes acting on the authority of the Lord Advocate enjoy the same absolute privilege as the Lord Advocate in relation to prosecutions on indictment.[90] Quoad summary proceedings there is at common law no distinction in the law applicable in an action directed against a public or a private prosecutor.[91] By statute, however, actions against the former arising out of proceedings under Part II of the Criminal Procedure (Scotland) Act 1975 are subject to a statutory time limit, and are competent only where the pursuer has suffered imprisonment and the proceedings have been quashed; express provision is moreover made that it is a defence to such an action that the pursuer was guilty of the offence in question and had undergone no greater punishment than was assigned by law.[92] "A man has probable cause if, in giving the information, he is acting in a way in which a reasonable man, swayed by no illegitimate motives, would act."[93] A letter, intimating the charge, and followed by a prosecution, is to be taken as part of the prosecution, and its actionability to be judged by the same standards.[94]

24. Unfounded Litigation.[95]—No damages can be claimed for bringing a civil action, even if it proves to be unfounded. It would seem a doubtful point whether averments that the action in question was brought maliciously would make a claim for damages relevant.[96] It is not wrong to take a decree irregularly, as where a decree in absence was obtained when the defender had not been properly cited, provided that no diligence has followed on the decree. If it has, averments and proof of malice will found a claim for damages.[97]

25. Wrongful Diligence.[98]—The use of diligence may found a claim for damages either because it has been carried out irregularly, or because it was used on some untenable claim. Irregular diligence of any kind is a wrong which is in no way privileged. It may be irregular either because it proceeds on an insufficient warrant,[99] or because the statutory forms have not been observed. In either case the creditor who sets the diligence in motion is personally liable, though the actual fault or mistake may be on the part of the solicitor,[1] messenger-at-arms, or sheriff officer.[2] Probably the solicitor is only liable for his own act or omission,[3] not for a mistake on the part of the

[89] *Chalmers* v. *Barclay, Perkins & Co.,* 1912 S.C. 521.
[90] *Hester* v. *Macdonald,* 1961 S.C. 370.
[91] *Chalmers,* supra.
[92] The time allowed is two months, 1975 Act (c. 21), s. 456; *Graham* v. *Strathern,* 1924 S.C. 699.
[93] Per Lord President Dunedin in *Mills* v. *Kelvin & White,* supra, 1913 S.C., at p. 528.
[94] *Chalmers,* supra.
[95] See Walker, pp. 851-62
[96] See *Hallam* v. *Gye* (1835) 14 S. 199.
[97] *M'Gregor* v. *M'Laughlin* (1905) 8 F. 70.
[98] See Walker, at pp. 862-74.
[99] See *M'Gregor* v. *M'Laughlin* (1905) 8 F. 70, as to the distinction between taking a decree irregularly and using diligence upon it.
[1] *Smith* v. *Taylor* (1882) 10 R. 291; *Clarke* v. *Beattie,* 1909 S.C. 299, per Lord President Dunedin, at pp. 303-4.
[2] *Le Conte* v. *Douglas* (1880) 8 R. 175.
[3] *M'Robbie* v. *M'Lellan's Trs.* (1891) 18 R. 470.

officials he employs.[4] A messenger-at-arms or sheriff officer is not liable unless he knew, or should have known, that the diligence was irregular.[5]

Where the ground for an action of damages is that diligence has been done on an unfounded or untenable claim, the law depends on the nature of the diligence. Certain forms of diligence, of which arrestment and poinding are examples, can be carried out on the appropriate warrant without any special application to the Court. In these cases there is no liability for a mere mistake, as in the case where property is arrested or poinded for a debt which has in fact been paid. In order to found action there must be averments and proof of malice and want of probable cause.[6] Other forms of diligence, including landlord's sequestration[7] and certain statutory warrants for arrestment,[8] are granted, as is interim interdict,[9] only on an ex parte statement of facts which render them necessary. Such forms are granted periculo petentis, and the person who applies for them is responsible for the truth of the statement he makes, and will be liable in damages if that statement proves to be untrue. No privilege is involved, and therefore there is no necessity for averments of malice or of want of probable cause.[10]

[4] *Henderson* v. *Rollo* (1871) 10 M. 104; Graham Stewart, *Diligence*, p. 799.
[5] *Clarke* v. *Beattie*, 1909 S.C. 299.
[6] *Wolthekker* v. *Northern Agricultural Co.* (1862) 1 M. 211; *Grant* v. *Magistrates of Airdrie*, 1939 S.C. 738, 758.
[7] *Gray* v. *Weir* (1891) 19 R. 25; *Shearer* v. *Nicoll*, 1935 S.L.T. 313.
[8] *Gray* v. *Magistrates of Airdrie*, supra.
[9] *Kennedy* v. *Fort-William Commissioners* (1877) 5 R. 302; *Glasgow District Ry.* v. *Glasgow Coal Exchange* (1885) 12 R. 1287; *Clippens Oil Co.* v. *Edinburgh Water Trustees*, 1907 S.C. (H.L.) 9 (measure of damages).
[10] *Wolthekker*, supra; *Grant*, supra.

CHAPTER XXXVI

PROPERTY: HERITABLE AND MOVEABLE

Erskine's *Institutes*, II; Bell's *Principles*, §§ 1470-1505; Dobie's *Manual of the Law of Liferent and Fee*.

1. Property or Ownership.—In the Civil Law property was analysed into three rights: usus (or right of use); fructus (or right of enjoying its fruits); and abusus (or right of using and disposing of it). Erskine speaks of property as "the right of using and disposing of a thing as our own."[1] It is seldom, if ever, that these rights are enjoyed without restriction. The owner of a house, for example, nowadays finds himself restrained in the exercise of his powers at various points, not only by the necessity for respecting the rights of others, but also by State and municipal regulations of the widest range and complexity.[2] Or it may be, as in the case of an heir of entail, that the conditions of his title disable him from exercising one or other of these rights. But despite such restrictions, the right in the subjects may nevertheless be such as is regarded in law as property. Erskine recognises this, for he qualifies the words quoted above by adding "except in so far as we are restrained by law or paction."

It is clear, therefore, that a person may have a right of property in a subject although he does not possess all the above powers to their full extent. One or more of the constituent rights which go to make up the aggregation which constitutes property in the fullest sense may be detached and enjoyed apart from the residue without necessarily reducing the sum of the remaining rights below the measure of what is recognised as property. It is not uncommon, for example, for the right of possession and enjoyment of the fruits to be severed from the other rights in the subject. B has a liferent of property inherited by A, or is tenant under a lease of part of A's estate. In each of these cases B has a limited right in the estate, but A's right would remain a right of property. Or, again, it may be that A holds lands in common with others. Here also his right is one of property, although his power over the land is necessarily limited by the rights of his co-owners.

Property is the largest right which can be possessed in a subject. As the illustrations given above indicate, there may be more limited rights. The owner of a liferent or servitude over another's estate has a right in that estate; the liferent and servitude belong to the class of jura in re aliena, but they are not rights of property, nor would their owner be described as proprietor of the estate. "Two different persons cannot have each of them the full property of the same thing at the same time,"[3] but these inferior rights may exist consistently with the right of property in another person. Subject to the

---

[1] *Inst.*, II, 2, 1; see *Anstruther* v. *Anstruther* (1836) 14 S. 272, at 286.
[2] See, e.g. Town and Country Planning (Scotland) Act 1972 (c. 46), passim.
[3] Erskine, *Inst.*, II, 1, 1.

existence of such rights the owner or owners of a subject have an exclusive right which enables them to prevent others from interfering with it.[4] The owner of land may interdict others from trespassing on it, and the owner of rights may prevent others from infringing these rights.

2. Classification of Property.—"Property," in Erskine's definition, is used as meaning ownership. But the term is also employed with another significance. It is commonly used to denote the subjects of ownership: such things as are owned and have material value. The citizen has certain rights as regards his person, reputation and liberty, but these are not considered to be property as they have no patrimonial value. Nor can there be property in a person,[5] or in such things as the air, or the sea, or the water flowing in a stream, although the water may become property when it is appropriated.[6]

Property, when it is used as meaning the subjects of ownership, may be classified in various ways. Thus there is corporeal property, consisting of things such as a house, or book, or money; and incorporeal property, consisting of rights. Typical instances of incorporeal property are patent rights, copyright, goodwill, and a jus crediti or right to a debt due by another. Jura in re aliena are always incorporeal. These rights may be of great value and will be included among the assets of the owner if he becomes bankrupt, and will pass on his death to his representatives or heirs. Another distinction is between fungibles and non-fungibles. Fungibles are such things as are estimated by weight, number or measure, and which can be replaced by equal quantities and qualities, e.g., money and grain. It is clearly a matter of indifference to a lender whether he receives repayment of his loan in the actual coin lent or others of like value. On the other hand, a horse or a picture is not fungible because "their values differ in almost every individual."[7] But of all the classifications, the most important is that which divides property according as it is heritable or moveable.

3. Heritable and Moveable Property.—The nomenclature here is not beyond criticism. "Heritable" points to succession; "moveable" refers to the nature of the subject. "Anything is called moveable, which, by its nature and use, is capable of motion"; immoveables "are called heritable, because they descend not to executors, to whom only moveables befall, but to heirs, and so the distinction cometh ordinarily of moveables and heritables."[8] This distinction applies to both corporeal and incorporeal property. It is now of

---

[4] "Correctly speaking, property imports dominium—the entire and exclusive dominion over the thing spoken of—the proprietor being the dominus and having the sole disposal of it,"—Bell, *Comm.*, I, 177.

[5] *Reavis* v. *Clan Line Steamers,* 1925 S.C. 725.

[6] *Morris* v. *Bickel* (1864) 2 M. 1082, per Lord Neaves; affd. 4 M. (H.L.) 44.

[7] Erskine, *Inst.*, III, 1, 18.

[8] Stair, II, 1, 2. In English law the term corresponding to "heritable" is "real," to "moveable," "personal." But the words "real" and "personal" are used in a different sense in Scots Law. A "real" right is one which affects the subject itself; a "personal" is one which is founded in obligation (Erskine, III, 1, 2; IV, 1, 10). A person having a right to lands has a "real" right if he has completed his title by the appropriate legal procedure (e.g. infeftment); his right is "personal" if he has not done so. A burden on lands is said to be "real" if it is so imposed that

less significance than formerly, since by virtue of the Succession (Scotland) Act 1964 both heritable and moveable property fall to be administered by the executor; but it remains important in questions relating to testate succession and legal rights.[9]

4. Land and its Pertinents.—The typical instance of heritable (or immoveable) property is land with its pertinents. Stones and minerals, as constituents of the land, are heritable until they are removed from the land, when they become moveable.[10] Trees also, as partes soli, while unseparated from the ground are heritable[11]; cut timber, on the other hand, is moveable. The natural fruits of the land which do not require seed and cultivation are also, while unseparated, heritable. It is laid down in the institutional writers that industrial crops are considered to be moveable as they "go with the property of the seed and labour as manufactures in which the productive powers of the soil are employed"[12]; but it is explained in *Chalmers's Tr.* v. *Dick's Tr.*[13] that the true position is that the crop before separation is pars soli, and, therefore, heritable, but that the tenant who has sown it is allowed by the law to separate and remove it unless he has contracted not to do so.

5. Fixtures.—When a moveable thing is brought into connection with heritage, the question may arise in a variety of circumstances as to the effect of this connection upon the moveable. On this matter a mass of decisions (not always reconcilable) has accumulated, embodying the law of fixtures.[14] The word "fixture" is used in more than one sense. It has been authoritatively defined as meaning anything annexed to heritable property, that is, fastened to or connected with it, and not in mere juxtaposition,[15] and it is in this sense that the term is used here. The annexation may be either to the soil directly or to something, such as a building, which itself has become annexed to the soil. In the case of a building the term "fixture" signifies something which has been affixed as accessory to the house, and does not include things, such as windows, which were made part of the structure of the house when it was constructed.[16] In accordance with the maxim "Inaedificatum solo, solo cedit"

---

it attaches to the lands, whoever the owner of them may be. Similarly, a vitium reale or "real" defect is one which affects the subject, into whosesoever hands it may come; thus, if goods be stolen, the theft is said to be a vitium reale, i.e. a defect in the title not only of the thief but of anyone who acquires them from the thief. See General Law of Obligations, Ch. III, supra, § 10.

[9] See Legal Rights, Ch. XL, infra § 1; Intestate Succession, Ch. XLI, § 4.
[10] *Bruce* v. *Erskine* (1707) M. 14092.
[11] *Paul* v. *Cuthbertson* (1840) 2 D. 1286; see also *Burns* v. *Fleming* (1880) 8 R. 226 (ornamental shrubs planted by a tenant). See Sale of Goods, Ch. XVII, supra, § 2.
[12] Erskine, *Inst.*, II, 2, 4; Bell, *Prin.*, § 1473; see also McLaren on *Wills and Succession*, I, p. 197.
[13] 1909 S.C. 761. Cf. *English Hop Growers* v. *Dering* [1928] 2 K.B. 174, per Scrutton and Sankey L.JJ.
[14] See Rankine on *Landownership*, 4th ed., pp. 116 et seq.; Amos and Ferrard on *Fixtures* (3rd ed., 1883); Adkin and Bowen's *Law relating to Fixtures* (1923); *Elwes* v. *Maw* (1802) 2 Smith's *Leading Cases* (12th ed.), p. 188; Smith, *Short Commentary*, p. 500.
[15] *Brand's Trs.* v. *Brand's Trs.* (1876) 3 R. (H.L.) 16, per Lord Chelmsford, at p. 23. The word is also used as meaning removable fixed things, *Re de Falbe* [1901] 1 Ch. 523, per Rigby and Stirling L.JJ., at 530 and 538; Amos and Ferrard, p. 2.
[16] *Boswell* v. *Crucible Steel Co.* [1925] 1 K.B. 119.

all buildings and things annexed to the soil "are accounted as parts of the ground."[17] To this rule, as Lord Cairns points out in *Brand's Trs. v. Brand's Trs.*,[18] there is no exception. The owner of the moveable before it was annexed to the heritable loses on annexation his right of property in it; and, while it is annexed, it must, as part of the heritage, belong to the owner of the heritage. It has been held to be a legal impossibility, apart from statute, to sever property in land from property in pipes and drains traversing the land.[19] A second general rule is that what has once become part of the heritage cannot lawfully be severed and removed by a limited owner. But to this rule exceptions are allowed. In certain circumstances the limited owner has the right to sever and remove that which he has annexed to the heritage. Two questions, therefore, usually arise:—First, has the thing been so affixed to the heritage as to become part of it? Secondly, assuming this to be so, can the thing, in a question with the owner of the heritage, be removed?

In the solution of these questions the test which has been applied in the more modern cases is the purpose and object of the annexation: was it the improvement of the heritage or the more complete and better enjoyment of the thing annexed that was the object and purpose?[20] This is to be discovered from the circumstances of the case.[21] And the matters to which attention is mainly directed are the mode and degree of the annexation and the effect of the removal, that is, whether the thing can or cannot be removed without injury to itself and to the heritable property. As a rule, there must be some physical attachment between the thing and the heritage. Prima facie, an article which is unattached is not a fixture; there may, however, be circumstances in virtue of which, despite its non-attachment, an article is regarded as part of the heritage, but the onus lies on those who assert that this is so.[22] Thus, articles retained in position merely by their own weight may be so specially adapted to a building or to their surroundings as to become fixtures.[23] So also articles accessory to a principal, which is heritable, may be fixtures, although there is no physical connection between the principal and the accessory. Such things are known as constructive fixtures. Thus the keys of a house, the bell of a factory,[24] and the loose articles which are necessary for the use of fixed machinery, provided these articles are so constructed as to form part of the

---

[17] Stair, II, 1, 40.
[18] Supra. This was followed in *Miller* v. *Muirhead* (1894) 21 R. 658, and *Howie's Trs.* v. *McLay* (1902) 5 F. 214. There are observations in English cases inconsistent with it; see *Wake* v. *Hall* (1883) 8 App.Cas. 195, and *Re Hulse* [1905] 1 Ch. 406. In *Dowall* v. *Miln* (1874) 1 R. 1180, Lord Justice-Clerk Moncreiff discusses the law of fixtures.
[19] *Crichton* v. *Turnbull*, 1946 S.C. 52.
[20] *Spyer* v. *Phillipson* [1931] 2 Ch. 183; *Re de Falbe* [1901] 1 Ch. 523, affd. sub nom. *Leigh* v. *Taylor* [1902] A.C. 157; *Hobson* v. *Gorringe* [1897] 1 Ch. 182; *Simmons* v. *Midford* [1969] 2 Ch. 415.
[21] *Hobson* v. *Gorringe*, supra.
[22] *Holland* v. *Hodgson* (1872) L.R. 7 C.P. 328, per Blackburn J. See *Assessor for Glasgow* v. *R.N.V.R. Club (Scotland)*, 1974 S.L.T. 291.
[23] *Niven* v. *Pitcairn* (1823) 2 S. 270; *D'Eyncourt* v. *Gregory* (1866) L.R. 3 Eq. 382 (unattached vases and statues forming part of architectural design); *Monti* v. *Barnes* [1901] 1 K.B. 205 (heavy dog-grates substituted for fixed grates). See also *Christie* v. *Smith's Exr.*, 1949 S.C. 572, a summer-house remaining in position by weight alone: *Oman* v. *Ritchie*, 1941 S.L.T. (Sh. Ct.) 13.
[24] *Barr* v. *McIlwham* (1821) 1 S. 124.

particular machine and are not equally capable of being applied in their existing state to other machines of the same kind, are notionally fixtures.[25]

On the other hand, the mere fact that there is some attachment to the heritage is not conclusive. Things so slightly attached as carpets nailed to the floor, or pictures hanging from a nail in the wall of a house, or a tent placed on the land, are not fixtures.

Questions as to fixtures may arise between parties standing to each other in various relationships and the right in the fixtures is affected by the nature of the relationship. In the cases which most commonly occur the conflicting interests are those of (1) (prior to the Succession (Scotland) Act 1964) the heir and executor as to fixtures added by their ancestor; (2) the seller and the buyer of heritage; (3) a heritable creditor maintaining that fixtures added by the debtor are included in the heritage covered by his security, and the general creditors of the debtor; (4) a liferenter of the heritage and his representatives, on the one hand, and the owner of the fee on the other; and (5) a tenant and his landlord.

Where the rival claimants were the heir and the executor the rule which sinks the fixture in the heritage was applied with most rigour.[26] As both derived their title from the deceased owner of the heritage, there was no reason for favouring the latter at the expense of the former. The problem remains, although the executor now administers both the heritable and the moveable estate of the deceased, in deciding whether an item is heritable or moveable for the purposes of legal rights. Where the fixture has been annexed by one who was owner of the heritage, the question is not whether he has lost, for the benefit of another, the right to recover the property in the fixture, but whether, as his property, it would have passed in one or the other line of his succession. The question depends, therefore, on the character of the fixtures whether they are or are not part of the heritage.[27] In the case of a bequest of heritage the terms of the will may indicate the extent of the bequest; otherwise, the legatee is in the same position as the heir-at-law under the previous law of intestate succession.

In the case of the seller and purchaser of heritage, the terms of the contract may show what is included. If this is not so, although there may be room for allowing greater weight to the element of intention,[28] the rule appears to be the same as in that of heir and executor. The question is one of fact, viz. has the article been so permanently affixed as to become part of the heritage or, on the other hand, is it so attached that it can be removed without injury to itself and the heritage?[29] On the sale of a house it was held (after a remit to a reporter) that built-in grates, lustres, gas-brackets, and mirrors were removable by the seller.[30]

[25] *Fisher* v. *Dixon* (1845) 4 Bell's App. 286; *Brand's Trs.* v. *Brand's Trs.*, supra.
[26] *Elwes* v. *Maw* (1802) 2 Smith's *Leading Cases* (12th ed.) p. 188; *Norton* v. *Dashwood* [1896] 2 Ch. 497.
[27] *Brand's Trs.* v. *Brand's Trs.*, supra, per Lord Chelmsford.
[28] *Cochrane* v. *Stevenson* (1891) 18 R. 1208, per Lord Kyllachy.
[29] Ibid., per Lord Kinnear; *Jamieson* v. *Welsh* (1900) 3 F. 176.
[30] *Nisbet* v. *Mitchell-Innes* (1880) 7 R. 575; see also *Cowans* v. *Assessor for Forfarshire*, 1910 S.C.

The same rule applies in a question between a heritable creditor and the general creditors, or a trustee in bankruptcy,[31] in valuation cases,[32] and in determining the appropriate diligence to be used with reference to fixtures.[33]

When the question arises between a landlord or fiar on the one hand, and the tenant or liferenter on the other, considerations of public policy have led to a more liberal admission of the right to remove the fixture. Both the liferenter and the tenant have no more than a temporary right in the heritage, and if a fixture cannot be removed the result is that the property in it is irrevocably transferred to the owner of the heritage. This being so, it is for the general advantage that the liferenter and the tenant should not be discouraged from making additions to the heritage by the operation of a rule of law which would make these for all time the property of the owner of the heritage.

It has long been settled, therefore, that a tenant may remove fixtures attached by him for the purposes of his trade[34]; and he may also remove such articles as he has annexed for ornament or for the better enjoyment of the article itself.[35] There is this limitation on that right, that the articles must be such as can be removed without material injury to the heritage and without being destroyed or losing their essential character or value.[36] But it will not prevent plant and machinery being removable that it is necessary for this purpose to take them to pieces, provided they can be fitted together in the same form in another place.[37]

In leases of agricultural subjects the common law was less favourable to the tenant[38]; but in holdings to which the Agricultural Holdings (Scotland) Act 1949[39] applies, the matter is now regulated by section 14 of that Act. Any engine, machinery, fencing or other fixture affixed by a tenant, and any building erected by him remain (under certain conditions specified in the section), the property of the tenant and removable by him up to six months from the expiry of the lease.

The case of the liferenter or his representatives has not been regarded as so strong as that of the tenant; but the tendency has been to place them in very much the same position as the tenant.[40] A liferenter may remove articles annexed for the purpose of trade or ornamentation under the same limitations as apply in the case of the tenant.

---

810. Electrical off-peak storage heaters were held to be heritable: *Assessor for Fife* v. *Hodgson,* 1966 S.C.30 (but, as to valuation for rating, see Local Government (Scotland) Act 1966 (c. 51), s. 20).

[31] *Reynolds* v. *Ashby & Sons* [1904] A.C. 466; *Holland* v. *Hodgson,* supra, *Monti* v. *Barnes,* supra, and *Howie's Trs.* v. *McLay* (1902) 5 F. 214.

[32] *Weir* v. *Assessor for Glasgow,* 1924 S.C. 670, at 682; but see *Assessor for Fife* v. *Hodgson,* 1966 S.L.T. 79.

[33] Stewart on *Diligence,* p. 70.

[34] *Syme* v. *Harvey* (1861) 24 D. 201; *Marshall* v. *Tannoch Chemical Co.* (1886) 13 R. 1042.

[35] *Spyer* v. *Phillipson* [1931] 2 Ch. 183.

[36] Amos and Ferrard, pp. 71, 72.

[37] *Whitehead* v. *Bennett* (1852) 27 L.J.Ch. 474; *Pole-Carew* v. *Western Counties Manure Co.* [1920] 2 Ch. 97.

[38] Hunter on *Landlord and Tenant* (4th ed.), 312; Rankine on *Leases* (3rd ed.), 301.

[39] 12 & 13 Geo. VI, c. 75; see *Leases,* Ch. XXXII, supra, § 25.

[40] *Re Hulse* [1905] 1 Ch. 406; *Fisher* v. *Dixon* (1845) 4 Bell's App. 286, per Lord Cottenham, at 356.

The right to remove a fixture as it exists under the above rules of the law may be modified by agreement. The person affixing the article may do so on the terms that he is to be entitled to remove it, although under the general law it might not be removable, and an agreement to this effect will be binding on the parties who have entered into it. But seeing that the right rests upon contract it does not bind those who are strangers to the contract. Thus in *Hobson* v. *Gorringe*[41] an engine was supplied on the hire-purchase system by the plaintiff to King, the owner of a saw-mill, on the terms that it was not to become his property until all 'he instalments had been paid, and that on default in payment of any instalment it was to be removable by the plaintiff; and the engine was so attached to the heritage as to become part of it. King did not complete the required payments, and therefore never became owner of the engine in terms of the agreement with the plaintiff. He granted a mortgage over his property in favour of the defendant who was unaware of the terms of the agreement, and who on King's bankruptcy entered into possession of the premises. In a competition between the plaintiff and the defendant, it was held that the former could not remove the engine: it had become part of the heritage, and, as such, was included in the mortgage, and the right of removal reserved under the agreement was not enforceable as against a creditor who had in ignorance of it taken a security over the heritage. So also an agreement of this kind would not be effectual as against a bona fide purchaser of the heritage. A purchaser has an opportunity of forming his own judgment as to whether a fixture is or is not removable under the general rules of the law, but cannot be affected by contracts which have not been brought to his knowledge.

6. Destination.—Even without actual annexation, corporeal moveables may, by destination, become part of the heritage in questions of succession, if the deceased has unequivocally manifested an intention to unite them to the heritage. Thus window-frames and building material collected on the ground for use in a building in the course of erection by a deceased person[42] and the funds required to complete it[43] have been held to be heritable quoad the succession to his estate.

In a question as to the succession to a tenant of a farm, the dung made on the farm was held to belong to the heir, as the tenant was under an obligation to apply it to the land, and it was to be presumed that his intention was to fulfil that obligation.[44]

7. Rights.—Passing from corporeal property to rights, the general rule is that these are heritable or moveable according to the nature of the subject

---

[41] [1897] 1 Ch. 182; see also *Reynolds* v. *Ashby* [1904] A.C. 466, and *Ellis* v. *Glover & Hobson* [1908] 1 K.B. 388.
[42] Erskine, *Inst.*, II, 2, 14; *Johnston* v. *Dobie* (1783) M. 5443; *Gordon* v. *Gordon*, 1806, Hume 188; cf. *Stewart* v. *Watson's Hospital* (1862) 24 D. 256.
[43] *Bank of Scotland* v. *White's Trs.* (1891) 28 S.L.R. 891; *Malloch* v. *McLean* (1867) 5 M. 335; see *Fairlie's Trs.* v. *Fairlie's Curator Bonis*, 1932 S.C. 216, per Lord President Clyde.
[44] *Reid's Executors* v. *Reid* (1890) 17 R. 519.

matter. Rights connected with land (such as leases and servitudes) are heritable; a claim to money is, on the other hand, moveable. Thus, even claims for indemnification against the loss of, or injury to, heritable property are moveable.[45] Shares in companies[46] and the interest of a partner in a firm and its property, are moveable although the property may include heritable subjects[47]; so are rights of patent and copyright.[48] It is a question of circumstances whether the goodwill of a business is so connected with the premises in which it is carried on as to be heritable; otherwise it is moveable.[49]

8. Feu-Duties and Rents.—These, as the produce of heritable subjects, are heritable. But in a question of succession the arrears are moveable, for the law "suffers not chance to govern but supposes everything to be performed which ought to have been performed and will not put it in the power of a dilatory debtor to hurt the executor." In other words, the arrears are treated as being in the pocket of the creditor.[50] The liability for arrears of feu-duty is primarily a burden on the moveable and not on the heritable estate of the deceased vassal.[51]

9. Heritable Securities.—From their connection with lands, sums secured over heritage were under the common law heritable as regards both the creditor's and debtor's succession. By section 117 of the Titles to Land Consolidation (Scotland) Act 1868,[52] such securities are made moveable as regards the general succession of the creditor, but by express provision of the statute they remain heritable as to the fisc (i.e., the Crown's right to the moveable estate of a person denounced rebel), and as regards the legal rights of spouses and issue (i.e. are not now subject to legal rights at all).[53] It is no longer possible to make a bond heritable for all purposes by taking a destination excluding executors.[54] The 1868 Act altered the law with reference only to the succession of the creditor; and such debts still remain heritable in a

---

45 *Heron* v. *Espie* (1856) 18 D. 917, at 951; *Caledonian Ry.* v. *Watt* (1875) 2 R. 917; *Kelvinside Estate Co.* v. *Donaldson's Trs.* (1879) 6 R. 995. A right of freshwater fishing is heritable: Freshwater and Salmon Fisheries (Scotland) Act 1976 (c. 22), s. 4.
46 Companies Act 1948, s. 73; *Hog* v. *Hog* (1791) M. 5479.
47 Partnership Act 1890, s, 22; *Lord Advocate* v. *Macfarlane's Trs.* (1893) 31 S.L.R. 357; *Murray* v. *Murray* (1805) M., "Heritable and Moveable," App. No. 4; *Minto* v. *Kirkpatrick* (1833) 11 S. 632; see also *Irvine* v. *Irvine* (1851) 13 D. 1267.
48 *Advocate-General* v. *Oswald* (1848) 10 D. 969; Patents Act 1977, s. 31 (2); Copyright Act 1956 (4 & 5 Eliz. II, c. 74), s. 36 (1).
49 *Muirhead's Trs.* v. *Muirhead* (1905) 7 F. 496; see Moveable Property—Incorporeal, Ch. XXXVIII, infra, § 27.
50 *Martin* v. *Agnew* (1755) M. 5457, 5 Brown's Sup., 830; *Logan's Trs.* v. *Logan* (1896) 23 R. 848; *Watson's Trs* v. *Brown,* 1923 S.C. 228.
51 *Johnston* v. *Cochran* (1829) 7 S. 226.
52 31 & 32 Vict., c. 101, as amended by Succession (Scotland) Act 1964, Sch. 3. For the definition of "heritable security," as used in the Act, see s. 3. It does not include "securities by way of ground annual, whether redeemable or irredeemable, or absolute dispositions qualified by back bonds or letters." Securities by way of real burden are moveable quoad succession (Conveyancing (Scotland) Act 1874 (37 & 38 Vict., c. 94) s. 30, as amended by Succession (Scotland) Act 1964, Sch. 3). Section 117 of the 1868 Act applies to a standard security (Conveyancing and Feudal Reform (Scotland) Act 1970 (c. 35), s. 32).
53 See Legal Rights, Ch. XL, infra, § 1.
54 See Meston, *Succession (Scotland) Act 1964* (2nd ed., 1969), p. 46.

question between the debtor's heirs and representatives.[55] If a creditor in a heritable security in his will makes different dispositions of his heritable and moveable estate, without referring specifically to the security, it will fall under the disposition of the moveable estate.[56]

10. Personal Bonds.—The veneration which the feudal system commanded in ancient times led to the inclusion under heritable property of rights which had no connection with heritable property. Rights were so treated for no better reason than that they had a certain degree of permanence, and, therefore, should be given to the heir in heritage. This is illustrated in the case of the rights noticed in this and the next paragraph. Under the common law "contracts and obligations for sums of money" containing clauses for payment of interest were from the first heritable if the date of payment were uncertain or distant, and became in any case heritable after the first term at which the interest or capital was payable.[57]

But the Bonds Act 1661 (c. 32) (re-enacting an earlier statute[58]) altered this and made such contracts and obligations moveable. The statute contains a provision that if the bond contains an express obligation to infeft the creditor in security of the debt, or excludes the executors of the creditor, it is to remain heritable. The statute also expressly left such bonds heritable quoad fiscum, and the widow's jus relictae, but the latter exception has been abolished by the Conveyancing (Scotland) Act 1924.[59]

11. Rights Having a Tract of Future Time.—"These are rights of such a nature that they cannot be at once paid or fulfilled by the debtor, but continue for a number of years, and carry a yearly profit to the creditor while they subsist, without relation to any capital sum or stock, e.g. a yearly annuity or pension for a certain number of years."[60]

An annuity is heritable and, as such, a burden on the heritable succession of the person liable to pay it, although the termly payments as they become due are moveable.[61] So also where a liferent right was assigned, it was held that this passed to the heir, and not the executor, of the assignee.[62] But where there is a capital sum or stock, its character will determine that of its fruits or income. Thus the income of a sum of money is always moveable.[63]

12. Conversion.—The character of property may be altered by conversion, actual or constructive. Thus the quality of the beneficial right in subjects held

---

[55] *Bell's Trs.* v. *Bell* (1884) 12 R. 85.
[56] *Hughes' Trs.* v. *Corsane* (1890) 18 R. 299.
[57] See *Heath* v. *Grant's Trs.,* 1913 S.C. 78, and cases there cited.
[58] 1641, c. 57.
[59] 14 & 15 Geo. V, c. 27, s. 22.
[60] Erskine, *Inst.,* II, 2, 6.
[61] *Hill* v. *Hill* (1872) 11 M. 247; *Reid* v. *McWalter* (1878) 5 R. 630; *Marquis of Breadalbane's Trs.* v. *Jamieson* (1873) 11 M. 912; *Countess de Serra Largo* v. *De Serra Largo's Trs.,* 1933 S.L.T. 391.
[62] *Allan* v. *Williamson,* 1741, Elchies' *Heritable,* No. 12; *Drummond* v. *Ewing,* 1752, Elchies' *Heritable,* No. 16.
[63] *Hill* v. *Hill,* supra.

in trust depends on the nature of these according as they are heritable or moveable; but that quality may be constructively converted from heritable into moveable, or vice versa, by the terms of the truster's directions or by what is found to be necessary in the course of the trust administration. So also rights in the succession may be affected by contracts entered into by the deceased for the purchase or sale of heritage, the completion of which by the necessary deed of conveyance has been interrupted by his death. These questions are considered elsewhere.[64]

[64] See Intestate Succession, Ch. XLII, infra, § 8, and Executors, etc., Ch. XLIV, § 11.

CHAPTER XXXVII

MOVEABLE PROPERTY: CORPOREAL

Temperley: *Merchant Shipping Acts* (7th ed., 1976) (British Shipping Laws, Vol. II).

1. Possession.—From the long controversy among jurists as to the nature of possession various theories have emerged, an account of which may be found in works on general jurisprudence. In this place it is necessary to refer only to the views of the institutional writers in our law, and among these there is substantial agreement on this matter. According to Stair, possession is the holding or detaining of anything by ourselves or others for our use. "To possession there must be an act of the body which is detention and holding; and an act of the mind which is the inclination or affection to make use of the thing detained."[1] The material element, the detention, must depend to some extent on the nature of the thing possessed; since it is obviously impossible, for example, to require the same kind of acts in regard to heritage as in regard to moveables. "By possession is meant possession of that character of which the thing is capable."[2] The mental element, the act of the mind, is the intention to hold the thing for one's own benefit. This is presumed from the fact of detention unless the holding of the thing as his own would infer a crime on the part of the holder.[3] The person who holds or detains the thing is not required to prove that he does so with this intention; it rests on him who disputes it to establish its absence. The absence of the animus possidendi distinguishes custody from possession. A servant in charge of his master's property is not regarded as possessing it; he has the custody, but not the possession of it.[4] It is not necessary, however, that the subject should be held on a rightful title; a thief holding the goods stolen is possessor of these, as both elements of the definition are satisfied.

Possession is divided into natural and civil.[5] Natural possession is actual possession of the subject. Thus the owner of a moveable is in natural possession if he keeps it in his hands or repositories; the owner of land if he cultivates it; the owner of a house if he occupies it. Civil possession is possession through an intermediary or representative. Thus a person possesses things through his servants or agents or custodiers for his behoof; a landlord through his tenant[6]; trustees owning a house through a liferenter in possession.[7]

---

[1] Stair, II, 1, 17; see also Erskine, *Inst.*, II, 1, 20; Bankton, I, 510. See Smith, *Short Commentary*, p. 461.
[2] *Young* v. *N.B. Ry.* (1887) 14 R. (H.L.) 53, per Lord Fitzgerald, at p. 56.
[3] Erskine, *Inst.*, II, 1, 20.
[4] Stair, Erskine and Bankton, supra; *Barnton Hotel Co.* v. *Cook* (1899) 1 F. 1190. For observations as to the distinction between custody and possession, see *Sim* v. *Grant* (1862) 24 D. 1033.
[5] Erskine, *Inst.*, II, 1, 22; Bell, *Prin.*, § 1312.
[6] *Union Bank* v. *Mackenzie* (1865) 3 M. 765.
[7] *Mitchell's Trs.* v. *Gladstone* (1894) 21 R. 586.

Possession is exclusive. Two persons cannot each have the full possession of the same subject at the same time. But there may be concurrent possession by two or more persons having different rights which are not antagonistic. Thus a subject may be possessed by several persons in common; a tenant possesses for his own interest and at the same time the landlord possesses through him; a pledgee possesses the thing pledged and the proprietor also possesses so far as necessary to support his right of property.[8]

2. Presumption of Ownership.—Seeing that "there use not witnesses or writ to be adhibited in the commerce of moveables," the possessor of a corporeal moveable is, in a question with a wrong-doer or a person asserting an adverse title, presumed to be its owner.[9] This presumption may be displaced by proof; but the possessor is entitled to stand upon his possession and require his adversary to establish his right of property.[10] The latter must show not only that he lost possession but that he did so in some way consistent with the retention of the ownership, as, for instance, that the goods were stolen from him or that they passed from him by "some title not alienative of property as loan or the like."[11] In certain circumstances however, the presumption, if it exists at all, is but slight; there is little ground for presuming ownership from possession in the case of one, such as a carrier, whose avocation requires the possession by him of goods entrusted to him by others.[12]

3. Reputed Ownership: Effect of Possession.—The object of the doctrine of reputed ownership was to afford protection to creditors who had been misled by the false credit acquired by their debtor owing to his having been permitted to possess as apparent owner property which belonged to another; and its effect was to preclude the true owner from asserting his right against these creditors.[13] Owing to changes in the law this doctrine is no longer of much importance.[14] The occasions on which the possession of, and the property in, goods may be separated are so frequent that creditors and others transacting with the possessor are not warranted in assuming that he is the owner. Possession does not give the possessor even an apparent authority to dispose of the property; and the mere fact that the true owner has allowed another to be in possession of his property will not preclude him from asserting his right as against those who purport to have acquired the property or rights over it from the possessor.[15] Other circumstances must be present if the owner is to

---

[8] Erskine, *Inst.*, II, 1, 22-23.
[9] *Scot* v. *Elliot* (1672) M. 12727; Stair, II, 1, 42; III, 2, 7; IV., 30, 9; Erskine, II, 1, 24; *Macdougall* v. *Whitelaw* (1840) 2 D. 500. See also *Glenwood Property Co.* v. *Phillips* [1904] A.C. 405, at 410.
[10] *Brownlee's Exr.* v. *Brownlee,* 1908 S.C. 232, per Lord President Dunedin, at p. 239.
[11] *Russel* v. *Campbell* (1699) 4 Brown's Sup. 468; *Heriot* v. *Cunninghame* (1791) M. 12405.
[12] *Warrander & Stirling* v. *Alexander & Thomson* (1715) M. 10609. Sed quaere if a carrier has possession.
[13] See *Shearer* v. *Christie* (1842) 5 D. 132; Bell's *Comm.*, I, 269.
[14] *Robertsons* v. *McIntyre* (1882) 9 R. 772, per Lord Justice-Clerk Moncreiff.
[15] *Lamonby* v. *Foulds,* 1928 S.C. 89; *Mitchell* v. *Heys & Sons* (1894) 21 R. 600; *Robertsons* v. *McIntyre* (1882) 9 R. 772. Cf. *Jones* v. *Waring & Gillow* [1926] A.C. 670, per Lord Sumner, and *Mercantile Bank of India* v. *Central Bank of India* [1938] A.C. 287.

be personally barred from vindicating his property.[16] The possession by a liferenter will not entitle his creditors to carry away the goods to the prejudice of the fiar,[17] nor the creditors of a tenant to attach moveables held by him under a contract with his landlord, the true owner.[18]

4. Acquisition of Property: Occupation.—Property may be acquired either by an original title, as e.g. by occupation, or by a derivative title from the former owner. Occupation is the taking possession of a thing with the intention of becoming owner of it.[19] "Quod nullius est fit occupantis." This mode of acquisition is not applicable to heritage, because under the feudal system the sovereign is the original proprietor of all the land within his dominions, nor to things which once have had an owner. Property in things which have never had an owner, such as wild animals, may be acquired in this way. Without specific appropriation a wild animal, although protected and preserved on private property, does not belong to anyone,[20] and it will become the property of him who takes or kills it, although he may be a trespasser or acting in contravention of the law. A poacher acquires the property in the animals which he takes unless these are forfeited by statute.[21] If such animals have once been appropriated and possession of them is retained by him who has thus become their owner, they are not capable of being acquired by another by occupation. But if the animal escapes and reverts to its original liberty "the property is lost so soon as the owner ceaseth to pursue for possession,"[22] and it may again be acquired by this means. Domesticated animals, or such as have a homing instinct (pigeons, bees) or carry a mark indicating private property, are not acquired by one who seizes and detains them and thereby prevents their returning to their owner.[23]

5. Treasure-Trove; Lost Property; Wrecks.—Treasure discovered hidden in the ground, the ownership of which cannot be traced, belongs not to the finder or to the owner of the ground, but to the Crown.[24] Erskine[25] and Bell[26] state that goods lost, abandoned and ownerless (bona vacantia) also fall to the Crown under the rule "Quod nullius est fit domini regis." The Burgh Police Act 1892 provides that things which are found must be deposited with the chief constable or other officer acting for him, and, if unclaimed within six months, they may be awarded by the district court to the finder, and, if the

---

[16] *Bryce* v. *Ehrmann* (1904) 7 F. 5. See Agency, Ch. XXII, *supra* § 29, for the Factors Acts.
[17] *Scott* v *Price* (1837) 15 S. 916, per Lord Mackenzie.
[18] *Hogarth* v. *Smart's Tr.* (1882) 9 R. 964.
[19] Stair, II, 1, 33; Erskine, *Inst.*, II, 1, 10; Bell, *Prin.*, §§ 1287-94.
[20] *Wilson* v. *Dykes* (1872) 10 M. 444, per Lord Justice-Clerk Moncreiff.
[21] *Scott* v. *Everitt* (1853) 15 D. 288; see also *Leith* v. *Leith* (1862) 24 D. 1059, at 1062 and 1077; *Livingstone* v. *Breadalbane* (1791), 3 Pat. App. 221.
[22] Stair, supra.
[23] Erskine, *Inst.*, II, 1, 10; Bell's *Prin.*, § 1290. There are special rules applicable to whale-fishing— see *Sutter* v. *Aberdeen Arctic Co.* (1862), 4 Macq. 355; Bell's *Prin.*, § 1289.
[24] Stair, II, 1, 5; Erskine, II, 1, 12; *Gentle* v. *Smith*, 1 Bell's *Illustrations*, 184; cf. *Cleghorn & Bryce* v. *Baird* (1696) M. 13524; *Sands* v. *Bell & Balfour*, May 22, 1810, F.C.; *Lord Advocate* v. *University of Aberdeen*, 1963 S.C. 533.
[25] II, 1, 12.
[26] *Prin.*, § 1291 (3); but cf. Stair, I, 7, 3.

owner does not prove his ownership and the finder cannot be found within six months, they may be sold by order of the court and the proceeds applied to the purposes of the Act.[27] In England it has been held that bank-notes accidentally dropped in a shop by an unknown person belonged not to the shopkeeper, but to the finder[28]; articles embedded in the soil and discovered in the course of operations were held to belong not to the discoverer, but to the owner of the soil.[29] Strayed cattle, Erskine says, do not belong to the finder; he must give public notice, and if within a year and a day the proprietor does not claim his goods, they become escheat and fall to the Crown, sheriff, or other person to whom a grant has been made of such escheats. Under the Winter Herding Act 1686 (c. 11), the owner of "horses, nolt, sheep, swine or goats" straying on another's lands is made liable, in addition to his liability for any damage done, in a penalty of half a merk for each beast, and the beasts may be detained till this and the expenses of keeping them are paid.[30] Wrecks, which belonged to the Crown, but could be claimed by the owner of the ship if a living thing were found on board,[31] are now placed under the general superintendence of the Board of Trade, which has power to appoint receivers, to whom any person finding or taking possession of the wreck must give notice. Provision is made for the disposal of the wreck whether claimed or unclaimed by the owner.[32]

6. Accession.—In this way a person becomes owner of something of an accessory nature by reason of his ownership of another, the principal, subject.[33] "Accessorium sequitur principale." Thus the proprietor of an animal becomes proprietor of its offspring[34]; and things affixed to heritable property become part of that property.[35] On this ground also the interest produced by a fund and not otherwise disposed of has been held to belong to the owner of the fund.[36] This method of acquiring property is illustrated in the case of heritable rights. The imperceptible addition made to one's ground, as by the retreat of the sea or the shifting of a river bed or by what is washed by a river from other grounds (alluvio), accrues to the owner of the ground

[27] 55 & 56 Vict., c. 55, s. 412. (The Act is repealed from the end of 1982: Local Government (Scotland) Act 1978 (c. 4), s. 5.) "If the finder at once, or within a short period, appropriate the article, theft is committed": Macdonald's *Criminal Law* (5th ed.), p. 32; contra, Hume, I, 62, and Alison, I, 360-1. See also *Lawson* v. *Heatly,* 1962 S.L.T. 53; Gordon, *Criminal Law* (2nd ed., 1978), pp. 464 et seq. As to the finder's right to recover what he may have expended on the goods, see the opinion of Scrutton L.J. in *Jebara* v. *Ottoman Bank* [1927] 2 K.B. 254.
[28] *Bridges* v. *Hawkesworth* (1851) 15 Jur. 1079; see Smith, *Short Commentary,* p. 464.
[29] *Elwes* v. *Brigg Gas Co.* (1886) 33 Ch.D. 562; *South Staffordshire Water Co.* v. *Sharman* [1896] 2 Q.B. 44. See also *Att.-Gen.* v. *Trustees of British Museum* [1903] 2 Ch. 598, and Goodhart's *Essays in Jurisprudence,* p. 75.
[30] Erskine, II, 1, 12, and III, 6, 28; Rankine on *Landownership,* p. 611; *Fraser* v. *Smith* (1899) 1 F. 487; *McArthur* v. *Jones* (1878) 6 R. 41. The Act applies to gardens—*McArthur* v. *Miller* (1873) 1 R. 248.
[31] Bell's *Prin.,* § 1292.
[32] Merchant Shipping Act 1894 (57 & 58 Vict., c. 60), ss. 510 et seq.; *Lord Advocate* v. *Hebden* (1868) 6 M. 489.
[33] Erskine, II, 1, 14-15.
[34] *Lamb* v. *Grant* (1874) 11 S.L.R. 672.
[35] See Property, Heritable and Moveable, Ch. XXXV, supra, § 5.
[36] *Gillespies* v. *Marshall* (1802) M. "Accessorium" No. 2. Cf. *Stewart* v. *Stewart* (1669) M. 50. See McLaren on *Wills,* I, 329.

receiving the addition. On the other hand, where there is avulsio, a sudden and sensible addition to land as contrasted with alluvio, there is no transference of property. An island formed in a river belongs to the owner of the alveus at that spot.[37]

7. Specification.—This is the making of a new subject by one person with materials belonging to another. Apart from the works of the institutional writers, there is little authority either on this matter or on the kindred modes of acquiring property dealt with in the next section. In a passage[38] which was cited with approval in a modern case,[39] Bell (agreeing with Erskine) states the rules in these terms: "If the materials, as a separate existence, be destroyed in bona fide, the property is with the workman; the owner of the materials having a personal claim for a like quantity and quality, or for the price of the materials; if still capable of restoration to their original shape, the property is held to be with the owner of the materials; a claim against him for work and indemnity in quantum lucratus being competent to the workman." In the former case the operation has resulted in the creation of a new subject; but the equitable doctrine by which its ownership passes to the workman cannot be invoked if the materials or part of them were stolen by the workman from their rightful owner.[40]

8. Confusion of Liquids and Commixtion of Solids.—These "raise a common property, if the commodities be of the same kind; and of such property pro indiviso the shares are in proportion to quantity and value, where either the union is by common consent, or where, having been made by accident or without fault, the commodities are inseparable. The property is unchanged if the articles be capable of separation. If the union be of substances different, so as to create a tertium quid, the property is (according to the rule in specification) with the owner of the materials, or with the manufacturer, according to the possibility or impossibility of restoring the original substances."[41]

But, where two or more persons have agreed to contribute to the production of a new subject, either materials or skill and labour, or both, the subject will belong to them as common property in shares corresponding to the value of their respective contributions.[42]

9. Voluntary Transference of Property.—The law of Scotland requires for the voluntary transmission of property in corporeal moveables, both the

---

[37] Erskine, supra; Bell's *Prin.*, § 934; Rankine on *Landownership* (4th ed.) p. 112.

[38] Bell's *Prin.*, § 1298; see also Stair, II, 1, 41; Erskine, II, 1, 16. For the Civil Law, see *Inst.*, II, 1, 25 et seq.; Girard, *Manuel de Droit Romain*, 3, 2, 3, 4; Buckland's *Text Book of Roman Law*, (3rd ed.), p.215. The doctrine does not apply to the situation in which a motor vehicle has been sold to a "private purchaser" so as to give him a good title under the Hire-Purchase Act 1964: *North-West Securities* v. *Barrhead Coachworks*, 1976 S.L.T. 99; cf. *F. C. Finance* v. *Langtry Investment Co.*, 1973 S.L.T. (Sh. Ct.) 11.

[39] *International Banking Corporation* v. *Ferguson, Shaw & Sons*, 1910 S.C. 182.

[40] *McDonald* v. *Provan*, 1960 S.L.T. 231.

[41] This passage is taken from Bell's *Prin.*, § 1298 (2). Cf. Lord Moulton's speech in *Tyzack & Branfoot S.S. Co.* v. *Sandeman & Sons*, 1913 S.C. (H.L.) 84.

[42] *Wylie & Lochhead* v. *Mitchell* (1870) 8 M. 552.

intention or consent of the owner to the transmission and delivery of the subject in pursuance of that intention.[43] A contract to transmit the property is in itself ineffectual for that purpose; it creates nothing more than an obligation, on the one hand, to give, and a right, on the other, to receive, delivery. "A mere assignation of corporeal moveables retenta possessione is nothing whatever but a personal obligation"[44]; without delivery, the property or real right in the subject does not pass. "Traditionibus non nudis pactis transferuntur rerum dominia." This rule applies to all forms of contract for the transference of moveables. Thus in the case of donation inter vivos[45] it must be established that there were both the animus donandi and delivery of the thing which is gifted and clear proof is required, as the presumption is against donation.[46] "The donor must divest himself of, and, invest the donee with the subject of the gift."[47] Although a person has come under obligation to give a thing to one party, if he delivers it to another, the latter becomes the proprietor of the thing.[48] An exception to the rule has, however, been made by statute in the case of the sale of goods.[49] The necessity for, and the effect of tradition and the various modes of delivery, actual, symbolical and constructive,[50] have been considered in the earlier chapters dealing with the different classes of contracts. It has also been seen that contracts regarding moveables do not run with these moveables.[51] In *Leitch & Co.* v. *Leydon*[52] it was held that the pursuers, manufacturers who issued their goods in receptacles (of which they retained the property), could not interdict the defender from helping a member of the public in lawful possession of one of these receptacles to put it to a use which, although not injurious to it, was objected to by the pursuers.

10. Property in Ships.—Ships are moveable property, but are subject to special rules which require separate notice.[53] Considerations of national policy led the English Parliament, in the seventeenth century, to legislate in regard to shipping, and this legislation was copied in Scotland after the Restoration. The regulation of shipping thus introduced has been continued in modern times. The leading statute now in force is the Merchant Shipping Act 1894,[54] as amended in certain details by later statutes.

11. Registration of Ships.—Every British ship[55] (except river boats or

---

[43] Erskine, *Inst.*, II, 1, 18; Stair, III, 2, 5; Bell's *Comm.*, II, 11.
[44] *Clark* v. *West Calder Oil Co.* (1882) 9 R. 1017, per Lord President Inglis.
[45] See Testate Succession, Ch. XLII, infra, § 36.
[46] *Brownlee's Exrx.* v. *Brownlee*, 1908 S.C. 232; *Milne* v. *Grant* (1884) 11 R. 887; *Thompson* v. *Dunlop* (1884) 11 R. 453; *Grant's Trs.* v. *McDonald*, 1939 S.C. 448. See *Newton* v. *Newton*, 1923 S.C. 15.
[47] *McNicol* v. *McDougall* (1889) 17 R. 25, per Lord Young.
[48] Erskine, III, 3, 90.
[49] Sale of Goods Act 1893; see Sale of Goods, Ch. XVII, supra, §§ 7, 14 et seq.
[50] Rights in Security, Ch. XVIII, §§ 18-20.
[51] Title to Sue, Ch. X, § 14.
[52] 1931 S.C. (H.L.) 1. See also *Wilson* v. *Shepherd*, 1913 S.C. 300.
[53] Temperley's *Merchant Shipping Acts*, (7th ed.), 1976.
[54] 57 & 58 Vict., c. 60. The references hereafter to sections are to this Act.
[55] See s. 742 and Merchant Shipping Act 1921 (11 & 12 Geo. V, c. 28), s. 1; Merchant Shipping (Liability of Shipowners and Others) Act 1958 (6 & 7 Eliz. II, c. 62), s. 4 (1).

coasters not exceeding 15 tons burthen and certain Canadian boats of larger size[56]) must be registered.[57] The term "ship" includes every description of vessel used in navigation not propelled by oars. If a ship is not registered, it is not recognised as a British ship. A British ship is one owned wholly by (a) British subjects, including those who have become British subjects by naturalisation[58]; and (b) corporate bodies established under and subject to the laws of some part of Her Majesty's dominions, and having their principal place of business in those dominions.[59] An alien is not qualified to be owner of a British ship.[60]

12. Effect of Registration.—The register is the evidence of title to a ship. Possession of a ship does not prove the title to it, nor does the ship pass by delivery.[61] Before registration the ship must be surveyed by a surveyor,[62] she must be marked as prescribed in the statute,[63] and a declaration must be made as to the qualifications of the applicant to own a British ship, the time and place of building of the ship, the name of the master, the number of shares of which the applicant is entitled to be registered as owner, and that no unqualified person is entitled as owner to any legal or beneficial interest in the ship or any share of it.[64] The entry in the register gives the name and description of the ship, the names of those in whom the title to the ship or its shares is vested, and the port to which she belongs (i.e., the port at which she is registered).[65] After registration the registrar grants a certificate of registry.[66] Provision is made for registration anew, and for indorsation of alterations in the above particulars.[67] Change of the vessel's name can be made only with leave of the Board of Trade, must enter the register and the certificate, and must be marked on the vessel.[68]

In the register no notice is taken of trusts.[69] The registered owner of a ship or a share of it has an absolute power of disposition in the manner provided by the Act, and can give an effectual receipt for money paid or advanced as consideration.[70] But, without prejudice to this, "interests arising under contract or other equitable interests may be enforced by or against owners and mortgagees of ships in respect of their interest therein in the same manner as in respect of any other" moveable property.[71]

---

[56] s. 2.
[57] s. 3.
[58] See British Nationality Act 1948 (11 & 12 Geo. VI, c. 56), s. 1.
[59] s. 1.
[60] See Status of Aliens Act 1914 (4 & 5 Geo. V, c. 17) s. 17.
[61] *Hooper* v. *Gumm* (1867) L.R. 2 Ch. 282, per Lord Justice Turner.
[62] s. 6.
[63] s. 7.
[64] s. 9.
[65] s. 11.
[66] s. 14.
[67] ss. 20, 48-54; Merchant Shipping Act 1906 (6 Edw. VII, c. 48), ss. 53 and 85.
[68] s. 47.
[69] s. 56.
[70] Ibid.
[71] s. 57. See Rights in Security, Ch. XVIII, supra, §§ 21-2, as to mortgages of ships.

13. Shares.—The property of a ship is divisible into sixty-four shares.[72] No one can be registered for a fraction of a share, and not more than sixty-four owners can be registered at the same time. A corporate body or not more than five persons may be registered as owning a share, these persons holding jointly as one person.[73] Where a registered share passes by operation of law on the marriage, death or bankruptcy of the registered owner, or by lawful means other than a transfer under the Act, to more persons than one, these persons are for the purposes of registration counted as one person.[74] Sea-fishing boats are owned in sixteen shares by sixteen individuals at the most, and otherwise under the same rules.[75]

14. Transfer.—The deed by which a registered ship or a share therein is transferred to a person qualified to own a British ship is a bill of sale,[76] "the universal instrument of transfer of ships in the usage of all maritime countries."[77] A form of bill is given in the statute; it contains the names of the parties, the consideration for the transfer, and a description of the vessel. It must be witnessed[78] and must be produced to the registrar at the port of registry along with a declaration of transfer setting forth the qualification of the transferee to own a British ship.[79] It is the duty of the registrar to enter in the register the name of the transferee and to endorse the fact on the bill itself[80] and until the register is thus altered the former owner remains in a position to dispose of the ship or his shares in it.[81] These provisions relate to the mode of transfer of the property in a ship or shares of a ship; a contract for the sale of these is valid although made without writing.[82]

---

[72] s. 5.
[73] Ibid.
[74] s. 27.
[75] Sea Fishing Boats (Scotland) Act 1886 (49 & 50 Vict., c. 53).
[76] s. 24.
[77] *The Sisters* (1804) 5 Ch. Rob. 159; *Chasteauneuf* v. *Capeyron* (1882) 7 App.Cas. 127.
[78] First Schedule.
[79] ss. 25 and 26.
[80] s. 26.
[81] s. 56.
[82] *McConnachie* v. *Geddes,* 1918 S.C. 391.

CHAPTER XXXVIII

MOVEABLE PROPERTY: INCORPOREAL

Terrell, *Law of Patents* (12th ed., 1971); Blanco White, *Patents for Inventions* (4th ed., 1974); Kerly, *Law of Trade Marks and Trade Names* (10th ed., 1972); Copinger and Skone-James, *Law of Copyright* (11th ed., 1971); Carter-Ruck and Skone-James, *Copyright* (1965); Russell-Clarke, *Copyright and Industrial Design* (4th ed., 1968); Gow, *Mercantile Law* (1964).

WITHIN the category of incorporeal moveable property are included subjects so diverse as rights to debts (nomina debitorum) or obligations, claims ex contractu and ex delicto, rights to shares in companies, goodwill, patents, copyright and trade marks and names. Some of these are dealt with in other parts of this book. Patents, copyright and trade marks are noticed in the concluding paragraphs of the present chapter. The law on these matters is statutory, and as any question which may arise can be determined only by reference to the precise language of the statutes, nothing more than a brief reference to their leading provisions has been attempted. The main topic for consideration here is the mode and effect of the transference of incorporeal moveable property.

1. Assignations.—Corporeal moveables, as was shown in the preceding chapter, are transferred by delivery or possession. This is impossible in the case of incorporeal property; and, therefore, some deed by which it may be made clear that the right in the property has passed from the owner to another is required. The deed by which this is accomplished is known as an assignation. This term is applied to deeds conveying either such moveable rights or rights in heritage which are either incapable of infeftment or on which infeftment has not followed. If the subject is heritage, and the deed is granted by one who is infeft in that heritage, it is styled a disposition.[1] The grantor of an assignation is known as the cedent; the grantee as the assignee or (less commonly) cessionary. It is a general rule that unilateral deeds are not effective unless they are delivered.[2]

As a general rule anyone in right of a subject may at pleasure convey it to another. The exceptions to this are few. An alimentary provision and rights which are personal to the creditor from the delectus personae or choice made of him by the grantor of the right cannot be assigned.[3] Strictly speaking, a liferent is not assignable, but its profits may be assigned.[4] A conditional obligation, or spes successionis, may be assigned, and the assignation will

[1] Stair, III, 1, 1 and 16; Erskine, *Inst.*, II, 7, 2, and III, 5, 1. Erskine's view that a particular moveable subject is transmitted by assignation and not by disposition is controverted by Ross (*Lects.*, I, 189) and Menzies (*Conveyancing*, p. 270).
[2] *Connell's Trs.* v. *Connell's Tr.*, 1955 S.L.T. 125.
[3] Erskine, *Inst.*, III, 5, 2; see Title to Sue, Ch. X, supra § 18.
[4] See Liferent and Fee, Ch. XL, infra, § 11.

become effectual if the condition is purified or the spes comes to be vested in the cedent.[5]

2. Form of Assignation.—In the earliest times it was considered that a creditor could not substitute another as creditor in his place without the consent of the debtor; and, consequently, a direct assignation of a debt was impossible. Hence the device was hit upon of making the assignee the mandatory of the cedent for the purpose of exacting and discharging the debt but without any obligation to account to the cedent. The older bonds were in the form of mandates, but in course of time deeds of direct conveyance came into use and have long been sanctioned. The Transmission of Moveable Property (Scotland) Act 1862,[6] without prohibiting the use of the forms then in existence, provides short forms of assignation.

But no particular form need be adopted.[7] "If anything is settled in the law of Scotland it is that no words directly importing conveyance are necessary to constitute an assignation but that any words giving authority or directions, which if fairly carried out will operate a transference, are sufficient to make an assignation."[8] Thus a bill of exchange drawn by a beneficiary for whom trustees held funds on these trustees in favour of another was treated as constituting an assignation in his favour[9]; and a writing containing the words "I hand over my life policy to my daughter," was held to be a valid assignation of the grantor's right in the policy.[10]

3. Obligations of Cedent.—In assignations the law implies that the cedent confers on his assignee everything which is necessary to make the assignation effectual.[11] It is also implied that the cedent warrants that the debt is subsisting: that the bond, decree or other deed assigned is such as can never be reduced: and that the cedent has undoubted right to the debt.[12] But there is no implied warranty of the solvency of the debtor.[13]

4. Intimation.—As between the cedent (or his executor) and the assignee the execution and delivery of the assignation is sufficient to give the latter a valid right.[14] But for the purpose of giving the assignee a right effectual as against all parties, intimation of the assignation to the debtor or holder of the fund is necessary. By this means the assignation is brought to the knowledge of the debtor or holder so as to interpel him from paying the debt or making over the fund to the original creditor or to any other assignee; and if thereafter he chooses to do so, this will afford him no defence to the claim by

[5] *Bedwells & Yates* v. *Tods*, Dec. 2, 1819, F.C.; *Kirkland* v. *Kirkland's Tr.* (1886) 13 R. 798, at p. 805.
[6] 25 & 26 Vict, c. 85
[7] In regard to special subjects there may be statutory provisions as to the mode of transfer.
[8] *Carter* v. *McIntosh* (1862) 24 D. 925, per Lord Justice-Clerk Inglis. See Bills of Exchange, Ch. XXVI, supra, § 27.
[9] *Carter* v. *McIntosh*, supra.
[10] *Brownlee* v. *Robb*, 1907 S.C. 1302.
[11] *Miller* v. *Muirhead* (1894) 21 R. 658.
[12] *Barclay* v. *Liddel* (1671) M. 16591; *Reid* v. *Barclay* (1879) 6 R. 107.
[13] Ibid.; Erskine, *Inst.*, II, 3, 25.
[14] *Thome* v. *Thome* (1683) 2 Brown's Sup. 49; Stair, III, 1, 15.

the assignee who gave him intimation.[15] Further, it has long been settled that intimation is necessary to complete the assignee's right. "The assignation itself is not a complete valid right till it be orderly intimated to the debtor."[16] It is the point from which the passing of the right is dated and also the criterion by which the right of the assignee is determined in a question with other assignees or claimants to the fund or debt. If A, having assigned a debt due to him to B, subsequently assigns it to C, the assignation to C, although later in date, will, if it is first intimated, carry the debt. So also an arrestment prior in date to the intimation, though subsequent to the assignation itself, will prevail over the assignation; but if it is later in date than the intimation, the assignation will be preferred.[17] Further, the intimation of the assignation of a debt will prevent the debtor X from pleading compensation against the assignee B, in respect of a debt due by the cedent A, which X has acquired after the date of the intimation; the right to the debt having passed from A with the intimation, there is no proper concourse of credit and debt between the same persons.[18] But if prior to the intimation the right to compensate was vested in the debtor X, then it will be available to him against the assignee B.[19] The intimation also has the effect of making it incompetent to prove any exception against the debt, whether of payment or otherwise, by the oath of the cedent unless the subject has been rendered litigious before intimation or the assignee admits on reference to his oath that the assignation is gratuitous or in trust for the cedent.[20]

5. Forms of Intimation.—The old, and still competent, form of regular intimation was that a procurator for the assignee delivered to the debtor in the presence of a notary and witnesses a copy of the assignation and took instruments in the notary's hands.[21] But by the Transmission of Moveable Property Act 1862 alternative forms are introduced. These are:—(a) delivery by a notary of a certified copy of the assignation, or (b) transmission by the holder of the assignation or his agent of a certified copy by post, the first being vouched by the notary's certificate of intimation, the second by the debtor's written acknowledgment. The latter mode was valid at common law. Of a complex deed only a copy of the part containing the assignation need be sent. Where there are several obligants, as in the case of trustees, or joint debtors, intimation should be made to all unless some one or more of them take the whole management; for otherwise, while intimation to one would complete the assignation, it would not interpel the others from paying the cedent.[22] An

---

[15] See *McGill* v. *Laureston* (1558) M. 843; *McDowal* v. *Fullerton* (1714) M. 576, 840.
[16] Stair, III, 1, 6; Erskine, *Inst.,* III, 5, 3; Bell, *Comm.,* II, 16; *Liquidator of Union Club* v. *Edinburgh Life Assurance Co.* (1906) 8 F. 1143, per Lord McLaren.
[17] Stair, III, 1, 43 and 44; Erskine, *Inst.,* III, 6, 19; *Liquidator of Union Club* v. *Edinburgh Life Assurance Co.* (1906) 8 F. 1143.
[18] See Extinction of Obligations, Ch. XV, supra, § 13; *Macpherson's J. F.* v. *Mackay,* 1915 S.C. 1011; *Wallace* v. *Edgar* (1663) M. 837; *Chambers' J. F.* v. *Vertue* (1893) 29 R. 257.
[19] *Shiells* v. *Ferguson, Davidson & Co.* (1876) 4 R. 250.
[20] *Lang* v. *Hislop* (1854) 16 D. 908.
[21] For details see Bell's *Lectures on Conveyancing,* (3rd ed.), I, 311.
[22] Erskine, *Inst.,* III, 5, 5; *Jameson* v. *Sharp* (1887) 14 R. 643. See *Browne's Tr.* v. *Anderson* (1901) 4 F. 305.

absentee may be notified in the statutory modes, or at the edictal citation office. According to the common law, a corporation is notified through its treasurer; a bank, through the manager and the agent of the branch where the fund lies; and a firm, through all its partners, or a manager, if such there be, formally appointed.[23] In the Companies Act 1948,[24] it is provided that documents may be served on a company by delivery at, or posting to, the company's registered office.

6. Equivalents of Intimation.—The law admits equivalents of intimation where the notice of the assignation given to the debtor is equally strong. Thus, diligence or a suit against the debtor founded on the assignation at the instance of the assignee, or a claim in a multiplepoinding to which the debtor is a party supplies the want of intimation, as these are judicial and public acts which bring the assignation to the eyes of the public and of the debtor.[25] The assignee's possession of the right by entering into enjoyment of the rents or interest is also equal to an intimation, for it imports not only notice to, but actual compliance by, the debtor.[26] An assignation of a lease, or of the rents and profits of land, is perfected by intimation to the landlord and the assignee's possessing the ground or levying the rents. Assignations to heritable bonds, real burdens, registered leases and securities over these are completed by registration in the Register of Sasines[27]; but the registration of assignations of personal rights as bonds, contracts, etc., in the Books of Council and Session or of the Sheriff Courts does not suffice, as these are merely for preservation and diligence and not for publication.[28] Notice to the common debtor's factor in entire control of the estate, followed by entry thereof in his books,[29] and an assignee's attending and voting at the meeting of a company in virtue of the share assigned to him[30] have also been held sufficient proof of intimation.

In a competition between an unintimated assignation and other claims, the defect in the assignee's title due to the absence of intimation will not be cured by the fact that the debtor was aware of the assignation.[31] But the following have been held to be equivalents of intimation:—a written promise by the debtor, to pay the debt to the assignee[32]; payment by him of part of the

---

[23] *Hill* v. *Lindsay* (1846) 8 D. 472; but see Partnership Act 1890, s. 16.
[24] 11 & 12 Geo. VI, c. 38, s. 437.
[25] *Whyte* v. *Neish* (1622) M. 854; *Dougall* v. *Gordon*, (1795) M. 851.
[26] Erskine, *Prin.*, III, 5, 3.
[27] *Edmond* v. *Mags, of Aberdeen* (1858) 3 Macq. 116.
[28] *Tod's Trs.* v. *Wilson* (1869) 7 M. 1100; see *Cameron's Trs.* v. *Cameron*, 1907 S.C. 407.
[29] *Earl of Aberdeen* v. *Earl of March*, 1730, 1 Pat. 44.
[30] *Hill* v. *Lindsay* (1847) 10 D. 78.
[31] *Lord Rollo* v. *Laird of Niddrie* (1665) 1 Brown Sup. 510. It would seem (although the point is not altogether clear) that, according to the decisions even where there is no such competition, the debtor's knowledge of the assignation will not render him liable to the assignee if he pay the debt to the cedent while no intimation has been given. See Stair, II, 1, 24, and More's Note CCLXXXI; Bell, *Comm.*, II, 18; *Dickson* v. *Trotter*, (1776) M. 873, Hailes' *Decs.*, 675; *Faculty of Advocates* v. *Dickson*, (1718) M. 866; *L. Westraw* v. *Williamson & Carmichael*, (1626) M. 859; *Adamson* v. *McMitchell* (1624) M. 859; and cf. *Leith* v. *Garden*, (1703) M. 865, and Erskine, *Inst.*, III, 5, 5.
[32] *Home* v. *Murray*, (1674) M. 863.

capital, or the interest, of the debt[33]; the participation by him as a party[34] (not as a witness[35]) to the assignation.

If the assignation is granted to the debtor in the obligation, or to or by the person to whom intimation would in the ordinary course fall to be made, intimation is unnecessary. Thus, where the beneficiary under a trust was also the sole trustee, it was held that intimation of an assignation by him was not required, seeing that he intimated it to himself as trustee when he granted the deed.[36]

7. Effect of Assignation.—The effect of an assignation is to place the assignee in the shoes of the cedent. He may sue and do diligence to enforce the right which has been assigned to him. But that right is vested in him subject to all the contingencies which affected the author. "Assignatus utitur jure auctoris."

No higher right can be conferred by the cedent than that which he himself possesses. "Nemo plus juris ad alium transferre potest quam ipse habet."[37] Thus a person who has a temporary right, or one which is liable to be withdrawn or defeated, cannot give to his assignee a permanent or absolute right; if the right comes to an end or is withdrawn or defeated, the assignee's right falls.[38] In *Johnstone-Beattie* v. *Dalziel*[39] a sum was settled by a father in his daughter's marriage-contract in trust to pay a sum on his death to the husband. The husband assigned this sum in security to creditors. Subsequently he was divorced and thereby forfeited his right to the sum, and it was held that the right of his assignees was resolved by this forfeiture. So also, if trustees have a discretionary power to withdraw or reduce the interest of a beneficiary the exercise of that power will be effectual in a question with one to whom the beneficiary has assigned his interest.[40]

Moreover, the right passes to the assignee subject to all the pleas and exceptions pleadable by the debtor against the cedent. As against the assignee the debtor may avail himself of every defence which would have been competent to him against the cedent; and it matters not that the assignee is a bona fide purchaser.[41] Thus, if a person who takes out an insurance on his life is guilty of misrepresentations which render the policy reducible in a question with him, this is pleadable by the insurance company against an onerous assignee of the insurer.[42] And if one party to a contract assigns it, the other may maintain against the assignee the claims arising out of the contract or in

---

[33] *Livingston* v. *Lindsay*, (1626) M. 860.
[34] *Turnbull* v. *Stewart*, (1751) M. 868.
[35] *Murray* v. *Durham*, (1622) M. 855.
[36] *Browne's Trs.* v. *Anderson* (1901) 4 F. 305; *Russel* v. *Breadalbane* (1831) 5 W. & S. 256.
[37] Dig., 50, 17, 54.
[38] "Resoluto jure dantis, resolvitur jus accipientis."
[39] (1868) 6 M. 333.
[40] *Chambers' Trs.* v. *Smiths* (1878) 5 R. (H.L.) 151; *Train* v. *Clapperton*, 1907 S.C. 517; affd. 1908 S.C. (H.L.) 26.
[41] Stair, I, 10, 16, III, 1, 20, and IV, 40, 21; Erskine, *Inst.*, III, 5, 10; *McDowells* v. *Bell & Rennie* (1772) M. 4974.
[42] *Scottish Widows' Fund* v. *Buist* (1876) 3 R. 1078, 5 R. (H.L.) 64; *Shiells* v. *Ferguson, Davidson & Co.* (1876) 4 R. 250.

respect of its breach which would have been available against the cedent.[43] Thus, in *Arnott's Trs.* v. *Forbes*,[44] a vassal was held entitled to retain his feu-duty in respect of a breach of contract by his superior in a question with a heritable creditor to whom the superiority had been disponed in security.

This rule is without exception in the sphere in which it is applicable—the assignation of personal obligations. It does not apply to the transmission of heritable estate "for there the disponee rests upon the faith of the records and so may disregard all rights granted by his author upon which an infeftment has not been taken before that which proceeded on his own disposition"; or to the sale of corporeal moveables, or to negotiable instruments, because "a free course of commerce" must be secured.[45]

But a person may waive his rights under the law, and so the debtor in an obligation may undertake in express terms that the pleas and counterclaims between the original parties shall not be pleadable in a question with assignees.[46] This undertaking will receive effect; and, according to a series of cases in England concerned with such documents as debentures and letters of credit, even without express stipulation the same result will follow when it appears from the nature or terms of the contract that it must have been intended to be assignable free from and unaffected by such pleas and counterclaims.[47] Moreover, the debtor may by his behaviour towards the assignee be precluded from urging pleas which otherwise would have been open to him. Thus, if an insurance company, in the knowledge that there were clear objections to the validity of an insurance policy, continued to receive the premiums from an assignee of the policy, this might deprive them of the right to challenge the policy.[48]

8. Latent Trusts and Claims.—The general rule that an assignee takes subject to all the pleas which would have been available against the cedent must not be understood as meaning that he is necessarily exposed to all the latent claims to which the cedent is open. This is brought out in the case of *Redfearn* v. *Somervail*.[49] There one who appeared to the world as owner of a share in a private company, but in reality had acquired it as trustee for a firm of which he was a partner, assigned it to a creditor in security of a private loan. The assignation was taken by the creditor in the honest belief that the cedent was the absolute owner of the share and it was duly intimated. A competition then ensued between the firm claiming the share as partnership property and the creditor as assignee, in which it was held that the latter's

---

[43] Elchies' *Annotations*, 62; *Government of Newfoundland* v. *Newfoundland Ry.* (1887) 13 App.Cas. 199.
[44] (1881) 9 R. 89; see also *Duncan* v. *Brooks* (1894) 21 R. 760.
[45] Erskine, *Inst.*, III, 5, 10; *Scottish Widows' Fund* v. *Buist*, supra, per Lord President Inglis; see § 9, post.
[46] See *Bovill* v. *Dixon* (1854) 16 D. 619, per Lord Rutherford, affd. 3 Macq. 1; *Re Goy & Co.* [1900] 2 Ch. 149.
[47] Pollock on *Contracts*, 13th ed., pp. 180 et seq.
[48] *Scottish Equitable Life Assurance Society* v. *Buist* (1877) 4 R. 1076, per Lord President Inglis; *Bovill* v. *Dixon*, supra.
[49] 1813, 1 Dow 50; see also *Burns* v. *Laurie's Trs.* (1840) 2 D. 1348. Contrast *Scottish Widows' Fund* v. *Buist*, supra.

claim must prevail. The ground on which this decision proceeded was that the question was not between the debtor in the obligation, the company, and the assignee "but between the assignee and a person setting up a collateral claim in the nature of that of a cestui que trust."[50] Under the rule assignatus utitur jure auctoris the assignee was obnoxious to all the pleas which would have been available to the company against the cedent; but that rule had no application to the case of another party intervening to set up a right to the subjects as beneficiary under a latent trust.

The principle established in this decision is that if an assignation is onerous and is taken in good faith, the assignee takes the subject free from all latent trusts or equities affecting the cedent's right. It is otherwise if the assignee is aware of the equity, or does not take the assignation in the honest belief that the cedent is entitled lawfully to enter into the transaction; or, if the assignee, although taking in good faith, does not give any valuable consideration for the assignation. Gratuitous assignees are not protected. Nor does the principle of *Redfearn* v. *Somervail* apply to the case of a general body of creditors under a sequestration who take the rights of the bankrupt tantum et tale as they stand in his person.[51] Thus, where a bankrupt appeared on the Register of Sasines as owner of heritable property, but had executed an unregistered declaration that he held this property as trustee for a company, it was held that the property did not pass to the trustee in his sequestration, for the trustee merely represented creditors who had no dealings with the bankrupt in relation to that property and who had given no value for the interest in it which he claimed. The trustee was not therefore in a position to found on the principle which protects onerous bona fide alienees.[52]

9. Negotiable Instruments.—Any person obtaining money in good faith and for valuable consideration is entitled to retain it notwithstanding that it has been lost or stolen from a former owner.[53] A different rule, as has been shown, prevails in regard to the assignation of rights and claims; the holder of the assignation is affected by infirmities in the title of his author. But there is a class of documents which the law, following mercantile usage, assimilates to money and treats as in effect part of the currency. The documents belonging to this class are known as negotiable instruments.[54]

A negotiable instrument is a document containing an obligation to pay money and possessing two distinguishing characteristics. The document must be such that (1) delivery of it will transfer to the transferee the right to the obligation contained in it, and (2) a bona fide holder for value will acquire a

---

[50] The English term for a beneficiary under a trust.
[51] *Gordon* v. *Cheyne* (1824) 2 S. 675.
[52] *Heritable Reversionary Co.* v. *Millar* (1892) 19 R. (H.L.) 43. In his speech Lord Watson refers to "the well-known principle that a true owner who chooses to conceal his right from the public, and to clothe his trustee with all the indicia of ownership, is thereby barred from challenging rights acquired by innocent third parties for onerous consideration under contracts with his fraudulent trustee." See also *Bank of Scotland* v. *Liquidators of Hutchison, Main & Co.,* 1914 S.C. (H.L.) 1.
[53] Bell's *Prin.,* § 528.
[54] See generally Gow, *Mercantile Law,* pp. 394 et seq.

title valid against all the world notwithstanding any defect in the title of the transferor or prior holders.

Both of the above characteristics must be present, otherwise the document is not a negotiable instrument.[55] In the first place the document must be such that when transferred it will pass in its own corpus the thing it represents without intimation.[56] If, for this purpose, a deed of transfer and not simple delivery of the document is required, the document is not a negotiable instrument[57]; and even in the case of documents which transfer the right by mere delivery they must, to be negotiable, be in a state in which this can be accomplished. Thus if a bill of exchange or cheque is so drawn as to require indorsement for its transference it is not negotiable until it has been indorsed.

The second characteristic is the more important. If a document is negotiable a valid title may be acquired to it, although it was stolen from, or passed out of the possession of, the owner or was delivered to the holder without the owner's consent. "The general rule of the law is, that where a person has obtained the property of another from one who is dealing with it without the authority of the true owner, no title is acquired as against that owner, even though full value be given, and the property be taken in the belief that an unquestionable title thereto is being obtained, unless the person taking it can show that the true owner has so acted as to mislead him into the belief that the person dealing with the property had authority to do so. If this can be shown, a good title is acquired by personal estoppel[58] against the true owner. There is an exception to the general rule, however, in the case of negotiable instruments. Any person in possession of these may convey a good title to them, even when he is acting in fraud of the true owner, and although such owner has done nothing tending to mislead the person taking them."[59]

This protection is given only to one who has taken the bill for value and in good faith.[60] A bona fide holder is one who takes the instrument honestly and without knowledge of any defect in the title of the transferor. Negligence or foolishness in not suspecting that there is something wrong in that title when there are circumstances which might lead to that suspicion is not inconsistent with good faith; but if suspicion or doubt is in fact created and the bill is taken without any inquiry, or if on inquiry the suspicion or doubt is not removed, the holder would not be in good faith.[61]

Documents may be made negotiable either by statute or by mercantile usage recognised by the law. But it is not within the power of private persons to give by stipulation this privilege to a document. Such a stipulation may be

---

[55] *London Joint Stock Bank* v. *Simmons* [1891] 1 Ch. 270, per Bowen L.J., at 294; [1892] A.C. 201. See Gloag and Irvine's *Law of Rights in Security,* pp. 544 et seq.

[56] *Connal & Co.* v. *Loder* (1868) 6 M. 1095, per Lord Neaves.

[57] *London & County Banking Co.* v. *London & River Plate Bank* (1887) 20 Q.B.D. 232; 21 Q.B.D. 535.

[58] I.e. personal bar.

[59] *London Joint Stock Bank* v. *Simmons* [1892] A.C. 201, per Lord Herschell, at p. 215; *Walker & Watson* v. *Sturrock* (1897) 35 S.L.R. 26.

[60] *Banque Belge* v. *Hambrouck* [1921] 1 K.B. 321.

[61] *Jones* v. *Gordon* (1877) 2 App.Cas. 616, per Lord Blackburn; *London Joint Stock Bank* v. *Simmons,* supra, per Lord Herschell.

good as between the immediate parties, but it cannot affect the rights of
subsequent holders so as to place these at the mercy of any thief who can find
a bona fide purchaser or to give them a right to sue on the document.[62]
"Independently of the law merchant and of positive statute...the law does
not either in Scotland or in England enable any man by a written engagement
to give a floating right of action at the suit of anyone into whose hands the
writing may come and who may thus acquire a right of action better than the
right of him under whom he derives title."[63]

Among the class of British negotiable instruments are bills of exchange,
cheques and promissory notes[64] (except in so far as they are restrictively
indorsed or have lost the character of negotiability through being overdue or
otherwise), bank notes, exchequer bills and bonds (unless registered), treasury
bills, dividend warrants, debenture bonds of a British company payable to
bearer, scrip certificates to bearer for shares, and share warrants to bearer.
The class is not, however, stereotyped; and if the Court is satisfied that other
documents have, by general usage of traders and merchants, come to be
treated as negotiable instruments, it will recognise and give effect to this
usage.[65] Post Office money orders and postal orders are not negotiable
instruments.[66] A bill of lading is not strictly a negotiable instrument, as the
transferee does not get a better title than the transferor[67]; nor are documents
of title under the Factors Act. A deposit receipt is not a negotiable
instrument.[68]

10. Trade Names and Marks: Passing Off.—Apart from statute there can
be no right of property in a name or mark,[69] but the common law has always
recognised the right of a trader who uses a name or mark to prevent other
parties from making use of it or of a colourable imitation of it in such a way
as to mislead the public into thinking that the business carried on, or the
goods sold, by these parties are his.[70] "No man is entitled to represent his
goods as being the goods of another man, and no man is permitted to use any
mark, sign or symbol, device or other means whereby, without making a direct
false representation himself to a purchaser who purchases from him, he
enables such purchaser to tell a lie, or to make a false representation, to

62 *Crouch* v. *Credit Foncier of England* (1873) L.R. 8 Q.B. 374, per Lord Blackburn.
63 *Bovill* v. *Dixon* (1856) 3 Macq. 1, per Lord Cranworth L.C.
64 See Bills of Exchange, Ch. XXVI, supra.
65 *Goodwin* v. *Robarts* (1875) L.R. 10 Exch. 337; 1 App.Cas. 476; *Bechuanaland Exploration Co.* v. *London Trading Bank* [1898] 2 Q.B. 658.
66 *Fine Art Society* v. *Union Bank of London* (1886) 17 Q.B.D. 705.
67 Scrutton on *Charterparties and Bills of Lading* (18th ed.), p. 181; Carver's *Carriage by Sea* (12th ed.), § 1047.
68 *Barstow* v. *Inglis* (1857) 20 D. 230; *Wood* v. *Clydesdale Bank*, 1914 S.C. 397. As to the nature of a deposit receipt, see *Dickson* v. *National Bank of Scotland*, 1917 S.C. (H.L.) 50.
69 *Kinnell & Co.* v. *Ballantine & Sons*, 1910 S.C. 246, per Lord President Dunedin and Lord Skerrington.
70 *Williamson* v. *Meikle*, 1909 S.C. 1272, per Lord Skerrington at p. 1278. The product of a particular industry may be protected: *Bollinger (J.)* v. *Costa Brava Wine Co.* [1960] Ch. 262 (champagne); *Vine Products* v. *Mackenzie & Co.* [1969] R.P.C. 1 (sherry); *Walker (John) & Sons* v. *Henry Ost & Co.* [1970] 1 W.L.R. 917 (whisky); *John Walker & Sons* v. *Douglas McGibbon & Co.*, 1972 S.L.T. 128 (whisky).

somebody else who is the ultimate customer."[71] In an action by a trader seeking to prevent the use by another of a name or device in connection with goods it is incumbent on the pursuer to prove that that name or device has become so associated with the goods made or sold by him as to denote in the market that they are his.[72] If the name is an invented or fancy word this proof is much easier than in the case of an ordinary word descriptive of the quality or place of manufacture of the article, but even such a descriptive word may acquire a secondary significance as denoting an article made or sold by a particular trader so as to make its use without qualification by a rival trader misleading.[73] It is not necessary to prove fraud on the part of the defender[74] or that any member of the public has been actually deceived[75]; but it must be shown that the defender's use of the name or device is likely to deceive the public.[76] An individual cannot be restrained from carrying on business or selling his goods under his own name unless it appears from his conduct that he is seeking to take advantage of the similarity of his name with that of a rival trader for the purpose of passing off his own goods as those of his rival[77]; but a newly formed limited company may be prohibited from using a name which is liable to be confused with that of another established business in the same line of trade, although the name selected is or incorporates the personal name of one of the directors or shareholders.[78] Where a trader makes false representations as to his goods amounting to a fraud on the public, he is thereby disentitled to protection for the name used by him in regard to these goods.[79] A professional designation such as C.A. or W.S. may be protected from use by unqualified persons.[80]

11. Registration of Trade Marks.—While the right to protect a trade name is left to depend on the common law, trade marks have since 1875 (the date of the first Act[81]) been afforded further protection by a series of statutes. The present statutory provisions are contained in the Trade Marks Act 1938.[82] But these in no way affect the common law rights and remedies against anyone for passing off goods.[83]

The Act makes provision for the registration of trade marks in a register

---

[71] *Singer Co.* v. *Loog* (1880) Ch.D. 395, 412; *Cellular Clothing Co.* v. *Maxton & Murray* (1899) 1 F. (H.L.) 29; *Haig & Co.* v. *Forth Blending Co.* 1954 S.C. 35 (whisky bottle of peculiar shape protected).
[72] *Kinnell & Co.* v. *Ballantine & Sons,* 1910 S.C. 246.
[73] *Reddaway* v. *Banham* [1896] A.C. 199; *Cellular Clothing Co.* v. *Maxton & Murray* (1899) 1 F. (H.L.) 29.
[74] *Singer Machine Manufacturers* v. *Wilson* (1877) 3 App.Cas. 376, per Earl Cairns L.C. at p. 391.
[75] *Kinnell & Co.* v. *Ballantine & Sons,* supra.
[76] *Dunlop Pneumatic Tyre Co.* v. *Dunlop Motor Co.,* 1907 S.C. (H.L.) 15.
[77] *Dunlop Pneumatic Tyre Co.* v. *Dunlop Motor Co.* (1906) 8 F. 1146, per Lord Kyllachy; *Reddaway* v. *Banham,* supra, per Lord Herschell; *Dorman & Co.* v. *Henry Meadows* [1922] 2 Ch. 332; *Jaeger* v. *Jaeger Co.* (1927) 44 R.P.C. 437.
[78] *John Haig & Co.* v. *John D. D. Haig.,* 1957 S.L.T. (Notes) 36; *Kingston, Miller & Co.* v. *Thomas Kingston & Co.* [1912] 1 Ch. 575; see also Goodwill, § 27, infra.
[79] *Bile Bean Manufacturing Co.* v. *Davidson* (1906) 8 F. 1181.
[80] *Society of Accountants in Edinburgh* v. *Corporation of Accountants* (1893) 20 R. 750.
[81] Trade Marks Registration Act 1875 (38 & 39 Vict., c. 91).
[82] 1 & 2 Geo. VI, c. 22. See Kerly's *Trade Marks and Trade Names,* (10th ed., 1972).
[83] s. 2.

kept at the Patent Office.[84] By registration of his trade mark the proprietor obtains a statutory title and is relieved of the burden which rested on him under the common law of establishing his title to the mark by proof of user.[85] No one now can recover damages for infringement of an unregistered trade mark.[86] The registration is for a period of seven or fourteen years according to the date of registration, but may be renewed.[87] A trade mark must be registered for particular goods or classes of goods; it cannot, for instance, be registered in respect of a repairing process.[88]

The register is divided into two parts, A and B.[89] For registration in Part A severer tests of distinctiveness are applied, and registration in this part gives the owner the exclusive right to the use of the trade mark in relation to the goods in respect of which it is registered.[90] On the other hand, registration in Part B is only prima facie evidence that the person on the register has the exclusive right of use of it.[91] For registration in Part A the mark must contain or consist of at least one of five essential particulars specified in section 9.[92] To be registrable in Part B a trade mark must be capable, in relation to the goods in respect of which it is registered or proposed to be registered, of distinguishing goods with which its proprietor is or may be connected in the course of trade from goods in the case of which no such connection subsists.[93] Provision is made for preventing the registration in either part of a trade mark "the use of which would, by reason of its being likely to deceive or cause confusion or otherwise, be disentitled to protection in a court of justice, or would be contrary to law or morality, or any scandalous design".[94] A descriptive word may be registered provided it is distinctive,[95] but ordinary laudatory epithets are not registrable.[96]

[84] "Mark" and "Trade mark" are defined in these terms:—" 'Mark' includes a device, brand, heading, label, ticket, name, signature, word, letter, numeral, or any combination thereof; a 'Trade mark' means a mark used or proposed to be used in relation to goods for the purpose of indicating, or so as to indicate, a connection in the course of trade between the goods and some person having the right either as proprietor or as registered user to use the mark, whether with or without any indication of the identity of that person" (s. 68). The mark may cover the whole visible surface of the goods: *Smith Kline & French Laboratories* v. *Sterling-Winthrop Group* [1975] 1 W.L.R. 914.

[85] *Champagne Heidsieck et Cie Monopole Société Anonyme* v. *Buxton* [1930] 1 Ch. 330; *Boord & Son* v. *Thom & Cameron,* 1907 S.C. 1326, 1342.

[86] s. 2.

[87] s. 20.

[88] s. 3; *Aristoc* v. *Rysta* [1945] A.C. 68.

[89] s. 1.

[90] s.4.

[91] s.5.

[92] These are:—"(a) The name of a company, individual, or firm, represented in a special or particular manner; (b) the signature of the applicant for registration or some predecessor in his business; (c) an invented word or invented words; (d) a word or words having no direct reference to the character or quality of the goods, and not being according to its ordinary signification a geographical name or a surname; (e) any other distinctive mark, but a name, signature, or word or words, other than such as fall within the descriptions in the foregoing paragraphs (a), (b), (c) and (d), shall not be registrable under the provisions of this paragraph, except upon evidence of its distinctiveness" (see 1938 Act, s. 9). For the purposes of s. 9, "distinctive" means "adapted…to distinguish goods with which the proprietor of the trade mark is or may be connected in the course of trade from goods in the case of which no such connection subsists…"

[93] s. 10; *Davis* v. *Sussex Rubber Co.* [1927] 2 Ch. 345.

[94] s. 11. See *Berlei (U.K.)* v. *Bali Brassiere Co Inc.* [1969] 1 W.L.R. 1306.

[95] *Re Joseph Crossfield & Sons* [1910] 1 Ch. 130

[96] Ibid. The word "Perfection" as applied to soap was held not to be registrable.

12. Applications for Registration.—These are made to the registrar and are advertised.[97] Within one month of the advertisement notice of opposition may be given by any person.[98] The registrar has a discretion and is not bound to accept any application.[99] There is an appeal to the Court or the Board of Trade from the decision of the registrar.[1] A registration must be taken as valid after seven years, unless it was obtained by fraud or the trade mark offends against the provisions of section 11.[2]

13. Assignation of Registered Trade Mark.—A registered trade mark can be assigned subject to conditions intended to prevent deception or confusion[3]; but a registered user cannot assign or transmit his right of use.[4] There are provisions with respect to the rectification of, and removal of marks from, the register.[5] It is an offence punishable by fine for anyone to represent an unregistered trade mark as being registered.[6]

14. Patents.—Patents are granted by the Sovereign in the exercise of the royal prerogative. The right which the patentee acquires by the grant is one of monopoly in an invention, enabling him to exclude others from manufacturing in a particular way, and using, that invention.[7] The foundation of the law is the English Statute of Monopolies[8]—extended to Scotland at the Union[9]— by which monopolies were declared to be illegal, but exception was made of "letters-patent and grants of privilege for the term of fourteen years or under, hereafter to be made, of the sole working or making of any manner of new manufactures within this realm to the true and first inventor or inventors of such manufactures which others at the time of making such letters-patent and grants shall not use so as also they be not contrary to the law nor mischievous to the state by raising prices of commodities at home, or hurt of trade, or generally inconvenient."[10]

The law is now contained in the Patents Act 1977[11] which implements the obligations of the United Kingdom under the Convention for the European Patent for the Common Market, the Convention on the Grant of European Patents and the Patent Co-operation Treaty signed at Washington on 19th June 1970. In addition to establishing a new "domestic" patent system, the

---

[97] s. 17.
[98] s. 18.
[99] s. 17 (2); see *Cheryl Playthings* [1962] 1 W.L.R. 543.
[1] s. 17 (4). The Court of Session has no jurisdiction to entertain an appeal against the registrar's refusal to register a trade mark: *J. & J. Buchanan* v. *Comptroller-General of Patents*, 1928 S.C. 692.
[2] s. 13.
[3] s. 22.
[4] s. 28 (12).
[5] ss. 32-36.
[6] s. 60.
[7] Bell, *Prin.*, § 1349; *Steers* v. *Rogers* (1893) 10 R.P.C. 245, per Lord Herschell; *Edwards & Co.* v. *Picard* [1909] 2 K.B. 903.
[8] 21 Jac. 1, c. 3.
[9] *Neilson* v. *Househill Coal and Iron Co.* (1842) 4 D. 470, per Lord Cunningham at p. 475; Bell's *Comm.*, I, 103.
[10] 21 Jac. I, c. 23, s. 6.
[11] Certain provisions of the Patents Act 1949 still govern patents granted under that Act.

Act gives effect in the United Kingdom to European patents (U.K.), incorporates the provisions of the Common Market Convention into United Kingdom law, and provides for the treating of international applications under the 1970 Treaty as domestic applications. The incorporation of the Common Market Convention involves the recognition in the United Kingdom of "Community patents" granted by the European Patent Office.

In Scotland, proceedings relating primarily to patents are competent in the Court of Session only; the sheriff court has patent jurisdiction only in relation to incidental questions.[12]

15. Subject-matter of the Patent.—Patents are granted for inventions which are new, involve an inventive step and are capable of industrial application.[13] An invention is new if it does not form part of the state of the art, the state of the art being all matter which has at any time before the date of application for the patent been made available to the public in the United Kingdom or elsewhere by written or oral description, by use or in any other way.[14] An invention involves an inventive step if it is not obvious to a person skilled in the art.[15] An invention is capable of industrial application if it can be made or used in any kind of industry, including agriculture, but methods of treatment or diagnosis practised on the human or animal body are not capable of industrial application.[16] The following are not inventions for purposes of the Act: a discovery, scientific theory or mathematical method; literary and other works which can be protected by copyright; schemes, rules or methods for performing a mental act, playing a game or doing business or a program for a computer; the presentation of information.[17] A patent will not be granted for an invention the publication or exploitation of which would be expected to encourage offensive, immoral or anti-social behaviour nor for animal or plant varieties or biological processes for the production of animals or plants other than micro-biological processes.[18] Behaviour is not regarded as offensive, immoral or anti-social only because it is prohibited by law.[19]

16. Grant of Patent.—An application for a patent may be made by any person who claims to be the actual deviser of an invention to the Comptroller-General of Patents, Designs and Trade Marks at the Patent Office in London. The application must contain a request for the grant of a patent and a specification describing the invention in a manner clear enough and complete enough for the invention to be performed by a person skilled in the art. The specification must also contain a claim or claims which define the matter for which the applicant seeks protection.[20] After publication in the journal

[12] s. 98.
[13] s. 1 (1).
[14] s. 2.
[15] s. 3.
[16] s. 4.
[17] s. 1 (2).
[18] s. 1 (3).
[19] s. 1 (4).
[20] s. 14.

published by the comptroller the application is referred by the comptroller to an examiner who makes first a preliminary examination and search to determine, if possible, whether the invention is new and involves an inventive step.[21] Subsequently, on a request by the applicant, the examiner makes a substantive examination and reports whether the application complies with the requirements of the Act.[22]

Any person may make observations in writing to the comptroller on the question of whether the invention is patentable and the comptroller shall consider the observations.[23] If the examiner reports that the application complies with the requirements of the Act, the comptroller may, on payment of the prescribed fee, grant the patent.[24] Notice of the grant is published in the journal as is the specification.[25]

17. Term of Patent: Transmission.—The term during which the monopoly in the patent is secured to the inventor is now 20 years.[26] A patent is incorporeal moveable property[27] and may pass to the proprietor's representatives on his death or on his sequestration. It may be assigned and a security can be granted over it.[28] The person becoming entitled to a patent is required to register his title in the register of patents. The register is prima facie and sufficient evidence of anything required or authorised by the Act or rules to be registered.[29] A licence may be granted under a patent for working the invention.[30] If a proprietor desires to make his patent available, as a matter of right, to any person seeking a licence and that on such terms as may be settled by agreement or, in default of agreement, by the comptroller, he may apply to the comptroller for an entry to be made in the register to the effect that licences are to be available as of right and the comptroller shall make that entry.[31] In certain circumstances compulsory licences may be granted.[32]

18. Revocation of Patent: Abuse.—The Court or the comptroller may, on the application of any person, revoke a patent on any of the following grounds: that the invention was not patentable; that the grantee was not the only person entitled to it; that the specification does not disclose the invention clearly and completely enough; that the matter disclosed in the specification extends beyond that disclosed in the application; that the protection conferred by the patent has been extended by an inadmissible amendment.[33] The

[21] s. 17.
[22] s. 18.
[23] s. 21.
[24] s. 18 (4).
[25] s. 24.
[26] s. 25. Under the 1949 Act the period was 16 years.
[27] s. 31 (2).
[28] s. 31 (3).
[29] s. 35.
[30] s. 31 (4).
[31] s. 46.
[32] s. 48.
[33] s. 72.

grounds are also available as defences to an action for infringement. In patent disputes the nature of the invention for which the patent was granted must be ascertained from the specification, which falls to be construed by the Court.[34]

19. Infringement.—A person infringes a patent if, without the consent of the proprietor, he makes, disposes of, offers to dispose of, uses or imports the product or keeps it whether for disposal or otherwise, or, where the invention is a process, uses the process or offers it for use in the United Kingdom, or he disposes of, uses, imports, or keeps any product obtained directly by the process.[35] Infringement of the patent entitles the proprietor to interdict against the infringer, and also to damages[36] unless the latter proves that at the date of the infringement he was not aware, and had not reasonable grounds for supposing that the patent existed.[37] The proprietor is entitled to an account of profits made by the infringer in lieu of damages.[38] Where infringement is widespread he has been held entitled to damages on a royalty basis.[39] The defender may not only deny the infringement, but may counterclaim for revocation of the patent.[40]

20. Designs.—Under the Registered Designs Act 1949 any person claiming to be the proprietor of any new or original design not previously published in the United Kingdom may apply to the comptroller to have it registered in the Register of Designs kept at the Patent Office.[41] "Design" is defined as meaning "features of shape, configuration, pattern or ornament applied to an article by any industrial process or means, being features which in the finished article appeal to and are judged solely by the eye, but does not include a method or principle of construction or features of shape or configuration which are dictated solely by the function which the article to be made in that shape or configuration has to perform."[42] The comptroller may, subject to appeal to the Appeal Tribunal, refuse to register a design.[43] On registration the proprietor obtains a copyright in the design for five years, which may be extended for two further periods of five years by the comptroller.[44] As a result, the proprietor enjoys the exclusive right in the United Kingdom of making, importing, selling, hiring or otherwise using the article of registered design.[45]

[34] See *Lyle & Scott* v. *Wolsey,* 1955 S.L.T. 322 ("Y-front" case), for Lord Hill Watson's observations on the construction of specifications and the function of expert witnesses.
[35] s. 60.
[36] s. 61. As to damages, see *United Horse Shoe Co.* v. *Stewart & Co.* (1888) 15 R. (H.L.) 45.
[37] s. 62 (1).
[38] s. 61 (2).
[39] *British Thomson-Houston Co.* v. *Charlesworth, Peebles & Co.,* 1923 S.C. 599.
[40] s. 74 (1).
[41] Registered Designs Act 1949, ss. 1 (1), 17 (1).
[42] Ibid., s. 1 (3). See *Amp. Inc.* v. *Utilux Pty* [1972] R.P.C. 103.
[43] Ibid., ss. 3 (3), 28.
[44] Ibid., s. 7 (1), (2). As to the position after the expiry of the 15 years, see Copyright Act 1956, s. 10, as amended by Design Copyright Act 1968 (c. 68), s. 1.
[45] Ibid., s. 7 (1).

21. Copyright.—The law of copyright is now embodied in the Copyright Act 1956,[46] which repealed most of the pre-existing legislation and made important changes in the law as contained in the Copyright Act 1911. It is provided that nothing in the 1956 Act is to affect the actionability of breaches of trust or confidence,[47] but with this exception there is no right of copyright otherwise than by virtue of the Act.[48]

Copyright has been defined, in its most elementary form, as "the right of multiplying copies of a published writing."[49] The 1911 Act defined it[50] as "the sole right to produce or reproduce the work or any substantial part thereof in any material form whatsoever, to perform, or in the case of a lecture to deliver, the work or any substantial part thereof in public; if the work is unpublished, to publish the work or any substantial part thereof." The 1956 Act, which extended the scope of copyright to include the use of modern media, contains no express definition, but provides[51] that it is, in relation to a work, "the exclusive right to do and to authorise other persons to do certain acts in relation to that work in the United Kingdom, or in any other country to which the relevant provision of the Act" has been extended by Order in Council. It provides in Part I[52] for copyright in original works, and in Part II[53] for copyright in sound recordings, cinematograph films, broadcasts and in published editions of works. The restricted acts in relation to each of these media are not identical, separate provision being made in each case.

22. Copyright in Original Works.—The subject matter dealt with in Part I of the Act under the heading of original works comprises original literary, dramatic, musical and artistic works, as these terms are defined by the Act,[54] whether published or unpublished. Originality in this connection refers to the form or expression of thought and not to the thought expressed.[55] The material on which the author has worked may not be new, but the result of his skill and labour as applied to that material must be to produce an original work.[56] Nor need the expression be in a novel form so long as it is not copied from another work but originates from the author.[57] The acts restricted by the copyright include those of reproducing the'work or any adaptation of it in any

---

[46] 4 & 5 Eliz. 2, c. 74. See Copinger and Skone-James, *Law of Copyright* (11th ed., 1971); Carter-Ruck and Skone James, *Copyright* (1965); Gow, *Mercantile Law*, p. 682 et seq. For the common law and earlier statutes, see Bell's *Comm.*, I., 111.

[47] s. 46 (4).

[48] s. 46 (5). But see Performers' Protection Acts 1958 to 1972 (6 & 7 Eliz. II, c. 44; 1963 c. 53; 1972 c. 32) which penalise the making of records, films or broadcasts or the relaying of a performance without the consent in writing of the performers.

[49] Per Lord Davey, in *Walter* v. *Lane* [1900] A.C. 539, at p. 550.

[50] 1 & 2 Geo. V, c. 46, s. 1 (2).

[51] 4 & 5 Eliz. II, c. 74, s. 1 (1).

[52] ss. 2–11.

[53] ss. 12–16.

[54] ss. 3 (1), 48. As to "artistic craftsmanship", see *George Hensher* v. *Restawile Upholstery* (*Lancs*) [1976] A.C. 64.

[55] *Harpers* v. *Barry, Henry & Co.* (1892) 20 R. 133.

[56] E.g. *Joy Music* v. *Sunday Pictorial* [1960] 2 Q.B. 60.

[57] *Macmillan & Co.* v. *Cooper* (1924) 93 L.J.(P.C.) 113, approving the judgment of Peterson J, in *University of London Press* v. *University Tutorial Press* [1916] 2 Ch. 601, and Lord Kinloch's opinion in *Black* v. *Murray* (1870) 9 M. 341, at 355; *Leslie* v. *Young & Sons* (1894) 21 R. (H.L.) 57; *G. A. Cramp & Sons* v. *Frank Smythson* [1944] A.C. 329.

material form, i.e., publishing,[58] performing or broadcasting the work or causing it to be transmitted to subscribers to a diffusion service, and making any adaptation of the work.[59] The copyright is also infringed by any person who imports or trades in an article without the licence of the owner of the copyright, where to his knowledge the making of that article was an infringement of the copyright or would have been if it had been made in the place into which it is so imported, or by a person who permits a place of public entertainment to be used for a performance in public of the work where the performance constitutes an infringement of the copyright[60]; but "fair dealing" with a work will not constitute an infringement.[61] To obtain the benefit of copyright under the Act the work, if published, must have been first published within the copyright area, that is, the United Kingdom or another country to which the Act has been extended,[62] or the author must have been a "qualified person" within the meaning of the Act,[63] that is, in the case of an individual, a British subject, a British protected person or a person domiciled or resident in the copyright area; if the work is unpublished, the requirement is that the author should have been a qualified person at the time when the work was made.[64] The term for which copyright subsists in an original work is the lifetime of the author, and then a period of fifty years from the end of the calendar year in which he died; but if the author had died before the work or an adaptation of it was first published, performed in public, offered for sale or first broadcast, the fifty-year period will begin to run from the end of the calendar year which includes the earliest occasion on which one of those acts is done.[65]

23. Copyright in Sound Recordings, Films, Broadcasts, etc.—Copyright subsists in every sound recording of which the maker was a "qualified person"[63] at the time when the recording was made, or if the first publication of the recording took place in the copyright area; the period for which it subsists in every sound recording of which the maker was a "qualified was first published.[66] The maker of the sound recording or the person who commissioned it is the person primarily entitled to the copyright.[67] The restricted acts, subject to certain exceptions,[68] are making a record embodying the recording, causing it to be heard in public or broadcasting it. Copyright also subsists in every cinematograph film of which the maker was a "qualified person"[68] or which was first published in the copyright area.[69] In the case of films registrable under Part II of the Films Act 1960, the copyright subsists

[58] As to what is meant by "publication," see s. 49 (2) (3).
[59] ss. 2 (5), 3 (5). See *Performing Right Society* v. *Rangers F.C. Supporters Club, Greenock,* 1974 S.L.T. 151.
[60] s. 5.
[61] See s. 6.
[62] s. 2 (2).
[63] See s. 1 (5).
[64] s. 2 (1).
[65] s. 2 (3).
[66] s. 12.
[67] s. 12 (4).
[68] See s. 12 (6), (7).
[69] s. 13.

until the film is registered thereunder and thereafter for a period of fifty years; in the case of non-registrable films it subsists until publication and then for fifty years thereafter.[70] The copyright belongs to the makers of the film, and the acts restricted are the making of a copy of the film, causing it to be seen or heard in public or broadcasting it. In the case of television and sound broadcasts by the B.B.C. or I.T.A. and by the B.B.C. respectively, copyright belongs to the broadcasting corporation or authority and subsists for a period of fifty years from the end of the calendar year in which the broadcast was made.[71] The acts restricted in this case include the making of a film or sound recording of the broadcast otherwise than for private purposes, re-broadcasting it, or in the case of television causing it to be seen or heard in public by a paying audience.[72] Finally, copyright subsists in every published edition of a literary, dramatic or musical work which does more than reproduce the typographical arrangement of a previous edition of the same work, and has been published by a "qualified person"[63] or within the copyright area.[73] The copyright belongs in the first instance to the publisher, and subsists for a period of twenty-five years from the end of the calendar year in which the edition was first published. The restricted act in this case is the making by any photographic or similar process of a reproduction of the typographical arrangement of the edition.

24. Ownership of Copyright.—The author or maker of a work is, in the absence of any agreement on the matter, the owner of any copyright subsisting in that work.[74] In the case of an engraving, photograph or portrait the person who orders and pays for the plate or other original is, in the absence of agreement to the contrary, the person entitled to the copyright.[75] In the absence also of agreement, where a literary, dramatic or artistic work is made by the author in the course of his employment by the proprietor of a newspaper, magazine or similar periodical for the purpose of publication therein, the proprietor is entitled to the copyright in the work in so far as the copyright relates to publication of the work in any newspaper, magazine or similar periodical; but in all other respects the author is entitled to the copyright.[76]

25. Transference of Copyright.—Copyright is transmissible by assignation, by testamentary disposition or by operation of law as moveable property.[77] The assignation may be total or partial[78]; but it will be ineffective unless it is in writing signed by or on behalf of the assignor.[79] Prospective ownership of copyright is assignable, and when it comes into existence it vests in the

[70] s. 13 (3); as to newsreels, see s. 13 (8).
[71] s. 14.
[72] s. 14 (4).
[73] s. 15.
[74] s. 4 (1); see also ss. 12 (4), 13 (4), 14 (2), 15 (2).
[75] s. 4 (3).
[76] s. 4 (2).
[77] s. 36 (1).
[78] s. 36 (2).
[79] s. 36 (3).

assignee or his successor in title without further procedure.[80] Unlike the gift or
sale of such a work,[81] the bequest of a literary, dramatic, musical or artistic
work which was not published before the testator's death carries with it such
copyright in it as the testator had at his death.[82] The owner of the copyright
may also grant a licence in respect of it, which is binding upon his successor in
title except a purchaser in good faith and for value.[83]

26. Infringement of Copyright.—Where copyright is infringed the owner
thereof, except as otherwise provided in the Act, is entitled to all such relief,
by way of interdict, damages, accounts or otherwise, as is available in
corresponding proceedings in respect of infringements of other proprietary
rights.[84] The Court may, having regard to the flagrancy of the infringement
and any benefit accrued to the defender thereby, award additional damages of
an exemplary nature.[85] If, however, the infringer proves that at the date of the
infringement he was not aware and had no reasonable ground for suspecting
the existence of copyright, the pursuer is not entitled to damages, but to an
accounting and payment of profits.[86] The owner is also entitled, subject to the
defence of ignorance,[87] to all such rights and remedies in respect of the
intromission by any person with any infringing copy as he would be as if he
were the owner of the copy.[88] The Act also provides that certain offences
under it shall be punishable on summary conviction by fine or by
imprisonment.[89]

27. Goodwill.—The goodwill of a business was said by Lord Eldon to be
"nothing more than the probability that the old customers will resort to the
old place."[90] This is an important element in goodwill, but as a definition the
statement is too narrow.[91] The goodwill of a business is the whole advantage,
whatever it may be, of the reputation and connection of the firm. "It is the
connection formed, together with the circumstances, whether of habit or
otherwise, which tend to make it permanent, that constitutes the goodwill of a
business. It is this which constitutes the difference between a business just
started, which has no goodwill attached to it, and one which has acquired a
goodwill. The former trader has to seek out his customers from among the
community as best he can. The latter has a custom ready made. He knows
what members of the community are purchasers of the articles in which he
deals, and are not attached by custom to any other establishment."[92]

[80] s. 37.
[81] *Cooper* v. *Stephens* [1895] 1 Ch. 567.
[82] s. 38.
[83] s. 36 (4).
[84] s. 17 (1); see Gow, *Mercantile Law*, p. 687.
[85] s. 17 (3).
[86] s. 17 (2); see *G. A. Cramp & Sons* v. *Frank Smythson* [1944] A.C. 329.
[87] s. 18 (2); but see *John Lane, The Bodley Head* v. *Associated Newspapers* [1936] 1 K.B. 715.
[88] s. 18.
[89] s. 21.
[90] *Cruttwell* v. *Lye* (1810) 17 Ves. 335.
[91] *Trego* v. *Hunt* [1896] A.C. 7.
[92] *Trego* v. *Hunt*, supra, per Lord Herschell at p. 17; *Inland Revenue Comrs.* v. *Muller & Co's
Margarine* [1901] A.C. 217, per Lord Macnaghten at 223.

Goodwill may be sold, and the vendor thereby bars himself from representing that he is continuing the old business; he therefore cannot use the firm name[93] or trade mark, nor can he solicit the customers of that business to transfer their custom to him.[94] The vendor may, however, set up for himself in the old trade under his own name, and even in close proximity to the premises in which the business he has sold is carried on; and he may deal with customers of the old business who come to him of their own accord without solicitation.[95] The executor carrying through a contract for the sale of a business concluded by the deceased was held not entitled to solicit the customers of that business.[96] Where a sale of the debtor's business is effected by the trustee in his sequestration or by a trustee for creditors, the debtor, it has been held, cannot be prevented from soliciting the customers of that business.[97] Where the firm name is sold alone and not as an element in the goodwill of the business, the ambit of the vendor's obligation is much more restricted, and no question of the goodwill of the business itself is involved.[98]

The Partnership Act 1890[99] provides that the mere receipt of part of the profits of a business by a person, in respect of the sale by him of the goodwill, does not make him a partner, but contains no other provision on the subject. If the matter is not dealt with in the contract of copartnery, the goodwill of the business is part of the assets of the firm, and, on its dissolution, any partner, or the representative of a deceased partner, can insist on its being sold.[1] A provision in a contract of copartnery whereby one partner undertakes not to carry on the same business after the dissolution of the firm is not a mere personal contract between the partners, but passes with the goodwill, and may be enforced by a purchaser thereof.[2]

In the case of a professional business depending on the personal qualities of the practitioner, the goodwill of the practice is not considered to have the value which belongs to the goodwill of a commercial business.[3]

Goodwill may be moveable or heritable. This is a question of fact depending on whether the goodwill is associated with the premises in which the business has been carried on or with the reputation of the trader.[4] In some cases both of these elements may be present, and if so, the goodwill is treated as partly heritable and partly moveable.[5]

---

[93] *Smith* v. *McBride & Smith* (1888) 16 R. 36.
[94] *Dunbarton Steamboat Co.* v. *Macfarlane* (1899) 1 F. 993; *Curl Bros.* v. *Webster* [1904] 1 Ch. 685.
[95] *Re David & Matthews* [1899] 1 Ch. 378; but see Passing Off, § 10 supra.
[96] *Boorne* v. *Wicker* [1927] 1 Ch. 667.
[97] *Walker* v. *Mottram* (1881) 19 Ch.D. 355; *Farey* v. *Cooper* [1927] 2 K.B. 384; *Melrose Drover* v. *Heddle* (1902) 4 F. 1120.
[98] *Barr* v. *Lions* 1956 S.C. 59, per Lord President Clyde at p. 64.
[99] 53 & 54 Vict. c. 39, s. 2 (3) (*e*).
[1] Bell's *Prin.*, § 379; *Re David & Matthews*, supra.
[2] *Townsend* v. *Jarman* [1900] 2 Ch. 698.
[3] *Bain* v. *Munro* (1878) 5 R. 416; *Rodger* v. *Herbertson*, 1909 S.C. 256; *Thatcher* v. *Thatcher* (1904) 11 S.L.T. 605; see *May* v. *Thomson* (1882) Ch.D. 705, per Jessel M.R. at 718.
[4] *Muirhead's Trs.* v. *Muirhead* (1905) 7 F. 496; *Graham* v. *Graham's Trs.* (1904) 6 F. 1015; *Hughes* v. *Assessor for Stirling* (1892) 19 R. 840.
[5] *Murray's Tr.* v. *McIntyre* (1904) 6 F. 588; *Assessor for Edinburgh* v. *Caira & Crolla*, 1928 S.C. 398.

CHAPTER XXXIX

LANDOWNERSHIP

Rankine on *Landownership* (4th ed., 1909).

1. Introductory.—This students' text-book is not the place for a dissertation on the fetters which have been placed upon the ownership of land in recent years. How much of the restrictive legislation which now crowds the statute-book has come to stay it is impossible to say but certain it is that the numerous Rent Acts, the Town and Country Planning Acts and the Acts permitting the requisition of land have amongst them so affected landownership as to cause genuine doubt as to the appropriateness of the word "ownership" in such a context.[1] Practically important as it may be, this legislation must here yield pride of place to consideration of the legal principles with which we are primarily concerned.

The law of heritable property is largely bound up with questions of conveyancing, which do not fall within the scope of this work. But as it is impossible to understand the questions dealt with in this chapter without some knowledge of the elementary principles of land tenure, a brief reference to these is necessary.

The cardinal feature of Scots conveyancing is the system of registration of titles to heritage. In 1617 there was instituted the Register of Sasines.[2] This is open to the public; and for the purpose of ascertaining the ownership of land and the burdens which have been imposed on it recourse must be had to this register. A person who enters into a contract to purchase land has a right as against the seller to have the bargain implemented and may sue him for damages if he fails to implement it. But he has not a real right against all and sundry; he is not in fact the owner until the conveyance to him has been placed on the register. Hence if another party purchasing the same land under a later contract should first register the conveyance in his favour he would (in the absence of fraud) acquire a right to the land to the exclusion of the earlier purchaser. So also, in order that a burden may form a charge on the land, no matter what changes occur in its ownership, it must appear on the register. The current form of security over land is the standard security which has superseded the bond and disposition in security.[3] The owner of land who has borrowed money binds himself to repay the loan and grants a standard security over the land, so that the lender may not only sue the borrower but

---

[1] See for example the Acquisition of Land (Authorisation Procedure) (Scotland) Act 1947 (10 & 11 Geo. VI, c. 42): Agricultural Land (Removal of Surface Soil) Act 1953, forbidding sale of soil of agricultural land by its "owner"; Community Land Act 1975 (c. 77); Offshore Petroleum Development (Scotland) Act 1975 (c. 8).
[2] Registration Act 1617 (c. 16).
[3] Conveyancing and Feudal Reform (Scotland) Act 1970 (c. 35).

may have recourse against the land for payment of his debt.[4] But unless the standard security appears on the register it would not form an effectual charge on the land as against a purchaser. On the other hand, if the standard security is registered, it will affect the lands, whoever may be the owner and whatever be the title by which he has acquired it.

A person who appears on the register as the owner of land is said to be infeft. In the earliest times, in conformity with the principle that delivery was the sole means of transmitting property, the transference of heritage was effected by the only possible form of delivery, viz. symbolical delivery. If heritable subjects were sold, appropriate symbols such as earth and stone for land, a clap and happer for a mill and a net for a salmon fishing, were handed over by the seller to the purchaser in the presence of witnesses. This constituted Sasine. The transaction was then recorded in a deed known as an Instrument of Sasine which described the subjects and detailed the ceremony; and this instrument was registered in the Register of Sasines, thereby enabling the public to learn of the change in the ownership of the land. By this means the buyer became infeft, or, in other words, obtained a real right to the subjects. In course of time it was recognised that the important feature was the appearance of the transaction on the register. The cumbrous proceeding of delivering symbols dropped out. It came to suffice that the record (the instrument of sasine), although what was recorded in it had not actually taken place, should be entered in the register; and finally the record has disappeared and all that is necessary is that the deed of conveyance itself should be registered. Infeftment now depends on the registration of the deed transferring the land. The purchaser of land is infeft when, and only when, his title is recorded; and the owner of a security over land, by registering the deed showing the existence of the security in the register, acquires a charge on the land effectual against all who may have rights of property in it.

In dealing with the law of land ownership, apart from conveyancing, it is proposed to consider first the rights of the Crown, the regalia; then the effects of possession of heritable property; and, lastly, the incidents of ownership, including such matters as the law of minerals, game, natural rights and servitudes.

I. REGALIA

2. Regalia: Majora and Minora.—The rights of the Crown in heritable property fall into two classes. The first consists of those rights which the Crown holds in trust for the public and which cannot be alienated; the second, of proprietary rights which belong to the Crown without restriction either as to their exercise or as to their alienation. "These two ideas [of sovereignty and of property in the Crown] are perfectly separate and distinct. ... The Crown, if it has not granted it out, has a right of property in the

---

[4] For example, a statutory standard condition normally incorporated in the standard security empowers the creditor, upon the debtor's default, to sell the land in satisfaction of the debt.

foreshore which may be alienated, and also a right of sovereignty as guardian of the public interests for navigation, fishing, and other public uses which cannot be alienated."[5] The inalienable rights are called regalia majora; the others are the regalia minora. They are indeed distinct, but there are cases, e.g. the foreshore, in which, as the above quotation shows, they are both found existing in regard to the same object.

3. The Sea.—The sea below the foreshore and within the three-mile limit belongs to the Crown in trust for the public rights of navigation[6] and white fishing. Whether the actual bed of the sea can be alienated is doubtful, but no right in it which, if exercised by the grantee, would interfere with the rights of the public, can be granted without the sanction of Parliament.[7]

4. The Foreshore.—The foreshore is the shore between the high and low water marks of ordinary spring tides.[8] In the foreshore the Crown has, as already noticed, a double right—a right of sovereignty and a right of property. In virtue of the former right the foreshore is vested in the Crown for the benefit of the public.[9] More than one public right is included. Of these, the two most important are the right of navigation and the right of white fishing. The former includes the right to anchor, to load and discharge goods, to embark and disembark, and to take in ballast.[6] The latter includes the right to dry nets and (with the exception of oysters and mussels which belong to the Crown[10]) to take shellfish.[11] Both these rights are inalienable by the Crown.[12] In addition, the public probably has a right to go on the foreshore for recreation.[13]

The foreshore itself, however, may be alienated, and an adjacent proprietor is held to own it if he has from the Crown either a specific grant of it, or a title habile to include it which has been followed by possession for the prescriptive period.[14] Such possession need not be, and indeed cannot be, such as to exclude the public entirely, for the rights of the public cannot be impaired.[15] The owner has the exclusive use of taking sea-ware and other materials from the foreshore, provided he does nothing to hinder the public in the exercise of its rights.

[5] *Smith* v. *Lerwick Harbour Comrs.* (1903) 5 F. 680, at p. 691.
[6] *Crown Estate Commissioners* v. *Fairlie Yacht Slip,* 1977 S.L.T. 19.
[7] *Lord Advocate* v. *Wemyss* (1899) 2 F. (H.L.) 1, at pp. 8 and 9.
[8] *Agnew* v. *Lord Advocate* (1873) 11 M. 309; *Fisherrow Harbour Comrs.* v. *Musselburgh Real Estate Co.* (1903) 5 F. 387.
[9] See *Burnet* v. *Barclay,* 1955 J.C. 34; Smith, *Short Commentary,* p. 64.
[10] *Parker* v. *Lord Advocate* (1904) 6 F. (H.L.) 37.
[11] Balfour's *Practicks,* 626; *Hall* v. *Whillis* (1852) 14 D. 324.
[12] *McDouall* v. *Lord Advocate* (1875) 2 R. (H.L.) 49.
[13] *Hope* v. *Bennewith* (1904) 6 F. 1004; *Mather* v. *Alexander,* 1926 S.C. 139 (erecting hut on foreshore); *Burnet* v. *Barclay,* supra. But see *Alfred F. Beckett* v. *Lyons* [1967] Ch. 449. As to the power of islands or district councils in regard to the foreshore, see s. 303 of the Burgh Police (Scotland) Act 1892 (55 & 56 Vict., c. 55) as amended by Schedule 28 to the Local Government (Scotland) Act 1973 (c. 65) and cf. *Mags. of Buckhaven & Methil* v. *Wemyss Coal Co.* 1932 S.C. 201.
[14] Prescription and Limitation (Scotland) Act 1973 (c. 52), s. 1 (1) and (4). See Prescription Ch. XVI supra.
[15] *Marquis of Bute* v. *McKirdy & McMillan,* 1937 S.C. 93.

5. Navigable Rivers.—Rivers which are tidal and navigable are regarded as part of, and subject to the same rule as, the sea. The solum belongs to the Crown, subject to the public rights of navigation and fishing.[16]

On the other hand, if the river is navigable but non-tidal, the solum belongs not to the Crown but to the riparian proprietors. The public have a right of navigation,[17] but no other rights in regard to the river. The banks are private property and cannot be used by the public except for purposes incidental to navigation.[18] The right of public navigation is not a servitude and cannot be lost through disuse.[19] It follows, from the right of navigation, that a member of the public can prevent any interference with the bed of the river which affects that right; but he has no title to object to any structure being put in the river unless it obstructs navigation. His right is one of passage; and there may be many operations in a river to which an opposite heritor would have a title to object, but which are quite lawful in a question with the public.[20] The Harbours Act 1814 prohibits the throwing of rubbish into a navigable river.[21]

6. Ferry: Port and Harbour.—These rights are classed as regalia, though in certain respects they differ from the other regalia. They are rights belonging to the Crown, which may be acquired from it by grant or prescription.[22]

A right of ferry is an incorporeal heritable right.[23] It is the right to carry persons by water across a narrow sea, river or loch, from one definite place to another. The place is not necessarily confined to a particular spot, but may be a stretch of shore. It involves the right to charge a fee for services and to exclude others from carrying passengers within the limits of the ferry, and the duty of receiving any person for carriage at reasonable times. Neighbouring proprietors may keep boats for the ferrying of their own families and servants, but may not, by carrying strangers for hire, interfere with the right of ferry.[24] Ferries are the responsibility of regional or islands councils.[25] A council may acquire, maintain and operate ferries; lease or hire ferries; make arrangements for their operation; fix fares and charges; and subsidise ferries from the local rates.

Harbours are either private or public. The former belong to individuals and are used for their own purposes, and the public have not right to resort to them, except with the permission of the proprietor.[26] Public harbours are those which anyone may use on payment of the proper dues. The right of port and harbour may be granted by the Crown to an individual or a

---

[16] *Orr Ewing* v. *Colquhoun's Trs.* (1877) 4 R. (H.L.) 116.
[17] *Wills' Trs.* v. *Cairngorm Canoeing and Sailing School* 1976 S.C. (H.L.) 30.
[18] *Leith-Buchanan* v. *Hogg,* 1931 S.C. 204.
[19] *Wills' Trs.* v. *Cairngorm Canoeing and Sailing School,* supra.
[20] *Orr Ewing* v. *Colquhoun's Trs.,* supra; *Campbell's Trs.* v. *Sweeney,* 1911 S.C. 1319.
[21] s. 11. See *National Coal Board* v. *Forth Conservancy Board,* 1947 S.N. 89.
[22] See *L.M. & S. Ry.* v. *Macdonald,* 1924 S.C. 835.
[23] *Baillie* v. *Hay* (1866) 4 M. 625; *Duke of Montrose* v. *Macintyre* (1848) 10 D. 896.
[24] *Weir* v. *Aiton* (1858) 20 D. 968.
[25] Local Government (Scotland) Act 1973 (c. 65), s. 153.
[26] *Colquhoun* v. *Paton* (1859) 21 D. 996.

corporation,[27] and confers the right to exact dues. The corresponding duty of the grantee of the right is to maintain the harbour so far as the dues received are sufficient for that purpose.[28] The Secretary of State has power to develop, maintain and manage harbours made by or maintained by him by virtue of an Act or order.[29] He may make loans to harbour authorities.[30] Regional councils have general responsibility for harbours.[31] They may acquire compulsorily any harbour in a poor state of repair, or a harbour whose maintenance is to be discontinued by its owner.

7. Precious Metals: Forestry: Highways.—These subjects are pure regalia minora. They are part of the patrimony of the Crown, but they may be alienated, and the public has no rights in any of them. Precious metals are dealt with elsewhere.[32]

The chief privilege flowing from a right of forestry was that one-third of the value of cattle forfeited for straying into the forest went to the forester, the other two-thirds going to the Crown. The right is of no practical importance in modern times.

Highways are included in the regalia.[33] They belong to the Sovereign. The solum of a highway belongs, unless it has been acquired from him, to the proprietor of the lands, the highway being merely a right of passage over the soil.[34]

8. Salmon Fishings.—Salmon fishing is a separate feudal right, which is vested in the Crown. It is among the regalia minora,[35] and the right of salmon fishing may, therefore, be granted by the Crown to a subject. The title is either an express grant of the salmon fishings,[36] or a barony title[37] or a charter cum piscationibus coupled with possession for the prescriptive period.[38] The possession must, as a rule, be by fishing by net and coble, but fishing by rod may be enough,[39] at least in cases where fishing by net and coble is impossible.[40] Where a grant or lease of salmon fishing is made by the Crown, it carries with it, unless it is specifically limited, the exclusive right to fish by all lawful and legitimate means.[41]

---

[27] *Earl of Stair* v. *Austin* (1880) 8 R. 183; *Macpherson* v. *Mackenzie* (1881) 8 R. 706.
[28] *Firth Shipping Co.* v. *Earl of Morton's Trustees*, 1938 S.C. 177.
[29] Harbours Development (Scotland) Act 1972 (c. 64).
[30] Harbours (Loans) Act 1972 (c. 16).
[31] Local Government (Scotland) Act 1973 (c. 65), s. 154.
[32] Infra, § 15.
[33] Bank., I., 3, 4; II., 1, 5; Ersk., II., 6, 17. There has been extensive legislation in relation to highways.
[34] *Galbreath* v. *Armour* (1845) 4 Bell's Apps. 374; *Waddell* v. *Earl of Buchan* (1868) 6 M. 690.
[35] Except in Orkney and Shetland (*Lord Advocate* v. *Balfour*, 1907 S.C. 1360).
[36] The conveyancing phrase "parts and pertinents" does not include salmon fishing: *McKendrick* v. *Wilson*, 1970 S.L.T. (Sh. Ct.) 39.
[37] Land is held on a barony title when it is held direct from the Crown and has been erected by the grant in liberam baroniam, i.e. into a freehold barony. A grant of barony carries with it various special rights and advantages: *Lord Advocate* v. *Cathcart* (1871) 9 M. 744.
[38] Prescription and Limitation (Scotland) Act 1973 (c. 52), s. 1 (1) and (4); cf. *Maxwell* v. *Lamont* (1903) 6 F. 245; Tait's *Game and Fishing Laws of Scotland* (2nd ed.), p. 122.
[39] *Warrand's Trs.* v. *Mackintosh* (1890) 17 R. (H.L.) 13 at p. 23; *Maxwell* v. *Lamont*, supra, per Lord Kinnear.
[40] *Sinclair* v. *Thriepland* (1890) 17 R. 507.
[41] *Joseph Johnstone & Son* v. *Morrison*, 1962 S.L.T. 322.

If the owner of the salmon fishings owns the land on both banks he has the whole fishings. But if the banks are owned by different proprietors, the fishing rights depend on the terms of the titles. If each proprietor has a right of salmon fishing ex adverso of his lands, and the stream is broad enough to allow a clear sweep of the nets without crossing the medium filum, each proprietor must keep to his own half. Where the stream is not sufficiently broad to admit of this, the Court will make the necessary arrangement.[42] These rules apply only if neither of the parties has established by immemorial possession a higher right.[43] Where the owner of the salmon fishings is not a riparian proprietor, the presumption is that he has a right to the whole fishings unless one of the riparian proprietors has an adverse right.[44] He has a right of access to the river and a right to moor boats, dry nets, fix posts, and do anything necessary for the exercise of his right, provided he pays due regard to the rights of the owner of the bank.[45]

Many statutes from the fourteenth century onwards have been passed to regulate salmon fishing. The exact terms of such of the older Acts as survive are not important, because they have been so much extended and interpreted by decision that there is almost a second common law based on the early statutes. The modern statutes are the Salmon Fisheries (Scotland) Acts 1828,[46] 1862[47] and 1868,[48] the Salmon and Freshwater Fisheries (Protection) (Scotland) Act 1951,[49] the Sea Fish (Conservation) Act 1967[50] and the Freshwater and Salmon Fisheries (Scotland) Act 1976.[51] The Acts deal chiefly with three subjects: (1) close time for salmon; (2) prohibition of fixed engines and certain other methods of fishing; and (3) restrictions on the erection of obstructions to the free passage of the fish up and down the river. The Secretary of State has now general superintendence of salmon fisheries except in the Tweed. The fisheries and the adjoining sea have been divided into districts, each district being under the charge of a District Board elected by the fishery proprietors of the district. Protection orders in relation to catchment areas of rivers may be made, and wardens appointed to secure compliance with the orders.[52] Water authorities have a general duty to maintain, improve, and develop the salmon fisheries in their areas.[53]

Under the 1868 Act the annual close time for each district is 168 days.[54] No person may fish or take salmon during Sunday, and under the 1951 Act the weekly close time, except for rod and line, is from 12 noon on Saturday to

---

[42] See *Gay* v. *Malloch*, 1959 S.C. 110.
[43] *Earl of Zetland* v. *Tennent's Trs.* (1873) 11 M. 469; *Campbell* v. *Muir*, 1908 S.C. 387.
[44] *Lord Monimusk* v. *Forbes* (1623) M. 14264.
[45] *Berry* v. *Wilson* (1841) 4 D. 139.
[46] 9 Geo. IV, c. 39.
[47] 25 & 26 Vict., c. 97.
[48] 31 & 32 Vict., c 123.
[49] 14 & 15 Geo. VI, c. 26.
[50] c. 84.
[51] c. 22.
[52] 1976 Act, ss. 1 and 2.
[53] Water Act 1973 (c. 37), ss. 18, 40; Local Government (Scotland) Act 1973 (c. 65), s. 148 (2).
[54] 1868 Act, s. 9 (1).

6 a.m. on Monday.[55] The Secretary of State may vary the annual close time for any district on petition of the District Board.

Salmon fishing by cruives is lawful in rivers above the highest point at which the ebb and flow of the tide is perceptible, where the right is derived from an express grant of cruives by the Crown or from possession for the prescriptive period proceeding on a habile title from the Crown. Except rod fishing, the only other lawful method of fishing for salmon in Scottish rivers, other than the tributaries of the Solway, is by net and coble.[56] Cruives have now practically disappeared. The tests of the legality of the method of fishing by net and coble are these:—(1) That when the net is in the water it is constantly in motion; (2) that one end never leaves the hand of the fisherman; and (3) that the fish are surrounded by the whole net and drawn ashore with it.[57]

Obstructions are regulated by by-laws, which provide, inter alia, that no mill dam shall be so altered as to create a greater obstruction to the passage of fish than already existing, and that every dam, weir or cauld shall be provided with a salmon ladder.

Salmon fishing in the Tweed and the Solway is regulated by special statutes. The Esk is regulated by the Salmon and Fresh Water Fisheries Act 1975.[58]

The right of salmon fishing in the sea is obtained in the same way as the right of fishing in rivers, i.e. by Crown grant, express or implied.[59] The prohibition of fishing by fixed instruments does not extend to the seashore.[60] Stake nets, for example, are therefore legal. Fishing for salmon at sea is regulated.[61]

II. POSSESSION OF HERITAGE

9. Effects of Possession.—In the law of heritable property possession has three practical effects. First, a possessor has the right to maintain or recover possession by availing himself of the possessory remedies. Secondly, possession in good faith, even by one who has no valid title, gives the possessor certain advantages. Thirdly, possession is an essential factor in positive prescription. The last of those points has been considered elsewhere,[62] and only the two others need be noticed here.

10. Possessory Remedies.—These are of two kinds, according as they are designed to repel encroachment and retain possession or to recover possession

[55] 1951 Act, s. 13.
[56] Tait's *Game Laws*, p. 161. 1951 Act, s. 2 (1).
[57] Tait's *Game Laws*, p. 179; *Hay* v. *Magistrates of Perth* (1863) 1 M. (H.L.) 41.
[58] c. 51, s. 39. See *Haddon* v. *Craig* 1967 S.L.T. (Sh. Ct.) 25.
[59] *McDouall* v. *Lord Advocate* (1875) 2 R. (H.L.) 49.
[60] Tait's *Game Laws*, p. 162.
[61] Sea Fish (Conservation) Act 1967 (c. 84); Salmon and Migratory Trout (Prohibition of Fishing) (No. 2) Order 1972 (S.I. 1973 No. 207).
[62] See Prescription, Ch. XVI, supra.

which has been lost.[63] The remedy of interdict is designed to maintain the existing state of possession and to prevent any threatened or attempted disturbance of that possession. Removing is the remedy available for recovering possession which has been lost. In either case some prima facie title is required.[64] Infeftment is obviously the best of all titles, but a lease is sufficient,[65] or a title which, though not expressly including the subject, is prima facie applicable thereto.

The possession required must be for not less than seven years,[66] and it must be open, peaceful and exercised as a matter of right. Thus, if the assertion of a right is constantly challenged and active steps are taken to prevent its exercise (as, e.g., where fences are erected by the owner of property across a footpath over it which another or the public claim a right to use), the possession is not of the peaceful kind required.[67] Or if a person holds a subject under contract his possession will probably be ascribed rather to his right under the contract than to an independent right of possession.[68]

A judgment in a possessory action does not settle any question of heritable right. It decides merely that the existing state of possession is not to be inverted. The parties to the possessory action may have no title to raise questions of heritable right, and if they have a title and wish to have such questions settled, the appropriate process is an action of declarator or of reduction. But, standing a possessory judgment in his favour, the holder has the rights of a bona fide possessor,[69] and is entitled to retain possession until he is ousted by an action challenging his title on its merits.

11. Bona Fide Possession.—A bona fide possessor is one who, though not in fact proprietor, believes himself proprietor on probable grounds and with a good conscience.[70] It is necessary that the possession should have been on a colourable title and in bona fides. An obvious case of a colourable title is one ex facie regular but which is subsequently reduced because granted "a non domino." Of bona fides there is an excellent instance in the undernoted case,[71] where the holder took the advice of counsel as to his rights, and in accordance with the opinion continued to exercise the rights of a proprietor.

A bona fide possessor, however, is put in mala fide when the true owner vindicates his right. This may happen if the true owner produces clear and irrefutable evidence of his right. Otherwise, the possessor is put in mala fide only by the decree of a Court. It depends on circumstances whether the judgment of a Lord Ordinary will have this effect. In a case of great difficulty the possessor may be protected until judgment in the Inner House, or even in some exceptional cases in the House of Lords.

[63] Mackay's *Manual of Practice*, p. 176; Burn Murdoch on *Interdict*, p. 75.
[64] *Carson* v. *Miller* (1863) 1 M. 604, per Lord Justice-Clerk Inglis, at 611; cf. Stair, IV, 3, 47.
[65] *Galloway* v. *Cowden* (1884) 12 R. 578.
[66] *Colquhoun* v. *Paton* (1859) 21 D. 996.
[67] *McKerron* v. *Gordon* (1876) 3 R. 429.
[68] *Calder* v. *Adam* (1870) 8 M. 645.
[69] Infra, § 12.
[70] Erskine, *Inst.*, II, 1, 25.
[71] *Huntly's Trs.* v. *Hallyburton's Trs.* (1880) 8 R. 50; see also *Menzies* v. *Menzies* (1863) 1 M. 1025.

12. Effects of Bona Fide Possession.—The effect of bona fides is threefold. In the first place it affords the possessor a defence to a demand by the true owner of the subject for restoration of the fruits drawn by the possessor. Under the strict rule of law one who has, without a valid title, been in possession and drawn the fruits of a subject might be required by the true owner to restore both the subject and these fruits. But where the possession has been held by a bona fide possessor he is allowed the benefit of an equitable plea in defence to the claim for restoration, the effect of which is that he is permitted to retain, not indeed the subject,[72] but the fruits which he has drawn.[73] Of this plea Stair observes that as it "is in favour of the innocent possessor, so it is in hatred of the other party not pursuing his right."[74]

Fruits while still growing belong to the owner of the soil, but when severed they become moveable and the property of the bona fide possessor.[75] In terms this applies to natural fruits, but the rule extends to industrial fruits, and to civil fruits, such as rents.[75] Everything severed while the possessor is in bona fide belongs to him.

The second advantage which accrues to a bona fide possessor is that he is entitled to recompense for improvements made by him on the subject possessed in the belief that he was enhancing the value of his own property. The true owner must repay him the amount of his expenditure, in so far as, and to the extent to which, it has benefited the subjects. But, if a liferenter executes improvements on the subject liferented he has no such claim, as presumably he was led to do so for his own benefit while his right subsisted.[76]

Lastly there is no liability for violent profits. A possessor in bad faith is responsible for violent profits. "Violent profits are profits acquired by violence—by an intruder without colour of law, who must account on the strictest footing."[77] They include not only all the profits which the owner could have made if he had been in possession, but also all damage which the subject may receive at the hands of the possessor.[78] Violent profits in the case of houses and other urban subjects in burghs were customarily double the rent.[79]

III. INCIDENTS OF OWNERSHIP

13. Right to Use Property.—The right of property in land entitles the proprietor to make what use of it he pleases, subject only to such restrictions as may be imposed by the common law or by statute or by the necessity for observing the rights of his neighbours or of the public generally. In addition to

---

[72] *Darling's Trs.* v. *Darling's Trs.,* 1909 S.C. 445.
[73] *Menzies* v. *Menzies* (1863) 1 M. 1025, per Lord Ardmillan.
[74] Stair, II, 1, 24.
[75] *Duke of Roxburghe* v. *Wauchope* (1825) 1 W. & S. 41.
[76] *Wallace* v. *Braid* (1900) 2 F. 754; see Quasi-Contract, Ch. XIV, supra, § 7.
[77] *Houldsworth* v. *Brand's Trs.* (1876) 3 R. 304, per Lord Justice-Clerk Moncreiff.
[78] *Gardner* v. *Beresford's Trs.* (1877) 4 R. 1091, per Lord President Inglis; see *Inglis' Trs.* v. *Macpherson,* 1910 S.C. 46.
[79] Erskine, *Inst.,* II, 6, 54; Bell, *Prin.,* § 1268 (c); *Jute Industries* v. *Wilson & Graham,* 1955 S.L.T. (Sh. Ct.) 46. But see Local Government (Scotland) Act 1973 (c. 65), s. 1 (5).

such general restrictions he may also be limited in his right of use by the conditions of his title or by rights which have been created in favour of other persons.

Of these general restrictions that which has probably most engaged the attention of the Courts is the restraint laid upon a proprietor by the law of neighbourhood. The law acknowledges "the undoubted right of the proprietor to the free and absolute use of his own property, but there is this restraint or limitation imposed for the protection of his neighbour, that he is not so to use his property as to create that discomfort or annoyance to his neighbour which interferes with his legitimate enjoyment."[80] "Sic utere tuo ut alienum non laedas." It is laid down by the institutional writers that a proprietor may be restrained from operations on his property, otherwise lawful, if these are in aemulationem vicini, i.e. for the sole purpose of inconveniencing or injuring his neighbour.[81] The presumption is that the proprietor is not acting emulously[82]; and, if the operations have been undertaken by him with a view to his own convenience or benefit, however inconsiderable, they cannot be restrained.[83] Although little has been heard of it in recent years, there is frequent reference to "this valuable rule of our law"[84] in the older cases,[85] and, but for the decisions in *Mayor of Bradford* v. *Pickles*,[86] and in the cases which have followed it,[87] there would be no reason to think that it had disappeared from our law.

14. Right to Exclusive Possession.—The right of property in land extends, subject to what is said in the next paragraph, "a caelo usque ad centrum." There are at common law no limits in the vertical direction except such as physical conditions impose.[88] A conveyance of land, therefore, in unqualified terms will give the disponee not merely a right to the surface but also to everything beneath the surface.[89] It follows from the exclusive nature of the right of property[90] that a proprietor is entitled to prohibit trespass on his lands. The legal remedy available to the proprietor against trespass is interdict, which will not, however, be granted in the absence of any actual trespass or of an explicit threat of trespass, or if there is no reasonable probability of a trespass being repeated.[91] But "the exclusive right of a

---

[80] *Fleming* v. *Hislop* (1886) 13 R. (H.L.) 43, per Lord Fitzgerald.
[81] Ersk., II, 1, 2; Bankton, IV, 45, 112; Bell's *Prin.*, § 964. Cf. the German Code, § 226—"The exercise of a right which can have no purpose except the infliction of injury on another is unlawful"; Smith, *Short Commentary*, p. 530; *More* v. *Boyle*, 1967 S.L.T. (Sh. Ct.) 38.
[82] Bankton, supra.
[83] *Dunlop* v. *Robertson*, 1803, Hume's Decs. 575; *Somerville* v. *Somerville* (1613) M. 12769. The doctrine applies only to active operations: *Graham* v. *Greig* (1838) 1 D. 171.
[84] *Ritchie* v. *Purdie* (1833) 11 S. 771, per Lord Gillies.
[85] These are collected in Rankine on *Landownership*, p. 381, and *Encyclopaedia of Scots Law*, Vol. XII, p. 497. *Weir* v. *Aiton* (1858) 20 D. 968.
[86] [1895] A.C. 587. See *Young & Co.* v. *Bankier Distillery Co.* (1893) 20 R. (H.L.) 76 at 77; *Campbell* v. *Muir*, 1908 S.C. 387.
[87] See Reparation, Ch. XXXIV, supra, § 6.
[88] *Glasgow City and District Ry.* v. *MacBrayne* (1883) 10 R. 894, per Lord McLaren, at 899. But see Carriage by Air, Ch. XXXI, supra, § 1.
[89] See *Campbell* v. *McCutcheon*, 1963 S.C. 505.
[90] See Property, Heritable and Moveable, Ch. XXXVI, supra, § 1.
[91] Bell, *Prin.*, § 961; Rankine on *Landownership*, 140; see also *Inverurie Mags.* v. *Sorrie*, 1956 S.C. 175.

landowner yields wherever public interest or necessity requires that it should yield."[92] Thus property may be entered for the purpose of extinguishing a fire, in pursuit of a criminal, or by a constable for the purpose of ascertaining whether a crime or offence is being committed[93]; and a right to enter premises without the proprietor's permission may be conferred by statute.[94]

As the proprietor may prevent trespass on the surface of his lands, so may he prevent any encroachment below[95] or above the surface. Thus he has been held entitled to insist on the removal of a cornice on his neighbour's house which projected a few inches beyond the boundary[96]; he is not bound to submit to the branches of his neighbour's trees overhanging his ground, and may remove such branches[97]; he may prevent the jib of a crane passing over his property.[98]

15. Minerals.—Mines[99] of gold and silver, and mines of lead of such fineness that three halfpennies of silver may be got out of the pound of lead, belong to the Crown.[1] The Crown, however, is not merely entitled, but is bound, when required, to make a grant of these precious minerals to the proprietor of the lands in which they are found in consideration of payment of a royalty.[2] Coal is vested in the National Coal Board.[3] All other minerals belong to the owner of the land in which they are found. A lease of minerals differs from the ordinary lease of urban or agricultural subjects. "The true nature of a mineral lease seems to be rather a grant of a temporary privilege— a privilege during a period of removing and appropriating so much of the substance of the minerals within a certain area as the grantee may be able or may choose to excavate, and that for a consideration or price calculated according either to the duration of the privilege or the amount appropriated."[4] What is called a mineral lease is really, when properly considered, a sale out and out of a portion of the land.[5] The consideration under the lease is either rent or royalties (i.e. a payment on the amount of minerals won by the

---

92 Bell, *Prin.*, § 956.
93 *Shepherd* v. *Menzies* (1900) 2 F. 443; *Southern Bowling Club* v. *Ross* (1902) 4 F. 405.
94 Thus the Health and Safety at Work etc. Act 1974, s. 20, authorises inspectors to enter upon premises without the permission of the owner, and the Burgh Police (Scotland) Act 1892, s. 118, as amended by the Local Government (Scotland) Act 1973, Schedule 28, authorises the proper officer of the islands or district council to enter dwellinghouses where he has reason to believe that they are not in a cleanly condition, and to cleanse and purify them. Other instances are all too common. In the 1952 statutes, for example, two examples are listed, under the Customs and Excise, and Hypnotism Acts of that year.
95 *Davey* v. *Harrow Corporation* [1958] 1 Q.B. 60.
96 *Milne* v. *Mudie* (1828) 6 S. 967; *Hazle* v. *Turner* (1840) 2 D. 886.
97 *Halkerson* v. *Wedderburn*, 1781 M. 10495; *Lemmon* v. *Webb* [1895] A.C. 1.
98 *Brown* v. *Lee Constructions*, 1977 S.L.T. (Notes) 61; but see *Woollerton and Wilson* v. *Richard Costain* [1970] 1 W.L.R. 411.
99 There has been much controversy as to whether particular substances such as freestone, whinstone, clay, oil-shale, are or are not minerals; see *N. B. Ry.* v. *Budhill Coal Co.*, 1910 S.C. (H.L.) 1; *Cal. Ry.* v. *Symington*, 1912 S.C. (H.L.) 9; *Borthwick Norton* v. *Paul*, 1947 S.C. 659; *Secretary of State for Scotland* v. *Assessor for Inverness-shire*, 1948 S.C. 334.
1 Royal Mines Act 1424 (c. 12).
2 Mines & Metals Act 1592 (c. 31); *Earl of Hopetoun* v. *Officers of State* (1750) M. 13527; *Earl of Breadalbane* v. *Jamieson* (1875) 2 R. 826.
3 Coal Industry Nationalisation Act 1946 (9 & 10 Geo. VI, c. 59), s. 5.
4 *Fleeming* v. *Baird* (1871) 9 M. 730, per Lord Justice-Clerk Moncreiff.
5 *Gowans* v. *Christie* (1873) 11 M. (H.L.) 1, 12.

lessee) or it may be both. But the term "rent" is figurative, as the payment is not for the use of the soil but for the consumption or taking away of part of it.[6]

16. Minerals under Railways, the Foreshore, the Sea or Highways.—Special questions arise in regard to minerals thus situated.

When, towards the middle of the nineteenth century, the railways were being constructed, difficulties emerged in connection with land rights. If, under their powers as to the acquisition of land, no provision had been made as to the minerals, the railway companies would have found themselves compelled to take the minerals as included in the land; and, apart from other difficulties, as the value, or even the existence, of minerals was in many cases uncertain, it would have been impossible to fix a fair value for lands compulsorily acquired. The Railway Clauses Consolidation (Scotland) Act 1845[7] was passed to deal with this situation, and the statutory provisions are now contained in sections 70 to 78 of that Act, as amended by sections 15 to 17 of the Mines (Working Facilities and Support) Act 1923.[8] The railway is not to be entitled to minerals under the land purchased, except so much as must be dug out or carried away or used in its construction, unless it shall have been expressly purchased. With these exceptions all minerals are deemed to be excepted from the conveyance. If the party in right of the minerals lying under the "area of protection" desires to work them, he must give notice to the railway and to the royalty owner (if any); and the railway has then the right to prevent the working of the minerals on paying compensation to the mine owner and the royalty owner. By the "area of protection" is meant the area comprising any railway or works and such lateral distance therefrom on all or both sides thereof as is equal at each point along the railway to one-half the depth of the seam at that point, or forty yards, whichever be the greater. Minerals under the foreshore belong to the Crown as owner of the foreshore, but may be alienated in favour of a subject, provided the rights of the public are not interfered with.[9] Subject to the permission of the local coast protection authority, the excavation of minerals on or under the seashore (other than minerals more than 50 feet below the surface) is prohibited.[10]

Minerals under the sea within the three-mile limit also belong to the Crown. The opinion has been expressed that, in so far as they are capable of being worked without causing disturbance, they may be alienated in favour of a subject.[11]

Minerals under roads may be excavated by the owner. Road trustees and

---

[6] *Nugent* v. *Nugent's Trs.* (1899) 2 F. (H.L.) 21, 22.
[7] 8 & 9 Vict., c. 33.
[8] 13 & 14 Geo. V, c. 20; see also the Mining Industry Act 1926 (16 & 17 Geo. V, c. 28), ss. 9, 24 (1); Coal Industry Nationalisation Act 1946 (9 & 10 Geo. VI, c. 59), s. 65; Railway and Canal Commission (Abolition) Act 1949 (12, 13 & 14 Geo. VI., c. 11); Mines (Working Facilities and Support) Act 1966 (c. 4); Mines (Working Facilities and Support) Act 1974 (c. 36).
[9] Supra, § 4.
[10] Coast Protection Act 1949 (12 & 13 Geo. VI, c. 74), s. 18; see *British Dredging (Services)* v. *Secretary of State for Wales and Monmouthshire* [1975] 1 W.L.R. 687.
[11] *Wemyss* v. *Lord Advocate* (1899) 2 F. (H.L.) 1, per Lord Watson.

other authorities have no right to them, but may prevent workings which endanger the road.[12]

17. Game.[13]—Game falls within the class of animals which are not the subject of property until appropriated.[14] "If we were at liberty to go to the law of nature we perhaps might not see our way to draw a distinction between those birds and animals ferae naturae that are game and those that are not so. But the law of Scotland has always, or at least for a long period, recognised such a distinction."[15] The various Game Acts are elsewhere[16] referred to, and each Act must be consulted to find what birds and animals are classed as game under it. There is no general definition, but hares, pheasants, partridges and grouse are included in all the Acts.

The right to kill game is an incident of the right of landed property; a privilege sui generis, which has nothing to do with the ordinary use of land.[17] A tenant as such has no right to take the game, since it is a right belonging to the proprietor alone.

The Game (Scotland) Act 1772[18] protects grouse from December 10 to August 12, blackgame from December 10 to August 20, partridges from February 1 to September 1, and pheasants from February 1 to October 1.

18. Fishing.[19]—Fish belong to no one while they are in their natural state, but if enclosed in a fish-pond they become the property of the person having right to, and enclosing them in, the pond.[20] The right of angling for trout in private streams is an accessory to the right of property in the adjoining lands, and there is no common right of fishing for trout belonging to the public at large or to such members of the community as may have access to the water by virtue of a right of passage along the banks.[21] The same rule applies to lochs[22] and to rivers which are navigable but not tidal.[23] With regard to the rights of opposite proprietors, each has a right to fish up to the middle of the stream, and, at least in small rivers, each has a common interest in that part of the river which flows between their estates.[24]

IV. NATURAL RIGHTS OF PROPERTY

19. Natural Rights and Servitudes.—Ownership of property carries with it certain rights against, and obligations towards, owners and occupiers of

---

[12] *Waddell* v. *Earl of Buchan* (1868) 6 M. 690.
[13] Tait's *Game and Fishing Laws of Scotland,* 2nd ed..
[14] See Moveable Property, Corporeal, Ch. XXXVII, supra, § 4.
[15] *Welwood* v. *Husband* (1874) 1 R. 507, at p. 511.
[16] See Criminal Law, Ch. L, infra, Part II, § 35, and Leases, Ch. XXXIII, supra, §§ 22 and 28.
[17] *Welwood* v. *Husband,* supra.
[18] 13 Geo. III, c. 54, as amended by the Protection of Birds Act 1954 (2 & 3 Eliz. II, c. 30).
[19] Tait's *Game and Fishing Laws of Scotland,* 2nd ed. For salmon fishing, see § 8 ante.
[20] *Copland* v. *Maxwell* (1871) 9 M. (H.L.) 1. The Theft Act 1607 (c. 3) provides that whosoever takes fish "in proper stanks and lochs" shall be liable to a fine. The taking of fish from a stank is theft—*Pollok* v. *McCabe,* 1910 S.C. (J.) 23.
[21] *Fergusson* v. *Shirreff* (1844) 6 D. 1363.
[22] *Montgomery* v. *Watson* (1861) 23 D. 635.
[23] *Grant* v. *Henry* (1894) 21 R. 358.
[24] *Arthur* v. *Aird,* 1907 S.C. 1170.

neighbouring property. Some of these rights arise ex lege from the relative situations of the properties: these may be called natural rights. Other rights, which are created by prescription or agreement, express or implied, are known as servitudes, and are dealt with hereafter under that head.[25] The former are necessary for the comfortable enjoyment of property, and are real rights of the same nature as ownership itself. They are incidents of the title to the property. They may be modified by the operation of contract, express or implied, e.g. by a servitude; but they cannot properly be said to be discharged or extinguished by contract, seeing that, if the contractual superimposed right comes to an end, the original natural right revives in full force.[26]

Certain of these rights are sometimes described as natural servitudes, but it seems better to reserve the term servitude to denote rights which do not arise ex lege, but from grant or prescription.

Natural rights of property may be considered with reference to (a) the right of support to land; (b) rights in water incidental to property in land; and (c) the rights of enjoyment of property which are protected by the law of nuisance.

20. Right of Support.—Land in general requires support both from below and from the surrounding land; if the necessary subjacent or adjacent support is withdrawn, it subsides with or without surface cracking. And here it is necessary to distinguish between land in its natural state and land carrying buildings. Obviously land carrying buildings requires greater support than it would if in its natural state, and a neighbouring owner may be bound to afford sufficient support for the land itself, but not bound to support the additional burden of the buildings.

An owner of land has an unqualified right to such support as is necessary to uphold the land in its natural state.[27] Questions regarding support generally arise where underlying supporting strata have been removed by mining.[28] "If A conveys minerals to B reserving the property of the surface, or if A conveys the surface to B reserving the property of the minerals below it, A in the one case retains, and B in the other gets, a right to have the surface supported unless the contrary shall be expressly provided or shall appear by plain implication from the terms of the conveyance."[29] Where the right of support is not displaced by provision or implication, and a subsidence occurs, it is an actionable wrong, involving liability in damages independent of negligence; but this liability is owed only to the landowner as an incident of ownership in

---

[25] See infra, § 25.

[26] Rankine, *Landownership*, p. 385.

[27] *Dalton* v. *Angus* (1881) 6 App.Cas. 740; *Bank of Scotland* v. *Stewart* (1891) 18 R. 957.

[28] For right of support for pipes laid under statutory authority, see *Edinburgh and District Water Trs.* v. *Clippens Oil Co.* (1900) 3 F. 156, and *Midlothian County Council* v. *N.C.B.*, 1960 S.C. 308; and for liability of National Coal Board for damage caused by subsidence of workings vested in it, see Coal Industry Nationalisation Act 1946, s. 48 (1); Coal Mining (Subsidence) Act 1957 (5 & 6 Eliz. II, c. 59), as amended by the Statute Law (Repeals) Act 1973 (c. 39), Schedule 1, and the Local Government (Scotland) Act 1973 (c. 65), Schedule 27.

[29] *White* v. *Wm. Dixon* (1883) 10 R. (H.L.) 45, per Lord Watson; *Cal. Ry.* v. *Sprot* (1856) 2 Macq. 449; *Butterknowle Colliery Co.* v. *Bishop Auckland Industrial Co-operative Co.* [1906] A.C. 305. The principles governing the decisions are applicable in both England and Scotland; *Caledonian Ry.* v. *Sprot* (1856) 2 Macq. 449 at 461; *Buchanan* v. *Andrew* (1873) 11 M. (H.L.) 13 at 16.

respect of damage to his property, and not to other parties for personal injury.[30] Each fresh subsidence is a new wrong allowing of a further action of damages, even though no further mining has taken place between the earlier and the later subsidence.[31] This right to bring more than one action of damages is not an exception to the general rule that the whole damages resulting from one wrong must be sued for in one action, for the ground of action in this case is not the mining but the subsidence, and each fresh subsidence is a new and independent infringement of the surface owner's rights.

Somewhat similar questions may arise between adjacent owners. Where there is rock close to the surface little adjacent support may be necessary, but where the ground is friable considerable subsidence might be caused by a neighbour digging or quarrying right up to the edge of his property: in such a case the neighbour is bound to stop excavating at such a distance from his boundary as will leave sufficient support for the neighbouring land.

Where buildings are placed on the lands there can be no natural right of support for the surface thus altered. In England the right of support of buildings is regarded as of the nature of a servitude. In Scotland the law is not so clearly developed. The right of support for buildings may be acquired in various ways. Thus it may be obtained by express grant, but it more usually arises from implied grant.[32] Where the ownership of the minerals is severed from that of the surface after buildings have been erected, it will be held that the mineral owner is bound to afford sufficient support for the enjoyment of the surface with buildings as they exist when the severance takes place, for parties cannot be held to have contemplated that existing buildings were not to be supported. On the other hand, it cannot be implied that the mineral owner has undertaken to support and to be liable for damage to all buildings, however extensive, which may afterwards be erected, for this might subject him to heavy claims for damages in respect of property which the parties never had in contemplation.[33] But if, at the time of the severance of the ownership of the minerals from that of the land, the land was conveyed expressly with a view to the erection of buildings or to any other use which might render increased support necessary, there is an implied right to such support as the contemplated use of such land requires.[34]

The right of the surface owner to support may, however, be modified by the terms of his title or by agreement. The mineral owner may be entitled to bring down the surface on payment of damages,[35] or even without paying damages.[36] The Mines (Working Facilities and Support) Act 1966[37] gives

---

[30] *Angus* v. *N.C.B.*, 1955 S.C. 175.

[31] *Darnley Main Co.* v. *Mitchell* (1886) 11 App.Cas. 127.

[32] *Dalton* v. *Angus*, supra, at 792, 830.

[33] *Hamilton* v. *Turner* (1867) 5 M. 1086 at 1095, 1099, 1100.

[34] *Caledonian Ry.* v. *Sprot* (1856) 2 Macq. 449; *North British Ry.* v. *Turner's* (1904) 6 F. 900; *Dalton* v. *Angus*, supra, at 792.

[35] *Anderson* v. *McCracken Brothers* (1900) 2 F. 780.

[36] *Buchanan* v. *Andrew* (1873) 11 M. (H.L.) 13; *Bank of Scotland* v. *Stewart* (1891) 18 R. 957; *Pringle* v. *Carron Co.* (1905) 7 F. 820.

[37] c. 4, as amended by the Mines (Working Facilities and Support) Act 1974 (c. 36).

power to the Court of Session[38] to grant to a person having the right to work minerals various ancillary rights provided these are required for the proper and convenient working of the minerals. These ancillary rights include a right to let down the surface on payment of compensation.

The support due by the owner of a building to a contiguous building or to the upper storey of the same building is noticed under the heading of Common Interest.[39]

21. Rights in Water: Water not in a Definite Channel.[40]—Surface water, or water percolating through the ground, may be appropriated by the owner of the land where it is found. It cannot be conveyed as property separately from the land itself.[41] A neighbouring proprietor may have a right to object to the appropriation of water from a definite stream or water course, but until water has reached such a stream it is entirely at the disposal of the person in whose land it is found. So an owner may appropriate underground percolating water by sinking a well, notwithstanding that this may cause his neighbour's well to dry up; his neighbour has no right to object, even if he enjoyed for the prescriptive period the well now rendered useless.[42] But, in the general case, an owner desires not to appropriate but to get rid of surface water. Such water may drain directly into a stream, and in that case no difficulty arises. On the other hand it may drain naturally on to lower land owned by a different proprietor, and in that case, the owner of the lower land is bound to receive it.[43] But the owner of the higher ground is not entitled to increase this burden on his neighbour by draining in such a way as to send down to the neighbouring land water which would not naturally run that way, or by sending down water artificially brought to the surface by pumping operations or conveyed from a distant stream.[44] It is otherwise in the case of ordinary agricultural drainage. This may alter the natural run-off of surface water, and may thereby considerably increase the burden on the adjacent owner. Nevertheless the latter is bound to receive it. It might be thought that the inferior owner should not be bound to suffer any increase of the natural burden, but it has long been settled that, as agricultural drainage is a necessary operation, the adjacent owner has no right to object to it and is bound to submit to the consequent alteration of the natural flow of water on to his land.[45] Provision for regulating such drainage on application to, and under the authority of, the sheriff is made by the Land Drainage (Scotland)

---

[38] Formerly the Railway and Canal Commissioners: Part I of the Mines (Working Facilities and Support) Act 1923 (13 & 14 Geo. V, c. 20), until s. 1 of the Railway and Canal Commission (Abolition) Act 1949 (12 & 13 Geo. VI, c. 11) substituted the Court of Session.

[39] Liferent and Fee, Ch. XL, infra, § 17.

[40] See Ferguson's *Law of Water and Water Rights of Scotland.*

[41] *Crichton* v. *Turnbull*, 1946 S.C. 52.

[42] *Chasemore* v. *Richards* (1859) 7 H.L.C. 349; *Mayor of Bradford* v. *Pickles* [1895] A.C. 587; *Milton* v. *Glen-Moray Glenlivet Distillery Co.* (1898) 1 F. 135; *Bradford Corporation* v. *Ferrand* [1902] 2 Ch. 655; *Langbrook Properties* v. *Surrey County Council* [1970] 1 W.L.R. 161.

[43] *Campbell* v. *Bryson* (1864) 3 M. 254.

[44] *Young* v. *Bankier Distillery* (1893) 20 R. (H.L.) 76; contrast *Anderson* v. *Robertson*, 1958 S.C. 367. Different considerations arise where an artificial embankment has been constructed to protect land from the sea: *McLaren* v. *British Railways Board*, 1971 S.C. 182.

[45] *Campbell* v. *Bryson*, supra.

Act 1930.[46] The obligation of an inferior owner to receive the natural run-off may also arise in connection with mining. A mineowner is entitled to work his minerals right up to his boundary, although this may cause water to drain into adjacent workings. The neighbouring mineowner has no right to object to this; if he requires protection he must protect himself by leaving an adequate barrier of his own minerals.[47] The Secretary of State has power to make schemes for the drainage of agricultural land.[48]

22. Streams.—Once water has reached a watercourse, however small it may be[49] and whether it be above or below the surface, very different principles apply. Such water is no longer subject to the sole control of the owner on whose land it happens to be. All the riparian proprietors, from the source to the mouth of the stream, have a common interest in it, and are entitled to object if their particular interests are infringed. Members of the public have no right to interfere in any case except where a stream is navigable.[50]

The bed or alveus of a non-tidal stream belongs to the proprietor of the land through which it flows, and if the stream separates the lands of two proprietors, each is prima facie owner of the soil of the bed up to the medium filum or middle line of the stream.[51] But although the bed of the stream may belong to a proprietor, he has no right to interfere with it in any way which may result in injury to the interest of any other riparian proprietor.[52] A proprietor may, however, acquire, by the operation of prescription, certain rights which prejudice other riparian proprietors.

Apart from fishing questions, an upper heritor is not concerned with the operations of a lower heritor except in so far as these cause, or are likely to cause, the water to regurgitate and prevent it from flowing freely away from the upper heritor's land.[53] But the position of the lower heritor exposes him to greater risk that his rights in the water may be prejudiced by the interference of the upper heritor with the quantity or quality of flow of the stream.

A riparian proprietor has a right to take water from the stream for what are known as the primary uses, i.e. drink for man and beast and ordinary domestic purposes, even though the result should be to exhaust the water altogether. He may be entitled to draw off water for other purposes, e.g. irrigation or manufacturing operations, but he can do so only if no other riparian proprietor's interest is thereby infringed.[54] "A riparian proprietor is entitled to have the water of the stream on the banks of which his property lies flow down as it has been accustomed to flow down to his property, subject to

---

[46] 20 Geo. V, c. 20.
[47] *Durham* v. *Hood* (1871) 9 M. 474.
[48] Land Drainage (Scotland) Act 1941 (4 & 5 Geo. VI, c. 13).
[49] *Cruikshanks & Bell* v. *Henderson*, 1791 Hume's *Decisions* 506.
[50] See § 5 ante.
[51] *Menzies* v. *Marquess of Breadalbane* (1901) 4 F. 55.
[52] *Morris* v. *Bicket* (1866) 4 M. (H.L.) 44.
[53] *Hope* v. *Heriot's Hospital* (1878) 15 S.L.R. 400.
[54] *McCartney* v. *Londonderry & Lough Swilly Ry.* [1904] A.C. 301; *Young* v. *Bankier Distillery Co.* (1893) 20 R. (H.L.) 76, per Lord Macnaghten; *Rugby Joint Water Board* v. *Walters* [1967] Ch. 397.

the ordinary use of the flowing water by upper proprietors, and such further use, if any, on their part in connection, with their property as may be reasonable under the circumstances. Every riparian proprietor is thus entitled to the water of his stream in its natural flow without sensible diminution or increase, and without sensible alteration in its character or quality. Any invasion of this right causing actual damage, or calculated to found a claim which may ripen into an adverse right, entitles the party injured to the intervention of the Court."[55] If the natural speed or direction of flow of the stream as it comes down to the lower proprietor's land is altered, this may injure him by requiring him to strengthen the banks of the stream in his property, or it may have the effect of altering the channel of the stream when it reaches him. So also if the natural flow of the stream is altered (e.g. if it is stored up and released at intervals), the inferior heritor who is injured by the resulting intermittent flow of the stream, may object.[56] But a lower heritor has in general no interest to object to an upper heritor diverting a part, or even the whole of, the stream, provided that the water is returned to the stream without sensible diminution in quantity or deterioration in quality before the stream reaches the property of the lower heritor.[57] Whilst obviously the natural overflow of a stream involves nobody in liability, an overflow of one which has been converted to use as a public sewer by, e.g., a local authority, may render the authority liable.[58]

A riparian proprietor has also an interest to prevent any interference with the stream by the proprietor of the land on the opposite side. No riparian proprietor is, even on his own portion of the alveus, entitled to do anything which prejudicially affects the common interest in the flowing water or from which such a result may reasonably be apprehended: any such operation may be prevented unless the Court is satisfied that there is not, and will not at any future time be, any injury resulting from it.[59] A heritor is entitled to put an embankment on his own lands, if this is necessary to prevent their being flooded, although it has the effect of increasing the flood on the lands of the opposite heritor[60]; but he has no right to obstruct the regular channels through which the river flows in time of flood, even if these are dry at other times.[61] In a question with an opposite heritor an owner is not entitled to divert water for any purpose even though he returns it before the stream leaves his property, for any such diversion must diminish the stream flowing past the opposite heritor's property.[62]

A heritor may also prevent any operations which cause appreciable change in the quality of the water flowing past his property. Discharge of sewage or

---

55 Per Lord Macnaghten in *Young* v. *Bankier Distillery Co.*, supra.
56 *Hunter & Aitkenhead* v. *Aiken* (1880) 7 R. 510.
57 *Orr Ewing* v. *Colquhoun's Trs.* (1877) 4 R. (H.L.) 116, per Lord Blackburn, at p. 127.
58 See *Greyhound Racing Trust* v. *Edinburgh Corporation*, 1952 S.L.T. 35. See too the Control of Pollution Act 1974 (c. 40).
59 *Morris* v. *Bicket*, supra; *Orr Ewing* v. *Colquhoun's Trs.*, supra, per Lord Blackburn; *McGavin* v. *McIntyre Brothers* (1890) 17 R. 818, per Lord Trayner; *Kensit* v. *Great Eastern Ry.* (1884) 27 Ch. D. 122, per Cotton L.J.
60 *Farquharson* v. *Farquharson* (1741) M. 12779; *Gerrard* v. *Crowe* [1921] A.C. 395.
61 *Menzies* v. *E. Breadalbane* (1828) 3 W. & S. 235.
62 *White & Sons* v. *White* (1906) 8 F. (H.L.) 41.

other matter into a stream is not prohibited at common law so long as no appreciable pollution results. Perhaps the most frequently adopted criterion of pollution is whether or not the addition of the material objected to unfits the water of the stream for use for any of the primary purposes, but this is not in all cases the proper test. An upper heritor's operations may leave the water fit to drink but may unfit it for some special use to which the lower heritor has been putting it, e.g. distilling: in such a case the lower heritor is entitled to object.[63] The fact that a certain amount of pollution may have already existed apart from the operations complained of does not entitle any heritor to increase the amount of pollution if such increased pollution causes any damage to lower heritors.[64] Some degree of pollution may have become legalised by continuing for the prescriptive period, and in that case the heritor causing the pollution is entitled to continue his operations, but not to increase the amount of noxious matter which he discharges into the stream. The common law has, however, been substantially replaced on the question of river pollution by statutory provisions, the current ones being contained in the Rivers (Prevention of Pollution) (Scotland) Acts 1951 and 1965,[65] and the Control of Pollution Act 1974.[66] The 1951 Act[67] provided for the establishment of river purification boards with functions to prevent the pollution of rivers. It is an offence to cause[68] or knowingly to permit to enter a stream any poisonous, noxious or polluting matter; to impede the proper flow of the water of a stream in a manner leading to a substantial aggravation of pollution; to permit to enter a stream any solid waste matter[69]; or to discharge, without the consent of the river pollution authority, trade or sewage effluent into a stream; or to discharge into a stream any matter other than trade or sewage effluent from a sewer.[70] Where any sewage effluent is discharged into a stream from any works or sewer vested in a local authority and the authority was bound to receive into the works or sewer matter included in the discharge, the authority is guilty of an offence whether or not it caused or knowingly permitted the discharge.[71]

23. Lochs.—Lochs fall into two classes. First, there are those which are entirely surrounded by the lands of one proprietor. In that case the whole loch (water and solum) belongs to the owner of the surrounding land and is under his sole control. If a stream runs out of it, however, he is limited in his use of the loch by the necessity for respecting the rights of the riparian owners in the stream. Secondly, the loch may be one on which the lands of several owners abut. In this case there is a presumption of a joint right of property in all. The

---

[63] *Young* v. *Bankier Distillery* (1893) 20 R. (H.L.) 76.
[64] *McIntyre Brothers* v. *McGavin* (1893) 20 R. (H.L.) 49.
[65] 14 & 15 Geo. VI, c. 66; 1965, c. 13. These Acts replaced the Rivers Pollution Prevention Acts 1876 and 1893.
[66] c. 40, Part II.
[67] Now read with the Local Government (Scotland) Act 1973 (c. 65), s. 135.
[68] *Impress (Worcester)* v. *Rees* [1971] 2 All E.R. 357; *Alphacell* v. *Woodward* [1971] 2 All E.R. 910; *Price* v. *Cromack* [1975] 1 W.L.R. 988.
[69] 1974 Act, s. 31; cf. *Gavin* v. *Ayr County Council*, 1950 S.C. 197.
[70] 1974 Act, s. 32.
[71] 1974 Act, s. 32 (2), (5), (6).

titles or the titles coupled with the state of possession may, however, be such as to give one owner the exclusive right.[72] When there are joint rights each proprietor has an exclusive right to the solum from his own shore up to the middle of the loch.[73] But he must not interfere with the enjoyment by the other owners of their right to the water, which is common to all.[74] All proprietors have the right to sail and fish upon the loch, but the Court may restrict or regulate the number of boats each proprietor may put on it.[75] The common law rights of owners of lands surrounding an artificial loch or reservoir are not clearly settled.[76] There are statutory provisions concerning pollution.[77]

24. Nuisance.—This is the term commonly used to denote the infringement of a natural right of property.[78] But the term is used by Bell in a wider sense:—"Whatever obstructs the public means of commerce and intercourse whether in highways or navigable rivers; whatever is noxious, or unsafe, or renders life uncomfortable to the public generally or to the neighbourhood; whatever is intolerably offensive to individuals in their dwelling-houses, or inconsistent with the comfort of life, whether by stench, by noise or by indecency is a nuisance." This definition includes what are in England called public nuisances which have nothing necessarily to do with the law of neighbourhood at all, but concern the public generally. Thus, the owner of a traction engine travelling on the highway has been held to commit a nuisance if he allows sparks to be emitted whereby the trees or houses of people living near the highway are injured.[79] Noise, vibration, and fumes from a launderette may amount to nuisance.[80] Again, there are many statutory nuisances which do not depend on the law of neighbourhood.[81] But the most common instances of nuisance are those referred to in the latter part of Bell's definition, which consist in the disturbance of an owner of property in his use and enjoyment thereof. The owner has a right to the comfortable enjoyment of his property, and the law of nuisance is designed to protect this right. As was said in a recent case, the proper approach to a case of alleged nuisance is rather from the standpoint of the victim of the loss or inconvenience than from the standpoint of the alleged offender.[82] Where the operations complained of interfere with the complainer's comfort and enjoyment the circumstances of the locality must be taken into account.[83] What is a nuisance

---

[72] *Scott* v. *Lord Napier* (1869) 7 M. (H.L.) 35.
[73] *Cochrane* v. *Earl of Minto* (1815) 6 Pat. 139.
[74] *Menzies* v. *Macdonald* (1854) 16 D. 827; affd. 2 Macq. 463.
[75] *Menzies* v. *Wentworth* (1901) 3 F. 941.
[76] *Kilsyth Fish Protection Association* v. *McFarlane*, 1937 S.C. 757.
[77] See, e.g. the Control of Pollution Act 1974 (c. 40), s. 32 (1) (*a*) (iii).
[78] *Prin.*, § 974; *Fleming* v. *Hislop* (1886) 13 R. (H.L.) 43.
[79] *Slater* v. *McLellan*, 1924 S.C. 854; see also *Ogston* v. *Aberdeen Tramways Co.* (1896) 24 R. (H.L.) 8.
[80] *MacNab* v. *McDevitt*, 1971 S.L.T. (Sh. Ct.) 41.
[81] See for example the Control of Pollution Act 1974 (c. 40), s. 58 (8); the Public Health and Burgh Police Acts; *Tontine Hotel (Greenock)* v. *Greenock Corporation*, 1967 S.L.T. 180; *Rae* v. *Burgh of Musselburgh*, 1974 S.L.T. 29.
[82] *Watt* v. *Jamieson*, 1954 S.C. at p. 57, per Lord President Cooper.
[83] But not so, according to English law, where actual injury to property is caused—*St. Helens*

in a residential neighbourhood would not necessarily be one in an industrial district. But an addition to the existing noises or smells in a district may be such as to give a cause of action.[84] If a nuisance exists it will not avail the wrongdoer to plead that it was in existence, and was known by the complainer to exist, when he purchased his property or came to the neighbourhood.[85] Nor is it any defence that other parties or even the complainer himself is contributing to the nuisance,[86] or that the public or a large number of people benefit by that which causes the nuisance,[87] or that the defender has taken all reasonable care to prevent it,[88] or that the defender was merely making a normal and familiar use of his own property.[89] But there is substantial authority to the effect that the owner or occupier of property from which a nuisance originates will be liable only if he had created or caused the nuisance, or if he had knowledge or the means of knowledge that actual nuisance was likely to be committed by other persons.[90] The right to object to a nuisance will be excluded if it has existed without challenge for the period of the negative prescription[91]—20 years[92]; but no shorter period will suffice, and even after the lapse of that period any increase in the extent of the nuisance may be challenged. Further, the objection may be met by showing consent on the part of the complainer, which may be either express agreement or acquiescence or such rei interventus as will create a personal bar. Moreover, what would otherwise be an actionable nuisance may be legalised by statute. If a statute gives an absolute authority to do that which is complained of, irrespective of its consequences in creating a nuisance, no action to prevent it will lie; but it may, on the other hand, be that the statutory authority is provisional in the sense that it is given on the express or implied condition that what is authorised can be done without injury to the rights of others, and in this case the right to complain would not be cut off. Nor will statutory authority afford a defence if the nuisance is due to negligence in carrying out the operation authorised if without such negligence it would be unobjectionable.[93]

Smelting Co. v. *Tipping* (1865) 11 H.L.C. 642; *Shotts Iron Co.* v. *Inglis* (1882) 9 R. (H.L.) 72. It has been held in England that the victim of a continuing nuisance causing damage to his property is entitled to recover the cost of remedying such damage, including that which occurred prior to his acquiring an interest in the property: *Masters* v. *Brent London Borough Council* [1978] 2 W.L.R. 768.

[84] *St. Helens Smelting Co.* v. *Tipping,* supra; *Maguire* v. *Charles McNeil,* 1922 S.C. 174; *Polsue & Alfieri* v. *Rushmer* [1907] A.C. 121.

[85] *Fleming* v. *Hislop* (1886) 13 R. (H.L.) 43.

[86] *Duke of Buccleuch* v. *Cowan* (1866) 5 M. 214.

[87] *Shotts Iron Co.* v. *Inglis* (1882) 9 R. (H.L.) 78.

[88] In other words the action in respect of a nuisance is not based on negligence; *Slater* v. *McLellan,* supra, per Lord President Clyde, at 859; *Rapier* v. *London Tramways Co.* [1893] 2 Ch. 588, per Lindley L.J. at 599.

[89] *Watt* v. *Jamieson,* supra.

[90] See *Gourock Ropework Co.* v. *Greenock Corporation,* 1966 S.L.T. 125; cf. *Smith* v. *Scott* [1973] Ch. 314.

[91] Prescription and Limitation (Scotland) Act 1973 (c. 52), ss. 7 and 8; and cf. *Harvie* v. *Robertson* (1903) 5 F. 338.

[92] See Prescription, Ch. XVI, supra.

[93] *Metropolitan Asylum District* v. *Hill* (1881) 6 App.Cas. 193; *Rapier* v. *London Tramways Co.,* supra; *Manchester Corporation* v. *Farnworth* [1930] A.C. 171; see Reparation, Ch. XXXIV, supra, § 30.

V. SERVITUDES

25. Definition.—A "'servitude' is a burden on land or houses, imposed by agreement—express or implied—in favour of the owners of other tenements; whereby the owner of the burdened or 'servient' tenement, and his heirs and singular successors in the subject, must submit to certain uses to be exercised by the owner of the other or 'dominant' tenement; or must suffer restraint in his own use and occupation of the property. Presupposing those extensions or restraints of the exclusive or absolute right of use which naturally proceed from the situation of conterminous properties, a servitude is a further limitation of that right in favour of the owner of another subject."[94]

Servitudes may be classified in various ways, but the classification of most practical importance is that which divides them into positive and negative servitudes. The quotation from Bell indicates the distinction between positive and negative. A positive servitude is one by which the owner of the dominant tenement is entitled to exercise certain rights over the servient tenement, and which is capable of possession in the sense of being actively exercised by the owner of the dominant tenement. Thus, a right of way or of access over the servient tenement is a positive servitude, as it enables the owner of the dominant tenement to pass over the servient tenement. On the other hand, a negative servitude consists in a restraint on the rights of the owner of the servient tenement and cannot be so possessed. A typical instance of this class is a servitude by which the owner of the servient tenement is restrained from building so as to injure the light of the dominant tenement.

The institutional writers also distinguish servitudes as urban and rural, and personal and praedial. Urban are such as relate to buildings (whether in the town or the country); rural to lands. The distinction between praedial and personal servitudes is of little practical importance as the only personal servitude is liferent,[95] and all other servitudes are praedial.

26. Characteristics of Servitudes.—A servitude exists for the benefit of the dominant tenement: it is a right annexed to that tenement, and no one can have any claim to a servitude except as proprietor of the tenement. It is inalienable and inseparable from the dominant tenement, and the proprietor cannot make it over to anyone not connected with that tenement or set up a right to it independently of the right to the tenement.[96] Moreover, it is for the use and benefit of the dominant tenement and not for purposes unconnected with that tenement. Hence a servitude of way in favour of one estate cannot be used for the benefit of another[97]; and a servitude of digging for slates and stones does not entitle the dominant owner to use his right for the purpose of selling the slates and stones to others.[98]

[94] Bell, *Prin.*, § 979.
[95] See Liferent and Fee, Ch. XL, infra, § 1.
[96] *Drummond* v. *Milligan* (1890) 17 R. 316, per Lord McLaren; *Patrick* v. *Napier* (1867) 5 M. 683, per Lord President Inglis and Lord Ormidale.
[97] *Scotts* v. *Bogles*, July 6, 1809, F.C.; *Irvine Knitters* v. *North Ayrshire Co-operative Society*, 1978 S.L.T. 105.
[98] *Murray* v. *Mags. of Peebles*, Dec. 8, 1808, F.C.

It is a further characteristic of servitudes that the burden imposed on the owner of the servient tenement is not to do anything active but merely to suffer the restraint of his rights involved in the servitude. Thus, as was pointed out in a leading case, an obligation on a vassal to provide and uphold a boat for the use of the superior could not be a servitude because it consisted in faciendo not in patiendo.[99] So also in the case of a servitude of way the owner of the servient tenement is under no obligation to repair the way.[1]

In the exercise of the servitude the owner of the dominant tenement must use his right civiliter, that is to say, in the way which, consistently with its enjoyment, is least burdensome to the servient tenement, and the owner of the latter tenement may make use of his property as he pleases provided he respects the servitude right.[2] Hence, the owner of a moor, over which there exists a servitude of digging and winning peat, is free to plough the moor so long as he leaves what is sufficient for the servitude unploughed[3]; the proprietor of a stream subject to a servitude of watering cattle may cover over the stream if he leaves open so much as is required for the use of the cattle[4]; and the proprietor of land over which is a servitude of footpath may erect swing gates across the path.[5]

27. Constitution of Servitudes.—As a general rule burdens on heritage do not affect singular successors unless they appear in the Register of Sasines.[6] But this is not necessary in the case of servitudes; and heritage may be subject to a servitude although there is no reference to it in the titles of the dominant or of the servient tenement. This being so, it has been held essential that they should be limited "to such uses or restraints as are well-established and defined, leaving others as mere personal agreements. What shall be deemed a servitude of a regular and definite kind is a secondary question, as to which the only description that can be given generally seems to be that it shall be such a use or restraint as by law or custom is known to be likely and incident to the property in question, and to which the attention of a prudent purchaser will in the circumstances naturally be called."[7] But the class of servitudes is not rigid and stereotyped; and there is authority for the view that a burden on property which satisfies the requirements of the law as to the nature and conditions of a servitude may be allowed as a servitude, although there is no precedent specifically recognising it as such. "The habits and requirements of life varying and extending with advancing civilisation, improved agriculture, and multiplying necessities, may render the introduction of a new servitude possible and legitimate. But it must, in my opinion, be of a truly praedial

[99] *Tailors of Aberdeen* v. *Coutts* (1840) 1 Robin.App. 296, per Lord Corehouse, at 310.
[1] *Allan* v. *MacLachlan* (1900) 2 F. 699.
[2] Erskine, *Inst.*, II, 9, 34.
[3] *Watson* v. *Dunkennar Feuars* (1667) M. 14529.
[4] *Beveridge* v. *Marshall*, Nov. 18, 1808, F.C.
[5] *Sutherland* v. *Thomson* (1876) 3 R. 485; *Orr Ewing* v. *Colquhoun's Trs.* (1877) 4 R. (H.L.) 116, at 121, 137.
[6] *Ante*, § 1.
[7] Bell, *Prin.*, 979; approved by Lord Watson in *N.B. Ry.* v. *Park Yard Co.* (1898) 25 R. (H.L.) 47; *Murray's Trs.* v. *Trs. for St. Margaret's Convent* (1906) 8 F. 1109, per Lord Kinnear; 1907 S.C. (H.L.) 8; *Marquis of Huntly* v. *Nicol* (1896) 23 R. 610, per Lord Kinnear.

character, similar in nature and quality to the praedial servitudes which the law has already recognised."[8] There are various modes in which servitudes may be created; and in this matter the distinction between positive and negative servitudes is of importance.

28. Express Grant or Reservation.—Both positive and negative servitudes may be created in this way,[9] and this is the only method of creating a negative servitude.[10] The grant must be made in favour of the owner of the dominant tenement[11] by one who either at the time, or subsequently comes to be, owner of the servient tenement.[12] No servitude can be created by express reservation where the granter remains the owner of the alleged servient tenement.[13] As in the case of other heritable rights, the grant must be contained in a probative writing. It may appear in the titles of the tenements or may be contained in a separate deed. It is not essential that it should appear in the Register of Sasines.[14]

But if it does not enter the Register, the grant of a positive servitude is not effectual against singular successors unless it is followed by possession, so that its existence may be advertised and purchasers put on their guard.[15] If there is possession for a continuous period of twenty years openly, peaceably and without any judicial interruption, and the possession was founded on and followed the execution of a deed which is sufficient in respect of its terms expressly to constitute the servitude, the validity of the servitude as so constituted becomes unchallengeable.[16] In the case of negative servitudes possession is not possible; and these occupy, therefore, a rather anomalous position, as their existence is not disclosed either on the Register or by any acts which may come to the knowledge of a purchaser. The Court tends to interpret more strictly a servitude created by grant than one created by prescription.[17]

Besides express grant or reservation there are two other means by which positive servitudes may come into existence.

29. Implied Grant or Reservation.—The constitution of a servitude by implication may occur when the owner of a heritage severs it into two or more parts and alienates one or more of these parts. A, the proprietor of an estate,

---

[8] *Patrick* v. *Napier* (1867) 5 M. 683, per Lord Ardmillan; *Dyce* v. *Hay* (1849) 11 D. 1266, 1 Macq. 312, per Lord St. Leonards; *Harvey* v. *Lindsay* (1853) 15 D. 768, per Lord Ivory; Rankine, *Landownership*, p. 419.

[9] Erskine, *Inst.*, II, 9 35; *Inglis* v. *Clark* (1901) 4 F. 288; *Metcalfe* v. *Purdon* (1902) 4 F. 507.

[10] Rankine, p. 426.

[11] *Safeway Food Stores* v. *Wellington Motor Company (Ayr)*, 1976 S.L.T. 53.

[12] *Stephen* v. *Brown's Trs.*, 1922 S.C. 136.

[13] *Hamilton* v. *Elder*, 1968 S.L.T. (Sh. Ct.) 53.

[14] Bell, *Prin.*, § 994; *Cowan* v. *Stewart* (1872) 10 M. 735; *McLean* v. *Marwhirn Developments*, 1976 S.L.T. (Notes) 47.

[15] Erskine, *Inst.*, II, 9, 3; *Campbell's Trs.* v. *Glasgow Corporation* (1902) 4 F. 752.

[16] Prescription and Limitation (Scotland) Act 1973 (c. 52), s. 3 (1).

[17] *Crawford* v. *Lumsden*, 1951 S.L.T. (Notes) 62 (reversing the Lord Ordinary: 1951 S.L.T. 64); *Moyes* v. *McDermott* (1900) 2 F. 918; see also *Hunter* v. *Fox*, 1964 S.C. (H.L.) 95; *Robson* v. *Chalmers Property Investment Company*, 1965 S.L.T. 381; *Walker's Exrx.* v. *Carr*, 1973 S.L.T. (Sh. Ct.) 77; *McEachen* v. *Lister*, 1976 S.L.T. (Sh. Ct.) 38; *Irvine Knitters* v. *North Ayrshire Co-operative Society*, 1978 S.L.T. 105.

for example, dispones a portion to B and retains the other portion. B claims that, although there are no words in the disposition creating a servitude over the retained portion, such a servitude has been created by implication. This is a claim to a servitude constituted by implied grant.[18] On the other hand, the proprietor A may claim that the retained portion has by implication a servitude over the portion granted to B. This is a claim to a servitude constituted by implied reservation. These two cases are distinct, and are ruled by different considerations.

In the first case, where the claim is to an implied grant of servitude, the principle that "when anything is granted all things are understood to be granted therewith that are necessary thereto"[19] applies, and, therefore, the grant will include such servitudes as are necessary for the use of the property. Hence, if the only means of access to the land disponed to B is over A's retained portion, a servitude of way over that portion will be implied, for "it is of the essence of property in the soil that the proprietor should have access to and from it."[20] But the law goes further than this. "When two properties are possessed by the same owner and there has been a severance made of part from the other, anything which was used and was necessary for the comfortable enjoyment of that part of the property which is granted shall be considered to follow from the grant if there are the usual words in the conveyance. I do not know whether the usual words are essentially necessary; but where there are the usual words I cannot doubt that this is the law."[21] It is not required that the servitude claimed should be so essential that the property could have no value without it; it is enough that it is necessary for "the convenient and comfortable enjoyment of the property as it existed before the time of the grant." Thus in the leading case of *Ewart* v. *Cochrane* the owner of a tanyard and house with a garden adjoining it constructed a drain from the former to a cesspool in the garden, and thereafter sold the tanyard, retaining the house and garden. In a question between the persons who had come to be in right respectively of the two properties, it was held that the drain could not be removed, as there had passed by implication on the sale of the tanyard a right to keep the drain in the position which it occupied.

Here the servitude claimed was in support of the grant. It is more difficult to establish that a servitude has been impliedly reserved. "If the grantor intends to reserve any right over the tenement granted, it is his duty to reserve it expressly in the grant."[22] This is the general rule. There is an admitted exception where the servitude is one of necessity in the sense that the retained property would be useless without it, as, e.g., a way forming the only access to the property; but it is not enough for this purpose to show merely that the

---

[18] However where there has been an express grant of servitude, the possibility of an implied grant may be precluded: *McEachen* v. *Lister*, 1976 S.L.T. (Sh. Ct.) 38.

[19] Stair, II, 7, 6.

[20] *McLaren* v. *City of Glasgow Union Ry.* (1878) 5 R. 1052, per Lord Justice-Clerk Moncrieff; *Walton Bros.* v. *Mags. of Glasgow* (1876) 3 R. 1130; Stair, II, 7, 10.

[21] Per Lord Campbell in *Cochrane* v. *Ewart* (1861) 4 Macq. 117; see also *Wheeldon* v. *Burrows* (1879) 12 Ch.D. 31; *Gow's Trs.* v. *Mealls* (1875) 2 R. 729; *Costagliole* v. *English* [1969] C.L.Y. 1158.

[22] *Shearer* v. *Peddie* (1899) 1 F. 1201.

servitude claimed as reserved is necessary for the comfortable enjoyment of the reserved portion.[23] If English authorities can be relied on—and there has been frequent reference to these in the Scottish cases—a servitude by implied reservation is allowed where there are reciprocal rights as between the property conveyed and the property retained, as in the case of two adjoining houses originally built together by a common owner and dependent each on the other for support,[24] and it is said that "the law will readily imply the grant or reservation of such easements as may be necessary to give effect to the common intention of the parties to a grant of real property, with reference to the manner or purposes in and for which the land granted or some land retained by the grantor is to be used. But it is essential for this purpose that the parties should intend that the subject of the grant or the land retained by the grantor should be used in some definite and particular manner. It is not enough that the subject of the grant or land retained should be intended to be used in a manner which may or may not involve this definite and particular use."[25]

If a positive servitude has been possessed for a continuous period of twenty years, openly, peaceably and without any judicial interruption, and the possession was founded on, and followed the execution of, a deed which is sufficient in respect of its terms by implication to constitute the servitude, then on the expiry of the twenty years the validity of the servitude as so constituted becomes unchallengeable, except on the ground that the deed is ex facie invalid or was forged.[26]

30. Prescription.—Negative servitudes cannot be acquired or constituted by prescription, and the mere enjoyment of a state of things existent on a neighbour's estate for the prescriptive period does not give a right to demand its continuance or to prohibit its being altered.[27] A positive servitude on the other hand may be constituted by prescription. If a positive servitude has been possessed for a continuous period of twenty years openly, peaceably and without judicial interruption, the existence of the servitude as so possessed becomes unchallengeable.[28] Infeftment in the dominant tenement is no longer a prerequisite, possession alone being sufficient.[29]

The acts of possession must be overt in the sense that they must in themselves be of such a character or be done in such circumstances as to indicate unequivocally to the proprietor of the servient tenement the fact that a right is asserted and the nature of that right; and it must be shown that they either were known or ought to have been known, to the owner of the servient

---

[23] *Murray* v. *Medley*, 1973 S.L.T. (Sh. Ct.) 75.
[24] See Rankine, *Landownership*, p. 438; *Union Lighterage Co.* v. *London Graving Dock Co.* [1902] 2 Ch. 557; see also *Ferguson* v. *Campbell*, 1913 1 S.L.T. 241.
[25] *Pwllbach Colliery Co.* v. *Woodman* [1915] A.C. 634, per Lord Parker; *Cory* v. *Davies*, [1923] 2 Ch. 95; *Wong* v. *Beaumont Property Trust* [1964] 2 W.L.R. 1325.
[26] Prescription and Limitation (Scotland) Act 1973 (c. 52), s. 3 (1).
[27] Rankine, p. 426; *Anderson* v. *Robertson*, 1958 S.C. 367; but see *McLaren* v. *British Railways Board*, 1971 S.C. 182.
[28] 1973 Act, s. 3 (2). See Prescription, Ch. XVI.
[29] 1973 Act, s. 3 (4).

tenement or to the persons to whom he intrusted the charge of his property.[30]

Where a servitude is thus acquired, the possession affords the measure of the right acquired. "Tantum praescriptum quantum possessum."[31] According to Erskine, however, a servitude by prescription may sometimes justly be extended beyond former usage; but the extension would apparently be admitted only where it was such a development of the use as might be held to be involved in the possession.[32]

31. Extinction of Servitudes.—A servitude may be extinguished in one or other of the following six ways: (1) By a change of circumstances. Thus, if land is acquired under compulsory powers, it is taken free of all servitudes unless it be otherwise provided in the special Act authorising its acquisition.[33] So also, if either the dominant or the servient tenement is destroyed, the servitude is extinguished, for in that case nothing remains to be the subject of a servitude. But, if the dominant is only temporarily rendered unfit for the servitude, the servitude is suspended for the time but is not extinguished.[34] (2) It may be extinguished confusione, i.e. by both tenements passing into the ownership of the same person, for when one person is the absolute owner of two estates it is impossible to speak of his having, in respect of his ownership and possession of one of them, any rights over the other. "Res sua nemini servit."[35] If the tenements thereafter come to belong to different persons, the servitude does not thereupon revive, but requires to be constituted de novo.[36] There is an exception to this in the case where the estates are held on distinct titles, and a separation of the titles, independently of the will of the proprietor, may be anticipated[37]; as, for example, where one estate is held under an entail and the other in fee-simple, or where they are held under entails with different destinations. It has already been shown that on the severance of the unity of a property a servitude may be impliedly granted or reserved.[38] (3) It may be renounced by the proprietor of the dominant tenement. (4) It may be lost through the operation of the negative prescription. And here it is necessary to attend to the distinction between the two classes of servitude. As a positive servitude entitles the owner of the dominant tenement to exercise certain rights over the servient tenement, it will be lost by mere non-exercise of these for twenty years.[39] This period will run from the midnight following upon the last occasion on which the dominant owner exercised his right.[40] But in the case of

---

[30] McInroy v. Duke of Atholl (1891) 18 R. (H.L.) 46, per Lord Watson; McGregor v. Crieff Co-operative Society, 1915 S.C. (H.L.) 93; cf. Diment v. N. H. Foot [1974] 1 W.L.R. 1427.
[31] Kerr v. Brown, 1939 S.C. 140.
[32] Erskine, Inst., II, 9, 4; Rankine, Landownership, p. 50.
[33] Magistrates of Oban v. Callander and Oban Ry. (1892) 19 R. 912.
[34] Erskine, Inst., II, 9, 37.
[35] Baird v. Fortune (1861) 4 Macq. 127, per Lord Cranworth; Donaldson's Trs. v. Forbes (1839) 1 D. 449.
[36] Erskine, supra: Union Bank v. Daily Record (1902) 10 S.L.T. 71.
[37] Bell, Prin., § 997; Donaldson's Trs. v. Forbes (1839) 1 D. 449.
[38] Supra. § 29; see Walton Bros. v. Mags. of Glasgow (1876) 3 R. 1130, per Lord President Inglis.
[39] Prescription and Limitation (Scotland) Act 1973 (c. 52), ss. 3 (5) and 7; see Prescription, Ch. XVI; cf. Walker's Exrx. v. Carr, 1973 S.L.T. (Sh. Ct.) 77.
[40] 1973 Act, ss. 8, 14.

a negative servitude, as there is no active use of these by the dominant owner but merely a restraint laid on the servient owner, there is no room for prescription unless the latter does something which is inconsistent with the restraint laid upon him. Thus the owner of land subject to the servitude Altius Non Tollendi cannot plead that it has been lost by prescription unless he has erected buildings in contravention of the servitude; but, if he has done so, prescription will operate if the contravention has remained unchallenged for a period of twenty years since its date.[41] The operation of prescription will not be averted by the fact that the servitude appears in the title of the servient tenement.[42] (5) A servitude may also be lost if there is conduct on the part of the dominant owner showing an intention to relinquish it or of such a nature as to raise a plea of personal bar, by acquiescence or otherwise, against its enforcement.[43] (6) A servitude may be discharged by the Lands Tribunal where changes in the neighbourhood have made the servitude unreasonable or inappropriate.[44]

32. Particular Servitudes.—The nature of the servitudes recognised by the institutional writers may be briefly indicated. They may be grouped under the headings of urban and rural servitudes. The third of the urban servitudes is negative: the others are all positive servitudes.

33. Urban Servitudes.—These are Support, Stillicide, and Light or Prospect.

(1) SUPPORT includes the servitudes known in the Civil Law as Tigni Immittendi and Oneris Ferendi. The former is the right to let a beam or other structural part of the dominant building into the wall of the servient tenement and to keep it there; the second is the right to have a building supported.[45] These servitudes are noticed by the institutional writers, but there is little to be found in the reported decisions regarding them.[46]

(2) STILLICIDE. No proprietor can build so as to throw the rainwater falling from his own house immediately upon his neighbour's ground; but this servitude of stillicide or eavesdrop entitles him to do so.[47]

(3) LIGHT OR PROSPECT. The negative servitudes Non Aedificandi, Altius Non Tollendi, and Non Officiendi Luminibus restrain proprietors from building on their ground, or from raising their buildings beyond a certain height, or from building so as to hurt the light or prospect of the dominant tenement. The institutional writers refer also to another form of servitude of

[41] 1973 Act, ss. 7, 3 (5); cf. Erskine, supra; *Wilkie* v. *Scott* (1688) M. 11189.
[42] *Graham* v. *Douglas* (1735) M. 10745. Only a real right of ownership in land is imprescriptible: 1973 Act, Schedule 3, para. (*a*).
[43] Bell, *Prin.*, § 999; Rankine, *Landownership*, p. 441; *Mags. of Rutherglen* v. *Bainridge* (1886) 13 R. 745; see also *Millar* v. *Christie*, 1961 S.C. 1.
[44] Conveyancing and Feudal Reform (Scotland) Act 1970 (c. 35), s. 1; see, e.g. *Devlin* v. *Conn*, 1972 S.L.T. (Lands Tr.) 11.
[45] Erskine, *Inst.*, II, 9, 7; Bell, *Prin.*, § 1003; Rankine, *Landownership*, p. 656.
[46] *Murray* v. *Brownhill* (1715) M. 14521; *Troup* v. *Aberdeen Heritable Securities Co.*, 1916 S.C. 918.
[47] Stair, II, 7, 7; Erskine, *Inst.*, II, 9, 9; Bell, *Prin.*, § 1004.

light which prevents the making in the servient tenement of windows and other openings which would interfere with a neighbour's privacy.[48]

34. Rural Servitudes.—These include Way, Aquaehaustus, Aqueduct, Pasturage and Fuel, Feal and Divot.

(1) WAY.—The way may not be a footpath, a horse road or a carriage road, and the terms of the grant or the extent of possession during the prescriptive period will determine to which category the way belongs.[49] The more burdensome servitude will include the less.[50] The destination of the road may impose a limitation on its use by confining it to traffic for certain purposes, as in the case of a church road or a road to a market, but the opinion has been expressed that, if a servitude of way is acquired by prescription, there is no restraint on its use by the dominant tenement as a road of one or other of the above descriptions by reference to the purpose of the traffic passing over it; the road may be used generally by the dominant owner irrespective of whether the traffic is for agricultural or building or any other particular purpose.[51] As has been already noticed, the owner of the servient tenement is not bound to repair the road, and he may erect on it gates so long as these do not interfere with the enjoyment of the servitude.[52] The servient owner has, in the case of a way acquired by prescription, been allowed to alter its line where the new line would be equally convenient to the dominant owner, but this is not possible where the servitude has been constituted by a grant in which the line of road has been laid down.[53]

(2) AQUAEHAUSTUS gives the right to take water from or to water cattle at a well or stream in the servient tenement. It involves the right of access by the dominant owner and a right to clean out or repair the well.[54]

(3) AQUEDUCT is the right to convey water by pipes or canals through the servient tenement.[55] The duty of maintaining the aqueduct in proper condition is on the dominant owner, and he is entitled to access to it for this purpose. Similar to this servitude is that of a dam or damhead by which one acquires a right of gathering water on his neighbour's land and of building banks or dykes for containing the water.[56]

(4) PASTURAGE is the right to feed cattle or sheep on another's ground or on a common.[57] It is usually found as a right enjoyed in common with others. If the extent of the right is not expressly defined, it is the amount of stock the servient tenement can winter.[58] The servient owner is entitled to use the

---

[48] Stair, II, 7, 9; Erskine, *Inst.*, II, 9, 10; Bell, *Prin.*, §§ 1005-7; Rankine, p. 461.
[49] Prescription and Limitation (Scotland) Act 1973 (c. 52), s. 3 (2); cf. Stair, II, 7, 10; Erskine, *Inst.*, II, 9, 12; Bell, *Prin.*, § 1010; *Malcolm* v. *Lloyd* (1886) 13 R. 512, per Lord President Inglis.
[50] Stair, supra.
[51] *Carstairs* v. *Spence*, 1924 S.C. 380, per Lord President Clyde.
[52] Supra, § 26. But see *Lanarkshire Water Board* v. *Gilchrist*, 1973 S.L.T. (Sh. Ct.) 58.
[53] *Hill* v. *Maclaren* (1879) 6 R. 1363; *Moyes* v. *Macdiarmid* (1900) 2 F. 918; Bell, *Prin.*, § 1010.
[54] Erskine, *Inst.*, II, 9, 13; Bell, *Prin.*, § 1011; Rankine, *Landownership*, pp. 571 et seq.
[55] See, e.g. *More* v. *Boyle*, 1967 S.L.T. (Sh. Ct.) 38.
[56] Erskine, supra.
[57] Stair, II, 7, 14; Erskine, II, 9, 14; Bell, *Prin.*, § 1013; Rankine, p. 454; *Fraser* v. *S. of State for Scotland*, 1959 S.L.T. (Notes) 36.
[58] *L. Breadalbane* v. *Menzies* (1741) 5 Br. Supp. 710; but see *Ferguson* v. *Tennant and Ors.*, 1976 S.L.T. (Notes) 51; 1978 S.L.T. 165.

surplus pasturage. The dominant owner may interdict the servient owner from carrying out operations which might damage the pasture or detract from the value of the servitude even where the dominant owner is not in fact exercising the right of pasturage.[59]

(5) FUEL, FEAL AND DIVOT is a servitude which gives the right to cut and remove peat for fuel and turf for fences.[60]

Other servitudes which have been recognised are the right to use ground for the purpose of bleaching clothes,[61] and of taking stone from the servient for the use of the dominant tenement.[62]

35. Public Right of Way.—This differs from the servitude of way in that it exists for the benefit of the public and may be vindicated by a member of the public. A servitude of way, on the other hand, is for the use and benefit of the dominant tenement alone, and it is only the proprietor of that tenement who has a title to sue in regard to it.[63]

A public right of way is a right in the public to pass from one public place to another public place.[64] And the road must follow a definite route.[65] "It will not do for people to enter the ground of a proprietor, and walk about in it as much as they choose, and come out where they entered. That will not make a right of way. The line of road must be a marked line. Persons will never make a line of footpath by straying in fifty different lines over a man's property."[66] Like a servitude of way, it may be a footpath, a horse road or a carriage road,[67] or indeed a motor road.[68]

This right of way may be acquired by grant, but almost invariably it has been created by possession or use for the prescriptive period of twenty years.[69] The use must be by the public, and not such as can be reasonably ascribed to a private servitude; it must be of such a character as to indicate that a right to use the track is asserted, for a use which is due to the permission or tolerance of the proprietor will not suffice; and it must be continuous, open and peaceable and without any judicial interruption.[69] The amount of unrestricted public use which must be proved varies with circumstances; in a thinly populated district use by a small number of persons may be sufficient.[70] If the right of way is established, the use is not limited to passage from one end to the other; a member of the public is entitled to use it for part of its course, as, e.g., for the purpose of reaching his own property.[71] As in the case of a

[59] *Ferguson* v. *Tennant and Ors.*, supra.
[60] Stair, II, 7, 13; Bell, *Prin.*, § 1014; Rankine, p. 456.
[61] *Home* v. *Young* (1846) 9 D. 286.
[62] *Murray* v. *Mags. of Peebles*, Dec. 8, 1808 F.C.
[63] *Thomson* v. *Murdoch* (1862) 24 D. 975, per Lord Deas; *Jenkins* v. *Murray* (1866) 4 M. 1046, per Lord Curriehill.
[64] *Campbell* v. *Lang* (1853) 1 Macq. 451; *Young* v. *Cuthbertson* (1854) 1 Macq. 455; *Marquis of Bute* v. *McKirdy & McMillan*, 1937 S.C. 93 (foreshore).
[65] *Mackintosh* v. *Moir* (1871) 9 M. 574; (1872) 10 M. 517.
[66] *Jenkins* v. *Murray*, supra, per Lord Curriehill.
[67] *Mackenzie* v. *Bankes* (1868) 6 M. 936.
[68] *Smith* v. *Sexton*, 1927 S.N. 92.
[69] Prescription and Limitation (Scotland) Act 1973 (c. 52), s. 3 (3); see Prescription, Ch. XVI.
[70] *Macpherson* v. *Scottish Rights of Way Society* (1888) 15 R. (H.L.) 68.
[71] *McRobert* v. *Reid*, 1914 S.C. 633.

servitude road, the proprietor of the lands over which the way runs is not debarred from dealing with his property in any lawful manner which does not interfere with the right of the public.[72]

A right of way constituted by use will be lost by disuse for the prescriptive period,[73] or it may be in a shorter period if the proprietor without challenge openly carries out operations on his land which make the use of the way impossible.[74]

An action for vindication of a right of way may be brought by any member of the public,[75] or by a regional, islands or district council.[76] When the question of the existence of a particular right of way has been properly raised and decided, the decision is res judicata in any subsequent action even when raised by a different party. So also an action of declarator that there is no right of way may be defended by any member of the public or by the local authorities mentioned above,[77] and here also a judgment will be res judicata. The same result follows if the action is raised or defended by a society formed to defend rights of way.[78]

---

[72] *Reilly* v. *Greenfield Coal and Brick Co.*, 1909 S.C. 1328, per Lord President Dunedin, at p. 1338.
[73] 1973 Act, s. 8.
[74] Rankine, *Landownership*, p. 337.
[75] *Potter* v. *Hamilton* (1870) 8 M. 1064.
[76] Local Government (Scotland) Act 1973 (c. 65), ss. 189, 235.
[77] cf. *Alston* v. *Ross* (1895) 23 R. 273; *Alexander* v. *Picken*, 1946 S.L.T. 91.
[78] *Macfie* v. *Scottish Rights of Way Society* (1884) 11 R. 1094.

CHAPTER XL

LIFERENT AND FEE: COMMON PROPERTY AND INTEREST

Rankine, *Landownership*; McLaren, *Wills and Succession* (3rd ed., 1894, and Supplement 1934); Dobie, *Manual of the Law of Liferent and Fee* (1941).

I. LIFERENT AND FEE

1. Nature of Liferent: Annuities.—A liferent is a right to use and enjoy a subject during life without destroying or wasting its substance (salva rei substantia).[1] It is described in the institutional writers as a personal servitude, the only personal servitude known in our law[2]; but in modern times the tendency is to regard it as a separate right or interest in property. It is to be distinguished from an annuity. An annuity is a right to receive from year to year a certain sum, and it is not necessarily limited to the lifetime of the recipient, for it may be given for a number of years or even in perpetuity.[3] A liferenter can claim only the fruits of the subject liferented, whereas an annuitant is entitled to the amount of his annuity, and (unless the deed creating it shows that it is to be charged on income only) can exact payment out of capital if the income falls short.[4]

The law does not recognise an interest intermediate between those of liferent and of fee,[5] which is the full and unlimited right in the capital or the subject itself.[6]

2. Creation of Liferents by Constitution and Reservation: Limitations.— Liferents were formerly divided into legal liferents or those "constituted by the law,"[7] namely, terce and courtesy,[8] and conventional liferents "constituted by the deeds of men"[9]; but with the abolition of terce and courtesy[10] this distinction is now obsolescent. Conventional liferents may be created by reservation or constitution. A liferent by reservation is that which a proprietor reserves to himself when conveying the fee to another. In the case of heritage no title to a reserved liferent requires to be completed, for the grantor's former title to the land (which included the right to its fruits) still subsists as to the reserved liferent.[11] A liferent by constitution is one created by the proprietor

---

[1] Stair, II, 6, 4; Erskine, *Inst.*, II, 9, 39.
[2] Erskine, supra; *Patrick* v. *Napier* (1867) 5 M. 683, per Lord President Inglis at 699.
[3] *Fleming* v. *Reuther's Exrs.*, 1921 S.C. 593; see also *Reid's Exx.* v. *Reid*, 1944 S.C. (H.L.) 25.
[4] *Kinmond's Trs.* v. *Kinmond* (1873) 11 M. 381; *Knox's Trs.* v. *Knox* (1869) 7 M. 873; *Colquhoun's Trs.* v. *Colquhoun*, 1922 S.C. 32.
[5] See Testate Succession, Ch. XLIII., infra, §§ 20, 29; *Cochrane's Exx.* v. *Cochrane*, 1947 S.C. 134; Smith, *Short Commentary*, p. 487.
[6] As to "fiduciary fee," see Bell, *Prin.*, §§ 1713-1715; see also Trusts (Scotland) Act 1921, s. 8 (2).
[7] Stair, II, 6, 2.
[8] See Legal Rights, Ch. XLI, § 2.
[9] Stair, supra.
[10] Succession (Scotland) Act 1964, s. 10 (1).
[11] Erskine, *Inst.*, II, 9, 42.

in favour of another, with or without a grant of the fee to others; familiar instances of such liferents are those created in testamentary deeds.

There are statutory limitations on the creation of liferents in favour of persons who are not living nor in utero at the time when the deed creating the liferent comes into operation.[12]

3. Proper and Beneficiary Liferents.

—A liferent may be constituted by a direct disposition or gift of a subject to a liferenter and fiar without the interposition of a trust. A liferent of this kind has been termed a proper liferent.[13] The possession belongs to the liferenter, who may hold either by himself or his servants; and the rights pertaining to the liferenter in a question with the fiar are determined by the law.[14] Proper liferents were more common in former times, and it is to such liferents that the attention of the institutional writers appears to have been mainly devoted. In modern times the advantages of a trust as obviating certain conveyancing difficulties in regard to the lodgement of the fee and also as securing impartial administration as between the liferenter and the fiar have led to the adoption in most cases of trust machinery. Where a subject is placed in the hands of trustees with directions to pay the income to one beneficiary and to hold the fee for another, the first of these has what has been termed a beneficiary liferent; he has not a direct right in the subjects, but a jus crediti under the trust.[15] Where the bequest takes the form of a direction to trustees to pay the income of a trust estate to a beneficiary, the terms of the deed may show that the income was intended to comprise either more or less than would have fallen to a proper liferenter.[16] If, however, there is given a liferent simpliciter, it has been laid down that the obligations resting on the liferenter are the same whether the liferent is given directly or through the medium of a trust.[17]

A proper liferent cannot be constituted over fungibles which perish in the use, but may be constituted over subjects which, though they wear out in time, yet waste by such slow degrees that they may continue fit for use for the full course of a ordinary life.[18] In *Rogers* v. *Scott*[19] it was held that the effect of a direction to trustees to allow the testator's widow the liferent of his farm and stock was to place on her the obligation to maintain the stock and leave it substantially of the same description, value and extent as it was when she received it. Where a liferent of a house along with its furniture is given, it has been held that the furniture, as an accessory to the possession of the house, cannot be removed from the house and used elsewhere.[20]

---

[12] See Testate Succession, Ch. XLIII, infra, § 31.
[13] Erskine, *Inst.*, II, 9, 56; *Inland Revenue* v. *Wemyss*, 1924 S.C. 284; *De Robeck* v. *Inland Revenue*, 1928 S.C. (H.L.) 34, per Lord Dunedin; *Miller* v. *Inland Revenue*, 1930 S.C. (H.L.) 49, per Lord Dunedin.
[14] *Ferguson* v. *Ferguson's Trs.* (1877) 4 R. 532, per Lord President Inglis.
[15] *Ker's Trs.* v. *Justice* (1868) 6 M. 627.
[16] *Miller's Trs.* v. *Miller*, 1907 S.C. 833, per Lord McLaren.
[17] *Johnstone* v. *Mackenzie's Trs.*, 1912 S.C. (H.L.) 106, at 109.
[18] Erskine, *Inst.*, II, 9, 40; *Miller's Trs.* v. *Miller*, supra.
[19] (1867) 5 M. 1078.
[20] *Cochran* v. *Cochran*, 1755 M. 8280; 2 Bell's *Illustrations*, p. 141.

4. Capital or Income.—The liferenter is entitled to the fruits of the subject but not to anything which is part of the corpus or capital. As between the liferenter and the fiar, a receipt will fall to, and a charge will be borne by, one or other according as these are of the nature of capital or of income. Although no general rule can be laid down, certain tests have been suggested as to use in determining to which category a receipt or charge belongs. In *Ross's Trs.* v. *Nicoll* [21] Lord McLaren observed: "In general I should be disposed to hold that every payment to be made from a trust estate which does not involve a diminution of capital ought to be regarded as a payment out of income, whether that payment is made yearly or half-yearly or periodically at longer intervals. All such payments when made to the trust estate are to be regarded as part of the profit as distinguished from the corpus of the estate, and therefore, fall to be made over from the estate to the person who is beneficially entitled to the income." Another suggested criterion (which is only a rough one and not decisive in every case) is "that capital expenditure is a thing that is going to be spent once and for all, and income expenditure is a thing that is going to recur every year." [22] Apart from such general considerations, there is a series of cases regarding timber and minerals which not only rule the right of the liferenter as to these but have been referred to as affording guidance by analogy in questions as to items of receipt of expenditure of a different kind. [23]

5. Rights in Timber.—The wood growing on an estate belongs as part of the corpus to the fiar. He has the right to thinnings and to all trees blown down in an "extraordinary storm"; and he may cut wood but not so as to interfere with the amenity and shelter of an estate and thus affect the liferenter's enjoyment of it. [24] The liferenter, on the other hand, is entitled to ordinary windfalls, and, in the case of copse-wood cut periodically on reaching maturity, he has the benefit of the cutting when the proper time for it arrives. He may also cut wood at the sight of the fiar for repairing fences and other purposes of the estate. [25]

6. Rights in Minerals.—The returns from mineral workings are not strictly fruits of the soil which could be claimed as such by a liferenter, but "if the owner of the soil, the fiar, creates a mineral estate by working or letting a particular seam of minerals, he thereby brings the proceeds of the minerals so worked or let within the category of fruits and within the right of usufruct." [26] Accordingly, it is settled that a gift of liferent or direction to trustees to pay the income of the estate to a beneficiary includes the rents and royalties from mines either worked, or let although not worked, in the lifetime of the grantor or truster. On the other hand, returns from mines opened by his trustees after

---

[21] (1902) 5 F. 146.
[22] *Vallambrosa Rubber Co.* v. *Farmer*, 1910 S.C. 519, per Lord President Dunedin; *British Insulated and Helsby Cables* v. *Atherton* [1926] A.C. 205, per Viscount Cave L.C. and Lord Atkinson.
[23] See, e.g. in *Davidson's Trs.* v. *Ogilvie*, 1910 S.C. 294 (copyright royalties).
[24] *Dickson* v. *Dickson* (1823) 2 S. 152; *Tait* v. *Maitland* (1825) 4 S. 247.
[25] *Macalister's Trs.* v. *Macalister* (1851) 13 D. 1239.
[26] *Campbell* v. *Wardlaw* (1883) 10 R. (H.L.) 65, per Lord Watson.

his death are not included unless the truster has directed his trustees to work the minerals.[27]

7. Bonuses: Price of Shares.—Where the subject liferented comprises shares in a company the dividends on these declared in the liferenter's lifetime are payable to him.[28] If a company, which has power under its constitution to increase its capital, pays a bonus out of accumulated profits which have been carried to reserve, it will depend on the action of the company whether the bonus falls to the liferenter or to the fiar. The accepted rule is that "when a testator or settler directs or permits the subject of his disposition to remain as shares or stock in a company, which has the power either of distributing its profits as dividend or of converting them into capital, and the company validly exercises this power, such exercise of its power is binding on all persons interested under him, the testator or settlor, in the shares, and consequently what is paid by the company as dividend goes to the tenant for life,[29] and what is paid by the company to the shareholder as capital, or appropriated as an increase of the capital stock in the concern, enures to the benefit of all who are interested in the capital."[30] A cash payment out of accumulated profits prima facie belongs to the liferenter.[31] But in cases where a company declares a bonus and at the same time offers its shareholders additional shares to be paid up to an amount equivalent to the bonus, it is a question of fact, looking to the form and substance of the particular transaction, whether the real intention of the company was to distribute cash or to capitalise the profits by effecting a distribution of shares. Unless the fund from which the payment is made has been in fact capitalised the payment is income and falls to the liferenter, and a mere statement by the company that the payment is made as a capital payment will not alter its character.[32]

In the less usual case of companies which have no power to increase their capital, if the company accumulates profits and uses them for capital purposes, it may be regarded as having appropriated the profits to capital, so as to make the distribution of them among the shareholders a distribution of capital.[33]

When company shares belonging to a liferented estate are sold in the interval between two dividends, the liferenter is entitled to the portion of the

---

[27] *Ranken's Trs.* v. *Ranken*, 1908 S.C. 3; *Naismith's Trs.* v. *Naismith*, 1909 S.C. 1380; *Campbell* v. *Wardlaw*, supra.

[28] *Re Wakley* [1920] 2 Ch. 205; *Re Marjoribanks* [1923] 2 Ch. 307. But there may be a question of apportionment as regards current dividends.

[29] This is the English equivalent of liferenter.

[30] *Bouch* v. *Sproule* (1885) 29 Ch.D. 635, at 653; approved L.R. 12 App.Cas. 385, at 397; *Blyth's Trs.* v. *Milne* (1905) 7 F. 799; *Howard's Trs.* v. *Howard*, 1907 S.C. 1274; *Hill* v. *Permanent Trustee Corporation* [1930] A.C. 720. The question was also discussed in connection with super-tax; see *Inland Revenue Commissioners* v. *Blott* [1921] 2 A.C. 171; *Inland Revenue Commissioners* v. *Fisher's Exrs.* [1926] A.C. 395.

[31] *Forgie's Trs.* v. *Forgie*, 1941 S.C. 188.

[32] *Re Bates* [1928] Ch. 682; *Hill* v. *Permanent Trustee Corporation*, supra.

[33] *Bouch* v. *Sproule*, supra. There are also a number of decisions as to casualties, of which *Macdougall's Factor* v. *Watson*, 1909 S.C. 215; *Edgar's Trs.* v. *Edgeware*, 1915 S.C. 175; and *Stewart's Trs* v. *Stewart*, 1931 S.C. 691, are the most recent. In view of the Feudal Casualties (Scotland) Act 1914, it is unnecessary to do more than refer to these.

price paid in respect of such part of the future dividend as has accrued at the date of the sale, but this portion is to be estimated in accordance with the dividend expected at the date of the sale and not with the dividend ultimately paid.[34]

8. Burdens affecting Liferent.—Liferenters bear the annual and ordinary burdens on the subjects, such as feu-duties, taxes, repairs,[35] the premiums for insurance against fire,[36] and interest on bonds charged on the property.[37] They are not answerable for ordinary wear and tear, nor for loss due to accident or vis major. While ordinary repairs are chargeable against revenue, the cost of extraordinary repairs or of rebuilding or of executing work of a permanent nature the benefit of which will at the expiry of the liferent accrue to the fiars is chargeable against capital.[38]

9. Right of Occupancy.—This is to be distinguished from a liferent. In *Clark* v. *Clark*[39] a testator directed his trustees to give "the use of" his house to his widow, and it was held that she had not a liferent of, but a right to occupy, the house; and being merely an occupant she had no right to let it, but, on the other hand, was liable only for rates and assessments in respect of occupancy and not for those burdens such as feu-duty, repairs or landlord's taxes which fall upon a liferenter. Whether a liferent of a house or this more limited right is given depends on the language used by the testator, but it has been thought to point to a gift of liferent that under the testator's directions no funds are left in the hands of the trustees to meet the annual burdens on the house.[40]

10. Alimentary Liferents.—A provision for the aliment of an individual is from its nature personal to him and not assignable by him or attachable by his creditors.[41] No man can effectually make an alimentary provision in favour of himself, for it is against the policy of the law that a person should have the beneficial enjoyment of his property and yet put it beyond the reach of his creditors.[42] Nor is it possible to make a right of fee alimentary[43]; if, therefore,

[34] *McLeod's Trs.* v. *Mcleod*, 1916 S.C. 604; *Cameron's Factor* v. *Cameron* (1873) 1 R. 21.
[35] *Johnstone* v. *Mackenzie's Trs.*, 1912 S.C. (H.L.) 106; Erskine, II, 9, 61; Bell, *Prin.*, § 1061.
[36] *Brown* v. *Soutar & Meacher* (1870) 8 M. 702; *Glover's Trs.* v. *Glover*, 1913 S.C. 115.
[37] *Glover's Trs.* v. *Glover, supra.*
[38] *Shaw's Trs.* v. *Bruce*, 1917 S.C. 169; *Preston* v. *Preston's Trs.* (1853) 15 D. 271; *Templeton* v. *Mags. of Ayr*, 1912 1 S.L.T. 421.
[39] (1871) 9 M. 435.
[40] The cases are reviewed in *Johnstone* v. *Mackenzie's Trs., supra; Milne's Trs.* v. *Milne*, 1920 S.C. 456; see also *Montgomerie-Fleming's Trs.* v. *Carre*, 1913 S.C. 1018; and *Countess of Lauderdale*, 1962 S.C. 302.
[41] Stewart, *Diligence*, p. 93. The English equivalent of a wife's alimentary liferent, the "restraint upon anticipation," has been abolished; Married Women (Restraint upon Anticipation) Act 1949. The protection has been held to apply only to the extent of a reasonable provision for the beneficiary, the excess being open to diligence: *Livingstone* v. *Livingstone* (1886) 14 R. 43.
[42] "That were to impose a condition contrary to law, that a man should at the same time be fiar, and yet not have power to affect the fee."—*Creditors of Primrose* v. *Heirs*, 1744 M. 15501, at 15504; *Kennedy* v. *Kennedy's Trs.*, 1953 S.C. 60; but see infra for ante-nuptial settlement by a woman.
[43] *Wilkie's Trs.* v. *Wight's Trs.* (1893) 21 R. 199, per Lord Rutherfurd Clark: *Watson's Trs.* v. *Watson*, 1913 S.C. 1133; *Miller* v. *Miller's Trs.*, 1953 S.L.T. 225.

trustees are directed to hold a subject or fund for, or to make it over to, a beneficiary in fee, any declaration that it is alimentary is of no effect. But a person may confer on another a liferent or annuity on the condition that it is to be alimentary. The proper mode of effecting this is to declare expressly that what is given is alimentary; but equivalents have been admitted as, e.g., where the right was declared to be exclusive of the beneficiary's acts and deeds and the diligence of creditors[44] or for his maintenance and support.[45] A mere exclusion of the rights of creditors without any restraint on the beneficiary's power to assign is ineffectual.[46] Further, in order to make the right alimentary, there must be a continuing trust under which the trustees are empowered to retain in their hands the subject out of which the liferent or annuity is given.[47] The law does, however, recognise one exception to the rule that prohibits any person from settling money so as to secure the income to himself and at the same time place it beyond the reach of his creditors, namely, that a woman may in her antenuptial marriage contract create an alimentary interest in her own favour in property derived from herself[48] or from her father's estate.[49] This alimentary protection continues during the subsistence of the marriage, but terminates with the dissolution of the marriage, unless effective provision has been made in the deed constituting the liferent for the continuation of its alimentary character thereafter.[50]

An alimentary liferent, once accepted,[51] cannot be assigned or discharged nor can the administration of the trustees in whom the liferented subject is vested be terminated by any act or deed of the liferenter.[52] Moreover, if the liferenter acquires the fee of the subjects, his alimentary liferent does not merge in the fee; but the liferent and fee continue to subsist as separate rights. Hence, where a widower who had under his marriage contract an alimentary liferent in his wife's estate became entitled under her will to the fee it was held that he could not compel the marriage contract trustees to denude in his favour.[53]

It was formerly the rule that, even where a liferent provision made by a married woman in her antenuptial contract in her own favour out of her own funds was not declared to be alimentary, she could not, stante matrimonio,

---

[44] *Dewar's Trs.* v. *Dewar,* 1910 S.C. 730; see also Stewart, *Diligence,* p. 95. An interesting and instructive decision is that in *Textile Pensions Trust* v. *Custodian of Enemy Property,* 1947 S.C. 528.

[45] *Arnold's Trs.* v. *Graham,* 1927 S.C. 353; followed in *Miller* v. *Miller's Trs.* 1953 S.L.T. 225.

[46] *Douglas, Gardner & Mill* v. *Mackintosh's Trs.,* 1916 S.C. 125.

[47] *Forbes's Trs.* v. *Tennant,* 1926 S.C. 294. As to alimentary rights in a question with creditors, see Diligence, Ch. XLVIII, infra, § 9.

[48] *Dempster's Trs.* v. *Dempster,* 1949 S.C. 92; *Sturgis's Tr.* v. *Sturgis,* 1951 S.C. 637.

[49] *Martin* v. *Bannatyne* (1861) 23 D. 705; see also *Neame* v. *Neame's Trs.,* 1956 S.L.T. 57; *Strange,* 1966 S.L.T. 59.

[50] *Dempster's Trs.,* supra; *Sturgis's Tr.,* supra; *Pearson etc.,* 1968 S.L.T. 46; *Sutherland etc.,* 1968 S.C. 200.

[51] *Douglas-Hamilton* v. *Duke and Duchess of Hamilton's Trs.,* 1961 S.C. 205; as to a testamentary provision, see *Ford* v. *Ford,* 1961 S.C. 122.

[52] *White's Trs.* v. *White* (1877) 4 R. 786; *Hughes* v. *Edwardes* (1892) 19 R. (H.L.) 33; *Cuthbert* v. *Cuthbert's Trs.,* 1908 S.C. 967; *Coles Petr.,* 1951 S.L.T. 308; *Kennedy* v. *Kennedy's Trs.,* 1953 S.C. 60. But see Executors, etc., Ch. XLIV, infra, § 14.

[53] *Main's Trs.* v. *Main,* 1917 S.C. 660; *Howat's Trs.* v. *Howat,* 1922 S.C. 506; *Anderson's Trs.,* 1932 S.C. 226.

bring that provision to an end.[54] But in *Beith's Trs.* v. *Beith*[55] this authority was held to have been superseded as a result of supervening legislation as to the status and capacity of married women; and a married woman who had no issue and was admittedly past the age of child-bearing was held entitled to demand repayment of the funds provided by her, although her husband was still alive. There is no room for the extension of that decision to a case where the liferent is alimentary[56]; but under the Trusts (Scotland) Act 1961[57] the Court may now, if certain conditions are satisfied, authorise an arrangement varying or revoking an alimentary liferent and making new provisions in its place.

11. Transmission and Extinction of Liferents.—Where the liferent is not alimentary, it may be transmitted by the liferenter to another by means of an assignation followed by intimation. The assignee will then become entitled to the fruits and income of the liferented subjects in place of the liferenter. "The proper right of liferent is intransmissible, *ossibus usufructuarii inhaeret*. When the profits of the liferented subject are transmitted to another, the right becomes merely personal, for it entitles the assignee to the rent, not during his own life, but his cedent's, and is therefore carried by simple assignation without seisin."[58]

A liferent is extinguished by the liferenter's death, by consolidation with the fee where the liferent and fee come to be vested in the same individual, unless the liferent is alimentary, and by discharge by the liferenter.

12. Apportionment of Income.—Under the common law, while the interest of money and the profits of subjects "arising from continual daily labour" (such as "fishings, collieries, saltworks") were held to vest de die in diem, annuities, rents and payments connected with land did not vest till the term of payment arrived.[59] Accordingly, if an annuitant entitled to an annuity payable at the usual terms for the preceding half-year died between terms, his representative could claim no part of the payment due at the next term after his death, although that might have taken place on the day preceding the term. But the common law has been altered by statute. The Apportionment Act 1870[60] (which supersedes an Act passed in 1834[61]), provides that all rents, annuities (which include salaries and pensions), dividends (including bonuses) and other periodical payments in the nature of income "shall, like interest on money lent, be considered as accruing from day to day, and shall be apportionable in respect of time accordingly." The Act applies equally to the liability to make, as to the right to receive, such payments.[62] The dividends to

---

54 *Menzies* v. *Murray* (1875) 2 R. 507.
55 1950 S.C. 66.
56 *Kennedy* v. *Kennedy's Trs.*, 1953 S.C. 60; *Chrystal's Trs.* v. *Haldane*, 1960 S.C. 127.
57 s. 1 (4); see Executors, etc., Ch. XLIV, infra, § 14.
58 Erskine, *Inst.*, II, 9, 24; *Ker's Trs.* v. *Justice* (1868) 6 M. 627, per Lord Curriehill.
59 Erskine, *Inst.*, II, 9, 64-66; Bell's *Comm.*, II, 8; see also *Balfour's Exrs.* v. *Inland Revenue*, 1909 S.C. 619.
60 33 & 34 Vict., c. 35.
61 4 & 5 Will. IV, c. 22.
62 *Learmonth* v. *Sinclair's Trs.* (1878) 5 R. 548; *Bishop of Rochester* v. *Le Fanu* [1906] 2 Ch. 513.

which it applies are those of public companies, which include all companies registered under the Companies Acts[63]; the profits of a partnership do not fall under the Act.[64] A bonus, although occasional and not periodical, is apportionable[65]; but payments by a company to its shareholders which are not declared or expressed to be made in respect of some definite period have been held not to be so, as they cannot be considered as accruing from day to day.[66] Independently of the statute it has been held that where a testator directs his trustees to pay to a liferenter the free income of the universitas of a mixed estate, this is to be regarded as equivalent to the gift of the income from a fund and accordingly that the right to the income vests de die in diem.[67]

The Act does not apply to sums payable under policies of assurance[68] or to any case in which it is expressly stipulated that no apportionment shall take place.[69] Thus, where a testator bequeathed shares in a company with the declaration that these should carry the dividend accruing thereon at the testator's death[70] or that the dividends should be paid to the legatee as received,[71] apportionment was held to be excluded for the benefit of the legatee. The Act will not, however, be excluded merely by inference.[72]

II. COMMON PROPERTY AND INTEREST

13. Nature of Right.—Property may be vested in two or more persons either jointly or in common. Where property is held jointly the owners have no separate estates but only one estate vested in them pro indiviso, not merely in respect of possession but also in respect of the right of property. The right of a joint owner accresces on his death to the others and cannot be alienated or disposed of either inter vivos or mortis causa. Instances of this mode of holding are found in the ownership of trustees, the rights of members in the property of a club, and joint liferents.

In the case of property held in common each proprietor has a title to his own share which he may alienate or burden by his separate act. On the death of one of the common owners his share will pass under his will or transmit to his heirs.[73] An example of this holding is that of heirs-portioners under the former law of intestate succession.[74]

[63] Re Lysaght [1898] 1 Ch. 115; Re White [1913] 1 Ch. 231.
[64] Jones v. Ogle (1872) L.R. 8 Ch. 192; Re Cox's Trusts (1878) 9 Ch.D. 159.
[65] Re Griffiths (1879) 12 Ch.D.655.
[66] Re Jowitt [1922] 2 Ch. 442.
[67] Andrew's Trs. v. Hallett, 1926 S.C. 1087, and cases there cited.
[68] s. 6. In Inland Revenue v. Henderson's Exrs., 1931 S.C. 681, it was held that the Act did not apply in a question as to income tax.
[69] s. 7.
[70] Re Lysaght, supra. See Re Edwards [1918] 1 Ch. 142.
[71] Macpherson's Trs. v. Macpherson, 1907 S.C. 1067.
[72] Tyrell v. Clark (1852) 2 Drewry 86.
[73] Cargill v. Muir (1837) 15 S. 408, per Lord Moncreiff; Johnston v. Craufurd (1855) 17 D. 1023, per Lord Curriehill; Schaw v. Black (1889) 16 R. 336, per Lord Shand. On the distinction between common property and joint property see Magistrates of Banff v. Ruthin Castle Ltd., 1944 S.C. 36, at p. 64, Munro v. Munro, 1972 S.L.T. (Sh. Ct.) 6. Smith, Short Commentary, p. 479.
[74] See Intestate Succession, Ch. XLII, infra, § 3.

14. Management of Common Property.—All the proprietors are entitled to a voice in the management of the property, and no one of them has a right to a greater measure of control than another. Any one of them may, therefore, prevent any alteration of the condition of the property or any "extraordinary use" of the subject,[75] and the purported creation of a right of servitude over the property at the instance of one owner will be null if the others do not consent.[76] The rule is: "in re communi melior est conditio prohibentis." An exception to this rule is admitted in regard to necessary operations in rebuilding and repairing; these are not to be stopped by the opposition of any of the owners.[77]

It is also a general, although not universal, rule that all the proprietors must concur in actions against other parties relative to the common property.[78] One proprietor alone has no title to bring a declarator of property in regard to the subjects, for a decree in the action would not be res judicata as against the other common proprietors[79]; nor can one prosecute an action of removing against a tenant possessing under a lease granted by all.[80] But any one of the proprietors may take proceedings for the purpose of protecting the subject from encroachment or trespass.[81]

15. Division of the Property.—No one is bound to remain indefinitely associated with another or others in the ownership of common property. Any one of the proprietors may, even against the wish of the others, insist on a division of the property.[82] This right to have the property divided is a necessary incident of common property, and it is in law impossible to create common property and at the same time to exclude this right.[83] But the right must be exercised with due regard to the interests of all the proprietors. While the right of the proprietor who wishes to terminate the community is to have the subject divided,[84] where division is impracticable or would entail a sacrifice to an appreciable extent of the interests of the parties (as was found in the case of a feuing estate), a sale of the whole and division of the price will be ordered.[85] An action of ejection by one common owner against another is probably incompetent.[86]

16. Commonty: Runrig.—Commonty is a species of common property, once highly important, but now almost extinct, held as an accessory of the private estates of the commoners. Originally it was regarded as of value only

75 Bell, *Prin.*, § 1075.
76 *W.V.S. Office Premises* v. *Currie*, 1969 S.C. 170.
77 Bell, *Prin.*, supra; *Deans* v. *Woolfson*, 1922 S.C. 221.
78 *Lade* v. *Largs Bakery Co.* (1863) 2 M. 17, per Lord Deas.
79 *Millar* v. *Cathcart* (1861) 23 D. 743.
80 Erskine, *Inst.*, II, 6, 53; *Aberdeen Station Committee* v. *N.B. Ry.* (1890) 17 R. 975, at 984.
81 *Warrand* v. *Watson* (1905) 8 F. 253; *Aberdeen Station Committee* v. *N.B. Ry.*, supra, at 981 and 984.
82 *Brock* v. *Hamilton* (1852) 19 D. 701; *Anderson* v. *Anderson* (1857) 19 D. 700.
83 *Grant* v. *Heriot's Trust* (1906) 8 F. 647, at 658.
84 *Morrison* v. *Kirk*, 1912 S.C. 44.
85 *Brock* v. *Hamilton*, supra; *Thom* v. *Macbeth* (1875) 3 R. 161; *Campbells* v. *Murray*, 1972 S.L.T. 249 (sale by private bargain competent).
86 *Price* v. *Watson*, 1951 S.C. 359.

for pasturage and other uses of the surface, but it has been held to carry right to the minerals. Difficulty has been experienced in distinguishing this right from a servitude of pasturage. In questions as to the uses to which a commonty may be put, the rule "melior est conditio prohibentis" applies, and nothing which is not sanctioned by usage may be done without the consent of all the commoners.[87] No action of division of commonty lands was competent till the Division of Commonties Act 1695 (c. 38), whereby it is enacted "that all commonties, except the commonties belonging to the King and royal burghs may be divided at the instance of any having interest by summons raised against all concerned before the Lords of Session who are hereby empowered...to value and divide the same according to the value of the rights and interests of the several parties concerned." Under the statute where the commonty is divided among the common proprietors each receives a share of the commonty next to, and corresponding to the value of, his lands.[88] Where the value of the subjects in dispute is small, the action may now be brought in the Sheriff Court.[89]

Runrig lands are those which are in alternate or intermixed patches and belong to different proprietors. The Runrig Lands Act 1695 (c. 23) authorises the division of such lands.[90]

17. Common Interest.—In a passage[91] which has been accepted as an authoritative exposition of the meaning of this term[92] Bell says that "a species of right differing from common property takes place among the owners of subjects possessed in separate portions but still united by their common interest. It is recognised in law as 'common interest.' It accompanies and is incorporated with the several rights of individual property. In such a case a sale or division cannot resolve the difficulties which may arise in management, but the exercise and effect of the common interest must, when dissensions arise, be regulated by law or equity." Riparian proprietors have a common interest in the water of the stream[93]; so where a square is laid out in a town with a central garden for the use of the owners of the houses forming the square, these, in the general case, have a common interest in the garden, although they may have no right of property in it[94]; and so also feuars or neighbouring owners may have a common interest in a passage giving a common access or in an area reserved for light or common use.[95] But it is in the case of flatted houses that the most frequent illustration of this interest is to be found.

---

[87] *Campbell* v. *Campbell,* Jan, 24, 1809 F.C.; *Innes* v. *Hepburn* (1859) 21 D. 832.
[88] See *Macandrew* v. *Crerar,* 1929 S.C. 699.
[89] Sheriff Courts (Scotland) Act 1907 (7 Edw. VII, c. 51), s. 5.
[90] For fuller particulars as to commonty and runrig see Rankine, *Landownership,* pp. 598 et seq., and Bell, *Prin.,* §§ 1087-99.
[91] *Prin.,* § 1086.
[92] See *Grant* v. *Heriot's Trust* (1906) 8 F. 647, at 658; *Smith* v. *Giuliani,* 1925 S.C. (H.L.) 45, at 57.
[93] See Landownership, Ch. XXXIX, supra, § 22.
[94] *George Watson's Hospital* v. *Cormack* (1883) 11 R. 320; *Grant* v. *Heriot's Trust,* supra.
[95] *Mackenzie* v. *Carrick* (1869) 7 M. 419; *Grant* v. *Heriot's Trust,* supra. As to the common interest of the inhabitants of a burgh in a street and the space above it, see *Donald & Sons* v. *Esslemont & Macintosh,* 1923 S.C. 122.

18. Flatted Houses.—Where different floors or storeys of the same house belong to different persons, there is no common property among the proprietors of the several floors or storeys, but the respective rights of property in them are qualified by the common interest of all. The titles may contain express provision as to the rights and obligations of the proprietors, but, apart from such provision, the law of the tenement is as follows[96]:—The owners of the lower storeys must uphold them for the support of the upper; and the owner of the highest storey must uphold it as a cover for the lower. But there is no absolute duty of support or protection, and to establish liability to make reparation the relevant proprietor must be shown to have been negligent.[97] The roof belongs to the owner of the highest storey, but he may be compelled to keep it in repair and to refrain from injuring it. If that storey is divided among several proprietors, each must uphold that portion of the roof which covers his property.[98] A local Act which requires owners of roofs to repair them does not apply to the owners of the lower storeys where there are no provisions in the titles imposing that duty on them.[99] A garret may not without consent be converted into an attic storey.[1] The solum on which the flatted house is erected, the area in front, and the back ground are presumed to belong to the owner of the lowest floor, or to the owners thereof severally, subject to the common interest of the other proprietors to prevent injury to their flats, especially by depriving them of light.[2] The external walls belong to each owner in so far as they enclose his flat; but the other owners can prevent operations on them which would endanger the security of the tenement. The gables are common to the owner of each flat, so far as they bound his property, and to the owner of the adjoining house, but he and the other owners in the tenement have cross-rights of common interest to prevent injury to the stability of the building.[3] The floor and ceiling of each flat are divided in ownership by an imaginary line drawn through the middle of the joists; they may be used for the ordinary purposes, but may not be weakened or exposed to unusual risk from fire.[4] The common passages and stairs are the common property of all to whose premises they form an access, and the walls which bound them are the common property of these persons and the owners on their further side.[5]

19. Common Gables.—For the purpose of economising space a gable may be built originally, or may come afterwards to stand, on a boundary. It may be, or may be held to have been, erected one-half on each side of the boundary

[96] *Smith* v. *Giuliani*, 1925 S.C. (H.L.) 45; and see *Wells* v. *New House Purchasers*, 1964 S.L.T. (Sh. Ct.) 2.
[97] *Thomson* v. *St. Cuthbert's Co-operative Association*, 1958 S.C. 380; *Kerr* v. *McGreery*, 1970 S.L.T. (Sh. Ct.) 7; *Doran* v. *Smith*, 1971 S.L.T. (Sh. Ct.) 46.
[98] *Sanderson's Trs.* v. *Yule* (1897) 25 R. 211.
[99] *Duncan Smith & McLaren* v. *Heatly*, 1952 J.C. 61; see also *Musselburgh Town Council* v. *Jameson*, 1957 S.L.T. (Sh. Ct.) 35.
[1] *Sharp* v. *Robertson*, 1800 M. "Property" App. No. 3; *Watt* v. *Burgess' Tr.* (1891) 18 R. 766.
[2] *Boswell* v. *Mags. of Edinburgh* (1881) 8 R. 986.
[3] *Gellatly* v. *Arrol* (1863) 1 M. 592. See *Todd* v. *Wilson* (1894) 22 R. 172.
[4] *McArly* v. *French's Trs.* (1883) 10 R. 574.
[5] Rankine, *Landownership*, p. 677.

so as to accommodate the houses erected, or to be erected, on each side. The right to encroach beyond the boundary is founded on the custom of burghs and of other populous places where houses are erected streetwise. Much discussion has arisen with regard to the right of the first builder and his successors in the ownership to recover one-half of the cost from the owner of the adjoining stance. It seems to be settled that, in the absence of stipulation to the contrary, this right cannot be enforced till the adjacent owner for the time being actually begins to make use of the wall. Each of the parties has a right of property in his own share while each has a common interest in the whole.[6] The customary uses to which the gable may be put are mainly the insertion of joists, dooks, fireplaces and chimneys, and the binding into it of front and back walls.[7] A fence or division wall cannot, without agreement, be converted into a house gable.[8]

20. March-Fences.—Under the March Dykes Act 1661 (c. 41),[9] a proprietor of lands is enabled to compel the owner of conterminous lands to bear half the expense of erecting, repairing, or where necessary rebuilding[10] the march dyke or fence between their lands. The Act applies only to lands exceeding five or six acres.[11] The fence must be advantageous to both proprietors, but the advantage need not be equal[12]; and the court will refuse an application under the Act if the circumstances are such as to make the pursuer's demand oppressive or unfair.[13] The application is usually made in the Sheriff Court, but the jurisdiction of the Court of Session is not excluded.[14] The neighbouring proprietor cannot be made liable for the expense of the fence unless he has given his consent to its erection or has been made a party to proceedings under the Act.[15]

The Act has been supplemented by the March Dykes Act 1669 (c. 17), dealing with straightening of the marches. "Where the marches are crooked and unequal" or unfit for a dyke or ditch, the sheriff, on application by the proprietor of the lands, is empowered to visit the marches, to adjudge, where necessary, parts of one estate to the other, and where the parts transferred hinc inde are not of equal value "to decern what remains uncompensated of the price to the party to whom the same is wanting." It is imperative that the sheriff should visit the marches.[16] As in the case of applications under the

---

[6] *Jack* v. *Begg* (1875) 3 R. 35; *Glasgow Royal Infirmary* v. *Wylie* (1877) 4 R. 894; *Berkeley* v. *Baird* (1895) 22 R. 372; *Robertson* v. *Scott* (1886) 13 R. 1127; *Baird* v. *Alexander* (1898) 25 R. (H.L.) 35; *Wilson* v. *Pottinger*, 1908 S.C. 580.
[7] *Lamont* v. *Cumming* (1875) 2 R. 784.
[8] *Grahame* v. *Mags. of Kirkcaldy* (1882) 9 R. (H.L.) 91.
[9] Stair, II, 3, 75; Erskine, *Inst.*, II, 6, 4; Bankton, I, 10, 153-4; Rankine, *Landownership*, pp. 613 et seq.
[10] *Paterson* v. *MacDonald* (1880) 7 R. 958.
[11] *Penman* v. *Douglas*, 1739 M. 10481; *Secker* v. *Cameron*, 1914 S.C. 354.
[12] *Blackburn* v. *Head* (1904) 11 S.L.T. 521, per Lord Kyllachy.
[13] *Earl of Peterborough* v. *Garioch*, 1784 M. 10497; *Secker* v. *Cameron*, supra.
[14] *Pollock* v. *Ewing* (1869) 7 M. 815. In this case and in *Graham* v. *Irving* (1899) 2 F. 29, the application of the Act where the estates were bounded by a stream or burn was considered; see Rankine, *Landownership*, p. 615.
[15] *Ord* v. *Wright*, 1738 M. 10479.
[16] *Lord Advocate* v. *Sinclair* (1872) 11 M. 137. See *Earl of Kintore* v. *Earl of Kintore's Trs.* (1886) 13 R. 997, as to the sheriff's powers under the Act.

earlier Act, the Court will refuse an application which would result in oppression or unfairness.

Without having recourse to these statutes adjoining heritors may agree to erect a fence at the common expense; or it may be that, without express agreement, a fence has been recognised and treated as a march-fence; and in such cases there is a common obligation on the part of the heritors to maintain and repair it.[17]

[17] *Strang* v. *Steuart* (1864) 2 M. 1015.

CHAPTER XLI

LEGAL RIGHTS OF SPOUSES AND ISSUE

M'Laren, *Wills and Succession* (3rd ed., 1894, and Supplement, 1934); Fraser, *Husband and Wife* (2nd ed., 1876); Clive and Wilson, *Husband and Wife* (1974); Meston, *Succession (Scotland) Act 1964* (2nd ed., 1969).

THE following two chapters deal with the law of succession; but before entering on this subject it is necessary to notice the legal rights of the surviving spouse and issue of a deceased person in his or her estate. Although this chapter is principally concerned with the present state of the law, it is necessary to note certain aspects of the law as it existed in respect of deaths occurring before September 10, 1964, when the Succession (Scotland) Act 1964 took effect. In the case of deaths before that date the legal rights which could be claimed were (1) terce and courtesy, legal rights of liferent accruing to a widow and widower respectively in the heritable estate of the deceased spouse; (2) jus relictae and jus relicti, the share of moveables accruing to a widow and widower respectively; and (3) legitim, or bairn's part, which was the portion of moveables falling to the surviving children. As a result of the changes introduced by the 1964 Act in respect of deaths on or after that date the only legal rights now available are those exigible from moveables, the rights of terce and courtesy having been abolished; the right to claim legitim now extends to the issue of the predeceasing children[1] and by the Law Reform (Miscellaneous Provisions) (Scotland) Act 1968 is extended to illegitimate children and their issue.[1a]

1. Nature of the Rights.—Certain characteristics are common to all of these rights. They are not strictly rights of succession, but rather are claims in the nature of debts due from the deceased's estate. The claimants cannot, however, compete with creditors of the deceased; their claims attach to the free moveable estate remaining after these debts have been met,[2] and, in a case of intestacy, after satisfaction of the prior rights of a surviving spouse.[3] The spouse, parent or grandparent, as the case may be, remains free to deal with his property in his lifetime. During his life he may defeat or diminish the claims on his moveable estate by converting it in whole or in part into heritage; similarly, by selling his heritage and investing the proceeds, he could defeat or diminish the claims of terce or courtesy on it; or he may alienate his estate (either gratuitously or for onerous consideration) so as to leave nothing

---

[1] Succession (Scotland) Act 1964 (c. 41), s. 11.

[1a] 1968 (c. 70), ss. 2 & 3 & Sched. 1, §§ 3, 4, 5 & 7. While an illegitimate child and, in the event of his predecease, his lawful issue have a right to legitim, illegitimate issue of a predeceasing child, whether the child be legitimate or illegitimate, do not.

[2] *Naismith* v. *Boyes* (1899) 1 F. (H.L.) 79, per Lord Watson, at p. 81, 82, applied in *Petrie's Trs.* v. *Manders's Tr.,* 1954 S.C. 430; *Russel* v. *Att.-Gen.,* 1917 S.C. 28; *Cameron's Trs.* v. *MacLean,* 1917 S.C. 416.

[3] 1964 Act, s. 10 (2); see Intestate Succession, Ch. XLII, *infra*, §§ 2, 5.

to meet the claims. But he cannot defeat or diminish the claims by any testamentary or mortis causa disposition, and his will can receive effect only after satisfaction of these claims. If a deed of alienation, although appearing ex facie to divest him of the property in his lifetime, in fact leaves it under his command, or, if there is any trust or understanding whereby the benefit of the property is retained by him or he is entitled to call for its re-conveyance to him, it will not be effectual to exclude the claims of the spouse and issue.[4] This is so, for example, if the fruits or income of the property are to be paid to him or applied for his benefit. But, as rights of fee and liferent are recognised by the law as distinct interests, it is competent to exclude the claims by a deed alienating the property notwithstanding that a liferent is reserved to the grantor.[5] The mere circumstance that the deed was executed for the express purpose of shutting out the legal claims will not render it ineffectual[6]; and the fact that the beneficial right may in certain circumstances revert to the grantor of the deed does not make the deed revocable so long as the circumstances do not arise.[7] A person claiming legal rights may be required to elect between those rights and a testamentary provision.[8]

In the past a spouse's legal rights might be claimed on divorce. The 1964 Act abolished that system, and introduced a more flexible arrangement whereby financial provision is made at the discretion of the Court.[9]

2. Legal Rights in Heritable Estate.—The legal rights of terce and courtesy, exigible from the heritable estate of a deceased spouse, were abolished in the case of deaths on or after September 10, 1964.[10] To the extent, however, that these rights may still be claimed in respect of deaths before that date, certain parts of the former law are still significant.

Terce was the widow's right to a liferent of one-third of the heritage owned by her husband at the date of his death, whether by infeftment or by reason of a personal right[11]; heritable securities were heritable quoad terce and courtesy.[12] There were certain subjects out of which terce was not due. These were subjects incapable of infeftment, such as leases, the mansion house of the estate and its appurtenances, or its rent if it was let,[13] superiorities and feu-duties,[14] or the revenue derived from minerals.[15] The widow was not entitled

---

[4] Fraser on *Husband and Wife*, II, 1000; Bell, *Prin.*, §§ 1584, 1585; *Lashley* v. *Hog* (1804) 4 Pat. 581; *Nicolson's Assignee* v. *Hunter*, March 3, 1841, F.C.; *Buchanan* v. *Buchanan* (1876) 3 R. 556; *Drysdale's Trs.* v. *Drysdale*, 1940 S.C. 85.

[5] *Collie* v. *Pirie's Trs.* (1851) 13 D. 506.

[6] *Boustead* v. *Gardner* (1879) 7 R. 139; *Skinner* v. *Beveridge* (1872) 10 S.L.R. 12; *Scott* v. *Scott*, 1930 S.C. 903; *Campbell* v. *Campbell's Trs.*, 1967 S.L.T. (Notes) 30.

[7] See *Scott* v. *Scott*, supra, per Lord President Clyde, at pp. 915-6; also *Campbell* v. *Campbell's Trs.*, supra.

[8] See infra, § 7; Testate Succession, Ch. XLIII, §§ 32-34.

[9] See Husband and Wife, Ch. XLVI., infra. § 25; Divorce (Scotland) Act 1976 (c. 39), ss. 5, 6.

[10] 1964 Act, s. 10 (1); references in any other enactment to courtesy or terce no longer have effect: Schedule 2, para. 2.

[11] Conveyancing (Scotland) Act 1924 (14 & 15 Geo. V, c. 27), s. 21 (4), as amended by Conveyancing Amendment (Scotland) Act 1938 (1 & 2 Geo. VI, c. 24), s. 5.

[12] Titles to Land Consolidation (Scotland) Act 1868 (31 & 32 Vict., c. 101), ss. 117 and 3 (10).

[13] *Constable's Trs.* v. *Constable* (1904) 6 F. 826.

[14] *Nisbett* v. *Nisbett's Trs.* (1835) 13 S. 517.

[15] *Constable's Trs.* v. *Constable*, supra; *Grosset* v. *Grosset*, 1959 S.L.T. 334.

to terce in competition with any creditor of the husband.[16] Property subject to terce could not be sold free of the burden of terce without the wife's consent, whether her claim arose on death or on divorce.[17] When terce was due out of lands burdened with a prior terce still subsisting, the second tercer had a right to lesser terce, i.e., to a third of the two-thirds unaffected by the first terce; and when the death of the prior tercer disburdened the lands of her terce, the lesser terce became enlarged as if the first had never existed.[18]

As the burden of terce could not be discharged without the widow's consent, it tended to create difficulties in transactions as to the burdened lands. To remedy this, it was provided[19] that the widow or the proprietor or a security-holder (postponed to the widow) might bring an action to have the annual amount of the terce fixed for the future[20]; and, on the amount being so fixed, the proprietor or security-holder was entitled to redeem the terce at a capital sum to be determined by the Court. These provisions were applicable also to lesser terce.

Courtesy was the liferent of a wife's heritable estate given by law to her surviving husband. It attached to the whole of the heritage capable of infeftment (including conquest[21]) which belonged to the wife at the date of her death.[22] It was due to the husband, however, "rather as father to an heir than as husband to an heiress,"[23] and it was a condition of the right that a child, who had been heard to cry, had been born of the marriage, and that the child would have been, if he survived, the mother's heir. If, therefore, the wife left a child by a former marriage who succeeded to her heritage, her surviving husband had no right of courtesy. As in the case of terce, the husband had no right in competition with creditors of the wife.[24]

3. Legal Rights in Moveable Estate.—The rights which are available to the surviving spouse and issue of a deceased person out of his moveable estate are full rights of fee. These are jus relictae and jus relicti, in the case of the widow and widower respectively, and legitim, which is the portion of moveables falling to issue.

In the computation of the proportion of the free moveable estate falling to each of these rights, the deceased's moveables are divided in two or three parts according to the circumstances of the case.[25] The possible units are: (1) the

---

[16] Conveyancing (Scotland) Act 1924, s. 24 (4) (c); *Countess de Serra Largo* v. *de Serra Largo's Trs.*, 1933 S.L.T. 391.

[17] *Macnaughton* v. *Lindores*, 1940 S.C. 441.

[18] Erskine, *Inst.*, II, 9, 47.

[19] Conveyancing (Scotland) Act 1924, s. 21.

[20] Where the action was defended the amount had to be ascertained by proof, not remit; *Dickson* v. *Dickson*, 1931 S.L.T. 75.

[21] *Walker* v. *Walker's Trs.*, 1917 S.C. 46. "Conquest" in the law of succession meant those heritable rights which a deceased had acquired by singular title, (e.g., purchase or gift) as distinguished from those to which he had succeeded. The distinction which formerly obtained in the law of succession between heritage and conquest was abolished by the Conveyancing (Scotland) Act 1874 (37 & 38 Vict., c. 94), s. 37.

[22] See Conveyancing (Scotland) Act 1924, s. 21(4)(a), as amended by Conveyancing Amendment (Scotland) Act 1938, s. 5.

[23] Erskine, *Inst.*, II, 9, 53.

[24] See 1924 Act, s. 21.

[25] See table set out in Meston, op. cit., Appx. 1, reproduced in *Parliament House Book*, Division H.

surviving spouse's share (jus relictae or jus relicti as the case may be); (2) the share falling to issue (legitim); and (3) the dead's part, which is free to pass under the deceased's will or, in a case of intestacy, according to the ordinary rules of succession. If the deceased is survived by his spouse and by issue, the moveables fall to be divided into three parts, one-third passing to each unit.[26] If he is survived by his spouse only and not by issue, or by issue only, the division is into two, one half going to the dead's part and the other passing as a legal right to the spouse or issue as the case may be. If the deceased is survived by neither spouse nor issue, there are, of course, no legal rights, and the whole of his free moveable estate will fall to be dealt with as dead's part.

The right to jus relictae or jus relicti and to legitim vests on the death of the spouse or ancestor. The amount of the shares of the free moveable estate due in virtue of these rights is determined according to the value of that estate as at that time,[27] except that, if there has been realisation of the estate in ordinary course, it is the actual realised value and not the estimate as at the date of death which determines the amount of the estate for the purpose of calculating the legal rights.[28] It is the free moveable estate actually left by the deceased which is valued for this purpose and so where a partner's contingent right to the goodwill of a partnership was, in terms of the partnership agreement, extinguished on his death, it was held that the value of the goodwill did not require to be taken into account in determining the fund available for payment of legal rights.[29] It has been decided that a discretionary death gratuity paid after death to personal representatives must, however, be brought into account in the computation of legal rights,[30] but that income falling into intestacy through the operation of the Thellusson Act is excluded.[31] Sums lent on heritable security, although now moveable in the general succession of the creditors, are heritable for the purposes of legal rights, as also are ground annuals, and are not included in the computation of the estate for the purpose of their ascertainment.[32] Personal bonds bearing interest, although made moveable by the Bonds Act 1661 (c. 32), as regards the general succession and legitim, remained heritable quoad jus relictae and jus relicti, but are now moveable as regards these rights also.[33] Claims to jus relictae, jus relicti or legitim may be extinguished by the long negative prescription, though in certain cases the plea of non valens agere may be competent.[34]

In competition with creditors the spouse and issue have no right to any

[26] See Succession (Scotland) Act 1964, c. 41, s. 11 (4).
[27] *Gilchrist* v. *Gilchrist's Trs.* (1889) 16 R. 1118; *Russel* v. *Att.-Gen.*, 1917 S.C. 28; see also *Milne* v. *Milne's Trs.*, 1933 S.L.T. 336.
[28] *Alexander* v. *Alexander's Trs.*, 1954 S.C. 436.
[29] *Ventisei* v. *Ventisei's Exrs.*, 1966 S.C. 21.
[30] *Beveridge* v. *Beveridge's Exx.*, 1938 S.C. 160; and see Superannuation Act 1977, (c. 11), s. 4.
[31] *Lindsay's Trs.* v. *Lindsay*, 1931 S.C. 586. For Thellusson Act, see Testate Succession, Ch. XLIII, § 30, infra.
[32] Titles to Land Consolidation (Scotland) Act 1868 (31 & 32 Vict., c. 101), s. 117, as amended by Succession (Scotland) Act 1964, s. 34 and Sched. 3.
[33] Conveyancing (Scotland) Act 1924, s. 22; see Heritable and Moveable, Ch. XXXVI supra, § 10.
[34] *Campbell's Trs.* v. *Campbell's Trs.*, 1950 S.C. 48; *Pettigrew* v. *Harton*, 1956 S.C. 67; cf. *Mill's Trs.* v. *Mill's Exrs.*, 1965 S.L.T. 375, a case of intestacy supervening.

part of the estate which is required to meet the debts of the deceased. But in a question as to the incidence of a debt as between the heritable and the moveable estate, only moveable debts may be deducted, the principle being that in fixing the amount of the legal claims there can be deducted only those debts which, had they been assets and not liabilities of the deceased, would have gone to increase the amount of these claims.[35] Among such deductions are funeral charges, the expense of confirming and realising the estate,[36] estate duty,[37] and ante-nuptial marriage contract provisions.[37] There is authority for saying that a "rational" or reasonable provision to a widow may diminish the legitim fund, and that a similar provision to children may diminish the jus relicti or jus relictae, if these provisions are made in inter vivos deeds notwithstanding that their operation is suspended till the grantor's death.[38]

4. Jus Relictae: Jus Relicti.—By virtue of these rights the widow or widower, as the case may be, is entitled either to one-half or one-third of the free moveable estate, depending on whether there are issue to take legitim. The right of the widower to jus relicti was introduced by section 6 of the Married Women's Property (Scotland) Act 1881,[39] which enacts that the husband shall take the same share and interest in his wife's moveable estate which is taken by a widow in her deceased husband's moveable estate, and subject to the same rules "in relation to the nature and amount of such share and interest and the exclusion, discharge or satisfaction thereof, as the case may be." The Act does not affect contracts between spouses made either before or during the marriage.[40] These rights are available to a surviving spouse only, and a decree of judicial separation pronounced in favour of a wife precludes a claim for jus relicti on her death.[41]

5. Legitim.—As in the case of jus relictae and jus relicti, legitim is either one-third or one-half of the ancestor's moveable estate; one-third if there is a surviving spouse entitled to his or her legal rights, and one-half if there is no surviving spouse or if his or her legal rights have been renounced.

The right to claim legitim was, prior to the 1964 Act, limited to the surviving children of the deceased; it was divided equally among those children, including posthumous children, who were not forisfamiliated. "By a child forisfamiliated is to be understood one who, by having already received from his father his share of the legitim, and discharged it, or by his renouncing it even without real satisfaction, is no longer accounted a child in the family and is therefore excluded from any further share of it."[42] The 1964 Act

---

[35] See Conveyancing (Scotland) Act 1924, s. 22.
[36] *Russel* v. *Att.-Gen.*, 1917 S.C. 28. As to mourning and aliment to the widow, see *Baroness de Blonay* v. *Oswald's Reps.* (1863) 1 M. 1147; *M'Intyre* v. *M'Intyre's Trs.* (1865) 3 M. 1074; *Griffiths' Trs.* v. *Griffiths*. 1912 S.C. 626.
[37] *Bell* v. *Bell* (1897) 25 R. 310. Capital transfer tax is now deductible as previously was estate duty.
[38] Fraser, *Husband and Wife*, II, 1011; Bell, *Prin.*, § 1585; *Lawrie* v. *Edmond's Trs.*, 1816 Hume 291; *M'Leod* v. *Love*, 1914 S.C. 983.
[39] 44 & 45 Vict., c. 21.
[40] *Murray's Trs.* v. *Murray* (1901) 3 F. 820.
[41] Conjugal Rights (Scotland) Amendment Act 1861 (24 & 25 Vict., c. 86), s.6.
[42] Erskine, *Inst.*, III, 9, 23; see infra, §§ 6, 7.

introduced to claims for legitim in respect of deaths on or after September 10, 1964, the principle of representation, which had hitherto only applied to the intestate succession to moveable estate.[43] Accordingly, where a person dies predeceased by a child who has left lawful issue, however remote, who survive the deceased, and the child would, if he had survived the deceased, have been entitled under any rule of law to legitim out of the deceased's estate, such issue have the like right to legitim as the child would have had if he had survived the deceased. Division among such issue, if more than one, is per stirpes at the level of the class nearest in degree to the deceased of which there are surviving members.[44] For all purposes relating to the succession to any person who has died on or after September 10, 1964 (whether testate or intestate), adopted children are treated as legitimate children of the adopter, and as such are entitled to claim legitim from his moveable estate or represent the adopting parent in a claim for legitim to which he would have been entitled by survivance.[45] The only circumstances in which an adopted child now has a claim for legitim against the estate of a natural parent is when that parent died on or after September 10, 1964, and the adoptive parent or parents died before that date.[46] Illegitimate children may now claim legitim as, in the event of their dying before the parent from whose estate the legitim is claimed, may their lawful issue, but an illegitimate person cannot claim by representation.[47]

6. Collation Inter Liberos.[48]—This doctrine is designed to preserve equality among the claimants on the legitim fund. "Collation" is in Scots law a technical term meaning "the right which belongs to persons interested in a succession to have the particular part of the estate in which one of them has acquired a separate right thrown into the common fund in order to provide an equal division of the whole."[49] If a child entitled to legitim has received advances from the parent in his lifetime, these must (as a general rule) be collated by that child when the fund comes to be distributed among the issue; the effect of this is that the advances are brought in to augment the total amount of the legitim fund and are then, in its division, set against the share of the fund falling to that child. This principle now applies to legitim claims made not only by children but also by remoter issue representing deceased children. Such issue must collate any advances made to them by the person whose estate is being distributed, and also the appropriate proportion of any advances made to the person whom they represent.[50] Whether a provision does or does not fall to be collated depends on its nature and the circumstances in which it is made.[51] Advances "made for the purpose of

---

[43] Succession (Scotland) Act 1964, s. 11 (1).

[44] 1964 Act, s. 11 (2).

[45] 1964 Act, s. 23 (1).

[46] Law Reform (Misc. Provs.) (Scotland) Act 1966 (c. 19), s. 5.

[47] Law Reform (Miscellaneous Provisions) (Scotland) Act 1968 ss. 2 & 3 & Sched. 1, §§ 3, 4, 5 & 7. See also § 1 and footnote 1a supra.

[48] See M'Laren, I, §§ 316 et seq.; cf. Collation inter haeredes, as to which see Intestate Succession, Ch. XLII, infra, §§ 3 (c) and 4.

[49] *Young* v. *Young's Trs.*, 1910 S.C. 275, per Lord Kinnear, at p. 288.

[50] See 1964 Act, (c. 41), s. 11 (3).

[51] Stair, III, 8, 45; Erskine, *Inst.*, III, 9, 24; *Duncan* v. *Crichton's Trs.*, 1917 S.C. 728.

setting the child up in trade or for a settlement in the world or for a marriage portion" must be collated.[52] On the other hand, sums lent to the descendant are not the subject of collation, as these are, like other debts, due to the whole estate (and not merely to the legitim fund) and recoverable for its behoof[53]; nor are payments by way of remuneration for services rendered by the descendant,[54] or made by the ancestor in discharge of his natural duty to maintain and educate the descendant.[55] There is no ground for requiring the collation of a provision of a heritable right[56] or of a legacy to the descendant, as these do not affect the legitim fund,[57] heritable subjects not being included in that fund and legacies being due only from the dead's part after that fund has been fixed. It has been held that a provision for a child in a marriage-contract which contains no reference to discharge of legal rights must be collated if that child is to participate in the legitim fund.[58] Although an advance is of such a nature that it would fall to be collated, collation is excluded if it appears that it was the ancestor's intention that the descendant should have the advance in addition to a share of the legitim.[59]

Collation inter liberos arises only between children or issue of predeceasing children claiming legitim. If there is only one claimant for legitim, neither the other descendants of the deceased who have accepted provisions in lieu of legitim nor the testator's trustees have any title to insist that that claimant shall collate advances; nor, on the other hand, can that claimant require the other descendants, who are not claiming legitim, to collate advances received by them.[60] So also there is no place for collation in a question between issue and the surviving spouse.[61] A parent may, however, bargain with a child receiving an advance, that the advance is to be taken as a payment to account of that child's share of legitim, so as to entitle the parent's executors to set off the amount of the advance in accounting to that child or his issue for his legitim.[62]

7. Satisfaction of Legal Rights.—Where advances made by the deceased during his lifetime require to be collated inter liberos, these will satisfy, in whole or part, the recipient's claim to legitim. But a spouse or descendant may also be required to elect between a legacy made in his favour by the deceased and the legal rights themselves, where the legacy is made in lieu or satisfaction of the legatee's legal rights. In accordance with the principle of approbate and reprobate the legatee cannot take both such a legacy and his legal rights, but must elect between them. If he chooses to take the legacy, he forfeits his legal

[52] Bell, *Prin.*, § 1588.
[53] *Webster* v. *Rettie* (1859) 21 D. 915.
[54] *Minto* v. *Kirkpatrick* (1833) 11 S. 632.
[55] Erskine, *Inst.*, III, 9, 24.
[56] Erskine, *Inst.*, III, 9, 25.
[57] Ibid.
[58] *Elliot's Exx.* v. *Elliot*, 1953 S.C. 43. Note that legitim may no longer be discharged by an ante-nuptial marriage contract: Succession (Scotland) Act 1964, s. 12; infra, § 8.
[59] Erskine, *Inst.*, III, 9, 24; *Douglas* v. *Douglas* (1876) 4 R. 105.
[60] *Coats' Trs.* v. *Coats*, 1914 S.C. 744; *Gilmour's Trs.* v. *Gilmour*, 1922 S.C. 753.
[61] Erskine, *Inst.*, III, 9, 25.
[62] *Young* v. *Young's Trs.*, 1910 S.C. 275; see also *Gilmour's Trs.* v. *Gilmour*, supra.

rights, which are held to have been satisfied by the testamentary provision; if he takes his legal rights, he loses the legacy.[63]

Formerly the legacy, for this principle to operate, required to be expressly stated to be in lieu of legal rights; if this was not so, a claim for legal rights did not necessarily involve a complete forfeiture of the testamentary provisions.[64] In the case of testamentary dispositions made on or after September 10, 1964, however, in which provision is made in favour of the spouse or any issue of the testator, a declaration that it is made in full and final satisfaction of legal rights will, in the absence of an express provision to the contrary, be implied.[65] A claim for legal rights does not involve forfeiture of testamentary provisions in favour of issue of the claimant unless these provisions are dependent on the forfeited right of the claimant.[66]

By accepting the testamentary provision a spouse or descendant is not necessarily barred from claiming legal rights in any estate which has fallen into intestacy, or may subsequently do so; the bar operates only in so far as the claim for legal rights conflicts with the testamentary settlement.[67] But an express discharge of legal rights in absolute and unqualified terms excludes the right to claim legal rights out of estate falling into intestacy.[68]

The acceptance of a testamentary provision in lieu of legal rights, unlike a prior discharge thereof, benefits the dead's part, out of which the testamentary provision is paid.[69]

8. Prior Discharge of Legal Rights.—Legal rights may be discharged during the lifetime of the ancestor or spouse by the person prospectively entitled thereto. In the case of spouses, the ante-nuptial contract may contain a renunciation of jus relictae and jus relicti. This is usually done by express words of discharge,[70] but, even without such words, a settlement in the contract of the whole estate which may belong to the settlor at the date of his death on his spouse, being inconsistent with the assertion of such a claim, will exclude it.[71] Acceptance by a wife in her husband's lifetime of a liferent provided to her in a post-nuptial contract or other deed will exclude her claim to jus relictae out of the fund burdened with the liferent, because the acceptance of a liferent is inconsistent with a claim to carry off part of the fee.[72] In the case of children it was possible, prior to the 1964 Act, for

---

[63] See further, Testate Succession, Ch. XLIII, infra, §§ 32-35.
[64] Ch. XLIII, § 34.
[65] 1964 Act, s. 13. *Munro's Trs.,* 1971 S.C. 280. "Any issue of the testator" includes any illegitimate children of the testator and issue of any such children (Law Reform (Miscellaneous Provisions) (Scotland) Act 1968, (c. 70), s. 3, Sched. 1, para. 6).
[66] *Munro's Trs.,* supra.
[67] *Naismith* v. *Boyes* (1899) 1 F. (H.L.) 79; *Petrie's Trs.* v. *Manders's Tr.,* 1954 S.C. 430. But note that income falling into intestacy through the operation of the Thellusson Act is not subject to legal rights: *Lindsay's Trs.,* v. *Lindsay,* 1931 S.C. 586; see Testate Succession, Ch. XLIII, § 30, infra.
[68] *Melville's Trs.* v. *Melville's Trs.,* 1964 S.C. 105; contrast *Petrie's Trs.,* supra.
[69] See further, infra, § 8.
[70] *Maitland* v. *Maitland* (1843) 6 D. 244.
[71] *M'Laren,* I, 136; *Home* v. *Watson* (1757) 5 Brown's Supp., 330; *Fisher's Trs.,* v. *Fisher* (1844) 7 D. 129.
[72] *Riddel* v. *Dalton* (1781) M. 6457; *Edward* v. *Cheyne* (1888) 15 R. (H.L.), 33; *Smart* v. *Smart,* 1926 S.C. 392.

intending spouses to discharge prospectively the right of any child of the marriage to claim legitim, even if the provision in favour of children in the ante-nuptial marriage contract was made in such a way that some of them would take no benefit from it.[73] Where the trust constituted under such an ante-nuptial contract was brought to an end during the lifetime of the parties it was held that the termination of the trust did not by operation of law revive legal rights.[74] Since the 1964 Act, however, the right of a child or remoter issue cannot be discharged without that person's consent; nothing contained in an ante-nuptial marriage contract executed on or after September 10, 1964, will operate so as to exclude that right.[75] Where provisions are made in his favour, the child or his issue will have the usual right to elect between these testamentary provisions and the right to legitim; in other words, it is now a question only of satisfaction, no longer of prior discharge. A descendant may, should he himself desire to do so, renounce his right to claim legitim during the ancestor's lifetime, if it is made clear in the deed that this is his intention; ambiguous expressions will not be construed as having this effect.

The effect of a prior discharge of legal rights is that the grantor of the discharge is treated as dead. If a spouse has during the marriage renounced his or her legal right, then the estate of the predeceaser is divisible equally between dead's part and legitim, or, if there are no issue entitled to legitim, the whole is dead's part.[76] In the case of legitim, if one child has discharged his right, the entire fund is divided among the other claimants just as if that child had predeceased the parent; and if all the children have discharged their rights, the moveable estate becomes divisible equally between jus relicti or jus relictae and dead's part; or, if the claim for these rights is not exigible, the whole becomes dead's part.

[73] E.g., *Galloway's Trs.* v. *Galloway,* 1943 S.C. 339.
[74] *Callender* v. *Callender's Trs.,* 1972 S.C. (H.L.) 70. There might, however, be revival of legal rights if the deed terminating the trust showed an intention to that effect.
[75] 1964 Act, s. 12.
[76] Erskine *Inst.,* III, 9, 20. Under the common law rule that donations between spouses were revocable, a spouse might revoke a discharge of legal rights if it was in effect a donation to the other spouse (see Fraser, *Husband and Wife,* II, 927), but such donations are not now revocable (Married Women's Property (Scotland) Act 1920 (10 & 11 Geo. V, c. 64), s. 5).

CHAPTER XLII

INTESTATE SUCCESSION

M'Laren, *Wills and Succession* (3rd ed., 1894 and Supplement, 1934); Walker, *Law of Intestate Succession in Scotland* (1927); Meston, *Succession (Scotland) Act 1964* (2nd ed., 1969).

1. Presumption of Life.—At common law a person is, in the absence of proof of his death, presumed to continue in life for a reasonable time.[1] No precise period has been fixed, but Stair speaks of 80 or 100 years.[2] In cases where evidence was adduced which satisfied the Court that the explanation of the disappearance of a missing person was his death, he has been presumed to be dead although under that age.[3] Where a number of persons perished in a common calamity, there was, prior to the Succession (Scotland) Act 1964,[4] no presumption based on age or sex as to which was the last survivor.[5] The general rule which was introduced by that Act for the purposes of succession is now that, where two persons have died in circumstances indicating that they died simultaneously or rendering it uncertain which of them survived the other, the younger person is presumed to have survived the elder[6]; but this rule is subject to two exceptions. Where the two persons were husband and wife, there is a presumption that neither survived the other[7]; the result is that the husband, having failed to survive, fails to qualify as a beneficiary in the division of the wife's estate, and vice versa. This exception is intended to avoid situations in which the estate of the elder spouse would pass to the younger and then to the younger spouse's relatives to the exclusion of those of the elder, which might be contrary to the wishes of the elder spouse. The other exception to the general rule arises where the elder person has left a testamentary provision which contains a provision in favour of the younger, whom failing in favour of a third person; if the younger person has died intestate the effect of the survivorship clause is preserved, so as to prevent the legacy passing to the younger person's relatives against the declared wishes of the elder, by a presumption, for the purposes of that provision only, that the elder person survived the younger.[8] No presumption arises for consideration if there is proof that one person survived the other and such proof may be on a balance of probabilities.[9]

---

[1] Dickson on *Evidence,* § 116; Stevenson's *Presumption of Life* (1893); *Greig* v. *Merchant Co. of Edinburgh,* 1921 S.C. 76.
[2] IV., 45, 17.
[3] *Greig* v. *Merchant Co. of Edinburgh,* supra.
[4] 1964, c. 41.
[5] *Drummond's J.F.* v. *H.M. Advocate,* 1944 S.C. 298; applied in *Ross's J.F.* v. *Martin,* 1955 S.C. (H.L.) 56.
[6] s. 31 (1) (*b*).
[7] s. 31 (1) (*a*).
[8] s. 31 (2).
[9] *Lamb* v. *Lord Advocate etc.,* 1976 S.L.T. 151.

A statutory presumption of death which applied where a person had disappeared and had not been heard of for seven years or more was introduced by the Presumption of Life Limitation (Scotland) Act, 1881[10] and, although it did not supplant, substantially reduced the importance of the common law rule. Both the common law and the previous statutory provisions have now been replaced by the Presumption of Death (Scotland) Act 1977 which provides for the granting of declarator of death if the court is satisfied on a balance of probabilities that a person who is missing—

(1) has died, or

(2) has not been known to be alive for a period of at least seven years.[11]

The court in granting declarator must find the date and time of death. If that is uncertain it will be taken to be the end of the period to which the uncertainty relates or, where the missing person has not been known to be alive for a period of seven years or more, the end of the day occurring seven years after the date on which he was last known to be alive.[12] The court may also determine the domicile of the missing person at his death and any question relating to an interest in property arising as a consequence of his death, and may appoint a judicial factor on his estate.[13] At the expiry of the time for appeal or, if an appeal is made, on the refusal or withdrawal of the appeal, the decree of declarator is conclusive of all the matters contained in it and effective against any person and for all purposes including the acquisition of rights to or in property belonging to any person.[14] The decree may, nonetheless, be afterwards varied or recalled[15] (e.g. where the missing person reappears or fresh evidence pointing to a different date of death comes to light) but such variation or recall affects property rights only if the application for variation or recall is made within five years of the date of decree.[16] If the application is within that time, the court may make such order in relation to property rights as it considers fair and reasonable in all the circumstances of the case. The order does not, however, affect income accruing between the date of decree and the date of variation or recall nor does it affect rights acquired by third parties in good faith and for value. If no order is made, property rights remain unaffected by the recall or variation of the decree.[16] In considering what order should be made the court must, so far as practicable in the circumstances, have regard to restricting any rights which, as a result of the order, emerge under a trust, to rights in undistributed property plus the value, as at the date of distribution, of rights in property which has been distributed. The court must also have regard, if the facts in respect of which the decree was varied or recalled justify such a course, to the repayment to an

[10] 44 & 45 Vict., c. 47. This Act was repealed and replaced by the Presumption of Life Limitation (Scotland) Act 1891, (54 & 55 Vict., c. 29), which remained in force until repealed by the 1977 Act. See *Barr* v. *Campbell*, 1925 S.C. 317, as to the effect of a decree under the Act on the construction of a trust disposition and settlement.
[11] 1977, (c. 27), s. 1.
[12] Ibid., s. 2 (1).
[13] Ibid., s. 2 (2).
[14] Ibid., s. 3.
[15] Ibid., s. 4.
[16] Ibid., s. 5.

insurer of any capital sum paid as a result of the decree.[16] Trustees are required, on the granting of decree of declarator, to effect insurance against any claims which may arise if the decree is varied or recalled and insurers may, before paying any capital sum as a result of a decree of declarator, require the payee to effect insurance against any claim which the insurer may have in the event of variation or recall.[16]

2. Succession on Death.—On the death of a person his property, so far as it is not regulated by deed, devolves on his heir or heirs according to the rules of intestate succession; but it is only to the balance after deduction of legal and prior rights, referred to as the free estate, that the rules of succession apply. There are, in effect, three sets of rules of division, which require to be considered in turn. First, after the debts and other liabilities of the estate have been met, the prior rights of a surviving spouse, if any, must be satisfied.[17] There then fall to be deducted from any moveable estate which remains such legal rights as may be due to the surviving spouse or to issue.[18] The final division of the balance of the deceased's moveable and heritable estate is made according to the rules of intestate succession applicable to the free estate.[19] The extent of the free estate will thus vary from case to case; where the intestate died survived by neither spouse nor issue no prior or legal rights will arise, and the rules of succession will apply to the whole of his estate after payment of debts, whereas in other cases all or most of the deceased's estate may be exhausted by the rights of his surviving spouse and issue. Those who succeed to property on the owner's death, whether by testate or intestate succession, are called universal successors, in contradistinction to singular successors who acquire the property of the owner in his lifetime by singular title, such as contract, conveyance or diligence.

Under the common law only those of legitimate relationship were entitled to succeed on intestacy. Limited exceptions were introduced by the Legitimacy Act 1926[20] and substantially re-enacted in the Succession (Scotland) Act 1964. A more radical change has, however, now been effected, by way of amendment of the 1964 Act, by the Law Reform (Miscellaneous Provisions) (Scotland) Act 1968 which, so far as succession to, and legal rights in, their parents' estate and succession by parents to the estates of their children are concerned, equiparates illegitimate with legitimate children.[21] Beyond that, there is, however, no succession through illegitimate relationship and, accordingly, an illegitimate child still cannot represent its predeceasing parent in a succession opening after the parent's death.[22] Illegitimate children cannot therefore succeed by representation to, for example, their grandparents' estate. For the purposes of succession to the estate of an illegitimate person, that

[17] Infra, § 5.
[18] See previous chapter.
[19] For a convenient table of the three rules of division, see Meston, *Succession (Scotland) Act 1964*, Appx. 1, pp. 83 et seq., reproduced in the *Parliament House Book*, Division H.
[20] 16 & 17 Geo. V, c. 60, s. 9; repealed by 1964 Act.
[21] 1968 (c. 70), ss. 1, 2 & 3 & Sched. 1.
[22] 1964 Act, s. 4 (4) as amended by 1968 Act s. 1.

person is presumed not to be survived by his father unless the contrary is shown.[23]

Under the previous law an adoption order did not deprive the adopted child of his rights in succession to the estate of his natural parents, nor did he acquire any in the estate of the adopter.[24] The 1964 Act[25] reversed this position in relation to the succession to any person who has died on or after September 10, 1964, and provided that an adopted person is to be treated for all purposes of succession as a child of the adopter, and not as the child of any other person. He is entitled to legitim, and to represent his adopter as one of his issue. The only circumstance in which an adopted person is entitled to succeed to the estate of his natural parent, or to claim legitim in that estate, when that parent died on or after September 10, 1964, is where the adoptive parent or parents died before that date.[26] In relation to his collaterals an adopted person adopted by two spouses jointly is treated as a brother or sister of the full blood of any other child or adopted child of both spouses. In any other situation where the relationship between an adopted child and another child or adopted child of the adopter is in issue the children are treated as brothers or sisters of the half blood only.[27]

Where there are no relatives entitled to succeed to the intestate estate, it falls to the Crown as ultimus haeres.[28]

The Scottish rules of succession apply to the moveable estate of a person who dies domiciled in Scotland, and to the devolution of heritable property situated in Scotland whatever the domicile of the deceased.

3. The Previous Law of Intestate Succession.—Important changes were made in the law of intestate succession by the Succession (Scotland) Act 1964[29]; but it is still necessary to consider briefly the previous law both as a background to the changes themselves, and because the Act, for obvious reasons, was not retrospective.[30]

The general scheme of succession as applied to heritable and moveable estate prior to the Act bore a basic similarity. The order of succession, with its emphasis on the blood relationship, was in each case the same. The estate devolved in the first instance on descendants of the deceased, first children, failing these on grandchildren, and so on ad infinitum. If there were no descendants, it devolved on relatives in the collateral line, i.e., brothers and sisters of the deceased; and failing these it passed to ascendants, the father and his collateral relatives, whom failing the grandfather and his collaterals, and

---

[23] Ibid. s. 4 (3).
[24] Adoption Act 1958, s. 18.
[25] s. 23(1).
[26] Law Reform (Misc. Provs.) (Scotland) Act 1966 (c. 19), s. 5.
[27] 1964 Act, (c. 41), s. 24.
[28] Stair, IV, 13, 1; Erskine, *Inst.,* III, 10, 2; *Rutherford* v. *Lord Advocate,* 1932 S.C. 674; Law Reform (Miscellaneous Provisions) (Scotland) Act, 1940 (3 & 4 Geo. VI, c. 42), s. 6; Succession (Scotland) Act 1964, s. 7.
[29] 1964, c. 41. Note that the transmission of titles and honours is excluded from the operation of this Act (s. 37 (1)); the previous law remains applicable to these items. Tenancy of crofts is now included (Law Reform (Misc. Prov.) (Scot.) Act 1968, (c. 70), s. 8).
[30] s. 37 (2).

so on in the line of ascent. But in matters of detail there were important and fundamental differences between succession in heritage and succession in moveable property.

(a) SUCCESSION IN HERITAGE: The basic, and characteristic, rule of succession in heritage was that the heritage passed, if possible, to one individual only, who as the heir-at-law, or heir-of-line, succeeded to the whole heritable property owned by the deceased at his death. Throughout the whole course of succession males were preferred to females, and among males, except in the collateral line, the older was preferred to the younger; throughout the succession also there was an unlimited common law right of representation. Thus, if the deceased's eldest son predeceased him leaving issue, his issue took in preference to the deceased's younger sons; and amongst his issue sons and the issue of sons were preferred to daughters and the issue of deceased daughters. The mother of the deceased and her relatives had no right of succession in heritage.

In the selection of the heir-at-law the rule was that the heritage should always, if possible, descend. In the event of the succession opening to the collateral line, therefore, if the deceased was survived by both elder and younger brothers, the younger brothers and their issue succeeded in the first instance in order of seniority, whom failing the succession passed from the younger to the older of the elder brothers. Failing collaterals of the full blood those of the half-blood consanguinean (i.e., those having the same father as the deceased but a different mother) could succeed; but, following the rule that the mother had no right of succession, collaterals of the half-blood uterine were completely excluded.

In the event of there being males to whom the heritage could pass, the heir was always one individual. But where females succeeded, all those females in the same degree to the deceased, known as heirs-portioners, took the estate equally between them, though a preference was allowed to the eldest heir-portioner in that she was entitled to certain subjects as her praecipuum.[31] Heirs-portioners were not joint proprietors, each having a title to her own share which she might burden or alienate; on her death that share did not accresce to the other heirs-portioners, but passed to her own representatives or heirs.[32] If one who would have succeeded as an heir-portioner predeceased the intestate, her issue, with a preference for males, took her share by right of representation.

(b) SUCCESSION IN MOVEABLE ESTATE: In the case of moveables the rule was that all those who were related in the same degree to the deceased as his next-of-kin were entitled to participate, irrespective of age and sex. At common law the surviving members of the class nearest in degree to the deceased shared equally in his moveable estate to the exclusion of the issue of a predeceasing member of that class; there was no right of representation. In

---

[31] Stair, III, 5, 11; Erskine, *Inst.*, III, 8, 5. These were titles of honour, the principal mansion-house with its necessary adjuncts, and a superiority with its casualties.
[32] *Cargill* v. *Muir* (1837) 15 S. 408.

each case relatives of the full blood were preferred to those of the half-blood consanguinean, but the half-blood of a nearer took in preference to the full blood of a more distant class. The mother, the maternal relations and relatives of the half-blood uterine had no right of succession in moveables.

These common law rules were altered in several respects by the Intestate Moveable Succession (Scotland) Acts of 1855 and 1919.[33] The 1855 Act introduced the principle of representation to the ascertainment of the heirs in mobilibus, but only to a limited extent.[34] Representation was extended only to the line of descent and to brothers and sisters of the intestate and their issue; it was not applicable to ascendants or their collaterals.[35] The right only emerged where there were surviving members of the class nearest in degree, in which case the issue of the predeceasing members could take per stirpes the shares which would have fallen to them had they survived; where all the heirs stood in the same degree of relationship to the deceased, e.g., as nephews and nieces, the division was per capita among each of them.[36] Where the intestate died without issue but was survived by his father and brothers and sisters, the father enjoyed under the 1855 Act[37] the right to take one-half of the estate in preference to the brothers and sisters. If the intestate was predeceased by his father but survived by his mother in similar circumstances, she too was entitled to succeed to part, fixed by the 1919 Act[38] at one-half also, of his estate in preference to the rights of the brothers and sisters. Finally, the 1855 Act[39] extended the succession to collaterals-uterine by giving them a right to succeed to one-half only of the estate where the intestate died without issue or other collaterals and predeceased by both parents.

(c) COLLATION INTER HAEREDES: Where the intestate's estate consisted of both heritable and moveable property, the heir-at-law taking the heritage was excluded from participating in the succession to moveables, whether as dead's part or legitim, except on condition of collating the heritage. It was in the heir's option to throw the heritage into the common stock with the moveable property so as to bring about a division of the whole equally between him and the other persons entitled to the moveables. It was a doctrine which arose to prevent the inequality which would otherwise have resulted if the heir-at-law, where he was among those who by their relationship to the deceased would be entitled to a share in the moveables, were to be given both the heritage and his share of the moveables.[40] The heir was required to collate not only what he took by intestate succession but also whatever he received by gift or deed, provided he would otherwise have succeeded to it as heir; a younger son, not alioqui successurus, was not obliged to collate heritage bequeathed to him by his father. If the heir-at-law was also the sole heir in mobilibus there was no

---

[33] 18 & 19 Vict., c. 23, and 9 & 10 Geo. V, c. 61.
[34] s. 3.
[35] *Ormiston* v. *Broad* (1862) 1 M. 10.
[36] *Turner* v. *Couper* (1869) 8 M. 222.
[37] s. 4.
[38] s. 1.
[39] s. 5.
[40] Erskine, III, 9, 1; *Anstruther* v. *Anstruther* (1836) 14 S. 272 at 282, affd. 2 S. & M'L. 369. See also *Gilmour's Trs.* v. *Gilmour*, 1922 S.C. 753 at 767.

place for collation; nor would the question of collation arise if the intestate left no heritable estate.

4. The Succession (Scotland) Act 1964.—The law of intestate succession in Scotland was extensively altered by the 1964 Act, which introduced with respect to deaths on or after September 10, 1964 changes which had long been thought overdue.[41] The most fundamental change was the assimilation, after the satisfaction of prior and legal rights, of the deceased's heritable and moveable estate for the purposes of succession. The rules which now fall to be applied without distinction as between heritage and moveables are similar to those which regulated the division of moveables under the previous law, but with wider possibilities of representation; thus all the persons in the class nearest in degree to the deceased, or their representatives per stirpes, share equally in the whole free estate. With the disappearance of the heir-at-law the doctrine of collation inter haeredes was rendered unnecessary. The special characteristics of certain items are preserved by their exclusion from the Act; the previous law still regulates the succession to titles, honours, and coats of arms.[42] Significant improvements were made in the position of the surviving spouse, both as regards prior rights and in the succession to the free estate in which previously she took no part. In the line of ascent and the collateral line the emphasis of the blood tie was removed by equating the rights of the mother and her relations with those of the father, and of the collaterals of the half-blood uterine with those consanguinean.

The law as regulated by the Act will now be considered in more detail.

5. Surviving Spouse's Prior Rights.—Where the deceased died intestate, but only then, the surviving spouse is entitled to certain valuable rights in the other's estate, known as prior rights.[43] Quoad these rights the surviving spouse ranks next after the creditors of the deceased, and the rights must be satisfied before the estate becomes available to the claimants for legal rights and intestate heirs.[44] Intestacy for this purpose arises where the deceased leaves the whole or any part of his estate undisposed of by testamentary disposition[45]; and in a case of partial intestacy the surviving spouse is only entitled to receive prior rights out of the intestate part of the estate. There are two separate rights, under section 8 of the 1964 Act to the dwelling-house with furniture and plenishings, and under section 9 to a financial provision out of the remainder of the intestate estate.

The right under section 8 falls into two parts. As far as the dwelling-house is concerned, the surviving spouse is entitled to receive the deceased's interest

---

[41] See Meston, op. cit., pp. 7-9.
[42] 1964 Act, s. 37 (1); note that the exclusion extends to the Act as a whole, including its provisions as to illegitimate and adopted children. See footnote 29, supra.
[43] Note that a decree of judicial separation obtained by a wife extinguishes all the rights of the husband in her intestate succession: Conjugal Rights (Scotland) Amendment Act 1861 (24 & 25 Vict., c. 86), s. 6.
[44] See 1964 Act, ss. 1 (2), 10 (2).
[45] s. 36 (1). Tehere may therefore be an intestacy where the sole beneficiary under a will renounces his or her rights (*Kerr, Petr.*, 1968 S.L.T. (Sh. Ct.) 61; *Munro's Trs.* v. *Munro*, 1971 S.C. 280).

in the house, including any garden or other ground attached, in which the surviving spouse was ordinarily resident at the date of the intestate's death[46] up to a value of £30,000; it is not a requirement that the deceased should have been resident in the house at his death. The interests available to the surviving spouse under this right are those of ownership or of tenancy under a lease, other than one to which the Rent Acts[47] apply, subject in either case to any heritable debts secured over the interest.[48] If the surviving spouse was ordinarily resident in more than one house an interest in which is included in the deceased's intestate estate, he or she has the right to elect within six months of the intestate's death which one to take under this section.[49] If the value of the interest in the house exceeds £30,000, the surviving spouse is entitled instead to a payment of £30,000 in cash; if it is less, the entitlement is to the interest in the house itself, with two exceptions where the entitlement is to the value of the interest only. These exceptions arise where the house forms only part of the subjects comprised in one tenancy of which the intestate was the tenant, or where it forms the whole or part of subjects falling into the intestate estate used by him for carrying on a trade, profession or occupation and the likelihood is that the value of the estate as a whole would be substantially diminished if the house were to be disposed of otherwise than with the assets of that trade, profession or occupation.[50] The second right under section 8 is to the furniture and plenishings falling within the deceased's intestate estate, up to a maximum of £8,000.[51] This is an entirely independent right, which exists even if the dwelling-house in which they are contained does not fall within the deceased's intestate estate. It is expressly provided[52] that the term "furniture and plenishings" does not include any article or animal used at the date of the intestate's death for business purposes, or money or securities for money, or any heirloom. Where the intestate estate comprises the furniture and plenishings of two or more dwelling-houses, the surviving spouse is limited to the furniture and plenishings of any one of them; the right to elect must be exercised within six months, and is in no way dependent on the right to elect between the dwelling-houses themselves.

The right to a financial provision out of the intestate estate under section 9 is exigible only after the claims under section 8 have been satisfied. If the intestate was survived by lawful issue in whatever degree, the right is to the sum of £8,000[53] out of the remainder of the intestate estate; if no issue survive the intestate the sum is £16,000[53], with interest in each case at the rate of 4 per cent. per annum. If the surviving spouse is entitled to receive any payment or benefit, other than a bequest of the house or furniture, by virtue of a

---

[46] s. 8 (4), and s. 8 (1) as amended by the Succession (Scotland) Act 1973, c. 25, s. 1.
[47] See Leases, Ch. XXXIII, supra, § 39; for statutory transmission on death under the Rent Acts see Ch. XXXIII, § 42.
[48] s. 8 (6) (d).
[49] Proviso to s. 8 (1).
[50] s. 8 (2).
[51] s. 8 (3) as amended by the Succession (Scotland) Act 1973 (c. 25), s. 1.
[52] See s. 8 (6) (b).
[53] s. 9 (1) as amended by the Succession (Scotland) Act 1973 (c. 25), s. 1 and the Prior Rights of Surviving Spouse (Scotland) Order 1977 (S.I. 1977 No. 2110).

testamentary disposition out of the deceased's estate, the amount or value of the legacy must be deducted from the appropriate figure due under section 9. If the intestate estate is less than the amount which the surviving spouse is entitled to receive, the right is to a transfer of the whole of that estate; in some cases, therefore, the whole of the balance of the intestate estate may pass to the surviving spouse under this right, leaving nothing upon which the legal rights of issue or the rules of succession to the free estate can operate. If the estate exceeds the entitlement, there is a division of the entitlement among the heritage and moveable property respectively in proportion to the respective amounts of those parts so that a proper balance is preserved prior to the deduction from the moveables of legal rights.[54]

6. Order of Succession to the Free Estate.[55]—The free estate is that part of the intestate's estate which remains after the deduction of prior and legal rights. The order of succession to this part is set out in section 2 of the 1964 Act, by means of a statutory list. This list follows, broadly speaking, the same general pattern as that which applied under the previous law; those who are nearer in relationship to the intestate and so higher on the list are preferred to and exclude those lower down. Separate sections[56] deal with representation, and the division of the intestate estate among those entitled to it. Representation is applied throughout the succession, except in relation to a parent or spouse of the intestate. The division is equally per capita among those who are in the same degree of relationship to the intestate, while the representatives of predeceasing members of that class take per stirpes.

In the first instance the succession descends to the surviving children of the intestate, including adopted children, and the issue of predeceasing children. Failing issue the succession opens to collaterals or their issue; if the intestate is survived by one or both of his parents, the parent or parents equally have right at this stage to participate to the extent of one half of the free intestate estate. Failing issue of collaterals of the whole blood, collaterals of the half-blood are entitled to succeed, without distinction between those related through the mother (uterine) and those related through the father (consanguinean).[57] Failing collaterals the succession passes to the parents, who are entitled to share the whole available estate between them; if only one survives, the whole free estate goes to the survivor. In the absence of any prior relative—that is, issue, collaterals or parents—of the intestate, the succession passes to the surviving spouse; in such a situation, there being no issue to take legitim, the surviving spouse would be entitled to take the entire intestate estate after payment of the deceased's debts. Failing a surviving spouse, the succession opens to ascendants, the relatives of the intestate's mother being placed on an equal footing with those of the father. The succession passes in the first instance to uncles or aunts of the intestate, then to grandparents, and then to collaterals of grandparents. Finally, it passes to remoter ancestors of

[54] s. 9 (3); see previous chapter.
[55] See Meston, op. cit., Appx. 2, for examples of the division of particular estates.
[56] ss. 5, 6.
[57] s. 3.

the intestate of whatever degree, before falling to the Crown as ultimus haeres.[58]

7. Vesting of the Right of Heirs in Intestacy.—At common law the succession, unlike legal rights,[59] did not vest in the heir-at-law or next of kin by their mere survivance of the intestate. The heir-at-law acquired no transmissible right in the lands until he took the appropriate steps to establish his right; this he might do by service, that is, by means of proceedings in which, on proving his right of succession, he obtained a decree of Court serving him as heir, or in certain cases by applying to the superior of the lands and obtaining from him a writ acknowledging his right as heir. The common law rule with regard to heritage was altered by the Conveyancing (Scotland) Act 1874, which provided that a personal right to every estate in land descendible to heirs should thereafter, without service or other procedure, vest in the heir entitled to succeed thereto by his survivance of the person to whom he was entitled to succeed.[60] The heir-at-law was thus enabled immediately to dispose of the estate, and it would transmit on his death to his heir or representative. The procedures of service and acknowledgement remained in use as the means whereby the heir completed title and acquired a real right in the heritage, but they were no longer necessary in order to give him a personal right. In the same way, at common law confirmation was necessary, although certain exceptions were allowed,[61] before vesting took place in the next of kin; if the next of kin died before confirmation was expede, the right opened to those who were next in the order of succession. This common law rule was altered by the Confirmation of Executors Act 1823,[62] to the effect of giving the heirs in mobilibus a vested right in the succession immediately on the death of the intestate. Accordingly, since that date, although confirmation remains necessary for the purpose of conferring on the executor a title to recover and administer the estate, it has not been required in order to enable an heir to transmit his right to assignees or creditors, or to his legal representatives.[63]

The assimilation of heritage and moveables effected by the 1964 Act[64] extends to the administration and winding-up of the deceased's estate; and the previous arrangements for moveables now apply, with modifications, to the whole estate without distinction between heritable and moveable property.[65] Thus the whole of the deceased's estate,[66] whether he died testate or intestate, vests in his executor by virtue of the confirmation. But the right of the intestate heirs to participate in the estate vests, by virtue of the 1823 Act, by their survivance of the intestate.[67]

[58] s. 7.
[59] See Bell, *Lectures on Conveyancing*, p. 1139.
[60] s. 9; *M'Adam* v. *M'Adam* (1879) 6 R. 1256.
[61] These are given in Erskine, III, 9, 30, and M'Laren, *Wills and Succession*, 11, § 1604.
[62] 4 Geo. IV, c. 98, s. 1; *Webster* v. *Shiress* (1878) 6 R. 102.
[63] *Frith* v. *Buchanan* (1837) 15 S. 729; *Elder* v. *Watson* (1859) 21 D. 112. For confirmation of executors, see Executors, Ch. XLIII, infra, § 3.
[64] Succession (Scotland) Act 1964, s. 1 (1).
[65] s. 14 (1).
[66] Note however the exceptions in s. 37 (1).
[67] See *Webster* v. *Shiress*, supra, per Lord Justice-Clerk Moncreiff at p. 106.

8. Incidence of Liabilities.—The whole of the deceased's estate is liable for his debts, even before the deduction of legal rights.[68] Formerly a creditor could sue either the heir-at-law or the executor,[69] but as between the heir and the executor the rule was that the former was liable in debts which were heritable or secured over heritage, and the latter in those that were moveable.[70] Hence, an heir who was required to pay a moveable debt had a right of relief against the executor, and the executor paying a heritable debt was entitled to relief from the heir.[71] Although the heir-at-law and the distinction between heritable and moveable for the purposes of succession to the free estate have disappeared, the 1964 Act expressly saved[72] the existing law whereby particular debts fall to be paid out of a particular part of the estate. The incidence of liabilities remains of significance in computing the moveable estate for the purposes of legal rights.

The moveable estate is liable under personal contracts entered into by the deceased. If, therefore, the deceased has concluded a contract for the purchase of lands, but dies before obtaining a disposition, the lands fall into the estate as heritage, but the price is payable out of moveables.[73] On the other hand, if the deceased has sold heritage but dies before granting a disposition, the contract must be implemented, but the price received will fall to be added to the moveable estate.[74] Liability attaches to heritage where the estate is liable under a heritable security, for such securities remain heritable quoad the debtor's succession,[75] and also for annuities granted by the deceased as these are heritable rights.[76]

In the case of testate succession the same rules hold as to the incidence of liabilities unless the testator has evinced a different intention. If trustees are directed to convey heritage burdened with debt to a beneficiary, that beneficiary is liable in the debt, and a general clause directing the trustees to pay all debts is not sufficient to relieve the beneficiary.[77] It is not clear whether this rule applies to the case of a bequest of a specific moveable subject which has been pledged or assigned in security by the testator.[78]

---

[68] See *Naismith* v. *Boyes* (1899) 1 F. (H.L.) 79, per Lord Watson at p. 82.
[69] *British Linen Co.* v. *Lord Reay* (1850) 12 D. 949; *Carnousie* v. *Meldrum* (1630) M. 5204.
[70] Erskine, III, 9, 48; *Duncan* v. *Duncan* (1882) 10 R. 1042.
[71] Act 1503, c. 76; Erskine, III, 9, 48.
[72] s. 14 (3).
[73] *Ramsay* v. *Ramsay* (1887) 15 R. 25; *Fairlie's Trs.* v. *Fairlie's Curator Bonis*, 1932 S.C. 216, per Lord President Clyde at 220.
[74] *Chiesley*, (1704) Mor. 5531; *Heron* v. *Espie* (1856) 18 D. 917; *M'Arthur's Exrs.* v. *Guild*, 1908 S.C. 743.
[75] *Bell's Trs.* v. *Bell* (1884) 12 R. 85.
[76] *Breadalbane's Trs.* v. *Jamieson* (1873) 11 M. 912. See Heritable and Moveable, Ch. XXXVI, supra, § 11.
[77] *Douglas's Trs.* v. *Douglas* (1868) 6 M. 223; *Macleod's Trs.* (1871) 9 M. 903.
[78] *Stewart* v. *Stewart* (1891) 19 R. 310; *Heath* v. *Grant's Trs.*, 1913 S.C. 78; *Reid's Trs.* v. *Dawson*, 1915 S.C. (H.L.) 47, per Lord Dunedin, at p. 50.

CHAPTER XLIII

TESTATE SUCCESSION

M'Laren's *Wills and Succession* (3rd ed., 1894 and Supplement, 1934); Henderson's *Principles of Vesting* (2nd ed., 1938); Murray's *Law of Wills in Scotland*.

A WILL is a declaration of what a person wishes to be done with his estate after his death.[1] In order that the declaration may be effectual the law (with an important exception[2]) requires that it shall be expressed in writing executed in certain prescribed modes, but otherwise allows almost complete freedom of testamentary disposition. A certain degree of restriction is imposed by the existence of the legal rights of spouses and issue,[3] and, as will hereafter be noticed,[4] there are purposes to which, on grounds of public policy, the law will not permit property to be devoted by testamentary deed.

It is essential to the validity of a will that the testator had sufficient capacity to test, and that it satisfies the requirements of the law in point of form.[5]

1. Capacity to Test: Reduction of Will.—A pupil has not sufficient understanding to test.[6] A married woman can, and always could, test without her husband's consent.[7] A minor has always been able to dispose of his moveable property by will, with or without his curator's consent,[8] and he may now test on his heritable estate as well.[9]

A testament executed by a person who is at the time insane is ineffectual. It is necessary to the exercise of the power of testing that the testator should be capable of comprehending the nature and effect of the testamentary act; and, in the absence of such capacity, the deed is null. If a person who is insane has a lucid interval, a will made in that interval may be sustained.[10] Where there is no general insanity on the part of the testator but merely delusions, it must appear that these delusions influenced the dispositions made in the will in order to deprive them of effect.[11] The law also recognises the existence of a state known as facility, in which, while there is no incapacity to test, there is

---

[1] Erskine, *Inst.*, III, 9, 5.
[2] Infra, § 2.
[3] See Legal Rights of Spouses and Issue, Ch. XLI, supra; note that a surviving spouse's prior rights emerge only in a case of intestacy: Ch. XLII, § 5.
[4] § 29, infra.
[5] As to formal validity of wills executed furth of Scotland, see Wills Act 1963 (c. 4), ss. 1, 2.
[6] Stair, III, 8, 37.
[7] M'Laren, *Wills and Succession*, I, 261 (in this chapter cited as M'Laren). The leading English books are Theobald's *Law of Wills* (13th ed., 1971) and Jarman on *Wills* (8th ed., 1951).
[8] M'Laren, 262.
[9] Succession (Scotland) Act 1964 (c. 41), s. 28.
[10] *Nisbet's Trs.* v. *Nisbet* (1871) 9 M. 937.
[11] *Sivewright's Trs.* v. *Sivewright*, 1920 S.C. (H.L.) 63; *Ballantyne* v. *Evans* (1886) 13 R. 652.

such weakness or pliability as exposes the testator to improper practices and solicitations by interested parties.[12] This facility may be due to natural disposition, or to old age, or to ill-health. It is not in itself fatal to the will; but, if, in addition, either fraud or circumvention has been used to impetrate the will, it will be reduced.[13]

Apart from cases of mental weakness, a will may be set aside on the ground that it was executed under error induced by misrepresentation,[14] or that it was obtained by undue influence (that is, an influence exercised by fraud or coercion[15]). The law regards with grave suspicion a will in favour of the solicitor who prepared it, and requires that he shall clear himself from the suspicion that it was got by deception or undue influence or that the testator did not know what he was about when making the will.[16]

2. Execution of Wills.—A nuncupative or verbal legacy is effectual to carry property not exceeding £100 Scots (£8.33), and if the legacy be of a larger sum it will be sustained to that amount.[17] It is not settled whether the Roman law in favour of the testamentum militare, which dispenses with formalities, is part of the law of Scotland.[18] Otherwise, wills and legacies must be in writing, and the writing must be probative,[19] i.e., either (1) a deed subscribed[20] and attested in accordance with the rules as to the execution of deeds,[21] or, where the testator is blind or cannot write, executed on his behalf by a notary, law agent, or justice of the peace, or by a parish minister (or his assistant and successor) acting as notary within his own parish[22]; or (2) a holograph writing, i.e., a document in the handwriting of, and signed by, the testator; or (3) a document to which the testator has appended in his own handwriting[23] the words "adopted as holograph" or similar words.

In holograph documents of a testamentary character subscription by the granter is essential to satisfy the requirements of a completed testamentary

---

[12] *Morrison* v. *Maclean's Trs.* (1862) 24 D. 625.

[13] *M'Dougal* v. *M'Dougal's Trs.*, 1931 S.C. 102; as to fraud and circumvention in the law of contract, see *Mackay* v. *Campbell,* 1966 S.L.T. 329; 1967 S.L.T. 337 (H.L.).

[14] *Munro* v. *Strain* (1874) 1 R. 522.

[15] *Weir* v. *Grace* (1899) 2 F. (H.L.) 30, per Lord Halsbury, at 31; *Forrest* v. *Low's Trs.*, 1907 S.C. 1240, per Lord Kinnear, at 1256; 1909 S.C. (H.L.) 16; *Williams* v. *Philip*, (1907) 15 S.L.T. 396; see also *M'Kechnie* v. *M'Kechnie's Trs.*, 1908 S.C. 93; *Gray* v. *Binny* (1879) 7 R. 332; *Ross* v. *Gosselin's Exrs.*, 1926 S.C. 325. For undue influence in contracts, see Agreements Improperly Obtained, Ch. VIII, *supra*, § 4.

[16] *Stewart* v. *M'Laren*, 1920 S.C. (H.L.) 148; *Forrest* v. *Low's Trs.*, *supra*; *Weir* v. *Grace*, *supra*.

[17] *Kelly* v. *Kelly* (1861) 23 D. 703; M'Laren on *Wills*, I, 573.

[18] *Stuart* v. *Stuart*, 1942 S.C. 510.

[19] Note that there are statutory provisions as to the disposal by a member of a registered Friendly Society of sums payable by the Society and not exceeding £1500 (Friendly Societies Act 1974 (c. 46), s. 66; (S.I. 1975 No. 1177); *Morton* v. *French*, 1908 S.C. 171) and as to sums, under the same limit, by members of Industrial and Provident Societies. As to nominations by depositors of sums in the National Savings Bank and Trustee Savings Banks, see National Savings Bank Act 1971 (c. 29), s. 8 and Trustee Savings Bank Act 1969 (c. 50), s. 28.

[20] See *Baird's Trs.* v. *Baird*, 1955 S.C. 286; *Ferguson*, 1959 S.C. 56.

[21] See Rules of Evidence, Ch. XII, *supra*, § 5.

[22] Conveyancing Act 1874, s. 41; Conveyancing (Scotland) Act 1924, s. 18. See *Finlay* v. *Finlay's Trs.*, 1948 S.C. 16; *Hynd's Tr.* v. *Hynd's Trs.*, 1954 S.C. 112; 1955 S.C. (H.L.) 1. See Ch. XII, *supra*, §§ 4-7.

[23] But see *M'Beath's Trs.* v. *M'Beath*, 1935 S.C. 471.

act.[24] Subscription by initials or by Christian name alone or by a familiar or pet name has been held to be sufficient if that was the writer's ordinary method of signing comparable communications or can on other grounds be taken as indicating that what is written above the subscription is the concluded expression of the writer's intention.[25] If a number of writings can be read together as one document they are sufficiently authenticated by subscription of the last of them.[26] There must, however, be subscription, and it will not do to sign the deed in the middle,[27] in the margin[28] or on the back.[29] It is enough for the validity of the deed that the essential parts should be holograph; if a portion only of the document is written by the testator, as where a printed form of will is filled up, that portion will be allowed effect provided that it is in itself and apart from the other parts of the document sufficient to constitute a testamentary disposition.[30] A testamentary writing has been held to be holograph when it was typed by the granter, that being his method of writing,[31] but the document must in gremio state that it was typed by the granter.[32] A statement in the writing that it is holograph of the granter has no evidential value unless the subscription is admitted or proved to be genuine[33]; and proof of genuineness is now a prerequisite for confirmation of executors-nominate under a holograph will.[34]

Writings which are not in themselves capable of effect may be validated by adoption. Thus if the testator appends to an informal document a signed note in his own handwriting adopting the document as holograph, it will thus be made effectual.[35] This is the case also if the testator in a properly executed deed refers to, and adopts, prior informal writings; and it will be sufficient for this purpose if the later deed, without expressly adopting the earlier writings, recognises them and demonstrates that the testator intended that they should form part of his will.[36] Moreover, a testator may by anticipation provide in his settlement that future writings, although neither tested nor holograph, or even, it may be, unsigned,[37] shall be received as valid, and a direction of this kind imparts to writings which come within the description given in the settlement the same efficacy as if they actually formed part of that deed.[38] But

[24] *Taylor's Exix* v. *Thom*, 1914 S.C. 79; *M'Lay* v. *Farrell*, 1950 S.C. 149; *Lorimer's Exr.* v. *Hird*, 1959 S.L.T. (Notes) 8.
[25] *Speirs* v. *Home Speirs* (1879) 6 R. 1359; *Draper* v. *Thomason*, 1954 S.C. 136; *Rhodes* v. *Peterson*, 1971 S.C. 56.
[26] *Lowrie's J. F.* v. *M'Millan, etc.*, 1972 S.L.T. 159.
[27] *M'Lay* v. *Farrell*, supra.
[28] *Robbie* v. *Carr*, 1959 S.L.T. (Notes) 16.
[29] *Boyd* v. *Buchanan*, 1964 S.L.T. (Notes) 108.
[30] *Bridgeford's Exr.* v. *Bridgeford*, 1948 S.C. 416; *Tucker* v. *Canch's Tr.*, 1953 S.C. 270; *Gillies* v. *Glasgow Royal Infirmary*, 1960 S.C. 438.
[31] *M'Beath's Trs.* v. *M'Beath*, supra.
[32] *Chisholm* v. *Chisholm*, 1949 S.C. 434.
[33] *Harper* v. *Green*, 1938 S.C. 198.
[34] See 1964 Act, s. 21; an affidavit by each of two persons that the writing and signature are in the testator's handwriting is sufficient.
[35] *Gavine's Tr.* v. *Lee* (1883) 10 R. 448; *Macphail's Trs.*v. *Macphail*, 1940 S.C. 560; *Hogg's Exr.* v. *Butcher*, 1947 S.N. 141, 190.
[36] *Callander* v. *Callander's Trs.* (1863) 2 M. 291; *Cross's Trs.* v. *Cross*, 1921 1 S.L.T. 244.
[37] As in *Crosbie* v. *Wilson* (1865) 3 M. 870; *Taylor's Executrices* v. *Thom*, 1914 S.C. 79, per Lord Skerrington.
[38] *Lowson* v. *Ford* (1866) 4 M. 631, per Lord Cowan.

if the testator has directed that the future writings are to be "under my hand," a writing to be effective must be subscribed, unless he has made it plain that it need not be.[39]

3. Other Writings with Testamentary Effect.—Besides deeds which are in their nature mortis causa, other deeds may contain provisions which are regarded as testamentary. An instance is to be found in marriage-contracts. Provisions in these conceived in favour of parties who are to take on the death or failure of the spouses and issue of the marriage are generally treated as testamentary and, therefore, revocable.[40] Again, a special destination in the title to heritage will carry the property on the death of the proprietor to the person named in the destination. If a party acquiring property in his own right chooses to take the title in such terms as to himself and A or the survivor of them, this will operate as a nomination of A as successor to that party in the right to the property.[41] And the same effect is allowed to special destinations occurring in documents of title, such as bonds, debentures, certificates of debt, and stock or share certificates of public companies.[42] On the other hand, no such effect is given to the terms of deposit-receipts; a deposit-receipt cannot operate as a will[43] and instructions attached to or written on a deposit-receipt do not receive testamentary effect unless they are indicative of an intention to bequeath.[44]

4. Intention to Test.—The law does not require that a will shall be in any particular form or that it shall be expressed in technical language. However imperfect the language, a document will receive effect as a will if it can fairly be construed as meaning that the author intended thereby to bequeath his estate in whole or in part.[45] A letter to the intended beneficiary may have this effect.[46] On the other hand, a mere list of names and sums of money is not sufficient for this purpose.[47]

If on the face of a writing there be something which raises a doubt whether it was meant to be a testament or, on the other hand, merely a memorandum or note of instructions for the preparation of a formal deed, evidence will be admitted for the purpose of determining the character of the writing. Thus, in *Munro* v. *Coutts*[48] a testator, who had executed a formal settlement, sent to his agent a letter containing a holograph signed document beginning "I wish a

[39] *Waterson's Trs.* v. *St. Giles Boys' Club*, 1943 S.C. 369, overruling *Ronald's Trustees* v. *Lyle*, 1929 S.C. 104. See too *Russell's Exr.* v. *Duke*, 1946 S.L.T. 242 (list of bequests on one side of used envelope and signature on other held a valid will).
[40] See *Lord Advocate* v. *Stewart* (1906) 8 F. 579, at 589; *Barclay's Trs.* v. *Watson* (1903) 5 F. 926; and *Law, Petr.*, 1962 S.C. 500.
[41] *Dennis* v. *Aitchison*, 1923 S.C. 819, per Lord President Clyde, at 824; 1924 S.C. (H.L.) 122. Contrast contractual destinations, §, 8, infra.
[42] *Connell's Trs.* v. *Connell's Trs.* (1886) 13 R. 1175; *Dennis* v. *Aitchison*, 1924 S.C. (H.L.) 122; *Drysdale's Trs.* v. *Drysdale*, 1922 S.C. 741; *Duff's Trs.* v. *Phillips*, 1921 S.C. 287.
[43] *Dinwoodie's Exr.* v. *Carruther's Trs.* (1895) 23 R. 234.
[44] *Gray's Trs.* v. *Murray etc.*, 1976 S.L.T. 105.
[45] *Colvin* v. *Hutchison* (1885) 12 R. 947; *Draper* v. *Thomason*, 1954 S.C. 136.
[46] *Rhodes* v. *Peterson, supra.*
[47] *Waddell's Trs.* v. *Waddell* (1896) 24 R. 189; *Cameron's Trs.* v. *Mackenzie*, 1915 S.C. 313.
[48] (1813) 1 Dow 437.

codicil to be made to my last will and settlement in the following manner," and containing a number of bequests. There being doubt regarding this document, extrinsic evidence was admitted; and, on considering the terms of the correspondence between the testator and his agent and the other facts proved, the House of Lords came to the conclusion that the document, although not defective in form, was intended to be no more than instructions to the agent and not a final testamentary writing. The same conclusion has been reached in cases where the doubt as to the effect of the document was created by the language of a letter with which the document was forwarded to the writer's law agent.[49] The effect of a title or heading placed on a deed may be such as to cast doubt on the deed, and to allow of evidence as to the circumstances attending its execution. The fact that a writing, which was in other respects a perfect will, was headed "Notes of Intended Settlement," was held, where the evidence was inconclusive, not sufficient to deprive the writing of effect.[50] But deeds entitled "Drafts" have been rejected.[51]

5. Revocability of Will.—A will is in its nature revocable at any time by the testator. It matters not that the will has been delivered; and a statement in a testamentary deed that it is irrevocable is of no effect. A person may, however, bind himself to leave his estate by will to another; and in that case a will made in contravention of the contract or promise may be reduced.[52]

6. Revocation of Will.—A will may be revoked in whole or in part in various ways. Thus (1) the testator may destroy, or tear up, the deed or may obliterate or cancel the writing. When it is shown that a man duly executed a will and had it at one time in his custody, but it is not forthcoming at his death, the presumption will be that he destroyed it animo revocandi.[53] But, if it be shown that the destruction or obliteration occurred without animus revocandi on the part of the testator, as, e.g., if it were accidental or were due to insanity, or were done without his consent the will would not be revoked.[54] Unauthenticated cancellations are of no effect, unless they render the original indecipherable[55]; but the authenticated cancellation of a residue clause has been held to be valid, notwithstanding the apparent misapprehension of the testator that there would be no residue.[56] Where a second will was executed by a testatrix and an earlier one destroyed in accordance with professional practice by her solicitor, and later it was found that the second was invalid, it was held that the earlier will had not been revoked by its destruction, but that

---

49 *Young's Trs.* v. *Henderson*, 1925 S.C. 749; *MacLaren's Trs.* v. *Mitchell & Brattan*, 1959 S.C. 183.
50 *Hamilton* v. *White* (1882) 9 R. (H.L.) 53.
51 *Sprot's Trs.* v. *Sprot*, 1909 S.C. 272; *Forsyth's Trs.* v. *Forsyth* (1872) 10 M. 616.
52 *Curdy* v. *Boyd* (1775) M. 15, 946; *Paterson* v. *Paterson* (1893) 20 R. 484; *Smith* v. *Oliver*, 1911 S.C. 103, per Lord President Dunedin, at p. 111. The promise can be proved only by writ or oath; *Gray* v. *Johnston*, 1928 S.C. 659.
53 *Bonthrone* v. *Ireland* (1883) 10 R. 779, per Lord Young at 790; *Clyde* v. *Clyde*, 1958 S.C. 343.
54 Bell, *Prin.*, § 1866; M'Laren, I, 409; *Fotheringham's Tr.* v. *Reid*, 1936 S.C. 831.
55 *Manson* v. *Edinburgh Royal Institution*, 1948 S.L.T. 196; *Hogg's Exr.* v. *Butcher*, 1947 S.N. 141, 190.
56 *Thomson's Trs.* v. *Bowhill Baptist Church*, 1956 S.C. 217.

its effective revocation was conditional upon the valid execution of a later will.[57] (2) He may revoke the will by a subsequent testamentary writing. This may be express, the testator declaring that earlier wills are revoked; but even an express general revocation of prior wills does not necessarily revoke a bequest of a specific subject, at least if it is contained in a separate writing delivered to the beneficiary.[58] Revocation may be implied from the circumstance that the two deeds are inconsistent, in which case the later will prevail. But it is only in so far as the two deeds are inconsistent that the earlier one is revoked by implication; and if the two are only partially inconsistent, there is revocation only to the extent of that inconsistency. In so far as the deeds can be brought into harmony, they will be read as together forming the testator's will.[59] Where a testamentary writing has been revoked by a subsequent testamentary writing which is itself cancelled by the testator, the general rule is that the earlier will revive and receive effect as if it had never been revoked; but it has been suggested that this rule may, in certain circumstances, suffer exception.[60]

7. Conditio si Testator sine Liberis Decesserit.—A settlement which makes no provision for children nascituri is presumed to be revoked by the subsequent birth of a child whether legitimate or illegitimate[61] to the testator. This presumption rests upon the supposition that in the altered circumstances the testator would not have desired that his will should remain in force; and the presumption may be rebutted by circumstances showing his intention that the will should stand notwithstanding the birth of the child.[62] The strongest case for the application of this rule is that of a testator who was childless when the will was made and died without having a reasonable opportunity of altering it. But it is not enough to displace the presumption that there were children in life at the date of the will[63] or that the testator survived the birth of the child for a considerable period without revising the will.[64] If the will is revoked, it is revoked in toto, but earlier wills expressly revoked by it are not revived.[65] If, however, the revocation of the earlier will was merely by implication, as in the case of a universal settlement, the earlier will becomes operative on the revocation of the later will by a subsequent birth.[66] The right to found on the conditio is personal to the after-born child, and no other party can challenge the will on this ground.[67]

[57] *Cullen's Exr.* v. *Elphinstone*, 1948 S.C. 662.
[58] *Clark's Exr.* v. *Clark*, 1943 S.C. 216.
[59] *Stoddart* v. *Grant* (1852) 1 Macq. 163; *Scott* v. *Sceales* (1864) 2 M. 613; *Gordon's Executor* v. *Macqueen*, 1907 S.C. 373; *Mitchell's Administratrix* v. *Edinburgh Royal Infirmary*, 1928 S.C. 47.
[60] See *Bruce's J.F.* v. *Lord Advocate*, 1964 S.L.T. 316, 1968 S.L.T. 242, 1969 S.L.T. 337, 1969 S.C. 296, cf *Scott's J.F.* v. *Johnston*, 1971 S.L.T. (Notes) 41.
[61] Law Reform (Miscellaneous Provisions) (Scotland) Act 1968 (c. 70), ss. 6 (2) and (3) and 22 (5). The birth of an illegitimate child does not have this effect in the case of a deed executed before 25th November 1968.
[62] *Elder's Trs.* v. *Elder* (1895) 21 R. 704, 22 R. 505; *Millar's Tr.* v. *Millar* (1893) 20 R. 1040; *Stuart Gordon* v. *Stuart Gordon* (1899) 1 F. 1005.
[63] *Knox's Trs.* v. *Knox*, 1907 S.C. 1123.
[64] *Nicolson* v. *Nicolson's Tutrix*, 1922 S.C. 649; *Rankin* v. *Rankin's Tutor* (1902) 4 F. 979.
[65] *Crown* v. *Cathro* (1903) 5 F. 950; *Elder's Trs.* v. *Elder* (1895) 22 R. 505.
[66] *Nicolson* v. *Nicolson's Tutrix*, cit. supra; M'Laren, Supplement, p. 106.
[67] *Stevenson's Trs.* v. *Stevenson*, 1932 S.C. 657.

8. Revocation of Special Destinations.—As has been pointed out above,[68] a special destination may have testamentary effect. There are cases in which such a destination is contractual as between the parties who have created it, so as to exclude the possibility of revocation except by their joint consent.[69] This is the case when property is held in joint names, each party having contributed an equal share of the purchase price[70]; but, if one of the parties has paid the whole purchase price, he is entitled to revoke the special destination quoad his own share.[71] Where there is no contractual element in a special destination, it may be expressly or impliedly revoked by testamentary deed. It cannot, however, be impliedly revoked by a testamentary deed executed on or after September 10, 1964. By statute such a deed is only effective to evacuate a special destination if it contains a specific reference to the destination and a declared intention on the part of the testator to evacuate it.[72] In determining the effect on a special destination of a testamentary deed executed prior to September 10, 1964, which makes no specific reference to that destination, the following principles apply:—(a) If a testator holds property on a destination created by a third party, that destination is presumed to be revoked by a general settlement of the testator which is dated after the destination and is inconsistent with the terms thereof.[73] (b) If a testator holds property on a destination created by him in favour of himself and another or others after the date of his testamentary general settlement, the terms of that destination must receive effect as the last expression of the testator's intention in relation to that property.[74] (c) If the special destination was granted by the testator in favour of himself and others before he made his will, there is a presumption that it was not revoked by the subsequent general settlement.[75] The destination and the settlement must be read together as expressions of the testator's intention. If, therefore, the purposes of the settlement are irreconcilable with the terms of the destination, the presumption is rebutted and the destination is held to have been revoked by implication.[76] But a clause in the subsequent settlement which revokes all prior testamentary writings without reference to special destinations will not per se revoke a prior destination made by the testator, because a special destination is not a writing of a testamentary nature, although it may have testamentary effect.[77]

---

[68] § 3, ante.
[69] *Renouf's Trs.* v. *Haining,* 1919 S.C. 497.
[70] *Perrett's Trs.* v. *Perrett,* 1909 S.C. 522; *Chalmers' Tr.* v. *Thomson's Exr.,* 1923 S.C. 271; and see *Shand's Trs.* v. *Shand's Trs.,* 1966 S.L.T. 306.
[71] *Brown's Trs.* v. *Brown,* 1943 S.C. 488; *Hay's Tr.* v. *Hay's Trs.,* 1951 S.C. 329.
[72] Succession (Scotland) Act 1964 (c. 41), s. 30; *Stirling's Trs.,* 1977 S.L.T. 229.
[73] *Thoms* v. *Thoms* (1868) 6 M. 704.
[74] *Perrett's Trs.,* supra.
[75] *Campbell* v. *Campbell* (1880) 7 R. (H.L.) 100; *Perrett's Trs.,* supra, per Lord President Dunedin, at p. 527.
[76] *Perrett's Trs.,* supra, and *Dennis* v. *Aitchison,* 1924 S.C. (H.L.) 122: see also *Brown's Trs.* v. *Brown* and *Hay's Tr.* v. *Hay's Trs.,* supra, where the settlements expressly included the conveyance of all estate held under special destinations.
[77] *Murray's Exrs.* v. *Geekie,* 1929 S.C. 633. Note that, on implied revocation, this case is distinguishable from *Brown's Trs.* and *Hay's Trs.,* supra, because there is here no express reference in the dispositive clause of the settlement to estate held under special destinations.

9. Mutual Wills.—A mutual settlement is a deed in which two or more parties give directions as to the disposal of their estates after their deaths. The question which has most commonly arisen in regard to this unfortunate form of deed is whether it is contractual, so as to debar the survivor of the parties from altering it as regards his or her estate after the death of the other party or parties, or is merely testamentary, leaving the survivor free to do so. The decisions show that this question must be solved on the terms of the particular deed, but the following rules may be extracted:— (1) As a rule a mutual settlement is no more than two wills contained in one deed, and as wills are revocable, the survivor may revoke the deed quoad his own estate; (2) where the parties are spouses, it is easier to hold that the provisions in favour of the spouses themselves or their children are contractual than it is in the case of provisions in favour of other parties; (3) the survivor may be debarred from altering the deed notwithstanding that, under its terms, he is given the fee of the whole estate,[78] but it is more difficult to hold that this is so in that case than where his interest in the estate of the predecessor is limited to a liferent.[79] If there is a clause in the deed dealing with revocation by the parties or the survivor, the terms in which it is expressed have great weight in determining the character of the deed.[80] It is very difficult to establish that a mutual will is irrevocable stante matrimonio.[81]

10. Interpretation of Wills: Extrinsic Evidence.[82]—In construing a testamentary deed it is the object of the Court to ascertain and give effect to the intention of the testator. That intention is to be collected from the language of the deed read in the light of those circumstances (such as the state of the testator's family and property) known to the testator and with reference to which he has written his deed[83]; and it is not permissible to search for his intention apart from the terms of his deed. Evidence of the testator's own opinion of the effect of his will is incompetent,[84] and it is doubtful whether revoked writings can be used as an aid to construction.[85]

The cases in which extrinsic evidence in aid of the interpretation of a will is admitted are all of an exceptional nature. The rules on this point may be summarised thus.[86] (a) A testator is always presumed to use words in their strict and primary acceptation, unless it appears from the context that he has used them in a different sense. (b) In the absence of such a context, the words must have their strict and primary sense, if, so interpreted, they are sensible

---

[78] As in *Duthie* v. *Keir's Exr.*, 1930 S.C. 645.
[79] *United Free Church of Scotland* v. *Black*, 1909 S.C. 25; *Lawrie's Exrs.* v. *Haig*, 1913 S.C. 1159; *Corrance's Trs.* v. *Glen* (1903) 5 F. 777.
[80] *Lawrie's Exrs.* v. *Haig* and *Duthie* v. *Keir's Exr.*, supra; *Craig's Trs.* v. *Craig's Trs.*, 1927 S.C. 367; *Thomson's Trs.* v. *Lockhart*, 1930 S.C. 674, at 678.
[81] *Saxby* v. *Saxby's Exrs.*, 1952 S.C. 352.
[82] See Walkers, *Evidence*, Ch. XXI.
[83] *Trs. of the Free Church of Scotland* v. *Maitland* (1887) 14 R. 333; *Hannay's Trs.* v. *Keith*, 1913 S.C. 482; *Dunsmure* v. *Dunsmure* (1879) 7 R. 261, per Lord Gifford.
[84] *Devlin's Trs.* v. *Breen*, 1945 S.C. (H.L.) 27.
[85] *Devlin's Trs.*, at p. 32.
[86] The rules are formulated in Sir James Wigram's book on *Extrinsic Evidence in Aid of the Interpretation of Wills* (5th ed., 1914), and are quoted in M'Laren, I, 374.

with reference to extrinsic circumstances; if not so sensible, extrinsic evidence is admitted. (c) If the characters in which a will is written need deciphering, or the language requires to be translated, evidence is admitted to declare what the characters are or to inform the Court of the meaning of the language. (d) For the purpose of determining the object of the testator's bounty or the subject of disposition or the quantity of interest given, the Court may inquire into all the material facts as to the person or property or the circumstances of the testator and his family and affairs. In accordance with the maxim, "falsa demonstratio non nocet dummodo constet de persona (re)," a mistake in the description of the subject or object is not fatal to the bequest, and extrinsic evidence is admissible in order to determine the person or thing intended. Thus, where a legacy was bequeathed to "William Keiller, confectioner, Dundee," and there was no such person, the Court allowed evidence in order to determine whether the legatee was William Keiller, a confectioner in Montrose, or James Keiller, a confectioner in Dundee.[87] Evidence of statements by the testator as to his intention is not, however, allowed except in one case, viz., where the description of the legatee, or of the thing bequeathed, is equally applicable in all its parts to two persons, or to two things.[88] If, after all competent evidence has been received, the subject or object of the legacy is uncertain, it will fail on the ground of uncertainty.[89]

Where two clauses of a settlement are contradictory and cannot be reconciled, then, in the absence of any reason for preferring the one to the other, the latter will receive effect as presumably embodying the latest expression of the testator's intention.[90]

11. Testamentary Disposition of Heritage.—Prior to the Titles to Land Consolidation (Scotland) Act 1868,[91] there could be no valid testamentary disposition of heritage unless it was in the form of a conveyance de praesenti taking effect at death, and the word "dispone" had to be used.[92] But by section 20 of that statute it is enacted that the succession to lands may be settled by testamentary deed and that the word "dispone" need not be used; it is enough if the deed contains, with reference to lands, "any word or words which would, if used in a will or testament with reference to moveables, be sufficient to confer upon the executor of the grantor, or upon the grantee or legatee of such moveables, a right to claim and receive the same."[93]

12. Uncertainty: Delegation of Power of Testing.—If it is impossible, on the construction of the deed, to ascertain the subject-matter, or the object, of

---

87 *Keiller* v. *Thomson's Trs.* (1826) 4 S. 724; *Macfarlane's Trs.* v. *Henderson* (1878) 6 R. 288; *Johnstone's Exrs.* v. *Johnstone* (1902) 10 S.L.T. 42; *Cathcart's Trs.* v. *Bruce,* 1923 S.L.T. 722. Cf. also *Shairp* v. *Henderson,* 1930 S.L.T. 743.
88 *Charter* v. *Charter* (1874) L.R. 7 H.L. 364, per Earl Cairns, L.C.; *Re Ray* [1916] 1 Ch. 461.
89 See § 12, infra.
90 M'Laren, I, 354.
91 31 & 32 Vict. c. 101.
92 *Kirkpatrick's Trs.* v. *Kirkpatrick* (1874) 1 R. (H.L.) 37; *Duke of Argyll* v. *Riddell,* 1912 S.C. 694, per Lord President Dunedin, at 741.
93 The series of cases dealing with this section depend on the terms of the particular wills considered.

the bequest, the legacy will fail from uncertainty.[94] This ground of objection has been much considered in connection with cases in which a testator places his estate in the hands of trustees with a power to them to select the beneficiaries. The law does not admit of the delegation of the power of testing. A direction, therefore, to trustees to dispose of the testator's estate as they think proper is ineffectual.[95] But, on the other hand, a testator may confer on his trustees, or on a selected individual, power to choose the beneficiaries from among a class of persons or objects, and, provided this class be sufficiently definite, the bequest will be sustained.[96] If the class is not a definite one,[97] or if the testator omits to appoint a trustee or executor,[98] the testator's directions will fail on the ground of uncertainty.

13. Residue: Intestacy.—In well-drawn testaments the bequest of legacies is usually followed by a clause disposing of the residue of the testator's estate. Residue comprises the whole of the testator's estate, capital and income, not required for the antecedent purposes of the testamentary deed or deeds.[99] The residuary legatee is regarded by the law as taking the estate subject to the burden of the prior purposes of the will[1]; and if, and to the extent to which, a legacy fails, the subject of the legacy enures to residue. If the residue is given at the testator's death, it matters not that the failure of the legacy is not ascertained until a later date, the subject will fall to the residuary legatee. When a testator makes a bequest of the "free residue" of his estate, and legal rights are claimed, these as well as debts and legacies are prima facie to be deducted before the "free residue" is ascertained.[2]

The right of the heirs ab intestato is displaced only in so far as the estate is effectually disposed of in favour of others. If, therefore, there be no residuary bequest, the subject of any testamentary disposition which fails of effect will fall into intestacy; and similarly, if the residuary bequest fails, the residue to the extent of that failure will devolve on the heirs ab intestato. These heirs are ascertained at the date of the testator's death and acquire right then to any portion of the estate which may be found not to have been disposed of.[3]

14. Classification of Legacies.—Legacies may be classified as General or Special.[4] A general legacy is one in which the subject given is "bequeathed indefinitely without any character distinguishing it from others of the same

---

[94] M'Laren, I, 349; *Magistrates of Dundee* v. *Morris* (1858) 3 Macq. 134, per Lord Wensleydale; *Robertson's J.F.* v. *Robertson*, 1968 S.L.T. 32.
[95] *Bannerman's Trs.* v. *Bannerman*, 1915 S.C. 398, per Lord Skerrington; *Anderson* v. *Smoke* (1898) 25 R. 493.
[96] See *Crichton* v. *Grierson* (1828) 3 W. & S. 323, and *Hill* v. *Burns* (1826) 2 W. & S. 80, and cases there cited. See § 28 infra.
[97] As in *Blair* v. *Duncan* (1901) 4 F. (H.L.) 1; *Turnbull's Trs.* v. *Lord Advocate,* 1918 S.C. (H.L.) 88. The cases are discussed in *Reid's Trs.* v. *Cattanach*, 1929 S.C. 727. As to the effect of a bequest for "charitable" purposes see Public Trusts, Ch. XLV, infra, § 6.
[98] *Angus' Exx.* v. *Batchan's Trs.*, 1949 S.C. 335.
[99] *Sturgis* v. *Campbell* (1865) 3 M. (H.L.) 70, per Lord Westbury.
[1] *Storie's Trs.* v. *Gray* (1874) 1 R. 953.
[2] *Samson* v. *Raynor*, 1928 S.C. 899.
[3] *Lord* v. *Colvin* (1865) 3 M. 1083.
[4] Erskine, III, 9, 11; Bell, *Prin.*, §§ 1876, 1877; M'Laren, I, 575.

kind belonging to the deceased,"[5] as, e.g., a sum of money or a certain quantity or amount of things falling under some generic description. In this case the legatee has no more than a right of personal action against the executor or trustee for implement of the legacy. A special legacy, on the other hand, is the bequest of a determinate subject: "where some individual is left"[6] as, e.g., a certain horse, or a debt due to the testator by a particular person, or some particular investment belonging to the testator. This has the effect of a mortis causa assignation to the legatee, who may bring an action against any person in possession of the subject after the death of the testator in order to compel him to make it forthcoming; and, although the executor must be called in this action, this is only to obviate the risk of the subject being carried off by the legatee, while the rest of the testator's estate may be insufficient to pay his debts so that the subject of the specific legacy is required for this purpose.[7] Demonstrative legacies are those in which the testator indicates the source from which the legacy is to be provided.[8] Where the legacy takes this form, the question may arise whether it is dependent on the existence or sufficiency of the funds denoted as the source of payment, or whether the legatee has, in the event of these funds disappearing or proving insufficient, a claim against the general estate of the testator. Thus in *Douglas's Exrs.*[9] the testator bequeathed sums of money "to be paid out of the arrears of income due to me from the Monteath trust estate," and, these arrears being insufficient, it was held that the balance must be made up out of the residue of the estate.

15. Ademption of Special Legacies.—Where the subject of a special legacy has ceased to form part of the testator's estate at the date of his death the legacy is adeemed, and nothing is due to the legatee. The intention of the testator is not considered in this matter. The only inquiries necessary are (a) whether the legacy is a special one, and, if so (b) whether the thing bequeathed does or does not remain part of the testator's estate.[10] Thus, if the testator has alienated the thing bequeathed, or if it has perished, or if a debt due to the testator and bequeathed by him has been paid up in his lifetime,[11] or if an investment bequeathed has been realised and the money reinvested,[12] or if money in a particular bank is bequeathed and the account is transferred to another bank,[13] or if heritage bequeathed has been taken from him under compulsory powers,[14] in all these cases the legacy is adeemed. But it is not adeemed where the testator has transferred the subject of the legacy but at the testator's death something remains to be done to perfect the transferee's

---

[5] Erskine, III, 9, 13.
[6] Stair, III, 8, 38.
[7] Erskine and Bell, supra.
[8] M'Laren, I, 575.
[9] (1869) 7 M. 504.
[10] *M'Arthur' Exrs.* v. *Guild*, 1908 S.C. 743, per Lord Kinnear.
[11] *Cobban's Exrs.* v. *Cobban*, 1915 S.C. 82; *Pagan* v. *Pagan* (1838) 16 S. 383.
[12] *Anderson* v. *Thomson* (1877) 4 R. 1101; *Maclean* v. *Maclean's Exx.*, 1908 S.C. 838. See also *Thomson's Trs.* v. *Lockhart*, 1930 S.C. 674.
[13] *Ballantyne's Trs.* v. *Ballantyne's Trs.* 1941 S.C. 35.
[14] *Chalmers* v. *Chalmers* (1851) 14 D. 57.

title.[15] Where the subject of bequest is shares in a company, and these shares are subdivided or converted into stock or otherwise altered by the act of the company, it seems that there is no ademption if the change is in name or form only, and the subject remains substantially the same at the testator's death.[16] The test is whether the subject of the testator's bequest has remained substantially the same thing at his death; if it has, there is no ademption.[17]

16. Abatement of Legacies.—If the testator's estate should prove insufficient to satisfy in full all his bequests, the classification of these is of importance, because on this depends the order in which they shall abate. A testator may provide for this contingency in his will, but in the absence of such a provision, the following rules hold. The residuary legatees have no right to receive anything until the prior legacies are paid in full. As between these prior legatees, a special legatee is entitled to be paid his legacy in full though nothing should remain for the general legatees. General legacies abate pari passu.[18] The order or numbering of the legacies does not give an earlier legacy priority over a later.[19]

17. Cumulative and Substitutional Legacies.—Testamentary writings may contain more than one legacy to the same legatee, so that a doubt arises whether he is entitled to one only or to both. The testator may make his intention on this point clear by an express provision; and in all cases the Court will examine his deed or deeds for the purpose of discovering indications of what was intended. It may be said that differences in the bequests will be favourable to the claim that both are due, as, for example, where a motive is stated for the one bequest which is not stated as to the other.[20] Assuming, however, that the testator's intention cannot be ascertained, there are certain well-settled rules or presumptions which will be applied. A distinction is taken between legacies to the same legatee left in the same deed and legacies left in separate deeds. In the first case, i.e., where the legacies are contained in the same writing, when exactly the same amount is given twice, the presumption is that this is a mere repetition arising from some mistake or forgetfulness.[21] On the other hand, where the legacies are not of the same amount, they are presumed to be cumulative. Where the same amount is bequeathed to the same legatee in two distinct testamentary writings, both legacies are presumed to be due,[22] and a fortiori this is also so where the legacies are of different amounts.[23] These rules proceed on the

---

[15] *Tennants' Trs.* v. *Tennant,* 1946 S.C. 420.
[16] *Macfarlane's Trs.* v. *Macfarlane,* 1910 S.C. 325; *Re Clifford* [1912] 1 Ch. 29; *Re Leeming* [1912] 1 Ch. 828.
[17] *Ogilvie Forbes' Trs.* v. *Ogilvie Forbes,* 1955 S.C. 405, per Lord President Clyde, at p. 411.
[18] Erskine, *Inst.,* III, 9, 12; M'Laren, I, 586.
[19] *M'Connel* v. *M'Connel's Trs.,* 1931 S.N. 31.
[20] *Horsburgh* v. *Horsburgh* (1848) 10 D. 824.
[21] But see *Gillies* v. *Glasgow Royal Infirmary,* 1960 S.C. 438, where legatee appeared twice in residue clause.
[22] *M'Lachlan* v. *Seton's Trs.,* 1937 S.C. 206.
[23] *Hooley* v. *Hatton* (1773) 1 Brown's Chancery Cases 390; *Royal Infirmary of Edinburgh* v. *Muir's Trs.* (1881) 9 R. 352; *Fraser* v. *Forbes' Trs.* (1899) 1 F. 513.

assumption that both writings are operative and that the second does not revoke or supplant the earlier.[24]

18. Legatum Rei Alienae.—Whether effect can be given to the bequest of a subject which does not belong to the testator depends upon his knowledge. If he knew that the subject did not belong to him, then, as it is not to be supposed that the testator intended a derisory bequest, effect is given to the legacy by requiring the executor to purchase the subject for the legatee, or, if it cannot be purchased, to pay its value to him. But if the testator believed the subject to be his own (which is presumed to be the case until the contrary is proved), then the legacy fails; for it may be assumed that he would not have made the bequest had he been aware that the subject did not belong to him.[25]

19. Terms Descriptive of Legatee.—The meaning of such terms depends in each case on the context in which they appear, but some of the more frequent of them have acquired a recognised prima facie meaning in legal interpretation. Thus the word "issue" includes all direct descendants,[26] unless the context demands a more restricted meaning[27]; and "children" does not normally include grandchildren.[28] In the case of a gift to a class of relatives followed by a provision that in the event of the predecease of any of such relatives the issue is to take, the issue of one who predeceases the making of the will does not take.[29] When a bequest is made to "heirs," the rule prior to the Succession (Scotland) Act 1964 was that the heir-at-law was entitled to the subject if it was heritable, the heirs in mobilibus if it was moveable, and, if it was mixed, the heritage went to the heir-at-law and the moveable portion to the heirs in mobilibus,[30] but this distinction will not apply to bequests to "heirs" made on or after September 10, 1964.[31] Further it is thought that, in the absence of clear indication to the contrary, a reference in a private deed to the "heir" or "heirs" of a person dying on or after September 10, 1964, must be construed as a reference to those entitled to succeed on intestacy under the 1964 Act[32]; prima facie such a bequest must be construed as a reference to those who have rights of succession in that person's estate, and the heirs of that person cannot be ascertained until he dies.[33] However, "heirs" has a different meaning from "next-of-kin": the former does, the latter does not,

[24] *Beattie* v. *Thomson* (1861) 23 D. 1163.
[25] Erskine, *Inst.*, III, 9, 10; *Meeres* v. *Dowell's Exr.*, 1923 S.L.T. 184.
[26] *Stewart's Trs.* v. *Whitelaw*, 1926 S.C. 701; *Murray's Trs.* v. *Mackie*, 1959 S.L.T. 129.
[27] See *Stirling's Trs.* v. *Legal and General Assurance Soc.*, 1957 S.L.T. 73, and cases cited therein.
[28] *Adam's Exx.* v. *Maxwell*, 1921 S.C. 418; cf. *Lindsay's Trs.*, 1954 S.L.T. (Notes) 51.
[29] *M'Kinnon's Trs.* v. *Brownlie*, 1947 S.C. (H.L.) 27.
[30] *Blair* v. *Blair* (1849) 12 D. 97; *Grant's Trs.* v. *Slimon*, 1925 S.C. 261. For an unusual case of applying the rules of heritable succession to a bequest of moveables see *Paton's Trs.* v. *Paton*, 1947 S.C. 250.
[31] Succession (Scotland) Act 1964, s. 1 (1); but note exceptions in s. 37 (1).
[32] Note that the 1964 Act, Sched. 2, paras. 1 and 2, expressly provide that references in any enactment to the heir-at-law or heirs of a deceased person are to be construed as references to the persons who are entitled by virtue of that Act to succeed on intestacy to that person's estate.
[33] See *Black* v. *Mason* (1881) 8 R. 497, per Lord President Inglis at p. 500; M'Laren, II, pp. 757, 762.

include the heirs who come in by representation.[34] Where the bequest is made to a person's "heirs and executors" this expression is held to mean heirs in intestacy, and executors-nominate are not included.[35] The term "blood relations" covers all those who can show a traceable relationship by blood, and is not restricted to next-of-kin.[36] "Assignees" in a destination-over means those to whom the legatee may have assigned the subject, provided he acquires a vested right, but not otherwise.[37] When a testator makes a bequest in favour of his own heirs or next-of-kin, these are normally ascertained at the date of his death.[38] When terms of relationship are used to point out the legatee, the common law rule is that only legitimate relations, as a general rule, take and that the words "child", "children" and "issue" are not normally to be interpreted so as to include illegitimate children.[39] In respect of all deeds executed and provisions made on or after 25th November 1968 it is, however, now provided by statute that the descriptive term is, unless the contrary intention appears, to be taken to include illegitimate relations[40] and references to "children" and "issue" are to be interpreted accordingly. In the case of deeds executed after the making of an adoption order and on or after September 10, 1964, any reference to the child or children of the adopter is unless the contrary intention appears to be construed as including a reference to the adopted person and similarly any reference to a person related to the adopted person is to be construed as if the latter were a child of the adopter.[41] There is no presumption in Scotland, where the word "wife" is used in a testamentary family provision, in favour of the wife who existed at the date of the will[42]; but a testamentary provision may be construed as made in favour of a person in her capacity as the testator's wife, in which case divorce subsequent to the date of the will will disqualify her from taking it.[43] A bequest to "dependants" has been held to be void from uncertainty.[44]

20. Interest of Legatee: Destinations-Over.—Under the more usual forms of bequest the benefit conferred on the legatee is an annuity or an interest in liferent or in fee in the subject of the bequest. It is now clear that an interest

[34] *Gregory's Trs.* v. *Alison* (1889) 16 R. (H.L.) 10; *Steedman's Trs.* v. *Steedman*, 1916 S.C. 857; *Borthwick's Trs.* v. *Borthwick* 1955 S.C. 227. See Intestate Succession, Ch. XLII, supra, §§ 3 (b), 6.
[35] *Lady Kinnaird's Trs.* v. *Ogilvy*, 1911 S.C. 1136, but see also *Scott's Exrs.* v. *Methven's Exrs.* (1890) 17 R. 389, and *Montgomery's Trs.* v. *Montgomery* (1895) 22 R. 824.
[36] *Cuninghame* v. *Cuninghame's Trs.*, 1961 S.C. 32.
[37] *Bell* v. *Cheape* (1845) 7 D. 614.
[38] *Anderson's Trs.* v. *Forrest*, 1917 S.C. 321; *Grant's Trs.* v. *Crawford's Tr.*, 1949 S.L.T. 374; but see Henderson, *Vesting*, pp. 228-9, and at pp. 92-7, for bequests to heirs of legatees.
[39] *Scott's Trs.* v. *Smart*, 1954 S.C. 12.
[40] Law Reform (Miscellaneous Provisions) (Scotland) Act 1968, ss. 5 and 22 (5). As to legitimated persons see Ch. XLVII, § 3, infra, and Legitimation (Scotland) Act 1968 (c. 22), ss. 3, 2 and 8.
[41] Succession (Scotland) Act 1964, s. 23 (2); mortis causa deeds are deemed for the purposes of this provision to have been executed on the adopter's death. Note that where the adopter died before September 10, 1964, and the natural parent died on or after that date, the adopted child retains his rights of succession to the estate of his natural parent: Law Reform (Misc. Provs.) (Scotland) Act 1966 (c. 19), s. 5.
[42] *Burn's Trs.*, 1961 S.C. 17. Cf. *Couper's J. F.* v. *Valentine*, 1976 S.L.T. 83.
[43] *Pirie's Trs.* v. *Pirie*, 1962 S.C. 43; but see as to "fiancée," *Ormiston's Exr.* v. *Laws.* 1966 S.L.T. 110.
[44] *Robertson's J.F.* v. *Robertson*, 1968 S.L.T. 32.

intermediate between fee and liferent is a conception which the law does not recognise.[45] Certain forms of bequest raise a doubt as to the legatees entitled to take. A direction that residue shall "be equally divided between my nephews and nieces and their children" may mean either that nephews and nieces and their children are to take equal shares or that each nephew and niece is to take an equal share, the children of any predeceaser taking their parent's share. In *Clow's Trustees* v. *Bethune*,[46] after considerable diversity of judicial opinion, the decision was for the latter construction, and the case illustrates the relevant considerations.

Destinations-over are frequently attached to bequests, e.g., to A, whom failing B. Here A is the institute and B may be either a conditional institute or a substitute. If the former, then, if and when A acquires right to the legacy, the destination-over to B at once flies off. But this is not so if B is a substitute. B will take in succession to A on his death if the substitution is not defeated by A.[47] A has the unrestricted right of fee and may after acquiring right to the subject consume it or dispose of it by either inter vivos or mortis causa deed thus defeating the substitution; but, if the substitution is not defeated, the subject will pass to B on A's death. A substitution includes a conditional institution so that, where B is called as a substitute he will take in place of A if A does not acquire right to the subject. Although it is possible to have a substitution in moveables,[48] there is a very strong presumption against this.[49] On the other hand, where the subject is heritage the presumption is that the destination is a substitution,[50] though the presumption may yield to the terms of the will.[51] The fact that a disposition of estate is made after the death of a legatee will not suffice to restrict his interest to a liferent if there are no other features of the deed pointing to this restriction.[52]

21. Vesting of Legacies.—A legacy is said to vest in a legatee when he acquires right to it. It then becomes his property; he may dispose of it by inter vivos or mortis causa deed; it may be made available to meet his debts; and on his death intestate it will transmit as part of his estate. It is not necessary that the legatee should be entitled to payment or possession of the legacy, for vesting may, and often does, take place although the legatee has no right to possession. Nor are the circumstances that the bequest is made through the instrumentality of a trust, or that it is subject to a liferent or annuity, inconsistent with immediate vesting in the fiar.[53] Thus, if trustees are directed

---

[45] *Cochrane's Exx.* v. *Cochrane*, 1947 S.C. 134, overruling *Heavyside* v. *Smith*, 1929 S.C. 68. Followed in *Innes' Trs.* v. *Innes*, 1948 S.C. 406.
[46] 1935 S.C. 754; and see *Boyd's Trs.* v. *Shaw*, 1958 S.C. 115, where a destination-over to issue of a named beneficiary "equally amongst them" was similarly construed.
[47] M'Laren, *Wills*, p. 623; *Cochrane's Exr.* v. *Cochrane*, supra.
[48] *Dyer* v. *Carruthers* (1874) 1 R. 943.
[49] *Crumpton's J.F.* v. *Barnardo's Homes*, 1917 S.C. 713, per Lord President Strathclyde; *Greig* v. *Johnstone* (1833) 6 W. & S. 406.
[50] *Watson* v. *Giffen* (1884) 11 R. 444. There may be indefeasible clauses of return in favour of the grantor of the deed or his heirs but the instances of this in modern cases are not numerous—see *Robertson* v. *Hay-Boyd*, 1928 S.C. (H.L.) 8.
[51] *Simpson's Trs.* v. *Simpson* (1889) 17 R. 248.
[52] *Turner's Trs.* v. *Turner*, 1961 S.L.T. 319.
[53] *Carleton* v. *Thomson* (1867) 5 M. (H.L.) 151.

to hold a fund for A in liferent, and, on his death, to hold it for or pay it to B, B will acquire a vested interest on the death of the testator.[54] Nor will a power in the trustees to encroach on capital operate so as to postpone vesting of the capital in the legatees.[55]

The date of vesting is to be determined in accordance with the testator's intention as disclosed in his testament. This is the governing principle, and the further rules which have been developed in the course of the decisions are all subject to this qualification, that they must yield to clear expressions of the testator's intention.[56] There is sometimes inserted in a testament an explicit declaration as to the time at which a legacy is to vest, and this usually settles the question, but not invariably, for such a declaration has been disregarded where it was irreconcilable with the terms of the bequest[57] and indeed it has been observed that the Courts have in general shown little enthusiasm for artificial vesting dates.[58] There are also two general considerations which influence the Court. In the first place, there is a presumption in favour of early vesting; that is to say, in a case of doubt the Court is favourable to that construction which will give the legatee a vested interest at the earliest date. As a will cannot come into effect until the testator's death, there can be no vesting prior to that time; and the presumption is, therefore, for vesting a morte testatoris.[59] Secondly, where a testator purports to dispose of his whole estate, the Court is disinclined to adopt a construction which will involve total or partial intestacy, although it may be compelled to do so.

The question must always depend mainly on the terms in which the particular bequest is made. If it be given to the legatee unconditionally, vesting will take place immediately. A legacy which is payable on a dies certus, i.e., a time or event which must arrive sooner or later (as, e.g., the death of a liferenter or other person), is regarded as an unconditional legacy.[60] On the other hand, if it is uncertain whether the event contemplated will ever happen, it cannot be known in the meantime whether the legacy will ever become due, and, in accordance with the maxim "dies incertus pro conditione habetur," the legacy is regarded as conditional.[61]

22. Vesting of Conditional Bequests.—In the case of conditional legacies a distinction is drawn between suspensive (precedent) and resolutive (subsequent) conditions.[62] The former operate to prevent vesting until the

[54] Henderson on *Vesting*, p. 24.
[55] *MacGregor's Trs.* v. *MacGregor*, 1958 S.C. 326.
[56] *Carleton* v. *Thomson*, supra; *Bowman* v. *Bowman* (1899) 1 F. (H.L.) 69, per Lord Halsbury, L.C. *Barclay's Trs.* v. *Inland Revenue*, 1975 S.L.T. 17.
[57] See *Croom's Trs.* v. *Adams* (1859) 22 D. 45.
[58] See *Carruthers' Trs.* v. *Carruthers' Trs.*, 1949 S.C. 530, per Lord President Cooper at p. 545. This case is concerned with an attempt, by the application of the maxim quod fieri debet infectum valet, to frustrate a testator's express direction as to vesting.
[59] *Carleton* v. *Thomson*, supra; *Taylor* v. *Gilbert's Trs.* (1878) 5 R. (H.L.) 217, per Lord Blackburn.
[60] See, e.g., *Mowbray's Trs.* v. *Mowbray's Exr.*, 1931 S.C. 595; *Fraser's Trs.* v. *Cunninghame*, 1928 S.L.T. 425.
[61] M'Laren, II, 783, 796; see Lord Skerrington's opinion in *Wylie's Trs.* v. *Bruce*, 1919 S.C. 211, at 240.
[62] See General Law of Obligations, Ch. III, supra, § 13.

fulfilment of the condition, the latter do not prevent vesting, but render it liable to be defeated if the event occur—that is, there is vesting subject to defeasance. There is little trace of the doctrine of vesting subject to defeasance in regard to legacies prior to the decision of the House of Lords in *Taylor* v. *Gilbert's Trs.*,[63] but since then the doctrine has been considerably developed. As a general rule conditions which are personal to the legatee have the effect of suspending vesting pendente conditione. The more usual of such conditions are those relating to the age of the legatee, or to his survivance of some time or event. If a testator leaves a bequest, or directs his trustees to pay a legacy, to A in the event of his attaining majority, there is no vesting in A while he is in minority. In this case the condition as to age is adjected to the substance of the gift: A becomes the object of the testator's bounty only when he reaches the age of 18. But if a bequest takes the form of a bequest to A with a provision that it is to be paid to him when he attains majority the bequest will vest in A at once although he is not major. The gift here is made without qualification, and the provision as to majority refers to payment, and was presumably introduced only for the protection of A while he is under age.[64]

Where the qualification of the legacy consists of words of survivorship (to A, B and C and the survivors or survivor of them), the vesting of the legacy will depend on the determination of the time to which these words refer. The testator may point out the time or event which the legatee must survive in order to acquire right to the legacy. Where he fails to do so, the rule laid down in the leading case of *Young* v. *Robertson*[65] is as follows:— The words of survivorship are to be referred to the period appointed by the settlement for payment or distribution of the subject-matter of the gift. If a testator gives a sum of money or the residue of his estate to be paid or distributed among a number of persons and refers to the contingency of any one or more of them dying, and then gives the estate or the money to the survivor in that simple form of gift which is to take effect immediately on the death of the testator, the period of distribution is the period of death, and accordingly the contingency of death is to be referred to the interval of time between the date of the will and the death of the testator. Vesting in this case will take place a morte testatoris. On the other hand, if the testator gives a liferent in a sum of money or in the residue of his estate, and at the expiration of that liferent directs the money to be paid or the residue to be divided among a number of objects, and then refers to the possibility of some one or more of those persons dying, without specifying the time, and directs in that event the payment or distribution to be made among the survivors, it is understood by the law that he means the contingency to extend over the whole period of time that must elapse before the payment or distribution takes place. The result, accordingly, is that in such a case the survivors are to be ascertained in like manner by a reference to the period of distribution, namely the expiration of the liferent;

[63] (1878) 5 R. (H.L.) 217.
[64] *Alves' Trs.* v. *Grant* (1874) 1 R. 969.
[65] (1862) 4 Macq. 314.

and vesting is, therefore, suspended till that event.[66] A survivorship clause may, however, be so worded, notwithstanding the subsistence of a liferenter, as to import only survivorship of the legatees inter se; in that event vesting is suspended until only the survivor is left, and the right then vests in him whether or not he survives the liferenter.[67] But this doctrine of "intermediate" vesting cannot, it is thought, be extended to a case where the fee is destined to more than two persons and the words "survivors or survivor" are used.[68]

A similar rule holds in regard to destinations-over (to A, whom failing to B). When trustees are directed to pay a legacy to a beneficiary on the occurrence of an event, and, failing him, to another or to other persons, then, if he does not survive that event, he takes no right under the settlement.[69] In the case of a simple bequest without postponement of payment, the destination-over is read as providing for the contingency of the legatee's predeceasing the testator, and as the destination-over ceases to be operative on the testator's death, the legacy vests at that date; but if the legacy is to be paid at a subsequent date, there is no vesting till that date. A destination-over to another person nominatim may take the form of a bequest to "A whom failing B," or to "A or B." At one time it was thought that the general rule did not apply where the persons called under the destination-over were described as the heirs of the institute, but it is now settled that under a destination-over to heirs vesting is suspended. Hence, if a legacy is bequeathed on the expiry or termination of a liferent to A or his heirs, it vests in A only at the death of the liferenter[70]; vesting will not be accelerated by a renunciation of the liferent by the liferenter before that date.[71] But such a renunciation, coupled with the valid exercise by the liferenter of a power to appoint the fee by inter vivos deed, will enable immediate payment of the capital to be made to the appointee.[72]

The rule as to the effect of words of survivorship or a destination-over on vesting in the legatee called in the first place is well settled. Somewhat different considerations affect the vesting in the person or persons called on that legatee's failure. If a testator directs his trustees to hold his estate for a person in liferent, and on his death, to divide it among such of certain persons as may then be alive, the issue of any of these who may predecease being entitled to their parent's share, do the issue of one who predeceases the liferenter take a vested right on their parent's death or is vesting in them suspended (as in the case of their parent) until the death of the liferenter? Or, if the bequest on the termination of the liferent be to A, whom failing to B, and A predeceases the

---

[66] *Laing's Trs.*, 1965 S.L.T. 215; cf. *Stirling's Trs.*, 1977 S.L.T. 229. Forfeiture of the liferent on the liferenter's election to claim legal rights does not accelerate vesting (*Muirhead* v. *Muirhead* (1890) 17 R. (H.L.) 45; *Munro's Trs.*, 1971 S.C. 280).

[67] *Lindsay's Trs.* v. *Sinclair* (1885) 12 R. 964; *Macfarlane's Trs.* v. *Macfarlane's Curator Bonis*, 1934 S.C. 476.

[68] *Playfair's Trs.* v. *Stewart's Trs.*, 1960 S.L.T. 351.

[69] *Bryson's Trs.* v. *Clark* (1880) 8 R. 142.

[70] *Wylie's Trs.* v. *Bruce*, 1919 S.C. 211; *Mackenzie's Trs.* v. *Georgeson*, 1923 S.C. 517.

[71] *Middleton's Trs.* v. *Middleton*, 1955 S.C. 51; *Chrystal's Trs.* v. *Haldane*, 1960 S.C. 127. Distinguish *Hurll's Trs.* v. *Hurll*, 1964 S.C. 12 (forfeiture).

[72] *Stainton* v. *Forteviot Trust*, 1948 S.C. (H.L.) 115; *Neame* v. *Neame's Trs.*, 1956 S.L.T. 57; and see § 28, infra.

liferenter, does B acquire a vested interest on A's death although he (B) may subsequently also predecease the liferenter? In a well-drawn settlement this should be made clear; but in the absence of express provision the question will depend on whether the conditions which affect the institute are by implication to be held to affect also the conditional institute. As a rule, if the gift-over to the issue of the legatee is substitutional the condition of survivance of the termination of the liferent expressed with reference to the parent is held to apply to the issue also,[73] but if the gift to the issue is an original one, they may acquire a vested right notwithstanding that they predecease the liferenter.[74]

23. Vesting Subject to Defeasance.[75]—There are three types of cases in which the application of this doctrine is now definitely recognised, and beyond which it will not readily be extended.[75a]

(1) FOR A IN LIFERENT AND HIS ISSUE IN FEE, WHOM FAILING TO B.—If trustees are directed to hold a fund for A in liferent and for his or her issue in fee, and failing issue of A, then for B in fee, B will, if there are no such issue in existence at the testator's death, take a vested right subject to defeasance if A subsequently has issue.[76] Should A never have issue, B's right is treated as having been from the first absolute, and it matters not that he predeceases the liferenter. On the other hand, if the bequest to A's issue comes into effect, B's right is wholly defeated. It is a condition of immediate vesting in B that his right can only be defeated by A having a child.[77] If the destination-over to B is framed so as to take effect on the death of A without leaving issue, the fee remains vested in B unless A is survived by issue.[78] If, however, the gift to B is qualified by conditions which in themselves suspend vesting, as, for example, by a destination-over to his heirs or to another person nominatim (e.g., to A in liferent and his issue in fee, whom failing to B, whom failing to C), or by words which show that his survivance of the expiry of the liferent is required, there is no room for vesting in him prior to that event, because the gift to B is not solely dependent upon A having no issue; in other words, it is subject to a double contingency.[79] But a contingency that issue may emerge to several liferenters (e.g., to A in liferent and his issue in fee, whom failing to B in liferent and his issue in fee, whom failing to C) is not such a double contingency as will suspend vesting in the ultimate beneficiary, C.[80]

(2) FOR A IN FEE, WITH A DIRECTION TO HOLD FOR A IN LIFERENT AND HIS ISSUE IN FEE.—If a bequest be made to A with a further direction that the

---

[73] *Todd's Trs.* v. *Todd's Exx.*, 1922 S.C. 1; *Banks' Trs.* v. *Banks' Trs.*, 1907 S.C. 125.
[74] *Campbell's Tr.* v. *Dick*, 1915 S.C. 100; but see *Robertson's Trs.* v. *Mitchell*, 1930 S.C. 970, per Lord President Clyde, at p. 976.
[75] See Henderson on *Vesting*, and Smith, *Short Commentary*, pp. 436 et seq.
[75a] Approved per Lord Reid in *Barclay's Tr.* v. *Inland Revenue*, 1975 S.L.T. 17 at 19. The word "readily" is to be stressed (ibid.).
[76] *Taylor* v. *Gilbert's Trs.* (1878) 5 R. (H.L.) 217.
[77] *Steel's Trs.* v. *Steel* (1888) 16 R. 204.
[78] *Gregory's Trs.* v. *Alison* (1889) 16 R. (H.L.) 10. Note that in *Taylor* v. *Gilbert's Trs.*, supra, vesting in A's issue was dependent upon one or more of them (a) surviving A and (b) attaining majority. See also *Munro's Trs.* v. *Monson*, 1962 S.C. 414.
[79] *Lees' Trs.* v. *Lees*, 1927 S.C. 886; *Nicolson's Trs.* v. *Nicolson*, 1960 S.C. 186.
[80] *Taylor* v. *Gilbert's Trs.*, supra; *G.'s Trs.* v. *G.*, 1937 S.C. 141; *Moss's Tr.* v. *Moss's Trs.*, 1958 S.C. 501.

trustees shall hold for him in liferent and for his issue in fee, it has been held in a series of cases that the fee will remain with A if he has no issue.[81] The ground for this construction is that the testator, having made a gift to A, is not to be taken to have intended by the further direction to revoke that gift, but rather to subordinate it to the bequest to the issue. In the event of there being issue, A's right is reduced to a liferent out of favour to the issue who are to have the fee; but if there are no issue, then A is to remain in enjoyment of the fee. It is essential in this case that there should be language sufficient to confer a right of fee upon A, for if, on the construction of the deed, it appears that nothing more than a liferent was in any circumstances given to him, the doctrine is inapplicable.[82]

(3) FOR A IN LIFERENT AND B IN FEE, WHOM FAILING TO B'S ISSUE.—If trustees are directed to hold a fund for behoof of a legatee with a provision that, if he predeceases the expiry of a liferent or other event leaving issue, such issue shall take their parent's share, the legatee will take a vested right subject to defeasance if he predecease the event and leave issue. If he does not so predecease (whether he has issue or not), or if he predecease but does not leave issue, his right is not defeated. The only event on which divestiture of his right takes place is if he does predecease and is survived by issue.[83]

In all these cases there is this common feature, that the legatee's interest is liable to be defeated only by the contingency that there may be issue born to the liferenter or legatee. There are, however, other cases of rather exceptional nature and not capable of classification, in which vesting subject to defeasance has been held to take place.[84]

24. Vesting of Class-Gifts.—The general rule is that (unless the will provides otherwise) those members only who are in existence when the time appointed for payment of the bequest arrives are entitled to participate in it. Hence, under a simple bequest to the children of A, where there is nothing to postpone payment beyond the testator's death, the children then alive take the bequest to the exclusion of children born later.[85] A child in utero is treated as if already born.[86]

But if the time of payment is postponed, as, for example, if the gift be to A

---

[81] *Tweeddale's Trs.* v. *Tweeddale* (1905) 8 F. 264; *Donaldson's Trs.* v. *Donaldson*, 1916 S.C. (H.L.) 55; *Aitken's Trs.* v. *Aitken*, 1921 S.C. 807; *Livingston's Trs.* v. *Livingston's Trs.* 1939 S.C. (H.L.) 17. Distinguished in *Riddoch's Trs.* v. *Calder's Tr.*, 1947 S.C. 281, where there was held to be initial gift of fee.

[82] *Muir's Trs.* v. *Muir's Trs.* (1895) 22 R. 553; *Nicol's Trs.* v. *Farquhar*, 1918 S.C. 358; *Smith's Trs.* v. *Clark*, 1920 S.C. 161.

[83] *Allan's Trs.* v. *Allan*, 1918 S.C. 164; *Gibson's Trs.* v. *Gibson*, 1925 S.C. 477; and see *Coulston's Trs.* v. *Coulston's Trs.*, 1911 S.C. 881, where two contingencies were held to be alternative and not cumulative so as to suspend vesting.

[84] See, e.g., *Yule's Trs* v. *Deans*, 1919 S.C. 750, per Lord Skerrington; *M'Call's Trs.* v. *M'Call*, 1957 S.L.T. (Notes) 16; *Martin's Trs.* v. *Milliken* (1864) 3 M. 326; *Bruce's Trs.* v. *Bruce's Trs.*(1898) 25 R. 796.

[85] *Stopford Blair's Exrs.* v. *Heron Maxwell's Trs.* (1872) 10 M. 760; *Hayward's Exrs.* v. *Young* (1895) 22 R. 757; *Wood* v. *Wood* (1861) 23 D. 338, per Lord Cowan. Where the bequest is to children, illegitimate children are included in the class unless the contrary intention appears (Law Reform (Misc. Provs.) (Scotland) Act 1968 (c. 70), s. 5—applicable only to deeds executed on or after 25th November 1968).

[86] *Cox's Trs.* v. *Cox*, 1950 S.C. 117.

in liferent and to his children in fee, all the children who are born prior to the death of the liferenter are included.[87] In this case the gift vests in the children alive at the testator's death, or if there are none, in the child first born, subject to partial defeasance to the extent necessary to allow of children born later receiving equal shares.[88] The fact that the class is liable to be enlarged does not suspend the vesting. Where the bequest is to children, as and when they respectively attain majority and the shares are then to be paid over, it has been held that the bequest is limited to the children alive when the eldest child reaches majority and so becomes entitled to demand payment of his share, as otherwise the share to be paid to the eldest child could not be fixed.[89]

In the case of *Hickling's Trs.* v. *Garland's Trs.*[90] the testator directed his trustees to hold a sum for a daughter in liferent, and on her death leaving issue to divide it among her issue. On the daughter's death two children were alive and two had predeceased her. It was held that the sum had vested in all four children. The bequest was dependent on the contingency of the daughter leaving, that is, being survived by, children; but that contingency was not imported into the description of the class so as to confine the gift to those children who survived their mother. If, through the survivance of certain members of the class the bequest came into effect, it operated in favour of all the members of the class. It is otherwise if the bequest is so framed as to show that only those children who survive the contingency are meant to share in the fund, or if there is a destination-over in the case of the liferenter dying without leaving issue.[91]

25. Division Per Capita or Per Stirpes.—Where a bequest is made to a number of individuals, although there are no words indicating the share to be taken by each, there is no room for doubt as to the mode of division: each will take an equal share. But if the legatees are called under a term or terms descriptive of a group, there may be doubt as to whether the fund is to be divided among all the beneficiaries as individuals (per capita) or according to the group or groups (per stirpes). It is clear that under a gift of residue to the children of A and the children of B either the family division may be disregarded so that each child of the two families receives an equal share, or the residue may be divided into halves and one-half distributed among the members of each family. It is within the power of the testator to use expressions which will remove all doubt on this point. The general presumption is in favour of per capita distribution, unless the language of the will or the frame of the bequest indicates the other mode of division.[92] There

---

[87] *Hickling's Trs.* v. *Garland's Trs.* (1898) 1 F. (H.L.) 7, per Lord Davey; *Christie* v. *Wisely* (1874) 1 R. 436; *Ross* v. *Dunlop* (1878) 5 R. 833; *Potter's Trs.* v. *Allan,* 1918 S.C. 173; *Murray's Tr.* v. *Murray,* 1919 S.C. 552.

[88] *Douglas* v. *Douglas* (1864) 2 M. 1008; *Carlton* v. *Thompson* (1867) 5 M. (H.L.) 151.

[89] *Scott's Trs.* v. *Scott,* 1909 S.C. 773.

[90] (1898) 1 F. (H.L.) 7; cf. *Primrose's Trs.* v. *Gardiner etc.,* 1973 S.L.T. 238.

[91] *Graham's Trs.* v. *Lang's Trs.,* 1916 S.C. 723; *Craik's Trs.* v. *Anderson,* 1932 S.C. 61.

[92] M'Laren, II, 780; *Hay Cunningham's Trs.* v. *Blackwell,* 1909 S.C. 219; *Robertson's Trs.* v. *Horne,* 1921 S.C. 817; *Campbell's Trs.* v. *Welsh,* 1952 S.C. 343; cf. *Boyd's Tr.* v. *Shaw,* 1958 S.C. 115; *Bailey's Trs.* v. *Bailey,* 1954 S.L.T. 282.

is, however, a presumption that where a bequest is given severally to parties in liferent and their issue in fee, the connection between the liferent and the fee implies stirpital division of the fee.[93]

26. Accretion.—Another question which may arise in regard to a legacy in favour of a number of legatees is whether the legacy is joint or several. If the legacy be given to the legatees jointly, or without words importing that they are to take separate shares, then, if any of these die without acquiring a vested right, the survivors will be entitled to the whole of the fund or subject bequeathed. A legacy to A and B simply will, if A predecease the testator, give B right to the whole of that sum.[94] But if words of severance, such as "equally" or "share and share alike," are used, accretion is excluded, and the share of a predeceaser will, in the case of a legacy, fall into residue (if there be a residuary bequest), or in the case of residue, lapse into intestacy. The rule has been authoritatively stated in these terms:—"When a legacy is given to a plurality of persons named or sufficiently described for identification 'equally among them,' or 'in equal shares,' or 'share and share alike,' or in any other language of the same import, each is entitled to his own share and no more, and there is no room for accretion in the event of the predecease of one or more of the legatees. The rule is applicable whether the gift is in liferent or in fee to the whole equally, and whether the subject of the bequest be residue or a sum of fixed amount or corporeal moveables. The application of this rule may, of course, be controlled or avoided by the use of other expressions by the testator importing that there shall be accretion in the event of the predecease of one or more of the legatees."[95] The most important exception to this rule occurs in bequests to a class, where notwithstanding the use of such terms as "equally," "share and share alike," the share of a predeceaser accresces to the survivors.[96]

If it is intended that accrescing shares shall be subject to the same conditions as the original share, as, e.g., where the original shares are settled on the beneficiaries in liferent, this should be made clear in the settlement, as there is no implication that the conditions apply to more than the original gift. Where the issue of the predeceaser take by virtue of the conditio si institutus sine liberis decesserit or a clause calling issue, it is only the parent's original share and not what would have accresced to him had he survived that can, as a general rule, be claimed by the issue, unless the will provides otherwise,[97] or adherence to the rule would result in intestacy.[98] In respect of provisions made on or after 25th November 1968 accretion operates for the benefit of an illegitimate person or of a person whose right is traceable through an

---

[93] *Home's Trs.* v. *Ramsay* (1886) 12 R. 314, *Bailey's Trs.* v. *Bailey,* supra, *Primrose's Trs.* v. *Gardiner,* supra.

[94] Stair, III, 8, 27; *Andrew's Exrs.* v. *Andrew's Trs.,* 1925 S.C. 844.

[95] *Paxton's Trs.* v. *Cowie* (1886) 13 R. 1191; applied in *Cochrane's Trs.* v. *Cochrane,* 1914 S.C. 403; *White's Trs.,* 1957 S.C. 322; but see *Young's Trs.* v. *Young,* 1927 S.C. (H.L.) 6 and *Mitchell's Trs.* v. *Aspin,* 1971 S.L.T. 166.

[96] *Muir's Trs.* v. *Muir* (1889) 16 R. 954; *Robert's Trs.* v. *Roberts* (1903) 5 F. 541.

[97] *Henderson* v. *Henderson* (1890) 17 R. 293; *Young* v. *Robertson* (1862) 4 Macq. 337; *Crosbie's Trs.* v. *Crosbie,* 1927 S.C. 159; *Miller's Trs.* v. *Brown,* 1933 S.C. 669.

[98] *Beveridge's Trs.* v. *Beveridge,* 1930 S.C. 578.

illegitimate person as it would for someone who is legitimate, unless the contrary intention appears.[99]

27. Conditio si Institutus sine Liberis Decesserit.[1]—In certain cases this condition is read into a bequest, including a bequest of revenue.[2] The effect is that, if the legatee die without acquiring a vested interest leaving issue,[3] the issue (although they are not mentioned in the will) have right to the legacy in preference (as the case may be) to the conditional institute, or the residuary legatee, or the heirs ab intestato of the testator. In the case of a bequest of income it applies so as to enable the payment of income to the issue of a beneficiary who before his death has entered into and enjoyed the bequest.[4] It is applicable only to bequests by a testator to his own descendants or to his nephews and nieces,[5] including those whose relationship to him is illegitimate,[6] but not to a step-child[7]; and where the legatees are nephews or nieces it is necessary that the testator should by the terms of his will have placed himself in loco parentis to them, which means that he should have made a settlement in their favour similar to that which a parent might be supposed to make.[7a] In such circumstances the presumption is that the conditio applies, in the absence of a contrary intention expressed or clearly implied in the deed itself or in other operative testamentary writings.[8] These limits to its application are now settled; but within these limits it is always a question of construction whether in any particular case the conditio is to be admitted.[9] It is favourable to its admission that the settlement is a universal one, that the beneficiaries are a class, and that the provision is of the nature of a family settlement.[10] On the other hand, the conditio does not apply if the bequest proceeds purely from delectus personae apart from the fact of relationship[11]; and, as its justification is the presumption that the failure to mention issue was due to the testator having overlooked the contingency of the legatee's predecease leaving issue, it does not apply if the terms of the will afford evidence that this is not so; and such evidence is found where the testator in other legacies has made express provision for the issue of predeceasing legatees.[12] It applies although the parent was called as a conditional

[99] Law Reform (Misc. Prov.) (Scotland) Act 1968 (c. 70), ss. 6 (1) (b), 6 (3) and 22 (5).
[1] M'Laren, I, Ch. XL; Henderson on *Vesting*, Ch. XVII.
[2] *Pattinson's Trs.* v. *Motion*, 1941 S.C. 290.
[3] Including, in provisions made on or after 25th November 1968, illegitimate issue. (Law Reform (Misc. Prov.) (Scotland) Act 1968 (c. 70) ss. 6 (1) (a) 6 (3) and 22 (5)).
[4] *Reid's Trs.* v. *Reid etc.*, 1969 S.L.T. (Notes) 4.
[5] *Hall* v. *Hall* (1891) 18 R. 690.
[6] Except in provisions made before 25th November 1968. (Law Reform (Misc. Prov.) (Scotland) Act 1968 (c. 70), ss. 6 (1) (a), 6 (3) and 22 (5)).
[7] *Sinclair's Trs.* v. *Sinclair*, 1942 S.C. 362.
[7a] *Bogie's Trs.* v. *Christie* (1882) 9 R. 453; See *Waddell's Trs.* v. *Waddell* (1896) 24 R. 189 and *Alexander's Trs.* v. *Paterson*, 1928 S.C. 371.
[8] *Knox's Exr.* v. *Knox*, 1941 S.C. 532; *Devlin's Trs.* v. *Breen*, 1945 S.C. (H.L.) 27, per Lord Thankerton, at p. 35; *Reid's Trs.* v. *Reid*, 1960 S.L.T. (Notes) 5.
[9] *Devlin's Trs.*, supra, at p. 32.
[10] *Blair's Exrs.* v. *Taylor* (1876) 3 R. 362; *Devlin's Trs.*, supra.
[11] *Keith's Trs.* v. *Keith* (1908) 16 S.L.T. 390.
[12] *Greig* v. *Malcolm* (1835) 13 S. 607; *M'Nab* v. *Brown's Trs.*, 1926 S.C. 387, approved in *Paterson* v. *Paterson*, 1935 S.C. (H.L.) 7. See *Alexander's Trs.* v. *Paterson*, supra, and *Reid's Trs.* v. *Reid*, supra.

institute,[13] but it cannot apply if the legatee was dead when the will was executed.[14] It admits the issue of a legatee who has either predeceased the testator or died after the testator without having acquired a vested right.[15] It applies in marriage-contracts as well as in testamentary deeds,[16] but not in the case of any other inter vivos deed.[17] As already mentioned, the issue take only the parent's original share.[18]

28. Powers.—A power or faculty is an authority reserved by or conferred upon a person to dispose, either wholly or partially, of property either for his own benefit or for that of others.[19] Such powers may be general, by which is meant a power to dispose of the property at pleasure, or special, by which is meant a more limited power. The typical instance of a special power is that of appointing a fund among members of a specified class. The person from whom the power issues is known as the donor of the power and the recipient as the donee of the power.

Where a person settles his property, or takes a disposition, in favour of himself in liferent and at the same time reserves to himself a general power of disposing of the property, this is equivalent to a fee. He has right to the property independently of the settlement or disposition, and if he reserves to himself the enjoyment of the fruits of the property and the power to dispose of the property at pleasure, he remains substantially the proprietor.[20] In that situation he is both donor and donee of the power and is outwith the ambit of the ordinary rule that the donee of a power cannot delegate the exercise thereof.[21]

If the donor confers on the donee a liferent with a power of disposal, both in unqualified terms, that is a gift of the fee,[22] and the donee may demand immediate payment or conveyance thereof. But if the liferent is declared to be alimentary, whatever may be the extent of the power,[23] or, although the liferent be unqualified, if the power is to be exercised in a particular manner, as by will or mortis causa deed only, or otherwise falls short of a general

[13] *Greig's Trs.* v. *Simpson*, 1918 S.C. 321.
[14] *Rhind's Trs.* v. *Leith* (1866) 5 M. 104; *Low's Trs.* v. *Whitworth* (1892) 19 R. 431; but see *Miller's Trs.* v. *Miller*, 1958 S.C. 125 (conditio applied where the bequest was confirmed by a codicil executed after the institute's death).
[15] *Young* v. *Robertson* (1862) 4 Macq. 337, per Lord Chancellor (Westbury), at p. 340; *Grant* v. *Brooke* (1882) 10 R. 92; *Alexander's Trs.* v. *Paterson*, supra; cf. *Mitchell's Exrs.* v. *Gordon's J.F.*, 1953 S.C. 176, where Lord President Cooper suggested, obiter, that its applicability was dependent upon the institute predeceasing the testator; sed contra: *M'Gregor's Trs.* v. *Gray*, 1969 S.L.T. 355.
[16] *Hughes* v. *Edwardes* (1892) 19 R. (H.L.) 33.
[17] *Halliday* (1869) 8 M. 112; *Crichton's Tr.* v. *Howat's Tutor* (1890) 18 R. 260; *Trs. of Gwendolen Beatrice Thomson's Trust*, 1963 S.C. 141.
[18] Supra, § 26.
[19] Farwell on *Powers* (3rd ed., 1916), p. 1. The subject of Powers is treated in M'Laren on *Wills and Succession*. The English books are Farwell on *Powers* (3rd ed.), and Sugden (Lord St. Leonards) on *Powers* (8th ed. 1861).
[20] *Morris* v. *Tennant* (1855) 27 Sc.Jur. 546; 30 Sc.Jur. 943; *Baillie* v. *Clark*, Feb. 23, 1809 F.C.
[21] *Cuninghame* v. *Cuninghame's Trs.*, 1961 S.L.T. 194, per Lord Ordinary (Mackintosh), at p. 197, and Lord President Clyde, at p. 201; *Monies* v. *Monies*, 1939 S.C. 344.
[22] *Rattray's Trs.* v. *Rattray* (1899) 1 F. 510; *Mackenzie's Trs.* v. *Kilmarnock's Trs.*, 1909 S.C. 472; *Baird* v. *Baird's Trs.*, 1956 S.C. (H.L.) 93.
[23] *Ewing's Trs.* v. *Ewing*, 1909 S.C. 409.

power, in either case the donee of the power is not in right of the fee of the property.[24]

The power must be exercised in accordance with the terms on which it is given. If the deed which confers it prescribes that it shall be exercised by will, it cannot be exercised by an inter vivos deed; but a power to appoint by "any writing under her hand" has been held wide enough to include inter vivos as well as testamentary deeds.[25] A mere reference in the power to the death of the donee of it, e.g., the postponement of payment to the fiars until the expiry of the donee's liferent, does not restrict him to choosing persons who survive him as the objects of the power, or suspend the vesting of indefeasible interests in the person chosen until the death.[26] In that event the power may be validly exercised by inter vivos deed. In interpreting a power there is no presumption that the objects should be the persons who would take failing its exercise.[27] It is not necessary to support a deed as an exercise of a power that it should make reference to the power; if there is no such reference, it becomes a question on the terms of the deed whether the donee intended to exercise the power.[28] It has long been recognised that words of general conveyance in a settlement are, unless a contrary intention appears, to be construed as including any estate which the testator had power to dispose of in any manner he might deem proper.[29] Thus, in *Hyslop* v. *Maxwell's Trs.*,[30] a power given by a testator to his niece, who enjoyed the liferent of a sum under his will, to dispose of that sum by will or deed after her death as she might think fit, was held to be exercised by her general settlement although it made no reference to the power and was executed before the death of the testator. As the power in this case was a general one, it fell under the rule. It is not yet finally settled whether a special power is to be held to be exercised by a general settlement which does not notice the power or purport to include subject to disposal by the testator,[31] but the prevailing opinion is that it is.[32] The law to be applied to determine whether or not a power has been validly exercised by a testamentary writing is that of the domicile of the donee at the date of his death.[33]

The exercise of a power is open to objection if it amounts to what is termed a fraud on the power[34] or is ultra vires. The term "fraud" in this connection does not denote dishonest or immoral conduct on the part of the appointer; it means that power has been exercised for a purpose, or with an intention, beyond the scope of, or not justified by, the deed creating the power.[35] Thus, it is a fraudulent exercise if the donee of a special power makes

---

[24] *Alves* v. *Alves* (1861) 23 D. 712; *Howe's Trs.* v. *Howe's Judicial Factor* (1903) 5 F. 1099.
[25] *Stirling's Trs.* v. *Legal & General Assurance Soc.*, 1957 S.L.T. 73.
[26] *Stainton* v. *Forteviot Trust*, 1948 S.C. (H.L.) 115; *Neame* v. *Neame's Trs.*, 1956 S.L.T. 57.
[27] *Stainton* v. *Forteviot Trust*, supra.
[28] *Smart* v. *Smart*, 1926 S.C. 392.
[29] *Bray* v. *Bruce's Exrs.* (1906) 8 F. 1078.
[30] (1834) 12 S. 413.
[31] *Alexander's Trs.* v. *Alexander's Trs.*, 1917 S.C. 654; but see *Tarratt's Trs.* v. *Hastings* (1904) 6 F. 968.
[32] *Burns' Trs.* v. *Burns' Trs.*, 1935 S.C. 905; *Gemmell's Trs.* v. *Shields*, 1936 S.C. 717.
[33] *Drurie's Trs.* v. *Osborne*, 1960 S.C. 444.
[34] M'Laren, II, 1107; Farwell on *Powers*, 457.
[35] Per Lord Parker in *Vatcher* v. *Paull* [1915] A.C. 372, at p. 378; *Re Simpson*, [1952] Ch. 412.

an appointment with the intention of benefiting himself or some other person not an object of the power[36]; or if the fund subject to the special power is appointed wholly to one object of the power in consequence of a bribe.[37] So also a parent cannot in exercising a power of appointing a fund among his children bargain with them for the purchase by him of other interests belonging to them.[38] But where the donee's purpose and intention in making the appointment was to benefit the objects of the power, the mere presence of an incidental benefit to himself, e.g., under an arrangement for the variation of trust purposes, will not be sufficient to constitute a fraud on the power.[39] Appointments in fraud of the power are voidable at the instance of an interested object of the power but challenge may be barred by homologation.[40]

The rule as to an ultra vires exercise has been thus stated: "If you cannot disconnect that which is imposed by way of condition or mode of enjoyment from the gift, the gift itself may be found to be involved in conditions so much beyond the power that it becomes void. But where that is not so, where you have a gift to an object of the power, and where you have nothing alleged to invalidate the gift but conditions which are attempted to be imposed as to the mode in which that object of the power is to enjoy what is given to him, then the gift may be valid and take effect without reference to those conditions."[41] In the case of a power to apportion a fund among a class, it is, since the Powers of Appointment Act 1874[42] (which alters the former law), no longer an objection to the exercise that certain members of the class are omitted or received only illusory shares; the whole of the fund may validly be appointed to one of the class. But in so far as the exercise purports to give any share of the fund to one who is not a member of the class it is bad.[43] A power to apportion under restrictions and conditions is validly exercised by a gift of liferent of a share with an unqualified power of testamentary disposal, or by a gift of a share to one member of the class in liferent and to another in fee.[44] If the deed should appoint the fund to the children on condition that they forgive a certain debt or pay a certain sum, the condition could be severed from the substance of the appointment with the result that the deed would be good as an appointment to the children, and the condition would be treated as void.[45] Partial invalidity in the exercise of a power is not necessarily fatal to

---

[36] *Stein* v. *Stein* (1826) 5 S. 101; *Craig* v. *Craig's Trs.* (1904) 12 S.L.T. 136, 620; *Dick's Trs.* v. *Cameron*, 1907 S.C. 1018.
[37] *Re Wright* [1920] 1 Ch. 108.
[38] *Smith Cunninghame* v. *Anstruther's Trs.* (1872) 10 M. (H.L.) 39.
[39] *Pelham Burn*, 1964 S.C. 3.
[40] *Callander* v. *Callander's Exr.*, 1976 S.L.T. 10.
[41] *M'Donald* v. *M'Donald's Trs.* (1875) 2 R. (H.L.) 125, per Earl Cairns, L.C.; *Dalziel* v. *Dalziel's Trs.* (1905) 7 F. 545, per Lord Dunedin; *Re Holland* [1914] 2 Ch. 595.
[42] 37 & 38 Vict., c. 37.
[43] See, e.g., *Moubray's Trs.* v. *Moubray*, 1929 S.C. 254, where the earlier cases are reviewed. Illegitimate persons are taken to be proper objects of a special power of appointment created by deed executed on or after 25th November 1968 unless the contrary appears (Law Reform (Miscellaneous Provisions) (Scotland) Act 1968 (c. 70), ss. 5 (3) and 22 (5)).
[44] *Moubray's Trs.* v. *Moubray*, 1929 S.C. 254; *Gemmell's Trs.* v. *Shields*, 1936 S.C. 717; *Angus's Trs.* v. *Monies*, 1939 S.C. 509.
[45] Farwell on *Powers*, p. 343.

the whole exercise. The question is whether the appointer, if aware of the partial invalidity, would have left the rest of the appointment as it stands.[46]

The existence of a power of appointment over a fund bequeathed to a class does not suspend vesting in the members of the class; they take a right to an equal share of the fund, which may be defeated in whole or in part by an exercise of the power.[47] If the power is not exercised, or if the exercise is wholly invalid, the members of the class remain vested in equal shares of the fund. The donee of a power may validly bind himself that he will not exercise the power so as to exclude or reduce below a certain amount the share of an object of the power. A liferent and power of disposal may be renounced, whereupon the fee vests in the objects in terms of the deed creating the power.[48]

29. Ineffectual Conditions and Directions: Repugnancy.—If a bequest is made subject to a condition which is in its nature impossible, uncertain,[49] illegal, or contra bonos mores, the condition is held pro non scripto, and the bequest is effectual.[50] Thus, a legacy given ob turpem causam,[51] or subject to a condition amounting to an absolute and general restraint of marriage by the legatee[52] or to a wife on condition that she ceases to live with her husband,[53] or to a young child on condition that he shall not reside with his parents (of unobjectionable character),[54] receives effect as an unconditional legacy as these conditions are not sanctioned by the law; and testamentary directions requiring that the testator's estate should be disposed of in an unreasonable manner which conferred no benefit on any person or on the public have been refused effect as involving an abuse of the power of testation.[55] A legacy to an enemy alien remains legally incapable of payment during the war.[56]

Further, on the ground "that an act which, if done, can be at once undone by the person having an interest, will not be directed by the Court to be done," it has been held in a series of cases that if trustees are directed to purchase an annuity payable to a person, that person (seeing that he could sell the annuity if it were purchased) may claim the purchase price of the annuity in lieu of it.[57] And where a vested, unqualified, and indefeasible right of fee in

---

[46] Coat's Trs. v. Tillinghast, 1944 S.C. 466; Monies v. Monies, 1939 S.C. 344; Middleton's Trs. v. Borwick, 1947 S.C. 517; Torrance's Trs. v. Weddel, 1947 S.C. 91; Cathcart's J.F. v. Stewart, 1948 S.C. 456; Maclaren's Trs. v. Wilkie, 1948 S.C. 652; Wight's Trs. v. Milliken, 1960 S.C. 137. Ford's Trs. v. Calthrop etc., 1971 S.C. 115.

[47] Sivright v. Dallas (1824) 2 S. 643; Watson v. Marjoribanks (1837) 15 S. 586; Romanes v. Riddell (1865) 3 M. 348.

[48] Lawson v. Cormack's Trs., 1940 S.C. 210.

[49] In Veitch's Exr. v. Veitch, 1947 S.L.T. 17, a condition that the legatee "occupy" a house was held not to be uncertain. See also Hood v. Macdonald's Tr., 1949 S.C. 24.

[50] Bell, Prin., § 1785; M'Laren, I, 600.

[51] Johnston v. M'Kenzie's Exrs. (1835) 14 S. 106; Young v. Johnston & Wright (1880) 7 R. 760.

[52] Ibid.; Sturrock v. Rankin's Trs. (1875) 2 R. 850; Aird's Exrs. v. Aird, 1949 S.C. 154.

[53] Wilkinson v. Wilkinson (1871) L.R. 12 Eq. 604.

[54] Grant's Trs. v. Grant (1898) 25 R. 929; Fraser v. Rose (1849) 11 D. 1466.

[55] Aitken's Trs. v. Aitken, 1927 S.C. 374; Lindsay's Exr. v. Forsyth, 1940 S.C. 568. M'Caig v. The University of Glasgow, 1907 S.C. 231; M'Caig's Trs. v. Lismore United Free Kirk Session, 1915 S.C. 426; Sutherland's Trs. v. Verschoyle, 1968 S.L.T. 43.

[56] Weber's Trs. v. Riemer, 1947 S.L.T. 295.

[57] Dow v. Kilgour's Trs. (1877) 4 R. 403; Dempster's Trs. v. Dempster, 1921 S.C. 332; contrast Branford's Trs. v. Powell, 1924 S.C. 439.

a bequest is given in a trust disposition and settlement to a beneficiary of full age, he is entitled to payment of the bequest notwithstanding any direction to the trustees to retain the capital and to pay over the income to him or to apply the capital or income in some way for his behoof.[58] Such a direction is considered to be repugnant to the right of fee vested in the beneficiary and, therefore, nugatory. But it is otherwise if there are other trust purposes which require that the subject of the bequest shall be retained by the trustees, or if the trustees are not merely directed to retain the bequest but are given power in their discretion to withdraw the fee from the beneficiary and to settle the bequest on him in liferent and on others in fee.[59] In such circumstances the beneficiary cannot put an end to the trust management.

30. The Thellusson Act.—By the Accumulations Act 1800[60] (commonly known as the Thellusson Act), the legislature interposed to check the mischief which, it was anticipated, might arise from directions for the accumulation of income for prolonged periods. By that statute accumulation of income was prohibited beyond one or other of four periods. The 1800 Act was re-enacted with modifications by the Trusts (Scotland) Act 1961[61]; and two further periods were added in respect of deeds taking effect after August 3, 1966[62] bringing the total number of periods now available to six. These are:—(1) the life of the grantor of the deed; (2) a term of twenty-one years from the death of the grantor; (3)[63] a term of twenty-one years from the date of the deed[64]; (4)[63] the duration of the minority or respective minorities of any person or persons living or in utero at the date of the deed; (5) the duration of the minority or respective minorities of any person or persons living or in utero at the death of the grantor; and (6) the duration of the minority or respective minorities of any person or persons who, under the terms of the deed directing accumulation, would for the time being, if of full age, be entitled to the rents or income directed to be accumulated.

Of these, period (1) can, by definition, only apply in the case of inter vivos deeds under which accumulation is directed during the grantor's lifetime[65]; but that period will not operate so as to prevent accumulation under periods (3), (4) or (6) continuing beyond the date of the grantor's death.[66] With this exception, however, the periods are alternative, not cumulative, and it is not

---

[58] *Yuill's Trs.* v. *Thomson* (1902) 4 F. 815; *Miller's Trs.* v. *Miller* (1890) 18 R. 301; *Dowden's Trs.* v. *Governors of Merchiston Castle School*, 1965 S.C. 56; *Smith's Tr.* v. *Michael*, 1972 S.L.T. 89; *Graham* v. *Graham's Trs.*, 1927 S.C. 388; contrast *Ford's Trs.* v. *Ford*, 1940 S.C. 426, where the later direction disposed of the fee.

[59] *Chambers' Trs.* v. *Smiths* (1878) 5 R. (H.L.) 151.

[60] 39 & 40 Geo. III, c. 98.

[61] 9 & 10 Eliz. II, c. 57, s. 5.

[62] 1966 (c. 19), s. 6.

[63] This period was added by the 1966 Act.

[64] As to whether an arrangement under the Trusts (Scotland) Act 1961 may amount to a new settlement so as to introduce a new terminus a quo see *Aikman Petr.*, 1968 S.L.T. 137.

[65] *Stewart's Trs.* v. *Stewart*, 1927 S.C. 350; *Union Bank* v. *Campbell*, 1929 S.C. 143.

[66] 1961 Act, s. 5 (4); 1966 Act, s. 6 (1) proviso. It is, however, essential that where under an inter vivos deed an accumulation period has begun during the life of the granter, any additional period beyond the granter's death should be a period "directed" by the granter (*M'Iver's Trs.* v. *Inland Revenue*, 1974 S.L.T. 202).

permissible to add one period to another.[67] Period (6) is available in a case where an accumulation is directed from a period subsequent to the date of the grantor's death,[68] it not being required that the minor should be in life at that date.[69] But where the direction is to accumulate income from the date of the grantor's death, the restriction under periods (2) or (5) will apply, whether or not accumulation has in fact taken place during that period.[70]

The statutory restrictions are not confined to cases in which accumulation of income is expressly directed. If a settlement is so framed that accumulation of income beyond the permitted period necessarily results, the Act will apply. Thus, where trustees were directed to convey the residue of the testator's estate to the children of M, and at the expiry of twenty-one years from the testator's death M was alive but had no children, it was held that, while it was the duty of the trustees within that period to accumulate the income for behoof of the residuary legatees, the income thereafter accruing could not be accumulated.[71] The statutory restrictions apply also in a case where the power to accumulate is merely discretionary, and there is no duty to exercise it.[72]

While the statutes put an end to accumulation after the prescribed periods, they do not otherwise affect the dispositions of the deed.[73] The deed is to be read as if it had expressly declared that the accumulation directed should then end, and for the rest it receives effect exactly as it stands.

The 1961 Act provides that the income directed to be accumulated contrary to its provisions shall "go to, and be received by, the person or persons who would have been entitled thereto if such accumulation had not been directed."[74] Accordingly, if there is a present gift of the income-bearing subject and the direction for accumulation is merely a burden on that gift, so that apart from it the legatee would have taken the income, the income released by the statute will go to the legatee.[75] On the other hand, if the gift is a future one, the statute does not operate to accelerate or enlarge the right of the legatee.[76] Thus, if the gift is to be made over to the legatee at the termination of an annuity, any income accruing during the annuitant's lifetime, but after the period of twenty-one years from the testator's death, will not go to the legatee.[77] If the subject of the gift were residue, the income in that case would fall into intestacy.[78] Renunciation of a liferent would have the

---

[67] *Union Bank* v. *Campbell*, supra.
[68] See *Carey's Trs.* v. *Rose*, 1957 S.C. 252.
[69] *Re Cattell* [1914] 1 Ch. 177.
[70] *Campbell's Trs.* v. *Campbell* (1891) 18 R. 992; *Carey's Trs.* v. *Rose*, supra.
[71] *Lord* v. *Colvin* (1860) 23 D. 111; *Barbour* v. *Budge*, 1947 S.N. 100. See also *Gibson's Trs.*, 1963 S.C. 350.
[72] 1966 Act, s. 6 (2).
[73] *Elder's Trs.* v. *Treasurer of the Free Church of Scotland* (1892) 20 R. 2, per Lord Kyllachy; *Maxwell's Trs.* v. *Maxwell* (1877) 5 R. 248, per Lord Justice-Clerk Moncreiff.
[74] 1961 Act, s. 5 (3).
[75] *Maxwell's Trs.* v. *Maxwell*, supra; *Mackenzie* v. *Mackenzie's Trs.* (1877) 4 R. 962; *Stewart's Trs.* v. *Whitelaw*, 1926 S.C. 701; M'Laren, I, p. 313.
[76] *Russell's Tr.* v. *Russell*, 1959 S.C. 148; cf. *Young's Trs.* v. *Chapelle etc.*, 1971 S.L.T. 147.
[77] *Smith* v. *Glasgow Royal Infirmary*, 1909 S.C. 1231; *Wilson's Trs.* v. *Glasgow Royal Infirmary*, 1917 S.C. 527; *Pyper's Trs.* v. *Leighton*, 1946 S.L.T. 255; cf. *Dowden's Trs.* v. *Governors of Merchiston Castle School*, 1965 S.C. 56.
[78] *Elder's Trs.*, and *Wilson's Trs.*, supra; *Carey's Trs.* v. *Rose*, 1957 S.C. 252. Legal rights are not claimable out of the income thus brought into intestacy; *Lindsay's Trs.* v. *Lindsay*, 1931 S.C. 586.

same effect. Where the income is that accruing on a legacy, the result of the statute is that the income will fall into residue if there be a residuary bequest which by means of present gift gives to the residuary legatee everything not otherwise disposed of and its terms allow of the income being paid away (for the retention of the income for behoof of residuary legatees would be equivalent to accumulation) or otherwise into intestacy.[79] A person in whom a fund has vested subject to defeasance is not entitled to the income under the statutory provision as the right of fee is not absolute.[80]

The Accumulations Act 1892[81] prohibits the accumulation of income by will for the purchase of land only.[82]

31. Limitation on the Creation of Liferents.—The Law Reform (Miscellaneous Provisions) (Scotland) Act 1968,[83] sec. 18 provides that where, by any deed executed on or after 25th November, 1968, there is created a liferent interest in any property, that interest is converted into a right of fee if anyone of full age becomes entitled to it who was not living or in utero at the date of the coming into operation of the deed.[84] In the case of someone not of full age, the conversion into a right of fee is postponed until he attains majority and is subject to the proviso that he should then still be entitled to the liferent interest. The conversion does not affect rights created independently of the deed or rights of security holders or superiors of heritable property. These provisions re-enact with some variations the substance of section 9 of the Trusts (Scotland) Act 1921[85] and sec. 48 of the Entail Amendment Act 1848[86] which continue to apply to liferent interests created by deeds executed before 25th November, 1968. Under the latter Act which applies to heritage, whereas the 1921 Act applies to moveables, there is no automatic conversion into a right of fee but the liferenter is enabled, if he so chooses, to acquire the fee by petitioning the Court for that purpose.[87] The section does not apply to annuities.[88]

32. Approbate and Reprobate or Election.—The doctrine known in Scots Law as Approbate and Reprobate is the same as that of Election in the law of England. It has been authoritatively stated in these terms:—

"It is equally settled in the law of Scotland and of England that no person can accept and reject the same instrument. If a testator gives his estate to A and gives A's estate to B, Courts of Equity hold it to be against conscience

---

[79] *Smith* v. *Glasgow Royal Infirmary*, per Lord President Dunedin at 1236; *Cathcart's Trs.* v. *Foresterhill Hospital*, 1977 S.L.T. 114.
[80] *Russell's Tr.* v. *Russell*, supra, per Lord President Clyde and Lord Russell (obiter).
[81] 55 & 56 Vict., c. 58.
[82] *Robertson's Trs.* v. *Robertson's Trs.*, 1933 S.C. 639.
[83] 1968, c. 70.
[84] A mortis causa deed comes into operation on the death of the testator and the execution or coming into operation of a special power of appointment is referable to the date of execution or, as the case may be, coming into operation of the deed creating the power (s. 18 (5)).
[85] 11 & 12 Geo. V, c. 58; Conveyancing (Scotland) Act, 1924 (14 & 15 Geo. V, c. 27), s. 45.
[86] 11 & 12 Vict., c. 36.
[87] *Crichton-Stuart's Tutrix*, 1921 S.C. 840, per Lord President Clyde; *Earl of Moray*, 1950 S.C. 281.
[88] *Drybrough's Tr.* v. *Drybrough's Tr.*, 1912 S.C. 939.

that A should take the estate bequeathed to him and at the same time refuse
to effectuate the implied condition in the will of the testator. The Court will
not permit him to take that which cannot be his but by virtue of the
disposition of the will and at the same time to keep what by the same will is
given or intended to be given to another person."[89] In the leading modern
case[90] children taking provisions made by a testatrix out of her own estate
claimed also to be entitled to challenge her appointment of a fund made in the
same deed and to take that fund as in default of valid appointment; but the
Court, applying the doctrine, held that acceptance of one part of the deed was
inconsistent with rejection of another part.

The most familiar illustration of the doctrine is to be found in cases where
a bequest is made to a spouse or descendant who has a legal right in the estate
of the testator.[91] A descendant or spouse cannot be deprived of that right by
testament,[92] but he or she may be required to elect between it and a
testamentary provision. A case for election will arise if a provision in a
testament is made with an express declaration that it is given in satisfaction of
the legal rights,[93] or if the provision is contained in a universal settlement, for
a legatee cannot, by claiming under a deed which was intended to dispose of
the whole estate, approbate it and at the same time reprobate it by
withdrawing a portion of the estate to meet his or her legal rights.[94] On the
other hand, if the settlement is a partial one and disposes only of dead's part,
a claim for legal rights would not disturb it, and, therefore, children or their
issue might take both these rights and provisions under the deed.[95]

33. Conditions of Election.—It is stated by Lord President Inglis, in
Douglas's Trs. v. *Douglas*,[96] "that, to make a proper case of election, the facts
of the case must be such as to satisfy three conditions. In the first place, I
think the party who is put to his election must have a free choice, and that
whichever alternative he chooses, he shall have a right absolutely to that
which he has chosen, without the possibility of his right being interfered with
or frustrated by the intervention of any third party. In the second place, the
necessity of making the election must arise from the will, express or implied,
of some one who has the power to bind the person put to his election. And, in
the third place, the result of the election of one or other of the alternatives
must be to give legal effect and operation to the will so expressed or implied."
In making an election a person should have information as to the alternative
rights open to him; and there are numerous cases in which an election made in

---

[89] Per Lord Eldon in *Ker* v. *Wauchope* (1819) 1 Bligh 1.
[90] *Crum Ewing's Trs.* v. *Bayly's Trs.*, 1911 S.C. (H.L.) 18.
[91] The issue of predeceasing children now share in the division of legitim: Succession (Scotland)
Act 1964 (c. 41), s. 11.
[92] See Legal Rights, Ch. XLI, § 1, supra.
[93] Such a declaration is implied in all testaments made on or after September 10, 1964: Succession
(Scotland) Act, s. 13 as amended by the Law Reform (Misc. Prov.) (Scotland) Act 1968 (c. 70),
s. 3 & Sched. I, para. 6.
[94] *Henderson* v. *Henderson* (1782) M. 8191; M'Laren, I 139.
[95] *White* v. *Finlay* (1861) 24 D. 38; M'Laren, I, 140.
[96] (1862) 24 D. 1191, at 1208; *Brown's Trs.* v. *Gregson*, 1920 S.C. (H.L.) 87.

ignorance or in circumstances which show that it does not represent a free and deliberate choice, has been held not to be binding.[97]

34. Equitable Compensation: Forfeiture.—A person who elects to claim against a will (e.g., a spouse or descendant enforcing legal rights) loses in any event any benefit given him by the will, so far as is necessary to indemnify those who have been prejudiced by his election, by restoring to the estate what has been taken as jus relictae or legitim. Thus, in *Macfarlane's Trs.* v. *Oliver*,[98] a testator directed his trustees to hold his whole estate for behoof of his son and daughter equally in liferent and for their issue respectively in fee. The daughter having claimed her legitim, the trustees accumulated the share of income which would have been payable to her as liferentrix until it reached a sum which enabled them to make good to her brother and to the grandchildren the loss occasioned to them by her claim of legitim; and it was held that, compensation having thus been made, the daughter was entitled to the future income of the share bequeathed to her and her children. But if a conventional provision is made for a spouse or child on the express condition that it is to be taken in satisfaction of her or his legal rights, the assertion of these rights normally involves total forfeiture of the provision. In testamentary settlements executed prior to September 10, 1964, the doctrine of equitable compensation operates in the absence of a clause of satisfaction; but such a clause is now implied in all wills made on or after that date.[99] Accordingly, a claim for legal rights will result in forfeiture of all provisions made for the claimant in such a deed unless the will contains a statement to the contrary. Not infrequently the provision in favour of a child is in the form of a liferent to him and the fee to his issue or a destination-over of the liferent to his spouse. Where the clause of satisfaction includes also a provision for forfeiture, it may expressly declare the forfeiture of their rights as well as those of the claimant; but if it does not, the fate of their rights depends on whether there is a separate and independent gift to them. If there is, their rights are not forfeited[1]; but if there is not, and on a construction of the deed it appears that the right of the issue or spouse is dependent on the liferent taking effect, forfeiture of their right is involved in the child's election to take legitim.[2] Where the clause of satisfaction does not contain an express forfeiture, it is doubtful whether forfeiture of the conventional provision by any person other than the actual claimant will be inferred.[3] Where there is forfeiture, any balance of the forfeited provision after indemnification falls either into residue

---

[97] See *Inglis* v. *Breen* (1890) 17 R. (H.L.) 76; *Stewart* v. *Bruce's Trs.* (1898) 25 R. 965; *Dawson's Trs.* v. *Dawson* (1896) 23 R. 1006; *Walker* v. *Orr's Trs.*, 1958 S.L.T. 220.
[98] (1882) 9 R. 1138. And see *Thomson's Trs.* v. *Thomson*, 1946 S.C. 399.
[99] Succession (Scotland) Act 1964, c. 14, s. 13, as amended by the Law Reform (Misc. Prov.) (Scotland) Act 1968 (c. 70), s. 3 & Sched. I, para. 6. *Munro's Trs.*, 1971 S.L.T. 313, 1971 S.C. 280.
[1] *Fisher* v. *Dixon* (1831) 10 S. 55, affd. 6 W. & S. 431; *Jack* v. *Marshall* (1879) 6 R. 543; *Brown's Trs.* v. *Gregson*, 1916 S.C. 97; *Hurll's Trs.* v. *Hurll*, 1964 S.C. 12. *Munro's Trs.*, supra.
[2] *Campbell's Trs.* v. *Campbell* (1889) 16 R. 1007; *M'Caull's Trs.* v. *M'Caull* (1900) 3 F. 222; *Ballantyne's Trs.* v. *Ballantyne*, 1952 S.C. 458; *M'Cartney's Trs.* v. *M'Cartney*, 1951 S.C. 504.
[3] See *Nicolson's Trs.* v. *Nicolson*, 1960 S.C. 186, per Lord President Clyde at 193; *Hurll's Trs.*, supra, per Lord Justice-Clerk Grant, at 19.

or into intestacy. It falls into intestacy if the provision was itself a gift of residue or part thereof, into residue if the provision was one of the prior purposes such as a legacy.[4] Thus a son claiming legitim may in the end take the balance of a gift or residue qua heir in intestacy.[5] If, however, a forfeiture clause is combined with a destination-over in the event of forfeiture and the destination-over fails, e.g., because there is no one to take under it, the forfeiture does not take effect.[6]

35. Satisfaction of Legitim.—As was shown in Chapter XLI,[7] a descendant's discharge of legitim *in the ancestor's lifetime* is equivalent in its effect to the descendant's death. It is otherwise when a descendant elects *after the ancestor's death* to accept a bequest in place of legitim. When a parent dies the right to legitim vests, and each child (or the issue of a predeceasing child) becomes a creditor with a claim on the executry for his or her share; and, if the child chooses rather to accept the bequest than to demand legitim, the debt to that child is extinguished. But the extinction of the debt benefits, not the legitim claimants, but the dead's part out of which the accepted bequest has been paid.[8]

A declaration by a testator that a legacy is given in satisfaction of legal rights will debar a legatee accepting the legacy from advancing any claim for these which conflicts with the scheme of the testator's settlement.[9] Whether the declaration has or has not a wider effect is a question of circumstances. The declaration may be read as intended to exclude such claims only in so far as necessary for the protection of the settlement. If this is so, then the legatee will not be debarred from asserting his or her legal rights against any portion of the estate which may fall into intestacy. Thus where a testator bequeathed a liferent of his estate to his widow in lieu of her legal rights and the residue to his children, and, by reason of the death of all the children, the estate fell into intestacy, it was held that the widow's acceptance of the liferent did not exclude her claim for her legal rights from the intestate estate.[10] But if it appears that the declaration was meant to safeguard the interests not only of the beneficiaries under the settlement but of the heirs ab intestato also, then the claim for legal rights would be completely debarred.[11]

36. Donation Mortis Causa.—This was defined by Lord President Inglis in *Morris* v. *Riddick*[12] as "conveyance of an immoveable or incorporeal right, or a transference of moveables or money by delivery, so that the property is immediately transferred to the grantee, upon the condition that he shall hold for the grantor so long as he lives, subject to his power of revocation, and,

---

[4] *Wingate* v. *Wingate's Trs.*, 1921 S.C. 857.
[5] As in *Tindall's Trs.* v. *Tindall*, 1933 S.C. 419.
[6] *Macnaughton* v. *Macnaughton's Trs.*, 1954 S.C. 312.
[7] Legal Rights, supra, § 8.
[8] *Fisher's Trs.* v. *Dixon* (1842) 2 D. 1121; per Lord Fullerton, affd. 2 Bell's App. 63.
[9] See n. 99 supra, and § 34 supra.
[10] *Naismith* v. *Boyes* (1899) 1 F. (H.L.) 79; *M'Gregor's Trs.* v. *Kimbell*, 1911 S.C. 1196; contrast *Sim* v. *Sim* (1902) 4 F. 944. *Naismith* applied: *Petrie's Trs.* v. *Manders's Tr.*, 1954 S.C. 430.
[11] Ibid.
[12] (1867) 5 M. 1036.

failing such revocation, then for the grantee on the death of the grantor." It has been said[13] that three essentials must occur: (1) the donor must act in contemplation of his death, (2) the subject of the donation must be delivered to the donee, and (3) the donor must manifest his intention to make in favour of the donee a de praesenti gift, consistent with the double resolutive condition stated above. Where there has been no delivery of the subject said to have been gifted, there is difficulty in establishing donation; but it has been laid down in a series of cases that delivery is not in all circumstances indispensable. In the case of a document such as a deposit-receipt[14] the fact that it was not delivered to the person alleging donation will not prevent the donation being effectual, if the intention to make it is otherwise established,[15] but there must be an equivalent to delivery.[16] There is, as in the case of donation inter vivos, a presumption against donation which has to be overcome.[17]

The effect of the donation is that the right of property in the subject passes at once to the donee. But during the lifetime of the donor that right is only a qualified one. Not only is the gift revocable by the donor, but it falls by the donee's predecease.[18] While the gift must have been made in contemplation of the donor's death, it is not required that he should have been under an immediate apprehension of death: and, although the gift may have been made at a time when he was dangerously ill, it is not ipso facto revoked by his recovery.[19]

Donations mortis causa "savour much indeed of legacies."[20] Thus, they remain under the power of the donor during his lifetime, and it is only on his death that the donee acquires an effectual right[21]; they are chargeable with the donor's debts if there is a deficiency of funds for their payment; and they do not affect the legal rights of the donor's spouse or issue.[22] But they differ from legacies in respect that there is an immediate, though conditional, transference of property and that, however valuable the gift may be, it does not require to be constituted by writing but may be proved by parole evidence. "Where they become good by the grantor's death, they are effectual against his heir or executor in the same manner as other deeds delivered at the date," and the donee is entitled to the subject of the gift although nothing is left for the legatees.[23]

---

[13] *Macpherson's Exx.* v. *Mackay*, 1932 S.C. 505, per Lord President Clyde at 513; see also *Graham's Trs.* v. *Gillies*, 1956 S.C. 437, at 448 and *Forrest-Hamilton's Tr.* v. *Forrest-Hamilton*, 1970 S.L.T. 338.

[14] "There must be delivery or its equivalent in the case of cash or bank notes"—Lord Mackenzie in *Hutchison's Exr.* v. *Shearer*, 1909 S.C. 15; see also *Crosbie's Trs.* v. *Wright* (1880) 7 R. 823, per Lord Deas.

[15] *Carmichael* v. *Carmichael's Exr.*, 1920 S.C. (H.L.) 195, at 203 and 205; *Scott's Trs.* v. *Macmillan* (1905) 8 F. 214; *Macfarlane's Trs.* v. *Miller* (1898) 25 R. 1202, and cases there cited; *Macpherson's Exx.* v. *Mackay*, 1932 S.C. 505; *Graham's Trs.* v. *Gillies*, supra. Contrast the case of an inter vivos donation, *Brownlee's Exx.* v. *Brownlee*, 1908 S.C. 232.

[16] *Gray's Trs.* v. *Murray etc.*, 1970 S.L.T. 105.

[17] *Macpherson's Exrx.* v. *Mackay*, supra.

[18] See *Morris* v. *Riddick*, supra; *Lord Advocate* v. *Galloway* (1884) 11 R. 541.

[19] *Blyth* v. *Curle* (1885) 12 R. 674.

[20] Bankton, I, 9, 16.

[21] Ibid.

[22] *Morris* v. *Riddick*, supra.

[23] Bankton, I, 9, 18; *Morris* v. *Riddick*, supra, per Lord Deas, at 1044.

CHAPTER XLIV

EXECUTORS: TRUSTEES: JUDICIAL FACTORS

M'Laren, *Wills and Succession* (3rd ed., 1894, and Supplement, 1934); Mackenzie Stuart, *Law of Trusts* (1932); Menzies, *Trustees* (2nd ed., 1913); Wilson and Duncan, *Trusts, Trustees and Executors* (1975); Currie, *Confirmation of Executors* (7th ed., 1973); Thoms, *Judicial Factors* (2nd ed., 1881); Irons, *Judicial Factors* (1908); Walker, *Judicial Factors* (1974).

I. EXECUTORS

1. Vitious Intromission.—The title to ingather and distribute the estate, both heritable and moveable,[1] of a deceased person belongs to the executor nominated by the deceased, or appointed by the Court, and in either case authorised to do so by confirmation by the Court. An unauthorised intromitter may incur liability for the whole debts of the deceased, even if there was no fraudulent intention.[2] But the Court has regard to the character and circumstances of the intromission and may relieve the vitious intromitter of the penal consequences of his actings. Thus, if the intromitter had a probable title for intromitting, e.g., if he was general disponee of the deceased (although this is not a competent title to intermeddle with the estate without confirmation), or if the circumstances show that he acted in good faith, he may escape universal liability.[3] Intromission, either necessary or custodiae causa by the wife and children of the deceased holding possession for the purpose of preserving the estate for the benefit of all concerned, does not infer liability; and there is clearly no place for it if the goods intermeddled with did not belong to the deceased.[4]

This rule was introduced for the benefit of creditors of the deceased and it is not available as a ground of action to heirs or legatees.[5] It cannot be pleaded against the heirs of a deceased vitious intromitter, the heir being liable only in so far as he is lucratus through succession to the intromitter. Where several are concerned in the intromission, each is liable in solidum and may be sued without calling the others; but the intromitter who pays the debt has relief against his fellow-intromitters. An intromitter who confirms before action is brought against him, or within year and day, thereby subjecting himself to liability to account, purges the vitiosity of his prior intromissions; but confirmation merely as executor-creditor[6] does not suffice for this purpose.[7]

[1] Succession (Scotland) Act 1964, (c. 41), s. 14 (1). Note that the executor had no title to ingather heritage in the case of persons dying before 10th September 1964.
[2] *Forbes* v. *Forbes* (1823) 2 S. 395; *Wilson* v. *Taylor* (1865) 3 M. 1060.
[3] *Adam* v. *Campbell* (1854) 16 D. 964; *Simpson* v. *Barr* (1854) 17 D. 33; *Greig* v. *Christie*, 1908 S.C. 370.
[4] *Greig* v. *Christie*, supra.
[5] Erskine, *Inst.*, III, 9, 54.
[6] See § 5 infra.
[7] Erskine, *Inst.*, III, 9, 52.

2. Appointment of Executor.—An executor is appointed either expressly or impliedly by the deceased (executor-nominate) or by the Court (executor-dative). Into the first class falls first the executor nominated[8] by the deceased, whom failing the testamentary trustees, whom failing any general disponee or universal legatory or residuary legatee.[9]

Where the deceased dies intestate or there is no executor-nominate, the executor is appointed by decerniture of the sheriff on an application for this purpose. The Court in which the application should be made is that of the sheriffdom in which the deceased was domiciled, or, if he had no domicile in Scotland or no fixed domicile, in the Sheriff Court of Edinburgh as the commune forum. The order of preference[10] observed in making the appointment is—(1) Next-of-kin and, if these do not claim, the representatives of next-of-kin who have died after the deceased but before confirmation is expede[11]; (2) the widow; (3) the children or descendants of such persons as would have been next-of-kin had they survived the deceased but who have predeceased him; (4) creditors; (5) legatees; and (6) the procurator-fiscal of court or a judicial factor. Where the father or mother of the deceased have right to a share of the estate they rank pari passu with the next-of-kin in a competition for the office.[12] The husband, if he is entitled to jus relicti, has right to the office, but not in competition, with his wife's next-of-kin.[13] Where the deceased has died intestate survived by a spouse, and the intestate estate is less than the amount which the surviving spouse is entitled to receive under prior rights, the surviving spouse has the right to be appointed executor[14]; otherwise the preference of the surviving spouse's right to the office will depend on the extent to which the deceased's estate exceeds the value of these rights.[15] An executor appointed by the Court is known as an executor-dative. All applicants having an equal right in the estate are entitled to be conjoined in the office. It is not settled to what extent the Court is entitled to take into consideration the capacity or incapacity of an applicant.[16]

3. Confirmation of Executors.—The appointment of a person as executor does not in itself confer on him authority to intromit with the estate of the deceased. In order to obtain such authority he must expede confirmation, that is, he must apply for, and obtain from the sheriff, a sentence or decree authorising him to "uplift, receive, administer and dispose of" the estate and to act in the office of executor; and an executor who intromits with the estate without confirmation is a vitious intromitter.[17] Confirmation in favour of an

---

8 *Tod* (1890) 18 R. 152.
9 Executors (Scotland) Act 1900 (63 & 64 Vict., c. 55), s. 3.
10 See Currie, *Confirmation of Executors*, pp. 98 et seq.
11 Confirmation of Executors (Scotland) Act 1823 (4 Geo. IV, c. 98), s. 1; Succession (Scotland) Act 1964, s. 5 (2).
12 *Webster* v. *Shiress* (1878) 6 R. 102; *Muir* (1876) 4 R. 74.
13 *Campbell* v. *Falconer* (1892) 19 R. 563.
14 1964 Act, s. 9 (4). See Intestate Succession, Ch. XLII, § 5.
15 Currie, op. cit., p. 108.
16 *Crolla*, 1942 S.C. 21.
17 *Cunningham & Bell* v. *M'Kirdy* (1827) 5 S. 315.

executor-nominate is called a testament-testamentar; in favour of an executor-dative a testament-dative. The office of executor is purely administrative.[18]

As a condition of confirmation an executor-dative must find caution to make the estate forthcoming to parties interested, but this is not required in the case of an executor-nominate.[19] All executors must give up on oath a full and true inventory of the whole estate, heritable and moveable, known to have belonged to the deceased, including property outwith Scotland.[20] A confirmation noting the Scottish domicile of the deceased is treated for purposes of the law of England and Wales as a grant of representation to the executors named therein in respect of the property of which in terms of the confirmation they are executors.[21] There is a corresponding provision for Northern Ireland.[22]

Confirmation to part only of the estate known to exist is prohibited by statute (except in the case of an executor-creditor) and is of no effect.[23] If an executor discovers that any part of the estate has been omitted or undervalued, he may by an eik have the same confirmed in addition to the estate originally confirmed; and it is also open to a creditor or other party interested to apply for confirmation ad omissa vel male appretiata. On such an application, if there has been no fraud on the part of the original executor, the sheriff will ordain the omitted subjects or the difference in value to be added to the original confirmation, or, if there be fraud, will grant a confirmation of the subjects to the exclusion of the original executor.

4. Confirmation in Small Estates.—Modern statutes have introduced a simple mode of obtaining confirmation in small estates. Where the value of the whole estate of the deceased does not exceed £10,000 an application may be made to the sheriff clerk, who fills up an inventory, takes the applicant's oath thereto, gets caution, if necessary, and expedes confirmation for a small fee. This procedure applies to both testate and intestate estates.[24]

There are statutory provisions permitting payments of certain kinds and under a specific amount without the exhibition of confirmation.[25]

5. Executor-Creditor.—A creditor may sue the executor who has confirmed to the debtor's estate to make payment of the debt. If there has been no confirmation, the creditor himself may apply for the office and may be confirmed as executor-creditor; and, when one creditor so applies, every co-

---

[18] *Smart* v. *Smart,* 1926 S.C. 392.
[19] Confirmation of Executors (Scotland) Act 1823, s. 2; Succession (Scotland) Act 1964, s. 20, proviso. See *Harrison* v. *Butters,* 1969 S.L.T. 183.
[20] Probate and Legacy Duties Act 1808 (48 Geo. III, c. 149), s. 38. It is competent to include in the inventory of the estate of a person dying domiciled in Scotland any real estate of the deceased in England and Wales or Northern Ireland: Administration of Estates Act 1971, s. 6.
[21] Administration of Estates Act 1971 (c. 25), s. 1.
[22] s. 2.
[23] Confirmation of Executors (Scotland) Act 1823, s. 3; *Elder* v. *Watson* (1859) 21 D. 1122.
[24] Intestates' Widows and Children (Scotland) Act 1875 (38 & 39 Vict., c. 41), Small Testate Estates (Scotland) Act 1876 (39 & 40 Vict., c. 25), as amended by Confirmation to Small Estates (Scotland) Act 1979 (c. 22), s. 1; Currie, *Confirmation of Executors,* p. 223 et seq.
[25] Administration of Estates (Small Payments) Act 1965 (c. 32), Sched. 1.

creditor may apply to be conjoined with him in the office. This confirmation is truly a form of diligence[26] and, as the creditor resorts to it solely for his own behoof, he is not required to confirm to more than the amount of his debt.

Confirmation is, however, available only to a creditor whose debt has been constituted by decree during the debtor's lifetime. If the debt is not so established, the procedure open to the creditor is to charge the next-of-kin to confirm. These may renounce the succession within twenty days after the charge, and if they fail to do so, they become liable, as vitious intromitters, for the debt. Should they renounce, the charger may constitute his debt and obtain a decree cognitionis causa against the haereditas jacens and, having thus constituted the debt, may obtain confirmation as executor-creditor.[27]

6. Effect of Confirmation.—Every part of the deceased's estate, heritable and moveable, falling to be administered under the law of Scotland to which confirmation has been obtained vests for the purposes of administration in the executor by virtue of the confirmation[28]; the confirmation confers on him full power to ingather, administer and dispose of the estate contained in the inventory. Before confirmation an executor may indeed sue for a debt due to the deceased[29]; but, without it, he cannot obtain an extract of decree for, or enforce, payment or grant an effectual discharge, of the debt. A debtor of the deceased is not bound to pay his debt to anyone except an executor who has confirmed to it[30]; and, if he chooses to pay to anyone else, this does not discharge him of his debt in a question with the executor who has confirmed. The executor alone has a title to sue those indebted to the deceased. Except in very special circumstances an heir or residuary legatee has no such title[31]; but, if the executor is unwilling to raise an action against a debtor and the legatee desires to do so, he may require the executor to give him the use of his name as pursuer of the action on condition of securing the executor against any risk of liability for the expenses of the action.

The confirmation itself, in the case of deaths on or after September 10, 1964, constitutes a valid title in the executor to the heritage contained in the inventory to it, and which has vested in him thereunder.[32] The executor may then transfer the heritage to the beneficiary entitled thereto by means of a statutory form of docket which is endorsed on the confirmation.[33] A person

[26] *Smith's Trs.* v. *Grant* (1862) 24 D. 1142, at p. 1169.
[27] Erskine, *Inst.,* III, 9, 34-35; Stewart on *Diligence,* p. 441; *Smith* v. *Tasker,* 1955 S.L.T. 347; *Stevens* v. *Thomson,* 1971 S.L.T. 136. It may be noted that under s. 163 of the Bankruptcy (Scotland) Act 1913 (3 & 4 Geo. V, c. 20), where a deceased person has left no settlement appointing trustees or persons having power to manage the estate, or in the event of such persons not accepting office or acting, a judicial factor may be appointed on the application of a creditor of the deceased or any person having an interest in the succession. This provision is applicable as well to solvent as to insolvent estates.
[28] Succession (Scotland) Act 1964, s. 14 (1).
[29] *Chalmer's Trs.* v. *Watson* (1860) 22 D. 1060; *Bones* v. *Morrison* (1866) 5 M. 240; *Mackay* v. *Mackay,* 1914 S.C. 200.
[30] *Fraser* v. *Gibb* (1784) M. 3921; *Buchanan* v. *Royal Bank of Scotland* (1843) 5 D. 211.
[31] *Morrison* v. *Morrison's Exr.,* 1912 S.C. 892.
[32] s. 15 (1). The inventory to the confirmation must contain such a description of the heritage as will be sufficient to identify the property or interest therein as a separate item in the estate: A. of S. (Confirmation of Executors Amendment) 1966 (S.I. 1966 No. 593).
[33] s. 15 (2); Sched. 1. The docket may be used as a link in title in any deduction of title.

who in good faith and for value subsequently acquires title to any interest in the heritage which was vested in the executor directly or indirectly, whether from the executor himself or from a person deriving title from the executor, is protected under the Succession (Scotland) Act 1964, in that no challenge may be made to that title on the ground that the confirmation was reducible or has been reduced, or that the title should not have been transferred to the person deriving title from the executor.[34]

7. Duties of the Executor.—The executor is not, in a question with creditors, to be regarded as a trustee for their behoof. He is proprietor of the executry burdened with the debts chargeable against it. As the deceased was debtor to his creditors, so is the executor who comes in his place, with this limitation, that the executor's liability does not extend beyond the estate committed to his charge. The executor is "eadem persona cum defuncto."[35]

Under the common law an executor might pay creditors according to the rule applicable to diligence, "prior tempore potior jure". Creditors who lived at a distance or who were late in learning of their debtor's decease were thus liable to be prejudiced; and, accordingly, in order to provide a remedy for this the Act of Sederunt of February 28, 1662, was passed. By this Act all creditors using legal diligence by citation of the executors or by obtaining themselves confirmed executors-creditors, or citing other executors-creditors, within six months after their debtor's death, come in pari passu with those who have used more timely diligence. Hence an executor cannot be compelled to pay away any part of the estate until after the expiry of the six months, nor (unless the solvency of the estate is assured) is he in safety to do so, seeing that until that period has elapsed it cannot be known for certain how many creditors may have claims on the fund in his hands. There is an exception in the case of privileged debts, i.e., debts which have preference over all other debts and must in any case be paid, under which term are included deathbed and funeral expenses, mourning for the widow and family, the wages of domestic and farm servants for the current term, taxes and rates.[36]

After the expiry of the six months the executor may proceed to pay primo venienti and is not answerable for so doing to creditors who appear afterwards. This rule protects executors acting fairly in the discharge of their duties; but there may be circumstances, e.g., if it became plain that the estate was insolvent, in which it would not be proper for the executor to pay off certain debts without regard to the claims of other creditors.[37] Even after the period of six months has expired a creditor citing the executor while funds remain in his hands is entitled to participate in the division of these funds.[38]

---

[34] s. 17.
[35] *Globe Insurance Co.* v. *Scott's Trs.*, (1849) 7 Bell's App. 296; *Stewart's Trs.* v. *Stewart's Exr.* (1896) 23 R. 739; *Mitchell* v. *Mackersy* (1905) 8 F. 198; *Tait's Exx.* v. *Arden Coal Co.*, 1947 S.C. 100. See also Succession (Scotland) Act 1964, s. 19.
[36] Erskine, III, 9, 43; *Barlass's Trs.*, 1916 S.C. 741.
[37] *Taylor & Fergusson* v. *Glass's Trs.*, 1912 S.C. 165, per Lord Dunedin; *Stewart's Trs.* v. *Evans* (1871) 9 M. 810.
[38] *Russel* v. *Simes* (1790) Bell's Oct. Cases 217.

Where the validity of a creditor's claim is doubtful the executor may require the creditor to constitute it by decree.[39]

After the claims of creditors have been met, it is the executor's duty (unless he himself is alone interested in the estate) to account for and distribute what remains of the estate to those who have right to it. These parties are not entitled to receive any benefit from the estate until the claims of creditors have been satisfied; and, if, in the knowledge that there are outstanding debts, the executor chooses to distribute the whole estate to the beneficiaries, he may be made personally liable to an unsatisfied creditor unless the latter has consented to the payment or has so acted as to be personally barred from objecting to the executor's conduct.[40]

The Succession (Scotland) Act 1964 provides that an adopted person is to be treated for the purposes of succession as the child of the adopter; but an executor is not obliged, before distributing the estate, to check whether an adoption order has been made which would entitle a person to an interest in the estate.[41] Similarly, the executor is not obliged to ascertain whether an illegitimate person exists, or has existed, the fact of whose existence is relevant to the distribution of the estate.[42] Where an interest in a lease forms part of the deceased's estate at his death in relation to which the deceased has not made a valid bequest or has made a bequest which has failed, the executor is entitled to transfer it, without the consent of the landlord, to any of the persons having rights of succession on intestacy in or towards the satisfaction of that person's claim.[43]

Although the office of the executor is distinct from that of trustee, both are governed by the general principles which apply to the administration of an estate by one person for behoof of others. In formal testamentary deeds trustees are usually also nominated executors, and in this case it is not easy to mark the point of differentiation between the respective duties of the two offices. Executors-nominate, as defined in the Executors (Scotland) Act 1900[44] are included in the definition of trustee for the purposes of the Trusts (Scotland) Acts 1921[45] and 1961,[46] and this definition was extended by the Succession (Scotland) Act 1964[47] so as to include executors-dative. Thus executors have the same powers, privileges and immunities and are subject to the same obligations, limitations and restrictions as gratuitous trustees under those Acts,[48] except that an executor-dative does not have power to resign or to assume new trustees.[47]

Removal of an executor from office for failure to co-operate with another

---

[39] M'Gaan v. M'Gaan's Trs. (1883) 11 R. 249, per Lord President Inglis.
[40] Lamond's Trs. v. Croom (1871) 9 M. 662; Heritable Securities Investment Association v. Miller's Trs. (1893) 20 R. 675; Campbell v. Lord Borthwick's Trs., 1930 S.N. 156.
[41] See s. 24 (2).
[42] Law Reform (Miscellaneous Provisions) (Scotland) Act 1968 (c. 70), s. 7.
[43] 1964 Act, s. 16; see Leases, Ch. XXXIII, supra, § 19.
[44] 63 & 64 Vict., c. 55.
[45] 11 & 12 Geo. V, c. 58, s. 2.
[46] 9 & 10 Eliz. II, c. 57, s. 6.
[47] c. 41, s. 20
[48] See in particular 1921 Act, ss. 4 and 5; 1961 Act, ss. 2 and 4.

executor in the administration, whilst a great rarity, is illustrated in at least one reported case.[49]

8. Failure of Executors by Death: Confirmation ad non executa.—Executry is an office and does not descend to heirs. Where, therefore, there is but one executor, the office dies with him; if there are two or more, it accrues to the survivor. The Executors (Scotland) Act 1900[44] contains provisions for the cases (a) where any sole or last surviving trustee or executor has died with any property (heritable or moveable) in Scotland vested in him as trustee or executor; and (b) where a confirmation has become inoperative by the death or incapacity of all the executors in whose favour it has been granted. In the first case the executor of the sole or last surviving trustee or executor may confirm, and this will enable him to recover and transfer the property[50]; in the second case no title to intromit with the estate confirmed transmits to representatives of the executors, but confirmation ad non executa may be granted to those parties to whom confirmations ad omissa are granted and is a sufficient title to continue and complete the administration of the estate.[51]

It has never been in use for an executor to obtain a discharge, for there could be no discharge until the administration of the estate was completed, and after the whole estate has been administered the executor's office has terminated and no discharge is needed.[52]

II. TRUSTEES

9. Statutes.—The doctrine of Trusts has long been familiar to Scots lawyers, but no detailed treatment of this subject is to be found in the Institutional writers. In the nineteenth century a great development, in which the influence of English law may be traced, took place in this branch of the law; and between 1861 and 1910 various statutes dealing with the administration of trusts were passed. These were all repealed by the Trusts (Scotland) Act 1921,[53] which, as amended by the Trusts (Scotland) Act 1961,[54] is the statute now in force. Many of the sections of the 1921 Act merely re-enact (in some cases with amendments) the provisions of the earlier statutes; but it also contains new sections which made important alterations to the former law. These Acts are not confined in their application to trustees in the strict sense of the term, for section 2 of the 1921 Act defines "trustee" as

---

[49] *Wilson* v. *Gibson,* 1948 S.C. 52.
[50] s. 6. If a note of property in England and Wales or Northern Ireland held in trust by a deceased person dying domiciled in Scotland is set forth in the inventory and is contained in or appended to the confirmation of Scottish estate which notes the domicile, the confirmation has the effect of a grant of representation in those countries in relation to the property specified in the note: Administration of Estates Act 1971, s. 5.
[51] s. 7.
[52] Erskine, III, 9, 47; *Johnston's Executor* v. *Dobie,* 1907 S.C. 31.
[53] 11 & 12 Geo. V, c. 58.
[54] 9 & 10 Eliz. II, c. 57.

including "any trustee ex officio, executor-nominate, tutor, curator, and judicial factor,"[55] and by the Guardianship of Infants Act 1925[56] a parent acting as tutor of a pupil under the common law or the Guardianship of Infants Acts, is also a trustee within the meaning of the Trusts Act. The Acts do not, however, apply to trusts constituted by a public general statute.[57]

10. The Trustee.—Erskine speaks of a trust as "of the nature of deposition, by which a proprietor transfers to another the property of the subject entrusted, not that it should remain with him, but that it may be applied to certain uses for the behoof of a third party."[58] This is an apt description of a familiar form of trust, but as a definition it is not sufficiently comprehensive.[59] A trust, for instance, may arise by implication of law as well as by express constitution; and a person may find himself bound as a trustee without his assent or even against his wishes.[60] But Erskine's statement is useful as directing attention to what is of the essence of the position of a trustee, viz., that, while he has the legal title to the property held in trust, he is under obligation to use his powers as legal owner for the benefit of some person other than himself (or it may be for a number of persons of whom he is one) or for some object not his own. The title to the property affected by the trust belongs to the trustee. "The property of the thing intrusted, be it in land or in moveable, is in the person of the intrusted, else it is not proper trust."[61] But the trustee, as such, does not enjoy the benefits derived from proprietorship, but must hold and apply the property for the purposes of the trust.

11. The Beneficiary: Conversion.—The person or persons for whose benefit the trust exists are known as the beneficiary or beneficiaries[62]; and their interest is termed the beneficial interest or jus crediti. This beneficial interest may (subject to the trustees' right to possess and administer the trust in terms of the truster's directions) be transmitted by the beneficiary's deed or attached by his creditors; and, if the beneficiary die vested in the beneficial interest, it will form part of his estate to be disposed of in terms of his testamentary or other deeds or in accordance with the law of intestate succession.

In these circumstances a question may arise as to the character of the beneficial interest, whether it is heritable or moveable. This will depend upon the nature of the subject held in trust, for the jus crediti partakes of the nature and quality of that subject. But in this matter the nature of the subject and,

[55] As to judicial factors, see § 25 infra. Executors-dative are now included: 1964 Act (c. 41), s. 20.
[56] 15 & 16 Geo. V, c. 45, s. 10.
[57] *Board of Management for Edinburgh Royal Infirmary,* 1959 S.C. 373.
[58] Erskine, *Inst.,* III, 1, 32.
[59] On the other hand, Lord Westbury's statement in *Fleeming* v. *Howden* (1868) 6 M. (H.L.) 113, at 121, that "an obligation to do an act with respect to property creates a trust" is too general; see *Bank of Scotland* v. *Liquidators of Hutchison, Main & Co.,* 1914 S.C. (H.L.) 1.
[60] See, e.g., *Stevenson* v. *Wilson,* 1907 S.C. 445; *National Bank of Scotland Nominee Co.* v. *Adamson,* 1932 S.L.T. 492.
[61] Stair, I, 13, 7.
[62] In English law the beneficiary is known as the cestui que trust.

consequently, of the beneficial interest, may be affected by the provision of the trust deed. If the truster has *directed* his trustees to sell the heritable property which is the subject of the trust and to make over the proceeds to the beneficiaries, then, as the truster's intention is that the beneficiaries shall receive not the heritage but the proceeds, the right of the beneficiaries is regarded as moveable, whether the sale has or has not been effected. This is known as constructive conversion. If, on the other hand, there is given to the trustees merely a *power* to sell, then until that power is exercised there is no conversion. So also if the right to sell is to arise only in case of necessity, or is limited to particular purposes, as, for example, to pay debts, or is not indispensable to the execution of the trust, then unless the necessity arises and is acted on, or after the particular purposes are answered, or if the sale is not indispensable, there is no change in the quality of the subjects.[63] The sale of heritage authorised by the Court on the ground of expediency will not effect conversion if this was not the truster's intention.[64]

If the effect of the directions in the trust deeds is constructively to convert the property, the beneficiaries (if capable of electing) may nevertheless, before there has been actual conversion, elect to take the property in its existing state. Thus, for example, where trustees, who are directed to sell heritage and pay the proceeds to A, have not effected a sale, it is open to A to intimate his intention to take the heritage rather than its price; and, as he could at once re-invest the price in the purchase of heritage, it would be futile to insist on a sale being carried out by the trustees. This is known as re-conversion. The election may be express or may be inferred from circumstances. It has been said that in order to effect re-conversion there must be either an overt act by the party in right of the succession or such lapse of time as, coupled with surrounding circumstances, imports unequivocally a determination to take the property as it stands.[65]

Where there is a direction in a will for conversion, this direction is held to have been given for the purposes of the will. It takes effect so far as is necessary to carry out these purposes. If, and in so far as, these purposes fail, the rights of those who are entitled to the estate independently of the will are not affected by the direction. The heir-at-law was entitled to the heritage which belonged to the testator unless it was effectually alienated in favour of others, and his right was not displaced merely by a direction to convert the heritage into moveable property. In *Cowan* v. *Cowan*[66] a testator directed his trustees to realise the whole estate but, beyond giving certain legacies, did not dispose of it in favour of anyone. The estate, therefore, fell into intestacy. It was held that the funds must be divided between the heir-at-law and the heirs in mobilibus in the proportions in which they had been derived from the heritable and moveable estate respectively as at the testator's death.

63 *Buchanan* v. *Angus* (1862) 4 Macq. 374; *Sheppard's Trs.* v. *Sheppard* (1885) 12 R. 1193; see also *Taylor's Trs.* v. *Tailyour*, 1927 S.C. 288.
64 *Taylor's Trs.* v. *Tailyour*, 1927 S.C. 288.
65 *Bryson's Tr.* v. *Bryson*, 1919, 2 S.L.T. 303, per Lord Sands; *Hogg* v. *Hamilton* (1877) 4 R. 845; M'Laren I, 237; *Mackintosh's Exr.* v. *Mackintosh*, 1925 S.L.T. 674.
66 (1887) 14 R. 670; *M'Conochie's Trs.* v. *M'Conochie*, 1912 S.C. 653.

12. Constitution of the Trust.—A trust may be constituted either by the act of the truster or by operation of law. No technical language is required for the creation of a trust.[67] A bequest to a person followed by precatory words expressive of the testator's wish or recommendation or confidence that the legatee will apply the subject bequeathed for behoof of other persons may be regarded as imposing a trust for this purpose on the legatee. Whether in such a case there is a trust depends on the intention of the testator as disclosed in the language of the bequest; and if it appears that that language, although not in form imperative, was intended to impose a duty on the legatee he will be deemed to be a trustee. A trust created in this way is known as a precatory trust.[68]

Where the purposes of a private trust[69] fail either in whole or in part, or if the purposes do not exhaust the trust-estate, then the estate, or so much of it as is not required for the trust purposes, must be accounted for to the creator of the trust or his representatives. In the case of a mortis causa trust, the truster being dead, the estate not required for the purposes of the trust will fall to be disposed of as part of the deceased's estate and will belong to his representatives or heirs; for example, if a testator by his trust-disposition and settlement conveys his estate to trustees with directions to settle the estate on his children and dies without leaving issue, the estate, in that event, would have to be accounted for to his heirs ab intestato. Where, on the other hand, the trust is an inter vivos one, the truster retains a reversionary interest in the trust-estate, which is called the "radical right" in the property. The truster is divested of his right in the funds conveyed in trust only in so far as these are required for carrying out the trust purposes; to the extent to which they are not so required they belong to the truster and are subject to his disposition. Thus, if in a marriage contract or other trust deed, funds are settled on the truster's issue, and there are no issue, then in the absence of any further trust purpose, the funds revert to the truster.[70] Where the trustees fail, the truster, in virtue of his radical right, may appoint new trustees.[71]

13. Revocability of Trust.—An inter vivos trust may or may not be revocable by the truster. If the trust is set up voluntarily for the purpose merely of the administration of the estate for behoof of the truster or if there are no other beneficiaries in existence, or if all the purposes in favour of these other beneficiaries are of a testamentary nature and are to take effect only on the truster's death, the trust is revocable. On the other hand, if the deed confers rights (and not mere spes successionis) on other parties, although these rights may not be vested but may be subject to contingencies, the terms of the deed thus show that it was intended that the trustees should hold the estate

---

[67] *Gillespie* v. *City of Glasgow Bank* (1878) 6 R. (H.L.) 104, per Earl Cairns, L.C., at p. 107; *Leitch* v. *Leitch*, 1927 S.C. 823.
[68] M'Laren, I, 345; *Garden's Exr.* v. *More*, 1913 S.C. 285.
[69] See Ch. XLV, § 7, infra, as to public trusts.
[70] *Smith* v. *Stuart* (1894) 22 R. 130; *Montgomery's Trs.* v. *Montgomery* (1895) 22 R. 824; *Higginbotham's Trs.* v. *Higginbotham* (1886) 13 R. 1016.
[71] *Glentanar* v. *Scottish Industrial Musical Association*, 1925 S.C. 226.

against the truster and the deed is regarded as irrevocable.[72] The question depends, however, on the terms and purposes of the trust deed, and in dubio a declaration that it is irrevocable will probably be decisive.[73] A marriage-contract may contain testamentary provisions, which are always revocable notwithstanding that the deed is declared to be irrevocable.[74] A truster may make himself the sole trustee of his own property but to make the trust irrevocable he must do something equivalent to delivery or transfer of the trust fund. Intimation to one of several beneficiaries will make the whole trust irrevocable[75]; as will, apparently, intimation to someone who was regarded as acting on behalf of the beneficiaries.[76]

14. Variation of Trusts.—At common law the powers of varying the purposes of a trust once it had taken effect, and where, in the case of inter vivos trusts, it could not be revoked by the truster, were very limited.[77] Where all the beneficiaries interested in the trust estate concur in asking the trustees to denude at a date prior to that contemplated by the truster, and if they are all legally capable of giving their consent, the trustees are bound to do so on being exonered and discharged.[78] But where by reason of non-age or otherwise one or more of the beneficiaries was incapable of giving his consent, or where there was a contingent right in unborn issue, the concurrence of all those interested in the trust estate could not be obtained. Furthermore, where one of the interests was an alimentary right properly constituted,[79] and accepted,[80] it could not at common law be renounced by the beneficiary as part of such an arrangement. The Trusts (Scotland) Act 1921 empowered the Court to authorise trustees to do certain acts although these were at variance with the terms or purposes of the trust, where expedient for its execution.[81] But it was not until the Act of 1961 that it became possible to surmount the common law obstacles to the formal variation of the purposes of the trust themselves.

Section 1 of the 1961 Act affords machinery whereby the Court may give effective approval to the variation of trust purposes on behalf of beneficiaries[82] who owing to non-age or other incapacity are incapable of assenting thereto, and may also authorise the variation or revocation of alimentary provisions. This machinery is invoked by means of a petition

---

[72] *Walker* v. *Amey* (1906) 8 F. 376; *Scott* v. *Scott*, 1930 S.C. 903; *Ross* v. *Ross's Trs.*, 1967 S.L.T. 12 (O.H.); *Campbell* v. *Campbell's Trs.*, 1967 S.L.T. (Notes) 30; *Bulkeley-Gavin's Trs.* v. *Bulkeley-Gavin's Trs.*, 1971 S.C. 209; *Lawrence* v. *Lawrence's Trs.*, 1974 S.L.T. 174. See § 14, infra.
[73] *Scott* v. *Scott*, supra.
[74] *Barclay's Trs.* v. *Watson* (1903) 5 F. 926; *Law*, 1962 S.C. 500.
[75] *Allan's Trs.* v. *Lord Advocate*, 1971 S.C. (H.L.) 45.
[76] *Clark's Trs.* v. *Inland Revenue*, 1972 S.C. 177.
[77] See Mackenzie Stuart, *Trusts*, pp. 346 et seq.
[78] See *Earl of Lindsay* v. *Shaw*, 1959 S.L.T. (Notes) 13, per Lord Justice-Clerk Thomson.
[79] Liferent and Fee, Ch. XL, supra, § 10.
[80] A renunciation before entering into enjoyment of the alimentary liferent is effective: *Douglas-Hamilton* v. *Duke and Duchess of Hamilton's Trs.*, 1961 S.C. 205.
[81] s. 5; see infra, § 19.
[82] See s. 1 (6); *Countess of Lauderdale*, 1962 S.C. 302.

presented to the Inner House of the Court of Session by the trustees or any of the beneficiaries.[83] Subsection (1) enables the Court to grant approval of an arrangement varying or revoking all or any of the trust purposes, or enlarging the powers of the trustees of managing or administering the estate,[84] on behalf of (a) any of the beneficiaries who by reason of non-age or other incapacity cannot assent, or (b) any person who may become a beneficiary at a future date,[85] or (c) any person as yet unborn; it is a condition of its granting approval that the Court should be of the opinion that the carrying out of the arrangement would not be prejudicial to the persons on behalf of whom its approval is sought.[86] The interests of such persons may be protected by insurance.[87] This may not be necessary if the liferenter has a power to appoint the fee which includes power to fix the date of vesting of the appointed shares,[88] or to protect negligible interests of remote beneficiaries.[89]

Under subsection (4) the Court may authorise an arrangement whereby alimentary provisions are varied or revoked and, it may be, replaced by other provisions which may dispose of the whole or part of the capital of the trust estate; but such an authorisation may only be granted if the arrangement is approved either by the alimentary beneficiary or by the Court on his behalf under subsection (1) and the Court is satisfied that the carrying out of the arrangement would be reasonable, having regard to the whole income of the alimentary beneficiary and any other material factors.[90] Applications under subsection (4) have been refused as unnecessary on the following grounds:— (a) that a liferenter was entitled ex proprio motu to renounce a contingent alimentary liferent[91]; (b) that the liferent had ceased to be alimentary[92]; and (c) that the liferent created by a wife in favour of herself by a post-nuptial marriage contract was not a valid alimentary liferent.[93] The Court will approve and authorise an arrangement under this section which is only made possible by the exercise of a power of appointment so long as the donee does not obtain any exclusive advantage thereby.[94]

---

[83] See the following cases for judicial observations on this procedure: *Colville*, 1962 S.C. 185; *Robertson*, 1962 S.C. 196; *Gibson's Tr.*, 1962 S.C. 204; *Findlay*, 1962 S.C. 210; *Tulloch's Trs.*, 1962 S.C. 245; also *Clarke's Trs.*, 1966 S.L.T. 249, re jurisdiction. Note that a declaration of irrevocability in an inter vivos trust deed does not preclude variation of its terms under this section: *Ommaney*, 1966 S.L.T. (Notes) 13.

[84] But see *Inglis*, 1965 S.L.T. 326.

[85] See *Buchan*, 1964 S.L.T. 51.

[86] The introduction of additional beneficiaries in a discretionary trust is prejudicial to the existing beneficiaries: *Margaret Jean Patricia Pollok-Morris*, 1969 S.L.T. (Notes) 60. As to prejudice to the beneficiaries, see also *John Sutherland Aikman*, 1968 S.L.T. 137.

[87] See *Robertson*, supra; cf. *Young's Trs.*, 1962 S.C. 293, where no insurance proposed and petition refused. Alternatively an appropriate fund may be set aside.

[88] See *Colville*, supra, and *Dick*, 1963 S.C. 598.

[89] *Phillips*, 1964 S.C. 141.

[90] *Gibson's Tr.*, 1962 S.C. 204; *Dick*, supra, per Lord President Clyde at p. 602; cf. *Bergius' Trs.*, 1963 S.C. 194, where liferent was contingent and application refused.

[91] *Findlay*, 1962 S.C. 210; *Smillie*, 1966 S.L.T. 41.

[92] *Strange*, 1966 S.L.T. 59; *Pearson*, 1968 S.C. 8; see also *Law*, 1962 S.C. 500, where the liferent had ceased to be alimentary on the death of the husband and the other provisions of an ante-nuptial marriage contract for which approval of variation was sought were testamentary and revocable by the wife. cf. *Sutherland*, 1968 S.C. 200.

[93] *Cargill*, 1965 S.C. 122.

[94] *Pelham Burn*, 1964 S.C. 3.

15. Proof of Trust.—In the case of testamentary trusts the existence and terms of the trust are almost invariably to be found recorded in some writing. But in inter vivos transactions there may be cases of trust which are not evidenced by any writ. A person may convey his estate to another in absolute terms but under a verbal agreement that it is to be held in trust; or property may be purchased by one party and by arrangement the title may be taken in the name of another who is to hold it not for his own benefit but for the benefit of the purchaser or subject to his directions. In such cases the ostensible owner of the property is truly merely a trustee for another. At one time the law allowed trusts to be established by parole evidence; but this was altered by the Blank Bonds and Trusts Act 1696 (c. 25),[95] which enacts that "no action of declarator of trust shall be sustained as to any deed of trust made for hereafter except upon a declaration or backband of trust lawfully subscribed by the person alleged to be the trustee and against whom or his heirs or assignees the declarator shall be intended, or unless the same be referred to the oath of party simpliciter." As regards this statute it is settled[96]—(1) that it applies only to actions by the truster or his representatives against the trustee or his representatives, and has no application in the case of third parties who may be affected by the trust or who may have an interest in establishing its existence; (2) that it applies only where the form of proceeding is that of a declarator of trust; (3) that it applies wherever there is a deed declaring in absolute terms that a right of property exists in one party, which right is claimed by another as being held in trust for him.[97] But where there is no such deed the Act does not apply. Hence where a person sought declarator that the sum contained in a deposit-receipt in the names of others truly belonged to him, proof at large was allowed on the ground that such a receipt was not a "deed of trust"[98]; (4) that it does not apply unless the absolute title to the property has been taken by the alleged trustee with the consent of the person who alleges that the property is held in trust for him; "the statute only applies when one man alleges that he has trusted another to take the title in his own name."[99] Thus if the title to property has been taken in name of one party through his own fraud and without the consent of the other the statute does not apply[99]; (5) that it does not apply unless a full right to the property, including the jus disponendi, is vested in the alleged trustee.[1] The Act has no application to cases based on mandate.[2] While there is authority to the effect that it is also inapplicable in questions between spouses,[3] this has not been followed in the more recent

---

[95] The occasion of this statute was the litigation between *Higgins* and *Callender* in (1696) M. 16182.

[96] See *Marshall* v. *Lyall* (1859) 21 D. 514; *Dunn* v. *Pratt* (1898) 25 R. 461; *Newton* v. *Newton*, 1923 S.C. 15.

[97] *Laird* v. *Laird & Rutherford* (1884) 12 R. 294, per Lord President Inglis, at p. 297.

[98] *Cairns* v. *Davidson*, 1913 S.C. 1054; *Beveridge* v. *Beveridge*, 1925 S.L.T. 234.

[99] Lord President Inglis in *Horne* v. *Morrison* (1877) 4 R. 977. See also *M'Connachie* v. *Geddes*, 1918 S.C. 391, and *Galloway* v. *Galloway*, 1929 S.C. 160.

[1] *M'Nair's Exix.* v. *Litster*, 1939 S.C. 72; *Weissenbruch* v. *Weissenbruch*, 1961 S.C. 340.

[2] *Dunn* v. *Pratt*, supra; *M'Connachie* v. *Geddes*, supra; *Galloway* v. *Galloway*, supra.

[3] *Anderson* v. *Anderson's Tr.* (1898) 6 S.L.T. 204; see also *Galloway*, supra, per Lord Justice-Clerk Alness, at p. 166.

cases in the Outer House.[4] It has been stated that the Act does not apply where a partner is alleged to hold property, heritable or moveable, on behalf of his firm[5]; but the sounder view appears to be that mandate or agency is excluded on the ground that it is not trust and that the Act applies to all actions of declarator of trust founded upon "a deed of trust."[6] The writing need not be probative: even unsigned holograph entries in business books have been held sufficient.[7] If the writing is unambiguous, it cannot be qualified or varied by parole evidence.[8]

When the fact that property is held in trust has been admitted or proved by writ or oath, the terms and purposes of the trust may be proved by parole.[9]

16. Trusts Arising by Operation of Law.—Besides those cases in which a trust is constituted either expressly or impliedly by the actings of parties, there are circumstances in which the law imposes on a person the duties and liabilities which attach to a trustee expressly appointed. The trust in such cases arises by operation of law. Thus where a trustee has acquired any property or benefit which (although not part of the estate to which the trust under which he acts expressly attaches) he is not entitled to retain for his own benefit but must communicate to the beneficiaries under that trust, he is regarded as holding this property or benefit subject to a trust for behoof of these beneficiaries.[10] Similarly a stranger to the trust, who obtains property belonging to the trust in circumstances which do not permit of his withholding it from the beneficiaries under the trust, is regarded as a trustee, i.e., as subject to the duty of restoring it to the trust. In both of these cases the trust is known as a "constructive" trust and is created by the operation of the law and not by any intention on the part of the parties concerned that a trust shall be constituted. It is, however, to trusts expressly or impliedly constituted that the great body of trust law relates; and it is to such trusts that attention is mainly devoted in the following sections of this chapter.

17. Acceptance of Office: Assumption and Resignation of Trustees.—No one can be compelled to accept office as a trustee. Acceptance may be proved in any form—by written or verbal acceptance—and may be inferred from the fact that the person has acted as trustee. It is a question of fact whether the office has or has not been accepted.

The estate and office vest in the trustees jointly where more than one is appointed; and, in the absence of anything to the contrary in the trust deed, the right of survivorship is implied; so that if a trustee dies the ownership and

---

[4] *Inglis* v. *Smyth's Exix.*, 1959 S.L.T. (Notes) 78; *Weissenbruch*, supra; *Adam*, infra.
[5] *Forrester* v. *Robson's Trs.* (1875) 2 R. 755, per Lord Justice-Clerk Moncreiff, at p. 759; *Galloway*, supra, per Lord Justice-Clerk Alness, at p. 167.
[6] *Laird* v. *Laird & Rutherford* (1884) 12 R. 294; *Adam* v. *Adam*, 1962 S.L.T. 332; Bell, *Prin.*, § 1995 (1), note (1). As to what is a "deed of trust," see dissenting opinion of Lord Kinnear in *Dunn* v. *Pratt* (1898) 25 R. 461, at p. 469.
[7] *Thomson* v. *Lindsay* (1873) 1 R. 65.
[8] *Pickard* v. *Pickard*, 1963 S.L.T. 56.
[9] *Livingstone* v. *Allan* (1900) 3 F. 233, per Lord President Kinross.
[10] See *Laird* v. *Laird* (1858) 20 D. 972. See infra, § 20 (3rd par.).

administration of the trust remain with the survivors. The law reads into all trusts (unless the contrary be expressed) a provision that a majority of the accepting and surviving trustees shall be a quorum.[11] There is also tacitly included a power to the trustee, if there be only one, or to the quorum, to assume new trustees[12]; and a statutory form of assumption which may be used for the assumption of new trustees is given in the 1921 Act.[13]

There is further included in all trusts, unless the contrary is expressed in the trust deed, a power to any trustee to resign office.[14] But a sole trustee is not entitled to resign unless he has assumed new trustees who have accepted office, or new trustees or a judicial factor have been appointed by the Court.[14] A conveyance to named persons and the heir of the last survivor as trustees entitles the heir to act as trustee.[15] Moreover, a trustee who has accepted a legacy bequeathed on condition that he accepts office or who is appointed on the footing of receiving remuneration for his services may not resign unless it is otherwise provided in the trust deed; but such trustees may apply to the Court for authority to resign. The effect of resignation is that the resigning trustee is divested of the trust-estate, which thereupon accrues to the remaining trustees without the necessity for any conveyance thereof.[16] If the trustee who resigns, or the representatives of a deceased trustee, cannot obtain a discharge from the remaining trustees and the beneficiaries refuse, or are unable, to grant a discharge, a petition may be presented to the Court for a judicial discharge.[17] And where the body of trustees are unable otherwise to get exoneration they may for this purpose bring an action of multiplepoinding, the rule which requires double distress as the ground of this action being in this case relaxed.[18]

18. Removal of Trustees.—Under the common law the Court has power to remove a trustee from office. But the Court is reluctant to exercise this power unless the trustee has been guilty of malversation of office or has shown by his conduct that he is unfit to discharge its duties[19]; in cases where there has been merely disagreement between the trustees, or the trustee has in good faith committed some irregularity or breach of trust, these circumstances have not been deemed sufficient to require that the trustee should be removed.[20] There is statutory provision for the cases where a trustee is either insane or incapable of acting by reason of mental or physical disability, or has been absent from

---

[11] Trusts (Scotland) Act 1921 (11 & 12 Geo. V, c. 58), s. 3 (c).
[12] Ibid., s. 3 (b).
[13] Ibid., s. 21.
[14] Ibid., s. 3 (a); see also s. 19. At common law trustees had no power to resign.
[15] *Glasgow Western Infirmary* v. *Cairns*, 1944 S.C. 488. See as to the machinery for formal recognition of the character of the heir, *Harry J. C. R. Skinner*, 1976 S.L.T. 60.
[16] 1921 Act, s. 3 (a); see also s. 20.
[17] Ibid., s. 18.
[18] *Taylor* v. *Noble* (1836) 14 S. 817; M'Laren's *Court of Session Practice*, 666.
[19] *Cherry* v. *Patrick*, 1910 S.C. 32; *Stewart* v. *Chalmers* (1904) 7 F. 163; *MacGilchrist* v. *MacGilchrist's Trs.*, 1930 S.C. 635.
[20] *Gilchrist's Trs.* v. *Dick* (1883) 11 R. 22; *Hope* v. *Hope* (1884) 12 R. 27. In *Taylor*, 1932 S.C. 1, where there was a deadlock owing to the two trustees disagreeing, the Court appointed an additional trustee.

the United Kingdom continuously for a period of at least six months.[21] In the case of incapacity it is enacted that the trustee shall be removed on the application of a co-trustee or beneficiary or anyone interested in the trust-estate; and on a like application the absent trustee may be removed.

In the case of such disability or absence of the person who is the sole trustee, or where trustees cannot be assumed under a trust deed, the Court may, in terms of section 22 of the 1921 Act, appoint a new trustee. This section comprehends all cases in which the trust cannot be kept up by means of powers within the trust deed.[22] A trust does not fail although all the trustees nominated in the trust deed should decline office or become unable to act; and under the common law the Court could, where necessary, appoint a trustee.[23] The statutory power does not exclude this power.[24] The Court has also power to appoint a judicial factor on a trust-estate, who administers the estate under the supervision of the Accountant of Court and in accordance with the provisions of the Judicial Factors Acts.[25]

19. Administration of the Trust: Powers and Duties of Trustees.—It is the duty of the trustee to administer the estate in accordance with the directions given by the truster. He must do what he is enjoined to do so far as it is lawful and possible. He may do what he is authorised by the truster to do; and he must refrain from doing what the truster has forbidden him to do. In many respects his duty coincides with that of an executor: thus he is bound to ingather the estate with due dispatch, pay the debts of the truster, and when the time for distribution of the estate arrives distribute it as may be directed in the trust deed.

Certain general powers are conferred on trustees by section 4 of the Trusts (Scotland) Act 1921.[26] These powers, which may be exercised where such acts are "not at variance with the terms or purposes of the trust,"[27] include, inter alia, those of selling, feuing, excambing or granting leases of any duration of the heritable estate; of borrowing money on the security of the trust estate; and of acquiring with the trust funds any interest in residential accommodation reasonably required to enable the trustees to provide a suitable residence for occupation by any of the beneficiaries.[28] Where the trustees enter into a transaction in the purported exercise of certain of these powers, in particular with regard to heritage, the validity of the transaction and of any title acquired by the second party under it cannot be challenged by the second party or any other person on the ground that the act in question was in fact at

---

[21] 1921 Act, s. 23.
[22] *Graham* (1868) 6 M. 958, per Lord President Inglis.
[23] *Campbell* v. *Campbell* (1752) M. 16203; *Grant* (1790) M. 7454.
[24] *M'Aslan* (1841) 3 D. 1263; *Glasgow* (1844) 7 D. 178; *Aikman* (1881) 9 R. 213; *Lamont* v. *Lamont*, 1908 S.C. 1033.
[25] See infra, § 25.
[26] As amended by the 1961 Act, s. 4.
[27] See, as to the meaning of this expression, *Marquis of Lothian's C.B.*, 1927 S.C. 579, at 585; *Leslie's J.F.*, 1925 S.C. 464; *Cunningham's Tutrix*, 1949 S.C. 275; *Christie's Trs.*, 1946 S.L.T. 309; *Bristow*, 1965 S.L.T. 225.
[28] s. 4 (*ee*), added by 1961 Act.

variance with the terms or purposes of the trust[29]; a purchaser of heritage from trustees, for example, is completely protected by this provision and need not look behind the purported exercise of the power under section 4. But this provision affords only a limited protection to the trustees themselves, for it leaves open any question of liability between them and co-trustees or the beneficiaries.[30] Where the trustees wish to exercise any of the powers listed in section 4 but the act in question would or might be at variance with the terms or purposes of the trust, they may present an application to the Court under section 5; under that section the Court is empowered to grant authority to the trustees to do any of these acts notwithstanding that such act is at variance with the terms or purposes of the trust, on being satisfied that such act is in all the circumstances expedient for the execution of the trust.[31] It is also provided that the Court may, under certain circumstances, authorise an advance of part of the capital of a fund destined either absolutely or contingently to beneficiaries who are not of full age.[32]

In certain cases also trustees who desire to exercise powers which neither the settlement[33] nor the statute provide may apply for authority to the Court in the exercise of the nobile officium, as, for example, for authority to make advances to major beneficiaries.[34] Cases of this kind are exceptional and cannot be classified; but the nobile officium has been exercised to supply the deficiency "where something administrative or executive is wanting in the constituting document to enable the trust purposes to be effectually carried out,"[35] or where there was an obvious casus improvisus under the scheme of the trust or to relieve the trust of conditions which made it unworkable or tended to defeat its purpose,[36] or, in the case of trusts subject to the jurisdiction of a foreign court, to facilitate by means of an auxiliary jurisdiction the carrying out of an order of the foreign court.[37] Trustees have no power to buy heritage, other than as residential accommodation for the use of the beneficiaries,[38] unless given by the trust instrument, but in very special circumstances they may be given power through the nobile officium.[39] While the Court has power in the exercise of the nobile officium to give retrospective sanction to ultra vires acts of administration by trustees, this power will only be exercised in exceptional circumstances and for compelling reasons[40]; and, where the trustees have acted contrary to the express terms of the trust or an

---

[29] 1961 Act, s. 2 (1).
[30] 1961 Act, s. 2 (2); see *Barclay* (*Mason's C.B.*), 1962 S.C. 594.
[31] This section does not apply to trusts constituted by private or local Acts of Parliament; see *Church of Scotland General Trustees*, 1931 S.C. 704.
[32] 1921 Act, s. 16; *Macfarlane* v. *Macfarlane's Trs.*, 1931 S.C. 95; *Craig's Trs.*, 1934 S.C. 34; *Anderson's Trs.*, 1957 S.L.T. (Notes) 5.
[33] *Moss's Trustees*, 1952 S.C. 523.
[34] *Frew's Trs.*, 1932 S.C. 501; *Craig's Trs.*, supra.
[35] *Anderson's Trs.*, 1932 S.C. 226.
[36] *Hall's Trs.* v. *M'Arthur*, 1918 S.C. 646; see also observations in *Gibson's Trs.*, 1933 S.C. 190.
[37] *Lipton's Trs.*, 1943 S.C. 521; *Campbell-Wyndham-Long's Trs.*, 1951 S.C. 685.
[38] 1921 Act, s. 4 (*ee*), added by 1961 Act.
[39] *Fletcher's Trs.*, 1949 S.C. 330.
[40] *Dow's Trs.*, 1947 S.C. 524; *East Kilbride District Nursing Assn.*, 1951 S.C. 64; *Horne's Trs.*, 1952 S.C. 70 (application in each case refused).

interlocutor of the Court, retrospective approval will usually be refused.[41] If trustees, or any one of their number, desire to place the trust under the administration of the Accountant of Court, an application may be made to the Court for this purpose.[42] The superintendence of the Accountant is limited, however, to the administration of the trust in so far as it relates to the investment of the trust funds and the distribution thereof among the creditors interested and the beneficiaries under the trust.[43]

Trustees under a trust deed as defined by the Trusts (Scotland) Act 1921[44] may obtain from the Court directions on questions relating to the investment, distribution, management or administration of the trust-estate, or as to the exercise of any power vested in, or as to the performance of any duty imposed on them.[45]

Where discretionary powers are conferred on trustees the Court cannot, unless definite and precise averments of bad faith can be made, review or even examine the grounds on which trustees have exercised their discretion.[46] The question whether the discretionary powers are given only to the original trustees or, on the other hand, can be exercised by assumed trustees depends on the terms of the deed, but the tendency of the recent decisions is to hold that they may be so exercised unless they are given in terms which clearly disclose a delectus personae.[47] Where a power of selection amongst charities is not expressly or impliedly given to named trustees personally, it may probably be exercised by assumed trustees, but not by a judicial factor, between whom and the testator there is no real nexus.[47]

20. Auctor in Rem Suam.—Apart from what is to be found in the trust deed or in the statutory provisions, there are certain principles recognised by the common law as regulating the administration of trusts and binding all trustees. Thus it has long been established that the trustee must not be auctor in rem suam; that is to say, he must not place himself in a situation in which his interest as an individual may conflict with his duty as a trustee.[48] It is a rule of universal application that a person having fiduciary duties to discharge (as, for example, an executor, guardian, judicial factor, agent, promoter or director of a company as well as a trustee in the strict sense) is not allowed to enter into engagements in which he has or can have a personal interest conflicting, or which may possibly conflict, with the interest of those whom he is bound to protect; and so strictly is this principle enforced that no question

---

[41] But see *Campbell-Wyndham-Long's Trs.*, 1962 S.C. 132.
[42] 1921 Act, s. 17.
[43] *Coulson* v. *Murison's Trs.*, 1920 S.C. 322 (the law as to the competency of an application by one trustee is now altered); *Liddell's Trs,* v. *Liddell*, 1929 S.L.T. 169; *Donaldson's Trs.*, 1932 S.L.T. 463.
[44] In *Leven Penny Savings Bank, Petitioners,* 1948 S.C. 147, the petitioning trustees failed to bring their trust deed within the definition.
[45] Administration of Justice (Scotland) Act 1933 (23 & 24 Geo. V, c. 41), s. 17 (vi); Rules of Court (1965) Ch. IV, Rules 232-233; *Peel's Tr.* v. *Drummond*, 1936 S.C. 786.
[46] *MacTavish* v. *Reid's Trs.* (1904) 12 S.L.T. 404.
[47] *Angus's Exx.* v. *Batchan's Trs.*, 1949 S.C. 335; but see *Leith's J.F.* v. *Leith*, 1957 S.C. 307.
[48] *Aberdeen Ry.* v. *Blaikie Brothers* (1854) 1 Macq. 461. See also *The York Buildings Co.* v. *Mackenzie* (1795) 3 Pat. 378; *Hamilton* v. *Wright* (1842) 1 Bell's App. 574; *Huntingdon* v. *Henderson* (1877) 4 R. 294, per Lord Young; *Wright* v. *Morgan* [1926] A.C. 788.

is allowed to be raised as to the fairness or unfairness of a contract so entered into.[49] It is not necessary to prove that the trustee obtained some advantage in the transaction. "It is quite enough that the thing which he does has a tendency to injure the trust, a tendency to interfere with his duty."[49]

Hence, under this rule, a sale of trust property by trustees to, or a loan by them to, one of their number (however fair the terms of the transaction may have been) are all open to challenge at the instance of the beneficiary.[50] The transaction is not indeed void, but is voidable.[51] The rule is not, however, extended to the case of a trustee buying from a beneficiary his interest in the trust property. This is not forbidden to the trustee, but the law casts upon him the onus of proving that he gave full value and that all necessary information was afforded to the beneficiary at the time of the sale.[52]

It is also settled that a trustee may not make profit out of his office, unless this is authorised by the truster or agreed to by all the beneficiaries.[53] If a trustee, for example, acts as solicitor or factor for the trust, or manages a business on its behalf, he is not entitled to any remuneration for his services unless such authority or consent is given.[54] Nor is a trustee permitted to make profit for himself by means of his office. Whenever a person holding a fiduciary position gains by reason of availing himself of that position any advantage he must communicate that advantage to the trust. As already mentioned, the law regards him as holding the advantage as constructive trustee for behoof of the beneficiaries.[55] Thus in *Wilsons* v. *Wilson*[56] a tutor who renounced the lease of a farm held for behoof of the pupils, and obtained a lease in his own name was held bound to account to the pupils for all the profits which he had obtained from the farm under the lease in his own favour. In *Magistrates of Aberdeen* v. *University of Aberdeen*,[57] the town council purchased from themselves certain lands which they held as trustees. Afterwards they applied to the Crown for a grant of the salmon fishing opposite these lands on the representation that they were the owners of these lands, and obtained the grant. It was decided that the town council still held the lands in trust, and that moreover, as they had obtained the grant of the fishing in virtue of their possession of these lands they were bound to hold the fishing as trustees for the benefit of the trust.

So, if a trustee in breach of his duty employs funds belonging to the trust in trade, although any loss thereby incurred must be made good by him to the

---

[49] *Hamilton* v. *Wright*, supra, per Lord Brougham.
[50] *Ritchies* v. *Ritchies' Trs.* (1888) 15 R. 1086; *Croskery* v. *Gilmour's Trs.* (1890) 17 R. 697. A creditor of the beneficiary is also entitled to challenge the transaction—*Meff* v. *Smith's Trs.*, 1930 S.N. 162.
[51] *Fraser* v. *Hankey & Co.* (1847) 9 D. 415.
[52] *Dougan* v. *Macpherson* (1902) 4 F. (H.L.) 7.
[53] *Sleigh* v. *Sleigh's J.F.*, 1908 S.C. 1112; *A.B.'s Curator Bonis*, 1927 S.C. 902; *Williams* v. *Barton* [1927] 2 Ch. 9.
[54] *Mackie* v. *Mackie's Trs.* (1875) 2 R. 312; *Mills* v. *Brown's Trs.* (1901) 3 F. 1012. If a truster empowers his trustees to appoint one of their number as law agent, this implies that he may be remunerated by the trust; *Lewis' Trs.* v. *Pirie*, 1912 S.C. 574.
[55] See § 16, supra.
[56] (1789) M. 16376. See also *M'Niven* v. *Peffers* (1868) 7 M. 181.
[57] (1877) 4 R. (H.L.) 48.

estate, any profit earned may be claimed by the beneficiaries; it is not enough that he makes the funds forthcoming with any interest that might have been obtained from proper trust investments.[58]

The law requires further that the trustee shall act in the administration of the trust with a due measure of prudence and diligence. He is bound to exercise that degree of diligence in the exercise of his office which a man of ordinary prudence would exercise in the management of his own private affairs.[59] His responsibility is tested by this average standard and not by reference to the intelligence or prudence exhibited by the particular trustee in the management of his own affairs. If the trustee fails to administer the estate with the required degree of care he is guilty of negligence and may be made liable for loss occasioned through his negligence.

21. Investment of Trust Funds.—One of the usual duties of trustees is to find suitable investments for the trust funds. Trust deeds commonly contain clauses specifying the investments which the trustees may make; sometimes it is provided that the trustees may retain stocks in which the truster has already invested, and a general power to do so authorises the trustees to keep these stocks.[60] General provision is also made by the Trustee Investments Act 1961[61] for the investment by trustees of the trust funds in their hands unless specially prohibited by the constitution or terms of the trust[62]; the powers contained in the Act are in addition to and not in derogation from any special power of investment which may otherwise have been conferred on the trustees.[63] The Act divides the investments in which the trustees have authority to place the funds into three categories[64]: narrower-range investments not requiring advice (e.g., defence bonds, national savings certificates, trustee savings bank deposits), narrower-range investments requiring advice (e.g., gilt-edged and certain other fixed-interest securities, debentures and other deposits), and wider-range investments (which always require advice, and include equity shares, shares in building societies and unit trusts). Where advice is required, trustees must obtain and consider proper advice given or confirmed in writing by a person who is reasonably believed to be qualified to give such advice by his ability and experience of financial matters.[65] When the trustees wish to place trust funds in wider-range investments, they must divide the trust estate into two parts of equal value as at the time of the division. The first part must be confined to narrower-range investments, and while property falling into the second part may be invested in wider-range investments the division is permanent; no transfer may be made from one part of the fund to the other unless a compensating transfer is

[58] *Cochrane* v. *Black* (1855) 17 D. 321; *Laird* v. *Laird* (1855) 17 D. 984; (1858) 20 D. 972.
[59] *Buchanan* v. *Eaton*, 1911 S.C. (H.L.) 40; *Raes* v. *Meek* (1889) 16 R. (H.L.) 31; *Knox* v. *MacKinnon* (1888) 15 R. (H.L.) 83.
[60] *Robinson* v. *Fraser's Trs.* (1881) 8 R. (H.L.) 127, per Lord Watson, at p. 138.
[61] 9 & 10 Eliz. II, c. 62.
[62] See s. 1 (3).
[63] s. 3 and Second Sched.
[64] First Sched.
[65] s. 6 (4), (5).

made at the same time.[66] The investments mentioned in the trust deed and those mentioned in the statute (unless excluded by the trust deed) are authorised investments. The Court will normally refuse to widen trustees' powers of investment, whether in the course of a variation by means of a cy près scheme or by giving its approval to an arrangement under the Trusts (Scotland) Act 1961, beyond those authorised in the original deed and by the statute.[67]

It is the duty of trustees to confine themselves to these authorised investments[68]; to make investments outside them is a breach of trust. But their duty goes further than this. Within the class of authorised investments they must exercise discretion in selecting their investments, and must avoid those which are attended with hazard.[68] If a trustee makes the investment negligently or in bad faith he will be held responsible for loss thereby occasioned to the trust-estate. In the exercise of his powers of investment under the statute it is the trustee's duty to have regard to the need for diversification of investments, and to the suitability of proposed investments to the particular trust, and to obtain and consider advice where it is required.[69] And it has been clearly laid down that despite directions by a settlor to retain investments, it is the duty of trustees, where necessary for the safety of the trust, to sell those investments.[70]

In the cases of loans on the security of heritage a trustee is not chargeable with breach of trust by reason only of the proportion borne by the amount of the loan to the value of the property at the time of the loan, provided (a) that the trustee acted upon a report as to the value of the property made by an able, practical valuator instructed and employed independently of any owner of the property, and (b) that the amount of the loan by itself or in combination with prior or pari passu loans does not exceed two-thirds of the reported value.[71] If a heritable security for money lent by a trustee would have been a proper investment for a less sum than was advanced by him, the trustee is liable only for the excess with interest.[72]

22. Breach of Trust: Beneficiary's Remedies.—A trustee who has been guilty of a breach of trust may be required to make good all the loss thereby occasioned to the estate. Where the breach consists of an unauthorised investment of trust funds, the beneficiaries may either adopt the investment or may repudiate it and have the sum invested restored to the trust with interest.[73] If the breach consists of the employment of the trust funds for his private purposes, the trustee may be required to account for the capital and

[66] s. 2.
[67] *Mitchell Bequest Trs.*, 1959 S.C. 395; *Inglis*, 1965 S.L.T. 326.
[68] *Learoyd* v. *Whiteley* (1887) 12 App.Cas. 727, per Lord Watson, at p. 733; *Brownlie* v. *Brownlie's Trs.* (1879) 6 R. 1233, per Lord President Inglis, at p. 1236.
[69] Trustee Investments Act 1961, s. 6.
[70] *Thomson's Trs.* v. *Davidson*, 1947 S.C. 654.
[71] 1921 Act, s. 30; *Boyd* v. *Greig*, 1913, 1 S.L.T. 398; *Shaw* v. *Cates* [1909] 1 Ch. 389.
[72] 1921 Act, s. 29.
[73] *Douglas* v. *Douglas's Trs.* (1864) 2 M. 1379; *Cochrane* v. *Black* (1855) 17 D. 321; *Laird* v. *Laird* (1885) 17 D. 984.

also, at the option of the beneficiary, either for the profit he has made by its use, or for interest at a rate fixed by the Court.[73] For breach of trust the trustees are jointly and severally liable, and one or more of them may be sued without calling all of them.[74]

Moreover, the beneficiary has a right to "follow the trust property" as against the trustee or his creditors or others claiming through him; that is to say, if the trustee has, in breach of his trust, parted with trust property—whether it be money or specific items—or has converted it into some other form, that property, or the property into which it has been converted, may be claimed as belonging to the trust. "All property belonging to a trust, however much it may be changed or altered in its nature or character, and all the fruits of such property, whether in its original or in its altered state, continues to be subject to, or affected by, the trust."[75] There are, however, limitations on this right to follow the property. It cannot be asserted against one who has acquired the property for value in good faith and without notice of the trust[76]; and it is necessary that the property which the beneficiary claims to follow can be traced and identified either as having been acquired with, or as representing, the original trust estate or some part of it.[77]

So, if a trustee mixes the trust funds with his own money, the Court will separate the trust from the private moneys and will award the former specifically to the beneficiaries. This principle has been applied to those in a fiduciary position, although not trustees in the ordinary sense. Thus, where a law agent, who had, without the knowledge of his client, sold shares which she had entrusted to him and lodged the price in his bank account, subsequently became bankrupt, a sum equivalent to the amount of the price of the shares was, by order of the Court, taken out of the sequestration and restored to the client.[78]

Where trust moneys are thus mixed with the trustee's private funds, and the trustee thereafter draws cheques on the account for his own purposes, the rule of Clayton's Case[79] does not apply in a question between the trustee and the beneficiary. Although the trust funds may have been paid in first, it is assumed that the trustee meant to act honestly and he is taken to have drawn out his own money rather than that belonging to the trust,[80] unless the circumstances exclude this assumption, as in the case where, after the trust

---

[74] Allen v. M'Combie's Trs., 1909 S.C. 710.

[75] Pennell v. Deffel (1853) 4 De G. M. & G. 372, per Turner, L.J., at p. 388; Re Hallett's Estate (1879) 13 Ch.D. 696; Sinclair v. Brougham [1914] A.C. 398; Banque Belge v. Hambrouck [1921] 1 K.B. 321; Taylor v. Forbes & Co. (1830) 4 W. & S. 444; Magistrates of Airdrie v. Smith (1850) 12 D. 1222. See also Aluminium Industrie Vaassen B.V. v. Romalpa Aluminium [1976] 1 W.L.R. 676.

[76] Somervails v. Redfearn (1813) 1 Dow 50 (the facts of which are stated in Moveable Property—Incorporeal, Ch. XXXVIII, supra, § 8); London and Canadian Loan and Agency Co. v. Duggan [1893] A.C. 506; see also Thomson v. Clydesdale Bank (1893) 20 R. (H.L.) 59; Bertram Gardner & Co's Tr. v. King's Remembrancer, 1920 S.C. 555, per Lord Skerrington, at 562. See also Trusts (Scotland) Act 1961, s. 2 (1), for sale of heritage at variance with the terms or purposes of the trust; § 19 supra.

[77] Re Hallett's Estate, supra; Bell, Comm., I, 286, 295, 296; James Roscoe (Bolton), Ltd. v. Winder [1915] 1 Ch. 62.

[78] Jopp v. Johnston's Tr. (1904) 6 F. 1028; Macadam v. Martin's Tr. (1872) 11 M. 33.

[79] See Extinction of Obligations, Ch. XV, supra, § 7.

[80] Re Hallett's Estate, supra.

funds are paid into bank, the whole of the moneys in the bank account are drawn out before further money is paid in.[81]

23. Breach of Trust: Protection to Trustees against Liability therefor.— There is not infrequently to be found in trust deeds a clause designed to alleviate the responsibility of the trustees in the administration of the estate. Thus, in the case of *Knox* v. *Mackinnon*[82] it was declared that the trustees "should not be liable for omissions, errors or neglect of management, nor singuli in solidum, but each shall be liable for his own actual intromissions only." It was held that clauses of this kind do not protect against positive breach of duty. Lord Watson observed: "I see no reason to doubt that a clause conceived in these or similar terms will afford a considerable measure of protection to trustees who have bona fide abstained from closely superintending the administration of the trust or who have committed mere errors of judgment while acting with a single eye to the benefit of the trust and of the persons whom it concerns; but it is settled in the law of Scotland that such a clause is ineffectual to protect a trustee against the consequences of culpa lata, or of gross negligence on his part, or of any conduct which is inconsistent with bona fides. I think it is equally clear that the clause will afford no protection to trustees who, from motives however laudable in themselves, act in plain violation of the duty which they owe to the individuals beneficially interested in the funds which they administer."

The 1921 Act contains the following provisions relative to the protection of the trustees. By section 3 it is provided that all trusts, unless the contrary be expressed, shall be held to include a provision that each trustee shall be liable only for his own acts and intromissions and shall not be liable for the acts and intromissions of co-trustees and shall not be liable for omissions; but this section does not afford protection to a trustee who neglects his duties or who authorises or acquiesces in breaches of trust committed by his co-trustees.

Again, where a trustee has committed a breach of trust at the instigation or request or with the consent in writing of a beneficiary, it is provided that the Court may, if it thinks fit, order that all or any part of the interest of that beneficiary shall be applied in indemnifying the trustee.[83] This section does not give the trustee a right to be indemnified but leaves the matter to the decision of the Court, and to raise a case for indemnity the beneficiary must have known the facts which made what was done a breach of trust and his concurrence must have been "clear and direct."[84]

Lastly, the 1921 Act introduced two new provisions borrowed from the law of England.[85] If it appears to the Court that a trustee who has committed a breach of trust has acted honestly and reasonably and ought fairly to be excused for the breach of trust, then the Court may relieve the trustee from

---

[81] *Roscoe* v. *Winder* [1915] 1 Ch. 62; *Re Stenning* [1895] 2 Ch. 433.
[82] (1888) 15 R. (H.L.) 83; *Ferguson* v. *Paterson* (1900) 2 F. (H.L.) 37; see also *Inglis*, 1965 S.L.T. 326.
[83] 1921 Act, s. 31.
[84] *Henderson* v. *Henderson's Trs.* (1900) 2 F. 1295.
[85] These provisions now appear in ss. 4 and 61 of the Trustee Act 1925 (15 & 16 Geo. V, c. 19).

personal liability[86]; and a trustee is not liable for breach of trust merely by continuing to hold an investment which has ceased to be an authorised investment.[87]

The following obligations of a trustee are imprescriptible:—(a) the obligation to produce accounts of his intromissions with any of the trust property; (b) the obligation to make reparation or restitution in respect of any fraudulent breach of trust to which the trustee was party or was privy; (c) the obligation to make furthcoming to any person entitled thereto any trust property, or the proceeds of any such property, in the possession of the trustee, or to make good the value of any such property previously received by the trustee and appropriated to his own use.[88] The obligation of a third party to make furthcoming to any party entitled thereto any trust property received by the third party otherwise than in good faith and in his possession is also imprescriptible. It would seem that a trustee's obligation to make reparation for an ultra vires or negligent breach of trust is subject to the quinquennial prescription.[89]

24. Trustees: Liability to Creditors.—For debts incurred by the truster trustees are not liable beyond the amount of the trust-estate. But if the trustees contract debts or incur liabilities in the course of their administration, they are personally liable for these in a question with the creditors, unless the creditors transacted with them on the terms that the trust-estate alone was to be responsible. Accordingly if trustees choose to continue the truster's, or enter into another, business, they are personally liable to the trade creditors[90]; and if they conduct an unsuccessful litigation they are, as a general rule, so liable in expenses to the successful litigant.[91] But in entering into a contract it is open to the trustees in the general case to stipulate that the trust-estate alone shall be liable, and this stipulation may be effectual. Thus in one case[92] where trustees borrowed money on a heritable bond in which they bound themselves "as trustees" it was held that their liability was limited to the amount of the trust-estate. The nature of the transaction may, however, be such as to prevent any effective limitation of their liability, as is exemplified in the case of trustees being registered as the proprietors of shares of a company incorporated under the Companies Acts. As shareholders, the trustees are and must be personally liable, for it is not within the power of a company to differentiate between those shareholders who are trustees and those who are not, to the effect of enabling the former to hold on any other terms than would apply if the holders were individuals holding for their own behoof.[93] In Scotland trusts

[86] s. 32; *Clarke* v. *Clarke's Trs.*, 1925 S.C. 693; *Re Allsop* [1914] 1 Ch. 1.
[87] s. 33; *Re Pauling's Settlement Trusts (Younghusband* v. *Coutts & Co.)* [1964] 1 Ch. 303.
[88] Prescription and Limitation (Scotland) Act 1973, Sched. 3.
[89] Ibid., Sched. 1 para. 1 (*d*).
[90] *Ford & Sons* v. *Stephenson* (1888) 16 R. 24.
[91] *Anderson* v. *Anderson's Tr.* (1901) 4 F. 96.
[92] *Gordon* v. *Campbell* (1842) 1 Bell's Apps. 428; see *Brown* v. *Sutherland* (1875) 2 R. 615.
[93] *Lumsden* v. *Buchanan* (1865) 3 M. (H.L.) 89; *Muir* v. *City of Glasgow Bank* (1879) 6 R. (H.L.) 21.

may be noticed in the register of the company,[94] but notice of the trust, while it may be useful as earmarking the shares for the trust, does not affect the liability of the trustees. While the trustees as shareholders are personally liable, they are entitled to be indemnified out of the trust-estate, unless they were in breach of trust in holding the shares.[95]

Under section 76 of the Companies Act 1948[96] executors are enabled to transfer shares belonging to the deceased without being registered as the holders of the shares, and may thus avoid incurring the risk of personal liability.

III. JUDICIAL FACTORS

25. Grounds of Appointment.—The Court of Session has long been in use, in the exercise of the nobile officium, to appoint judicial factors to manage and administer estates in cases where this is necessary to afford protection against loss or injustice which cannot be prevented by means of the ordinary legal remedies. No limit can be set to the circumstances in which this power may be exercised[97]; but the more familiar instances of such appointments are:—(1) The appointment of a factor on a trust-estate, as, e.g., where there is a total failure of trustees, or there has been misconduct on their part, or where there is a deadlock in the administration of the trust.[98] (2) The appointment of a factor on the estate of a deceased person in terms of section 163 of the Bankruptcy (Scotland) Act 1913,[99] or under section 14 of that Act on an estate sequestrated or threatened with sequestration pending the appointment of a trustee in the sequestration. (3) The appointment of a factor loco tutoris on the estate of a pupil without guardians,[1] or of a curator bonis to minors or persons who, by reason of mental or physical incapacity, are unable to manage, or provide for the management of, their property.[2] (4) The appointment of a factor loco absentis on the property of an absent person either where he is ignorant of his interests, or these are unprotected, or where the interests of third parties require that the appointment shall be made.[3] (5) The appointment of a factor on partnership estates.[4] (6) The appointment of a factor on property which is the subject of judicial competition, where circumstances render it expedient that provision should be made in this way

---

[94] This is not permitted in the case of companies registered in England or Ireland: Companies Act 1948, s. 117.

[95] *Buchan* v. *City of Glasgow Bank* (1879) 6 R. (H.L.) 44; *Wishart* v. *City of Glasgow Bank* (1879) 6 R. 1341, per Lord Shand.

[96] 11 & 12 Geo. VI, c. 38.

[97] *Leslie's Judicial Factor*, 1925 S.C. 464.

[98] See, e.g., *Stewart* v. *Morrison* (1892) 19 R. 1009.

[99] Note that the office of judicial factor under this section is not assimilated to that of a trustee in a sequestration: *Reid's J.F.* v. *Reid* 1959 S.L.T. 120.

[1] See Parent and Child, Ch. XLVII, infra, § 16. Such a factor being an officer of the Court may not be appointed to act jointly with a mother: *Speirs,* 1946 S.L.T. 203.

[2] Ch. XLVII, §§ 17, 23. As to the nature of the office of curator bonis, see *I.R.* v. *M'Millan's Curator Bonis,* 1956 S.C. 142.

[3] Stair, IV, 50, 28; Bell's *Prin.,* § 2120; *Peterson & Co.* (1851) 13 D. 951.

[4] *Dickie* v. *Mitchell* (1874) 1 R. 1030; *Carabine* v. *Carabine,* 1949 S.C. 521; see Partnership, Ch. XXIV, supra, § 29.

for the custody of the estate pending the issue of litigation. Factors may also be appointed on estates held pro indiviso in certain cases where the co-proprietors are unable to agree in regard to its administration,[5] and, on the application of the liferenter and fiduciary fiar, where the fee of the estate has been conveyed to a person in liferent and in fee to persons who are, when the conveyance comes into operation, unborn or incapable of ascertainment.[6]

26. Sequestration of Estate.—In addition to appointing a judicial factor the Court may sequestrate the estate. Sequestration is defined by Bell[7] as "a judicial assumption by the Court of possession of property which is in competition before it, that it may be placed in the custody of a neutral person, accountable in Court for his management, and sufficiently responsible, in order to be preserved and properly managed for the benefit of those who shall be preferred in the competition." It may be resorted to in cases where the Court deems it necessary that the person in possession of property shall be superseded as regards its custody and management.

27. Duties and Powers of Factor.—A judicial factor is an officer of Court, not subject to the control of parties,[8] and his duties are largely regulated by statutes and Acts of Sederunt.[9] He must find caution for the due performance of the office, and must lodge with the Accountant of Court a rental of the lands and an inventory of the moveable property belonging to the estate. He administers the estate under the superintendence of the Accountant, who may make such orders as he considers proper,[10] and with whom the factor must lodge annual accounts.

By virtue of the definitions of "trustee" and "judicial factor" in the Trusts (Scotland) Act 1921,[11] as amended by the Trusts (Scotland) Act 1961,[12] the provisions of these Acts extend to any person holding a judicial appointment as a factor or curator on another person's estate.[13] Accordingly judicial factors may exercise the general powers conferred on trustees by section 4 of the 1921 Act where such an exercise would not be at variance with the terms or purposes of the trust; and where the factor desires to do something which would be at variance with the terms or purposes of his appointment he may apply to the Court for special powers under section 5.[14] The function of a judicial factor is, generally speaking, to conserve and manage the estate under

---

5 *Bailey* v. *Scott* (1860) 22 D. 1105; *Allan* (1898) 36 S.L.R. 3; 6 S.L.T. 152.
6 1921 Act, s. 8 (2); *Napier* v. *Napiers*, 1963 S.L.T. 143; see also *Gibson*, 1967 S.L.T. 150.
7 *Comm.*, ii, 244.
8 *M'Culloch* v. *M'Culloch*, 1953 S.C. 189.
9 A.S., February 13, 1730; Judicial Factors Act 1849 (Pupils Protection Act), 12 & 13 Vict., c. 51; Judicial Factors (Scotland) Act 1880, 43 & 44 Vict., c. 4; Judicial Factors (Scotland) Act 1889, 52 & 53 Vict., c. 39; Trusts (Scotland) Act 1921, 11 & 12 Geo. V, c. 58; Trusts (Scotland) Act 1961, 9 & 10 Eliz. II, c. 57; Trustee Investments Act 1961, 9 & 10 Eliz. II, c. 62; Rules of Court (1965), Rules 199-201; Codifying Act of Sederunt (S.R. & O., 1913/638) Bk. L, Ch. VIII; A.S. (Appointment of Judicial Factors) 1967.
10 1849 Act, ss. 19 and 20.
11 s. 2.
12 s. 4.
13 Esp. 1921 Act, ss. 2, 4, 5; 1961 Act, ss. 2, 4, See § 19, supra.
14 *Tennent's J.F.* v. *Tennent*, 1954 S.C. 215.

his charge, and it may not be easy to decide whether the exercise of a
particular power, e.g., to sell or purchase heritage, would be at variance with
his appointment; each case must be decided on its own facts, and in a case of
doubt a petition for special powers would be justified.[15] Section 2 of the 1961
Act, which guarantees the validity of any title acquired by a person who enters
into a transaction with trustees purporting to act under section 4, extends to
judicial factors; and a purchaser of heritage from a factor need not look
behind the purported exercise of the power under that section.[16]

The voluntary acts of a judicial factor in the administration of the estate,
as, for example, the sale of heritage, do not affect the rights of succession to
the estate, although it is otherwise where the act was a necessary one.[17] In the
case of a trust-estate the judicial factor takes the place of the trustees and
administers the estate in accordance with the provisions of the trust.[18] He has
no higher powers than those allowed by the truster to the trustees.[19] He may
do what the truster has directed shall be done,[20] and may even in certain cases
exercise discretionary powers conferred on the trustees.[21]

At the conclusion of his administration the judicial factor may obtain a
discharge from the Court on presenting a petition for that purpose.[22]

[15] *Cunningham's Tutrix*, 1949 S.C. 275; *Bristow*, 1965 S.L.T. 225.
[16] See further, § 19, supra.
[17] *Moncrieff* v. *Miln* (1856) 18 D. 1286; *Macfarlane* v. *Greig* (1895) 22 R. 405; *Macqueen* v. *Tod*
    (1899) 1 F. 1069; *M'Adam's Exr.* v. *Souters* (1904) 7 F. 179; *Macfarlane's Trs.* v. *Macfarlane*,
    1910 S.C. 325.
[18] *Orr Ewing* v. *Orr Ewing's Trs.* (1884) 11 R. 600, per Lord President Inglis, at p. 627; *Browning's
    Factor* (1905) 7 F. 1037, per Lord Johnston.
[19] He does not have the powers of investment conferred on the trustees and, unless wider powers
    are granted by the court, he must administer the estate in accordance with the Trustee
    Investments Act 1961: *Carmichael's J.F.* v. *Accountant of Court*, 1971 S.C. 295.
[20] *Stirling's Judicial Factor*, 1917 1 S.L.T. 165.
[21] See supra, § 19; *Leith's J. F.* v. *Leith*, 1957 S.C. 307.
[22] *Campbell* v. *Grant* (1870) 8 M. 988.

CHAPTER XLV

LAW OF ASSOCIATIONS: PUBLIC TRUSTS

1. Legal Position.—Unincorporated associations, commonly referred to as voluntary associations, occupy an anomalous position in the eye of the law. Corporate bodies[1] and, in Scotland, partnerships or firms,[2] are recognised as possessing legal personality; but, although the Courts may be called on to take cognizance of, and adjudicate on, matters relating to a voluntary association, it is not regarded as having a legal existence distinct from that of its members. Hence such an association cannot at common law sue or be sued in its collective name alone; the names either of all the members, or of responsible members such as office-bearers, must be added.[3] But in the Sheriff Court an association may sue or be sued in its descriptive name without the addition of the names of any individuals.[4]

Further, the Court will not take any concern with the actions or resolutions of such bodies except in so far as these affect civil rights. Unless such rights are involved, an action for determining questions between a member and the association will not be entertained.[5] "Agreements to associate for purposes of recreation, or an agreement to associate for scientific or philanthropical or social or religious purposes, are not agreements which Courts of law can enforce. They are entirely personal. Therefore, in order to establish a civil wrong from the refusal to carry out such an agreement, if it can be inferred that any such agreement was made, it is necessary to see that the pursuer has suffered some practical injury either in his reputation or in his property."[6]

2. Classes of Associations.—Voluntary associations include bodies of such varied character as social clubs, dissenting churches, and societies formed for charitable or religious or scientific purposes. In practice trading associations are not found among them, as section 434 of the Companies Act 1948 forbids the formation of unregistered associations of more than 20 persons for the purpose of carrying on business for the acquisition of gain.[7]

As the instances given suggest, there is a broad distinction between two types of association. In the case of the ordinary social club the funds are

---

[1] Capacity to Contract, Ch. VI., supra, § 7.
[2] Partnership, Ch. XXIV, supra, § 9; Partnership Act 1890, s. 4 (2).
[3] *Renton Football Club* v. *M'Dowall* (1891) 18 R. 670; *Pagan & Osborne* v. *Haig*, 1910 S.C. 341; *Bridge* v. *South Portland Street Synagogue*, 1907 S.C. 1351.
[4] Sheriff Courts (Scotland) Act 1907 (7 Edw. VII, c. 51), Rule 11, as amended by Sheriff Courts (Scotland) Act 1913 (2 & 3 Geo. V, c. 28).
[5] *Forbes* v. *Eden* (1867) 5 M. (H.L.) 36; *Skerret* v. *Oliver* (1896) 23 R. 468; *Drennan* v. *Associated Ironmoulders of Scotland*, 1921 S.C. 151, per Lord Dundas; *Marshall* v. *Cardonald Bowling Club*, 1971 S.L.T. (Sh. Ct.) 56.
[6] *Murdison* v. *Scottish Football Union* (1896) 23 R. 449, per Lord Kinnear.
[7] Certain exceptions to this rule were introduced by Companies Act 1967, s. 120. See Ch. XXIV, supra, § 4.

contributed by the members and are to be applied for their benefit. Any questions which may arise are solved, therefore, by the application of the law of contract and joint property. Another type of association is that which exists for the promotion of some further purpose or object. Here the element of trust is to be discovered, and the general principles of trust law will control the application of the funds contributed or subscribed.

3. Clubs.—Most clubs are governed by rules drawn up by the members, and any member who joins is understood to agree to be bound by those rules; they form part of the contract between him and the other members.[8] If the rules contain a provision for their alteration, any alteration made bona fide and in accordance with the rules is binding on all the members unless the alteration is incompatible with the fundamental purpose of the association.[9] But where the rules make no such provision, they cannot be altered without the consent of all the members.[10]

The property of the club belongs to all the members, each member having a right with all the other members.[11] "The right of a member of a club in the property of the club is of a peculiar description. While the club exists as a going concern he is not entitled to insist on a sale and a division of the price. When he dies his right, such as it is, does not pass to his representatives, and if he retires from the club his whole interest therein ceases. But as long as he remains a member of the club his right is one of common property."[12] Hence it has been held that, while the wish of the majority of the members will rule in the ordinary administration of the property of the club, it is not competent for the majority gratuitously to alienate club property against the protest of a minority where there is nothing in the constitution of the club giving such a power.[13] If the club comes to an end the property remaining after all the debts and liabilities have been met is distributable among the members at the time.[14]

No member of the club, as such, is liable to pay to it or to anyone else any money beyond his subscription[15]; and if he is to be made liable by a creditor of the club, his liability must be established on the ground that he has undertaken liability or has so acted as to render himself liable under the ordinary rules of the law of agency.[16] He has the unilateral right, not

---

[8] *Lyttelton* v. *Blackburne* (1875) L.J. Ch. 219.

[9] *Thellusson* v. *Viscount Valentia* [1907] 2 Ch. 1; *Morgan* v. *Driscoll* (1922) 38 T.L.R. 251.

[10] *Harrington* v. *Sendall* [1903] 1 Ch. 921; *Dawkins* v. *Antrobus* (1881) 17 Ch.D. 615, per Jessel, M.R. But see the observations of Lords Guthrie and Skerrington in *Wilson* v. *Scottish Typographical Association*, 1912 S.C. 534. See also *Martin* v. *Scottish Transport & General Workers Union*, 1952 S.C. (H.L.) 1.

[11] *Graff* v. *Evans* (1881) 8 Q.B.D. 373.

[12] *Murray* v. *Johnstone* (1896) 23 R. 981, per Lord Moncreiff at p. 990.

[13] Ibid.; Contrast *Hopwood* v. *O'Neill*, 1971 S.L.T. (Notes) 52.

[14] *Baird* v. *Wells* (1890) 44 Ch.D. 661, per Stirling, J.; cf. *In re Sick and Funeral Society of St. John's Sunday School Golcar* [1973] Ch. 51. These rules do not, however, apply to a proprietary club, that is, one in which the club premises and what is necessary for the members belong to and are provided by the proprietor, who receives the fees of the members. In this case the members have no right in the property.

[15] *Wise* v. *Perpetual Trustee Co.* [1903] A.C. 139.

[16] *Thomson* v. *Victoria Eighty Club* (1905) 43 S.L.R. 628; *Flemyng* v. *Hector* (1836) 2 M. & W. 172; *Todd* v. *Emly* (1841) 7 M. & W. 427.

dependent on acceptance by the club, to resign his membership at any time, even though the rules contain no provision as to resignation.[17]

A member who has been expelled from a club may apply to the Court to have the resolution of the club set aside; and the Court will entertain the action if the club possesses property, for the effect of the expulsion is to deprive the member of his right in that property. The Court will not, however, review the merits of the club's decision, and will interfere only if it is not authorised by the rules, or if it is contrary to natural justice (as for example if no opportunity were afforded to the member of defending himself against the charge on which the decision is founded), or if the decision was not arrived at in good faith.[18]

4. Religious and other Associations.—Where subscriptions are contributed to an association or society formed for the promotion of a certain object, the sums so contributed are held in trust for that object.[19] Every contribution is an irrevocable appropriation of the donor's money to the purposes of the association, and, so long as these purposes are capable of being effected, the donor is not entitled to repayment of his contribution.[20] Unless it is otherwise provided in the rules of the association or the terms on which subscriptions were invited, the purposes to which the money is to be applied cannot be altered without the consent of all the subscribers.[21]

If it becomes impossible to carry out the purpose for which the subscriptions were given, the disposal of the funds of the association may present great difficulty. Where that purpose is of a public or charitable nature, it would appear from the decision in *Anderson's Trs.* v. *Scott*[22] that the proper course is that a scheme should be prepared by the Court in the exercise of the jurisdiction which it possesses in regard to such trusts. Otherwise the funds would apparently fall, as a rule, to be repaid to the subscribers. "Where parties join in a subscription to effect a particular object, and place the money subscribed in the hands of certain persons to carry out that object, I think the quasi trust, thereby created, is for the alternative purpose of either carrying out the object of the subscription, or, if that cannot be done, of paying back the money."[23] There may be great practical difficulties in this course: and if a subscriber could not be traced it is possible that his share would fall to the Crown as bona vacantia.[24] The terms on which the funds were contributed

[17] *Finch* v. *Oake* [1896] 1 Ch. 409.
[18] *Anderson* v. *Manson,* 1909 S.C. 838, per Lord Dundas; *Dawkins* v. *Antrobus* (1881) 17 Ch.D. 615; *Burn* v. *National Amalgamated Labourers' Union* [1920] 2 Ch. 364; *Young* v. *Ladies Imperial Club* [1920] 2 K.B. 523; *Maclean* v. *The Workers' Union* [1929] 1 Ch. 602.
[19] *Ewing* v. *M'Gavin* (1831) 9 S. 622; *Connell* v. *Ferguson* (1857) 19 D. 482, per Lord Deas.
[20] *Ewing* v. *M'Gavin,* supra; *Peake* v. *Association of English Episcopalians* (1884) 22 S.L.R. 3; 8 S.L.T. 236.
[21] *M'Caskill* v. *Cameron* (1840) 2 D. 537; *Steedman* v. *Malcolm* (1842) 4 D. 1441.
[22] 1914 S.C. 942; see infra, § 7; see also *Gibson* (1900) 2 F. 1125; *Davidson's Trs.* v. *Arnott,* 1951 S.C. 42.
[23] Per Lord Deas in *Connell* v. *Ferguson,* supra, and *Mitchell* v. *Burness* (1878) 5 R. 954; *Bain* v. *Black* (1849) 11 D. 1287, per Lords Mackenzie and Fullerton, at 1307 and 1310; affd. 6 Bell's Apps. 317; *Re British Red Cross Balkan Fund* [1914] 2 Ch. 419.
[24] This was the decision of the Lord Ordinary (Cullen) in *Anderson's Trs.* v. *Scott,* supra; see also Lord President Dunedin's opinion in *Incorporated Maltmen of Stirling,* 1912 S.C. 887, and Lord Sands' opinion in *Caledonian Employees' Benevolent Society* 1928 S.C. 633.

may, however, be such as to negative any quasi trust as, e.g., where the contributions are not purely gratuitous but have been finally paid over by the contributors as the consideration for benefits to be received by them, and in that case they would have no claim for the return of their contributions.[25]

In the case of a dissenting church the funds contributed to it are held in trust, and in case of division among its members any question as to the right to these funds is determined by inquiring which of the parties is adhering to the original principles professed by the church. The constitution of the church may provide for the disposal of the property in the event of a schism or may give the church the power of altering its principles; but, in the absence of such provisions, where the property is claimed by different sections of those who formed the church, the property will be held to belong to those who adhere to those principles.[26]

If a clergyman wrongfully expelled from a church or a member from an association applies to the Court for redress he must show that he has suffered some patrimonial loss; but under such loss is included the deprivation through the expulsion of some particular status, i.e., the capacity to perform certain functions or to hold certain offices.[27] The Court will award damages for any wrong done in this way, but will not pronounce decree ordaining the church or association to re-admit the expelled member.[28] The Court will not interfere with the judgments of an ecclesiastical tribunal, unless the tribunal has acted clearly beyond its constitution and has affected the civil rights and patrimonial interests of a church member, or its proceedings have been grossly irregular.[29]

5. Societies Regulated by Statute.—There are certain associations which hold an intermediate position between corporate and unincorporated bodies. They have no corporate existence, but the legislature has intervened for their regulation and assistance. The more important of these are Friendly Societies—which means, broadly speaking, societies constituted for the maintenance and relief of members and their families in sickness or old age or distress, and also to a limited extent for certain methods of insurance[30]—and Trade Unions.[31] The former are regulated by the Friendly Societies Act 1974, a consolidating enactment which contains elaborate provisions whereby such societies may register and thus acquire the privileges and duties attached by the statutes to registration. But there are still some friendly societies which are not registered; their status is not altogether clear.

At common law a trade union, if its rules and objects were open to

---

[25] *Smith* v. *Lord Advocate* (1899) 1 F. 741; *Cunnock* v. *Edwards* [1895] 1 Ch. 489.
[26] *Free Church of Scotland* v. *Lord Overtoun* (1904) 7 F. (H.L.) 1.
[27] *Skerret* v. *Oliver* (1896) 23 R. 468, per Lord Kincairney; *Bell* v. *The Trustees,* 1975 S.L.T. (Sh. Ct.) 60.
[28] Ibid.; *Gall* v. *Loyal Glenbogie Lodge of the Oddfellows' Friendly Society* (1900) 2 F. 1187, per Lord Trayner.
[29] *M'Donald* v. *Burns,* 1940 S.C. 376.
[30] For the definition of these see the Friendly Societies Act 1974 (c. 46), s. 7 (1).
[31] Building societies are incorporated under the Building Societies Act 1962 (10 & 11 Eliz. II. c. 37). There is said to be one unincorporated Scottish building society, and there can be no new ones. Societies regulated by the Industrial and Provident Societies Act 1965 are incorporated on registration (1965 (c. 12), s. 3).

objection as being in restraint of trade, was an illegal association in the sense that it could not sue or enforce contracts,[32] or be sued in respect of an alleged breach of contract with a member.[33] By the Trade Union Act 1871[34] it was enacted that the purposes of any trade union should not be illegal on this ground so as to render any member liable to criminal prosecution, or any agreement or trust void or voidable. This dispensation has been preserved in subsequent legislation,[35] and extended so as to cover any rule of a trade union. Any such rule is not to be held to be unlawful or unenforceable by reason only that it is in restraint of trade.[36] A major reform of the law relating to trade unions was attempted by the Industrial Relations Act 1971,[37] which gave preferential treatment to organisations registered under its provisions and accorded to them corporate status.[38] That Act was however repealed, following a change of government, by the Trade Union and Labour Relations Act 1974[39] by which the unincorporated status of trade unions was restored. Trade unions and employers' associations within the meaning of that Act[40] have however certain attributes and privileges in consequence of which, although unincorporated, they may be said to have a legal entity.[41] For instance they are capable of making contracts and, subject to certain immunities, of suing and being sued in their own name, and any judgment, order or award made against them is enforceable against any property held in trust for them as if they were bodies corporate.[42] Statutory rights[43] not to be excluded or expelled from a trade union by way of arbitrary or unreasonable discrimination have been repealed[44] but in some circumstances protection may be afforded at common law.[44a] A member of a trade union has the right, on giving reasonable notice and complying with any reasonable conditions, to terminate his membership.[45]

6. Public and Charitable Trusts.—While the Court has jurisdiction over the administration of all trusts, it exercises wider powers over trusts instituted for

---

[32] *Wilkie* v. *King,* 1911 S.C. 1314, per Lord Dunedin; *Shanks & M'Kernan* v. *United Operative Masons Society* (1874) 1 R. 453 and 823. Not all trade unions were illegal—*Russell* v. *Amalgamated Society of Carpenters and Joiners* [1910] 1 K.B. 506.

[33] *Bernard* v. *National Union of Mineworkers,* 1971 S.C. 32.

[34] 34 & 35 Vict. c. 31, ss. 2 and 3. See further, Capacity to Contract, Ch. VI., supra, § 14.

[35] See Industrial Relations Act 1971 (c. 72), s. 135; Trade Union and Labour Relations Act 1974 (c. 52), s. 2 (5).

[36] Trade Union and Labour Relations Act 1974, s. 2 (5); see *Faramus* v. *Film Artistes Association* [1964] A.C. 925; *Edwards* v. *Society of Graphical and Allied Trades* [1971] Ch. 354.

[37] c. 72.

[38] s. 74.

[39] c. 52. That Act has, in turn, been amended by the Trade Union and Labour Relations (Amendment) Act 1976 (c. 7). See also Trade Union Act 1913 (2 & 3 Geo. V, c. 30) and Trade Union (Amalgamation etc.) Act 1964 (c. 24) as amended. Certain trade unions which are "special register bodies" may be incorporated (1974 Act, s. 2 (1)).

[40] For definition of these expressions, see 1974 Act, s. 28.

[41] *Taff Vale Rly. Co.* v. *Amalgamated Society of Railway Servants* [1901] A.C. 426; *Bonsor* v. *Musicians Union* [1956] A.C. 104.

[42] 1974 Act, ss. 2 (1), 3 (2) and 14.

[43] 1974 Act, s. 5.

[44] Trade Union and Labour Relations (Amendment) Act 1976, s. 1.

[44a] E.g. on grounds of natural justice, of *ultra vires* or of a public policy against arbitrary exclusion: *Nagle* v. *Feilden* [1966] 2 Q.B. 633.

[45] 1974 Act, s. 7, as amended (1976 (c. 7), s. 3 (1)).

the benefit of the public, frequently described as "charitable."[46] The law of Scotland makes no precise definition of the expression "charity" in this context; "charitable trust" is merely a convenient general term. "There is no distinction either as to construction or principles of administration between gifts to charitable trusts, properly so called, and gifts to purposes which, though not charitable, are lawful and useful. The true distinction is between private trusts or bequests, in which only individuals named or designed can claim an interest, and those which are intended for the benefit of a section of the public, and which may be enforced by *popularis actio*."[47] This statement of the law[48] was accepted in *Anderson's Trs.* v. *Scott*,[49] and, therefore, in considering earlier decisions and dicta as to the powers of the Court over "charitable" trusts, the term "charitable" must now, it would appear, be understood as including public trusts in general and not those only which are eleemosynary.

But although, according to this decision, no distinction need be drawn between charitable and public trusts as regards the jurisdiction of the Court, the terms "charitable" and "public" have by no means the same effect when used by a testator to describe the objects of his bounty. If a testator leaves his estate to trustees in trust to divide it among such "charitable" purposes as they may think proper, the descriptive word "charitable" is, out of favour for charities,[50] held by itself to denote a sufficiently definite class of beneficiaries, and the gift is sustained. On the other hand, if the purposes are described merely as "public," this description is held to be so vague as to invalidate the bequest. Instructions to trustees to divide the estate among "charitable or public,"[51] "charitable or religious"[52] and "charitable or social"[53] objects have been held void from uncertainty in respect that two classes of beneficiaries were favoured, and that the words "public," "religious" and "social" used without further detail to describe the second class were too vague a direction to receive effect. But a conjunction of the words "charitable" and "benevolent" does not impair the peculiar virtues of "charitable."[54] If the trust purposes are in themselves uncertain, the fact that the benefit of the trust is confined to a particular locality will not save the trust.[55] And a gift to

---

[46] *Dundas* (1869) 7 M. 670, per Lord President Inglis.
[47] I.e., an action on behalf of the public. Any person possessing an interest, either existing or contingent, under the trust purposes of the trust has a title to enforce its due execution: *Ross* v. *Governors of Heriot's Hospital* (1843) 5 D. 589; *Murray* v. *Lord Cameron*, 1969 S.L.T. (Notes) 76.
[48] In M'Laren, *Wills and Succession*, II., 917.
[49] 1914 S.C. 942.
[50] *Magistrates of Dundee* v. *Morris* (1858) 3 Macq. 134.
[51] *Blair* v. *Duncan* (1901) 4 F. (H.L.) 1; *Turnbull's Trs.* v. *Lord Advocate*, 1918 S.C. (H.L.) 88; *Campbell's Trs.* v. *Campbell*, 1921 S.C. (H.L.) 12; *Reid's Trs.* v. *Cattanach's Trs.*, 1929 S.C. 727. There are numerous decisions as to the effect of various forms of bequest.
[52] *Macintyre* v. *Grimond's Trs.* (1905) 7 F. (H.L.) 90; but see *Brough* v. *Brough's Trs.*, 1950 S.L.T. 117; and Testate Succession, Ch. XLIII, supra, § 10.
[53] *Rintoul's Trs.* v. *Rintoul*, 1949 S.C. 297; contrast *Milne's Trs.* v. *Davidson*, 1956 S.C. 81.
[54] *Wink's Exrs.* v. *Tallent*, 1947 S.C. 470; Lord Keith (p. 484) treats the words as synonymous. See also *Pomphrey's Trs.* v. *Royal Naval Benevolent Trust*, 1967 S.L.T. 61, per Lord Fraser, at p. 63.
[55] *Turnbull's Trs.* v. *Lord Advocate*, supra; *Harper's Trs.* v. *Jacobs*, 1929 S.C. 345.

"charities" generally will fail if the testator does not appoint a particular person as trustee or executor to make a choice.[56]

Neither of the questions discussed above requires a precise definition of the word "charitable," which is treated as being sufficiently specific in itself. It is a different matter, however, where the construction of Income Tax statutes is concerned. In *Baird's Trs.* v. *Lord Advocate*[57] an attempt was made to achieve a definition of "charitable purposes" in a taxing statute so as to produce uniformity between England and Scotland; but the Court refused in that case to apply the technical definition of English law, and insisted that the words should be given their popular and ordinary meaning. It was laid down in *Baird's Trs.* that in their popular meaning the words were confined to the relief of poverty; but this definition has in most subsequent cases been considered to be too narrow.[58] In *Income Tax Commissioners* v. *Pemsel*,[59] however, Lord Watson[60] pointed out that the word "charity" had been employed in the legislative language of the Scottish Parliament, and of the British Parliament when legislating for Scotland, in substantially the same sense as that in which it had been interpreted by the English Courts; and it was held that for the purposes of the Income Tax Acts "charitable purposes" should be given the technical meaning of English law,[61] based on the statute of Elizabeth and the decisions of the Court of Chancery. Finally in *Inland Revenue* v. *Glasgow Police Athletic Association*[62] it was emphasised that for tax purposes the English law of charities is part of the law of Scotland and not foreign law. The position is the same in deciding whether an organisation is established "for charitable purposes only" so as to be entitled to rating relief on the subjects it occupies.[63] But the limited and technical meanings given to the words in *Baird's Trs.* or *Pemsel* have never been applied in a question as to the construction or administration of a Scottish testamentary trust.[64]

The general principles of trust administration[65] are as applicable to public as to private trusts, and the definition of trust in the Trusts (Scotland) Act 1921 is so drawn as to include both types. There are, however, certain principles which are peculiar to public trusts. The Court is said to apply a

---

[56] *Angus's Exix.* v. *Batchan's Trs.*, 1949 S.C. 335.

[57] (1888) 15 R. 682.

[58] *Anderson's Trs.* v. *Scott*, 1914 S.C. 942; *Allan's Exr.* v. *Allan*, 1908 S.C. 807, per Lord Kinnear; see Lord Halsbury's and Lord Davey's speeches in *Blair* v. *Duncan* (1901) 4 F. (H.L.) 1; *Chalmers' Trs.* v. *Turriff School Board*, 1917 S.C. 676, per Lord Justice-Clerk Dickson; *Wink's Exrs.* v. *Tallent*, 1947 S.C. 470, per Lord President Cooper.

[59] [1891] A.C. 531; see also *Jackson's Trs.* v. *Inland Revenue*, 1926 S.C. 579; *Inland Revenue* v. *Glasgow Musical Festival Association*, 1926 S.C. 920; *Scottish Woollen Technical College* v. *Inland Revenue*, 1926 S.C. 934.

[60] At pp. 558, 560.

[61] In *Pemsel's Case* Lord Macnaghten, with reference to English law, observes: " 'Charity,' in its legal sense, comprises four principal divisions: trusts for the relief of poverty; trusts for the advancement of education; trusts for the advancement of religion; and trusts for other purposes beneficial to the community, not falling under any of the preceding heads." But this does not mean that all trusts which are beneficial to the community are regarded in English law as charitable.—*Att.-Gen.* v. *National Provincial Bank* [1924] A.C. 262.

[62] 1953 S.C. (H.L.) 13.

[63] See Local Government (Financial Provisions, etc.) (Scotland) Act 1962, s. 4 (10); *Scottish Burial & Cremation Society* v. *Glasgow Corporation*, 1967 S.C. (H.L.) 116.

[64] *Anderson's Trs.* v. *Scott*, supra; *Wink's Exrs.* v. *Tallent*, supra, per Lord Keith, p. 482.

[65] See preceding chapter, §§ 9 et seq.

more lenient standard in its dealing with those who administer a trust of this kind than with private trustees. It does not press severely on them if in good faith they err in their management of the trust, and if their administration, although mistaken, has been honest and unconnected with any corrupt practice, they will not be punished for their actions in the past.[66] But the most striking distinction between public and private trusts is to be found in the power which the Court possesses to act on the principle of cy près in the case of trusts of the former description.

7. Cy Près.—Where the intention of the founder of a charitable or public trust cannot be carried into effect in the precise manner directed by him, it is within the power of the Court to direct that the funds shall be applied in a manner as nearly akin as possible to that directed. The principle has been authoritatively stated in these terms:—"In both countries (England and Scotland) this principle has prevailed, namely, that there shall be a very enlarged administration of charitable trusts. You look to the charity which is intended to be created—that is to say, the benefit of the beneficiary—and you distinguish between the charity and the means which are directed to the attainment of that charity. Now the means of necessity vary from age to age... and the Courts of Equity have always exercised the power of varying the means of carrying out the charity from time to time, according as by that variation they can secure more effectually the great object of the charity, namely, the benefit of the beneficiary."[67] According to this doctrine, known as cy près or approximation, the Court has power to vary the means by the substitution for a particular form of charity of another form approximating as closely as may be to the old one; but the Court cannot change a charity, or sanction the application of the funds to a wholly different purpose. Some cases disclose a strict approach to the question whether there has been a failure so as to admit of a cy près scheme, and it has been said that it is not a legitimate ground for the application of the doctrine that, through the changing circumstances of society, the administration of a charity has become increasingly arduous and discouraging in its results.[68] On the other hand, the Court has shown itself ready to exercise its power in a case of strong expediency falling short of impossibility of performance, where it is clear that the circumstances of the trust or the arrangements for its administration are such that its carrying out would be seriously hampered unless the means were varied.[69]

This principle is not, however, applicable in all cases where there is a charitable bequest; in the case of bequests which lapse before they take effect, there must be, either expressed or implied, a general charitable intention. In

[66] *Andrews* v. *Ewart's Trs.* (1886) 13 R. (H.L.) 69.
[67] *Clephane* v. *Magistrates of Edinburgh* (1869) 7 M. (H.L.) 7, at 15; see also *Trs. of Carnegie Park Orphanage* (1892) 19 R. 605, and *Grigor Medical Bursary Fund Trs.* (1903) 5 F. 1143, per Lord M'Laren; *Gibson's Trs.*, 1933 S.C. 190.
[68] *Glasgow Domestic Training School*, 1923 S.C. 892, per Lord President Clyde at 895; *Scotstown Moor Children's Camp*, 1948 S.C. 630.
[69] *Gibson's Trs.*, supra; *Glasgow Y.M.C.A.*, 1934 S.C. 452, per Lord Blackburn at 458; *Clutterbuck*, 1961 S.L.T. 427; *Magistrates of Forfar*, 1975 S.L.T. (Notes) 36.

Burgess's Trs. v. *Crawford*[70] Lord President Dunedin distinguished between three classes of bequest. The first is where there is a gift for a charitable purpose, but the means by which it is to be carried out are not indicated; here the Court will, out of the favour which it has always shown to charitable bequests, supply the means cy près so as to enable the purpose to be carried out.[71] The second class is where there is a gift to a society or institution which does not exist and never has existed, in which case, from the mere non-existence of the object, there is spelled out a general charitable intention.[72] The third class is that in which the gift is in form made to a particular charitable institution which has ceased to exist, or for a particular purpose which cannot be effected; here the question arises in each case whether, on a fair construction of the deed, there is a general charitable intention with a direction as to the method in which that intention is to be effected,[73] or whether the gift is meant only for that particular institution[74] or that particular purpose.[75] If it is the latter, the doctrine of cy près has no place, and the gift fails with the failure of the institution or purpose. In *Burgess's Trs.*[70] the Court, applying these rules, held that a bequest for the purpose of establishing an industrial school for females, which had become impossible of fulfilment owing to supervening legislation, lapsed as no intention beyond this particular object was disclosed in the settlement.

There is, however, an important difference between the cases discussed above, where there is a failure before the trust opens, and where the failure occurs after the bequest has actually taken effect[76] in favour of a charity.[77] In the latter case it is not necessary to consider whether or not there is a general charitable intention. Although the trust or bequest may be for a particular charitable institution, the Court will not allow the trust to lapse because of the subsequent failure of the object. The funds will in such a case be applied under a cy près scheme, unless a resulting trust or destination over is brought into effect by the lapse.[78]

Where the principle of cy près falls to be applied, this is done by means of a scheme for the administration of the trust settled by the Court.[79] The power of sanctioning the settlement of a scheme belongs to the nobile officium, and is

---

[70] 1912 S.C. 387, following Lord Herschell's opinion in *Re Rymer* [1895] 1 Ch. 19; see also *Cumming's Exr.* v. *Cumming*, 1967 S.L.T. 68, per Lord Avonside, at p. 69.

[71] E.g. *Ballingall's Judicial Factor* v. *Hamilton*. 1973 S.L.T. 236.

[72] E.g., *Tod's Trs.* v. *The Sailors' & Fishermen's Orphans' and Widows' Society*, 1953 S.L.T. (Notes) 72; *Pomphrey's Trs.* v. *Royal Naval Benevolent Trust*, 1967 S.L.T. 61; *Cumming's Exrs.*, supra. Contrast *MacTavish's Trs.* v. *St. Columba's High Church*, 1967 S.L.T. (Notes) 50, where the expression of intention failed for uncertainty.

[73] E.g., *Macrae's Trs.*, 1955 S.L.T. (Notes) 33; *Shorthouse's Trs.* v. *Aberdeen Medico-Chirurgical Society*, 1977 S.L.T. 148.

[74] E.g., *Connell's Trs.* v. *Milngavie District Nursing Association*, 1953 S.C. 230; *Fergusson's Trs.* v. *Buchanan*, 1973 S.L.T. 41.

[75] E.g., *Burgess's Trs.*, supra; *Pennie's Trs.* v. *R.N.L.I.*, 1924 S.L.T. 520; *Tait's J.F.* v. *Lillie*, 1940 S.C. 534; *Hay Memorial J.F.* v. *Hay's Trs.*, 1952 S.C. (H.L.) 29; *M'Robert's Trs.* v. *Cameron*, 1961 S.L.T. (Notes) 66.

[76] As to failure to take effect, see *Cuthbert's Trs.* v. *Cuthbert*, 1958 S.C. 629; *Edinburgh Corporation* v. *Cranston's Trs.*, 1960 S.C. 244.

[77] *Anderson's Trs.* v. *Scott*, 1914 S.C. 942; *Re Slevin* [1891] 2 Ch. 236; *Davidson's Trs.* v. *Arnott*. 1951 S.C. 42.

[78] *Young's Trs.* v. *Deacons of the Eight Incorporated Trades of Perth* (1893) 20 R. 778.

[79] For procedure, see *Forrest's Trs.* v. *Forrest*, 1960 S.L.T. 88.

exercisable only by the Inner House of the Court of Session.[80] It must be borne in mind that where a settlor's directions are sufficient to enable trustees to prepare a scheme for themselves and where it is not impracticable to carry them out and there is no lack of machinery prescribed by the settlor, it is unnecessary for the trustees to apply to the Court at all.[81]

[80] See Trusts (Scotland) Act 1921, s. 26; *Ossington's Trs.*, 1966 S.L.T. 19.
[81] *Robertson's Trs.*, 1948 S.C. 1; *Galloway* v. *Elgin Magistrates*, 1946 S.C. 353.

CHAPTER XLVI

HUSBAND AND WIFE

Clive and Wilson: *Husband and Wife* (1974).

MARRIAGE is said by Erskine[1] to be truly a contract; but although this is true in the sense that it is founded on the consent of the parties, it is much more than a contract. It differs indeed in many important respects from other contracts. Thus, the conditions of marriage and the rights and duties created by it are not left to be regulated by the parties, nor can it be dissolved at their pleasure; and it affects the status both of the parties and of their issue. Hence it is recognised that the general rules of the law of contract cannot be applied indiscriminately to the relationship of marriage.[2]

1. Impediments to Marriage in General.—Under the common law a pupil could not marry, although if the married pair cohabited after puberty this gave force to the marriage.[3] But the Age of Marriage Act 1929[4] enacted that a marriage between persons either of whom is under the age of sixteen is void. So also there can be no valid marriage if one of the parties was at the time of the marriage, by reason of insanity[5] or intoxication,[6] incapable of understanding the nature of the engagement entered into. Moreover, although a party may appear to have consented to marriage, yet, if it be proved that, through error, fraud, duress or design,[7] there was no true consent to marry, or to marry the other party to the ceremony, the marriage will be declared null. But the error must be such as to exclude the consent to marriage; error, however grave, inducing the marriage, but not excluding such consent, does not afford ground for annulling it.[8] Thus, the fact that a wife has either concealed from her husband that she was pregnant at the date of the marriage or has induced him to marry her by fraudulently stating that her condition was due to him does not entitle him to have the marriage declared null.[9] The fact that one party is disabled by a rule of his religion from entering into the marriage does not render it void.[10] If consent be given, marriage is thereby perfected

---

[1] *Inst.*, I, 6, 2; and see Walton, *Husband and Wife* (3rd ed., 1951), Ch. 1.

[2] *Lang* v. *Lang*, 1921 S.C. 44.

[3] Erskine, *Inst.*, I, 6, 3; Fraser, I, 53; and see *A.B.* v. *C.D.*, 1957 S.C. 415, for effect of cohabitation after impediment of nonage removed.

[4] 19 & 20 Geo. V, c. 36; now Marriage (Scotland) Act 1977 (c. 15), s. 1.

[5] Erskine, *Inst.*, I, 6, 2; *Park* v. *Park*, 1914 1 S.L.T. 88; *Graham* v. *Graham* (1907) 15 S.L.T. 33.

[6] *Johnston* v. *Brown* (1823) 2 S. 495, and in Fergusson's *Consistorial Law*, 229.

[7] *Orlandi* v. *Castelli*, 1961 S.C. 113.

[8] See Clive and Wilson, pp. 75 et seq.

[9] *Lang* v. *Lang*, 1921 S.C. 44. See *MacDougall* v. *Chitnavis*, 1937 S.C. 390. Contra in England: Nullity of Marriage Act 1971 (c. 44) s. 2 (*f*).

[10] *MacDougall* v. *Chitnavis, supra*. But religious belief regarding the prerequisites of marriage may preclude consent (*Mahmud* v. *Mahmud*, 1977 S.L.T. (Notes) 17). As to capacity and conflict of laws, see Clive and Wilson, Ch. 6, and *Bliersbach* v. *M'Ewen*, 1959 S.C. 43.

although the parties may never cohabit. "Consensus non concubitus facit matrimonium."

2. Forbidden Degrees.—Marriage is forbidden within certain degrees of relationship. These are now defined by the Marriage (Scotland) Act 1977, but it is necessary to consider the law in force prior thereto, as it will continue to govern the validity of all marriages contracted before January 1, 1978.

(a) *Marriages before January 1, 1978.*

Two modes of computing the degrees of relationship require to be considered for this purpose. By the Roman Law method of calculation, which differs from that of the Canon Law in this respect, the relationship in the collateral line between two persons is computed by counting from one to the common ancestor and thence downwards to the other party: thus uncle and nephew are held to be related in the third degree, and cousins-german in the fourth degree. By Canon law it is computed by counting from either of the parties to the common ancestor, and, where the parties are not equally removed from that ancestor, the longer line of descent from him is taken: thus uncle and nephew are held to be related in the second degree (the nephew being two degrees removed from his grandfather) as also are cousins-german. By the Act 1567, c. 15[11] (which refers to the eighteenth chapter of the Book of Leviticus), it was enacted that seconds in blood—by which was meant cousins-german according to the computation of the Canon Law—and all more distantly related might lawfully marry, and no distinction was made between the full-blood and the half-blood. Further, the same degrees as were forbidden in consanguinity (relationship between parties descended from a common ancestor) were forbidden in affinity (the relationship between one of the married parties and the blood relations of the other).[12] Marriage was moreover forbidden, by an extension beyond the terms of the Act, where the relationship of blood or affinity was, no matter how remote the degree, such that one of the parties might be deemed to stand in loco parentis to the other, as grand uncle and grand niece.[13] On these rules exceptions were engrafted by various Acts which were repealed and re-enacted to permit marriage after divorce by the Marriage (Enabling) Act 1960,[14] which permitted marriage between a man and a woman who was the sister, aunt or niece of the whole or half blood of a former wife of his (whether she was living or not) and between a man and a woman who was formerly the wife of his brother, uncle or nephew of the whole or half blood (whether living or not), provided that such a marriage was not invalid by the law of the domicile of either party thereto. Illegitimate relationship within the second degree was equally with legitimate a bar to marriage,[15] but the prohibition which depended on the fact that one of the parties stood in loco parentis to the other was based on a legal fiction and

[11] See *H.M. Advocate* v. *Martin & Aikman,* 1917 J.C. 8.
[12] *Purves' Trs.* v. *Purves* (1895) 22 R. 513.
[13] Erskine, *Inst.,* I, 6, 9.
[14] 8 & 9 Eliz. II, c. 29. Now repealed but still applicable to marriages before 1st January 1978.
[15] *Robertson* v. *Channing,* 1928 S.L.T. 376. See Clive and Wilson pp. 89-90, sed contra Fraser, I, pp. 131-132. Opinions were reserved in *Philp's Trs.* v. *Beaton,* infra.

did not extend to cases where the relationship was merely a natural one.[16] For the purpose of the law relative to marriage the adopter of a child and the child itself were deemed to be within the prohibited degrees of consanguinity and that notwithstanding a subsequent adoption of the child by another.[17]

(b) *Marriages on or after January 1, 1978.*

For these marriages the previous law on forbidden degrees is replaced by a statutory code which includes an exhaustive list of relationships within which parties may not marry.[18] The effect is that marriage is forbidden between parties related within the third degree of consanguinity whether in direct line of ascent and descent or, according to the Roman law (not the Canon law) method of calculation, in the collateral line. As before no distinction is made in consanguineous relationships between the full blood and the half blood.[19] In affinity the prohibition is confined to relationships within the second degree of ascent and descent. Both in consanguinity and affinity the relationship exists although traced through or to any person of illegitimate birth.[20] The law on adoptive relationships is unchanged.

3. Subsisting Prior Marriage.—A marriage with one who is at the time married to a third party is ipso jure null, although either, or both, of the contracts are irregular.[21]

4. Impotency.[22]—Where either of the parties, being of suitable age, is incapable of sexual intercourse, the marriage may be declared null.[23] It is not essential that there should be structural incapacity; invincible repugnance may amount to impotency. Impotency is not, however, an absolute bar to marriage, but only affords ground on which it may be annulled[24]; and there may be circumstances which so plainly imply a recognition of the existence and validity of the marriage by the complaining spouse as to make it inequitable and contrary to public policy that he or she should be permitted to impugn it.[25] The defender in the action is entitled to an opportunity of undergoing remedial medical treatment.[26] The action may be brought by the

---

[16] *Philp's Trs.* v. *Beaton*, 1938 S.C. 733.

[17] Adoption Act 1958 (7 Eliz. II, c. 5), s. 13 (3); cf Adoption Act 1950 (14 Geo. VI c. 26) s. 10 (1), Adoption of Children Act 1949 (12, 13 & 14 Geo. VI, c. 98), s. 11 (1).

[18] Marriage (Scotland) Act 1977 (c. 15), ss. 2 and 27 (3). Schedule 1 contains an exhaustive list of the forbidden relationships, to which reference should be made.

[19] s. 2 (2) (*a*).

[20] s. 2 (2) (*b*).

[21] See Clive and Wilson, pp. 80-86; Marriage (Scotland) Act 1977, s. 2 (3) (*b*).: as to the crime of bigamy, see Criminal Law, Ch. L, infra, Part II, § 19.

[22] See Clive and Wilson, pp. 47-58.

[23] *G.* v. *G.* 1924 S.C. (H.L.) 42. As to what does and does not constitute physical consummation, see *Baxter* v. *B.* [1948] A.C. 274; *Cackett* v. *C.* [1950] P. 253; *W.* v. *W.* [1967] 1 W.L.R. 1554 and *J.* v. *J.* 1978 S.L.T. 128.

[24] See *Administrator of Austrian Property* v. *Von Lorang,* 1926 S.C. 598, per Lord President Clyde, at 616; 1927 S.C. (H.L.) 80; *S.G.* v. *W.G.,* 1933 S.C. 728; as to onus, see *M.* v. *W. or M.,* 1966 S.L.T. 152.

[25] *C.B.* v. *A.B.* (1885) 12 R. (H.L.) 36, per Lord Selborne L.C. at p. 38, Lord Watson, at p. 45; *L.* v. *L.,* 1931 S.C. 477; *A.B.* v. *C.B.,* 1961 S.C. 347. A.I.H. and adoption of child generally have this effect (but see Clive and Wilson, pp. 56-57 on effect of fecundation *ab extra*).

[26] *W.Y.* v. *A.Y.,* 1946 S.C. 27.

impotent spouse on the ground of his own irremediable impotency.[27] It has
been held that an action of declarator of nullity on the ground of impotency
was not out of time 24 years after the pretended marriage.[28]

5. Constitution of Marriage: Regular Marriage.—A marriage is regular or
irregular according to its mode of constitution. A regular marriage may be
either a religious or a civil marriage.[29] In either case each party to the
marriage must submit to the Registrar of the district in which the marriage is
to be solemnised a notice of intention to marry accompanied by a birth
certificate, and where either party has previously been married, evidence of
the dissolution of the previous marriage.[30] There are special provisions where
a party to a marriage intended to be solemnised in Scotland is residing in
another part of the United Kingdom or is not domiciled in any part of the
United Kingdom and also for marriages outside Scotland where a party
resides in Scotland.[31] After receipt of the notice, the Registrar, if satisfied that
there is no legal impediment, or if so informed by the Registrar General, issues
a marriage schedule which is the authority for the solemnisation of the
marriage.[32] The schedule may not, however, be issued before the expiry of
fourteen days from receipt of the notice unless on the written request of a
party to the marriage and with the authority of the Registrar General.[33]

At any time before the solemnisation of a marriage any person may submit
an objection in writing to the Registrar.[34] Where the objection relates to a
matter of misdescription or inaccuracy the Registrar may, with the approval
of the Registrar General, make any necessary correction. In any other case he
must, pending consideration of the objection by the Registrar General,
suspend the completion or issue of the marriage schedule or, if a marriage
schedule has already been issued for a religious marriage, notify the celebrant
of the objection and advise him not to solemnise the marriage.[35] If the
Registrar General is satisfied, on consideration of an objection, that there is a
legal impediment to the marriage he must direct the Registrar to take all
reasonable steps to ensure that the marriage does not take place. If, on the
other hand, he is satisfied that there is no legal impediment, he must so inform
the Registrar and the marriage schedule may then be completed and issued, if
that has not already been done, so that the marriage may proceed.[36] There is a
legal impediment for this purpose where the parties to the marriage are within
the forbidden degrees of relationship or are of the same sex or where either of
them (a) is already married, (b) will be under the age of sixteen on the date of
solemnisation of the intended marriage, (c) is incapable of understanding the

---

[27] *S.* v. *F.*, 1945 S.C. 202; *H.* v. *H.*, 1949 S.C. 587.
[28] *Allardyce* v. *A.*, 1954 S.C. 419; 1954 S.L.T. 334. See this case too on the subject of expenses in
      an action of nullity.
[29] Marriage (Scotland) Act 1977, s. 8.
[30] ibid. s. 3 (1).
[31] s. 3 (6) and (5).
[32] s. 6.
[33] s. 6 (4).
[34] s. 5 (1).
[35] s. 5 (2).
[36] s. 5 (3), and 6, (1).

nature of a marriage ceremony or of consenting to marriage, or (d) is not domiciled in Scotland and his marriage in Scotland to the other party would be void ab initio according to the law of his domicile.[37]

A religious marriage may be solemnised by a minister of the Church of Scotland, a minister, clergyman, pastor or priest of a religious body prescribed by regulations or other approved celebrant.[38] The marriage schedule must be produced to the celebrant and the parties to the marriage and two witnesses (who must be persons professing to be sixteen years or over) must be present. Failure in any of these respects renders the marriage void.[39] Where the celebrant belongs to the Church of Scotland or a prescribed religious body, the marriage must be in accordance with a form recognised as sufficient by the Church or body to which the celebrant belongs.[40] In any other case the statutory requirement is that the form of solemnisation must include a declaration by the parties, in the presence of each other, the celebrant and the witnesses, that they accept each other as husband and wife and a declaration thereafter by the celebrant that they are husband and wife.[41]

A civil marriage is solemnised by an authorised Registrar. No form is prescribed. A marriage schedule must be available and the parties and witnesses must be present. There is, however, in contrast with a religious marriage, no provision that failure in these respects renders a civil marriage void.[42]

It is an offence for anyone, who is not within the classes of persons authorised under the Act to solemnise marriages, to conduct a marriage ceremony in such a way as to lead the parties to believe that he is solemnising a valid marriage, or for the celebrant of a religious marriage to solemnise it without at the time having the marriage schedule available to him, or for either the celebrant of a religious marriage or an authorised Registrar to solemnise a marriage without both parties being present.[43]

6. Irregular Marriage.—Before 1940 an irregular marriage might be constituted by any one of three modes: (1) declaration de praesenti, i.e. consent to marriage there and then, (2) promise subsequente copula, and (3) cohabitation with habit and repute. No marriage can be contracted by the first two modes since July 1, 1940,[44] but the law relating to them may remain of importance for some time to come as questions of legitimacy and rights of succession may depend on the validity of an irregular marriage contracted many years before.[45] The statement of the law relating to all three modes is therefore retained, although only the third is now valid.

[37] s. 5 (4).
[38] s. 8 (1). See also Marriage (Prescription of Religious Bodies) (Scotland) Regulations 1977 (S.I. 1977 No. 1670).
[39] s. 13.
[40] s. 14 (a).
[41] ss. 14 (b) and 9 (3).
[42] s. 19.
[43] s. 24.
[44] Marriage (Scotland) Act 1939 (2 & 3 Geo. VI, c. 34), s. 5 now repealed; Marriage (Scotland) Act 1939 (Commencement) Order 1940. cf. Marriage (Scotland) Act 1977, s. 21.
[45] Ibid., s. 8.

7. Declaration de Praesenti.—Declaration de praesenti meant the consent by the parties to present marriage.[46] It was sufficient that such consent be proved to have been given, whether in writing or orally, although no witnesses were present[47] and although the actual time and place at which the consent was given were not proved.[48] But the Court had to be satisfied that the parties truly intended to contract marriage. Hence, although there was a writing expressing the parties' consent to marriage, the question might arise whether it was drawn up for the purpose of marriage or for some other purpose, and, if so, the Court would investigate the whole facts of the case, including the circumstances in which the consent was given and the subsequent conduct of the parties, in order to determine whether there was truly consent to present marriage.[49] But a person who had signed a mutual declaration of marriage was not allowed to plead that he had signed it with a mental reservation, where his conduct induced the other party to believe that he was consenting to marriage.[50] No such marriage was valid unless one of the parties had his or her usual place of residence in Scotland or had lived in Scotland for twenty-one days preceding the marriage.[51]

8. Promise Subsequente Copula.—Here there was promise of marriage, followed by intercourse permitted upon the faith of the promise.[51a] The promise could not be proved by parole evidence. At one time it was established that the promise might be proved by writ or oath,[52] but in *Longworth* v. *Yelverton*[53] the opinion was expressed in the House of Lords that section 36 of the Court of Session Act 1830,[54] made reference to the defender's oath incompetent. Where the promise was to be proved by writ, the writing need not contain an express promise: it was sufficient that there could be collected from its terms that a promise was given.[55] There was no limitation on the mode of proof of intercourse. It must have been allowed on the faith of the promise, otherwise there was no marriage; but if it followed the promise this would generally be presumed.[56] This presumption, however, and the presumption that there was present consent to marriage might be rebutted as, e.g., by some inference to be drawn from the subsequent conduct of the parties.[57] It was formerly doubted whether a declarator was not necessary to constitute the marriage, but it was latterly settled that the promise and

---

[46] *Dalrymple* v. *Dalrymple* (1811) 2 Haggard 54; *Walker* v. *Macadam* (1813) 1 Dow 148, 5 Pat. 675; Clive and Wilson, pp 108-113.
[47] *Dysart Peerage Case* (1881) 6 App.Cas. 489; *Petrie* v. *Petrie*, 1911 S.C. 360; Fraser, I, 295.
[48] *Leslie* v. *Leslie* (1860) 22 D. 993.
[49] *Davidson* v. *Davidson*, 1921 S.C. 340; *Imrie* v. *Imrie* (1891) 19 R. 185; *Dunn* v. *Dunn's Trs.*, 1930 S.C. 131; *Courtin* v. *Elder*, 1930 S.C. 68.
[50] *Duran* v. *Duran* (1904) 7 F. 87.
[51] Marriage (Scotland) Act 1856 (19 & 20 Vict., c. 96), s. 1 (repealed by Marriage (Scotland) Act 1939, s. 8); see *Gray* v. *Gray*, 1941 S.C. 461.
[51a] See Clive and Wilson, pp. 113-122.
[52] Fraser, I, 386; Bell's *Prin.*, § 1518; Dickson on *Evidence*, § 545.
[53] (1867) 5 M. (H.L.) 144.
[54] 11 Geo. IV, & 1 Will. IV, c. 69.
[55] *Ross* v. *Macleod* (1861) 23 D. 972; *Lindsay*, 1927 S.C. 395.
[56] *Morrison* v. *Dobson* (1869) 8 M. 347; *Maloy* v. *Macadam* (1885) 12 R. 431.
[57] *N.* v. *C.*, 1933 S.C. 492.

intercourse in reliance on it in themselves constituted the marriage.[58] It was not, however, recognised by the law until it had been judicially affirmed, but once affirmed the marriage dated from the intercourse.[59] The declarator might be brought at the instance of the man[60] or of a child of the parties.[61]

9. Cohabitation with Habit and Repute.[62]—This is the only form of irregular marriage now recognised by the law. The consent by which marriage is constituted may be proved by the cohabitation, or living together at bed and board, of a man and woman who are generally reputed husband and wife. The repute must be general and consistent, so preponderating as to leave no substantial doubt.[63] The fact that the cohabitation was at the outset adulterous is not fatal to the constitution of marriage by continuance of the cohabitation with repute after the parties become free to marry[64]; nor is the fact that at the beginning of the cohabitation there was no intention of marriage.[65] But, although there have been the requisite cohabitation and repute, there is no marriage if it be shown that the parties had not in fact any matrimonial intention.[66] In all the cases in which marriage has been thus established the cohabitation has continued for a considerable period.[67]

10. Registration of Marriages.—In the case of religious marriages there is a statutory provision requiring that the marriage schedule be signed by the parties, the witnesses and the celebrant and transmitted to the district Registrar within three days of the marriage. The Registrar must then cause particulars of the marriage to be entered in the register of marriages.[68] Similar provisions apply to a civil marriage.[69] Irregular marriages are registered following intimation to the Registrar General by the Principal Clerk of Session of the decree of declarator.[70]

11. Legal Effects of Marriage: Adherence.—It is the duty of spouses to adhere to each other. To the husband, as head of the household belongs the right of regulating it and fixing the place of residence, and, in the absence of just cause absolving her from that duty,[71] the wife must follow her husband

---

[58] *Mackie* v. *Mackie,* 1917 S.C. 276.
[59] *N.* v. *C.,* supra, per Lords Johnston and Morison.
[60] *Hardie* v. *Boog,* 1931 S.L.T. 198; see *Lindsay* v. *Lindsay,* supra.
[61] *X.* v. *Y.,* 1921, 1 S.L.T. 79.
[62] See Clive and Wilson, pp. 116-122.
[63] See *Petrie* v. *Petrie,* 1911 S.C. 360, per Lord Johnston, at p. 367; *Hamilton* v. *Hamilton* (1839) 2 D. 89, per Lord Fullerton.
[64] *Campbell* v. *Campbell* (1867) 5 M. (H.L.) 115; *De Thoren* v. *Wall* (1876) 3 R. (H.L.) 28. Cf. *Low* v. *Gorman* 1970 S.L.T. 356.
[65] *Hendry* v. *Lord Advocate,* 1930 S.C. 1027; see also *A.B.* v. *C.D.,* 1957 S.C. 415, cohabitation after void marriage.
[66] *Bairner* v. *Fels,* 1931 S.C. 674.
[67] Fraser, I, 400; *Wallace* v. *Fife Coal Co.,* 1909 S.C. 682. A modern case, mainly concerned with assessing the evidence available, is *Nicol* v. *Bell,* 1954 S.L.T. 314 (cohabitation for 22 years).
[68] Marriage (Scotland) Act 1977, s. 15.
[69] Ibid., s. 19 (3) and (4).
[70] Ibid., s. 21.
[71] As to which, see § 21, infra.

wherever he is.[72] A spouse may exclude the other from his or her house but may at any rate in the case of the husband, put himself in desertion by doing so.[73] A spouse may be relieved of the duty of adherence by decree of judicial separation or if the other spouse is unwilling to adhere or if there is reasonable cause for non-adherence.[74] The Court cannot, however, compel a spouse to adhere; and in modern practice actions for adherence are virtually unknown,[75] except when aliment is also sought. So essential to the married state is the duty of adherence that violation of that duty is recognised as a ground for divorce[76]; and for the same reason the Courts will not lend their aid to enforce a contract for voluntary separation.[77] Such contracts are revocable by either spouse at any time,[78] but the uncorroborated evidence of the pursuer is not sufficient to establish revocation.[79] A revocation is not effectual unless the party seeking to revoke is genuinely willing to adhere.[80] The contract may be revoked by deed or letter or by the institution of an action of divorce or separation, and falls if the parties resume cohabitation. If parties have been living separate under a contract of separation, the Court will grant decree for arrears of aliment which have become due in terms of the contract in the past but not for aliment in the future.[81]

The law formerly refused an action of reparation by one spouse against the other on the ground of the intimate relationship between them, but each may now sue the other in respect of a wrongful or negligent act or omission[82]; and a spouse may sue the other's employer for damages on the basis of vicarious liability.[83] An action of removing by one spouse against the other is competent, if they stand in the relation of landlord and tenant,[84] and an action based on contract is also competent.[85]

12. Aliment.—A husband is bound to aliment his wife if she is willing to live with him,[86] even if she is a confessed adulteress.[87] It is sufficient that he maintain or offer to maintain her at bed and board, but if she is voluntarily living apart his obligation to aliment her persists unless he is willing to cohabit with her and she does not have reasonable cause for non-cohabitation.[88] The

---

[72] *Stewart* v. *Stewart*, 1959 S.L.T. (Notes) 70.
[73] *MacLure* v. *MacLure*, 1911 S.C. 200; *Millar* v. *Millar*, 1940 S.C. 56. In *Burgess* v. *Burgess*, 1969 S.L.T. (Notes) 22, it was accepted, apparently without hesitation, that a wife who excluded her husband from the matrimonial home was in desertion. A wife, however, has ordinarily no obligation to aliment her husband and so no obligation to provide a home.
[74] See Divorce (Scotland) Act 1976 (c. 39), s. 7.
[75] But see *Stirling* v. *Stirling*, 1971 S.L.T. 322.
[76] See § 21, infra.
[77] *Macdonald* v. *Macdonald's Trs.* (1863) 1 M. 1065.
[78] Erskine, *Inst.*, I, 6, 30; Fraser, II, 911 et seq.; *Drummond* v. *Rollock* (1624) M. 6152; *Macdonald* v. *Macdonald's Trs.*, supra.
[79] *Barr* v. *Barr*, 1939 S.C. 696.
[80] *Palmer* v. *Bonnar*, January 25, 1812, F.C.; *Hood* v. *Hood* (1871) 9 M. 449; *Dickson* v. *Hunter* (1831) 5 W. & S. 458, per Lord Brougham L.C.
[81] *Livingston* v. *Begg*, 1666 M. 6153; *Bell* v. *Bell*, February 22, 1812, F.C.; *Hood* v. *Hood*, supra.
[82] Law Reform (H. & W.) Act 1962 (c. 48), s. 2: superseding *Harper* v. *Harper*, 1929 S.C. 220.
[83] *Webb* v. *Inglis*, 1958 S.L.T. (Notes) 8.
[84] *Millar* v. *Millar*, 1940 S.C. 56; see *Labno,* v. *Labno*, 1949 S.L.T. (Notes) 18 re ejection.
[85] *Horsburgh* v. *Horsburgh*, 1949 S.C. 227.
[86] *Beveridge* v. *Beveridge*, 1963 S.C. 572.
[87] *Donnelly* v. *Donnelly*, 1959 S.C. 97.
[88] Divorce (Scotland) Act 1976, (c. 39), s. 7.

amount of aliment which will be awarded by the Court depends on the rank and manner of life of the spouses.[89] An action for aliment without any conclusion or crave for divorce, separation or adherence is one of "interim" aliment and is competent in the Sheriff Court.[90] All awards of aliment are subject to variation or recall, and the jurisdiction of the Sheriff Court has recently been extended to include the power to recall or vary all final awards of inter alia aliment made by the Court of Session.[91] If the wife has been able to support herself, the Court will not grant decree for aliment in the past[92]; but the husband is liable to tradesmen who may have supplied goods necessary for her aliment.[93] The Married Women's Property (Scotland) Act 1920[94] for the first time places on a wife, who has a separate estate or has a separate income more than reasonably sufficient for her own maintenance, the obligation of providing her husband with maintenance if he is unable to maintain himself. A wife suing for divorce who states a prima facie case is entitled to apply for interim aliment at the earliest stage of the case.[95] It is now competent for the Court to grant decree of interim aliment to a pursuer who is voluntarily living apart from the defender except where the defender is willing to cohabit with her and she has no reasonable cause for non-cohabitation.[96] The Court now has the same powers to prevent alienations of property made wholly or partly for the purpose of defeating a claim for aliment made in any action of separation and aliment, adherence and aliment and interim aliment as it has in relation to claims for financial provision in divorce.[96a]

13. Jus Mariti.—The effect of marriage under the common law on the position and property of the wife has been profoundly modified by a series of statutes beginning in the middle of last century and concluding with the above-mentioned Act of 1920.[94] Many points formerly of importance have ceased to be of more than historical interest, and are, therefore, not dealt with in the succeeding paragraphs.

Of the rights accruing to the husband on marriage, the most important was the jus mariti. This was the right of property in the wife's moveable estate vested by law in the husband. Marriage had the effect of an assignation to him

---

[89] Erskine, *Inst.,* I, 6, 19; *Thomson* v. *Thomson* (1890) 17 R. 1091; *Scott* v. *Scott* (1894) 21 R. 853; and see *Alexander* v. *Alexander,* 1957 S.L.T. 298, where the husband's regular expenditure of capital was taken into account.

[90] *Donnelly* v. *Donnelly,* 1959 S.C. 97.

[91] Law Reform (M.P.) (Scotland) Act 1966 (c. 19), s. 8. Note the distinction between interim orders for aliment and actions of interim aliment; see *Donnelly* v. *Donnelly,* supra.

[92] *Macmillan* v. *Macmillan* (1871) 9 M. 1067. This may not apply if the wife is living apart under agreement to separate or after judicial separation; see Walton, pp. 205 and 124.

[93] See Clive and Wilson, pp. 263-265.

[94] 10 & 11 Geo. V (c. 64), s. 4. The earlier Acts are:—Conjugal Rights (Scotland) Amendment Act 1861 (24 & 25 Vict. c. 86), and the amending Act of 1874 (37 & 38 Vict. c. 31); Married Women's Property (Scotland) Act 1877 (40 & 41 Vict., c. 29); Married Women's Policies of Assurance (Scotland) Act 1880 (43 & 44 Vict., c. 26); Married Women's Property (Scotland) Act 1881 (44 & 45 Vict., c. 21). See *Beith's Trs.* v. *Beith,* 1950 S.C. 66 for an interesting review of the changes and their effect.

[95] *Fyffe* v. *F.,* 1954 S.C. 1; and see Walton, pp. 145 et seq., on aliment pendente lite: also *Barbour* v. *Barbour,* 1965 S.L.T. (Notes) 67.

[96] Divorce (Scotland) Act 1976, c. 39, s. 7.

[96a] Ibid., s. 6.

of the whole moveable estate belonging to the wife at the date of the marriage or which she might acquire during its subsistence. The husband became ipso jure owner of this property; he might sell or dispose of it at his pleasure; and his creditors might attach it for his debts.[97] But the jus mariti might be excluded by a renunciation or discharge in an ante-nuptial marriage-contract; and a provision in a conveyance or bequest of property to a wife by a third party that it should belong to the wife exclusive of the jus mariti was effectual. There were also certain goods known as paraphernalia which did not fall under the right; these consisted of the wife's wearing apparel, her personal ornaments, the receptacles in which these were kept, and things given to her as paraphernalia by the husband at or before marriage.[98]

Since the husband became entitled to the wife's moveable estate, he was liable for the whole of the moveable debts contracted by her before the marriage. This liability, originally unlimited, was by the Married Women's Property (Scotland) Act 1877 limited to the property received by the husband from or in right of his wife, at, before, or after, the marriage. Finally, by the Married Women's Property (Scotland) Act 1881,[99] the jus mariti was abolished in the case of marriages contracted after the date of the passing of the Act, July 18, 1881.

14. Jus Administrationis: Wife's Obligations.—Under the common law the husband became curator of the wife, and his consent to her acts in regard to her property was necessary. In the case of property falling under the jus mariti, the husband as owner might dispose of it as he pleased; but where that right did not apply (as in the case of heritable property), or where it was excluded, the jus administrationis had the effect of disabling the wife from effectually disposing of it without her husband's consent.

Further, as has already been noticed,[1] all obligations undertaken by a wife without her husband's consent were (with some exceptions) null[2]; and all personal obligations, even if undertaken with his concurrence, were (again with some exceptions) also null.[3] With some minor exceptions the wife could not sue without her husband being conjoined as her curator, and, if she were sued, it was necessary that he should be called along with her as a defender.

In these matters the Act of 1920 effected a radical alteration of the law. A married woman is no longer (unless she is a minor) under the curatory of her husband; the jus administrationis is wholly abolished, and she has the same power of disposing of her estate as if she were unmarried; she is capable of entering into contracts and incurring obligations, and may sue and be sued, as if she were unmarried, and her husband is no longer liable under contracts or obligations entered into or incurred by her on her own behalf. If the wife is

---

[97] *Fraser* v. *Walker* (1872) 10 M. 837.
[98] Erskine, *Inst.,* I, 6, 15; Fraser, I, 770; Clive and Wilson, p. 286.
[99] 44 & 45 Vict., c. 21.
[1] Capacity to Contract, Ch. VI, supra, § 5.
[2] Erskine, *Inst.,* I, 6, 20-24; Fraser, I, 519, 802.
[3] Erskine, *Inst.,* I, 6, 25; *Harvey* v. *Chessels,* 1791, Bell's *Cases,* 255; *Jackson* v. *MacDiarmid* (1892) 19 R. 528; *Galbraith* v. *Provident Bank* (1900) 2 F. 1148. Clive and Wilson, pp. 245-246.

deserted by, or living apart from, her husband, her contracts for the supply of goods to herself or her children bind her estate, but without prejudice to the right of the creditor to recover the price from the husband if he would have been liable under the former law.

15. Wife's Praepositura.—Where spouses are living together the wife is presumed to be praeposita negòtiis domesticis, and, as such, authorised to pledge her husband's credit for the price of goods necessary for the family (such as food, clothing, medicine, medicinal attendance and furniture) purchased by her.[4] This presumption rests on the fact that the ordering of household necessities is usually entrusted to the wife; and where the house of a widower was managed by his daughter, the father was on similar grounds held liable on contracts for such goods entered into by the daughter.[5] The goods must be of the kind suitable to the husband's position in life; and if the tradesman supplies the goods in reliance upon the wife's credit alone, he cannot hold the husband liable. Apart from this implied mandate, a husband may give his wife express authority to make contracts on his behalf, in which case he will be liable, on the ordinary principles of agency, on contracts within the scope of the authority conferred.

The husband may at his pleasure terminate the praepositura. He may do so formally by means of Inhibition. This is a writ in the Sovereign's name inhibiting the wife on the one hand from disposing of the husband's goods or contracting debts to his prejudice, and the lieges on the other from receiving from her such goods or advancing money or furnishing goods to her without her husband's special authority.[6] It is obtained by presenting a petition to the Outer House (which is granted as a matter of course) and on being registered in the General Register of Inhibitions it has the effect of terminating the praepositura in a question with all persons, whether they were or were not aware that it had been obtained.[7] Thereafter the husband is free from liability under the wife's contracts, with the exception that if he fails to provide her and his family with what is necessary for their maintenance, he remains liable to a tradesman who has supplied such goods.[8] Without resorting to inhibition, a husband may, by notification to a tradesman, free himself from liability to that tradesman; but public advertisement does not have this effect unless the tradesman was aware of the advertisement.

A wife is bound to account to her husband for her intromissions with money received as praepositura,[9] but the Married Women's Property Act 1964[10] has altered the law that savings made by the wife from such money remained the husband's property.[11] The Act[10] provides that money derived from any allowance made by the husband for the expenses of the matrimonial

---

[4] Erskine, *Inst.*, I, 6, 26.
[5] *Hamilton* v. *Forrester* (1825) 3 S. 572; see also *Debenham* v. *Mellon* (1880) 6 App.Cas. 24.
[6] *Juridical Styles* (3rd ed.), III, 280.
[7] *Topham* v. *Marshall*, 1808 M. "Inhibition" App. No. 2.
[8] Erskine, *Inst.*, I, 6, 26.
[9] *Ireland* v. *Ireland*, 1954 S.L.T. (Notes) 13.
[10] 1964, c. 19.
[11] See *Preston* v. *Preston*, 1950 S.C. 253, and cases cited therein.

home or for similar purposes, or property acquired out of such money, shall, in the absence of agreement to the contrary, be treated as belonging to the husband and wife in equal shares. This has been judicially construed as embracing football pool prize money won by a wife whose husband averred that she had taken the stake money from her housekeeping allowance.[12]

16. Donations between Spouses.—Under the common law a donation by one spouse to the other during marriage was revocable by the donor. This is no longer so,[13] but the right of creditors to revoke such a donation, if completed within a year and day before the sequestration of the donor's estate, is preserved.[14]

17. Policies of Assurance.—By the Married Women's Policies of Assurance (Scotland) Act 1880,[15] passed before the abolition of the jus mariti and jus administrationis, a married woman was enabled to effect a policy on the life of herself or her husband for her separate use and exclusive of these rights. The statute also contains a provision now of more practical importance that a policy, effected by a married man on his own life and expressed on the face of it to be for the benefit of his wife or children or both, shall be deemed a trust for these. "Children" includes adopted children.[16] Delivery of the policy is not required,[17] as it is enacted that when effected it is to vest in the husband and his representatives, or any other trustee nominated, in trust for the purposes so expressed, "and shall not otherwise be subject to his control, or form part of his estate, or be liable to the diligence of his creditors, or be revocable as a donation, or reducible on any ground of excess or insolvency." If, however, the policy was effected with intent to defraud creditors, or if the person insured is made bankrupt within two years from its date, the creditors are entitled to repayment of the premiums out of the proceeds of the policy.[18] This Act has been held to apply to a policy taken out by a widower for behoof of his children,[19] and to an endowment policy under which the sum was payable at a fixed date to the husband, whom failing his widow, where the husband had predeceased that date.[20] The trust is for the interest of the wife or children as that interest is expressed in the policy; it may be an interest vesting at once in the beneficiaries or, on the other hand, contingent on their surviving the husband.[21] If the interest has vested in the wife, then although she predeceases her husband, the proceeds of the policy on his death will form

---

[12] *Pyatt* v. *Pyatt*, 1966 S.L.T. (Notes) 73.
[13] Married Women's Property (Scotland) Act 1920, s. 5.
[14] Ibid.
[15] 43 & 44 Vict., c. 26.
[16] Children Act 1975 (c. 72), Sched. 2, § 1.
[17] *Jarvie's Trs.* v. *Jarvie's Trs.* (1887) 14 R. 411.
[18] 43 & 44 Vict., c. 26, s. 2; but see 10 & 11 Geo. V, c. 64, s. 5 (*b*).
[19] *Kennedy's Trs.* v. *Sharpe* (1895) 23 R. 146. It does not apply to a policy taken out by an unmarried man for his future wife on the eve of his marriage: *Coulson's Trs.* v. *Coulson* (1901) 3 F. 1041, per Lord Justice-Clerk Macdonald.
[20] *Chrystal's Trs.* v. *Chrystal*, 1912 S.C. 1003.
[21] *Chrystal's Trs.* v. *Chrystal*, supra, per Lord Johnston.

part of her estate,[22] but his estate is entitled to receive out of the proceeds of the policy repayment of the amount of the premiums paid since the wife's death.[23] The policy may be surrendered by the trustee with, and it may be even without, the consent of the beneficiary,[24] but the trust created by the policy cannot stante matrimonio be revoked or put an end to by the husband even with the consent of his wife and children.[25] The terms of settlement of such a policy may now be varied by the Court on divorce.[26]

18. Judicial Separation.—The grounds recognised by the common law as entitling a spouse to a decree of judicial separation were adultery and cruelty. The Licensing (Scotland) Act 1903[26a] added a third ground, viz. habitual drunkenness, by which was meant such drunkenness as rendered the person "at times dangerous to himself or herself or others or incapable of managing himself or herself and his or her affairs." The grounds justifying judicial separation are, however, now equiparated with the grounds for divorce.[27]

19. Dissolution of Marriage.—By the law of Scotland marriage cannot be dissolved till death, except by divorce. Until January 1, 1977 the grounds of divorce were adultery, wilful desertion, incurable insanity, cruelty, sodomy and bestiality. Divorce for adultery was introduced at the Reformation and rested on common law. Wilful desertion was first enacted as a ground of divorce in 1573 and re-enacted by the Divorce (Scotland) Act 1938[28] which also added the other four grounds. The previous grounds of divorce are, however, all now abolished by the Divorce (Scotland) Act 1976[29] which purports to substitute irretrievable breakdown of marriage as the sole ground of divorce. The question of jurisdiction in divorce and other consistorial causes has already been considered.[30] In all such actions the summons must be served on the defender personally, unless he or she cannot be found, in which case there must be edictal service and also service on the children of the marriage and on one or more of the next-of-kin, if these are known and are resident in the United Kingdom. These, whether cited or not, may enter appearance and state defences.[31] Decree will not be granted if there is collusion between the parties, and collusion is a ground for reducing a decree but the requirement that the pursuer take the oath of calumny, swearing that there has been no collusive agreement with the defender, has been abolished.[32] It is competent in this connection for the Lord Advocate to appear and lead

---

22 *Cousins* v. *Sun Life Assurance Society* [1933] 1 Ch. 126.
23 *Bilham* v. *Smith* [1937] 1 Ch. 636.
24 *Schumann* v. *Scottish Widow's Fund* (1886) 13 R. 678.
25 *Scottish Life Assurance Co.* v. *Donald* (1901) 9 S.L.T. 348; *Edinburgh Life Assurance Co.* v. *Balderston,* 1909 2 S.L.T. 323; cf. *Barras* v. *Scottish Widows' Fund* (1900) 2 F. 1094.
26 Divorce (Scotland) Act 1976, c. 39, s. 5.
26a 3 Edw. VII. c. 25, s. 73. See *Cox* v. *Cox.* 1942 S.C. 352; *Hutchison* v. *Hutchison,* 1945 S.C. 427; and *Rooney* v. *Rooney,* 1962 S.L.T. 294.
27 Divorce (Scotland) Act 1976, c. 39, s. 4.
28 1 & 2 Geo. VI, c. 50.
29 c. 39.
30 Courts and Jurisdiction, Ch. II, supra, § 10; and see Clive and Wilson, pp. 862 et seq.
31 Conjugal Rights (Scotland) Amendment Act 1861 (24 & 25 Vict. c. 86), s. 10.
32 1976 (c. 39), s. 9.

proof.[33] Collusion means "permitting a false case to be substantiated or keeping back a just defence."[34] "Mutual desire that a decree...should be obtained, and mutual action to facilitate this end, are not collusion, if there be no fabrication or suppression."[35] In all consistorial actions the facts must be proved: proof of admissions alone is not enough,[36] and, in proof of adultery a confession by a wife supported by production of an extract birth certificate purporting to be signed by herself and a paramour has been held insufficient.[37] Uncorroborated evidence of some acts may be accepted provided they form part of a pattern of conduct in which there is corroboration of other acts.[38] A finding of adultery in any previous proceedings and, in relation to the other grounds of divorce, an extract decree of separation if granted to the pursuer on substantially the same facts, may afford sufficient proof provided the evidence of the pursuer is also received.[39]

The Divorce (Scotland) Act 1976 provides that decree of divorce may be granted if, but only if, it is established in accordance with the provisions of the Act that the marriage has broken down irretrievably.[40] The seeming concentration on irretrievable breakdown as the sole ground of divorce is, however, misleading. The provisions of the Act on establishing irretrievable breakdown enact that on proof of any one of a series of matters, the marriage is to be taken to have broken down irretrievably with the result that irretrievable breakdown as such does not require to be proved. Each of these matters is, therefore, in effect, a distinct ground of divorce. The grounds so considered are—

(1) the adultery of the defender,
(2) behaviour of the defender of such a kind that the pursuer cannot reasonably be expected to cohabit with him,
(3) desertion of the pursuer by the defender for a period of two years,
(4) non-cohabitation for a period of two years combined with the defender's consent to divorce, and
(5) non-cohabitation for a period of five years.[41]

If, at any time before granting decree in an action of divorce, it appears to the court that there is a reasonable prospect of reconciliation it must continue the action to enable reconciliation to be attempted. Cohabitation during such a continuation is not to be taken into account for the purposes of the action and does not therefore, whatever its length, constitute condonation of adultery nor

---

[33] Conjugal Rights (Scotland) Amendment Act 1861, s. 8.
[34] *Walker* v. *Walker,* 1911 S.C. 169; *Fairgrieve* v. *Chalmers,* 1912 S.C. 745.
[35] *Administrator of Austrian Property* v. *Von Lorang,* 1926 S.C. 598, per Lord Sands, at p. 628; 1927 S.C. (H.L.) 80. See *Riddell* v. *Riddell,* 1952 S.C. 475.
[36] *Smith* v. *Smith,* 1929 S.C. 75.
[37] *MacKay* v. *MacKay,* 1946 S.C. 78; *Macfarlane* v. *Macfarlane,* 1956 S.C. 472. As to the need for expressly pleading an admission, see *MacColl* v. *MacColl,* 1948 S.C. 500.
[38] *Walker* v. *Walker,* 1953 S.C. 297; 1953 S.L.T. 170.
[39] Law Reform (Miscellaneous Provisions) (Scotland) Act 1968, s. 11; Divorce (Scotland) Act 1976 (c. 39), s. 3. and Sched. I, § 4. cf. Divorce (Scotland) Act 1938, s. 4 (2); *Wilson* v. *Wilson,* 1939 S.C. 102; *McInnes* v. *McInnes,* 1954 S.C. 396; *Burnett* v. *Burnett,* 1955 S.C. 183; *Hall* v. *Hall,* 1958 S.C. 206.
[40] s. 1 (1).
[41] s. 1 (2).

bar divorce for desertion.[42] Any ground of divorce, including adultery, may now be established by proof on a balance of probabilities.[43]

20. Divorce for Adultery.[44]—Carnal connection is necessary to constitute adultery. Artificial insemination by a donor is not adultery.[45] The Court will not order a wife or child to submit to blood tests for the purpose of obtaining evidence relevant to allegations of adultery.[46] It is no defence to an action of divorce for adultery that there has been adultery on the part of the pursuer: cross actions of divorce are competent.[47] Condonation or forgiveness of the offence by the aggrieved spouse is, however, a good defence.[48] In order that there may be condonation there must have been genuine belief that the adultery alleged to have been condoned has been committed.[49] Mere suspicion of infidelity will not found the plea.[50] Condonation will not be inferred from anything less than cohabitation, by which is meant living together as man and wife.[51] Verbal forgiveness or even sexual intercourse will not alone suffice. It is not essential to the plea of condonation that the spouses should have shared the same bed.[52] Section 2 (2) of the Divorce (Scotland) Act 1976 (c. 39) now permits continuance or resumption of cohabitation after knowledge of adultery provided cohabitation is confined to a period of three months from the date of continuation or resumption. Cohabitation within that period does not amount to condonation.[53] A condition attached to condonation is inept. If the offence is condoned, it can never thereafter be founded on as a ground of divorce but, if there is alleged to have been subsequent adultery, it may be used in evidence as throwing light on suspicious conduct with the same, or even a different, paramour.[54]

Another plea in defence to an action of divorce for adultery is lenocinium or connivance.[55] If a husband gives facilities, and creates opportunities, for adultery by his wife, he cannot obtain divorce for the offence at which he has thus connived. But this plea will not be applicable if the husband has done no more than refrain from dissuading his wife: there must be active facilitation of, or encouragement to, commission of the offence.[56] Delay, however long, to

---

[42] s. 2 (1).
[43] s. 1 (6).
[44] See Clive and Wilson, Ch. 16.
[45] *Maclennan* v. *Maclennan*, 1958 S.C. 105.
[46] *Whitehall* v. *Whitehall*, 1958 S.C. 252.
[47] See, for example, *Connell* v. *Connell*, 1950 S.C. 505.
[48] 1976 (c. 39), s. 1 (3). As to onus of proof, see *Andrews* v. *Andrews*, 1961 S.L.T. (Notes) 48; also *Mitchell* v. *Mitchell*, 1947 S.L.T. (Notes) 8.
[49] *Paterson* v. *Paterson*, 1938 S.C. 251; as to knowledge of the extent of the adultery, see *Ralston* v. *Ralston* (1881) 8 R. 371, and *Steven* v. *Steven*, 1919, 2 S.L.T. 239.
[50] *Collins* v. *Collins* (1882) 10 R. 250, and (1884) 11 R. (H.L.) 19.
[51] 1976 c. 39, ss. 1 (3) and 13 (2).
[52] *Edgar* v. *Edgar* (1902) 4 F. 632, per Lord M'Laren, at p. 635.
[53] Ibid, 1976 c. 39, s. 2 (2).
[54] *Collins* v. *Collins*, supra; *Robertson* v. *Robertson* (1888) 15 R. 1001; also *Nicol* v. *Nicol*, 1938 S.L.T. 98.
[55] 1976 Act, s. 1 (3).
[56] *Thomson* v. *Thomson*, 1908 S.C. 179; *Wemyss* v. *Wemyss* (1866) 4 M. 660. See also *Gallacher* v. *Gallacher*, 1928 S.C. 586, 1934 S.C. 339; *Hannah* v. *Hannah*, 1931 S.C. 275. Lenocinium, most inappropriate if the term is used precisely, has been regarded as attributable to a wife: *Riddell* v. *Riddell*, 1952 S.C. 475.

take proceedings will not, without other circumstances pointing to acquiescence or condonation, operate as a bar to an action for divorce on the
grounds either of adultery[57] or desertion.[58]

21. Divorce for Behaviour Justifying Non-cohabitation.—It is a ground of
divorce that, since the date of the marriage, the defender has at any time
behaved (whether or not as a result of mental abnormality and whether such
behaviour has been active or passive) in such a way that the pursuer cannot
reasonably be expected to cohabit with the defender.[59] This ground
comprehends cruelty, including statutory habitual drunkenness, and also
sodomy and bestiality under the previous law,[60] but it is broader than these
grounds and is not to be equiparated with them. While it is competent to
found on behaviour at any time since the date of the marriage, that behaviour
must be such that the pursuer cannot, at the date of the proof, reasonably be
expected to cohabit with the defender. Accordingly, behaviour in the remote
past, especially if followed by continued cohabitation, will normally be
relevant only in so far as it is part of, or throws light on, more recent conduct.
There is, however, no requirement that the behaviour should be extensive in
time, and a single serious incident may suffice. Although the behaviour need
not have been aimed at the pursuer, the defender's intention is not irrelevant
because it may affect the reasonableness of expecting continued cohabitation.
Behaviour suggests something more than a state of affairs or a mental or
physical condition[61] but, as the behaviour may be passive, it may consist in
neglect or inactivity. It is immaterial that the defender's conduct is
conditioned by insanity or mental deficiency, but a purely automatic reaction
or an action or state of inactivity which is determined by unavoidable physical
constraint is probably not behaviour for the purposes of the Act. There will
normally be a close relation between the reasonableness of the defender's
conduct and the reasonableness of expecting the pursuer to cohabit with him,
but if in any case that relation should be lacking it is only the latter which
requires to be considered.

22. Divorce for Desertion.[62]—The Divorce (Scotland) Act 1938,[63] by
section 7, repealed the Act 1573, c. 55, which was the foundation of divorce
for desertion, and section 11 of the Conjugal Rights (Scotland) Amendment
Act 1861,[64] which amended it. The 1938 Act has in turn been repealed by the
Divorce (Scotland) Act 1976 which provides for divorce where the defender
has wilfully and without reasonable cause deserted the pursuer and (1) during

[57] *Johnstone* v. *Johnstone,* 1931 S.C. 60; *Macfarlane* v. *Macfarlane,* 1956 S.C. 472, at p. 476. As to
    delay in bringing nullity proceedings, see *Allardyce* v. *Allardyce,* 1954 S.L.T. 334.
[58] *Monahan* v. *Monahan,* 1930 S.C. 221.
[59] 1976 Act, s. 1 (2) (*b*).
[60] See 7th ed. of this book Ch. XLV, §§ 23 and 24.
[61] See *Katz* v. *Katz,* [1972] 1 W.L.R. 955, per Sir. George Baker P. at p. 960. cf. *Thurlow* v.
    Thurlow [1975] 2 All E.R. 979; *H.* v. *H.,* 1968 S.L.T. 40; *Grant* v. *Grant,* 1974 S.L.T. (Notes) 54.
[62] See Clive and Wilson, Ch. 17, but note the modifications introduced by the Divorce (Scotland)
    Act 1976.
[63] 1 & 2 Geo. VI, c. 50.
[64] 24 & 25 Vict., c. 86.

a continuous period of two years thereafter the parties have not cohabited and (2) the pursuer has not refused a genuine and reasonable offer by the defender to adhere.[65] Until 1964 the law had required the pursuer to prove not only the initial wilful desertion but also the pursuer's willingness to adhere throughout the period necessary to qualify for a right to divorce.[66] That rule is now abrogated and the pursuer's state of mind after the date of the initial separation is no longer a relevant consideration except only for the purpose of assessing the credibility and reliability of the pursuer with a view to ascertaining inter alia whether or not the pursuer was truly a consenting party to the initial separation.

"Desertion is a bilateral transaction which involves a spouse who deserts and a spouse who is simultaneously willing to adhere."[67] The 1976 Act does not alter the meaning of "desertion" as used in the 1938 Act, which "connotes a parting from the deserted spouse in breach of matrimonial duty."[68] Accordingly, the pursuer must still prove that the defender separated from the pursuer against his or her will and not by agreement. Conversely, the defence of voluntary separation is open to the defender. Refusal of sexual intercourse per se is not desertion.[69] There must be something akin to a complete withdrawal from the society of the other spouse; but there may be desertion although the spouses continue to reside under the same roof.[70]

There must be a deliberate intention to desert and the desertion dates from the time when the intention to desert is established, provided that there is at that time de facto separation, whether voluntary or compulsory.[71] It is not desertion where the absence arose from some necessary cause or duty, nor where a wife refuses to live with relatives of her husband with whom he does not propose to live.[72] Refusal by the pursuer of a genuine and reasonable offer of adherence by the defender will terminate desertion.[73] Insanity may preclude the formation of the animus deserendi.[74]

"Reasonable cause" for non-adherence includes all such grave and weighty conduct of the pursuer as would make it unconscionable to ordain the defender to adhere.[75] It probably extends, exceptionally, to a condition for which the other spouse is not responsible and to behaviour before marriage.

[65] s. 1 (2) (c).
[66] *Macaskill* v. *Macaskill*, 1939 S.C. 187; *Borland* v. *Borland*, 1947 S.C. 432. This rule was modified by the Divorce (Scotland) Act 1964 (c. 91).
[67] *Burrell* v. *Burrell*, 1947 S.C. 569, per Lord President Cooper at p. 578.
[68] *Wilkinson* v. *Wilkinson*, 1942 S.C. 472, per Lord President Normand at pp. 476 et seq.
[69] *Lennie* v. *Lennie*, 1950 S.C. (H.L.) 1.
[70] Ibid., per Lord Normand at p. 5, and per Lord Reid at p. 16; see also Walton, p. 79.
[71] *Trondsen* v. *Trondsen*, 1948 S.L.T. (Notes) 85; see also *Beeken* v. *Beeken* [1948] P. 302 (C.A.); as to the inference to be drawn from the silence of the absent spouse, cf. *Lough* v. *Lough*, 1930 S.C. 1016, with *Lench* v. *Lench*, 1945 S.C. 295.
[72] *Young* v. *Young*, 1947 S.L.T. 5; cf. *Stewart* v. *Stewart*, 1959 S.L.T. (Notes) 70.
[73] 1976 Act, s. 1 (2) (c) (ii); as to bona fides, see *Martin* v. *Martin*, 1956 S.L.T. (Notes) 41; as to reasonableness, see *Burnett* v. *Burnett*, 1958 S.C. 1; and see Clive and Wilson, pp. 501-502.
[74] *Mudie* v. *Mudie*, 1956 S.C. 318; and see *Crowther* v. *Crowther* [1951] A.C. 723, per Lord Reid at 736.
[75] *Richardson* v. *Richardson*, 1956 S.C. 394; *M'Millan* v. *M'Millan*, 1962 S.C. 115, conduct suggestive of adultery; *Hamilton* v. *Hamilton*, 1953 S.C. 383, confession of adultery; *A.B.* v. *C.B.*, 1959 S.C. 27, murder, while insane, of a child of the marriage; *Cameron* v. *Cameron*, 1956 S.L.T. (Sh. Ct.) 21, intolerable conduct held to fall short of legal cruelty; *Hastings* v. *Hastings*,

The remedy of divorce is not available until the expiry of two years from the date of the initial act of desertion, after which the pursuer acquires a vested right to divorce and any offer of adherence thereafter comes too late.[76] The only relevance of privy admonition is to show that the pursuer did not acquiesce in the initial separation.[77] Section 2 (4) of the 1976 Act permits spouses to resume cohabitation for a period or periods not exceeding six months in all without interrupting the continuity of the period of non-cohabitation required by the Act, but such periods of cohabitation cannot count towards the required period of non-cohabitation. Cohabitation for any greater length of time will interrupt the statutory period of non-cohabitation and so terminate the emergent right to divorce. Since sexual intercourse per se does not amount to cohabitation, an act or, it may be, acts of sexual intercourse without resumption of cohabitation have no effect. After expiry of the qualifying period of non-cohabitation, a resumption of cohabitation will bar divorce unless the cohabitation is confined to the period of three months following the resumption.[78] The adultery of the pursuer before or at the time of separation, if uncondoned, affords reasonable cause for non-adherence by the defender and so bars divorce. Adultery of the pursuer thereafter is irrelevant.

23. Divorce of Consent.—There is ground for divorce if there has been no cohabitation between the parties to the marriage at any time during a continuous period of two years after the date of the marriage and immediately preceding the bringing of the action and the defender consents to the granting of decree of divorce.[79] Consent must be indicated in the prescribed manner and may be withdrawn at any time before decree is granted.[80] Failure to defend or even known absence of objection is not enough. There is no provision for dispensation with consent, and so this ground of divorce is not available where the defender lacks capacity. The period of non-cohabitation is calculated and allowance made for intervening periods of cohabition on the same principle as described in the next paragraph.

24. Divorce for Non-cohabitation.—It is a ground for divorce that there has been no cohabitation between the parties at any time during a continuous period of five years after the date of the marriage and immediately preceding the bringing of the action.[81] The right to bring an action emerges on the day after the fifth anniversary of the separation.[82] Periods of cohabitation not

---

1941 S.L.T. 323, fraud on defender; cf. *Brown* v. *Brown,* 1955 S.L.T. 48, where Lord Wheatley held embezzlement not to be "reasonable cause" but suggested that indecent practices might be; see also *White* v. *White,* 1966 S.L.T. 288.

[76] *Bell* v. *Bell,* 1941 S.C. (H.L.) 5; see also *Scott* v. *Scott,* 1908 S.C. 1124, re insanity of defender.

[77] See *Woodhouse* v. *Woodhouse,* 1936 S.C. 523, per Lord President Normand, at p. 530.

[78] 1976 Act, s. 2 (3).

[79] 1976 Act, s. 1 (2) (*d*). On the meaning of cohabitation and whether or not a mental element is required, see § 24 and footnote 85 infra.

[80] Ibid., s. 1 (4); cf. *Beales* v. *Beales* [1972] 2 All E.R. 667 at 674; *M'Gill* v. *Robson* [1972] 1 W.L.R. 237; *Mason* v. *Mason* [1972] Fam. 302.

[81] Ibid. s. 1 (2) (*e*).

[82] i.e. by the civilis computatio; cf. *Warr* v. *Warr* [1975] 1 All E.R. 85.

exceeding six months in all do not interrupt the continuity of the non-cohabitation but are left out of account in measuring its length.[83] Cohabitation means that the spouses are in fact living together as man and wife.[84] It is undecided whether a mental element is required for non-cohabitation, so as to exclude cases where the separation is involuntary or without intention of breaking the consortium, as in absence because of imprisonment, illness or the exigencies of military, professional or other duties.[85]

The court has a discretion to refuse decree in an action on this ground, if to grant it would result in grave financial hardship to the defender. Hardship for this purpose includes the loss of the chance of acquiring any benefit.[86]

25. Effect of Divorce on Property.—Prior to the Succession (Scotland) Act 1964[87] a decree of divorce granted on any ground other than incurable insanity had the same effect as regards the property of the parties and their rights and interests in any property as if the decree had been granted on the ground of adultery.[88]

Part IV of the Succession (Scotland) Act[89] 1964 introduced new provisions governing the financial rights and obligations of spouses on divorce, except for incurable insanity, and terminated the right of the innocent spouse to claim legal rights in actions commenced on or after September 10, 1964. The relevant law is now contained in section 5 of the Divorce (Scotland) Act 1976. The Court, on granting decree of divorce, may now order either spouse to pay to the other such periodical allowance as it thinks fit, having regard to the means of the parties and to all the circumstances of the case.[90] An application for such an order after decree of divorce is competent only if there has been a change in the circumstances of either party.[91] Such an order, being alimentary, is subject to variation or recall by the Court of Session or by the Sheriff Court,[92] may be enforced under the Maintenance Orders Act 1950,[93] and terminates on the remarriage or death of the person in whose favour it was made.[94] The Court also has power to make an order for payment by one spouse to the other of such capital sum as it thinks fit.[95] The terms of any marriage settlement, so far as taking effect on or after termination of the

[83] 1976 Act, s. 2 (4).
[84] Ibid., s. 13 (2).
[85] Cf. *Santos* v. *Santos* [1972] Fam, 247. The 1976 Act is, however, stronger against a mental element in non-cohabitation than is the corresponding wording of the Divorce Reform Act 1969 in England and Wales.
[86] 1976 Act, s. 1 (5).
[87] 1964, c. 41.
[88] 1 & 2 Geo. VI, c. 50, s. 2 (1). As to that effect, see 6th ed. of this book, p. 615, Clive and Wilson, p. 540, and *Coats' Trs.* v. *Inland Revenue*, 1965 S.L.T. 145.
[89] 1964, c. 41, ss. 24, 33 (2) and 38 (3).
[90] s. 5 (1) (*a*) and (2).
[91] s. 5 (3).
[92] s. 5 (4) and Law Reform (M.P.) (Scotland) Act 1966, c. 19, s. 8 (1) (*c*) and (*e*).
[93] 1976 Act, Sched. 1, § 1.
[94] s. 5 (5) (*b*).
[95] s. 5 (1) (*b*) and (2).

marriage, may also be varied by the Court on the application of either party.[96] The Court is also given power to prevent a spouse from alienating any of his property by settlement or disposition in favour of a third party when it is satisfied that alienation has been or is to be made wholly or partly for the purpose of defeating in whole or in part any claim by the other spouse for a periodical allowance or capital payment.[97] Reduction is available only where the alienation is by instrument or deed but interdict may be granted against the alienation of property or its transfer out of the jurisdiction or other dealing with it by whatever means.[98] It is not normally necessary in an undefended action for the pursuer to seek to recover detailed evidence of the defender's means by diligence.[99]

26. Dissolution of Marriage on Presumed Death of Spouse.—Where a person who is missing is thought to have died or has not been known to be alive for a period of at least seven years, any person having an interest, including a spouse of the missing person, may raise an action of declarator of his death.[1] Decree will be granted on the court's being satisfied either (1) that the missing person has died, or (2) that he has not been known to be alive for a period of at least seven years.[2] In the latter event he is deemed to have died at the end of the day occurring seven years after the date on which he was last known to be alive.[2] Once the time for appeal has expired or, if an appeal is taken, once the appeal is withdrawn or refused, the decree is effective for all purposes including the dissolution of a marriage to which the missing person was a party.[3] The marriage is not revived if the decree is subsequently recalled or varied, or if it appears that the missing person was in fact alive.[4]

---

[96] s. 5 (1) (c) and (2).
[97] s. 6; see *Johnstone* v. *Johnstone*, 1967 S.L.T. 248.
[98] *Maclean* v. *Maclean*, 1976 S.L.T. 86.
[99] *Gould* v. *Gould*, 1966 S.L.T. 130; cf., where issue is joined as to the amount of the defender's means, *Douglas* v. *Douglas*, 1966 S.L.T. (Notes) 43.
[1] Presumption of Death (Scotland) Act 1977, c. 27, s. 1. See Ch. XLII, supra, § 1.
[2] Ibid., s. 2 (1).
[3] Ibid., s. 3 (1).
[4] Ibid., s. 3 (4).

CHAPTER XLVII

PARENT AND CHILD: GUARDIANSHIP

Fraser, *Parent and Child* (3rd ed., 1906); Bevan, *The Law Relating to Children* (1973); Bevan and Parry, *Children Act 1975* (1978).

I. PARENT AND CHILD

1. Legitimacy.—In accordance with the brocard "pater est quem nuptiae demonstrant," the child born of a married woman during the subsistence of the marriage is presumed to be legitimate.[1] This presumption holds also in the case of a child born after the dissolution of the marriage if its birth takes place at a date which allows of conception while the marriage subsisted.[2] But the presumption applies only where the child may have been conceived during the marriage,[3] and it is, therefore, inapplicable where the child is born within so short a period after the celebration of the marriage, or at a date so long after its dissolution, as to make it impossible that it was conceived in wedlock.[4] There is also authority to the effect that the presumption does not hold where the marriage is irregular;[5] and it is not applicable where the question at issue is whether there ever was marriage between the parents of the child.[6]

The presumption in favour of legitimacy is very strong, but it may be overcome. The mere fact that the mother was guilty of adultery during the period when the child must have been conceived is not sufficient for this purpose.[7] It is otherwise if it is proved that the husband is impotent or that he was absent from the wife at the date of the child's conception, but the proof of his absence must be "special and circumstantiate that there remaineth no doubt that he could not have been present."[8] According to the more recent authorities, the law does not insist on proof that access by the husband to the wife was impossible[9]; but the Court must be satisfied that intercourse did not take place between the spouses at any time during the period in which the

---

[1] Stair, III, 3, 42; Erskine, *Inst.*, I, 6, 49; Bell, *Prin.*, § 1626.
[2] Fraser, *Parent and Child*, 2. This work is hereafter referred to as Fraser.
[3] See the opinions in *Gardner* v. *Gardner* (1876) 3 R. 695.
[4] Stair, supra; *Lepper* v. *Watson*, 1802 Hume 488; *Aitken* v. *Mitchell*, 1806 Hume 489.
[5] *Swinton* v. *Swinton* (1862) 24 D. 833; *Baptie* v. *Barclay* (1665) M 8431; but cf. Stair, III, 3, 42, and IV, 45, 20.
[6] *Deans' Judicial Factor* v. *Deans*, 1912 S.C. 441.
[7] Stair, supra; *Routledge* v. *Carruthers*, May 19, 1812, F.C.
[8] Stair, supra.
[9] For weight to be given to the presumption in affiliation actions at the instance of a married woman, see *Ballantyne* v. *Douglas*, 1953 S.L.T. (Notes) 10. *Quaere* if dicta in that case on the standard of proof in rebuttal apply outwith the context of affiliation actions. The standard is usually taken to be proof beyond reasonable doubt (*Imre* v. *Mitchell*, 1958 S.C. 439 at 462; *Brown* v. *Brown* 1972 S.L.T. 143 at 145). It is undecided whether this is affected by the lowering of the standard of proof of adultery in actions of divorce (Divorce (Scotland) Act 1976, s. 1 (6)).

child might have been conceived.[10] In a question as to the legitimacy of a child, the direct evidence of a parent is admissible.[11] Moreover, extrajudicial "statements of the parents made without reference to present or prospective litigation, and especially if these statements were made under circumstances which naturally called for explanation" are receivable in evidence.[12] But where the parents have once acknowledged the child as lawful, their testimony cannot afterwards be used to overcome the presumption in favour of its legitimacy.[13]

Where a child is born before the marriage there is no presumption, arising from the fact of the subsequent marriage, that the husband is the father of the child.[14] On the other hand, if a man marries a woman in the knowledge that she is pregnant, and there have been opportunities for intercourse prior to the marriage, these circumstances raise a very strong presumption that he is the father of the child.[15]

2. Children of Putative Marriage.—A putative marriage is one contracted in the bona fide belief on the part of one, or both, of the parties that they are free to marry, whereas there is in fact an impediment to the marriage. In these circumstances, although there is no marriage, yet by reason of the good faith of one or both of the parties, the children procreated before the impediment is discovered are entitled to the status of legitimacy[16]; according to Lord Fraser the marriage must be a regular one and the error must be one of fact and not of law.[17] In *Purves' Trs.* v. *Purves*[18] an averment by the parents of a child, the mother being the niece of the father's deceased wife, that they had married in ignorance that parties so related were forbidden to marry was held irrelevant as an averment of such bona fides as would save the legitimacy of the child.

By the Law Reform (Miscellaneous Provisions) Act 1949, section 4 (1),[19] it is provided that where a voidable marriage is declared null, any child who

---

[10] *Brodie* v. *Dyce* (1872) 11 M. 142; *Steedman* v. *Steedman* (1887) 14 R. 1066; *Coles* v. *Homer & Tulloh* (1895) 22 R. 716. What the possible maximum duration of pregnancy is has not yet been determined. In *Currie* v. *Currie*, 1950 S.C. 10, 336 days was not ruled out, but such a period was held to go far towards entitling the Court to infer adultery. In *Wood* v. *Wood* [1947] 2 All E.R. 95, 346 days was accepted. But doctors differ and this has been denounced as impossible: see *British Medical Journal* of Nov. 27, 1948. In *Preston-Jones* v. *Preston-Jones* [1951] A.C. 391 the House of Lords decided that 360 days was excessive, at least in the absence of acceptable medical evidence. See Glaister and Rentoul, *Medical Jurisprudence* (12th ed), p. 359.

[11] *Imre* v. *Mitchell*, 1958 S.C. 439; *Burman* v. *Burman*, 1930 S.L.T. 120. Dicta by Lord M'Laren in *Tennant* v. *Tennant* (1890) 17 R. 1205 to the effect that it was contrary to principle to allow the legitimacy of a child to be taken away by such evidence can be accepted, if at all, only in the sense that evidence of this kind may not amount, if it stands alone, to full legal proof.

[12] *Tennent* v. *Tennent* supra; see *Burman* v. *Burman*, supra.

[13] Bankton, I, 2, 3; *Imre* v. *Mitchell* supra, per Lord President Clyde, at p. 464.

[14] *Brooke's Executrix* v. *James*, 1971 S.C. (H.L.) 71.

[15] Ibid. In *Imre* v. *Mitchell*, supra, Lord President Clyde at p. 462, following Lord Blackburn in *Gardner*, describes the presumption as "almost irresistible."

[16] Stair, III, 3, 41; Erskine, *Inst.*, I, 6, 51; see *Brymer* v. *Riddell*, 1811, Bell's Report of a case of Legitimacy; Fraser, 27; *Smijth* v. *Smijth*, 1918 1 S.L.T. 156; *Petrie* v. *Ross* (1896) 4 S.L.T. 63.

[17] Fraser, 33 and 34, sed quaere. See Bankton, I, 5, 51, on the significance of regular marriage and *Purves' Trs.* v. *Purves*, supra, on dubium jus and error in law supported by popular sentiment. In *Philip's Trs.* v. *Beaton*, 1938 S.C. 733, opinions were expressly reserved on the question of error juris.

[18] (1896) 22 R. 513.

[19] 12, 13 & 14 Geo. VI, c. 100; and see Walton: *Husband and Wife* (4th ed.) p. 235.

would have been the legitimate child of the parties had the marriage been dissolved, and not annulled, on the date of the decree is to be deemed to be legitimate notwithstanding the annulment.

3. Legitimation per Subsequens Matrimonium.—An illegitimate child is legitimated by the subsequent intermarriage of the parents. At common law that is subject to the proviso that they were free to marry at the time when the child was conceived.[20] The grounds on which this rule is based are discussed in *Kerr* v. *Martin*,[21] where the question was whether the marriage of the father of an illegitimate child in the interval between the birth of the child and his marriage to the mother excluded the legitimation of the child. It was held by a narrow majority that it did not, but it was indicated in the opinions of the Court that the legitimation of this child could not have the effect of prejudicing the rights of succession of the children of the father's earlier marriage. The offspring of an adulterous or incestuous connection are not legitimated by the marriage of their parents.[22]

The common law rules will continue to apply to cases in which it is necessary to rely on legitimation before June 8, 1968. For all other cases the common law is superseded by the Legitimation (Scotland) Act 1968.[23] Under that Act legitimation takes place from the date of the marriage, or from June 8, 1968 if the marriage was before then, whether or not the parents were free to marry when the child was conceived.[24] Legitimation may be effected by a putative or voidable marriage as well as by a valid marriage and, if a child has died before the marriage of his parents, the rights and obligations of persons alive at the date of the marriage are to be determined as if the child had been legitimated.[25]

4. Pupillarity and Minority.—A person under the age of 18 is in minority.[26] But this period is subdivided into pupillarity,[27] which continues until the age of 14 in males and 12 in females, and minority, which continues in both sexes till the age of 18. "A pupil has no person in the legal sense of the word. He is incapable of acting or even of consenting."[28] Minors, on the other hand, can legally act. The difference between pupils and minors as regards the power to test[29] and of entering into contracts[30] has already been noticed; and

---

[20] Erskine, *Inst.*, I, 6, 52; Bankton, V, 57-8.
[21] (1840) 2 D. 752; see also *M'Neill* v. *M'Gregor* (1901) 4 F. 123.
[22] Erskine and Bankton, supra; Bell, *Prin.*, § 1627.
[23] 1968, (c. 22).
[24] Ibid., ss. 1, 4.
[25] Ibid., ss. 8 (1) and 3.
[26] Age of Majority (Scotland) Act 1969, (c. 39), s. 1.
[27] "Pupillarity" may by statute be given an extended meaning: see e.g. *Wilson* v. *Wilson*, 1954 S.L.T. (Sh. Ct.) 68.
[28] Erskine, *Inst.*, I, 7, 14; *Hill* v. *City of Glasgow Bank* (1879) 7 R. 68, per Lord President Inglis at p. 74; *Sinclair* v. *Stark* (1828) 6 S. 336, per Lords Craigie and Cringletie. These dicta must, however, be read subject to some qualification. A pupil has passive capacity and probably may bind others in a negotium claudicans (discussed in relation to minors by T. B. Smith, *Short Commentary*, p. 795, but the principle is also applicable to pupils). He may also invite criminal and delictual liability (for criminal liability he must be 8 or over).
[29] Testate Succession, Ch. XLIII, supra, § 1.
[30] Capacity to Contract, Ch. VI, supra, §§ 2-4.

it is necessary here only to consider the rights and obligations which exist between parent and child and the provisions of the law as to the custody and guardianship of pupils and minors. In these matters there is a distinction, less marked than it once was, in the treatment of legitimate and of illegitimate children, and the position of the latter will be considered separately.[31]

5. Parental Authority.—At common law the parental authority over a legitimate child belonged exclusively to the father. Such powers as the mother had during the father's lifetime arose by delegation or, in the absence of the father, by principles akin to those on which powers may be vested in loco parentis. By the Guardianship Act 1973 it is, however, provided that the rights and authority of a mother and father shall be equal and exercisable by either without the other.[32] Previous references to the patria potestas and to the authority of the father must therefore now be read as referring to the authority of each parent.

Parental authority over a pupil child is such as may be described as a right of dominion.[33] The parent is entitled to govern the person of the child and to order its upbringing. But when the child on attaining puberty acquires legal capacity, a change in this authority takes place. The parental authority does not come to an end, for the parent still retains authority over the child, but it is weakened.[34] To what extent precisely the parent retains control over a child in puberty has never been defined. In *Harvey* v. *Harvey*[35] these propositions were formulated—"(1) That the control to which a minor pubes is subjected does not proceed on any notion of his incapacity to exercise a rational judgment or choice, but rather arises, on the one hand, from a consideration of the reverence and obedience to parents which both the law of nature and the divine law enjoin, and, on the other hand, from a regard to the inexperience and immaturity of judgment on the part of the child, which require friendly and affectionate counsel and aid. (2) That the power of a father at this age is conferred not as a right of dominion, or even as a privilege for the father's own benefit or pleasure, but merely, or at least mainly, for the benefit, guidance and comfort of the child. (3) That, therefore, the father's authority and right of control may at this age of the child be easily lost, either by an apparent intention to abandon it and leave the child to his own guidance, or by circumstances or conduct showing the father's inability or unwillingness to discharge rightly the parental duty towards his child. (4) That in all questions as to the loss of the parental control during puberty from any of these causes, the wishes and feelings of the child himself are entitled to a degree of weight corresponding to the amount of intelligence and right feeling which he may exhibit."

---

[31] §§ 8, 9, infra.

[32] 1973, (c. 29), s. 10 (1).

[33] Stair, I, 5, 13; *Harvey* v. *Harvey* (1860) 22 D. 1198, per Lord Justice-Clerk Inglis.

[34] *Greenock Parish Council* v. *Kilmarnock and Stirling Parish Councils*, 1911 S.C. 570, per Lord Dunedin; *Fisher* v. *Edgar* (1894) 21 R. 1076, per Lord M'Laren. See § 7, infra.

[35] Supra; see also *Craig* v. *Greig & Macdonald* (1863) 1 M. 1172, per Lord Justice-Clerk Inglis, Lords Benholme and Mackenzie.

The parental authority is subject to control, in the interest of the children, by the Court of Session and terminates when the child attains majority. It may terminate earlier on the death of the parents or if the child is forisfamiliated while in minority. What is meant by forisfamiliation in this connection is that the child has, with parental consent, set out on an independent course of life.[36] It is inferred by the child's marriage, at least in the case of a daughter; or by the child, with parental assent, setting up house for himself on his own resources. So a parent by his conduct may forfeit his power if he deals unnaturally with his children, either by cruelty or by unwillingness to provide them with means suitable to their condition.[37] An action of reparation founded on delict or quasi-delict is competent at the instance of a minor child against his parents.[38]

6. Aliment.—A father is under a natural obligation to support his child, and his is the primary obligation.[39] The amount of aliment which he may be required to afford is no more than will support the child beyond want[40]; but "want" is a relative term to be interpreted in accordance with the social position of the parties.[41] The obligation subsists not only during minority but even after the child has become major. But there is a distinction between the claim of a son who has completed his professional or business training and of one who has not: in the former case the Court is not so ready to award aliment, but will do so if the father has sufficient means and the son has become indigent through physical or mental incapacity or through inability to obtain suitable employment which will afford him maintenance.[42] The father may discharge his obligation in the manner which is least burdensome to himself; and accordingly an offer by him to receive and maintain the child in his house is an answer to a claim for an award of aliment, unless by his conduct he has forfeited his right to this alternative.[43] If the father does not maintain the child in family or make him an allowance for his support, and he is not otherwise provided for, the father will be liable to tradesmen who supply the child with necessary furnishings.[44] Under the Education Acts a father is bound to have his children educated, and may be punished for failure to do so.

If the father is dead or unable to afford aliment, his child is entitled to

---

[36] "Forisfamiliation" is used in a rather different sense as regards a claim for legitim; see Legal Rights, Ch. XL, supra, § 5.

[37] Stair, I, 5, 13; Erskine, *Inst.*, I, 6, 53.

[38] *Young* v. *Rankin*, 1934 S.C. 499.

[39] Stair, I, 3, 3, and I, 9, 1, and Erskine, III, 1, 9, speak of this as an "obediential," i.e. a natural obligation; *Fairgrieves* v. *Hendersons* (1885) 13 R. 98; *Dickinson* v. *Dickinson*, 1952 S.C. 27. See too National Assistance Act 1948 (c. 29), s. 42.

[40] *Maule* v. *Maule* (1825) 1 W. & S. 266.

[41] *Thom* v. *Mackenzie* (1864) 3 M. 177; *Smith* v. *Smith* (1885) 13 R. 126. In *Dickinson* v. *Dickinson*, supra, the Court increased the amount of aliment upon a consideration of the income tax exigible.

[42] Erskine, *Inst.*, I, 6, 56; *Reid* v. *Moir* (1866) 4 M. 1060; *Whyte* v. *Whyte* (1901) 3 F. 937; *Watson* v. *Watson* (1896) 33 S.L.R. 771.

[43] Erskine, *Inst.*, I, 6, 56; *Bell* v. *Bell* (1890) 17 R. 549.

[44] Stair, I, 5, 7; Erskine, *Inst.*, I, 6, 57; as to the child's liability, see Sale of Goods Act 1893, s. 2.

aliment from the following relatives in this order:—(1) the mother[45]; (2) the paternal ascendants in their order; and (3) the maternal ascendants in their order[46]; and the obligation is reciprocal, for these relatives may require aliment from him. But a person cannot claim to be alimented by his father or ascendants if he has himself descendants, unless these are unable to afford him aliment. A father is not bound to support his daughter-in-law,[47] nor a stepmother her stepson[48]; nor is a man bound to support his parents-in-law, except in so far as he has been lucratus by his marriage.[49]

There is no natural duty of aliment as between brothers and sisters or other collaterals.[50] But there may be liability on the ground of representation. The father's obligation will be transmitted with his estate, and if one child takes the estate he does so with the corresponding liability to aliment his brothers and sisters out of that estate. There would be no such liability, however, if in the division of the estate among the children equality or substantial equality had been observed.[51] It is not clearly settled whether the liability does or does not devolve on the representatives of more distant relatives such as grandparents[52]; but at all events it does so devolve if the obligation has been acknowledged by the relative in his lifetime.[53]

If a child has separate estate and is alimented by a parent, the latter is entitled to be reimbursed out of the income of that estate.[54] And indeed in a proper case a parent, when one of ample means, may be entitled to be recompensed for the maintenance and education of children out of the capital belonging to those children.[55]

Where the Supplementary Benefits Commission has given relief to one who has a claim for aliment against a relative, it may obtain from the Court an order upon that relative to pay "such sum, weekly or otherwise as the Court may consider appropriate."[56] And a father who, being able to do so, persistently neglects to maintain his children may be prosecuted and punished by fine or imprisonment.[57]

7. Custody of Children.—Under the common law the father of a pupil child, or the mother after the father's death, was entitled to its custody. This

[45] See National Assistance Act 1948, (11 & 12 Geo. VI, c. 29), s. 42 (1); Supplementary Benefits Act 1976 (c. 71), s. 17 (1).
[46] Fraser, 100; see *Cooper* v. *Fife Coal Co.,* 1907 S.C. 564, and *Ewart* v. *R. & W. Ferguson,* 1932 S.C. 277.
[47] *Hoseason* v. *Hoseason* (1870) 9 M. 37; *Mackay* v. *Mackay's Trs.* (1904) 6 F. 936.
[48] *Macdonald* v. *Macdonald* (1846) 8 D. 830.
[49] *M'Allan* v. *Alexander* (1888) 15 R. 863.
[50] Fraser, 102.
[51] *Mackintosh* v. *Taylor* (1868) 7 M. 67; *Beaton* v. *Beaton's Trs.,* 1935 S.C. 187; *Hutchison* v. *Hutchison's Trs.,* 1951 S.C. 108.
[52] Contrast Lord Ivory's note to Erskine, I, 6, 58, quoted in *Spalding* v. *Spalding's Trs.* (1874) 2 R. 237, and *Anderson* v. *Grant* (1899) 1 F. 484, with *Smith* v. *Smith's Trs.* (1882) 19 S.L.R. 552, and Fraser, 129. See also *Parish Council of Leslie* v. *Gibson's Trs.* (1899) 1 F. 601; *Gay's Tutrix* v. *Gay's Trustee,* 1953 S.L.T. 278.
[53] *Parish Council of Leslie* v. *Gibson's Trs.* (1899) 1 F. 601.
[54] *Ker's Trs.* v. *Ker,* 1927 S.C. 52; *Duke of Sutherland, Petitioner* (1901) 3 F. 761; *Hutcheson* v. *Hoggan's Trs.* (1904) 6 F. 594.
[55] *Pollard* v. *Sturrock's Exrs.,* 1952 S.C. 535.
[56] National Assistance Act 1948 (11 & 12 Geo. VI, c. 29), s. 43; Supplementary Benefits Act 1976 (c. 71), s. 18 (1). The section is obscure, but seems to entitle the Court to order the defender to make up for past default.
[57] 1948 Act, s. 51; 1976 Act, s. 27. *Cullen* v. *Maclean,* 1960 S.L.T. (Notes) 85.

right was subject to control by the Inner House of the Court of Session in the exercise of the nobile officium, but the Court would not interfere with the father's right unless it could be shown that the child's health or morals would be endangered by his remaining in the father's custody.[58] The common law has been substantially modified by legislation, and questions of custody brought under any Act of Parliament are dealt with, as the case may be, in the Outer House of the Court of Session[59] or the Sheriff Court within whose jurisdiction the respondent resides.[60] Most applications for custody, including all custody disputes between parents, are brought under statute. Until 1970 those applications for custody which were not brought under statute required to be made by way of petition to the Inner House.[61] Although all such applications involve the exercise of the nobile officium they are now, however, presented to the Outer House.[62]

In 1861 jurisdiction was conferred on the Court in actions of divorce or judicial separation to pronounce orders as to the custody, maintenance and education of the pupil children of the marriage[63]; this power now extends to children up to the age of sixteen.[64] The Act of 1861 gave the Court in such actions a wide discretion in dealing with these matters, the paramount consideration being the welfare of the children.[65] The custody jurisdiction of the Outer House in actions of divorce and separation was extended in 1958 to actions of nullity,[66] and also to cover any child who is the illegitimate child of both parties to the marriage, or is the child of one party (including any illegitimate or adopted child) and has been accepted as one of the family by the other party.[67] Where the action is dismissed or decree of absolvitor is granted, the Court may nevertheless make provision for the children of the marriage as if the action were still before the Court.[68] The Court also has statutory jurisdiction on the application of either parent to deal with questions arising independently of actions of divorce, nullity or separation as to the custody of or right of access to a child of the marriage under sixteen.[69] In each case the Court has power to vary or revoke its order by a subsequent order.[70]

The Guardianship of Infants Acts 1886–1925[69] provide that where in any

[58] *Lang* v. *Lang* (1869) 7 M. 445; *Nicholson* v. *Nicholson* (1869) 7 M. 1118.
[59] Rules of Court of Session (1965), Rule 189 (a) (xx).
[60] As to the jurisdiction of the Sheriff Court, see the Sheriff Courts (Scotland) Act 1907 (7 Edw. VII, c. 51), s. 5 (2) as amended by the Sheriff Courts (Scotland) Amendment Act 1913 (2 & 3 Geo. V, c. 28), Sched. 1. See also *Campbell* v. *Campbell*, 1956 S.C. 285.
[61] See *Sanderson* v. *Sanderson*, 1921 S.C. 686; *Curran*, 1957 S.L.T. (Notes) 47.
[62] Act of Sederunt (Rules of Court Amendment No. 2) 1970. These cases, which comprehend most applications by persons other than parents, will be statutory when s. 47 of the Children Act 1975 is brought into force and, as they will no longer involve the exercise of the nobile officium, will be competent in the Sheriff Court.
[63] Conjugal Rights (Scotland) Amendment Act 1861 (24 & 25 Vict., c. 86), s. 9.
[64] Custody of Children (Scotland) Act 1939 (2 & 3 Geo. VI, c. 4). See *Wilson* v. *Wilson*, 1954 S.L.T. (Sh. Ct.) 68.
[65] *Symington* v. *Symington* (1875) 2 R. (H.L.) 41.
[66] Matrimonial Proceedings (Children) Act 1958 (6 & 7 Eliz. II, c. 40), s. 14.
[67] 1958 Act, s. 7.
[68] 1958 Act, s. 9.
[69] Guardianship of Infants Acts 1886-1925 (49 & 50 Vict., c. 27; 15 & 16 Geo. V, c. 45), as amended by Administration of Justice Act 1928, s. 16, and Custody of Children Act 1939. See also Children and Young Persons (Scotland) Act 1932 (22 & 23 Geo. V, c. 47), s. 73 (3).
[70] 1958 Act, s. 14 (3); 1925 Act, s. 3.

proceeding before any Court the custody or upbringing of a child or the administration of any property belonging to, or held for, it , or the application of the income thereof, is in question, the Court in deciding that question must regard the child's welfare as the first and paramount consideration and may not take into consideration whether from any other point of view the claim or right of the father is superior to that of the mother, or vice versa.[71] Furthermore, in actions for divorce, nullity or separation the Court may not, under the Matrimonial Proceedings (Children) Act 1958, grant decree unless and until it is satisfied either that arrangements have been made for the care and upbringing of every child for whose custody, maintenance and education it has jurisdiction, and that those arrangements are satisfactory or are the best which can be devised in the circumstances, or that it is impracticable for the party or parties appearing before the Court to make any such arrangements.[72] In appropriate circumstances a wife divorced for adultery[73] or for desertion[74] may be allowed the custody of her young children. The Court will require that the child in its formative years be given the opportunity of a religious upbringing, and only in special circumstances award its custody to a father who is an atheist.[75]

Where in an action of divorce, nullity or separation the Court considers that there are exceptional circumstances making it impracticable or undesirable for the child to be entrusted to either of the parties of the marriage, it may, if it thinks fit, make an order committing the care of the child to any other individual, e.g. a grandparent, or to the local authority.[76] Alternatively it may, where it considers this desirable, make an order placing the child under the supervision of the local authority.[77] The Court may also, in pronouncing decree of separation or divorce, declare the culpable spouse unfit to have the custody of the children, and in that case that parent is not on the death of the other entitled as of right to the custody or guardianship of the children.[78] A tutor appointed by a deceased parent[79] may, if he considers the surviving parent unfit to have the custody of the pupil, apply to the Court for an order regarding his custody and for payment of a sum towards his maintenance.[80] An award of custody may on the application of either parent be made in favour of one of the parents or of a third party notwithstanding that the parents are then still residing together. In that event an award of aliment may

---

[71] 1925 Act, s. 1; Hume v. Hume, 1926 S.C. 1008; M. v. M., 1926 S.C. 778; Christison v. Christison, 1936 S.C. 381. In Douglas v. Douglas, 1950 S.C. 453, the claims of both parents being otherwise equally good, custody was given to the innocent parent; see also Stevenson v. Stevenson, 1967 S.L.T. (Notes) 7. Dicta to the effect that ceteris paribus the father should be preferred as head of the family will, it is thought require reconsideration in the light of the Guardianship Act 1973 (c. 29), s. 10 (1).
[72] 1958 Act, s. 8 (1).
[73] Johnston v. Johnston, 1947 S.L.T. (Notes) 26.
[74] M'Lean v. M'Lean, 1947 S.C. 79; but see Brown v. Brown, 1948 S.C. 5.
[75] M'Clements v. M'Clements, 1958 S.C. 286; but see Mackay v. Mackay, 1957 S.L.T. (Notes) 17.
[76] 1958 Act, s. 10; and see Smith v. Smith, 1964 S.C. 218, as to third party claim by way of minute.
[77] 1958 Act, s. 12.
[78] 1886 Act, s. 7.
[79] See infra, § 14.
[80] 1925 Act, s. 5 (4).

be made against the parent or parents excluded from custody. Where custody is awarded to a parent no such order for custody or aliment is, however, enforceable while the parents are residing together and if they continue to reside together for three months after the making of the order it ceases to have effect.[81]

Where a child is withheld from the person having right to his custody, he may obtain from the Court an order for the delivery to him of the child.[82] The test to be applied in such an application is what is in the best interests of the child in the whole circumstances having regard to the parent's prior right to custody.[83] But, where the Court is of opinion that a parent applying for such an order has abandoned or deserted the child, or has so conducted himself that his right of custody ought not to be enforced, it may decline to make the order[84]; and, if an order for delivery of the child is made, the parent may, in the discretion of the Court, be ordered to pay the whole or part of the money which has been spent on the child.[85] The Court may also take steps to secure that the child, when it is not delivered to the parent, shall be brought up in the religion in which the parent has a legal right to require that it shall be brought up.[86]

ACCESS.—The Court has power to make provision for access by a parent[87] to children whose custody is awarded to someone else, and may do so in actions of divorce, nullity or separation whether or not provision is made for the legal custody of the children.[88] As a rule some measure of access is allowed, even in favour of the parent who has been guilty of the matrimonial offence which has led to dissolution of the marriage. But the matter is within the discretion of the Court and access may be refused if the circumstances, character or conduct of the parent render it undesirable in the child's interests that access should be allowed.[89] The Scottish Courts have jurisdiction where divorce is granted in Scotland but the child of the marriage is resident in England,[90] but the fact that the right to apply for a variation of the order is reserved does not confer a continuing jurisdiction thereafter.[91]

---

[81] 1886 Act, s. 5, and 1925 Act, s. 3, as amended by the Guardianship Act 1973, (c. 29), s. 11 (6) and Sched. 4.

[82] *Leys* v. *Leys* (1886) 13 R. 1223; *Campbell* v. *Campbell,* 1920 S.C. 31; *Begbie* v. *Nichol,* 1949 S.C. 158 (order made).

[83] *Macallister* v. *Macallister,* 1962 S.L.T. 385.

[84] Custody of Children Act 1891 (54 & 55 Vict., c. 3), s. 1. "Parent" includes any person liable to maintain the child or entitled to his custody (s. 5). See *Woods* v. *Minister of Pensions,* 1952 S.C. 529 (mother's application refused); *Gibson* v. *Hagen,* 1960 S.L.T. (Notes) 24 (parents' application granted).

[85] Ibid., s. 2. Order to pay was refused in *Begbie* v. *Nichol, supra.* Note that the 1891 Act is concerned with issues arising not between parents, but between the parents and a third party: *Campbell* v. *Campbell,* 1956 S.C. 285.

[86] It should be noticed that the Children and Young Persons (Scotland) Acts 1937-1963 contain elaborate provisions for the protection of children and for the punishment of certain offences by their custodiers.

[87] Note that it is competent to grant access to someone other than the child's parent: see *S.* v. *S.,* 1967 S.L.T. 217—access granted to paternal grandparent.

[88] 1958 Act, s. 14 (2); *Huddart* v. *Huddart,* 1960 S.C. 300.

[89] See e.g., *M'Allister* v. *M'Allister,* 1947 S.N. 41 (refused); *Murray* v. *Murray,* 1947 S.N. 102 (allowed); *Urquhart* v. *Urquhart,* 1961 S.L.T. (Notes) 56 (refused); *Gray* v. *Gray,* 1961 S.L.T. (Notes) 83 (refused).

[90] *Hamilton* v. *Hamilton,* 1954 S.L.T. 16; Courts and Jurisdiction, Ch. II., supra, § 10.

[91] *M'Shane* v. *M'Shane,* 1962 S.L.T. 221.

8. Illegitimate Children.—A bastard is often described as being in the contemplation of the common law filius nullius. It has been said that both parents are to be regarded as strangers in blood to him.[92] He who is proved to be the father has none of the powers which belong to the father of a legitimate child. He has, subject to what is said in the following paragraph, no right to the custody of the child or to act as his administrator-in-law. The natural relationship is recognised at common law only for the purpose of imposing on him the duty in certain circumstances of alimenting the child.[93] The illegitimate child has at common law no claim to legitim nor right to inherit the estate of either of his parents if they die intestate. He has no relations unless he marry and have issue. The surviving spouse of one who is illegitimate has the ordinary legal rights of a spouse in the estate of the deceased; and the lawful children are his or her heirs ab intestato, and, as such, entitled to his or her estate. If he dies intestate and without leaving lawful issue, the common law rule is that he has no heirs, "for there is no collateral or ascendant succession of the bastard,"[94] and, subject to the legal claim of the surviving spouse, his estate falls to the Crown as ultimus haeres.[95]

These common law rules, stemming from the basic proposition that the bastard is filius nullius, have been abrogated to a substantial extent by legislation. The position of an illegitimate child has now been assimilated to that of a legitimate child so far as claims to legitim and rights of succession to the estate of a parent dying intestate are concerned, and the parents of an illegitimate child now have rights of succession to his estate if he dies intestate.[96] In construing deeds relationships are to be taken to include illegitimate relationships unless the contrary intention appears and the conditiones si institutus and si testator sine liberis decesserit and the principle of accretion may now operate in favour of illegitimate persons.[97] Another statutory concession relates to title to sue for damages for loss of society and loss of support. An illegitimate child is for these purposes to be treated as if he were the legitimate child of his mother and reputed father.[98]

9. Aliment and Custody of Illegitimate Children.—Both parents are liable to aliment the illegitimate child,[99] and the child's claim therefor against his parents transmits on their death against their representatives.[1] The Illegitimate Children (Scotland) Act 1930[2] enacts that this obligation shall endure until the

---

[92] *Clarke* v. *Carfin Coal Co.* (1891) 18 R. (H.L.) 66, per Lord Watson; see *Philp's Trs.* v. *Beaton,* 1938 S.L.T. 530. Such dicta and the brocard that the illegitimate child is filius nullius are to be read subject to the limited legal recognition which the common law gives to the natural relationship in questions of custody, aliment and forbidden degrees for intermarriage (see § 9, infra, and Ch. XLIV, § 2, supra).

[93] *Corrie* v. *Adair* (1860) 22 D. 900, per Lord Justice-Clerk Inglis.

[94] *Ld. of Halcro* v. *Somervel* (1626) M. 16395.

[95] *Brock* v. *Cochrane,* Feb. 2, 1809, F.C.

[96] See Intestate Succession, Ch. XLII, supra, § 2.

[97] See Testate Succession, Ch. XLI, supra, §§ 7, 19, 24, 26 and 27.

[98] Damages (Scotland) Act 1976 (c. 13), Sched. 1, § 2 (*b*).

[99] Erskine, I, 6, 56; National Assistance Act 1948, s. 42.

[1] *Oncken's Judicial Factor* v. *Reimers* (1892) 19 R. 519; *Hare* v. *Logan's Trs.,* 1957 S.L.T. (Notes) 49.

[2] 20 & 21 Geo. V, c. 33, s. 1. By the Affiliation Orders Act 1952 (15 & 16 Geo. VI, & 1 Eliz. II, c.

child is sixteen; but this is without prejudice to the common law obligation under which the child is entitled to be alimented until he is able to earn subsistence. If he is mentally or physically incapable of doing so, the duty of alimenting him will continue during his lifetime.[3] Where the mother has supported the child she has a claim of relief against the father for his share of their joint debt.[4] If the paternity of the child is disputed, this claim may be enforced by means of an action of affiliation and aliment in which the question of paternity will be submitted to the decision of the Court.[5] Even before the child is born, but not more than three months before the expected date of its birth, the mother may, on certain conditions, raise an action of affiliation and aliment against the alleged father, but no declarator of paternity or decree for payment can be pronounced, and no proof can be taken, before the birth of the child, except that, where the action is undefended or paternity is admitted, decree for a sum towards inlying expenses and for aliment after birth may be pronounced.[6] Under the National Assistance Act 1948 and the Supplementary Benefits Act 1976, the Supplementary Benefits Commission has an equal right with the mother to bring an action of affiliation and aliment, and the Court may order the money to be paid to the Commission and not to the mother.[7] Furthermore, the Commission is empowered to enforce a decree by diligence, including imprisonment.[8]

Under the common law the mother is the person primarily entitled to the custody of the child. The father[9] might, when the child reached the age of seven or ten, offer to take it into his charge or to place it in a suitable home, and if this was refused the mother lost her right to claim any contribution from the father[10]; but such an offer no longer enables him to escape liability.[11] Under the 1930 Act, however, any person entitled to the custody of the child may apply to the Court for an order for payment to him by the father or mother, or both, of a sum in respect of aliment of the child[12]; and the Court may, on application by the father or mother in any action of aliment, "make such order as it may think fit regarding the custody" of the child and the right of access thereto, "having regard to the welfare of the child and to the conduct of the parents and to the wishes as well of the mother as of the father and may

41), the period is extended for certain purposes and subject to certain exceptions to the age of 21.

[3] *Oncken's Judicial Factor* v. *Reimers* (1892) 19 R. 519; *A.B.* v. *C.D.'s Exr.* (1900) 2 F. 610.

[4] *Oncken's Judicial Factor* v. *Reimers, supra.*

[5] For the specialities of evidence in actions of affiliation and aliment, see Walker and Walker, *Evidence,* §§ 170-175; *Macpherson* v. *Beaton,* 1955 S.C. 100; *Roy* v. *Pairman,* 1958 S.C. 334.

[6] 1930 Act, s. 3.

[7] National Assistance Act 1948, s. 44 (7) (*a*) and (*b*); Supplementary Benefits Act 1976, (c. 71), s. 19.

[8] Ibid., s. 44 (7) (*c*).

[9] *Walter* v. *Culbertson,* 1921 S.C. 490; *Macpherson* v. *Leishman* (1887) 14 R. 780.

[10] *Moncrieff* v. *Langlands* (1900) 2 F. 1111; *Shearer* v. *Robertson* (1877) 5 R. 263; *Macdonald* v. *Denoon,* 1929 S.C. 172.

[11] 1930 Act, s. 2 (2).

[12] s. 1 (3). See also Children and Young Persons (Scotland) Act 1937, s. 92, as to orders for payment of sums due under a decree for aliment.

on the application of either parent recall or vary such order."[13] This, of course, makes a substantial modification of the mother's common law right, here as elsewhere the modern law recognising the paramountcy of the child's welfare.[14] In awarding aliment or a sum for the mother's inlying expenses the Court is required to have regard to the means and position of both parents and the circumstances of the case as a whole[15]; there is, in Scotland, no statutory limitation on the quantum of such an award.[16]

If the child becomes chargeable to supplementary benefit in consequence of persistent neglect to maintain it by the person responsible, that person is liable to be fined or imprisoned.[17] The parents are liable for the expenses of burial in the event of its death.[18]

An illegitimate child is not bound to aliment either of its parents. "To impose upon illegitimate children, to whom the law denies the status of blood-relationship, and all rights of succession, a liability to maintain parents, who in the most charitable view have done them a great wrong, would be harsh and inequitable."[19]

10. Adoption of Children.—The contract of adoption is not recognised in Scots law and, however solemn may be the agreement by which a parent hands over his child to another, it is always open to the parent to reclaim the child.[20] Adoption is a purely statutory process, introduced by the Adoption of Children (Scotland) Act 1930[21] and now governed by the Adoption Act 1958[22] and the Children Act 1975,[23] and is effected not by contract but by an order of the Court.[24] The law is consolidated in the Adoption (Scotland) Act 1978.[24a] Provided certain statutory requirements are met an adoption order may be made extinguishing the parental rights and duties of the natural parents and vesting them in the adopters.[25] The child is then treated in law as if he had been born as a legitimate child of the adopters.[26] Accordingly he has the same rights of aliment and to sue for damages for the death of an adoptive parent as a legitimate child would have, and the adopters have corresponding

---

[13] s. 2 (1).
[14] See e.g. *Duguid* v. *M'Brinn*, 1954 S.C. 105.
[15] s. 1 (2); *Mottram* v. *Butchart*, 1939 S.C. 89; (see *Fraser* v. *Campbell*, 1927 S.C. 589, for prior law); *Terry* v. *Murray*, 1947 S.C. 10.
[16] Note that the limitation in the Affiliation Orders Act 1952 (c. 41), s. 1, does not apply to Scotland. See *Halkett* v. *M'Skeane*, 1962 S.L.T. (Sh. Ct.) 80.
[17] National Assistance Act 1948, s. 51; *Cullen* v. *Maclean*, 1960 S.L.T. (Notes) 85. Supplementary Benefits Act 1976 (c. 71) s. 25.
[18] Under the general section (50) relating to burial in the National Assistance Act 1948.
[19] *Clarke* v. *Carfin Coal Co.* (1891) 18 R. (H.L.) 66, per Lord Watson.
[20] *Kerrigan* v. *Hall* (1901) 4 F. 10.
[21] 20 & 21 Geo. V, c. 37.
[22] 7 Eliz. II, c. 5; see also Adoption Act 1964, c. 57.
[23] 1975, c. 72.
[24] *J. & J.* v. *C.'s Tutor*,1948 S.C. 636.
[24a] 1978, c. 28, not yet commenced.
[25] Ibid., s. 8. For procedure in Court of Session, see Rules of Court (1965), Ch. IV, rules 219-230; and in Sheriff and Juvenile Court, see Act of Sederunt (Adoption of Children) 1959 (printed in Parliament House Book, Division H).
[26] Ibid., Sched. 2, § 1 (1). On the death of the adoptive parent the obligation to aliment will now transmit as in the case of a legitimate child and the law as laid down in *Hutchison* v. *Hutchison's Trs.*, 1951 S.C. 108, is superseded.

rights. Adoption has, however, no effect on the prohibited degrees of relationship for the purposes of the crime of incest and affects them so far as the law relating to marriage is concerned only in that the adopted child and the adopters are deemed for all time coming to be within the prohibited degrees.[27] Formerly an adoption order did not deprive the child of his legal rights in his parents' estates or of any right under any intestacy or disposition which he would otherwise have taken; nor did it confer on the child any right in property as a child of the adopter. But under the Succession (Scotland) Act 1964[28] an adopted person is now to be treated as the child of the adopter and not of any other person for all purposes relating to the succession to a deceased person and the disposal of property under an inter vivos deed. The adopted person loses all rights in the estate of his natural parents,[29] and any reference in a deed to the child or children of the adopter is construed as including a reference to the adopted person.[30] An adopted child takes the British nationality of its adoptive parent or adoptive male parent where there are two.[31] An adopted children register (with an index) is maintained in which entries, as directed by adoption orders, are to be made, and the word "adopted" is to be inserted in the register of births, deaths and marriages.[32]

11. Conditions of Adoption.—Any person who has not attained the age of eighteen, and who is not and has not been married, may be adopted.[33] The adoption order may be made on the application either of a married couple[34] or of one person.[35] In the latter event the applicant must be unmarried or, if married, the Court must be satisfied that the applicant's spouse cannot be found, or is separated from the applicant and living apart and likely to remain separated permanently, or is incapable, by reason of physical or mental ill-health, of applying for an adoption order.[36] Adopters must be twenty-one or over.[37] There are provisions forbidding adoption by the mother or father of the child alone unless the other natural parent is dead or cannot be found or there is some other reason justifying his exclusion[38]; and requiring agreement to the adoption (which must be in writing[39]) of parents or guardians of the child,[40] and the consent of the child himself if a minor.[41] The father of an illegitimate child is not a parent of the child for this purpose, and his agreement to an adoption of the child is not required.[42] The agreement of a

---

[27] Ibid., Sched. 2, § 1 (3).
[28] c. 41, s. 23 (1); see Intestate Succession, Ch. XLII, supra, § 2; Testate Succession, Ch. XLIII, § 19.
[29] But see Law Reform (Miscellaneous Provisions) (Scotland) Act 1966 (c. 19), s. 5.
[30] 1964 Act, s. 23 (2).
[31] 1958 Act, s. 19.
[32] Ibid., s. 23.
[33] 1975 Act ss. 8 (1) and (5) and 107 (1); see *M, Petitioner,* 1953 S.C. 227.
[34] Ibid., s. 10.
[35] Ibid., s. 11.
[36] Ibid., s. 11 (2).
[37] Ibid., ss. 10 (1) and 11 (1).
[38] Ibid., s. 11 (3).
[39] A. of S., 1959, para. 1 (a); Rules of Court 219 (b). And see s. 6 of 1958 Act.
[40] 1975 Act, s. 12 (1).
[41] Ibid., s. 8 (6).
[42] *A. v. B.,* 1955 S.C. 378; *Re O.,* [1965] Ch. 23.

parent or guardian must be unconditional and given freely and with full understanding of what is involved, but it is not necessary for this purpose that the parent or guardian should know the identity of the applicants.[43] The Court may on certain grounds dispense with the agreement of a parent or guardian[44] but it may dispense with the consent of a minor who is to be adopted only if it is satisfied that the child is incapable of giving his consent.[45] It has been held competent for a husband and wife to adopt the wife's legitimate child by a former marriage.[46] In reaching any decision relating to the adoption of a child, a court or adoption agency must give first consideration to the need to safeguard and promote the welfare of the child throughout his childhood and must also give due consideration to the child's wishes having regard to his age and understanding.[47] The Act of 1958 imposes a probationary period of three consecutive months, during which the child should be continuously in the care and possession of the applicant.[48] A curator ad litem must be appointed to the child,[49] and all proceedings in the petition are heard in camera unless the Court otherwise orders.[50]

II. GUARDIANSHIP

12. Tutors and Curators.—As there is a difference in the legal position of pupils and minors,[51] so there is a distinction in the office of their respective guardians. The guardian of a pupil is a tutor; as the pupil has no legal personality, the tutor acts for him, and his duties consist in protecting the person and managing the estate of the pupil. A curator, as the guardian of a minor pubes is styled, does not act for, but with, the minor; the minor is himself capable of acting, and the curator does no more than consent to his actions and deeds. This is the sense in which the maxim "tutor datur personae, curator rei" is to be understood.[52] In most other particulars the nature, powers and duties of the two offices are the same.

13. Parents as Administrators-in-law.—At common law the father is the natural guardian or administrator-in-law of his legitimate child while in minority. As such he is tutor to his pupil and curator to his minor child. By

---

[43] Ibid., s. 12 (1). see A, Petitioner, 1936 S.C. 258.
[44] Ibid., s. 12.
[45] Ibid., s. 8 (6).
[46] I. v. I., 1947 S.C. 485.
[47] 1975 Act, s. 3.
[48] 1958 Act ss. 3 (1), 13; see M, Petitioner, 1953 S.C. 227; G, Petitioner, 1955 S.L.T. (Sh. Ct.) 27. Notice must be given to the social work department of the local authority within whose area the applicants reside (1958 Act, s. 3 (2)) unless the applicant or one of them is a parent or the child is over the upper limit of compulsory school age (see A, Petitioners, 1958 S.L.T. (Sh. Ct.) 61). When s. 9 of the 1975 Act comes into force, the requirement of continuous care and possession will be replaced by a requirement that the child should during the 13 weeks preceding the making of the order have had his home with the applicants or one of them.
[49] s. 11 (4); for duties of curator ad litem, see A. of S., 1959, paras. 6-8; Rules of Court 221.
[50] A. of S., 1959, para. 11; Rules of Court 227.
[51] See § 4, supra.
[52] Erskine, Inst., I, 7, 14.

the Guardianship Act 1973 the mother has the rights and authority of a guardian equally with the father and these are exercisable by either parent without the other.[53] The effect of the Act is to make the mother an administrator-in-law as well as the father. As such they cannot strictly be said to hold any office for their position is inseparable from the relation of parent and child.[54] Under the common law the father alone could nominate a person to act after his death as tutor or curator to his child, but this power may now be exercised by either parent. A stranger making a bequest to a pupil may nominate tutors to him, but the duties of such tutors are confined to the administration of the subject of the bequest, and they have no further powers.[55]

As administrators-in-law the parents manage the estate of the pupil, and are entitled to recover sums due to the pupil and to grant discharges therefor. A parent's discharge is, as a rule, a sufficient protection to those who make payment of a sum due to the child; but there are circumstances—as, e.g., if they are aware that the parent is insolvent—in which it would be their duty to protect the child's interest by taking such steps as requiring the parent to find caution or refusing to make payment except under a decree of the Court.[56] Where it is necessary in the interests of the child, the Court may supersede a parent in the exercise of his guardianship and appoint a factor loco tutoris.[57] As administrator-in-law of his child a parent is a tutor within the meaning of the Judicial Factors Act 1849,[58] and a trustee within the meaning of the Trusts (Scotland) Acts 1921 and 1961.[59]

14. Nominated Guardians.—Under the common law the mother was never guardian of her children, nor could she nominate a tutor to them. But even before the Guardianship Act 1973 put her on an equality with the father the Guardianship of Infants Acts had altered this rule. Under these Acts on the death of the father the mother became guardian of her pupil child.[60] Except in so far as superseded by the 1973 Act these rules remain in force. If the father has appointed a guardian, the mother acts jointly with him; if no guardian has been appointed, or if the appointed guardian is dead or refuses to act, the Court may appoint a guardian to act with the mother.[61] The mother may appoint a person as guardian of the pupil after her death[62]; and there are similar provisions as to her nominee acting jointly with the father.[63] Where

[53] 1973, (c. 29), s. 10.
[54] *Robertson* (1865) 3 M. 1077.
[55] Erskine, *Inst.*, 1, 7, 2.
[56] *Stevenson's Trs.* v. *Dumbreck* (1861) 4 Macq. 86; *Wardrop* v. *Gossling* (1869) 7 M. 532.
[57] *Robertson*, supra; *Johnstone* v. *Wilson* (1822) 1 S. 558; *Allan* (1895) 3 S.L.T. 87.
[58] 12 & 13 Vict, c. 51 (commonly referred to as the Pupils Protection Act); Judicial Factors Act 1889 (52 & 53 Vict., c. 39); Guardianship of Infants Act 1886, s. 12.
[59] Guardianship of Infants Act 1925, s. 10; altering the law as laid down in *Shearer's Tutor*, 1924 S.C. 445. See *Linton* v. *Inland Revenue*, 1928 S.C. 209, per Lord President Clyde, at 214; *Cunningham's Tutrix*, 1949 S.C. 275. See Executors etc., Ch. XLIV, supra, § 27.
[60] Guardianship of Infants Act 1925, s. 4 (1). The Act repeals ss. 2 and 3 of the 1886 Act.
[61] Guardianship of Infants Act 1925, s. 4 (1).
[62] s. 5 (2).
[63] s. 4 (2).

both parents nominate guardians, these act jointly after the death of the survivor of the parents.[64]

A surviving parent may, however, refuse to act with the nominee of the deceased spouse, and in that case the parent is the sole guardian unless the nominee obtains an order from the Court that he is to act either jointly or as sole guardian.[65] When joint guardians other than both parents are unable to agree they may apply to the Court for its direction and the Court may make an order regarding the matter in dispute,[66] including, where one of the guardians is a parent, an order as to the custody and payment for the maintenance of the child.[67]

By the Social Work (Scotland) Act 1968[68] where a child has no parent or guardian, or where the parents have abandoned him or are on grounds specified in the Act, incapable or unfit to have care of him, power is conferred on a local authority to resolve that parental rights and powers with respect to a child in its care or in the care of a voluntary organisation should vest in the authority or organisation as the case may be. The resolution so to proceed remains in force until the child attains the age of 18,[69] unless rescinded[70] or determined by the Sheriff.[71]

15. Tutor-Testamentar.—A tutor-testamentar, or nominated tutor, is preferred to all others, and is entitled to the office by virtue of the nomination and without any other form of appointment such as is required in the case of other tutors. As the parents may be assumed to exercise a wise discretion in the selection of a tutor, the tutor-testamentar is not required to take the oath de fideli administratione[72] or to find caution "unless the Court, upon the application of any person having interest, shall so direct."[73]

Where more than one tutor has been nominated, on the declinature or death of one or more of these, the remaining tutor or tutors may act. This is not so, however, if the nomination is stated to be a joint one, in which case if one fails the other cannot act, or if one be appointed sine qua non, in which case on his failure the nomination will fail.[74]

16. Tutor-of-Law: Tutor-Dative.—Where a pupil has no tutor—which can, since the above-mentioned legislation, occur only where both parents are dead

---

[64] s. 5 (5).
[65] s. 5 (3) and (4).
[66] s. 6.
[67] Children and Young Persons (Scotland) Act 1932, s. 73 (1). These provisions are not it is thought applicable to disagreements between parents which are governed except on questions of custody and access by the 1973 Act, s. 10 (3). For custody and access disputes between parents see § 7, supra.
[68] 1968 Act (c. 49), s. 16, as amended by 1975 Act (c. 72), ss. 74 and 75.
[69] 1968 Act (c. 49), s. 18 (1).
[70] Ibid., s. 18 (2).
[71] Ibid., s. 18 (3).
[72] Stair, I, 6, 6; Erskine, *Inst.*, I, 7, 3.
[73] Ibid.; Guardianship of Infants Act 1886, s. 12.
[74] Erskine, *Inst.*, I, 7, 15; Fraser, 243. The rule under the common law as to tutors-dative is different; the office is in its nature a joint one, and the death of one vacates the appointment—*Stewart* v. *Scott* (1834) 7 W. & S. 211.

and there is no nominated tutor or no nominated tutor prepared to act—the common law affords means for the appointment of a tutor, known as a tutor-of-law or a tutor-dative. In modern practice an officer of the Court, known as a factor loco tutoris (who will not be appointed jointly with the mother),[75] is almost invariably appointed; but the appointment of a tutor under the provisions of the common law is still competent.[76]

17. Curators.—There are only two cases in which a curator is imposed on a minor.[77] (1) Where the parents are alive they are ipso jure curators to the child. If, however, a parent gives his consent,[78] or, even without his consent, if he has acted in violation of his duty, or there is a conflict of interest between him and the child,[79] another curator may be appointed for the management of the child's property. (2) Under the Tutors and Curators Act 1696 (c. 8), the father may by a deed executed in liege poustie (i.e. not on deathbed) nominate a curator. A factor loco tutoris becomes ipso facto curator of the child when he attains puberty, but the office terminates if he chooses curators.[80]

If the parents are dead and there is no curator nominated and acting, the minor, if he desires to have a curator, may obtain one by presenting a petition to the Court.[81]

18. Administration by Tutors, Factors Loco Tutoris and Curators.—All tutors and factors loco tutoris must lodge with the Accountant of Court a rental of the lands and a statement of the moveable property belonging to the pupil. In their administration they are subject to the provisions of the Judicial Factors Acts[82] and act under the superintendence of the Accountant of Court.

The position of the curator is different. "The law gives no right or title of management of a minor's estate to his curators, further than giving him their advice and concurrence to assist himself in managing"[83]; and an act by the curator alone, such as the discharge of a debt or the pursuit of an action, is null.[84] But, although the curators have not complete control, as tutors have, of the management of the estate, they are responsible for seeing that it is properly administered. "Their duty is to see to the minor's affairs, that they get no detriment; and so they must answer, not only for the deeds wherewith

---

[75] *Spiers*, 1946 S.L.T. 203.

[76] *Dick* v. *Douglas*, 1924 S.C. 787.

[77] Erskine, *Prin.*, I, 7, 6. By the Guardianship Act 1973, s. 10 (1), the mother is curator of her minor child with the same rights and authority as the law allows to the father.

[78] Erskine, *Inst.*, I, 6, 54; *Robertson* (1865) 3 M. 1077; *Graham* (1881) 8 R. 996; *Balfour Melville* (1903) 5 F. 347.

[79] *M'Nab* v. *M'Nab* (1871) 10 M. 248. Such appointments may not now be necessary since the Guardianship Act 1973, s. 10 (1), made the mother a curator as well as the father, except in the event of the failure of both parents.

[80] Judicial Factors Act 1889, s. 11; *Ferguson* v. *Blair* (1908) 16 S.L.T. 284.

[81] Administration of Justice (Scotland) Act 1933 (23 & 24 Geo. V, c. 41), s. 12. The application will normally be to the Outer House of the Court of Session (R. of C., 189 (a) (xiii)); but a petition to the Sheriff Court under s. 12 has been held competent, *Maclean*, 1956 S.L.T. (Sh. Ct.) 90.

[82] 12 & 13 Vict., c. 51; 43 & 44 Vict., c. 4; 52 & 53 Vict., c. 39; see Executors etc., Ch. XLIV, supra, § 27.

[83] *Allan* v. *Walker*, 1812 Hume's Decs., 586, per Lord Meadowbank.

[84] Erskine, *Inst.*, I, 7, 14; *Bute* v. *Campbell* (1725) M. 16338.

they consent, but for their omission, and for any detriment the minor suffereth by their negligence"[85]; and, if the curator finds that the minor will not follow his advice or do what is necessary for the proper maintenance of the estate, he may apply to be relieved of his office.[86] The Judicial Factors Acts do not apply to a curator to a minor; but the word "trustee" is defined for the purposes of the Trusts (Scotland) Acts 1921-1961 as including factors and curators and a "judicial factor" as including, for those purposes, any person holding a judicial appointment as a factor or curator on another person's estate.[87]

19. Termination of Office.—The offices of tutory and curatory terminate when the child attains puberty or majority respectively, or by the death of the tutor or curator or the minor. The rules when more than one tutor or curator have been appointed have already been noticed. After a tutor or curator had accepted office the common law did not permit him to resign without sufficient cause shown to the Court.[88] But section 31 of the Judicial Factors Act 1880 empowers the Court to accept the resignation of a tutor and to appoint a factor in his place; and a tutor or curator has power to resign office as a trustee under the Trusts (Scotland) Act 1921.[89]

Under the common law a tutor or curator who failed in his duty, or was unsuitable through mental or physical incapacity or on moral grounds, might be removed by the Court from his office.[90] The above-mentioned Act of 1880 provides for the removal of a tutor on similar grounds,[91] and the Guardianship of Infants Act 1886[92] empowers the Court, "on being satisfied that it is for the welfare" of the pupil, to remove any testamentary tutor or any tutor appointed or acting by virtue of the Act and to appoint another guardian in his place.

At the termination of the guardianship an action is competent to the minor for the purpose of calling the guardian to account and to the guardian for recovering what has been profitably expended for the minor in the course of the administration.[93] These actions formerly prescribed if not raised within ten years of the majority or of his death in minority[94] but are now imprescriptible[94a]. In modern practice tutors and factors loco tutoris obtain their discharge by means of a petition to the Court.[95]

20. Curator Ad Litem.—This is a guardian appointed by the Court to

---

[85] Stair, I., 6, 36.
[86] Bell, *Prin.*, § 2096.
[87] Trusts (Scotland) Act 1921 (11 & 12 Geo. V, c. 58), s. 2 as amended by Trusts (Scotland) Act 1961 (c. 5), s. 3.
[88] Fraser, 408, 480.
[89] 11 & 12 Geo. V, c. 58, s. 3.
[90] Erskine, *Inst.*, I, 7, 29; Fraser, 411.
[91] ss. 5, 6, 20 and 21.
[92] s. 6.
[93] Erskine, *Inst.*, I, 7, 31 and 32.
[94] 1696, c. 9.
[94a] Prescription and Limitation (Scotland) Act 1973 (c. 52), ss. 7, 16 & Scheds. 3 and 5.
[95] Judicial Factors Act 1849 (c. 51), s. 34.

protect the interests of a minor in a litigation. Where a pupil has no tutor, or the tutor refuses to concur, or the action is one in which the tutor is the defender or has an adverse interest, the pupil may institute the action and apply to the Court for the appointment of a curator ad litem.[96] A minor may prosecute an action without the concurrence of a curator. But in either case the defender, for his own security, is entitled to object to the action proceeding until the guardian concurs or a curator ad litem is appointed.[97] If a pupil is called as defender in an action, a curator ad litem to him may be appointed by the Court, although appearance has not been entered for him in the action.[98] Curators of this sort have no right to administer the minor's estate; they are appointed for the special purpose of the action and with the conclusion of the action their office terminates.

Curators ad litem may be appointed to other persons under legal disability, such as insane persons.[99]

21. Pro Tutor and Pro Curator.—This is the name applied to one who assumes to act as a tutor or curator without a legal title to the office. Such a one has none of the active powers or privileges, but is liable to all the obligations of a duly appointed tutor or curator.[1]

22. Curatory of the Insane: Cognition.—Every person above majority and capable of managing his property has a natural right to do so, and before he can be deprived of this right some procedure is necessary for the purpose of establishing that he is not in a condition properly to exercise it. The method in former times was cognition.[2] Under this process a jury was summoned, and if, after inquiry, the person was found to be "furious or fatuous or labouring under such unsoundness of mind as to render him incapable of managing his affairs,"[3] the nearest agnate was appointed curator, except where the father or husband of the person was alive, in which case they were preferred to the agnate. The procedure is now regulated by the Court of Session Act 1868, and may still be used; and, without cognition, the nearest male agnate may be appointed tutor-dative on a petition supported by medical certificates which satisfy the Court.[4] The customary course now is to apply by petition in the Outer House craving the Court, in the exercise of the power which it has long used, to nominate a curator bonis. Statutory provisions are contained in the Mental Health (Scotland) Act 1960[5] for the admission of persons suffering from mental disorders to hospital and for their detention.

[96] *Ward* v. *Walker*, 1920 S.C. 80.
[97] M'Laren, *Court of Session Practice*, p. 172.
[98] *Drummond's Trs.* v. *Peel's Trs.*, 1929 S.C. 484.
[99] M'Laren, p. 185. See also Divorce (Scotland) Act 1976, (c. 39), s. 11.
[1] Erskine, *Inst.*, I, 7, 28; Fraser, 561; *Fulton* v. *Fulton* (1864) 2 M. 893; *Dunbar* v. *Wilson & Dunlop's Tr.* (1887) 15 R. 210.
[2] Erskine, *Inst.*, I, 7, 49.
[3] Court of Session (Scotland) Act 1868 (31 & 32 Vict., c. 100), s. 101. The earlier procedure was under the Act 1585, c. 18.
[4] *Dick* v. *Douglas*, 1924 S.C. 787.
[5] 8 & 9 Eliz. II, c. 61, s. 23.

23. Curator Bonis.—The petition for appointment of a curator bonis may be at the instance of anyone interested (such as his next-of-kin, or other relative, or his solicitor) or, where it is satisfied that no such arrangements are being made, by the local authority.[6] It must appear that the person is incapable of managing his own affairs, not necessarily from insanity, for it may be due to the loss of sight or speech or hearing or to senility,[7] and this must be borne out by the certificates on soul and conscience of two medical men. The petition must be served on the party unless the Court sees fit in the light of medical certificates to dispense with this. When the petition is opposed on the ground that there is no incapacity, the Court may determine what inquiry is necessary for further information on this point. The party has no right to insist on a cognition; and the course usually followed is that of a remit to experts.[8]

Interdiction, a means by which persons who were not insane but were liable to be imposed upon were restrained from signing any deed (not being a rational or onerous deed) affecting heritage to their prejudice without the consent of their interdictors,[9] has been abolished.[10]

24. Powers of Curator Bonis.—The appointment of a curator bonis does not divest the incapax of his estate, but his management thereof is superseded in favour of the curator.[11] It is the duty of the curator to manage the estate, and he does so as an agent for the incapax rather than as a trustee.[12] He has no power over the person of the incapax,[13] although his position may entitle him to apply to the Court where necessary for the protection of the incapax.[14] The powers of a curator bonis are those of a judicial factor, and he is subject to the rules laid down in the Judicial Factors Acts and is a trustee under the Trusts Acts.[15]

25. Termination of Office.—The appointment of a curator bonis is superseded by the appointment of a curator under a cognition or of a tutor-dative and it may, on a petition to the Court, be recalled if the incapax recovers his power of managing his estate.[16] The curator obtains his discharge by presenting a petition for that purpose.

[6] Ibid., s. 91.
[7] *Kirkpatrick* (1853) 15 D. 734; *Dowie* v. *Hagart* (1894) 21 R. 1052; *Duncan*, 1915, 2 S.L.T. 50.
[8] *C.B.* v. *A.B.* (1891) 18 R. (H.L.) 40; *Brown*, 1960 S.C. 27.
[9] Erskine, *Inst.*, II, pp. 7, 53; Fraser, pp. 692 et seq.
[10] Conveyancing (Scotland) Act 1924 (14 & 15 Geo. V, c. 27), s. 44 (3) (*b*).
[11] *Yule* v. *Alexander* (1891) 19 R. 167; *Mitchell & Baxter* v. *Cheyne* (1891) 19 R. 324; *I.R.* v. *Macmillan's C.B.*, 1956 S.C. 142.
[12] *I.R.* v. *Macmillan's C.B.*, supra, at p. 147; *Burns' C.B.* v. *Burns' Trs.*, 1961 S.L.T. 166.
[13] *Robertson* v. *Elphinstone*, June 28, 1874, F.C.; *Bryce* v. *Grahame* (1828) 6 S. 425, 3 W. & S. 323.
[14] See *Gardiner* (1869) 7 M. 1130; *Robertson* v. *Elphinstone*, supra, per Lord Robertson.
[15] See Executors etc., Ch. XLIV, supra, § 27.
[16] *Forsyth* v. *Forsyth* (1862) 24 D. 1435.

CHAPTER XLVIII

DILIGENCE[1]

Graham Stewart, *Diligence* (1898).

1. Meaning and Forms of Diligence.—Diligence has been defined as "the legal procedure by which a creditor attaches the property or person of his debtor, with the object of forcing him either (1) to appear in Court to answer an action at the creditor's instance, or (2) to find security for implement of the judgment which may be pronounced against him in such an action, or (3) to implement a judgment already pronounced."[2] Various forms of diligence of creditors[3] are recognised, according to the nature and situation of the property to be attached, or according to the nature of the claim in respect of which diligence is to be used. The following forms require notice: (1) Civil Imprisonment; (2) Arrestment; (3) Personal Poinding; (4) Adjudication; (5) Inhibition; (6) Poinding of the Ground; (7) Maills and Duties; (8) Sequestration for Rent. The last has been considered in the chapter on leases.[4]

I. CIVIL IMPRISONMENT

2. Imprisonment.—Imprisonment for debt was recognised in the law of Scotland on the theory that after a charge for payment had been given in the royal name, and had not been implemented, the defaulter was in rebellion.[5] The power to imprison for debt has however been considerably restricted by statute, and is now rarely exercised. By the Debtors (Scotland) Act 1880[6] imprisonment for debt was abolished, except in the case of taxes, fines or penalties due to the Crown, rates and assessments, and sums decerned for aliment. For these debts imprisonment was limited to twelve months. The Crown Proceedings Act 1947[7] abolished imprisonment for the non-payment of taxes except in relation to death duties, which must now be construed as including capital transfer tax,[8] and purchase tax. The saving in respect of purchase tax was repealed by the Finance Act 1972 by which that tax was

---

[1] All diligence is subject to the provisions of the Reserve and Auxiliary Forces (Protection of Civil Interests) Act 1951 (14 & 15 Geo. VI, c. 65), ss. 7-9.

[2] Stewart, *Diligence*, p. 1.

[3] Contrast diligence for such matters as citation of witnesses and commission and diligence to examine witnesses and to recover documents: see Maclaren, *Court of Session Practice*, pp. 342, 1029, 1058.

[4] Ch. XXXIII, supra, § 12. The diligence known as interdiction was abolished by the Conveyancing (Scotland) Act 1924, s. 44.

[5] See Stair, IV, 47.

[6] 43 & 44 Vict., c. 34, s. 4.

[7] 10 & 11 Geo. VI, c. 44, ss. 26 (2), 49.

[8] Finance Act 1975 (c. 7), Sched., 12, para. 1.

abolished.[9] By the Civil Imprisonment (Scotland) Act 1882[10] the period of imprisonment for failure in payment of rates[11] and assessments was limited to six weeks. The general power to imprison for sums decerned for aliment was also abolished by the 1882 Act, but the sheriff is empowered to inflict imprisonment for a period not exceeding six weeks, in the case of wilful failure to pay sums decerned for as aliment (including expenses), or such instalments thereof as the sheriff shall appoint.[12] Failure to pay is deemed to be wilful unless the debtor proves want of means, but a warrant for imprisonment may not be granted unless the sheriff is satisfied that the debtor has not possessed or been able to earn the means of paying the sum in question since the commencement of the action in which the decree was pronounced.[13] To render imprisonment competent under this provision there must be a direct claim for aliment; not merely a claim by a local authority for reimbursement of money expended in aliment,[14] or a claim for arrears after the right to aliment has ceased.[15] Imprisonment does not operate as a satisfaction or extinction of the debt or interfere with the creditor's other rights and remedies for its recovery.[16] The abolition of imprisonment for debt leaves untouched the power of the Court to imprison for failure to implement a decree ad factum praestandum.[17] By the Law Reform (Miscellaneous Provisions) (Scotland) Act 1940,[18] however, no person may be imprisoned on account of his failure to comply with a decree ad factum praestandum unless the Court is satisfied that he is wilfully refusing to comply with the decree. In the case of wilful refusal the term of imprisonment is limited to six months, but the Court is required to order immediate liberation if satisfied that the person undergoing imprisonment has complied or is no longer wilfully refusing to comply with the order.[19] Such imprisonment does not operate to extinguish the obligations imposed by the decree on which the application for imprisonment proceeds.[20]

II. ARRESTMENT

3. Nature of Arrestment.[21]—Arrestment is the appropriate diligence for the attachment of a debtor's moveable property which is in the custody of a third

[9] c. 41, s. 54 (8) and Sched. 28, Part II.
[10] 45 & 46 Vict., c. 42, s. 5.
[11] The power to imprison for non-payment of rates is now contained in the Local Government (Scotland) Act 1947, s. 247 (5).
[12] 1882 Act, s. 4.
[13] 1882 Act, s. 4 (3). As regards means, certain state benefits are not to be taken into account: see National Assistance Act 1948 (c. 29), ss. 44 (7) (c) and 51; National Insurance (Industrial Injuries) Act 1965 (c. 52), s. 28 (2); Family Allowances Act 1965 (c. 53), s. 10 (2) and (3); Social Security Act 1975 (c. 14), s. 87 (3).
[14] Mackay v. P.C. of Resolis (1899) 1 F. 521.
[15] Glenday v. Johnston (1905) 8 F. 24; cf. Tevendale v. Duncan (1882) 10 R. 852.
[16] 1882 Act, s. 4 (5).
[17] Debtors (Scotland) Act 1880, s. 4.
[18] 3 & 4 Geo. VI, c. 42, s. 1.
[19] 1940 Act, s. 1 (1) (ii).
[20] 1940 Act, s. 1 (1) (iii).
[21] For arrestment to found jurisdiction, see Courts and Jurisdiction, Ch. II., supra.

party.[22] If the creditor is a seller of goods the property in which has passed to the debtor he may by virtue of a special statutory provision[23] arrest the goods while in his own hands or possession. If the property is in the debtor's own custody personal poinding is the appropriate diligence, except in the case of a ship.[24] Arrestment operates not in rem but in personam, amounting to a prohibition against the arrestee from parting with the property and rendering him liable to a penalty if he does so.[25] In order to transfer the property arrested to the creditor and thus to complete the diligence it is necessary that the arrestment be followed by a process of furthcoming.[26] It is used either in security on the dependence of an action, so that the debtor's property may be secured for the benefit of the creditor before judgment is obtained, or in execution. If the ground of debt is liquid, as in a bond or bill, but the term of payment has not yet come, a warrant for arrestment in security may be obtained by letters of arrestment on averments that the debtor is vergens ad inopiam or in meditatione fugae.

4. Arrestment on the Dependence.—This is the usual form of arrestment in security. To render it competent there must be conclusions for payment of money, other than the conclusion for expenses.[27] Arrestment on the dependence of an action for payment of a future debt, including the payment of a periodical allowance or capital sum on divorce, is competent, but only in special circumstances such as averments that the defender is vergens ad inopiam or in meditatione fugae.[28] In an action in the Court of Session application for a warrant for arrestment on the dependence may be inserted in the summons before it is signetted[29]; in the Sheriff Court it should be craved in the initial writ.[30] The procedure for execution of the arrestment is similar to that for arrestment in execution.[31] An arrestment on the dependence used prior to service of an action in the Court of Session or an ordinary action in the Sheriff Court falls unless the action is served within twenty days of the execution of the arrestment.[32] If arrestments on the dependence are duly laid, and decree in the action is ultimately obtained, the arrester has a preferable right over the subjects arrested, even although the debtor may have been sequestrated before the decree was obtained, provided that the arrestment was used more than sixty days before sequestration[33] and that the action was

[22] Stewart, *Diligence*, p. 105.
[23] Sale of Goods Act 1893, s. 40.
[24] *Clan Line Steamers* v. *Earl of Douglas S.S. Co.*, 1913 S.C. 967.
[25] Stair, III, 1, 25-26.
[26] See *Lord Advocate* v. *Royal Bank of Scotland*, 1978 S.L.T. 38.
[27] See *Stafford* v. *M'Laurin* (1875) 3 R. 148; *Ellison* v. *Ellison* (1901) 4 F. 257; *Fisher* v. *Weir*, 1964 S.L.T. (Notes) 99.
[28] *Gillanders* v. *Gillanders*, 1966 S.C. 54; *Brash* v. *Brash*, 1966 S.C. 56.
[29] Rules of Court, 74. A warrant for arrestment on the dependence may also be obtained on a counter claim or a third party notice in the Court of Session: Rules of Court, 84 (*e*), 85 (*b*).
[30] Sheriff Courts (Scotland) Act 1907 (7 Edw. VII, c. 51) Sched. I, Rules 4 & 7.
[31] See § 5 below.
[32] Debtors (Scotland) Act 1838 (1 & 2 Vict., c. 114), s. 17; Sheriff Courts (Scotland) Act 1907, Sched. I, Rule 127. For summary causes in the Sheriff Court the period is 42 days: Summary Cause Rules, 47.
[33] Bankruptcy (Scotland) Act 1913 (3 & 4 Geo. V, c. 20), s. 10; see Bankruptcy, Ch. XLIX, infra, § 21.

carried on without undue delay.[34] At common law all personal debts due to the common debtor, i.e. the defender in the action for payment, or moveable property belonging to him in the hands of an independent third party may be arrested on the dependence.[35] By statute however it is no longer competent to arrest on the dependence of an action any earnings or any pension.[36] For this purpose "earnings" means any sums payable by way of wages or salary, and "pension" includes any annuity in respect of past services and any pension or allowance payable in respect of disablement or disability.[37]

5. Arrestment in Execution.—Arrestment in execution may proceed (1) on an extract of a decree of any court; (2) on a warrant endorsed on an extract from the Books of Council and Session or Sheriff Court Books, in which has been registered either a deed such as a bond, lease or other agreement with pecuniary conclusions containing a clause consenting to registration for execution, or a protest by a notary public of a bill for non-payment[38]; and (3) on a summary warrant for the recovery of rates obtained by the collector of rates of a rating authority on application to the Sheriff.[39] Warrant to arrest in execution of a decree may be granted by the issue of letters of arrestment on presentation of the extract decree or of letters of horning and poinding and arrestment, but an extract of a decree of the Court of Session or Sheriff Court is itself now a sufficient warrant for this purpose,[40] and in modern practice the other forms of obtaining authority to arrest are rarely used. A schedule of arrestment is served on the arrestee, who must be subject to the jurisdiction of the Court from which the warrant to arrest has been obtained specifying the debt or other subject arrested, and arresting generally all goods, debts, rents, and every other thing in the hands or custody of the arrestee pertaining and belonging to the debtor. If a decree from one Sheriff Court is to be enforced in another Sheriffdom a warrant of concurrence is required.[41] When the arrestee is a body of trustees a schedule should be served on each trustee[42]; in the case of a corporate body service at its place of business is sufficient.[43] If the arrestee has no liability to account to the common debtor at the date when the arrestment is served on him the arrestment will fall.[44]

Warrants for arrestment emanating from the Court of Session can be executed only by messengers at arms,[45] except that in any county in which

---

[34] *Mitchell* v. *Scott* (1881) 8 R. 875; *Benhar Coal Co.* v. *Turnbull* (1883) 10 R. 558 (liquidation).
[35] See § 8, infra.
[36] Law Reform (Miscellaneous Provisions) (Scotland) Act 1966 (c. 19), s. 1.
[37] 1966 Act, s. 1 (2).
[38] Writs Execution (Scotland) Act 1877 (40 & 41 Vict., c. 40) s. 3; Conveyancing (Scotland) Act 1924 (14 & 15 Geo. V, c. 27) s. 10 (5). As to protest of bills, see Bills of Exchange, Ch. XXVI, supra, § 23.
[39] Local Government (Scotland) Act 1947, s. 247 (2) and (3).
[40] Debtors (Scotland) Act 1838 (1 & 2 Vict., c. 114), ss. 2 & 9; As regards decrees of the Court of Session as Court of Exchequer, see Exchequer Court (Scotland) Act 1856, Sched. G.
[41] 1838 Act, s. 13. A warrant of concurrence is not necessary in the case of a warrant to arrest on the dependence: 1907 Act, Sched. I, Rule 10.
[42] *Gracie* v. *Gracie*, 1910 S.C. 899. The schedule should state that the arrestment is served on the arrestee as trustee, not as an individual; *Burns* v. *Gillies* (1906) 8 F. 460.
[43] *Campbell* v. *Watson's Tr.* (1898) 25 R. 690.
[44] See § 9, infra.
[45] Debtors (Scotland) Act 1838, Sched. 1.

there is no resident messenger at arms, or in any of the islands of Scotland, a Sheriff Officer duly authorised to practise there has all the powers of a messenger at arms in regard to the execution of or diligence on any decree, warrant or order.[46] Warrants for arrestment in execution emanating from the Sheriff Court may be executed either by a Sheriff Officer or by a messenger at arms,[47] but a warrant for arrestment on the dependence and warrants for arrestment on decrees of the Exchequer Court can be executed only by a Sheriff Officer.[48] It is competent to serve schedules of arrestment proceeding on any warrant or decree of the Sheriff in a summary cause by registered post or by recorded delivery.[49] An officer must not act in a case in which he has a personal interest.[50] If the Sheriff is satisfied that no messenger at arms or Sheriff Officer is reasonably available to execute an extract decree or warrant, he may grant authority to any person whom he may deem suitable to execute such decree or warrant, and the person so authorised shall have all the powers of a messenger at arms or Sheriff Officer as regards any diligence or execution competent on such decree.[50a]

6. Preference Secured by Arrestment.—Arrestments, whether in security or in execution, are preferred inter se according to their date of service,[51] the date of any decree of furthcoming being irrelevant for this purpose. Where two or more arrestments are served on the same date they rank pari passu. A Crown arrestment however is preferred to an ordinary arrestment which has not been followed by a decree of furthcoming by the date when the Crown arrestment is executed.[52] In order to secure a preference to the arresting creditor in competition with a poinding the arrestment must have been followed by a decree of furthcoming prior in date to the completion of the poinding.[53] Arrestments used within 60 days prior to the constitution of notour bankruptcy and within 4 months thereafter are ranked pari passu as if they had all been used of the same date.[54] Arrestments executed within 60 days of sequestration or the commencement of a winding up are ineffectual to secure any preference to the arresting creditor in competition with other creditors.[55] Where a receiver is appointed to a company an arrestment which has not been followed by a decree of furthcoming will not be effective so as to exclude the power of the receiver to take possession of the property of the company.[56] The

---

[46] Execution of Diligence (Scotland) Act 1926 (16 & 17 Geo. V, c. 15), s. 1.
[47] 1838 Act, Sched. 6.
[48] Dobie, *Sheriff Court Practice*, p. 263; Exchequer Court (Scotland) Act 1856, s. 29 and Sched. G.
[49] Execution of Diligence (Scotland) Act 1926, s. 2 as amended by Sheriff Courts (Scotland) Act 1971, Sched. 1; Recorded Delivery Service Act 1962, s. 1.
[50] *Dalgleish* v. *Scott* (1822) 1 S. 506; *Lawrence Jack Collections* v. *Hamilton*, 1976 S.L.T. (Sh. Ct.) 18; *British Relay* v. *Keay*, 1976 S.L.T. (Sh. Ct.) 23.
[50a] Execution of Diligence (Scotland) Act 1926, s. 3.
[51] *Hertz* v. *Itzig* (1865) 3 M. 813.
[52] Exchequer Court (Scotland) Act 1865 (c. 56), ss. 30, 42.
[53] Stewart, *Diligence*, p. 159.
[54] Bankruptcy (Scotland) Act 1913, s. 10; see further Bankruptcy, Ch. XLIX, infra, § 7.
[55] Bankruptcy (Scotland) Act 1913, s. 104; Companies Act 1948, s. 327 (1) (a).
[56] Companies (Floating Charges and Receivers) (Scotland) Act 1972, c. 67, s. 15; *Gordon Anderson (Plant)* v. *Campsie Construction*, 1977 S.L.T. 7; *Lord Advocate* v. *Royal Bank of Scotland*, 1978 S.L.T. 38.

service of a schedule of arrestment confers on the arrester a personal right to the subject arrested preferable, where there is no question of bankruptcy, to an inchoate right granted by the debtor, such as an unintimated assignation[57] or a delivery order for goods in a store not completed by intimation to the storekeeper.[58] The rights of the debtor are transferred to the arresting creditor, so that, in the case of the arrestment of an illiquid claim, the arrester may vindicate it by action.[59] An arrestment prescribes in three years from its date, if not pursued or insisted on within that time or, in the case of the arrestment of a future or contingent debt, from the date when the debt became due or the contingency was purified.[60] An arrestment in security prescribes in three years from the date of the decree which constitutes the debt.

7. Breach of Arrestment.—Arrestments which have been regularly executed render the subject arrested litigious so far as the arrestee and other parties who have knowledge of the arrestment are concerned.[61] An arrestee who in the knowledge of an arrestment parts with the funds or subject arrested to the prejudice of the arresting creditor is liable to him for the value of the funds or subject arrested up to the limit of the amount secured by the arrestment, or, if the value of the funds or subject cannot be ascertained, for payment of the amount of the debt owed to the arresting creditor.[62] A party to an action who had received payment of funds from an arrestee in breach of an arrestment on the dependence of the action was ordained to repay the funds to the arrestee, on the ground that it had accepted the funds in the knowledge of the arrestment and to the prejudice of the arresting creditor.[63] An arrestee who acts in breach of an arrestment is also theoretically in contempt of court and liable to a fine or imprisonment.[64]

8. Action of Furthcoming.—An arrestment is not a perfected diligence, and does not give the arrester a complete right to the subject arrested unless it is followed by decree in an action of furthcoming. "An arrestment and furthcoming is an adjudication preceded by an attachment, and the essential part of the diligence is the adjudication."[65] Where a liquid debt has been arrested an action of furthcoming may proceed as soon as the arrestments are laid; if the debt is future or contingent the furthcoming, if brought, will be sisted until the debt becomes liquid.[66] The purpose of the action is to ascertain precisely the nature and extent of the obligation to account which has been arrested and to adjudge to the arrester so much as may be required to make

---

57 *Gracie* v. *Gracie*, 1910 S.C. 899.
58 *Inglis* v. *Robertson & Baxter* (1898) 25 R. (H.L.) 70.
59 *Boland* v. *White Cross Insurance Co.*, 1926 S.C. 1066.
60 1838 Act, s. 22; *Jameson* v. *Sharp* (1887) 14 R. 643.
61 Stewart, *Diligence*, p. 127; see also *High Flex (Scotland)* v. *Kentallan Mechanical Services Co.*, 1977 S.L.T. (Sh. Ct.) 91.
62 Stewart, *Diligence*, p. 222.
63 *High Flex (Scotland)* v. *Kentallan Mechanical Services Co.*, supra.
64 See *Inglis & Bow* v. *Smith* (1867) 5 M. 320.
65 *Lucas's Trs.* v. *Campbell* (1894) 21 R. 1096, per Lord Kinnear at p. 1103.
66 *Boland* v. *White Cross Insurance Co.*, supra.

payment to him of the principal debt with interest and expenses.[67] Where the subjects are not a debt but consist of corporeal moveable property or incorporeal moveable property such as rights under an insurance policy or shares, the arresting creditor may conclude for a sale of the property and payment out of the proceeds.[68] If there are competing claims on the same fund an action of multiplepoinding may be necessary.[69] The expenses of arrestment and furthcoming may be recovered out of the subjects arrested.[70] In a question with the arrestee the arrester takes no higher right than the debtor, and any defence available against the debtor may be pleaded against the arrester in an action of furthcoming.[71]

9. Subjects Arrestable.—It has been laid down that the subject attachable by arrestment is "an obligation to account."[72] It includes debts unless they are heritably secured (when the proper diligence is adjudication); funds held by a bank in name of the debtor; shares in a company[73]; interests in a trust estate[74]; a policy of insurance, although premiums may have to be paid upon it before it becomes due[75]; and corporeal moveable property belonging to the debtor which is in the hands of an independent third party. Arrestment of wages is in current practice much the most used and most effective form of diligence.[76] Assuming an obligation to account, it is no objection that the debt is contingent and that it may turn out that nothing is due by the arrestee to the debtor.[77] It has been held that a claim of damages for wrongful dismissal might be arrested although at the time of the arrestment the debtor had neither raised an action nor asserted a claim.[78] But in principle it would appear that a claim of damages, whether arising from breach of contract or delict, is not arrestable until it has been asserted and thus made the subject of a claim by the injured party.[79] A debt payable in future (e.g., wages or instalments of rent or interest not yet due) cannot be arrested, because there is no present obligation either to pay or to account.[80] Bills of exchange cannot be arrested[81]; any goods or other moveables may be, unless they are in the hands of the debtor himself or held by somebody, e.g. a bank, on his behalf for safekeeping only with no right of lien over them when poinding is the

---

[67] Bell, *Comm.*, II, p. 63.
[68] *Lucas's Trs.* v. *Campbell*, supra; cf. *Stenhouse London* v. *Allwright*, 1972 S.C. 209.
[69] Stewart, *Diligence*, pp. 140-141.
[70] Sheriff Courts (Scotland) Act 1907, Sched. I., Rule 129.
[71] *Chambers' Trs.* v. *Smith* (1878) 5 R. (H.L.) 151.
[72] Bell, *Comm.*, II, p. 71; *Shankland* v. *M'Gildowny*, 1912 S.C. 857; *Agnew* v. *Norwest Construction Co.*, 1935 S.C. 771.
[73] *American Mortgage Co.* v. *Sidway*, 1908 S.C. 500.
[74] *Learmont* v. *Shearer* (1866) 4 M. 540.
[75] *Bankhardt's Trs.* v. *Scottish Amicable* (1871) 9 M. 443.
[76] See Report of the M'Kechnie Committee on Diligence (1958) (Cmnd. 456), 60; see also § 10, infra.
[77] *Boland* v. *White Cross Insurance Co.*, 1926 S.C. 1066; *Park, Dobson & Co.* v. *Taylor*, 1929 S.C. 571.
[78] *Riley* v. *Ellis*, 1910 S.C. 934.
[79] *Caldwell* v. *Hamilton*, 1919 S.C. (H.L.) 100, per Lord Dunedin at p. 109; *Shankland* v. *M'Gildowny*, supra, per Lord Kinnear at p. 867.
[80] *Smith & Kinnear* v. *Burns* (1847) 9 D. 1344; *Kerr* v. *Ferguson*, 1931 S.C. 736.
[81] Bell, *Comm.*, II, p. 68.

proper diligence.[82] Private books and papers, of no commercial value, cannot be arrested, either in execution or to found jurisdiction.[83] When the subject to be arrested is a ship, it is usual, though probably not necessary, to obtain a special warrant from the Court. Should it be apprehended that the captain will sail in disregard of the arrestment, a warrant to dismantle the ship, by removing some necessary part of her equipment, may be obtained.[84]

10. Alimentary Debts.—It is a general principle of Scots law that funds held for a debtor are not arrestable to the extent that they are alimentary. A debt may be alimentary either by some rule of law or by express provision. Among debts which were alimentary at common law were all salaries and wages payable by the Crown (including any Department of State), irrespective of the amount or grade of service, or of the character of the debt on which the arrestment was based[85]; but this privilege has now been removed, except in the case of the pay of serving members of the armed forces, and with this exception the wages of Crown servants are now arrestable.[86] Salaries enjoyed by parties holding a munus publicum, such as those of a professor[87] or of a parish minister,[88] are arrestable, subject to the beneficium competentiae, i.e., in so far only as they exceed what the Court may consider a reasonable amount for maintenance of the debtor. It would appear that this rule may extend to any salary,[89] and that at common law wages are only arrestable beyond what is a necessary aliment for the employee.[90] By the Wages Arrestment Limitation (Scotland) Act 1870, most recently amended by the Wages Arrestment Limitation Amendment (Scotland) Act 1960,[91] the wages of labourers, farm servants, manufacturers, artificers and workpeople are arrestable only to the extent of one-half of the wages earned by the debtor in excess of £4 per week.[92] This does not apply to arrestments used in virtue of a decree for alimentary allowances or payments, or for rates and taxes, provided that the arrestment sets forth the nature of the debt for which it has been used. By other statutes certain specific debts are entirely excluded from arrestment, as for example the wages of any seaman or apprentice in the merchant service,[93] family allowances and Social Security benefits[94] and certain pensions.[95]

---

[82] Stewart, *Diligence*, pp. 107–109.
[83] *Trowsdale's Tr.* v. *Forcett Ry.* (1870) 9 M. 88.
[84] *English's etc., Shipping Co.* v. *British Finance Co.* (1886) 14 R. 220; *Borjesson* v. *Carlberg* (1878) 5 R. (H.L.) 215.
[85] *Mulvenna* v. *The Admiralty*, 1926 S.C. 842.
[86] Law Reform (Miscellaneous Provisions) (Scotland) Act 1966 (c. 19), s. 2; Provisions for deductions from the pay of members of the Armed Forces in respect of judgment debts are contained in the Armed Forces Act 1971 (c. 33), ss. 59 & 61.
[87] *Laidlaw* v. *Wyld* (1801) M. App. Arrestment No. 4.
[88] *Learmonth* v. *Paterson* (1858) 20 D. 418.
[89] *Caldwell* v. *Hamilton*, 1919 S.C. (H.L.) 100, Lord Dunedin.
[90] *Shanks* v. *Thomson* (1838) 16 S. 1353.
[91] 33 & 34 Vict., c. 63; 8 & 9 Eliz. II, c. 21.
[92] Note that the amount of wages excepted from arrestment may now be varied by Order in Council: see Law Reform (Miscellaneous Provisions) (Scotland) Act 1966 (c. 19), s. 3.
[93] Merchant Shipping Act 1970 (c. 36), s. 11. There is no exemption from arrestment under a maintenance order: Merchant Shipping Act 1579 (c. 39), s. 39 (2).
[94] Family Allowances Act 1965, s. 10 (1); Social Security Act 1975, s. 87.
[95] e.g. under Education (Scotland) Act 1962, Sched. 3, para. 23.

Subject to the conditions that the capital must be vested in trustees,[96] and must be provided by some person other than the liferenter or annuitant himself,[97] a liferent or annuity may be declared to be alimentary. The effect of such a declaration is that the liferent or annuity is protected from the diligence of creditors in so far as it is a reasonable provision in relation to the beneficiary's station in life.[98] But it remains arrestable in virtue of alimentary debts, such as rent, food and clothing suitable to the debtor's condition in life.[99] It is no objection that the debt was incurred before the instalment of the alimentary fund which is arrested became due.[1] Arrears of an alimentary fund are arrestable.[2]

11. Recall and Loosing of Arrestments.—In certain cases arrestments may be recalled or loosed by the Court. A recall extinguishes the diligence: a loosing entitles the arrestee to pay to the debtor, but in case he does not do so preserves the security obtained by the arrestment.[3] In the case of arrestment in execution recall or loosing requires payment or consignation. In the case of arrestments on the dependence of an action the debtor may have the arrestments recalled or loosed on caution or consignation.[4] He may have them recalled or loosed without caution on the ground that they are nimious or oppressive,[5] or that the subjects are not arrestable.[6] A third party, who alleges that the subjects belong to him, has no title to petition for recall.[7] The arrestee cannot obtain the recall of an arrestment where the subject arrested is a debt, even on averment that no debt is due; where it is some corporeal moveable property it is not enough that he alleges that he has claims over it in a question with the debtor, but if he maintains that the property in question is his own he may have the arrestment recalled unless the arrester can show a prima facie case for holding that it really belongs to the debtor.[8]

III. Personal Poinding

12. Nature and Warrants for Poinding.—Personal poinding is the diligence by which moveable property in the possession of the debtor or of the creditor is attached and sold for behoof of the creditor, or if not sold made over to him to the extent or to account of his debt.[9] Until followed by a sale of the

[96] *Forbes's Trs.* v. *Tennant,* 1926 S.C. 294.
[97] *Lord Ruthven* v. *Drummond,* 1908 S.C. 1154.
[98] *Cuthbert* v. *Cuthbert's Trs.,* 1908 S.C. 967; see also *Weir* v. *Weir,* 1968 S.C. 241.
[99] *Lord Ruthven* v. *Pulford,* 1909 S.C. 951.
[1] Ibid.
[2] *Muirhead* v. *Miller* (1877) 4 R. 1139.
[3] *Graham* v. *Bruce* (1665) M. 792.
[4] Stewart, *Diligence,* p. 202; see also Rules of Court, 74 (*g*); *Fisher* v. *Weir,* 1964 S.L.T. (Notes) 99.
[5] *Magistrates of Dundee* v. *Taylor* (1863) 1 M. 701; *Radford & Bright* v. *Stevenson* (1904) 6 F. 429; *Levy* v. *Gardiner,* 1964 S.L.T. (Notes) 68.
[6] *Lord Ruthven* v. *Drummond,* 1908 S.C. 1154.
[7] *Brand* v. *Kent* (1892) 20 R. 29.
[8] *Laing* v. *Barclay, Curle & Co.,* 1908 S.C. (H.L.) 1.
[9] Stewart, *Diligence,* p. 274.

pointed effects poinding, like arrestment, is an inchoate or incomplete diligence. It confers on the creditor no real security in the effects, but prohibits the debtor from parting with them to the prejudice of the creditor. It is competent in execution only; not in security or on the dependence of an action. The warrant for poinding may be obtained by the issue of letters of horning and poinding, but in modern practice this procedure is rarely used. An extract decree of the Court of Session or Sheriff Court is itself now sufficient warrant to charge and poind,[10] as is an extract from the Books of Council and Session or Sheriff Court Books in which has been registered either a deed containing a clause consenting to registration and execution or a protest by a notary public of a bill for non-payment.[11] A summary warrant for the recovery of rates or taxes by poinding may also be obtained by the collector of rates of a rating authority or the collector of taxes on application to the Sheriff.[12]

13. Charge for Payment.—A poinding must be preceded by a charge, or formal requisition for payment. The charge, for which there is no statutory form, is executed by delivery of a schedule of charge by an officer of Court.[13] It may be given to the debtor personally, or at his dwelling-place, or, if he is furth of Scotland, may be left at the office of the Keeper of the Records of Edictal Citations.[14] After the charge has been given certain days of charge within which payment may be made, known as induciae, must elapse before the poinding is executed. The number of days depends partly on the nature of the warrant, partly on the residence of the debtor.[15] In those cases where summary diligence is competent, as on an extract registered bond or protested bill or promissory note, the days of charge are six.[16] The days of charge are also six in the case of decrees of the Court of Session as Court of Exchequer, such as those for payment of tax due and not paid.[17] In the case of decrees of the Court of Session they are fifteen days if the debtor is within Scotland, and fourteen days if he is furth of Scotland. A charge following on a decree granted in a summary cause in the Sheriff Court is for a period of fourteen days,[18] but in the case of decrees of the Sheriff Court in ordinary actions the days of charge are seven when the debtor is within Scotland.[19]

14. Execution of Poinding.—On the expiry of the days of charge, if no payment is offered, the poinding may be executed by the officer. He appoints two parties as valuators, who must then examine the effects which have been

[10] Debtors (Scotland) Act 1838, ss. 3, 4 and 9; As regards decrees of the Court of Session as Court of Exchequer, see Exchequer Court (Scotland) Act 1856, Sched. G.
[11] Writs Execution (Scotland) Act 1877, s. 3; Conveyancing (Scotland) Act 1924, s. 10 (5).
[12] Local Government (Scotland) Act 1947, s. 247 (2); Taxes Management Act 1970, s. 63.
[13] For persons empowered to execute a warrant to charge and poind, see § 5, supra; Debtors (Scotland) Act 1838, Scheds. 1 & 6; Execution of Diligence (Scotland) Act 1926.
[14] Sheriff Courts (Scotland) Act 1907, Sched. I., Rule 15; Stewart, *Diligence*, p. 290.
[15] See table of days of charge in Stewart, *Diligence*, p. 314.
[16] See Bills of Exchange, Ch. XXVI, supra § 25.
[17] Exchequer Court (Scotland) Act 1856, s. 28.
[18] Summary Cause Rules, 91.
[19] Sheriff Courts (Scotland) Extracts Act 1892, s. 7.

poinded and fix their value.[20] The effects are left with the debtor, with a schedule specifying the effects which have been poinded and the values which have been placed upon them.[21] Anyone who unlawfully intromits with them or carries them off is liable to imprisonment until he returns them or pays double the appraised value.[22] The poinding must be reported to the Sheriff within eight days, and he may give orders for the security of the goods poinded, and for their immediate disposal if they are of a perishable nature.[23] If required, the Sheriff grants warrant for the sale of the poinded effects by auction.[24] If there is undue delay on the part of the creditor in following out his diligence by a sale of the poinded effects, the poinding may be held to be inoperative.[25] The sale must be advertised, and must take place no sooner than eight nor more than twenty days after publication of the notice of sale.[26] The goods are exposed at prices not less than the appraised value fixed by the valuators. The poinding creditor is entitled to bid. If no offer is received the effects, or such portion as, at the appraised value, will satisfy the debt and expenses, are to be delivered to the creditor.[27] But if the goods belong to a third party such delivery does not give the creditor a right of property in them, except in the improbable event that he can found on the doctrine of reputed ownership.[28] The result of the sale, if effected, is reported to the Sheriff, and the creditor is entitled to payment of his debt and expenses out of the proceeds.[29] The creditor attaches the goods tantum et tale as vested in the debtor and subject to all the conditions legally attaching to them, such as lien, pledge or landlord's hypothec. Should a third party maintain that the goods which have been poinded belong to him, he may interdict the sale, or lodge a minute of objections with the Sheriff.[30] Where goods have been sequestrated by the landlord under hypothec, it is still competent to poind them, so as to attach any balance that may remain after the landlord's claim is satisfied, but the poinding creditor cannot sell or remove them.[31]

15. Preference Secured by Poinding.—As with arrestments, poindings used within sixty days prior to the constitution of notour bankruptcy and within four months thereafter are ranked pari passu as if they had all been used of

[20] Debtors (Scotland) Act 1838, s. 23; *Le Conte* v. *Douglas* (1880) 8 R. 175; *Scottish Gas Board* v. *Johnstone,* 1974 S.L.T. (Sh. Ct.) 65.
[21] 1838 Act, s. 24.
[22] 1838 Act, s. 30.
[23] 1838 Act, ss. 25, 26.
[24] But see *Scottish Gas Board* v. *Johnstone,* supra, where the Sheriff refused to grant a warrant for sale on the ground that the appraisal of the value of the effects had not been properly carried out.
[25] *Henderson* v. *Grant* (1896) 23 R. 659; *New Day Furnishing Stores* v. *Curran,* 1974 S.L.T. (Sh. Ct.) 20.
[26] 1838 Act, s. 26.
[27] 1838 Act, ss. 27, 29.
[28] *George Hopkinson* v. *Napier & Son,* 1953 S.C. 139, where opinions were reserved as to the rights of a bona fide purchaser at a judicial sale. As to reputed ownership, see Moveable Property, Corporeal, Ch. XXXVII, supra, § 3.
[29] 1838 Act, s. 28. See *Cantors* v. *Hardie,* 1974 S.L.T. (Sh. Ct.) 26, in which the procedure to be followed on a sale of poinded goods is discussed; *J. Ratcliff & Co.* v. *M'Kelvie,* 1977 S.L.T. (Sh. Ct.) 64.
[30] *Lamb* v. *Wood* (1904) 6 F. 1091.
[31] *Wylie* v. *Fisher,* 1907 S.C. 686.

the same date.[32] Sequestration or the winding up of a company are equivalent to an executed or completed poinding, and poindings executed on or after the sixtieth day prior to the date of the sequestration or winding up are ineffectual to secure any preference to the poinding creditor except for the expenses bona fide incurred by him in using the diligence.[33] The preference of poinding in competition with a completed diligence depends upon the date when the poinding has been completed by a sale or the handing over of the goods to the creditor.[34] In competition with other inchoate diligences it is determined by priority in date of execution. A poinding which has not been completed before the appointment of a receiver will not be effective so as to exclude the power of the receiver to take possession of the property of the company.[35] Claims by a rating authority for arrears of rates and by the Inland Revenue for arrears of any tax, in each case for not more than one year's arrears, are accorded a preference by statute over the goods and effects belonging to the debtor at the time the rates or tax became in arrear or were payable, and are recoverable from the poinding creditor.[36] In the case of claims for arrears of rates, the poinding creditor is entitled when accounting to the rating authority to deduct the expenses of and incidental to the taking of the goods and effects and their preservation and sale.[37]

16. Subjects Poindable.—In general any corporeal moveable property which is of commercial value, and capable of being sold by auction under warrant from the Sheriff, may be poinded. By established practice however the debtor's wearing apparel and the working tools of his trade are exempt.[38] When the exemption in favour of working tools has been founded on by professional men it has been held to be a question of degree, depending on their value and necessity, how far articles in professional use could be poinded.[39] Beds or bedding material, chairs, tables and furniture or plenishings providing facilities for cooking, eating or storing food or facilities for heating which are at the time of the poinding in a dwelling house in which the debtor is residing are also exempt from poinding, if reasonably necessary to enable him and any person living in family with him in that dwelling house to continue to reside there without undue hardship.[40] Bills of exchange, cheques, certificates and other such documents cannot be attached by private diligence, and the competency of poinding money or notes is doubtful. Any of these may be poinded, however, when the diligence is at the instance of the

---

32 Bankruptcy (Scotland) Act 1913, s. 10.
33 Bankruptcy (Scotland) Act 1913, s. 104; Companies Act 1948, s. 327 (1) (a).
34 Stewart, *Diligence*, p. 365; see also § 6, supra.
35 Companies (Floating Charges and Receivers) (Scotland) Act 1972, c. 67, s. 15 (2); *Lord Advocate* v. *Royal Bank of Scotland*, 1978 S.L.T. 38.
36 Local Government (Scotland) Act 1947 (c. 43), s. 248; Taxes Management Act 1970 (c. 9), s. 64.
37 1947 Act, s. 248 proviso, added by Valuation and Rating (Scotland) Act 1956, s. 34.
38 Stewart, *Diligence*, p. 345.
39 *Macpherson* v. *Macpherson's Tr.* (1905) 8 F. 191 (dentist's instruments); *Pennell* v. *Elgin*, 1926 S.C. 9 (solicitor's law library).
40 Law Reform (Diligence) (Scotland) Act 1973 (c. 22), s. 1.

Crown.[41] By the Diligence Act 1503 (c. 98), plough goods, i.e., implements and animals used in ploughing, cannot be poinded during the ploughing season, unless there are no other poindable goods available.[41a] Growing crops may be poinded.[42]

IV. ADJUDICATION

17. Nature and Grounds of Adjudication.—Adjudication is the diligence by which heritable property may be attached either in payment or in security of debt. It operates so as to bind the property which is attached by it until the whole debt on which it proceeded has been satisfied. It is based on the Adjudications Act 1672 (c. 19), by which it is substituted for the earlier process of apprising, thereby abolished.[43] In form an action, adjudication in execution may be founded on any decree or liquid document of debt. Adjudication in security may be used where the debt is future or contingent, but it is competent only where the debtor is vergens ad inopiam or has had other adjudications led against him.[44] The action must be raised in the Court of Session.[45]

18. Subjects Adjudgeable.—Any right to land, whether infeftment has been taken or not, and whether in liferent or fee; leases, where judicial assignees are not excluded; heritable securities, although moveable in succession[46]; the stock of a chartered body where the charter excludes arrestment—not the shares of a company under the Companies Act[47]—are adjudgeable.

19. Effect of Adjudication.—The service of a summons of adjudication, if followed by a registration of a notice in a statutory form in the General Register of Inhibitions and Adjudications,[48] renders the subjects litigious, that is to say, it impliedly prohibits voluntary alienation, and any disponee takes subject to the diligence. Such a notice prescribes, and is of no effect after five years, and litigiosity is not pleadable and cannot be founded on to any effect, after the expiry of six months from and after final decree in the action creating it.[48] Decree in the action is equivalent to a conveyance of the subjects and, when followed by recording of the decree in the appropriate Register of Sasines[49] vests them in the creditor, subject to the right of redemption. The adjudger takes the subjects tantum et tale as they are vested in the debtor and

[41] Exchequer Court Act 1856, s. 32.
[41a] See Rankine, *Leases* (3rd ed.), p. 705.
[42] *Elder* v. *Allen* (1833) 11 S. 902.
[43] See *Lord Adv.* v. *Marquess of Zetland*, 1920 S.C. (H.L.) 1.
[44] Stewart, *Diligence*, p. 665; Bell, *Comm.*, I, 752.
[45] Bell, *Comm.*, I, 714. The rule is preserved by the Sheriff Courts (Scotland) Act 1907, s. 5 (4).
[46] See Titles to Land Consolidation Act 1868 (32 & 33 Vict., c. 116), s. 117; *Hare* (1889) 17 R. 105.
[47] *Sinclair* v. *Staples* (1860) 22 D. 600.
[48] Conveyancing (Scotland) Act 1924 (14 & 15 Geo. V, c. 27), s. 44.
[49] 1924 Act, s. 44 (5).

subject to all the conditions and qualifications which attach to them.[50] In a competition between adjudgers all adjudications prior to that first made effectual, i.e. by recording in the General Register of Sasines, and all those subsequently led within a year and a day, rank pari passu.[51] Those outwith the year and a day rank according to the date of the recording of the decree. Sequestration is equivalent to a decree of adjudication of the bankrupt's heritable estate as at the date of the first deliverance, and any adjudications which have not been made effectual more than a year and a day before that date confer no preference on the adjudger.[52]

20. Right of Redemption.—A decree of adjudication vests the property adjudged, subject to redemption within a period of ten years, known as the "legal." After that period has expired the creditor may raise an action of declarator of expiry of the legal, decree in which excludes the right of redemption. Should no such proceedings be taken, the subjects remain redeemable although the legal has expired.[53] If, however, the title of the adjudger has been duly recorded in the Register of Sasines and possession has followed thereon for ten years from the date of the expiry of the legal, positive prescription applies, and the debtor's right of redemption is excluded.[54]

V. Inhibition

21. Nature of Inhibition.—Inhibition has been defined as "a personal prohibition, prohibiting the party inhibited to contract any debt, or grant any deed by which any part of his lands may be alienated, or carried off, to the prejudice of the creditor inhibiting."[55] It is competent on any liquid debt, such as a decree,[56] bond or bill, or on the dependence of an action containing conclusions for payment of money alleged to be presently due, other than the conclusion for expenses.[57] If used for a debt payable in future (e.g., future instalments of sums decerned for as aliment) an application for inhibition requires averments that the debtor is vergens ad inopiam or in meditatione fugae.[58] The procedure is either by letters of inhibition passing the Signet,[59] or by warrant for inhibition implied in the summons of an action raised in the

[50] Stewart, *Diligence*, p. 620.
[51] Diligence Act 1661 (c. 62).
[52] Bankruptcy (Scotland) Act 1913, s. 103; cf. Companies Act 1948, s. 327 (1) (*b*) as regards winding up.
[53] *Govan* v. *Govan* (1759) 2 Paton 27.
[54] *Hinton* v. *Connell's Trs.* (1883) 10 R. 1110; Prescription and Limitation (Scotland) Act 1973, c. 5, s. 1 (1) and (3).
[55] Erskine, II, 11, 2.
[56] But not a decree obtained under the Small Debt Acts: see *Lamont* (1867) 6 M. 84. By analogy inhibition would seem not to be competent on a decree obtained in a summary cause in the Sheriff Court.
[57] *Burns* v. *Burns* (1879) 7 R. 355.
[58] *Symington* v. *Symington* (1875) 3 R. 205. In such cases procedure must be by petition, not by warrant inserted in the will of the summons.
[59] Titles to Land Consolidation Act 1868, s. 156; for form of letters of inhibition, see Sched. QQ.

Court of Session on the dependence of which an inhibition is sought.[60] The letters or summons must be served on the debtor, and a notice of inhibition registered in the General Register of Inhibitions and Adjudications. Without such registration an inhibition has no effect.[61] It prescribes in five years from the date of registration of the notice.[62]

22. Effect of Inhibition.—The effect of an inhibition, if duly registered, is to render any voluntary deed affecting the debtor's heritable property, whether he has a completed title to it or not,[63] voidable at the instance of the inhibitor (ex spreta inhibitione) in so far as his interests are prejudiced, and no further.[64] Heritable property acquired after the date of the inhibition is not affected, unless it was destined under a prior indefeasible title, as in the case of an entail.[65] An inhibition strikes at any sale, or heritable security, not at a lease, unless its terms are such as in substance to amount to an alienation.[66] It has no effect on prior debts, and therefore where heritable security had been given for a cash credit bond before the inhibition, advances made after it were not affected.[67] It does not affect rights which are not due to any voluntary act of the debtor. So it is no bar to adjudication; and when the debtor in a bond paid the sum due and obtained an assignation to a third party, it was held that as the creditor in a bond is bound to accept payment and grant an assignation the fact that he was subject to a prior inhibition did not invalidate the transaction.[68] Likewise it is no bar to the exercise of a power of sale conferred on a heritable creditor prior to the inhibition. Such a creditor is entitled to be paid in full from the proceeds of the sale if there are sufficient funds. But an inhibition subsequent in date to the heritable security will secure for the inhibitor a ranking to the free proceeds of sale preferential to that of ordinary creditors who have taken no steps to secure their debts and also to that of other creditors who have sought to obtain a preference, e.g. by arrestment, but whose preferences postdate that of the inhibitor.[69] Similarly a receiver appointed to a company which has granted a floating charge over its heritable property may take possession of and sell that property even although affected by an inhibition, provided the floating charge was granted prior to the date of registration of the inhibition.[70]

23. Inhibition when Debtor Sequestrated.—Inhibition is only a negative or prohibitory diligence; it precludes the party inhibited from contracting any

[60] Rules of Court, 74. A warrant for inhibition on the dependence may also be obtained on a counter-claim or third party notice in the Court of Session: Rules of Court, 84 (c), 85 (b).
[61] Titles to Land Consolidation Act 1868, s. 155; Conveyancing (Scotland) Act 1924, s. 44.
[62] 1924 Act. s. 44 (3) (a).
[63] Dryburgh v. Gordon (1896) 24 R. 1.
[64] See Lennox v. Robertson (1790) Hume 243.
[65] Titles to Land Consolidation Act 1868, s. 157.
[66] Earl of Breadalbane v. M'Lachlan (1802) Hume 242.
[67] Campbell's Tr. v. De Lisle's Executors (1870) 9 M. 252.
[68] Mackintosh's Trs. v. Davidson & Garden (1898) 25 R. 554.
[69] Bank of Scotland v. Lord Advocate and others, 1977 S.L.T. 24.
[70] Companies (Floating Charges and Receivers) (Scotland) Act 1972 (c. 67), ss. 15 and 21; cf. Lord Advocate v. Royal Bank of Scotland, 1978 S.L.T. 38.

debt, or granting any voluntary deed by which any part of his heritable property may be alienated or otherwise affected to the prejudice of the inhibitor; it has no positive effect in giving the inhibitor any real right in any part of the debtor's estate. Its effect is to preserve the heritable property as part of the debtor's estate, and therefore attachable by the inhibitor by adjudication. If there is no question with other creditors, but only with persons who have acquired rights to the debtor's heritable estate, the inhibitor is entitled to any preference which adjudication would confer without the actual use of that diligence.[71] If the debtor is sequestrated the act and warrant in favour of the trustee has the effect of an adjudication for the benefit of all creditors, including the inhibitor.[72] In such cases the principle of ranking has been decided to be that as a first step all creditors should be ranked pari passu on the proceeds of the heritable estate; that the right to participate in that ranking of creditors whose debts were contracted anterior to the inhibition is not affected by inhibition; and that the inhibitor is entitled, at the expense of the ranking awarded to posterior creditors, to the difference between an equal dividend to all and the dividend which he would have drawn had there been no debts contracted subsequent to the inhibition.[73]

24. Recall of Inhibition.—An inhibition duly registered forms an in-cumbrance to title which a seller of lands under the ordinary obligation of warrandice is bound to remove by procuring a discharge, and, in a question with the purchaser, it is immaterial that the inhibition may be open to objection.[74] When an inhibition is used on the dependence of an action, and the defender is ultimately assoilzied, the Court, on motion to that effect, will grant an order on the Keeper of the Register to have the inhibition marked as recalled.[75] When the debt on which the inhibition is used has been paid the creditor is bound, at the debtor's expense, to clear the record by recording a discharge. Should he refuse to do so, the party inhibited may present a petition for recall, and the creditor will be liable for the expenses of the petition and for all expenses necessarily incurred in having the inhibition completely removed.[76] The creditor is not entitled to recover the expense of using the diligence.[77] An inhibition may be recalled, with or without caution, if the Court is satisfied that in the circumstances its use is nimious or oppressive.[78] An inhibition on the dependence of an action will usually be recalled on caution or consignation.[79]

[71] *Lennox* v. *Robertson* (1790) Hume 243.
[72] Bankruptcy (Scotland) Act 1913, s. 103; cf. Companies Act 1948, s. 327 (1) (*b*) as regards winding up.
[73] Bell, *Comm.*, II, 408; *Baird & Brown* v. *Stirrat's Tr.* (1872) 10 M. 414; *Scottish Waggon Co.* v. *Hamilton* (1906) 13 S.L.T. 779.
[74] *Dryburgh* v. *Gordon* (1896) 24 R. 1.
[75] *Barbour's Trs.* v. *Davidson* (1878) 15 S.L.R. 438.
[76] *Robertson* v. *Park, Dobson & Co.* (1896) 24 R. 30; *Milne* v. *Birrell* (1902) 4 F. 879.
[77] *Milne* v. *Birrell*, supra.
[78] *Mackintosh* v. *Miller* (1864) 2 M. 452; *Burns* v. *Burns* (1879) 7 R. 355.
[79] For procedure, see Rules of Court, 74 (*g*) and (*h*); cf. *Fisher* v. *Weir*, 1964 S.L.T. (Notes) 99.

VI. POINDING OF THE GROUND

25. Title to Poind the Ground.—Poinding of the ground is a real diligence for attaching moveables. In form it is an action, competent either in the Court of Session or Sheriff Court.[80] It is open only to a creditor holding a debitum fundi, that is who has his debt secured upon land. Such a creditor is a superior for his feu duty, a heritable creditor unless under an ex facie absolute disposition, the creditor in a real burden secured over land[81] or the creditor in a ground annual,[82] but not the creditor under an assignation in security of a lease registered under the Registration of Leases Act 1857.[83] No one whose title is that of a proprietor, as in the case of the holder of an ex facie absolute disposition qualified by a back bond, can poind his own ground,[84] but a creditor who has obtained a decree of maills and duties, and is therefore to a certain extent in possession, retains the right to poind.[85] The action, which is competent both in the Court of Session and the Sheriff Court, is for warrant to poind and distrain all moveables belonging to the debtor, or to his tenants or possessors of the lands, which are on the lands over which the debitum fundi is constituted. Unlike personal poinding, it does not require a charge for payment before the extract decree is executed.[86] It may be carried into effect by procedure similar to that in personal poinding.[87]

26. Subjects Poindable.—The subjects attached by a poinding of the ground are all moveables in fact situated on the ground at the date of service in the action, and belonging to the proprietor of the lands. He need not be the debtor, if he is proprietor of the lands over which the poinder's bond extends.[88] Moveables belonging to tenants may be attached, in so far as their value does not exceed rents due and unpaid.[89] Moveables belonging to a third party cannot be poinded[90]; but where lands belonged to a firm, and the title was in the name of the two partners, it was held that moveables belonging to one of them, as he was in substance a proprietor, might be attached.[91] The right to poind the ground in effect amounts to a floating charge over moveable property, but until it is put in force by action it does not give the creditor a nexus over any particular articles, and consequently it does not give any right over articles which have been removed before the action was raised.[92] If they have been removed unlawfully the creditor may have an action of damages

---

[80] Bell, *Prin.*, § 2285. For history of this form of diligence see opinion of Lord Deas, *Royal Bank v. Bain* (1877) 4 R. 985.
[81] *Scottish Heritable Security Co.* v. *Allan Campbell & Co.* (1876) 3 R. 333; *Scottish Union & National Insurance Co.* v. *James* (1886) 13 R. 928.
[82] *Bell's Trs.* v. *Copeland* (1896) 23 R. 650.
[83] *Luke* v. *Wallace* (1896) 23 R. 634.
[84] *Scottish Heritable Security Co.* v. *Allan Campbell & Co.* (1876) 3 R. 333.
[85] *Henderson* v. *Wallace* (1875) 2 R. 272.
[86] Bell, *Prin.*, § 2285.
[87] Supra, § 14.
[88] Erskine, IV, 1, 13; *Millar's Trs.* v. *Miller & Son's Tr.* (1886) 13 R. 543.
[89] Diligence Act 1469 (c. 36).
[90] *Thomson* v. *Scoular* (1882) 9 R. 430.
[91] *Kelly's Tr.* v. *Moncreiff's Tr.*, 1920 S.C. 461.
[92] *Traill's Trs.* v. *Free Church*, 1915 S.C. 655.

against the party responsible; he cannot maintain that his poinding covers goods not in fact on the ground, or insist on their being restored.[93] Service of the summons or initial writ completes the nexus of the creditor over the moveables on the ground, and he has a preferable right to them, or to their proceeds, if sold in a question with anyone who may have obtained possession of them.[94]

27. Poinding in Competition with Other Rights.—Questions as to the preference obtained by a poinding of the ground are to be decided on the principle that the creditor, in poinding, is not acquiring any new right but merely putting in force a right which is immanent in the charge on land which constitutes the debitum fundi and in respect of which he poinds. On this principle it is held that the date of the poinding is the date when that charge was completed by infeftment, not the date when the action of poinding of the ground was raised.[95] In a competition between creditors, both using the diligence, a superior poinding for feu duty is preferable to any bondholder, because feu duty is a charge upon land necessarily prior in date to any right granted by the vassal.[96] Between bondholders the holder of the prior bond is preferred irrespective of the date of their diligence.[97] There is no race of diligence between poinding of the ground and personal poinding; the former dates from the constitution of the real right, the latter from the date of the diligence.[98] The same rule applied at common law to sequestration: if a creditor had a real right completed before the sequestration, his right to poind the ground was not affected by it.[99] But in this particular the law has been altered by legislation. By section 114 of the Bankruptcy (Scotland) Act 1913 (repeating earlier legislation), it is provided that no poinding of the ground which has not been carried into execution by sale of the effects sixty days before the date of the sequestration shall be available in any question with the trustee, with the proviso that no creditor holding a right over the heritable estate preferable to that of the trustee shall be prevented from executing a poinding after the sequestration, but that such poinding shall be available in competition with the trustee, to the extent only of the interest on the debt for the current half-yearly term, and one year's arrears. A similar provision applies to the liquidation of a company.[1]

28. Liability of Poinder for Rates and Taxes.—As with personal poinding, claims by a rating authority for arrears of rates and by the Inland Revenue for arrears of any tax, in each case for not more than one year's arrears, are accorded a preference by statute over the goods and effects belonging to the debtor at the time the rates or tax became in arrear or were payable, and are

[93] *Urquhart* v. *Macleod's Tr.* (1883) 10 R. 991.
[94] *Lyons* v. *Anderson* (1880) 8 R. 24.
[95] *Athole Hydropathic Co.* v. *Scottish Provincial Assurance Co.* (1886) 13 R. 818.
[96] Bankton, II, 5, 22; *Royal Bank* v. *Bain* (1877) 4 R. 985, opinion of Lord Deas.
[97] *Bell* v. *Cadell* (1831) 10 S. 100; *Nicol's Tr.* v. *Hill* (1889) 16 R. 416.
[98] *Bell* v. *Cadell*, supra.
[99] *Royal Bank* v. *Bain* (1877) 4 R. 985.
[1] Companies Act 1948, s. 327 (1) (*d*).

recoverable from the poinding creditor.[2] In the case of claims for arrears of rates, the poinding creditor is entitled when accounting to the rating authority to deduct the expenses of and incidental to the taking of the goods and effects and their preservation and sale.[3]

VII. MAILLS AND DUTIES

29. Maills and Duties: Title.—An action of maills and duties[4] is the diligence by which the creditor in a heritable security may attach rents due by the tenants of the subjects over which his security extends. The action may be brought by the holder of a real right in lands if he has the right to enter into possession, but not by the creditor in a real burden, who has no such right.[5] The clause of assignation of rents in a bond and disposition in security provides the legal basis for the creditor's right in the event of the debtor's default to enter into possession and uplift the rents.[6] The creditor in a standard security has a statutory right under Standard Condition 10 (3) to enter into possession of the security subjects and to recover the rents where the debtor is in default.[7] It is settled that this diligence is not open to a superior,[8] though he may obtain the same result by an action of poinding of the ground followed by an arrangement with the tenants under which they agree to pay their rents to him rather than have their effects sold under the poinding.[9] The creditor in a ground annual may raise an action of maills and duties,[10] but it is not competent for the creditor under an assignation in security of a registered lease to do so since the Registration of Leases (Scotland) Act 1857 provides a special procedure whereby the creditor may enter into possession and uplift the rent.[11] The holder of a disposition ex facie absolute qualified by a back bond has a direct right to exact the rents, and an action of maills and duties by him is unnecessary, and probably incompetent.[12]

30. Procedure.—In its earlier form an action of maills and duties was directed against the tenants, the proprietor being called for his interest. This procedure is still competent, but has been superseded in practice by the forms introduced by the Heritable Securities Act 1894.[13] Under that Act the action is

[2] Local Government (Scotland) Act 1947 (c. 43), s. 248; Taxes Management Act 1970 (c. 9), s. 64.
[3] 1947 Act, s. 248 proviso, added by Valuation and Rating (Scotland) Act 1956, s. 34.
[4] See, on this subject, Rankine, *Leases* (3rd ed.), p. 360. The expression "maills and duties" is the old form for "rents", "maills" being the money payment and "duties" the personal services.
[5] Stair, IV, 35, 24.
[6] Titles to Land Consolidation (Scotland) Act 1868, s. 119; Conveyancing (Scotland) Act 1924, s. 25 (1) (a); see *M'Ara* v. *Anderson*, 1913 S.C. 931.
[7] Conveyancing and Feudal Reform (Scotland) Act 1970, c. 35, ss. 20, 24.
[8] *Prudential Assurance Co.* v. *Cheyne* (1884) 11 R. 871; *Nelson's Trs.* v. *Tod* (1896) 23 R. 1000.
[9] *Aberdeen Corporation* v. *British Linen Bank*, 1911 S.C. 239.
[10] *Somerville* v. *Johnston* (1899) 1 F. 726.
[11] *Dunbar* v. *Gill*, 1908 S.C. 1054.
[12] *Scottish Heritable Securities Co.* v. *Campbell* (1876) 3 R. 333; *Crichton's Trs.* v. *Clarke*, 1909 1 S.L.T. 467.
[13] 57 & 58 Vict., c. 44, s. 3.

directed against the proprietor of the lands covered by the security, and the tenants need not be called as defenders. Instead, notice of the raising of the action may be given to the tenants by registered letter in a statutory form (Schedule B), and this has the effect of interpelling them from making payment of their rents to the proprietor. When decree is obtained, a similar notice (Schedule C) gives the creditor the right to the rents. Neither the original nor the statutory form is available against a proprietor who is in personal occupation of the subjects,[14] but the Act contains a separate provision under which he may be ejected if he is in default.[15]

31. Effect of Decree.—The effect of the decree in an action of maills and duties is to transform the preference over the rents given to the holder of the heritable security into an active right to uplift the rents. After service in such an action, or a notice under the Heritable Securities Act 1894, he, and not the proprietor, is the creditor of the tenant, and the latter therefore cannot plead compensation on a debt due by the proprietor, and incurred after the date of the service or notice.[16] He has the same right of hypothec that the proprietor possessed, and may sequestrate for rent, whether the tenant be the recipient of the original notice or an assignee.[17] He is so far in possession of the lands that he may remove tenants,[18] and grant leases,[19] but he was held not to be a possessor of the subjects so as to render it incompetent for him to raise an action of poinding of the ground.[20] If a creditor enters into the actual possession and management of the subjects he incurs the liabilities of a proprietor to third parties for injuries resulting from their defective state, but this would probably not apply if all that he did was to obtain a decree of maills and duties and to uplift the rent.[21]

32. Effect of Bankruptcy.—On the analogy of cases relating to poinding of the ground, and on the principle that an action of maills and duties merely puts in force a right already conferred by the heritable security, the right of the creditor in the security to use this form of diligence is not affected by the fact that the debtor has been sequestrated.[22]

---

[14] *Smith's Trs.* v. *Chalmers* (1890) 17 R. 1088.
[15] 1894 Act, s. 5.
[16] *Chambers' Factor* v. *Vertue* (1893) 20 R. 257.
[17] *Robertson's Trs.* v. *Gardner* (1889) 16 R. 705.
[18] *Forsyth* v. *Aird* (1853) 16 D. 197.
[19] Heritable Securities Act 1894, ss. 7, 8; see, as regards standard securities, Conveyancing and Feudal Reform (Scotland) Act 1970, Standard Conditions 10 (4) and (5).
[20] *Henderson* v. *Wallace* (1875) 2 R. 272. See § 25, supra.
[21] *Baillie* v. *Shearer's Factor* (1894) 21 R. 498; see opinion of Lord Trayner.
[22] Stewart, *Diligence*, p. 524.

CHAPTER XLIX

LAW OF BANKRUPTCY

Goudy, *Bankruptcy* (4th ed., 1914); Wallace, *Bankruptcy* (2nd ed., 1914).

1. History of the Law.—In the earlier history of the law of Scotland there was no provision whereby a party who had become insolvent might obtain a discharge from his debts without actual payment, or the favour of his creditors. And, while creditors as a body might be ranked on the heritable estate by the process, which is still competent, of ranking and sale, the moveable estate was open to the diligence of the individual. Where a debtor was imprisoned, release was attainable by the process known as cessio bonorum, whereby the debtor, on giving up all his property, was released from imprisonment, and could not be afterwards imprisoned in respect of pre-existing debts. He did not, however, obtain a discharge, and any property which he might afterwards acquire could be attached by his creditors by the use of the appropriate diligence. Sequestration, a process under which the bankrupt's estate is transferred to a trustee, was introduced in 1772, by a statute confined to living debtors who were engaged in trade. By subsequent Acts, the most important being the Bankruptcy Act 1856, the process was extended to all debtors and to the estates of those deceased. The law now depends mainly on the Bankruptcy (Scotland) Act 1913,[1] and certain earlier statutes relating to the effect of bankruptcy on prior transactions by the bankrupt. The process of cessio bonorum was preserved in name until it was abolished by the Act of 1913, though it had been transformed into a species of sequestration adapted to small estates. The Act of 1913 has substituted a process termed summary sequestration.

In dealing with the existing law, three stages have to be distinguished, each having separate legal results, namely, insolvency, notour bankruptcy, and sequestration. Any of these may be denoted by the word "bankruptcy," which has no technical meaning.

2. Insolvency.—Insolvency may mean that at a particular date the bankrupt's assets, if realised, would not meet his liabilities, although he may have been able to meet all debts which were presented for payment; or it may mean inability to meet debts of which payment is demanded, although, when the assets are realised, they may exceed the liabilities. In questions between creditors as to the validity of deeds granted by a party alleged to be insolvent, insolvency usually has the first meaning; in questions between the debtor and his creditors, e.g., as to his notour bankruptcy, it always has the second.[2]

---

[1] 3 & 4 Geo. V, c. 20.
[2] See Goudy, *Bankruptcy*, p. 17.

Insolvency in the first sense, which is known as absolute insolvency, is proved by a report as to the bankrupt's assets and liabilities at the material date; insolvency in the second sense, which is known as practical insolvency, by his refusal or failure to pay a debt admittedly due and presented for payment. As a general rule insolvency does not in either sense affect the capacity or the rights and duties of the debtor or terminate any legal relations which may have arisen from contract with him. In itself it is not a bar to a debtor pursuing or defending an action, although he may in certain cases be required to find caution for expenses. It does not prevent a debtor from entering into contracts or from continuing with his business with the purpose and intention of recovering his commercial position.[3] It may however affect the rights and obligations of parties to contracts such as those of sale, partnership and lease which may according to their terms become altered once insolvency has occurred. An unpaid seller may exercise the right of stoppage in transitu against a buyer who has become insolvent,[4] and insolvency may give rise to an irritancy under a lease.[5] In addition insolvency has special effects in relation to gratuitous alienations by the debtor and voluntary transactions between him and his creditors.[6]

3. Notour Bankruptcy.—Notour bankruptcy originally designated the condition of a man who, to avoid imprisonment for debt, had retired to the sanctuary, the Abbey of Holyrood. His insolvency thereby became notorious or notour.[7] It has now a statutory meaning.[8] It is constituted, in the case of individuals—(a) by sequestration, or by the issuing of an adjudication of bankruptcy or the granting of a receiving order in England or Ireland; (b) by insolvency,[9] concurring (1) with a charge for payment,[10] followed by the expiry of the days of charge without payment; (2) when a charge is not necessary, with the lapse without payment of the days which must elapse before poinding or imprisonment can follow on a decree or warrant for payment of money[11]; (3) with a poinding or seizure of any of the debtor's moveables for payment of rates or taxes; (4) with a decree of adjudication of any part of the heritable estate for payment or in security; or (5) with sale of any effects belonging to the debtor under a sequestration for rent. In the case of a company, notour bankruptcy may be constituted in any of the foregoing ways, or by any of the partners being rendered notour bankrupt for a company debt.[12] "Company" is defined as including bodies corporate or partnerships.[13] A company registered under the Companies Acts may be made

---

[3] *Ehrenbacher & Co.* v. *Kennedy* (1874) 1 R. 1131.
[4] Sale of Goods Act 1893, s. 44.
[5] Leases, Ch. XXXIII, supra, § 21.
[6] See §§ 4 and 5, infra.
[7] Bell, *Comm.*, II, 192.
[8] Bankruptcy Act 1913, s. 5.
[9] Meaning practical insolvency, i.e. inability to meet current obligations, *Teenan's Tr.* v. *Teenan* (1886) 13 R. 833; or refusal to do so, *Scottish Milk Marketing Board* v. *Wood,* 1936 S.C. 604.
[10] For evidence of execution of charge, see *I. R.* v. *Gibb,* 1963 S.L.T. (Notes) 66.
[11] See Diligence, Ch. XLVIII, supra, § 13.
[12] Bankruptcy Act 1913, s. 6.
[13] s. 2.

notour bankrupt,[14] although such companies cannot be wound up except under the special provisions of those Acts.[15]

Important consequences flow from the constitution of notour bankruptcy. It is a pre-requisite to sequestration when applied for by creditors.[16] It has the effect of equalising diligences used within sixty days prior to its constitution or within four months thereafter,[17] and it enables creditors to reduce preferences struck at by the Bankruptcy Act 1696 (c. 5).[18] Notour bankruptcy is held to commence from the time when its several requisites concur, and once constituted it continues in the case of a sequestration until the debtor obtains his discharge, and in other cases until his insolvency has ceased.[19]

4. Reduction of Gratuitous Alienations.—It is a general principle at common law that from the moment of his insolvency a debtor is bound to administer his estate for behoof of his creditors. While he may continue with his trade with the intention of making gain for his creditors and for himself, his funds are no longer his own to give away as caprice or affection may dictate.[20] Accordingly every voluntary alienation of property by a debtor while in a state of insolvency to the prejudice of his creditors is fraudulent and may be the subject of challenge at common law. Thus an alienation of goods or money, if it was in the nature of a gift,[21] or a gratuitous surrender of rights,[22] or a purchase at an exorbitant price[23] is reducible either at the instance of creditors, prior or posterior,[24] or of the trustee in his subsequent sequestration.[25] The onus of proof that the transaction was in substance gratuitous and that the debtor was insolvent at the date of the alienation rests upon the challenger. It is not however necessary to prove that the alienation was made with fraudulent intention. A presumption of fraud, in the sense of breach of trust, is created by proof that the alienation was made without onerous consideration when the debtor was insolvent.[26]

Where the alienation was made to a conjunct or confident person it may also be challenged under statute. The Bankruptcy Act 1621, c. 18, provides that all alienations made by a debtor of any of his lands, debts or goods to any conjunct or confident person without true just and necessary causes and without a just price really paid after the contracting of lawful debts from true creditors are null if subjected to challenge. The Act has been held to apply to every kind of deed by which property or obligations are transferred,[27] but it

---

[14] *Clark* v. *Hinde, Milne & Co.* (1894) 12 R. 347.
[15] *Standard Property Investment Co.* v. *Dunblane Hydropathic Co.* (1884) 12 R. 328; see Company Law, Ch. XXV, supra, § 41.
[16] Bankruptcy Act 1913, s. 11 (B).
[17] s. 11; see § 7, infra.
[18] See § 6, infra.
[19] Bankruptcy Act 1913, s. 7.
[20] Bell, *Comm.*, II, 170; Goudy, p. 22.
[21] Bell, *Comm.*, II, 184; *Wink* v. *Speirs* (1867) 6 M. 77; *Main* v. *Fleming's Trs.* (1881) 8 R. 880.
[22] *Obers* v. *Paton's Trs.* (1897) 24 R. 719; *Thomson* v. *Spence*, 1961 S.L.T. 395.
[23] *Abram S.S. Co.* v. *Abram*, 1925 S.L.T. 243.
[24] Opinion of Lord Justice-Clerk, *Wink* v. *Speirs*, supra.
[25] Bankruptcy Act 1913, s. 9.
[26] *M'Cowan* v. *Wright* (1852) 14 D. 901.
[27] *Thomas* v. *Thomson* (1865) 3 M. 1160; *Obers* v. *Paton's Trs.* (1897) 24 R. 719.

does not apply to a transaction which consists merely of a payment in cash.[28] Conjunct persons are those who are nearly related to the bankrupt, by blood or affinity; confident persons are those with whom he has an intimate or confidential relationship, such as a partner in business, an intended spouse or a confidential adviser, servant or factor.[29] The onus of proof that the receiver of the deed is conjunct or confident with the debtor and of insolvency at the date of the challenge rests on the challenger. Once this is done however insolvency at the date of the alienation is presumed, and it lies on the defender to prove either the onerosity of the alienation or that he was solvent at the time.[30]

The Act provides that if the disponee, a conjunct or confident person, has transferred the subject to a bona fide third party, it cannot be recovered, but the disponee is liable for its value. It is also provided in a separate part of the Act that alienations during insolvency in defraud of diligence may be cut down in favour of the creditor who used the first lawful diligence, but in view of the provisions for the equalisation of diligences on notour bankruptcy this provision is now of little practical importance.

It is a good answer to a reduction, either at common law or under the Bankruptcy Act 1621, that the deed in question was granted for some true, just and necessary cause. The fulfilment of an obligation, undertaken during solvency, is not struck at.[31] Provisions in ante-nuptial marriage contracts or other alienations made for the purpose of securing the party to be benefited against the financial risks of marriage are regarded as having been made for a true and just cause and not reducible merely because the granter was insolvent, although they may be reduced if the party to be benefited was aware of the insolvency.[32] A provision for a wife by a post-nuptial marriage contract may be sustained, though made at a time when the husband was insolvent, provided that it is reasonable in amount and is not to take effect until after the dissolution of the marriage.[33]

5. Reduction of Fraudulent Preferences at Common Law. — Also challengeable on the ground of insolvency are any transactions which have the effect, whether directly or indirectly, of conferring a benefit on one creditor in preference to others. Although a creditor has a legal claim on the debtor, it is the duty of the debtor once he is insolvent to abstain from any act which interferes with the preferences or rights of the creditors inter se.[33a] Such transactions are not pacta illicita,[34] but they are reducible at the instance of other creditors, the trustee in a sequestration or the liquidator of a company. Examples of such transactions are where during his insolvency a debtor gives

---

[28] *North British Railway Co.* v. *White* (1882) 20 S.L.R. 129; *Gilmour Shaw & Co.'s Tr.* v. *Learmonth*, 1972 S.C. 137.
[29] *Edmond* v. *Grant* (1853) 15 D. 703; *M'Lay* v. *M'Queen* (1899) 1 F. 804; *Bank of Scotland* v. *Gardiner* (1907) 15 S.L.T. 229.
[30] *Bolden* v. *Ferguson* (1863) 1 M. 522; *Dawson* v. *Thorburn* (1888) 15 R. 891.
[31] *Pringle's Tr.* v. *Wright* (1903) 5 F. 522.
[32] *M'Lay* v. *M'Queen* (1899) 1 F. 804; *Gilmour Shaw & Co.'s Tr.* v. *Learmonth*, supra.
[33] *Robertson's Tr.* v. *Robertson* (1901) 3 F. 359.
[33a] Bell, *Comm.*, II, 226; *M'Ewen* v. *Doig* (1828) 6 S. 889.
[34] *Munro* v. *Rothfield*, 1920 S.C. (H.L.) 165.

security for what was formerly an unsecured debt or an obligation to grant a security is undertaken,[35] or where he facilitates a creditor's efforts to exercise diligence or to obtain a decree against him.[36] Once it has been proved that the transaction was entered into voluntarily, during insolvency and while the debtor was conscious of his insolvency, fraud is presumed and it is unnecessary to prove an intention of fraud on his part or any collusion or concert on the part of the favoured creditor.[37] All such voluntary transactions are liable to be reduced unless they fall within one or other of the following classes: (1) payments in cash of debts due and payable, (2) transactions in the usual course of trade, and (3) nova debita or transferences for a consideration given at the time.[38]

A payment in cash includes, besides currency, cheques drawn by the debtor on his banker. The transfer of a cheque received by the debtor from a third party, and indorsed by him, was held, where it was used as a method by which one dealer paid another, not to be protected as a payment in cash.[39] But it has since been explained that the decision proceeded on the ground that such a method of payment was unusual in the trade, and a similar payment, but made to a banker to meet an overdraft, was held good.[40] The transfer of a bill of exchange, in which the primary debtor is a third party as acceptor, and which is not instantly payable, is not a payment in cash, and is not safeguarded as a transaction in the usual course of business, by proof that it was the method of paying his business debts usually adopted by the particular trader.[41] As a general rule payment of a debt before it is due is not protected.[42] Payment in cash of a debt which is due is reducible only if collusion or consent between the debtor and the favoured creditor (with the object of defrauding the equal rights of the debtor's other creditors) is proved.[43] The fact that both parties were aware of the insolvency or impending bankruptcy does not, by itself, infer collusion[44]; the decisions leave it in doubt what further evidence is necessary.[45]

Transactions in the usual course of trade include payments for goods supplied on credit, or delivery of goods already paid for,[46] if, in the latter case, the transfer is in fulfilment of a definite obligation, and does not amount to an

---

[35] M'Cowan v. Wright (1853) 15 D. 494; Thomas v. Thomson (1866) 5 M. 198.
[36] Lauries' Tr. v. Beveridge (1867) 6 M. 85.
[37] M'Cowan v. Wright, supra per Lord Justice-Clerk Hope at p. 504; Whatmough's Tr. v. British Linen Bank, 1932 S.C. 525 per Lord President Clyde at p. 543; see also M'Dougall's Tr. v. Ironside, 1914 S.C. 186.
[38] Bell, Comm., II, 201.
[39] Carter v. Johnstone (1886) 13 R. 698.
[40] Whatmough's Tr. v. British Linen Bank, 1934 S.C. (H.L.) 51.
[41] Horsburgh v. Ramsay (1885) 12 R. 1171.
[42] Blincow's Tr. v. Allan & Co. (1828) 7 S. 124; Whatmough's Tr., supra, per Lord Thankerton at p. 59; Goudy on Bankruptcy (4th ed.), p. 85.
[43] Whatmough's Tr., supra, per Lord President Clyde, 1932 S.C. at p. 543; 1934 S.C. (H.L.) 51.
[44] Coutts' Tr. & Doe v. Webster (1886) 13 R. 1112; Pringle's Tr. v. Wright (1903) 5 F. 522.
[45] See Jones' Tr. v. Jones (1888) 15 R. 328; Craig's Tr. v. Macdonald, Fraser & Co. (1902) 4 F. 1132; Newton & Son's Tr. v. Finlayson, 1928 S.C. 637, where the payment was reduced; Crockart's Tr. v. Hay, 1913 S.C. 509; Angus' Tr. v. Angus (1901) 4 F. 181; Whatmough's Tr. v. British Linen Bank, 1932 S.C. 525; 1934 S.C. (H.L.) 51, where it was sustained.
[46] Taylor v. Farrie (1855) 17 D. 639.

attempt to complete a security under which the creditor had no real right.[47] Where goods were sent to be bleached, and thereby subjected, according to the established usage of the trade, to a lien for a balance due on prior transactions of the same kind, a challenge of the lien, as in substance a security for a prior debt, failed.[48] And an auctioneer, conducting a displenishing sale for a farmer, is entitled to retain enough of the money received to satisfy the prior balance due by the farmer, unless some unusual procedure can be founded on to take the transaction out of the ordinary course of trade.[49]

Nova debita include transactions where the bankrupt and the party whose right is challenged incurred reciprocal obligations at the same time, or with an interval so short as to admit of the application of the term "unico contextu."[50] To these, though the party may have been insolvent at their date, or may have become notour bankrupt within six months thereafter, neither the common law nor the Act of 1696, as amended, constitutes any objection. So a party lending money, and taking a security for it duly completed in the way appropriate to the particular subject, obtains a good security, although he may have known that the borrower was insolvent, or although the loan may have been granted within six months of the borrower's bankruptcy.[51] Where a bank had, within sixty days of their debtor's bankruptcy, taken an assignation in security of the overdraft standing against him, but thereafter that overdraft was paid and it was arranged that a new advance should be covered by the assignation, it was held that as at the date of the ultimate bankruptcy the bank held the assignation for the new advance, a novum debitum, it was not open to challenge under the 1696 Act.[52]

6. Reduction of Fraudulent Preferences under Statute.—Preferences granted by a debtor on the eve of or during his notour bankruptcy are reducible under the Bankruptcy Act 1696 (c. 5). That Act, as amended by the Companies Act 1947, section 115 (3), declares that all voluntary dispositions, assignations or other deeds made and granted, directly or indirectly, by the bankrupt either at or after his becoming notour bankrupt or within six months[53] beforehand in favour of his creditors, either for their satisfaction or further security in preference to other creditors, are to be void and null. Every form of alienation by which any right to heritable or moveable property may be transferred from one person to another, whether directly or indirectly, may be the subject of challenge under the Act. Such transactions include for example the delivery or disposition of property in security of a prior debt,[54] the indorsation of a bill or cheque for a payment not yet due[55] and an arrangement with a debtor to pay

---

[47] *Jones & Co's Tr.* v. *Allan* (1901) 4 F. 374.
[48] *Anderson's Tr.* v. *Fleming* (1871) 9 M. 718.
[49] *Crockart's Tr.* v. *Hay*, 1913 S.C. 509, distinguishing *Craig's Tr.* v. *Macdonald, Fraser & Co.* (1902) 4 F. 1132.
[50] See *Cowdenbeath Coal Co.* v. *Clydesdale Bank* (1895) 22 R. 682.
[51] *Price & Pierce* v. *Bank of Scotland*, 1910 S.C. 1095, affd. 1912 S.C. (H.L.) 19.
[52] *Robertson's Tr.* v. *Union Bank*, 1917 S.C. 549.
[53] Previously the period was sixty days.
[54] *Stiven* v. *Scott & Simpson* (1871) 9 M. 923; *T.* v. *L.*, 1970 S.L.T. 243.
[55] *Blincow's Tr.* v. *Allan* (1828) 7 S. 124; *Carter* v. *Johnstone* (1886) 13 R. 698, distinguished in *Whatmough's Tr.* v. *British Linen Bank*, 1934 S.C. (H.L.) 51.

a creditor direct.[56] Any transaction which results in giving a creditor or class of creditors, until then unsecured or imperfectly secured, a security for his or their debt is reducible; for instance, a trust deed for the benefit of creditors to which some have not acceded.[57]

A mere acknowledgement of an existing debt, which enables a creditor to obtain no more than ordinary ranking and does not confer on him any preference is not struck at by the Act.[58] Nor is an act which the debtor is legally bound to perform, such as the payment of an existing debt as it falls due or the specific implement of an obligation as it becomes prestable.[59] Nor is the substitution for an existing security of another of equivalent value.[60] Where a security has been given or promised at the time when an advance was made, or more than six months before notour bankruptcy, but has not been completed so as to form a preferable right till within six months, the security is not reducible if the act by which it was completed was that of the creditor. So an assignation may be intimated, a bond and disposition in security may be recorded in the Register of Sasines.[61] Although the cases are somewhat difficult to reconcile, it is probably the law that when money is advanced on the face of a specific security to be immediately granted, the Act will not apply, although the security is not completed until after an interval of time.[62] On the other hand, if an act by the debtor is required, the transaction will generally be reducible. So if, under a mere obligation to transfer goods as a pledge the goods are actually transferred within six months,[63] or a bond and disposition in security over heritage is granted in implement of a purely verbal agreement made outside the six month period[64] or of an obligation which was not contemporaneous with the original loan[65] the security cannot stand. The same rule was applied where share certificates were deposited in security, and the right of the creditor was subsequently completed by a transfer and registration.[66] In order to maintain a successful challenge under the Act it is necessary to aver and prove that the debtor is notour bankrupt, that the deed was granted voluntarily and in satisfaction of, or in further security of prior debt and that it was granted either at or after notour bankruptcy or within six months before it.[67] Three classes of transaction are however recognised as being outside the operation of the Act, namely: (1) payments in cash of debts due and payable; (2) transactions in the ordinary course of trade; and (3)

---

[56] *Newton & Sons' Tr.* v. *Finlayson & Co.*, 1928 S.C. 637.
[57] *Mackenzie* v. *Calder* (1868) 6 M. 833.
[58] *Matthew's Tr.* v. *Matthew* (1867) 5 M. 957.
[59] *Taylor* v. *Farrie* (1855) 17 D. 639; *Stiven* v. *Scott & Simson* (1871) 9 M. 923.
[60] *Roy's Tr.* v. *Colville* (1903) 5 F. 769.
[61] *Scottish Provident Institution* v. *Cohen* (1888) 16 R. 112. And see infra, § 22.
[62] *Cowdenbeath Coal Co.* v. *Clydesdale Bank* (1895) 22 R. 682, per Lord Low at p. 689. See also Bell, *Comm.*, II, 211; *Cranstoun* v. *Bontine* (1832) 6 W. & S. 79; *Taylor* v. *Farrie*, supra; *Price & Pierce* v. *Bank of Scotland*, supra.
[63] *Jones & Co.'s Tr.* v. *Allan* (1901) 4 F. 374; *Stiven* v. *Scott & Simson*, supra. See cases of sale intended to operate as securities, supra, Ch. XVII., § 12.
[64] *Barclay* v. *Cuthill*, 1961 S.L.T. (Notes) 62.
[65] *T.* v. *L.* 1970 S.L.T. 243.
[66] *Gourlay* v. *Mackie* (1887) 14 R. 403. Contrast *Guild* v. *Young* (1884) 22 S.L.R. 520.
[67] Goudy on *Bankruptcy*, p. 104; *Barclay* v. *Cuthill*, supra.

nova debita. These exceptions, which apply also in the case of challenges made at common law, have been dealt with in the previous paragraph.

7. Effect of Notour Bankruptcy on Diligence.—Notour bankruptcy, in addition to affording a ground for the reduction of securities for prior debts, has the effect of equalising diligence. Arrestments and poindings used within sixty days prior to the constitution of notour bankruptcy, and within four months thereafter, rank pari passu as if they had all been used of the same date; and any creditor judicially producing in a process relative to the subject of such arrestment or poinding liquid grounds of debt or decree of payment, is entitled to rank as if he had executed an arrestment or a poinding.[68] Put otherwise, since sequestration is equivalent to an arrestment on behalf of all creditors, if sequestration occurs within sixty days before or four months after notour bankruptcy, an arrester within that period ranks pari passu with the other creditors.[69]

8. Sequestration: Parties and Petition.—The estates of any person who is subject to the jurisdiction of the Courts of Scotland may be sequestrated. So may the estates of a party deceased, if he was subject to the jurisdiction at the date of his death.[70] The estate of a partnership, or of a chartered body, such as a royal burgh,[71] may be sequestrated, but the process is not applicable to a company registered under the Companies Act,[72] nor to an unincorporated association,[73] or, probably, any body established by private Act of Parliament.[74] Any order made by a Court having jurisdiction in bankruptcy in Scotland is enforceable in England and Northern Ireland in all respects as if the order had been made by the Court required to enforce it, and reciprocal provisions apply to the enforcement in Scotland of orders of the Courts in England and Northern Ireland.[75] A petition for sequestration may be presented either in the Court of Session or in the Sheriff Court of the county in which the debtor has resided or carried on business for the year preceding the date of the petition, or preceding his death, in the case of a deceased debtor.[76] There are statutory provisions to meet the case where a petition is presented, or sequestration awarded, in more than one Court.[77] The petition may be at the instance of the debtor himself, with the concurrence of one or more creditors whose debts in all amount to not less than two hundred pounds. The debts may be liquid or illiquid, provided they are not

---

[68] Bankruptcy Act 1913, s. 10; *Clark* v. *Hinde, Milne & Co.* (1884) 12 R. 347.
[69] *Stewart* v. *Jarvie*, 1938 S.C. 309.
[70] Bankruptcy Act 1913, s. 11. As to jurisdiction, see Courts and Jurisdiction, Ch. II., supra, § 11.
[71] *Wotherspoon* v. *Magistrates of Linlithgow* (1863) 2 M. 348. Royal burghs do not now exist but there are other kinds of chartered body.
[72] *Standard Investment Co.* v. *Dunblane Hydropathic* (1884) 12 R. 328. As to winding up of companies, see Company Law, Ch. XXV, supra, § 38.
[73] *Pitreavie Golf Club* v. *Penman*, 1934 S.N. 15.
[74] *Haldane* v. *Girvan, etc., Ry.* (1881) 8 R. 1003.
[75] Bankruptcy Act 1914 (4 & 5 Geo. V, c. 59), s. 121.
[76] Bankruptcy Act 1913, s. 16; see *Burness & Son* v. *Anderson*, 1959 S.L.T. (Sh. Ct.) 47.
[77] Ibid., ss. 16-19; see *West of Scotland Refractories*, 1969 S.C. 43.

contingent.[78] In the case of a petition[78] by the debtor with concurrence, the only requisite is jurisdiction. The petition may also be presented by one or more creditors, who are qualified as for concurrence, provided the debtor is notour bankrupt, and has within the year preceding resided or had a dwelling-house or place of business in Scotland; in the case of a company, if it is notour bankrupt, and has within the year carried on business in Scotland and any partner has so resided or had a dwelling-house, or if the company has had a place of business in Scotland.[79] Unless the debtor, if alive, concurs in the creditor's petition, his notour bankruptcy must have been constituted not more than four months before the date of the petition.[80] In the case of a deceased debtor the petition may be by a mandatory to whom he had granted a mandate to apply for sequestration; or by creditors. In the latter case the petition may be presented immediately after the debtor's death, but sequestration cannot be awarded until six months after the death, unless the debtor died notour bankrupt, or unless his successors concur in the petition or renounce the succession.[81] In all cases a petitioning or concurring creditor must lodge with the petition an oath,[82] in which he swears to the verity of his debt, and specifies the securities he holds for it, and any other obligants who may be liable. He must also produce vouchers affording prima facie evidence of his debt.[83] It is rather implied than expressed in the Act that where the debtor is not a party to the petition evidence of his notour bankruptcy must be produced or a diligence for the recovery of such evidence applied for.[84]

9. Effect in Interrupting Prescription.—The presentation of or concurrence in a petition for sequestration has the effect of interrupting the prescription of the debt of the creditors petitioning or concurring. The same result follows from lodging a claim with the trustee, the Sheriff or the preses at any meeting of creditors. The interruption is effectual even if the sequestration is recalled.[85]

10. Preservation of Estate.—On the presentation of the petition measures may be taken for the preservation of the estate by the appointment of a judicial factor. The Sheriff has power to grant warrant to put under safe custody any banknotes, money, bonds, bills, cheques, drafts or other moveable property, and, if necessary, to open lock-fast places, and search the premises and the person of the debtor. At any time after sequestration is granted, and before the election of a trustee, the Sheriff may cause the books and papers of the bankrupt to be placed under safe custody, and his shop, warehouse or other repository to be locked up.[86]

[78] ss. 11, 12, as amended by Insolvency Act 1976 (c. 60), Sched. 1; *Forbes* v. *Whyte* (1890) 18 R. 182.
[79] s. 11.
[80] s. 13; see *Burgh of Millport*, 1974 S.L.T. (Notes) 23.
[81] Bankruptcy Act 1913, ss. 11, 13.
[82] Ibid., ss. 20-24; *Blair* v. *North British, etc., Insurance Co.* (1889) 16 R. 325.
[83] Ibid., s. 20; *Simpson* v. *Myles* (1881) 9 R. 104; *Ballantyne* v. *Barr* (1867) 5 M. 330.
[84] Bankruptcy Act 1913, s. 25; *Arrol* v. *Christie* (1901) 4 F. 262; *Drummond* v. *Clunas Tiles Co.*, 1909 S.C. 1049.
[85] Bankruptcy Act 1913, s. 105; see also Prescription and Limitation (Scotland) Act 1973, s. 9 (1) (*b*).
[86] Ibid., ss. 14, 15.

11. Award.—Where the petition is presented by the debtor, or with his concurrence, or, in the case of a deceased debtor, with the concurrence of his successors, sequestration must be awarded forthwith, the Court having no discretion in the matter.[87] Where the petition is by the creditors, without the concurrence of the debtor, the first deliverance is an order for intimation and service on the debtor. On the expiry of the induciae, if the debtor does not appear and show cause why sequestration cannot competently be awarded, or pay the debt in respect of which he was made notour bankrupt, and the debts of the petitioning creditor, and any other creditors appearing or concurring, sequestration must be awarded.[88] In all questions where the date of the sequestration is material, it is to be taken as that of the first deliverance, though the actual award may be later.[89] The interlocutor awarding sequestration must declare that the debtor's estate belongs to his creditors for the purposes of the Act.

12. Petition for Recall.—The award of sequestration is not subject to review, but a petition for recall may be presented to the Outer House, at any time within forty days of the award, by the debtor or his successors, if he or they have not consented to the petition, or by any creditor. The Act does not specify the grounds on which a petition for recall may be founded. If the objection is any ex facie irregularity in the procedure by which it was obtained, the sequestration must be recalled[90]; if the objection is latent, e.g., failure by the petitioning creditor to specify a security, the Court has a discretion in the matter, and will not recall the sequestration if the recall would prejudice the other creditors.[91] The award will not be recalled because the debtor is able, but refuses, to pay the debt.[92] More than forty days after the award a petition for recall may be presented (and must be granted, unless cause is shown to the contrary) by nine-tenths in number and value of the creditors[93]; or, at any time within three months of the date of sequestration, on the ground that a majority in number and value of the creditors resides in England or Ireland and that the estate ought to be distributed under the insolvency laws there.[94]

13. Recording Abbreviate.—The party applying for sequestration is bound, within two days of the first deliverance, to present an abbreviate of the petition and first deliverance to the Keeper of the Register of Inhibitions and Adjudications, and insert a notice in the London and Edinburgh Gazettes. The recording of the abbreviate has the effect of an inhibition and citation in an adjudication at the instance of the creditors afterwards ranked on the estate.[95]

[87] Bankruptcy Act 1913, s. 28.
[88] s. 29; *Stuart & Stuart* v. *Macleod* (1891) 19 R. 223.
[89] s. 41.
[90] *Ballantyne* v. *Barr* (1867) 5 M. 330.
[91] *Nakeski-Cumming* v. *Gordon*, 1924 S.C. 217.
[92] *Scottish Milk Marketing Board* v. *Wood,* 1936 S.C. 604.
[93] Bankruptcy Act 1913, s. 31.
[94] s. 43.
[95] s. 44, as amended by s. 44 of the Conveyancing (Scotland) Act 1924.

14. Trustee: Qualification.—The Lord Ordinary or Sheriff must, in the deliverance awarding sequestration, fix a day for a meeting of creditors to elect a trustee.[96] The following persons are ineligible: the bankrupt; any conjunct or confident person[97]; any person who holds an interest opposed to the general interests of the creditors; any person whose residence is not within the jurisdiction of the Court of Session.[98] A minor is not eligible[99]; and collusive transactions entered into in order to secure election may disqualify.[1] The judgment of the Sheriff, declaring the person elected to be the trustee, is final.[2] A trustee may be removed by a majority in number and value of the creditors, at a meeting called for that purpose, or by the Court on the application of one-fourth of the creditors in value.[3] Where the statutory machinery for the election of a trustee has broken down the Court may in the exercise of its nobile officium appoint a fresh meeting of the creditors to be held for this purpose.[4]

15. Valuation and Deduction of Securities.—The trustee is elected by a majority in value of the creditors present, or represented by a mandatory, at a meeting.[5] A person who has acquired a debt after the date of the sequestration, otherwise than by succession or marriage, and the wife of the bankrupt, cannot vote.[6] In order to entitle any other creditor to vote he must produce at the meeting the account and vouchers necessary to prove his debt and either a notice of claim to the debt in the prescribed form[7] or, in any case in which the trustee so requires, an oath to the verity of his debt as required of creditors petitioning for sequestration.[8] He must also value and deduct any securities he may hold for his debt over any part of the bankrupt's estate, specifying the balance, on which he is entitled to vote.[9] "Security" is defined as including "securities, heritable or moveable, and rights of lien, retention or preference."[10] The creditor must also value and deduct the obligation of any co-obligant bound with, but liable in relief to, the bankrupt e.g., if the bankrupt is liable as a cautioner, the obligation of the principal debtor.[11] Where a debt is payable in future interest must be deducted; when it depends on a contingency, or consists of an annuity granted by the bankrupt, application must be made to the Sheriff to have a value put upon it.[12] In the case of a claim on the estate of a firm, it is not necessary to value and deduct

[96] s. 63.
[97] See § 4, supra.
[98] s. 64.
[99] *Threshie*, May 30, 1815, F.C.
[1] *Mann* v. *Dickson* (1857) 19 D. 942; Goudy, *Bankruptcy* (4th ed.), 199.
[2] s. 67; *Grierson* v. *Ogilvy's Tr.*, 1908 S.C. 959.
[3] s. 71.
[4] See *W. & A. Gilbey* v. *Franchitti*, 1969 S.L.T. (Notes) 18.
[5] ss. 65, 66, 96.
[6] s. 60.
[7] Bankruptcy (Amendment No. 2) Rules 1977 (S.I. 1977, No. 1394).
[8] s. 45, as substituted by Insolvency Act 1976, s. 5 (3).
[9] s. 55; *University of Glasgow* v. *Yuill's Tr.* (1882) 9 R. 643; *Clydesdale Bank* v. *Allen & Co.*, 1926 S.C. 235.
[10] s. 2.
[11] s. 56.
[12] ss. 48-50.

the claim on the estates of individual partners; in a case of a claim for a firm's debt on the estate of a partner, it is necessary to value and deduct the claim on the estate of the firm, and also the claim against the other partners in so far as they are bound to relieve the bankrupt.[13] The trustee, or the majority of the creditors present at a meeting, may demand an assignation to the trustee of any security or claim at the value which the creditor has put upon it, plus twenty per cent.[14]

16. Commissioners.—At the meeting for the election of a trustee, commissioners fall to be elected. They are three in number—creditors, or mandatories of creditors.[15] Their duties are to advise the trustee.[16] Their consent is necessary in fixing an upset price for the sale of heritable property[17]; in declaring or postponing a dividend[18]; in the compromise of any claim.[19] It is their duty to audit the trustee's accounts, and (subject to appeal) to fix his commission.[20]

17. Deed of Arrangement.—Instead of electing a trustee, it is competent for the creditors to decide that the estate shall be wound up by a deed of arrangement. This requires the consent of a majority in number and three-fourths in value of the creditors, and must be reported to and approved by the Lord Ordinary or the Sheriff, who must be satisfied that the arrangement is reasonable.[21] The sequestration is then at an end.[22]

18. Vesting of Estate in Trustee.—The interlocutor of the Sheriff confirming the election of a trustee is declared to be final, and not subject to review in any Court whatever.[23] The sheriff-clerk is then directed to issue to the trustee an act and warrant in the form of schedule D of the Act. This act and warrant forms the title of the trustee to recover any property belonging to or debt due to the bankrupt, and to maintain actions.[24] It ipso jure vests in the trustee for behoof of the creditors, absolutely and irredeemably, as at the date of the sequestration, the whole property of the debtor; in the case of heritable property occupied by him, it reduces the debtor to the position of a squatter in that property without any title to remain there.[25] The vesting clauses, applicable to moveable and heritable property, are printed below.[26] The generality of their expression is controlled in two respects: (a) The "whole

[13] s. 57.
[14] s. 58.
[15] s. 72.
[16] s. 81.
[17] s. 110.
[18] ss. 121, 127, 131.
[19] s. 172; *Hamilton's Exr.* v. *Bank of Scotland*, 1913 S.C. 743.
[20] ss. 121, 176.
[21] *Stone* v. *Woodhouse Hambly & Co.*, 1937 S.C. 824.
[22] ss. 34-39.
[23] s. 67; *Grierson* v. *Ogilvy's Tr.*, 1908 S.C. 959.
[24] s. 70.
[25] *White* v. *Stevenson*, 1956 S.C. 84.
[26] s. 97.—"(1) The moveable estate and effects of the bankrupt, wherever situated, so far as attachable for debt, or capable of voluntary alienation by the bankrupt, to the same effect as if

property of the debtor" is confined to property to which he had a beneficial interest; it does not include, and therefore the trustee cannot claim, property to which the debtor had merely a formal title even if ex facie absolute which is held, not for himself, but in trust for third parties.[27] There is an exception where the beneficiary is the bankrupt's wife; she cannot claim, in sequestration, property which she has lent or entrusted to her husband, or allowed to be immixed with his funds.[28] If the debtor has paid money held by him in the trust into an account which is not earmarked with the trust, and also keeps private money of his own in the same account, the Court will if it can disentangle the account, separate the trust funds from the private monies and award the former specifically to the beneficiaries.[29] (b) The trustee takes the estate tantum et tale as it stood in the bankrupt,[30] and cannot maintain a right to property which is reducible on the ground of the bankrupt's fraud.[31] But in the absence of fraud there is no rule, in Scotland, that the trustee, as an officer of Court, cannot assert a claim which it would have been dishonourable for the debtor to make.[32] The provision that the moveable estate shall vest in the trustee, so far as "capable of voluntary alienation," was not contained in the corresponding section of the Bankruptcy Act 1856, but does not, apparently, entitle the trustee to the tools of the bankrupt's trade, which were exempt on the ground that they were not attachable for debt.[33] A spes successionis, i.e., any non-vested contingent right under a will, marriage-contract, or deed of an irrevocable nature, which the earlier Acts did not touch, is now vested in the trustee.[34] A right of or interest in copyright vests in the trustee, but on the terms, as to payment of royalties or a share of profits to the author, which were binding on the bankrupt.[35] Any alimentary right vested in the bankrupt may, on the trustee's application to the Lord Ordinary or the Sheriff, be reduced to a suitable aliment to the bankrupt, in view of his

---

actual delivery or possession had been obtained, or intimation made at that date, subject always to such preferable securities as existed at the date of the sequestration and are not null or reducible."

"(2) The whole heritable estate belonging to the bankrupt in Scotland, to the same effect as if a decree of adjudication in implement of sale, as well as a decree of adjudication for payment and in security of debt, subject to no legal reversion, had been pronounced in favour of the trustee, and recorded at the date of the sequestration, and as if a poinding of the ground had then been executed, subject always to such preferable securities as existed at the date of the sequestration, and are not null and reducible."

Provision is also made for the vesting of real property in England, Ireland and other British Dominions.

[27] *Heritable Reversionary Co.* v. *Millar* (1892) 19 R. (H.L.) 43; *Forbes' Trs.* v. *Macleod* (1898) 25 R. 1012; *Bank of Scotland* v. *Hutchison, Main & Co.*, 1914 S.C. (H.L.) 1. The beneficiary in such cases may recover his property by a petition under s. 99.

[28] Married Women's Property (Scotland) Act 1881 (44 & 45 Vict., c. 21) s. 1 (4). And see infra, § 28.

[29] *Macadam* v. *Martin's Tr.* (1872) 11 M. 33; *Smith* v. *Liqr. of James Birrell*, 1968 S.L.T. 174. As to following trust money, see Executors, Trustees, etc., Ch. XLIV, supra, § 22.

[30] *Davidson* v. *Boyd* (1868) 7 M. 77.

[31] *Colquhoun's Tr.* v. *Campbell's Trs.* (1902) 4 F. 739; *Gamage* v. *Charlesworth's Tr.*, 1910 S.C. 257.

[32] *Clyde Marine Insurance Co.* v. *Renwick*, 1924 S.C. 113.

[33] *Pennell* v. *Elgin*, 1926 S.C. 9.

[34] Bankruptcy Act 1913, s. 97 (4).

[35] s. 102.

existing circumstances.[36] Government pay or pension may, with the sanction of the department concerned, be made available to the trustee.[37]

19. Acquirenda.—The Act provides that all property which the bankrupt may acquire before he obtains his discharge shall ipso jure fall under the sequestration. The trustee is directed to present a petition to the Lord Ordinary or Sheriff for an order declaring that all right and interest in such property is vested in him.[38] The order may cover instalments of the property to be received in future.[39] Where no such order was pronounced, and the bankrupt, still undischarged, carried on business, it was held that creditors in debts incurred in that business were preferable to the trustee.[40] The property which passes to the trustee includes any salary which the undischarged bankrupt may receive, and any earnings in a profession or trade, subject (at least in the case of a salary) to a reasonable allowance for the bankrupt's support.[41] The position of the trustee in regard to contracts in which the bankrupt was engaged has been considered already.[42]

20. Actions in which Bankrupt Engaged.—A trustee in a sequestration has a title to be sisted as a party in any action in which the bankrupt may be engaged, if the result of success would be to enlarge or preserve the estate, but not in a purely personal action, such as an action for divorce.[43] By sisting himself as a party, the trustee risks personal liability for any expenses which may be found due to the opposite party.[44] If the trustee refuses to sist himself, the bankrupt retains his title to sue, unless the other party can satisfy the Court that under no circumstances can the sequestration result in a surplus.[45] It is in the discretion of the Court whether a party who is bankrupt will be allowed to proceed with an action without finding caution for expenses, but as a general rule that condition will be imposed where the bankrupt is a pursuer, not where he is a defender.[46]

21. Effect of Sequestration on Diligence.—Sequestration, as from the date of the first deliverance, is equivalent to an arrestment in execution and decree of furthcoming, and to an executed or completed poinding. No arrestment or poinding executed on or after the sixtieth day before the sequestration is effectual, and any funds or effects attached must be given up to the trustee. The creditor, who is thus deprived of the benefit of diligence executed before

---

[36] s. 98.
[37] s. 148.
[38] Ibid., s. 98; *Lord Napier's Tr.* v. *De Saumarez* (1899) 1 F. 614.
[39] *Caldwell* v. *Hamilton*, 1919 S.C. (H.L.) 100; *Birrell's Tr.* v. *Birrell*, 1957 S.L.T. (Sh. Ct.) 6.
[40] *Grant* v. *Green's Tr.* (1901) 3 F. 1016.
[41] *Caldwell* v. *Hamilton*, supra.
[42] Title to Sue, Ch. X, supra, § 22.
[43] *Thom* v. *Bridges* (1857) 19 D. 721.
[44] *Cowie* v. *Muirden* (1893) 20 R. (H.L.) 81.
[45] *Whyte* v. *Forbes* (1890) 17 R. 895.
[46] *Crichton Bros.* v. *Crichton* (1902) 5 F. 178; *Neil* v. *South East Lancashire Insurance Co.*, 1930 S.C. 629.

the sequestration, is entitled to his expenses.[47] In the case of the sequestration of a deceased debtor, dated within seven months of his death, arrestments and poindings executed within sixty days before the death, or any time subsequent to it, are cut down.[48] The effect of sequestration on adjudication, inhibition, poinding of the ground, maills and duties,[49] and the landlord's sequestration,[50] has been noted already.

22. Effect of Sequestration on Personal Rights.—A party who has an incomplete or personal right to any property falling under the sequestration, cannot, as a general rule, complete his right after the date of the first deliverance. The statutory effect of the act and warrant, as vesting in the trustee the whole property of the bankrupt, forms an impediment. Thus, in the case of moveable property the trustee is vested with a right completed by possession or intimation, as the nature of the property may demand. The vesting clause in the case of heritable property gives the trustee an immediate and completed right to a lease held by the bankrupt, preferable to the right of any assignees who have not entered into possession.[51] But there is an exception in the case of property where the title of a transferee or disponee is completed by entry in a register. So it was held that a party who, at the date of the sequestration, held a transfer of shares duly executed by the bankrupt, might complete his right by sending in the transfer for registration after the sequestration, provided that he did so before the trustee had been registered as the owner of the shares.[52] In the case of heritable property, sequestration is not a bar to the completion of title by recording a disposition in the Register of Sasines. The right of a party so recording, in competition with the trustee depends, not on the date of the sequestration, but on priority of registration.[53]

23. Duties and Position of Bankrupt.—The bankrupt, to whom the trustee may be authorised to pay an allowance for his sustenance,[54] is bound to deliver to the clerk of the meeting for the election of the trustee a state of his affairs[55]; to grant all deeds requisite for the recovery or disposal of his estate[56]; and to submit himself for examination.[57] The Sheriff may issue an order for the examination of the bankrupt's wife and family, clerks, servants, factors and law agents, who, on failure to appear, may be apprehended.[58] As the bankrupt is deprived of his estate, no act or deed of his is effectual without the consent of the trustee, but a party who has purchased and received goods in ignorance of the bankruptcy, if ready to pay the price, is not bound to

[47] Bankruptcy Act 1913, s. 104; *Stewart* v. *Jarvie*, 1938 S.C. 309.
[48] Ibid., s. 106.
[49] Diligence, Ch. XLVIII, supra.
[50] Leases, Ch. XXXIII, § 12.
[51] *Clark* v. *West Calder Oil Co.* (1882) 9 R. 1017.
[52] *Morrison* v. *Harrison* (1876) 3 R. 406.
[53] *Cormack* v. *Anderson* (1829) 7 S. 868; *Clark* v. *West Calder Oil Co.*, supra.
[54] s. 74.
[55] s. 77.
[56] Ibid.
[57] ss. 83-89.
[58] s. 86.

restore them, and a debtor who, in ignorance of the bankruptcy, has paid a debt bona fide to the debtor, is not bound to pay again to the trustee.[59] Failure by a bankrupt to fulfil the duties laid upon him; concealment of his property or destruction of any writing relating to his estate; failure, if in business, and if his debts exceed two thousand five hundred pounds, to keep business books[60]; obtaining credit to the extent of fifty pounds without stating that he is an undischarged bankrupt; are offences for which he may be imprisoned for a period not exceeding two years.[61] He is disqualified from sitting or voting in Parliament; from being elected a member of the House of Commons or any local authority; and from holding certain specified offices.[62]

24. Realisation of Assets.—With regard to the realisation of the estate, it is provided that where heritable property is subject to a bond it may be sold by the bondholder with the concurrence of the trustee, by the trustee with the concurrence of the bondholder, or by the trustee alone, if that course is determined at a meeting of creditors before the bondholder has taken proceedings for sale.[63] A sale of the heritable estate by private bargain requires the concurrence of a majority of the creditors in number and value; of the bondholders, if any; and of the Accountant of Court.[64] When any estate is sold publicly a creditor may purchase, but the trustees, the commissioners, a law agent employed by the trustee, and his partners are disqualified.[65] Book debts cannot be sold until a year after the sequestration.[66] With the consent of the commissioners any question that may arise in the sequestration may be compromised or referred to arbitration.[67]

25. Payment of Dividends.—The Act has provisions as to the dates for the payment of the first and subsequent dividends, which, however, may be accelerated or postponed with the consent of the commissioners.[68] Creditors must lodge their claims for ranking, and must be prepared to prove them by the appropriate evidence.[69] It is not competent to refer to the oath of the bankrupt.[70] A written acknowledgement, if dated after the commencement of the sequestration, is not competent as proof of a loan.[71] Securities must be valued and deducted. The rules in this respect, and with regard to the valuation of future and contingent debts, are the same as those which apply in lodging claims for voting purposes, except that the trustee has the right to

---

[59] s. 107.
[60] s. 178; *Adair* v. *Isaacs*, 1946 J.C. 84.
[61] ss. 178, 182, as amended by Insolvency Act 1976, Sched. 1. See *Kaye* v. *H.M.A.*, 1957 S.L.T. 357.
[62] Bankruptcy Act 1883 (46 & 47 Vict., c. 52), s. 32, as applied to Scotland by Bankruptcy (Sc.) Act 1913, s. 183; Local Government (Sc.) Act 1973 (c. 65), s. 31.
[63] Bankruptcy Act 1913, ss. 108-110.
[64] s. 111.
[65] s. 116.
[66] *Stewart* v. *Crookston*, 1910 S.C. 609, and see s. 133.
[67] s. 172.
[68] ss. 117-132.
[69] See s. 45, as substituted by Insolvency Act 1976, s. 5 (3).
[70] *Adam* v. *Maclachlan* (1847) 9 D. 560.
[71] *Carmichael's Tr.* v. *Carmichael*, 1929 S.C. 265.

demand an assignation of any security at the value which the creditor has put upon it.[72] A creditor may revalue his security at a lower figure and he is then entitled to a further dividend even if he has received one hundred pence in the pound on the balance originally brought out.[73] The creditor is not bound to value and deduct the obligation of a co-obligant, except in the case of a claim on the estate of a partner for a firm debt, when the trustee is to value and deduct the claim against the estate of the firm.[74] It is the duty of the trustee to decide on the validity of any claim, and to notify the creditor.[75] If no appeal is taken within fourteen days of a Gazette notice of the date of payment of the dividend the trustee's decision is final.[76]

26. Creditors Holding Securities.—When the trustee does not take over a security at the value which the creditor has put upon it the creditor may realise it himself. The subject over which it extends does not become his property; and if by the realisation of the security and the dividend paid on his claim he obtains more than full payment of his debt, he is bound to account for the surplus to the trustee, or, if the sequestration is at an end and the bankrupt reinvested in his estates, to the bankrupt.[77] When the security was unrealisable, and became a source of expense, it was held that the bankrupt, although he had obtained a discharge, was bound to accept a reconveyance.[78]

27. Preferential Debts.—Creditors may be ranked as preferred, ordinary and postponed creditors. The Act gives a list of preferential debts (s. 118, as amended),[79] which are inter se to rank equally. They are (a) all local rates due by the bankrupt at the date of the award of sequestration, and having become due within twelve months before that date, all assessed taxes, including income tax, assessed on the bankrupt up to April 5 next before the said date, and not exceeding in the whole one year's assessment; (b) all wages or salary of any clerk or servant in respect of service rendered to the bankrupt during four months before the said date, not exceeding eight hundred pounds to any one clerk or servant; (c) all wages of any workman or labourer not exceeding eight hundred pounds to any one, in respect of services rendered to the bankrupt during four months before the said date; and (d) subject to similar limitations as to time, any sums owed on account of social security contributions, contributions to occupational pension schemes and in respect of state scheme premiums.[79] It is provided (s. 118 (5)) that nothing in the section shall affect the provisions of the Friendly Societies Act 1896,[80] or the preference attaching

[72] Bankruptcy Act 1913, s. 61; and see supra, § 15; *Maclachlan* v. *Maxwell*, 1910 S.C. 87.
[73] *Wood* v. *Mackay's Tr.*, 1936 S.C. 93.
[74] s. 62.
[75] s. 123.
[76] s. 124.
[77] *Kinmond, Luke & Co.* v. *Finlay & Co.* (1904) 6 F. 564.
[78] *Clydesdale Bank* v. *M'Intyre*, 1909 S.C. 1405.
[79] For an up to date version of s. 118 incorporating the amendments, see Parliament House Book, Division I.
[80] See now Friendly Societies Act 1974 (c. 46), s. 59 of which gives the Society, in the bankruptcy of an official, a right to any money or property held in his hands and belonging to the Society, "in preference to any other debt or claim."

at common law to death-bed and funeral expenses. The Crown has no general preference,[81] and a law agent, who has given up to the trustee papers over which he has a lien, is entitled to be ranked as a preferred creditor.[82]

28. Postponed Creditors.—Postponed creditors, entitled to be ranked after all other creditors have been paid in full, are the bankrupt's wife, claiming in respect of property which has fallen under the sequestration because she had lent or entrusted it to her husband, or allowed it to be immixed with his funds[83]; and parties who have lent money to a firm, or sold the goodwill of a business, on terms which involve the receipt of a share in the profits of the firm's business, or interest at a rate varying with such profits.[84]

29. Rule against Double Ranking.—The rule that no debt can be ranked twice on a sequestrated estate is of practical importance in the case where a principal debtor and cautioner are bankrupt. The creditor may then rank on each estate; but the cautioner's estate has no ranking on the estate of the principal debtor. To allow such a ranking would mean that a higher dividend would be paid on the debt in question than is paid on the other debts. Nor can the cautioner's estate obtain the result of a ranking by deducting the amount paid from separate claims in which the principal debtor was a creditor of the cautioner.[85] The rule rests on the theory that when a debt is ranked in sequestration it is, so far as the sequestrated estate is concerned, to be treated as paid. It does not apply where the principal debtor is not sequestrated but compounds with his creditors.[86]

30. Discharge, on Composition.—A bankrupt may obtain his discharge with or without a composition with his creditors. An offer of a composition may be made, by the bankrupt or his friends, at the meeting for the election of the trustee. It requires a bond of caution, signed by the bankrupt and a cautioner. It must be approved by a majority in number and three-fourths in value, and accepted by the same majority at a subsequent meeting. It must thereafter be approved by the Lord Ordinary or the Sheriff.[87] Similar provisions apply to an offer of composition made at any subsequent meeting.[88] The bankrupt must declare, on oath, that he has made a full and fair surrender of his estate, and has not entered into any collusive arrangement with any creditor. Creditors must value and deduct their securities.[89] On approval of the offer an interlocutor is pronounced declaring the sequestration at an end, and the bankrupt reinvested in his estate.[90] Neither the bankrupt nor the cautioner can object to the claim of any creditor, nor to the security

---

[81] *Admiralty* v. *Blair's Tr.*, 1916 S.C. 247.
[82] Rights in Security, Ch. XX, supra, § 35.
[83] Married Women's Property (Scotland) Act 1881 (44 & 45 Vict. c. 21) s. 1 (4).
[84] Partnership Act 1890 (53 & 54 Vict., c. 39), s. 3; and see supra, Ch. XXIV, § 5.
[85] *Anderson* v. *Mackinnon* (1876) 3 R. 608.
[86] *Mackinnon* v. *Monkhouse* (1881) 9 R. 393.
[87] *Stone* v. *Woodhouse Hambly & Co.*, 1937 S.C. 824.
[88] Bankruptcy Act 1913, ss. 134-136.
[89] *Macbride* v. *Stevenson* (1884) 11 R. 702.
[90] Bankruptcy Act 1913, s. 137.

held by any creditor, unless such debt or security was stated in the offer of composition as objected to.[91] No person who has not produced an oath as creditor can claim against the cautioner after the lapse of two years from the date of the deliverance approving the composition, but his claim for the composition against the bankrupt is not affected.[92] If an offer of composition has been rejected, or has become ineffectual, any subsequent offer requires the consent of nine-tenths in number and value of the creditors.[93]

31. Discharge, without Composition.—Without a composition a discharge may be obtained by petition to the Lord Ordinary or the Sheriff. The petition cannot be presented until a report on the bankrupt's conduct has been obtained from the trustee. This report the trustee is bound to furnish, without demanding any fee from the bankrupt.[94] In addition to lodging this report, the bankrupt, if he petitions for discharge before two years have elapsed from the date of the sequestration, must obtain the concurrence of a majority, in number and value, of his creditors.[95] After two years the concurrence of creditors is not required. In certain circumstances, where the statutory machinery has broken down, the Court may grant a discharge in the exercise of its nobile officium.[96]

32. Conditions of Discharge.—A bankrupt is not entitled to a discharge, with or without composition, unless one of two alternative conditions has been fulfilled: (1) that a dividend or composition of twenty-five pence in the pound has been paid, or security found for it to the satisfaction of the creditors; (2) that the failure to pay twenty-five pence in the pound has, in the opinion of the Court, arisen from circumstances for which the bankrupt cannot justly be held responsible.[97] On this latter point it has been held that a discharge should not be refused on the ground of mere improvident trading.[98] In a case where the bankrupt was the petitioner and the estate failed to pay the expenses of the sequestration, though from causes for which the bankrupt was not responsible, a discharge was refused, on the ground that no one was entitled to the benefit of sequestration unless he could pay the expenses involved.[99] No lapse of time gives a bankrupt an absolute right to a discharge. It has been refused, on an unfavourable report by the trustee as to the bankrupt's conduct ten years after the sequestration, and although no creditor opposed.[1] A discharge may be granted on the condition that a portion of an alimentary fund be given up to the creditors.[2]

[91] s. 140.
[92] s. 141.
[93] s. 142.
[94] s. 143; *White* v. *White's Tr.* (1879) 6 R. 854.
[95] s. 143. The requisite majority depends on the date when the petition is presented.
[96] *Aitken* v. *Robson*, 1914 S.C. 224; *Laing*, 1962 S.C. 168; *Black*, 1964 S.L.T. 308; *Fraser* v. *Glasgow Corporation*, 1967 S.C. 120.
[97] s. 146; *Inglis*, 1928 S.N. 58; 1937 S.L.T. 619; *Greer*, 1960 S.L.T. (Sh. Ct.) 13.
[98] *Phillips* (1885) 13 R. 91. See *Gemmell* (1902) 4 F. 441.
[99] *M'Carter* v. *Aikman* (1893) 20 R. 1090.
[1] s. 149; *Millar* (1877) 5 R. 144.
[2] *Hamilton* v. *Caldwell*, 1916 S.C. 809.

33. Effect of Discharge.—A discharge frees the debtor from all debts, except debts due to the Crown (when the consent of the Treasury is required)[3]; debts incurred after the first deliverance; debts arising on obligations depending on contingencies too remote to admit of their valuation, such as an obligation of warrandice when, during the sequestration, no eviction has been threatened,[4] or the obligation to aliment relatives in the event of their becoming indigent.[5] The bankrupt, however, in the case of a discharge without composition, is not reinvested in his estate, which remains with the trustee,[6] and to which, after the trustee is discharged, his creditors have right. They may make their right effectual, in the case where some property has been recovered, by a petition to the Court of Session under its nobile officium, praying for an order for holding a meeting of creditors for the election of a new trustee.[7] A similar application is competent at the instance of the bankrupt, if undischarged, and prepared to pay his creditors in full or in part.[8] The bankrupt, after his own discharge and that of the trustee, has a title to sue on a claim which the trustee has not chosen to pursue, and the defender in such an action cannot insist on caution for expenses.[9]

34. Discharge of Trustee.—On a final distribution of the funds the trustee, whether the bankrupt has obtained a discharge or not, after calling a meeting of creditors, may apply to the Sheriff or Lord Ordinary for his discharge.[10] Any creditor may object, on the ground that there are assets still to be recovered.[11] The sederunt book of the sequestration, and a deposit receipt for any unclaimed dividends, are lodged with the Accountant of Court, who is directed, seven years thereafter, to transmit the deposit receipt to the King's Remembrancer.[12] The trustee is entitled to take credit for the expenses of the sequestration, and for a fee or commission, to be fixed by the commissioners before declaring the first dividend, with an appeal to the Accountant of Court, and from him to the Lord Ordinary or the Sheriff, at the instance of the trustee, any creditor, or the bankrupt.[13]

35. Collusive Agreements with Creditors.—It is a general principle of common law that any contract by which one creditor in a sequestration may obtain a share of the assets larger than that which the law would allot to him is a pactum illicitum.[14] When it takes the form of a collusive bargain between the bankrupt and a particular creditor the parties are not in pari delicto, with

3 s. 147.
4 *Garden* v. *M'Iver* (1860) 22 D. 1190.
5 *Marjoribanks* v. *Amos* (1831) 10 S. 79; *Downs* v. *Wilson's Tr.* (1886) 13 R. 1101.
6 *Flett* v. *Mustard*, 1936 S.C. 269.
7 *Whyte* v. *Northern Heritable Securities Investment Co.* (1891) 18 R. (H.L.) 37. The bankrupt cannot object that the asset or claim in question was known to the trustee, and not insisted on by him. And see *Cockburn's Trs., Petrs.*, 1941 S.C. 187.
8 *M'Duff* v. *Baird* (1892) 20 R. 101.
9 *Cooper* v. *Frame* (1893) 20 R. 920.
10 Bankruptcy Act 1913, s. 152.
11 *Hamilton's Tr.* v. *Caldwell*, 1918 S.C. 190.
12 Bankruptcy Act 1913, s. 153. See *Scott* v. *King's Remembrancer*, 1920 S.C. 555.
13 ss. 121, 122.
14 *Thomas* v. *Waddell* (1869) 7 M. 558; *Farmers' Mart* v. *Milne*, 1914 S.C. (H.L.) 84.

the result that while the creditor cannot enforce payment the bankrupt may recover what he has paid.[15] The Bankruptcy Act 1913[16] provides that any agreement or consideration made for facilitating, or concurring in, the bankrupt's discharge, shall be null and void; that any creditor implicated shall forfeit his debt and be liable to pay to the trustee double the consideration that he has received or been promised; that the bankrupt, if personally concerned, shall forfeit all right to a discharge, and that his discharge, if granted, shall be annulled. If the facts come to light after the sequestration has been closed, any creditor not fully paid may raise a multiplepoinding in the name of the creditor implicated, who will be ordered to consign double the amount he has received or been promised, together with any dividend he may have received, to be divided among the creditors ranked in the sequestration.

36. Summary Sequestration.—A summary sequestration is competent where the debtor's assets do not in the aggregate exceed £4000 in value.[17] Where the bankrupt is the petitioner he must lodge with his petition a state of his affairs: where the petition is by creditors the first deliverance contains an order on the debtor to lodge such a state within six days. The judge to whom the petition is presented may make an order for summary sequestration, or may refuse it. In either case his decision is final, but the sequestration, if awarded, may be recalled on the conditions applicable to ordinary sequestration. The petition may be presented by the debtor alone, without the concurrence of any creditor; or by a creditor or creditors whose claims in all amount to one hundred and twenty pounds or upwards, if the debtor is notour bankrupt, and the notour bankruptcy has been constituted within four months. There is no provision for the summary sequestration of a company, or of the estates of a deceased debtor. The forum is the Sheriff Court of the sheriffdom within which the debtor has resided or carried on business during the year preceding the petition; but if the petition is by creditors, and they do not know what sheriffdom is applicable, or if the debtor is furth of Scotland, the petition may be to the Outer House of the Court of Session.[18] In carrying on a summary sequestration there are a number of details in procedure, for which reference must be made to the Act,[19] differing from the rules applicable to ordinary sequestration.

37. Private Trust Deeds for Creditors.—Without resorting to sequestration the estates of a party who has become insolvent may be wound up by some private arrangement with his creditors. The methods usually selected are a private trust-deed for creditors,[20] or a composition contract. The Bankruptcy Act 1913 has no provision for such arrangements, with the exception of a clause under which, in the absence or failure of any express provision on the

[15] *Macfarlane* v. *Nicoll* (1864) 3 M. 237.
[16] ss. 150, 151.
[17] s. 174, as amended by Insolvency Act 1976, Sched. 1.
[18] s. 175, as amended by Insolvency Act 1976, Sched. 1.
[19] s. 176.
[20] For form of trust deed, see Burns, *Conveyancing Practice* (4th ed.), p. 151.

subject, the trustee in a trust-deed for creditors is bound to submit his accounts for audit to the Accountant of Court.[21] There is no statutory provision in Scotland, as there is in England,[22] for the registration of a trust-deed for creditors in a public register.

A trust-deed for creditors is carried out by a conveyance by the debtor to a trustee, with the accession of some, or all, of the creditors. Such a trustee has no statutory title, and must complete his right to the various subjects conveyed to him by the appropriate methods. Should he fail to do so, the subjects left in the debtor's possession may be attached by diligence at the instance of creditors who have not acceded to the trust-deed or of creditors to whom the debtor may have subsequently become indebted.[23] When the trustee has completed his title nothing is left with the debtor which can be attached by diligence. A non-acceding creditor may render the debtor notour bankrupt, and, should he do so within six months of the granting of the trust-deed, that deed will be open to reduction, under the Bankruptcy Act 1696 (c. 5),[24] as a security for prior debts.[25] When more than six months have expired the trust-deed is not open to reduction by non-acceding creditors.[26] But it is no bar to sequestration, which may be applied for by a non-acceding creditor[27]; by the debtor, with concurrence of a non-acceding creditor[28]; or by a creditor who has acceded, in the event of non-acceding creditors taking proceedings which might result in giving them preferential rights.[29] Where sequestration is awarded, the trust-deed falls without any reduction, the estate must be wound up by the trustee in the sequestration, and any rights acquired under the private trust-deed must be asserted in the bankruptcy proceedings.[30] The trustee under the private trust-deed has, in the event of sequestration, a lien for any expenses he may have incurred.[31] But, like other liens, this requires possession; where the trustee in a private trust-deed granted by a farmer had advanced money for the administration of the farm, but had not obtained a completed assignation of the debtor's lease, it was held that as he had no possession he had no lien, and that there were no grounds on which he could claim any preferential ranking in the ensuing sequestration.[32]

In dividing the estate the trustee in a trust-deed for creditors is bound to provide for all claims intimated to him. He was held personally liable when he rejected a claim which the creditor was able to prove to be well founded.[33] Even although a particular creditor may not have acceded to the trust-deed, he is entitled to be ranked in the distribution of the estate.[34] The trustee under

21 s. 185.
22 Deeds of Arrangement Act 1914 (4 & 5 Geo. V, c. 47).
23 *Gibson* v. *Wilson* (1841) 3 D. 974.
24 As amended by the Companies Act 1947, s. 115 (3).
25 *Mackenzie* v. *Calder* (1868) 6 M. 833.
26 *Lamb's Trs.* v. *Reid* (1883) 11 R. 76.
27 *Kyd* v. *Waterson* (1880) 7 R. 884.
28 *Macalister* v. *Swinburne* (1874) 1 R. 958; *Salaman* v. *Rosslyn's Trs.* (1900) 3 F. 298.
29 *Jopp* v. *Hay* (1844) 7 D. 260. See *Munro* v. *Rothfield,* 1920 S.C. (H.L.) 165.
30 *Salaman* v. *Rosslyn's Trs.*, supra.
31 *Thomson* v. *Tough's Tr.* (1880) 7 R. 1035.
32 *Mess* v. *Sime's Tr.* (1898) 1 F. (H.L.) 22.
33 *Cruickshank* v. *Thomas* (1893) 21 R. 257.
34 *Ogilvie* v. *Taylor* (1887) 14 R. 399.

a private trust-deed has no title to challenge illegal preferences granted by the debtor, unless a creditor entitled to challenge has acceded to the trust, and has assigned his title to sue to the trustee.[35]

An insolvent estate may, alternatively, be wound up without depriving the debtor of his estates, through the medium of a composition contract. Under its usual form the debtor agrees to pay so much in the pound to each creditor, and grants bills payable in instalments for that amount, thereby conferring on each creditor, in the event of failure in payment, a liquid debt on which diligence may at once proceed. In the absence of any provision to the contrary, the full debt revives on failure in payment of any instalment.[36] As the debtor under the process is not deprived of his estate it remains open to the diligence of any creditor who is not barred by his accession to the composition contract. Each creditor who accedes does so on the implied condition that the accession of all is obtained.[37]

[35] *Fleming's Trs.* v. *M'Hardy* (1892) 19 R. 542.
[36] Bell, *Comm.*, II, 400.
[37] Bell, *Comm.*, II, 395, 400.

CHAPTER L

CRIMINAL LAW[1]

Hume's *Commentaries on the Law of Scotland respecting Crimes* (3rd ed., with Bell's Notes as supplement, 1844); Macdonald's *Practical Treatise on the Criminal law of Scotland* (5th ed., 1948); Alison's *Criminal Law of Scotland* (1833); Anderson's *Criminal Law* (2nd ed., 1904); Trotter's *Summary Criminal Jurisdiction* (1936); Renton and Brown's *Criminal Procedure* (4th ed., 1972); Smith's *Short Commentary on the Law of Scotland* (1962), pp. 116-238; Gordon's *Criminal Law* (2nd ed., 1978).

PART I

THE NATURE OF CRIME

1. Definition.—A crime may be defined generally as a wrongful act, attempt or omission the consequences of which are actually, or are deemed to be, harmful to the community, which is punishable by the State and in respect of which proceedings are now conducted in the name of someone representing the State.[2] Judicial opinion and writers of textbooks have sometimes distinguished "offences" from "crimes" but, as is expressed by the author of the leading Scots text book: "the terms are not clearly distinguished, and indeed are often used interchangeably, and even statutory uses and definitions are unhelpful."[3] It is not necessary in a charge to specify the crime by any *nomen juris*; it is enough to set forth facts relevant and sufficient to constitute a crime.[4] The conception of a crime involves three essentials: (1) An overt act. (2) Dole or criminal intention. (3) Liability to punishment.

2. Overt Act.—The State does not punish a mere wicked intention.[5] The intention must be manifested by some overt act. The offender must do some

---

[1] It is not intended in this general outline of the criminal law to cover the field of criminal procedure and evidence although incidental reference will be made where necessary to the relevant statutory provisions with regard to procedure. For a detailed treatment of criminal procedure in Scotland see Renton and Brown's *Criminal Procedure* (4th ed., 1972) which must now, of course, be read in the light of the consolidating Criminal Procedure (Scotland) Act 1975 (c. 21) and the amending provisions to that Act in the Criminal Law Act 1977 (c. 45), Sched. 11. In the citation of cases at the instance of H.M. Advocate the name of the prosecutor is omitted, and only that of the accused is given. In this chapter the works of Hume and Macdonald are referred to as Hume and Macd. As to the method of citing the Justiciary Reports, see the *Citation of Cases, ante* p. x.

[2] Bankton (I-X. i.) defines it tersely as "an unlawful act that merits punishment."

[3] Gordon, *op. cit.*, p. 16. See, by way of illustration, the definitions in the Criminal Procedure (Scotland) Act 1975, s. 462 (1).

[4] 1975 Act, s. 44; *Strathern* v. *Seaforth*, 1926 J.C. 100; *Dalton*, 1951 J.C. 76. For a discussion of the inherent power of the High Court of Justiciary to declare new crimes see Smith, pp. 125-131. It is unlikely that this power would be invoked today. Cf. *Shaw* v. *D.P.P.* [1962] A.C. 220, re law of England.

[5] *Cameron*, 1911 S.C. (J.) 110; *Morton* v. *Henderson*, 1956 J.C. 55.

act which it is a crime to do, or fail to do some act which it is criminal for him to omit to do. If he is guilty of such criminal conduct, the wicked intent is presumed.[6]

3. Dole is an expression which may be used in a general or in a particular sense. In its general sense it has been defined as that corrupt and evil intention which is essential to the guilt of any crime. It exists when the act is attended with "such circumstances as indicate a corrupt and malignant disposition, a heart contemptuous of order, and regardless of social duty."[7] This intention need not be directed against anyone in particular, or against the person who, or thing which, actually suffers, for the result may not square with the intent.[8] The presence or absence of dole in this general sense is relevant to some questions of criminal responsibility (as in theft by finding, in the accused's state of mind in relation to consent to assault and in distinguishing culpable homicide from murder) and also to mitigation of penalty. It is, however, in the sense of the mental element necessary before guilt will be affirmed in relation to a particular crime, that dole, or mens rea, has its main application. There is no common mental element required for all crimes but for most common law crimes intention to commit the actus reus (which in turn generally connotes knowledge of all the material elements of fact) is usually necessary, although recklessness may often be equiparated with intention and for some crimes negligence is sufficient.[9] It will not avail the offender, in the absence of mental illness, to prove that he did not know that the acts libelled against him were punishable.[10] A man is presumed to intend the natural consequences of his acts, and although the crime actually committed is not the one intended, the perpetrator is guilty of the former if it be the "near and natural result" of his act.[11] An exception to the rule that dole is an essential element is to be found in the case of those statutory offences which are by the statute made punishable irrespective of the presence or absence of dole[12] or for which a master may be held responsible although they have been committed by his servants without his knowledge.[13] It has been held accordingly that a bye-law imposing vicarious criminal liability is not on that account bad.[14] The master, however, may avoid liability if he can show that the servant acted contrary to express and particular instructions or for some purpose of his own.[15] There is

---

[6] Hume, I, p. 22; Macd., p. 1.

[7] Hume, I, p. 21; cf. *Gray* v. *Hawthorn,* 1964 J.C. 69; *Cawthorne,* 1968 J.C. 32, per Lord Guthrie at 36-7.

[8] Hume, I, p. 23.

[9] For a general discussion see Gordon, *Criminal Law* (2nd ed.), pp. 213-267. See also *Sutherland* (1856) 2 Irv. 455. See Macd., p. 101; *Cranston,* 1931 J.C. 28; *Paton,* 1936 J.C. 19.

[10] *Clark* v. *Syme,* 1957 J.C. 1; cf. *Dewar,* 1945 J.C. 5.

[11] *Fraser and Rollins,* 1920 J.C. 60.

[12] See especially *Mitchell* v. *Morrison,* 1938 J.C. 64 (a Full Bench decision); *Duguid* v. *Fraser,* 1942 J.C. 1; *Fraser* v. *Heatly,* 1952 J.C. 103.

[13] *Gair* v. *Brewster,* 1916 S.C. (J.) 36, 7 Adam 752; *M'Aleer* v. *Laird,* 1934 J.C. 79; *Macmillan* v. *Western S.M.T. Co.,* 1933 J.C. 51; *Duguid* v. *Fraser,* 1942 J.C. 1. But the Court drew the line in *Napier,* 1944 J.C. 61. See for a discussion of vicarious responsibility *Gardner* v. *Akeroyd* [1952] 2 Q.B. 743.

[14] *M'Kenna* v. *Sim,* 1916 S.C. (J.) 24.

[15] *Ferguson* v. *Campbell,* 1946 J.C. 28.

a presumption that dole is an essential ingredient of every offence, and the burden rests upon the Crown to show that the words of the statute creating the offence or the subject matter with which it deals impose an absolute obligation, so as to rebut this presumption.[16] If the statute provides that the offence can be committed only "knowingly," the Crown must establish actual knowledge on the part of the accused.[17]

4. Criminal Responsibility.—Dole is absent so that what would otherwise be criminal is not so where the accused (a) is insane or (b) is under age or (c) acts under necessity or compulsion.

5. Insanity; Intoxication.—Insanity on the part of the accused may be pleaded either in bar of trial, on the ground that it deprives the accused of power to instruct a defence; or to escape conviction, where it can be shown to have existed at the date of the act charged. Where a prisoner in custody awaiting trial is found to be insane, the Court may order, on the application of the Secretary of State, that the accused be detained in hospital till Her Majesty's pleasure be known.[18] Similar procedure is available when the accused is found unfit to plead, on grounds of insanity.[19] The question, which may be raised by the prosecutor, by the defence or by the Court, is determined either on a preliminary enquiry by the Court before the accused is called on to plead,[20] or by the jury.[21] In the latter case, if the jury find that the accused is insane, they do not consider the question of guilt or innocence.[21] There must be insanity; an abnormal mental state short of that is not enough.[20] If the accused is able to instruct his defence, but the jury acquit on the ground that he was insane when he committed the act, he is ordered to be detained till Her Majesty's pleasure be known.[22] The burden of proving insanity is on the accused, but the standard of proof is on a balance of probabilities.[23] That someone is prevented by mental disease from knowing the nature and quality of his act or from knowing that the act is legally or morally[24] wrong is an element in determining insanity but is not an exhaustive test. The general rule is rather that no-one is responsible for the commission of a crime whose reason has been so overpowered on account of some mental defect that he has been rendered incapable of controlling his conduct.[25] That rule admits of exception where the absence of the power of control is due to temporary

[16] *Mitchell* v. *Morrison* (supra) at p. 71; *Fraser* v. *Heatly*, supra; *Macleod* v. *Hamilton*, 1965 S.L.T. 305; cf. *Lim Chin Aik* v. *The Queen* [1963] A.C. 160.
[17] *Noble* v. *Heatly*, 1967 J.C. 5.
[18] Mental Health (Scotland) Act 1960 (8 & 9 Eliz. II, c. 61), s. 65.
[19] 1975 Act, ss. 174 and 375. Other grounds are available to show that the accused is unfit to plead: cf. *Wilson*, 1942 J.C. 75, where accused was a deaf mute.
[20] *Russell*, 1946 J.C. 37; cf. *Kidd*, 1960 J.C. 61, for effect of amnesia.
[21] *Brown*, 1907 S.C. (J.) 67, 5 Adam 312.
[22] 1975 Act, ss. 174 and 375.
[23] *Braithwaite*, 1945 J.C. 55; *Mitchell*, 1951 J.C. 53.
[24] *Gibson* (1844) 2 Broun 332, per Lord Justice-Clerk; *Dingwall* (1867) 5 Irv., at p. 475; *Kidd*, 1960 J.C. 61, where the rules laid down in *M'Naghten* (1843) 10 C.P. and F. 200 were expressly excluded from the law of Scotland.
[25] *Kidd*, supra; cf. *Breen* v. *Breen*, 1961 S.C. 158.

dissociation produced (e.g. through drink or drugs) by the accused's own fault. There must to constitute insanity be an alienation of reason in relation to the act committed. It may be limited to the particular subject-matter of the charge, as where a man otherwise sane had the insane idea that he must kill his children.[26]

Mental weakness or aberration of mind not amounting to insanity has been held to reduce the guilt of a person charged with murder to guilty merely of culpable homicide.[27] The defence of diminished responsibility applies only to murder and the Court is not likely to extend the scope of such defences.[28] A special defence that the accused was not responsible for his actions on account of the incidence of temporary dissociation owing to an epileptic fugue or other pathological condition has been held incompetent.[29] Such a condition is only relevant when considering sentence.[29] If the Court is satisfied that a convicted person is a mental defective it may, instead of pronouncing sentence, order his removal to hospital.[30]

Voluntary, self-induced intoxication, whether by drink or drugs or a combination of both, does not found the plea of temporary insanity; nor will it support the plea of diminished responsibility in cases of murder whatever the degree of impairment of the accused's mental faculties.[31] Involuntary intoxication, on the other hand, does excuse, although it also will not constitute in law a state of temporary insanity. If an accused person suffers from a total alienation of reason in relation to the act committed[32] amounting to mental disorder, whether or not it is caused by alcoholism or drug addiction, the pleas of insanity in bar of trial or of insanity at the time may be established.

6. Nonage.—It is a conclusive presumption that no child under the age of eight years can be guilty of any offence.[33] No child between the ages of eight and sixteen may be prosecuted for any offence except on the instructions or at the instance of the Lord Advocate, and no Court other than the High Court of Justiciary and the Sheriff Court has jurisdiction over a child for an offence.[34] But if the Lord Advocate does not instruct proceedings to be taken, such a child may be brought before a children's hearing on the ground that he has committed an offence.[35]

---

[26] *Sharp,* 1927 J.C. 66.
[27] *Savage,* 1923 J.C. 49; *Muir,* 1933 J.C. 46; *Kirkwood,* 1939 J.C. 36. The allegedly illogical nature of this rule was pointed out by Lord Johnston in *Higgins,* 1914 S.C. (J.) 1 but it is capable of defence on both practical and jurisprudential grounds. See Smith op. cit., pp. 153-163.
[28] *Carraher,* 1946 J.C. 108; *Cunningham,* 1963 J.C. 80; see 1963 S.L.T. (News) 166.
[29] *Cunningham,* 1963 J.C. 80; *Clarks,* 1968 J.C. 53; *Murray,* 1969 S.L.T. (Notes) 85.
[30] 1975 Act, ss. 175 and 376.
[31] *Brennan* (seven judges), 1977 S.L.T. 151, overruling *Campbell,* 1921 J.C. 1 and *Kennedy,* 1944 J.C. 171.
[32] Hume, I, p 37, quoted with approval in *Brennan* as the foundation of the modern law of insanity.
[33] Children and Young Persons (Scotland) Act 1937 (1 Edw. VIII, & 1 Geo. VI, c. 34), s. 55.
[34] Social Work (Scotland) Act 1968 (c. 49), s. 31.
[35] 1968 Act, s. 32 (2) (g).

7. Necessity or Compulsion.—Necessity imposed by circumstances may mitigate penalty but is not in general an excuse in law for causing an innocent person to suffer. According to Hume you may not commit theft although you are starving, and you may not kill and eat a companion even to avert certain death by hunger.[36] There is however, no Scottish authority in point and necessity as a defence to a criminal charge is probably a question of fact and degree. Extreme necessity, it is thought, may justify an act which would otherwise constitute a minor offence.[36a] Compulsion by a human being to commit crime is a possible excuse, as, for example, where an individual is concussed under threat of death by a large body of persons or a young child is forced to commit a crime by a parent.[37]

8. Self-Defence: Provocation.—Homicide or assault may be justified if committed in self-defence. To establish this special defence in a case of homicide there must be reasonable grounds to fear imminent danger to life or the act must be done to prevent rape[38]; there must be no means of escape or retreat; and the retaliation must not be excessive.[39] Depending upon the particular circumstances it may be excessive to retaliate with a lethal weapon such as a firearm or knife, when the assault being perpetrated or threatened is with fists. It is a defence which may be pleaded in justification of acts committed in defence of others.[40] Homicide in defence of property interests is probably not justifiable.[41] In cases of assault it will be sufficient to sustain this special defence that there was imminent danger of physical harm or of injury to property; the same rules as to means of escape and proportionality of retaliation apply as in homicide. Self-defence is distinguishable from provocation which is relevant only as a mitigating factor and does not, procedurally, constitute a special defence. Provocation may be effective to reduce murder to culpable homicide,[42] but as a plea is not restricted to cases of murder.[43]

9. Crimes by Accession.—Scots law makes no distinction between commission of a crime and accession to it.[44] Criminal responsibility and liability to punishment are thus incurred not only by the perpetrator, but by any person who has aided the execution of a crime. Such indirect participation

---

[36] Hume I, p. 55; *Reg.* v. *Dudley* (1884) 14 Q.B.D. 273.
[36a] See Gordon, *Criminal Law* (2nd ed.), pp. 420-429.
[37] Hume I, pp. 49, 50, 51; Macd., p. 11.
[38] *Owens,* 1946 J.C. 119; *Crawford,* 1950 J.C. 67; *M'Cluskey,* 1959 J.C. 39. Imminent danger of demembration may be sufficient (see Crawford at 71) but such cases can be explained on other grounds (Gordon; *Criminal Law* (2nd ed.) p. 761).
[39] *Kizileviczius,* 1938 J.C. 89; *Doherty,* 1954 J.C. 1; cf. *M'Cluskey* where a threat to commit an indecent assault was held to be insufficient to justify violent retaliation resulting in death in self-defence.
[40] *Carson,* 1964 S.L.T. 2.
[41] Gordon, pp. 761-2.
[42] *Kizilevicius; Crawford; McDermott,* 1973 J.C. 8.
[43] *Callander,* 1958 S.L.T. 24.
[44] Macd., pp. 2-8. This applies to statutory offences: 1975 Act, ss. 216, 428.

is known as art and part. Accomplices may be tried separately, and the charge does not need to state whether an accused is principal or accessory.[45] A person is guilty art and part who incites or procures a person to commit the crime[46] or who assists the actual perpetrator in its execution. And instigation by itself is criminal even although the crime suggested is never committed.[47] In the case of accession by incitement, retraction or repentance by the instigator before the commission of the crime is a valid defence. If the offence committed has more serious consequences than the instigator intended, he is· nevertheless guilty art and part unless the result was an unlikely one. Thus the instigator of a robbery with violence would be guilty of murder if the victim died.[48] Actual assistance may be given before the execution of the crime by furnishing the perpetrator with the means, such as poison or weapons, in the knowledge that these are intended to be used for a particular criminal purpose. Accession at the actual commission of the crime may be inferred from what occurs at the time.[49] A person accused as art and part cannot be convicted where the prosecution has failed to bring home the crime to the principals charged. Thus where A, not being a director, was charged along with certain company directors as "art and part" with them in a fraudulent allotment of shares and the directors were acquitted, it was held that A could not be convicted.[50] Accession *after* the fact may afford evidence from which previous participation may be inferred.[51] Otherwise it is not recognised as a crime, save in the case of treason.[52] It is, however, a separate offence to harbour a criminal.

10. Attempt.—An attempt to commit an indictable offence is punishable as a crime.[53] But there must have been more than preparation for the offence; perpetration must have begun. Even when no harm ensues, the law takes cognisance of and will punish a step taken towards the carrying out of the offence.[54] It has been held in one case no crime to attempt the commission of an impossible crime, viz., to attempt to procure abortion in a woman who is not pregnant.[55] On the other hand, there may be an attempt to steal where there was nothing to steal.[56]

---

[45] 1975 Act, s. 46.
[46] But see *Johnstone*, 1926 J.C. 89, where, upon a charge of causing abortion, the mere communication of the operator's name to the interested parties was held not to be an accession to the crime.
[47] *Tannahill and Neilson*, 1943 J.C. 150.
[48] Hume, I, p. 280; Macd., p. 4; *Lappen*, 1956 S.L.T. 109.
[49] *Kerr*, 1871, 2 Coup. 334; cf. *Webster* v. *Wishart*, 1955 S.L.T. 243.
[50] *Young*, 1932 J.C. 63.
[51] Macd., p. 8; Hume I, pp. 281, 282.
[52] Macd., p. 8.
[53] 1975 Act, s. 63.
[54] *Cameron*, 1911 S.C. (J.) 110; *Tannahill and Neilson*, 1943 J.C. 150; *Coventry* v. *Douglas* 1944 J.C. 13; Hume I., p. 27; *Morton* v. *Henderson*, 1956 J.C. 55.
[55] *Semple*, 1937 J.C. 41.
[56] *Lamont* v. *Strathern*, 1933 J.C. 33.

PART II

Particular Crimes

1. Classification.—Crimes may be conveniently classified as (1) against the State; (2) against the person; and (3) against property.

Section I

CRIMES AGAINST THE STATE

2. Treason.—After the Union in 1707 the law of treason then in force in England was adopted by statute as the law of Scotland.[57] The principal forms of treason, as contained in the Act 25 Edw. III. st. 5, c. 2, afterwards amended, principally in 1796, are as follows: To compass or imagine the death of the King, Queen-Consort, or of the eldest son, being heir-apparent, of the Sovereign, or serious bodily harm or restraint of the Sovereign; and to levy war against the King or adhere to his enemies. The "compassing and imagining" must be shown by some overt act, such as publication of writings. The "war" referred to is to be distinguished from rioting caused by some local grievance. A person cannot be a traitor unless he is the child of a British father, or is resident in the realm and subject of a State at peace with it, or in some other way under the King's protection, e.g., by being the holder of a passport.[58] A British subject cannot naturalise himself as a subject of a foreign State at war with this country so as to exempt himself from criminal liability for treason.[59] The traitor need not be within the King's realm at the time of his treason.[60]

3. Treason-Felony.—The crime of treason-felony was formulated with the object of punishing as treasonable such acts as devising the deposition of the Sovereign, levying war against him to force a change of counsels or to intimidate Parliament, and the stirring up of invasion.[61] The guilty intention has to be shown by overt act or deed, including writing, advised speaking, and conspiracy.[62]

4. Sedition.—The crime of sedition consists in all those practices, whether by deed, word, or writing, or of whatsoever kind, which are suited, though not perhaps intended, to disturb the tranquillity of the State, for the purpose of producing public trouble or commotion, and moving Her Majesty's subjects to the dislike, resistance, or subversion of the established government and law,

[57] Treason Act 1708.
[58] *Joyce* v. *Director of Public Prosecutions* [1946] A.C. 347.
[59] *R.* v. *Lynch* [1903] 1 K.B. 444.
[60] *R.* v. *Casement* [1917] 1 K.B. 98; *Joyce,* supra.
[61] Treason-Felony Act 1847.
[62] *Cumming,* 1848, J. Shaw 17.

or the settled frame and order of things.[63] The crime being one which is greatly affected by the state of public opinion at any given time, the strict enforcement of the law is more an administrative than a legal question. Modern prosecutions are rare.

5. Piracy.—Piracy consists of hostilities at sea by anyone who holds no commission from a recognised Government, or by one who holds such a commission and commits depredations on vessels of his own or a friendly country; or the unlawful taking possession of a vessel; or the feloniously carrying off of property or persons on board. The essential elements of the crime are the same as those requisite to a relevant charge of robbery where that crime is committed in respect of property on land and within the ordinary jurisdiction of the High Court.[64] It is punished by the law of any realm wherein the offenders are found, and in Scotland by the Court of Justiciary with any penalty short of death. In international law the crime is now defined in the Tokyo Convention Act 1967.[65]

6. Mobbing and Rioting.—The crime consists in combining to the alarm of the lieges either for an illegal purpose or in order to carry out a legal purpose by illegal means, e.g., violence or intimidation.[66] It is the common purpose which distinguishes mobbing and rioting from breach of the peace. The concourse need not be large; the number required to constitute a mob depends on what the persons composing it do, the violence they show, and the threats they use.[67] The combination may have been lawful at first, and may then have taken up an unlawful purpose or proceeded to attain a lawful end in an illegal way.[68] The intimidation may have been the result of overwhelming numbers without the use of violence. The ring-leaders are usually selected for prosecution, but every member of the mob willingly present is liable to punishment for all the acts done by the mob, both those which it set out to commit and those which it might naturally be expected to commit in carrying out its purpose, except those which occur after he has voluntarily quitted it.[69]

7. Breach of the Peace embraces a large number of unruly acts, which are usually dealt with summarily.[70] The crime is committed where something is done in breach of public order or decorum which might reasonably be expected to lead to the lieges being alarmed or upset or tempted to take reprisals at their own hand.[71] There is no limit to the kind of conduct which

---

[63] Hume, I., p. 553; explained in *Grant*, 1848, J. Shaw 68. See Incitement to Disaffection Act 1934.
[64] *Cameron*, 1971 J.C. 50.
[65] See also Hijacking Act, 1971 (c. 70).
[66] Macd., 131; *Nicolson*, 1887, 1 White 307, per Lord Young; *Robertson*, 1842, 1 Broun 152, per Lord Justice-Clerk, at 192.
[67] *Sloan* v. *Macmillan*, 1922 J.C. 1.
[68] *Blair*, 1868, 1 Coup. 168.
[69] *Orr* (1856) 2 Irv. 502.
[70] Macd., 137; *Hutton* v. *Main* (1891) 19 R. (J.) 5; 3 White 41.
[71] *Raffaelli* v. *Heatly*, 1949 J.C. 101; *Young* v. *Heatly*, 1959 J.C. 66, where the incidents complained of took place in private.

may give rise to a relevant charge of breach of the peace.[72] It may be committed in an attempt to prevent such a breach being committed.[73] It is a statutory offence for anyone to have an offensive weapon with him in a public place.[74]

8. Deforcement: Obstructing Police.—The crime of deforcement consists in resistance, active or passive, successfully made to messengers or other officers while they are employed in executing the law. The requisites of the crime are that the act or acts must be forcible, there being such violence or show of violence as to alarm a man of ordinary courage and presence of mind[75]; that the act or acts shall have succeeded in preventing the officer from doing his duty; that the person deforced was a proper executor of the warrant in question, or an assistant[76]; that the act prevented was a formal or solemn proceeding and the officer in actu proximo[77]; and that the warrant was ex facie regular and adapted to the purpose for which it was used. The comparable offence of obstructing the police in the execution of their duty is punishable under statute,[78] and requires for its constitution an element of physical obstruction such as assault.[79]

9. Revenue Offences.—Revenue officers are similarly protected by statute in the execution of their duty.[80] Smuggling is penalised by the Customs and Excise Act 1952.[81] Revenue Acts providing for payment of taxes and Government duties prescribe the appropriate penalties for the crime of fraudulent evasion of tax.[82] The law as to counterfeiting and the uttering of base coins has been codified by statute.[83]

10. Prison-Breaking.—Escapes and attempts to escape from prison are criminal, even when they are accompanied by no other form of crime.[84] To abscond from a working party outside prison would be a different offence, namely that of attempting to hinder the course of justice and frustrate its ends.[85] Breaking into prison for the purpose of a rescue is also a crime.[86]

11. Perjury: Subornation of Perjury: Prevarication.—Perjury is the judicial affirmation of a falsehood on oath, or in an affirmation equivalent to oath. To

---

[72] *Montgomery* v. *McLeod,* 1977 S.L.T. (Notes) 77.
[73] *Palazzo* v. *Copeland,* 1976 J.C. 52.
[74] Prevention of Crimes Act 1953.
[75] *Nicolson* (1887) 1 White 307, at 314.
[76] *Cunningham* v. *Wilson* (1901) 3 F. (J.) 65, 3 Adam 243.
[77] *Maclean* (1886) 14 R. (J.) 1; 1 White 232.
[78] Police (Scotland) Act 1967, s. 41.
[79] See *Curlett* v. *M'Kechnie,* 1938 J.C. 176.
[80] Customs and Excise Act 1952, s 10.
[81] Notably by ss. 70-74.
[82] For a treatment see Gordon, pp. 944-952.
[83] Coinage Offences Act 1936 (26 Geo. V. & 1 Edw. VIII, c. 16); and Coinage Act 1971 (c. 24); see also Macd., 78.
[84] *Smith,* 1863, 4 Irv. 434.
[85] *Turnbull,* 1953 J.C. 59; *Martin* 1956 J.C. 1.
[86] *Urquhart,* 1844, 2 Broun. 13.

constitute this crime, the violation of truth must have been deliberately intended by the accused; and, therefore, reasonable allowance ought to be made for forgetfulness or misapprehension, according to his age, health, and other circumstances. The falsehood must be explicitly and absolutely affirmed. It is essential that the false statement should have been made as part of evidence which was competent. Otherwise, even if no objection was taken to the evidence, there can be no conviction.[87] An accused who gives false evidence at his trial may be guilty of perjury like any other witness.[88] The affirmation must be made in a judicial proceeding before a person competent to receive it.[89] A proceeding before a court of the Church of Scotland or an arbiter is undoubtedly judicial. It is not enough to prove mere discrepancy between two statements made by the accused, one of them having been made on oath[90]; the truth must be established and shown to be inconsistent with the testimony.[91] The false statement usually relates to external fact, but it is not incompetent to prove a perjured statement of opinion. The falsehood must be wilful and corrupt, i.e., promulgated by one who knows the truth and deliberately tells lies. The purport of the false evidence is spoken to, as a rule, by the judge who presided on the occasion, with the help of notes taken at the time, and by other officials then present; but judges of the Supreme Court are apparently not competent to give evidence in these cases. The real facts may be proved, though they may instruct some other crime of which the accused has been acquitted. Falsehoods uttered under an oath in which there is no appeal to the Deity, or under an affirmation not held by law to be equivalent to an oath imprecating the Deity, may competently be punished as fraud.

Subornation of perjury consists in tampering with persons who are to swear, and counselling or procuring them to commit perjury.[92]

Prevarication consists in attempting while giving evidence to mislead the Court, a kind of unsuccessful perjury. It may be punished at once by the presiding judge.[93] There is statutory power to punish prevarication in a summary trial.[94]

A false statement on oath is a statutory offence.[95]

12. False Information of Crime.—To give false information to the police and so cause them to institute an investigation with a view to criminal proceedings being taken is a crime and one seriously regarded by the Court.[96]

---

[87] *Smith,* 1934 J.C. 66. In *Angus,* 1935 J.C. 1, a subornation case, the Justiciary Court seemed doubtful, but the point was not really before it, since the evidence was plainly competent. See also *Graham,* 1969 S.L.T. 116.
[88] *Cairns,* 1967 J.C. 37.
[89] *Barr,* 1839, 2 Swin. 282, and especially at 294-310. See *Hastie,* 1863, 4 Irv. 389, where the judge was absent during part of the proceedings.
[90] *Bole* (1883) 11 R. (J.) 10, 5 Coup. 350.
[91] *Sanderson* (1899) 1 F. (J.) 87; 3 Adam 25; but see *Roberts* (1882) 10 R. (J.) 5; 5 Couper 118.
[92] Hume I, 384; Macd., 166; *Angus,* supra; *Scott,* 1946 J.C. 96.
[93] *Macleod* v. *Speirs* (1884) 11 R. (J.) 26; *Wylie,* 1966 S.L.T. 149.
[94] 1975 Act, s. 344.
[95] False Oaths (Scotland) Act 1933 (23 & 24 Geo. V. c. 20); *Waugh* v. *Mentiplay,* 1938 J.C. 117.
[96] *Kerr* v. *Hill,* 1936 J.C. 71; *Gray* v. *Morrison,* 1954 J.C. 31.

SECTION II

CRIMES AGAINST THE PERSON

13. Generally.—Offences against the person may be directed against the life, personal safety, liberty, chastity or reputation of a particular individual.

14. Homicide: Murder.—The generic term for an act which results in death is homicide. It occurs when a human being is killed by a human being. The victim must be self-existent, not an unborn child.[97] Homicide is causing the death of a person by an act or omission[98] but for which the person killed would not have died when he did, and which is directly connected with his death. In cases where the act or omission is not the sole cause of the death, if the accused has inflicted a dangerous bodily injury he takes the risk (1) of the necessary surgical or medical treatment, though not of mal-regimen[99]: (2) of the state of health of his victim at the time[1]: (3) of any disease which arises in a usual and natural way from the injury, such as erysipelas or lockjaw, though not of the consequences of the wilful folly of his victim.[2] Moreover, one who accelerates the death of a moribund person commits homicide.

Homicide is not necessarily criminal. It loses its criminal character if it is either (a) casual, or (b) justifiable. It is casual, and therefore innocent, if it proceeds from pure misadventure without gross negligence and without any act of the killer's will directed either to homicide, or to doing bodily harm, or to doing any wrong or unlawful act.[3] It is justifiable and accordingly innocent, when it is done in the necessary prosecution of that which the killer is bound or has a right to do, as in the cases of a judge who was empowered to sentence to death, the officials who carried out the warrant, magistrates and others engaged in suppressing a dangerous riot, officers of the law (at least criminal officers) in cases of violent and dangerous resistance, and soldiers and sailors on duty if acting on reasonable grounds and in accordance with proper military or naval practice. It may also be justifiable as an act of self-defence against attempted murder or serious assault[4] or, in the case of a woman, against an assault upon her chastity.[5] The murder of or assault upon a third party may be similarly prevented.[6]

Criminal homicide is divided into (a) murder, and (b) culpable homicide. The sentence for murder is imprisonment for life.[7] In the case of culpable homicide there is an absence of that wilful intent or utter recklessness of consequences upon which a murder charge depends. Obviously the distinction between murder and culpable homicide may in some cases be a narrow one.

---

[97] Hume I, 186; *M'Allum*, 1858, 3 Irv. at p. 200; *Scott* (1892) 19 R. (J.) 63; 3 White 240.
[98] See *M'Phee*, 1935 J.C. 46; murder by exposure.
[99] *Williamson*, 1866, 5 Irv. 326. cf. *Heidmeisser* (1879) 17 S.L.R. 266 at 267.
[1] *Rutherford*, 1947 J.C. 1.
[2] *Norrises*, 1886. 1 White 292.
[3] *A.B.* (1887) 15 R. (J.) 30; 1 Wh. 532; *Rutherford*, supra.
[4] See supra, Part I § 8.
[5] Alison, vol i., p. 132; *McCluskey*, 1959 J.C. 39 per L.J-G. Clyde at pp. 42-3.
[6] *Carson*, 1964 S.L.T. 21.
[7] 1975 Act, s. 205.

Murder is the wilful taking away of a person's life without just cause, whether the act was intended to kill or displayed such utter and wicked recklessness as to imply a disposition depraved enough to be wholly regardless of consequences.[8] The latter alternative covers the cases of intent to cause dangerous bodily injury to the actual victim, of intent to cause death or such injury to a third party, of an act done with an unlawful object and known to be likely to cause death, though there was no intention to hurt anyone, and of intent to inflict grievous bodily injury in order to facilitate the commission of a serious crime or the escape of the offender. The consent of the victim is no defence[9] equally in murder[10] as in assault.

Culpable homicide embraces all sorts of homicide which are neither casual nor justifiable, on the one hand, nor murderous, on the other. Death which results from an assault or comparable criminal act is at least culpable homicide: the offence cannot be reduced to simple assault only.[11] In some cases an intention to kill is present, and the crime is reduced from murder to culpable homicide by the weakness of the offender's intellect,[12] by its having taken place in the course of duty where the circumstances did not justify the taking of life,[13] or by the existence of provocation, either in the form of violence[14] or of a gravely disturbing event such as the discovery of a wife in adultery[15] or circumstances analogous to adultery in the case of those living together and regarded as man and wife.[16] In other cases there is no intent to kill, and the accused may at the time be engaged in an otherwise lawful act. The question for the jury then is whether he has been rash, grossly negligent, or reckless.[17] The number of fatalities due to the reckless driving of motor vehicles has led to a considerable number of prosecutions. The driver of a motor vehicle who inflicts injury may be guilty of culpable homicide if his conduct is notably and seriously negligent or displays utter disregard for the safety of others.[18] The prosecution must prove "gross and palpable carelessness."[19] In modern practice, however, proceedings are normally taken for the statutory offence of causing death by reckless driving.[20]

Attempt to murder is a crime chargeable at common law. The intent necessary for the establishment of the crime is the same as that necessary for murder, namely a deliberate intention to kill or such wicked recklessness as to imply a disposition depraved enough to be regardless of consequences. The

[8] Macd., 89; *Rutherford*, 1947 J.C. 1. See Part I., § 3, supra.
[9] *Rutherford*, supra.
[10] *Smart*, 1975 S.L.T. 65.
[11] *McDermott*, 1973 J.C.‧8 (disapproving the directions given by the presiding judges in *Gilmour*, 1938 J.C. 1 and *McCluskey*, 1959 J.C. 39).
[12] See Part I., § 5, supra. but see also Gordon, (1976) 21 Jo. Law Soc. Scot, 168.
[13] *Sheppard*, 1941 J.C. 67. Reasonable belief in facts that would have justified the action may, however, constitute sufficient defence.
[14] *M'Guinness*, 1937 J.C. 37; *Kizileviczius*, 1938 J.C. 60.
[15] *Hill*, 1941 J.C. 59; cf. Part I., § 7, supra.
[16] *McDermott*, supra.
[17] Macd., 101; *Wood*, 1903, 4 Adam 150; *Sheppard*, supra; *Bird*, 1952 J.C. 23.
[18] *Drever*, 1885, 5 Coup. 680, per Lord Young, *Waugh* v. *Campbell*, 1920 J.C. 1, per Lord Salvesen; Macd., 101.
[19] *Cranston*, 1931 J.C. 28; *Paton*, 1936 J.C. 19; See also *Dunn* 1960 J.C. 55.
[20] Road Traffic Act 1972 (c. 20), s. 1, as amended by the Criminal Law Act 1977 (c. 45), s. 50.

only difference between the two is that in attempted murder the killing is not brought off and the victim escapes with his life.[21]

15. Concealment of Pregnancy.—A presumptive or statutory murder was constituted by the Act 1690, c. 21, by which any woman who should conceal her pregnancy during its whole course, and should not call for or make use of help in the birth, was to be reputed the murderer, if the child was dead or missing. The punishment for this offence was in 1809 reduced to a maximum penalty of two years' imprisonment.[22] The Act applies to married as well as to unmarried women. Concealment means non-disclosure, not merely active deception.[23] If disclosure has taken place, it is immaterial what was the object and who was the recipient. It is also of no consequence that the birth was premature, provided it occurred at such a time as made live birth possible.

16. Abortion.—Subject to the conditions provided in the Abortion Act 1967, it is criminal to cause or procure abortion with felonious intent. The accused may be the woman to whom the drugs are administered or on whom the operation is performed, as well as the actor and his accessories.[24] In a charge of attempting to procure abortion the indictment must set forth that the woman was at the time pregnant.[25] It is no crime to supply abortifacients to a woman who is not pregnant: such conduct cannot be treated as an attempt to procure abortion.[26] An abortion is not criminal if two registered medical practitioners are of the opinion formed in good faith—"(a) that the continuance of the pregnancy would involve risk to the life of the pregnant woman, or of injury to the physical or mental health of the pregnant woman or any existing children of the family, greater than if the pregnancy were terminated; or (b) that there is a substantial risk that if the child were born it would suffer from such physical or mental abnormalities as to be seriously handicapped;"[27] and the operation is carried out under the conditions specified in the Act.

17. Cruelty.—Cruelty exercised on certain of the lower animals is penalised by statute, and may be described as treatment causing pain without adequate motive.[28] To establish cruel ill-treatment in contravention of the Protection of Animals (Scotland) Act 1912 it is not necessary to show a deliberate intention to cause pain.[29] Cruel conduct towards persons, such as wives and lunatics, who have no adequate power to resist, is indictable, though it may not amount to assault. The exposure of infants and unnatural

21 *Cawthorne,* 1968 J.C. 32.
22 Concealment of Birth (Scotland) Act 1809.
23 *Gall,* 1856, 2 Irv. 366.
24 *Reid,* 1858, 3 Irv. 235; *Graham,* 1897, 2 Ad. 412.
25 *Anderson,* 1928 J.C. 1.
26 *Semple,* 1937 J.C. 41. See Part I., § 10, supra.
27 Abortion Act 1967, s. 1 (1).
28 Cruelty to Animals Act 1876; Protection of Animals (Scotland) Act 1912 and 1934; Protection of Animals (Cruelty to Dogs) Act 1933; Protection of Animals (Amendment) Act 1954; Abandonment of Animals Act 1960.
29 *Easton* v. *Anderson,* 1949 J.C. 1.

treatment of children were sufficiently dealt with at common law,[30] but statute has also stepped in for their protection, and is more commonly resorted to. In particular the Children and Young Persons (Scotland) Act 1937[31] renders criminal various forms of ill-treatment of children and young persons. So also does section 95 of the Mental Health (Scotland) Act 1960 in the case of patients in mental hospitals.

18. Assault.—Assault, though used loosely as meaning any act of violence to the person, means technically an attack threatened, if serious, or accomplished, whether serious or not, and intentionally directed to take effect physically on the person attacked. Where the assault does not involve another crime, such as, for example, sodomy, consent may be a good defence provided the accused did not intend to inflict bodily harm.[32] The greatest difficulty in practice arises where there has been provocation. Words do not justify blows, but may mitigate the punishment for assault. Blows justify corresponding retaliation, but not cool, or repeated, or otherwise excessive reprisals.[33] The interval during which the provocation may be assumed to continue is longer if the insult be written than if it be verbal.[34] One may be placed by natural or other relationship in a position involving the power to inflict chastisement on another which, without that position, would be assault. Thus parents have the right to chastise their children, within moderate limits; a master may inflict moderate chastisement on his apprentice, and a teacher on his pupils.[35]

19. Bigamy.—The crime of bigamy is committed by one who feloniously, during the life of his or her spouse, enters into what, but for the prior contract, would be a marriage with a third party. But the accused cannot be convicted if he can prove that at the date of the second marriage he had a reasonable belief in the death of the former spouse.[36] The aggrieved husband or wife is a competent witness either for prosecution or defence.[37]

20. Incest.—Carnal intercourse between persons who stand within the degrees of kindred forbidden in the eighteenth chapter of Leviticus is, with certain statutory exceptions, incest. Section 2 and Schedule 1 of the Marriage (Scotland) Act 1977 now provide a comprehensive list of all the persons who are forbidden to marry by reason of relationship. Expressed broadly, the effect of the Act is that prohibition against marriage does not extend beyond great-grandchildren, and between collaterals is limited to siblings and uncle and niece or aunt and nephew.[38] The prohibition extends to all relations in the

---

[30] *M'Intosh* (1881) 8 R. (J.) 13; 4 Coup, 389.
[31] 1 Edw. VIII & 1 Geo. VI, c. 37.
[32] *Smart,* 1975 S.L.T. 65; See also Gordon, p. 828.
[33] See *Hillan,* 1937 J.C. 53; *Callander,* 1958 S.L.T. 24 as to defences of provocation and self-defence, and Part I., § 8, *supra.*
[34] *Gallocher* v. *Weir* (1902) 4 F. (J.) 93; 3 Adam 665.
[35] *M'Shane* v. *Paton,* 1922 J.C. 26; *Gray* v. *Hawthorn,* 1964 J.C. 69.
[36] *Macdonald,* 1842, 1 Broun 238. Cf. the Presumption of Death (Scotland) Act 1977, s. 13.
[37] Criminal Justice Administration Act 1914, s. 28 (3); Criminal Procedure (Scotland) Act 1975, c. 21, ss. 143 and 348.
[38] See Gordon, p. 898.

degrees specified whether of the full blood or half blood, and continues despite the dissolution by death or divorce of the marriage that created it. If the relationship comes within the forbidden relationships by consanguinity or affinity specified in Schedule 1, marriage between the persons is void even where traced through or to any person of illegitimate birth. It is unclear whether any connection between such persons would now be incestuous. It has, however, been held that sexual intercourse between a man and his wife's illegitimate daughter did not constitute incest on the view that there can be no incest between bastard relations, except perhaps between mother and bastard son.[39] Similarly, in relationships by adoption it is not incest for an adoptive parent to have sexual intercourse with the adopted child,[40] but a marriage between such persons is void.[41] Provided that they are not blood brothers or sisters, adopted siblings may marry each other. Extra-marital intercourse is not incestuous between a man and woman who is the sister, aunt or niece of a former wife of his (whether living or not), or who was formerly the wife of his brother, uncle or nephew (whether living or not).[42]

21. Rape, etc.—Rape is the carnal knowledge of a woman effected by forcibly overcoming her will. Penetration, even to the slightest extent, is enough. A prostitute is not shut out from the protection of the law, but proof that the act was committed against her will is more difficult than in the ordinary case. The force used must be such as to overcome physical resistance, and the degree of physical resistance offered is important as evidence of the victim's unwilling state. Her will may, of course, be overcome by threats of violence, particularly with a weapon.[43] Carnal knowledge of a woman when asleep and without her consent by one who is not her husband, though probably not rape, is an indictable offence.[44] Nor is it rape when connection is had with a woman rendered insensible by drinking unless either the drink has been doctored or she was plied with it in order to overcome her resistance.[45] Such behaviour amounts to indecent assault only. Rape (often referred to as constructive rape) may be committed without any force or overcoming of the victim's will: (1) where the victim is a girl below thirteen years of age[46]; (2) where the victim is an idiot[47]; (3) by impersonating the woman's husband.[48]

The Sexual Offences (Scotland) Act 1976 consolidates almost all the statutory provisions of Scots law relating to sexual offences. In particular it re-enacted much of and clarified to a certain extent the Criminal Law Amendment Acts of 1885, 1912, 1922 and 1951. It deals inter alia with procuring, whether by threats and the like or not; abduction of unmarried

---

[39] *McKenzie*, 1969 J.C. 52; Hume, I, 452; Alison, I, 565; McDonald, 148. Fraser: *Parent and Child* I, 131 included father and bastard daughter.
[40] *McKenzie, supra*; Children Act 1975, Sched. 2, para. 1.
[41] 1977 Act, Sched. 1, para 3.
[42] Criminal Procedure (Scotland) Act 1938, s. 13.
[43] E.g. *Yates*, 1977 S.L.T. (Notes) 42.
[44] *Sweenie*, 1858, 3 Irv. 109; *Thomson*, 1872, 2 Coup. 346.
[45] *Logan*, 1936 J.C. 100.
[46] Sexual Offences (Scotland) Act 1976 (c. 67), s. 3.
[47] *Sweenie, supra*; *Mack*, 1959 S.L.T. 288; See also Gordon, pp. 890-2.
[48] 1976 Act, s. 2 (2).

girls under 18 with intent to have sexual intercourse; detention of women in brothels; and brothel keeping. It is an offence for any person to have intercourse with any girl of or above the age of 13 and under the age of 16 years, unless he had reasonable cause to believe the girl was his wife or, being under 24 years of age, and not having been charged with a like offence (as defined in the 1976 Act), he had reasonable cause to believe the girl was of or above the age of 16 years.[49]

22. Sodomy and Bestiality.—Sodomy is the unnatural connection between human males. The crime is prosecuted at common law. Acts of gross indecency between male persons are prosecuted under section 7 of the Sexual Offences (Scotland) Act 1976. Bestiality, or unnatural connection with animals, is dealt with at common law.

23. Lewd, Indecent and Libidinous Practices.—These are criminal when used towards children under the age of puberty. In the case of females above that age there must be the element of assault to constitute a crime under the common law. It is a statutory offence to use any lewd, indecent or libidinous practice or behaviour towards a girl of or above the age of 12 and under the age of 16, which, if used towards a girl under the age of 12, would have constituted an offence at common law, whether or not the girl consents.[50] Indecencies between males are made punishable by statute.[51] Indecent exposure is also an offence if done to the annoyance of persons mentioned in the charge; not otherwise.[52] To publish, circulate or expose for sale obscene publications is also criminal, whatever be the motive.[53]

24. False Accusation: Threats: Blackmail.—A false accusation to be criminal must impute crime or gross immorality.[54] A threat to do serious injury to a person or his property or reputation is a crime, whatever the motive of the threat,[55] but the charge must specify the nature of the threat.[56] Where the purpose is to obtain money or other advantage, threats of a less grave character are criminal, unless they are recognised as legitimate forms of pressure.[57] Legal process is legitimate and pressure by one contracting party on another may be[58]; where the threat is unlawful it is no defence that the money demanded is in fact due,[59] and if the threat is to expose unlawful or improper conduct, it is no defence that the charge is true.[60]

---

[49] 1976 Act, s. 4.
[50] 1976 Act, s. 5.
[51] See supra § 22 and e.g., *Ogg*, 1938 J.C. 152.
[52] *Mackenzie*, 1864, 4 Irv. 570.
[53] *Robinson*, 1843, 1 Broun 643.
[54] *Robertson*, 1870, 1 Couper 404.
[55] *Miller*, 1862, 4 Irv. 238; *Edmiston*, 1866, 5 Irv. 219; *Silverstein*, 1949 J.C. 160, 163.
[56] *Kenny*, 1951 J.C. 104; *Donoghue*, 1971 S.L.T. 2.
[57] *Miller; Silverstein; M'Ewan* v. *Duncan & M'Lean*, 1854, 1 Irv. 520.
[58] *Silverstein; Thorne* v. *Motor Trade Assn.* [1937] A.C. 797.
[59] *Crawford* (1850) J. Shaw 309; *Macdonald*, 1879, 4 Couper 268.
[60] *M'Ewan*, supra.

25. Intimidation.—The Conspiracy and Protection of Property Act 1875[61] deals mainly with illegal modes of conducting and settling trade disputes, but the seventh section is not confined to such cases. It provides for the punishment of every one who, with a view to compel any other person to abstain from doing or to do any act which such other person has a legal right to do or abstain from doing, wrongfully and without legal authority uses violence or intimidation, persistently follows him about, hides his property or hinders him in the use of it, besets his dwelling or place of business, or follows him with two or more other persons in a disorderly manner.[62] But it is lawful for one or more persons, in contemplation or furtherance of a trade dispute, to attend near a place where a person works or carries on business or where he happens to be, provided it is not a place where he resides, for the purpose only of peacefully obtaining or communicating information or of peacefully persuading any person to work or abstain from working.[63]

SECTION III

CRIMES AGAINST PROPERTY

26. Theft.—This crime is committed when property is feloniously taken or appropriated without the consent of its owner or possessor. A thing may be stolen which is at the time in the hands of the thief with the owner's consent and this occurs as soon as he appropriates it feloniously to his own use.[64] But it may be a question whether the crime is in these circumstances theft or breach of trust and embezzlement. The distinction between these two forms of crime, in many cases a narrow one, depends on the terms on which the property came into the accused's possession. If he received it for a specified purpose,[65] the crime is theft. A watchmaker who appropriates a watch left with him to be repaired[66] or a soldier who sells part of his uniform commits theft.[67] If, on the other hand, the accused had a power of administration, if, for example, he was entitled to dispose of property and account for the price[68] or to spend money entrusted to him and account for it,[69] the crime is embezzlement. Fortunately, the distinction is of little importance, since a person charged with the one crime may be convicted of the other[70] and sentence depends on the facts disclosed rather than on the technical name of the crime.

[61] 38 & 39 Vict., c. 86.
[62] *Agnew* v. *Munro* (1891) 18 R. (J.) 22; 2 White 611; *Clarkson* (1894) 22 R. (J.) 5; 1 Adam 466; *M'Kinlay* (1897) 25 R. (J.) 7; 2 Adam 366.
[63] Trade Unions and Labour Relations Act 1974, s. 15. For the definition of "trade dispute" see TULRA 1974, s. 29; *Wilson* v. *Renton*, 1910 S.C. (J.) 32.
[64] *Smith*, 1838, 2 Swin., at p. 56.
[65] *O'Brien* v. *Strathern*, 1922 J.C. 55, per Lord Justice-General, at p. 57.
[66] *Brown*, 1839, 2 Swin, 394.
[67] *O'Brien* v. *Strathern*, supra.
[68] *M'Minn*, 1859, 3 Irv. 312.
[69] *Kent*, 1950 J.C. 38.
[70] 1975 Act, s. 60 but see *Kent*, supra.

The thing stolen must be the property of another and capable of appropriation. Wild animals cannot, therefore, be stolen as they are the property of no one until they are appropriated by capture.[71] But animals ferae naturae, if caught or killed or under control, so that they may be taken at pleasure, may be subjects of theft. The mere transient use of a thing, without intent to deprive the owner permanently of his property (sometimes called furtum usus), is not a crime according to the law of Scotland, but taking possession of the property of another and using it without his consent and in the knowledge that permission to do so would not have been obtained, may constitute a crime.[72] Where the property is a motor-car this has now been made a statutory offence.[73] A dead body before, though not after, burial may be the subject of theft.[74] Illegal removal of a body after burial constitutes the crime of violating sepulchres.[75] Child-stealing or plagium is theft of a child below the age of puberty from the possession of its parents or guardians.

In theft (subject to the explanation that the use of violence may make it robbery) the mode of appropriation is immaterial. The felonious purpose is not necessarily the acquisition of gain; it is sufficient if there be an intent to deprive another of his property in the knowledge that the act is wrongful. Whether this knowledge is disproved by the possession of colourable title is a question of circumstances.[76] Probably a person cannot steal his own property, in the hands, for example, of custom house officers at the time. A wife can steal from her husband and a husband from his wife.[77] It is no longer necessary to state in the indictment who was the owner or possessor of the stolen article.[78] Theft is committed although the thing be taken from one who had not lawful possession of it, as, e.g., another thief. A resetter[79] is not a thief, since he gets the goods with the consent of the thief who is in possession. The essence of the crime is the felonious appropriation. Plagium accompanied with violence to the child is still theft and not robbery, for the force is not used towards the possessor. So is a stealthy taking, though followed by violence in the effort to retain possession. Any violence used to effect the theft is, however, sufficient to raise the crime to robbery. A person may be convicted of an attempt to steal, although it is shown that there was nothing to steal as when, for example, the victim's pocket contained nothing.[80] Possession of recently stolen property without reasonable explanation may be sufficient evidence for conviction of theft.[81] Under the Burgh Police (Scotland) Act 1892, the possession by a known or reputed thief of property for whose

[71] Wilson (1872) 10 M. 444; 2 Couper 183.
[72] Strathern v. Seaforth, 1926 J.C. 100. See also Murray v. Robertson, 1927 J.C. 1; cf. Herron v. Best, 1976 S.L.T. (Sh. Ct.) 80.
[73] Road Traffic Act 1972, s. 175.
[74] See Dewar, 1945 J.C. 5, which deals primarily with the theft of coffins; Herron v. Diack, 1973 S.L.T. (Sh. Ct.) 80.
[75] Soutar (1882) 5 Couper 65; Dewar, 1945 J.C. 5, at p. 11.
[76] Kilgour (1851) J. Shaw, 501.
[77] Harper v. Adair, 1945 J.C. 21; Kilgour, supra.
[78] 1975 Act, s. 52; Costello v. Macpherson, 1922 J.C. 9.
[79] See § 28, infra.
[80] Lamont v. Strathern, 1933 J.C. 33. See Part I, § 10, supra.
[81] Macd., p. 336; Christie, 1939 J.C. 72; Fox v. Patterson, 1948 J.C. 104, as explained in Brannan, 1954 J.C. 87. See also Cryans v. Nixon, 1955 J.C. 1; Wightman, 1959 J.C. 44.

possession he cannot account is itself an offence. To be a known thief a man must have the established character of one.[82]

27. Housebreaking.—This is the leading aggravation of theft or the attempt to commit that crime. It involves entry of a house which is secured.[83] The entry need not be with the whole body or any part of it; it is enough if with some implement some article has been removed. The house may be any building—at all events any roofed building—finished or unfinished,[84] or any part of a building used as a separate dwelling. Not merely the sanctity but the strength or security of the house must have been overcome. This rule is illustrated in great detail by the decided cases in regard to doors, windows, and other apertures. It is not housebreaking if the house is entered through an open door or an open window near the ground; but it is if entrance is obtained by connivance with an inmate or by tampering with the fastenings at some earlier date. It is sufficient merely to mention the analogous aggravations of shopbreaking[85] and opening lockfast places.

28. Reset.—Reset is the felonious receiving or retaining of goods, obtained by theft, robbery, swindling, or embezzlement, by one who knows that they have been dishonestly appropriated by any of these means.[86] The felonious intent is to deprive the owner or possessor for however short a time. The receiving is the taking from the depredator or a third party, no matter on what terms, or the retaining after knowledge that the property has been stolen. Reset is also established when the accused connives at a third party possessing or retaining the stolen goods, but some positive act consistent with the intention to deprive the true owner of possession is required.[87] The crime applies only to specific articles, and does not extend to the proceeds of the sale or to the pledging of goods improperly obtained or to money got in exchange for stolen money.[88] There must be knowledge that the goods were stolen: mere suspicion is not enough.[89] Possession of recently stolen property in criminative circumstances may be sufficient evidence for conviction.[90]

29. Robbery.—As already indicated, the felonious appropriation of property by means of personal violence is robbery. The property does not require to be upon the person at the time; it is enough that it should be in the care or custody of the victim, e.g., sheep in charge of a shepherd.[91] The violence may be constructive, rather than actual.[92] It is enough if there be such

[82] *Moir* v. *Mitchell*, 1939 J.C. 81; *Lyon* v. *Robertson*, 1955 J.C. 16; *Johnston* v. *Heatly*, 1960 J.C. 26.
[83] *Alston*, 1837, 1 Swin., at p. 468.
[84] Hume I, 103.
[85] *Guthrie*, 1867, 5 Irv. 369.
[86] 1975 Act, s. 59.
[87] *Clark*, 1965 S.L.T. 250; Macd., p. 67; cf. *McNeil*, 1968 J.C. 29.
[88] See Macd., p. 30.
[89] Hume I, 114.
[90] *Fox* v. *Patterson*, 1948 J.C. 104, as explained in *Brannan*, 1954 J.C. 87.
[91] Hume I, 106.
[92] See *O'Neill*, 1934 J.C. 98.

conduct as causes reasonable fear of immediate bodily injury for the purpose of extortion.[93] It is important to distinguish between robbery, assault followed by theft and theft followed by assault.

30. Breach of Trust and Embezzlement.—The nature of this one and indivisible offence has been already sufficiently indicated in the description of theft. The term "embezzlement" is now used alone in describing the crime in indictments. Its main characteristic is the felonious appropriation of what has been entrusted to the accused with certain general powers of administration and only under obligation to account.[94] The law has developed in the direction of enlarging the ambit of the crime of theft and diminishing that of embezzlement and fraud.[95]

31. Falsehood, Fraud, and Wilful Imposition.—This nomen juris was, so long as such terms necessarily appeared in indictments, the technical name in Scotland for swindling. It had the advantage of detailing what the prosecutor has to establish, namely, some falsehood, by word of mouth or writing or conduct; a fraud, that is to say, that the falsehood has been uttered with the intent to cheat; and wilful imposition, that is, that the intention has been successful. In order to establish the crime it is not necessary that the person defrauded should have suffered loss of any kind, or that the accused should have gained anything.[96] An attempt to swindle is now also indictable, like other attempts at crime.[97] The forms of swindling are endless. The greatest difficulty in libelling has arisen in the case of "long-firm frauds," where it is necessary to bring out not merely that the accused never intended to pay for goods ordered, but that the merchant was induced by some falsehood, express or clearly implied, to send them on.[98]

32. Forgery: Uttering Forged Writings.—Forgery per se is not a crime.[99] The crime is uttering, i.e., using as genuine a fabricated writing falsely intended to represent and pass for the genuine writing of another person. The fabrication may be achieved either by appending a false signature or by bringing a false writing to a true signature.[1] It is immaterial whether the person whose signature or writ the writing purports to be exists or is fictitious, whether the forgery is adroit or clumsy, and whether the writing was forged by the utterer or another.[99] The uttering must be such surrender or possession as puts the false writing out of the control of the accused, e.g., by posting it. It is immaterial that the falsity has been at once detected. There is uttering if the writing has been registered for execution, or for publication, or perhaps for

[93] *Templeton* (1871) 2 Couper 140; Hume I, 106.
[94] See *Allenby*, 1938 J.C. 55, for a decision that using the funds of others, in special circumstances, did not constitute embezzlement.
[95] *O'Brien* v. *Strathern*, 1922 J.C. 55.
[96] *Adcock* v. *Archibald*, 1925 J.C. 58.
[97] *Cameron*, 1911 S.C. (J.) 110; 6 Adam 456.
[98] *Witherington* (1881) 8 R. (J.) 41; 4 Couper 475.
[99] *Barr*, 1927 J.C. 51; for the weight to be attached to expert evidence relating to handwriting, see *Richardson* v. *Clark*, 1957 J.C. 7; *Campbell* v. *Mackenzie*, 1974 S.L.T. (Notes) 46.
[1] *Fraser*, 1859, 3 Irv. 467.

preservation. The uttering must also be felonious, that is to say, it must be seriously made, with the knowledge that it is false, and not in jest. Otherwise the motive is a matter of no moment. It is of no consequence whether the writing reached its destination or not, and whether if genuine it would or would not have served the ends of the accused.[2]

33. Fire-Raising.—This crime consists in wilfully or recklessly setting on fire a building, growing or stored cereals, growing wood, coalheughs, or certain other forms of property. Its gravity depends upon a consideration of whether the act was done recklessly or wilfully, e.g., for revenge or to defraud insurers.[3] The crime is not complete unless the fire has taken effect, has caught and not merely by heat charred the premises.[4] Some difficulty arises where the accused is himself the owner or possessor of the things set on fire.[5] If his purpose be to ignite neighbouring premises or to defraud insurers there is undoubtedly an offence.[6] The law regarding intention to cause damage to the property of tenants, landlords, or bondholders has not been settled.[7] But a person is not guilty of fire-raising who burns his own property which is not insured and who does not by his act endanger the life or property of others.[8]

34. Poaching and Trespass.—Poaching is principally struck at by the Night Poaching Act of 1828 (9 Geo. IV, c. 69), as amended in 1844 (7 & 8 Vict., c. 29), and the Day Trespass Act of 1832[9] (2 & 3 Will. IV, c. 68). The first of these statutes prescribes penalties for any person who shall by night unlawfully take or destroy any game (defined in the Act to include hares, pheasants, partridges, grouse, heath or moor game, black game and bustards) or rabbits in any land, whether open or enclosed, or shall by night unlawfully enter or be on any land, whether open or enclosed, with any gun, net, engine or other instrument, for the purpose of taking or destroying game. The poaching of salmon and deer are struck at by the Salmon and Freshwater Fisheries (Protection) (Scotland) Act 1951[10] and the Deer (Scotland) Act 1959[11] respectively. Under the 1951 Act only certain methods of fishing are permitted.[12] "Night" is defined as the period between one hour after sunset and one hour before sunrise, according to local time.[13] The being on land with instruments applies not only to the person who has the instrument, but to all who are with him and participating.[14] If any such person resists apprehension, or offers violence with any offensive weapon, the gravity of the offence is

[2] *Myles*, 1848 Ark. 400.
[3] *Smillie* (1883) 10 R. (J.) 70; 5 Couper 287.
[4] *Grieve* (1866) 5 Irv. 263; *Pollock* (1869) 1 Coup. 257.
[5] Hume I, 131-3.
[6] *Bell*, 1966 S.L.T. (Notes) 61.
[7] *Arthur* (1836) 1 Swin. 124.
[8] *Black* (1856) 2 Irv. 575, 583.
[9] Game (Scotland) Act 1832 is the title under the Short Titles Act 1896.
[10] 14 & 15 Geo. VI, c. 26.
[11] 7 & 8 Eliz. II, c. 40, ss. 21-25.
[12] See section 2, and *Porteous* v. *McNaughton* 1971 J.C. 12.
[13] See *MacKinnon* v. *Nicolson*, 1916 S.C. (J.) 6.
[14] *Granger* (1863) 4 Irv. 432.

greatly increased. The use of such a weapon tells against all concerned if they knew of its presence.[15] The most serious form of night poaching, by a band of three or more persons who are armed, may be visited with any penalty up to fourteen years' imprisonment.[16] The Day Trespass Act prescribes penalties on summary conviction for any person who commits trespass by day in pursuit of game. Daytime is from one hour before sunrise to one hour after sunset. The Poaching Prevention Act 1862 (25 & 26 Vict. c. 114), gives power to a police constable to search any person in any highway, street or public place, if he has good reason to suspect him of coming from land where he has been unlawfully in pursuit of game, and having in his possession any game, gun or net. A similar power is given to stop and search any conveyance. The penalty on conviction is a fine not exceeding £5 and forfeiture of the game, gun or net.[17] An agricultural tenant, when there is no stipulation to the contrary in the lease, may kill rabbits, and may authorise anyone else to do so.[18] Under the Ground Game Act of 1880[19] he has the right, of which he cannot deprive himself by contract, to kill hares and rabbits. While the principal importance of the laws relating to trespass is in regard to poaching, the Trespass Act of 1865[20] imposes penalties upon persons who occupy private land or premises or who light fires on or near a private road or cultivated land without consent of the owner or legal occupier.

35 Malicious Mischief.—This may be described as destruction of or injury to property without the direct intention of taking it away from its owner or possessor, but with some other evil intention, such as the indulgence of cruelty or malice.[21] It is not essential that there should be a deliberate wicked intent to injure; it will suffice if a deliberate disregard of or even indifference to the property rights of others is shown.[22] The mischief must have taken effect in some way, though not perhaps to the prejudice of the person or to the full extent intended.[23] Intent should not be confused with motive, and if the necessary intent is shown, it is irrelevant, except in mitigation, to advance in defence a belief held bona fide by the accused that he was entitled to act as he did.[24] Cases of malicious mischief and poaching offences are now almost invariably dealt with summarily.

36. Bankruptcy Frauds.—These are dealt with by the Bankruptcy (Scotland) Act 1913 (3 & 4 Geo. V. c. 20), sections 178-184, and are referred to in the chapter on Bankruptcy.[25]

---

[15] *Mitchell* (1877) 1 White 321.
[16] Act, 9 Geo. IV, c. 69, s. 9, as modified by 20 & 21 Vict., c. 3, s. 2.
[17] *Gray* v. *Hawthorn*, 1961 J.C. 13; cf. *Aitchison* v. *Bartlett*, 1963 J.C. 27, a case under a comparable section in the 1951 Act.
[18] *Crawshay* v. *Duncan*, 1915 S.C. (J.) 64.
[19] 43 & 44 Vict., c. 47.
[20] 28 & 29 Vict., c. 56. See *Paterson* v. *Robertson*, 1944 J.C. 166.
[21] *Forbes* v. *Ross* (1898) 25 R. (J.) 60; 2 Adam 513.
[22] *Ward* v. *Robertson*, 1938 J.C. 32, per Lord Justice-Clerk Aitchison; *Clark* v. *Syme*, 1957 J.C. 1.
[23] *Thomson* (1874) 2 Couper 551.
[24] *Clark* v. *Syme,* supra; Gordon, pp. 713-4. *Speid* v. *Whyte* (1864) 4 Irv. 584.
[25] Ante, Ch. XLIX, § 23.

INDEX

833

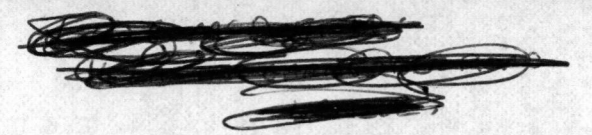

INTRODUCTION
TO THE
LAW OF SCOTLAND